SELECTIV
GUIDE
to
Colleges

also by Edward B. Fiske

The Best Buys in College Education

SELECTIVE GUIDE to Colleges

by Edward B. Fiske

EDUCATION EDITOR OF

The New York Times

WITH

AMY STUART WELLS

AND

SELECTIVE GUIDE TO COLLEGES STAFF

Times
BOOKS

To Pouce

Index by State

The colleges in this guide are listed alphabetically and cross-referenced for your convenience. Below is a list of the selected colleges listed by state. Following this listing you will find a second listing in which the colleges are categorized by the yearly cost of attending each school.

ALABAMA

Alabama, University of—Tuscaloosa
Auburn University
Birmingham–Southern College
Tuskegee Institute

ARIZONA

Arizona State University
Arizona, University of

ARKANSAS

Arkansas, University of

CALIFORNIA

California Institute of Technology
California State University and Colleges
California, University of—Berkeley
California, University of—Davis
California, University of—Irvine
California, University of—Los Angeles
California, University of—Riverside
California, University of—San Diego
California, University of—Santa Barbara
California, University of—Santa Cruz
Claremont–McKenna College (Claremont Colleges)
Deep Springs College
Harvey Mudd College (Claremont Colleges)
Mills College
Occidental College
Pacific, University of the
Pepperdine University
Pitzer College (Claremont Colleges)
Pomona College (Claremont Colleges)
Redlands, University of
San Francisco, University of
Santa Clara University
Scripps College (Claremont Colleges)
Southern California, University of

Stanford University
Whittier College

COLORADO

Colorado College
Colorado School of Mines
Colorado, University of—Boulder
Denver, University of

CONNECTICUT

Connecticut College
Connecticut, University of
Fairfield University
Trinity College
Wesleyan University
Yale University

DELAWARE

Delaware, University of

DISTRICT OF COLUMBIA

American University
Catholic University of America
George Washington University
Georgetown University
Howard University

FLORIDA

Eckerd College
Florida Institute of Technology
Florida State University
Florida, University of
Miami, University of
Rollins College
South Florida, University of (including New College)
Stetson University

GEORGIA

Agnes Scott College
Clark College (Atlanta University Center)
Emory University
Georgia Institute of Technology
Georgia, University of
Morehouse College (Atlanta University Center)
Morris Brown College (Atlanta University Center)
Spelman College (Atlanta University Center)

IDAHO

Idaho State University

ILLINOIS

Chicago, University of
DePaul University
Illinois Institute of Technology
Illinois, University of, at Urbana–Champaign
Knox College
Lake Forest College
Northwestern University
Principia College
Wheaton College

INDIANA

DePauw University
Earlham College
Indiana University at Bloomington
Notre Dame, University of
Purdue University
Rose–Hulman Institute of Technology
Wabash College

IOWA

Cornell College
Grinnell College
Iowa State University
Iowa, University of

KANSAS

Kansas, University of

KENTUCKY

Centre College
Louisville, University of

LOUISIANA

Louisiana State University
Loyola University
Tulane University
Xavier University of Louisiana

MAINE

Atlantic, College of the
Bates College
Bowdoin College
Colby College
Maine, University of

MARYLAND

Goucher College
Hood College
Maryland, University of
St. John's College
St. Mary's College of Maryland
The Johns Hopkins University

MASSACHUSETTS

Amherst College
Babson College
Boston College
Boston University
Bradford College
Brandeis University
Clark University
Gordon College
Hampshire College
Harvard University
Holy Cross, College of the
Massachusetts Institute of Technology
Massachusetts, University of—Amherst
Mount Holyoke College
Northeastern University
Smith College
Tufts University
Wellesley College
Wheaton College
Williams College
Worcester Polytechnic Institute

MICHIGAN

Albion College
Alma College
Calvin College
Hope College
Kalamazoo College

Michigan State University
Michigan, University of

MINNESOTA

Carleton College
Macalester College
Minnesota, University of—Twin Cities
St. John's University
St. Olaf College

MISSISSIPPI

Millsaps College

MISSOURI

Missouri, University of—Columbia
St. Louis University
Washington University

MONTANA

Montana College of Mineral Science and
Technology

NEBRASKA

Nebraska, University of, at Lincoln

NEW HAMPSHIRE

Dartmouth College
New Hampshire, University of

NEW JERSEY

Drew University
Fairleigh Dickinson University
New Jersey Institute of Technology
Princeton University
Rutgers University
Seton Hall University
Stevens Institute of Technology

NEW MEXICO

New Mexico Institute of Mining and Technology
New Mexico, University of
St. John's College

NEW YORK

Adelphi University
Alfred University
Bard College
Barnard College (Columbia University)
CUNY—Brooklyn College
CUNY—City College of New York
CUNY—Community Colleges
CUNY—Hunter College
CUNY—John Jay College of Criminal Justice
CUNY—Lehman College
CUNY—New York City Technical College
CUNY—Queens College
Colgate University
Columbia College (Columbia University)
Cooper Union
Cornell University
Fordham University
Hamilton College
Hartwick College
Hobart and William Smith Colleges
Hofstra University
Houghton College
Ithaca College
Manhattanville College
New School for Social Research
New York University
Pratt Institute
Rensselaer Polytechnic Institute
Rochester Institute of Technology
Rochester, University of
St. Lawrence University
Sarah Lawrence College
Skidmore College
Southampton College
SUNY—Albany
SUNY—Binghamton
SUNY—Buffalo
SUNY—Purchase
SUNY—Stony Brook
Syracuse University
Union College
Vassar College
Wells College
Yeshiva University

NORTH CAROLINA

Davidson College
Duke University
North Carolina State University
North Carolina, University of, at Chapel Hill
North Carolina, University of, at Greensboro
Wake Forest University

OHIO

Antioch College
Case Western Reserve University
Cincinnati, University of
Dayton, University of
Denison University
Hiram College
Kent State University
Kenyon College
Miami University
Oberlin College
Ohio State University
Ohio University
Ohio Wesleyan University
Wittenberg University
Wooster, College of

OKLAHOMA

Oklahoma, University of
Tulsa, University of

OREGON

Lewis and Clark College
Oregon State University
Oregon, University of
Reed College
Willamette University

PENNSYLVANIA

Allegheny College
Bryn Mawr College
Bucknell University
Carnegie–Mellon University
Chatham College
Dickinson College
Drexel University
Duquesne University
Franklin and Marshall College
Gettysburg College
Haverford College
Lafayette College
Lehigh University
Muhlenberg College
Pennsylvania State University
Pennsylvania, University of
Pittsburgh, University of
Swarthmore College
Ursinus College
Villanova University
Washington and Jefferson College

RHODE ISLAND

Brown University
Rhode Island, University of

SOUTH CAROLINA

Charleston, College of
Clemson University
Furman University
South Carolina, University of

TENNESSEE

Fisk University
Rhodes College
South, University of the—Sewanee
Vanderbilt University

TEXAS

Austin College
Baylor University
Dallas, University of
Houston, University of
Rice University
Southern Methodist University
Southwestern University
Texas A & M University
Texas Christian University
Texas, University of, at Austin
Trinity University

UTAH

Brigham Young University
Utah, University of

VERMONT

Bennington College
Marlboro College
Middlebury College
Vermont, University of

VIRGINIA

Hollins College
Randolph–Macon Woman's College
Richmond, University of
Sweet Briar College
Virginia Polytechnic Institute and State
  University
Virginia, University of

Washington and Lee University
William and Mary, College of

WASHINGTON

Evergreen State College
Puget Sound, University of
Washington, University of
• Whitman College

West Virginia University

WISCONSIN

Alverno College
Beloit College
Lawrence University
Marquette University
Ripon College
Wisconsin, University of—Madison

Index by Price

PUBLIC COLLEGES AND UNIVERSITIES

INEXPENSIVE — $

Alabama, University of—Tuscaloosa, AL
Arizona State University, AZ
Arkansas, University of, AK
Auburn University, AL
Charleston, College of, SC
CUNY—Brooklyn College, NY
CUNY—City College of New York, NY
CUNY—Hunter College, NY
CUNY—Queens College, NY
Florida State University, FL
Houston, University of, TX
Idaho State University, ID
Iowa State University, IA
Kansas, University of, KS
Louisiana State University, LA
Massachusetts, University of—Amherst, MA
Montana College of Mineral Science and
   Technology, MT
New Mexico Institute of Mining and
   Technology, NM
North Carolina State University, NC
North Carolina, University of, at Greensboro,
   NC
Oklahoma, University of, OK
Utah, University of, UT
Virginia Polytechnic Institute and State
   University, VA
Washington, University of, WA
West Virginia, WV

MODERATE — $ $

Arizona, University of, AZ
Cincinnati, University of, OH
Clemson University, SC
Delaware, University of, DE
Georgia Institute of Technology, GA
Georgia, University of, GA
Indiana University at Bloomington, IN
Iowa, University of, IA
Kent State University, OH
Louisville, University of, KY

Maine, University of, ME
Michigan State University, MI
Minnesota, University of—Twin Cities, MO
Missouri, University of—Columbia, MO
Nebraska, University of, at Lincoln, NE
New Mexico, University of, NM
North Carolina, University of, at Chapel Hill,
   NC
Ohio State University, OH
Oregon State University, OR
Oregon, University of, OR
Purdue University, IN
Rutgers University, NJ
St. Mary's College of Maryland, MD
South Carolina, University of, SC
South Florida, University of (including New
   College), FL
SUNY—Albany, NY
SUNY—Binghamton, NY
SUNY—Buffalo, NY
SUNY—Purchase, NY
SUNY—Stony Brook, NY
Texas A&M University, TX
Texas, University of, at Austin, TX
Wisconsin, University of—Madison, WI

EXPENSIVE — $ $ $

California, University of—Davis, CA
California, University of—Los Angeles, CA
California, University of—Santa Barbara, CA
California, University of—Santa Cruz
Colorado School of Mines, CO
Connecticut, University of, CT
Evergreen State College, WA
Illinois, University of, at Urbana–Champaign, IL
Maryland, University of, MD
Miami University, OH
New Hampshire, University of, NH
New Jersey Institute of Technology, NJ
Ohio University, OH
Pennsylvania State University, PA
Rhode Island, University of, RI
Virginia, University of, VA

VERY EXPENSIVE — $ $ $ $

California, University of—Berkeley, CA
California, University of—Irvine, CA
California, University of—Riverside, CA
California, University of—San Diego, CA

Colorado, University of—Boulder, CO
Michigan, University of, MI
Pittsburgh, University of, PA
Vermont, University of, VT
William and Mary, College of, VA

PRIVATE COLLEGES AND UNIVERSITIES

INEXPENSIVE — $

Agnes Scott College, GA
Alverno College, WI
Atlantic, College of the, ME
Austin College, TX
Baylor University, TX
Birmingham–Southern College, AL
Brigham Young University, UT
Calvin College, MI
Centre College, KY
Cooper Union, NY
Dallas, University of, TX
Dayton, University of, OH
Deep Springs College, CA
DePaul University, IL
Duquesne University, PA
Fairleigh Dickinson University, NJ
Fisk University, TN
Florida Institute of Technology, FL
Hofstra University, NY
Hope College, MI
Houghton College, NY
Howard University, DC
Loyola University, LA
Marquette University, WI
Millsaps College, MS
Morehouse College (Atlanta University Center),
  GA
Rice University, TX
Richmond, University of, VA
St. John's University, MN
St. Louis University, MO
St. Olaf College, MN
Seton Hall University, NJ
Southwestern University, TX
Spelman College (Atlanta University Center),
  GA
Stetson University, FL
Texas Christian University, TX
Tulsa, University of, OK
Tuskegee Institute, AL
Wabash College, IN
Wake Forest University, NC
Wheaton College, IL
Xavier University of Louisiana, LA

MODERATE — $ $

Adelphi University, NY
Albion College, MI
Allegheny College, PA
Alma College, MI
Antioch College, OH
Beloit College, WI
Bradford College, MA
Carleton College, MI
Chatham College, PA
Colorado College, CO
Cornell College, IA
Cornell University, NY
Davidson College, NC
DePauw University, IN
Drexel University, PA
Earlham College, IN
Eckerd College, FL
Emory University, GA
Fairfield University, CT
Fordham University, NY
Furman University, SC
Gordon College, MA
Grinnell College, IA
Hartwick College, NY
Hiram College, OH
Hollins College, VA
Illinois Institute of Technology, IL
Ithaca College, NY
Kalamazoo College, MI
Knox College, IL
Lawrence University, WI
Macalester College, MN
Notre Dame, University of, IN
Ohio Wesleyan University, OH
Puget Sound, University of, WA
Randolph–Macon Woman's College, VA
Rhodes College, TN
Ripon College, WI
Rollins College, FL
Rose–Hulman Institute of Technology, IN
San Francisco, University of, CA
Santa Clara University, CA
South, University of the—Sewanee, TN
Southern Methodist University, TX
Sweet Briar College, VA

Trinity University, TX
Ursinus College, PA
Villanova University, PA
Washington and Jefferson College, PA
Washington and Lee University, VA
Whitman College, WA
Whittier College, CA
Willamette University, OR
Wittenberg University, OH
Wooster, College of, OH
Yeshiva University, NY

EXPENSIVE — $ $ $

Alfred University, NY
American University, DC
Babson College, MA
Bryn Mawr College, PA
Case Western Reserve University, OH
Catholic University of America, DC
Clark University, MA
Colby College, ME
Denison University, OH
Denver, University of, CO
Dickinson College, PA
Drew University, NJ
Duke University, NC
Franklin and Marshall College, PA
George Washington University, DC
Georgetown University, DC
Gettysburg College, PA
Goucher College, MD
Holy Cross, College of the, MA
Hood College, MD
Kenyon College, OH
Lafayette College, PA
Lake Forest College, IL
Lewis and Clark College, OR
Manhattanville College, NY
Marlboro College, VT
Miami, University of, FL
Mills College, CA
Muhlenberg College, PA
New School for Social Research, NY
Northeastern University, MA
Oberlin College, OH
Pratt Institute, NY
Principia College, IL
Redlands, University of, CA
Reed College, OR
Rochester Institute of Technology, NY
St. John's College, MD and NM
St. Lawrence University, NY
Scripps College (Claremont Colleges), CA
Stevens Institute of Technology, NJ
Syracuse University, NY

Trinity College, CT
Union College, NY
Vanderbilt University, TN
Washington University, MO
Wells College, NY
Wheaton College, MA
Worcester Polytechnic Institute, MA

VERY EXPENSIVE — $ $ $ $

Amherst College, MA
Bard College, NY
Barnard College (Columbia University), NY
Bates College, ME
Bennington College, ME
Boston College, MA
Boston University, MA
Bowdoin College, ME
Brandeis University, MA
Brown University, RI
Bucknell University, PA
California Institute of Technology, CA
Carnegie–Mellon University, PA
Chicago, University of, IL
Claremont–McKenna College (Claremont
    Colleges), CA
Colgate University, NY
Columbia College (Columbia University), NY
Connecticut College, CT
Dartmouth College, NH
Hamilton College, NY
Hampshire College, MA
Harvard University, MA
Harvey Mudd College (Claremont Colleges), CA
Haverford College, PA
Hobart and William Smith Colleges, NY
Johns Hopkins University, MD
Lehigh University, PA
Massachusetts Institute of Technology, MA
Middlebury College, VT
Mount Holyoke College, MA
New York University, NY
Northwestern University, IL
Occidental College, CA
Pacific, University of the, CA
Pennsylvania, University of, PA
Pepperdine University, CA
Pitzer College (Claremont Colleges), CA
Pomona College (Claremont Colleges), CA
Princeton University, NJ
Rensselaer Polytechnic Institute, NY
Rochester, University of, NY
Sarah Lawrence College, NY
Skidmore College, NY
Smith College, MA
Southern California, University of, CA

Stanford University, CA
Swarthmore College, PA
Tufts University, MA
Tulane University, LA
Vassar College, NY

Wellesley College, MA
Wesleyan University, CT
Williams College, MA
Yale University, CT

Introduction

The fourth edition of the *Selective Guide to Colleges* is an expanded and revised version of a book that has been a best-seller since it first appeared in the early 1980s and is generally recognized as the definitive book of its type.

Half a dozen new colleges have been added to the new edition, bringing the total to nearly three hundred. The revised write-ups have taken special note of the electronic revolution, the building boom and the curricular reforms that are sweeping the nation's campuses. With tuitions rising at double the rate of inflation, we've made a point of noting which colleges offer merit scholarships, subsidized loans, prepayment plans or other ingenious weapons for fighting the cost-of-education battle.

Picking the right college—one that will coincide with the needs, goals, interests, talents and personality of each individual—is one of the most important decisions that any young person will ever make. It is also a major investment. One year of college now costs at least $5,000 at a typical public university and $10,000 at a typical private college, and the tab at the most selective and expensive schools is fast approaching $20,000. Obviously, college-bound students and their families will want to learn as much as they can about potential alma maters before making such a major decision and such a major investment.

Fortunately, the college-bound student and his or her family have some important things going for them. Because of the declining birthrate, the number of high school graduates is now declining and will continue to do so throughout the rest of the 1980s and the 1990s. This basic demographic fact—coupled with the increasing cost of higher education—means that colleges are finding it increasingly difficult to fill their classes or, in the case of highly selective ones, to maintain the academic quality of their freshmen classes. The net result is that—with the exception of relatively few highly prestigious institutions—it is increasingly the student, not the college, who is in the position to determine where he or she will go to school.

That's where the *Selective Guide to Colleges* fits in.

The *Guide* is designed as a tool to help you make the most intelligent educational investment you can. It is a buyer's guide for the buyer's market.

WHAT IS THE *SELECTIVE GUIDE TO COLLEGES*?

The *Guide* is essentially a journalistic, or reporting, effort that duplicates a process familiar to any college-bound student and his or her family. If you are wondering whether to consider a particular college, it is logical to seek out friends or acquaintances who go there and ask what it's like. What we have done is exactly this—but on a far broader and more systematic basis than any individual or family can do alone.

We began by asking students, guidance counselors, and admissions directors: What is it that students really want to know about a college or university when deciding where to apply? We then went out and asked these questions of the people most likely to know the answers: students who are already there.

In using the *Guide,* some special features should be kept in mind:

The *Guide* is, as the title declares, selective. We have not tried to cover all four-year colleges and universities. Rather, we have taken nearly three hundred of the best and most interesting institutions in the nation—the ones that students in a buyer's market most want to know about—and written essays of 1,000 to 2,500 words about them.

Since choosing a college is a matter of making a calculated and informed judgment, this guide is also subjective. Based on what persons familiar with the colleges and universities tell us about their experience, it makes judgments about the strengths and weaknesses of each institution and contains a unique set of ratings of each college or university on the basis of academic strength, social life, and overall quality of life. No institution is right for every student. The assumption underlying the *Guide* is that each of the colleges chosen for inclusion is the right place for some students. Like finding the right husband or wife, college admissions is a matching process. You know your own interests and needs; the *Guide* will tell you something about those that each college seems to serve best.

Finally, the *Guide* is systematic. Each write-up is carefully constructed to cover specific topics, from the academic climate and the makeup of the student body to the social scene, in a systematic order. This means that you can easily take a specific topic, such as the level of academic pressure or the role of fraternities and sororities on campus, and trace it through all of the colleges that interest you.

HOW SHOULD THE *GUIDE* BE USED?

Students will find the *Guide* useful at a variety of points in the college-selection process—from deciding whether to visit a particular campus to formulating some key questions to ask during an admissions interview. To make it easy to find a particular college, the write-ups are arranged in alphabetical order, with an Index by State provided at the beginning.

While most people are not likely to start reading at Adelphi and keep going until they reach Yeshiva (though some tell us they have), we would encourage browsing. This country has an enormously rich and varied network of colleges and universities, and there are dozens of institutions out there that can meet the needs of any particular student. Too many students approach the college-selection process wearing blinders—limiting their sights to local institutions, or the pet schools of their parents or guidance counselors, or to schools they know only by possibly outdated reputations.

One of the benefits of the buyer's market, though, is that we need not be bound by such limitations. Once you have decided on the type of school you want—a small liberal arts college, an engineering school or whatever—we hope you will thumb through the book looking for similar institutions that might not have occurred to you. Many students have found this worthwhile, and, quite frankly, we view the widening of students' horizons about American higher education as one of the most important purposes of the book. Perhaps the most gratifying remark we hear comes when the admissions director at some small college tells us, as several have, that he or she has freshmen who first heard about the institution in the *Selective Guide to Colleges*.

HOW THE COLLEGES WERE SELECTED

How do you single out "the best and most interesting" of the nearly two thousand four-year colleges in the United States? Obviously there are many fine institutions that are not included. Space limitations simply required that some hard decisions be made.

The selection was done with several broad principles in mind, beginning with academic quality. Depending on how you define the term, there are about 175 "selective" colleges and universities in the nation, and by and large these constitute the best institutions academically. All of these are included in the *Guide*. In addition, an effort was made to achieve geographical diversity and a balance of public and private schools. Special efforts were made to include a good selection of three types of institutions that seem to be enjoying special popularity at present: engineering and technical schools, those with an evangelical or other religious emphasis and those located on the West Coast or along the Sunbelt, where the cost of education is considerably lower than at their northern counterparts. The current edition includes several colleges that in recent years have significantly increased their academic quality and appeal to students.

Finally, in a few cases we exercised the journalist's prerogative of writing about schools that are simply interesting. The tiny College of the Atlantic, for example, would hardly qualify on the basis of superior academic program or national significance, but it offers an unusual and fascinating brand of liberal arts within the context of environmental studies. Likewise, Deep Springs College, the only two-year institution in the *Guide,* is a unique institution.

HOW THE *GUIDE* WAS COMPILED

Each college or university selected for inclusion in the *Selective Guide to Colleges* was sent a packet of questionnaires. The first was for the administration and covered topics ranging from their perception of the institution's mission to the demographics of the student body. They were also asked to distribute a set of questionnaires to a cross section of students.

The questions for students, most of which were open-ended and required short essays as responses, covered a series of topics ranging from the accessibility of professors and the quality of housing and dining facilities to the type of nightlife and weekend entertainment available in the area. By and large students responded enthusiastically to the challenge we offered them. The quality of the information in the write-ups is a tribute to their diligence and candor. American college students, we learned, are a candid lot. They are, by and large, proud of their institutions— but also critical in the best sense of the word.

Other sources of information were also employed. Administrators were invited to attach to their questionnaires any catalogues, in-house research, or other documents that would contribute to an understanding of the institution, and to comment on their write-up in the last edition. Staff members have visited many of the colleges, and in some cases additional information was solicited through telephone interviews and other contacts with students and administrators.

The information from these various questionnaires was then collated by a staff of more than a dozen persons, mostly young journalists and freelance writers, and edited by Edward B. Fiske, the education editor of *The New York Times.*

THE FORMAT

Each essay covers certain broad subjects in roughly the same order. They are as follows:

Academics
Student body
Financial aid
Housing
Food
Social life
Extracurricular activities

Certain subtopics are covered in all of the essays. The discussions of academics, for example, always deal with which departments (or, in the case of large universities, schools) are particularly strong or weak, while the sections on housing contain information on whether the dorms are coed or single-sex and how students get the rooms they want. Other topics, however, such as class size, the need for a car or the number of volumes in the library, are mentioned only if they constitute a particular strength or a problem at that institution.

The drinking age has recently risen in several states, and we paid particular attention to what effect that has on campus life. Also, we noted particular efforts some schools' administrations were making to change or improve the social and residential life on campuses by such measures as outlawing fraternities, clustering dorms in residential colleges, banning alcohol from campus and the like.

STATISTICS

Although the point of the *Guide* is to offer an interpretative essay on each of the colleges, we have included some basic statistics in the margin of each write-up. These include the address, type of location (urban, small town, rural, etc.), enrollment, male-female ratio, median SAT scores, percentage of students on financial aid, relative cost, and number of students who apply and the percentages of those who are accepted and enroll. For convenience, we have also added the telephone number of the admissions office. Unlike some guides, we have intentionally not given precise figures on the student-faculty ratio because colleges use different—and often self-serving—methods to calculate the ratio and thus make them virtually meaningless.

SAT scores are an imprecise measure of academic ability, and comparisons of scores that differ by less than fifty or sixty points on a scale of 200 to 800 have little meaning. According to the laws of statistics, there is a chance of only one out of three that the SAT score you receive is within about thirty points—either higher or lower—of your "real score," or the average score that you would receive if you took the test an infinite number of times. On the other hand, median scores offer some indication of your chances to get into a particular institution and the intellectual level of company you will be keeping—or, if you prefer, competing against. For this reason median SAT scores for colleges have been included, but rounded to the nearest ten, and ACT scores to the nearest full point. Keep in mind, though, that the range of SAT (or ACT) scores for freshmen at any college is wide. Moreover, the most competitive schools have the largest and most sophisticated admissions staffs and are well aware of the limitations of standardized tests. A strong high school average or achievement in a field such as music will usually counteract the negative effects of modest SAT or ACT scores.

Tuition and fees are constantly increasing at American colleges, but by and large the cost of various institutions in relation to one another does not change. Rather than put in specific cost figures that would immediately become out of date, we have classified colleges into four groups ranging from inexpensive ($) to very expensive ($$$$), based on estimated costs of tuition, room and board, for the 1986–87 academic year. Separate scales were used for public and private institutions, and the ratings for the public institutions are based on cost for residents of the state; out-of-staters should expect to pay more. If a public institution has a particularly low or high surcharge for out-of-staters, this is noted in the essay. The categories were defined as follows:

	PUBLIC	PRIVATE
$$$$	Over $7,000	Over $15,000
$$$	$6,000–$7,000	$13,000–$15,000
$$	$5,000–$6,000	$11,000–$13,000
$	Under $5,000	Under $11,000

We also include an index that groups colleges by their relative cost.

SCHOLARSHIP INFORMATION

Since the first edition of the *Selective Guide to Colleges* appeared, the problems of financing college have become increasingly critical, mainly because of the rising cost of college and the withdrawal of federal loans from many middle-class students.

In response to these developments, many colleges and universities have begun to devise their own plans for paying for college. These range from subsidized loan programs to "merit" scholarships that are awarded without reference to financial need. Most of these programs are aimed at retaining the middle class.

In updating the *Guide,* we have asked each college and university to tell us what steps it has taken to help students pay their way, and their responses are incorporated in the write-ups. Also indicated is whether a candidate's inability to pay the full tuition, room and board charges is a factor in admissions decisions. Some colleges advertise that they are "need-blind" in their admissions, meaning that they accept or reject applicants without reference to their financial situation and then guarantee to meet the "demonstrated financial need" of all students whom they accept. Others say they are need-blind in their admissions decisions but do not guarantee to provide the financial aid required of all those who are accepted. Still others agree to meet the demonstrated financial need of all students, but they package their offers so that students whom they really want receive a higher percentage of their help in the form of outright grants rather than repayable loans.

The phrase *demonstrated financial need* is itself a slippery term. In theory, the figure is arrived at when students and families fill out a need-analysis form—normally the Financial Aid Form (FAF) from the College Board or the Family Financial Statement (FFS) of the American College Testing Program—that leads to an estimate of how much the family can afford to pay. Demonstrated need is then calculated by subtracting that figure from the cost at a particular institution. In practice, however, various colleges make their own adjustments to the standard figure.

Students and parents should not assume that because their family has even a six-figure income, they are automatically disqualified from some kind of subsidized financial aid. In cases of doubt, they should fill out a Financial Aid Form or the Family Financial Statement or some similar need-analysis form to determine their eligibility. Whether they qualify or not, they are also eligible for a variety of awards made without regard to financial need.

Inasmuch as the need-based awards are universal at the colleges in this guide, the awards generally singled out for special mention in the write-ups are the merit scholarships. We have not mentioned awards of a purely local nature—restricted to residents of a particular county, for example—but all college applicants should search out these awards through their guidance offices and the bulletins of colleges that interest them. Similarly, we have not duplicated the information on federally guaranteed loan programs that is readily available through high school and college counseling offices, but we cite novel and often less expensive variants of the federal loan programs offered by individual colleges.

RATINGS

In each case the ratings—Academics, Social Life and Quality of Life—are done on a system of one to five, with three considered normal for colleges included in the *Guide.* If a college receives a rating higher or lower than three in any category, the reasons should be apparent from the narrative description of that college.

Students and parents should keep in mind that these ratings are obviously general in nature and inherently subjective. No complex institution can be described in terms of a single number or other symbol, and different people will have different views on how various institutions should be rated in the three categories. They should not be viewed as either precise or infallible judgments about any given college.

On the other hand, the ratings are a helpful tool in using the book. They represent a summary—an index, if you will—of the write-ups. Our hope is that each student, having decided on the kind of configuration that suits his or her needs, will then thumb through the book looking for other institutions with a similar set of ratings.

The categories are defined as follows:

Academics. This is a judgment about the overall academic climate of the institution, including its reputation in the academic world, the quality of the faculty, the level of teaching and research, the academic ability of students, the quality of libraries and other facilities, and the level of academic seriousness among students and faculty members.

Although the same basic criteria have been applied to all institutions, it should be evident that an outstanding small liberal arts college will by definition differ significantly from an outstanding major public university. No one would expect the former to have massive library facilities, but one would look for a high quality faculty that combines research with a good deal of attention to the individual needs of students. Likewise, public universities, because of their implicit commitment to serving a broad cross section of society, might have a broader range of curriculum offerings but somewhat lower average SAT scores than a large private counterpart. Readers may find the ratings most useful when comparing colleges and universities of the same type.

In general, an academics rating of three stars suggests that the institution is a solid institution that easily meets the criteria for inclusion in a guide devoted to the top 10 percent of colleges and universities in the nation.

An academics rating of four stars suggests that the institution is above average even by these standards and that it has some particularly distinguishing academic feature, such as especially rich course offerings or an especially serious academic atmosphere.

A rating of five stars for academics indicates that the college or university is among the handful of top institutions of its type in the nation. Those in the private sector will normally attract students with combined SAT scores of at least 1200, and those in the public sector are invariably magnets for the top students in their states. All can be assumed to have outstanding faculties and other academic resources.

Social Life. This is primarily a judgment about the amount of social life that is readily available. A rating of three telephones suggests a typical college social life, while four telephones means that students have a better than average time socially. It can be assumed that a college with a rating of five is something of a party school, which may or may not detract from the academic quality. Colleges with a rating below three have some impediment to a strong social life, such as geographic isolation, a high percentage of commuting students or a disproportionate number of nerds who never leave the library. Once again, the reason should be evident from the write-up.

Quality of Life. This category grew out of the fact that schools with good academic credentials and plenty of social life may not, for one reason or another, be particularly wholesome places to spend four years. The term *quality of life* is one that has been gaining currency in social-science circles, and in most cases the rating for a particular college will be similar to the academic and/or social ratings. The reader, though, should be alert to exceptions to this pattern. A liberal arts college, for example, might attract bright students who study hard during the week and party hard on weekends and thus earn high ratings for academics and social life. If the academic pressure is cutthroat rather than constructive, though, and the social system manipulative of women, this college might get an apparently anomalous two asterisks on Quality of Life. By contrast, a small college with modest academic programs and relatively few organized social opportunities might have developed a strong sense of supportive community, have a beautiful campus and be located near a wonderful city—and thus be rated four asterisks for Quality of Life. As in the other categories, the reason can be found in the essay to which the ratings point.

Picking a college is a tricky business. But given the current buyer's market, there is no reason why any student should not be able to find the right college for him or her. That's what the *Selective Guide to Colleges* is designed to help you do.

Happy college hunting.

Consortia

Students unsure about attending a small college because they feel it might limit their college experiences should realize that many of these schools have banded together to offer unusual programs that they could not support on their own. Offerings range from exchange programs—trading places with a student on another campus—to a semester or two anywhere in the world—one of the five continents or somewhere out at sea.

Following is a list of some of the largest and most established of these programs, some sponsored by groups of colleges and others by independent agencies. An asterisk (*) after the name of a college indicates that the institution is the subject of a write-up in the *Guide*. An asterisk following the name of a program in the college write-ups means that it is described below.

The **Associated Colleges of the Midwest** comprises thirteen independent institutions in five states: Beloit,* Lawrence* and Ripon* in Wisconsin; Carleton,* Macalester* and St. Olaf* in Minnesota; Knox,* Lake Forest* and Monmouth in Illinois; Coe, Cornell* and Grinnell* in Iowa; and Colorado College.*

The consortium offers to its members' students semester-long programs to study art in London and Florence; culture and society in Florence, Yugoslavia or the Soviet Union; and tropical field research in Latin America. Yearlong programs include Chinese studies (in Hong Kong or the People's Republic of China), India studies and study in Japan. By and large the arts of London and Florence are the most popular with students. The only requirement overseas prospects face for any programs is a general knowledge of Spanish for the Latin-American tropical field program. Students journeying to Japan must participate in a language orientation before they leave, while those en route to Hong Kong can get some training after they land.

Domestic off-campus programs include Humanities at the Newberry Library (an in-depth research project) and urban education and urban studies, both based in Chicago. Energy-related scientists can study at the Oak Ridge National Laboratory in Tennessee, and there's a wilderness field station in northern Minnesota. Those interested in health-related professions can spend their first two years in college and then complete their degrees at Rush University in Chicago.

Living arrangements in the domestic programs vary with the program and region. Chicago visitors, for instance, are offered places in residential hotels; Minnesota's wilderness enthusiasts must rough it in cabins, and Oak Ridge scientists are essentially on their own. There are no comprehensive costs for any of the ACM programs, domestic or foreign, and tuition is based solely on the "home" school's standard fees. The programs are open to sophomores, juniors and seniors majoring in all fields, and the only programs that tend to be especially strict with admissions are the Oak Ridge and Newberry arrangements.

The **Great Lakes Colleges Association** comprises twelve independent institutions in three states: Antioch,* Denison,* Kenyon,* Oberlin,* Ohio Wesleyan* and the College of Wooster* in Ohio; DePauw,* Earlham* and Wabash* in Indiana; and Albion,* Hope* and Kalamazoo* in Michigan. Like ACM, the Great Lakes group offers students off-campus opportunities both in the U.S. and overseas. The only major difference is that each GLCA program has a flat price (ranging from $2,750 for the cheapest semester program to $12,390 for the most expensive one-year program) regardless of the home school's tuition.

For adventures abroad, there's a yearlong African studies program in four different countries. Students can spend a year studying in Scotland, a semester at GLCA's very own center in

Colombia, or a semester comparing the urban systems of Yugoslavia, England and the Netherlands (European Term in Comparative Urban Studies).

GLCA also cosponsors five programs mentioned in the ACM write-up above, but these also cost more: a fall semester exchange at a People's Republic of China university, study in Hong Kong or Yugoslavia, and programs at the Newberry Library in Chicago and Oak Ridge lab in Tennessee. Other domestic programs include a one-semester arts internship in New York City and a multifaceted urban semester in Philadelphia.

Primarily juniors participate, but the programs are open to sophomores and seniors as well. New York and Philadelphia are the most popular domestic plans, and Colombia is the biggie with those heading abroad. There are language requirements to meet in several of the programs, such as a year of Mandarin for China, a year of Japanese for Japan and two years of Spanish for Colombia. Often, however, an intensive summer language program can be substituted.

The **Lehigh Valley Association of Independent Colleges** is a cooperative effort among six colleges in the same area of Pennsylvania: Allentown College of St. Francis de Sales, Cedar Crest College, Lafayette College,* Lehigh University,* Moravian College and Muhlenberg College.*

The newest opportunity available through this consortium is a six-week summer study abroad program that takes students of member schools to England, France, Germany, Spain, Israel and Switzerland. But the most frequently used service of the association is its interlibrary-loan program, which permits students at one institution to use the research facilities of the others. There is some sharing of faculty members and cross-registration among students, although the bulk of both occurs between schools that are the closest to each other, notably Cedar Crest–Muhlenberg and Lafayette–Lehigh. A Jewish studies program is headquartered at Lehigh, but all member schools have at least one professor who lends a different expertise in this field. These faculty members travel from college to college in order to offer students at each institution a variety of courses in this field. The association also sponsors cooperative cultural programs, the best of which are symposiums in the natural sciences that move from campus to campus. Students at each college are also eligible for reduced-rate tickets at plays and other events on campuses of association schools.

The **Twelve-College Exchange Program** comprises a dozen small, highly selective schools in the Northeast: Amherst,* Bowdoin,* Connecticut College,* Dartmouth,* Mount Holyoke,* Smith,* Trinity,* Vassar,* Wellesley,* Wesleyan,* Wheaton (MA)* and Williams.*

Effectively, students enrolled in any schools of the federation can "visit" for a semester or two (usually the latter) with a minimum of red tape. Approximately three hundred students utilize the opportunity each year; most of them are juniors. Placement is determined mainly by available space, but students also need to display good academic standing. While the home college arranges the exchange, students must meet the fees and standards of the host school. Financial-aid holders can usually carry their packages with them.

The **Christian College Coalition** is made up of more than seventy liberal-arts schools from across the nation, including Calvin,* Gordon,* Houghton,* Oral Roberts and Wheaton (IL),* that "are accredited, committed to academic excellence, hire only committed Christian administrators and faculty and possess a clear Christ-centered element in their missions." The colleges are further fused by a central office, several publications and a dedication to integrating faith with academics and daily life.

Also in Washington is an American studies program that permits forty students to spend a semester in the hub of earthly power. Those sophomores, juniors and seniors who are selected from the member colleges live in a dorm on the small campus and are taught by three professors and several adjunct instructors from the Washington area. Many also take part in government internships. The standard cost of the program, plus room and board, is $3,900. Special arrangements can be made for students whose home school tuition is less. Admissions priority is usually given to those from membership colleges.

The **Christian College Consortium** comprises thirteen of the nation's top evangelical liberal arts schools: Asbury, Bethel (MN), George Fox, Gordon,* Greenville, Houghton,* Malone, Messiah, Seattle Pacific, Taylor, Trinity (IL), Westmont and Wheaton (IL).*

The consortium offers a visitors program whereby their students can spend a semester—with little paper pushing—at any of the member schools. More than a hundred students (no freshmen) participate each year, and they pay the home school's regular fees. Other than a reasonably good grade average, there are no special requirements. The consortium sponsors a guest lecturer each year who speaks on the integration of faith and learning at each of the schools. There are also combined programs and workshops for faculty.

The **Washington Semester** of American University takes an unlimited number of students from hundreds of colleges across the country (who meet minimum academic qualifications of a 2.75 GPA) and gives them unbeatable academic and political opportunities in the nation's capital. The program is the oldest of its kind in Washington.

Admitted students take part in a semester of seminars with policymakers and lobbyists, an internship and a choice between an elective course at the university or a self-designed in-depth research project. Students live in dorms on the campus and are guided by a staff of eighteen American University professors.

Ninety percent of the students are drawn from 192 affiliated schools. Although admissions competition depends on the home school and how many it chooses to nominate, the average GPA hovers around a 3.3. Most who participate are juniors—but second-semester sophomores and seniors get equal consideration—and the cost is either American University's tuition, room, board and fees or that of the home school (check with the individual school for details). Just over a third of the affiliated colleges are profiled in the *Guide*.

The **Venture Program** operates out of Brown University but has at various times counted many of the most prestigious East Coast and midwestern colleges and universities in its membership. The six current member institutions include Bates,* Brown,* Connecticut College,* Hobart and William Smith,* Vassar* and Wesleyan.*

The mission of the program is to place students who desire a leave of absence into full-time, paid, temporary employment in all sectors of the economy and the nation. Venture's aim is to provide students with the experience they desire and will often "develop" positions if they don't already exist. There are no requirements, no credits granted, and no cost for either party, and the entire deal is paid for with a hefty foundation grant and by the individual schools themselves—another plus, since the participating schools enjoy good reputations, businesses and organizations are often eager to please.

Usually about three hundred students apply to the program, and half are accepted, mostly juniors. Jobs range in length from four to twelve months. Venture officials say they attract "a different breed" of students; those "exceptional, independent thinkers" who are looking for both a legitimate escape from the walls of academia and a convenient ticket into the world of what's to come.

Money can't buy you love, but it sure can hoist the anchor off a four-year grind. For between $8,195 and $9,875 plus another couple grand for personal expenses, qualified students from any college in the nation can take a **Semester at Sea** and whisk around the globe on a study/cruise odyssey.

Based at the University of Pittsburgh, this nonprofit group takes 450 students each term (from second-semester freshmen to grads) and puts them on a ship bound for almost everywhere. The vessel itself is practically a college campus in its own right. Sixty courses are taught by two dozen professors in subjects ranging from anthropology to marketing and usually stressing "the international scene" as well as the sea itself. What's more, art, theater, music and other extras can be found on board. When students aren't at sea, they're in port in any of twelve foreign countries throughout the world—India, the Middle East, Soviet Union, the Far East and the Mediterranean—and it's not uncommon for leaders and diplomats to meet them along the way.

Students must be in good standing at their home colleges to be considered, which often means a GPA of 2.5 or better. Some financial aid is available in the form of the usual federal grants and loans, and thirty eligible students can use a work/study plan to pay for half the trip. Most colleges do recognize the Semester at Sea program and will provide participating students with a full term's worth of credits. Information may be obtained by writing to Semester at Sea, Forbes Quad, University of Pittsburgh, Pittsburgh, PA 15260.

Sea Semester (not to be confused with the Semester at Sea) is a similar venture for water lovers, but it is designed for students more geared toward the "theoretical and practical" applications of the subject. Six twelve-week sessions are offered each year (obviously, overlapping), and there are twenty-four students in each session. Two prerequisites for the program are courses in college-level math and lab science. All majors are considered, as long as they're in good academic standing, submit transcripts and recommendations, and have an interview with an alumnus in their area. About two out of three are accepted.

Students spend the first half of the term living with families in the Woods Hole area and studying oceanography, maritime and nautical studies. Independent-study projects begun ashore are completed during the "sea component" aboard a 125-foot sailing research schooner, which cruises along the eastern seaboard and out into the Atlantic, North Atlantic or Caribbean, depending on the season. Six weeks on the ocean is when theory becomes reality, and the usual "mission" consists of enough navigation, oceanographic data collection, and record keeping to keep even Columbus on the right course.

Students from affiliated colleges (American,* Boston University,* Colgate,* College of Charleston,* Cornell,* Eckerd,* Franklin and Marshall,* the University of Pennsylvania* and Rice University*) receive a semester's worth of credit directly through their school. Students from other schools must receive credit through Boston University. The cost is around $6,800 (including room and board) and need-based financial aid is available. Usually, three-quarters of the financial aid requests are filled, and awards average about $2,000. Federal financial aid is transferable. Write to the Sea Education Association, P.O. Box 6, Woods Hole, MA 02543.

Don't get seasick yet—here comes one more. The **Williams College—Mystic Seaport Program in American Maritime Studies** enrolls twenty-one students each semester for studies in "man's relation with the sea; past, present, and future." Participants take four courses (American maritime history, maritime literature, a marine-policy seminar and oceanography or marine ecology) and journey ten days on a research vessel. In the fall semester, students sail from Woods Hole to the Gulf of Maine. In the spring, students fly to St. Petersburg, and their voyage takes them around the Florida peninsula to Miami.

Students live in small houses at the seaport, are responsible for their own cooking and cleaning, and must choose one of many maritime skills to develop under the supervision of the seaport staff. Juniors with a B average or higher are the norm, although "strong" sophomores are also considered. Since space is limited, half who apply to the program are turned away.

Most students are drawn from schools in the Twelve College Exchange* as well as Bates,* Colby,* Colgate,* Hamilton,* Middlebury,* Tufts* and Union,* but students from all four-year liberal-arts colleges are encouraged to apply. The cost of the entire deal is about $6,850. Write to the Williams–Mystic Program, Mystic Seaport Museum, Mystic, CT 06355.

The **Five College Consortium** is a nonprofit organization comprised of Amherst,* Hampshire,* Mount Holyoke,* Smith* and the University of Massachusetts at Amherst,* that is designed to enhance the social and cultural life of the thirty thousand students attending these Connecticut Valley colleges. Legally known as Five Colleges Inc., this cooperative arrangement allows any undergraduate at the four private liberal arts colleges and UMass to take courses for credit and use the library facilities of any of the other four schools. A free bus service shuttles among the schools.

The consortium sponsors a joint department of dance and a major in astronomy as well as a number of interdisciplinary programs, including black studies, East Asian language, coastal and marine studies, and international relations. Students from the four smaller colleges benefit from the large number of course choices available at UMass, especially in the hard sciences. The undergrads from UMass, in turn, take advantage of the small college atmosphere as well as particularly strong departments like art at Smith and sculpture at Mount Holyoke. There is also a Five College Orchestra and an open-theater auditions policy that allows students to audition for parts in productions at any of the colleges.

The social and cultural aspects of the Five College Consortium are more informal than the academic structure. The consortium, coordinated by an independent office, puts out a calendar listing art shows, lectures, concerts, films at the five schools, as well as the bus schedules. In addition, student-sponsored parties are advertised on all campuses, and there is a good deal of informal meeting of students from the various schools.

For those students taking courses on other campuses, one's home school meal ticket is valid on any of the five member campuses for lunch. Dinners are available with special permission. Taking classes in other schools is encouraged, but not usually for first-semester freshmen, and the consortium is a big drawing card for all schools involved.

The **Seven-College Exchange** consists of four women's schools (Hollins,* Mary Baldwin, Randolph–Macon Woman's* and Sweet Briar*) and one men's school (Hampden–Sydney) and two coed (Randolph–Macon and Washington and Lee*).

The exchange program was more popular when it began almost two decades ago and was utilized mainly for social reasons. Today, no more than a few dozen students participate, and officials say that they use the plan "strictly for academic reasons." Whatever and wherever, students must have at least a 2.0 average. Home school tuitions are the rule, and both sophomores and juniors are eligible. Students can utilize the foreign study programs at any of the seven colleges, and there is also some sharing of libraries and other resources.

The **Southern College/University Union,** established in 1969, currently comprising eight prestigious southern schools (Birmingham–Southern,* Centenary, Centre,* Fisk,* Millsaps,* Rhodes,* University of the South* and Vanderbilt*).

In addition to faculty development, the union sponsors two six-week summer study programs in England. Both cost students about $3,000 (travel not included). While students from nonmember institutions can apply, priority and financial aid are reserved for those of member schools. The first program, run through Rhodes College, is British Studies at Oxford, a high-quality English education experience for approximately 150 students. The second is International Studies in London, a political economy program for about seventy-five students run by Vanderbilt.

For the cost of a semester at their home institution, Southern College/University Union students can participate in the Oak Ridge lab semester (see the **Associated Colleges of the Midwest**).

The **Worcester Consortium** is made up of ten institutions nestled in and about Worcester, Massachusetts: Anna Maria, Assumption, Becker Junior, Central New England, Clark University,* Holy Cross,* Quinsigamond Community, the University of Massachusetts Medical Center, Worcester Polytechnic Institute* and Worcester State.

Member schools coordinate activities ranging from purchasing light bulbs to sharing libraries, and a bus transports scholars to the various campuses as well as public libraries. Academic cross-registration is offered, as are two special programs: a health studies option and a certificate in gerontology. The consortium also provides free academic and financial aid counseling to potential first-generation, low-income college students. Write the Educational Opportunity Center, 819 Main Street, Worcester, MA 01610.

SELECTIVE
GUIDE
to
Colleges

Adelphi University

Garden City, NY 11530

Location Suburban
Total Enrollment 10,490
Undergraduates 5,760
Male/Female 30/70
SAT V/M 490/530
Financial Aid 51%
Expense Pr $ $

Applicants 2,840
Accepted 62%
Enrolled 42%
Academics ★ ★
Social ☎ ☎
Q of L ● ●
Admissions (516)663-1100

Adelphi likes to think of itself as a place on the move—which may be the reason it has become famous for offering continuing-education courses on commuter trains. But Adelphi-on-Wheels is also a good way to describe life on this campus, where three-quarters of the students commute in and leave after class.

Adelphi students are generally native Long Islanders with a preprofessional bent, and its best schools are in preprofessional fields, notably nursing, social work, business, and banking. Students also speak highly of the departments of speech and hearing, theater, dance and communications. Other liberal-arts offerings, like art history and music, are nothing to sing about at the moment, but changes may be on the horizon—at least if Adelphi's new president has his way. With increasing competition for a shrinking pool of college-age students, Adelphi hopes to outdistance its rivals with a back-to-basics approach giving renewed emphasis to the undergraduate liberal arts. Part of that initiative will be to replace the current "embarrassing proliferation of courses and programs" with a unified core curriculum required for freshmen and sophomores.

Adelphi is proud of its small classes and personalized education. Though the school has almost 5,800 undergraduates, the largest classroom seats only sixty-five, and most classes enroll about twenty-five students. On the other hand, freshmen, who are among the last to register, sometimes must wait a year or two before they can get into all of the courses they want. The academic climate is mild and even those with the toughest majors "don't have to contend with a high-pressure environment," one premed student says. All students must take freshman English, and other requirements vary among departments.

A number of special options, such as independent study, an honors program, and study abroad (Israel is popular), are offered; and since Adelphi is so close to New York City, there is a good selection of internships, from one day a week to nearly full-time. Dentistry students can take advantage of a seven-year joint degree program with Georgetown University. In addition to its standard undergraduate fare, Adelphi offers all sorts of unusual programs—for middle-aged housewives, those seeking credits for life experience and commuters. The library boasts a computerized card catalogue for easy reference.

The relatively small number of Adelphi students who do not come from Long Island itself are likely to hail from one of the five boroughs of New York City, or from upstate—with a few immigrants from neighboring states thrown in. The campus atmosphere is casual and friendly, and as for the students, well, being in New York, Adelphi gets everything "from new wave liberal to conservative future businessman to athletic all-star," according to one junior. About 15 percent of the student body is Hispanic or black.

Never known as an intellectual's college, Adelphi is now actively recruiting top

3

high school graduates with a generous scholarship program. Financial aid, in fact, "is what holds many students here," one art and design major notes. Tuition is slashed an average of $2,000 for students who rank in the top 10 percent of their high school class or who have a B average and a combined SAT score of 1000. For high school valedictorians and a limited number of students who have attained academic records "of exceptional merit," awards range from half to full tuition. There also are one hundred athletic scholarships, forty of which are reserved for women. A relatively low endowment keeps Adelphi hustling for students, since tuition fees are the only thing that keep the coffers full.

Parking, which is the bane of life at many commuting schools, is no less a problem at Adelphi. Freshman commuters must park off campus and take a shuttle bus, which runs every ten minutes, the rest of the way. In theory, upperclassmen can park on campus, but actually finding a space is another story. Those who get a dorm room—usually students from relatively far away—find that they will be tripled up, at least for the first one or two semesters. There is one all-female dorm, and the rest are coed "by floor or by door." Freshmen and sophomores have priority for rooms. Squatters' rights prevail for upperclassmen, though most seniors choose to live off campus in nearby apartments. Dormies must take either two or three meals a day at one of several university cafeterias, where the food is usually edible, if not gourmet. The dining facilities provide one of the few places outside of class where commuters, boarders, and faculty can mingle.

Since many students trek home on weekends, Thursday and Friday nights are reserved for parties. The Rathskeller is the most popular place to hang out, especially during the weekly "Thursday Night Live" program for those twenty-one and older. When it closes, students head for local bars. Students fill in the time between classes at the campus arcade, or at various events sponsored by the Student Activity Board. The fraternities and sororities keep busy with their fund-raising events, beer blasts and carnivals. All are welcome at the festivities, which provide most of the on-campus weekend fun, though the 10 percent of students who are Greek tend to be clubby. Adelphi enjoys the benefits of a prime Long Island location; according to one student, "Adelphi has the best of both worlds—the excitement of New York City, and the closeness to many of Long Island's beaches." The city is about a half an hour away by train.

Adelphi has no football team, but the "much-adored" lacrosse team, along with the soccer and baseball teams, which all do well, help rally a bit of school spirit. Dorm teams usually play against each other in intramurals. While students complain about a lack of camaraderie because of all the commuters, those left on campus do find it easy to get to know one another. The modest number of boarders, as well as the small class size, helps give Adelphi a "small school atmosphere with large school advantages," one student notes.

Still, in part because Adelphi *is* primarily a commuter university, it lacks the cohesiveness, spirit, and unified sense of purpose found at many other schools. For students who want to commute in, learn a professional skill, and go home, Adelphi could be an ideal choice. Others should be wary—at least for the moment. The new president, who took office in 1986, has already instilled new life into the university, and the future looks promising for Adelphi's previously neglected liberal arts' offerings. Adelphi is on the move again, and in the right direction.

Agnes Scott College

Decatur, GA 30030

Location Suburban
Total Enrollment 520
Undergraduates 520
Male/Female N/A
SAT V/M 530/540
Financial Aid 51%
Expense Pr $ $

Applicants 350
Accepted 85%
Enrolled 49%
Academics ★ ★ ★
Social ☎ ☎
Q of L ● ● ●
Admissions (404)371-6285

"Aren't women's colleges slowly going out of business?" proposes an Agnes Scott College admissions brochure with seeming innocence. As one might guess, the answer is an emphatic "No," and Agnes Scott women would be the first to tell you so. With the fourth largest endowment per student in the nation and a seven-to-one student/faculty ratio, ASC boasts high-quality academics in an intimate learning environment—and the financial backing to keep it that way. Women and their potential for growth are taken seriously here.

Since its founding in 1889, Agnes Scott has been the best women's college south of Virginia. Secluded in Decatur, a quiet suburb of Atlanta about twenty minutes from downtown, ASC's wooded hundred-acre campus offers a mix of Gothic and Victorian buildings arranged around a central quadrangle. Despite the outward tranquility, academic life at ASC is far from serene. The work is rigorous and challenging, so much so that one student described the academic climate as "high pressure—about 220 degrees." And you know courses are taken *seriously* when students complain about the reduced library hours on weekends. Some of ASC's best departments include English, economics, biology and languages. The fine and performing arts have their own modern facility, while scientists can easily make their way to the school's own small observatory. Creative writers have the chance to rub elbows with real live practitioners of the art every springtime when the college sponsors a writers festival; would-be Heideggers can philosophize at ASC's own regional Undergraduate Philosophy Conference. Classes are rarely larger than twenty-five (most are fewer than fifteen), and students are lavished with personal attention from the faculty. "I have chatted at great length with professors I have never had in class," says a senior English major. The down side of ASC's size is that some courses are only taught every other year, and scheduling conflicts are sometimes a problem.

The emphasis here is mainly on the liberal arts. Freshmen must take two semesters each of English and physical education, and everyone must take a foreign language to the intermediate level in order to graduate. Other requirements include four semesters of humanities and fine arts, three in math and the natural sciences, and one in the social sciences. ASC is affiliated with the Presbyterian Church, and one course in either the Bible or philosophy is also mandatory. For those looking to get a leg up on the corporate ladder, ASC offers a prebusiness program with a full selection of internships. Upon graduation, over two-thirds of Agnes Scott graduates head directly for real-world jobs.

The popular "Return to College" program at Agnes Scott enables women of any age to complete an interrupted degree, sharing classes with the younger students. Students can spend their summers in Europe with one of several faculty-led adventures or participate in a marine or desert biology trip. Southerners who want a taste of the

5

California life-style can spend a semester at Mills College in Oakland, California, while engineers may complete their degree in a 3-2 program with Georgia Tech. The library has about 180,000 volumes, a daily courier service that retrieves needed books from other nearby schools, and even a cozy spot on the main floor where students can curl up in front of a fireplace. As part of the University Center of Georgia, Agnes Scott shares facilities and resources with fourteen other Atlanta-area schools.

The student body hails mainly from the Southeast, with 40 percent native Georgians. Most students share conservative upbringings and are "somewhat apathetic southern women who come from upper-middle-class to upper-class families," according to one. Nevertheless, over 85 percent of them are from public high schools, and blacks and Hispanics make up almost 10 percent of the student body. "We run the gamut from the independent women who have been on their own all the way to daddy's girls," says a senior English major. Nearly half ranked in the top 10 percent of their high school class, and almost all were in the top half. A strictly enforced honor system, which allows for self-scheduled exams and unmonitored tests, is frequently cited as the cornerstone of the college and is a big reason for the sense of community spirit that pervades the campus. Agnes Scott is need-blind in admissions and prides itself on meeting the demonstrated financial need of all its students. It also awards merit scholarships—ranging from $100 to $7,185—based on academic performance or musical ability and a personal interview.

Linked by tree-lined brick walks, dorms at Agnes Scott are large, spacious, and well maintained. The three older dorms, prized for their high ceilings and hardwood floors, have recently undergone renovation, but their lovely Gothic facades have been preserved. Upperclassmen, who draw rooms in a lottery, often get double rooms to themselves. Freshmen are assigned to places in three of the six dorms, which tend to be more "chummy" than the upperclass houses. No one lives off campus unless she is married or living at home. The food served in the cathedral-like dining hall is "adequate but not terrific," and students who want some fresh air can dine al fresco on an adjacent patio area when the weather is nice.

The honor system forbids the consumption of alcohol both on and off campus—Georgia's drinking age is nineteen—but many students admit to violating it a time or two during the course of their four years. ASC women generally spend their weekends "trying to meet guys," at monthly TGIFs (a euphemism for "beer blasts"), or quarterly proms at an Atlanta hotel. Nevertheless, be prepared for weekend traveling, more often than not to "that little trade school down on North Avenue," aka Georgia Institute of Technology, where many women attach themselves to a Tech fraternity as a "Lil Sis." Agnes Scott has no sororities because with only about 520 students, the college itself is a close-knit sisterhood. For stay-at-home types, a student activities center now under construction should improve the campus social scene somewhat.

One student claims that "there should be a direct rapid transit line from ASC to Georgia Tech and Emory University, because so many girls go there automatically." Atlanta's public transport is, in fact, convenient to campus and occasionally lures students in to the symphony or art museum, as well as to haunts where students can socialize with males. All in all, the bustling city of Atlanta is a "big plus" to this little college in Decatur, which the administration bills as "A Green Grove Near a Great City." Aside from a standout tennis team, varsity sports are underdeveloped. The administration has recently taken steps to bolster the athletic program by adding volleyball, basketball and soccer teams, as well as a new physical activities center and an outdoor track. Intramural activities range from studio dance to synchronized swimming.

The prescription for happiness at Agnes Scott is pretty straightforward: a small-town southern heritage, an interest in Georgia Tech football and Emory U beer, and above all, a desire to learn. Summarizes a sophomore: "Agnes Scott offers the best of the old and the new in a spirit of friendship and achievement."

University of Alabama—Tuscaloosa

Tuscaloosa, AL 35486

Location Suburban	**Applicants** 6,190
Total Enrollment 15,980	**Accepted** 75%
Undergraduates 13,300	**Enrolled** 60%
Male/Female 51/49	**Academics** ★★★
SAT V/M 470/510	**Social** ♨♨♨
ACT 22	**Q of L** ●●●
Financial Aid 46%	**Admissions** (205)348-5666
Expense Pub $	

In the popular psyche, the University of Alabama is synonymous with Bear Bryant, the late, legendary coach who led the Crimson Tide to bowl games for twenty-four consecutive years and racked up more total victories than any previous coach in NCAA history. Alabama's football team has a long tradition of gridiron glory, but unfortunately, its academic team isn't in the same league. To avoid getting thrown for a loss, students must pick and choose carefully among Alabama's many programs. Those who do will find strong offerings in a number of professional fields and several innovative interdisciplinary programs.

Designed to resemble Thomas Jefferson's famous University of Virginia campus, Alabama looks like a page out of history—amid the dogwoods and magnolias, it's hard to find a building that looks like it was built since the War Between the States. The beautiful, historical main quad is a must-see on every campus tour. "It is a friendly campus, with deep roots in tradition and a slower, more interesting life," is one public relations major's take. "I came here for a summer honors program during high school and was hooked."

The University of Alabama at Tuscaloosa supports eight undergraduate colleges and schools and a number of graduate divisions, including a law school. The most interesting is New College, an experimental unit founded in 1970 that enrolls two hundred students. Faculty members at New College teach in seminars only, and students are granted much flexibility in designing their courses of study. Emphatically not an honors college only, the school enrolls students with a wide range of academic abilities and interests, many of whom have yet to choose a major. New College was designed to be "a catalyst for change within the university," and already some of its programs—women's studies, career exploration, and the business internship, for example—have been incorporated into the larger schools and colleges. Innovative courses have spilled over into the Weekend College, a division of continuing education that has attracted a large undergraduate following, and also the popular interim terms (in January and June), where students may take one in-depth course for credit.

7

The School of Commerce and Business, popular among students, offers excellent programs in accounting and marketing. Engineering is also strong, though most of the state's top talent generally heads to Auburn. Alabama recently increased its emphasis on research, spurred in part by a joint venture between the university, General Motors and the United Auto Workers, which gives students the chance to "apply broad theoretical knowledge to real-world solutions to real-world problems." Twenty lucky students enroll in the Computer Based Honors Program, in which they are paid as research fellows to devise computer applications in their field of study. The university's relatively new core curriculum requires all students to take designated courses in writing, math, humanities, social and laboratory sciences, and foreign language or computer science.

The College of Arts and Sciences is uneven. The better programs include the natural sciences, English (especially creative writing), and history (note the southern history and culture program). Students in the liberal arts would be wise to enroll in the honors program, open to those who scored 1220 on the SAT or 27 on the ACT, or ranked in the top 10 percent of their high school class. Alabama also offers course work in four other schools—communications, education, home economics, and social work. The latter three are havens for women seeking an MRS. degree. Teaching assistants are no strangers to the classroom, and introductory lecture courses number well into the hundreds.

Though the university reaches across the country to recruit all-Americans for its football team, it has less success luring academic superstars. Over 70 percent of the students come from Alabama, though the state places no limit on the number of out-of-staters and does not hold them to stiffer admission requirements. Most students are conservative, laid back, and friendly, and want nothing more than to "get jobs (or husbands) and to make money," according to one undergrad. Several of Alabama's other state colleges are predominantly black, which may be part of the reason only 10 percent of Tuscaloosa's student body is black. For a publicly supported institution, 'Bama goes in for scholarship grants in a big way. Almost three hundred are earmarked for athletes, and the university awards another 2,500, at an average of $650, for academic achievement. National Merit Scholars automatically qualify, and 150 Presidential Scholars receive full scholarships.

Most university students live in apartments in the Tuscaloosa area or in the Greek houses, but about a quarter of them (with women outnumbering men) live in campus dorms. Since "this is the Bible Belt, we have no coed dorms, nor will we ever," according to a senior. Most halls have recently been renovated and boast new carpet and furniture, as well as computer facilities and study areas. Six of the dorms also have cafeterias, and the student union building also has a number of dining facilities. About 15 percent of students live in Greek houses, and many dine there as well.

Students spend their free time about evenly between the town (decent shopping facilities and bars) and the campus, where fraternity and sorority parties provide most of the action, especially when it comes to celebrating football victories. About 20 percent of the student body is Greek affiliated; and though individual organizations vary in exclusivity, few people are turned away who want to join the system. The range of other campus organizations is impressive: everything from the Society for Creative Anachronism (medievalists), to Bible study groups, to the sailing club. "The intramural program is a big part of our college life," one woman claims. As for varsity sports? "Are you kidding? This is Alabama. Football is king!" enthuses a senior. Basketball, baseball and swimming programs are understudies to the gridiron Crimson Tide. A recently built student recreation center includes racquetball and an indoor track. When all else fails, students are content to "just sit around, watch TV, and shoot the bull," according to a finance major.

Alabama is a B-grade university that in recent years has instituted some innovative programs in an effort to attract better students. The administration clings to the assertion that football is a "social *and* academic focal point of the whole university"—the reason, one assumes, that Bear Bryant received an honorary Doctor of Laws degree at the 1981 commencement. While there are still many students who care more about football and partying than anything else, the university's recent push for academic excellence has made 'Bama a viable choice for serious students. Says one marketing major, "It's a growing influential university."

Albion College

Albion, MI 49224

Location Small town	**Applicants** 1,520
Total Enrollment 1,640	**Accepted** 91%
Undergraduates 1,620	**Enrolled** 34%
Male/Female 48/52	**Academics** ★★★
SAT V/M 530/570	**Social** ☎☎
Financial Aid 50%	**Q of L** ●●●
Expense Pr $ $	**Admissions** (517)629-5920

Academic excellence, personal attention and a congenial atmosphere characterize Albion College, long ranked as one of Michigan's best private colleges. Founded in 1835, Albion continues to attract a mainly ambitious, bright, pink-cheeked and conservative bunch of students (although "lately, quite a few liberals are sneaking into the freshman classes"). And its historical affiliation with the Methodist Church has little present-day effect on campus life. Instead, Albion places its emphasis on providing students with preprofessional experience within the context of liberal arts.

The college resides in its namesake town, which is small, industrial, economically depressed and, in the words of one student, "dry of resources." But the Albion campus is heavy on charm with a beautiful central quad enclosed by buildings of "Ivy League" architectural style. There's plenty of open space, a gorgeous Nature Center and lots of statuesque pines. "Even through the addition of new facilities, the college has kept a very traditional setting," states one student.

Albion integrates its required liberal-artsy core of courses with popular professional programs such as that of the Gerald R. Ford Institute for Public Service (prelaw), which includes a one-semester internship in a government-related position. Also requiring an internship, and another favorite with the students, is the professional management program (aka prebusiness). The premedical biology/chemistry program continually draws dedicated undergrads, and economics and English garner respect from students. With all these top-notch preprograms, it's not surprising that almost all Albion graduates who apply are accepted into law, business, and medical schools. Psychology, music, education and physical education departments are small and definitely in the need-improvement category. Physics is reported by students to be nothing to write home about, and the cuts in the number of history professors has "definitely weakened that department," says one junior.

The college maintains a separately endowed Center for the Study of Ethics, which "focuses attention on ethical concerns central to liberal learning and leadership within society." Another recent addition is the new Women's Studies Center. Students with superior academic backgrounds are selected to enter into an honor's program that includes special seminars, classes and a thesis. Albion also allows students to design their own majors. No religious study is required, and, according to one student, "You couldn't guess that Albion is a Methodist college—in fact, many students don't realize it."

Academic pressure at Albion is ranked as medium to high. Many students put pressure on themselves to make the grade, partly in an effort to get into graduate school, and partly in a "need to get your $11,000 out of it." Still, this sum is considered a bargain by some, primarily due to the low professor/student ratio. Class size can range anywhere from three to one hundred, but the average class has about twenty students. Professors are interested not only in students' academic performance but also in their emotional well-being, and are apt to hold classes in their homes or invite students to dinner. There are two adjoining campus libraries complete with computer facilities, a listening lab for foreign language or music study and a helpful staff. The interlibrary-loan service is also useful, as are weekly bus trips to the University of Michigan libraries in Ann Arbor.

Most Albion students are from Michigan and the surrounding states, with a few from other regions of the country and abroad. In general, the students are a pretty homogeneous bunch: white, upper middle class, conservative. "It's easy to pick out students who don't quite fit into the 'Albion Mode,'" proclaims a senior. "Many do not stay, but it's great when they do—they give a little push to challenge the predominate conservative attitude." While its small size is often cited as an important benefit of Albion, sometimes the college seems too small to students who claim that rumors spread fast and that everyone knows (or claims to know) what everyone else is up to. A third of incoming freshmen rank in the top tenth of their high school graduating class, and 95 percent are in the top half. Need-based financial aid packages can be hefty, and 28 percent of all undergrads receive merit scholarships based on academic records, test scores and demonstrated leadership abilities. Athletic scholarships are a no-no.

Few students live off campus in Albion, largely due to the comfortable and well-maintained campus dormitories. By far the favorite dorm is Wesley Hall (a "fabulous, newly renovated dorm, which even has microwave ovens") where the entire freshman class lives. Dorms are coed by hall or floor, and rooms are assigned by lottery. Other housing options are a limited number of annexes and co-ops, the beautiful on-campus home of a past college president, and the fraternity houses. (Sororities do not have houses but hold their meetings in lodges.) Two large, recently remodeled dining rooms feed all campus residents on an inflexible twenty-one-meal-a-week plan. Those who live in annexes may cook for themselves, but the food service is considered to be better than college-average. And oh what a salad bar—"it would give Ponderosa a run for its money!"

Since the town of Albion is often less than exciting, on the weekend many students travel to one of the nearby larger towns, Jackson or Battle Creek, or make the hour-long trek to Ann Arbor or Lansing, homes of the U. of M. and Michigan State University, respectively, for a taste of big-campus social life. Lake Michigan beaches are an hour-and-a-half drive; but closer still is the Kalamazoo River, and canoes are available for students to use free of charge. Horseback riding, cross-country skiing, plays, sporting events, concerts (featuring such name groups as the Romantics) also keep students occupied in their spare time. More than half of the students belong to one of Albion's six national fraternities and six sororities. (After all, this is the school where, seventy-five years ago, two fraternity brothers composed a well-known tune—"The Sweetheart of Sigma Chi"—that inspired the little sister fraternity tradition.) Greek parties draw large crowds—Greek and non-Greek—and are the social center of the campus. The varsity football team has enjoyed recent success, and basketball games are usually well attended. Intramural sports are also popular (and competitive) and should get better with improvements to the indoor athletic facilities on the near-future agenda.

In general, Albion students are quite happy with the "personalized education" they receive. Professors are accessible and interested, academics are challenging without overwhelming pressure, and students are easygoing and friendly. Although one student complains that "sometimes I feel like I'm in a bubble—like it's not the real world," a classmate brags that she has gotten to know "a lot of people on a level that is deeper than 'Hi, how are you.'" At Albion, anonymity can never be a problem.

Alfred University

Alfred, NY 14802

Location Rural	**Applicants** 1,800
Total Enrollment 2,430	**Accepted** 80%
Undergraduates 1,880	**Enrolled** 36%
Male/Female 56/44	**Academics** ★ ★ ★
SAT V/M 500/580	**Social** 🏛 🏛 🏛
Financial Aid 65%	**Q of L** ● ● ●
Expense Pr $ $ $	**Admissions** (607)871-2116

Alfred University is conspicuously uncategorical. It's awfully small to be called a university, and it's not exactly a private school either (one third of its students are enrolled in its public ceramics program and pay public school tuition). The academic community consists of artists and engineers, nurses and scientists, accountants and psychologists. Yet while outsiders may be perplexed about how to define this energetic, multifaceted community, a junior sums it up in one word: "Excelsior."

A charming, close-knit group of modern and old brick buildings along with a stone castle peacefully coexist in a small valley of upstate New York's hilly wilds. Alfred bills itself as an educational village in which students can pursue their studies in a locale where not only the school, but also the whole town, is dedicated to "the industry" of higher education. The town of Alfred consists of two colleges (the other is Alfred Tech, a junior college), a main street with one stoplight, and little else. "The quiet atmosphere does allow for better study habits," says a business major. "But students who need big city excitement should avoid Alfred."

The university and its students share a no-nonsense approach to education. Half of all requirements for a bachelor's degree must be earned in the liberal arts college. Oral and written communications, math and computer literacy competencies are all necessary for graduation.

Alfred is actually the "host" school for the New York State School of Ceramics, which is a unit of the state university system. Ceramic engineering (the development and refinement of ceramic materials) is the undisputed king of the academic castle at Alfred, for it is the one program that brings international recognition to the college. The ceramic art department, with its programs in glass, printmaking, sculpture, video, and teacher certification, is also well regarded. The School of Art and Design, a recent addition to the College of Ceramics, receives less enthusiastic review from students, but does offer an unusual graphic design major in which students use electronic and computer equipment. The business administration school provides undergraduates with work experience through a small business institute where students have real clients. The nursing school is one of the best in the state, with students getting a year's worth of clinical experience in a Rochester hospital, and graduates getting excellent scores on the licensing exam. Many majors offer a co-op program that alternates work and study.

The science and humanities programs are the weakest links in Alfred's curricular chain, but psychology, gerontology and biology are meritorious majors. Other interesting opportunities include a performing arts major with an internship in a professional symphony, theater or dance company as well as a new major in foreign language and culture that sponsors trips abroad. Exchange programs are available with European colleges and technical schools. The Track II honors program enables students to do independent interdisciplinary work with close personal attention from top faculty members.

The university stresses its commitment to help indecisive undergrads plan their future, and career planning, academic services, and advisement are all strong enough for Alfred to deliver on the promise. Even the library staff is reported to be quite helpful—"if they don't have the required materials, they will scour the country for them."

More than two-thirds of the students are from New York State, 84 percent from public schools, and 52 percent from the top fifth of their high school classes. "Students are basically conscious and academically oriented," assesses an applied clinical psychology major, "though there is a sincere effort to reach out to other people and be cooperative rather than competitive." Another student contends that "the main interests are having 'other interests' to complement the academics." Alfred attempts to enroll freshmen regardless of their financial need, but there are no workable aid package guarantees. A whopping 20 percent of the students are awarded merit scholarships, ranging from $500 to $4,000. Entering freshmen with good academic records are eligible.

No one minds the two-year on-campus residency requirement, since the rooms are large and comfortable and the dorms well equipped with lounges, kitchens, laundry facilities, and some even have such extras as computers and saunas. Upperclassmen have a choice of coed-by-room dorms, one of which has only single rooms, while freshmen enjoy their own coed-by-floor housing divided into doubles or suites for six people. About 16 percent of the students rent apartments in Alfred's small downtown area, with another 16 percent in the frats. The school has two dining halls (one for six hundred people, another three hundred) and a choice of the fifteen- or twenty-one-meal plans. Freshmen and sophomores are required to dine on cafeteria cuisine, which renders an enormous variety of regular buffets, plus a salad bar, a deli line, and daily international lines.

Alfred's location in Finger Lakes territory, almost two hours from Buffalo and Rochester, is so isolated that the only escape from campus life is into the hills. Students are dedicated to outdoor activities: skiing, hunting, camping and rock climbing. Varsity men's and women's soccer and basketball, as well as men's football and swimming are the top athletic squads. Fraternities and sororities (ten organizations, all told) provide most of the spark for Alfred's social life, and one-third of the students are members. The Student Senate Activities Board plans more events than a single student could hope to attend, and other extracurricular activities are always looking for a few good organizational-type undergrads.

"Alfred gives you exposure to a whole different way of life," comments a senior.

Those who can't abide cold winters or who feel that life can't exist in a rural setting should not consider this upstate school. Although students are active and take their studies seriously, one student notes, "there isn't a fast-paced 'rush hour' atmosphere." Such a juxtaposition makes Alfred and its students simply indescribable.

Allegheny College

Meadville, PA 16335

Location Small town	**Applicants** 2,190
Total Enrollment 1,870	**Accepted** 82%
Undergraduates 1,840	**Enrolled** 30%
Male/Female 50/50	**Academics** ★ ★ ★
SAT V/M 540/570	**Social** ☎ ☎ ☎
Financial Aid 57%	**Q of L** ● ● ●
Expense Pr $ $	**Admissions** (814)724-4351

Tucked away in Pennsylvania's northern hinterland ninety minutes from both Pittsburgh and Cleveland, Allegheny College has built a strong regional reputation on its low student-faculty ratio and the high placement rate seniors enjoy at professional schools and in the business world. While catering to students' preprofessional demands, the college has not strayed from the liberal arts ideals that shaped its beginnings in 1815.

The competitive premed program weeds out many early hopefuls but ends up placing 75 percent of its students in medical school. Acceptance rates at law and business schools are even higher. Biology, chemistry, English, history and political science are traditionally strong, and current students also praise psychology, the earth sciences and foreign languages. The arts and communications divisions, however, could be better. There are five-year BA/MA programs in engineering, forestry, medical technology, nursing and education. Whatever the department, you can count on close contact with faculty members. The average class has only about twenty students, and almost one-third of the courses enroll fewer than ten. The faculty is very accessible and committed to teaching. "The 'top profs' teach introductory courses as well as higher level ones," says one junior. Undergraduates must take three courses each in natural sciences, social sciences and humanities. The college also places great emphasis on writing, a skill that is incorporated into most courses and departments. Juniors take a special seminar in their major, which is followed by the grueling "senior project"—an independent study culminating in a presentation, written or performed, and an oral exam. The comp is the climax of any Allegheny student's career, and undergraduates react to the challenge with a mixture of awe, dread, and satisfaction. Though Allegheny is affiliated with the Methodist Church, there is no religion requirement.

Allegheny runs on trimesters: three ten-week terms with a long break from Thanksgiving to New Year's. Exams are given more frequently than on a conventional calendar—"Ten week terms keep you on your toes," a senior notes—but students take only three courses a term, which allows greater attention to each one. The library is adequately stocked for a college of Allegheny's size, but for in-depth research students must sometimes resort to an interlibrary loan from other schools. Perhaps the library's most attractive feature is its microcomputer lab that includes about fifty personal computers for student use. For a break from the standard grind, Allegheny offers study in Washington or abroad, a popular on-campus independent-study option, and term-length internships or "externships" (a chance to observe a professional at work during the winter vacation).

Allegheny attracts serious-minded students who are willing to work extremely hard to get good grades. "It's a very high-pressure, competitive environment," reports one senior. Most students have professional goals in mind from the beginning. Almost 60 percent head directly into the business world after graduation, while another quarter move on to professional school. About half the student body hails from Pennsylvania (especially Pittsburgh and its environs) and sizable contingents come from nearby upstate New York and New England. There is a cohesive minority-group community on campus that makes up about 5 percent of the student body. The college has an honor code that allows students to take exams unproctored. Allegheny is need-blind in admissions and meets the demonstrated need of practically everyone who applies on time. Three programs offer eighty merit scholarships a year, ranging from $1,500 to $5,000. One is based on a competitive exam given to all applicants, another is awarded for academics and extracurricular activities, and the third is reserved for bright students with "strong values and ethical convictions."

Situated on 165 acres of hills, trees, flowers, benches and walkways, Allegheny's campus is so pretty that area residents often use it as a backdrop for their wedding pictures. A dozen dorms accommodate its undergraduates in relative style and comfort (complete with TV and study rooms) and offer a variety of living situations: all-freshmen dorms, coed and single-sex halls, small houses, and single, double and triple rooms. Everyone who wants a dorm room can have one, although a sizable minority of upperclassmen move into off-campus apartments. Three dining halls, one of them for upperclassmen only, serve average college cuisine. Another option is the coed Allegheny Men's Dining Club, which offers an independent (or, as they put it, "relevant") alternative to fraternity-house dinners. The architectural styles range from modern to Federalist era buildings full of old-world charm.

Unfortunately, the architecture at Allegheny isn't the only thing reminiscent of the old world. The weather in Meadville—aka "Mudville" to students—is soggy enough to make any Briton feel right at home. According to the college viewbook, "There is an old joke about Meadville that states: 'How do I get to Meadville?' 'Drive until you hit rain and then look for the signs.'"

Greek organizations are a powerful force on Allegheny's campus and provide a great deal of the nightlife. The seven fraternities enjoy their own housing, while the five sororities are relegated to special dorm suites. Downtown Meadville is ten minutes from campus but offers little in the way of excitement. Even the bars are off-limits to all but the oldest students because of Pennsylvania's drinking age of twenty-one. Off-campus parties provide some relief, but the drinking age is enforced at dorm parties. And frequent Saturday classes tend to put a damper on the double-dose weekend social life. Nevertheless, "Allegheny graduates are creative and know how to have a good time," a journalism major asserts. The nearest getaway is Lake Erie, and there are ski areas, beaches, and shopping malls within an hour's drive. In athletics, men's golf and swimming and women's basketball, softball and swimming are the leading sports, but Allegheny teams give their Division III competitors a run for their money on almost every field and court. The recent addition of four playing fields has increased the space available for outdoor sports.

Allegheny has two major drawbacks: It is not widely known outside the region, and the campus is "somewhat isolated from the rest of the world." What it does have are strong academic programs, lots of personal attention, and a highly motivated student body with its sights set squarely on the job market. Those looking to combine the liberal arts with preprofessional training should thrive in this out-of-the-way corner of the world.

Alma College

Alma, Michigan 48801

Location Rural	**Accepted** 90%
Total Enrollment 1,030	**Enrolled** 38%
Undergraduates 1,030	**Academics** ★ ★ ★
Male/Female 46/54	**Social** 🐾 🐾 🐾
ACT 25	**Q of L** ● ● ●
Financial Aid 72%	**Admissions** (800)292-9078
Expense Pr $ $	in Michigan, (800)292-9267 out of state
Applicants 870	

Though it sprouts out of farmland some distance from even a minor urban area, Alma College specializes in preparing its customers for the real world. A trained professional staff provides career-planning workshops and individual counseling throughout a student's college years, and numerous top firms visit the campus to recruit seniors. In fact, over the last five years Alma has seen to it that more than 94 percent of its graduates have been placed in a job or graduate school within ninety days of graduation. Now *that's* an Alma Mater.

Small but beautiful describes the campus that has been plunked down in the exact geographical center of Michigan's lower peninsula. Trees and open grassy space abound. All the buildings wear the same red brick "for consistency," and most have been either built or renovated in the past three decades. In addition to physical improvements, Alma has made a conscious and determined effort in the past several years to significantly raise its academic standards.

Liberal arts distribution requirements account for more than a third of the degree requirements. The premed sciences, as well as math and computer science, are considered among the strongest offerings, and the abundance of prelaw types flock to the superb history and social science programs. One-third of the students choose to major in business administration or international business, the latter linking foreign language study and travel with preparation for the multinational corporate world. Speech, journalism, theater and dance all need revitalization. But the college has added performance scholarships for talented students and plans to build a new performing arts facility.

One Alma program designed to address the realities of the contemporary job market is exercise and health science, which deals with corporate fitness and health maintenance as well as opportunities in the medical setting. A public affairs institute that offers a peacemaking and conflict resolution minor also attracts student interest. Foreign language offerings on Alma's Michigan campus are limited; still the school has managed to develop strong international programs. Students may take advantage of study-abroad programs in France, Germany, Spain and Mexico or use their month-long spring term to do field work or take an intensive course in such exotic spots as Jamaica, Portugal, and Israel. Three-two programs in engineering, forestry, and wildlife are offered in conjunction with the University of Michigan, as is occupational therapy with Washington University.

Faculty members rate high "not only as instructors, but as friends and resources." Class size verges on the intimate, but getting into a required course is seldom a major problem. "If a student really needs a class," explains one woman, "the prof invariably enlarges the class." The recently renovated library provides more study space as well as shelf space for books previously in storage. But in-depth research usually requires a trek to the library of one of Michigan's larger schools.

In keeping with the school's high hopes for their professional success, Alma students are an ambitious lot, their attention honed on "where they are going after Alma," according to a prelaw student. The campus is overwhelmingly conservative, "although the liberal voice is coming out a little." Blacks and Hispanics account for less than 2 percent of the students, and while out-of-state recruiting is increasing, a whopping 93 percent of the students are Michiganers. The financial aid department is described as "not as eager to help students as it is to help prospective students," by an empty-pocketed upperclassman. But Alma does award a large number of merit scholarships, from $200 to $4,000, on the basis of academic achievement and artistic talent.

Alma's location "in the middle of nowhere" means that almost all students have to live on campus. Freshmen are assigned rooms in single-sex and coed dorms, while upperclassmen play the lottery and generally end up in suites. A coed international house and several small single-sex housing units (including frats and sororities) round out the housing choices. Everyone subcribes to one meal plan and imbibes at the Commons, "which makes things hectic at times." The quality of the meals is standard institutional, but for the most part, Alma students seem indifferent to their culinary education.

Fraternity and sorority members make up about 50 percent of the campus, but according to one senior, "The Greek life's in trouble right now." It seems the new campus alcohol policy has cramped the frat style, and students have been heading away from the dry frat parties and into the bars. Says a history major, "Social life on campus is very restricted and closely monitored. The policies tend to ignore the fact that we are legally adults." The Union Board oversees regular social and entertainment events, movies are shown every weekend, and residence events are sponsored by the dorms.

Alma College is less than an hour from Lansing (translate Michigan State) and about fifteen minutes from Mt. Pleasant (Central Michigan University). There is mutual respect between the town of Alma and the college itself: "Local merchants love us," explains one student. Ski slopes are an hour away, and for warm weather diversion, students can always hit the "pits"—old gravel pits filled with water and surrounded by sandy beaches. Intramural as well as varsity sports are a major part of life at Alma, with the women's teams often stealing the thunder from the men's. Many students are attracted to Alma because of its excellent intercollegiate standing in sports such as basketball, cross-country, softball, track, field hockey and volleyball.

For the individual who does not want to give up history and literature for preprofessional training, Alma offers a compromise. Its curriculum integrates the traditional liberal arts with the practical considerations of establishing a career in the waning years of the twentieth century. If one is somewhat unclear about what career avenue to pursue, Alma might be a good place to sort it all out. The remoteness of the school certainly provides a proper setting for introspection, and the upbeat social life won't let you get too serious. Like the farmland that surrounds it, Alma is, according to the analysis of a psychology major, "Friendly, personal, down-to-earth—a good place to grow."

Alverno College

Milwaukee, WI 53215

Location Suburban	**Applicants** 920
Total Enrollment 1,830	**Accepted** 72%
Undergraduates 1,830	**Enrolled** 73%
Male/Female N/A	**Academics** ★ ★ ★
ACT 18	**Social** ☎
Financial Aid 75%	**Q of L** ● ● ● ●
Expense Pr $	**Admissions** (414)382-6100

In the early 1970s, a small Roman Catholic women's college located in a residential area of southside Milwaukee began asking itself an intriguing question: How do you provide a relevant liberal arts and preprofessional education to highly motivated local women who are, for the most part, already employed full-time? The answer: You devise a competency-based curriculum emphasizing mastery of specific skills and areas of understanding, rather than simply offering run-of-the-mill courses with letter grades. The result: Alverno College has established itself as one of the most innovative colleges in the country. "Here," explains one student, "learning is a process."

Alverno's cozy, park-like campus has three main academic buildings that feature brick and stone exteriors and stained glass windows. The school organizes its unique curriculum around eight abilities, ranging from logical and critical thinking, to understanding the arts and humanities, to global awareness and cross-cultural understanding. These skills are integrated into traditional courses. There are no grades in the traditional sense, and students move through interdisciplinary, progressive levels toward a degree by being "validated" in the eight areas. For example, a course in sociology might contribute to validation in communication and social interaction, as well as to validation in making independent value judgments. Students demonstrate their competence all the while in a noncompetitive but intense atmosphere that emphasizes the relationship between liberal and religious traditions and everyday life. If it sounds confusing, that's because it is. "Coming from a letter-grading system, it seems frightening and highly ambiguous—but after your first semester, things fall into place," an art therapy major assures. "It's a very exciting awakening."

Alverno is really two colleges rolled into one. There is a regular weekday program that attracts traditional college-age women, the majority of them from Milwaukee. Many in this group are the first in their family to enroll in college. Then there is the Weekend College, which allows working women, most of them older, many divorced, to earn a degree in four years by attending classes every other weekend. About eight hundred students enroll in the Weekday College, while just over a thousand opt for the weekend sessions. Sixty percent of the students have full- or part-time jobs. Students may also earn credit by spending four to eight hours a week in internships related to their field of study. Alverno's nursing, business and music programs are solid and well established. Education is strong and gaining popularity. Students also praise the professional communication and business management programs. The library holds a modest ninety thousand titles—mainly in nursing, education and psychology—and for major research projects students must often make interlibrary loans or trek to Marquette or the University of Wisconsin.

Enrollment has increased in recent semesters, "and some classes are large enough to approach being unwieldy," states a business management student. Still, faculty members are teaching-oriented and concerned about students. "All the instructors I've had so far have asked us to call them by their first name," says one senior. Academic counseling and individual attention are offered throughout a student's academic career. Career-advising services are good, too, and Alverno graduates are extremely successful in getting into graduate and professional schools, though many work for several years before applying.

Many students are older than typical college age, and quite a few have children. Students "hold conservative values but are liberal in their attitude about a woman's place in today's society," a nursing major explains. Only 14 percent ranked in the top tenth of their high school classes; almost three-quarters were in the top half. The vast majority of the students are on financial aid, and academic scholarships of up to $4,920 are awarded to almost a quarter of them, based on a personal evaluation of each incoming student. Though only a tenth of the students live on campus, the dorms are clean and comfortable with a sink in each room. Roommates are paired based on questionnaires. Male visitors are allowed, but they must sign in and be out by 11 PM on weekdays and 2 AM on weekends; they can stay overnight in a guest room for $2. Most of the women who live in the dorms are Weekday College students. The dormies are required to buy the meal plan at the dining commons, which features half-portions and a salad bar. Students must fend for themselves on the weekend when the dining room closes. Meals are the focus of the school's social life and provide a good chance to mingle with professors.

The city of Milwaukee has many attractions: a myriad of parks and shopping centers, a performing arts center, ethnic festivals in the fall, free outdoor concerts; most students prefer the social life of the city to the college. Alverno is ten minutes by bus from the city center. Just as it emphasizes lifetime learning, Alverno promotes "lifetime sports" and sponsors a Wellness Center and such courses as aerobics and modern dance. There are no organized athletics, varsity or intramural per se, but the school has a jogging track and gymnasium and plenty of opportunity for tennis and cross-country skiing. The college also sponsors dance and theater groups.

Alverno is no place to look for a husband, nor much of a place for a social life. There is an on-campus pub but students frequent fraternities at a nearby engineering school for a real party. Although Alverno was founded by the School Sisters of St. Francis, the religious atmosphere is low-key. The teaching sisters wear street clothes and are called by their first names. Forty percent of the students are actually non-Catholic. Religious studies aren't required. However, for those who seek it, there is a lovely chapel with masses every other Saturday evening.

Perhaps the most striking quality about Alverno, other than its unique curriculum, is its quiet feminism. By background and training, Alverno students are not political activists, but there is among both teachers and students an underlying determination to further the lot of women in American society and to support one another in the process. "Alverno's sense of sincere caring and individual learning philosophies have greatly contributed to the self-assured woman I have become," says a senior. "And I believe the end product tells it all."

The American University

Washington, DC 20016

Location Suburban
Total Enrollment 11,000
Undergraduates 5,360
Male/Female 40/60
SAT V/M 540/560
Financial Aid 60%
Expense Pr $ $ $

Applicants 6,820
Accepted 62%
Enrolled 26%
Academics ★ ★ ★
Social ☎ ☎ ☎
Q of L ● ● ●
Admissions (202)885-6000

The best thing about The American University is its location in a suburb of Washington, D.C. With an extensive government internship program, courses on every topic even remotely related to politics, and a guest speaker list that reads like a Who's Who of American political life, the university unabashedly caters to students who have set their sights on a career inside the beltway. Without the city, there would be little reason for American's existence, nor any for students to attend.

Situated in an affluent residential district at the far end of Embassy Row, the university has built a reputation for bringing the "resources of the nation's capital to the campus." More than 1,500 students a year take three- to six-credit internships as part of their course load, and the university has established ties with more than nine hundred private, nonprofit, or government institutions. It also uses these connections in its Washington Semester* and the co-op program, available in a wide range of majors. Another benefit of the university's location is the impressive list of lecturers and speakers streaming to campus—everyone from Gerald Ford to Dr. Ruth has visited at one time or another.

Most if not all of the university's strongest programs have some connection to life in D.C., including public policy, communications, government and international service. Related subjects of foreign languages and economics enjoy a well-deserved reputation, and the business program also is strong. Students interested in the performing arts, sciences and education would be well advised to look elsewhere. The university offers a wide range of study-abroad programs, in cities from Bonn to Buenos Aires, as well as an exchange with Leeds University in England, which allows six top political science majors to spend part of their junior year as interns in the British Parliament. American's location helps draw top-notch professors to its faculty, which is replete with adjunct professors who divide their time between American and jobs in Washington and offer a wealth of real-world experience. Despite some of their off-campus obligations, many of the professors remain accessible to students. American is affiliated with the Methodist Church, but no mixing of religion and politics is required.

Though the university has never enjoyed a stellar academic reputation, standards have risen substantially in the 1980s. In the past three years alone, applications have jumped 50 percent, while enrollment has gone up by nearly a third. Median SAT scores are also up, and undergraduates now must follow a general education program requiring thirty credit hours in English, the arts and humanities, science and social science. A new library has been a welcome addition on campus and students report that the study lounges are becoming increasingly crowded. Nevertheless, the academic scene is still far from competitive. "There is very little pressure among students," one business major says. "It is understood that everyone does well."

AU boasts a diverse population, drawing students from every state and 120 foreign countries. A little under 10 percent are black or Hispanic and about 12 percent are foreign. While the university justifiably prides itself on being a national and international hub, there's a significant contingent of middle- and upper-class students from New York and its environs. The prevailing social and political mode is liberal, and students, for the most part, are career-oriented. Over half graduate in the top fifth of their high school class but about 12 percent come from the bottom half.

Recognizing the problems that many families have with an annual college bill that exceeds $12,000, AU provides about 450 merit scholarships of up to $4,467 each year for outstanding students. Minimum requirements include a 3.3 high school GPA and a combined SAT score of 1150. Nearly one hundred athletes in eight sports are awarded athletic scholarships, and there is even a fund for children of Methodist ministers. Because of a housing crunch, the university only guarantees dorm rooms to freshmen, and many students move into group houses in the surrounding suburban area as upperclassmen. The dorms are equipped with "the bare essentials" for living and all are coed, except for one women's dorm, which is less rowdy than the others. Leonard Hall, the international dorm, is considered one of the best places to live on campus. Boarders may choose from a range of meal plans or cook on their own using dorm kitchen facilities.

A prominent feature in AU's dorms is the noise level. Although most students consider socializing an essential part of undergraduate life, there is the occasional student who complains "I'm paying for an education, not a party." On weekends the revelry continues up and down the streets of swanky Georgetown, which is loaded with bars, restaurants and punky boutiques. Transportation in and around D.C. is easy and cabs are affordable. AU men's basketball, soccer and golf teams are decent, but sports are not the center of attention here. The university currently lacks a decent athletic facility, although a sports and convocation center is in the works. Only a small percentage of the students join fraternities and sororities, and on-campus parties are more likely to start at AU's popular Tavern.

Students agree that the main reasons they come to AU are location, location and location. All who want to capitalize on Washington's resources will find American an invigorating home base.

Amherst College

Amherst, MA 01002

Location Small town	**Applicants** 1,580
Total Enrollment 1,560	**Accepted** 21%
Undergraduates 1,560	**Enrolled** 42%
Male/Female 57/43	**Academics** ★ ★ ★ ★ ★
SAT V/M N/A	**Social** ☎ ☎ ☎
Financial Aid 37%	**Q of L** ● ● ●
Expense Pr $ $ $ $	**Admissions** (413)512-2328

This is not the Amherst that Grandpa and Dad knew. Women are in, frats are out. A new free-wheeling curriculum has been instated, and there's a new gymnasium with not one but two swimming pools. Yet some things never change, and this quintessential

New England school has remained staunchly devoted to excellence in undergraduate education.

Variations on traditionalism have also permeated the campus architecture. While Amherst's predominant style is still nineteenth-century academia—"red brick is the key," says one student—everything from a "pale yellow octagonal structure to a garish, modern new dorm" can be found here. But whether or not students approve of the structural growth, no one complains about the ideal setting of lusciously green knolls and valleys and enough large, healthy trees to drop a thick, multicolor blanket of leaves each fall.

In keeping with the school's established emphasis on the inquiring mind, Amherst's new curriculum is guided by the philosophy that education is an activity, not a body of knowledge. The only college-wide required course, Introduction to Liberal Studies, encompasses several seminar classes from which students choose one. The seminars are taught by two or more professors from different disciplines and designed to foster thinking across many lines of traditional study. Other than that, students pick a major, fulfill the departmental program requirements and perform satisfactorily on comprehensive exams in the major field. The administration says of this approach to college education that "a student should be free at this stage to make choices—even foolish choices."

Particularly noteworthy departments include Russian, neuroscience and music. ("They don't call this 'the singing college' for nothing," says a senior.) The most popular offerings—English, political science, economics, psychology and history—are top-notch, and students are able to mix and match among these subjects to create their own dual-degree, interdisciplinary programs. Pioneering in the field of American studies was done here, and the program remains strong. Two new programs in international and women's studies are gaining interest and enthusiasm, but students are critical of the romantic languages and fine arts. Computer science courses benefit from sleek facilities. Amherst has more than its share of prelaw, prebusiness and premed candidates, and the last group reports that the natural science departments are strong but cruel. Even pre-nothings find the workload demanding. "People here think about classes a lot (probably too much) and work hard, but aren't cutthroat," claims a senior.

Besides its bright and motivated student body, Amherst's strongest asset is its faculty. The emphasis is on teaching ability, supported and enriched by research and scholarship. Moreover, students have the opportunity to work closely—"face to face, eyeball to eyeball," in the words of one administrator—with their professors. "Total access to all professors" is a much-treasured fact of life at Amherst, one student reports. "The only exception would be in the chemistry department, which is known for its unfriendly, stingy profs," adds an English major.

Amherst's course offerings are greatly enhanced by its membership in the Five College Consortium.* Student opportunities to take basic accounting at UMass or "something experimental" at Hampshire often seem like a godsend round about the middle of sophomore year. Amherst offers several study-away-from-home options, including one in Kyoto, Japan, where one of the college's colonial-style buildings has been duplicated. During the three-week January inter-term, there are no formal courses offered and no grades or academic credits given, but the college keeps its facilities open so that students may pursue individual research projects or even teach courses to fellow students if they wish. Some choose to leave Amherst for January and pursue fieldwork in a foreign country, archeological site or marine research station.

While ethnic diversity has never been one of Amherst's strong points, geographical distribution is wide. And although a majority of the students are from New York and Massachusetts, others hail from as far away as California and the Midwest. A smattering represent foreign countries. Amherst students come from affluent families more often than not: "Those of us who do not come from the top 5 percent of the socioeconomic scale learn a good deal about life-styles of the rich and famous," one student attests. A third of the students come from private schools, and 85 percent were in the top tenth of their high school classes. As for politics, it depends on who you talk to—liberals say Amherst is very conservative; conservatives think it's very liberal. "But I would say the 'silent majority' are conservative, traditional types," divulges an English major. Any he-versus-she stigma left over from the infancy of coeducation has subsided. "I think it gets better every year," remarks one woman. "In the past, there was a lot of trouble with sexism and chauvinism, but Amherst has definitely made an effort to make women feel better here." Generous alumni help Amherst provide more than a third of its students with scholarships or loans of some sort.

Half of the freshmen choose to live in freshman dorms, which are crowded but offer the chance to get to know your classmates. Upperclassmen have several options, including suites in nicer and less noisy residence halls and apartment-like social dorms. "Ex–fraternity houses are the most desirable dorms—beautiful, recently renovated houses," a sophomore reports. All of these on-campus options are coed, either by floor or room. The few off-campus students fend for themselves; some are lucky enough to stay in houses of professors who are on leave. But everyone who lives on campus, and anyone else who wants to, eats in Valentine Hall, which contains five dining rooms. "Each room has a different personality—people are often described by where they eat," claims a content vegetarian. "There's herbal tea, rice cakes and natural peanut butter in the veggie room." Everyone must take a twenty-one-meals-a-week plan, and for that one special one, a birthday cake is provided. "A nice touch," one grateful student notes.

"Contrary to what you may have heard about the by-product of our abolition of fraternities, social life here is excellent," a senior states. Others confess that fraternities do indeed still exist in an underground sort of fashion. There is a system of social groups or societies called "deme," which one student contends is just plain "queer." Usually there is at least one all-school party a week, complete with kegs and dancing, where "people go in order to see and be seen." Small, private cocktail parties are popular as is live entertainment at The Backroom campus club/café. Otherwise, students use the weekends to sleep, eat, drink, go to the game (especially if the opponent is Williams), see a movie, catch up on their work or hit the road. Good snow skiing is not far, and Boston (an hour and a half) and New York (almost four) are close enough to make them worth a trip or two a semester.

With Amherst's idyllic small-town setting bringing out the athlete in everyone, sports are taken seriously. Amherst competes in Division III, but the strong baseball team takes on Division I opponents as well. In addition to baseball, other strong teams include men's football and lacrosse and women's tennis, soccer and volleyball. The intramural program attracts a healthy number of participants, and there's a wealth of aspiring organizations, i.e., "struggling liberal political organizations and a strong Hunger Action Committee."

Amherst is a college in transition. Its willingness to review and revamp its fine educational program and cast off decades worth of social traditions, though, is a signal that the ultimate goal is to make a good thing even better. "Amherst," reports one student, "encourages questioning everything."

Antioch College

Yellow Springs, OH 45387

Location Rural	**Applicants** 380
Total Enrollment 490	**Accepted** 70%
Undergraduates 490	**Enrolled** 55%
Male/Female 45/55	**Academics** ★ ★ ★
SAT V/M 560/500	**Social** ☎ ☎ ☎
Financial Aid 75%	**Q of L** ● ● ● ●
Expense Pr $ $	**Admissions** (513)767-7047

In its heyday in the late 1960s, Antioch was the closest thing to anarchy in higher education. As a much-storied haven for radical nonconformists, Antioch became the epitome of every straitlaced parent's worst nightmare about the rebellious younger generation. Though times have changed, Antioch hasn't. The college still educates to "empower," and still offers full scholarships earmarked especially for student activists. Though enrollment has dwindled from a peak of about 2,000 in the early 1970s to only 490 today, Antioch remains a highly tolerant, caring and individualistic place for the few hardy souls with the courage to thumb their noses at the status quo.

Founded in 1852 by abolitionist and social reformer Horace Mann, Antioch has long been at the forefront of educational reform. With all the fuss that many universities are making today about cooperative education, you'd never guess that way back in the 1920s Antioch pioneered the idea that students should alternate time in the classroom with jobs in the real world. Under the college's famous co-op program, students spend nearly half of their college years out in the real world, be it selling fresh-squeezed orange juice on a street corner in California, studying Buddhism in India, or working in a Fortune 500 company in New York City. The campus in Yellow Springs is more reminiscent of a 1960s commune than a small midwestern college. Students with long hair and jeans, many of them products of "alternative" high schools, discuss feminism, gay rights, and nuclear proliferation over vegetarian meals, and they are more likely to take road trips to Washington for an antinuke rally than show up at a neighboring school's fraternity party. In class, evaluations written jointly by the student and professor take the place of grades, and everyone, from the students to the president, is on a first-name basis. Whether in the classroom or off on a job, students at Antioch don't just learn. They "develop."

Students say that the co-op program is one of the big reasons why they're here. Antioch operates on a trimester system, enabling students to graduate in either four or five years. Students usually spend two quarters on academic work and the remaining quarter plus the summer on a co-op job. The college helps place students, and co-op credit is awarded for just about anything as long as students submit a paper or a project and prove they learned something. For those students who do not earn enough money at these jobs and are still in financial need, the college helps out within the limits of its meager resources.

Antioch has recently revised its general education program. Students now spend their freshman year pursuing a "core" of courses that blend the traditional liberal arts with examination of the "social, historical, philosophical, and economic" nature of work. In addition, there are distribution requirements in the humanities, social sciences, and natural sciences, and skill requirements in nine areas. Physical education is also required. "The academic climate is at once very casual and very intense," says one student; academic competition is all but nonexistent, but because classes are usually no larger than twenty, students must always be prepared to participate. Close personal relationships often develop between students and faculty, and representatives of both groups sit on the committees that pick new professors. Academic advising is excellent, and each student is also assigned a co-op adviser to help with the nearly continuous job hunt. A network of alumni offering jobs is one major resource that students can depend on in their search. A major drawback to the co-op system is that students must constantly keep their bags packed, not knowing from one month to the next where they'll be. Friendships at the Yellow Springs campus often suffer because of the on-again, off-again attendance schedules, as does involvement in extracurricular groups. With so many people in far-flung locations, there are rarely more than a couple hundred students on the campus at any given time, severely limiting the social options.

Antioch's traditional academic programs are somewhat uneven, and the special-ized programs that can be found in many research universities are unavailable here. The sciences, especially biology, have traditionally been strong, as have political science and psychology. Environmental studies is excellent, in part because of the close proximity of a thousand-acre forest preserve and a nature museum. Chemistry, however, is weak, and students complain about languages and art. The administration says it is "rebuild-ing" in the arts and humanities. Communications gets mixed reviews from journalism majors, but Antioch does operate a major public radio station that gives students experience in the broadcast field. According to one senior, some students take all the courses Antioch offers in their field before transferring to a larger university. One thing students at Antioch don't lack is a good library; with about 254,000 volumes, Antioch's is huge for a college of its size.

Almost all departments suffered from the financial crisis that threatened the very survival of the college in the late 1970s. The problem stemmed in part from Antioch's failed attempt a decade ago to become a "national" university by setting up more than two dozen branch campuses across the nation. (Seven of these remain.) In the wake of this expansion and ensuing troubles, enrollment at the Yellow Springs campus shrunk drastically. Today, however, under the direction of a new president, Antioch is making a comeback. Since the fall of 1985, student enrollment has gone up 12 percent and the budget deficit has been replaced with a $600,000 surplus. Faculty salaries have been raised and new professors have been hired.

Antioch's desire to serve the "culturally disadvantaged" has enriched the diver-sity of a campus that is already of an individualist bent. In fact, being different may be the only thing students here have in common. "I feel that however weird an idea I might have about a topic," one woman explains, "it will be accepted at Antioch. (Unless of course it is a conservative view.)" Most students are outspoken achievers attracted by Antioch's academic freedom, and the majority retain what one woman calls "a lovely radical streak." As another sums up, "We are brainy, artsy-fartsy, druggy, avant-garde, often neurotic, gifted outcasts." Less than 20 percent of the students come from Ohio, and the rest hail from points throughout the nation. About 18 percent of the students—roughly thirty per year—receive merit scholarships ranging from $1,500 to $8,200.

Housing accommodations vary in quality, and maintenance is poor, due to lack of funds. In contrast to the college's democratic creed, room assignments are deter-mined by the whim of "a much-courted administrator." All the dorms are coed and equipped with kitchens. Everyone is guaranteed housing if he or she wants it, and students can choose from a number of special options that include a quiet hall, a moderate noise hall, and even a chemical-free hall that bars smoking, drinking, and yes, nonprescription drugs. There is also special housing for married students and cohabitat-ing couples. Seven and nineteen meal per week plans are available at the Caf, which boasts vegetarian entrees, a salad bar, and a popcorn machine. (Popcorn flavored with tamari and brewer's yeast is reputedly an Antioch favorite.) Since the dorms all have kitchens, many people choose the seven meal plan and form a co-op with friends for the rest. Only 4 percent of the students live off campus.

Superimposed on the heartland of rural Ohio is the town of Yellow Springs, which grew up around Antioch and reminds at least one student of "a little piece of Greenwich Village that fell into Ohio." Students don't seem to mind the isolation, and most are content if they can get "a cheery hello and granola from town." Urbanites can always work in a big city during their co-op period, and if they get desperate, Dayton is only thirty minutes away. A car can be useful for long-distance travel, but students generally remain on campus. The town offers a variety of health food stores, an artsy theater and a pizza joint that makes its pies with wholewheat crusts, as well as an assortment of bars and restaurants. For a relaxing walk in the woods, a campus-owned thousand-acre glen with forests and streams is waiting nearby.

"Fraternities and sororities—yuck! How about the Gay-Lesbian Alliance?" Without Greek organizations, social life tends to be spontaneous and mellow. There is a student coffee house "where people hang out, drink coffee, eat, play music, and read poetry," while stargazers frequently congregate on the roof of the science building and dance aficionados cut the rug twice a week at campus dances. Many student organizations, such as, in no particular order, the Women's Center, Peace Center, Green Peace, American Friends Service, Earth First!, No Business As Usual, Gay-Lesbian Alliance, Third World Alliance, Green Politics Study Group, etc., draw widespread student interest. Most students take a hostile view towards organized religion—one can only guess what Jimmy Swaggart would think of Antioch—but there is a Quaker meeting hall on campus, and many students take an interest in Eastern religions. Like fraternities, varsity sports are taboo, though a few odd intramural teams "pick up, disband, re-form." Popular sports include soccer, softball and Ultimate Frisbee, and gym classes are offered in kayaking, rafting, and horseback riding. A nearby reservoir is a popular place for swimming and windsurfing, and Clifton Gorge, adjacent to the glen, offers rock climbing. In keeping with its communal character, Antioch's Community Government runs social events, and students on the Administrative Council, which includes faculty members and administrators, take part in decisions on tenure and the budget.

Students who choose Antioch are taking a risk, and they know it. The Antioch brand of liberal activism goes against the grain in these conventional times. For the few who take the plunge, Antioch offers a unique opportunity to discover yourself in both the working world and among the college's bright and opinionated student body. Horace Mann once implored his students to "be ashamed to die until you have won some victory for humanity." Antioch students take the motto to heart.

Arizona State University

Tempe, AZ 85287

Location Urban	**Applicants** 11,158
Total Enrollment 41,540	**Accepted** 82%
Undergraduates 31,090	**Enrolled** 50%
Male/Female 52/48	**Academics** ★ ★
SAT V/M 450/510	**Social** 🎭🎭🎭🎭
Financial Aid 60%	**Q of L** ●●●●●
Expense Pub $	**Admissions** (800)252-ASU1

You've got to wonder about a university with palm trees and a bright orange sun smiling up at you from its admissions booklet, about an administration that tries to lure students by citing lower clothing costs as one benefit of attending. Is it a resort or a college you're applying to? Is this a promotion for sun, relaxation and recreation or four years of education at one of the country's largest public universities? The answer is yes, er uh—both.

Picture a beautiful, contemporary campus deep in the heart of the Sunbelt. Add state-of-the-art sports facilities and a nearby man-made beach complete with wave-maker, and more cinemas, bars and nightclubs than any human needs. Now place all of this adjacent to the growing and exciting Phoenix metropolitan area and within a few hours of fine snow skiing. Sounds too good to be true? It sounds like ASU.

The modern cement-and-brick campus complete with bike paths and a fitness trail is enough to make any northerner weep. "ASU basks in a pleasant climate almost year-round," brags a telecommunications major. The landscape is always green, the sun is ever present, there are flowers in January, and outside studying is always possible. Temperatures reach 115 degrees in August and September, but the twenty species of palm trees live through it, as do most students—especially when they occasionally sneak a dip in one of the many campus fountains.

But underneath every beach towel there's sure to be a book or two; someone must be attending the more than 150 programs available at this garden of earthly delights. Although a fourth of the students enter the college of business administration, the largest in the country, there are eight other undergraduate schools—liberal arts and sciences, engineering and applied sciences, architecture and environmental design, education, fine arts, nursing, public programs (criminal justice, leisure studies, mass communication) and social work (the only school of its kind in the state). The best bets in terms of quality are business, fine arts, and public programs, which include the Walter Cronkite School of Journalism and Telecommunications. Engineering programs—especially microelectronics, robotics and computer-assisted manufacturing—are sure bets; the facility for high resolution microscopy allows students to get a uniquely close-up view of atomic structures.

In the liberal arts, the sciences (including solar energy, physical science, geology and biology) and social sciences are strong. The less technically minded may enjoy the interdisciplinary opportunities in such areas as film studies, urban planning, medieval and Renaissance studies, and Islamic studies. Under a new general studies program, all students must meet core requirements by choosing courses from five disciplines: literacy and critical inquiry, numeracy, traditional humanities, global awareness, and historical awareness.

Undergraduates who are more interested in their education than their tans may find more obstacles than just the temptations of Tempe. To get into many particular courses—and not just the exotics, such as scuba diving—you might have to wait a semester or two. Required introductory courses in the larger schools fill up quickly, and are usually huge. "It affects your performance when you're continuously placed in courses in excess of five hundred persons," claims a poli-sci major. But upperclassmen generally enjoy smaller classes and have fewer registration strifes. The library, a noteworthy facility, contains more than two million volumes, including just about every word Barry Goldwater ever wrote. Top students can take advantage of a five-year BA/MBA program. Anyone who can tear him- or herself away from ASU for a semester or a year may choose to experience Latin America, Yugoslavia, West Germany or numerous other domestic and foreign special programs. ASU also administers an honors program packed with interdisciplinary courses and polished off with a capstone senior seminar.

Arizona State's admissions policy is a high school senior's dream. Those from the Midwest or East Coast intent upon a life in the land of sun and fun need only rank in the top half of their class or have a cumulative SAT score of 1010 or ACT of 23. (More than a third of each freshman class comes from out of state, including many Chicagoans fleeing their miserable winters.) In-state students should have the same rank or total SAT score of 930 or ACT of 21. The process of rolling admissions enables students to get an answer between two and three weeks after their files are completed. There are 335 athletic scholarships available, nearly 40 percent for women. More than 8,550 academic merit scholarships, ranging up to $6,000, are awarded.

Despite the high predominance of the "laid-back West Coast crowd," ASU undergrads are considered "generally conservative, economically concerned individuals." Yet one senior warns that "snooty people would be happier elsewhere." Hispanics make up the largest minority group—5 percent of the student body—if you don't count the sizable number of over twenty-five students returning for their degree. Many ASU students work at least twenty hours a week, and one-third of them are married.

The single-sex, coed, graduate and married dorms are generally well maintained and spacious, but they only accommodate about a tenth of the student body. Freshmen who want rooms must apply at least six months in advance because returning students receive priority. Off-campus living possibilities are made more accessible through a special service known as the ASU Tenants Association, which puts out updated vacancy information and will forward it to out-of-staters. Sun Devil Village is a square-mile complex of apartment buildings, bars, restaurants and laundromats just east of campus, which many inhabitants refer to as "Sin City" for one reason or another. About ten thousand students enjoy the cheaper rents, nightly parties, and independence afforded by this off-campus haven. One other housing alternative is the Greek system. Brothers live off campus in their own houses, while sororities are housed in one large dorm.

The university's Grand Marketplace, a collection of eight "theme" dining centers, may well have the best institutional food in the country. Students can roller-skate into the Grill for charcoal-broiled burgers or the Cafe Olé for Mexican fare, or they can line up elsewhere for salads, health foods, ice cream, or delicatessen fare. Meal plans are available in residential hall cafeterias and Greek houses.

Nearly everyone owns a car, and for this reason the university recently added a multilevel parking garage with over 1,500 spaces. A car also puts Colorado mountains, California beaches, Vegas slots and real Mexican food only hours away.

With nearly three dozen societies, the Greek system is strong but not overpowering. There are plenty of Greek and non-Greek parties to go around for those who aren't road tripping on the weekends. Another favorite pastime is cheering on various Sun Devil teams. The men's baseball, badminton, golf, and women's gymnastics and swimming teams are national powerhouses. The Sun Devils routinely turn out top National Football League draft picks, and basketball is also popular. Intramurals alone feature more than sixty different sports.

Despite the university's massive size and burgeoning population, the atmosphere is not overbearing. Most students at this campus seem to have their suntanned arms open to welcome just about anyone. So while ASU may not go down in history as the most academically challenging institution, students who choose this warm weathered, warmhearted school are in for four unforgettable years. If Walt Disney had built a "College World," he might have modeled it after Arizona State.

University of Arizona

Tucson, AZ 85721

Location Urban	**Applicants** 10,900
Total Enrollment 31,080	**Accepted** 86%
Undergraduates 22,100	**Enrolled** 45%
Male/Female 52/48	**Academics** ★ ★ ★
SAT V/M 470/520	**Social** ☂ ☂ ☂ ☂
ACT 21	**Q of L** ● ● ● ●
Financial Aid 60%	**Admissions** (602)621-3237
Expense Pub $ $	

Twenty-five years before Arizona achieved statehood, the federal government authorized a tiny land-grant university on the edge of its sand- and dust-covered frontier. Today, the University of Arizona serves more than thirty thousand students with thirteen colleges, six schools, and 186 degree programs. The hot, dry weather, with day after day of cloudless sunshine, encourages students to spend their time baking in the sun, not stewing in the library, and even the administration keeps academics in perspective. Classes are canceled each spring when the rodeo comes to town.

The city of Tucson, flanked on four sides by the impressive Santa Catalina mountain range, is a beautiful natural oasis in the Sonora desert. Architecturally the U of A campus distinguishes itself from the city's regiment of adobe buildings by a design that seems a study in the versatility of red brick. Old Main, the university's first building, is now heading into its second century, but there are several more modern structures. Although the palm trees, sage brush and cactus are staples of the regional flora, the campus does have plenty of shady trees, lush green lawns, and many opportunities to plop down in the sun to read or snooze. "To me it really looks like a university," says one native Arizonian, "but my friends from back East tell me they feel like they're studying in a resort."

Sciences are unquestionably the school's forte, and the clear, clean Arizona skies help make the astronomy department among the nation's best. Students have access not only to leading astronomers but also to the most up-to-date equipment, including a huge 176-inch telescope, operated jointly by the university and the Smithsonian. Servicing all this fancy equipment is the school's renowned Optical Science Center. Both UA's labs for environmental research and the surrounding desert contribute to the excellent work in studies of arid land. The colleges of mines, engineering, and earth science are all first-rate, as are those of nursing, pharmacy, and health-related professions, which make use of the university's medical school. The fact is, you can't go wrong with any of the sciences, though computer resources could do with some expansion.

In the College of Arts and Sciences, the architecture, history and English departments stand out, as do anthropology and sociology. Eager shutterbugs can pore through photographer Ansel Adams's personal collection, while budding musicians play in the hundred or so performances put on by the School of Music. Areas getting low marks from students are the language programs, psychology, and the radio and television department.

General education and core requirements vary from college to college, but everyone takes freshman English, and almost everyone takes intro math. Most departments outside the health fields offer cooperative education programs that provide early work experience for those interested. With regard to research spending, the university ranks in the top twenty among public institutions, and this emphasis on scholarship can be frustrating for students looking for student-faculty interaction. "UA is not the place for someone dependent on a lot of individual attention." Underclassmen in many of the colleges will have to deal with crowded introductory classes and courses taught by teaching assistants rather than professors. And, recent state cutbacks in U of A's budget have caused frustrating increases in class size and reduced library hours. The university's huge bureaucracy has also rendered the academic counseling services inadequate. Yet, because the academic pressure is usually inversely proportional to that of the barometer, this is not so serious a problem as it might be elsewhere. "The academic climate is, above all, casual, but within the various colleges and departments the competition can be tough," says one nursing student.

The administration cites a sharp increase in freshman applications over the past few years, especially from out-of-staters, and in-state admissions standards are being toughened. The competition has always been much tougher for those who hail from beyond the sunny Arizona boundaries, and some colleges—like nursing, pharmacy and architecture—are virtually closed to them. Still, a quarter of the student body comes from out of state—mainly Californians, Midwesterners and New Yorkers—and about 8 percent more from overseas. Many out-of-staters end up establishing residency before their school years are out. In addition to need-based financial aid, an amazing 5,500 merit awards and all the athletic scholarships allowed by the NCAA are available.

Dorm rooms tend to be small but well maintained; the major problem is actually getting a room. "There is a huge demand for rooms," reports one senior. "A lot of people were unable to find university accommodations last year." The most recently built dorms are the most comfortable, and the pace of renovations on the older ones has picked up. When it comes to coed housing, the administration "is still in the dark ages," sighs one student. The two dorms billed as coed actually have separated male and female wings with a common lounge area and strict "visitation rules" tend to put a damper on things. Students recommend the dorms mainly for freshmen and transfer students unfamiliar with the area. Upperclassmen flock to the abundant and inexpensive apartments near the school. What U of A lacks in housing it makes up for in its excellent meal service. The best way to enjoy the food at the student union's seven restaurants is to use the university-issued All Aboard credit card which helps students take advantage of the wealth of different gustatory options and frees them from carrying cash.

Despite the high percentage of off-campus residents, students stream back onto campus most weekends for parties, sports and cultural events. About three thousand undergraduates belong to fraternities and sororities, and though the campus is technically alcohol-free, a Greek party dweller reveals that "the frats haven't realized it yet." Campus organizations are plentiful and diverse. An active and popular student government runs a free legal service, a tenants' complaint center, and "a very accessible gripe committee," all of which provide relief from an administration that is well meaning but mired in bureaucracy.

The university's fine athletic facilities support quality intramural and varsity programs. The basketball Wildcats were PAC 10 champs in 1986. Division I football and baseball enjoy national prominence, generate lots of money for other men's and women's sports teams, and provide great weekend entertainment for students and city residents alike. The women's sports programs tend to lag behind the men's, but the basketball and volleyball teams are strong contenders. For those who consider catching rays a sport, Mexico's beaches are not too far for a road trip, and popular Mt. Lemmon, where one can ski in the winter when it's seventy degrees on campus, is only eighty miles away.

The University of Arizona renders a wide variety of academic opportunities as well as academic diversions, and it is no place for "those who need coddling or individual guidance." As for the spectacular weather, prospectives are warned to honestly evaluate how it will affect their ability to concentrate. Assuming your self-control checks out, says one satisfied senior, "one needs only the desire to learn and a bit of initiative to really excel here."

University of Arkansas

Fayetteville, AR 72701

Location Small city	**Applicants** 4,397
Total Enrollment 13,980	**Accepted** 85%
Undergraduates 11,460	**Enrolled** 67%
Male/Female 55/45	**Academics** ★ ★
ACT Comp 21	**Social** 🐗 🐗 🐗 🐗
Financial Aid 52%	**Q of L** ●●●
Expense Pub $	**Admissions** (501)575-5346

The state of Arkansas has two conspicuous problems—an underdeveloped economy and no athletic teams in the major leagues—but the University of Arkansas is doing its best to address both of them. A comprehensive state institution that provides instruction both in technical areas and in the liberal arts, it also fields a top-ranked football team. Unfortunately, it's easier to go hog-wild over the Razorbacks on the field than in the classroom.

The 329-acre campus is located amid the mountains, lakes and streams of the Ozarks, a popular vacation area in the extreme northwest corner of the state. Cowpath shortcuts across grassy lawns connect most of the modern concrete and WPA-vintage buildings, while a bit of Hollywood Boulevard–style nostalgia can be found on the Senior Walk, the concrete sidewalk that bears the engraved name of every student who made it through to graduate. "It is truly a southern school," says one student. "People smile and speak to other people whether they know them or not."

Established as a land-grant institution in 1871, the University of Arkansas has since expanded its scope of educational responsibilities from solely agricultural and mechanical arts to a broad spectrum of academic offerings in eight colleges and professional schools. Attempting to upgrade the campus academic atmosphere, the university has abandoned its open admissions policy for Arkansas high school graduates and mandated that students without a 2.5 high school GPA, an ACT score of 18, three or four credits in math, English, social science and natural sciences, or a combination thereof, need not apply. In addition to reigning as the premier research institute in Arkansas (with specialties in agricultural law, alternative energy, and rehabilitation), U of A offers more than one hundred undergraduate degree programs. The school boasts a fine English department with a nationally recognized writing program and a history department strong in southern history. Other academic strengths include physics (especially laser technology), chemistry, engineering and architecture.

The Fulbright College of Arts and Sciences offers a degree program in computer science, and many computer terminals were recently added. A recently completed $16-million Center for the College of Engineering is one of the finest such facilities in the country, and a new fine arts center is slated for construction in the near future. Theater buffs can re-create their heritage in the full-scale replica of a Greek theater. Each college has its own required core curriculum courses in the humanities and social and natural sciences, though students in every program must take both freshman- and junior-level composition. Arts and sciences students must achieve proficiency in a foreign language. The honors program gives undergraduates a chance for independent study, self-designed courses, and individual research. One of Arkansas' most innovative academic entrees is the Sack Lunch Symposium, which brings in speakers during the lunch hour for a mixed audience of students and professors.

The level of academic seriousness among undergraduates varies widely, and despite a recent tightening of admission requirements, the academic climate is fairly casual. Nevertheless, many departments retain high standards, and grading can be stiff. An accessible faculty, genuinely interested in teaching, helps ease whatever academic pressure there is. One man praises "the care most of my instructors have taken to make sure I go away with more than I came with." Even the president has office hours for students every day from noon to one. Large lectures are common, though, and underclassmen should get used to seeing teaching assistants not necessarily much older than themselves.

Students are of the small-town, 1950s Main Street variety. Although their worldview may be formed by sports, cliques and cruising the local burger joints, there is a cosmopolitan influence exerted upon the campus from the community of writers, artists and intellectuals that has grown up around the university and earned it a reputation as a hotbed of liberalism in the state's more conservative quarters. Arkansas residents make up 86 percent of the student body, and most of the rest come from nearby states, especially Texas and especially the Dallas area. The 6 percent of students who are black or Hispanic tend to function as a tightly knit subsociety. Because Arkansas is prime Bible Belt territory, vocal fundamentalist groups are in no short supply. In addition to limited need-based financial aid, five exceptional students receive scholarships of up to $10,000 for each year they attend, and over one thousand others receive smaller awards in varying amounts.

All freshmen must live in on-campus housing, which is abundant and relatively well maintained. Most is single-sex, though coed housing is available. There is usually no problem getting a room, but that doesn't stop about three-quarters of the students from looking for greener pastures off campus. Some students move into fraternities or sororities after they pledge in October, while about half commute from home or apartments in Fayetteville. The university operates a free bus service between the campus and parts of Fayetteville with large student concentrations. Dining facilities are adequate, and there are a few prize salad bars to be found on campus for those willing to seek them out. Each Greek house has its own kitchen.

Fayetteville is a quiet, reasonably crime-free town that provides most of the necessities of student life—including nice restaurants, fast-food joints, bowling alleys, miniature golf, shopping malls and, of course, a bar or two. Bluegrass festivals, craft fairs and good hunting and fishing are among the regional charms. The more than thirty Greek societies have a prominent presence on campus, but they're not universally respected. "Fraternities and sororities, while providing ample party life for their members, tend to be not much more than finishing schools for the young, upwardly mobile students from Little Rock and Fort Smith," says one senior. Campus-sponsored activities include theme parties, such as Casino Night or Holiday on the Hill, but a recent crackdown on campus drinking has staunched the flow of alcohol. The university often attracts the likes of Steve Winwood, Cyndi Lauper and Willie Nelson for on-campus concerts.

And then there's sports. "The Hogs rule" is how one student describes their role on campus. There are Razorback logos on T-shirts, napkins, book covers, license plates and on game day on the cheeks of ecstatic fans. The influx of spectators on game weekends in the fall "makes the campus look like downtown New York," one man comments. Winning men's basketball, baseball, track and tennis teams are also big-time on campus, while most students agree that women's sports get short shrift.

The cost of living in Arkansas is low, and so is the cost of an education at its state university. Football and partying are definitely more prominent than academics in many students' minds, but serious students determined to eke out a high-quality education could well spend a prosperous four years in Razorback country.

ATLANTA UNIVERSITY CENTER

Atlanta is viewed as the preeminent city in the country for bright, talented and successful blacks. It became the capital of the civil rights movement in the 1960s—the town whose leaders said it was "too busy to hate"—and today it is a place where middle-class blacks can savor what is known locally as "the black experience."

At the center of this extraordinary culture is the Atlanta University Center, the largest cluster of private black institutions of higher learning in the world. The six component institutions have educated generations of black leaders. The Reverend Dr. Martin Luther King, Jr., went to Morehouse College, his grandmother, mother, sister and daughter to Spelman College. Graduates spread across the country in a pattern that developed when these were among the best and only colleges to which talented blacks could aspire. Even now, when the options are almost limitless, they continue to send their children back for more.

The Center consists of four undergraduate colleges and two graduate institutions on adjoining campuses in the center of Atlanta. Students at these affiliated schools can enjoy the quiet pace of their beautiful magnolia-studded campuses or plunge into all the culture and excitement of this most dynamic of Deep South cities. There are discos, concerts, plays, films and sporting events in town and plenty of parties to be found on each of the campuses.

The six schools became affiliated in 1929, using the model of California's Clare-mont Colleges, but they remain fiercely independent. Each has its own administration, board of trustees and academic specialties, and each maintains its own dorms, cafeterias and other facilities. Students at one of the units may cross-register at any of the other five.

The governing body of the consortium is the Atlanta University Center, Inc. Two trustees from each of the six schools sit on its board along with outside members. AUC, Inc., administers a Center-wide dual-degree program in engineering in conjunction with Georgia Tech—and it runs campus security, a student crisis center, and a joint institute of science research. There is also a Center-wide service of career planning and placement where recruiters may come and interview students from all six of the institutions. A brand new $15-million library is shared by all six.

Dating and social life at the coeducational institutions tend to take place within the individual schools. On the other hand, Morehouse, an all-male college, and Spel-man, a women's college, maintain a close academic and social relationship. The More-house–Spelman Glee Club takes its abundance of talent around the nation, and its annual Christmas concert on the Spelman campus is standing room only.

Two of the six schools are graduate institutions. Atlanta University began as a primary and secondary school, conducting its first classes in a railroad boxcar in 1865. Today it encompasses five graduate and professional schools—education, business, library information studies, social work and arts and sciences—and it makes its re-search facilities and faculty members available to the undergraduate colleges, many of whose graduates go on to AU for further education. The Interdenominational Theolog-ical Center is a federation of six Protestant seminaries that turn out a third of all seminary-trained candidates for the ministry.

A relatively new element at the Atlanta University Center is the Morehouse College of Medicine, which was founded in 1978 as a graduate school offering the first two years of medical education. Graduates would then complete their medical training at a variety of southern medical schools. Beginning with the incoming students of 1981, the medical school evolved into a four-year institution and, in 1982, it became indepen-dent of Morehouse, making it the seventh school to join the Atlanta University Center.

Among the undergraduate colleges, Morehouse and Spelman are clearly the academic leaders. Following are sketches of Clark and Morris Brown and write-ups on Morehouse and Spelman:

Clark College. Founded in 1869 by the Methodist Episcopal Church, Clark is a coed institution and the largest of the colleges. It has traditionally been known for its programs in the health professions, public policy and mass communications, but busi-ness administration now heads the list of most popular majors. In second place is mass communications, which offers excellent training in print journalism, radio and televi-sion production and filmmaking. The school owns radio station WCLK. Less than a quarter of Clark students graduated in the top two-fifths of their high school class, but a third go on to graduate school. A quarter of Clark students come from outside the South. Enrollment: 600 men/1,220 women. Median SATs: 330V/330M.

Morris Brown College. More vocational in emphasis, Morris Brown was founded in 1881 by the African Methodist Episcopal Church and continues to receive support from it. Its most popular programs are education and business administration. Students receive considerable personal attention, and those coming with poor academic prepara-tion are provided with special help. Morris Brown also offers evening courses for employed adults as well as a program of co-op work-study education. Only a small percentage of Morris Brown graduates continue their formal education beyond the baccalaureate. Enrollment: 600 men/870 women. Median SATs: 300V/350M.

Morehouse College

Atlanta, GA 30314

Location Urban	**Applicants** 1,200
Total Enrollment 2,120	**Accepted** 87%
Undergraduates 2,120	**Enrolled** 55%
Male/Female N/A	**Academics** ★ ★
SAT V/M 400/430	**Social** ☎ ☎ ☎
Financial Aid 70%	**Q of L** ● ● ●
Expense Pr $	**Admissions** (404)681-2800

Founded in 1867 in the basement of Springfield Baptist Church, Morehouse is a liberal arts institution known for its tradition of academic excellence and black leadership. In addition to the Reverend Dr. Martin Luther King, Jr., alumni include Julian Bond, and Maynard Jackson, a former Atlanta mayor. "The House" leads all predominantly black four-year colleges in the percentage of faculty members with a doctorate, and it is one of four Georgia colleges with a Phi Beta Kappa chapter.

Several historical brick buildings grace the wooded, well-kept campus, to which thirteen new buildings have been added in as many years. The general studies program includes not only normal distribution requirements but study of "the unique African and Afro-American heritage on which so much of our modern American culture is built." The Morehouse curriculum includes the traditional liberal arts majors in the humanities and social and natural sciences, but it also offers increasingly popular concentrations in accounting, insurance, business administration, computer science. Counseling, including career counseling, is considered quite strong, and, says a finance major, "The relationship between faculty and students can best be described as extended brotherhood."

If its sister school Spelman was once the "Vassar of black society," Morehouse was the Harvard or Yale, attracting male students from the upper echelons of black society around the country. Georgia is the number one source of students, but New York and California are next. Now that they are welcomed to bigger schools with better national reputations, the men of Morehouse choose the school for the same reasons Spelman women choose theirs: They want an institution with a strong academic program and supportive atmosphere in which to cultivate their success orientation and leadership skills. At Morehouse they can concentrate on achievement first, without facing the additional challenges and barriers of a predominantly white institution. More than two-thirds of students get need-based financial aid, and one-fifth qualify for merit scholarships ranging from $775 to a full ride (requirements are 1050 composite SATs and a top-quarter class rank). About half of them continue to graduate and professional schools.

There is a considerable shortage of housing, leaving half the student body to make do on their own. According to one student, the administration does assist students in finding housing up to a point, "but other schools have better programs." The meal plan at Morehouse is mandatory for students living on campus and draws plenty of complaints. (Morris Brown and Spelman colleges are said to have the best cafeteria food of all the Atlanta Center schools.)

Homecoming is a joint effort between Morehouse and Spelman. The homecoming queen elected by Morehouse men has traditionally been a Spelman woman, as are the cheerleaders and majorettes. Socially, Morehouse men are seldom found far from Spelman women. The four fraternities, which attract about 10 percent of the men as members, hold popular parties. Going out on the town in Atlanta is a popular evening activity, and on-campus football games, concerts, movies and religious programs all draw crowds. In its early years Morehouse sometimes left much to be desired in the area of varsity sports, but it now competes well in NCAA Division II. Track, cross-country, tennis, basketball, football, and baseball are all strong, but it is the strong intramural program that "allows students a chance to become that Dr. J. or OJ lurking inside us all," notes one resident of The House.

The future of Morehouse looks as bright as its past. In recent years the college has strengthened the board of trustees, enriched the academic program, conducted a successful multimillion-dollar national fund-raising campaign, increased student scholarships and faculty salaries, doubled its endowment, improved its physical plant and acquired twelve additional acres of land. Thus it is well equipped to serve the modern heirs of a distinguished tradition. If you're thinking of attending Morehouse, says one student, you should be serious about studying, know where you are heading, and, above all, be prepared to "help uplift black society and give something back when you leave."

Spelman College

Atlanta, GA 30314

Location Urban	**Accepted** 52%
Total Enrollment 1,770	**Enrolled** 52%
Undergraduates 1,770	**Academics** ★ ★
Male/Female N/A	**Social** ☪ ☪ ☪
SAT V/M 430/430	**Q of L** ● ● ● ●
Financial Aid 85%	**Admissions** (800)282-2625
Expense Pr $	in Georgia, (800)241-3421 out of state
Applicants 1,860	

Spelman College is a flourishing educational anachronism. Founded in 1881, it traditionally turned out teachers, nurses and other leaders of the emerging black middle class. It's one of only two surviving black women's colleges in the country, which until recently enjoyed a monopoly on its distinct student market.

Spelman now finds itself competing head-on with the Seven Sisters in the Northeast and other prestigious and predominantly white institutions that are eager to recruit the talented black women who traditionally lined up at Spelman's doors. Yet it still offers something special: an environment where black women can develop self-confidence and leadership skills before venturing into a world where they will once again be in the minority. "My college manages to blend southern hospitality, sisterly love and outstanding education—it's a good place for any woman interested in becoming something, or at least improving herself," a biology major reports.

Set around a classic collegiate green, Spelman's campus is cozy and compact with a mixture of new and gracious older buildings. The college offers a well-rounded liberal arts curriculum complete with rigorous distribution requirements. Traditional strengths are in the natural sciences, both of which have strong faculties. Reflecting new trends in the job market, the college has turned professional with a vengeance. Many students have discarded the popular majors in humanities and the fine arts of the early seventies in favor of premed and prelaw programs, psychology, education and engineering (through the Georgia Tech program). The school is also developing career-oriented programs in such fields as computer science and management and organization. The new Women's Research and Resource Center specializes in black women's studies and community outreach to black women. Of the faculty members, about 65 percent have doctorates, and many are black and/or female—and thus excellent role models. Except for required core courses, classes are small; individual attention is the hallmark of a Spelman education. Students who want to spread their wings can venture abroad through a program with Syracuse University or try one of the domestic exchange arrangements with Wellesley, Mt. Holyoke, Vassar or Mills.

Spelman's reputation continues to attract black women from all over the country, including a high proportion of alumnae children. More than two-thirds of the students come from outside Georgia. Spelman cultivates distinct constituencies: high achievers looking for a supportive environment (and rewarded with a challenging honors program), average students and a few women with high potential who performed relatively poorly in high school. These students blend well inside and outside the classroom, for they come with similar goals. They believe they can enjoy more leadership positions and a more natural social life than at predominantly white schools. "I wanted to be in a place where I could choose my friends, not where there were fifteen blacks who *had* to be my friends," explains one Spelmanite. Spelman responds favorably to about 90 percent of accepted applicants who demonstrate financial need, and two hundred students with 3.0 GPAs qualify for merit awards of $750 to $3,600.

Housing is in short supply, with the ten dorms serving about two-thirds of the student body. Some freshmen complain about the condition of their older dorms and look forward to the time when they can live in the more modern dorms reserved for upperclassmen. The meal plan is mandatory for boarders, though there are no restrictions about moving off campus.

Generations of young women have been sent to Spelman with the hopes that they would "meet a Morehouse man," and today's students still date the young men of Morehouse that they meet in classes or through extracurricular activities. Until 1978, sororities were not allowed at Spelman for fear that they would divide the student body, but the administration has relented.

All Spelman women take at least two hours of physical education, and for those who want more, the school boasts fine volleyball, basketball and tennis teams; synchronized swimming is the specialty, however. Athletic facilities are poor, but there are several organized intramurals, including flag football and bowling.

Spelman College has spent a century furthering the education and opportunities of black women, who have suffered for generations under a double handicap of race and sex. It has adapted its curriculum to meet the career aspirations of today's youth, and it has begun to meet the challenge of institutional survival posed by affirmative action in other universities. With several generations of support from the Rockefeller family apparently coming to an end (the school was named out of gratitude to John D. Rockefeller's wife, Laura Spelman), it is taking steps toward independent financial security. A recent fund-raising push almost doubled its endowment.

Spelman, once an elite institution in black society, is staking its future on its ability to provide a unique kind of education that can compete with any other institution. As one administrator puts it, "We are ready to take the risk of being judged by both worlds."

_____

College of the Atlantic

Bar Harbor, ME 04609

Location Small town
Total Enrollment 140
Undergraduates 140
Male/Female 50/50
SAT V/M 510/530
Financial Aid 60%
Expense Pr $

Applicants 60
Accepted 80%
Enrolled 80%
Academics ★ ★ ★
Social ☎ ☎
Q of L ● ● ●
Admissions (207)288-5015

College of the Atlantic is a child of the Woodstock generation that appears to be coming of age. Founded in the fall of 1969, while the dust was still settling on Max Yasgur's farm, this tiny college in northern Maine provides "an alternative to traditional higher education," built around communal living and the study of humankind's relation to the environment. Times have changed and so has College of the Atlantic, yet the school retains a slightly psychedelic flavor. The Grateful Dead is still the band of choice on campus, and COA is undoubtedly the only school in the nation where students can get academic credit for studying "Bread, Love, and Dreams."

In the best Dead tradition, the college has "kept trucking on" in the aftermath of a disastrous fire that destroyed its library and dining hall in the summer of 1983. Resourcefulness is, however, the name of the game at this unusual institution of environmental higher education, and a tremendous group effort quickly produced an almost complete replacement collection of books. Ground will be broken in the fall of '87 on a new library building to include a larger dining hall.

The college was established on Maine's scenic Mount Desert Island as "an experiment in the ecology of human relationships and in the meaning of cooperative living." The college offers only one degree—a BA in human ecology, the study of "the relationships between humans and their natural and social environments." Most courses focus on some angle of this topic and are offered not in departments but in three broad resource areas: environmental science, environmental design and applied human studies. "We feel that departments are excuses to set up educational barriers," one student states. Students are required to take two core courses in each of the three areas.

The approach is holistic, but the sciences still stand out as the ruling orientation. Excellent instruction is offered in ecology, zoology and marine biology. The design program runs a close second in quality and offers one of the best undergraduate programs in alternative energy in the nation. Students in the program built Maine's first solar-heated house. Unfortunately, aside from environment-related topics, the courses are skimpy. Public policy is the lone offering in a nonscientific preprofessional field, and students complain about the lack of any professors or courses in philosophy or music. In the latter, "all we have is a student-run choir." Lack of traditional courses and adequate lab equipment partially explain a low 50 percent acceptance rate at schools of medicine.

While there are only a handful of required courses here, there are many required experiences, starting with a rugged five-day wilderness orientation before a student's first semester. Students must also complete a ten-week off-campus internship, participate in a student-run problem-solving workshop, and support at least one "campus-building" activity, such as the student government or newspaper. During January term they take an intensive look at one subject. Juniors must write a human ecology essay and build on it the next year in the senior project, a major work of independent study reflecting their main interests.

With fewer than twenty-five full-time professors, students develop close relationships with their teachers. "There are no titles here," one man reports; "I have anatomy with Butch and art with Joanne and Eric." Students receive written evaluations of their work, not grades, and they must reciprocate with their own evaluation of the course and their performance in it. The unusual advising system (a three-person faculty/student team chosen by the advisee) also promotes close student-faculty contact. The thirty-acre campus has adequate facilities and inspirational beauty. New class and lab space have recently been added. For now, using the library is a real headache. Students must walk a half an hour to get to the building now in use, and for any real research, must drive an hour to the University of Maine at Orono. The campus is adjacent to Acadia National Park and stretches along the glorious Maine coast. "It's hard to talk about it without sounding like a travel brochure," one woman sighs.

Most people attracted to the College of the Atlantic and its unique curriculum are bright, disillusioned members of the upper middle class. Virtually all of them come from the top half of their high school class, and a large percentage transfer from other schools, after growing "tired of trying to beat the traditional large university system." They come not for a degree, but for the educational experience. One sophomore believes that people "who feel a concern for the earth and man's diverse interaction with it are ideal candidates for the kind of education COA offers." The college enrolls a sizable percentage of older than average students. COA "generally" follows a need-blind admissions policy and assists as many applicants as it can. Don't be surprised if the relative amount of your financial aid package covered by loans is high. No merit scholarships are offered.

College of the Atlantic is run by the All-College Meeting, a government comprising the college's entire community—everyone serves on a committee or two—with virtually ultimate authority on all policy decisions. A majority of students live in nearby Bar Harbor; those on campus live in small cooperative houses with five to twenty others, two of which were once servant wings of turn-of-the-century summer mansions. Many students—particularly the older ones—prefer to "seek out special places to live" in the nearby countryside. The college provides a cheap vegetarian lunch for all students (often featuring local farm produce) and daily snack sessions with coffee, juice and whole-grain muffins. At other times students fend for themselves. More options will be available when the new dining facility is completed. In the meantime, potluck dinners are frequent. "Social life revolves around nature and the seasons, biking, hiking, boating, cross-country skiing, rock climbing etc.," according to one man. Dating—"except perhaps to climb Mount Cadillac"—is rare. Video movies and square dances are more popular than pot parties or beer bashes. "I think our social skills may be lacking as far as cocktail party conversations go, but everyone loves to dance," one woman reports. Unfortunately, she says she would like to hear something besides the Grateful Dead every once in a while. Sports facilities are limited to the volleyball net on campus, the pool at the local Y and the jogging trails in the nearby national park. Cooperative games are more popular than competitive ones, as the frequency of hackeysack sessions and hiking and climbing expeditions proves. Although many students have cars, few emigrate on the weekends. (Boston, the nearest urban center, is five and a half hours away.) In general, students prefer a more laid-back "adult" life-style to the often frenetic pace of undergraduate social life. "We watch a lot of birds and tourists; both have frequent mass migrations to this area," says one student.

Although the school is many students' idea of institutional Utopia, certain gripes do crop up. The resource shortage, both personal and physical, is galling but unavoidable at such a young and small school. With one faculty member per subject, specialization is virtually impossible, and support for job placement is meager. The intensity bred by such close quarters can lead to introspection and a compulsion for "talking it out" that can eventually become draining rather than supportive. Not only will you soon know everyone on campus; you'll know everything about them.

Nevertheless, dedicated environmentalists who seek a close-knit community of like-minded individuals should not be dissuaded. Though in many ways COA is a throwback to the late '60s, rising enrollments and an improving physical plant attest to its continuing vitality in the '80s.

Auburn University

Auburn, AL 36849

Location Small town
Total Enrollment 19,360
Undergraduates 17,440
Male/Female 55/45
SAT V/M 500/570
ACT Comp 24
Financial Aid 25%
Expense Pub $

Applicants 7,750
Accepted 83%
Enrolled 49%
Academics ★ ★
Social ☎ ☎ ☎
Q of L ● ● ●
Admissions (205)826-4080

Throughout most of its 130-year history, Auburn was a school where Alabama farm boys came to learn the latest tricks of their trade. The corps was mandatory in those days, and with "War Eagle!" as its rallying cry, Auburn was a bastion of white male camaraderie. Though "girls" now make up almost half the student body, Auburn remains an institution steeped in southern traditionalism. Students who share that heritage will find Auburn a warm and friendly place to get excellent training in agricultural and technical fields.

"On the rolling plains of Dixie, 'neath the sun-kissed skies," begins Auburn's alma mater, and most students think the campus couldn't be lovelier. Huge mossy trees, lush lawns, and majestic colonnades grace the thousand sprawling acres, though most of the main red-brick Georgian and modern academic buildings are grouped in a compact central location. The town of Auburn, depicted in an Oliver Goldsmith poem as the "loveliest village of the plains," grew up amid miles of forest and farmland solely to serve the university and bubbles over with "warm southern atmosphere," one student reports. "Auburn is the friendliest village on the plains, and the girls are the prettiest," says another student.

As a land-grant institution, Auburn's traditional academic strengths have been in the agricultural sciences. Architecture, engineering and veterinary medicine are also among the finest undergraduate programs of their kind in the Deep South. Pharmacy is also regarded as strong, but the business school is more popular than it is academically solid. Otherwise the university's academics are uneven, partly because of the severe financial difficulties that have plagued Auburn for several years but also, some say, because of the university's priorities. While library services were slashed despite increasing demand, the university added ten thousand seats to the football stadium; the same week that faculty were told there was no money for raises, the alumni association purchased the football coach's house for him. Exam dates and first days of classes are changed for bowl games.

Academic intensity varies from program to program. While engineering is "very high pressure," most other areas are fairly casual. Students are generally "concerned with but not devoted to academics." The general education program, required of all students, includes courses in English composition, world history, art history or literature, natural science, mathematics or philosophy. A co-op option, which provides pay and credits in several professional fields, is increasingly popular, as is the campus ROTC program. A relatively new honors program offers a greater academic challenge to the few who want it. Students assert that some of Auburn's best professors have left because of the financial squeeze, and professors get mixed reviews on their accessibility. Where one finds them "genuinely interested in teaching," another thinks they are "far-removed" from students.

Though more diverse than it once was, Auburn is hardly a melting pot. Almost two-thirds of the undergraduates are homegrown Alabamians, and Auburn has taken some heat from the courts recently because it is unable to attract significant numbers of blacks, who account for only 4 percent of the undergraduates. The conservative tone of this Bible Belt campus fosters many fundamentalist Christian groups, and Auburn is home to one of the largest branches of the Campus Crusade for Christ movement in the United States. Campus politics follow suit. "If you are a radical, a liberal, or a minority, you'd be happier elsewhere," says a senior.

Each year, Auburn awards over a thousand scholarships ranging from $200 to $6,000 to students with outstanding scholastic records. It also offers about 270 athletic scholarships and its own non-need-based loan program. Housing is provided for less than a quarter of the students, most of them women, in twenty-five dorms. The men's dorms are reportedly the pits, so most exercise the option of joining one of the thirty fraternities or moving to one of the nearby apartments or trailer parks. Women have slightly better pickings, especially if they belong to one of the eighteen sororities, which have space in the choicest dorms. Freshmen must request housing when they apply for admission, and even then they receive last pick. Those hoping to strike up a romance with that boy or girl across the hall can forget it. "Of course we don't have coed dorms," observes a journalism major. "That's 'sinful.'" Visiting hours are restricted to the weekends. The meal plan gives students a novel option called the Chef's Club, in which students charge meals on a magnetic card and are billed only for what they eat. There are five cafeterias and several snack bars on campus, and fraternity men have the option of eating in their houses.

Despite the friendly feeling of community, some students note the drawbacks to small-town life: Town merchants have been known to raise their prices around term time, and there's virtually no nightlife. One virtue everyone agrees upon is the proximity of I-85, which puts Montgomery (where Auburn has a branch campus) just an hour away, and Atlanta, Birmingham and the inviting Gulf coast beaches just a couple of hours farther off.

Seldom, however, are students so bored by their bucolic surroundings that they have to hightail it out of town the minute their last Friday class ends. Once they set aside their books, Auburn students react to the prospect of partying with unabashed, good-ole-boy gusto. "Auburn is said to come alive Thursday night and not die out until

Monday night," reports one partyer. Most students make their social rounds by way of the local bars, supper clubs, dances and the many fraternity parties. Despite the lack of coed dorms, one need not sit in a bar crying into a glass of beer while listening to "Your Cheatin' Heart," for the healthy male-female ratio puts a date within the reach of nearly every wallflower. What to do is not much of a problem, for plays, concerts, pep rallies, parties and the Wreck Tech Pajama Parade are all held on campus.

Auburn is traditionally a football powerhouse, and the time-honored rallying cry "War Eagle!" still reverberates through the stadium every time an Auburn back runs for daylight. "It's the pulse of the campus, uniting each and every student in a common bond," enthuses one student. Although basketball, swimming and track draw nowhere near the rabid crowds of their pigskin-crazy peers, these sports sometimes produce more impressive teams. Women's athletics deserve much more attention than they receive; many squads are the cream of the Southeastern Conference. Intramurals are popular, especially so among Greeks, who compete for the coveted all-sports trophy every year.

Auburn offers some of the Deep South's best technical training in an atmosphere of southern hospitality. Auburn students love the conservative, small-town—and yes, conformist—ethos of their school, and few feel any need to change it. "My parents met at AU; they remained AU supporters through the years, and it was assumed I would attend without question," a public relations major relates. "I'm glad—it's an embracing environment, a place to call home."

Austin College

Sherman, TX 75090

Location Rural	**Accepted** 83%
Total Enrollment 1,180	**Enrolled** 48%
Undergraduates 1,180	**Academics** ★ ★ ★
Male/Female 53/47	**Social** ☎ ☎ ☎
SAT V/M 510/540	**Q of L** ● ● ●
Financial Aid 50%	**Admissions** (800)442-5363
Expense Pr $	in Texas, (214)892-9101 out of state
Applicants 760	

Good private liberal arts colleges are few and far between in this state where bigger is better. But tiny Austin College, located an hour north of Dallas in the Red River Valley (no, it's not in Austin, as everyone assumes), turns isolation and small size into virtues by offering a highly personalized education. Students here believe they get more out of secluding themselves on sixty attractively landscaped acres than by living it up anyplace else.

Located on the outskirts of the downtown area, Austin's self-contained campus is architecturally diverse but consistently beige in color. The students who occupy it have no problem believing that they are the college's primary concern. Everyone is assigned a faculty mentor, who watches over his or her progress both inside and outside the classroom during all four years. Each semester, students write an Individual Development Report that is reviewed by these mentors. There is considerable opportunity for independent learning on and off campus, and a six-course core curriculum provides a solid common base in Western thought from "Plato to present." Most classes are small, and even the required freshman courses are broken down into small discussion sections. Reports one student: "The academic climate could be classified as high pressured, but there is a great support system that helps students deal with it."

Preprofessional areas are undoubtedly Austin's specialties. When it comes time to apply to professional schools, premed and predental students at this little college have the highest acceptance rate of any Texas school, and aspiring legal eagles also do well. Austin's five-year teaching program has been a model for recent reforms at other institutions. For obvious reasons, science and education receive high marks from students. The administration claims that the foreign language faculty are noted for "innovative pedagogy," and students are inclined to agree. One senior recounts, "it's not atypical for a professor to take his class out into the sunshine to discuss Spanish verb conjugations." Business lacks enough variety to suit some, and art has "exceptional teachers" but limited resources. Students can earn double majors or combine three of the schools twenty-six majors into an interdisciplinary degree. A cooperative engineering program links Austin with other Texas schools.

During the January Term students can take an "experiential learning" course, usually outside their major, on a pass/fail basis. Those students who need a break from campus altogether can quickly and easily find themselves "scuba diving in Cozumel, Mexico, or reviewing plays in London," a communications arts major notes. Austin also offers its students independent study, junior year abroad, and college or departmental honors programs. A $6-million library expansion has more than doubled the capacity of the old, formerly inadequate facility. For some reason, Austin is home to the country's "largest collection of Alexander the Great" materials.

The student body is more than 90 percent Texan and mostly suburban, with a decided career orientation and a comfortable share of family money. Still, a strong feeling of egalitarianism pervades the campus. "Students are usually conservative when they arrive," reports a political scientist. "But many become more liberal by the time they graduate." Though the school has been tied to the Presbyterian Church in the United States since 1849, chapel is optional and the church affiliation manifests itself only in the emphasis on values in the core courses, the restrictions on the use of alcohol on campus and the limited dormitory visitation hours.

Austin provides a good portion of financial aid, but does not promise to assemble a workable financial package for all admitted students. Close to one-fourth of the student body receives some sort of meritorious award, either for academic or artistic talent, and stipends range from $500 to $9,000 a year.

Most students live in the five dorms; freshmen and sophomores have no choice in the matter. But the situation could be worse—at least Austin's dorms receive the students' stamp of approval. Two are coed, and each has its own distinctive character. Nearly all students take advantage of the three-meals-a-day plan, and Austin's unlimited eats generally merit going back for seconds. The Green Room off to one side of the main cafeteria provides a restaurant atmosphere for students three nights a week. Reservations and appropriate dress are required, and waiters serve the meals.

One-third of the students belong to the ten fraternities and five sororities, all local chapters, which offer weekend parties and occasional formal dances. The town of Sherman offers little to do and, thanks to the conservative Southern Baptist influence, nothing to drink. "A lot of big city kids are disillusioned at first by the small size of the town," reports one urbanite. A popular weekend excursion is the one-hour drive to the Dallas–Fort Worth Metroplex, and the college's twenty-eight-acre recreational spot on Lake Texoma (a half hour north). Even without athletic scholarships, varsity sports seem to be generating increasing campus support. The football and the men's tennis teams are tough Division II contenders and are usually good for a championship now and then. There's overwhelming enthusiasm for intramurals, and students rave about the excellent gymnasium facilities, complete with sauna.

The atmosphere can seem a little dull and claustrophobic at times (and smell quite awful when the wind is blowing from the direction of the salad dressing plant down the street). But for the career-minded and academically motivated student looking for a personalized, well-rounded education, Austin College is a good choice. "This place has so much to offer," reassures a sophomore. "And if it doesn't have what you're looking for, you can always make it happen."

Babson College

Wellesley, MA 02157

Location Suburban	**Applicants** 1,690
Total Enrollment 3,160	**Accepted** 43%
Undergraduates 1,550	**Enrolled** 46%
Male/Female 65/35	**Academics** ★ ★ ★
SAT V/M 500/595	**Social** ☎ ☎
Financial Aid 37%	**Q of L** ● ● ●
Expense Pr $ $ $	**Admissions** (617)239-5521

Even in New England, 450 wooded acres with classic white-pillared brick buildings do not a liberal arts college make. Founded in 1919 by Roger W. Babson (famous for predicting the stock market crash of 1929), Babson College alumni include top executives from Pepsi Cola, Ford Motor Company and Dunn & Bradstreet. This is a school that takes its business learning seriously and subscribes to a philosophy of educating students for free enterprise leadership. It's a bastion of the American capitalistic work ethic, an institution that thrives on Junior Achievement types. Never mind the recent trend toward a stronger liberal arts emphasis; "Babson Means Business."

Students at this small private institution face a rigorous work load and, as one marketing major points out, "there is always an analysis to piece together or a Wall Street Journal to read." Core courses introduce students to the fundamentals of economics and management, and then it's time to branch out into specialties. Accounting is said to be number one among majors (Babson graduates earn some of the highest scores on CPA exams). Other high-quality programs are finance, marketing and communications. The exclusive program of entrepreneurial studies, which brings prominent venture capitalists and entrepreneurs to campus for how-to lectures, is highly touted by administrators and students as well. Despite the administration's attempt to beef up the liberal arts department—offering more attractive electives and adding faculty members and a new chairman—students still say it's full of "blow-off classes." Even the college president admits, "This is not a place to come to major in literature or history." Still, 40 percent of every Babson student's curriculum is comprised of liberal arts courses.

Faculty members usually have hands-on experience in the business world and often continue a consulting practice on the side. But students don't feel neglected by busy professors; in fact they benefit from such outside interests. "Most professors integrate real life experiences into class discussions," reports a marketing major. Courses are usually taught by the case-study approach, in which specific business situations are covered in class and students perform in groups, or little pseudo-corporations. This type of learning requires frequent out-of-class group meetings and a lot of study schedule coordination. It also means grades can be based on group output so the pressure for each individual to produce is intense. Frequent class participation is a must and "competition among peers is high; everyone is trying to outdo everybody else," says a soon-to-be accountant.

Getting into necessary and desired classes can be a struggle in itself. "Not enough classes are offered and sometimes two necessary courses conflict," attests a senior. Thanks in part to a $2-million grant from the Olin Foundation, the school is expanding its computer facilities, and a telecommunications installation makes for more convenient voice and data access. The Horn Library is great for (you guessed it) business research, but leaves much to be desired in the liberal arts area. At any rate, its first two floors are most conducive to socializing; but serious students need only keep climbing the stairs. Two desperately needed facilities—a new gym for indoor sports and a student center—are on the school's wish list.

Babson can still be characterized as white, wealthy and extremely conservative. "It screams money," says an entrepreneurship major. Diversity is not a commodity for this otherwise affluent student body. "There's not a lot of respect for 'strange' people," advises one upwardly mobile student. One student describes his colleagues as "self-centered, leadership hungry and interested in money and opportunity." Another student adds, "Babson is not the place for indecisiveness." Students are goal-oriented, and their goals are specific: Take over Daddy's business or make one of their own. Although there is less need here than at most schools, need-based financial aid is available. There's no free lunch for athletes or academic high achievers, though. In fact, one student complains his personal scholarships from outside sources were subtracted from, rather than added to, his Babson grant.

Babson resides on a typically collegiate-looking campus of Georgian architecture, no-more-than-four-story buildings, neatly clipped lawns and full, well-groomed trees. Freshmen are guaranteed housing, but upperclassmen have to contend with the whims of a lottery. This system leaves some unlucky sophomores out in the cold because Babson can only house 85 percent of its students. There are four all-male and two all-female dorms. The remaining halls, students report, are coed and well maintained although they sometimes get overheated. Everyone uses one of three meal plans (nineteen, fourteen or ten meals a week) at the dining hall, which serves good but "schoolish-type" food. Every Wednesday is gourmet night when the menu fluctuates between such delicacies as fresh lobster, Italian cooking and turkey dinners. Saturday is steak-and-shrimp night.

Babson is only about twelve miles from Boston, in sedate Wellesley, where residents tend to "dislike students and their disturbances." The closest mass transit station is two miles away, but those with cars have easy access not only to Boston and its myriad schools and cultural offerings, but also to Cape Cod and the New Hampshire ski slopes. Understandably, the campus empties out quite a bit on weekends, but for those who stay, weekend highlights often include an all-school party at the auditorium or a semiformal sponsored by a residence hall or a Greek organization. The four fraternities and two sororities also host follow-ups (room parties) to the regular 9:00 PM–1:00 AM school events. The college strictly observes the Massachusetts drinking age of twenty-one—more so than its students, who conduct themselves "just like in the business world" and favor martinis and Bloody Marys to kegs of beer.

Lest you think the career-oriented students take too many study breaks, be informed that some of the best attended functions are sponsored by the marketing and finance clubs. Extracurricular activities are good practice for future managers and entrepreneurs. The groups tend to be *very* competitive and one marketing major contends that "if you aren't involved in at least five activities, you're a nobody."

Men's ice hockey and men's and women's skiing are the top varsity sports as far as the record books are concerned, but students turn out to watch basketball, lacrosse and soccer too, and women's field hockey is gaining popularity. Intramural athletics are moderately popular and, like everything else at this school, competitive.

If your politics are anything but conservative, i.e., if you don't have what one student calls "a positive attitude toward business and its importance in the economy," then you should probably look beyond Babson. But those who really mean business may invest in Babson and reap the untaxable capital gains.

Bard College

Annandale-on-Hudson, NY 12504

Location Rural	**Applicants** 1,240
Total Enrollment 890	**Accepted** 56%
Undergraduates 840	**Enrolled** 40%
Male/Female 48/52	**Academics** ★ ★ ★
SAT V/M 620/580	**Social** 🛋 🛋 🛋
Financial Aid 60%	**Q of L** ● ● ●
Expense Pr $ $ $ $	**Admissions** (914)758-6822

Bard College was one of the first small private schools in America to put the arts back into liberal arts, and it is still a place where students' imaginations are valued as highly as their academic abilities. Although it earned a reputation in the 1960s for funky intellectualism, Bard has fought a successful battle to resuscitate the classics and facilitate serious academic inquiry along both individualized and traditional lines. Now a respected institution with a distinctive identity, Bard seems to be coming closer to a day when the only flakes on campus are made of snow.

For more than two decades, creative types have flocked to Bard's isolated setting inside the endless terrain of the Hudson Valley, where the Catskills and Adirondacks serve as a backdrop. The hodgepodge of architectural styles includes everything from cottages and historical mansions to modern dorms "in the best of Howard Johnson modes." Students can start to appreciate Bard's beautiful surroundings and individualized approach to higher education before they are even admitted if they choose to participate in a daylong seminar/interview and receive an "instant" rejection or acceptance. More special attention before matriculation comes when freshmen are required to show up three weeks before classes start for the unusual Workshop in Language and Thinking, organized around the notion that good writing and clear thinking are necessary tools for what they will be doing for the next four years.

Bard has mild distribution requirements, and independent studies are really the soul of the school's curriculum. Any student can write his or her own course description, find a professor to sponsor it, and produce a custom-designed program. "Tutorials are something students expect to have, not something they hope to get," one literature major explains. Bard also makes a point of recognizing visual and performing arts as

45

equals among academic disciplines, and many faculty members in these areas are working professionals who teach part-time. In addition, the college has plans to construct a $5-million, fifteen-hundred-seat amphitheater on the campus to house a new Hudson Valley Summer Arts Festival of music, ballet and maybe even opera. There are good film and music courses to be found at Bard, including a rock 'n' roll workshop. The art department is strictly "fine" arts; commercial artists need not apply. The drama department has always been strong—after all, this is Chevy Chase's alma mater—but student criticism of this program seems to be on the rise.

The best division at Bard is unquestionably languages and literature. This assessment is based on the small classes, distinguished authors like Mary McCarthy teaching classes in creative writing, and student gratitude for having learned how to express themselves through their writing "with clarity, vigor and individuality." Natural sciences and physics are surprisingly good, although social sciences could stand improvement. Students say that the library, which has only 170,000 volumes, just doesn't stack up; with fluorescent lights that hum overhead, it is also an impossible place in which to try to study. Students can seek out resources at nearby Vassar, where they complain they are less than warmly received.

At the end of their second year, all students go through a process called moderation in which they write an educational autobiography and a statement of tentative academic objectives and declare a major. This paper and a major project are presented before a board of professors within the relevant department and discussed with the student. The junior year includes a conference of preparation for the senior project, usually a tutorial, and during the senior year students do the equivalent of an undergraduate dissertation, such as a critical analysis of literature, dance or a lab experiment. "Bard is the sound of one's footsteps," explains a senior. "Most students put themselves in a high-pressure situation—never in opposition to other students, but to themselves."

Bard offers combined programs with other schools in engineering, social work, business administration, public administration and forestry and environmental science. In the junior year, there are many opportunities to study abroad, through Bard's programs in France and Germany or almost anywhere in the world either independently or through another school. The winter field period comes at the end of December and lasts for six weeks: a chance to take in-depth courses on or off campus, pursue internships, travel or whatever. Bard also runs the Simons' Rock Early College in Massachusetts, a program that compresses the last two years of high school and first two years of college into a comprehensive two-year program. Simon's Rock graduates have the option of moving over to Bard or, more typically, transferring elsewhere as juniors.

The student body at Bard is cosmopolitan, chic, "politically liberal—not radical—bright, independent and usually very creative." They hail mainly from the East Coast and California, with a significant contingent of midwesterners thrown in. "There are those who wear Izods and flannel nighties, those with nose clips and purple hair," according to one people watcher. "You see everything from Arab robes to three-piece suits." Minority students constitute 16 percent of the student body. Although a sizable portion of the students matriculate from privileged and overprivileged homes, Bard's administration has made an effort to create socioeconomic diversity. The newly instituted Excellence and Equal Cost program allows public school students in the top ten of their class to attend Bard for the price of attending their home state university or college. Despite its traditionally small endowment, Bard manages to offer generous financial aid of all kinds to students with demonstrated need. Merit and athletic scholarships are zippo.

Freshmen are required to live on campus in dorms that range from a large cinder-block monstrosity to converted mansions to modular households for eight to fifteen people. A quarter of the other students rent rooms elsewhere (a move that requires a car). Most freshman rooms are doubles or triples, and most are coed, except for the all-female Blithewood mansion (aka the "virgin vault"). All residential students eat on campus, and aside from the fine salad bar, food quality is considered average at best. But far superior to any regular meals are the free midnight brunches—everything from cupcakes to eggrolls—served during finals.

Social life at Bard is far from an endless party. "Fraternities and sororities are dirty words at Bard," comments one Bardian. Students report, "There are some campus parties, but most of our socializing takes place around a six-pack in a dorm room." Even the usual bulk of campus clubs, societies, ensembles, and political groups tend to come and go on this campus. "Bard students aren't joiners," one woman explains. "You don't see too many of us together at one time. We don't like to have our sense of individuality threatened." But that doesn't mean there's nothing to do. *Au contraire,* the radio station and several student publications are currently hot extracurricular activities. Films and lectures are as well attended as the coffee shops where "people hang out."

Soccer, cross-country, and women's volleyball are popular team sports, but Bard is virtually devoid of dedicated jocks. "But there are plenty of pseudo-jocks, and intellectuals in good shape," reports one student. For what it's worth, adds another, "men's and women's athletics are equal in their misery." An intramural softball program captures the interest of more than half the students in the spring. Five miles of trails through the woods along the Hudson are perfect for a myriad of outdoor activity, from cross-country to raspberry picking to skiing, jogging or hiking.

Having a car on this gorgeous but isolated campus does much to prevent occasional attacks of claustrophobia. The local community is too small to offer much in the way of entertainment, but Bard is less than twenty miles from Woodstock, which is a good place for interesting shopping, and within striking distance of ski slopes in the Catskills or Berkshires. New York City, just two hours away, is visited often.

Most students seem relatively comfortable with Bard's strengths and peculiarities. Everyone goes by first names (the president is "Leon") and seems to realize he or she is sharing a rare experience: four years at a college that still believes in an education for its own sake.

Barnard College, NY—See COLUMBIA UNIVERSITY

Baruch College, NY—See CITY UNIVERSITY OF NEW YORK

47

Bates College

Lewiston, ME 04240

Location Small city	**Applicants** 2,990
Total Enrollment 1,500	**Accepted** 47%
Undergraduates 1,500	**Enrolled** 35%
Male/Female 50/50	**Academics** ★ ★ ★ ★
SAT N/A	**Social** 🐿 🐿 🐿
Financial Aid 40%	**Q of L** ● ● ●
Expense Pr $ $ $ $	**Admissions** (207)786-6000

The warmth, friendliness and closeness of the college community are what keep students at Bates College going through those long, cold Maine winters. But life in Lewiston is more than just a bowl of Cream of Wheat. Founded by active abolitionists in 1855, Bates was the first coeducational college in New England. True to its ancestry, this highly selective school remains active and innovative. It has eliminated SAT scores as a required part of the application and created a unique 4-4-1 calendar, which saves some of the most interesting, unconventional learning experience for the end of the school year—just the incentive students need during those long Maine winters to bundle up, crack the books and keep an eye out for spring.

Despite its willingness to experiment, this little liberal arts college is no academic softy. "Bates has the hardest grading in the United States," believes one victim. "It can be aggravating to spend so much time working just to get a B." Although the faculty is demanding, students say professors also give a lot in return. "Most profs can be found in their offices or reached at home, and they are always willing to help you out," a junior attests.

Bates, an intriguing mix of Georgian and Federal buildings and Victorian homes spreading out over its grassy campus, is an oasis in the New England industrial city of Lewiston. While it is not too far from Boston or Maine's gorgeous rock-bound coast (of which Bates owns a sizable strip), Lewiston, a "run-down milltown," is short on cultural advantages. The town does, however, provide plenty of internships and part-time jobs, a distinct vocational advantage not always found at such a small college.

The traditional liberal arts curriculum is as strong as the pressure to achieve within it. Students cite chemistry, biology and geology as solid among the sciences, and history and English as standouts on the humanities side. Foreign languages, astronomy, and philosophy continue to get low marks from students. But theater and the arts have been given a recent boost by the opening of the new Olins Arts Center, which houses a performance hall, gallery, recording studio, art studios, and practice rooms. Bates also boasts a rhetoric program and a national-level debate team that is great for prelaw students. These academic offerings are enhanced by a challenging independent-studies program, the junior year abroad for top scholars, and the Washington Semester.* Also for juniors, Bates offers Dana Foundations grants enabling students to assist professors in their research in return for financial aid covering the entire cost of their last two years of college.

The unusual 4-4-1 calendar at Bates is conducive to studies abroad at the end of the college year, and trips to China, India or South America are there for the taking. While the spring short-term courses may be more relaxed, students find them no less worthwhile. One student cites an Arts and Artists course, which took him to several major U.S. cities, as having greatly influenced his view of the art world. In addition, students have access to the ten-college Venture Program* and the American Maritime Studies Program at Mystic Seaport*—two unusual and attractive options for students seeking real-world experience. Students also benefit from the Ladd Library, which houses an all-night study room, a typing room and "an audio room with everything from Bach to Bruce Springsteen."

Seven of every eight students come from outside Maine, many from Massachusetts. They are bright, inquisitive, hardworking and generally affluent young men and women, many involved in political clubs. "Having always admitted women and minorities and never having had fraternities or sororities, there is a social continuity here that is unique," claims the administration. Although minorities are welcome and heavily recruited, they only make up 7 percent of the population. Skiing is a common passion, and excellent slopes are just over an hour away. Most students with financial need receive adequate packages, but being wait-listed is a real threat. No athletic or merit scholarships are awarded.

Campus dwellers are spread out among a freshman center, upperclass dorms and charming old Victorian houses for ten to thirty students. Upperclassmen who want singles will probably have to settle for the single-sex dorms or houses. All boarders eat in the Commons, where they enjoy above-average food. A few adventurous or penurious souls take to cheaper off-campus living as one way to beat the increasing cost of education at Bates.

Weekends are short; "Friday night till 10 PM and all day Sunday mean the library for most Batesies," explains a psych major. Most stay on campus, so there are always enough people around to create a "casual, easygoing, and often spontaneous" good time, whether at a private party, or an activity sponsored by one of the many student organizations. Lewiston's main contribution to social life at Bates is "the old standby bar: The Goose." Bates students are usually on hand to cheer their varsity teams—especially basketball, football and lacrosse—despite their unexceptional records. The Bates teams that do excel are the women's soccer and the men's and women's ski teams. Students agree that women's sports at Bates are on a par with men's. The intramural program, organized by the students and supervised by faculty members, is "strong and spirited," complete with lively dorm rivalries. A modern athletic and recreation facility offers track, tennis, swimming, squash and more.

Bates students sometimes complain that the academic pace is too grueling, the college too insular, and the students cut too much from the same cloth. But they are proud of their perseverance in this lonely and often cold location and share unusual respect for and camaraderie with their fellow academic exiles. As one student comments: "I work best when I'm doing 30,000 things at once, and I have plenty of chances to live this way here. The challenge, the push, the opportunities—that's what I love about Bates."

Baylor University

Waco, TX 76798

Location Center city
Total Enrollment 11,560
Undergraduates 10,180
Male/Female 46/54
SAT V/M 490/540
Financial Aid 35%
Expense Pr $

Applicants 4,640
Accepted 73%
Enrolled 70%
Academics ★ ★ ★
Social 🍷🍷🍷
Q of L ● ● ●
Admissions (817)755-1811

What do you get when you take a campus that is owned and supported by Southern Baptists, a bunch of above-average college students (many of whose parents are preachers or missionaries), a philosophy that discourages drinking and dancing, and plop them all down deep in the heart of Texas? You get a "Baylor Bubble" of course. And while most students here enjoy the academically and religiously oriented world of Baylor University, one student advises that "radical, nonconforming, big-time partiers might feel a little stifled here."

Baylor, the largest Baptist university in the world, sits upon 425 acres adjoining the historic Brazos River near downtown Waco (population: 110,000) in central Texas—right between Dallas and Austin, and about a hundred miles from each. The campus, "composed in the gracious tradition of the Old South," has held up surprisingly well considering the age of most of the buildings. "The central part of campus, called the Quadrangle, was built when Baylor moved from Independence, Texas, in 1885, and is characterized by Georgian architecture," explains one design student. Today, several new red-brick structures mix with the old on this well-landscaped campus, which is closed to traffic.

When it comes to academics, the atmosphere is tempered by a degree of pragmatism. All freshmen must enter the college of arts and sciences where they remain for two years in a core curriculum before moving into their majors—either in arts and sciences, or one of the more professional schools of business, education, music and nursing. But all degree students must take two religion courses (on the Old and New Testaments), as well as two semesters of "Forum"—a series of lectures and meetings on various issues or religious testimonials.

The Armstrong Browning Library houses the largest collection of books, papers and personal belongings of poets Robert and Elizabeth Barrett Browning, and there is even a huge collection of stained glass windows portraying themes from their poems. Special programs include church-state studies and museum studies. There are institutes of environmental studies, childhood learning disorders, and foreign and domestic affairs. The archeology and geology departments utilize fossil- and mineral-rich Texas prairies, but those who tire of southwestern scenery may migrate toward one of Baylor's programs in Europe, Mexico or Israel.

The friendly, family style atmosphere of the school is one of Baylor's biggest strengths. "Class sizes are small, and many professors know students by name," says a senior. "The faculty is concerned about students on more than an academic basis," adds an international business major. Even the university president sets aside time for students to come and chat with him.

Baylor has strong offerings in the business department, especially accounting and the fairly new entrepreneurship program. The school of music is also strong, and the education program is well regarded in the state. Due in part to Baylor's outstanding medical school, undergraduate premed majors are in good shape. And naturally, religious studies is a safe bet. Students are much less enthusiastic about the journalism offerings, as well as the math department. And although there are two programs in computer studies, some students complain there are not enough computers available.

Students are predominantly middle- to upper-middle-class Christian conservatives, and three-fourths are from the top quarter of their high school class. A majority of students are from the South—76 percent from Texas. Most are quite conservative ("You don't admit to being a member of the Baylor Young Democrats!" advises a business administration major). They tend to be "well-dressed, all-American types who enjoy good clean fun," according to several accounts. "It's called the Baylor Bubble," explains one student, "because everyone has a sort of naive, innocent look at the world. Sometimes it's exasperating, sometimes nice."

Baylor's tuition is meager compared to other small private schools, and the university administers more than $20 million in student financial aid. There are also $15,000 scholarships available to National Merit finalists who name Baylor as their first choice. All dorms are single sex; visitation is limited to three hours on Sundays. Freshmen are urged to live on campus and are assigned old but well-maintained rooms when they are admitted. Due to a lack of space, many upperclassmen move off campus, although some lucky students (mostly women) obtain a slot in the much-in-demand, spacious upperclass dorms. As for campus dining, "visiting students have always complimented our food service so it must be pretty good," concludes an elementary education major. There's even a "lite line" for students watching their weight.

Twenty-five percent of the students belong to a fraternity or sorority, although no houses are permitted. Despite several other student organizations, much of the school's social life revolves around the frats—"too much," some students believe. "If you are not a part of this system," reports a senior, "then you just aren't in the 'in' social aspect at Baylor." The university maintains a small marina for sunning, swimming, sailing, canoeing and paddle boating, and there are several lakes with good beaches and a city park nearby. As for nightlife, Waco "isn't a very exciting city; it's not adventuresome or even interesting," claims a future accountant. So, in wide-open Texas, where distances don't seem to matter, a big date usually means dinner and a movie in Austin or Dallas. Needless to say, a set of wheels is a big help, if not a necessity.

And what about football? C'mon, this is a Texas school—football dominates at Baylor. "Students love their team and there's great school spirit," attests one student. Baseball, track and basketball are also popular. There is an intramural program, but religious activities are participated in with a bit more vigor. There are national chapters of Campus Crusade and the Fellowship of Christian Athletes. The Baptist Students Union sponsors weekly concerts by religious singing groups, one-dollar movies, and Coke (soft drink) hours.

Baylor students apparently thrive within the strong sense of community—Baptist community—fostered by the school's traditional values. Although one student admits that "Baylor sometimes seems a little too sheltered or cut off from the outside world," another proclaims that "the atmosphere is so wonderful with so many neat Christians around who love the Lord and aren't afraid to show it." In other words, don't burst their bubble.

Beloit College

Beloit, WI 53511

Location Small city
Total Enrollment 1,040
Undergraduates 1,030
Male/Female 51/49
SAT V/M 520/530
Financial Aid 71%
Expense Pr $ $

Applicant 950
Accepted 79%
Enrolled 38%
Academics ★ ★ ★
Social 🐿 🐿 🐿
Q of L ● ● ● ●
Admissions (608)365-3391

Beloit won academic fame during the 1960s and '70s for the Beloit Plan, which had students learning on a year-round basis and sent them out for mandatory off-campus experiences, often abroad. The double whammy of a financial crunch and a more career-oriented student generation put an end to this experiment, but many vestiges of the progressive era remain—as Beloit continues to provide an innovative liberal arts atmosphere for those who may be dissatisfied with the New Traditionalism of the 1980s.

Beloit students agree that the ivy-covered brick and stone buildings and "delightful lack of cement" make the spacious campus lovely but strangely out of place in the blue-collar town of Beloit. One student points out: "Beloit's actual location, in a puny town in the middle of nowhere, does not reflect on the college itself." If anything, the rather drab, economically depressed surroundings have motivated more students to take advantage of Beloit's multitude of off-campus programs. For example, there's the highly popular Professional Exploration Program (PEP) that lets students flex their muscles, often for credit, in school-arranged jobs and internships, including summer positions through Beloit Internship Summer Employment Program. The World Outlook Program, though cut back sharply, offers faculty-led trips abroad, and special problems courses enable one to three students to work with professors on research in areas of common interest. The Fudan-Beloit Exchange Program allows five Beloit students and a faculty member to switch places with students and a professor from the Fudan University in China. Other options include student teaching in Britain or Australia, studying classics at the University of Chicago or politics at American University in Washington. Additional ventures abroad are available through the Associated Colleges of the Midwest.* Says one student, "Seldom does a student leave Beloit with merely four years of straightforward class instruction."

Beloit's anthropology and geology departments, often weak areas at small liberal arts colleges, are the stars of the school's forty-one standard majors. Excellent facilities, faculty and numerous field trips, are what make both departments strong. The school's location on prehistoric burial grounds also helps, as do the extensive museum collections of archeological and ethnographic artifacts. There's also a decent art museum on campus, giving Beloit, in the words of one man, "one of the best museum-student ratios in the country." For the professionally oriented, a museum studies minor is offered, as are prelaw advising, a master's in teaching program, and early-admission premed and predental programs. English is another strong area, and psychology, theater and economics are the departments that have experienced the greatest growth in the past decade, but students believe there is room for yet more improvement. Physics, music and religion draw criticism for lack of breadth or depth. The Center for Language Studies complements Beloit's good foreign language department programs with intensive summer study (based on the Middlebury College model) in Arabic, Chinese,

Japanese, Russian and English as a second language. In addition, the college has created an experimental ten-day language orientation program that gives incoming freshmen an opportunity to test-learn in any one of ten languages before choosing which to study. Beloit also runs a summer theater in its modernized performing arts complex. The library is the least adequate academic facility, greatly in need of updating and reorganization.

No student graduates from Beloit without demonstrating mastery of basic writing and reasoning skills and completing distribution requirements in the natural sciences, humanities, social sciences and interdisciplinary studies. Although pressure is largely self-determined, "it is not true to say that anyone can just waltz in here and get a degree without doing a day of work," contends a senior. Thirty-five percent of classes have ten students or fewer, and none have more than fifty. All but 4 percent of the faculty have doctorates or the highest appropriate degree in their field. And almost across the board teaching is the faculty's first priority. The atmosphere is friendly and nurturing— "You don't find a team of professors trying to outwit a team of students here," reports one senior. Students and faculty are on a first-name basis, with the use of the title "Doctor" strictly taboo. Opportunities for independent study abound and Beloit Track II (not a razor but a program) allows students to combine courses and independent study projects to form custom-made majors. (How about mythology, oral history or set design for educational television?)

Beloit's alternative programs and liberal educational strengths attract a student body of "independent, slightly hedonistic, sharing, intellectual individuals." About 75 percent are from outside Wisconsin, and foreign students make up about 13 percent of the enrollment. Beloit students vary widely in their background, interests, and outlooks, yet there exists a certain tolerance and all seem to get along. Although the student body is a tad more conservative and career oriented than it once was, conformity is still a low priority. Beloit was not designed for "students who want to learn their way directly into upper-middle-class comfort or those content with being given direction instead of finding their own," attests one independent thinker. Beloit has won national attention with its Moral Obligation Scholarship Program, under which about 35 percent of students in need receive grants that carry a moral, but not legal, obligation for students to repay them as gifts after they become alumni. The college also takes special note of academic merit among incoming students, offering forty-five scholarships, worth up to $3,000 a year for students with 3.5 high school GPAs, good test scores and a lofty class rank.

Housing and dining facilities are better than they were a decade ago, but are still nothing to rave about. The campus is physically split in two, with the academic and administrative buildings on one side and residence halls on the other. Dorms are either coed-by-floor, or completely coed—including bathrooms, where the "knock-first method" of entrance is protocol. Students must remain in campus housing and consume Chapin Hall's cafeteria food until their junior year—the ice cream and yogurt bars prevent starvation when the cooks are having a bad day. Upperclassmen often seek refuge in the fraternity, sorority or one of the specialty houses—foreign languages, music or veggie. Living off campus is also an option. Laundromats, drugstores, Italian restaurants and quiet country roads are all within easy walking or biking distance of the campus. And the college provides van service to Chicago, Milwaukee and the excellent college town of Madison, each approximately an hour away.

No matter where students spend their time indoors, much of their time outdoors is spent in the cold and frequent rain. Still, Beloit's on-campus pub, with its live bands and plentiful beer—"This is, after all, Wisconsin," explains one student—is a cozy place to escape the elements and there are several student-frequented bars in town. Fraternities and sororities are on the comeback, becoming increasingly popular since the school passed a policy that no student activity funds can be spent on alcohol. Fraternities have their own activity funds and thus throw the most intoxicating campus parties. Day trips to cities or more scenic outdoor areas are common on the weekends, but a large majority of students remain on campus where movies, dances and all-campus parties tie up Friday and Saturday nights. Sports here are played more for fun than glory, but the football team is on the way up, and basketball is already good, as are women's volleyball and tennis teams.

Beloit is a small community that for a while was in the process of getting even smaller. The administration, however, has apparently been able to stabilize the financial and enrollment situation and now the future shines brighter. Beloit remains a place where learning is taken seriously, but not confined to the protection of ivy-covered walls.

Bennington College

Bennington, VT 05201

Location Rural	**Applicants** 520
Total Enrollment 570	**Accepted** 79%
Undergraduates 560	**Enrolled** 46%
Male/Female 35/65	**Academics** ★ ★ ★
SAT V/M 510/490	**Social** 🐿 🐿 🐿
Financial Aid 59%	**Q of L** ● ● ● ●
Expense Pr $ $ $ $	**Admissions** (802)442-5401

Bennington is one of the last bastions of the progressive, unstructured approach to education that was pioneered by John Dewey in the 1930s and flourished again in the 1960s. Specializing in the arts and humanities, the college offers a highly personal education that emphasizes learning by doing, freedom of choice and diversity of opinion. There are barely six hundred students at Bennington, and it sometimes seems as if there are also six hundred different life-styles. As one denizen puts it, "To be conventional at Bennington is to stick out and be weird."

Situated on six hundred acres in the heart of Vermont's Green Mountains, Bennington has an appealing, white-houses-with-green-shutters New England serenity, with rows of cottages set on either side of a lawn with the student commons building at its head. The school has very little academic structure—no grades and few tests. "All the pressure's internal here," says one senior. "There are no external standards like grades to get in the way of a real search for excellence." The school's strong counseling program is what holds everything together. Each faculty member is assigned fewer than a dozen students, with whom he or she must meet for at least an hour a week. Wednesday is "universal counseling day," and in the afternoon all faculty members can be found in their offices. At Bennington, close faculty attention (the ratio is still less than 9 to 1) is intended to avert the need for any core curriculum or required courses. Students are given the opportunity to create their own programs of study according to their goals and interests, to be approved by their advisers.

Literature and language, with its emphasis on critical and creative writing and its strong faculty, is one of the school's two best divisions. Visual arts is the other. The new Visual and Performing Arts building supplies lots of studio space as well as galleries, workshops, theaters and classrooms; the music division requires composing as well as performing—remember, creating is at least as important as more traditional learning. Film and video are also offered. One weak spot in Bennington's artistic offerings is that because of its low endowment, the college is sometimes unable to afford state-of-the-art equipment. Enrollment in the dance department has been tapering off, possibly because, as one student reports "dance at Bennington means *only* modern dance." Though passable, the sciences lack high-technology research capabilities and have few faculty members.

One of Bennington's few academic requirements is that students sample courses in four of seven broad subject areas during their first two years. Students must also complete four nine-week "fieldwork terms," each beginning in January, that give students a chance to engage in special study or to work in fields related to their majors and thus to put items on their resumé that might appeal to potential employers. Study-abroad options of a more traditional kind are also available.

Individual evaluations (two per term) take the place of grades, but students who think they need grades to show graduate schools needn't be frightened off. Nearly half the students continue their schooling after graduation, and about three-quarters of those applying to professional schools are admitted. Anyway, if you really need one, the dean will provide an assurance of grade equivalency to another institution. The library, though it has only 100,000 volumes, is strong in theater and art, and librarians will buy books on student suggestion. However, students complain that the lighting is poor and the temperature is often uncomfortable. For serious research, students must use an interlibrary-loan system or make the half-hour trip to Williams College.

Like everything else at Bennington, the admissions process is creative. Says one student, "I loved Bennington's application, how personal it was and how it tried to get at who I was, not how I'd done in high school or on tests." Interviews are required, and students are encouraged to send in supplementary work—poems, stories, artwork, music, and the like.

"People who had a bad time in junior high fit in well here," one happy student observes. Creative, spontaneous and independent are words that pop up frequently when Bennington students talk about their school. Since most people are wrapped up in themselves and their work, "This place can sometimes be very hard and very cold," says one student. Only 2 percent of the student body is from Vermont, and though minorities are rare, one out of ten students is from another country. Students are admitted without regard to their financial need; Bennington, however, has the dubious distinction of being the most expensive college in the nation, and middle-class students just above the usual aid cutoffs may have a tough time. In all fairness, Bennington also spends more on each of its students than any other college, with lavish faculty attention and free extras like music lessons and art studios.

The majority of Bennington's students live in twelve white New England cottages and three modern row houses, all of which are coed. Freshmen are assigned to doubles, but most upperclassmen can get singles. The houses have their own living rooms and fireplaces, and each holds between two- and three-dozen students and elects a house chairperson. Increasing enrollment has tightened up the housing situation recently, and about 10 percent of the students live off campus. Though each house has its own kitchen, all on-campus students pay for the yummy meal plan whose offerings reflect the tastes of the many vegetarians and other health-conscious eaters. The spice rack is always out, and the salad bar includes seeds, nuts and tofu. The six small dining rooms are intimate and comfortable, and in warm weather, there are frequent cookouts.

Although the atmosphere of Bennington is sophisticated and cosmopolitan—like a bit of bohemian New York that took a wrong turn on its way to Greenwich Village—

the surroundings are rural New England at its best. Quaint towns, good hiking country and ski slopes are all close by, and just off campus students can meet for a "nice, quiet meal" at the Publyk House, or for breakfast at the Blue Benn Diner. Downtown Bennington offers little more than movies and ice cream, and some locals apparently resent the intrusion of Bennington's sophisticates. "The townspeople don't like us and we don't care that much for them either," says a double major in politics and drama. Albany, the nearest real city, is an hour away, but most students would rather head for New York or Boston. The college offers a gaggle of student performances, exhibitions and recitals. Three big social events, Oktoberfest, Winter Carnival and Springfest punctuate the year, and there is always an all-night theme party on Friday, a film on Saturday, and a coffeehouse on Sunday. Because there are so few men—Bennington was formerly a women's college—women often find the social life frustrating, and long-term relationships are rare. "Visitors from other colleges are apt to comment 'but all you do is sit around and talk,' " one student says.

There is a modest intercollegiate sports program, centering on soccer and tennis. For the most part, however, the athletic program depends on who can rustle up a volleyball, soccer or tennis game at any given time. "Most people prefer 'loner' sports like jogging, biking, or swimming anyway," says one student.

The Bennington philosophy is that "the process of choosing is more important to a student than the choices made." Not surprisingly, everyone is on a first name basis with everyone else, but the company and their accomplishments can be intimidating, even alienating. "Sometimes, you can get very, very, lonely," says a senior. Self-motivation, creativity, and confidence are musts for prospectives. According to one student, Bennington asks the difficult question: "Fine, you did well on tests, but who *are* you?" Relax: You've got four years to answer.

Birmingham–Southern College

Birmingham, AL 04901

Location Urban		**Applicants** 700	
Total Enrollment 1,720		**Accepted** 86%	
Undergraduates 1,630		**Enrolled** 56%	
Male/Female 50/50		**Academics** ★ ★ ★	
SAT V/M 520/540		**Social** 🐘 🐘 🐘	
Financial Aid 75%		**Q of L** ● ● ●	
Expense Pr $		**Admissions** (205)226-4686	

Birmingham–Southern was founded in 1918 when two smaller colleges merged, hence the name that gets parted in the middle. Since then, several national publications have touted it as the best educational buy in the region, offering good professional preparation and liberal arts education in an intimate, individual-oriented atmosphere. In addition to its scholastic credentials, BSC also claims sixteen Miss Alabamas among its alumni.

The campus of Birmingham–Southern is a green and shady oasis located in a depressed urban neighborhood and surrounded by a ten-foot fence. "For protection," explains a history major. Behind the gates on "the Hilltop," as the architectural hodge-podge of a campus is called, BSC maintains its reputation as one of the top academic institutions in the state. It boasts one of only two Phi Beta Kappa chapters in Alabama. Classes rarely have more than forty students and most are much smaller. Each student is assigned a faculty member who serves as his or her academic adviser and often becomes an important friend and mentor. "The caring attitude of faculty" and "nurturing, responsive atmosphere" on campus are much praised by students. "Profs even help you find summer jobs and scholarships," a junior says.

The number of students who go on to professional school in medicine, business, and law is high. Premeds cite the strong biology program as a major drawing card. About a quarter of the students major in business, a division that includes programs ranging from accounting to business law. Southern is a regional center for the fine and performing arts. The art, drama, dance and music programs are all among the best in the South, and the staff in each area includes well-known professionals. One group of students recently traveled to Florida to help the conceptual artist Christo "wrap" an island, while back at Southern students stage several major productions each year, often including American and world premieres. Weaker programs include nursing and physical fitness, although the administration says both are slated for improvements. A recent addition has brought the computer science facilities up to date. Since BSC is affiliated with the United Methodist Church, each student is required to take a religion course.

All liberal arts majors must complete a general education program that includes courses in writing, mathematics, and seven different liberal arts areas. BSC's library, which features "nothing special" in terms of offerings, is a good place to study and generally meets students' needs. Students also have free access to both the Birmingham Public Library and the one at nearby University of Alabama at Birmingham. The popular January term is a time for students to pursue individual projects or internships, from cooking lessons to travel in China. An honors program allows exceptional students to take small seminars with one or more professors. Freshmen participate in a series of extracurricular seminars designed to help them with course selection, career plans, etc.

Over 80 percent of the students are home grown Alabamians, and practically all the rest hail from Deep South states. Many have family ties to Southern; one student explained that "my sister and both my parents went to Birmingham–Southern, as did my senior minister and the owner of the grocery store where I worked in high school." Nonsoutherners should be prepared for massive culture shock. Though moderate by Alabama standards, the student body is quite conservative except for "fringe groups in the fine arts." About 38 percent of the students belong to the Methodist Church, and 9 percent are minorities. All types of academic backgrounds are represented: about 30 percent of the students rank in the top tenth of their high school class, 15 percent in the bottom half. Regardless of their past records, students who come to Southern will feel pressure to take their education seriously. "The very lazy belong here even less than the stupid," one student states. "Most students are concerned with their future careers," adds a classmate. In addition to need-based awards, BSC offers about two hundred merit scholarships ranging from $1,000 to $6,000. National Merit Scholars who list Southern as their first choice are apt to win a stipend of several thousand dollars, with additional help available if they need it.

Most students live on campus, including many of those whose families reside in Birmingham. "If you don't live on campus, you miss a lot," a junior explains. Dorms are single sex with various visitation policies, ranging from none at all to twenty-four hour, which students choose for themselves. Andrews and New Men's are generally the most desired men's dorms, while Hanson and Goodwin are the preferred residences for women. Whereas students seem generally pleased with residential accommodations, there is equally universal condemnation of the dining service. Everyone living on campus must purchase at least a fourteen-meals-per-week plan, the cost of which some students consider inordinately high. "The food service is only interested in large profits and cuts corners everywhere," an upperclassman complains. There are, however, numerous restaurants in Birmingham, if not in the surrounding neighborhood, to provide some relief.

The twelve Greek organizations are responsible for many of the social functions on campus, especially on weekends (only 5 percent of students actually live in fraternities, but about half are members). Most Greek parties are closed, and one student claims that "people are identified too much by their Greek affiliation." Private dorm parties are the main alternative for independents. The arts departments function almost as a community unto themselves and add a good deal of sparkle to campus life. "Debate, politics, religious groups and health classes are all really popular," one student comments. Many students take advantage of what the city of Birmingham has to offer in the way of nightlife—cultural events, bars, and the rather bohemian South Side. Beaches and mountains are less than five hours away, accessible for weekend trips.

In a state where the late Bear Bryant is practically a saint, BSC is a school without a football team. Men's basketball, usually a contender for the NAIA crown, partially fills the void; the baseball and soccer teams are also very competitive. Both the men's and women's tennis teams also do well. Each recently boasted an academic all-American. Beyond that, however, "Women's sports are virtually nonexistent," a junior complains. Intramurals are popular, though dominated by the Greeks.

BSC offers a career-oriented education in a fairly social setting. Because the vast majority of students are from the Deep South, those from other areas of the country run the risk of spending four years as outsiders. But for students who fit the mold, BSC's conservative and friendly climate can offer four happy and prosperous years.

Boston College

Chestnut Hill, MA 02167

Location Suburban		**Applicants** 14,990	
Total Enrollment 13,990		**Accepted** 33%	
Undergraduates 8,450		**Enrolled** 44%	
Male/Female 43/57		**Academics** ★ ★ ★	
SAT V/M 540/580		**Social** 🕿 🕿 🕿 🕿	
Financial Aid 73%		**Q of L** ● ● ●	
Expense Pr $ $ $ $		**Admissions** (617)552-3100	

Nationally, it's known as the school where Doug Flutie threw game-winning passes, but in its hometown—the city with more college campuses than McDonald's franchises—Boston College remains more closely tied to the local business and political world than any of its counterparts. Founded in 1863 by the Society of Jesus to provide an education for Boston's swelling Catholic population, the college, like the city, has since become more cosmopolitan. Today's Boston College has managed to maintain its religious aura without impinging on the social well-being of its gregarious, sports-oriented and politically minded students.

Don't let the name fool you, Boston College is actually a university with eight schools and colleges. In fact, it's the largest Catholic university in the nation and resides on not one but two suburban campuses: the main campus at Chestnut Hill and the Newton campus one and a half miles away. "Walking through the campus on a beautiful day with the bells of Gassen Hall ringing makes me just stop and appreciate the scenery around me," a junior says. The dominant architecture is Gothic revival, but as one student reports, "progress catches up with even the most harmonious of tones." In other words, modern structures are springing up all the time. There's lots of grass and trees, not to mention a large peaceful reservoir (just perfect to jog around) right in the front yard.

The college's stated purpose is to feed "the spiritual hunger of the young who search for meaning and value in a technological culture." And to assist students in satiating their spiritual appetites, BC requires each undergrad to take a heavy load of liberal arts core courses. Everything from theology to the natural sciences and a foreign language is covered in the core curriculum, but these courses may be taken at any time during the undergraduate years. (About one-third of the three thousand courses BC offers each year can be taken in fulfillment of core requirements.)

The four schools that dole out bachelor's degrees are arts and sciences, management, nursing and education. In the school of arts and sciences—the largest undergraduate division—theology and philosophy stand out. English, however, is the most popular major, and the history, chemistry and political science departments receive numerous compliments from students. Sociology and psychology are rated as weak, along with biology and some of the fine arts ("the music department is basically nonexistent," according to one student). But drama students enjoy a multimillion-dollar Theater Arts Center with state-of-the-art lighting and sound systems. As for the more preprofessional offerings, the school of nursing is one of the best around, and the education school is particularly strong in special education. The school of management is striving toward higher quality in its curriculum and faculty, and students praise the finance and accounting departments.

Students searching for out-of-the-ordinary offerings will also find their needs fulfilled at BC. An emphasis on developing students' well-rounded view of the world, is manifested in various interdisciplinary programs. The student-run PULSE program is particularly interesting because it provides participants with the opportunity to fulfill their philosophy and theology requirements while engaging in social service fieldwork. Those involved, half of whom are freshmen, take four courses over the year (two on personal and social responsibility) and spend twelve hours a week at any of about thirty-five service organizations in the Boston area. The Perspectives program (a four-part freshman program) attempts to illustrate how great thinkers from the past have made us who we are—"an open mind is requisite," according to the administration. Other such mind-broadening programs include Faith, Peace and Justice, and the International Jesuit Volunteers. BC also offers programs in Irish, Slavic, and American studies, urban affairs, and an immersion program is a big draw for the department of romance languages and literatures.

The Jesuits on BC's faculty (about eighty out of seven hundred) exert an influence out of proportion to their numbers, if only because they add an "air of discipline," one woman reports. Students praise the faculty's accessibility as well as their fair grading. Introductory classes may have several hundred students, while upper-level courses are sometimes difficult to get into—part of the hassle of attending the largest Catholic college in the country. Yet, one of the benefits to attending BC is the new O'Neill Library. (Yes, it's named after the former House majority leader, who is a BC alumnus.)

Students rave about the library's computerized card catalogue, reservable soundproof rooms, and typing rooms. "The hours of operation are more than adequate, except on the weekends," analyzes a philosophy major. "It's not conducive to study here until Sunday."

Obviously, BC students are serious about their work, but not excessively so. "The best way to deal with academic pressure is to put the books down for a while and crack open a beer," advises one student. "BC is a wee bit too laid-back for serious academics and bookworms," claims a junior. About a fourth of BC students come from the greater Boston area, with an additional third from nearby eastern states. Catholics comprise more than 80 percent of the student body, but the admissions office is attempting to increase the number of both non-Catholics and members of minority groups (currently around 14 percent). Three out of four students come from the top fifth of their high school class; most are fairly conservative. "Most are well-off financially," a psychology major observes. "A lot of gold is worn by both sexes." BC accepts students solely on their academic merit and awards financial aid based on the academic potential of student with financial need. Non-need scholarships are awarded only to athletes on six of the men's and nine of the women's teams.

While housing is plush compared to most institutionalized accommodations, obtaining it is chancy. Freshmen generally are put in Newton campus doubles. The upperclassmen who are lucky enough to get a slot are accommodated on the Chestnut Hill campus in larger suites or apartments with full kitchens, dishwashers, and even garbage disposals. There's a lottery to determine which freshmen are guaranteed four years of housing and which are guaranteed only three, and it's small consolation for the losers that they get to pick which year they will live off campus. Those who move off voluntarily will have trouble moving back. Luckily, there's Boston's fairly reliable bus and subway system to bring distant residents to campus; if they want to drive to school, there's another lottery for parking stickers. Meals operate on a rather expensive and unpopular point plan, which requires students to pay in advance for books of "Monopoly-type" coupons. (Breakfast, lunch and dinner are worth two, four and five coupons, respectively.) "This system is somewhat ridiculous, especially for girls," complains a senior. "Who eats $900 worth of food in one semester?"

The state's minimum drinking age of twenty-one has toned down the super-partying atmosphere of BC, but its students remain a convivial lot—they've merely moved their parties off campus to avoid "monitoring." And of course, there is certainly no shortage of college parties in the Boston area. "Beer to BC students is like honey to bees," one happy student explains. And although some romantic undergrads lament that there are "no real dates at BC because guys don't believe in asking girls out," the campus is replete with sporting events, movies, festivals, concerts and plays. But best of all, downtown Boston is just twenty minutes away, "and that's on a slow trolley," reports one student. Religion does not play a large part in student life, though the optional daily, and 10 PM Sunday night masses are well attended. "As far as social life is concerned," one woman explains, "Catholic morals are encouraged but no penalty is inflicted if they are not followed."

Athletic events become social events as well. Basketball and hockey are good, but it's the football team students really go crazy over—"The spirit of Flutie still lives here!" says a senior. Tailgate parties before and after games are popular. "Unfortunately, such enthusiasm is just starting to spread to soccer, lacrosse and baseball," reports a political scientist, "and it has yet to hit the women's sports. Intramural sports are real biggies here—"everyone loves a sport," sings a senior—and students rave about BC's marvelous recreational complex.

While it may be that "a BC football game is the largest college athletic event in New England," a BC graduate is certainly the best received in the local political and business communities. "A home for academically motivated, upper-middle-class beer drinkers" is one BC student's fond assessment of his school. With a "spiritual atmosphere for those who want to find it," and plenty of social and academic resources for everyone, boredom is seldom a problem here. As a junior aptly advises: "The student who is interested only in academics should not go to Boston College—it has too much to offer beyond that."

Boston University

Boston, MA 02215

Location Center city	**Applicants** 18,230
Total Enrollment 27,500	**Accepted** 64%
Undergraduates 13,880	**Enrolled** 35%
Male/Female 49/51	**Academics** ★ ★ ★ ★
SAT V/M 550/600	**Social** 🍺🍺🍺🍺
Financial Aid 46%	**Q of L** ● ● ●
Expense Pr $ $ $ $	**Admissions** (617)353-2300

Twenty years ago Boston University lacked wealth and prominence. It had succumbed to being the largest mass of financially unstable academic mediocrity ever to occupy sixty-eight urban acres. Today, BU is on its way back. Although it will probably never shake its dubious distinction as "the other university" in Boston after Harvard and MIT, things are looking much brighter on the south side of the Charles River.

BU's president, John Silber, the main catalyst in the school's resurrection, is an outspoken, pugnacious administrator who has challenged almost everyone on the campus—from the faculty union to a student who hung an anti-apartheid banner out his dorm window. Sometimes Silber wins; sometimes he loses. But he always makes for vigorous debates throughout the university, and even those who oppose his views respect what he has done to make BU the place where countless upper-middle-class students come to prepare for successful careers.

Depending on your temperament, life BU-style is either invigorating or intimidating. The mixture of older brownstones, large Gothic buildings and nondescript high rises are woven into the city streets alongside the Burger King and AMC car dealership. "Assertive, independent students who are used to managing their lives in a fast-paced city thrive here," says an up-and-coming electrical engineer. "BU has no neat and tidy confines like other schools," adds a senior. In other words, if you're into cement and enjoy dodging cars and trolleys on a six-lane thoroughfare between classes, this might be the setting for you.

Camouflaged amid the shops, restaurants and traffic, BU is one of the largest private universities in the nation, and its ten undergraduate schools provide an appropriately wide range of offerings. The College of Communications is popular and nationally known. Its curriculum comprises a healthy mixture of theory and hands-on training, and it houses the country's only center for the study of political "disinformation." The school for the arts contains a strong theater department and a renowned music program in which students are taught by members of the Boston Symphony Orchestra. Another top offering is the College of Engineering, which is now housed in a new

$110-million center with state-of-the-art facilities. The allied health, nursing and management programs deserve honorable mention. The college of liberal arts is the largest, with the sciences, developmental economics, African studies, philosophy and especially English its strongest areas; foreign languages garner some negative reviews. One unique offering is the well-known College of Basic Studies, which offers a rigorous two-year introduction to college academics for high school graduates with great potential but unimpressive paper credentials. Although there is a certain stigma attached to admitting you are a "CBS" student, the basic studies program has been a big success—most of its graduates transfer into other BU schools and have a higher graduation rate after four years than the national average.

The University Professors Program—BU's answer to an honors program—is where "students of great promise" take integrated core courses from professors whose expertise spans two or more disciplines and then propose a sharply focused course of study in their area of interest. Dual-degree possibilities abound at BU, including a five-year BA/MBA program, the highly selective six-year BA/MD or BA/JD options, and a seven-year liberal arts/dental program. Study abroad semesters and exchanges are available in many countries including Australia, Africa, England, Greece and Spain. Nautical enthusiasts can enroll in a Sea Semester at Woods Hole* on Cape Cod. A newly added culinary center makes instructors and kitchens available to those with epicurean inclinations.

At a university of this size, students pay heavily for procrastination and disorganization. "If you're not registered in time, you could get closed out of a desired course," veterans of the system warn. But one senior adds that "in some cases prolonged and insistent pleading may get a student into a desired course." Enormous lecture courses are usually accompanied by more manageable discussion sections, and good teachers and quality advising are generally the rule. "I believe BU rates highly on the faculty/ student relation scale," says a mass communications major. In any school, small seminars are assured by senior year. Students claim it's tough to define an academic climate at this huge, varied university, but one undergrad has found "lots of strict deadlines, an amazing amount of reading to be consumed, and lots of competition for A's." She adds, however, that "BU is very unlike Wellesley or Harvard where the 'air' seems very scholarly."

BU has one of the largest academic library systems in the country, and it comes complete with collections of famous writers, politicians and philosophers—Abraham Lincoln, Theodore Roosevelt and Robert Frost to name a few. The hours at the main, six-story library are generous (open twenty-four-hours before and during exams), but students claim it could be better organized—"Too often things aren't on the shelves"— and the notorious third-floor social area is "not conducive to serious academic pursuits."

"Contrary to popular belief, not everyone's from Long Island and New Jersey," one woman clarifies, although a large percentage are. More than three-quarters of the students hail from outside Massachusetts, and about nine hundred come from foreign countries. BU has a local reputation as a rich kids' school, full of "JAPPY" women who use too much makeup and hair spray and chew their gum loudly. Yet students are adamant that they, as a whole, are diverse. "There is such a mixture of students from so many different backgrounds that it makes meeting people enjoyable," a biomedical engineering major says. While Silber sets a pretty conservative tone to this campus with his views on Latin American policy and faculty unions, it has not permeated the student body. "Students here are not conservative, but I can't specifically state why they're liberal," reports a perplexed senior. Although BU was founded as a Methodist seminary (one of it's most distinguished alums is the Reverend Dr. Martin Luther King, Jr.), and maintains an outstanding theology department to this day, there is no prevailing faith here. "Campus life is rather colored by all the openness of religion here," explains a senior. "There are Hare Krishnas, Buddhists, Moonies . . . all types, all sorts, all over."

Each BU school handles its own admissions. Students apply to one school but many indicate a second—and usually less selective—choice. Competition for spots in most of the ten undergraduate schools are getting stiffer (the average incoming freshmen SAT score went up thirty points in the last three years), and the administration has made a calculated decision to maintain its new tough admission standards even if it means a smaller enrollment. Only about a third of BU's graduates head straight for jobs after graduation. Ninety-four percent of those who aspire to become attorneys are accepted into law school. Besides the two hundred athletic scholarships—a quarter for women, primarily in basketball, swimming, and track and field—the university awards more than four hundred non-need, renewable $500 to full-tuition scholarships for outstanding students as well as about fifty awards, ranging from $1,000 to full tuition, to entering freshmen in the School for the Arts. For those who miss out on merit scholarships VISA and MasterCard are accepted.

Freshmen are "guaranteed housing"—a laughable phrase because the dorms are always overbooked and BU has become infamous for spending large sums of money on hotel rooms for overflow freshmen. Most first-year students who get campus housing find themselves in Warren Towers, "a three-pronged monstrosity" that houses about 1,700 students. Sophomores move into the smaller dorms or three-story brownstones. Upperclassmen compete in separate lotteries for special-interest floors, rooms within their dorms, or for a room in another dorm. Due to the housing shortage, about 40 percent of the undergraduates live independently, although Boston's housing crunch makes finding a place tough. But life off campus in the "student slums" is relatively tranquil, and a little scrimping can even make it less expensive than the dorms. Flexible food plans are available to all, and there are a number of cafeterias to choose from including a slightly more expensive veggie dining room.

Social life is divided mainly between on-campus parties, local bars and nightclubs (many of which are just around the corner from the dorms), and parties at neighboring colleges. A Greek revival is in full swing, and there are well over three hundred clubs and organizations on campus. Fenway Park is just a short hop across Kenmore Square, and the green line of the Boston's subway system, which squiggles through the center of the campus, puts "the city itself right at our fingertips." In fact, one student promises, "The only way to be bored here is to lock yourself in your room and hide under the bed."

With a championship hockey team that produced four members of the Olympic team in 1980 and improving basketball and crew squads, varsity sports hold their own among BU's many diversions. The football team may have potential, but because of its past record, "it's actually a local joke," explains a remorseful fan. Hundreds of teams attest to the popularity of intramurals.

BU is so huge that it's easy to get lost in the crowd. "This is the kind of place where you may meet someone nice at the beginning of the semester and never see that person again," attests a senior. But for students who don't desire a peaceful, intimate educational setting, there is high quality instruction to be derived from this massive institution. Although BU has some drawbacks, the worst troubles seem part of the past. Most members of the campus community agree that their dark cloud now has a Silber lining.

Bowdoin College

Brunswick, ME 04011

Location Small town	**Applicants** 3,510
Total Enrollment 1,350	**Accepted** 24%
Undergraduates 1,350	**Enrolled** 46%
Male/Female 55/45	**Academics** ★ ★ ★ ★
SAT V/M N/A	**Social** ♟ ♟ ♟
Financial Aid 38%	**Q of L** ● ● ●
Expense Pr $ $ $ $	**Admissions** (207)725-3100

Bowdoin is proud of its independent spirit. It was one of the first liberal arts colleges to make SAT scores optional for applicants and to abolish letter grades, class rank and grade point averaging. Its fraternities were among the first in the nation to accept women as full members, and the excellent women's sports program not only fields almost as many teams as its male counterpart, but claims an Olympic gold medal winning alumna, marathoner Joan Benoit, as well. Such ability to change with—and occasionally ahead of—trends in higher education is one reason why Bowdoin, founded in 1794 and boasting Hawthorne and Longfellow as alums of the same class, remains one of the most prestigious and academically distinguished small colleges in the United States.

Bowdoin's is a compact campus, a tightly woven patchwork of pine groves, athletic fields and a congenial mix of traditional old brick buildings and more modern architecture of the 1960s. And Bowdoin's college community seems equally tight-knit—a factor many students attribute to a similarity of backgrounds (most students come from eastern prep schools and "comfortable" families) and the de-emphasis on grades. Says one student, "There is a definite feeling that everyone is on your side." The administration's decision to make SAT scores optional in admissions further reinforces this move away from evaluating a student empirically to assessing the total person.

While courses at Bowdoin don't produce cutthroat competition among the students, they remain, however, extremely challenging. Students agree that the most outstanding departments are economics, history, English and the sciences (especially chemistry). Religion and environmental studies also merit favorable reviews. The main criticism heaped upon several departments is that they are too small, and thus too limited in view. Romance languages, visual arts, music, sociology, psychology, computer science, and physics are considered most plagued by this lack of resources and faculty. Women's studies offerings are increasing, and some students predict a strong program in years to come.

Innovative programs are the rule rather than the exception, and self-designed and double majors are increasingly popular. Inexpensive study-abroad options include semesters at Bowdoin's own program in Sri Lanka and Beijing or elsewhere in Europe and the Far East. Other semesters off campus are scheduled through the Twelve-College Exchange,* Mystic Seaport,* S.E.A. Semester at Woods Hole Oceanographic Institution, independent study, and senior honors projects. All told, approximately 10 percent of the student body participates during any given semester in one of Bowdoin's off-campus programs. Also available are special engineering programs with Columbia and the California Institute of Technology which provide a BA/MS in five years.

Students are expected to select two courses each in natural science and math,

64

social and behavioral science, humanities and the arts, and foreign studies. Students can get into most courses without difficulty. And while the largest class may be an introductory level course of 175 students, more than 40 percent of the classes have ten or fewer students. As part of a campus-wide expansion program to adequately provide for the needs of a growing student body, Bowdoin has added thirteen faculty members to its teaching staff and plans are underway for a major science complex as well as the renovation of residential halls and dining facilities. Students are already enjoying the benefits of the new underground extension to the library, which cordons off special sections for serious study, yet maintains the traditional "social" get-together areas.

Bowdoin students tend to look alike (it's easy to guess that L. L. Bean's factory store, open twenty-four hours, is just down the road), and most are "clean-cut and somewhat conservative." Generally, preppie students seem to fit in best, according to student sources. "You have to be a people person to really feel a part of the Bowdoin mainstream," adds a gregarious senior. Bowdoin attempts to meet the estimated financial need of all students. Although no merit scholarships are offered, students, regardless of need, may work on campus, and a special program allows students working on independent projects to apply for aid doing research in lieu of a campus job.

Housing accommodations are varied, although often cramped. Upperclassmen who do well in the very competitive room lottery (based on seniority) make a beeline for on-campus apartments. Bowdoin's liberal housing policy includes coed suites with four rooms adjoining a common living room. Off-campus house-sitting accommodations along the scenic Brunswick coast are available at low, off-season rates, and some hardy souls even live on nearby islands. The food is prepared in the dining halls—"not shipped in"—and students give the cooks four stars. The word is everyone gains weight over the winter, which is not a short season up here in Maine. Administrators do want prospective students to know that the coastal influences give this southern corner of the state milder winters and less snow than the north. And, they might add, there is irrefutable evidence that this area of the Maine coast is indeed warming up. Point of fact: Cardinals have been sighted here for the first time, and some of these harbingers of warmth are canceling their flight plans south and choosing to "winter over" in Maine.

With a population of eighteen thousand, Brunswick is quaint and friendly, but decidedly not the place to go for cultural or social enrichment. Students have discovered the remedy for Brunswick blahs is Portland—only a half-hour drive away—which offers good shopping, restaurants, nightlife, an art museum and the symphony. Boston is only two and half hours away, and there are several ski slopes within an eighty-mile radius. "This is an outdoor enthusiasts' dream world," exclaims a trail-blazing econ major.

Some 40 percent of the student body pledges one of the nine coed fraternities, which have been a mixed success because of confusion over whether the new female "brothers" are full members, social members or just there to date. The Greek-sponsored beer-guzzling parties are usually the biggest social events of the week—a fact some students bemoan. One student points to the excessive on-campus drinking as one of Bowdoin's biggest negatives. Students admit that weekends can get boring around Bowdoin. "The cloudiness and somberness can sometimes get to a person," says one student. But things really liven up when hockey season rolls around. The Polar Bears, a longtime ECAC Division III winner, always play to a packed house. "Bowdoin really loves its hockey players!" gushes one student. Football and swimming teams have winning records and avid fans. The intramural program is well-organized but sometimes lacks participants. The completion of the $9-million field house with its sixteen-lane swimming pool, two-hundred-meter-track, tennis courts and exercise rooms should inspire more athletic endeavors. Otherwise, Bowdoin's extracurriculars encompass clubs and committees in just about everything from crew to poetry.

Bowdoin's excellence stems from its personalized approach to education and its ability to select students on the basis of their potential, not their test scores. Therefore, people of varied talents are admitted and thrive here. And, according to a student, "one of the most powerful differences about this school is that enthusiasm or spirit—indeed love for Bowdoin."

Bradford College

Bradford, MA 01830

Location Suburban
Total Enrollment 430
Undergraduates 430
Male/Female 48/52
SAT V/M 480/530
Financial Aid 40%
Expence Pr $ $

Applicants 600
Accepted 50%
Enrolled 41%
Academics ★ ★ ★
Social 🐭 🐭 🐭
Q of L ● ● ●
Admissions (617)373-1745

"The Life and Times of Bradford College" reads like a rags-to-riches, great-American-dream story. This Horatio Alger of higher education was a semisuccessful two-year women's college until 1971 when it turned into a very unsuccessful coed four-year institution with financial woes, student body boycotts and dismal faculty morale. But Bradford's luck changed around 1982 when it found a young, vital president and adopted the Bradford Plan for a Practical Liberal Arts Education. Suddenly, it's THE Bradford College, earmarked as one of the most innovative and up-and-coming schools of the '80s. Bright, sought-after high school students are knocking down Bradford's door, looking for a unique brand of education that fills them up with liberal arts but does not leave them empty-pocketed when it comes to career preparation, or, as they put it, "the practical liberal arts."

Set upon a hill overlooking the city of Haverhill, Bradford's seventy-acre campus of lawns and woods surrounds a tree-lined pond and crossover bridge. With only a dozen or so buildings, the campus manages to wear a range of architectural styles—from the Victorian elegance of Academy Hall, built in 1870, to the large modern library and arts center. An abundance of foliage, including the ivy draped across the older buildings, induce one student to comment that "there's a definite academic air about the place."

But what separates this teeny, tiny college from the plethora of small liberal arts schools is the Bradford Plan. This original curriculum stresses the importance of strong communication skills (writing, writing and more writing), interdisciplinary majors and skill-oriented minors. Under the guidelines of the Plan, all students begin their undergraduate program with two courses in expository writing and a class called the spirit of mathematics. At the end of their first year, students are required to participate in the Freshman Inquiry program, which means they write a two- to five-page paper on their aspirations and meet with a faculty and administrative adviser to design the best strategy for meeting these goals. Next are general education requirements that include unconventional courses such as the nature of work, global perspectives, ethics and values, and the human heritage. The capstone senior project requirement may take the form of a research paper, an exhibit, a theatrical production, etc.

But Bradford's unconventionality does not end with the Plan. For instance, SAT scores are not application requirements, and students don't major in any one specific degree program, but rather they have comprehensive, interdisciplinary majors to help them acquire lifelong intellectual tools. Practicality is reserved for the minors, which attempt to teach students such day-to-day skills as marketing, communications, public administration or arts management. Internships are encouraged, and students who decide to participate will take two related courses at the college during their internships, one on the literature of work and another that helps them react to their experiences on the job.

Students and administrators agree that the humanities (especially English, philosophy and history) are what Bradford does best. The creative arts department, with its superb facilities and excellent faculty, also offers several strong programs. But the thread that ties the entire curriculum together is the writing program. "Most professors realize that writing is a critical part of thinking and analyzing," comments one student who has had several writing assignments in his business classes. Computer science, foreign language and mathematics are the admitted Bradford shortcomings. "The science department is new and will require a few more years before the college can really sell it," notes a human development major.

Student reactions to life on the Bradford Plan varies. "It tends to push people to achieve," says a history/photojournalism major. But at the same time, "there aren't a lot of ivory tower intellectuals wandering around," reports a classmate. "Most of the pressure has to be self-inflicted." Class size is rarely a problem on this campus of 425, and some upperclassmen speak of seminars they share with no more than two or three classmates. Students sing the praises of the faculty—"even the physical education professors are published"—and claim they have no problems gaining access to any prof at any level. The library is well staffed, fairly well stocked and computerized. Bradford also boasts a computer center and a television studio.

The majority of Bradfordians hail from New England (22 percent from Massachusetts) and New York, but there are students from as far away as California, Texas and Wyoming. Ten percent are from foreign countries, and 11 percent represent minority groups. "Bradford tends to attract a different breed of cat," sasses a humanities major. Lots of outdoorsy types coexists with a lot of music and art students, but basically, "there are no crowds to follow at Bradford." Anyone attempting to stereotype these students would conclude that most are liberal, nonaggressive and tolerant of all types of people. About half come from public schools, and more than three-fourths rank in the top half of their high school class. "If you're serious about school but don't know what you want to do yet, then Bradford is perfect," corroborates one student. Merit scholarships, ranging from $1,000 to $8,000, are available for exceptional students who graduate in the top 20 percent of their high school class. Because the college has no varsity teams, there are, logically enough, no athletic scholarships offered.

Approximately 90 percent of Bradford students live on campus in three coed-by-floor dorms and two coed cluster houses. The dorms have their own laundry and cooking facilities, and the double and single rooms are not just spacious, "they're the largest dorm rooms anywhere," cheers an excited senior. The older Academy Hall is the most popular (juniors and seniors only on the fourth floor) possibly because it provides underground passages to most classrooms—"great in the winter!" Freshmen are assigned rooms based on questionnaires about basic living styles and upperclassmen play the lottery game. There is one old-fashioned and family-style dining hall, and one meal plan for three unlimited meals a day. The college has its own cooks and "since they're cooking for 400–500 people rather than 8,000, they tend to do a better job," assesses a junior. There are cookouts with live music, formal dinners, international nights and occasionally even fresh lobster. The student union sells sandwiches and snacks (hot and cold) after dinner for munchie attacks.

With no fraternities or sororities on campus, activities are aimed at the entire student body. Most students are interested in going to dorm parties and on-campus dances or taking in a flick. Clubs sponsor ski trips, whale-watching expeditions and sight-seeing trips to Newburyport or Salem. Students frequently hop on the train for the half-hour ride into Boston, or they head north to ski or east to the beaches depending on the season and amount of participation. "These escape routes are very important to the students," explains a business/creative arts major.

Bradford has four athletic clubs (men's lacrosse and soccer, women's volleyball and coed innertube water polo) that play other schools on a regular basis with much support from nonparticipating fellow students. But intramural sports are the prevailing activity, and the coed teams of flag football, wiffleball and floor hockey are the most popular. There is even a teensy ski slope five minutes from the campus, plus golf courses and acreage for cross-country skiing abound.

Bradford has found a good compromise between vocational education and studying the liberal arts. The college manages to help students develop practical professional options with an interdisciplinary approach. And while some students complain that the college is too small and often there is too much gossip, most students are loving every minute of personal attention. "I came here because I didn't want to be forgotten, or more specifically, because I wanted to be noticed," claims a humanities major. As soon as it started espousing individuality and open-mindedness, Bradford was an overnight success.

Brandeis University

Waltham, MA 02254

Location Suburban	**Applicants** 3,970
Total Enrollment 3,680	**Accepted** 60%
Undergraduates 2,900	**Enrolled** 35%
Male/Female 50/50	**Academics** ★ ★ ★ ★
SAT V/M 600/630	**Social** ☎ ☎ ☎
Financial Aid 38%	**Q of L** ● ● ●
Expense Pr $ $ $ $	**Admissions** (617)736-3500

The campus statue of Louis Brandeis, for whom Brandeis University is named, shows the great Supreme Court justice obviously in a hurry, striding determinedly forward, judicial robes streaming out behind him. It's a fitting representation for a university that is also on the move.

Despite the prestige that a larger graduate program could bring, the focus at Brandeis resolutely remains on its undergraduates, who in turn have shown their appreciation by solicitously attending to Louis Brandeis' welfare. Every winter his statue is supplied with a hat and scarf, and during campus construction, which is most of the time at this young university, he usually sports a hard hat.

Only ten miles west of Boston, this Jewish-founded but nonsectarian school is a mere baby compared to its academic neighbors. (As Harvard celebrated its 350th birthday, Brandeis had yet to see its 40th.) But the energetic institution has not lost any time becoming "the youngest major research university in the United States." It encourages serious undergraduate research in all fields, providing funds for students to work with faculty members in a variety of scholarly investigations. With an eight-to-one student/teacher ratio, "Professors are extremely accessible and often encourage student visits," comments one undergrad. Several students a year coauthor articles in academic journals.

Set atop a hill in a pleasant residential neighborhood—and thus affording a scenic view—Brandeis' attractively landscaped campus is made up mainly of modern but distinctive brick or cement buildings. (The music building is shaped like a grand piano; the theater looks like a top hat.) Several of its departments offer nationally ranked graduate programs including biochemistry, biology, English, history, physics and political science. Any of these departments would also be good bets for undergraduates and offer a special four-year BA/MA program for students energetic enough to take graduate-level courses and write a thesis in addition to completing undergraduate requirements. Dedicated premeds are catered to hand and foot with special advisers, internships, and their own Berlin Premedical Center, which houses specialized laboratories designed to provide the would-be physician with research opportunities. "Law and medicine are two main interests among the student population," a senior reports. Acceptance rates to such graduate programs are 95 percent and 80 percent respectively.

With the largest faculty in the field outside of Israel, the university is virtually unrivaled in Near Eastern and Judaic studies. And a wide variety of interdisciplinary programs, such as Latin American, medieval, Soviet or women's studies add spice to the list of possible majors. Computer science is a notable growth field, especially in the area of artificial intelligence, but students are down on the mathematics department, calling it "primarily a stepping stone for science and computer majors." Brandeis also maintains a commitment to the creative arts, with strong drama offerings and a theory-based music program founded by Leonard Bernstein. Up to a quarter of the junior class goes abroad each year to twenty countries in Europe, Asia and Latin America, through programs sponsored by other colleges and institutions. The only program Brandeis sponsors on its own is a summer dig for archeologists in Israel.

In addition to basic requirements in science and English, four semesters of a foreign language are mandatory before graduation. Freshmen must sign on for comprehensive University Studies courses in the humanities and history aimed at giving undergraduates a "shared understanding" of Western civilization through examination of a core group of classic texts; a surefire way to identify a Brandeis freshman is to look for a copy of the *Iliad* or *The Divine Comedy* under his or her arm.

Eighty percent of the students graduated in the top fifth of their high school classes, and most continue a strenuous regimen of academic achievement. "As long as you never let up on yourself, even for a moment, the pressure won't kill you," says one. Most spend three to five hours a day at the books, although one student confesses, "I do wish the library would be open later than 2:00 AM" If the pressure gets to you, try the Flex 3 option: three classes one semester, if an especially rough course is required, and five the next.

Brandeis is almost two-thirds Jewish, and, one student says, "Being of an upper-middle-class, Jewish background makes it easier to fit in." Yet one Baptist sees no problem. "On the contrary," he says, "having all the Jewish holidays off is great!" There are three chapels on the campus—Catholic, Jewish and Protestant—built so that the shadow of one never crosses the shadow of another. It's an architectural symbol that students say reflects the realities of the campus community. Hispanics and blacks make up 4 percent of the student body. Native New Yorkers and New Jersians make up the largest undergraduate contingent, but the many West Coast imports add their distinctive flair, as do a hundred or so foreign students.

The university seeks to package financial assistance to meet the calculated needs of all admitted students who apply on time. It also offers about one hundred merit scholarships of $4,000 or more to outstanding undergraduates.

Brandeis is the only school in the nation that offers you living quarters in a replica of a Scottish castle with pie-shaped rooms and stairways leading to nowhere. More pedestrian housing options include traditional coed-by-floor dormitory quadrangles, where freshmen and sophomores are housed in doubles, juniors in singles. There are also university-owned apartments, including the Foster Living Center, or the "Mods," which are coed townhouses reserved for seniors. As one lucky denizen puts it, "It's an honor to live in the Mods." Freshmen are guaranteed housing, but upperclassmen fend for themselves and play the lottery. A new 330-room quadrangle will help alleviate housing shortage blues. There is affordable off-campus housing nearby, and about 20 percent of the students go that route. Brandeis boasts the best college food in the Boston area, as well as the most appetizing setups: Your meal tickets can buy lunch or dinner in a fast-food joint, the pub (with sit-down service), a country store, a kosher dining hall, vegetarian selection and, finally, the regular cafeteria where "the salad bars are huge."

Like many colleges across the country, Brandeis is making concerted efforts to improve its social life. Weekends begin on Thursdays, with live entertainment at the on-campus Stein pub, and Friday night at the movies is a must. A Greek system as such is not recognized by the university, but students report unofficial fraternizing taking place in off-campus houses. Brandeis coeds also frequent their neighbor institutions, party-hopping throughout Boston and Cambridge. They can take Brandeis' own shuttle bus, the nearby commuter train, or try their luck on hitchhiker's row at the campus exit. As for Waltham, Brandeis' host town, "it's not exactly a booming metropolis, but it grows on you," says one senior.

Spared the annual gridiron follies, Brandeis has developed national Division III championship men's track and soccer teams as well as strong baseball, men's and women's cross-country, and tennis teams. "The Jury" is a new student club getting more students to sporting events, though Brandeis' sport facilities are nothing to cheer about and remain in desperate need of improvement.

Perhaps inevitably, Brandeis continues to struggle with the tension between its desire to maintain a prevalent Jewish atmosphere (the cafeterias don't serve pork) and its need to attract a well-rounded, eclectic group of students. Still, few private universities have come as far as Brandeis in such a short time, evolving from a bare 250-acre site with the leftovers of a failed veterinary school to a modern research university of ninety buildings and a $130-million endowment. And there are no signs that Louis Brandeis—or his namesake institution—is slowing down.

Brigham Young University

Provo, UT 84602

Location City outskirts
Total Enrollment 27,120
Undergraduates 24,790
Male/Female 52/48
ACT 24
Financial Aid 43%
Expense Pr $

Applicants 6,200
Accepted 91%
Enrolled 83%
Academics ★ ★ ★
Social 🐝 🐝 🐝
Q of L ● ● ● ●
Admissions (801)378-2507

The Church of Jesus Christ of Latter-day Saints, otherwise known as the Mormon Church, is about as all-American as any religion could be. It was born on the nineteenth-century frontier, has a prophet named Joseph Smith, and a scripture that describes the early history of North America. Brigham Young, its premier university, is as wholesome and squeaky clean as any in the country. Visitors are likely to think that they stumbled into the filming of a Coca-Cola commercial, except that Coke, along with all other artificial stimulants, is banned.

Brigham Young is, first and foremost, a university that knows what it stands for. Before you start classes, you must sign an honor code that makes it clear what you're *not* going to do. No drugs, alcohol, tobacco, coffee, or tea. No promiscuity, gambling, cutoff jeans, tank tops, beards, or unkempt hair, either. You don't have to be a Mormon to attend—though 97 percent of the students are—but you have to follow the Mormons' code of ethics, which can be tough without a corresponding religious commitment. Mormon values of prosperity, chastity and obedience pervade all aspects of life on the 616-acre campus, beginning at 6 AM when the tower on the upper campus peals off the first four bars of the Mormon hymn "Come, Come Ye Saints" to rouse the faithful for another day. "The church is campus life; standards of dress, morality, etc., are directly related to the church," explains one junior math major. A religion course is required each semester, and everyone must complete an extensive general education program that includes work in the natural sciences, social sciences, arts and letters, mathematics and foreign language. A number of religion courses, including extensive study of the Book of Mormon, are also required. Beyond career, beyond life, this place offers an "education for eternity."

With almost twenty-five thousand undergraduates enrolled, BYU has more full-time students than any other private university in the nation, and academic offerings run the gamut from traditional liberal arts courses to things like range management or tourism and travel. Premed, elementary education, engineering and business courses, especially accounting, are among the strongest. The foreign languages are highly praised by students, as are programs in design and manufacturing technology programs. When asked what departments need improvement, the administration responded with fitting humility: "All of them." Students were more specific and criticized Spanish for relying too much upon teaching assistants, classics for too narrow an approach, and music for general weakness. There is a large study-abroad program that offers the chance to work in Vienna, London, Jerusalem, and elsewhere at relatively low cost. About three-quarters of the men interrupt their studies to fulfill the traditional two-year stint as a missionary. This is typically done after the freshman year, leading one student to comment that BYU has "the oldest sophomore class in the world." About 10 percent of the women also take time off for missionary work.

Most classes are kept to twenty-five or thirty students, though required courses can be larger, and some in the social sciences can soar well into the hundreds. An honors program, open to students with a 29 or above on their ACT and a 3.8 high school GPA, offers small seminars and allows students "to be intellectual producers, not just consumers," in the words of one student. The faculty members, who are addressed as "Brother" and "Sister," are very accessible but draw mixed reviews on their attention to student concerns. Most professors stick strictly to mainline Mormonism both in and out of the classroom. Though BYU is a bona fide megauniversity, massive registration lines are one headache students are spared. While their counterparts at other schools are still camping out all night to get the classes they want, students here can relay their choices to a computer by merely dialing a touchtone phone. The libraries, which close on Sundays, are a little thin in medicine and modern literature but otherwise excellent. The campus bookstore also gets raves, but not from Culture Club fans: Boy George has been banned from the shelves. No shortage of Donny and Marie, though.

About one-third of BYU students are from Utah, another quarter are from California and Idaho, and the remainder includes about fifteen hundred foreign students, who speak a total of seventy different languages and testify to the effectiveness of the far-flung Mormon missionary effort. However, less than 3 percent of the students belong to minority groups. Mormons were vocal in their opposition to the rejected Equal Rights Amendment, and feminists as well as Third World organizations are virtually nonexistent. Despite their focus on the hereafter, BYU students aren't adverse to flaunting their worldly success: "Many students are from wealthy families and come here to show it," according to an English major. A popular Family Studies program gives credence to one female student's assertion that "many of the women are here to find husbands."

Brigham Young annually awards over five thousand scholarships ranging from $100 to $2,200 to outstanding students, as well as full-tuition loans to anyone, with terms similar to those for Guaranteed Student Loans. Tuition for church members is $770 lower than that for nonmembers because Mormon families contribute to the university through their church tithes. All freshmen live in the single-sex dorms, while most upperclassmen opt for less expensive apartments near the school, also single sex (remember the honor code?). To promote a more intimate social life, the campus is broken into geographic "wards," and then again into smaller "home evening groups" of about fifteen students. "It's an effective way of shrinking the big university atmosphere," a student explains. There are numerous eating facilities on campus, including three cafeterias, two candy shops and two ice cream parlors. Shopping is within walking distance, and for other needs there is a bus to the mall in Provo.

Aside from Provo, which isn't a swinging town by any stretch of the imagination, the nearest excitement is in Salt Lake City, an hour away. Campus buildings, like everything else at BYU, "are clean, modern, and orderly." The campus, which lies at an altitude of 4,600 feet in the foothills of the Wasatch Mountains, offers breathtaking sunsets and easy access to magnificent skiing, camping, and hiking areas. There are also plenty of school activities on the weekends, including dances in BYU's ballroom, movies, concerts, plays or sports events. Fast talkers will want to check out the debate team, which consistently ranks among the best in the nation. Dating is common, within Mormon bounds of proper behavior. There are some fraternities and sororities, but they "are more of a nuisance than anything else" according to one senior, and play a minor role in social life.

Brigham Young is committed to what its namesake, who led the early Morm[
into Utah, once referred to as the "harmonious working of the whole human or
nism." Thus, physical fitness is encouraged for everyone, and the intramural progr
is rated as one of the best in the country, with indoor and outdoor jogging tracks, ;
facilities for tennis, swimming, paddle tennis, handball, golf and just about any ot
sports activity you might want. Also important are varsity sports, and the philosophy
of obedience seems to work wonders on the football field. BYU, ranked number one
in 1984, always overpowers its Western Athletic Conference rivals. Ironically, it was
BYU that produced the Chicago Bears star quarterback Jim McMahon, known as
much for his outrageousness off the field as for his performances on it. In addition to
football, the basketball, wrestling and golf teams are also consistently good.

BYU students seem to appreciate the discipline required at their "clean, squeaky
clean" school. The combination of the social code and the tightness of the community
can make the school seem a little unreal and isolated from the rest of the world, but
most students see this as a small price to pay for an education that will serve them all
their lives . . . and then some.

Brooklyn College, NY
—See CITY UNIVERSITY OF NEW YORK

Brown University

Providence, RI 02912

Location City outskirts	**Applicants** 12,080
Total Enrollment 7,000	**Accepted** 20%
Undergraduates 5,600	**Enrolled** 51%
Male/Female 52/48	**Academics** ★ ★ ★ ★ ★
SAT V/M N/A	**Social** ☎ ☎ ☎ ☎
Financial Aid 50%	**Q of L** ● ● ● ● ●
Expense Pr $ $ $ $	**Admissions** (401)862-2378

With more applicants per seat than any other school in the nation, Brown is undeniably
the "hot" college of the '80s. At a university with no distribution requirements that
stipulates only twenty-eight credits for graduation, Brown students are accustomed to
freedom—academic and otherwise—and they relish it. Where else but Brown would
over a thousand students sponsor a referendum calling on the university to stock suicide
pills to be used in the event of nuclear war? And who could forget the spectacle of Amy
Carter, flanked by other Brown undergraduates, being dragged kicking and screaming
from the South African Embassy by riot police. And of course, university officials
would rather not be reminded of the brouhaha over nude photos of several Brown
students seized by police in connection with a prostitution ring near the campus. Is

73

there no end to what Brown students can dream up? Could it be, perhaps, that they're getting a little out of hand? Not on your life. "We are attracting independent students with high motivation," says one administrator. "At least we have the good sense to get out of their way."

Nearly two decades ago, Brown abandoned its traditional academic approach in favor of the unorthodox New Curriculum, a move that has won it the devotion of several generations of undergraduates, as well as skepticism from some of its stodgier Ivy League fellows. Gone are rigid distribution requirements, plus and minus grades, and sharply defined lines between academic disciplines. In their place, Brown offers students an education that is completely self-determined, with little grade pressure, few course prerequisites, and lots of experimentation. Students take their classes for marks of either A, B, C, or No Credit or simply Satisfactory or No Credit. In any case the NC disappears from the transcript, while the letter grade or Satisfactory can be supplemented by a written evaluation from the professor. The New Curriculum is the main reason students cite for choosing Brown. As one explains, "Brown does what no other school I'm aware of does: tells me that I'm the one who can concoct the best education for myself. It's a big responsibility, but it's an incredibly freeing responsibility."

There isn't much that's structured at Brown, least of all the architecture. Located atop College Hill in the East Side of downtown Providence, Brown's campus is made up of a mish-mash of old and new that one student labeled "somewhat uninspiring." Though far from idyllic, the campus has its share of grassy lawns that afford students refuge from the city streets beyond.

Among traditional departments, history, geology and religious studies (with an independent offshoot in Judaic studies) are among the university's best, and students also had praise for computer science and applied math. Other top-notch programs include comparative literature, classics, modern languages and the writing program in the English department. Among the sciences, engineering and the premed curriculum are standouts. "If you get through Brown, you'll get into med school," a junior says, backed up by a 92 percent placement rate. Future doctors can opt for an eight-year liberal medical education program that offers an MD for those who stick it out. Law and society is a popular undergraduate interdisciplinary program, and political science is said to be rapidly improving, as is the international studies concentration. Sociology and philosophy, however, still receive considerable criticism from students. Economics is condemned by many for being too conservative and closed-minded, while the "pseudo-business major called Organizational Behavior and Management has such flexible requirements that it's often manipulated into a no-thought, gut concentration," a senior believes.

Brown's faculty has successfully resisted the notion that somewhere in their collective wisdom and experience lies a core of knowledge that every educated person should possess. As a result, the only university-wide requirements for graduation are to demonstrate writing competency and complete twenty-eight semester courses (while paying for the normal and expected thirty-two). There may also be a few departmental requisites, depending on one's concentration—Brown's term for major. Those with interests in interdisciplinary fields will enjoy Brown's wide range of concentrations, self-style if you want, that cross departmental lines and cover everything from cognitive sciences to semiotics. Brown also offers group independent-study projects, which are just what the name implies. One woman explains: "If you and your friends want to have a class and find a faculty sponsor—it's all set!"

In an era when many schools are disavowing their 1960s experimentation in favor of stricter back-to-basics programs, Brown, after a two-year internal study, recently reaffirmed its commitment to the New Curriculum's unstructured style of education. As one dean put it, "If something ain't broke, you shouldn't try to fix it." But at least one professor takes issue with that conclusion, maintaining that the New Curriculum has made Brown popular among "those smart students who reject disciplined learning and do not want to work hard." He wonders aloud, "Why should our students not be happy, considering that, if they do not want to meet rigorous requirements they do not have to?"

Though Brown's computing facilities are excellent—the university is a national leader in academic computer applications—the library system could stand some improvement. "The Rock" and "SciLi," as the Rockefeller humanities library and the science library are known respectively, have uneven collections and lack attractive study spaces. "The library system at Brown is probably the weakest aspect of the university," says one student, and advanced research often sends students scurrying to Yale or Harvard. Off-campus offerings include internships through Venture,* limited cross-registration with the nearby Rhode Island School of Design, and study-abroad programs in Brazil, West Germany, East Germany, Great Britain, France, Tanzania, Japan, Spain and China.

Brown prides itself on undergraduate teaching and looks for skill in the classroom as much as the usual scholarly credentials when making tenure decisions. The administration's interest in interdisciplinary instruction and imaginative course design help cultivate high-quality instruction. Less impressive is Brown's record on academic advising. Though university's unstructured curriculum makes advising a critical component of the academic program, Brown has yet to implement an adequate system. "This, I think, is the Achilles heel of the Brown curriculum," says a senior history major. "The academic counseling system needs to be much, much stronger than it is." The university recently took a step in the right direction with a new program that matches a team of upperclassmen and faculty to each freshman, but more must be done if the advising system is to play its proper role in Brown's do-your-own-thing environment. Brown offers nearly a hundred interdisciplinary freshman seminars via the Curricular Advisory Program (CAP), and the professors in these courses officially serve as academic advisers for their students' first year. Most are highly praised by students for their abilities and availability. "They are very casual about open office hours and welcome students to pop in for a chat." Upper-level classes are usually in the teens, and CAP courses are limited to twenty, but many intro lectures can run well into the hundreds, and often there aren't enough teaching assistants to staff them effectively. As one student complains, "You can generally get into classes, but sometimes they're so huge that you wish you had been denied entrance."

Compared with the other Ivys, Brown's academic climate is relatively casual. With it's generous S/NC option, which can be used for all twenty-eight credits if the student so chooses, Brown students often lack the manic intensity found at other schools of comparable quality. Academic pressure is almost entirely self-generated, and "people don't feel like they have to step on other people to get ahead," says a senior history major. Even so, most students put in long hours to stay on top of their classes—sometimes longer than they care to admit. "A typical Brown student would sooner die," one student confides, "than be caught in the library on a Friday or Saturday night. This does not mean that we don't study on the weekends, we just take to our rooms surreptitiously." After all, they do have an image to keep up.

Brown students are cast from a different mold than most East Coast achievers. They are about as friendly and unharried as you can be and still enjoy a 90 to 95 percent acceptance rate at graduate schools. Some seniors say that recent freshmen are a little more intense and high-strung than their predecessors, but grinding geeks are still few and far between. With only 6 percent of the students hailing from Rhode Island, geographical diversity is one of Brown's hallmarks. Politically, there is also a lively mix. "Of course, Brown is full of liberals," writes one student, "but you'd be surprised how many conservatives (even reactionaries) are kicking around." Brown is one of the few remaining hotspots of student activism in the nation; nary a semester passes without at least one demonstration against C.I.A. recruitment on campus, U.S. involvement in Central America or some other current issue. Recently, the target was close to home: Minority students staged sit-ins and rallies until the administrators agreed to look into ways of improving life at Brown for blacks and Hispanics, who make up 7 and 2 percent of the student body, respectively.

Brown admits students on a need-blind basis, but a relatively low endowment means Brown can't be as generous with financial aid as most of the other Ivys. In a few cases near the end of the admissions process, the university "starts to give a higher priority to students with less than average financial need." Brown doesn't offer athletic or academic merit scholarships, but fifteen Starr National Service Scholarships, ranging from $1,000 to $2,000, are awarded each year to students who devote a year or more to volunteer public-service jobs. About fifty other "academically superlative" students, called National Scholars, will find their financial aid package sweetened with extra grant money.

About half the freshmen are assigned to one of the eight coed West Quad dorms in "loud and rambunctious" units of thirty to forty with several sophomore or junior dorm counselors. The other half live in the quieter Pembroke campus dorms or in a few other scattered locations. After freshman year, students seeking on-campus housing enter a lottery. The dorms themselves are fairly nondescript—"There are no fireplaces or engraved wood trim, à la Princeton," observes one student—but nevertheless there are many options to choose from, including apartment-like suites with kitchens, two sororities, two social dorms, and three coed fraternities. The lottery is based on seniority, and sometimes the leftovers for sophomores can be a little skimpy. A significant number of upperclassmen move into off-campus houses or apartments, most within walking distance. Brown's food service, which gets high marks from students for tastiness and variety, offers meal plans ranging from seven to twenty a week. All students on a meal plan get a credit card that allows them to go to one of the three snack bars on campus, open far into the evening, if they miss a meal in "The Ratty" or "V–W," Brown's two dining halls.

The university is situated in a part of Providence where the houses are old and the streets picturesque. "Downtown is a ten-minute walk, but why bother when you can buy anything from Cap'n Crunch to Bass Weejuns on Thayer Street, which runs through the east side of campus," a philosophy concentrator explains. Since Providence is Rhode Island's state capital, many internship opportunities in state government are available, as are a few good music joints, lively bars, and fine restaurants. Unfortunately, Providence is an industrial city that has seen better days, and despite some recent gentrification, one student advises prospectives to "be prepared to wear your proletarian disguise." For a change of scenery, many students head to Boston or the beaches of Newport, both an hour away.

The few residential Greek organizations are generally considered much too un-mellow for Brown's taste, and since freshmen and sophomores are their chief clientele, a recent rise in the state drinking age has crimped their beer-blasting style. (The several nonresidential black fraternities and sororities serve an altogether different function.) Off-campus parties have become increasingly important "since campus security started acting like the Gestapo, raiding and shutting down campus parties where beer was available to those under twenty-one." For those who don't mind the stricter drinking rules, the university sponsors frequent campus-wide parties, and Thursday Funk Night at the Underground, a campus pub, usually draws a crowd. During the daylight hours, strong theater and dance programs, a daily newspaper, a skydiving club, political organizations, "even a Scrabble club and a successful croquet team" represent just a few of the ways Brown students manage to keep themselves entertained. The campus student center recently underwent a thorough renovation. For those interested in community outreach, the university's Public Service Center helps place students in a variety of volunteer positions, a pet project of the president.

Brown isn't an especially sports-minded school, but a number of teams nevertheless manage to excel. "Our football team is known for choking, but that doesn't keep us from going out and having a grand ole time," says one student. Men's basketball, lacrosse, crew and water polo have recently brought home Ivy championships, as have women's swimming, soccer, basketball, softball, hockey and field hockey. Football and men's hockey are the biggest spectator sports, "but most students would rather be playing a sport than watching one," and a good intramural program helps them do just that. Athletic facilities include a new Olympic-size pool, a new indoor athletic complex with everything from tennis courts to weight rooms, and a basketball arena in the planning stages.

Ever since the days of Roger Williams, Rhode Island has been known as a land of toleration, and Brown certainly is a twentieth-century embodiment of this tradition. The education offered at this university is decidedly different from that provided by the rest of the Ivy League, or for that matter, by most of the country's top universities. Brown is content to gather a talented bunch of students, offer a diverse and imaginative array of courses, and then let the undergraduates make sense of it all. "You get four years of choice," says one student. "Deal with it."

Bryn Mawr College

Bryn Mawr, PA 19010

Location Suburban	**Applicants** 1,200
Total Enrollment 1,800	**Accepted** 58%
Undergraduates 1,100	**Enrolled** 45%
Male/Female N/A	**Academics** ★★★★★
SAT V/M 650/630	**Social** ☎☎☎
Financial Aid 55%	**Q of L** ●●●
Expense Pr $ $ $	**Admissions** (215)645-5152

Bryn Mawr College bills itself as a small women's college, but it's not. Much like its eclectic, individualistic student body, Bryn Mawr denies generalizations. With its students running around to several larger, coed schools for their classes and majors; men enrolled in the graduate schools; and men from neighboring Haverford College living in the dorms and taking classes here—Bryn Mawr doesn't quite fit the bill.

No matter how you define the school, "only one word comes to mind when describing the academic climate at Bryn Mawr—intense," according to a neuroscience major. It's no wonder the students at this school—the smallest of the Seven Sisters—call themselves Bryn Mawrters. As one student explains, "I suspect it would be a difficult place to blow off your work; you'd start to feel uncomfortable real fast." For the last several years the freshmen at Bryn Mawr have had among the highest average verbal SAT scores in the nation. And general education requirements include competence in English composition, a language other than English, and mathematics, plus a year's work in each of four areas: social sciences, laboratory sciences, literature and the humanities.

Most departments are strong, especially English, art history, archeology and Russian—"The C.I.A. wants to recruit us, that's how good we are," reports one senior. The arts, both fine and performing, and the philosophy department, rely heavily on coeducational Haverford, which is within walking distance for students who want to major or do serious work in these subjects. Swarthmore and the University of Pennsylvania offer several course list supplements. But Bryn Mawr has a rich variety of special programs, including a rare undergraduate concentration in classical and Near Eastern archeology that sponsors its own digs in Italy, Greece and Turkey. Other interdisciplinary programs include the study of global peace initiatives, the growth and structure of cities, and Hispanic studies. Conspicuously missing is a women's studies program, but it can be chosen as an independent major.

Bryn Mawr's coed graduate schools of social work and arts and sciences share faculty with the undergraduate departments, and professors are praised not only as scholars but also as teachers. "Profs always have time for the students, and promote an attitude of students first," boasts an undergrad. The school places a high premium on integrity and student autonomy. The honor code allows students to set their own exam schedules, and students sit in on the board of trustees and college-wide committee meetings. "The honor code plays a large role in our personal freedom," proclaims one student. "There are no rules here; there is only the understanding that you will not impinge upon the rights of others."

Bryn Mawr attempts to help all needy students obtain some sort of financial assistance, but does not offer athletic or merit scholarships. The student body comes from all over the country (50 percent from the Northeast), and all over the world (9 percent are foreign). More than 90 percent are from the top fifth of their high school classes, and three-quarters go on to graduate or professional school. Most are well read, ambitious, always ready for intellectual conversation, and impressively nonstereotypical. "A student body including a sheep rancher from Montana and a basketball star from Zimbabwe denies any generalization," insists one sophomore. Yet a colleague adds, "Bryn Mawr is, for the most part, liberal." In fact, a baffled senior reports that "the student government president is Republican, but this is a horrible mistake and no one is quite sure how it happened."

The community of Bryn Mawr (Welsh for "high hill") is part of suburban Philadelphia's wealthy Main Line (named after a railroad). "It's a quaint and charming town, with all the standard amenities like banks and drugstores," notes an English major, "however, the prices of clothing, food, etc., reveal that it's not exactly a college town." The attractive campus is a path-laced oasis—peaceful and self-contained, but within walking distance of the train station. The predominant architecture is collegiate Gothic, and most buildings are turreted gray stone. Variations on this theme include a sprinkling of modern buildings such as Louis Kahn's slate and concrete residence hall. All of this is scattered among trees, greens and hills. One student complains about midwinter depression, "when the rain turns the gray stone buildings into fortresses out of a gothic novel." But another adds, "Spring comes early and is gorgeous with azaleas, daffodils and flowering cherry trees."

Social life revolves around the eleven dormitories. Students have their choice of single-sex or coed (with Haverford men) dorms. The old dorms, despite their peeling paint and leaky roofs, are still the most popular—commonplace luxuries such as fireplaces, window seats, and stained glass windows could have something to do with it. Dorms have quotas for students from all four classes, so freshmen mix freely with upperclassmen. All those who live on campus must subscribe to the twenty-meal-a-week plan, where "if worse comes to worse, the yogurt machine, with flavors ranging from chocolate to piña colada, is almost always open." Students may eat at Haverford as well.

The college holds many traditional ceremonies and celebrations—the medieval-style May Day festivities, the presentation of lanterns in class colors on Lantern Night; afternoon teas are treasured complements to the otherwise contemporary social scene. Free films are shown every Friday, and each weekend sees one or two dorm bashes as well. "Most parties tend to be bi-college" (i.e., with Haverford), reports one student. But a classmate adds that the social relationship with recently-gone-coed Haverford isn't all it's cracked up to be: "The situation isn't ideal because the male/female ratio between Haverford and Bryn Mawr is one to three. This creates some people problems."

"The new gym put a spark to athletics here," reports one woman, "and people are beginning to value them more." Field hockey and lacrosse show the best inter-collegiate records, with swimming and gymnastics close behind. Several intramural games are run jointly with Haverford, including touch football and softball, "but they haven't really caught on well." Off campus, students amuse themselves with Philadelphia's theaters, shops, and restaurants—Bryn Mawr is a seventeen-minute train ride away.

Despite the males on campus, Bryn Mawr still sees itself as providing "an important balance in a society not yet free of sexism." Let the men study, eat and sleep here, but they'll never run the place. As a senior puts it, "Powered by women, supported by women—Bryn Mawr gives women a different vision of what is possible."

Bucknell University

Lewisburg, PA 17837

Location Rural	**Applicants** 6,250
Total Enrollment 3,450	**Accepted** 44%
Undergraduates 3,230	**Enrolled** 32%
Male/Female 51/49	**Academics** ★ ★ ★ ★
SAT V/M 560/630	**Social** 🍷 🍷 🍷 🍷
Financial Aid 60%	**Q of L** ● ● ●
Expense Pr $ $ $ $	**Admissions** (717)524-1101

Students at Bucknell are the academic embodiment of what Tom Wolfe might have called the We Generation. They take pride in their clean-cut, all-American image, their traditional values and the recognition that, as one puts it, "Bucknellians generally become good businessmen and women, i.e., the backbone of American society." Bucknell is a place where the people are "primarily concerned with having fun, passing, and getting a good job after graduation."

Set on three hundred wooded acres in the rolling hills of central Pennsylvania, Bucknell's campus is so well manicured that it's "almost too perfect," one student believes. With mainly white-trimmed brick buildings, the campus looks like a postcard, especially when spring brings its profusion of blooming cherry trees. Despite the tranquil setting, the academic atmosphere is intense during the week and even into the weekends. Students have easy access to faculty members—including the university president, who teaches a freshman biology course. "It's not uncommon to see faculty and students playing tennis or basketball together," says one biology major.

Students commend a variety of subjects, beginning with the extremely demanding engineering and natural science departments, which emphasize lab work and research. Other strong offerings include psychology, English, economics, foreign languages (particularly Japanese), philosophy, political science and international relations. Never among Bucknell's strongest offerings, music and the arts should benefit from a new facility now under construction. A recent expansion of the Bertrand Library has doubled its size and enhanced its aesthetic appeal. "The new library is the most beautiful you could imagine," sings a music major.

First-year students are in for a special academic treat known as the Freshman Humanities Semester, which introduces them to the highlights of Western culture and philosophy under the guidance of a dozen professors. "Few participants ever regret having done it," reports one student. "Values and ideas are challenged in a manner never offered again in one's remaining three and a half years." With a 4-1-4 academic calendar, Bucknell's optional Jan-Plans enable students to pursue between-semester internships, foreign study, volunteer work or other pet projects. Semesters in Florence, London and Vienna, led by Bucknell professors, are popular and encouraged for those with a strong GPA. An array of other study-abroad programs are also available. All BA candidates must fulfill distribution requirements that include four courses in the humanities and two each in science and social science. In addition, each student must complete a three-course writing requirement.

Chances of getting into Bucknell can depend on what you want to study, with accounting and management programs the most highly selective. The same thing can be said of staying. "It is easy to flunk out of engineering," declares one student, although "it would take a determined effort to flunk out of most other departments." Bucknell's students hail mostly from New England and Middle Atlantic public schools, and over three-quarters ranked in the top fifth of their classes. "There are those students who don't study and somehow get by, but most students have a good time," says a sophomore.

One political science student describes his fellow Bucknellians as "Caucasian, conservative, and career conscious." Though a new minority center is testament to the university's commitment to attracting minorities, blacks and Hispanics still account for a paltry 3 percent of the students. When total student financial need exceeds funds available, offers of aid are made on a competitive basis, comparing each candidate's academic record, extracurricular activities and special talents. The university has several generous loan programs but awards no athletic or academic merit scholarships (National Merit Scholars do receive a token $250).

Housing is guaranteed to all who request it, and several spacious new dorms have been added in recent years for both freshmen and upperclassmen. As part of an effort to improve intellectual life on campus, the administration recently unveiled a residential college option for first-year students as an alternative to regular dorm life and to beer bash socializing. Approximately half of each freshman class is housed in one of the two "colleges," Renaissance and International. In the coming years, upperclassmen will be integrated into the colleges, but for now they enter a lottery, based on seniority, for space in the dorms. Many seniors opt for the slightly more expensive university-owned apartments just a short stroll from campus. Except for a sorority dorm, all are coed by floor. Smaller special-interest houses accommodate students who share common interests like Judaic studies. About 9 percent of the students bolt university housing altogether, and another 10 percent opt for fraternity houses. Boarding students take their meals in a central dining hall, where the food is made on the premises and is well above average for institutional fodder. The Bison, a food and recreation center, provides another university-run dining option.

Bucknell's isolation means not only that it is safe and free of crime, but also that "civilization is three and a half hours by car." Civilization in this case means New York City, but the Poconos are half that distance for those who like to ski. Consequently, social life still revolves around fraternity parties, especially for upperclassmen. Sixty percent of the men join fraternities and 50 percent of the women join sororities, which do not have houses. Administration-sponsored alternatives to the Greek activities include visiting comedians, bands and plays.

Cross-country is Bucknell's most successful varsity team, though men's tennis, skiing, basketball and water polo, and women's cross-country, swimming and basketball all do very well. Intramurals are available in almost every imaginable sport, and participation is enthusiastic. The university has excellent athletic facilities, including a multimillion-dollar field house and an eighteen-hole golf course.

Bucknell is probably not the right place for "a free floating spirit seeking inner discovery," and while most students tend to view this as a virtue of the school, a few note drawbacks. Bucknell still lacks the diversity and intellectual life found at Ivy-type institutions, and according to one student, "It's like we're in a bubble. We seem to be studying, socializing, eating and never realize what's going on around us." In short, students who fit the Bucknell mold can spend four comfortable years working hard to prepare for success in the outer world, while rarely having to contend with its harshest realities.

California Institute of Technology

Pasadena, CA 91125

Location Suburban	**Applicants** 1,340
Total Enrollment 1,840	**Accepted** 31%
Undergraduates 850	**Enrolled** 46%
Male/Female 85/15	**Academics** ★ ★ ★ ★ ★
SAT V/M 650/760	**Social** ☎
Financial Aid 70%	**Q of L** ● ● ●
Expense Pr $ $ $ $	**Admissions** (818)356-6341

Small in size, gigantic in reputation, Caltech is in a league of its own. Just look at the numbers: undergraduate student body of just 850, student/faculty ratio of three to one, average combined SAT scores of 1410 for entering freshmen (tops in the nation), and a faculty with nearly twenty Nobel Prizes to its credit.

Check out the opportunities: rigorous training in math, science and engineering, research from sophomore year on with world-class professors, a phenomenally successful honor system that makes integrity the unbroken rule in and out of the Caltech classroom, and sure job offers at top dollar from private industry and the federal government at the end of four years. But also check out the catches: academic pressure unmatched at any other college, competition for grades that can crush students with the first C's of their lives, and a depressing social life spawned by an overwhelming ratio of males to females. Says one grizzled veteran, "The main reason I am here is that several people told me I would never survive."

Old Spanish-style buildings and a few "typical block institutional moderns" make up the Caltech campus, which is isolated from the show-biz/hot-tub scene that many people think of as California culture. "Pasadena is nestled right up against the beautiful San Gabriel mountains," says one woman. "Unfortunately the smog nestles up against the mountains, too." Despite the somewhat soupy atmosphere, the campus has lots of greenery, including olive trees, lily ponds and plenty of flowers.

Though it takes a while for students to get acclimated, most soon become devoted to Caltech and Caltechers. "Everyone is horribly bright here," says one senior, and it's taken as gospel on this campus that Caltech offers the best overall technical education in the country—no matter what students at a certain school in Massachusetts might think. Most of the first year and some of the second is devoted to fulfilling the school's core requirements—two years of calculus, two years of physics, one year of chemistry and a number of labs. Lectures are large, but break into recitations of about ten students each that are often led by other faculty members. The pass/fail curriculum in the freshman year goes a long way toward easing the high-powered atmosphere for new arrivals.

Caltech made its reputation in physics, and this subject is still a premier attraction. Engineering (especially electrical engineering), chemistry, biology, astronomy and geology are standouts, and just about everything outside of the humanities/social science division (in which students must take a fifth of their courses) is excellent. Most students can access the campus computer system from their dorm rooms, and one student boasts that Caltech has "the best computer/student ratio in the nation." The economics major, one student says, is surprisingly good: "Combined with good courses in mathematics, it's excellent preparation for graduate school in economics." Students seriously interested in the humanities or social sciences are often frustrated by the limited course offerings. ("Caltech is tops in science, not breadth," observes one student.) In spite of a few geniuses who are either impossible to understand or impossibly demanding, the professors tend to be good teachers. Of course, they are usually more interested in research than in classes, but so are most of their students. For many, summertime is the time to go SURFing, as in Summer Undergraduate Research Fellowships, which are grants that give about a hundred undergraduates a chance to get a head start on their own research under a faculty sponsor. With about 40 percent of the students destined to earn PhDs after graduation—one of the highest percentages in the nation—many Caltech students continue to follow in the footsteps of their faculty mentors long after graduation.

After four years in high school as the resident math/science genius, most freshmen show up at Caltech a little wet behind the ears. "A large number have inflated egos and are not used to talking with peers," says a seasoned hand, adding that "this attitude of superiority rarely survives the freshman year." Bragging about being first in your high school class will impress no one at Caltech—you're just joining the group. But Caltechers, despite their academic preoccupations, vociferously deny that they prefer computers to people. "We aren't a bunch of eggheads and nerds!" says one student emphatically. "People who want to spend their college careers stuck in their rooms need not apply." About a third of the student body comes from California's public schools, but the rest are drawn from all over the nation. Asian Americans account for about 20 percent of each class, blacks and Hispanics for 2 and 3 percent, respectively.

Perhaps the most distinctive attribute of Caltechers is their commitment to one another—a supportiveness sustained by an honor code based on the principle that "no Caltech student takes unfair advantage of another" and maintained through four years of grueling academic pressure and competition. Although the pressure is intense, the climate is, curiously enough, not competitive. "Pressure here is self-inflicted. We push ourselves to our individual limit, and then accept that limit," says one senior. In addition to need-based financial aid, Caltech awards thirty-six merit scholarships that range from $8,000 to $10,000.

There are no fraternities or sororities, but the seven coed on-campus houses inspire a loyalty worthy of the Greeks. The four older houses offer mostly single rooms, while the three newer ones have doubles; and Caltech will pay students for home improvements like carpeting or built-in bookshelves. Freshmen select their houses during Rotation Week, when they spend a day of partying at each one, indicating at week's end the four they like the most. Resident upperclassmen take it from there in a professional sport–type draft that places each freshman in one of his or her top choices. Each dorm's dining hall serves standard institutional food from a central kitchen, and these eating-living quarters serve as students' home bases, which they loyally support. About a third of the upperclassmen live in college-owned quarters adjacent to the campus, while 2 percent move off campus entirely.

The houses are the emotional center of Caltech life. Site of Caltech's infrequent parties, they are also the scene of innumerable practical jokes perpetrated on staff members and seniors. On Ditch Day seniors barricade their dorm rooms using everything from steel bars to electronic codes, leave clues as to how to dislodge them, and disappear from campus. Underclassmen spend the day figuring out how to break in and claim the awaiting alcoholic reward. Sidewalks in Pasadena roll up at 5 PM, but L.A. is the original all-night city for Caltechers with a car, and—more rare—a free evening.

It may come as a surprise that Caltech's football squad has played in the Rose Bowl more than any other team—but that's only because it's the school's home stadium. The classic student prank of the decade was orchestrated during the 1984 Rose Bowl game. UCLA was playing Illinois, and a group of Caltech whiz kids were playing with the scoreboard. They had spent months devising a radio control device that allowed them to take control of the scoreboard in the second half and flash pictures of their school's mascot, the beaver, as well as a new version of the score that had Caltech leading MIT by a mile.

When it comes to actually playing the game, however, varsity athletics are not Caltech's strong suit—"We show up. We compete. We lose," says one neo-Caesarian—and teams are therefore open to anyone who wants to play. Students enthusiastically recommend their losing teams as an excellent escape from academic work, "even if you're a horrible athlete." No one turns out to watch them compete, but students do manage a big bonfire if the expected rout turns into a victory. Intramural sports receive at least as much attention as the varsity.

"If you truly want to study science or engineering and you want to be the best at it, even at the expense of social life and free time, come here," says one junior. "Otherwise, don't." Unfortunately, a Caltech education also comes at the expense of something more important than a good collegiate social life. One student explains, "On one level the honor code works; we learn to act like real scientists, we will not cheat on exams, we will not fudge our results. But on another level it does not work. We do not think about our social responsibilities as scientists. We are never taught to question what our work is going to do to the world."

Yes, Caltech students have outside interests—"computers, video games, stereos, music, wargames, science fiction, girls" is one sophomore's list—but science and research are their great loves. High-powered, demanding, rewarding, Caltech is, as one student says, "a steep ladder: It gets you up there fast, but it's very risky."

CALIFORNIA PUBLIC COLLEGES and UNIVERSITIES

California's three-tier network of public higher education offers its citizens a wide variety of educational styles and services: nine combined research and teaching units of the University of California (UC), nineteen state universities and colleges (CSUC) that primarily emphasize undergraduate teaching, and a myriad of two-year community colleges that offer both terminal degrees and the possibility of transferring into four-year institutions. All told, the system is as varied as the state itself and provides tough competition to local private institutions in price and academic quality.

Admissions requirements to the three tiers and the institutions within them vary widely. Community colleges are open to virtually all high school graduates. The top third of California high school graduates (as measured statewide by a combination of SAT scores and grade-point average) may attend units of the state university and college system, though beginning in the fall of '88, all applicants must have taken a course in the fine or performing arts to be considered for admission. Students in the top 12.5 percent of their class are eligible to attend the University of California. Admissions standards vary within both the UC and state systems, and meeting the minimum requirements is no guarantee of admission to the campus of one's choice. Competition is particularly fierce at the most popular of the UC campuses, where the number of qualified applicants far outnumbers the places available. Out-of-state students pay more, face even more difficult entrance requirements and must compete for a limited number of spots.

The **California State University and Colleges** is totally separate from the University of California, and, in fact, the two institutions have historically competed for funds as well as students. The largest system of senior higher education in the nation, CSUC focuses on undergraduate education and, while its members offer master's degrees, they can award doctorates only in collaboration with a UC institution. Research in the state university system is severely restricted—a blow to CSUC's national prestige but a big plus for students. Unlike UC, where the mandate to publish or perish is alive and well, teachers in the state system are there to teach. CSUC's biggest problem is the success of UC, and its frequent lament, "Anywhere else we'd be number one," is not without justification.

The five state colleges and fourteen state universities cater to more than 310,000 students a year, most of them commuters, many already in the work force or married. While a solid liberal arts education is offered, the stress is usually on career-oriented professional training. Size varies dramatically, from about thirty thousand students at San Diego and Long Beach to under five thousand at several other branches. Each campus has its own specific strengths, although in most cases a student's choice of school is dictated by location rather than by academic specialties. For those with a wider choice, some of the more distinctive campuses are profiled below.

A few of the schools have built up residential populations. **Chico,** situated in the beautiful Sacramento Valley, draws the large majority of its students from outside a hundred-mile radius. The on-campus undergraduate life is strong and the partying is great. **Bakersfield** and **San Bernardino,** two of the smallest schools, boast residential "villages" along with more conventional dorms, the former's in a living-learning center with affiliated faculty members, the latter's with its own swimming pool.

California Polytechnic at San Luis Obispo is the toughest state university to get into. It provides excellent training in the applied branches of such fields as agriculture, architecture, business and engineering. Enrollment: 16,000.

Fresno is the place to go for wine and cheese. Situated in the verdant Central Valley, it has the only viticulture school in the state outside of Davis, and undergraduates can work in the school winery. Yosemite, King's Canyon, and Sequoia national parks are nearby. Enrollment: 16,500.

San Diego State is the biggest and balmiest of the campuses and, since it has a more residential and outdoorsy, campus-oriented social scene, appeals to traditional-age undergraduates. "You could go for the weather alone—some do," says one former student. Contrasted with other state schools, athletics are very important, and the academic offerings are almost as oriented to the liberal arts as at its UC neighbor at San Diego. Out-of-staters prefer this campus to the inland ones. Enrollment: 31,500.

Humboldt State is about five hundred miles north of San Diego, perched at the top of the state near the Oregon border in the heart of the redwoods. Humboldt's forestry and wildlife departments have national reputations, and the natural sciences are in general strong. Students have the run of excellent laboratory facilities and the Redwood National Park. Most in-staters come to get out of Los Angeles and enjoy the rugged coastline north of San Francisco that is for many the "real" California. Enrollment: 6,000.

Dominguez Hills in East Los Angeles is especially strong in management and business, fine arts and computer science. Individual attention is available through the Small College, a school-within-a-school in which students may design their own curriculums with the assistance of a faculty adviser. Primarily a commuter school, Dominguez Hills has opened a few dorms. Enrollment: 8,000.

The **University of California** is the undisputed star of the state's public-education system, comprising some of the nation's best research universities. Although technically one school, the nine campuses each do their own thing in the best Western tradition—and they do it extremely well.

Berkeley was founded first (in 1868) and remains best known. Most of the other schools began as specialized branches: San Francisco opened in 1873 as a graduate institution in the health sciences and remains so more than a hundred years later, San Diego focused on marine biology, Riverside was a citrus research station, and Davis ran a farm for agricultural students. Los Angeles and Santa Barbara joined the troupe in 1919 and 1944 respectively. In the '50s and '60s all these campuses gradually changed from strictly vocational schools into full-fledged universities. UC's great leap forward came in 1965, when the economic boom of the '60s and the Great Society ideals led to the opening of three more campuses: Irvine, Santa Cruz and San Diego.

Enrollment was expected to fall off after the last of the baby boom classes graduated, but instead applications have soared and enrollment has increased far beyond the administration's expectations. The university—all nine branches—has succeeded as a great research institution; but unfortunately, undergraduates are in some ways shortchanged. Students in all of the schools complain about the massive bureaucracy and impersonal education, and crowding on a number of the campuses is an on-going problem. On a more positive note, the state legislature has recently taken an attitude of benevolence toward the system, and university administrators say their funding is at an all-time high. While tuition at most schools continues to skyrocket, the UC system hasn't had a price hike in three years. Each UC campus receives a full-length summary below (except for graduate and health science–oriented San Francisco).

Whatever schools they choose, Californians attend their public universities because the opportunities for an excellent education, whatever their interest, are virtually boundless. They also assume that the Golden State is the only place to be. Out-of-staters might find this chauvinism a bit hard to swallow. On the other hand, they might convert.

UC—Berkeley

Berkeley, CA 94720

Location Urban	**Applicants** 20,300
Total Enrollment 31,500	**Accepted** 34%
Undergraduates 22,300	**Enrolled** 47%
Male/Female 55/45	**Academics** ★ ★ ★ ★
SAT V/M 550/630	**Social** 🐘 🐘 🐘 🐘
Financial Aid 30%	**Q of L** ● ● ●
Expense Pub $ $ $ $	**Admissions** (415)642-0200

At the University of California at Berkeley most students spend at least part of every day people watching, and the most frequently heard remark is "Look at that one." Leftist activists say it of the born-again Christians carrying the Pro-USA placards. Women in Shetland wool sweaters and blue jeans say it about sorority sisters who manage to walk the hilly campus in four-inch heels. Nearly everyone says it about the bums, the Hare Krishnas, the black man in a white sheikh outfit who drinks a bottle of champagne every afternoon in a courtyard just north of campus, and the mimes and comedians who regularly perform for free. Few students ever converse with the people they look at, but everyone seems delighted that everyone else is part of the scenery.

The scenery is what makes Berkeley delightfully different from most universities. The campus is located in a small city set on a hillside between the Berkeley hills and San Francisco Bay, with buildings that range from the stunning classical amphitheater to the modern University Art Museum draped in neon sculpture. Berkeley embraces 2,001 alternative life-styles and, so it seems, an equal number of Nobel Prize holders on the faculty. It includes a student government with eighty full-time employees and an annual budget of $1 million. At Berkeley everything is either big or odd, or both—all of which befits one of the nation's most prestigious public universities.

Like everything else, the academic side at Berkeley can be overwhelming. A student must contend with more than twenty thousand other undergraduates, an urban environment, and a high-pressure curriculum. Some introductory courses, particularly in the sciences, have as many as eight hundred students, and professors, who must publish or perish from the university's highly competitive teaching ranks, devote a great deal of time to research. Berkeley has made most of its reputation on its research and graduate programs, most of which rank among the best in the nation. And while the undergraduate education is excellent, younger students must take a gamble with the trickle-down theory that the intellectual might of those in the ivory towers will drip down to them eventually. Though the best professors often teach introductory courses, students generally have personal contact only with the teaching assistants who are brought in to read exams and papers. On the positive side, a new Division of Freshman and Sophomore Studies offers small seminars for first- and second-year students in the liberal arts.

Berkeley's academic requirements are not extensive, but they sustain the university's commitment to liberal arts education at a time when professional training is becoming ever more popular. There are requirements in English composition and literature, a foreign language and one term each of American history and American institutions. Each department maintains its own distribution requirements, though many of these can be fulfilled through advanced-placement exams in high school. Most of the departments are noteworthy, and some are just about the best anywhere. Sociology, mathematics, physics, chemistry, history, English and engineering (especially civil, chemical and electrical) are just some of the real stars. The performing arts department falls below par, and communications is definitely an underdeveloped area.

Special programs abound at Berkeley, though it's up to the student to find out about them. One student's favorite is the Political Economy of Industrial Societies, which combines history, political science and sociology. Students may study abroad on fellowships at one of fifty centers around the world, or spend time in various internships in cities like New York, Washington or Sacramento. The engineering college encourages students to take time off to work through a co-op program. If all you want to do is study, the library system, with 6.5 million volumes, is one of the largest in the nation and maintains open stacks.

Applications to Berkeley (or Cal, as it's also called) are at an all-time record level, and the acceptance rate has, accordingly, dropped sharply. In-staters account for about 78 percent of the students, and blacks and Hispanics make up a combined total of 11 percent. Today, the trend is away from the legacy of the Free Speech movement and the '60s, and business majors and fraternity members increasingly outnumber the young Communists and peaceniks. "Don't confuse the city of Berkeley with the student body, which is well balanced and not right- or left-leaning," says one junior. But although the move may be from radical to regular, the diversity among students is still greater than you will find almost anywhere else, and so is the tolerance. "*Anything* and *anyone* goes here," says one economics major. "After Berkeley nothing shocks you anymore."

Berkeley officials have good news regarding financial aid: that office's $30-million budget should be enough "to make up the difference between the average student costs and the family's ability to pay." Non-need merit scholarships are awarded to about 850 students every year, and Berkeley deals out about $1.5 million every year to about 300 promising athletes.

For many students, their first and worst experience at Berkeley is finding a place to live. The dormitories have room for only about 4,800 students, leaving the remaining 28,000 to scramble for expensive and scarce off-campus apartments, rooms in student-run cooperatives, or houses. Recently, the shortage of rooms in the Berkeley area reached crisis proportions, with the number of students seeking apartments far exceeding the available supply. "I've been staying in the living room of a friend's apartment for fourteen weeks while looking for other accommodations," reports one junior. About two-thirds of the university's highly prized dorm rooms are reserved for freshmen, and as the few singles go to resident assistants, doubles are likely to become crowded triples, albeit at a reduced fee. Losers in the May lottery automatically go on a long waiting list to vie for rooms in subsequent monthly lotteries. In the absence of a mandatory meal plan everybody eats "wherever and whenever they wish," including in the dorms.

Though the housing crunch can get you down, the beautiful California weather will probably take your mind off it in time. The BART subway system provides easy access to San Francisco, and that city remains a cultural—and countercultural—mecca. Outside the city, it just gets better. Whether you want to ski Lake Tahoe, hike Yosemite National Park, beachcomb in Big Sur or taste wine in the Napa Valley, all are within driving range. A car is only an asset when you want to go out of town: students warn that parking in Berkeley is difficult, to say the least.

Weekends are generally spent in Berkeley, hanging out at the many coffeehouses and sidewalk cafés, heading to a fraternity or sorority party, or taking advantage of the many events right on campus. Many students use the weekend to catch up on studying, and, of course, there's always the people-watching. More than a hundred student groups are registered on campus, which ensures that there is an outlet for just about any interest but that no one group will never dominate campus life.

Greeks have returned in force, with approximately 16 percent of the students in a fraternity or a sorority and a certain amount of tension between them and the other 84 percent. The minimum drinking age of twenty-one has no visible effect on anyone's behavior. Varsity athletics are also on the rise. Men's rugby and water polo recently brought home PAC 10 championships, basketball's popularity has surged, and just about everybody turns out for the Stanford football game. Intramurals are popular, and the personal fitness craze is fed by a new recreational facility.

The common denominator in the Berkeley community is academic motivation, and the self-reliance that emerges from trying to make your mark among twenty thousand peers. "I have had to learn to stand on my own here. Nobody holds my hand," one student reports. Beyond that, the diversity of town and campus make an extraordinarily free and exciting college environment for almost anyone. "It makes one feel free to dress, say, think, or do anything and not be chastised for being unorthodox," says one student. "At Berkeley it is worse to be dull than to be odd."

UC—Davis

Davis, CA 95616

Location Small city	**Applicants** 4,630
Total Enrollment 19,835	**Accepted** 92%
Undergraduates 14,600	**Enrolled** 66%
Male/Female 51/49	**Academics** ★ ★ ★
SAT V/M 490/560	**Social** ☎ ☎ ☎
Financial Aid 45%	**Q of L** ● ● ● ●
Expense Pub $ $ $	**Admissions** (916)752-2971

Davis is deceptive. Although it is within easy reach of a number of large cities, the town lies in the middle of a stretch of flat farmland that could easily be mistaken for the Kansas plains. Even more deceiving is the fact that beneath the apricot and walnut trees of this sleepy little town is one of the most intense and demanding of the University of California campuses. "Don't get tricked by the friendly and quiet atmosphere," one senior cautions. "Davis is an extremely competitive place."

Originally known as the University Farm, Davis was founded as an agricultural adjunct to UC–Berkeley in 1909. The campus features a blend of architectural styles, from traditional dairy barn to modern concrete. The hub of the university is a central area known as the Quad, one of many grassy open spaces on campus. Though it has added programs in many disciplines over the last four decades or so—including liberal arts, engineering and four professional schools—its aggie departments are still the ones that shine. The enology (study of wine making) department is the best in the country, which is appropriate for a school this close to the Napa Valley wine region. Animal science, agricultural economics and engineering are strong departments; in fact, all the sciences are strong. The school is "the number one choice for any prevet," and it isn't bad for premeds either. Humanities subjects such as history and English are generally good, but they are not up to par with the sciences. Noteworthy special programs include the Integrated Studies Program, which offers seminars and housing to a select group of freshmen, and the Experimental Farm, which gives ag students first-hand farm experience. Since internships and co-op programs are well established, it is the rare Cal Aggie that completes four years on campus in a row.

Faculty members at Davis are expected to do top-level research as well as teach, especially in the college of agriculture and environmental sciences. Many large introductory classes are taught by graduate students, but one student reports that "top profs are approachable if the student will make an effort." Though it has about two million volumes, the library lacks adequate study space, and students complain about the eleven PM closing time.

The academic demands are intense, and the students (95 percent of whom graduated in the top tenth of their high school classes) are high achievers. Adding to the pressure is the university's ten-week quarter system, which makes for shorter, more hectic terms and an extra set of exams each year. Students are highly grade conscious, and many covet a slot at a prestigious graduate or professional school. Davis has always been a fairly liberal campus, but lately "there is a trend for students here to be more conservative, religious, and materialistic," says a senior. Blacks and Hispanics together account for 7 percent of the students, while Asian Americans are roughly double that number. The university attempts to make sure all its on-time applicants receive the financial aid they need to attend, and late applicants are funded if money remains. More than 150 scholarships, from $100 to $1,500, are awarded on the basis of academic merit.

In between quizzes and cram sessions, the outlying countryside offers a welcome change of pace. The town of Davis itself is small, about forty thousand population, and students make up more than half of it. "Come here in the summer when the students are away and you have never seen a more boring place," says one agriculture major. But if some call it boring, others call its tree-lined streets and quiet nights peaceful, and everyone agrees it's safe. The relationship between college and town is one of rare cooperation (partly because the students are a significant voting bloc in local elections). Health and energy consciousness run high in town and on the vast, architecturally diverse campus, where bicycles—"hundreds, thousands of bicycles!" one woman exclaims—are the main form of transportation. The university has encouraged environmental awareness by banning cars on campus, sponsoring solar energy projects, and promoting such novelties as contests between dorms for the lowest heating and electric bills.

Housing space is in short supply; freshmen and transfers can usually get a room, but the vast majority of upperclassmen live off campus in nearby houses or apartments. Nineteen meals a week in the dining halls come included with the housing bill. A variety of nearby eating establishments serve the student clientele, but a car can come in handy if you are looking for a good meal in Sacramento (twenty minutes) or a great one in San Francisco (little more than an hour). Beaches are a two-hour drive from the campus and the ski slopes and hiking trails of Lake Tahoe and the Sierra Nevadas are a little closer. But if you feel, as most Davis students do, that studies are too important to be abandoned on weekends, the town has restaurants, activities, and entertainment enough to keep the stay-at-homes happy.

On-campus activities are varied. Active drama and music departments provide frequent entertainment, and there is plenty of room for homegrown talent in the coffeehouses, bars and restaurants, which offer mellow live entertainment and poetry readings on a regular basis. Fraternities and sororities stand out conspicuously in the easygoing life-style among the alfalfa fields, but they are growing in popularity. Intramurals are much more popular than organized varsity athletics (which include polo), and on this outdoor campus almost everyone does something athletic—jogging, softball, tennis, swimming or Frisbee—if only to break up the monotony of studies with a different kind of competition. A recent proposal for a new thirty-thousand-seat football stadium has created a flap on campus because the preferred sight is now occupied by the Experimental Farm.

Proud of its small-town atmosphere, Davis is not for the lazy or faint of heart. As one man says, "There's no free ride. You are going to have to work for everything you get." Nor is it for the faint of nose, since some of the things that do come free include hay fever, the hog barns and what one senior calls "the sordid smells of various fertilizers." But in spite of these olfactory annoyances, Davis is the ideal spot to combine high-powered work in science and agriculture with that famous easygoing California life-style.

UC—Irvine

Irvine, CA 92717

Location Suburban	**Applicants** 12,200
Total Enrollment 13,460	**Accepted** 25%
Undergraduates 11,880	**Enrolled** 94%
Male/Female 51/49	**Academics** ★ ★ ★
SAT V/M 450/550	**Social** 🛥 🛥 🛥
Financial Aid 20%	**Q of L** ● ● ●
Expense Pub $ $ $ $	**Admissions** (714)856-6703

On the playing field and court they are the Anteaters, their campus was the set for *Planet of the Apes,* and their favorite freshman dorm is called Middle Earth. But make no mistake: UC–Irvine is not a school for space cadets. Rather it is an up-and-coming branch of the University of California with two big-selling points: excellent opportunities for undergraduate research while you're in school, and a high job placement rate when you get out.

The newest of the UC campuses, Irvine was founded in 1965 with only twelve hundred students. That number is now multiplied by ten, but students point out that the school is still only a third of the size of UCLA or Berkeley. Although enrollment is up and the administration has dreams of further expansion, "it is a perfect size," says one English major. Located in the coastal foothills five miles from the Southern California shore, Irvine occupies 1,510 acres liberally supplied with trees and shrubs from all over the world. Irvine's modern buildings are arranged around a large park. "It's green everywhere you look, all willows and pines," says one woman. "It makes an atmosphere of harmonious serenity."

That serene mood is dispelled once you move indoors. A "premed mentality" reigns at Irvine, since the school of biological sciences is the best and most competitive academic division. "Students can be stepped on and crushed by the weight of their academic work load!" one reports. They can also be stepped on and crushed by their classmates at registration time; it's a tough fight into the science classes of choice as a freshman or sophomore. What one student calls the "playground" side of the campus is made up of the humanities and social sciences. These schools are reasonably good, especially the popular interdisciplinary social ecology program, which combines criminal justice, environmental studies, psychology, anthropology and sociology. But the pace is, as one student says, "much less pressure and more conducive to relaxed learning than the biological sciences." Languages are strong at Irvine, but mathematics is weak. Like most of the UC schools, Irvine is on the quarter system.

Strong in research, Irvine is still an excellent place for undergraduates to get a head start on their own or their professors' pet topic, though teachers can get a little carried away. "Relationships with professors are fairly restricted to the laboratory," says one biology major. "But we understand that research comes before teaching at this institution." One sociology major is a little more blunt. "Students are sometimes made to feel like a burden." The exception is in the social ecology department, where teacher-student relationships are emphasized. The "breadth requirement" means that students must take three courses each in writing, natural sciences, social and behavioral sciences and humanities in order to graduate. There is also a language requirement, though students can substitute linguistics, logic, math or computer science. Honors programs are available in humanities, economics and political science.

"Typical Reagan youth" is how one sophomore describes the Irvine student body. Over 90 percent are in-staters, the majority from Southern California and many of those from Orange County. The students are in general "much more conservative than at the other UC campuses," according to one applied math major. Eighty-five percent ranked in the top 10 percent of their high school class, and all of the rest were in the top fifth. Minorities account for nearly half the student body, with Asian Americans weighing in at a hefty 28 percent, while blacks and Hispanics combine for 10 percent of the undergrads. Need-based aid is available, and there are 425 merit scholarships awarded to freshmen. Men's basketball receives the bulk of the athletic scholarship money, though the sum available for women athletes has recently increased.

Condominium-style dorms are both single-sex and coed and "decent as dormitories go—if you can get in," says one engineering major. Plans for more housing, including buildings for the now homeless fraternities and sororities, are in the works, but currently almost three-quarters of the students live off campus—many on the beach.

The Greek scene is vigorous, but in general Irvine lacks the on-campus liveliness that some of the other UC schools provide. "There is no sis-boom-bah school spirit here" says one engineer. But if life on campus is slow, life off campus is not. That's because the campus is located just forty miles from L.A., five from the beach, a little over an hour from the ski slopes. Catalina Island, with beaches and hiking trails, is a quick boat trip off Newport Harbor. "The local community is stale," one woman says, but students over twenty-one can take advantage of the many bars and clubs in the neighborhood surrounding the campus; younger students must make do with frequent Greek-sponsored parties.

Irvine's men's basketball team has led the PCAA Division I for several years, and the water polo team is the country's best. There is no football team, but intramurals, including judo, karate and aikido, are extremely popular, and a new five-thousand-seat multipurpose gym was recently christened.

Some complaints center on the quarter system—"It is impossible to try to assimilate that much that fast!" claims one premed. But the size, combined with chances for research with top-name professors, means that with a lot of work, the rewards of this demanding education are great. Just don't come thinking it'll be easy. UC–Irvine students keep their heads in their books and their noses to the ground—you begin to see why they chose the anteater for their mascot.

UC—Los Angeles

Los Angeles, CA 90024

Location Urban	**Applicants** 21,570
Total Enrollment 34,420	**Accepted** 42%
Undergraduates 22,750	**Enrolled** 45%
Male/Female 48/52	**Academics** ★ ★ ★ ★
SAT V/M 600/580	**Social** ☙ ☙ ☙
Financial Aid 28%	**Q of L** ● ● ●
Expense Pub $ $ $	**Admissions** (213)825-3101

UCLA is education writ large, which is the best thing about it. With 13 schools and colleges, 70 departments, degrees offered in 200 disciplines, courses offered in nearly 100 languages, what does it matter that you have to share it all with 34,000 other students or that the waiting list for an on-campus parking permit is 5,000 names long?

Sandwiched between two of the most glamorous cities in the U.S., Beverly Hills and Bel Air, UCLA's beautifully landscaped 411 acre campus includes a range of architectural styles, from Gothic to baroque to postmodern high-rise. A wealth of gardens—botanical, Japanese and sculpture—add a touch of quiet elegance to the campus, but the prevailing atmosphere is far from tranquil. Berkeley may still be harder to get into than UCLA, but because UCLA has retained its ten-week quarter schedule (Berkeley is on semesters), it is more hectic, and possibly more demanding, than its cousin up north. "There is a lot of competition and people are really uptight about succeeding," testifies a senior.

What are the strongest programs? Not an easy question to answer on a campus with two colleges and eleven professional schools, many of which are among the best in the nation. The school of engineering and applied science is quite strong, with electrical generally regarded as the leading department. As befits a university next door to Hollywood, the motion picture and television department is first rate. In the College of Letters and Science, political science, psychology, economics, history and geology are particularly strong, and the catchall communication studies major is tough to get into and popular among those who do. The biological sciences are all excellent, and the programs in the College of Fine Arts are unsurpassed in dance and ethnic arts. Students may major in the liberal arts but add a business concentration to their majors, but aspiring Wall Streeters should be aware that there is no full-blown business major.

During their first two years, most students take required core classes that are usually jammed with two to three hundred people, although requirements vary among the different colleges. Freshmen are required to take a course involving quantitative reasoning unless they hit more than 600 on their math SAT, and a course in computer literacy is also among the requirements for a liberal arts degree. Getting into classes can be a real headache, but most students say that with persistence, you can get the ones you need (and you make friends fast on the registration lines). With a B average or better you can spend your junior year abroad at one of forty-four affiliated universities in twenty-three countries.

Grading is tough at UCLA, and counseling is as hard to come by as the easy A.

A three-day orientation session helps get new students off on the right foot, and a twenty-four-hour HELPline serves up psychological counseling. Professors get mixed reviews on their willingness to work with students. A senior in psychology says, "UCLA has some of the top researchers in the country but not the top teachers, and it is sometimes frustrating to try to get to know them." Others say that profs are accessible even to underclassmen "if the student is not intimidated." A remarkable UCLA institution is the professional note taker. The university hires students to take lecture notes for selected classes, and at the end of each week the students make a mad rush to the student union to buy them. A system of eighteen libraries with over five million volumes provides for almost every conceivable research need, and on the off chance that a material isn't available, there is even a research train that runs to several of the nearer UC campuses.

More than 95 percent of UCLA students are from California. As mandated by California's master plan for higher education, admission for in-staters is limited to those who graduated in the top 12.5 percent of their high school class, and out-of-staters get thumbs up only if they made the top 6.25 percent. Almost three-quarters are from public schools, while nearly 45 percent are members of minority groups. Asian Americans top the list at 18 percent, followed by Hispanics at 12 percent, blacks at 7 and Filipinos tally an impressive 4 percent of the students. Politically, "a trend toward conservatism with a handful of vocal liberals could summarize the student body," believes one senior. In addition to need-based financial aid, the university offers over thirteen hundred merit scholarships from $100 to $4,000, and anyone with a 3.85 high school GPA and 1100 on the SAT is eligible for consideration. UCLA also awards 415 athletic scholarships in 14 sports ranging from rugby to waterpolo.

Dormitories are situated at the foot of the Santa Monica mountains overlooking the campus. You must—you guessed it—put your name on a waiting list, since the dorms can handle only about a fifth of the undergrads and freshmen are not guaranteed housing. The most comfortable living arrangements are the new North and South dormitory suites, which have two bedrooms and a living room and house four people to a suite. The areas surrounding the dorms boast tall pines and well-kept flower gardens, and a short walk brings you to two huge swimming pools and adjacent tennis courts. About 10 percent of the students live in Greek houses, and most of rest either commute from home or take their chances in the housing market of nearby Westwood, where apartments are scarce and rents are astronomical. Ten dining halls serve average meals for those who remain on campus, while the Greek houses have their own cooks.

UCLA probably has the all-around best intercollegiate athletic program in the country, so weekends boast college athletic events galore. The basketball team has been on the skids since the glory days of Kareem Abdul-Jabbar and Bill Walton, but football has taken up the slack with several recent appearances in the Rose Bowl. Other outstanding teams include tennis, track and field and soccer for the men, and softball, track and field and volleyball for the women. If you would rather be a doer than a watcher, the facilities awaiting you are superb. The beach is close by and the mountains only a short drive away, and the proximity to all the good things in Los Angeles is also a major drawing card. Public transportation in the city is cheap but inconvenient, making a car almost a necessity. But parking is the bane of any commuter's existence, and for many students, the easiest solution is to live close to campus and bike it. The hopping suburb of Westwood, which borders the campus, has at least fifteen movie theaters and scores of restaurants all its own. On campus, UCLA's forty fraternities and sororities are the most popular and visible social groups. "Greeks tend to be the movers and shakers on campus," one communications major reports, and their parties and social events help create a solidarity that some say is the missing element at UCLA as a whole. Top-name entertainers, political figures and speakers of all kinds come to the campus; film and theater presentations are frequent and music is abundant.

In order to make the most of UCLA, students must have stamina, self-reliance and willpower. "There is so much here that I would like to be a part of and I must realize that I simply do not have the time!" moans one fine arts major. "There is too much to do and still pass your classes." It is not for those who are easily intimidated but once freshmen overcome their initial fears, there are plenty of ways to make UCLA "a family community." After that, almost anything is possible.

UC—Riverside

Riverside, CA 92521

Location City outskirts	**Applicants** 5,830
Total Enrollment 5,730	**Accepted** 74%
Undergraduates 4,250	**Enrolled** 27%
Male/Female 48/52	**Academics** ★ ★ ★
SAT V/M 470/550	**Social** ☎ ☎
Financial Aid 49%	**Q of L** ● ● ●
Expense Pub $ $ $ $	**Admissions** (714)787-3411

First the researchers at UC–Riverside decided the regular orange had too many seeds and was hard to peel, so they invented the naval orange. Now administrators at the former citrus station have done for a UC education what their forebears did for fruit—got rid of the hassle. With only thirty-five hundred students, life at Riverside is not plagued by the inconveniences that attend life at the other UC campuses. There is no standing in line, classes rarely close, students and professors recognize one another, and getting a parking permit is as easy as asking for one. As one woman says, "It is UC quality education, but with a personal touch."

Located in the flatlands of Southern California on the outskirts of a small city, Riverside's beautifully landscaped campus consists of mainly modern architecture, with a tall bell tower marking its center. Riverside still specializes in the plant sciences, but all the sciences, as well as math, statistics and computer science, are excellent. The most prestigious and demanding course of study sends twenty-four Riverside students to UCLA after three years to finish their MDs. Unique in California, this biological–medical sciences program loses many of its participants after a year or two to the intense workload and competition. Riverside calls itself the "Swarthmore of the West," and most of the liberal arts offerings are good, particularly history and political science. The department of administrative studies is one of the two business programs offered in the UC system. Academic weaknesses include economics, journalism and psychology. All students are required to meet extensive breadth requirements that include courses in English composition, natural sciences and math, humanities and social sciences.

The library has an impressive 1.2 million volumes, and what Riverside doesn't have can be gotten with ease from UCLA's massive collections. Or you can pick it up yourself—a daily shuttle bus runs books and students back and forth to the UCLA campus. Research is an institutional priority for faculty, but unlike other UC schools, Riverside professors dedicate most of their time and attention to their students. "Professor-student contact is one of UCR's best aspects," says one student. "We get a lot of support." Getting into the classes you want is a dream-come-true. "No problem ever," a student says, although first-year English and world history occasionally prove her wrong.

The doctors-to-be that make up the UCR student body are mainly from L.A., San Diego or the Bay Area and are basically conservative, with "radicals getting very little support," according to one history major. "Studying is number one for us, then having a good time." Though the student newspaper is known for its liberalism, the campus it writes about is politically conservative. Asian Americans account for 19 percent of the students, and Hispanics and blacks 10 percent and 5 percent respectively. Roughly half the student body receives need-based financial aid, and about two hundred merit scholarships, ranging from $100 to $4,000, are doled out every year. National Merit finalists and semifinalists are guaranteed a $1,000 award each year they attend. Housing is a breeze—reasonably priced and reasonably easy to obtain. About a third of the students live in the well-maintained dorms, a third live in reasonably priced off-campus apartments and a third commute from home. Dorms are clean and comfortable, and "provide a social context as well as a living atmosphere." Riverside's weather is wonderful three seasons a year (in summer the smog is terrible).

Social life is relatively tame, since so many of the students commute. The administration claims "a quiet atmosphere, conducive to serious study"; students say it's boring. "It is impossible to get the majority of the student body here interested in anything but academics," laments one bio-med major. Fraternities and sororities thrive, and usually hold campus-wide parties once a quarter, but in general "no wild party action here," says one senior. A campus hangout known as the Barn has live bands, comedy nights, and movies.

Despite the general lethargy, sports generate a considerable amount of interest. The karate teams are both among the best in the nation, and men's basketball recently turned in a championship season. Among women's sports, volleyball draws the biggest crowds. For weekend athletes, intramurals are a popular antidote to too many hours in the library. People have been known to camp outside the sign-up office for a night in order to make sure their team gets a place in the intramural league. In addition, "the escape opportunities are excellent." Los Angeles and the beach are about an hour away. The desert is somewhat closer, and Big Bear and Mammoth ski resorts are also within easy reach.

So why doesn't every student in California who likes a good personalized education and hates long lines come to UCR? Some students complain that course offerings are limited, and others of the school's "lack of history, tradition, and culture." Most, however, agree with the physics major who says "the thing I like least about Riverside is the city of Riverside." A suburb is about the nicest thing it gets called, although it is about an hour from anywhere interesting.

Coming to Riverside is a trade-off. There's no football team and not much variety, but the small, personalized style is unique in the UC system. Academics are serious and demanding, but on campus social life and extracurriculars are on a strictly do-it-yourself basis. It can't do what Berkeley or UCLA does, but then it doesn't try. Comparing Riverside to schools ten times its size really doesn't work—it's a little like comparing apples and, well, oranges.

UC—San Diego

La Jolla, CA 92093

Location Suburban
Total Enrollment 14,425
Undergraduates 12,110
Male/Female 55/45
SAT V/M 500/580
Financial Aid 40%
Expense Pub $ $ $ $

Applicants 4,600
Accepted 54%
Enrolled 91%
Academics ★ ★ ★ ★
Social ☎ ☎ ☎ ☎
Q of L ● ● ● ●
Admissions (619)534-3160

Situated in the suburbs on the beautiful Southern California Coast, UC–San Diego made its reputation years ago as a graduate research institution in the hard sciences. In the 1960s, when most schools were going coed, this university went undergraduate and set up four colleges, each with its own distinct style. Thanks to a high-tech curriculum, top-flight science faculty and some hotshot graduates, it has moved into the national limelight.

Set on a tree-lined campus with buildings that are "gray and cement-looking," UCSD's programs in science and engineering are top-notch—"not for the faint of heart," says one junior. Computer science and the premed program in biology are especially good, but you simply can't go wrong in any of the hard sciences. And if you do go wrong, you won't last, since these departments require a B-plus average in entry-level courses for acceptance into the major. The humanities and social sciences suffer by comparison. Although political science, anthropology, communications and psychology are far from weak, according to one student "they are almost a joke" compared to the sciences. The university lacks a full-fledged business program. Imaginative interdisciplinary offerings include computer music, urban planning, Chicano studies and a psychology/computer science program in artificial intelligence. The engineering programs can only get better after the completion of a new $48-million facility.

Westerners at San Diego can sample the East through an exchange program with Dartmouth or explore their own state with a visiting quarter at other California state schools. Getting into the popular education-abroad program is usually more difficult. Like most of the UC campuses, San Diego operates on the quarter system, which makes for a semester's worth of work crammed into ten weeks. Science students find the load intense and rush to enroll in entry-level math and science courses. "The pressure here is incredible," says a senior biology major. "People are so competitive that it makes you uncomfortable." The pace is fast right from the start, and according to another student, "Someone who is unsure of their interests or career should think twice before coming."

Most faculty members, including the five resident Nobel Prize holders, are perpetually involved in one research project or another, and students say that luring them away from the lab table requires persistence. Science students like the emphasis on research, but others get frustrated with the undergraduate's second-class status. "Publish or perish accurately describes faculty life; teaching is not emphasized in promotions," an anthropology major observes. Students have a choice of seven libraries, some good for research, others better for socializing.

San Diego's colleges, each of which has some two thousand students, offer a full range of majors but differ in their academic requirements and characters—they also cut down on the impersonality so common to large institutions. Revelle College, the oldest, is the most rigorous and mandates that students become equally acquainted with a certain level of course work in the humanities, sciences and social sciences. It is the only college with a language requirement, and the core humanities sequence is a two-year great books sequence taught by faculty from a number of departments. Muir, the most popular, allows more flexibility in both the major field and in the distribution requirements. Third College is a child of the sixties, founded to emphasize and encourage social awareness, and, like Revelle, it places equal weight on sciences, social sciences and humanities. Warren, the newest of the four, has developed a highly organized internship program that gives its undergraduates more practical experience than the others. The administration reports that a fifth college is on the drawing board, to open in 1988 with a curriculum devoted mainly to international and cross-cultural studies. Prospective freshmen apply to UC–San Diego—the admissions requirements are identical for each college—but students must indicate which one they want to enter.

"Nerds do well here, but anyone willing to work can survive," one UCSD student believes. A short walk to the beach, however, reveals the student body's non-nerd half—surfers and their groupies who celebrate the "kick back" (that's San Diego talk for laid-back) Southern California life-style. The Sun God, given tribute in a hideously loud and colorful statue on campus, is a fitting mascot for this sun-streaked student body. Yet, these beach babies are no scholastic slouches. All of them placed in the top fifth of their high school classes and came up with the 3.3 GPA or compensating SAT scores to qualify for admission. Many of the scientists continue their study after graduation; UCSD ranks sixth among American colleges and universities in the percentage of science graduates who go on to earn the PhD. Most of the 7 percent from out of state are from back East. Minority representation is high, with about 13 percent of the student body Asian American and another 10 percent black or Hispanic. Students who apply late for financial aid are advised to get a Guaranteed Student Loan, if they can, and a package is worked out to cover the winter and spring quarters. The university awards about thirty Regents Scholarships to freshmen each year, starting at $500.

Each of the university's colleges has its own housing complex, with both dorms and apartments, but space is tight. Warren's housing is the nicest with bigger rooms and lots of grassy area outside, while Muir and Revelle are cement city. Most freshmen live on campus, with all those coming from more than twenty miles away guaranteed housing, while sophomores compete by lottery for the much more desirable apartment suites. By junior year students usually decide to take up residence in La Jolla proper or nearby Del Mar, often in beachside apartments, where the rent is not cheap. Cars are, of course, an inescapable part of the Southern California life, and owning one will make off-campus living even more pleasant. Unfortunately, trying to park on campus can be a nightmare. Dorm residents are required to buy a meal card, which will let them into any of the four campus cafeterias as well as the campus deli and burger joints.

With most juniors and seniors off campus and no fraternities or sororities to speak of, social life at San Diego is hardly well structured. "UCSD can be lonely," one man notes. Alcoholic parties are banned in the residence halls, and students rely heavily on the surrounding area for their entertainment. Downtown San Diego, with the zoo and Balboa Park ("Take a walk on the wild side" is one senior's recommendation), is only fifteen minutes away. Mexico—and the $5 lobster—is a half-hour drive (even nearer than the desert, where many students go hiking), and the two-hour trip to Los Angeles makes for a nice weekend jaunt. Though the area's tourist industry provides lots of nightlife, the drinking age of twenty-one can cramp a student's style quite a bit. Opportunities for socializing on campus should increase with the completion of a new University Center.

Although San Diego's swimming and water polo teams are good, the students are indifferent to varsity sports and recently voted to transfer money for athletic scholarships to support their fabulous intramural program instead. Classes are available in windsurfing, sailing, scuba diving and kayaking at the nearby Marine Aquatic Center. Everyone participates in one league or another and if you're not on an intramural team, "you're not a true UCSD student."

The students at UCSD are exceptionally serious and out for an excellent education. But the pace—study, party, relax, study more—and the props—sun, sand, Frisbees and flip-flops—give UCSD's rigorous curriculum an inimitable flavor that current undergraduates would hate to see change. Indeed, many believe they have the best setup in higher education: "a beautiful beachfront environment that eases a life of academic rigor."

UC—Santa Barbara

Santa Barbara, CA 93106

Location City outskirts	**Applicants** 17,000
Total Enrollment 17,420	**Accepted** 64%
Undergraduates 15,280	**Enrolled** 37%
Male/Female 48/52	**Academics** ★★★
SAT V/M 480/540	**Social** 🐘🐘🐘🐘
Financial Aid N/A	**Q of L** ●●●●
Expense Pub $ $ $	**Admissions** (805)961-2881

This is the California the Beach Boys sing about: balmy weather, parties, palm trees and sun. Located just a five-minute walk from the beach, UC–Santa Barbara's campus is surrounded on three sides by the Pacific Ocean, and five miles to the north lie the Santa Inez mountains. "The impact of the sea and mountains combined is breathtaking—to put it mildly," says a senior. The weather is a near-guaranteed seventy degrees most of the year and one man's sole complaint about life at Santa Barbara is "Not enough brunettes." Tough luck, pal.

Santa Barbara's 815-acre campus, located between the ocean and a large nature preserve, features mainly 1960s Southern California architecture with a Southern California atmosphere to match. "It is easier to study in an environment where everyone is not cutthroat and you are not always stressed out," says one man. It's not that academics are ignored at UCSB—they are simply integrated into a mellow combination of work, play and sunshine. "People here really take time to enjoy life, and study too. There is a good balance between the two," another student says. The least mellow aspect of life at UCSB is the quarter system, which keeps students off their surfboards and in the library for exams three times a year rather than two. The education-abroad program for the entire UC system is based in Santa Barbara and many students take advantage of the opportunity to study at fifty host universities worldwide.

Not surprisingly, the marine biology department capitalizes on the school's aquatic resources and stands out among the university's departments. Engineering is also strong, and the high-tech offerings recently got a boost with the addition of a new engineering building and robotics center. History, English and communications are also strong, but there are weaknesses in the social sciences, notably political science and sociology. The College of Creative Studies, described as "great if you can get in," offers an unstructured curriculum to about a hundred self-starters ready for advanced and independent work in the arts, math or the sciences. A new interdisciplinary program, called the Global Peace and World Security Program, combines aspects of physics, anthropology and military science.

Besides possible earthquakes, overcrowding is Santa Barbara's biggest problem, and several students report it's getting worse all the time. Classes are big (as many as six hundred in some, according to the administration) and often hard to get into. The libraries are "overcrowded at midterms and finals—it is almost impossible to find a spot to study!" says one student. The same is true of access to computer terminals. "The only available times are between late night and early morning." Professors, however, attempt to make up for deficiencies in other areas by being readily available; many let students assist them in research.

Ninety-five percent of the UCSB student body comes from California, with most of them born and raised in either the Los Angeles or San Francisco Bay areas and educated in the public schools. There are still a few organics among the surfers and preppies, and "The majority are casual about way of dress, ways of life, academics." According to one student, "They are liberal on subjects like sex and parties and conservative on subjects like El Salvador." BMWs and Mercedes have replaced T-birds in this version of the California dream—UCSB's student body is the most well-to-do of any of the UC campuses. Minorities make up 19 percent of the student body, with Hispanics and Asian Americans the largest groups at about 7 percent each. About two hundred merit scholarships, ranging from $300 to $8,500, are available to National Merit finalists and Regents award winners, who are selected on the basis of all-around achievement and a personal essay.

Dorms are comfortable, well maintained and much sought after. "Mine was less than fifty yards from the beach," says a student. They are also scarce, housing only 2,500 of the 16,500 students. The rest, which include a number of hapless freshmen, must shift for themselves in the overpriced college towns of Isla Vista and Goleta. Meals in the dorms are available only to residents, and are, according to one student "reasonable, with four entrees and always a large salad bar—this is California, remember?" Overcrowded or not, UCSB students like the school's medium size. "It is small enough so that you know whomever you like but large enough so that you can quietly get lost in a crowd when you want to," says one introvert.

"Lots of parties!" is how one man describes the Santa Barbara social life. Fraternities and sororities are popular at UCSB, but " no one feels any pressure to join—there's a lot to do without feeling left out," says one junior. Off-campus parties in Isla Vista are a social staple, as are Thursday night live bands at the Pub on campus. The local bars are off-limits to those under twenty-one, but when the long-awaited birthday arrives, students celebrate with a quaint little ritual known as "The State Street Crawl," imbibing at all the numerous establishments up and down this main drag. Movies and concerts are also available, and the mountains, Los Padres National Forest, and L.A. are all an easy drive away. A never-ending rotation of intramurals is available on and off the beach. The most successful varsity teams include water polo, baseball, volleyball and men's basketball.

If asked what they like best about their college, most students would agree with the political science major who says, "Location, location, location." Warns a history major: "High-pressure students should definitely stay away because the mellowness of the school will drive them nuts." Consider yourself warned. Anyone who loves sun, beach, sports and fresh air can love some aspects of Santa Barbara, but the only totally happy UCSB student is one who can appreciate the school's "casual, kicked-back feeling towards life." And get along without brunettes.

UC—Santa Cruz

Santa Cruz, CA 95064

Location Suburban	**Applicants** 8,930
Total Enrollment 8,590	**Accepted** 73%
Undergraduates 7,870	**Enrolled** 32%
Male/Female 50/50	**Academics** ★ ★ ★ ★
SAT V/M 520/560	**Social** 🐿 🐿 🐿
Financial Aid 65%	**Q of L** ● ● ● ● ●
Expense Pub $ $ $	**Admissions** (408)429-4008

Students at UC–Santa Cruz are emphatic. "We are *not* just a mellow place where vegetarians hang out for four years without dealing with hassles like grades," says one. "Some of us do eat meat, and it is not all that mellow. Must we live with this image forever?" Administrators are also emphatic. "Political liberals are no longer in the majority," states their slick admissions brochure. But Santa Cruz has retained from its origins in the turbulent sixties its faith in the individual. People come here to do their own thing, and if their own thing has changed from Nehru jackets and organic farming to prebusiness and computer games, then so be it. The times have changed, and so has Santa Cruz.

It is a wonder how anyone gets any work done at all on this campus, set as it is on a two thousand–acre expanse of meadowland and forest overlooking the Pacific Ocean. Among the most beautiful in the nation, the Santa Cruz campus is laced with bike paths and hiking trails, and the beach is only a few minutes away. Each of the eight residential colleges was designed by a different architect in styles ranging from Mediterranean to contemporary concrete block, "but each blends in with the natural surroundings," says one junior. Due to a unique building code, nothing can be built taller than two-thirds the height of the nearest redwood tree.

"Students expecting laid-back academics don't last long here," warns one senior. Santa Cruz's academic offerings range as widely as its architecture, and feature both traditional and innovative programs. In its effort to become what one official calls a "near-perfect hybrid," between the large university and the small college, campus life revolves around the colleges, each of which includes about eight hundred students and specializes in a broad academic area. Whatever one's specialty, the curriculum is demanding. Led by environmental studies and marine biology, the sciences are Santa Cruz's strongest suit, and frequently give students the opportunity to coauthor published research with their professors. The Center for Coastal Marine Studies boasts one of the largest groups of experts on marine mammals in the nation, and for budding stargazers the Lick Observatory is nearby. Most subjects in the social sciences are rated highly by students, but politics, with a nationally renowned faculty, is the clear frontrunner. Third World studies and various ethnic studies programs are also praised. The humanities are less spectacular, and fine and performing arts are weak.

The curriculum at Santa Cruz has undoubtedly become less "alternative" over the years. Business and communications have become popular courses of study, as has computer engineering, which recently acquired a new facility. But while the majority of students now pursue traditional majors, the possibilities are still there for eclectically minded students to pursue just about anything they can get a faculty member to OK. UCSC boasts more than the average number of interdisciplinary programs, including environmental, community and women's studies, creative writing and modern society and social thought. Field and independent study are encouraged, and the cooperative education program, required in many majors, is extensive. Overall, the emphasis is on the liberal arts, and students will find few programs with a vocational emphasis.

Santa Cruz is one of the only universities in the country to require a senior thesis, although a comprehensive exam will also fill the bill. General education requirements are broad: Students must take three courses each in the humanities, social sciences and natural sciences. The main library, McHenry, could be better, but students have access to books at other UC campuses through an on-line catalogue system and interlibrary loans.

Students are increasingly receiving letter grades in their upper-level courses, but they still applaud the Narrative Evaluation System (NES) as one of Santa Cruz's true assets. "You work very hard here and are rewarded with a truly accurate assessment of your work, not just a letter grade," says one fan. Though the curriculum is demanding and the quarter system keeps the academic pace fast, the atmosphere is emphatically noncompetitive. Such competition as there is tends to be internalized—"The NES and the setting may appear casual, but there is a strong pressure for individual achievement," says one history major. About 70 percent of the students eventually go on to graduate study. All UC campuses insist on faculty research, but most Santa Cruz professors are there to teach. Most classes are small, and according to one student, "It is expected that you will deal with faculty on a first-name basis." Few TAs teach undergraduates, but that could change in the next few years as the university continues an ongoing policy of expansion. According to a recently released "Twenty-year Plan," the university will increase its undergraduate ranks, as well as its fledgling graduate programs, until total enrollment reaches twelve to fifteen thousand. Students attribute recent crowding in introductory courses to a higher total enrollment, which has already swelled to about two thousand since 1980.

Nowadays, students agree that entering classes, like the curriculum, are becoming more conservative. But it remains the most liberal of the UC campuses, and according to one student, "We are still a school with a social conscience." Eighty-eight percent of the students are Californians, though Santa Cruz has managed to lure easterners. About a fifth of the students belong to minority groups, with Asian Americans accounting for 11 percent of the students, Hispanics 7 percent, and blacks 3 percent. Just about anyone can find compatible colleagues. "There is a lot of opportunity for anyone to express his or her opinion—extreme left to extreme right," says one student. "What we don't have are playboys and jocks in the fraternity sense, because we don't have fraternities or sororities or a football team."

About half the students live in the residential colleges, which vary from traditional room-and-board dorms to group apartments with kitchens. Some have their own dining halls, with reasonably good food; students may also opt to join a food co-op. Freshmen must live on campus but are free to choose among the colleges. Upperclassmen can take their chances in the lottery or move off campus, though increasing enrollments mean that nearby apartments are becoming increasingly scarce and expensive. Students who opt to strike out on their own remain affiliated with one of the colleges.

The campus overlooks Monterey Bay and it is almost always warm and sunny. There are hiking trails on campus and in the nearby state forest. The beach and resort town of Santa Cruz, with its boardwalk and amusement park, are ten minutes away by ten-speed, and those looking for city lights will have no trouble getting to San Francisco (seventy-five miles distant) by public transportation. If you have a car, the proximity of places like Carmel, Big Sur, the Napa Valley and the Sierras could be a serious distraction.

With no fraternities or other established groups to dominate the social life, people tend to hang out with friends from their own college. "We don't need frats here because the college system provides an intimate atmosphere for making friends," says one communications major. "Because you have eight colleges you have eight times as many opportunities for concerts, dances, films, speakers, etc." As for varsity sports, "We do not have a football team and are not planning on having one," asserts a junior. Santa Cruz only fields five teams—including tennis, where it is nationally ranked in Division III—but participation in intramurals is widespread, with rugby in particular growing in popularity. The student recreation department sponsors everything from white water rafting to classes in East Asian cooking.

Santa Cruz is a place where the education of undergraduates has traditionally been the main priority, and students hope it stays that way. But Santa Cruz is also a school with an identity crisis. Even as students insist that the university isn't just for hippies anymore, they are also wary that Santa Cruz is forsaking its principles as it becomes more and more like a typical research university. "The current conventional administrators are trying to sell us as a kind of Cal-Tech-by-the-Sea," says one. "We don't need to be like everyone else, at least not without putting up a fight!" But in another, more cheerful, student's words, "The open minds still outnumber the closed," and as long as Santa Cruz retains its belief in "to each his or her own," it will remain uniquely Santa Cruz.

Calvin College

Grand Rapids, MI 49506

Location Suburban	**Applicants** 1,530
Total Enrollment 4,200	**Accepted** 95%
Undergraduates 4,010	**Enrolled** 70%
Male/Female 48/52	**Academics** ★ ★ ★
SAT V/M 500/550	**Social** 🛎 🛎 🛎
Financial Aid 60%	**Q of L** ● ● ● ●
Expense Pr $	**Admissions** (616)957-6106

Perhaps no other religious college is quite so sincere about putting Christianity in the classroom as Calvin College. It believes, as the president puts it, in the "sovereignty of God in every part of life," from the family, church and state to world affairs, economics, business and the arts. The educational organ of the Christian Reformed Church of North America, Calvin shares that denomination's great respect for intellect as well as old-style evangelical Protestantism. It's no miracle, then, that Calvin College ranks academically with Wheaton College in Illinois as the best of the country's evangelical colleges.

Founded in 1876 by Dutch farmers, Calvin occupies a campus with 165 acres of beautifully landscaped farmland, encompasses three ponds, playing fields, and a nature preserve. The college takes pains to preserve the wildlife and woodlands without forgetting that the campus exists for the students' enjoyment. A few of the historic homes of the settlers remain, but most activity at Calvin takes place in buildings built after 1960. "The school is only one mile from three shopping malls, fifteen movie theaters, and thirty-two restaurants," reports one future demographer. "But when you're on the campus itself, you feel like you're in your own world."

At Calvin the emphasis is less on enforcing rigid codes of conduct than on creating and conveying a Christian sense of scholarship. Every subject, the school believes, can be approached from a Christian perspective, integrating faith and learning. The first page of a Calvin brochure, for example, quotes a verse from Philippians: "There must be no competition among you, no conceit." In these days of cutthroat preprofessionalism, such appeals are rarely heard, but Calvin students are appreciative. "The religious approach enables me to develop my own set of values and beliefs," says a business administration major. "Calvin gives me a world and a life view."

Calvin undergrads going for a bachelor of art degree will face rigorous general education requirements in courses such as history, philosophy, theology and mathematics. Requirements for professional degree candidates are a bit less stringent and less liberal arts oriented. Traditionally, the school's strongest programs are history, philosophy and English, and the departments of music, math and the natural sciences are outstanding. Calvin graduates have few problems getting accepted to schools of law, medicine and business. The teacher-training program is justifiably popular, but the social sciences, as well as Calvin's newer professional offerings in business, nursing and engineering have not yet made their mark. Class size is comfortably small, and faculty members, all of whom must be committed to the Church's teachings, are especially helpful. Professors are expected to reserve about ten hours per week for advising outside of class, but most devote more time to their students. The faculty draws accolades from students for being personable, casual, friendly and open-minded, but they are also tough, demanding graders.

As a reprieve from the rigorous and somewhat structured curriculum, students use the interim month of January to pursue a variety of creative, low-pressure alternatives both on and off the campus. For those who opt for travel, there are opportunities for studying art and theater in England, history and culture in China, and languages in Germany, Canada, and the Dominican Republic. Students who stay on campus can take such courses as Shakespeare's Greatest Hits or the more provocative Toward a Theology of Wealth and Possessions. The library is excellent, but hard-core academics express chagrin that it is closed on Saturday nights and Sundays.

Almost three-quarters of Calvin students are members of the Christian Reformed Church. The proportion of nonmember students is way up from fifteen years ago, but seems to have leveled off in recent years. More than half the students are from Michigan, about one-quarter are from the Grand Rapids area. Quite a few students hail from Iowa and the parts of Canada that have large concentrations of Church members. As one classics major explains, "To fit in at Calvin, it's best to have some sort of religious commitment and a real willingness to work." Although the college maintains a competitive admissions policy, students with marginal academic records—about 5 percent of each freshman class—may be conditionally admitted under a special program where they take fewer credit units and join the academic-support program.

Calvin's admissions decisions are made without reference to a student's financial need, but the school does not guarantee a fully funded aid package. Some 20 percent of the students receive academic scholarships, ranging from $500 to $2,000. Grants ranging from $360 to $980 are provided to student members of the Christian Reformed Church to help defray travel costs from their hometowns, and more than two thousand of the undergraduates benefit from Michigan's Differential Grant Program, under which residents who attend private colleges in the state qualify for up to $500 a year.

While 35 percent of the student body commutes, those students under age twenty-one who do not live at home must live on campus. Men and women are housed in separate wings of the L-shaped residence halls. Visits between the sexes are limited to weekend evenings and Sundays, but the lounge and basement (equipped with everything from free washers and dryers to meditation chapels) are open to all. Campus housing is modern and comfortable, though a bit overcrowded due to increased enrollment. One dorm, Bolt Hall, has a computer room in its basement. The Knowlcrest apartment complex adjacent to campus houses upperclass students in suites of six, but most juniors and seniors move off campus to take advantage of cheaper and more private accommodations. Students can choose from a variety of meal plans, including a health food alternative.

The campus is only a couple of bus stops from downtown Grand Rapids, where restaurants and cinemas beckon students as much as the nearby ski slope and lake. Local residents go home on weekends, but for the 50 percent or more who stay on campus, the college provides a variety of spiritual and cultural offerings, as well as dances, pizza parties, retreats, and hayrides. There are no fraternities or sororities, but men and women tend to go out in groups. Students say it can be difficult to develop relationships. "If you are seen with a person of the opposite sex, people consider you to be married off," one senior complains. Alcohol and drugs are outlawed on campus (abuse brings fines and suspension), but beer consumption off the grounds is not unusual. In suggesting expectations rather than laying down strict rules, Calvin does put trust in students to "do what we want in a way that we see fit." There is a great deal of camaraderie on campus, although some students bemoan the lack of ethnic diversity among students. Despite the absence of a football squad, sports are very popular at Calvin, with men's soccer and basketball, and women's softball both strong and well supported. Intramural competition never fails to get those Calvinites' blood circulating.

For every student who finds some of the restrictions of a church-related school overwhelming, there is another who feels that Calvin's Christian dedication does not go far enough. No matter what their religious orientation, however, all students can expect from Calvin College a challenging education and a respected degree.

Carleton College

Northfield, MN 55057

Location Rural	**Applicants** 2,600
Total Enrollment 1,840	**Accepted** 48%
Undergraduates 1,850	**Enrolled** 39%
Male/Female 49/51	**Academics** ★★★★★
SAT V/M 630/650	**Social** ☎☎☎
Financial Aid 56%	**Q of L** ●●●
Expense Pr $ $	**Admissions** (507)633-4190

Really now, who on earth but Eskimos and polar bears would want to spend four hours—let alone four years—in the frozen tundra of rural Minnesota? Eighteen hundred and eighty hardy souls on the campus of Carleton College can tell you. Despite an unlikely location, Carleton happens to be one of the finest liberal arts colleges west of New England—or anywhere else for that matter—combining an intellectual atmosphere worthy of the Northeast's finest with an endearing unpretentiousness that is distinctly midwestern. Says one senior, "I like the freedom to be what I want to be and do what I want to do without being stereotyped or criticized."

Surrounded by miles of gently rolling farmland, Carleton's nine-hundred-acre campus in the tiny town of Northfield is a free spirit's paradise. There are lakes, woods and streams all around, plus twelve miles of hiking and cross-country skiing trails and even a four-hundred-acre arboretum put to good use by everyone from the jogging jock to the bird-watching nature lover. The architecture is eclectic—everything from Victorian to contemporary. No less varied are Carleton's top-notch academic programs; English, history, economics, chemistry and biology are all among the best in the nation. In the '70s, Carleton ticketed the second-highest number of undergraduate science students per capita destined for a PhD of any liberal arts college in the nation. Nevertheless, the administration admits that more lab space is much needed, and recent gifts will be used to bolster science and computer facilities. Engineers can opt for a 3-2 with Columbia University or Washington University in St. Louis, and for geologists seeking some fieldwork—and maybe a chance to thaw out after a Minnesota winter—there is a college-sponsored program in Death Valley. Closer to home at the Arb, as the arboretum is affectionately known, majors in environmental studies have their own wilderness field station which includes a prairie restoration site.

At the opposite end of the academic spectrum, the creative and performing arts also flourish. "Photography and film studies are getting more money all the time," notes one sophomore. Students in theater arts or design often take advantage of an option called the Morgan Major, in which students develop their own curriculum. No matter what their field, Carleton graduates are practically assured admission to top graduate or professional schools.

A number of distribution requirements ensure that students in Carleton's various majors are firmly grounded in the liberal arts. All must show proficiency in English composition and at least one foreign language while fulfilling requirements in four broad areas. A senior comprehensive project is required in every major field. In recent years Carleton has joined the trend toward interdisciplinary programs and offers Asian and Jewish studies, urban affairs and women's studies. Off-campus study is also popular—55 percent of the students do it at some point in their careers—with programs available either through Carleton or the Associated Colleges of the Midwest.* The well-stocked library is now bright and airy, due to a recent renovation, but students would like to see it stay open past midnight. That way they'd know where their friends are in the wee hours.

With high-powered students and a heavy workload, Carleton isn't your typical mellow midwestern liberal arts college. The trimester calendar means finals are only a couple of months apart, and students bemoan the recent elimination of the "President's Day" midterm break. Almost everyone feels the pressure, but it is "a pressure that comes from inside the students rather than competitive pressure," according to a senior history major. Nearly a third of all classes have ten students or fewer, so "Carls" are expected to participate actively. Carleton's faculty members are very committed to teaching; their interaction with students often spills over into the lunchroom, ballfields, and even professors' living rooms.

If Carleton's isolation poses problems for the admissions office, it's a well-kept secret among the students. Almost three-quarters hail from outside Minnesota, and nearly half are from outside the Midwest. Both coasts are heavily represented, and fifteen foreign countries send at least one student. Blacks and Hispanics account for 6 percent of the students. Three-fourths went to public schools, and two-thirds finished in the top 10 percent of their high school classes. Most Carls are, in no particular order, intellectual, fun-loving, and slightly rumpled. "Someone who cares a lot about money and clothes and making the 'right' friends might be better off elsewhere," one maintains. Students are openly disdainful of fraternities and rah-rah college spirit. "There are no cheerleaders at Carleton, and Carleton students are proud of that!" pipes up one senior. Despite a recent trend toward conservatism, Carleton is still a predominately liberal campus, though a group of vocal "hard-core Republicans" keeps things interesting. All students are admitted without regard to financial need, and about thirty-five students receive merit awards. A prepayment plan is available that allows parents to pay the comprehensive fee for all four years when a student first enrolls and thereby avoid later tuition increases.

Campus accommodations range from comfortable old dorms with working fireplaces—a godsend in a state where winters resemble a scene out of *Dr. Zhivago*—to modern hotel-like residence halls. Best of all are the nine college-owned off-campus "theme" houses for students with special interests such as foreign languages, the outdoors, or nuclear issues. With the exceptions of "The Farm House," an environmental studies house sitting on the edge of the Arb, all the theme houses are situated in an attractive residential section of town close to campus. Every student who wants one is guaranteed a room on campus, though sophomores sometimes end up in overflow housing. Dorms are coed by room, but for bashful types there are two halls with single-sex floors. Juniors and seniors have the option of moving off campus, and about 15 percent do. Everyone who stays on campus must be on a meal plan, the minimum being seven a week. Carleton's three dining halls offer passable institutional fare, but nothing to write home about. One of the nicest things about the dining halls is a tunnel system that connects them with many other campus buildings, including some of the dorms. On especially frigid days, students can eat and go to class without venturing outside, or even enjoy a leisurely brunch in their pajamas.

In the absence of a Greek system—"Thank God!"—the social life tends to be relaxed and informal. Student activities are organized by a group called "Co-op," which sponsors a dance every two weeks with a live band, Wednesday socials every two weeks, free movies, and special events like Comedy Night. In Northfield, a town of twelve thousand, students frequent the campus of cross-town rival St. Olaf's College and a night spot known as Reub'n'Stein. The Twin Cities, thirty-five miles to the north, are a popular destination for socializing, and since students aren't allowed to have cars on campus, the college charters buses twice daily and three times Saturdays and Sundays. There are numerous musical groups on campus, and at any given time three hundred students are in music instruction, according to administrators.

Even though intramural sports no longer fulfill the phys ed requirement, they still take precedence over varsity athletics. About a third of the students play on a varsity team, but about two-thirds play intramurals. Among the varsity squads, men's and women's tennis ranks near the top in Division III. The cross-country, track, and women's volleyball teams are very competitive, as are the championship cross-country ski teams. (The women took home the national championship in 1984.) A Frisbee game is likely to draw a crowd to Bald Spot (a playing field), and of course, there's even popular men's and women's "Rotblat" (keg softball—"named after an ineffectual White Sox pitcher," a student reports).

As one of the top liberal arts colleges in the nation, Carleton is a serious school that avoids taking itself too seriously. Intellectual but not stuffy, intelligent but not smug, Carleton is the ideal place for students seeking to immerse themselves in the life of the mind—and have some fun in the process. And after all, with sixty-nine flights to Minneapolis/St. Paul from the northeastern corridor every day, it isn't *that* isolated. Just don't forget your longjohns.

Carnegie–Mellon University

Pittsburgh, PA 15213

Location City outskirts
Total Enrollment 5,820
Undergraduates 4,130
Male/Female 65/35
SAT V/M 570/670
Financial Aid 65%
Expense Pr $ $ $ $

Applicants 6,440
Accepted 55%
Enrolled 35%
Academics ★ ★ ★ ★
Social 🐻 🐻 🐻
Q of L ● ● ●
Admissions (412)268-2082

Carnegie–Mellon likes to call itself "The Professional Choice." It is certainly no place for an amateur. Though C–MU students major in everything from fine arts to electrical engineering, the one thing they all have in common is a driving ambition to succeed in their chosen fields. Few linger to smell the roses. Most students specialize in a preprofessional area when they arrive as freshmen and never look back. Carnegie–Mellon students know what they want and are willing to work incredibly hard to get it. As one student explains, "If you are serious about what you do, and want to go to college for that reason, Carnegie–Mellon is for you."

Formed by the merger of the Carnegie Institute of Technology and the research-oriented Mellon Institute, Carnegie–Mellon's self-contained hundred-acre campus is attractively situated in the affluent Oakland section of Pittsburgh and borders on the city's largest park. With "nice" but "drab and functional" buildings that range from early 1900s vintage to contemporary, Carnegie–Mellon is divided into four undergraduate colleges: fine arts, humanities and social sciences, the Carnegie Institute of Technology, and the Mellon College of Science. Each has its own distinct character, but all share the university's commitment to what it calls a "liberal/professional" education. For most students, this catchword translates into a program that puts liberal arts into an extremely relevant context, stressing programs that develop technical skills and good job prospects. Even the humanities and social sciences types can major in "applied history," "professional writing" or public policy instead of traditional concentrations.

Most departments are strong, but exceptional ones include chemical and electrical engineering, biology, applied math and cognitive psychology. C–MU is a national leader in computer science, and not just for specialists. Freshmen in the humanities and social sciences are first introduced to computers in a required philosophy course (using them to work on problems of logic), and one drama major testifies that "students do everything and anything on the computers." Another nonscience type supports this emphasis with a typically pragmatic assessment: "C–MU does try to incorporate automation in every aspect of the university. Who can blame them when society is now in the 'Information Age'?"

Each freshman is assigned a personal computer workstation. The drama department, the first and still one of the best in the country, concentrates on performance, and its faculty is made up of highly regarded working professionals. Departments that students cite as not up to the university's otherwise high standards include music, foreign languages, and chemistry—although in the latter the administration says improvements are under way. Though most students cite the College of Humanities and

Social Sciences as the weakest at C–MU, it does have its merits. Students follow an unusual core curriculum of nine specified courses designed to equip them with a "portfolio" of skills necessary "to understand the complex relationships between human affairs, science and technology."

The logical extension of Carnegie–Mellon's professional focus comes in the form of numerous internships, and the five-year co-op program in metallurgical engineering and materials science places students in the metals industry. Engineers and science students may vie for a spot in the junior year in Switzerland program. Humanities and social sciences students can spend a semester in England, and majors in political science can go to Washington. There are also five-year BS/MS programs as well as a five-year MBA option.

Recently, Carnegie–Mellon introduced a university-wide core curriculum designed to counteract the tendency in many of its students toward a narrow, preprofessional focus. The idea is to give students with diverse interests a shared intellectual background. As Herbert Simon, the Nobel Prize–winning psychologist who helped design the core curriculum, puts it, "We want to provide some common topics of conversation besides sports, the weather, and sex." Nevertheless, Carnegie–Mellon remains one of the most fragmented campuses in the nation. Students divide themselves into the "fruits" (actors, dancers, and other artsy types) and the "veggies" (engineers and architects). According to one student, "The engineering students tend to be conservative while the fine arts students are free spirits." While the "fruits" and "veggies" are united in their quest of a good job after graduation, that seems to be all they have in common. With each group absorbed in its field of interest, there isn't much interaction between the different "types." One chemistry major reports, "The colleges seem at odds with each other. It's like they don't realize that arts and engineering are just two different ways to express yourself." In the words of another student, "Everyone is full speed ahead and they're not taking time to look into other ideas. . . . I think some eyes need to be opened."

Although its students come from all parts of the country, Carnegie–Mellon is still primarily a regional institution that draws one-third of its students from Pennsylvania. Seventy percent attended public schools, and about 20 percent are from minority groups. Whatever your major, you'll find "constant friendly competition" in your chosen field. But students say that the demanding work load prevents a cutthroat atmosphere. They "tend to pull together to get through," and study groups are common. To help combat academic stress among students, a new mental and physical health program was initiated in the fall of '86.

Carnegie–Mellon says it remains committed to need-blind admissions and meeting the demonstrated need of all acceptees. In devising its aid packages, the university provides larger proportions of outright grants to "academic superstars." In addition, the College of Humanities and Social Sciences annually offers merit-based scholarships of $1,000 or more, and there are also awards for music and engineering students of exceptional talent.

Student housing offers old and new buildings, with the most popular being university-owned apartments. Upperclassmen get the pick of the rooms, while freshmen are assigned rooms from the remainder. Although freshmen are guaranteed housing, quarters are a bit cramped. Most halls are coed, but a few are all male. Though students can remain in campus housing as long as they wish, many upperclassmen prefer the privacy—and price—of off-campus living. There are a variety of flexible meal plans available and five dining facilities that range from all-you-can-eat to "salad-plus."

The Greek system provides the most visible form of on-campus social life, though only about a fifth of the students belong. "If you want to be socially active year-round and have a common bond with others that goes beyond your college, then Greek is it," says one woman. Coffeehouses, inexpensive films, dances, and concerts, plus Pittsburgh itself (opera, ballet, symphony, concerts, sports) provide plenty of alternatives to frat parties for the less gregarious. There is a campus nightclub—Scotland Yard—and a new university student center is in the planning stages. The one event that manages to bring everyone together is the Spring Carnival, when the school shuts down for a day and a Big Top is constructed in a parking lot. Students set up booths with electronic games, and fraternities race in "buggies" made of lightweight alloys designed by future engineers. Students put on original "Scotch and Soda" presentations, one of which—*Pippin*—went on to become a Broadway hit. A bus ride to Pittsburgh's Golden Triangle section takes about twenty minutes, and Oakland offers plenty of restaurants, night-clubs, grocery stores, and discos. The lopsided male-female ratio prompts many men to learn the routes to nearby University of Pittsburgh, Duquesne University, and all-female Chatham College.

Pittsburgh is a sports-crazed town, and Carnegie–Mellon's Division III varsity teams have trouble competing for attention against the Steelers. One fan complains that "half the student body doesn't even know the football team was champs in their conference." Tartan squads also excel in men's cross-country and track and women's tennis and field hockey. The intramural program includes two dozen sports and attracts a wide enough following. The recreational athletic facilities, however, could stand some improvement.

Carnegie–Mellon is the Switzerland of American higher education—an unlikely combination of diverse academic types that somehow manages to function as a reasonably coherent whole. It has pioneered the use of computers in the classroom, but resisted the temptation to become "Computer U." It has remained a leader in preprofessional education, but taken steps to ensure that all students are exposed to the liberal arts. Yet the bottom line is still the fact that C–MU is an academic pressure cooker. "The pressure is continuous," says one student. "There's always a test, homework set, paper, etc., coming up—and the push to succeed, to be the best, is rough." For students who can make it at Carnegie–Mellon, the real world is a piece of cake.

Case Western Reserve University

Cleveland, OH 44106

Location Urban
Total Enrollment 7,940
Undergraduates 3,210
Male/Female 70/30
SAT V/M 550/630
ACT 26
Financial Aid 68%
Expense Pr $ $ $

Applicants 2,090
Accepted 88%
Enrolled 34%
Academics ★ ★ ★ ★
Social ☎
Q of L ● ● ●
Admissions (216)368-4450

In 1879, Cleveland became the first American city to light up its boulevards with electric streetlamps. In 1967, the revitalized city on the southern shore of Lake Erie became a bright spot in the nation's educational landscape, as the union of Case Institute of Technology and the adjacent Western Reserve University bridged the traditional gap between technical and liberal arts learning. Yet the significance of this marriage often goes unnoticed by the serious undergrads, many of whom are more intent on garnering one of CWRU's respected bachelor's degrees than in receiving a very well-rounded education.

Case Western Reserve is located on the eastern edge of Cleveland in "University Circle," a five hundred area of parks and gardens that is home to more than thirty cultural, educational, medical and research institutions. "It's very pretty for a city campus," observes a chem major. Students with a taste for architectural schizophrenia will delight in the differences in building styles that resulted from joining the older Western Reserve with newer Case Institute. Others, however, may agree with a bewildered business major who laments that "some of the campus is quaint; other parts are just plain ugly."

Case Institute of Technology is still the hub of engineering and physical sciences, while Western Reserve College administers the university's liberal arts programs. Students from both colleges are required to complete core programs that explore both spheres of intellectual inquiry. One new option for students at Western Reserve is a core program called LAMBDA (Liberal Arts Mathematics-Based Alternative), which grounds itself in mathematics but aims to provide ample training in the humanities as well. It's designed to appeal to students who like the math-science area but do not wish to pursue an engineering major.

The strongest academic programs in Western Reserve College are anthropology, art education (conducted with the adjoining Cleveland Museum of Art), history, music (linked with the nearby Cleveland Institute of Music) and psychology. WRC's language programs, on the other hand, are the weakest. Case Institute of Technology boasts one of the world's first departments in biomedical engineering. Other leading programs include mechanical engineering, metallurgy, mathematics and physics. There are majors in both computer engineering and computer science, and there is even a degree in polymer (macromolecular) science.

CWRU's facilities, though, are far less impressive than its offerings. "The libraries are dungeons. They need newer book collections—and the hours are really inadequate," complains one student. While computers have made their way into a variety of departments and there is a new computer lab, students find that there are still not enough terminals to go around.

Classes tend to be smaller and professors more accessible at WRC than at CIT, perhaps because of CIT's admitted emphasis on research. According to one student, "many of the professors in the sciences are absorbed in research, and few seem to care about other aspects of their students' lives besides academics." Yet this rather extreme focus on studies is often shared by the student body: "A good number of students are totally obsessed with their work," says one senior. There is no question that this is a highly motivated student body, and the competition is intense. "The standards of acceptance are surprisingly low for the caliber of student here," warns one biochemist. "You may be able to get in, but unless you're really good, you won't be here for long."

CWRU is a great school for those who know they want more than a BA: Five-year integrated BA/MA degree programs are available, and the Senior Year in Absentia program lets the enterprising student substitute the first year of professional school for the final year at Western Reserve. Also, the preprofessional scholars program makes a conditional commitment to its undergrads of admission to one of the university's medical, law or management professional schools upon graduation. Work and research opportunities for undergraduates are spectacular.

More than 85 percent of the freshmen come from the top fifth of their high school classes. And, according to one undergrad, "most of the students are from Ohio (50 percent) or a foreign country (15 percent)." Anyone not hailing from either of these places is probably from Pennsylvania, New York or New England. Asian–American students make up more than 10 percent of the student body, but other minorities are not so well represented. "I wish there were more black students on campus," says one senior. "Or at least administrative support for black students." Women also may have a tough time of it, given that they comprise only 30 percent of the student body. "The school really is dominated by the men," complains one senior woman. A prevailing conservative wind doesn't help matters, though one frustrated poli-sci major wails, "There is little political activity within the student body."

Case Western Reserve offers students a wide variety of possibilities for meeting costs, and last year four out of five students requesting aid received it. The university distributes merit scholarships, which range from $1,500 to full tuition, to a whopping 20 percent of the student body. The university also sponsors five creative achievement awards worth up to $6,000, a number of four-year awards for outstanding minority students, and fifty or more alumni and departmental scholarships.

Dorms are divided into two areas of campus. The Northside dorms offer doubles on a hall with a common bathroom, while Southside has small singles in six-person suites. Housing is well maintained and coed, save for one female dorm and several off-campus male fraternity houses. The only students who can technically move off campus are fraternity dwellers, local commuters, and students over the age of twenty-one. Apartments are available, but expensive, and are often a long trek from campus (students say the bus service is inadequate), and financial aid awards are trimmed if students move off campus. Every student living on campus must take meals—either two or three a day—in one of three cafeterias. The food runs the gamut from "bland" to "boring." The kosher options perk things up a bit, but one frustrated woman reveals, "It's really not possible to be a vegetarian and eat in the commons."

As with most urban schools, crime is a potential problem, and "the surrounding community is poor and often resentful of students," an undergrad reports. But university police and advanced electronic surveillance help students feel secure. In warm weather those looking for an escape need not go far: The sandy beaches of a rejuvenated

Lake Erie are just a few minutes away, and the university owns a farm that's perfect for picnics and overnights.

CWRU, as noted, is anything but a social school. "The campus has come a long way in the last few years," one student says, "but it's still not a 'party school' by a long shot." The growing Greek scene, with sixteen frats and four sororities, offers chances for students to let off steam, and the Film Society's weekend movies are popular, as are the frequent events sponsored by the University Program Board. The Flats, a waterside strip of student-oriented nightclubs and bars, is a favorite Cleveland hangout. "There is fun to be had," asserts one student, "but many students study in their rooms all week and then complain about the lack of social life—it's their own fault!"

Students have historically lamented the lack of school spirit at CWRU, but recently it has been on the rise. The Division III Spartans are now a winning football team, and soccer and cross-country have also done well. Though women's sports are still not on par with men's, they're definitely on the upswing. The dorm-centered intramural program commands a high level of participation and enthusiasm. The university recently added a new racquetball and squash complex, and a field house with an Olympic-size pool is currently under construction.

Despite these noticeable advances in the sports, extracurricular and Greek arenas, Case Western Reserve's rigorous academics continue to overshadow its social appeal. And while students don't always appreciate what the federation of technology and liberal arts affords them, they do realize that this is a school with the power to make dedicated preprofessional undergrads successful. "It's hard to escape the pressure," explains one senior. "Students here just don't know when to relax."

Catholic University of America

Washington, DC 20064

Location City outskirts	**Applicants** 3,000
Total Enrollment 6,000	**Accepted** 50%
Undergraduates 2,700	**Enrolled** 50%
Male/Female 50/50	**Academics** ★ ★ ★
SAT V/M 550/560	**Social** ☎ ☎ ☎
Financial Aid 50%	**Q of L** ● ● ●
Expense Pr $ $ $	**Admissions** (202)635-5305

Historically, financially and philosophically, Catholic University of America has close ties to the Roman Catholic Church (add geographically, since the Shrine of the Immaculate Conception, the largest Catholic church in America, is adjacent to the campus). As the only university in the nation chartered by the Vatican, CUA's mission is "to educate the Catholic community, and to serve the nation and the world." While that may sound a little ambitious for some tastes, the typical undergraduate is rarely roused by any such talk or by periodic squabbles with the Vatican over academic freedom in the theology department. Well insulated from differences of opinion or belief, CUA students spend four comfortable years enjoying low-pressure academics and generally carefree living. Says one senior, "The attitude of students is not at all 'pious.' But students have a good attitude about life, which I think is due to a 'religious' atmosphere."

An oasis of greenery and Gothic-style stone buildings in a lower-class Washington, D.C., neighborhood, Catholic is one of the few colleges in the country originally started as a graduate institution. Five of its ten schools now admit undergraduates: arts and sciences, engineering, architecture, nursing, and music, while three others (social service, education, and religious studies) provide undergraduate programs through arts and sciences. In the latter, history, psychology and religious studies are among the best departments in the arts and sciences. The School of Nursing is one of the best in the nation, and the School of Engineering and Architecture is also highly regarded. The physics department benefits from a vitreous state lab, a boon for both research and hands-on undergraduate instruction. The School of Music offers excellent training in vocal, organ and liturgical music, but "jazz is nearly unheard of here," one student cautions. The department of drama has sent students on USO tours and has produced several successful graduates, such as Susan Sarandon and Ed McMahon, but the current word around campus is that it's "riding on its reputation from the past and needs new blood."

CUA students must take at least forty courses in order to graduate. In the School of Arts and Sciences, twenty of these must be from a core curriculum—spread across the humanities, social sciences, philosophy, religion, and natural science—and an additional twelve must be from a major field. The dean of arts and sciences admits that many students find the core overly rigid. Double majors are common, and combined BA/MA programs are available in most fields. Super-talented students can enroll in a new twelve-course interdisciplinary honors program that offers sequences in philosophy, humanities and social sciences. Standard off-campus opportunities are augmented with internships at the British and Irish parliaments.

Academic facilities are generally adequate, and in strictly quantitative terms, CUA has Washington's second-largest library after you-know-what. Of course, the Library of Congress has all its books catalogued on a computer, something CUA has yet to accomplish, and students report that several departmental libraries are "comically" out-of-date.

Catholic University is research oriented, but most classes are small and faculty-student relations are excellent. "The academic climate is one of a quiet pursuit of excellence," states one student, and pressure is far from unbearable. Clergy are at the helm of certain graduate schools, but the School of Arts and Sciences has a primarily lay faculty, with priests occupying fewer than 10 percent of the teaching posts. The university is different from other major Catholic universities because of its direct ties to the Vatican and the American Catholic hierarchy, as opposed to an order like the Jesuits. Its chancellor is the archbishop of Washington, and Catholic churches across the country donate a fraction of their annual collections to the university. Theologically, the overall tenor is conservative, and the university recently disciplined one of its faculty members—a nationally respected moral theologian who was censured by the Vatican for his views on sexual issues. CAU denies any conflict between academic freedom and Catholic orthodoxy, but it's clear that, the university unlike every other major Catholic college and university in the United States, this pontifical institution has yet to fully resolve this issue.

Catholicism is clearly the tie that binds the student body. Sunday masses are so well attended that extra services must be offered in the dorms. Says one administrator, "We like students to leave with Catholic values, but most of them come here with those values in the first place." About 90 percent of the students belong to the faith. Most are from the Northeast, mainly of Irish or Italian stock, and a significant number are Washington area natives. About 7 percent of the students are black or Hispanic, while foreigners account for 10 percent. Politically, "it's so middle-of-the-road it's sickening," maintains one student, who nevertheless adds, "but it's what I wanted."

The university maintains a need-blind admissions policy. Thirty lucky students— one from each archdiocese in the nation—receive a full-tuition merit scholarship, and children and siblings of alumni receive a substantial reduction in tuition. The total number of applications to CUA are down from five years ago, and the administration says it needs more funds for merit scholarships to attract top students.

Eighty percent of the undergraduates live on campus in one of the dozen residence halls, four of which are coed by floor. A housing crunch was eased a few years ago when the university bought and renovated an old Holiday Inn, but space is still tight. The shortage should eventually be alleviated with the completion of several new dorms now in the planning stages. Freshmen are required to live on campus, but many upperclassmen flee CUA's restrictive visitation and alcohol policies and move into apartments of their own. Four fraternities and three sororities have chapters on campus, but they are nonresidential and have only a couple of hundred members. "Greeks are dead or dying," according to one man, and not too many students are in mourning. Several meal plans are available in the dining halls, which serve food that is rated fair to good. The Rathskellar, or "Rat," is the campus bar and grill where quick breakfasts and lunches can be purchased.

A Metro stop conveniently located on campus connects CUA with an abundance of entertainment and employment opportunities. Capitol Hill is a fifteen-minute subway ride, and the Georgetown area, with its chic restaurants and night spots, only a half hour away. Despite the decline of the Greeks, CUA students still indulge in some serious partying. According to one senior, "Many students, having gone to Catholic schools all their lives, really go nuts when they reach college and the reins are removed." Lower key alternatives to the party scene include coffeehouses, movies and theater, and for those eager to repent the weekend's excesses, student ministry retreats. Catholic's Hartke Theater is a modern, spacious facility, and the university choral groups are first-rate. Sports are popular on campus, both on the varsity and intramural levels. The teams compete in Division III, and while few teams are championship material, men's basketball does draw a loyal following. Intramural and varsity athletes alike benefit from the addition of a new $10-million sports complex.

The friendly campus makes Catholic University a pleasant place to be, and the core curriculum makes it a good place to get an education. Students should, however, remember what is implied in the name. "The university takes its Christian and Catholic heritage seriously," an assistant vice president reports, and so does the student body.

Centre College

Danville, KY 40422

Location Suburban	**Applicants** 840
Total Enrollment 740	**Accepted** 73%
Undergraduates 740	**Enrolled** 38%
Male/Female 55/45	**Academics** ★★★
ACT 26	**Social** ♨♨♨
Financial Aid 50%	**Q of L** ●●●
Expense Pr $	**Admissions** (606)236-6064

Kentucky is about as well known for liberal arts colleges as most other states are for purebred horses. But if you get out your magnifying glass and look amid the Bluegrass, smack in the middle of the state, you will find tiny Centre College, a fine century-and-a-half-old educational breeding ground. In a 1903 speech Princeton University president Woodrow Wilson referred to it as "a little college down in Kentucky which in sixty years has graduated more men who acquired prominence and fame than has Princeton in her 150 years." Since then, Princeton has made a comeback, but Centre has kept on turning out leaders—as well as most of Kentucky's Rhodes Scholars.

Centre's campus is a mix of old Greek revival and attractive modern buildings with the surrounding horse country providing a romantic backdrop. Since the many trees change colors lavishly with the seasons, "the campus is always beautiful," says more than one student. The school holds no classes on Wednesdays, and the library is closed on Saturday nights. The rest of the week there is a good education to be had from Centre, thanks mainly to its small size and highly accessible faculty. Most professors take a genuine, personal interest in their students, giving out home phone numbers and even inviting students over for an occasional meal. One senior reported that his four classes consisted of ten, twenty, six and twelve students, respectively. Of course, the flip side of all this personal attention is a heightened accountability; no falling asleep in the back row of a lecture at Centre. "The professors expect you to perform well," one student reports, and they are seldom disappointed. Most students have set their sights on graduate or professional school, and are willing to put in long hours to make the grades. Students aren't especially competitive among themselves, but there is a lot of self-generated pressure to succeed.

English and the premed sciences are generally considered the best departments by the students; English is the most popular major, with management and economics not far behind. Centre retains loose ties with the Presbyterian church, and requires two classes on the history or philosophy of religion—a rule most students are not especially fond of. Other general education requirements are extensive and designed to ensure proficiency (in writing, mathematics and one foreign language), breadth (through four courses each in three major divisions of humanities, social studies and science and mathematics) and integration (through one interdisciplinary junior or senior seminar). Courses in the latter category are among the most innovative at Centre. One student reported that a seminar entitled Death and Dying made a profound difference in his outlook on life. A new physical sciences building to be completed in 1988 should help bolster what has been a weak spot in the past. Glass-blowing enthusiasts will find one of the few fully equipped facilities in the region. The administration says it would like to develop its resources further in the social sciences, and especially in ethnic and minority studies. The art and drama departments are among the least popular with students. Perhaps the biggest academic drawback at Centre is the reality that, with only eight hundred students enrolled, course offerings in many areas are very limited.

Through the Southern College University Union,* Centre offers a number of study abroad programs, including a program in London that emphasizes the economic, social and political facets of contemporary international problems. There are also a number of month-long winter-term classes that involve group travel and study abroad in such places as France, China, Russia and the Bahamas. A 3-2 liberal arts and engineering program is offered with Columbia and Georgia Tech. A modest 125,000-volume library is "used more for socializing than for studying," a history major reports, and the computing facilities seem to be growing at an adequate pace to keep up with their increasing use in academic departments.

Most students come from white, middle- to upper-middle-class Kentucky families and are riding the tidal wave of conservatism that is washing through American colleges. More than one student echoes the complaint of an English major that "there is a pressure to conform socially that creates some tension, and not a great deal of toleration from some." A scant 3 percent of the students are from minority groups, and since Centre lacks a national reputation, nearly all of the students are from Kentucky and bordering states. Another common complaint is the lack of privacy. One student comments that since Centre is so small, "some people find it smothers them." Still, the majority of the student body seems satisfied with the Centre community, which after four years becomes almost like a second family. Academically, Centre students are an able group. More than two-thirds graduated in the top fifth of their high school classes.

Each student may attend free of charge all events at the separately endowed Norton Center for the Arts at Centre (including those by prominent visiting artists). An outstanding alumni-giving program also enables Centre to offer needy students generous financial aid, in which "outright grant makes up 65 to 75 percent of the package," the president claims. Academic scholarships are many, but consideration for the top awards requires supplementary application. But even those who have to pay the full price are getting a bargain relative to most other liberal arts colleges.

Virtually all of Centre's students live on campus. Freshmen occupy single-sex dorms while upperclassmen have the option of living in halls that are coed by floor. Hillside is divided into separate units where six people live in a unit with three bedrooms and a living room. Breckenridge and Wiseman are popular dorms "because they have character and larger rooms," comments one junior. Since none of the three sororities have their own houses, most upperclass women live on campus. Men have the option of living in one of the six frat houses. Everyone eats together three times a day in the main dining center, Cowan Hall. "You need to have a sense of humor to eat here," says another. There are two meal plans available and a sandwich line for lunch, as well as a calorie count for each dish. The surrounding community provides a few restaurants, when students really need a break.

Centre's bucolic setting fosters a fairly active, albeit insular, social life. Many students belong to Greek organizations, the chief social focus. Since the town of Danville is "dry," informal socializing in the dorms is the primary alternative to Greek parties, though Greeks and non-Greeks generally get on well. The college's social board sponsors movies and other events. Lexington, within an hour's drive, is a popular draw on weekends for dates and films, as well as for shopping, and fine state parks nearby provide great camping, swimming and hiking. Men's intercollegiate basketball and women's tennis are among the top sports, but the intramural program is usually more popular, with most students participating in at least one sport.

Over eighty years after receiving Woodrow Wilson's praise, Centre continues to relish its role as David in a world of academic Goliaths. Admissions literature boasts that Centre's latest fund raising drive broke the record previously held by Princeton for alumni participation. And old grads still talk about the time back in 1921 when the Centre football team knocked off then-mighty Harvard in one of the biggest upsets in the history of collegiate sports. With a recent flurry of publicity spotlighting its highly personalized approach to education, Centre has put the big boys on notice that they haven't heard the last from this up-and-coming small college.

College of Charleston

Charleston, SC 29424

Location Center city	**Applicants** 2,130
Total Enrollment 5,531	**Accepted** 79%
Undergraduates 5,150	**Enrolled** 54%
Male/Female 35/65	**Academics** ★ ★
SAT V/M 460/480	**Social** 🍸🍸🍸
Financial Aid 39%	**Q of L** ● ● ●
Expense Pub $	**Admissions** (803)792-5670

Steeped in antebellum grandeur, the College of Charleston is a public institution situated in the middle of the city's restored historic district and surrounded by plantations, mansions, gardens, moss-covered trees and old churches. Befitting the twelfth-oldest institution of higher learning in the country, much of its campus consists of restored eighteenth- and nineteenth-century houses, some of them used for student residences. Life at the College of Charleston is a reflection of its surroundings; relaxed and traditional, it provides a congenial atmosphere for South Carolinians who want an affordable education close to home.

The college's strongest academic area is the sciences, particularly biology. The fine premed program is connected to the nearby Medical University of South Carolina. Marine biology is exceptional because of numerous research facilities nearby, and the fine arts receive a boost from the Spoleto Festival of the Arts, held each summer in Charleston. Although students are critical of the computer science major, a campus-wide computer literacy requirement recently went into effect. Students must take at least fourteen core curriculum courses designed to introduce them "to the principal areas of intellectual inquiry" and to "teach basic intellectual skills." The college also offers programs in business and engineering, though students interested in either would do well to investigate the University of South Carolina in the former, and Clemson in the latter, before settling on C of C.

There are a number of interesting interdisciplinary options at C of C. Western civilization—the art, history and philosophy of the West—takes up twelve semester hours and is team-taught by three professors. Students have the option of enrolling in a Studia Humanitatis minor, in which they take their required humanities courses in one area of interest, complete with special seminar. A fast-paced honors program often compresses a yearlong course into a semester. Studious types may be less than enthused with the library—which houses less than 200,000 thousand volumes—though it does boast a collection on the history of blacks in South Carolina.

Faculty appear to be making a concerted effort to increase the diligence of C of C undergraduates. One reason is that admissions standards are far from stringent—

students need only produce a high school transcript and an SAT score to be considered—and though there is a suggested deadline for applications, the college will consider them right up until the beginning of classes. But while one student admits, "The academic climate is as high-pressure as the student chooses," others say that prospectives should not be fooled by the low entrance requirements. As one junior warns, "Too often incoming students don't realize the course demands until it's too late." Perhaps to make up for their tough classroom demeanor, many professors have taken to attending a Friday afternoon happy hour at a nearby bar to see students on a more informal basis.

Because the College of Charleston is a state school, almost all of its students (nearly 90 percent) are South Carolinians, with almost two-thirds from the greater Charleston area itself. About a quarter come from the top tenth of their class, though nearly as many were in the bottom half. Many are older students seeking a midlife career change, mainly women with a spouse at one of three nearby military bases. About 7 percent of the students are black. The college accepts all comers without reference to student financial need, but a small number are wait-listed when funds are depleted. About 185 academic scholarships, ranging from $100 to $2,200, are awarded yearly, as are ninety athletic scholarships in basketball, soccer, tennis and swimming.

Almost three-quarters of the C of C students are commuters, living either at home or in nearby apartments. It is best to live within walking distance, since on-campus parking spaces are expensive and off-campus ones impossible to find. For those who want to live on campus, accommodations are often limited. There are three dormitories, two converted hotels (good to avoid), and about two dozen restored houses. Most housing is coed—a recent change from predominantly single-sex accommodations—a single suite can house as many as ten students. The houses are scooped up quickly by upperclassmen, and kitchens inside enable residents to escape the extremely cramped confines of the one dining hall. Meal plans of seven, ten or nineteen meals a week are offered, and there is a campus snack bar, along with numerous fast-food restaurants, close at hand.

While the college's beautiful campus is situated in a run-down section of Charleston, the nicer parts of the city have great appeal, with downtown's cafés, shops, theaters and other tourist attractions not far from the campus. Beaches are only twenty minutes away, and South Carolina's mild climate also makes the campus "great for outdoor studying," not to mention outdoor parties.

A modern physical education center opened in the early '80s is the centerpiece of the college's athletic program. The sports teams compete in Division III, and many are highly successful. Sailing, men's basketball, and women's tennis have all won national championships in recent years, and women's basketball and men's tennis are also strong. Since C of C is two-thirds female, women's sports are more highly developed here than at most coed schools. The one thing the college doesn't have is a football team, but fearless physical types do not despair: It recently chartered a rugby club. On campus the fraternities provide many activities and sponsor frequent weekend parties. Women victimized by the skewed sex ratio often date cadets from the Citadel, the men's military school, also in Charleston.

Students at the College of Charleston enjoy their school's tranquil atmosphere and value its sense of southern elegance. Those from the immediate area should seriously consider whether a school farther away might not be more challenging and stimulating, but all who stick around will find plenty to do to pass the time.

Chatham College

Pittsburgh, PA 15232

Location Urban	**Applicants** 301
Total Enrollment 600	**Accepted** 64%
Undergraduates 600	**Enrolled** 74%
Male/Female N/A	**Academics** ★ ★ ★
SAT V/M 500/500	**Social** ☎ ☎ ☎
Financial Aid 65%	**Q of L** ● ● ● ●
Expense Pr $ $	**Admissions** (412)365-1290

The founding fathers (literally) of Chatham College were Pittsburgh businessmen who wanted to "give their daughters an education equivalent to that of their sons." Chartered in 1869, Chatham could be considered, in retrospect, a paternal boost to the early women's movement. As if to even out the score, this small, private women's college has become a strong maternal force in today's fight for female equality by playing an emotionally supportive role in the lives of its students—whether recent high school graduates, middle-aged women returning to college or single mothers.

Comfortably established in a lovely residential section of Pittsburgh, the college expects women to be leaders and encourages its students not to settle for stereotyped women's roles. With more than half its students coming from Pennsylvania (20 percent are Pittsburgh commuters), Chatham cannot boast the national prestige of a Wellesley or Smith, nor can it match their academic rigor. But for women who do not have the grades or the desire to go farther east, Chatham offers a sound liberal arts education with a slant toward professionalism and female success in the business world.

In accordance with the core curriculum, students take seven interdisciplinary courses dealing with themes such as The West and the World, Perspectives on Gender Roles, and Science and Technology. Through the Center for Professional Development, students also fulfill mandatory proficiency requirements in several areas including mathematics, writing, computer literacy and library research. Finally, each senior completes a two-semester tutorial project, usually a research thesis centered on her major and worked on with a faculty adviser.

Underlining Chatham's new approach to curriculum is the concept of "anticipatory learning"—or the conviction that a liberal arts education in our technological society should prepare students to handle ideas and jobs that do not yet exist. One device for providing career-oriented training has been the popular January internships (80 percent of the students take at least one internship), in which Chatham students fan out to work in institutions ranging from local steel companies to nonprofit organizations. Aside from internships, the January term offers intensive courses at Chatham or another 4-1-4 institution as well as foreign study groups led by faculty members. Through a mentor program, juniors and seniors devise contracted relationships with professional women in their intended fields. The Chatham cooperative dance program exposes students to professional training at the Pittsburgh Ballet Theatre School.

English is far and away the best department at Chatham, but political science, chemistry and biology are also strong. The more preprofessional side of Chatham is represented by popular majors such as economics, management, communications and international business. Information science and human services administration are newly established multifaceted majors and a taste of further such offerings to come. Nonmajor concentrations exist in areas such as black studies, women's studies and education certification. A shiny new computer center is sure to alleviate the no-access blues. And although students admit to weaknesses in the music, art, foreign language and theater departments, cross-registration with accredited colleges and universities in the Pittsburgh area helps fill gaps in Chatham's offerings.

Half the faculty are women, and with a nine-to-one ratio, student-professor relations are close. "Professors know you by your name, not by a number," says one student. Another boasts she had several faculty members help her find a summer job. Vocational and psychological counseling programs are strong at this institution. The college says it is willing to accept "capable, motivated students who need special personal and academic attention as freshmen." A special gateway program is designed as a support system for women who are returning to college—more than 10 percent of Chatham women are twenty-five years old or older.

An important factor in the admissions process at Chatham is the quality of the applicant's essay. Over half the students come from the top fifth of their high school class, and 25 percent of the students graduate from private schools. The student body is in many ways a reflection of the local steel industry, with the daughters of blue-collar workers and high-paid executives both represented. Chatham also maintains one of the best records among predominantly white liberal arts colleges for attracting minority students: Close to one in five undergrads is from a minority group. It's not surprising then that the overall social climate is one of healthy diversity. "There is an equal mix of liberals and conservatives and no one's attitude is held against her," a psychology major says.

In addition to need-based aid, Chatham offers freshman applicants an opportunity to compete for three scholarships in each academic division (humanities, social sciences, sciences and fine and performing arts) through on-campus examinations and interviews. Stipends for these renewable scholarships range from $1,800 to full rides.

Most of the noncommuting students live on campus, which is not exactly a hardship because several of the dorms are ivy-covered, renovated mansions donated to Chatham by prominent Pittsburgh families. These leftover mansions have all the comforts of home—and then some. "A beautiful spacious room with bay windows, a fireplace and a private bathroom," is how one lucky denizen describes her abode. In keeping with the school's innate maternal instincts, Chatham is the only college in the country where mothers and their children can live in affordable undergraduate housing. The dorm for single mothers has small apartments, each with a bedroom, bathroom and microwave oven. Freshmen are assigned rooms and roommates, while upperclass students play a housing lottery. One dorm is considered coed because it houses ten males from a neighboring college. Visitation rules in the two freshman dorms ban men after 2 AM. The other dorms can vote on visiting hours, and apparently most set no limits. Campus residents must purchase a full-time meal plan, but the dining hall serves good food "on most days," reports a biology major, "and the meat is real." Theme dinners add a bit of spice to holidays and special occasions. Although the library is not huge, students claim it is for the most part adequate and it houses a noteworthy women's issues collection. Students enjoy cooperative access to other libraries in the community and find their own a comfortable place to study.

Although Chatham is easily accessible to downtown Pittsburgh, its country-like atmosphere is removed from the hectic urban pace. Many of the buildings are composed of soft-red brick from yesteryear and detailed with intricately carved wood trimmings and stained glass windows. Trees are plentiful on campus, as are grassy hills and, "of course, squirrels." Social life is also on the quiet side. "If you're going to college to drink and date, Chatham is the wrong place to be," warns a junior. With no sororities on campus, Chatham has many extracurricular student groups to plan and create activities such as dances, plays and road trips. "But most fun is found off campus; Carnegie–

Mellon and Pitt are the hotspots," according to a business law major. The city also has a lot to offer in the way of cultural activities and shopping. Field hockey, volleyball and tennis rate as Chatham's best and most supported varsity sports and the intramural program isn't too shabby either.

For the most part, Chatham students seem pretty satisfied with their school. Although they do "tire of never seeing a male face," according to one junior, they praise the individual attention and the opportunities to gain "the confidence you need to be competitive in a male-dominated society." High-powered academic types should head for one of the Seven Sister schools, but for those women who need an extra boost, Chatham could be perfect.

University of Chicago

Chicago, IL 60637

Location Center city	**Applicants** 4,660
Total Enrollment 8,500	**Accepted** 44%
Undergraduates 3,100	**Enrolled** 43%
Male/Female 60/40	**Academics** ★ ★ ★ ★ ★
SAT V/M 630/660	**Social** ☎ ☎
Financial Aid 67%	**Q of L** ● ● ●
Expense Pr $ $ $ $	**Admissions** (312)702-8650

In the past, when people thought of the University of Chicago, what first came to mind was a collection of eggheads. This world-famous university near the shores of Lake Michigan was known for its eccentric and socially awkward intellectuals, its preoccupation with theory rather than practice, its disinterest in sports and, maybe, the semiannual Lascivious Costume Ball (the more titillating the costume, the cheaper the price of admission). In recent years, though, the administration has set out to loosen things up a bit. Athletic facilities and dormitories have been renovated, football has returned, social programming has expanded, and the quality of undergraduate life has improved at this intellectual pressure cooker of a school.

The University of Chicago is a first-rate research and teaching institution that occupies a self-contained and architecturally magnificent campus. The main quads are steel gray Gothic—gargoyles and all—and the newer buildings are by Saarinen, Van der Rohe and Wright. On the undergraduate level, the school is rigorously and unequivocally committed to the view that a solid foundation in the liberal arts is the best foundation for any walk of life. Consequently, there are no undergraduate courses in career-oriented subjects such as business, engineering, social work, or computer science. Music students study musicology, not the violin, and they learn the calculus along with everyone else.

Eighty percent of a student's courses at Chicago come as part of some requirement or other. Extending over the first two years of study is the common core, a much-emulated series of courses that was recently enhanced by the addition of new general education requirements. Under the new revised core, students take special yearlong courses in the humanities and social, biological and physical sciences as well as two courses in mathematics beyond precalculus, a foreign language, a year of

121

Western or non-Western civ, and a course in art or music. In addition, seniors are encouraged to undertake final-year projects, which need not be in a student's area of concentration.

Chicago's brilliant and distinguished faculty is certainly its greatest asset. And although the university was founded in the tradition of the German research universities, professors take their teaching role quite seriously. "Those who teach undergraduates do so because they want to," proclaims a well-attended-to biology major. "It's not unusual to have a freshman class taught by a Nobel Prize winner." In fact, these dedicated professors get more time to teach and do research than they would elsewhere, since Chicago is one of the few schools in the country with full-time advisers to help students with academic and other matters. Lecture courses, especially in the sciences or "really popular classes," can exceed seventy to one hundred students if the professor is indifferent to size. It's not unusual for students to camp out overnight the Sunday before registration to be first in line.

The economics department, academic home of Milton Friedman, is strong, as are English, history, anthropology, linguistics, math, physics, chemistry and evolutionary biology. Chicago was father to both sociology and political science as scholarly disciplines, and these two programs remain among the best anywhere. The university also prides itself on outstanding Eastern, South Asia, Middle Eastern and Slavic studies departments. The few weak areas include art, foreign languages and anything else that verges on the practical. The New Collegiate Division of the university offers popular interdisciplinary programs such as PERL (Politics, Economics, Rhetoric and Law) and Tutorial Studies, to which undergraduates may apply at the end of their first year. Students may study abroad in Paris, Lisieux, Bologna, Mexico City, Leningrad, Brazil, England and Israel. A combined degree program that allows students to earn a BA and an MD in seven years gets many takers; other students prefer to enter Chicago's law and business schools after their junior year. "Those who are ready can accelerate as fast as our faculty and facilities permit," explains an administrator.

Since Chicago is committed to the ten-week quarter system that it invented, the first term starts in late September and is over by Christmas. For practical purposes this means virtually uninterrupted work for the school year, a long summer vacation, and three exam weeks a year. All five libraries are excellent, containing one of the most extensive collections in the country—"much bigger than an undergrad would ever need," is how one student describes them. Regenstein, aka "The Reg," is the main library and the "unquestionable social center for the campus, with most conversation and trusting occurring in the A-level coffeeshop."

Chicago has more graduate students than undergraduates, so the climate reflects this. For some, this means high pressure, "a grind." Others like it and are even proud of it. "Students are always talking about ideas; academics are something we share," says a junior. Despite their common thirst for knowledge, students urge prospectives to recognize that the old stereotype U of Chicagoans as "one-dimensional geeks" no longer applies. "There's still a little of that," concedes one junior, "but the movement is toward the smart, well-rounded, middle-class set."

Less than a fourth of the student body comes from Illinois, and the rest from all over the country, with a high percentage from the East Coast and many raised in academic homes. Seventy-five percent graduated in the top tenth of their high school classes, and an *incredible* three-fourths go on to further study of some kind (the university is known as the "teacher of teachers"). Both conservatives and liberals are "ably present and vocal," and interests cover the gamut, from government and politics to playing the piano. "It's a tolerant school, socially speaking," says one man. In keeping with a long-standing tradition, Chicago will take some freshmen before they have graduated from high school. And in addition to need-based aid, the university awards twenty merit scholarships each year, ranging from $1,000 up to full tuition, for academically outstanding freshmen with impressive extracurricular involvement.

The tree-lined campus is located in the integrated neighborhood of Hyde Park, an old community on the South Side of Chicago surrounded by low-income communities on three sides and Lake Michigan on the fourth. Although the area has a high-crime history, it seems to be on the rebound. As one student describes it, "Hyde Park has a strong sense of community, and one never feels like he is surrounded by the fast pace and tension of a city." Of course, downtown Chicago, with its internationally acclaimed symphony, museums, and other cultural facilities, is easily accessible by public transportation. Cars are a nice luxury, but hard to park and a nuisance in the winter, which as you may have heard, is long and hard in the Windy City.

There are five dorm complexes on campus, some new and sterile, the rest old with a lot of character. Each dorm has its own personality; Shoreland, a former luxury hotel on the shore of Lake Michigan, is the largest and most social, but it's also a half mile from campus. With the exception of two single-sex dorms, all are coed by room or by floor, and some are equipped with kitchens and new computer facilities. Many upperclassmen move off campus, although housing is guaranteed all four years. Food in the dining halls is "the general cafeteria fare—mediocre, but plentiful." Freshmen and residents of certain dorms are required to be on a full meal contract, and others can buy a meal plan or purchase individual meal coupons.

The six fraternities and sororities don't play a very large role, although frat parties are reasonably well attended. Other weekend entertainment options on campus include low-cost flicks (in the new five-hundred-seat movie theater), dorm parties, and a plethora of cultural activities. "There are a decent number of official college events," relates a junior. "But they're usually hit or miss both with respect to popularity and quality." With one hundred-plus extracurricular clubs and programs, everyone can find something of interest. A student comments that it is easy to start new programs: "You can do pretty much whatever you want, because funds and resources generally exceed student interests."

As evidence of Chicago's new commitment to provide its students with opportunities to do much more than study, the university recently joined the new University Athletic Association, which includes other nonconformists like Johns Hopkins and New York University. The football program was resurrected after thirty years of absence and, to everyone's surprise, has already had a winning season. Women's soccer was also added to the roster, and new baseball, softball, and soccer fields have been built. University athletes are well respected (and, interestingly, have a higher overall GPA than the student body as a whole); according to one man, "interest in varsity sports is increasing as the university sheds its idiosyncrasies." Intramurals attract an excited three-fourths of the student body. The facilities for running, racquetball, squash, and tennis win student praise, and the gym boasts a sauna.

The University of Chicago comes highly recommended by its students, who use words such as challenging, enlightening and introspective to describe it. "One gets the feeling that he is constantly surrounded by very important research," remarks a senior. Of course, students do have to make some concessions. "If you like to sleep, try someplace else," advised one. "We study, converse, and party with great intensity," says another.

University of Cincinnati

Cincinnati, OH 45221

Location City outskirts
Total Enrollment 35,670
Undergraduates 28,510
Male/Female 50/50
SAT V/M 440/500
Financial Aid 48%
Expense Pub $ $

Applicants 8,600
Accepted 86%
Enrolled 58%
Academics ★ ★
Social 🐭 🐭 🐭
Q of L ● ● ●
Admissions (513)475-3425

Once a locally supported city university, the University of Cincinnati has been educating Cincinnati's sons and daughters for generations. Although it's now officially one of twelve state schools, it maintains a give-and-take relationship with one of Ohio's most attractive and livable cities. The compact campus sits quite contently nudged up against the edge of the downtown area and centered at the top of a hill. Ultramodern buildings rise up next to traditional ivy-covered Georgian halls, and considering this is an urban campus, there's an amazing amount of space, grass, and greenery.

One of UC's specialties is research. Faculty expertise ranges from the study of microbes in Antarctica to the songs of spiders in Mexico. Researchers at UC have given the world antiknock gasoline, the electronic organ, antihistamines, and the U.S. Weather Bureau. But most students from outside Cincinnati come to UC for professional degrees, and befitting the place where cooperative education was born in 1906, Cincinnati's overall co-op program is one of the largest in the country. Sixteen programs at UC now offer the popular five-year professional-practice option, during which students spend four quarters (forty weeks) working full-time, money-making jobs pertinent to their future careers.

The colleges of engineering; business administration; and design, architecture, art and planning (the schools with the most co-op students) are the best bets at UC. The university's music conservatory, one of the best state-run programs in the field, also offers broadcasting training. The schools of nursing and pharmacy are also well known and benefit from UC's health center and graduate medical school. The two-year University College is Cincinnati's open-admissions unit, which prepares less-qualified students to transfer into four-year programs and offers a variety of vocational degrees, including paralegal technology and cable-TV management. While technical and artsy programs are generally good, basic liberal arts areas like English, languages, communications and math are not strong at UC.

Academic pressure, determined by the student and the major, is on the whole, "rather casual." It's considered no major feat to slide by in certain majors, studying "an hour a day if you don't want to cram." Students don't necessarily get the courses they want here—"There are always difficulties in getting into courses in a university with thirty thousand students," says one senior—but petitioning the registrar is often worth the trouble. Some courses end up being quite large (two persons to a desk in popular design courses is not unusual). One fine asset is the school's huge library, which has more than a million volumes and is completely computerized. Lines can get long at computer terminals, but most other facilities are more than adequate.

A third of the faculty members hold outside jobs, bringing fresh practical experience to the classroom. Others, one student reports, "are absorbed in research and a bit more isolated than I would like." Freshmen and sophomores seem to accept the fact that they will see a lot of TAs at first, but will then have greater access to faculty as juniors and seniors. Undergraduate research assistantships are available in most science programs. Two-thirds of the undergraduates are from the city and surrounding county, and all but 5 percent come from within the state. Despite this geographical uniformity, UC students range from "the preppiest preps to the punkiest punks." Prospective freshmen apply to the college they wish to attend, not the university as a whole, and the requirements differ among the schools. Design and architecture and engineering are among the more selective; business, education and the University College are easier bets.

Financial aid packages for students with demonstrated need are typical combinations of grants, loans and work-study. A whopping 4,899 merit scholarships, ranging from $300 to $2,500, are awarded to outstanding freshmen in a wide range of programs on the basis of class rank, standardized test scores, and (sometimes) chosen course of study. Over three hundred athletic scholarships in nine men's and seven women's sports are awarded.

About 10 percent of UC students live on campus, so the lack of parking facilities is a bigger deal than the housing conditions. Noncommuting freshmen and athletes are required to live in the six coed and single-sex dorms. Many upperclassmen consider off-campus living far better than the crowded, noisy dorm life, especially when apartments can be had more cheaply. Still, about two hundred sophomores end up on the dorm waiting list each fall semester. Food in the two cafeterias located on opposite ends of the campus is "bland and unappetizing," and many students find stopping at the plastic village of fast-food joints surrounding the campus a cheaper and more convenient option. The student union also has extensive snack bar facilities.

Merchants have turned the area surrounding UC, called Clifton, into a mini–college town with plenty to do. A bus line running by the campus takes undergraduates into the heart of the "Queen City" of Cincinnati, which has definitely earned its fine reputation as a scenic and cultural mecca. It has museums, a ballet, professional sports teams, parks, rivers, hills and as many large and small shops as anyone could want. Caution and common sense are required in maneuvering through the urban neighborhood and the campus itself at night, especially for women, and an efficient escort service is provided by the university.

UC's varsity sports struggle along from year to year, and students have come to expect dismal records. Women's soccer is the most recent exception. Demonstrating their unwavering school spirit, undergraduates turn out regularly to encourage the football team and cheer on the more successful basketball squad. Fraternities and sororities are small-time at UC (only 10 percent of the students belong) but they are still the most active places to party on campus, usually opening their functions to everyone.

UC students, however, tend to be more interested in studying hard and getting a good education at a reasonable price than overindulging in extracurriculars. Cincinnati and its prime university are just waiting for eager, aggressive students who want an all-encompassing atmosphere where they can receive career training and a whole lot more.

City College of New York, NY
—See CITY UNIVERSITY OF NEW YORK

CITY UNIVERSITY OF NEW YORK

Situated in areas that range from the quiet of the Flatbush section of Brooklyn to posh Park Avenue, the nineteen campuses of the City University of New York provide the ultimate urban setting for those seeking the rich diversity of the nation's largest city. And while the university, like the city itself, had more than its share of problems during the 1970s, it has managed to regain a large measure of financial stability in the last few years as a result of a state takeover of most of the university's operating costs from the city.

New York City began operating a system of municipal colleges with the opening of City College in 1847, but a unified university did not begin to take shape until 1961. Today, CUNY, as it is known, makes up the third largest university in the nation, with eight four-year liberal arts colleges, eight two-year community colleges, a specialized technical college, a graduate center that coordinates doctoral study, a law school, a medical school and an affiliated medical school.

Probably no other institution of higher education in the nation had as dramatic or turbulent a history in the 1970s as the City University. In 1970, the university adopted a controversial open admissions policy that guarantees any New York State high school graduate a place in at least one of its undergraduate colleges. The ensuing rapid expansion created myriad administrative headaches as well as a heated debate about the degree to which the university had lowered its academic standards. By 1976, New York City's fiscal crisis forced the university to tighten its admissions policy and impose tuition for the first time. The number of students plummeted from 240,000 to 190,000 and the university lost 20 percent of its faculty members. Despite the extensive loss of students and professors, the institution's educational quality managed to hold up much better than might be expected. Today, the university's financial condition has much improved as a result of the greater state assumption of costs in 1979. A massive construction and renovation program has been resumed after having been halted during the city's fiscal crisis, and the university has even been able to increase in size within the last three years with the addition of a law school and a medical school.

With virtually no dormitory facilities, CUNY is the quintessential commuter institution. More than 90 percent of its diverse student body is drawn from the city's five boroughs. Extracurricular activities, while numerous, are usually limited to lunch hours and specially designated club periods during the day. Generally speaking, any high school graduate will be admitted to one of the university's community colleges, and those with a high school average of at least 80 or who are in the top third of their graduating class will be accepted into one of the four-year colleges. SATs are not required but can be used as a third avenue for admissions if the high school record is not good enough. However, many of the colleges, such as the engineering school at City College, offer special programs with more restrictive admissions requirements. Those wishing to apply to any unit of CUNY may do so through the university's office of admissions services.

CUNY offers an impressive variety of programs, ranging from career and vocational training in the community colleges to the traditional liberal arts education and highly specialized professional courses of study in the senior colleges. Quality, of course, varies from campus to campus and program to program. The oldest and largest of the four-year senior colleges—Brooklyn, City, Hunter and Queens—all have well-established national reputations and distinguished faculties. Some of the other senior units, such as New York City Technical College, Baruch and John Jay colleges, have also earned recognition in specific specialized fields. And the community colleges, by and large, make available substantial offerings in everything from engineering technology to bookkeeping and secretarial science. In addition, the university has developed a large and complex remedial program in the basic academic skills of reading, writing and mathematics to meet the needs of underprepared students enrolled through open admissions. While Brooklyn, City, Hunter and Queens colleges are described in detail below, the following is a thumbnail sketch of some of the university's other units:

Baruch College. Once the business school of City College, Baruch became a separate unit in 1968. Although it has a large liberal arts component, more than 70 percent of Baruch's students go there for its highly regarded specialized programs in business and public administration. Its accounting department has over the years trained approximately a third of the certified public accountants in New York City. The college also has offerings in journalism, arts administration, actuarial science, educational administration and a five-year combined BA/MA in business administration. Situated in Manhattan's fashionable Gramercy Park area, the college suffers from relatively poor facilities, crowded classes and a high student-faculty ratio—mainly because students are lining up at the doors for a quality education and surefire employment credentials. However, the college's facilities problems are expected to be solved within the next few years as a result of a $250-million building expansion program. Enrollment: 13,000.

John Jay College of Criminal Justice. Situated on Manhattan's West Side, John Jay is the largest college of criminal justice in the United States. With close ties to the New York City Police Department, the college offers fine programs in criminal justice, fire science, forensic science, forensic psychology and police science—all within the context of broadly based liberal arts requirements. In addition, the college offers internships in more than eighty federal, state and city agencies. An average of 75, not 80, is required for admission to the baccalaureate program. The college also offers a two-year associate's degree. The college is also undergoing a $250-million building program. Enrollment: 6,000.

Lehman College. This liberal arts college in the northern Bronx is sometimes overshadowed by its older and larger relatives, but it probably has not only the most attractive of the CUNY campuses but also some of its best facilities. Among its strongest disciplines are mathematics, biology, history, economics, English and chemistry. The college is recognized nationally as a leader in nursing education and has a very active performing arts center. Lehman also offers an individualized BA program that enables highly motivated students to design their own curriculum. Enrollment: 8,000.

New York City Technical College. This specialized unit, in downtown Brooklyn, offers a number of programs not readily available at other schools in the city or state, including the associate degree in dental hygiene. At present, most courses of study are two-year programs, but the college recently upgraded its nationally recognized hotel and restaurant program to the four-year bachelor's level. Other highly regarded programs include graphic arts and advertising technology, radiologic health, ophthalmic dispensing, and electrical technology. Admissions requirements vary from program to program. Enrollment: 11,000.

Community Colleges. These eight units, scattered from the southern tip of Brooklyn to the south Bronx, offer two-year courses of study in the liberal arts as well as vocational and career training. Students receiving their associate of arts or associate of sciences degrees are then eligible for transfer to one of the university's senior colleges to go on for a bachelor's degree. Kingsborough and Queensborough community colleges are probably strongest in the liberal arts, while La Guardia Community College, situated in Long Island City, Queens, is one of the national leaders in the field of co-op education. Hostos Community College, in the south Bronx, is the only institution in the nation that offers a college-wide bilingual option for Hispanic students who need intensive instruction in English as a second language while receiving subject matter instruction in Spanish.

Brooklyn College

Brooklyn, NY 11210

Location Urban	**Applicants** 4,100
Total Enrollment 14,270	**Accepted** 75%
Undergraduates 11,150	**Enrolled** 62%
Male/Female 44/56	**Academics** ★ ★ ★
SAT V/M N/A	**Social** ☎ ☎
Financial Aid 65%	**Q of L** ● ●
Expense Pub $	**Admissions** (718)780-5001

Traditionally a strong liberal arts institution, Brooklyn College remained a holdout in the 1970s against the trend toward vocationalism. But that does not mean the college did not change. Instead of narrowing its focus, the college developed an ambitious core curriculum for all students in their first two years that has become a national model.

Established in 1930 as an offshoot of City and Hunter colleges, Brooklyn quickly acquired a strong academic reputation that rivals those of its two parent institutions. It now ranks eleventh in the country, for example, in the number of graduates who have gone on to earn doctoral degrees.

Brooklyn consists of a college of liberal arts and sciences, with thirty-one academic departments, including an education school and a conservatory of music. Among the sciences the best departments are geology, biology, chemistry, computer and information science and physics, which has its own low-energy atomic accelerator. In the humanities, the art, music and theater departments boast impressive faculty members, and the television and radio department has the best studio facilities in CUNY. The English department has a strong creative writing program.

The college has attracted national attention for its new "common educational experience," under which all freshmen and sophomores take a sequence of ten courses for thirty-four credits in areas that include everything from Homer and Descartes to computers and African culture. Students' assessments of the program vary. "The mandatory core classes give a student the varied background and rounded education needed to be an intelligent, well educated individual," believes one student. Another man criticizes "silly required humanities, and for some, silly science courses, in an age where college is career/vocationally oriented." Students must also take three semesters of a foreign language (or test out of the requirement), and all freshmen and transfer students are required to undergo sessions of academic counseling.

Notwithstanding its emphasis on the liberal arts, the college has a strong track record in training students for business and the professions. The fifth largest producer of graduates with accounting degrees, Brooklyn recently began a new degree program in business, management and finance. A high percentage of applicants from the college are accepted into dental, medical and law schools. Each year a number of outstanding freshmen join a special scholars program in which they attend special classes and seminars and pursue independent study. The college also runs a seven-year combined BA/MD program with the New York Health Science Center in Brooklyn, along with joint BS programs in nursing and in allied health professions, and it has inaugurated a "2 plus 2" program in engineering with the Polytechnic University of New York, Pratt Institute and the City College of New York.

Brooklyn's campus, which occupies more than thirty acres in the residential Midwood section of Flatbush, is among the most attractive in the City University. When students are burnt out from activities in Brooklyn or across the river in Manhattan, there are grassy areas with flower gardens and goldfish ponds to give a respite. "It's like a small, quiet world in the midst of a nasty, horn-honking city," says one student.

Most of the college's students come from the borough, and about half are Jewish, more than 30 percent either black or Hispanic and almost 7 percent Asian Americans. Although a dormitory is in the planning stages, Brooklyn is a commuter school whose students live either with their parents or in their own apartments. More than two hundred students are eligible for renewable merit scholarships ranging from $250 to $2,000 if they have maintained a high school average of 90 and score in the top 10 percent on the SAT.

The college has a large six-story student center and three major eating facilities (including one kosher kitchen) on campus, and plenty of restaurants and fast-food places nearby. "Fraternities and sororities play a very small role on campus," says one junior, although "ethnic and academic clubs are very active." Intramural and varsity athletic programs are popular. Brooklyn has the only football team among CUNY colleges. It also boasts the only Division I men's basketball team, a Division I women's basketball team, and Division I teams in soccer and other sports. Weekends are usually enlivened by performances at the Brooklyn Center for Performing Arts.

This is New York, and it takes initiative and staying power just to do such things as register for classes, find out about student aid and scholarships. As far as one student is concerned, "Brooklyn offers an Ivy League education at one-tenth the cost."

City College of New York

New York, NY 10031

Location Urban	**Applicants** 3,350
Total Enrollment 12,793	**Accepted** 75%
Undergraduates 10,343	**Enrolled** 55%
Male/Female 60/40	**Academics** ★ ★ ★
SAT V/M N/A	**Social** ☎ ☎
Financial Aid 85%	**Q of L** ● ●
Expense Pub $	**Admissions** (212)690-6977

The oldest of the CUNY colleges and the one with the most distinguished history, City College is like "the United Nations," one student says. More than half the students are either recent immigrants or come from abroad to study, and at last count there were almost fifty different languages spoken on campus. At City College, it would be difficult to feel unaccepted.

For decades, City College offered high quality education at no cost and drew thousands of bright and ambitious New Yorkers who could not afford Ivy League tuitions. As a result City College has a list of illustrious alumni—including Ira Gershwin, Upton Sinclair, Bernard Malamud, Jonas Salk, Paddy Chayevsky and seven Nobel Prize winners—that few colleges can match. Although the college, like the other branches of CUNY, had to impose tuition in 1976, City has still provided an important avenue of upward mobility for the poor. The college now ranks first nationally in the number of minority graduates in engineering and third in the number of black graduates who go on to medical school.

City is the most educationally complex unit of CUNY, with five professional schools that make it virtually a university within a university. It leads the other branches of the university in supported research activity. The schools of engineering and architecture have recently received a major infusion of resources, and the Sophie Davis School of Biomedical Education has become part of a new City University Medical School at City College. The medical school offers an accelerated seven-year BS/MD program for highly motivated students interested in practicing in medically underserviced urban areas. The college has also begun a major thrust in the humanities, winning several major grants for curriculum development and related activities.

Among the individual departments, physics is outstanding, and the departments of English, history, biology and psychology, which is clinically oriented, are all good. The social sciences, which had been somewhat weak for a number of years, have gotten better since faculty and offerings have been beefed up.

There are a variety of special offerings for the top students. A solid legal studies program allows qualified students to earn a combined bachelor's and law degree in six years, and a center for performing arts offers a small number of qualified students training in dance, theater, film and music. The college also provides a freshman honors program and a research honors program for upperclassmen. The library, with over a million volumes, is the largest in the City University. Although it has been hurt badly by budget cuts, it has a new home in the college's new $100-million North Academic Center. The center also houses academic departments, dining halls and a student union. A multimillion-dollar renovation program is currently giving the college's distinctive group of Gothic buildings a badly needed facelift and $2.4 million has been allocated for a new athletic field. Students with an 80 average from high school can get into the liberal arts program, but those interested in the more competitive special programs or professional schools have to do even better than that. There are twenty renewable merit-based City College Scholar Awards worth $1,250 a year, and recipients are selected from those with a high school average of 90 or better and SAT scores of 1200 plus.

Set on a ridge in Harlem in northern Manhattan, the thirty-five-acre campus is easily accessible by public transportation. The area has a high crime rate, and the college has added more security police and a private bus service that shuttles students and faculty the few blocks between the campus and the subway. Student parking is available but inadequate. There are two new student dining halls that act as centers of social life. Of that social life, one student says, "There are numerous ethnic, academic, religious, political and social clubs that you may join. There is lots to do on campus, but," she adds, "large numbers of students go home and are not involved."

As might be expected from a New York school, food on campus is expensive, and the nonacademic parts of campus life, such as registration, can be a hassle—although students report the college is working hard to make things work better. But whatever

130

the problems with support services, the great strengths of City are its students and its programs. "I think any student could easily feel at home here because the student body is so diversified," one junior noted. "However, any student who is not fully prepared to work hard will be better off at another college."

Hunter College

New York, NY 10021

Location Urban	**Applicants** 4,140
Total Enrollment 19,570	**Accepted** 74%
Undergraduates 15,490	**Enrolled** 49%
Male/Female 30/70	**Academics** ★ ★ ★
SAT V/M N/A	**Social** ☎ ☎ ☎
Financial Aid 65%	**Q of L** ● ● ●
Expense Pu $	**Admissions** (212)772-4490

Hunter College was established in 1870 as a teachers' college and the women's counterpart to City College, which then admitted only men. In its first century, Hunter earned a reputation for turning out bright, aggressive professional women—more who went on for their doctoral degrees than any other college in the nation. Today, Hunter is essentially a strong liberal arts college, but it also has a graduate school of social work and schools of education, health sciences and nursing.

The college is located on the Upper East Side of Manhattan with a campus that is "made up only of the actual buildings themselves." Specifically, it consists of two large older stone buildings and two new wings (Hunter West and Hunter East), connected by glassed in walkways high above Lexington Avenue and East 68th Street.

In the liberal arts area, Hunter's strongest disciplines include English, art, French, urban planning, anthropology and sociology. The college also has a good premedical program, with three-quarters of its graduates making it into medical school. The Brookdale Health Sciences Center, situated farther downtown, houses both the Hunter–Bellevue school of nursing (the largest nursing program in the country) and the health sciences school with its outstanding programs in community health, gerontology and physical therapy. The education school, one of the college's major strengths, allows students to participate as interns at Hunter's own elementary and secondary schools for gifted children. The school also has excellent programs in special and bilingual education.

A "Junior Year in New York" program places students from other colleges into museums, theater companies, schools and other places depending on their interest. The college offers its own students an internship program in New York City government and has an exchange program with the University of Paris that enables students to study abroad for one or two semesters. It also has a special arrangement for music majors to take elective courses at the famed Mannes College of Music in Manhattan.

Hunter College's stated goal has long been "to educate those who are unwelcome in other higher educational institutions because of poverty, sexism, racism or ageism." As a result, the school has strong resources for underprepared and returning students, as well as those who have to work while taking classes. Thirty percent of Hunter students are black, 20 percent are Hispanic and 10 percent are Asian Americans.

Hunter's convenient East Side location makes it easily accessible from all five

131

boroughs. Students, however, usually live elsewhere than in this high-rent area, and parking facilities are barely adequate. Nevertheless, the college does boast the only residential dormitory in the CUNY system at its downtown Brookdale Health Sciences Center campus although it accommodates only a small number of students. In 1983, Hunter greatly expanded and improved its main campus facilities with the opening of two seventeen-story towers that include an ultramodern nine-floor library. A graduating senior says the "library is superb. Computerized equipment makes finding reference material elementary." Less than 10 percent of students come from out of state. Men have been admitted since the 1960s.

Hunter offers a variety of benefits available to high achievers. Those with 1200 SATs and high school grade averages in the 90s qualify for $1,000 yearly Scholars Awards, and those with 1000 SATs and 85 averages qualify for Merit Awards of half that much. There is an honors program with a series of freshman and sophomore colloquiums, after which students go on to design the rest of their own curriculums, and honors students are offered another prized possession—living space. Its dormitory scholarships, providing free room and board, are available to students with Scholars Awards credentials, while Merit Award credentials entitle students to priority in room assignments.

As at some of the other CUNY campuses, the red tape can add to the difficulties of New York City life. The financial aid counseling service, what there is of it, drives students up a wall, as does the search for housing. Commuters and residents congregate in the college's cafeteria or snack bars when they are not busy with schoolwork or one of the more than ninety student organizations on campus. Although athletics take a back seat to the arts and politics, team sports, particularly basketball, are important within the context of intramural CUNY competition. Students enjoy a multistory underground gym that "makes Jack La Lanne look primitive."

New York is a melting pot and so is Hunter College. It will, says a biology major, appeal to "mature students who are curious and willing to interact with people of varying backgrounds and ethnicity. The diversity of Hunter College greatly enhances the learning experience.

Queens College

Flushing, NY 11367

Location Urban	**Applicants** 5,400
Total Enrollment 15,532	**Accepted** 60%
Undergraduates 12,224	**Enrolled** 53%
Male/Female 42/58	**Academics** ★ ★ ★ ★
SAT V/M N/A	**Social** 🐦 🐦
Financial Aid 55%	**Q of L** ● ●
Expense Pub $	**Admissions** (718)520-7323

Faculty members and administrators at Queens College have long referred to the school as the jewel of the City University system. While other colleges within the university take vigorous exception to this opinion, more neutral observers acknowledge that Queens probably is now the strongest of the university's four-year colleges.

One reason is its location. The college draws many good students from the middle-class borough in which it is located, as well as from Long Island. Another factor is that Queens has been extremely aggressive in building a number of outstanding departments. The college's best departments—English, political science, music, sociology, anthropology and earth and environmental science—are in the humanities and social sciences: but the biology and chemistry departments are also considered excellent, and specialized areas such as accounting and computer science are the largest undergraduate programs in the state.

Queens, with an eighty-acre campus built on the highest point of the borough, has an inspiring view of the Manhattan skyline. Although the college's architecture is basically drab, a $200-million construction program is providing a marked improvement. Projects currently being completed include a new science building, a library and a permanent home for the recently opened City University School of Law. Work on a new facility for the school of music is expected to start shortly. Also, the college has opened an environmental research and training center in Suffolk County, Long Island, and lured an important biology research institute to the campus from St. Louis.

Several programs are designed to foster student-faculty interaction outside the traditional classroom setting. The scholars program offers the opportunity for independent study under the guidance of a faculty member, and there is also an individualized BA option. The special studies and honors program enables faculty members to offer new, experimental courses to small groups of students before they become officially part of the curriculum. Queens College offers day and evening continuing education programs and runs its own study programs in France, Italy and Israel.

Queens attracts most of its students from the New York City public school system, and those with a 90 high school average and a combined SAT of 1200 are eligible for full-tuition merit awards. With no dormitories on the Queens campus, most students live at home, although an increasing number are finding housing near campus. The student body reflects the ethnic makeup of the borough—a third of the students are Jewish and a heavy percentage Asian American.

Social life revolves around lunchtime and late afternoon encounters at the campus beer joint or one of the four cafeterias (two of them kosher). There are plenty of fast-food eateries a few steps away. Although five buses serve the campus, commuting by mass transit can be a bit of a hassle. Social life here can be whatever you want to make it—there's no pressure to become a real butterfly. And, yet, one student says, "The extracurricular life at Queens is probably the school's biggest selling point," with a very active student government and parties, concerts and other programs. The chief policy-making body on the campus, the academic senate, was established in the wake of student protests in the '60s and takes a distinctive form: A third of its voting members are students, the rest faculty members. There is not one administrative vote in the senate.

When budget cuts began in the mid-'70s, counseling and athletics were the first to go, but they've improved now that money is coming through. The Health Services Center has developed some new programs, including one on nutrition and weight control. Varsity teams were saved when students voted to add a sports fee to their tuition bill, and more money is being channeled into sports.

By choosing this first-rate commuter college, students sacrifice a traditional college experience in favor of a good, affordable education. "With its established educational quality, talented faculty and accessibility to the resources of New York City," says an economics major who ought to know, "Queens is an outstanding value."

THE CLAREMONT COLLEGES

The peaceful Los Angeles suburb of Claremont is a Southern California stereotype replete with palm trees, Spanish architecture and the San Gabriel Mountains in the background. The climate could only be called perfect were it not for the stifling smog that blankets the town from April through September. In the midst of it all stand the Claremont Colleges, a consortium of five undergraduate colleges with an adjoining graduate school, theological seminary and botanical gardens. From the point of view of undergraduates, the cluster of residential colleges, each with its own personality and academic specialties, offers one of the finest educational smorgasbords in the country.

The Claremont Colleges consortium provides the resources of a large university, but none of the five colleges—Claremont–McKenna College, Harvey Mudd, Pitzer, Pomona, and Scripps—is bigger than a medium-sized dorm at a state school. Each school retains its own institutional identity, with its own faculty, administration, admissions and curriculum, although the boundaries of both academic work and extracurricular activities tend to be flexible. Each of the schools tends to specialize in a particular area that complements the offerings of all the others. Claremont–McKenna caters mainly to students planning careers in business, law or government, while Harvey Mudd is the choice for future scientists. Pitzer, the most liberal of the five, excels mainly in the behavioral sciences, and Scripps' best offerings are in art and foreign languages. Pomona, which ranks as one of the top liberal arts colleges anywhere, is the one Claremont school that is strong across the board, with the humanities especially so.

The colleges collectively share many services and facilities, a computer system, art studios, a student newspaper, laboratories, a health center, auditoriums, book stores, a maintenance department and business office. The Claremont library system makes over 1.5 million volumes available to all students, though each campus has its own facility. The Claremont University Center, a separate entity, owns central facilities for the group. Faculties and administrations are free to arrange joint programs or classes between all or just some of the schools. Courses at any college are open to students from the others, but each college sets limits on the number of classes that can be taken at other schools. Perhaps the best example of academic cooperation is the team-taught interdisciplinary courses, organized by instructors from the different schools and appealing to a mix of different academic interests. If it sounds a bit haphazard and complicated, it is.

Students at the Claremont Colleges come mostly from California, with the balance from other western and northwestern states. Once only Pomona attracted sizable contingents from the East, although now all have about half from out of state, give or take 10 percent. Harvey Mudd and Claremont–McKenna in particular have begun to promote themselves nationwide. The tone at Claremont is decidedly intellectual—graduate school is a more common goal than business school—and premeds especially will find themselves a tiny minority.

The local community of Claremont, "Clareville" to students, is geared more to senior citizens than seniors, juniors, sophomores and freshmen. But "the Village," a quaint cluster of specialty shops (including truly remarkable candy stores) is an easy skateboard ride away from any campus; unfortunately the shades come down and the sidewalks roll up well before sunset. For hot times, L.A. and UCLA-dominated Westwood are within sniffing distance, and a new shuttle bus make them even closer for Claremont students without cars. Nearby mountains and beaches make this collegiate paradise's backyard complete. Mount Baldy ski lifts, for instance, are only fifteen miles away—you'll reach Laguna Beach before both sides of your favorite tape are played out. For spring break, Mexico is cheap and a great change of pace.

On campus, extracurricular life maintains a balance between cooperation and independence. Claremont–McKenna, Harvey Mudd and Scripps field joint athletic teams, with men's soccer, swimming and water polo nationally ranked and women's volleyball and track strong. Athletics are biggest at Pomona and C–MC. Each of the five colleges has its own dorms, and since off-campus housing is limited in Claremont proper, the social life of students revolves around their dorms. There are no fraternities, except at Pomona, where joining one is far from de rigueur. All cafeterias are open to all students, and most big events—films, concerts, etc.—are advertised throughout the campus. Large five-school parties are regular Thursday, Friday and Saturday night fare. Still, since students' hearts and minds remain for the most part with their own college, interaction among students at different schools, be it for meals or dates, is not what it might be. Students benefit from the nurturing and support within their own schools, each of which has its own academic or extracurricular emphasis, although they all share the same zip code and address.

Below are profiles of each of the undergraduate Claremont Colleges.

Claremont–McKenna College

Claremont, CA 91711

Location Suburban	**Applicants** 1,360
Total Enrollment 840	**Accepted** 49%
Undergraduates 840	**Enrolled** 34%
Male/Female 65/35	**Academics** ★ ★ ★ ★
SAT V/M 580/630	**Social** 🚻 🚻 🚻
Financial Aid 66%	**Q of L** ● ● ●
Expense Pr $ $ $ $	**Admissions** (714)621-8088

Founded as the Claremont Men's College with an emphasis on the study of political economy Claremont–McKenna College took its married name in 1976 when women were allowed to partake of the fine career preparation in business, government and the professions. Although small and "intensely competitive," CMC (the monograms on the towels didn't have to be changed) nonetheless offers a friendly atmosphere. Its fifty-acre campus with twenty-four buildings is described by students as "functional and no-frills," fitting right in with the pragmatic attitude that dominates at the school.

Economics and political science are CMC's specialties, and together they claim about thirty faculty positions. Philosophy, accounting, English and psych are also considered strong. About 75 percent of the students eventually go on for advanced degrees, primarily at professional schools. CMC's academic offerings are greatly enhanced by six campus research institutes specializing in strategic studies, business practices, demographics, political trends, environment and data processing. CMC's 3-2 programs in management engineering with Harvey Mudd and Stanford University, BA/MBA with the University of Chicago, and 3-3 law program with Columbia Univer-

135

sity are popular options. Constant communication between students and faculty is "definitely encouraged," in and out of class, and there are a number of special meals in the dining halls arranged to help students and faculty get acquainted. CMC's stiff work load makes for an intense academic climate, and according to one student, "it's not uncommon for students to study on weekend nights."

Almost 60 percent of the students are native Californians, and the majority of the rest are from west of the Mississippi. Most were raised in conventional upper-middle-class families; blacks and Hispanics make up about 8 percent of the students, and Asian Americans account for another 7 percent. "Most people here are very conservative and concerned about their futures in the job market," says one math senior. Student dedication to professional life after college makes another senior complain that CMC sometimes seems "like a stepping stone to a job rather than a place to broaden horizons." Indeed, alumni are successful in California commerce circles: "Most of the major banks in California are riddled with CMC alumni," an administrator boasts. Sixty-four lucky students get renewable academic merit scholarships of between $1,000 and $2,714 per year.

All but one dorm is coed, and one marketing engineering student dubbed the range of living styles as everything from "party dorms to quiet morgues." Upperclassmen have no trouble getting a room, but freshmen occasionally end up in lounges for the first semester when space runs out. About 12 percent of the students live off campus. The dining facilities are adequate—"though nothing to write home about unless it is to ask for care packages full of food"—and students can eat in dining halls at any of the other four colleges.

"For CMC, you have to be intelligent, that's a given. But you also must take initiative to get involved," says one of the lone literature majors. The work-hard, play-hard ethic is alive and well among this driven lot, although one senior says only about "20 percent are considered heavy party-goers." Despite over ten years of coeducation, CMC remains very much a male institution. Men still outnumber women by two to one, and male-female relations are somewhat strained, with CMC men dating women at the other Claremonts—notably Scripps—more often than those at CMC.

CMC is by far the most athletic of the Claremonts, with the men especially dominating the teams jointly fielded with Harvey Mudd and Scripps. Water polo, swimming, tennis, and baseball have all won championships in recent years, and soccer, a Division III powerhouse, is led by a coach who doubles as a professor of philosophy and religion.

"CMC is still not well known, especially on the East Coast," laments a CMC vice president. Though that isn't likely to change overnight, CMC's impressive list of alumni in positions of prominence in government, business and law are slowly bringing the school nationwide respect.

Harvey Mudd College

Claremont, CA 91711

Location Suburban
Total Enrollment 550
Undergraduates 540
Male/Female 80/20
SAT V/M 620/740
Financial Aid 63%
Expense Pr $ $ $ $

Applicants 890
Accepted 48%
Enrolled 35%
Academics ★ ★ ★ ★
Social 🕿 🕿 🕿
Q of L ● ● ●
Admissions (714)621-8011

Bet you always wanted to know who Harvey Mudd was and why there is a college in Southern California named after him? Well, just in case, he was a highly successful mining engineer and owned the Cyprus Mining Corporation, reportedly the largest of its kind anywhere. But more importantly he was one of the supporters of the group plan that led to the Claremont Colleges system and was a trustee for twenty-nine years. Naturally, after he left a pot of gold to Claremont, they started a small, elite science and engineering school bearing his name in 1955.

Today, Harvey would be proud of the school that carries on his tradition and mission, striving to "educate leaders in science and engineering who have a clear understanding of the impact of their work on society." Over the years it has sent 40 percent of its graduates on for PhDs—more than any college in the country.

HMC's mid-'50s vintage campus even "looks like an engineering college—it's very symmetrical and there's no romance." Adds a junior general engineering major, "It's classical American cinder block." While most technical schools tend to have a narrow focus, HMC has come up with the novel idea that even scientists and engineers "need to know and appreciate poetry, philosophy, and non-Western thought," in the words of an administrator. Students here take a third of their courses in the humanities—the most of any technical college. These courses are taken primarily from other Claremont schools. To ensure breadth in the sciences students take another third of their work in math, physics, chemistry, biology, engineering design and computations. Then, finally, the last third of a student's courses must be in one of four major areas: chemistry, physics, engineering or mathematics (including computer science). Chemistry is considered the strongest area by most students, with physics not far behind. Math comes in for the heaviest student criticism, and some students claim the engineering program is too general. A Freshman Project groups students to tackle "some real-life engineering problems." The Engineering and Mathematics Clinic provides more than thirty small groups of upperclassmen with more difficult research tasks, sponsored by major corporations and government agencies to the tune of $24,000 per project.

"HMC is very high pressured," says a sophomore. "The academic load is tremendous, but students help each other out. Study groups are imperative to academic survival." There are occasional problems getting popular courses, but relations with profs are excellent, "a great plus," says one student. "The campus-wide honor code actually works" says one woman in general engineering. "I've never seen anyone cheat." That trust extends to personal property as well.

These budding technicians are also top achievers. More than 90 percent graduated in the top 10 percent of their high school class, and every single one was in the top half. Almost 60 percent of the students are homegrown Californians, mainly from white upper-middle-class households. Blacks and Hispanics account for only 1 percent each of the student body, though Asian Americans weigh in at 18 percent. More than half the student body receives need-based aid and HMC offers fifty non-need-based academic scholarships of up to $1,500 per year. With an endowment that comes to roughly $100,000 per student, HMC's long-term financial future looks bright.

Five older dorms and a new modern one are all coed and mix the classes. "They're excellent for social integration," states one student. There are no fraternities, and most social life takes place in and around the dorms. Despite their heavy work load, most HMC students find abundant social outlets, even if it's just joining the parade of unicycles that has overrun the campus. "HMC students study hard, and party hard to let off the tensions," adds another student. Since there are no fraternities, most socializing takes place in and around the dorms, where there are parties every weekend. No one in the admissions office bothers to look at applicants' athletic achievements, and the results are evident in the laid-back athletic program. For the few students who are interested, Mudd does field varsity sports teams with Claremont–McKenna, the best of which include soccer, tennis, water polo and swimming, but there is little student interest. Intramurals—in conjunction with Scripps and CMC—are much more popular.

"The school is relatively new and buried in obscurity," complains one engineering sophomore. Nevertheless, HMC is right on the heels of Caltech as the best technical school in the West, and the public relations and admissions departments are working to get the word out. HMC doesn't guarantee that you'll be the owner of your own mining company within a decade of graduation—or president of anyone else's—but it does promise you a gem of a technical education.

Pitzer College

Claremont, CA 91711

Location Suburban	**Applicants** 790
Total Enrollment 770	**Accepted** 73%
Undergraduates 770	**Enrolled** 40%
Male/Female 45/55	**Academics** ★ ★ ★
SAT V/M 510/530	**Social** ☎ ☎ ☎
Financial Aid 55%	**Q of L** ● ● ●
Expense Pr $ $ $ $	**Admissions** (714)621-8129

Established in 1963 as a liberal arts college with an emphasis in the social and behavioral sciences, Pitzer is the newest and most unorthodox of the Claremont Colleges, the one with the "get out there and make your own way" attitude. It retains much of the alternative-school aura associated with that memorable era in which it grew up. It is run, for example, by a community government that puts students on all policy committees, including those on curriculum and faculty promotion, and its distinctive identity comes from its laid-back, do-your-own-thing style of living and the size and strength of its anthropology, psychology and sociology departments.

Even the campus is, well, different. The classroom buildings are modernistic octagons, and the grass-covered "mounds" that distinguish the grounds "are perfect for sunbathing and Frisbee," says a junior. Class size is generally small, promoting close interaction between students and faculty. "The small size makes Pitzer a great place to learn and live," says an English/psychology major.

There are no general education requirements, which suits everyone just fine. "I have a freedom to choose courses pertinent to my career objectives," says one student. "That requires sound judgment and independent thinking." A lively freshman seminar program sharpens students' learning skills, especially writing. Students select from thirty majors in sciences, humanities and social sciences. The social and behavioral sciences are the strongest, with political science and econ close behind. Interdisciplinary inquiry is encouraged. Original research is common, and Pitzer students take advantage of Claremont's abundant foreign study options.

Individualism is a prized characteristic among Pitzer students, more than half of whom are attracted from out of state. "Most students here are easy going, and the emphasis is placed on the individual's optimum development, as opposed to competition," explains an English lit major. Pitzer has a substantial minority community; blacks and Hispanics make up 18 percent of the student body and Asian Americans 9 percent, while foreigners account for another five. "We're liberal as far as dress, political and social views," one student claims. "Too many democrats," another complains. But lest anyone get the idea that Pitzer students are too out in left field, 70 percent of them eventually go on to graduate or professional school. Although adequate financial aid is awarded to most students with need, Pitzer doesn't have the financial resources to tempt outstanding students with pots of gold.

All freshmen that hail from beyond a ten-mile radius are required to live on campus, as do practically all upperclassmen. The accommodations are fairly posh for undergraduate dorms, with juniors and seniors virtually guaranteed singles, most with private bathrooms. Boarders can choose from a variety of meal plans in the dining hall (which never fails to have a vegetarian plate), join a food co-op, or cook on their own. One interesting campus curiosity is Grove House, a structure students saved from the wrecking ball seventeen years ago and moved to campus. It houses a dining room, study areas, and art exhibits. Pitzer has no Greek organizations—nor does it want any—and social life tends to be fairly low-key. Dances, cocktail parties and cultural events do much to occupy students' leisure time, but without a car things can get claustrophobic. Those who do have wheels enjoy a range of opportunities, from skiing in the nearby mountains to the cosmopolitan delights of Los Angeles and Hollywood forty-five minutes away. Aspiring jocks would be well-advised to look elsewhere for playmates; intramural inner-tube water polo is about as intense as the sports scene gets.

Pitzer attracts open-minded students looking for the freedom to go their own way. Notes a junior: "Students who are the type to think about their world on their own, rather than plug into the institutionalized way of thinking, might find this school is for them."

Pomona College

Claremont, CA 91711

Location Suburban	**Applicants** 2,790
Total Enrollment 1,330	**Accepted** 42%
Undergraduates 1,330	**Enrolled** 32%
Male/Female 48/52	**Academics** ★ ★ ★
SAT V/M 620/660	**Social** 🏛 🏛 🏛
Financial Aid 47%	**Q of L** ● ● ●
Expense Pr $ $ $ $	**Admissions** (714)621-8134

The largest and oldest of the Claremont Colleges, Pomona College is also the most prestigious of the five. With its demanding traditional liberal arts curriculum, the school lives up to the Ivy League vision of the California settlers who founded it. It remains, as one econ major puts it, "an East Coast oasis in a small Southern California community." Despite its excellent regional reputation, on a national level, Pomona's nemesis is its anonymity.

The architecture is variously described as California Mediterranean or pseudo-Italian. More than one stone building is cloaked in ivy and topped with a red-tile roof, and the campus abounds with eucalyptus trees and canyon live oaks and occasional "secretive courtyards lined with flowers." The most recent additions are a science building, a dining hall, and a new gym and field house and eight-lane track that give Pomona the best athletic facilities of the Claremont Colleges.

Classes at Pomona are rigorous and challenging. "The academic climate is characterized by an almost absurd pursuit of intellectual plateaus," reports a lit major. "The emphasis on grades is stifling," says an English major, but most students tend to compete against their own past performance, not other students. English, psychology, international relations, languages, biology, history, government and economics are particularly popular. Pomona's most obvious weakness lies in the behavioral sciences, and students with interests in those fields tend to cross-register at nearby Pitzer. Pomona students can spend a semester at Oxford University or travel with professors to other parts of Europe. Those who prefer America the beautiful can spend a semester at Colby or Swarthmore, pursue a 3-2 engineering plan with the California Institute of Technology, or spend a "Washington semester" with a congressman. A Liberal Arts Field Experience program offers internships.

The faculty makes a point of being accessible, and it's not uncommon for professors to hold study sessions at their houses. An ever popular "take-a-professor-to-lunch" program gives students free meals when they arrive with a faculty member in tow, and there is even a prof who leads aerobics classes open to all.

Pomona attracts "people who produce work of exceptionally high quality, but who know how to relax and are interested in the nonacademic," notes one senior. Forty-five percent of the students are native Californians, but a sizable percentage venture from the East Coast to enjoy a Pomona education. Four percent are black and 7 percent are Hispanic, while Asian Americans make up about 10 percent of the student body. There is a healthy mix of liberal and conservative on campus, though the leftists, especially the feminist wing, are much more vocal. The student government is active, and the administration is credited with respecting students' opinions. "It's great that we are involved in decision making that affects us," a senior says. Pomona is need-blind in admissions and meets the full demonstrated need of all those who attend. Eighteen students, chosen from those who designate Pomona as their first choice, are awarded

National Merit Scholarships, and two other students are chosen for $2,000 stipends. Admissions officers are on the lookout for anyone with special talents and are more than willing to waive the usual grade and score standards for such finds.

The vast majority of Pomona students live on campus all four years. The dorms are divided into two distinct groups: Those on South campus are fairly quiet and offer spacious rooms; those on the North end have smaller rooms with a livelier social scene. Freshmen must live on campus and are placed in a "sponsor group" with two guardian upperclassmen, creating a "quasi-family away from home." Upperclassmen generally get single rooms or spacious two-room doubles that sometimes have fireplaces—rather odd considering the only season around here is summer. "The rooms are fabulous," exclaims a German lit/biology major. "They have character." A handful of students isolate themselves in Claremont proper, where apartments are scarce and expensive. Boarders must buy at least partial meal plans. The food is good, with steak dinners on Saturday and ice cream for dessert every day, and diners can draw inspiration from a giant Orozco mural of Prometheus bringing fire from Mount Olympus in one of the dining halls. Students with common interests can occupy one of the large university houses; currently there is a vegetarian group and a "kosher kitchen," both of which serve meals to other undergraduates. Pomona has a well-established language dorm with wings for French, German, Spanish, Russian and Chinese speakers, as well as language tables at lunch.

Students often spend Friday afternoons relaxing with friends over a brew at The Greek Theater. That's about as hopping as things get on the weekends, when most students tend to curl up in their rooms beside the unlighted fireplace with a good textbook. "Doing academic work is still the most popular activity on campus," says an English lit major, "followed closely by dancing, wasting time at the Student Union and having small parties." There are movies five nights a week, and students also enjoy just tossing a Frisbee between kegs of beer set up on the lawn. Pomona is unique among the Claremont Colleges in that it has six nonnational fraternities (two coed) each with their own party rooms on campus. There in "no peer pressure to join frats," and no fraternity rivalry—the only thing nonmembers miss out on is the chance to duck easily under the twenty-one-year-old drinking age. For seeking an escape from campus, a car is all but essential to take advantage of the fabled surfing beaches, Hollywood's glamour, and skiing at nearby Mount Baldy.

Time was when Pomona was an athletic powerhouse; the football team even knocked off mighty USC on Thanksgiving Day back in 1899. But the college has long since deemphasized varsity sports and today a reasonably good high school team could beat the combined forces of Pomona and Pitzer. The sports scene is very low-key, though men's basketball and women's basketball and swimming have recently won championships. Women's athletics are on par—some say above par—with men's. Intramurals, including hotly contested inner-tube water polo matches, attract many participants, a new track and field complex is sure to please hard-core track stars and weekend jocks alike.

"The strength in every department, the uniqueness of every student, the ease with which one may approach a professor" are what one senior has come to appreciate most about Pomona. The strongest link in an extremely attractive chain, Pomona continues to symbolize the Claremont Colleges' rising status in the world of higher education.

Scripps College

Claremont, CA 91711

Location Suburban	**Applicants** 520
Total Enrollment 600	**Accepted** 81%
Undergraduates 600	**Enrolled** 81%
Male/Female N/A	**Academics** ★★★
SAT V/M 520/520	**Social** 🐾🐾🐾
Financial Aid 42%	**Q of L** ●●●●
Expense Pr $ $ $	**Admissions** (714)621-8149

Scripps is what you get when the Seven Sisters go West. It is the only single-sex college in the Claremont consortium and one of only two women's colleges on the entire West Coast. It provides a strong grounding in the humanities, as well as, according to one student, "an emphasis on women without being overly feminist."

The architecture at Scripps is Spanish and Mediterranean, with Roman roof-tiled buildings and elegant landscaping creating a tranquil, comfortable environment. "Students and professors are very close," notes an econ sophomore. "In fact, at 6:30 on the morning before Christmas break, staff and faculty sang us carols while we were still in bed!"

At the heart of the Scripps curriculum is the humanities program, a required sequence of interdisciplinary courses with topics that range from the role of women in antiquity to the modern concept of self. In addition, each student must demonstrate competency in writing, a foreign language and the natural sciences. Scripps is particularly strong in fine arts and languages, and history and psychology are also good. If none of these suit your fancy, suggests a psych/art major, design your own.

No matter what major they choose, all must complete a senior thesis or project in their field. About 20 percent of the students enroll in the yearlong Corporate Training for Liberal Arts Women Program, usually as sophomores or juniors, which gives future yuppies a chance to show their stuff at major companies, such as Xerox and Pacific Bell. Computers appear across the curriculum and are located in dorms for convenience, and there's usually no problem getting into the courses you want—most of which will be conducted in small, personal groups.

Scripps' women are mainly from affluent families—"I would classify some as snobs," says one woman—and nearly half are native Californians. They are by and large a conservative group, with a sprinkling of radical feminists. Blacks and Hispanics account for 9 percent of the student body, and Asian Americans make up another five. Most of the women were only average students in high school; just under a quarter were in the top 10 percent of their class, but 28 percent were in the bottom half.

The small, homestyle dorms are well maintained and luxurious, often boasting their own reflecting pools and inner courtyards. Freshmen should expect a roommate, or two if enrollment keeps increasing, but upperclasswomen usually get singles, often with a sink in the room. Each dorm has its own dining hall, as well as its own "antiquated kitchen" for those who want to fend for themselves. Students praise the dining facilities, which serve vegetarian alternatives at every meal.

Many Scripps women religiously cultivate their fashionable tans, and on weekends there's an exodus to the beach. For those who stay around, there's always the companionship found with coed students from the rest of Claremont's colleges, especially those from Claremont–McKenna.

Scripps has the appeal of being both a women's college, with its supportive environment, and part of the diverse academic and social university environment of the Claremont Colleges. That combination is what makes it, in the words of a psychology major, "socially and academically unlimiting."

Claremont–McKenna College, CA —See CLAREMONT COLLEGES

Clark College, GA—See ATLANTIC UNIVERSITY CENTER

Clark University

Worcester, MA 01610

Location Center city	**Applicants** 2,960
Total Enrollment 2,980	**Accepted** 65%
Undergraduates 2,240	**Enrolled** 30%
Male/Female 45/55	**Academics** ★ ★ ★ ★
SAT V/M 520/560	**Social** 🕿 🕿 🕿
Financial Aid 46%	**Q of L** ● ● ●
Expense Pr $ $ $	**Admissions** (617)793-7431

When Sigmund Freud visited America in 1909, the only university to invite him to lecture was Clark University in Worcester—not one of those name joints in Cambridge or New Haven. The foresight exhibited in that move remains evident in Clark's brave and untiring attitude. Though not as renowned as most of its New England competitors, Clark continues to fight with the best of the schools in the Northeast for recognition for, and students who can appreciate, a quality undergraduate education.

Clark was founded as a research-oriented graduate school—the second such institution after Johns Hopkins—and its researchers contributed to the discovery of the birth control pill, liquid-fueled rockets and the windchill factor. The school's focus has shifted toward undergraduate education in recent decades, but today many Clark students can still benefit from "elbow teaching"—working side by side on research projects with faculty members. The geography and psychology departments both have national reputations and are unquestionably Clark's biggest drawing cards. The social and natural sciences are, in general, strong; the Fuller Foundation Center for Music has been entirely renovated, offering state-of-the-art facilities in computer music. The humanities and foreign languages are weak, and the department of math and computer science is reported by students to be a complete joke.

Emphasis is placed on broad academic exploration during the first two years. A new freshman seminar program gets the neophytes ready for required courses in liberal studies, verbal expression and formal analysis (film studies or environmental issues will

143

suffice). Students must also take additional courses in five of six "perspective" areas: aesthetics, comparatives, history, science, language and culture, and values. Interdisciplinary programs are popular—women's studies is especially good—and students may design their own majors. Internships and study abroad programs are encouraged in all academic areas, and through the Worcester Consortium,* students may cross-register at any one of nine other colleges in Worcester, including Holy Cross* and Worcester Polytechnic Institute.* Students can get a visual arts degree in conjunction with the Worcester Art Museum.

More than half of all Clark students end up in graduate school, including 88 percent of all who apply to medical schools. Even with all the grad school goals, students are not cutthroat about grades; the academic pressure is much less intense than at other institutions of comparable quality. "Classes can be high pressure, but if you just want to cruise by, then it's very casual," explains one student. The main library houses adequate resources, but hasn't enough light or heat. And despite new library monitors who remind students to "button their lips," the word processors and computer terminals in the building make it annoyingly noisy.

The campus buildings, mixtures of red brick and dirty white concrete, range architecturally from "institutional boring" to a "glass deco science center," and there isn't a whole lot of green in between. One man bemoans the lack of a traditional college atmosphere that can be found at neighboring Holy Cross College, but a classmate adds, "new buildings pop up everywhere and so do lawns."

Clark students are a bright, earnest, independent group coming mainly from New York and New England. Two-thirds of them are from public schools, and close to half are Jewish; "It's very safe to be Jewish here," says a sophomore." Many students are upper-middle-class, "or at least they pretend to be." Personalities run the gamut from "yuppies to granola-heads," but each group tends to be goal oriented. And while some students still claim the school is very liberal, "looking the freshmen over—they get more conservative every year," observes a senior. All financial aid is need-based, but students with exceptional academic backgrounds are likely to be given a package with more grant and less loan.

Dorm space at Clark has gotten a little tighter of late, although most students who want rooms can get them through the "room roulette" lottery. All the dorms, except one, are coed by floor or wing, and the two freshman residence halls are said to be less tidy and less luxurious than the others. Freshmen must live on campus, but many juniors and seniors live in cheap triple-decker apartments nearby. The on-campus dweller must subscribe to one of three meal plans and, while one student says the food is just plain "terrible," another claims, "it's not the best, but they work at it." One cafeteria customer insists the kosher kitchen "is worth the extra cost regardless of your religion."

Worcester, a sort of homely, blue-collar city, is ignored and disowned by many New Englanders. Yet "Woosta" (as the natives call it) is New England's second-largest city and still growing. It offers numerous restaurants, dance clubs, concert halls, a resident symphony, theater companies, and good science and art museums. It's also home to the Centrum, a thirteen-thousand-seat arena where some of the country's best bands play. Clark, however, is situated in one what one student defines as "the armpit of the city," and for students nervous about walking alone at night there is a twenty-four-hour escort service. A car is helpful to students, but not good for town/gown relations: "A great deal of jealousy exists on the part of the townies toward Clark students who drive their BMW's, Saabs and Porsches around," observes a psych major. Buses will take the less-endowed students to places like the Berkshires, Boston, Springfield and Providence.

The general social pattern at Clark is to study hard until Thursday night and party hard until Sunday. The college sponsors movies, parties, concerts and the like, but the social life for many students is self-promoted—"Those who are waiting for things to happen will be waiting for a long time," one senior warns. The three non-national fraternities and sororities are not recognized by the administration, but seem to be gaining in popularity among students. Clark has never had a jock school reputation, but the men's and women's varsity basketball teams have been tops in their divisions. Other strong teams are men's tennis and soccer, and women's volleyball and field hockey. The new, multifunctional Student Athletic Center has given a boost to the intramural program and voluntary physical education courses such as aerobics, squash and scuba diving.

At Clark, the expectation is that undergraduates are serious, self-motivated, and open-minded, though perhaps the only quality not tolerated in this lenient environment is a lack of purpose. The students, like their school, are out to prove they are as good as their northeastern counterparts. "The people at Clark are almost too independent and self-assured," says one senior. "No one wants to show normal human weakness."

Clemson University

Clemson, SC 29631

Location Small town	**Applicants** 6,400
Total Enrollment 12,150	**Accepted** 69%
Undergraduates 10,490	**Enrolled** 50%
Male/Female 55/45	**Academics** ★ ★ ★
SAT V/M 480/550	**Social** ☎ ☎ ☎
Financial Aid 35%	**Q of L** ● ● ● ●
Expense Pub $ $	**Admissions** (803)656-2287

Clemson University has a way of bringing out the tiger in its students. "Tigermania," as it's known on campus, lasts throughout the year and reaches a fever pitch on fall Saturday afternoons, when the whole student body—plus sixty-six thousand extras— jams the football stadium to cheer the Tigers on. Unfortunately, while the spirit of athletic competition has always animated this friendly southern campus, lately Clemson has come to resemble a sports franchise with academic programs on the side, instead of vice versa. After a recent series of embarrassing recruiting scandals, capped off by revelations of drug use by Clemson athletes, the university president resigned when the board of trustees would not let him fire the athletic director. The student newspaper labeled the trustees' actions "totally ironic and outrageous," and serious questions remain about the university's priorities.

Still, though they don't generate as much enthusiasm as the sports teams, Clemson's academic programs are also excellent in many areas. Nestled in the foothills of the Blue Ridge Mountains, the university occupies the spacious grounds that were once the plantation of southern John C. Calhoun. All that room comes in handy, because Clemson is a land-grant state university that specializes in agricultural and technical fields. Electrical engineering is the university's largest department, and computer engineering leads the nation in research on large scale, integrated computer circuitry. One of Clemson's oldest and finest programs is agriculture, which enjoys the use of nearly twenty thousand acres of farms and woodlands surrounding the campus. The College of Architecture offers intensive semester programs at the Overseas Center for Building Research and Urban Study in Genoa, Italy. Highly motivated students should consider Calhoun College, Clemson's honors program, open to freshmen who scored 1200 or above on their SAT and ranked in the top 10 percent of their high school graduating class.

The graphic communications program in the industrial education department has a national reputation, and the program in textile science is noted for its sharp faculty. Other strong programs include applied math, the natural sciences and nursing. Because of the prevailing technical emphasis, most students interested in the liberal arts head "down country" to the University of South Carolina. Though undergraduate teaching has always been one of Clemson's strong points, institutional priorities have changed somewhat in recent years. There is a move afoot to make Clemson a major research university—à la Georgia Tech—and plans call for doubling the number of graduate students in the next ten years.

More than 70 percent of the undergraduates hail from South Carolina, and most of the rest come from neighboring states. Just over a third were in the top 10 percent of their high school graduating class. Blacks make up only 5 percent of the student body, and Hispanics and Asian Americans both count for less than 1. Students tend to be conservative, with jocks and John Deere types abounding, and though Clemson isn't affiliated with any church, there is a strong Southern Baptist presence on campus. But everyone can become part of the Clemson family, from southern belle to New Jersey Yankee, as long as they're friendly, easygoing, not overly intellectual, and enthusiastic about life in general and the Tigers in particular. Clemson students tend to take a casual attitude toward study habits, although the engineering programs can be high-pressured. At a school that is "mad for sports," there are 180 athletic scholarships given in twelve sports. The university also offers a full complement of academic scholarships; 350 awards, ranging from $75 to $5,000, are made each year without regard to need, ranging from $75 to $5,000. Even those who have to pay full price are getting a bargain compared to most schools because of Clemson's cheap tuition.

Clemson's architectural style ranges from early 1900s red brick to modern high rise, with the academic and administrative buildings clustered in the center of campus surrounded by the residence halls. Most of the dorms are single sex, though coed university-owned apartment complexes are also an option. Dorm rooms are assigned on the basis of seniority, so freshmen are urged to get their housing requests in early. Clemson House, the coed dorm, is considered one of the best places to be. About half the students—by choice or not—end up living off campus. The food is typical college fare, and students complain that the quality drops as the semester wears on. Fast-food restaurants provide relief when the food on campus "gets too unbearable," one accounting major notes. Upperclassmen can opt to cook for themselves; each dorm has cooking facilities.

After class, many students hop on their bikes and head to nearby Lake Hartwell. Early springs, long summers, and mild winters draw hordes there for water sports. The beautiful Blue Ridge Mountain range is also close by for hiking and camping, and beaches and ski slopes are both within driving distance. On weekends when the Tiger teams are playing, there are pep rallies, cookouts, dances, and parties for the mobs of excited fans. Aside from the sports teams, fraternities and sororities provide most of the campus social life, though students who don't pledge "are not committing social suicide," says one senior. There are plenty of off-campus parties where the main activity is drinking beer. Clemson is a small college town that offers a few bars and movie theaters for evening fun, but now that the drinking age is twenty-one, many former haunts are off limits to students.

Sports are what makes the world go 'round at Clemson, and on game days the campus dissolves into a sea of Tiger orange. The football team, winner of the national championship in 1981, is by far the most popular on campus, though basketball and soccer also draw large and enthusiastic followings. The baseball, cross country, and tennis teams likewise are consistent contenders. Though students live and die with the men's teams' every move, "unfortunately women's athletics are not on par with the men's at all," according to a female senior.

Not a haven for liberal arts or liberal politics, Clemson nevertheless provides a high-quality education to those whose interests lie in technical fields. Like SATs and Achievement Tests, love of big-time college sports is practically an admissions requirement. The sports teams foster a community spirit that is both friendly and infectious. Once here, alumni swear, your blood "runneth orange" forever.

Colby College

Waterville, ME 04901

Location Small town	**Applicants** 3,100
Total Enrollment 1,670	**Accepted** 41%
Undergraduates 1,670	**Enrolled** 34%
Male/Female 50/50	**Academics** ★ ★ ★ ★
SAT V/M 560/600	**Social** ☎ ☎ ☎
Financial Aid 34%	**Q of L** ● ● ●
Expense Pr $ $ $	**Admissions** (207)872-3168

It's no coincidence that Colby College sits atop a stretch of high ground known as Mayflower Hill; if ever there was a quintessential New England college, this is it. Rolling hills, majestic Georgian architecture, and hordes of outdoorsy students dressed to gladden the heart of any L. L. Bean retailer are all part of the Colby ambience.

A small college with a history of innovation and educational excellence, Colby boasts a faculty that is devoted to undergraduate teaching. Academic standards are high, especially in government, English, economics and the life sciences (which launch 90 percent of their premeds into medical school). Less traditional programs in creative writing, American and East Asian studies also get rave reviews. Not quite up to par are sociology, the arts and the quasibusiness field known as administrative science. ("Nobody's a business major at Colby.") Distribution requirements include course work in English, a foreign language, the natural sciences, social sciences, and humanities, and the Freshman Humanities Program offers interdisciplinary, team-taught courses to a maximum of fifteen students.

More than half the freshmen begin their Colby careers with a five-day orientation excursion by bicycle, canoe or foot through Maine's wilderness. Once they are back to civilization, curling up with their books seems to be the most popular activity, not only during the long and cold Maine winters, but even in balmier weather. The pressure is seldom intense and hardly ever cutthroat, but with five courses required each semester, it never really lets up. "Those who expect to get by on their good looks and charm should go elsewhere," one senior says. The library has plentiful resources for a school this size, and there are separate facilities for music and art and the sciences. At matriculation, each student gets an account number to facilitate paying for computer time.

An early harbinger of progressive education, Colby was the first college to establish a special January program. Motivated undergraduates find an internship or prepare an in-depth report during this short term, while others head for the Sugarloaf ski slopes an hour away and write a quick paper at the end of the month. The Senior Scholars program lengthens the Jan-Plan experience to a whole year for selected students. Despite the beautiful surroundings, four years on the outskirts of Waterville (population forty thousand) is more than many students can take. Freshmen wary of Maine winters can pack off for Cuernavaca, Mexico, or Florence, Italy, to fulfill their language requirement firsthand, delaying enrollment until the second semester. There are also Jan-Plan trips to everywhere from the Grand Canyon to the Soviet Union, and juniors regularly seek out foreign- or college-exchange opportunities. Popular targets are Bermuda (for biology), Connecticut's Mystic Seaport, Kyoto, the great cities of Europe, and even China is a possibility. For would-be engineers, there are joint 3-2 programs with Case Western Reserve and the University of Rochester.

Founded in 1813 as the nation's second Baptist college (after Brown), Colby has a long-standing tradition for harboring students and faculty "with a commitment to social justice." Colby students formed one of the earliest antislavery societies, and Colby was the first of the all-male colleges in the Northeast to admit women, in 1871. The student body today is somewhat preppy (L. L. Bean headquarters are an hour away in Freeport) and becoming more conservative. Students are predominantly Yankee and only 3 percent black ("It is a tough place to attract minorities to," one woman says), but college officials are working to enroll a more diverse population. Students are admitted without regard to their financial need, and Colby remains committed to meeting the full demonstrated need of all admitted applicants. National Merit Scholars garner token $200 honoraria, and outstanding upperclassmen and minority students may get up to $1,400 in extra grant money in lieu of loans. Colby runs its own parent loan program with favorable terms in addition to federal loan programs.

A major social change at Colby was the abolition of the well-entrenched fraternity and sorority system in 1984. The Greeks, who were criticized by many as being discriminatory and harmful to campus life, were expelled by the board of trustees after a protracted war of words that ultimately ended up in court. Hard feelings remain to this day, and the persistence of underground frats is a continuing source of controversy on campus. Under a new Residential Commons Plan, the campus is divided into four dorm groups, each with live-in faculty members, and a new $3.5-million student center opened its doors in the fall of 1985. Nevertheless, underground fraternities persist, and are a source of continuing controversy in the administration. One thing about the social scene hasn't changed: Beer is consumed in copious quantities. "Kegs are it!!" says one English major. Students have a lot of autonomy over their living conditions, even to the point of setting dining hall menus, and students can choose a "quiet" residence hall (never "dorm" at Colby) where there are posted hours for making noise. A tiny minority of upperclass students move off campus to neighboring farmhouses or to house-sit for a professor on sabbatical. The rest of the students are stuck with an uninspiring food plan whereby everyone pays for twenty-one meals a week.

Colby's nine-hundred-acre campus—complete with red-brick buildings, white trim, ivy and a wildlife preserve—is the place of choice for socializing, although many students do their midweek partying downtown at places like the Courthouse and You Know Whose. On weekends, some students head for the hills (half-price season tickets available at Sugarloaf), and others make the three-hour trip to Boston, but most stay put and frequent the all-campus parties, which have become more popular with the demise of the fraternities. Despite all the activity, Colby is somewhat isolated and students complain that the social life "can become repetitive."

An enthusiasm for outdoor sports is the major nonacademic credential needed to become a content Colby undergraduate. Athletics have come a long way since the first intercollegiate croquet game here back in 1860, and Colby's men and women excel at varsity basketball (especially the women), ice hockey and track. "People get psyched for these events," an English major explains. "We get to rag on Bowdoin and Bates—our friendly rivals!" Intramural winners wear their Colby "I Play" Champs T-shirts with pride, and the overwhelming majority of men and women take part in some fifteen different sports, including women's rugby. Others use the superb field-house facilities on an individual basis. Drama is probably the next most popular extracurricular activity, and numerous productions are mounted each semester.

Anyone already set on a particular career, technical or otherwise, might find the liberal arts training offered on this bucolic campus unsettling. For the most part, Colby undergraduates are more interested in their skis and their books than in any activity that smacks of the real world, including job hunting. They're in the north country for four years of stimulating and enjoyable contact with friendly professors and peers. As one freshman says, "It is the perfect setting for finding out what you want to do with your life and making lasting friendships." And just think, you wouldn't even have to order your L. L. Bean essentials by mail.

Colgate University

Hamilton, NY 13346

Location Rural	**Applicants** 5,790
Total Enrollment 2,700	**Accepted** 35%
Undergraduates 2,690	**Enrolled** 33%
Male/Female 54/46	**Academics** ★ ★ ★ ★
SAT V/M 600/640	**Social** 🏠 🏠 🏠
Financial Aid 64%	**Q of L** ● ● ●
Expense Pr $ $ $ $	**Admissions** (315)824-1000

Three pizzerias, five bars, one movie theater and a Burger King certainly aren't enough to lure 2,600 energetic, proven achievers to the tiny town of Hamilton in chilly upstate New York—but Colgate University is. A highly respected liberal arts college on a wonderland campus, Colgate stands out among the surrounding hills and farmhouses as a hotbed of academic and extracurricular activity.

Except for a few postmodern structures, Colgate's buildings are ivy-covered limestone classics connected by sloping lawns and tree-lined walks. The campus's location on a steep hill keeps the already athletic students in top shape. Those ski fanatics tuckered out by the rigors of academia, but not too tired to hit the slopes, need walk only a few hundred yards to the college's own ski run. (The cemetery's proximity to this run may or may not be testament to those Colgaters who just don't know when to stop.) Whatever your taste, Colgate's campus is beautiful. "Breathtaking," gasps one student.

The stars of Colgate's strong liberal arts curriculum are the geology department

("All geo majors love it and the profs"), philosophy, religion, history and English. Except for physics and computer science, students also praise the sciences, which enjoy great facilities and "large numbers of faculty who welcome contact and work with students." "The economics department wins most-improved," according to one math/econ major (the recent addition of five professors could have something to do with that). Though there are several dramatic and musical productions each year, there is no theater major at Colgate, and the arts in general tend to be weak. Social sciences are not impressive either.

Colgate works to keep its class sizes small, allowing valuable interaction between professors and students. And the students are quick to appreciate it: "Student-teacher relationships are probably the best thing about Colgate," says one. Yet a frustrating drawback to the more personalized classrooms is the difficulty students sometimes have in getting into all of the courses of their choice; a few may close, and students have to wait until next semester. The bachelor of arts curriculum includes various liberal arts components designed to provide students with a "big picture" perspective in addition to their fields of concentration.

The interdisciplinary freshman seminars give students an excellent introduction to the various departments as well as close, first-semester contact with top professors. The required general education program is spread over four years and organized into the "tier system," which simply means the courses (covering such broad topics as the Emergence of Western Culture and Contemporary Issues) are structured to build upon each other. Competency in a foreign language is required along with fairly standardized distribution requirements in humanities, social sciences and natural sciences. And when students are ready to delve into a major, they have thirty-eight established fields of concentration to choose from (unless they would rather design their own). A nice break from the routine, the January Special Studies term affords students a valuable way to explore career interests as well.

About half of every class takes advantage of Colgate's impressive array of off-campus study options. Cultural programs around the globe include English, history and economics in London, and language studies in France, Spain and Switzerland. Colgate students shy away from mundane junior-year-abroad stints: One student wrote radio shows for the Zambian government, and work-study on an Israeli kibbutz is a popular choice. Back home, geology students pursue fieldwork in the Northeast, political science majors spend time in Washington, and almost anyone can enter an internship with a Colgate alumnus, take a leave of absence on the Venture program* or sail away on a Sea Semester.*

Any evidence of Colgate's past financial woes has vanished in the dust of busy construction workers. The library recently received a much-needed expansion, although students complain that its facilities are still inadequate for major research. A beautiful new dining hall is a hit with students, but the renovation of the Student Union has attracted some criticism. "This aging-but-majestic granite building was completely gutted and now bears a striking resemblance to Bloomingdale's," one woman complains. Another building sports a pink and purple decor. Next project? A multimillion-dollar field house is currently under construction.

A bit less than half the student body comes from within the state, and mostly everyone else from northeastern suburban communities. Minority groups are eagerly recruited, and black and Hispanic students represent just over 7 percent of the student body. All of Colgate's financial aid programs are based on need; and while the college works hard to help any needy student, funds are limited.

Dorms come in both the single-sex and coed models and house freshmen and upperclassmen in doubles, triples, quads or larger suites with fireplaces. In addition, Colgate-owned apartments off campus offer one-year leases to an equal number of sophomores, juniors, and seniors who compete for the coveted places in the spring lottery. After freshman year, there's an exodus of men into fraternities and women into apartments. Theme housing is another highly touted alternative, and French and Spanish speakers, environmentalists, feminists, and majors in peace studies all have their own accommodations. Fraternity men eat in their own houses, while others use the three cafeterias, on either a nineteen- or ten-meal plan. A lunches-only option is used by many off-campus dwellers. The snack bar serves the most palatable fare but costs extra.

Almost everyone is a jock at Colgate, and their love of the outdoors enables them to survive the Chenango Valley's long winters in style. The rural area is ideal for jogging or bicycling and interested students can avail themselves of a golf course, the college's ski run ("It's small, but fun and cheap"), a trapshooting range, and sailing, crew and canoeing on scenic Lake Moraine. Varsity teams take on ambitious schedules, and hockey and football teams are perennial eastern powers. One student sums up the attitude toward athletics: "If you go to Colgate, you'll play a varsity sport. If not varsity, then a club sport, and if not a club sport, then intramurals. If you don't play intramurals then you work out on your own. And if you don't work out on your own—you probably don't go to Colgate."

With Hamilton hardly more than a hamlet with a few inexpensive bars, frats dominate the social life—as much by default as by desire. Sixty percent of the freshman males join the brotherhood, and with the addition of three new sororities (bringing the total to five), there is an increase in fraternal interest among women. "For those who want to venture beyond the 'frat-bar' formula, student organizations do provide options, and the Pub, W. A. Gorp Coffeehouse and Cecilies present an array of jazz bands and comedians on a regular basis," one student reports.

Colgate has long suffered from an identity crisis: It is constantly trying to decide whether it has more fun being a sports-and-party school or a Serious Academic Institution. The administration seems to be solving this problem by promoting both sides of the school's personality—by sponsoring intramural sports and intramural parties, by designing and maintaining a rigorous academic program, and by encouraging its students to play hard and work hard. Together.

Colorado College

Colorado Springs, CO 80903

Location Urban	**Applicants** 2,370
Total Enrollment 1,900	**Accepted** 51%
Undergraduates 1,880	**Enrolled** 40%
Male/Female 50/50	**Academics** ★ ★ ★
SAT V/M 550/590	**Social** 🏛 🏛 🏛 🏛
Financial Aid 45%	**Q of L** ● ● ● ●
Expense Pr $ $	**Admissions** (303)473-2233

Almost twenty years ago Colorado College went looking for a fresh approach to liberal arts education and came up with a novel method of scheduling known as the Colorado College Plan. Students here study one course as hard as they can for three and half

151

weeks, nine times a year. This innovation, coupled with the fact that the institution is the best small liberal arts college west of the Midwest and east of California, makes Colorado College a good bet for able students who are looking to alternate intense periods of study with skiing, hiking and sunny Rocky Mountain highs.

It works like this: Under the so-called Block Plan a student takes only one course during each of the nine blocks, and a faculty member teaches only one. At the end of each course is a four and a half day block break, during which students relax, head for the hills or take part in concerts, plays or other offerings scheduled for such periods.

The advantages of such a system are numerous. A student can get immersed in one subject and concentrate on it without the hassle of juggling a complicated schedule or letting one course slide in order to get caught up in another. There is no rushing from one class to another, and classes can be scheduled for odd times and places if there is a good reason (astronomy at midnight, Spanish over the border in Mexico). Students and faculty can give each other undivided attention and get to know each other on a more personal basis. "CC profs encourage you both academically and in other areas of your life," says an English major. "I like that kind of interest in the whole me." Class size is usually limited to twenty-five students and the method of doling out places in especially popular departments like English and political science is handled like an academic auction. At the beginning of each year students are given ninety points to bid on the classes they want. Those who bid the most for a particular class will get a spot.

There are also, of course, trade-offs to such an approach. Students say it is sometimes hard to integrate courses with each other when you are taking them one at a time, but professors are putting a renewed emphasis on interdisciplinary study. There's also the danger of students burning out because of the large amounts of material that is crammed into a short period of time and the intensity of focusing on a single subject with no diversions. Some courses last for two or three blocks, but prospective students who are seriously interested in the natural sciences or other areas in which courses build on one another or require something of an incubation period should probably ask some hard questions about the intensity of study—whether the block plan will give them what they want. "Just try to imagine learning organic chemistry or calculus in three and a half weeks and you'll see the problem. The block plan is the Achilles' heel of these departments," reports one student.

Academic standards at Colorado College are high, and the block plan makes it tough to bluff your way through courses without doing the required work. "Students usually get behind and then stress out while trying to catch up," recounts a senior; "that's when block breaks save your soul." Most students feel, though, that once you get the hang of the block plan, the level of academic pressure is "intense but not excessive." But a pass/fail option helps to ease the tension. As part of the general education program, all students are required to take courses in Western civilization, non-Western or minority cultures and field or laboratory science. They must also choose what is called a thematic minor, five closely related courses that examine an issue or theme, a cultural group, area of the world or time period.

The college offers unusual programs in southwestern, Native American, and Asian studies. Some of the safest bets here are in the art department, where art history and studio art are welded together to give future artists a broader understanding. Political science, history and mathematics win the praises of students and administrators alike. The department of economics and business is undergoing some changes, dropping the conventional business major and offering a business concentration within the economics major. Students have yet to be convinced that this is a good idea. For variety, students can design their own majors. In addition to sponsoring its own programs in Germany, France and Mexico, the college offers exchanges in Chicago, London and Rio, as well as several other study-abroad opportunities through the

Associated Colleges of the Midwest.* The library is long on hours (open until two AM) but occasionally short on books.

Students at Colorado College are a bright and fairly independent lot. Almost two-thirds are from outside Colorado, especially from California, Illinois, New York and Massachusetts, and most are from well-off families. "Studied casualness" is the desired trait, but CC students aren't too laid-back: Close to two-thirds graduated in the top fifth of their high school class. "Politically, I think there's been an influx of right-wingers," reports one disappointed senior. "But rest assured that there is a bastion of liberal peace-and-justice supporters here, too." Eight percent of the students are from minority groups, and the school tries to attract as many as it can. One thing students share: "The Colorado College healthy look," says one English major. "Everyone is interested in the outdoors." The admissions office places great weight on the essay, and 15 percent of each year's freshmen begin their work at summer school, take off the fall, and then settle into the regular routine in January. The college offers a handful of scholarships in several fields, without concern for need, to students with outstanding academic promise. Thirty athletic scholarships are awarded to either male ice hockey players (the school's only Division I team) or women soccer stars.

Most freshmen live in one of three large or several smaller dormitories (the smaller ones are nicer), and on-campus students usually subscribe to at least ten meals in the dining halls. "Meal plans may very well be the least attractive facet of campus life," quips a senior. Upperclassmen may choose to live in dorms (the more spacious houses are organized around foreign languages or other themes) or in one of the five fraternities. (There are also four sororities, but they are not residential.) Only seniors are regularly permitted to live off campus, others are given permission only when the dorms are fully occupied.

The school's appearance and location are big plusses. "Imagine a sunny day with no clouds or smog in the sky, sitting on a grassy slope, looking at a fourteen-thousand-foot snow-covered peak," says a studio art major. "It's absolutely breathtaking." The seventy-five-acre campus successfully combines modern architecture and century-old stone, "Ivy Leaguish" buildings in a sparkling clean setting at the foot of Pike's Peak. The college is just a few blocks from the center of Colorado Springs and near regional centers such as Denver and Santa Fe, New Mexico. The weather is excellent and outdoor sports abound—backpacking, skiing, mountain-climbing, hiking, rafting and bicycling. A student-built cabin resides on school-owned mountain property and is frequently used as a student campsite. Campus nightlife includes dorm-sponsored parties and fraternity parties based on themes such as Cave Man, Hollywood, Mardi Gras, Space Gig and Fiji Island. And scheduled parties with the Air Force cadets, "Zoomies," are also popular with Colorado women. Those who are twenty-one may hit the happy hours or Murphy's Tavern, and Tuesday night is $1 movie night at all local theaters.

The college runs an extensive leisure program, including lectures, concerts and excursions. In addition, adjunct courses can be taken side by side with a regular course in such areas as lifesaving or languages, and "intramural sports enjoy extreme devotion from participants," according to one student source. Hockey is the only sport that generates campus-wide enthusiasm, though the women's diving and volleyball, and men's and women's soccer teams are also good.

"Anyone who wants a liberal education will feel at home sitting under one of our trees," a philosophy major believes, and the possibilities are "exhilarating." But in the end, it is the block plan that makes or breaks Colorado College, and a decision to go there is a decision in favor of the college's academic agenda. "I would not recommend CC for students who procrastinate or who are nonenergetic couch potatoes," warns a senior. If it works for you, though, it works well.

Colorado School of Mines

Golden, CO 80401

Location Suburban
Total Enrollment 2,520
Undergraduates 1,730
Male/Female 80/20
SAT V/M 540/640
ACT 26
Financial Aid 50%
Expense Pub $ $ $

Applicants 940
Accepted 84%
Enrolled 40%
Academics ★ ★ ★
Social ☎ ☎
Q of L ● ●
Admissions (303)273-3220

The Colorado School of Mines has been described as "the Caltech of coal, the Oxford of oil shale, and the Princeton of petroleum." It is an engineering school with an admittedly narrow focus, offering degrees in only ten fields, all related to energy, petroleum or mineral technology. But given the sad state of the minerals and energy industries today, CSM may be pulling its head out of the mine shaft and looking at its focused curriculum in a different light.

A cluster of architecturally diverse buildings and shady lawns nestled up against the Rocky Mountains, Mines' campus can readily be mistaken for a peaceful, get-away-from-it-all kind of place. But a study of those who live and learn here will prove why they don't call this "the school of hard rocks" for nothing. "You have to be serious about studying and willing to sacrifice a lot of fun and extracurriculars for it," says one junior. Pass/fail grading is unheard of, although failing grades are not. And while some teachers win undying praise for their accessibility and concern, others are known to push too hard. "They are overzealous to make the students good engineers." Yet CSM's administration is working to change this intense preprofessional attitude by instilling a new philosophy that "emphasizes the education of engineering professionals for careers as opposed to training them for the first few years of a career." One new development is the Engineering Practices Introductory Course Sequence (EPICS), a four-semester sequence in the basics of problem solving, self-education and communication.

All undergraduate major fields—or "options," as they're called—are quite good; the eager student may pick from among such subjects as metallurgical, geophysical, geological, chemical or petroleum-refining engineering. Less prominent programs include chemistry, geochemistry and applied mathematics—all viewed as service departments for the engineering majors. Courses in a student's option start in the second semester of the sophomore year, and, by senior year, courses are taken almost exclusively in one's field. Minors can be earned in a number of fields, including computer science, environmental sciences and engineering ecology—good departments for minors, but not recommended for majors. Students complain about the recent short library hours and say the facility is well stocked with engineering and technical materials, but there is little in the way of literature. "If you are just looking for a book to read and let your mind wander, you best go elsewhere," says one mining engineer.

Besides the two regular semesters during the school year (fifteen weeks long, two weeks longer than semesters at most other schools), students in some subjects must spend one or two summers gaining hands-on experience in their field. Many vary the pace through the cooperative education program, which can provide a welcome breather. For superambitious students, there is the Guy T. McBride Honors Program in Public Affairs, which invites thirty to forty exceptional freshmen each year to a series of interdisciplinary seminars and tutorials to prepare them for leadership and management careers. Many students end up taking more than four years to complete their difficult programs.

Mines is a state school, and more than two-thirds of its students are from Colorado. The foreign student body mainly comes from Latin America or the Middle East, and everyone agrees Mines students are a conservative lot. One geophysical engineering student offered this breakdown of the population: "25 percent squids (those who study twenty-four hours) and the rest fun-loving and willing to work hard for satisfactory grades." Aside from the 285 athletic scholarships—a quarter of them for women—about one-fifth of the student body receives merit scholarships, which range from $700 to full tuition and are awarded on the basis of high school performance, board scores and extracurricular activities.

The location of Mines at the base of the Rocky Mountains assures students of gorgeous Colorado weather and easy access to skiing, mountain climbing, and other outdoor sports. Occasionally students make it into Denver, a half hour away, or to the University of Colorado at Boulder for some nights of partying. Golden, where Mines is located, has little to offer besides the Coors Brewery. (The three-thousand-foot pipeline that runs from the Coor's plant to the campus is used to convert excess steam from the brewery into heat for the school, not to supply the frats with party hops and barley.)

The school's dormitories are comfortable and most are coed, though the preponderance of men results in a few single-sex dorms. Many upperclassmen move off campus, but if they reserve a dorm room at least six months in advance, they will not get forced off. The one dining hall offers several meal plans; aside from the salad bar, the food receives less than rave reviews.

There is life outside of the library, although the Miners may not always remember to live it. One senior notes that "CSM is probably one of the last places where you will find true student athletes—we play for fun." But what the school lacks here in quality it makes up for in quantity, boasting more varsity sports than any other school in Colorado. Some students join one of the six fraternities or two sororities—in which they find places to eat, sleep and (sometimes) party. But given the high male-female ratio, relations between the sexes are a bit strained. Men complain that there are too few coeds, which means "a guy can spend too much time with his nose in the books." Women, on the other hand, maintain that "most male students feel the female population is very undesirable and refuse to date the girls." Both agree there is not much time for socializing anyway. "Mines is a school to be endured, not enjoyed," says one student.

But if endured, there is the pride of accomplishment that comes with a CSM degree. "Those who stay and finish are self-starters who are willing to work for what they want," sums up one student. And, despite the recent depressions in their prospective fields, chances are very good they will get it. As one student explains, "Our school is thought of highly by recruiters in the industries and that's the best evaluation."

University of Colorado—Boulder

Boulder, CO 80309

Location Suburban
Total Enrollment 23,130
Undergraduates 18,930
Male/Female 54/46
SAT V/M 500/560
Financial Aid 50%
Expense Pub $ $ $ $

Applicants 11,410
Accepted 76%
Enrolled 42%
Academics ★ ★ ★
Social 🐘 🐘 🐘 🐘
Q of L ● ● ● ● ●
Admissions (303)492-6301

The University of Colorado is, in many respects, a lot like other big state schools. Engineering and the sciences are excellent, and the liberal arts are respectable. The dorms are overcrowded, and the huge introductory classes can make an individual feel lost in the crowd. But Boulder has one attraction—or distraction—that distinguishes it from the rest of the pack: its spectacular location in the foothills of the Rocky Mountains. With one of the most gorgeous settings for a university in the country, Boulder has become a haven for eastern preppies, blond Californians, and even Coloradans seeking to pursue the life of the mind in a winter wonderland.

The best of the state's schools, CU–Boulder offers entering freshmen the choice of five colleges—arts and sciences, business administration, engineering and applied science, environmental design and music. Each has different entrance standards and requirements; music, for example, requires an audition of all prospective students. Molecular biology, with its state-of-the-art electron microscopes, is one of the best departments of its kind in the country. CU can also boast of its space satellite (the only student-run satellite in the U.S.) and its six astronaut graduates who have made it into space, creating a rather stellar alumni roster. Business, engineering, psychology and the "hard" sciences are strong at CU. But despite limitless course offerings (CU boasts four thousand courses covering 140 fields of study), students find the foreign language and humanities offerings lagging far behind. The administration has launched a major enrichment program to develop strength in these area.

The campus architecture is patterned after an Italian Renaissance village; buildings are composed of flagstone with red tile roofs. "The campus is both homogeneous and comfortable, and has the look and feel of an Ivy League school," notes an administrator. Yet while CU may look a little "Ivyish," the similarity stops abruptly at the door of one of many infamous five-hundred-student lecture classes. Freshmen commonly complain that classes are very large and often difficult to get into. But Boulder has managed to personalize things somewhat through its residential academic programs: 320 qualified freshmen take part in the Sewall Hall program, living together and studying in small seminars, while the Farrand Hall program offers other underclassmen a structured academic program, also in a residential setting.

Students can't say enough about the weather, the setting, and the beauty of Boulder. "It's awesome," says one senior. "The campus is covered with green in the summer, gold in the fall, and the winters are mild with lots of sun." It's not surprising, therefore, that the number of out-of-staters, which make up about 30 percent of the student body, is growing at an incredible rate. Students from all over the country, especially New York, Illinois, and California are paying the hefty out-of-state tuition surcharge, which is now close to $5,000, donning their Vuarnets and heading for those Rocky Mountain skies. And what do they all have in common? "Everybody runs, plays tennis, rides bikes, and SKIS."

First-year students are required to live in the dorms. The word from upperclassmen is that accepted freshmen want to make their reservations early, and they want to make them at Kittredge, the country club of dorms with pine paneling and vaulted ceilings. "Late applicants find themselves in very small temporary rooms and are put on waiting lists for permanent housing," reports an experienced freshman. After first year, finding a place to live gets even more complicated. There's stiff competition for rooms on campus, and students have been known to camp out in line the night before room selection to get the room they want. But the majority of students, 60 percent in fact, prefer to avoid the competition and look for off-campus alternatives, which are often more expensive. Another 25 percent find rooms in their fraternities or sororities.

One alternative to the "decent, but not great" school meal plan or the horrid slop at the frat houses is the student-run Alfred Packer Grill. This snack shop provides fast food under apparently innocent auspices, but Boulder students and historical trivialists know that Alfred Packer was convicted and sentenced in Colorado for cannibalism in 1883. Are you still hungry? If so, then the idea of a student-sponsored Alfred Packer Day won't be too hard to swallow either. This twenty-year tradition includes rib and raw meat eating contests and a red onion munch.

Though students protest that the party scene here doesn't live up to its reputation, life at CU still revolves around having fun. The drinking age is twenty-one (except for 3.2 beer), and bars check IDs rigorously, but liquor still flows at parties all over town on most nights of the week. "The student turnover and flunk-out rates are high due to the unlimited skiing opportunities and enormous social aspects of CU," claims a surviving junior. Fraternities have grown in recent years and, to the relief of many, have also changed. Students note that fraternities are breaking away from their traditional "drinking club" image and are becoming more diverse in membership and activity. An increasing number of Greek social functions are open to all comers.

For the culturally minded, both the university and the town offer all sorts of films, plays, and concerts by top rock bands. It is easy to get around by using the free bus service that runs on campus and through town. While as one woman says, "sex and drugs and rock and roll are still alive and well at Boulder," exercise is the leading extracurricular. The student rec center with its swimming pools, squash and racquetball courts, three weight rooms and ice skating rink "is well worth the extra $200 fee each year," one junior reports. In addition, the opportunities for outdoor recreation are virtually limitless. The ski resorts are just over a half hour away, and when there is no snow there is still hiking in the mountains and fishing in the streams. Organized sports vary in quality, ranging from the ski team, which is championship caliber, to the football team, which is . . . well, "coming back." This rebirth has caused the students to rally behind their Buffalos and enthusiastically cheer them on to their second bowl in two years. Women's sports are reportedly not in the same league with the men's. In fact, one student states that women's basketball is the only sport that gets any respect.

While CU offers a smorgasbord of academic courses in all its five colleges, students still find it hard to resist the ever present call of the Rockies—a call that literally tears them away from books and school for an hour, a day or even a whole semester. In the words of one student: "If you are serious about books and nothing else you do not belong here. The atmosphere lends itself to having a good time."

COLUMBIA UNIVERSITY

Until 1983, Columbia University was the lone member of the Ivy League that still maintained separate male and female colleges. Columbia College is now coed; but Barnard College is still all women. Although the two colleges remain separate entities, students from both schools are often discovered in the same classrooms, dormitories and dining halls. And women from both schools often find themselves vying for the attention of the same male undergraduates, of which, women from both schools will agree, there are proportionally far too few. Yet Barnard and Columbia Colleges manage to maintain a love/hate relationship from opposite sides of Broadway amid the grime and glory of human experiences found in New York City.

Emerging from the 116th Street IRT subway stop, the novitiate will find, in the words of Stevie Wonder, "New York—just like I pictured it." An abundance of people, storefront shops, cafes, taxis, litter and bicycles characterize the upper Manhattan neighborhood of Morningside Heights. To many students' surprise, Columbia also has a traditional campus, one of the most impressive spaces in the city: a huge quadrangle with the squat Butler Library at one end, the imposing administration building at the other, and grass in the middle presided over by a statue of Alma Mater. But in a real sense Columbia University extends from Yankee Stadium to Staten Island. Its campus is Manhattan itself.

What's it like to go to *the* school in *the* city? First off, it can be very distracting. With cultural, political and social diversions to dazzle the blahs out of any student, it's often difficult to concentrate on the books. But after the obligatory sightseeing, most have neither the drive nor the money to take on the town each weekend. Instead, undergraduates find their own individual hangouts—from the blue-blazer-and-tie preppie bars of the East Side to the new-wave-rock cellars and the artists' lofts of Tribeca and SoHo.

Like most Ivy League institutions, Columbia University's prestige derives both from its graduate and undergraduate schools, sixteen in all. Undergraduates can enroll in the excellent School of Engineering and Applied Sciences, the two-year School of Nursing, or the School of General Studies for older students. But for most undergraduates Columbia University means either Columbia College or Barnard College—both top-quality schools with independent histories, reputations, and administrations.

Barnard College was founded in 1897, with the blessing of the Columbia board of trustees, whose members had decided that Columbia itself should not admit women. Today, Barnard maintains its identity as an independent liberal arts college for women with its own curriculum, faculty, admissions standards and graduation requirements. Yet, because of its affiliation with the university, it can make use of Columbia's libraries, courses and recreational facilities.

In addition, the two colleges pool their resources in a majority of departments and in the interdisciplinary majors of East Asian and ancient studies, and they run the fine Reid Hall program at the university's Paris campus together. With few restrictions, students at both colleges can take courses at the other. Largely because of Columbia's laboratory facilities, much of the movement is from Barnard to Columbia; but Barnard has a strong art department, and Columbia has none. Students at both school are also able to enter the joint-degree programs with Columbia graduate schools.

Well, it took until 1982 before Columbia finally decided that what it really needed was a few good women. But by that time, Barnard wasn't ready to relinquish its independence, and after long negotiations, the president of the university decided that Columbia College would simply begin admitting women as matriculants and thus compete directly with Barnard to attract the best of them. At the same time, Barnard gained control over its faculty. But the two schools did become closer in some respects by merging their intercollegiate athletic programs and forming a consortium under which they now compete in the Ivy League as a single Division I competitor under the Columbia name and lion mascot. Currently it's easier to get into Barnard than it is to get into Columbia. The median SAT scores at Columbia are higher, and the majority of overlapping accepted applicants head for the Columbia side of the street. If there's any difference between women at the two schools, it may be that Columbia women are preppier, those at Barnard more artsy and typically New Yorkish.

The division between the two colleges is sharpest during the freshman year. Each college has its own general education requirements, which occupy much of the time of freshmen and, to some extent, sophomores. In some ways, the us-vs.-them attitude created during this first year can last until graduation, but most students find that the abundance of shared extracurricular activities—newspapers, glee clubs, the radio station—leads to more natural interaction between Columbia and Barnard students.

With combined offerings of both colleges, the university, and the city itself, finding something to do is never a problem, but finding a good place to live can be another story. Quite simply, demand far exceeds supply. Freshmen at both colleges are guaranteed dorm rooms for all four years, but upperclassmen who want to move off campus must go up against the odds and a tangled bureaucracy. Forget independent trailblazing: Nearby neighborhoods are too expensive or unsafe, and there probably aren't many available apartments in them in the first place.

Although Barnard maintains its commitment to be a separate and supportive institution for women, common trials and rewards continue to shape undergraduate life at both colleges. In fact, when they graduate, Barnard and Columbia students receive the same degree—tangible evidence that, however separate their schools are institutionally, their undergraduate experience is to a large extent the same.

Barnard College

New York, NY 10027

Location Urban	**Applicants** 2,026
Total Enrollment 2,200	**Accepted** 45%
Undergraduates 2,200	**Enrolled** 46%
Male/Female N/A	**Academics** ★★★★★
SAT V/M 610/620	**Social** 🐻🐻🐻
Financial Aid 65%	**Q of L** ●●●
Expense Pr $ $ $ $	**Admissions** (212)280-2014

Back when most of the other Seven Sisters were still sedately turning out genteel, well-spoken brides for Ivy League graduates, Barnard College was educating women who, dedicated to their careers, already embodied the ideals of the feminist movement. Today, bright and inquisitive young women still embark on a Barnard education with career goals uppermost in their minds. Nevertheless, now that their brother school is 45 percent female, they do admit they wouldn't mind a date now and then. In fact, Barnard undergraduates are finding they must be as socially aggressive as they are academically adept. "Relations with men take an effort here," warns a junior. "You can't just expect to meet men—you have to seek them out."

The tiny campus, dwarfed by its Manhattan surroundings, consists of a diverse collection of buildings that are notably more modern than Columbia's. Contrary to popular opinion, says one student, "there are some trees and green, wide-open spaces— far from the madding crowd." Springtime sunbathers on the lawn can look through a lovely iron fence into Broadway and, across the street, Columbia. As for the neighborhood, "technically it's Harlem," confesses a sophomore, "but the gentrification (a favorite Barnard word of scorn) has enabled the area to be called Morningside Heights."

Barnard offers a combination of the intimate attention of a small, independent women's college and the resources of a major research university. English, creative writing, political science, economics, art history, and the premed program are particularly strong subjects, and foreign languages are superb. Psychology is dubbed excellent, and the women's studies program ranks at the top, although majors in this field must have a concentration in another department as well. Barnard students still must trek across the street if they want to major in computer science, but the school does have an adequate computing center/classroom. Barnard has no math department, and anyone who has survived a math course here—"The professors don't speak English"— would not recommend this school for serious mathematicians. In most subject areas, Columbia's departments are usually larger and have more offerings, but, with cross-registration, Barnard students rarely feel shortchanged. Rather, the small size of most of the Barnard departments creates a pleasant camaraderie among majors.

Barnard also offers several interdisciplinary majors unique within the university, including medieval and Renaissance studies and urban affairs. The Program in the Arts offers women the chance to concentrate on their artistic specialty—dance, music, theater, visual arts or writing—while completing a program in liberal arts. The Experimental Studies program, a holdover from the '60s—"a gut," says one woman—offers classroom credit for off-campus internships.

The 1980s have brought to Barnard new curriculum requirements designed to reflect the changing nature of our technological society and the fact that more and more of its graduates are going into law, business and other professions rather than academic careers. The curriculum includes a traditional freshman writing course and a freshman seminar taught by a senior faculty member on some broad theme such as "the modern idea of freedom" or "the rise of possessive individualism." Other requirements include a lab science, two courses in the humanities and social sciences and a course called "quantitative reasoning," the latter which almost always involves making the acquaintance of a computer or two. While these requirements guarantee Barnard grads intellectual breadth, the mandatory senior thesis project or comprehensive examination assures them of academic depth. The Senior Scholars program enables academically advanced students to substitute a single extensive research project for a semester or year of classes. While Barnard's small library accommodates both "lookers and gabbers" and the more studious ("You can find quiet stacks and not see anyone for hours"), plentiful gaps in the collection are easily filled by trips to university's libraries across the street.

Barnard professors enjoy the proximity of a research institution almost as much as undergraduates. But students, not research, are given top priority by faculty members. "They seem to really care about us and about the material that they enthusiastically teach," explains a women's studies student. Freshmen can have access to top professors, and upper-level seminars guarantee intimate access once you're seriously into a subject. Students say they appreciate the high proportion of female faculty members and the good academic and career counseling services. Psychological counseling, however, is criticized.

Ninety percent of Barnard students are from the top fifth of their high school class. Thirty-five percent come from New York City—which is more of a guarantee of diversity than one might suppose. There are plenty of wealthy East Siders, and a hefty 48 percent went to private schools. Minority students, more than half of them Asian American, constitute 24 percent of the population. "We're definitely an eclectic bunch," a political science major reveals. "We have Orthodox Jews, prep-school WASPs, punk rockers with purple hair and lots of 'regular' college students too." But, as one woman explains, "New York is the great equalizer, and students accept each other at face value."

A long-awaited eighteen-story Barnard dormitory tower will soon adorn the Manhattan skyline and ease the living situation of those Barnard students who have been housed in a downtown hotel. "There is no reason why I must live in a roach motel on 79th Street when the college tuition is $16,000 and the campus is 37 blocks away," exclaims a furious biochem student. Until the tower's completion, the college has one all-female and two coed dorms on campus and five off-campus apartment buildings. With rents in New York higher than the skyscrapers, demand for Barnard housing is intense. The college guarantees housing for freshmen but will "sweeten its financial aid pot to you if you choose to commute," one woman reports. Students living within an hour and a half of the school are normally expected either to commute or to rent nearby apartments, but they can also qualify for housing on a space-available basis. Lest anyone attempt to exist on a diet of coffee, Sartre and de Beauvoir, men and women in Barnard's on-campus dorms must buy a full meal plan. Meal cards can also be used at Columbia's John Jay cafeteria, but women say the food is better at Barnard— especially the homemade blue cheese dressing and fresh-squeezed O.J. Columbia students who want kosher meals must come to Barnard.

Commuters often complain that they cannot participate much in campus life; students who live on campus complain there is not much campus life in which to participate. Since Columbia went coed, students report that the social life has taken a nosedive. "I think the relations between men and women are more tense here than they are at other schools," analyzes an English major. Another student confesses, "I wish I had known more about Barnard's and Columbia's attitudes toward each other. This school always seems to be on the defensive, and I truly don't think it should be."

Meanwhile, Barnard's presence in New York City continues to dominate its social and academic life. And there are opportunities to get involved in student government, the school philharmonia, newspaper and radio journalism and other extracurricular activities, as well as winning basketball, tennis, volleyball and swimming teams. Barnard women are welcome to take advantage of Columbia's marvelous gym and the numerous coed intramurals.

"Sometimes I feel like I'm missing out on the true collegiate experience," says a women's studies major. "People at Barnard don't often throw raucous beer bashes and don't get pumped up for big games." But that doesn't mean four years here aren't exceptional in their own way. Women who graduate from Barnard are well prepared for the challenges that lie ahead—intellectually as well as socially. And for this degree of strength, they are grateful—"I've grown to love the fact that Barnard is all women," says one woman. "And I didn't really care when I applied."

Columbia College

New York, NY 10027

Location Urban	**Applicants** 6,800
Total Enrollment 2,950	**Accepted** 27%
Undergraduates 2,950	**Enrolled** 42%
Male/Female 55/45	**Academics** ★ ★ ★ ★ ★
SAT V/M 640/660	**Social** 🏛🏛🏛
Financial Aid 45%	**Q of L** ●●●
Expense Pr $ $ $ $	**Admissions** (212)280-2521

With all the resources of a major university in a major city at its disposal, Columbia College serves many different needs and serves them well. Some students come because they are eager to live in New York after growing up elsewhere; others grew up in the city and couldn't imagine living anywhere else. Some are attracted by the quality of the education and spend four years oblivious to the city's riches; others appreciate the friendly student body and the dearth of social snobs. Women come because now they are allowed to. Men come because, between all the Barnard undergrads and the rapid increase in female classmates, they've never had it so good.

Although Columbia is the smallest college in the Ivy League, its atmosphere is not intimate. The university's size (seventeen thousand undergraduate and graduate students), its urban character, and its lack of school unity can be a bewildering experience for timid freshmen. Students find themselves "growing up" rather quickly in this environment—"with the inevitable demands from the bums on the street and no winning football team to make us feel good, we are self-conscious in a very uncollegiate way," explains one older-than-his-years student. The campus itself is often called a city within a city because the center of the great quadrangle remains isolated from the hustle and bustle of Manhattan. The red buildings with worn copper roofs are set in a "well thought out architectural plan that combines beautiful neo-classical buildings with economy of space," notes one undergrad with approval.

An affinity for academic work with an intellectual, not preprofessional, overtone will guarantee one plenty to do and plenty to enjoy at Columbia. Most of the departments that offer undergraduate majors are strong, especially English, history, political science, sociology and psychology. Chemistry is the best of the generally high quality science offerings. The geology department has two hundred acres of seismographic equipment set up in Rockland County. Students say foreign language offerings are comparatively weak, arts virtually nonexistent, and music facilities limited. The administration admits the economic and computer science departments are too oriented toward graduate students, but computer majors are benefiting from an increase in equipment. Interesting curricular options include combined majors, such as philosophy-economics and biology-psychology. Hardly a subject exists in which an undergraduate course is not taught by a prominent scholar in the field, and the depth of professorial talent is impressive. As at most research universities, scholarship is generally favored over teaching ability when faculty appointments are made, but students rarely complain about the teaching or accessibility of faculty.

The heart and soul of the undergraduate experience at Columbia is the college's renowned and challenging core curriculum. Laborious as they may sound, these required courses, focusing on cultural achievements of Western civilization, are applauded by most students—except for some of the female newcomers. "Much of the material covered in core curriculum courses is sexist and racist, very white-male-oriented," contends one emphatic sophomore who nonetheless is willing to admit that "the core is still very important and interesting." Two of the most demanding introductory courses in the Ivy League—Contemporary Civilization and Literature Humanities—greet freshmen and sophomores with their yearlong syllabi that cover, respectively, the great works of political philosophy from Plato to Freud and the masterpieces of Western literature from Homer to Dostoevski. Both are taught only in small sections, usually led by faculty members rather than graduate assistants. Art and music humanities requirements take one semester each, usually in the freshman year. Although these artistic requisites are not treated with the same reverence as their Western civ counterparts, they're eye-opening all the same. "Without the core music course, I would still think that Mozart is something only my mother can listen to," concedes a political science major. An elective course entitled The Theory and Practice of Science, taught by science and mathematics professors, exposes nonscience majors to the method, language and logic of modern science. Designed mainly for freshmen, this scientific theory class gives students enough technical background to read and understand classical scientific works such as the famous 1953 Crick/Watson paper laying out the chemical basis of heredity. Four semesters of a foreign language, and argumentative writing class, and two semesters of phys ed are also required. As part of a prestigious junior-year-abroad program, thirty students are selected to spend a year at Oxford or Cambridge University in England (Barnard has a similar program). Summer, semester and yearlong programs are available at the Barnard/Columbia Reid Hall campus in Paris.

With 45 percent of the students heading to medical, law or graduate business school (and enjoying 90, 95 and 100 percent acceptance rates, respectively), the atmosphere at Columbia is intense and the students, intellectually aggressive. "The academic climate is high pressure, but everyone is serious and competitive so it feels natural," summates a sociology major. A classmate adds that the pressure is highly individualized: "Some people choose to become uptight and others just do the work and don't worry about it."

Like the populace of New York City, Columbia's student body constitutes what another student calls "the most consistently diverse group since Noah's Ark." A fifth are from the city and nearly another fifth from elsewhere in the state, but the remainder come from all over the country and the world. Coeducation efforts are clipping right along, and since 1982 freshman classes have been almost equally divided between the sexes. Hispanics and blacks account for 15 percent of the student body. On the whole, the admissions office seeks "an urban type—or someone who wants to be." It's obvious that Columbia is looking for more than high test scores: The school rejects 40 percent of those applicants scoring over 1400 on their combined SATs. Columbia students share a seriousness of purpose that generally excludes the social elitism of more secluded Ivies. Despite recent flares of racially related confrontations between students, a tradition of liberalism continues on this, one of the '60s' most radical campuses. "I think the Columbia education has some liberalizing effects on most students," reports a less-conservative sophomore. Recently, a group of Columbia students took action that would make idealistic alumni proud: They padlocked the front doors of the administration building, Hamilton Hall, for more than three weeks, demanding the university remove its indirect interests in South Africa. Even when they're not demonstrating, Columbia students remain some of the most streetwise, socially aware students in the Ivies. "Snobby preps—please stay away," begs one student. "You won't survive in the real world." Following Ivy League policy, no athletic scholarships are awarded, nor are any given for academic merit.

Columbia, long known for ignoring the comforts of student life in general and that of undergrads in particular, has begun to introduce a few of the amenities that are taken for granted elsewhere. For instance, a political scientist tells that "dorms are improving year by year, and there's a notable lack of roaches and mice these days." The primary freshman dorm, Carman Hall, and three other rundown dormitories have been renovated. A new high rise provides more pleasant, albeit more expensive, apartment living—and some of the most spectacular views in New York City—for the students who occupy it. The new policy of four years of guaranteed, mostly coed dorm housing has yet to be tested, however, and a move off campus can still be a gamble.

Columbia's dining hall, which offers a number of meal plans, "has gotten better and better, and the food is actually quite good now," according to a satiated senior. At least one meal plan is mandatory the first semester, but most students turn down the institutionalized offerings or opt for the eight-meal-a-week plan after their freshman year. The student-activities center houses a small restaurant, but most upperclassmen prefer to cook in dorm kitchens (with food purchased at the low-cost student-run grocery) or eat out.

A small percentage of students belong to the seventeen fraternities (several of them coed) whose houses are situated near the campus. For most students they represent "places to go get free beer if there's nothing better to do," but one frat rat claims the Greek scene is rapidly expanding. Two fledgling Columbia-Barnard sororities have appeared on campus, as many predicted they would. "Social life at Columbia can be very unnerving if you worry about it," calculates a mathematics major. "No one is interested in making plans for the weekends—people just decide to do things impromptu."

One option is to hang out at the Entertainment Complex (call it "the Plex" if you want to be cool), the dancing joint in the basement of Ferris Booth Hall or the old standby King's Pub, which has tightened its scrutiny of IDs in light of New York's new drinking age of twenty-one. Lest the most popular pastime of Columbia students for decades be forgotten: sitting elbows back, legs crossed on the steps of Butler Library, "where the tanning is always great," and watching the world go by. On nice days, there's usually a free show—tennis, Frisbee or pickup football games—on the grassy field of the quad.

Columbia's football record is, to put it kindly, pathetic. One problem, of course, is that the football field is a thirty-minute subway ride away, and space to practice and play other sports is also limited. Nevertheless, Columbia excels at several varsity sports, including soccer, wrestling, tennis, baseball and men's and women's swimming and fencing, and a strong intramural organization always manages to find courts and fields for eager participants.

Columbia is a good school for individualists and urbanites, serious scholars and preprofessionals. Of course, it takes a certain mix of wit and stamina to confront Morningside Heights anew each day and bring it down to human size. "There are lessons of life taught here that cannot be learned at any other institution—Ivy or otherwise," says one streetwise undergraduate. But Columbia students don't appear to miss the ivory tower sense of security. As one student puts it: "When you walk down the street there are as many nonstudents as students, which provides a good sense of reality—older and younger people really do exist."

Connecticut College

New London, CT 06320

Location City outskirts
Total Enrollment 1,920
Undergraduates 1,650
Male/Female 40/60
SAT V/M 540/570
Financial Aid 52%
Expense Pr $ $ $ $

Applicants 3,000
Accepted 48%
Enrolled 32%
Academics ★ ★ ★ ★
Social ☎ ☎ ☎
Q of L ● ● ● ●
Admissions (203)447-7511

Contrary to what many think, Connecticut College is neither an all-women school (although it once was) nor an offshoot of the University of Connecticut. It is a highly selective, private, coeducational college that provides academic challenges and support to women who realize that any professional goal is attainable and men who wouldn't think of telling them differently.

Conn College's lovely stone Gothic and modern campus is located atop a hill and next to a 450-acre arboretum in the once-whaling, now-industrial city of New London. "A rural country school with an urban view" is how one junior describes it, and the campus provides a nice view of the Thames River (pronounced the way it looks, not like the "Temz" that Wordsworth so dearly loved) on one side and the Long Island Sound on another. Since its founding in 1911, Conn has been dedicated to the liberal arts. There are still general education requirements in eight areas, including philosophy, religious studies and foreign language.

Art, dance, and theater are superb. Talented dance students often take a few semesters off to study with professional companies, and theater majors have the chance to work with the Eugene O'Neill Theater Institute, named for New London's favorite literary son. Botany and zoology majors make use of the college's arboretum for field work. History, psychology and government departments are strong, and the fine Asian studies program features study-abroad opportunities in China, Japan and Hong Kong. English and math are less spectacular. And the once-strong music department has suffered from a lack of student interest, but the administration hopes to generate renewed enthusiasm through an innovative program in new music media.

Internships are encouraged, and about half the students leave for junior year. Some stay in New England through the Twelve-College Exchange Program,* while others head for Europe, Mexico or Washington, D.C. There are no teaching assistants at Connecticut College, and the faculty is generally "very concerned with the students'

165

academic and personal lives," a government major reports. Students appreciate the feeling of trust embodied in the school's honor code, which allows them to take self-scheduled, unproctored exams during finals week. According to a senior, the academic climate is moderate—"People really buckle down when it is time to study," reports a history major. "But when it's time to play, we play."

The student body at Conn College is a curious mixture of preppies and artsy-craftsy types, with a few jocks (computer and athletic) thrown in for good measure. A vast majority of the students come from New England or the Middle Atlantic states, about half from private schools, half from public. However tempting a target the nuclear submarine base across the river at Groton might seem, Conn College is definitely not a campus geared to political activism. Yet, according to a sophomore, students here are the uninhibited types who "feel free to express themselves emotionally and physically." Freshmen are admitted without reference to their financial ability to pay, but receive no guarantee that all or any of their need will be met. Low-interest loans are available, but athletic and academic merit scholarships are not.

The living conditions are among the finest to be found anywhere, a quality that some attribute to Connecticut's previous incarnation as an all-women's college ("the Eighth Sister"). In fact, after freshman year, almost everyone gets a single. This actually turns out to have a funny effect on campus traffic patterns: People stay home in the evening if they want to study and go to the library if they want to socialize. Ninety-eight percent of the students choose to live in the beautiful, old stone campus buildings, each of which has its own janitor and housekeeper. There are living rooms with baby grand pianos, fireplaces, and comfortable furniture. On weekends, everyone eats in a dining commons. But Monday through Friday, students eat in the small dorm dining rooms where the on-the-spot cooking sometimes lacks variety.

Students rather than the administration run the dorms, and most activities, including coed intramural sports, revolve around them. There are no fraternities or sororities on campus, but there are weekly parties—keg on Thursdays and all-campus on weekends—sponsored by dorms or other student groups. Though the male-female ratio is still not even, there is casual dating and lots of friendship between members of the opposite sexes. As in the olden days, some women students still date Coasties from the United States Coast Guard Academy across the street. The most serious of the school's varsity sports are sailing, men's and women's basketball, women's lacrosse and field hockey and men's ice hockey (the rink heats up like crazy if Wesleyan is being trounced). "One of my favorite pictures is of students sitting along 'the bump' that separates the two main playing fields and watching a guys' soccer game one minute then turning around to see our 'lady camels' in action with field hockey the next," a sophomore says.

Connecticut is notable among the high-quality eastern colleges for being located on the coast. There are gorgeous beaches and quaint towns within easy reach of the campus, and they make ideal playgrounds in the warmer months. New London itself receives mixed reviews. "It's a slow town," claims one man. "All the calendars in the city say 1971." Others find it friendly and enjoy the few good restaurants and "plenty of interesting bars." The campus is also an easy bus ride to Boston and New York (two and three hours respectively), as well as Hartford and New Haven (each less than an hour).

All in all, there are plenty of academic and extracurricular reasons for heading to the little college on the hill, but men who see the favorable male-female ratio as one of those reasons should guess again. "Conn College women are generally highly directed individuals," says one. "From its roots as a women's college, Conn gets a breed of women who can truly intimidate males. They are gutsy, strong-willed, and highly intelligent. Gentlemen, beware."

University of Connecticut

Storrs, CT 06268

Location Rural
Total Enrollment 23,060
Undergraduates 12,320
Male/Female 49/51
SAT V/M 500/540
Financial Aid 55%
Expense Pub $ $ $

Applicants 12,600
Accepted 59%
Enrolled 41%
Academics ★ ★ ★ ★
Social 🐾 🐾 🐾
Q of L ● ● ●
Admissions (203)486-3137

In a part of the country where many consider public education strictly taboo, the University of Connecticut presents a huge, hard-to-overlook disclaimer. Founded more than a century ago as an agricultural college—this is where America learned to get more eggs per chicken by leaving the lights on in the coops—UConn is now a comprehensive university with high-quality academic offerings in many areas. Never mind the fine herd of cows grazing on the rural campus; this is one northeastern public school to take seriously.

The campus is an architectural potpourri, with utilitarian modern and half-century-old red-brick structures dominating. The academic and administrative buildings are surrounded by the residence halls, and the entire package is engulfed in dense woods, miles away from city life of any sort. Preprofessional programs like engineering, economics, accounting and business administration are strong, as are nursing, pharmacy, physical therapy and, of course, agriculture. The Roper Center for Social Science houses the fine social science departments. The basic sciences, especially biology, are solid, and students compliment the history faculty for excellent teaching. By contrast, a junior reports that the communication sciences are weak—you can really slide through with minimal work. There is little to celebrate in the fine arts areas either, but computer science has been coming around slowly. A core curriculum plan, which will be required of all undergrads and will emphasize writing and philosophy, is in the works. The administration says it looks for teachers who can "excite interest and evoke a response from students," and students back that up. "Professors are responsive and helpful," says one woman. "They are involved in research but not to the exclusion of students." Academic advising, however, is minimal.

As in most state universities, classes are usually large—some meet in assembly halls or auditoriums—though students take this with a grain of salt and hold their questions for the much cozier discussion sections run by teaching assistants. Students in the rigorous honors program get more individual attention and have more demanding requirements. The futuristic library, with its computer terminals, video theater, and all-night study center, is a favorite place for both study and socializing. In fact, it's so popular that students complain because the "weekend hours were chopped, and on week nights you can't get a seat after 6:30 PM."

UConn's language departments run formal exchange programs in many countries, and business administration majors can participate in an exchange program with schools in France. Co-op programs for any major are negotiable and becoming more feasible options for students seeking to make contacts with city folk. There are several programs for disadvantaged or underprivileged students, including summer courses to improve basic study skills and special assistance to students in health science. UConn also has four branch campuses around the state that offer the first two years of the university's undergraduate program. Students who complete their work satisfactorily at these schools are automatically accepted at the Storrs campus for their last two years.

More than 90 percent of the students are from Connecticut, and nearly half of these in-staters live at home and commute to school. More than two-thirds were in the top fifth of their high school classes, and 70 percent of those classes were in public high schools—frequently in rural areas of the state. "The student body is very un-hip," claims a political science major. "They're conservative small towners who are apathetic and very uninspiring people." In spite of a low inspiration factor, the number of freshmen who complete four years and earn their degrees from UConn is high for a state school. Those who are in financial need generally end up receiving it, regardless of a long waiting list and "very unhelpful" financial aid counseling. In addition to five hundred athletic scholarships, the university awards about one hundred merit scholarships ($500 to $2,000) for a wide range of skills and abilities, regardless of need.

Housing is available to everyone who wants it, including transfers and "branchfers" (transfers from branch campuses). Though a few dorms are single sex, most are coed by floor, with the exception of the Independent Democratic Community, a communal housing unit that is fully coed. But dorm life at UConn is reported to be less than ideal: "The rooms are small and poorly maintained—the administration knows students don't have many options in middle or rural Connecticut." Students in the smaller dorms eat sit-down dinners (quality varies from chef to chef) served by student waiters, while those in the modern high rises dine together in one huge commons. Meals are not served on weekends, but many students would just as soon go out to the snack bar for some ice cream, freshly made with some help from those cows in the front yard.

Storrs is more like a large plot of farmland than a town; actually, "it's no college town whatsoever." There's no way to get to campus except to drive, but once there, a shuttle bus carries students around. "Social life is rotten here," one student bemoans. "The two (count 'em, two) bars in Storrs get old after a couple weeks." For road trips (few students spend their weekends in Storrs), Hartford is only a half hour away, and Boston, Cape Cod and New York are less than three hours. Only a minuscule percentage of the student body belongs to the fraternities or sororities, including, one woman says, those who can't get dates any other way. If there is one recreational activity available at UConn that most other college campuses can't offer it's "cow-tipping," that is, sneaking up on unsuspecting cows (which sleep standing up), and tipping them over. More orthodox sporting events are surprisingly popular for such a suitcase school. The basketball, soccer (both men's and women's), and women's field hockey teams draw a lot of support. Intramurals are, in the words of an English major, "crucial to students on a personal level because they're the best way to relieve tension."

UConn suffers because many of its wealthy state residents send their children to private, out-of-state schools. It also suffers from a serious location crisis—"Storrs is more rural than Iowa," exclaims a transplanted midwesterner who expected something different in an eastern school. But in the realm of academics, UConn does most things well and some things excellently. At a time of escalating private education costs, Connecticut residents might be well served by looking in their own backyard: The grass doesn't come much greener than in Storrs. And not just because of the cows.

Cooper Union

New York, NY 10003

Location Urban	**Applicants** 1,830
Total Enrollment 1,060	**Accepted** 17%
Undergraduates 990	**Enrolled** 66%
Male/Female 70/30	**Academics** ★ ★ ★
SAT V/M 480–590/520–730	**Social** ☎
Financial Aid 43%	**Q of L** ● ● ●
Expense Pr $	**Admissions** (212)254-2629

Ready to hear about one of the best bargains in American higher education? At Cooper Union for the Advancement of Science and Art, tuition is free. Students pay a fee of only a few hundred dollars to defray nonacademic expenses, such as athletic programming and the school newspaper. In return, they receive a high-quality, no-frills education in engineering, art, or architecture with all of the pleasures and hassles of being in downtown Manhattan.

This unusual situation came about in 1849 when Peter Cooper, an entrepreneur with no formal schooling who had made a fortune selling glue and railroad ties, opened a tuition-free school for poor students of "strong moral character." Other benefactors, notably J. P. Morgan, Frederick Vanderbilt and Andrew Carnegie, added to the endowment, which along with some real estate holdings, is enough to keep the place running. With no tuition revenues, some corners do have to be cut: Even the administration admits new engineering laboratories and equipment are needed, and students clamor for more light tables, copy cameras, and work spaces, as well as better computer graphics facilities. Still, Cooper Union maintains a reputation as one of the best undergraduate art and engineering schools in the country.

The academic climate here is intense, and the curriculum is highly structured. One liberal arts course is required each semester, but students say the pickings are slim. They are allowed to take free courses at nearby New York University, but many worry about graduating without strong backgrounds in the humanities and social sciences. Administrators claim that a recent grant from the National Endowment for the Humanities will help improve these areas. The engineering school, which has the largest enrollment, emphasizes applied engineering rather than theory and offers a 3-2 program leading to a master's degree. A high percentage of the faculty members are part time, mainly because the art and architecture programs draw heavily on practitioners in the field. Freshmen are just as likely as seniors to have full professors. Illustration and art history courses not offered at Cooper Union can be taken a few blocks across town at Parson's School of Design.

The Cooper Union library is small and closes on weekends, but students have access to New York University's magnificent Bobst Library and others nearby. Exams are for the most part open-book, and pass/fail grading is nonexistent. Classes are small and not difficult to get into, and student-faculty relationships are generally good. Some students cite academic, career and other counseling services as insufficient on this high-pressure, dispersed campus. "A great weakness of the school is that it doesn't offer enough psychological help for students to the city," one student says. The work load is enormous, but the result is camaraderie among students rather than competition. "Cooper alumni are just like people who have fought in the trenches together and survived," observes one veteran.

About 80 percent of the engineering students are from New York State, and more than half of those grew up in the city. Sixty percent of the architecture students and about 50 percent of those in art are also New Yorkers. Most are from public schools, and many are the first in their families to attend college. Twenty-one percent of the students are from minority groups, over half of them Asian Americans. A paltry 2 percent are black. Engineering students tend to be rather conservative, art and architecture students rather liberal, and "the mixture makes for a very interesting student body." Says one fine arts major: "An independent, organized, creative, and self-motivated student would fit in perfectly at Cooper." For students who demonstrate financial need, help with living expenses is available.

Cooper Union is what the president calls a "three-building, one-parking-lot college." There are no dorms. Unavailability of apartments and extremely high rents in the area force most students to move out to the boroughs or New Jersey, or simply commute from home. Food comes either in a brown bag from Mom, à la carte from the unexciting school cafeteria, or from one of the myriad delis and ethnic restaurants nearby. Picnics in the lounge are a center of social life, with New York's ubiquitous cockroaches presumably filling in for ants.

The combination of intense workload and no dorms means that campus social life is extremely limited. About a fifth of the students, mostly engineers, belong to a Greek society. The school sponsors a campus party about once a month. The intramural sports program is held in "a traveling gymnasium" of several different facilities in the city. Students organize clubs and outings around interests such as skiing, fencing, classical music, religion and drama. The colorful neighborhood is ideal for sketching and browsing. Greenwich Village, with its abundance of theaters, art galleries, and cafés lies just a few blocks to the west. One street over to the east is St. Mark's Place, the "hangout" strip of shops and restaurants where new wave has washed away almost all of past decades' bohemia. The Bowery is due south, and all of midtown Manhattan spreads to the northern horizon. There, in what one student calls "the center of everything good and bad" stands Cooper Union's stately brick main building, once the only skyscraper in New York.

Strong moral character is no longer a prerequisite for admission, but an outstanding high school academic average most certainly is. Median SAT scores are 590 verbal and 730 math for engineering students, 480 verbal and 600 math for artists, and 520 and 520 for would-be architects. Prospective applicants should note, however, that art and architecture students are picked primarily on the basis of a faculty evaluation of their portfolios. For engineering students, admission is based on a formula that gives roughly equal weight to the high school record, SAT scores, and the College Board achievement tests in mathematics and physics or chemistry.

Getting into Cooper Union is tough, and once admitted, students can expect very little help in dealing with the combined onslaught of city and school. As one student warns, those not ready to "play in the big league should switch teams." Surviving the school's academic rigors requires talent, self-sufficiency, and a clear sense of one's career objectives. Students who don't have it all can be sure that there are six or seven people in line ready to take their places.

Cornell College

Mount Vernon, Iowa 52314

Location Rural
Total Enrollment 1,160
Undergraduates 1,160
Male/Female 49/51
ACT 25
Financial Aid 75%
Expense Pr $ $

Applicants 1,040
Accepted 78%
Enrolled 41%
Academics ★ ★ ★
Social 🐵 🐵 🐵
Q of L ● ● ●
Admissions (319)895-8149

Ever get tired of juggling four or five courses at a time? Mixing up your hypotenuses and hyperboles? If so, perhaps the traditional academic prescription "Take four courses every two fifteen-week semesters and come back in the fall" is not for you. At Cornell College, students don't have to worry about consuming various subjects simultaneously; here, the eight-term year allows students to savor each subject, one course at a time.

At this teensy liberal arts college in Iowa (a much smaller place than its namesake university in New York), the school year is divided into nine three-and-a-half-week terms, each separated by a four-and-a-half-day break. Students are required to take a course during eight of the terms. They may elect to use the extra term for a vacation (often a ski trip) or else accelerate their studies by taking a ninth course at no extra charge. Another option is to take two "parallel courses" together for two terms. At the professors' discretion, courses will meet for either one long or two short sessions each day, but it doesn't really matter, students don't have any other classes to go to.

Cornell and Colorado College are the only two schools in the country to employ the one-course-at-a-time schedule (it's known as the block plan at Colorado), so it's tough to make a large-scale comparison to more traditional plans, but there are definitely pros and cons. "Because of the one-course-at-a-time format, I feel I am able to learn and concentrate better," says a psych major. "I don't have to worry about other courses and obligations." Other benefits include not having to put up with less enjoyable courses for more than a month, and being able to take a "blow-off" course (and *only* a blow-off course) when the weather is nice. Administrators, naturally, praise the program, claiming it improves the quality of a liberal arts education by allowing students increased contact with the faculty and total immersion in thought-provoking studies. They add that this pace of learning prepares students for the business world where "what needs to be done needs to be done quickly and done well."

The down side of this approach is that it can be difficult to pursue cumulative subjects like math and the natural sciences, and a one- or two-day absence can knock you right out of a term. But if you have the right temperament and attention span to deal with a highly concentrated method of learning, Cornell could be an enriching experience. In fact, many students here cite one-class-at-a-time as their biggest reason for choosing Cornell, and with enrollment up by 40 percent since 1982, it appears the OCAAT attraction factor is on the rise.

Cornell was the first college west of the Mississippi to admit both men and women. It stays true to its original liberal arts mission, with outstanding humanities departments including history, politics, foreign languages (especially Spanish) and English. Today, Cornell also boasts a rigorous premed program, supported by strong chemistry and biology departments. Economics and business (especially international business) are popular, as are geology and music. Students criticize the theater, psychology and computer science departments.

Cornell students can take advantage of annual faculty-led workshops held in all parts of the world—marine science research in the Bahamas or social development studies in Latin America, to name two—or spend a semester in any one of twenty countries through Associated College of the Midwest* programs. Domestic off-campus programs are offered to pre-politicos in Washington, D.C., to urban studies students in Chicago, and to geology and wilderness lovers in various field outposts. Combined degree and co-op programs are offered in several subjects. And the short, four-day breaks between courses are programmed by the Office of Student Affairs and include recreational and educational activities such as symposia, fine arts festivals, carnivals and athletic events.

"Not too competitive but extremely intense" is how one student describes the academic climate at Cornell. Because only a short time is spent in each class, there's no chance to slack off. Students have nothing but praise for Cornell's faculty, who are "willing to go to extremes" for the students' well-being; professors' home telephone numbers are standard information on course syllabi. Cornell does not employ teaching assistants, and class size rarely exceeds thirty students. Freshmen should expect to get closed out of the most popular courses—but there's always next month. Cornell's library could be better, and although channels exist through which to get additional materials, students complain this system takes too much time and money.

Two-fifths of the students are Iowans, and other midwestern states are also well represented. "But the campus population is really diverse, with small-town boys like me living with guys from Chicago or China or Denmark," a junior reports. "People accept each other for who they are rather than how many chemical equations they can spout, or how high their GPA is," says a political science major. In addition to need-based financial aid, Cornell awards a handful of academic merit scholarships ranging up to $2,500.

The campus is a collage of modern red-brick and sandstone Victorian-style buildings, some of which date back to the eighteenth century. The densely wooded and groomed-to-perfection campus is listed on the National Register of Historic Places, and violets cover the grassy expanses between buildings in the spring. Cornell perches on a hilltop and the view from the bell tower of the Gothic-style King Chapel is unequaled by any in the region.

Most students live on campus in small coed or single-sex dorms with "stark but quaint" rooms. Two apartment buildings are also available to upperclassmen. Everyone eats together in the Commons, where "the food is not exceptional, but is usually edible." Student waiters serve up family-style diners on weeknights. "Saturday is steak night, and we often have fun meals, like drive-in-movie night, California burgers, or southern-style," a sophomore reports.

One student describes Mount Vernon as "a community of about three thousand— other than that, it's cornfields." There exist a few local bars and a lot of peace, quiet and safety. Cedar Rapids and Iowa City lie less than half an hour away and boast more appealing nightlife. On campus, selective social clubs (nonnational fraternities) five male, five female and one coed) dominate the party scene—and not all students are happy about it. "I think the groups splinter the campus into cliques and are unnecessary at a school that only enrolls about a thousand students," a philosophy major theorizes. The spanking new $6-million multipurpose sports center is one-third complete. Cornell's football team is usually a contender for the conference title, and wrestling has pinned down a few national titles. Women do well in volleyball, and the intramural program is highly popular.

One course at a time is certainly not for everybody; neither, says one student, are "small towns in Iowa, winters in Iowa, and Iowa in general." But for students who can handle it, Cornell offers an intensive education in a supportive, naturally beautiful environment. Says a senior: "It's a great place in the middle of nowhere."

Cornell University

Ithaca, NY 14853

Location Small city	**Applicants** 21,030
Total Enrollment 17,900	**Accepted** 29%
Undergraduates 12,620	**Enrolled** 49%
Male/Female 55/45	**Academics** ★ ★ ★ ★ ★
SAT V/M 560/670	**Social** 🕿 🕿 🕿
Financial Aid 42%	**Q of L** ● ●
Expense Pr $ $	**Admissions** (607)255-5241

No one's going to tell you life at Cornell is easy. With rain, drizzle, slush and snow generally known as "the four seasons of Ithaca," just walking to class across the vast and hilly campus can be tough. And then there's the infamous academic pressure. A highly talented and highly competitive student body, demanding professors and a series of periodical "preliminary" tests leading up to finals are the main factors that prompted Cornell students to originate the communal primal scream in the '70s—an activity that quickly replaced streaking as the favored midnight study break on campuses across the country. Cornell may be, as one hearty denizen put it, "the only place where you walk up a 45 degree incline in 20 degree weather to get 30 percent on a prelim."

Though obstacles at Cornell are great, the rewards are greater. Physically dramatic, Cornell and its surroundings are breathtakingly scenic—or, as the saying goes, "Ithaca is gorges." Ravines, waterfalls and parks border all sides of Cornell's campus, which sits high atop a hill that commands a view of both Ithaca and Cayuga Lake below. The main academic quadrangle, presided over by a statue of Ezra Cornell, surely ranks as one of the most beautiful of any American college.

At the undergraduate level Cornell has four privately endowed colleges: the large and highly selective engineering and arts and sciences colleges, the tiny and elite five-year architecture, art and planning school, and a hotel administration college, with its own on-campus hotel, which teaches everything you always wanted to know about the hospitality industry. Curiously enough, Cornell is also New York State's land-grant university. Thus three more colleges are operated by Cornell under contract with New York State: agriculture and life sciences, human ecology, and industrial and labor relations (ILR). Three-quarters of the students in these contract colleges are residents of New York State who pick up their Cornell degrees for half the price at state university tuition levels.

The colleges of engineering and arts and sciences are the stars of the privately endowed campus. A&S boasts considerable strength in English, history, government and just about all the natural and physical sciences. Foreign languages, required for all A&S students, are also strong, and the performing arts, mathematics and most social science departments are currently receiving much-needed improvements. Among the public units, the agriculture college is one of the best in the nation, a good bet for anyone hoping to make it into a veterinary school (there's one at Cornell, with state support). ILR is strong in its specialty and comes as close as anything at Cornell to being an undergraduate business school. About a third of its graduates go to law school, a third to business school and a third directly into union, personnel or management positions. Human ecology is generally considered the easiest of the seven undergraduate schools, though any such statement should be seen as relative. Seventy-five percent of Cornell students ranked in the top 10 percent of their high school class.

Student-faculty relations at Cornell are far from ideal. Lower-level courses are generally large lectures (Introduction to Psychology draws more than a thousand students), though many are taught by charismatic profs who try to remain accessible despite the size of the class. But the impersonal atmosphere nettles many. "Most times I feel as if I am a statistic here," says a junior. First-year students have the opportunity for close interaction with faculty through freshman seminars, which are mandatory in the College of Arts and Sciences. In addition to their thematic focus, most of the seminars stress writing skills, and thanks in part to a recent $5-million grant, numerous programs to strengthen writing skills are available to all students. Classes in the Common Learning Program involve professors from several departments examining a modern issue. Small, popular upper-level courses are slightly more difficult to get into than the large introductory lectures, but diligent students who preregister correctly usually have few problems. Distribution requirements vary with school and program.

Cornell academics are notoriously demanding. "Here's the plan," says one seasoned veteran, "C if you do almost nothing. B if you sincerely try. A if you scurry like the devil and jeopardize your health." The results: A's are almost as rare as C's, but not quite, and B's are ubiquitous. According to a biology major, Cornell's intense competition is fed by a "combination of self-imposed and university-imposed pressure" that reaches its fiercest levels among premeds and other preprofessionals.

The library system is by any account superb. With fifteen branches around campus, Cornell students have access to more than five million volumes. "Few undergrads are able to exhaust the library's material while doing research, let alone have to go elsewhere for needed information," testifies one history major. "There is a free bus to take you home from the libes at night," a family studies major adds. With more than four thousand courses offered every year, Cornell is a massive potpourri of opportunities—"I've studied everything from organic chemistry to wine tasting and sex," says a senior. For those whose curiosity is still not satisfied, co-op programs are available to engineering and human ecology students, and Cornell-in-Washington is a popular semester program for public policy students. Students looking to study abroad can do so at nine locations in Western Europe and the Middle East, while those in the College of Art, Architecture and Planning have the benefit of a special Cornell-in-Rome program.

Potential students apply to one of the seven schools through the central admissions office; and though standards at the various units differ, no Cornell students are intellectual slouches. The mixture of public and private, vocational and liberal arts at one institution provides a diversity of students rare among America's colleges. Just over half the students are from New York State, and blacks and Hispanics account for about 9 percent of the students. Gays and feminists are also well represented and well organized. "The campus has both liberals and conservatives, although the liberals seem to shout a bit louder," a junior says. The state schools draw a large number of students from upstate New York, Ohio and other parts of the Midwest, while arts and sciences and engineering draw well from the tri-state metropolitan New York City area (including Lawn-Guy-Lind), and New England. Whatever their origin, all seem self-motivated and able to work hard. "Common sense and perseverance" serve you well at Cornell, a computer science major says.

Cornell is need-blind in admissions, and meets the demonstrated need of all accepted applicants. Cornell takes pride in the alumni-developed Cornell Tradition, a unique program of fellowships for students on financial aid who are willing to work extra hours each week. In addition to their salaries, the students receive up to $2,000 to partly replace loans, enabling them to be relatively free of debt after they leave the university. An effective job referral network also makes use of loyal alumni contacts to procure summer jobs and internships for students.

The university's housing comes in a wide variety of styles and quality divided between two areas. On west campus where most of the freshmen are quartered, the dorms tend to be old and a little run down (small and ugly doubles) but also the most social on campus. On the north campus, where most of the upper-class boarders reside, the halls are newer and quieter. There is a small number of highly coveted apartments with kitchens and a greater number of spaces in suites—six large double rooms with a common living area. Freshmen, sophomores and a few upperclassmen are spread out in countless other living arrangements. Every year, a few freshmen find themselves living in lounges until other accommodations open up, though some new residence halls now under construction should make space more plentiful. Upperclassmen who don't enter the housing lottery can try their luck in Collegetown, the blocks of apartments and houses within walking distance of the campus, where demand keeps the housing market tight and rents high. Cornell's food service is reputedly among the best in the nation. Students may choose among one of several meal plans or pay à la carte. Milk products and some meats come right from the agriculture school, and about twice a semester a Cross-Country Gourmet team—the staff of a famous restaurant—comes to campus and prepares its specialties en masse.

Fraternities and sororities draw just under half the students and are an important source of housing and dining as well as social activities. The more than fifty fraternities and twenty sororities each throw at least one large party a year to entice new enrollees. Though a recent rise in the drinking age has put a damper on the Greek scene, freshmen can still spend more than a month of Saturdays drifting from house to house. Collegetown bars are also an option, but they too are less lively now that all under twenty-one are barred. Weekends are about the only time people permit themselves to take a break from work, but during the fleeting hours when books are far from everyone's mind the campus metamorphoses. "Since Cornell students spend a lot of time studying they seem to indulge themselves on weekends by partying," explains one student in human ecology. A new $22-million performing arts center is currently under construction, and there are innumerable movies, concerts and sports events, both at the college and in Ithaca. In addition, more than a hundred extracurricular clubs ranging from "a tanning society to a society of women engineers make it very difficult to get bored." For the few who manage to, there is always nearby Ithaca College, a favorite haunt of Cornell men frustrated by the Cornell social scene.

Hockey is unquestionably the dominant sport on campus, and camping out in line for season tickets is an annual ritual. The Big Red football program, recently revived after years in the Ivy League cellar, has become a top contender for the league championship. Lacrosse and men's basketball are also strong, while gymnastics and volleyball are among the best women's teams. There are plenty of intramural activities, including more than a hundred hockey teams, organized around dorms, fraternities and other organizations. Athletes of all types are sure to benefit from the completion of another big construction project, a $26-million sports and recreation complex. Greek Peak Mountain is nearby for skiing, Cayuga Lake for boating and swimming and lots of areas exist for hiking and just watching the clouds roll by.

Yes, the clouds roll by the beautiful campus, but some Cornell students rarely see them; they are too busy proving to themselves, their parents and the rest of the Ivy

League that they are top students who, but for the luck of the draw, would be at Harvard or Yale. Some feel a parallel pressure to achieve socially: to put in a significant amount of "face-time" (Cornellian for meaning "having your face seen with the right people in the right place at the right time") at fraternities and campus functions. The happiest Cornell student is the sort who can set his or her own individual limits and standards and take any sort of pressure, or precipitation, in stride. This is the sort of student who finds the school stimulating, enlightening and rewarding. "Princeton was my first choice, but I'm glad I ended up at Cornell," says an engineering major. "The people are more diverse, less stuffy, and more real."

Depending on your own personality and goals, Cornell's demanding academic standards and eclectic grouping of buttoned-down preprofessionals and earthy New York vocational types are either good reasons to come to this particular ivy-covered campus on a hill, or good reasons to head in another direction.

University of Dallas

Irving, TX 75061

Location Suburban	**Applicants** 1,050
Total Enrollment 2,540	**Accepted** 85%
Undergraduates 1,040	**Enrolled** 25%
Male/Female 47/53	**Academics** ★ ★ ★
SAT V/M 590/610	**Social** ☎ ☎
ACT 27	**Q of L** ● ● ●
Financial Aid 47%	**Admissions** (214)721-5266
Expense Pr $	

Students considering the University of Dallas should have a passion for antiquity and a taste for pasta, as well as a valid passport. For while the education offered at the suburban Dallas campus is fine, it is this Roman Catholic university's satellite campus in Rome, Italy, that really sets UD apart from other small liberal arts colleges. Virtually the entire sophomore class—more than 85 percent—participates in the Rome program, and this mind-broadening experience is exemplary of what draws many UD students to the Southwest for a liberal arts education. Those who are interested in learning anything and everything thrive at UD, according to one student. "As long as they can come to terms with realizing how little they do know."

Any of the liberal arts–only majors at UD are enriched by the Italian semester, during which students study art, architecture, classical literature and the development of Western civilization. There are supervised side trips to Florence, Assisi and Greece, as well as many chances to interact with Romans and their culture. "Frankly, this was my most fruitful semester," a senior reflects. "I learned not only the course material but a lot about my life as an American in comparison with European life." The Rome semester is considered part of the UD core curriculum, which attempts to teach the Greco-Roman foundations of Western civilization, with the Church as the proper vessel of this heritage. "When you are a freshman, we whet your appetite with Homer, Aristotle, Dante and Milton," officials say. And then they send you to the Eternal City for an experience you're guaranteed not to forget.

Students looking for technical training or job assurances after graduation will not find them here; UD has a large graduate business school, but on the undergraduate level, enthusiasm for the traditional liberal arts has barely been dampened by the country's rising vocational tide. Political philosophy is a popular major, although students claim that most courses tend to be slanted toward the conservative view of politicking. The English department is highly praised for its "incredible strength" in both the presentation of literary criticism and its close examination of the literary cycle from Virgil through T. S. Eliot. Premed students are well served by the biology and chemistry programs, and more than 95 percent of them are accepted into medical schools. The elementary and secondary education majors, as well as the art and drama departments demonstrate a lot of potential. But physics, math and economics programs are less attractive, and the phenomenological psychology program is described by one student as "not exactly weak, but very unusual." There are no engineering or computer science programs at UD, and few computer terminals are available to students. Save for one overworked woman who tries to keep several choirs going, the music department is nonexistent.

In keeping with the Church-vessel philosophy, two religion courses (Understanding the Bible and Western Theological Tradition) are required of all students. Those inclined toward the sciences may take advantage of the John B. O'Hara Chemical Science Institute, which offers a hands-on nine-week summer program. This project is designed to prepare undergraduates for independent research early in their academic career. Some students may also qualify as Constantin Scholars and thereby structure an individual course of study. There is at least one aspect of the great tradition of Western civilization that is not fulfilled at UD: Student assessment of the library ranges from "minimally adequate," to "pitiful." But an interloan system has been set up with nearby SMU and the excellent Dallas Public Library, and the administration has made promises of new books to come.

The campus occupies a pastoral home adjacent to a Dallas suburb and is on top of "the closest thing this region has to a hill." According to one student's account, "the style of the campus is well suited to the natural landscape, which, unfortunately, is nothing to write home about." The primary tone of the buildings is brown, and the architecture, as described by a senior, is "post-1950s done in brick—typical Catholic-institutional." While it may not be a picture-perfect school, it does have a new, aesthetically pleasing chapel, and its students do not suffer from a lack of either fresh air or wide open space. There are also trees, grass and graceful stone landscaping.

Most students take their studies seriously, and almost all take advantage of the low student-teacher ratio by getting to know their professors. "In my four years here," reflects an English lit major, "I have never known of any professor being inaccessible to any student." About 30 percent of faculty are priests; over 90 percent hold doctoral degrees. Getting into the small, personal classes is usually not a problem—"When a class is 'full,' one just brings one's own chair," states a biochemistry major.

Nearly 70 percent of UD students are Catholic, and many choose this school specifically because of its religious affiliation. Slightly more than half of the student body is from Texas, but those who aren't could be from almost anywhere: New England, New York, California or Japan. Seven percent of students are Hispanic, and only about 1 percent are black. UDers tend to be pretty far to the right politically, and ahead of the crowd academically, though a philosophy major adds, "We welcome liberals for debates so that we don't lose touch with what we're fighting for." Rules governing dorms and conduct reflect a traditional religious orientation, with which students tend to feel comfortable.

More than half the student body receives some form of aid at an average of $6,400 a pop (that's more than the cost of tuition). UD also offers 230 merit scholarships, ranging from $750 to full tuition, to attract quality students. The university administers an annual exam for these scholarships, and also considers class rank, personal interviews and test scores, or a combination thereof. Virtually all students who need financial help can get it, although no athletic scholarships are offered. Many students list a generous award as one of their main reasons for deciding to attend UD.

There is one "spacious and comfortable dining hall, which has a wonderful view of North Dallas," and then there's the Rathskeller that serves snacks and fast food. The section of Irving that immediately surrounds UD does not offer a variety of haute cuisine, and most students eat on campus. The food is tolerable, "but not overly habit forming," explains one upperclassman. "The menu is based on what the students want and not on the whims of the meal service," adds another. All freshmen and sophomores, and the majority of upperclassmen as well, live on campus in single-sex dorms, "where visitation regulations are relatively strict," one student reports. There are no fraternities or sororities at UD; therefore, the dorms tend to serve as "houses," where "a great effort is made to maintain a sense of community." Although there is plenty of housing to go around, off-campus living is allowed, and many students reside in nearby apartments.

Though located right across the street from Texas Stadium, home of the Dallas Cowboys, the University of Dallas is fairly unique for a Texas school in that its entire population, including faculty, administration and janitorial staff, does not become rabid at the sight of a football. Intercollegiate sports are deemphasized—golf and baseball teams were disbanded—but the soccer team has done fairly well in competition with other small colleges, and the rugby club is not too bad. Intramural sports, on the other hand, are well organized and very popular. "This is not a school for athletics, but rather scholar athletes," reports a biochemistry major. Aside from the intramurals, one student states, "I don't know that we have any extracurricular activities."

Indeed, with no fraternities or sororities at UD—"and there never will be," declares a student—most on-campus entertainment is sponsored by the student government. Three free movies a week, dances, visiting speakers and colloquia are usually on the agenda. Church-related and religious activities provide fulfilling social outlets for a goodly number of students, and despite its lack of sports and fraternity enthusiasts, UD goes all out for Groundhog Day. "It's the largest celebration on campus," explains an English major. "Everyone gets up at 4 in the morning, goes to groundhog park, etc., etc. . . ." Irving is a dry town, which doesn't bother too many students, one of whom states, "Hippies and moral degenerates should go elsewhere." The Dallas–Ft. Worth "metroplex" offers almost unlimited possibilities, including a full agenda for barhopping in downtown Dallas (about ten minutes away), and one of the Southwest's finest art museums, the Kimball, in Fort Worth (only a bit farther). Public transportation, however, is notoriously deficient, and students who wish to avail themselves of the delights of the big city, Texas-style, or even the mild amusements of some of the smaller towns, will need their own set of wheels. The school itself provides some transportation to nearby shopping malls and to Dallas itself.

The Rome semester and the personal attention are what UD students like best, and the liberal arts and religious emphasis are happily embraced. Most arrive on campus already belonging there. "Those interested in memorizing enough to just get by would be happier elsewhere," notes a senior. This is a school where students actually enjoy what they're learning: "We're apt to discuss philosophy around a keg of beer, just as if we were in a classroom."

Dartmouth College

Hanover, NH 03755

Location Rural
Total Enrollment 4,720
Undergraduates 3,670
Male/Female 60/40
SAT V/M 640/690
Financial Aid 60%
Expense Pr $ $ $ $

Applicants 8,730
Accepted 22%
Enrolled 53%
Academics ★ ★ ★ ★ ★
Social 🐘 🐘 🐘 🐘 🐘
Q of L ● ● ●
Admissions (603)646-2875

Several years ago, a group of Dartmouth students led an emotional campaign to have the Indian reinstated as the college's official mascot. The Indian, you see, had been the mascot for over two hundred years, during which time Dartmouth had been doing just fine as a prestigious small college for young men of the northeastern elite. But in the early '70s, the administration did away with the Indian, claiming it was offensive to Native Americans, and things haven't been the same since.

The on-going dispute over the mascot is but one small manifestation of the institutional upheaval that has convulsed Dartmouth over the past two decades. In the '70s, with the coming of coeducation and diversification, a farsighted president wrought profound changes at this most conservative Ivy League school, and the Dartmouth of old became little more than a gleam in the eyes of nostalgic alumni. The '80s, however, have seen a resurgence of conservatism among students—hence the flap over the mascot. Today, the controversy over Dartmouth's course in the '80s continues; conservatives are angry, liberals are outraged, blacks and homosexuals are offended, a president of five years has resigned, and Dartmouth continues its attempts to reconcile a traditionalist past with its role as a leading center of liberal learning.

Much is questioned and considered at Dartmouth, but academic excellence is taken for granted. Set on a "little dreamland just inserted into the New Hampshire Valley, Dartmouth's small student body and outstanding teaching-oriented faculty make it far and away the most intimate of the Ivys. Three professional schools—business, engineering and medicine—provide additional resources, but Dartmouth's raison d'être is the undergraduate liberal arts. Departments that get the highest marks include religion, government, English and history. Students also praise geology, education and math, while only economics and biology draw complaints. Dartmouth is perhaps most renowned for foreign languages, which are taught through the Intensive Language Model, developed by John Rassias, a nationally known professor of romance languages and literature who occasionally shows up at a French class dressed like Montesquieu and smashes an egg on a student's head to illustrate a French proverb. Computer science is also among the best in the nation, thanks in no small part to John Kemeny, the former Dartmouth president who coinvented the BASIC language and now teaches freshman computer science. Computer literacy is a way of life at Dartmouth; indeed, Dartmouth has gone further than any other college in the country in extending computing and word processing to every aspect of the curriculum from physics to philosophy. Virtually every academic and residential room on campus is hard-wired to the college mainframe, and three-quarters of the freshman class of '88 bought their own PCs.

Students are generally enthusiastic about their professors—and little wonder. Dartmouth is the only Ivy League college that explicitly rates teaching ability over scholarship when granting tenure. "Dartmouth professors still maintain that old-fashioned belief in one-on-one contact with their students," an undergrad attests. The most senior faculty member carries the same teaching load as a beginning one. As a history major puts it, "You pay for professors, you get professors." Grading is consistently tough, and A's are rare. Peer pressure takes a funny guise at Dartmouth, where almost everyone wants to do well, but knows too much studying is definitely not cool. "A typical student will go without sleep for two nights while working on a paper and brag to his friends how little effort was put into it," a junior reports.

Incoming students receive immediate indoctrination to the written word at the college level: a composition course followed by a mandatory freshman seminar that focuses on developing research and discussion skills. Students must also take three terms of physical education, four courses each in the humanities, sciences and social sciences, and master a foreign language by sophomore year.

The school's most important innovation is the Dartmouth Plan, under which the school operates year-round with four ten-week terms a year, including one during the summer. The plan, which enabled the school to accept an extra 250 students a year without increasing its physical plant, was implemented over two decades ago when the school went coed. It was a way of placating alumni who feared that admitting any fewer than the traditional "1,000 men of Dartmouth" each year would weaken the football and other teams. Since then the ratio of men to women has evened out, but the decision to go coeducational remains a sore point for some Dartmouth alumni—who are, it seems, the only ones in the Ivy League who have yet to figure out that half of their children are girls.

Under the D-plan, freshmen must spend fall through spring terms on campus, but after that students may choose any enrollment pattern they wish as long as they spend the summer after their sophomore year on campus. Students use their time off for jobs, internships, the Twelve-College Exchange, or travel. More than half the student body enters one of Dartmouth's forty-five—that's right, forty-five—programs of foreign study, either for intensive language training (a nice way to fulfill the language requirement) or a departmental excursion (philosophy in Scotland, biology in the Caribbean, for example). Although students praise the flexibility of their "free-form four years," this revolving-door style of education can be rough on relationships, since friends, classmates and couples are not always on campus at the same time.

The quarter system creates a hectic academic pace, with hardly a break between classes and finals, although a few pass/fail courses relieve some tension. Exceptional students in most majors can join an honors track that emphasizes intensive independent and tutorial study. The library, with more than a million volumes, is one of the biggest undergraduate facilities in the nation and is the academic and social headquarters of the campus.

Set around a picturesque New England green with Baker Library at one end and a college-owned inn at the other, Dartmouth's compact campus is dominated by green copper-topped colonial-frame structures and a small number of more modern buildings, like the computer center. Although the nearest significant urban area (Boston) is two and a half hours away, the Hopkins Center for the Creative and Performing Arts and the Artist in Residence program add a touch of culture to the rural campus.

In many ways, Dartmouth is a different breed of Ivy from the Harvards and the Yales of the liberal establishment. With thriving fraternities and abundant school spirit, Dartmouth is a throwback to the days when penny loafers and college sweaters were a student's stock in trade. The college's powerful and intensely loyal alumni are the self-appointed keepers of the flame. This burgeoning family tree began to take root in the days before the interstate highway system, when Dartmouth males had nothing to do on Saturday nights but sit around developing camaraderie of the sort rarely seen outside beer commercials. Somehow, the tradition survived coeducation and continues to thrive, though some current students say it is sometimes confused with inertia.

When Dartmouth was the exclusive domain of wealthy frat brothers, the college was like a happy family; today the campus is about as peaceful as Archie Bunker's living room. In recent years, Dartmouth's more liberal elements—mainly women and minorities—have squared off against the 1980s heirs of the Dartmouth tradition, and the result has been "a strong radical left and right fighting each other," according to a junior. A key player in the controversy has been *The Dartmouth Review,* edited by a small band of ultraconservatives, which made headlines a few years ago for its blistering attacks on blacks and homosexuals. The war of words turned to violence several years later when a group of conservative students demolished an antiapartheid shanty inhabited by liberal protesters. This and a dispute with faculty over the restoration of R.O.T.C. led to the resignation of the president in 1986. It's no surprise that Dartmouth has a championship debate team: There are enough issues raised on this campus in a single week to keep scores of students arguing for months.

Dartmouth undergraduates are typically outgoing, gregarious types who managed to fit sports and parties into their schedule all high school and see no reason to stop in college. An astounding 25 percent play on intercollegiate teams. "It is not unusual for individuals to attend classes, go to sports practice, eat dinner, study for four or five hours and then go out for some beers—all in a relatively normal day," a senior reports. Most undergraduates are gearing up for remunerative careers—sometimes at the expense of the life of the mind. One student believes that "a school of this nature should have a wider variety of intellectual discussion going on." Dartmouth has a national student body, though southerners are notably fewer than those from other regions. Students generally fall into the conservative category, but only a relative few sympathize with the cadre of editorial reactionaries at *The Dartmouth Review.* Even so, "flaming liberals, if they are easily offended, will have difficulty fitting in," an engineering student believes. Blacks and Hispanics make up a combined total of 6 percent of the students, and while recent racial incidents caused problems in attracting minorities, a concerted recruiting effort now seems to be paying off.

Dartmouth, which is need-blind in admissions, meets the demonstrated financial need of all accepted students. It became the first of a growing number of privately financed institutions to go into the business of selling tax-exempt bonds through a state authority to underwrite loans to families at low interest rates. No athletic or merit scholarships are awarded.

To the city dweller, Hanover is halfway to the North Pole but to the outdoors lover it's nearly paradise. Dartmouth's own ski area is twenty minutes away, and the Connecticut River is even closer for canoeing and kayaking. More adventurous types take to the wilds of Dartmouth's twenty-seven-thousand-acre land grant in the northeast corner of the state, where cabins can be rented for $1 a night. Most freshmen begin their Dartmouth career with a camping trip led by an upperclassman or faculty member, and the outing club is the most popular student organization. Love of the outdoors life extends to athletics, and football, hockey and skiing are the strongest men's sports. With excellent crew, skiing and basketball teams, "women's sports are not on par with men's; they're better," a male junior acknowledges. Few Dartmouth students miss the biannual excursion to the Harvard football game, when thousands of Big Green devotees descend upon Cambridge, and few Dartmouth freshmen miss the chance to build the huge bonfire on Dartmouth Night, the college's equivalent of Homecoming.

If the outdoors is a second home to Dartmouth students, fraternities are a kind of second family. Dozens of Greek organizations, some coed, some all-female, most all-male, set the tone of the social life at Dartmouth: rowdy and just a bit obnoxious. Each fraternity has its own atmosphere: There is one for "computer jocks," another

181

for the hippie types "with drugs on tap instead of beer" and another is something akin to Animal House—the film, after all, written by a Dartmouth alumnus. Some professors pledge a fraternity and attend the parties, while others remain paradigms of maturity. Several years ago, maturity won out and the faculty voted to abolish the fraternities. After an outcry from—you guessed it—the alumni, the school compromised by putting them on one-year probation.

Unable to get rid of the fraternities entirely, the administration has set out on a long-range plan to provide social alternatives. New dorms are being built, and a number of rooms in old dorms are being torn out and replaced with social areas and kitchens. In addition, the thirty-seven dorms have been grouped into half a dozen clusters, which organize activities and programs, and provide a sense of community. Freshmen are divided equally among the dorms and have a choice of single-sex or coed halls. Rooms are large and well maintained, and some of the older ones have working fireplaces. The D-Plan makes assigning rooms a bureaucratic nightmare, and the Office of Residential Life (known to students as the Office of Ruining Your Life) takes a lot of heat from disgruntled boarders. Sophomores are sometimes bumped off campus, only to be forced to break their lease and move back on during their required residential summer after the sophomore year. Aside from that special case, the 10 percent of students who go off campus have low priority if they try to return to campus housing. However, a three-dorm complex now under construction will substantially increase the space available. Freshmen must buy a twenty-one-meal plan in Thayer Hall, where the most voracious are said to acquire a "Thayer layer." Upperclassmen can choose from a variety of plans, but prefer to fend for themselves or grab quick meals at various campus pubs and cafés.

The Dartmouth student pub closed when the drinking age went up to twenty in New Hampshire, and fraternities were subsequently forced to shut their doors to freshmen. Both events provided an impetus to diversify the social life, and now dances, parties and movies at the student center, opened about a decade ago complement Greek activities. In response to the excessive imbibing of some of the brothers, Dartmouth was one of the first to develop a counseling and educational program designed to combat the abuse of alcohol.

Though the campaign to "bring back the Indian" never really had a chance, the battle over the future of Dartmouth has only just begun. Much depends on the new president, and how he handles the continuing discord. At stake is whether the college can maintain its special character—and the loyalty and devotion that alumni feel so intensely—while incorporating women and minorities as full partners in the Dartmouth experience. Dartmouth has always been a place where lively debate was taken for granted. It still is.

Davidson College

Davidson, NC 28036

Location Small town	**Applicants** 2,060
Total Enrollment 1,400	**Accepted** 29%
Undergraduates 1,400	**Enrolled** 60%
Male/Female 60/40	**Academics** ★ ★ ★ ★
SAT V/M 610/620	**Social** 🐿 🐿 🐿
Financial Aid 35%	**Q of L** ● ● ●
Expense Pr $ $	**Admissions** (704)892-2000

Davidson likes to think of itself as the South's answer to the Ivy League. Long a top-notch regional college for southern WASPs, Davidson is now working to overcome its provincial past and emerge as a leading national liberal arts college. The school was founded under Presbyterian auspices, and today the work ethic is still alive and well. With an excellent faculty and fine facilities, Davidson lacks only a national student body to join the ranks of the Dartmouths and Princetons of American higher education. And for any of you Yankees thinking of coming south, remember this: When it comes time to pay the bills, Davidson is about $5,000 cheaper than its cousins to the north.

Despite its continuing push for national recognition, Davidson is old-fashioned enough to view the "formation of character" as the primary duty of a liberal arts college. Davidson operates under an honor code that allows students to take exams independently and leave doors unlocked. Every entering freshman agrees in writing to abide by the code, and all work handed in is signed with the word "pledged." There are extensive core requirements in all subject areas, and little academic flexibility. The college retains its Presbyterian tie, and two religion courses are required. The strongest departments are those that feed students into professional schools—biology, chemistry, economics and English. Acceptance rates at professional schools run above 80 percent. Among the humanities, history and religion are viewed as best. Departments that do not receive high marks include sociology/anthropology, classical studies, and speech and theater.

Davidson's two-year interdisciplinary humanities program offers an unusual opportunity to study Western civilization in a broad historical context while fulfilling much of the core requirement. The Center for Special Studies serves upperclass students who wish to pursue independent or combined majors. A 3-2 engineering program is available in conjunction with a number of excellent universities. The college is committed to foreign studies—a fifth of the students go abroad—and the new Dean Rusk Endowment for international studies has beefed up offerings in this field. Students can take theme trips to study classics in Greece and Rome and art in France, or trek through India. Armed with a Sloan Foundation grant, the college is attempting to integrate computers throughout its curriculum.

Class size is restricted; you'll have to look hard to find a room other than the cafeteria with more than fifty students in it. The faculty is very accessible outside the classroom, and "students and professors at Davidson are more like friends than anything else," according to a senior. The academic pressure is accentuated by a trimester system—three sets of finals a year instead of two—and by the fact that every class meets every day. With no nights off at Davidson, it is no wonder that the library is also the social headquarters.

If the arts are liberal, the students are not. Most come from affluent and otherwise

183

august southern families, the children of doctors, ministers and businessmen. About 80 percent of the students come from south of the Mason-Dixon Line, and almost a third from North Carolina. Considering their backgrounds, it isn't surprising that many students head into law and medical school, or into the banking and insurance fields. Students are mainly interested in "corporate careers, college hijinks and maintenance of the status quo," a senior notes. A tight-knit community, Davidson maintains a low tolerance for dissenters. Minorities are few, and one student complains about "the narrow-mindedness of many students vis-à-vis women, blacks, and other minorities." Although not very accommodating, students are bright, and only four other colleges this size have turned out as many Rhodes Scholars as Davidson. Students are proud of their moral character, "not in the sense of being priggish, but in the concern with doing right," a senior says. Some students, however, find all this southern, Christian hospitality oppressive, and, after a while, Davidson can seem "too small and too rigid," which may be why many students go abroad.

Davidson meets the full financial need of students and is attempting to woo otherwise Ivy League–bound students with generous scholarships. The school offers numerous merit awards, ranging from $100 to $1,500, as well as four all-expenses scholarships, awarded through a competition, and a couple of $500 scholarships for students interested in business or banking. Its only athletic scholarships (fifteen) are given to male basketball players.

Most students live on campus in coed or single-sex dorms. Freshmen of the same sex are housed together and get to eat in Vail Commons, which is rated high for food and socializing. Three new dorms have eased the housing shortage of recent years, but they are farther from the center of campus and the rooms are somewhat small. Sophomores, who have lowest priority in the housing lottery, usually wind up in the new halls or else off campus. Upperclassmen may live either in the dorms, off campus, or in college-owned houses on the campus perimeter that hold about ten persons each. Most upperclass students eat in one of ten eating clubs, which maintain their own cooks and serve meals family style.

Social life at Davidson is limited at best. Although the college went coed in 1972, there are still three males for every two females (a ratio set by the trustees for reasons that no one seems able to explain), and the situation can be difficult for both sexes. The six fraternities, three all-women's eating houses, and two coed eating houses are the focal points of social activity on campus. All but one are located in Paterson Court, a place where freshmen are not allowed for the first five weeks of school. The fees the houses charge go not only toward meals but also for parties and other campus-wide events. The fraternities are not much different from the other eating clubs, and freshmen simply sign up for the group they want to join, with no rushing allowed. Davidson adds to the egalitarianism by requiring that most parties be open to the entire community. Students also flock to the 900 Room, a nightclub-cum-bar in the student union.

There isn't much to the town of Davidson besides the college; the city of Charlotte and "civilization" is twenty miles away. The school's small-town setting is beautiful, and Davidson maintains facilities on nearby Lake Norman for sailing, swimming, horseback riding and water skiing. Myrtle Beach and skiing are several hours away, albeit in different directions. Most students spend a lot of time outdoors, and participate in intramural sports at some point during their Davidson careers. Basketball is the big varsity sport on campus and is usually a contender for conference championships. Men's soccer is also popular, but "forget football," a senior warns. "We're too small and the only reason we have a team is because of a few diehard trustees." The women's tennis team recently captured its divisional title, though many students feel that varsity women's athletics suffer from neglect. Most freshmen try their hand at intramural "flickerball." Sorry, you'll have to enroll to find out what it is. The sports facilities have recently been bolstered by the addition of an indoor tennis center, and a new sports complex is scheduled to open in 1988.

Being different at Davidson means being conspicuous, and for some prospective students its blend of southern accents and conservatism would be a mistake. But if you prize community diversity, you might fit in here; and if you fit in, you'll probably love it.

University of Dayton

Dayton, OH 45469

Location City outskirts
Total Enrollment 10,810
Undergraduates 7,120
Male/Female 55/45
SAT V/M 470/520
Financial Aid 46%
Expense Pr $

Applicants 4,920
Accepted 83%
Enrolled 41%
Academics ★ ★ ★
Social 🐿🐿🐿🐿🐿
Q of L ● ● ●
Admissions (513)229-4411

Variously known in the past as St. Mary's School for Boys, St. Mary's Institute and St. Mary's College, the University of Dayton might best be known as St. Merry's. This 140-year-old Roman Catholic institution makes a point of tending to the social as well as the academic and spiritual needs of its students. Without condoning rowdiness, Dayton's president asserts that "there is a crying need for a balance of celebration and hard work" in higher education. His philosophy is happily enacted by his charges. "UD is known for its enthusiastic parties," one honors student admits. Adds a classmate: "Einsteins with no personalities would be better off elsewhere."

Founded by the Society of Mary (Marianists), Dayton continues to emphasize that order's devotion to service. More than eight hundred students in twenty different public service groups volunteer their time to activities that include tutoring local kids, reading to the blind, or working with the terminally ill. And like many religiously affiliated schools, Dayton prides itself on the closeness and sense of community among its students and faculty members. "UD is just one big family, as hokey as it may sound," a marketing major says. While UD occupies a campus that is "architecturally uninspiring," it is nevertheless secluded from the traffic and bustle of downtown Dayton.

Despite the well-developed social and service scenes, UD students still find time for academics, and several of the school's programs are excellent. Strong offerings can be found in engineering, business and the sciences. The liberal arts are less distinguished, though students praise the religious studies department. Communication arts is widely regarded as a gut major, while art, theater and foreign language programs suffer from student disinterest. Daytonites say the library, which becomes a social gathering place in the evenings, has adequate resources in most areas except modern fiction. Students are supposed to use the limited number of computer terminals only for programming, but hijacking for word processing is an everyday offense.

Students satisfy Dayton's general education requirements by taking courses in five areas: history, natural sciences, social sciences, arts, and philosophy and religion. For high achievers, UD offers a self-directed learning option (working on self-paced or independent projects), internships, and an honors program that features small seminars and a required senior thesis. The Interdepartmental Summer Study Abroad program is a popular ticket to Europe's most exciting cities, while the Immersion Program in Third World countries is much praised by participants. Students in engineering, business administration, computer science, and biology can take advantage of the cooperative education opportunities. Back on campus, academic advising is adequate, class size is kept to human proportions, and students speak enthusiastically about contacts with their teachers outside of the classroom.

Students, almost four-fifths of whom are Roman Catholics, tend to be fun-loving products of middle-American families. Over 60 percent of Dayton's denizens are native Ohioans, and, to everyone's relief, preppies are about as scarce as radicals. Dayton isn't terribly selective, and the academic ability of its students varies widely. Twenty-two percent were in the top tenth of their high school classes, but about the same number were in the bottom half. Dayton is need-blind in its admissions and makes an "attempt to provide sufficient financial assistance to enable a student to attend." Its twenty-four athletic scholarships go to tall people, male and female, who play basketball. More than five hundred merit scholarships, ranging from $1,000 to full tuition, go to people of all sizes with superior academic credentials.

Freshmen who do not live at home must take rooms in single-sex dorms, and the admissions office continues acceptances until late spring when the allotted spaces for housing are filled. The dorms are well maintained but noisy. "The women's dorm is a prison: No unescorted males and no men after 2 AM are permitted inside," one student says. For obvious reasons, upperclassmen often enter the lottery for coveted university-owned coed apartments and off-campus houses. The nearby student "ghetto," filled with cheap apartments for UD undergrads, serves as a sort of continuous social center. Block parties are perennial warm weather favorites, but most smaller affairs are also popular. "When someone has a party, the whole university knows about it; word-of-mouth is an art at UD," one senior reports. Campus dining halls are as lively as the living quarters, although the fare is unexceptional. Freshman residents must take meals either five or seven days a week, and seconds are allowed at the salad bar. Upperclassmen have the option of cooking their own meals, while commuters can grab a bite at the campus snack bar.

Greek organizations draw a small percentage of UD men and women as members but play an active role in the social life. Sports are even more important, especially basketball, with the hoopsters often ranked in the nation's Top 20. The football team, which plays in Division III, always draws a flock of loyal fans, and a recent trip to the national playoffs was another cause for active celebration. When students aren't cheering, they can participate in an extensive intramural program. While not a major metropolis, the city of Dayton does offer something more than student bars. The art institute, aviation museum, symphony and ballet are all just minutes away from campus by bus, and a large shopping mall is also easily accessible. Those who hunger for a more cosmopolitan atmosphere can frequent Cincinnati and its restaurants, shops, and sports teams.

Dayton's attempts to provide its students with a high quality of life sometimes lead to excess, and "too many students put socializing ahead of studying," a senior claims. Still, as a midsize university where the undergraduates come first, Dayton offers an attractive combination of diversity and personal attention, as well as opportunities for spiritual growth—and a chance to have some fun on the side.

Deep Springs College

Deep Springs, CA
Via Dyer, NV 89010

Location Rural
Total Enrollment 25
Undergraduates 25
Male/Female N/A
SAT V/M 680/660
Financial Aid N/A
Expense Pr $

Applicants 50
Accepted 30%
Enrolled 80%
Academics ★★★★
Social ☎
Q of L ●●●
Admissions (619)872-2000

Set in the midst of an uninhabited desert valley, Deep Springs College offers one of the most remarkable educational experiences in all of higher education. Twenty-five students, all of them men, are enrolled at this tiny two-year college, which doubles as a ranch and comes complete with crops, cattle and fourteen thousand acres of grazing land. If that sounds to you like a haven for backwoods types with nicknames like "Hoss" and "Tex," guess again. Deep Springs lures some of the ablest students in the nation to its rustic California campus, many of whom shunned acceptances at Ivy League schools to partake of its unique approach to learning. As one man explains, "Deep Springs gives me the opportunity to think about my values and beliefs in an area free of materialistic distractions." Best of all for those on a tight budget, nobody at Deep Springs pays a penny of tuition, and room and board is also provided free of charge.

Founded in 1917 by an industrialist who made a fortune in the electric power industry, Deep Springs today remains true to its charter "to combine taxing practical work, rigorous academics, and genuine self-government." Academic learning is the primary activity here, but students are also required to perform twenty hours per week of chores, which can include everything from cattle drives to cooking dinner. Students help evaluate applications to the college and choose the college's faculty; they even elect one of their own to be a voting member on the board of trustees. The students themselves enforce a spartan community code that bans both drinking and drugs during the term, as well as a policy that forbids anyone from leaving the fifty square miles of desert that surround the campus while classes are in session during the college's six terms of about seven weeks each.

California's White Mountains provide a stunning backdrop for the Deep Springs campus, set on a barren plain near the only water supply for miles around. Made up of a cluster of trees, a lawn and a few "somewhat ramshackle" buildings, the campus is twenty-eight miles from the nearest town, a thriving metropolis known as Big Pine, population 950. The focal point of campus is the "Main Building," a venerable ranch house that includes a classroom, ten dorm rooms, the library and eating facilities. Faculty houses are across the lawn a few yards away, and the trappings of farm life surround the tiny settlement. The college has 170 acres under cultivation, mostly with alfalfa, and an assortment of barnyard animals.

It should come as no surprise that course offerings are limited. The faculty consists of four permanent professors, two each in the sciences and humanities, plus an average of four others who are hired on a temporary basis to teach for a term or two. The quality of particular academic areas varies as professors come and go, though students cite literature, philosophy, physics, geology, botany and math as strong points. One student feels the social sciences are neglected, and another bemoans the lack of lab space, noting that the science courses tend to be much more theoretical than experimental. Partly because the faculty is so small, second-year students often get to try their hand at teaching; one recently conducted his own calculus course, and others act as instructors in an interdisciplinary Common Course, which focuses on the great books and is required for first-year students. The experience serves them in good stead later on; over half of Deep Springs' students eventually earn a PhD, one of the highest percentages in the nation. In addition to the Common Course, all students must take public speaking both years they are enrolled, as well as a year of composition that focuses on writing across the curriculum. Students at Deep Springs tend to be academic Renaissance men with wide-ranging interests in many fields, and according to one student, "mere bookishness or math wizardry won't cut it here."

Between seven and ten courses are offered every term, and registration is a snap. Each student signs up for any course that strikes his fancy, and the schedule is then made up to accommodate everyone. A library with twenty thousand volumes is located down the hall from the dorm rooms, but for anything beyond literary classics and a few other odd volumes, students use the University of California interlibrary-loan system. With class sizes ranging from two to twelve, there is ample opportunity for close student-faculty interaction. All faculty are fully integrated into the life of the college, and everyone takes meals together in the main building. Students routinely visit their faculty mentors in their houses, literally a stone's throw away across the front lawn.

For anyone wondering why twenty-five perfectly healthy young men would want to spend two years cooped up together in the middle of a desert, students have a variety of responses. One maintains he came "in a burst of idealism. I wanted the unique, the unusual. I wanted something different." Others echo his sentiments, though a few admit that they came for the "wrong reasons," which according to one man include "the novelty of ranch life, to build my muscles, to enjoy desert life." After the novelty wears off, the students who end up thriving here find sustenance in the intellectual and pseudo-intellectual banter that pervades the campus at all hours of the day and night. Says one man, "You have to be pretty self-confident and willing to work, and a little uneasy about the cultural games and stereotypes that are at a normal college." At least one student, however, feels his mates go a little overboard in their self-conscious philosophizing and complains of a "sense of elitism and pretentious intellectualism." An average of one student per year decides that Deep Springs isn't his cup of tea and decides to go elsewhere.

Most DS students are from upper-middle-class families, and 90 percent ranked in the top tenth of their high school class. Many are transplanted urbanites, more often than not from the New York, Chicago, or Los Angeles metropolitan areas. The rest hail from points scattered across the nation, though there is a notable lack of southerners. An Asian American and an occasional Hispanic number among the students, but blacks seldom enroll. Political leanings range from "ever so slightly right to far left," and bearded earthy types make up a significant percentage of the student body. The college's single-sex status, the one thing students have no control over, is a source of much griping. As far as most students are concerned, the trustees are a bunch of old fuddy-duddies "afraid of what would happen out in the desert with unsupervised young people." Every year since 1970, the student body has voted in favor of accepting women, and rumor has it that the change will eventually occur. After their stint at Deep Springs, students routinely transfer to some of the most prestigious schools in the nation. "I was accepted at the University of Pennsylvania, Cornell University, Harvard University and St. John's College. I expect them to accept me again when I transfer," says a second year student. With no tuition or room and board fees, students pay only for books, travel and personal items.

The dorm rooms, mainly doubles and triples, are assigned by squatters' rights. The building hasn't been renovated since the '50s, and one student reports a few leaky spots in the roof. Each room has its own inside name, such as the sunshine room, the black hole, and Petrie's room, named after a three-legged cat. According to one resident, "As students are wholly free to choose where and how they live, some inevitably live in abject squalor, while others, next door, live in relative comfort and tidiness." Students all pitch in preparing the meals, from butchering the meat and milking the cows to washing the dishes. A vegetarian option is prepared in addition to the standard buffet fare.

"We are out of touch with 'social life' as it is defined at colleges elsewhere and we are glad," says one man. There are no women to chase nor any beer to swill, and, even worse for a generation weaned on MTV and "Miami Vice," there is no TV reception. "We sleep for fun. Life is hard here," claims a first-year student. Perhaps the most popular social activity on campus is conversation over a cup of coffee in the dining hall, where the chatter is usually lively until the wee hours of the morning. Chess and comic books have recently enjoyed a surge of popularity, Ping-Pong is a perennial favorite, and for the athletically inclined, popular pastimes include games of soccer, volleyball, and Ultimate Frisbee on the lawn. Other common activities are walks in the desert, hikes in the nearby mountains, and horseback riding. Occasionally, the college will leave campus en masse, usually to go skiing or backpacking in the nearby mountains. During term breaks, students are free to leave the campus, and the nearest large city is Reno, four hours away.

Perhaps more than any other school in the nation, Deep Springs is a community where students and faculty interact day to day on an intensely personal level. In such a small group, the actions of each person affect everyone, and all must quickly learn how to get along with one another in an interdependent community. As one student says, "I have learned about personal responsibility, authority, and the right and duty of taking control of my education and life."

Because of its special character, Deep Springs is the right choice for only a tiny fraction of high school seniors. Urban cowboys who dream of riding into the sunset are in for a rude awakening, but for a few, the camaraderie and soul searching fostered in this caring community can be tremendously rewarding. In the words of one student, "It is hard indeed to leave Deep Springs without having your mind considerably opened up and stimulated."

University of Delaware

Newark, DE 19711

Location Small city
Total Enrollment 18,630
Undergraduates 16,580
Male/Female 45/55
SAT V/M 490/540
Financial Aid 40%
Expense Pub $ $

Applicants 11,430
Accepted 65%
Enrolled 44%
Academics ★ ★
Social 🐿 🐿 🐿 🐿
Q of L ● ● ●
Admissions (302)451-8123

The major university in the tiny First State was founded in 1743—in neighboring Pennsylvania. Its name doesn't suggest that it's a private school, and it isn't—at least not completely.

Now to clarify things a bit. U of D is a privately controlled land-grant institution that is supported by the state and private sources—which in Delaware, of course, includes the Du Ponts. There are all the makings of a rah-rah state university experience, with parties, football, fraternities and more parties; but there are also some solid professional offerings and an honors program that attract out-of-staters, who constitute more than half of the student population and face higher admission standards.

Built around one of the country's largest elm groves, Delaware's campus is an attractive mix of Williamsburg-style brick and modern geometric buildings with a sufficient number of both shady and tanning areas. The academic menu includes 130 different majors ranging from the usual liberal arts and science departments to vocational programs like fashion merchandising. Engineering, especially chemical engineering, is generally agreed to be the specialty of the house, with business (most notably accounting, management and economics) as well as history and art history not far behind. Also strong are the natural sciences, physical therapy, nursing, medical technology and agricultural science. The music department is upwardly mobile, and a number of its faculty members have impressive professional performance credits. Criminal justice is considered a "cake" major, and students poo-poo the math and communications departments. The computer science department is still byte-sized. Students in all programs must take some combination of general education requirements that include delving into the creative arts and humanities, culture and institutions, human beings and their environment, and natural phenomena.

Work loads, grading standards and quality of instruction vary among departments. The outstanding honors program admits 250 students a year, including some exceptional high school juniors. All freshmen in honors are housed in a dorm of their own. The undergraduate research program and humanities semester programs also attract many of the university's best and brightest. Students complain that they are occasionally closed out of popular courses, and some introductory classes may have as many as 340 enrolled. Students can take one or two classes during the January term to reduce their course load during the regular semester. Most faculty members are accessible if students make the effort to approach them first, but science profs are notorious for finding lower forms of life on their microscope slides more interesting than the higher forms in their classrooms. A recently completed expansion and renovation has left the library with double the amount of seating and a computerized card catalogue system.

For a quasi–state school, Delaware has a wide variety of students. Close to 40 percent are residents of Delaware, and many of the rest are from neighboring Pennsylvania, Maryland, New Jersey, New York and Virginia, as well as other states up and down the eastern seaboard. Most are from public schools, and those who aren't jocks are probably sports fans. According to a chemistry major, "the conservative, suburbanite, academically successful, socially adept, football-loving kind of student" will do well here. Delaware offers athletic scholarships confined to football, men's and women's basketball, and women's field hockey. While most of these scholarships hinge on academic promise and/or financial need, the university now does offer awards based strictly on athletic merit. More than 1,300 academic scholarships, with awards ranging from $200 to $8,500, are also provided, and in order to get these awards in the hands of the most deserving, the university maintains a scholarship-search program that matches eligible Delaware students with potential scholarships.

Except for those commuting from home, freshmen are required to live on campus. Although the housing crunch has eased, some freshmen are still placed in what is termed extended housing, which means that doubles become triples and lounges become near-communes. Relief usually arrives at midyear when enough students move or leave school. For freshmen who get regular housing and upperclassmen who get lucky in the lottery, U of D provides a wide assortment of accommodations, including coed and single-sex dorms, dorms with restricted visiting hours, singles, apartments and suites. There are also special-interest houses, such as French House, Arts House, and International House. On-campus students must hold a meal contract, and commuters can buy a thirty-lunch meal ticket. Dining hall choices include diet meals, sandwich and salad bars, a taco bar, and vegetarian meals.

Thanks to the new drinking age of twenty-one, the administration has banned open campus parties, and IDs are checked in downtown bars. There is one nonalcoholic bar on campus and "dry" dances are held on Friday nights. Fraternities throw many of the parties, but their role on campus is limited, and the role of the sororities even more so. "Greek life is small and not very popular, except for freshman girls," one senior notes. The university sponsors movie screenings for a dollar, and the college town of Newark offers the typical college-town array of fast-food joints, bars, malls and movies.

The music and drama departments run trips to New York City and Washington on weekends. Depending on the season, ski slopes in Pennsylvania and the coastal playground of Rehoboth Beach offer diversion. On fall Saturdays, Blue Hen football is the big attraction, with tailgate picnics before the game and parties afterward. The women's lacrosse team has attracted fans and picked up a national title. Intramural sports come in both the single-sex and coed varieties, and student interest abounds.

The University of Delaware is a large school for such a small state, and the many programs have something for everyone. And as a communications major explains, "The school is big enough to get lost in when you want, yet small enough to allow you to make many different types of friends."

Denison University

Granville, OH 43023

Location Small town
Total Enrollment 2,120
Undergraduates 2,120
Male/Female 50/50
SAT V/M 510/550
Financial Aid 30%
Expense Pr $ $ $

Applicants 3,370
Accepted 57%
Enrolled 32%
Academics ★ ★ ★
Social 🐺 🐺 🐺 🐺 🐺
Q of L ● ● ●
Admissions (614)587-6276

"Denison's biggest problem may be in overcoming its reputation as a party school." This assessment comes not from a dean of students trying to placate nervous parents, but rather from one of an increasing number of Denison students who feel compelled to tell the world that their party reputation is old hat and their academic endeavors are as meritorious as any. Judging by a recent increase in freshman applications, more and more people are hearing about Denison. But whether it's the high life or the higher education that's attracting prospective students remains to be seen.

These days, an alumnus returning to campus with a ready beer stein may feel a bit out of place. The school's newfound devotion to the academic life is reflected as much in the high rate of grad school acceptances among seniors (over 95 percent to medical, law, and business) as in the number of impromptu study groups that spring up around campus. Though one econ major characterizes her classmates as "closet intellectuals," Denison's days of scholarly bashfulness are all but over.

A cluster of brick colonial buildings atop a hill form the center of the 1,100-acre campus, and the surrounding countryside is magnificent. Coos one student, "Denison is a beautiful bit of New England tucked into the rolling hills of central Ohio." Huge oaks shade well-kept lawns and sloping walkways in the balmy months, and in the fall, fiery colors wreath the university's hilltop enclave. Tiny Granville, with a population not much larger than the school's enrollment, offers students little in the way of diversion but still manages to win the hearts of students with its quaint and friendly charm.

For all those party-animals-turned-academics, Denison's host of commendable departments include economics, political science and psychology. English is a popular major that offers both a literature and writing concentration, and the film and theater departments are highly rated but underenrolled. The top-notch geology and biology departments attest to the administration's efforts to produce graduates who are scientifically literate. Denison admits its speech communications program is understaffed, and the math department leaves many students disappointed. It is rumored that some programs in the arts could be improved. ("A troupe of sixteen hippos could probably out-leap some of our dance majors," criticizes one aficionado.)

The college's newly revised general education requirements begin with freshman studies courses, which concentrate on basic skills such as writing and reading comprehension. Frosh must also navigate the esoteric waters of Aesthetic Inquiry and the Human Imagination. Other inquiry courses await sophomores and upperclassmen, as do courses in global studies, minority or women's studies, and oral communications. The faculty is strongly encouraged by the administration to engage in research, but this is not a problem for students. But the faculty remains accessible. Indeed, it's common for undergrads to act as research assistants, affording them both exposure to high-level academic study and more contact with the faculty. Says one student, "At Denison, a professor may be a scholar, your teacher, your mentor, and your role model, but most important, your friend."

In addition to the university's comfortable, well-stocked library with an impressive array of audiovisual resources, the computer facilities are also excellent for a small liberal arts college. Terminals exist alongside pianos in the dorms, and since the work on computer is incorporated into the curriculum of nearly every department, students are assured of obtaining some degree of computer literacy. Denison encourages internships and off-campus study through the programs of the Great Lakes Colleges Association.* Denison's January terms—students must enroll in at least two during their college career—can be used for study abroad, independent projects or courses for fun. During the regular school year, students may teach experimental courses (worth a half credit) in such fields as Chinese cookery, bartending or auto mechanics.

Denison is proud of its attempts to fully fund all enrolled students who apply for financial aid by the deadline, and many students report that the university's accommodating approach was a key factor in their decisions to attend. There are no athletic scholarships, but a considerable number of merit awards, ranging from $100 to $4,500, are granted. Twenty-five percent of the student body hails from Ohio, and many of the rest are drawn from the Northeast. Preppies from New York and Chicago's North Shore will find many with whom they can compare whale pants and duck shoes. According to one senior, "Denisonians tend to be very all-American; the kind of people you see on television commercials." They are also conservative (note the popular Investment Club, Entrepreneurs Society, and Republicans Club), but the existence of over ninety student organizations should allay the fears of diversity seekers.

All Denison students live on campus, with the exception of approximately two hundred seniors who are "released" each year. Living situations vary, with single-sex and coed dorms available. Says one satisfied poli-sci major, "You can find almost every possible living situation—short of cohabitation—here at Denison." Smith Hall, the freshman dorm, is specially geared to the needs of newcomers, with counseling, entertainment and information. Shepardson Hall (the Living/Learning Center) houses upperclassmen who commit themselves to organizing and participating in creative learning projects. The Homesteaders live in student-built, solar-paneled cabins on a farm a mile away from campus and raise much of their own food. There are two pleasant dining halls on campus and the food generally earns praise: "It's always fresh and often warm, and an attempt to make things appetizing can be seen." Students take either five- or seven-day meal plans.

Denison is a Division III school, and its students are enthusiastic athletes and spectators, especially when it comes to lacrosse (both men's and women's), men's football and soccer, and women's field hockey. Intramurals are not as strong as they have the potential to be, owing to an abundance of "high school athletes turned collegiate spectators."

Just over half of the men belong to fraternities; just under half of the women belong to sororities, which have nonresidential houses. Weekends for many students mean the ritual procession to fraternity row, but the fast and wild life is not for everyone. Freshmen, who are not allowed to have cars on campus, are heavy subscribers to the frat scene, but many juniors and seniors come to think of it as tiresome. But there are numerous social options to the Greek scene (other clubs and dorm-sponsored parties, etc.), which lend balance to Denison life; the best feature is the lack of pressure to do one thing or the other. "Denison may be 50 percent Greek, but it's not a matter of life or death—it's an added activity," claims a senior. The commercial and cultural facilities that Granville lacks can be found in Columbus, the state capital, just forty-five minutes away, or even in Newark, just six miles down the road. Cars come in handy since, other than the occasional bus, there really is no mass transportation.

Denison's notorious party image has been toned down, and prospectives should be ready for much more than Greek revelry. "You won't see people jumping out windows at exam time," says a history major, "but academics are taken very seriously here." Fortunately, the academic atmosphere is supportive, not cutthroat, and Denisonians work together to meet the rigorous demands. Inevitably, this cooperation leads them to realize that the people are the most important element in their idyllic hilltop community. Says one already-nostalgic senior, "All the physical beauty of the campus and the structures on it, all the incredible materials and facilities at one's disposal would mean nothing if not for the friends I've made here."

University of Denver

Denver, CO 80208

Location City outskirts	**Applicants** 2,070
Total Enrollment 6,920	**Accepted** 75%
Undergraduates 3,150	**Enrolled** 38%
Male/Female 50/50	**Academics** ★ ★ ★
SAT V/M 510/550	**Social** 🐘🐘🐘🐘
Financial Aid 43%	**Q of L** ● ● ● ●
Expense Pr $ $ $	**Admissions** (303)871-2036

The University of Denver is a century-old institution that is weathering a mid-life crisis. In 1985, the university was perched on the brink of financial disaster. Since then, a new chancellor has gotten DU back on its feet, but not without some severe belt-tightening that has resulted in the elimination of a number of programs and a lack of sufficient funding for many others. Recent construction has bolstered the university's aging physical plant, but much more remains to be done. Though the near future now appears stable, DU's long-term financial situation remains iffy.

Despite its financial woes, DU offers much to commend itself. Located in a quiet Denver residential neighborhood, DU is the only private university in Colorado and one of the few between St. Louis and the West Coast. Its technical and scientific programs turn out graduates that are sought by the high-technology industries springing up from Denver to Albuquerque, while its preprofessional programs are feeders for graduate schools and new businesses in the burgeoning Western economy.

DU is at its best in preprofessional areas. The well-known School of Hotel and Restaurant Management tops the list, followed closely by the business school, where accounting, management and finance are reported to be especially good. The well-known program in sports sciences (part of the department of physical education) trains students in everything from kinesthesiology to sports sociology. Early admittance to DU's graduate schools of law, business, international studies and social work is offered to outstanding undergrads. Future engineers, especially those interested in energy-related work, may elect a combined program with the nearby Colorado School of Mines. However, engineering at DU gets mixed reviews. Those interested in women's studies might consider the program after the university's recent absorption of the former Colorado Women's College.

While most of the emphasis—and most of the money—has gone to the preprofessional programs, budget cuts have taken their toll on the liberal arts. According to one student, "The School of Arts and Sciences often gets shoved out of the way when it comes to the allocation of funds." Even so, psychology and English (especially creative writing) remain quite good. On the other hand, the arts, notably theater, draw widespread criticism. One student explained that he enrolled as an art education major only to have the program axed by budget cuts before he could complete it.

Along with the streamlining of many areas, the new administration has instituted a back-to-basics approach for the student body as a whole with the recent implementation of a core curriculum required for every undergraduate in the university. Poets and engineers alike are required to take one course each in English, arts and humanities, social sciences, natural sciences, mathematical and computer sciences and oral communication. In addition, each student must show proficiency in a foreign language. University rules stipulate that all core courses must be taught by senior faculty. Course titles include The Making of the Modern Mind and Understanding Human Conflict. The stated purpose of the core is to counteract overspecialization at the expense of the liberal arts—a malady otherwise much in evidence at DU. Freshman classes usually range in size from twenty-five to sixty, although introductory courses in business, psychology and economics can be much larger. Courses in the popular field of mass communications are not only large but often all but impossible to get into. Otherwise, most first-year students have few problems getting into the courses they want or seeing their professors, most of whom make an effort to be accessible, though opinions differ on whether freshmen and sophomores have adequate access to top faculty. An honors program is available, as are numerous study-abroad options. Penrose Library has adequate space and materials for most student needs, as well as a noisy social scene on the top floor. The academic climate is generally pretty casual, which is due in part to the excellent ski climate and the nearby Rockies. There are definitely hard courses and competitive majors, and one student reiterates "any college is only as pressured as a student wants to make it."

"Graduating, skiing, and having fun" are the students' main interests, one woman reports, and not necessarily in that order. About 50 percent graduated in the top fifth of their high school class; 86 percent in the top half. The student population is mixed, and no one group dominates. The majority are from Colorado, but Chicago, the Northeast, and the West Coast are all well represented. Those from the two coasts—especially the northeasterners—tend to be more well-to-do than their counterparts from in-state. DU has long been known in some circles as a refuge for northeastern preps who couldn't make the Ivy League—an image the university is working to change. "There are a lot of spoiled kids, but most are just well-off," according to one student. Because it is one of the few private colleges in the West, DU is also among the most expensive in the region.

The university offers financial aid to all eligible applicants on a first-come, first-served basis "until our funds are totally committed." There are more than a hundred renewable athletic scholarships, worth in excess of $600,000, and several academic merit scholarships, ranging from $1,500 to full tuition. Unfortunately, the tight financial situation makes funds limited.

Students are required to live their first two years on campus, and fortunately housing is plentiful. The residence halls are comfortable, but a little short on atmosphere. A few singles can be found, and once in a room, you can retain it until graduation. Dorms are coed by wing or floor, and there's no visitation. Every dorm resident must sign up for fifteen- or twenty-meal plans, a requirement that helps make about a third of the students happy to live in on- or off-campus apartments. There are no restrictions concerning off-campus living, and decent quarters can be found within walking distance of campus. Greeks can live and dine together in their houses.

Students tend to have one thing in common—a love of the outdoors. With consistently beautiful sunny weather and great skiing and hiking less than an hour away in the Rockies, many of them head for the hills on weekends. The bus system ("terrific") makes it easy to get into downtown Denver. Ironically, some students feel that campus social life suffers from its ideal location. "At times, DU stands for 'Dead University,'" laments one. Luckily there are a number of on-campus attractions. About a quarter of the students join fraternities or sororities. They provide most of the weekend parties on campus, and most are open to all. Wednesday is pub night at the the new $7-million student center. Since Colorado is a "3.2 state," everyone under twenty-one is only allowed to drink 3.2 beer, a watered-down variety of the real thing. Varsity hockey games are perhaps the biggest source of campus social life. Each winter, throngs of enthusiastic DU rooters turn out to support the team, the only one on campus that plays in Division I. Other teams capable of drawing a crowd are men's basketball and soccer and women's gymnastics. Intramural participation is high, and there are the usual athletic facilities open to students. And then there's always Denver, full of great restaurants, bars and stores, many of which cater to students.

After a tense period in the mid-'80s, the University of Denver appears to have both feet back on the ground. The university's precarious financial situation has stabilized, at least for the time being. Still, given the university's small endowment, much will hinge on the latest fund-raising drive. Academically at least, DU is a university moving forward with renewed purpose. Already offering fine programs in many pre-professional fields, it may one day have a full complement of liberal arts programs to match.

DePaul University

Chicago, IL 60604

Location Urban	**Applicants** 2,180
Total Enrollment 13,130	**Accepted** 66%
Undergraduates 7,980	**Enrolled** 49%
Male/Female 45/55	**Academics** ★ ★ ★
ACT 23	**Social** ☎ ☎
Financial Aid 55%	**Q of L** ● ● ●
Expense Pr $	**Admissions** (312)341-8300

Basketball is not DePaul's only claim to fame, although the school's enrollment has soared since the Blue Demons began making regular appearances at the NCAA and NIT championships. But for whatever reason students choose this Roman Catholic institution, most are happy to rebound from the basketball stands into challenging academic programs offered in an atmosphere with a touch of religion.

DePaul has two campuses. The Frank J. Lewis center—the "vertical" campus—in Chicago's downtown Loop houses the law school and the College of Commerce in three twelve-story buildings. Most classes in the humanities and sciences are taken uptown on the Lincoln Park campus, where the dorms, the music school, and the DePaul Theatre School are situated on a four-block mix of old and modern in a ritzy suburb. A twenty-minute ride on the elevated train connects the two sites.

DePaul's name is closely associated with Midwest business, and undergraduates are welcomed as interns in local commercial institutions. The newly established school of accountancy is reported to be the most challenging department in the College of Commerce; economics is said to be the least. The theater school, with its shiny new facility, is renowned, as is the school of music. The department of computer science and information systems remains a national leader. It continually updates its software and maintains one of the largest Digital Equipment Corporation configurations available to academic institutions. The school of education and several of the science departments (including biology, chemistry and physics) are enjoying rejuvenation through increased enrollments and fresh new faculty members. DePaul's impressive prelaw and premed programs balance agreeably with the excellent liberal arts offerings. Foreign languages programs receive criticism from students; the art department, which the administration claims is underrated, is definitely underenrolled. The university recently dropped its music therapy, radiologic technology and art education programs, but added urban studies and women's studies.

Teaching ability is the first priority in faculty selection at DePaul, where courses are small and senior profs teach on all levels. "You never leave a class without understanding the subject," attests a senior. A number of social activities are designed to bring the undergraduates and the faculty together, and students are given a phone book with all the profs' home numbers. This faculty of practitioners is praised for savvy advisement. All students take proficiency tests in basic skills at the Assessment and Advisement Center and are given individual guidance in course selection. The required liberal studies program, which includes religion and philosophy, takes up about half of a student's work load—too much, according to the more career-minded students. A subcomponent of liberal studies is common studies—a sequence of history and writing courses. DePaul also has a military science department, which provides students with the opportunity to achieve commissions as Army officers in addition to their majors. The highly selective honors program includes interdisciplinary courses, a modern language requirement and a senior thesis. (Honor students must maintain a 3.4 grade average to graduate from the program.) The trimester system provides a fast academic pace, and classes are held Saturdays, Sundays and in the evening to accommodate working students.

Founded in 1898 by the Vincentian Fathers, DePaul is run by priests, who also teach some of the courses. But not all students appreciate the religious influence here. "There's a big controversy regarding whether DePaul is a Catholic or educational institution first," reports a communications major. Other students feel the religious aspects help create a sense of community among the dispersed student body. There is daily mass in the on-campus Catholic church, but the administration contends DePaul's main constituency is Chicago residents, and non-Catholics won't feel left out either in class or in social life.

Indeed, 47 percent of the students are non-Catholic, and less than 15 percent come from outside of the local area. Just about half of the students ranked in the top fifth of their high school classes; the administration says DePaul serves "the slightly above average to very good student who is career-oriented." Many are the first in their families to go to college, and more than 90 percent of the undergraduates are working their way through school, with half holding full-time jobs. Political persuasions appear to be prerequisites to choosing a major and a school—"The Loop campus is conservative with some suit-and-tie students; the Lincoln Park campus is liberal," analyzes a marketing major. Hispanics and blacks are well represented in the student body—about

20 percent—and DePaul wants to boost this figure by reaching out to disadvantaged inner-city inhabitants who show academic potential. DePaul puts up about seventy-five athletic scholarships and double that number for academic merit and talent. Employment opportunities are offered by the administration as a means of offsetting what cranky students describe as a "weak" financial aid program.

Only 5 percent of the students live on this campus of commuters. DePaul has four modern coed dorms; one's brand new. Three of these are for all students and one for juniors, seniors and married students only. The latter provides apartment living with furniture and built-in cooking facilities. The meal plan is run on a credit card system, and both residents and commuters can decide what their credit limit per semester will be. But the best option appears to be dining out.

In addition to men's basketball, the female Blue Demons also demonstrate a bit of finesse on the court. Men's track and golf, as well as women's volleyball and softball teams, are fierce competitors. There is a solid intramural program, where once again, basketball rules. Fraternities and sororities have few members, no houses, and therefore "don't play much of a role" in the social life of DePaul. The activities board programs a substantial number of events, which makes it the "predominate on-campus social factor." For off-campus things to do, there is all of Chicago for culture, commerce and entertainment. Students enjoy the beaches of Lake Michigan and the bars on Rush Street. The Lake Forest area has many attractive clubs and bars of its own.

Like the basketball team, DePaul students are of the come-from-behind order. While not all will be honored with a *Sports Illustrated* cover story, most will take advantage of the smaller-scale, more personalized attention they get from their professors and classmates. They may not like every aspect of this little Catholic school, but they know a sure shot when they see one.

DePauw University

Greencastle, IN 46135

Location Small town	**Applicants** 2,155
Total Enrollment 2,370	**Accepted** 75%
Undergraduates 2,310	**Enrolled** 41%
Male/Female 45/55	**Academics** ★ ★ ★
SAT V/M 520/580	**Social** 🎭 🎭 🎭
Financial Aid 40%	**Q of L** ● ●
Expense Pr $ $	**Admissions** (317)658-4006

More than a century ago DePauw students banded together to fight a nosy bunch of faculty members by establishing several fraternities and the first Greek letter sororities, and thereby setting their own standards of extracurricular conduct. Such a move is typical of DePauw's affluent and upwardly mobile students who like to have the best of all possible worlds—a liberal arts school with Ivy League traditions and a midwestern friendly atmosphere.

Though DePauw's College of Liberal Arts continues to uphold the value of a well-rounded education, the university is placing more and more emphasis on the career-oriented fields. But the administration has no problem with students getting a healthy dose of liberal arts while keeping their eyes on business careers—a unique music/business major is even offered. And the much-talked-about management fellows program, designed for honors students in any major, comprises intense managerial course work and a semester-long internship. An international business concentration evolves around three majors: political science, economics or foreign language. Students major in one of these areas while taking selected courses in the other two and participating in an internship abroad. The English, economics, psychology and music departments are students' favorites, while chemistry, education, sociology and anthropology are less strong. Students admit the communications and computer science departments pale in comparison to other schools, yet both are improving steadily. DePauw also has a school of music as well as a school of nursing in which students spend their last two years working and studying at a hospital in Indianapolis.

Students are required to take courses from each of six general areas (natural sciences and mathematics, social and behavioral sciences, literature and the arts, historical and philosophical understandings, foreign language and self expression) and demonstrate competence in writing, quantitative reasoning and oral communication. The obligatory January term—"a really creative time for both the students and faculty"—encourages independent study, internships, and exchanges with other schools. Close to half the students study abroad through programs of the Great Lakes Colleges Association* or at DePauw's own study centers in Athens, Barcelona, Freiburg, Nanzan and Vienna.

A $4.8-million renovation of the main library (a sore spot in the school's reputation) will update resources, computerize the card catalogue system and add a media center. Future plans for the updated library include a larger staff and substantial increases in money spent on books. Other facilities are outstanding: The multimillion-dollar Science and Mathematics Center contains a science library and plenty of computer terminals, and the magnificent four-building Performing Arts Center holds the music library, practice rooms, theater, auditorium, and recital hall.

Academic standards tailed off in the 1970s, but, today, after surviving its sesquicentennial and raising its admission and graduation requirements, DePauw is clearly on its way back. Competition for grades is keen among the many preprofessionals, but as one music/business major attests, "People do not kick and gouge to get the best grade or highest GPA." And a communications major adds that the perfect DePauwer should have "above average intelligence, yet should not be abnormally bright." Praise for the concern of faculty is widespread and because of a new registration system, more underclassmen are able to get classes with top professors. Students who have an eye toward a potential academic career of their own should know that DePauw ranks high as a producer of future PhDs in a variety of fields.

Variety, though, is what's hard to find among the mainly affluent, mainly white, almost always conservative and career-minded student body. In fact, a junior notes that "bloodlines run strong at DePauw—many students have a direct relative who attends or attended." While such a familiar atmosphere helps water down freshman year culture shock, one undergrad bemoans, "Living in a homogeneous society will not prepare me for today's world." On the other hand, a sophomore points out that the rich sense of camaraderie "can often cheer you up, even on a very down day." Forty percent of the undergrads receive need-based aid, and approximately 275 scholarships are awarded to those who demonstrate "truly outstanding qualities of scholarship." Some 150 other students with special talents and leadership abilities are also eligible for merit awards ranging from $500 to $8,200.

DePauw has only six dormitories, and students report they are well maintained but old, "which simply adds to their charm and livability." Greek rush takes place the first week of school, and male freshmen move right into their fraternity houses. (Freshman women are assigned to single-sex dorms and not allowed to inhabit their sorority houses until sophomore year.) A minuscule number of students are granted permission to move into town. Dining-hall food, required for dormitory students, is said to be surprisingly good with "exciting things like dessert tables full of multiple homemade desserts," according to one customer. Fraternities and sororities have their own cooks who aren't too bad themselves—"I think the food is too good, hence my need for a diet," admits an overcapacitated Greek.

Close to three-fourths of DePauw does go Greek, but students claim the system "is not the elitist club that it is on many campuses." Independents are not stigmatized as much as they once were. As one junior puts it, "independents are *not* geeks who study all the time." Popular diversions are house dances and the ubiquitous "keggers," as fraternity parties are called. Many upperclassmen prefer smaller group gatherings and the quieter atmosphere of what bars there are in town. (Marvin's is the place to go when craving a garlic cheeseburger.) Well-attended varsity athletic contests tend to turn into social events, especially the annual Monon Bell football game against arch-rival Wabash College, played for possession of a bell. Men's basketball and soccer teams religiously please their fans; women's field hockey and swimming teams are tough to beat. The new Lilly Athletic Center is finally providing decent athletic facilities for women. Lest you be confused, remember DePaul in Illinois is the basketball power-house; DePauw's fiercest games are played between frat teams on the frequently used intramural fields.

Founded as a Methodist college, DePauw has shed its strong identification with that denomination, in fact Roman Catholics now outnumber Methodists. "It is a Methodist school," says a premed student, "but this just keeps it conservative, that's about it." Missionary relief trips, which take students to impoverished areas of Central America and South Africa, are lingering reminders of religious ideology. Students are active in work projects with area churches and social-service agencies, in addition to several extracurricular activities on campus.

Flat, agricultural Indiana is neither the garden spot of the world nor a mecca of entertainment opportunities. A small ski slope, several state parks and a lake for the sailing club are nearby. For off-campus diversion, Indianapolis is less than an hour away, and several other colleges, including Indiana University and Purdue, are within visiting distance. Yet according to one estimate, 95 percent of the students stay "home" in Greencastle on weekends. Perhaps their college world is too comfy. "DePauw University is physically what I've always thought a college would look like," says one student. "There is green grass on every corner, which gives rise to beautiful, modern red-brick buildings," observes another. These unintimidating three- or four-story structures surround a well-kept park with fountains and a reflecting pool.

Diverse or not, DePauw students manage to remain lively. And while some students admit they desire a less homogeneous peer group and a more worldly environment, others enjoy the midwestern values, warmth and hospitality at DePauw. In fact one senior claims what he likes least about this Indiana ivory tower "is that I am only here for four years."

Dickinson College

Carlisle, PA 17013

Location Small town
Total Enrollment 1,940
Undergraduates 1,940
Male/Female 45/55
SAT V/M 540/570
Financial Aid 45%
Expense Pr $ $ $

Applicants 3,720
Accepted 50%
Enrolled 32%
Academics ★ ★ ★
Social 🐿 🐿 🐿
Q of L ● ● ●
Admissions (717)245-1231

Dickinson College is deporting students left and right. With an administration dedicated to the belief that the world is shrinking and global education is essential, the college has developed one of the most extensive programs for "injecting international dimensions into a full range of academics." Via classroom lectures and language studies, via airplanes and boats, Dickinson is "injecting" students all over the place—from Malaga to Moscow, from Bologna to Bremen. Funny thing is, the little liberal arts school has become so popular with its worldly curriculum and travel opportunities that it's attracting students at a faster pace than it can send them away.

With all this deportation and exploration going on, English has become a second (or third or fourth) language at Dickinson. Foreign language is not only required, it's worshipped. Part of the school's commitment to international study includes summer language immersion programs, in which students spend three fluent months in France, Germany, Spain, Italy or Russia. The college received a $1-million grant from the National Endowment for the Humanities to further expand its foreign language and international education. Today, more than one-fourth of all Dickinson graduates leave the campus for a summer, semester or year. The college sponsors programs in six countries and is affiliated with programs in institutes around the world, including Australia, China, Japan, South Africa and Yugoslavia.

Regardless of how many hemispheres its students visit while picking up credits, at home, Dickinson has well-established majors in several of the humanities—history, English, philosophy, political science, religion and classical studies. Biology is the strongest science major, followed by chemistry. Both students and administrators are reluctant to label any departments as weak. Says one senior: "Perhaps a better way to put it would be less pronounced." All right then, the less pronounced departments are fine arts and psychology, though more pronounced are the new buildings in which they're housed.

Dickinson's distribution requirements are not to be taken lightly: a freshman seminar; three courses in each of the main areas of study (humanities, social sciences, natural and math sciences); cross-cultural studies; and physical education. Each year forty-eight selected students named Nisbet Scholars are excused from all distribution requirements in order to structure their own liberal arts honors program. Double majors and interdisciplinary studies are quite the fashion at Dickinson, where students can combine a specific program with a more general "option," such as comparative civilizations, Latin American studies or teaching certification. Several academic disciplines are supplemented by opportunities for Dickinson to send away some two hundred more students each semester through internships and practical job experiences both in and out of state.

The academic climate is fairly intense. "There are no sleaze courses here—you

201

have to work," says one senior. Students warn that with Dickinson's increased popularity and so, increased enrollment, freshmen don't always get into the classes of their choice. "But continued interest (and a little buttering up of the professor) will allow you to get into a class sooner or later," contests an experienced political scientist. Dickinson provides a chance to get to know your teachers as well as your textbooks; upper-level classes rarely grow beyond thirty students. "An evening dinner at a prof's house is usually the rule, not the exception," says one well-fed senior. But according to another report, the faculty is a bit too obtrusive: "I feel many professors must learn their realm here is in the classroom—period."

Dickinson students tend to be white, upper-middle-class and from the Northeast (with about one-third from Pennsylvania itself). Most are well motivated toward good-paying jobs, and they are relatively conservative. Seventy-two percent graduate in the top fifth of their high school class; about the same percentage come from public schools.

Part of Dickinson's appeal is its effective preparation for postgraduate study. Those who buckle down can enjoy Dickinson's placement records of over 95 percent to law schools, 85 percent to medical schools, and a virtual money-back guarantee for business schools. Although the college provides no athletic or merit scholarships, it does attempt to meet the financial need of its students. For families no longer qualifying for Guaranteed Student Loans, it provides flexible financing planning through which parents may borrow from $2,500 to $7,000 a year at attractive interest rates.

Dickinson guarantees rooms to all its students (although sophomore males tend to get the bad end of the deal) and in the past has bought and renovated nearby houses to keep its word. The result is a varied array of campus architecture. But all the buildings appear to be carved from the same hunk of gray limestone (indigenous to the area), which gives the place a certain continuity. There's even a three-foot limestone wall that envelops the well-wooded, 110-acre Dickinson plot in the center of the small town. Freshmen have their own dorms (including two for women only). Most of the rest of the dorms are coed by floor except the "cream of the crop housing: the new eight-person townhouse suites." Special-interest houses, such as Spanish House, Arts House and Whole Earth House, are available a short distance from center campus, as are the fraternities. About 10 percent of the students, mostly seniors, move into houses and apartments lining Carlisle's pleasant neighborhood streets.

Dickinson campus residents, including Greeks, eat at one large dining hall, "which makes meals the social hub of the day," a senior says. While many campus munchers note the dining hall could use some renovating, the food's not bad. Breakfast and lunch run together on weekends, "so you can wake up at noon and still get scrambled eggs and bacon"—an important option since Dickinson's social life revolves around weekend late-night dancing and partying at the fraternities. "Most students blow off steam this way," says one woman. Fraternities also give daring students a chance to duck the legal drinking age of twenty-one, although college policy stipulates students are expected to abide by the law. Fifty percent of the men go Greek; 45 percent of the women join one of the six nonresidential sororities. The predominance of the Greek life draws some complaints ("Most of the guys won't take a girl anywhere except his frat house," bemoans a frustrated female), but independents are reportedly coming into their own. There are two weekend film societies, and the College Entertainment Board sponsors live dance bands and a Thursday night "coffeehouse" with student entertainers.

For off-campus adventures, Carlisle has good clean fun: a roller-skating rink, bowling alley and an authentic farmer's market. For road trips (although students report most stay put on the weekends, saving their travels for broader horizons),

Philadelphia, Pittsburgh and Washington, D.C., are reachable, not to mention Harrisburg, which is only forty miles away.

It rains a lot in Carlisle—"Cardrizzle" is the students' name for their adopted town's contribution to meteorology—but on clear days nature lovers will enjoy the nearby mountains and state parks. The Appalachian Trail passes by ten minutes from campus, and one student promises "the finest trout fishing in the East." Ski facilities are a half an hour away with a free daily shuttle bus to transport students. Intramurals are a favorite of the fraternities, but dorms also organize teams. For those interested in headier competition, Dickinson fields respectable varsity teams in women's field hockey, men's basketball, and men's and women's cross-country, soccer, swimming. According to some, "women's athletics are definitely on par with men's—in fact, they might even be better." For those who enjoy victories, devotion to the football team is not recommended. Club teams, organized by the students to compete with other schools are popular (especially the rugby team) as are a number of less physical campus clubs and organizations.

Dickinsonians have no problem reconciling their travel time and robust involvement in partying with similar application to their studies at home or abroad. The well-roundedness of a liberal arts education, they argue, begins in the classroom but by no means ends there, or in Pennsylvania, or in the U.S. . . . .

Drew University

Madison, NJ 07940

Location Suburban	**Applicants** 1,800
Total Enrollment 2,050	**Accepted** 77%
Undergraduates 1,510	**Enrolled** 27%
Male/Female 45/55	**Academics** ★ ★ ★
SAT V/M 550/590	**Social** 🛎 🛎 🛎
Financial Aid 51%	**Q of L** ● ● ●
Expense Pr $ $ $	**Admissions** (201)377-3000

Historians report that Daniel Drew, Wall Street wizard, scoundrel and philanthropist, invested a half million dollars in his own Methodist theological seminary in 1867 because he wanted to assure himself a place in heaven. No earthly creature knows for sure if his good deed—the largest single gift any school had ever received—achieved its divine purpose, but present-day students see "the house that Drew built" as an answer to their prayers. The university still supports a school of theology, but it is now more interested in undergraduates drawn to the altar of a broad liberal arts education.

Nestled in the homey town of Madison within striking distance of New York City (a mere thirty miles to the west), Drew's lush 186-acre woodland grounds squelch misconceptions people tend to have about northern New Jersey. Students sing the praises of a campus that is situated "within a stunning forest of oaks" (a quote straight from a public relations director's heart, since Drew has dubbed itself the "University in the Forest"). The forty-five buildings on campus, a harmonious blend of modern and traditional, include such standouts as Mead Hall, a Greek revival masterpiece, and Samuel W. Browne Hall, modeled after a building at Oxford.

Academic programs that receive high marks include biology, economics, English, political science, psychology and theater arts. The university has adopted a goal of "computer fluency" for all of its graduates, and freshmen are each issued a microcomputer and supporting software that they take with them upon graduation. (Who wants all those outdated computers lying around?) Workshops are offered on how to use the equipment, and the newly enlarged and improved Computer Center are tangible evidence of Drew's commitment to its Computer Initiative program. Foreign languages (especially German), music and philosophy appear to be the weakest departments. And while the physical education department has strong programs, it suffers from inadequate facilities. But things are looking up since a new tennis center has been opened and plans for a new field house are in the works.

Drew's commitment to a true liberal art's education is evident in its offerings both on and off campus. General ed requirements involve course work in the social sciences, natural/physical sciences, and the humanities. Students seem eager to take advantage of the seven programs for off-campus and foreign study: One in three students studies off campus at some point in their undergraduate career. Offerings include a semester at the United Nations, political studies in Washington, D.C., an art or theater semester in New York, a London semester on British government and politics, and the Brussels semester on the European community. Students can also move around the country or the world during the optional January term.

Drew's library complex, a cluster of three buildings, contains some 373,000 titles. Students rate the facilities from adequate to excellent, with the most common gripe being that they close too early on Saturday and Sunday nights. When Drew students list the strengths of their school, the faculty invariably tops the list. Students say that professors are always happily and readily available to meet with them. "Drew is very much a student-oriented school," says a sophomore. "All profs are teachers first." Student-faculty relations get off to a good start with the Freshman Seminar program, in which students choose from a large offering of seminars and then work closely with a top professor on both oral and written skills.

Just under half of Drew's students are from New Jersey, and 62 percent attended public schools. "Students are highly motivated, but there is little overt academic competition," reports a junior. Half of the freshmen ranked in the top tenth of their high school class. Politically, Drew students sway toward the conservative end of the spectrum. "People here are carnal, pre-yuppies," assesses an English major. "It's costing them a small fortune to come here, and they want to spend their time preparing for their future success—monetarily anyway." The Drew Scholars program awards fifty grants of up to $12,000 a year based on academic, civic and personal achievement, but there are no athletic scholarships offered.

About 90 percent of the students live on campus in dorms ranging from new and air-conditioned to old and run-down, with the latter perversely popular because of their spacious rooms. There are both single-sex and coed dorms, and each offers a Freshman Floor, Quiet Floor, or Traditional Floor. A circa-1880 house provides a spacious option for French and Spanish students. Although the dorms have kitchenettes, everyone must buy the meal plan. The foods tend to be rather pedestrian, except for the ice cream jubilees described by a drama student as follows: "A cart with a huge cast of flavors and all the sauces and goo to be dumped on top is wheeled into the middle of the main dining hall. Then someone blows a whistle and leaves the cart to be demolished."

Students give the social life on campus high marks, and many seem proud that there is so much to do despite the absence of fraternities and sororities and the presence of the twenty-one-year-old drinking age. A favorite gathering spot on campus is The Other End, a low-grade cellar that students and faculty transformed into an enticing, student-run bistro with a cabaret stage. Movies are shown on campus Thursday through Sunday, and student-run committees organize picnics, concerts, parties and always-popular trips to NYC. "Madison is a college town," a poli-sci major reports. "But New York is close enough to provide everything lacking in Madison." The New Jersey Shakespeare Festival is in residence part of every year and offers both performances and internships.

As for sports, a junior states, "Intramurals get five stars—the whole campus participates in something." Though students seem more interested in intramurals than the school's varsity teams, they are proud of their successful teams, which include men's soccer and tennis, women's field hockey and lacrosse by both sexes. Fencing and equestrian pursuits have a loyal following as well. Eighty-five percent of the students are involved in a varsity, club or intramural sport.

At a time when most colleges are gearing their courses more and more toward the job market, Drew—perhaps with a touch of madness in its Methodism—remains dedicated to the well-rounded intellect rather than the well-lined purse. If he were to visit his school today, robber baron Daniel Drew might feel a bit out of touch with what he created.

Drexel University

Philadelphia, PA 19104

Location City outskirts	**Applicants** 4,620
Total Enrollment 12,490	**Accepted** 81%
Undergraduates 7,370	**Enrolled** 43%
Male/Female 70/30	**Academics** ★ ★ ★
SAT V/M 490/570	**Social** ☎ ☎
Financial Aid 77%	**Q of L** ● ●
Expense Pr $ $	**Admissions** (215)895-2400

The motto of Drexel University is "Science, Industry, and Art," but whoever wrote this motto should update it to read "Science, Industry and the Art of Landing a Job." The science and industry aspects of this downtown Philadelphia school are vivid—in fact all freshmen are required to buy computers. Don't bemoan the idea of putting out $1,400 to buy a computer (that's a bargain for an Apple Mac Plus) because at Drexel the microcomputer is used in everything from psychology (analyze survey data) to chemistry (building models of molecular structures) to design (prepare computer-generated graphics). But for many Drexel students, the highest art form is a well-drafted, comprehensive resumé that communicates an abundance of technical experience and expertise.

Cooperative education, aka total education, is the hallmark of the Drexel curriculum, which alternates periods of full-time study and full-time employment for five years, providing students with twelve to twenty-one months of money-making job experience before they graduate. And the co-op possibilities are unlimited: Students can co-op in Philly or virtually anywhere in the country and several foreign countries. All but 2 percent of the undergraduates choose this route. Freshman and senior years of the five-year programs are spent on campus, and the three intervening years (sophomore, prejunior, and junior) usually consist of six months of work and six months of

205

school. A new precooperative education course covers such topics as skills assessment, ethics in the workplace and stress management. The administration claims that each co-oping student has the opportunity to earn from $7,000 to $30,000 while attending Drexel. And although some students complain jobs can turn out to be six months of make-work, most enjoy making important contacts in their potential fields and earning some tuition and spending money. "Co-op education is the greatest," announces an operational management major. "No textbook can teach you what you learn from being there in person."

To accommodate the co-op students, Drexel operates year-round. Even so, flexibility is not one of Drexel's lovable features. Once preregistered for a course, students complain that it is almost impossible to switch; and since course offerings differ each term, students must plan their school terms carefully to meet all requirements. The mandatory liberal arts core curriculum combines work in communications, English, history, mathematics, natural sciences, political science, psychology, sociology and microcomputer use.

Drexel's greatest strength lies in its engineering college, which churns out more than 1 percent of all the nation's engineering graduates, BS through PhD. The College of Science is well recognized for theoretical and atmospheric physics; chemistry and, not surprisingly, computer science are recommended. The Nesbitt College of Design Arts recently tightened up its programs in fashion and interior design, photography and technological publication production. The College of Business and Administration is the students' favorite, enrolling more than one-third of them. The College of Information Studies is okay, but no one seems able to take the College of Humanities and Social Science too seriously.

The pace is fast, and with the year-round calendar, co-opers go almost nonstop. "The ten-week quarters do not afford students any time to slack off," says a finance student. "The pressure can get to you sometimes, but it does teach you discipline." So it's a good thing the professors are the helpful types, diligent about keeping office hours. Also helpful is the new library with a computerized card catalogue, good hours and lots of room for studying.

Drexel's downtown campus is, in a word—stark. The buildings are simple and brick; most are modern and in good condition. Sitting just west of the center city, the campus is condensed into about a four-block radius. Students are encouraged to use a shuttle bus between library and dorm, and complaints about crime and the inadequate security patrols are high.

The performance-oriented student body is 64 percent Pennsylvanian. Forty-four percent of them graduated in the top fifth of their class. Drexel students tend to lean rightward politically—"When your future job depends on nukes, you don't protest against them," says one. "We believe in the work ethic," says another. In addition to need-based financial aid, a wide range of athletic and merit scholarships are offered.

"The dorm rooms," says one student, "remind me of a prison, with all the furniture fixed." The three high-rise and one low-rise dorms, sex-segregated by floor, are jammed. But a new fifteen-story, 429-bed dorm is reported by students to be quite spacious and luxurious. Nearby apartments or the fraternities are frequently cheaper and more private than the university housing. The recently enlarged cafeteria offers adequate food and plenty of hamburgers and hot dogs, but it's far away from the dorms. While freshmen are forced to sign up for a meal plan, most upperclassmen make their own meals—the dorms have cooking facilities on each floor. If all else fails, nomadic food trucks cruise the campus and provide quick lunches to many.

The co-op program often undermines any sense of class unity and adds strain to personal relationships. The activities that depend on some continuity of enrollment for success—music, drama, student government, athletics—suffer most. "It's hard to get

people involved because of the amount of schoolwork and co-ops," says one[ ]
There is no football team, but men's basketball and soccer, as well as the m[ ]
women's swimming generate some interest. An extensive intramural program[ ]
all the students, and joggers routinely head for the steps of the Philadel[ ]
Museum, just like Rocky does in the movies.

Since about half of the students commute, the campus tends to be a bit [ ]
on weekends. Friday night flicks are cheap and popular with those who stay[ ]
and dorms sponsor floor parties. The twelve fraternities also contribute to the party
scene, especially freshman year, but the four smaller sororities have little impact. When
nothing's doing at Drexel, the University of Pennsylvania is right next door. Students
take full advantage of their urban location by frequenting clubs, restaurants, cultural
attractions and shopping malls in Philadelphia. Public transportation provides easy
access to all of these. The Jersey shore and the Pocono ski areas are about two hours
away by car.

"If you're looking for a small university on acres of land in a small town, better
look elsewhere," warns a senior at this inverse of an ivory tower. In the words of one
student: "Drexel has a real-world approach to education. We are here to learn what
work is all about."

Duke University *good*

Durham, NC 27706

Location Small city
Total Enrollment 10,350
Undergraduates 6,160
Male/Female 55/45
SAT V/M 620/680
Financial Aid 35%
Expense Pr $ $ $

Applicants 12,680
Accepted 26%
Enrolled 48%
Academics ★ ★ ★ ★ ★
Social 🐿 🐿 🐿 🐿
Q of L ● ● ● ●
Admissions (919)684-3214

Harried Ivy Leaguers can be forgiven if they are more than a little puzzled by Duke
University. The professors at Duke are just as learned, the students just as bright, and
yes, their SAT scores are just as high as those at Duke's prestigious cousins to the north,
yet the aura of pressure and gloom that so often hangs heavy over the campuses of the
Ivy League is nowhere to be found at this equally renowned southern university.
"People here do the work with a smile and have a beer later," chirps one student. The
reason why Duke can be laid-back and high-powered at the same time lies in its unique
blend of North and South. Though distinctly southern, Duke is the one great university
below the Mason-Dixon Line that most resembles those in the North, both physically
and philosophically. Duke attracts nearly as many students from New York as North
Carolina, its campus is as neo-Gothic as Yale's, and ever since tobacco baron James
B. Duke charged the school with a mission of doing "great things for God and
humanity," Duke has been a university of national stature.

Founded in 1838 as the Union Institute (later Trinity College), Duke University
came into being in 1924 when it became the chief beneficiary of quite a stack of
tobacco-stained dollars called the Duke Endowment. Located in the lush foothills of

the North Carolina Piedmont, the university today consists of two schools: engineering and Trinity College, the latter a merger of previously separate men's and women's liberal arts colleges. Symbolic of Duke's national scope is the Institute of Policy Science and Public Affairs, founded in 1971. Similar to Harvard's Kennedy School of Government and Princeton's Woodrow Wilson School, the institute offers a first-rate undergraduate program in addition to graduate degrees. Public policy studies, an interdisciplinary mix of social science courses, case studies, and a mandatory internship, is one of the most rigorous undergraduate majors, as well as one of the best.

Duke's engineering program—particularly electrical—is top-notch, as are the natural sciences, most notably chemistry and physics. The history department stands out among the humanities, with the oral history program receiving special praise. Students also cite political science as particularly good. A relatively new program in computer science is popular, and computer literacy is encouraged campus-wide. Math is, by general consensus, the worst department at Duke—"a disgrace" one student believes. Economics receives only mixed reviews, but the English department, tired and traditional until recently, has received an infusion of innovative young faculty members that has transformed it into one of the most exciting anywhere. Duke's general education program is fairly straightforward, with undergraduates required to take courses in literature, history of civilization, the natural sciences, foreign language, and composition, as well as several "small group learning" seminars in a variety of areas. Students with special interests and talents can design their own curriculum under the Program II option.

Despite the laid-back aura, the academic atmosphere can be competitive, especially in the sciences. Student faculty relations are good—the university sponsors lunch several times a week for students and faculty—but steadily increasing enrollments in recent years appear to have cost Duke something in intimacy. Though upper level seminars still number fewer than fifteen students, freshman introductory courses can have enrollments of several hundred. With an estimated 3.3 million volumes and 5.5 million manuscripts, the library facilities are no less than outstanding. Though Duke was founded under Methodist auspices, there is no religion requirement.

Only 15 percent of Duke's undergraduates are from North Carolina. The South remains the most heavily represented region, but the northeastern corridor also sends its fair share of young minds to Duke. Duke's "fascinating variety of winners" are about 5 percent black, 2 percent Hispanic, and 3 percent foreign, though a majority are upper-middle-class suburbanites. Duke's campus is conservative politically, and pre-professionalism runs high. A tantalizing early-identification option gives premeds a chance to apply to Duke Medical School during their sophomore year, but only about a dozen applicants are accepted into the competitive program each year. For those who don't make it—and for that matter anyone else—Duke's Office of Counseling and Psychological Services offers a variety of helpful programs.

Duke admits students without reference to their financial need and guarantees to meet the full demonstrated need of all accepted applicants. Those without need are in the running for a total of 260 merit scholarships, ranging from $250 to full tuition, awarded annually. A small number of full-tuition awards for the best and brightest of the freshman class include six weeks of summer study at Oxford University. Other merit-based awards include twenty scholarships a year starting at $1,000 for outstanding black students, and Duke hands out over two hundred athletic scholarships annually.

Most undergraduates at Duke live on campus, with freshmen housed in various clusters that are both single-sex and coed. Duke's fraternities and sororities do not have their own houses, but members of the former live in designated areas of the college dorms. Because Duke guarantees four years of housing, there is some overcrowding, and freshmen and sophomores may find themselves living in triples. There is a bonanza of eating options on campus, including three dining halls, a soda shop, a full-service restaurant and on-campus pizza delivery. Students use a magnetic prepaid meal card to pay for all of this, and the amount of each purchase is deducted from the total. Full reimbursement for any unused money at the end of the semester is an unusual and much-appreciated policy.

Fraternities and sororities thrive at Duke, with close to 45 percent of men and women pledging. At least one student feels that the Greeks "are a bit too dominant in the social life," but another notes that going this route is "by no means the only way to have a good time." The fraternities, who take charge of kicking off the weekend with a Thursday night bash, are responsible for Duke's reputation as a good school for a great social life. Fraternity parties are open to everyone and often have live bands, but due to a recent policy change they are BYOB affairs. Beyond their doors, the social life betrays a tradition of southern gentility, and students claim that relations between the sexes are still somewhat formal. At least one student believes that hardcore studyers "often become frustrated with the highly visible social atmosphere."

Duke's beautiful, forested campus—where even tourists come to view the chapel—is actually split in two. The west campus, with its impressive Gothic architecture, is the more active and popular. It contains residential quads, classroom quads, the administration building, Perkins Library, and the student union, which includes the main dining hall known as "The Pits." The east campus, the site of the old women's college, is a quieter area done in Georgian architecture. Some classes are held at the east campus, and students who prefer a quieter life-style often choose to live there. The two campuses are connected by bus, though many students enjoy the mile or so walk along wooded Campus Drive. The 8,300-acre Duke Forest lies just a few minutes from west campus. Students head for the quarry and Jordan Lake for swimming and water sports, or drive four hours in either direction to get to the ocean or the ski slopes.

Durham is an old industrial city that grew up around tobacco but, more importantly, is now the site of Research Triangle Park, a huge complex of research institutions and light industry about fifteen minutes from campus. Preeminent among these is the Research Triangle Institute, cocreated by Duke, North Carolina State University at Raleigh, and the University of North Carolina at Chapel Hill for nonprofit, scientific and sociological research.

Duke is a culturally active campus, even if Durham is no hotbed of art and culture. Theater groups thrive, and the Freewater Film Society shows classic movies each week. Duke also has a cable-television system that undergraduates use for parodies of game shows and other entertainment. As for sports? Suffice it to say that Duke's official motto is *Eruditio et Religio* only to a few diehard administrators; everyone else knows it as *Eruditio et Basketballio*—which translates more or less as "To hell with Carolina—" the University of North Carolina, that is, Duke's archrival in basketball for supremacy of the Atlantic Coast Conference. Cameron Indoor Arena is packed to the rafters for every game, and Duke fans are every bit as manic as those of the Big Ten, only much more clever in their jibes at the opposition. The Blue Devils consistently rank among the nation's best teams, and one student advises that "if you plan to get good seats at a basketball game—buy a tent." Though less popular, football is still a "big money, big social, little-winning sport," one junior notes. Despite the fact that Duke sports are big-time, many students praise the tradition of scholar-athletes. "When I sit in the stands I'm cheering for friends of mine, not some nameless, faceless brutes," a political science major says. For part-time jocks, there are two intramural leagues, one for competitive types and one for strictly weekend athletes, which draw heavy participation from the Greeks. Both varsity and intramural athletes have benefited from the recent construction; there is a new locker/office complex for varsity sports, and intramurals have been bolstered by the addition of lighted fields and artificial turf.

Duke has been described as "an Ivy League school with decent weather." This description is not fair to Duke's southern heritage, nor does it account for the strong fraternity system. Nonetheless, there is something to it. A major research university with an emphasis on undergraduate education, "Duke may lack the powerful intellectual life of Harvard and Yale," one student surmises, "but it is a real close community of scholarly, well-rounded people destined for future achievement."

Duquesne University

Pittsburgh, PA 15282

Location Center city	**Applicants** 2,451
Total Enrollment 6,580	**Accepted** 78%
Undergraduates 4,210	**Enrolled** 48%
Male/Female 45/55	**Academics** ★ ★
SAT V/M 480/510	**Social** ☎ ☎
Financial Aid 78%	**Q of L** ● ●
Expense Pr $	**Admissions** (412)434-6220

After staging a death-defying comeback from last decade's financial woes, Duquesne University has tightened its belt. Today the little Roman Catholic university is marching on, attracting students by offering resourceful financial aid packages and managing to keep its private school tuition competitively low.

Raised on a bluff above the noise and bustle of Pittsburgh, Duquesne provides both a scenic view of the downtown area and the peace and quiet of the country. "We're in a world of our own," says one student who enjoys the secluded, grass-carpeted campus. Amid this calm, the university professes to offer a values-centered education and all that is needed to "help you realize your goals as a person and as a career professional." Yet students say liberal arts offerings have been somewhat slighted in recent years as precious funds have been directed toward more vocational and professional areas. "You can't educate the whole person, yet emphasize science and business more than the other areas," a political science major complains. To address this issue, the administration is promoting a new core curriculum plan that ensures all students, regardless of major, will be given a solid liberal arts base.

Undergraduates can enroll in any one of six schools: arts and sciences, business administration, music, education, pharmacy and nursing. The well-reputed pharmacy school—Duquesne's most intense and selective program—features one-on-one clinical experience while operating its own pharmacy. The school's strong ties with Pittsburgh employers often lead to internships and jobs for the journalism, law and business students. In the College of Arts and Sciences, the biology and chemistry departments are strong enough to produce graduates with a 100 percent acceptance rate at medical schools. Duquesne is one of the main centers of the phenomenological branch of philosophy and psychology in this country, and taking contemporary theology courses—especially Father Bushinski's Marriage—is the most popular way of fulfilling the three-course religion requirement. Students say the weakest departments are theater, classical literature and foreign languages.

Class sizes at Duquesne are successfully kept to manageable proportions, and students report little trouble getting into desired courses. Professors generally receive high ratings for their teaching and accessibility. While almost all faculty members are laymen, Duquesne's Catholicism does manifest itself in the nearly two-thirds Catholic student body and the school's official name—Duquesne University of the Holy Ghost. (In 1967, incidentally, Duquesne became the birthplace of the modern charismatic renewal movement in the Catholic Church, when four laymen on campus received the "baptism of the Holy Spirit" and began speaking in tongues.) Students can cross-register with the University of Pittsburgh and Carnegie–Mellon, the city's two other major colleges, and those interested in engineering may complete their degree program at Case Western Reserve. These institutions also provide resources for students who find Duquesne's library facilities inadequate (all six of Duquesne's undergraduate schools use the same library).

Seven of every ten undergrads are from Pennsylvania (40 percent commute), with most others coming from Ohio, West Virginia, and other nearby states. A new program to encourage enrollment of foreign students should add some diversity to the population. The majority of students, says one woman, "are interested in getting a good job—in fact, sometimes I think that's their only interest."

As the pioneer college to offer what are coming to be known as educational "futures" plans, Duquesne is selling four years of college tuition to parents of babies and small children for a fraction of the anticipated cost (the younger the child, the better the bargain). This innovative plan is a gambler's form of financial aid. If in 15, 16, or 17 years the "future" children decide Duquesne isn't the right school, or if they can't get in (they still have to apply), parents get back the initial deposit, but none of the interest earned on it. Yet if a child spends a full year at Duquesne, the value of that tuition guarantee can be transferred to another school. In addition, several of the athletic teams now offer athletic scholarships and more than one hundred University Scholars receive up to $2,000 a year. These merit awards are based exclusively on academic achievement and are renewable with a maintained 3.0 GPA.

Today's students choose between two upperclass and two underclass dorms. One large dorm, with separate male and female wings, is reserved for freshmen; upperclassmen may live in the modern, magnificent and noisy Towers complex, with its seventeen stories, huge cafeteria, lounges, TV rooms and pool. After their freshman year, students who want to live together in groups of ten to sixteen can apply for "interest wings" in the Towers. Many upperclassmen choose, however, to move into apartments in Pittsburgh—Rand McNally's "most liveable city"—and there is an apartment complex practically on campus that has housed much of the Duquesne community at one time or another. Meal plans provide "sort of fast-foodish food." As one psychology major puts it, "The food is not exactly a gourmet feast, but there is always a nice variety," which means the salad bar may be the only option for a choosy palate. Commuters have their own cafeteria, and fraternity and sorority members have special seating in dining halls.

A smorgasbord of campus architecture provides everything from older, established-looking to ultramodern buildings, with a lot of '50s and '60s design scattered throughout. Downtown Pittsburgh provides a view from the cliff and a great nightlife from a closer perspective. A good bus system zips students to the city in under five minutes, making major-league sports, concerts, opera, ballet and other aspects of a large metropolis accessible for everyone. In addition to its famous heavy industry and a large number of new corporate headquarters, Pittsburgh has the usual bars, stores and theaters. On campus, there are always parties and movies in the main dorm, and the fraternities and sororities play a large role in campus social life. Pennsylvania's drinking age is twenty-one, and some students complain that policies concerning alcohol on campus are unnecessarily restrictive. More than a hundred various organizations and clubs provide various extracurricular energy outlets. For example, the Tamburitzans, a unique folk music troupe that performs around the world, consists of approximately forty students, all on scholarship through the School of Music.

Since Duquesne is largely a commuter school, there is little sense of traditional college spirit other than what is mustered by the nationally ranked basketball team. Students go wild over the generally winning Division I Cagers—"the biggest crowd pleaser at Duquesne," says one senior—and to a lesser degree, over the football squad. Crew and outdoor track are recent additions to the athletic program. The intramural program is "the highlight of Duquesne social life," and students can participate in a variety of sports. Duquesne recently broke ground on a $10.1-million recreation complex, which includes a basketball arena, racquetball courts, weight training facilities and aerobics rooms.

Academically, socially, aesthetically and by most other measures, Duquesne isn't going to win any great awards. But few of its cheerful, home-grown students are complaining. While outspoken progressives and highly motivated scholars might want to look elsewhere, many conservative undergrads, especially those who appreciate Catholicism and a decent education at a not-too-outrageous price, will find this plateau overlooking Pittsburgh just fine for a four-year stop.

Earlham College

Richmond, IN 47374

Location City outskirts	**Applicants** 730
Total Enrollment 1,060	**Accepted** 85%
Undergraduates 1,060	**Enrolled** 48%
Male/Female 45/55	**Academics** ★ ★ ★
SAT V/M 550/550	**Social** 🏠 🏠 🏠
Financial Aid 60%	**Q of L** ● ● ● ● ●
Expense Pr $ $	**Admissions** (800)428-6958

Although Quakers make up only 18 percent of the student body at Earlham—and the football team has yet to adopt passive resistance as a defense strategy—Quaker values pervade all aspects of student life at Earlham. Mutual trust and a sincere interest in knowledge are the key notes of this small, liberal arts school. The students and professors and "even the president" are called by their first names, and alcohol is not allowed on campus. You don't just enroll in Earlham, you join a community committed to "peace, simplicity, honesty, integrity and compassion."

Sitting on eight hundred sprawling acres, the campus itself is cozy and not intimidating. "It's hard to feel overwhelmed when you can see every building from the center of the campus," explains a sociologist. The majority of the structures have nothing in common architecturally, and many are "remnants of the early Earlham days." With luscious wide-spread lawns and a huge wooded back campus, this southern Indiana school may seem isolated, but its approach to liberal arts education is far from provincial. There are more than twenty off-campus programs, including semesters in Japan, Scandinavia, Israel, Mexico, Kenya and the Canadian wilderness; about 50 percent of the students eventually take advantage of at least one of them. The school is also affiliated with the Great Lakes Colleges Association.*

On campus, degrees are offered in thirty-nine departments and interdisciplinary programs, with about 20 percent of the students involved in self-designed majors. Faculty members are selected for their excellence in teaching and their ability to cross curricular lines. After class, they share dorm life and student social activities. "Faculty members don't expect to teach their classes and then go home or do research," reports a human development student. "The assumption here is that professors can learn as much from students as the other way around."

Earlham operates on a trimester calendar in which students take only three classes each eleven-week term. There are rigorous core requirements in all divisions, including a freshman year humanities sequence, which stresses an encounter with classic texts, discussion and writing. All courses stress the development of library skills, and students praise the library facilities and staff. Cooperative and group learning are a vital part of the academic approach, and class discussion rather than lecture is the predominant learning style. Sciences, especially biology and geology, are strong, as are the social sciences, languages and philosophy. International studies (particularly Japanese), peace and global studies and human development and social relations win plaudits from students. The weakest offerings are in the academic extremes of art and business, while students refer to music and women's studies as insubstantial. About 40 percent of Earlham graduates eventually go on to some sort of graduate study, and both prelaw and premed students enjoy high acceptance rates at graduate school. For the adventurous student, a four-week program in the Galapagos Islands and a wilderness program are offered.

The student body at Earlham is probably more diverse than any other college in Indiana. A third of the students hail from the East, half from the Midwest, and only 17 percent from the Hoosier State. Earlham makes a strong commitment to minority students, whose enrollment is now 14 percent of the student body. "Sensitive, tolerant, and deeply caring" is how one student describes her peers. And at a time when the national climate is conservative, Earlham students are proud to call themselves "unabashedly liberal people who want to explore life—academically, politically and socially." Idealism runs high as does the percentage of graduates entering service-oriented professions. Students help make the rules at Earlham; they are responsible for following them and, if they don't like them, changing them. Professors, more often than not, hand out exams and leave the classroom unproctored. As one student observes, "There are more responsibilities to Earlham than just paying the bill."

A handful pay the bill with honors scholarships—forty per year worth $1,000 to $2,000. Earlham attempts to provide the requisite scholarship help for all its students who evidence need. The college also offers "short-term emergency" loans at low interest rates, but no athletic scholarships.

The five dorms on campus, all well maintained, vary in the living arrangements they offer. Some have larger rooms for doubles or triples, others have a majority of singles, but none of them are overcrowded. Freshmen are reserved space in each of the dorms, and upperclassmen divide up the remaining rooms by lottery. Students rate the dorms from "very livable" to "excellent." Interested upperclassmen may apply for the position of resident counselor, which entails organizing activities and providing support and counsel. A group of students may petition to live together, a popular option. Living off campus requires permission from the housing office, but juniors and seniors may move from the dorms into one of eighteen college-owned apartments and houses, including a working chicken farm. Most people eat at the college dining hall—"Not a four-star restaurant, but very clean and comfortable"—on one of the three available meal plans. A vegetarian main course and a salad and health-food bar are available in the large and noisy cafeteria.

Quaker beliefs plus Indiana's liquor laws add up to an extremely dry campus. "Parties are not a mainstay for students here," one notes. But alternatives to a rowdy social life abound, including a fine film and artists series and Breadbox, a student-run coffeehouse that features student performers. Almost all students participate in music or theater activities, and campus organizations range from Amnesty International to a sailing club. When all else fails, "We go out in small groups and listen to the corn grow or indulge in some cow tipping," quips one sarcastic senior.

Men's and women's varsity athletics receive equal support at Earlham, although "sports as a whole are not greatly emphasized," a political science major notes. Men's soccer and women's field hockey have done well of late and have been rewarded with new playing fields. A thriving intramural program has benefited from extensive, modern facilities.

"Few people come to Earlham because of Richmond," attests a social relations student. "In fact, most would say they came to Earlham in spite of Richmond." City-oriented people may have to make an adjustment to the slower life, but Richmond does boast a symphony and theater and is big enough to supply part-time jobs and volunteer activities for interested students. As a last resort, bigger, rowdier colleges and several major midwestern cities are only a couple of hours in any direction, and Indiana University and a national park in picturesque Brown County are but an hour or so to the southwest. Those lucky enough to have a car take a few such road trips each semester.

Earlham students seem very aware and appreciative of what is known as the Quaker experiment in education—a college experience extending far beyond the traditional constraints of a lecture and a textbook. It may not always succeed, but as one student explains, "Earlham is like an incubator; all aspects of the environment generate growth."

Eckerd College

St. Petersburg, FL 33711

Location City outskirts	**Applicants** 1,000
Total Enrollment 1,210	**Accepted** 70%
Undergraduates 1,210	**Enrolled** 44%
Male/Female 50/50	**Academics** ★ ★ ★
SAT V/M 500/530	**Social** ☎ ☎ ☎
Financial Aid 44%	**Q of L** ● ● ● ● ●
Expense Pr $ $	**Admissions** (813)867-1166

The setting is ideal: ten minutes from the heart of sunny St. Petersburg, a half hour from Tampa, a quick barefoot walk from the beaches of beautiful Boca Ciega Bay. Add to this a school-owned marina with facilities provided for students and faculty free of charge, and what do you have? A school for the terminal beach bum? Try again. Eckerd College, which occupies this remarkable setting, is in fact a church-related, values-oriented, incredibly innovative liberal arts school. Despite the outward appearance of most students—"We prefer shorts and sandals to skirts and ties"—this is a serious college full of undergrads with the energy and enthusiasm to enjoy an imaginative educational setting. Beach bums are advised to take their Coppertone elsewhere.

Founded in 1960 as Florida Presbyterian College and renamed a decade later after a generous, gift-giving Florida businessman, Jack Eckerd, the college is bordered on two sides by Old Tampa Bay, and provides "acre upon acre of waterfront campus area." The architecture is modern, and none of the buildings are more than two stories high. The chapel-in-the-round, the most interesting of all the structures, is surrounded by a pond with fountains—"very Floridian." And the entire campus remains green ("thanks to the weather") and immaculately kept all year round.

Close student-faculty relationships are emphasized at Eckerd. Every student has a faculty "mentor" who serves as an adviser, an inspiration, a guidance counselor and a friend. "Beefing with professors" and "pitchers with professors" are popular events sponsored by the campus snack bar and pub. Another unique opportunity for Eckerd students is cross-generational interaction with a subcommunity of senior citizens known as the Academy of Senior Professionals. Academy members come to Eckerd from all walks of life—they're retired doctors, lawyers, artists, bank presidents, writers, etc.—to become part of a shared learning process by taking classes with freshmen and seniors, working with professors on curriculum development, and leading workshops in their area of expertise. In addition, innovative Eckerd pioneered in the 4-1-4 academic year schedule where students spend the month of January, known as winter term, working on a single project for credit.

Freshmen arrive on this sunny campus three weeks early for an orientation, which includes a mandatory project to be completed for course credit under the supervision of an assigned mentor. During the fall and spring semesters freshmen take an interdisciplinary two-course sequence entitled Western Heritage, which focuses on great books. They must also meet a writing proficiency requirement as well as a quantitative methods requirement in mathematics or computer science. One year of foreign language study is also mandatory.

Sophomores and juniors take four courses from a list of options in each of four broad perspectives on human existence: aesthetic, cross-cultural, environmental, and social relations. Seniors take a course that focuses on contemporary issues from the Judeo-Christian perspective, and a capstone senior seminar in which they are asked to draw on what they've learned throughout college to find solutions to important issues.

Solid departments include celebrated programs in biology, chemistry, computer science, mathematics, physics and marine science. Business administration, education, creative writing, psychology and human resources are also top-notch offerings. The theater department does not receive much credit, and one senior reports "communications is Eckerd's absolute weakest department." Foreign languages are not the choice offerings on this campus either, but in compensation the school has developed a strong program of foreign study, including its own campus in London. Winter term may be taken there, or in Coventry, Vienna, Italy, Czechoslovakia/Poland, Israel or the Caribbean of the Dry Tortugas.

Eckerd considers itself Christian nonsectarian, but maintains an informal "covenant" with the two major Presbyterian denominations, from which they receive some funds. Only a small minority of the students are Presbyterian, but religion plays more than a peripheral role in their lives and classroom education. "You can accept or reject religion here, but you can't ignore it," reports a senior. The sense of campus community is, however, strong. The college president cares so much about student welfare that during exam time—that stressful period when no one eats well—he serves them late-night pizzas for sustenance.

Forty percent of Eckerd's students come from Florida, and 9 percent are foreigners. Most of the rest are northeasterners looking for warmer climes and a small school with a stimulating, distinctive curriculum. Eckerd goes after what it calls "competent givers"—men and women who can lead and are committed to human service rather than a lucrative career. "Students here want to excel at being good human beings," observes one student. Class standing isn't all that important (less than half made it into the top fifth of their high school class) but academic drive is. More than a third go on for higher degrees at some point after graduation. Overall, students are self-disciplined, motivated and politically uncategorical—"the campus enjoys a comfortable mix of liberals and conservatives."

Eckerd usually succeeds in working out a viable financial package for those who require financial help. Need-based and merit scholarship awards are often combined at this little southeastern school where fifty Presbyterian students are nominated each year by pastors for scholarships worth $2,400. Other merit scholarships—close to two hundred in total—range from $2,000 to full rides, and are based on transcripts, test scores and leadership/services accomplishments. Fifteen incoming freshmen are awarded up to $1,500, used to complete significant research with a faculty member.

About 80 percent of the students live in one of seven housing quads separated from the rest of the campus by Dorm Drive. Both single-sex and coed-by-floor dorms are available, with mostly double-rooms and some singles. Freshmen are assigned rooms with an eye toward compatible personal habits—pets or no pets, smoking or nonsmoking, etc. Rooms are fairly large and usually air-conditioned; there is no extra charge for the waterfront views and beautiful sunsets. The cafeteria won an award for being the "cleanest in the Southeast," and on top of that, the food's not half bad. Arrangements can be made with the food service company to equip student groups with cookout gear—food, plates, utensils and grills—for those who crave a beachfront view with their meals.

There are no Greek groups at Eckerd, but one elementary education major claims, "each dorm is very much like a small sorority or fraternity in that we are unified and plan activities together." When students aren't heading for the white sandy beaches, St. Petersburg (although it's viewed by most students as "a geriatric retirement city") provides entertainment in the form of museums, shops, restaurants and theaters. Basketball and soccer are popular at Eckerd, but the nationally ranked baseball team is the top banana. Baseball fever hits Eckerd early, and no wonder; six pro teams come down for spring training nearby. Other varsity sports of interest are sailing and boardsailing; intramurals range from flag football to the assassin game, in which students try to shoot each other with dart guns.

There's no denying that Eckerd is alluring in more ways than one—academic excellence and innovative programs, ideal location, and the near-perfect climate. Yet people are most important, and personal values are not taken lightly in this community by the sea. Says one student: "At Eckerd there's really no place for people who always seem to take, but never seem to give."

Emory University

Atlanta, GA 30322

Location Suburban
Total Enrollment 8,790
Undergraduates 4,870
Male/Female 47/53
SAT V/M 550/600
Financial Aid 52%
Expense Pr $ $

Applicants 4,550
Accepted 68%
Enrolled 40%
Academics ★ ★ ★ ★
Social ☎ ☎ ☎
Q of L ● ● ● ●
Admissions (404)727-6036

Maybe they should call it Woodruff–Chandler University, or just Coca-Cola U. The Woodruff and Chandler families have certainly donated a nice chunk of their family soft drink biz profits to build Emory University and its endowment—which now weighs in at a healthy $700 million. Since the school wasn't renamed after one gift of $105 million in 1979, it probably never will be. Not that it's necessary anymore: Full-tuition Robert W. Woodruff scholars already work out at the new George W. Woodruff Physical Education Center, study in the ten-story Woodruff Library, and take classes from professors in Woodruff-endowed chairs.

With its coffers overflowing from the recent gifts, Emory has set about the task of establishing itself as a southern university of the first rank—along with the likes of Duke, Vanderbilt and the University of Virginia. Yet in many ways, Emory has more in common with northern counterparts like Brown and the University of Pennsylvania than with any of its fellows south of the Mason-Dixon Line. It is only by a quirk of geography that Emory is located in the suburbs of Atlanta; with about half of its students from outside the South, and many of the rest transplanted southerners, Emory often seems like a little piece of New Jersey that somehow got lost on the way to Hackensack.

If Emory is a geographical anomaly, there is nothing strange about its academic programs. Serious instruction in an intimate learning environment has always been the hallmark of an Emory education. Emory's new funding has made more student scholarships and research grants available and vastly improved the need-based financial aid program. Set on 550 acres of woods and rolling hills, the campus is centered on an academic quad of marble-covered, red-roofed buildings, with more contemporary structures dotting the periphery of the lush, green grounds. Lately, the campus has been a beehive of activity, with new buildings sprouting up left and right. Along with all the Woodruff facilities, last year a new art and archeology museum opened, and a huge student center completed in 1986 is rapidly becoming the hub of the campus. Next on the agenda is a $42-million science research facility.

Emory's chemistry department is considered one of its strongest areas and may be one reason that the school sometimes seems overrun by premeds. The history department also earns high marks, as do political science, classics, English, psychology and the relatively new anthropology department. Art history is also strong, and the brand-new theater arts department seems to be off to a promising start. Music and fine arts departments, on the other hand, garner criticism from students both for poor course offerings and a lack of facilities. The math professors are "consistently unpopular," and even the administration admits that the geology department is in need of improvement. More than a third of every student's course work goes toward fulfilling rigorous and comprehensive distribution requirements in the liberal arts. This core

217

program is divided into six categories with names like Tools of Learning, and Aesthetics and Values. Health or physical education courses are also required. Freshmen who choose to take an Emory College seminar gain a structured introduction to the school, become part of a small social group, and establish contact with a faculty mentor. "Most professors are incredibly receptive to the students and their interests," believes one senior. A wide variety of degrees are available, including a 3-2 engineering program with Georgia Tech, early admission to Emory's graduate school of business or dentistry, and combination BA/MA degrees in nearly a dozen fields. The recently christened Jimmy Carter Presidential Library and Center, a boon for political science majors, offers internships for undergraduates.

Less than a quarter of the students are Georgians, and a little over half are from the Southeast. New York, New Jersey and Florida are all well represented, and the university has a large Jewish contingent that dwarfs that at any other southern university. The typical "Emeroid" is from an upper-middle-class family, dedicated to preparing for a career, and not overly concerned with the life of the mind. "People care not about what they are learning but rather about how their GPA will fit into their starting salary," says one political science major. Nevertheless, Emory takes pride in its ability to accommodate all types, and is far more accepting of racial and ethnic minorities than most southern universities. "We've got Jews, blacks, northerners, southerners, punk rockers, stoners, theater types, preprofessionals, etc., and they all feel relatively comfortable with each other . . . usually," a senior says. Outstanding freshmen will find the school most accommodating of all, since fully 18 percent of each entering class receives merit scholarships ranging from $750 to more than full tuition awarded on the basis of personal and academic achievement, regardless of need. Needy students also take note: The massive infusion of funds means that Emory is now need-blind in admissions, and the administration is anxious to get the word out.

Housing at Emory is guaranteed only for freshmen, though it is usually available for most others who want it. Most of the dorms are coed, though two are all female and one is all male, and vary in terms of spaciousness and sociability. Newcomers are housed together their freshman year, a time viewed with nostalgia by upperclassmen. "I lived in decrepit old Dobbs Hall with tiny rooms and no air conditioning," relates one, "and I wouldn't have missed it for the world." A recent freshman class that was larger than expected forced the university to move many upperclassmen into hotels and a nearby apartment complex—"a great deal"—while offering others $1,000 to live off campus. Almost half of the upperclassmen do so by choice anyway, with about 15 percent opting for Greek houses. The new dining hall inside the student center serves palatable meals with a variety of options. Students who live on campus are required to get some variation of the meal plan, which includes options in the dining hall, campus restaurant, kosher deli, snack bar—even at the ice cream and frozen yogurt shop. A new food service contract has improved the quality of cafeteria fare; fraternity members invariably eat at their houses.

About half of the students join a fraternity or sorority, and everyone acknowledges the Greek life to be the dominant social force on campus. The frats and sororities tend to attract the preppier members of the student body, while a flourishing off-campus community, comprised mainly of upperclassmen, provides a more independent lifestyle for nonjoiners. Lately, with the completion of the new student center, non-Greek social life on campus has picked up. "Outdoor band/beer parties every other Friday (called MOVE parties) are rapidly becoming an institution," one man reports. "Dooley's Week" a week-long spring festival is the most popular campus tradition. And whenever the campus gets slow, there's always Atlanta—hands down the most exciting city in the Southeast. Many students regularly make use of Atlanta's many entertainment resources—the downtown area is only ten minutes away—or take occasional trips to the Carolinas or the coast. Emory is Methodist affiliated, and its president is a theologian, but the religious atmosphere of the college is described by one student as "nil."

Sports at Emory are even more conspicuously absent. Emory does not field varsity teams in the traditional "big" areas of football, basketball, swimming or baseball, and at least one student thinks "it's a shame, too." School spirit may suffer, but an extensive intramural program doesn't. The school has built a huge $20-million gymnasium, and recently organized a Division III men's basketball team to compete in the newly chartered University Athletic Association, along with other top academic institutions, including the University of Chicago, Johns Hopkins University and Carnegie–Mellon University. In the meantime, men's and women's tennis, swimming, track and cross-country varsity teams regularly turn in winning seasons, and men's soccer is ranked in the nation's top twenty.

Emory has always been a fine school, and its future looks even better. While most schools in the region suffer from an endemic provincialism, Emory strikes a balance between North and South. Perhaps more importantly, at a time when many schools are scrounging for cash, Emory is knee-deep in it, and as a result everything from the physical plant to financial aid is improving by leaps and bounds. Meanwhile, undergraduate enrollment has shot up over 50 percent in the last five years and shows no signs of tapering off. After years of playing second fiddle to bigger and better-known southern universities, Emory is finally beginning to look like "the real thing."

Evergreen State College

Olympia, WA 98505

Location City outskirts
Total Enrollment 2,970
Undergraduates 2,830
Male/Female 47/53
SAT V/M 520/520
Financial Aid 38%
Expense Pub $ $ $

Applicants 940
Accepted 53%
Enrolled 73%
Academics ★ ★ ★
Social 🎭 🎭 🎭
G of L ● ● ● ●
Admissions (206)866-6000

Many colleges these days are picking up on bits and pieces of the nontraditional, decidedly alternative methods of education that Evergreen State College was born to provide. Founded in 1967, Evergreen was the first college in the nation to create its entire curriculum around interdisciplinary learning. Students here have been designing their own academic programs and helping to govern the institution for well over a decade. At a time when educators across the country are being awakened to the benefits of student autonomy, the message from Evergreen is, "We hate to say we told you so, but . . ."

Still one step ahead of the game, Evergreen remains comparably alternative in structure because there are no grades, no required courses and no traditional departments here. The college also "has a special interest in those students who have not been well served by traditional education." This group includes many older students (the average undergraduate age is twenty-four) and the creative types whose talents weren't nurtured in high school classrooms.

"Everything at Evergreen is unusual or especially imaginative," claims one student. A colleague describes the school's setting as "environmentally conscious, unobtrusive, functional as well as aesthetically pleasing." In less esoteric terms, the campus is "a prime example of modern cement and steel architecture with sculpture, murals and windows abounding." Snuggled in amidst a thousand acres of undeveloped forestry, far away from major highways and civilization, Evergreen is also aquatically equipped with 3,300 feet of undeveloped waterfront and beach on the southern end of Puget Sound.

Instead of signing up for a series of unrelated individual courses, students at Evergreen enroll in one coherent and integrated program at a time, many of which last up to a year. Freshmen and sophomores take "core programs," such as Origins of Life and Intelligence, Society and the Computer or Political Ecology. "The core programs," claims one junior, "offer students a chance to cooperatively pursue interesting subjects and simultaneously gain an understanding of the many diverse factors which affect that subject." Advanced students concentrate in one of eight specialty areas of interdisciplinary study, which cover everything from Applied Social Theory to Expressive Arts. "There has long been substantial agreement within the faculty that major issues facing civilization in the late twentieth century cannot even be conceived and named, let alone usefully examined, exclusively through the lenses of traditional academic disciplines," explains an Evergreen administrator. Thus, the school's unique academic structure aims not only to impart knowledge, but to develop each student's capacity for inquiry. There are no set syllabuses for these interdisciplinary study courses, and student input often constitutes the substance of the class. If none of the packaged programs meet a student's needs, special programs can be put together with the help of a faculty adviser. Students also help grade themselves by filling out self-evaluations. In turn, they receive detailed written evaluations from the faculty instead of letter or numerical grades.

Since there are no departments per se, and all the areas intertwine with other disciplines at one point or another, it's hard to say what's strong and what's weak. Students do emphasize that political science, management and the natural sciences—especially environmental studies—are excellent. Evergreen has led the nation in the number of grants awarded to undergraduates by the National Science Foundation. Even the administration admits the language study programs need to be expanded, and areas such as music, performing arts and photography suffer from a shortage of faculty, although they have great facilities that "are just crying out to be used." The library is modest, but it opens "very early in the morning." Students praise the librarians as "the best in the country," which presumably means they are adept in arranging interlibrary loans.

Faculty rotate from year to year in core programs, advanced programs and staff positions like academic advisers. "This movement keeps faculty members accessible and, for the most part, fresh," a creative writing major says. "Because there is no tenure here, professors do not have to operate under the pressure to 'publish or perish,'" an education major adds. "They are able to concentrate on teaching *and* learning that benefits them as well as the students." The emphasis at Evergreen is on seminars rather than on lectures; the work load can be heavy, but the atmosphere tends to be noncompetitive.

Individualism is stressed on this campus, although one student reports seeing many cliques—"the hippies, the punks, the yuppies and the people who just don't care." Despite the groupies, Evergreen students are an accepting, free-spirited and hardworking bunch. "There is a predominant feeling that we want to change the world, and not in a bad sense," conceptualizes a social science major. A classmate adds that "those who are willing to try and break through their conditioned training will enjoy this school." Although many assert that students vary politically, some worry about conservative influences. "Indeed, the overriding fear on campus is no longer whether the state legislature will continue support for the school, but whether Evergreen is becoming more traditional," claims one student.

Despite the administration's claim that high school academics are not the main criterion in Evergreen's selection process, 99 percent of the students come from the top half of their high school classes. Application numbers and average SAT scores have been creeping up in recent years. In addition to offering need-based financial aid and what one student calls "the best private school education at the best public school price," Evergreen awards a dozen athletic partial scholarships and about forty-seven, ranging up to $1,500, for academic merit.

Between the conventional dormitories and the modular housing units with kitchens for three to five students, the college manages to house about six hundred of its students. A shortage of housing both on and off campus is becoming more critical every year according to student reports, and sign-up is on a first-come, first-served basis. The dorms are coed, and singles are available at a slightly higher price. Off-campus options include apartments in town or a privately owned complex only ten minutes from campus. Evergreen's cafeteria offers "rather routine and repetitive" meals as well as a board plan and a deli.

Olympia has become home to the many Evergreen graduates who live and work there, and Seattle is only sixty miles down the road. But most nonacademic activity revolves around the breathtaking natural environment, kept green by Washington's infamous rain. "There's constant, gray drizzle," one student complains. "Chinese water torture." A junior agrees that while "it rains a lot, it's never too cold to ride your bike, if you don't mind getting damp." Students go skiing, watch the salmon jump, go backpacking or take advantage of the beautiful wild beach areas on the campus. The college rents out camping gear, and has sailboats, rowboats, and canoes. Men's and women's varsity soccer teams are successful, while the swimming, sailing and Ultimate Frisbee teams "have a great time"—what do you expect from a school that calls its teams the geoducks (pronounced *gooeyducks*) after the king clams found in Puget Sound. Several students sign up for leisure education courses, which encompass everything from dance and swimming to weaving and massage. Organized social life tends to center around movies, dances, political rallies and potluck suppers in different houses or programs.

So, it's pretty much business as usual at this far western school. Meanwhile, academics around the country are "introducing" reforms in undergraduate education, i.e., promoting the active approach to learning and increasing students' responsibility for their own education, practices that have been regular features of Evergreen's curriculum since its inception. Ideologically, this is still one of the best schools for students who think they were born twenty years too late; academically, it's way ahead of its time.

Fairfield University

Fairfield, CT 06430

Location Suburban
Total Enrollment 5,120
Undergraduates 2,910
Male/Female 45/55
SAT V/M 530/570
Financial Aid 60%
Expense Pr $ $

Applicants 5440
Accepted 40%
Enrolled 35%
Academics ★ ★ ★
Social 🐷 🐷 🐷 🐷
Q of L ● ● ● ●
Admissions (203)254-4100

Tucked into the academic corridor that runs between Boston and New York City, Fairfield University is a relatively young school that is fast building a reputation for academic excellence. As the university moves into its second century, Fairfield's synthesis of the Jesuit tradition of academic excellence and 1980s career training is winning converts at a clip even the most zealous missionaries would find hard to match.

With a campus boasting spacious, carefully manicured grounds, "Fairfield reminds me of a vacation resort," says one junior. Appearances notwithstanding, the only R&R students around here get is usually in the form of reading and research papers. All students, no matter what their major, must weather a stiff core curriculum in the liberal arts on top of the requirements in their major field. Less than fifty years after its founding, Fairfield is gaining a well-deserved reputation for its rigorous blend of traditional Jesuit academics and solid 1980s career training.

Though it has good programs in many areas, Fairfield's main strengths are in the natural and behavioral sciences. Biology and psychology are especially good, and students rave about the premed program. The accounting department in the business school is also outstanding, and newer programs in computer science and management information systems are gaining ground. The nursing school is highly respected and offers a variety of excellent clinical experiences. Fine arts is undeveloped, but the school is planning to build a comprehensive fine arts center complete with a theater, art gallery, TV station and classroom space. For those interested in social sciences, the programs in politics, American studies and communications are strong. Philosophy, however, needs to diversify its offerings.

In order to graduate, each student must complete extensive core requirements that include at least two semesters in eight academic areas ranging from natural sciences to religious studies to fine arts. The core curriculum consumes more than half of a student's total course load, leading to a common gripe that it is "very restrictive and repetitive." Others find it to be a necessary part of a complete education. The honors program offers upperclassmen a more flexible mode of learning in a yearlong, interdisciplinary course that examines selected time periods from a variety of perspectives. Engineering students may enroll in a joint five-year program with the University of Connecticut, and there is a seven-year dental program with Georgetown University. The library is considered too small, too hot and somewhat overcrowded. But the faculty members, the vast majority of whom are lay professors, are well liked and much respected, and one-to-one relationships between faculty and students are common. Classes are usually composed of fewer than forty students, though one notable exception is a psychology course called Death and Dying that usually attracts about seventy.

About 90 percent of Fairfield's students come from Roman Catholic families, and almost half graduated from parochial high schools. Some two-fifths of the students are native to Connecticut, and most others come from nearby states. Not surprisingly, Fairfield students tend to be "somewhat conservative and homogeneous in styles, background and general attitudes," one senior attests. Students are accepted without reference to their financial need, and the university tries to assemble an aid package to help as many as possible. The school offers 160 non-need scholarships annually, ranging from nine Presidential Scholars awards covering full tuition to token $500 gifts. In addition, Fairfield awards about forty full athletic grants-in-aid each year.

Since Fairfield's two-hundred-acre campus is situated on some of the choicest and most expensive real estate in the country—Connecticut's Gold Coast in Fairfield County—it's not surprising that the administration takes pains to preserve the special atmosphere of its sprawling lawns, ponds, and natural woodlands. Most buildings are modern, and the dorms are spacious, attractive and well maintained. Freshmen and sophomores are expected to live on campus, usually in one of the five coed dorms in the "quad," while juniors and seniors often opt for attractive and roomy university town houses nearby. Once students have a room, they can hold on to it for the following year if they choose. All boarders must sign up for a twenty-one-meal plan that offers three entrees, periodic special dinners, and an ice cream bar. While about 70 percent of the students live on campus, many upperclass men and women choose to rent beach houses along the Sound, which creates something of a split between those who live on campus and those who don't. There are two social atmospheres, with campus-sponsored events competing with off-campus beach parties. These worlds are connected by a university-run shuttle bus, which makes the short trip every half hour and also stops at the railroad station and downtown.

Despite the rift between campus and beach, Fairfield has an active social scene. Semiformal campus dances—numbering five a year—usually sell out, and there are usually several big name concert acts on campus every semester, among them the Hooters and Eurythmics. In between, numerous private parties and informal dances are thrown every weekend. Although Jesuits are very much in evidence, and often live in the dorms, students say they offer advice only when asked and do not hinder the social scene. Nevertheless, the campus ministry draws a large following, with masses every day and retreats about three times a semester. Except for a few local bars for those of age, well-to-do Fairfield is "dead," one student notes, and those who need a break from the campus and beach hop the train to New Haven (a half hour away) or New York (just over an hour) for an evening or weekend. Boston lies about three hours to the northeast.

Basketball, both men's and women's, is the sport of choice at Fairfield, although "sports are not this school's forte," one senior points out. Hockey and baseball are also popular, and students turn out to support the Stags in large numbers. Living up to the Jesuit motto of sound mind and sound body, many students play on intramural teams, whose exploits are copiously chronicled in the campus newspaper.

Fairfield is a congenial and friendly place that benefits from the Jesuit tradition of a "value-based liberal education." Students may grumble about the rigorous core requirements, but by graduation they are usually firm believers in Fairfield's stimulating mix of Catholicism and career training.

Fairleigh Dickinson University

Rutherford, NJ 07666

Location Suburban	**Applicants** 4,330
Total Enrollment 13,520	**Accepted** 63%
Undergraduates 8,730	**Enrolled** 31%
Male/Female 52/48	**Academics** ★ ★
SAT V/M 450/480	**Social** ☎ ☎
Financial Aid 68%	**Q of L** ● ●
Expense Pr $	**Admissions** (800)338-8803

Founded in 1942, Fairleigh Dickinson was, for a long time, an attractive alternative to New Jersey's underdeveloped public colleges. Since then, the state's system of higher education has come a long way, which is good for the people of New Jersey, but bad for old Fairleigh. Yet instead of crying over spilt enrollment, FDU decided to sharpen its competitive edge. It has tapered its liberal arts departments, placed more emphasis on career-oriented education, and begun offering more part-time and two-year programs. And if that doesn't lure vocationally minded undergrads, the buy-one-get-one-for-$2,500-less financing plan is bound to encourage some co-sibling attendance. But perhaps abolition of the much-hated nickname—Fairly Ridiculous—would be the most effective marketing maneuver.

Sprawled over three campuses—Madison, Rutherford and Teaneck—Fairleigh Dickinson is really three schools in one. Students apply to only one campus, usually the one closest to home, but each has its specialties. Madison is the campus for future accountants, students interested in health programs (physical and respiratory therapy, radiologic technology), and those seeking a five-year BA/MA psychology program. Rutherford's main attractions include a hotel, restaurant and tourism management major (with required internship), a program in clinical nursing, and extensive remedial offerings in writing, reading and mathematics. Teaneck, with the largest enrollment, is noted for its programs in science, engineering, communications and social work. It's also the home of Edward Williams College, a small two-year liberal arts college from which successful students may transfer into any of the four-year programs.

Overall, the college of business administration attracts half of the total FDU student population. The college of science and engineering is steadily growing in enrollment, resources and number of faculty. Education receives a lot of criticism from students (and has been discontinued at the Rutherford campus), but it does have a strong commitment to practical experience in city schools. Last and probably least in the minds of FDU's practicality-minded students (two-thirds of whom head straight for the job market) are the humanities and social science offerings. But everyone receives at least a minimum of exposure to the arts and sciences through a newly implanted core curriculum consisting of four integrated courses focusing on the areas of logical analysis and communication, understanding world perspectives, broadening personal perspectives and achieving appreciation of interrelationships.

The academic climate is generally relaxed, and any tension about intellectual matters tends to be limited to finals week. One marketing major on the Madison campus says the thing she likes best about FDU is "the informal college atmosphere and the fact that the faculty members go out of their way to help and get to know students." Classes are nicely sized—"You won't get lost in them, but you won't be lonely either"—and rarely difficult to get into. On the other hand, the libraries—with just more than a half million volumes among them—are barely adequate for a school this size. Interlibrary loan and access to Drew University's library help. Cooperative work/study programs are available in chemistry and toxicology, and outstanding students can pursue independent study projects through the honors program. The Rutherford Plan allows students to combine study with work experiences for academic credit.

Marine biology majors must spend one semester at FDU's West Indies Laboratory in the Virgin Islands (poor things), while other students may spend a semester at Wroxton College in England, which is also owned and operated by the university. The rest of the time, Madison campus undergraduates enjoy a 187-acre estate of picture-postcard beauty, featuring woods, grassy malls and English gardens. Rutherford's denizens frequent another beautiful campus, complete with a castle modeled after Château d'Amboise in France, only twenty minutes from Manhattan and a short trot from the Meadowlands sports complex. The Teaneck campus, with all of its foliage and color, stretches along the banks of the Hackensack River, near the main street of this uninspired suburb, but only ten minutes from the George Washington Bridge into New York City.

Location is obviously a big selling point for FDU: Only 21 percent of the students come from outside New Jersey, and they are mainly from Connecticut and New York. Foreign students make up 9 percent of the student body, minorities about 15 percent. The students are drawn from all ranks of their class, with more than a third from the bottom half. "We are not intellectually elite," one student modestly observes. A candid classmate adds: "Average students belong here. Those with higher standards belong elsewhere." A healthy balance between social and academic life seems to work best here, current students say. If the thought of bagging classes on the first sunny spring day to head for the Jersey shore horrifies you, this might not be your ideal school.

FDU boasts a many-sided program of financial aid, which attempts to offer "from 80 to 85 percent" of the computed need for students who apply for aid before March 15 and then deals with remaining applicants on a funds-available basis. There are more than a hundred renewable grants, which range from $3,000 to $4,000, available to incoming or transfer students with a minimum B-plus academic average and a combined SAT score of 1050. There are also about ninety-four athletic scholarships (nearly half for men's and women's basketball), and the FDU-pioneered bargain-pack Family Plan, which allows families with more than one person enrolled to get hefty tuition discounts, is especially helpful to students of large families.

Seniority dictates rooming choices on each campus, but those who wish to live on campus will always get a place in one of the single-sex dorms—along with membership in the mandatory food plan. Depending on the campus, just over or just under a half of full-time undergraduates live at school. Commuters disappear on weekends to family and friends, leaving boarders behind just to "stay around the dorm and drink, or see a movie." The relatively new fraternities and sororities—"existent, but largely unknown"—available on each campus add a bit more structure to residents' nightlife and are beginning to lure commuters to their Saturday parties. New Jersey's drinking-age minimum of twenty-one means that no school-sponsored event may serve alcohol. "Drugs are out," says one woman, and preppie clothes are in, although jeans and sweats will never be out of place. Soccer is the most popular and successful of more than a dozen varsity sports, and the strong intramural program breeds intense and lively rivalries. The new athletic/recreational center on the Teaneck–Hackensack campus, complete with racquetball courts and a six-lane indoor track, is sure to help FDUers get enough exercise.

Not likely to ever draw national attention for its academics or wild social scene, FDU has modest aims. It tries to keep its curriculum and programs in tune with developing industries in the state and its instruction is personal. And that's exactly what the pragmatic students seem to want. As one Hackensackian puts it, "Students at this institution are mainly concerned with getting an education so as to make themselves more marketable," which is not so ridiculous.

Fisk University

Nashville, TN 37203

Location Urban	**Applicants** 590
Total Enrollment 540	**Accepted** 43%
Undergraduates 520	**Enrolled** 45%
Male/Female 30/70	**Academics** ★ ★
SAT V/M 410/450	**Social** ☎ ☎
Financial Aid 71%	**Q of L** ● ● ●
Expense Pr $	**Admissions** (615)329-8665

There are still a few cracks in the walls of the historic buildings at Fisk University, and occasionally there's no hot water in the dormitories, but that's nothing compared to the real trouble this school has seen. Poor fiscal management and the rush of black students to previously all-white colleges spelled financial disaster for Fisk in the '70s and early '80s. But when the president made an unusual appeal to some ten thousand alumni for emergency contributions, suddenly half a million dollars landed on the university's doorstep. And when this gift was matched dollar-for-dollar by a prominent Nashville businessman, Fisk students, faculty and administrators were convinced that the future was once again bright at this, one of the best-known and most prestigious of the predominantly black colleges.

"Tradition," reads one brochure, "is the cement that has kept this university in the minds and hearts of generations of students—it's the fuel that will ignite our journey into the 22nd century." Examples of such tradition are seen in the Jubilee Hall (named after the Fisk Jubilee Singers who, in 1873, traveled the country singing spirituals to raise money for their school), an English-style dormitory, which is the oldest building to reside on the campus of a black college. The rest of Fisk's forty-six-acre campus portrays the growth of the urban school. There are white stone and red-brick buildings, with a bit of nineteenth-century English and a lot of twentieth-century American architecture on this tidy little academic spot on the map of inner-city Nashville.

Fisk's president has pushed for a stronger university commitment to the liberal arts; therefore, every undergrad takes prescribed courses during his first two years. General areas of study in this core curriculum include creative arts, communications (both oral and written), natural science and social science. By the end of sophomore year, most students squeeze in a few electives and begin to think about choosing a major. The best departments are biology, chemistry and physics. Music, sociology, math and English also rate well. The administration admits the department of management and economics is in considerable need of a well-trained, stable faculty. But then, business programs are not the essence of this university whose aim is to "prepare students to bridge the gap between the races and open dialogue between the children of prosperity and their cousins in need."

Fisk has a supportive, rather than competitive, honors program, designed to foster continued excellence from students who have maintained a 3.0 grade average in their first two years at the university. Some students design internships or co-op jobs with local business or government; others participate in one-for-one exchange programs with Boston College, Cornell University, or other American universities or a study-abroad program at Oxford University. There's also a well-regarded five-year joint engineering program with nearby Vanderbilt University. But sticking around the Fisk campus, where a supportive, family-like atmosphere cuts across all academic and extracurricular activities, isn't a bad option either. "Professors are always willing to help," an electrical engineering major reports. And because of the school's itty-bitty size, "all students normally have access to the teachers they want," according to a sophomore. The Fisk library is a good place to spend some time, even if you're not studying. It houses special collections of Langston Hughes, George Gershwin and W.E.B. DuBois (one of Fisk's most famous alums). And a stop at the university's newly renovated art gallery is an enriching study break—with paintings of Cézanne and Renoir, it's one of the most outstanding art galleries in any southern school.

Fisk admissions officers consider high school performance and recommendations over and above all other criteria, but they like to at least see SAT scores. About 15 percent of students come from the top tenth of their high school class. Ninety-six percent of the students are black, many are middle class, and they come from all over the nation. "Students have become mildly conservative," says a poli-sci major, "compared to earlier Fisk students, who were somewhat radical." Fisk makes financial-aid offers first to students who complete applications by April 1, and thereafter until the funds are exhausted. There are also thirty-four renewable merit scholarships for full rides awarded to National Achievement Scholarship Program winners and other honor students. Air Force, Army and Navy ROTC are additional options.

All the dorms are now single sex, with women getting the nicest of the formerly coed units. Maintenance could be better—"If something is broken, plan on waiting a long time to get it fixed," one woman says. Unfortunately for the playful Fisk students, when the money got tight, the leisure activities were the first to go. Every on-campus organization is limited to one party or major activity a month, and private dorm parties are forbidden without permission. Every dorm resident eats in the same cafeteria on a full meal plan, and monotony may make the food seem worse than it purportedly is. Despite all this, few students live off campus.

Men find it fairly easy to get dates, thanks to the favorable sex ratio. Half of Fisk's students join a fraternity or sorority, but after rush week these organizations settle down to civic-minded tasks. Volunteer work is a frequent activity for all students, especially at nearby Hubbard Hospital or Tennessee State Prison. Creative arts form another diversion. Several plays are produced by students each year, and the various choirs, along with visiting authors, dancers, and musicians, perform regularly and contribute to the annual arts festival. Fisk has no religious affiliation, but most students attend church every Sunday, either on campus or around the city. Fisk is on the edge of Nashville's poorer, high-crime area, and this, coupled with erratic bus schedules, can be a deterrent to off-campus activities. "There really is not very much you can do in the city without having your own car," attests one student. Still with seventeen other colleges as well as music ranging from country to classical, the city supplies plenty of diversion.

Varsity football fell under the budget-cut ax, but there's still a club team that plays other colleges. Varsity basketball games draw crowds, and the women's team wins more often than the men's. Women's volleyball is another top female sport. Track is traditionally strong for both sexes, and men's baseball has been doing OK of late. Fisk supplies tennis courts and one playing field, but swimmers and runners have to use facilities at other schools. A new intramural program seems to be off to a promising start.

Despite the turmoil of the last decade, Fisk still has vestiges of the fine black academic institution it was once widely celebrated to be. "Fisk allows black students to reap what has been denied to them for so long—culture," one student contends. The new boost in applications may be a signal that young blacks are not just looking to predominantly white schools these days. And for those who realize and appreciate all the traditional and spiritual advantages of a top-notch black college, Fisk is an ideal choice.

Florida Institute of Technology

Melbourne, FL 32901

Location City outskirts	**Applicants** 2,500
Total Enrollment 7,070	**Accepted** 70%
Undergraduates 3,960	**Enrolled** 50%
Male/Female 80/20	**Academics** ★ ★ ★
SAT V/M 500/600	**Social** ☎ ☎ ☎
Financial Aid 65%	**Q of L** ● ● ●
Expense Pr $	**Admissions** (800)352-8324

The Florida Institute of Technology was founded in 1958 to offer continuing education opportunities to the scientists, engineers and technicians who had gathered at Cape Canaveral to put an earthling on the moon. Needless to say, changes in the space program prompted diversification of FIT's academic programs, and today's prospective students need not have their eyes on the clouds to succeed at FIT. While the flight school is still the institute's best and the varsity precision flying team still wins national titles, the fine engineering and ocean science programs also attract competent men and women to this relaxed alternative to the high-powered technical institutions of the Northeast and the West Coast. Although barely a quarter of a century old, FIT is fast reaching the point where its graduates are as sought after as their less-tanned counterparts.

Engineers can choose among seven solid majors (electrical, computer and mechanical engineering are standouts), and their fellow students interested in oceanography and marine biology also enjoy excellent facilities and equipment. The admissions office advises that prospective students have a strong background in math and science (especially chemistry and physics) and have their career-planning act together. Few students choose to major in the humanities or in the less practical sciences, although those who do venture into these departments, psychology in particular, are often pleasantly surprised. Math offerings draw the most complaints from students, while chemistry and environmental science departments are seriously undersubscribed. A four-story library with excellent computer facilities and an abundance of study spaces is the showplace on this contemporary campus, which has more than two hundred species of palm trees spread across its 146 acres.

If walking across campus is like taking tropical horticulture lab at FIT, scheduling courses can be the trickiest problem set at the school. Class sizes, especially laboratory classes, have strict ceilings, and many courses are not offered each semester. After freshman year, difficulties let up a bit. "Upper-level courses are generally ten or fewer students per instructor," a senior reports. Graduate teaching assistants are not overused, and while some prestigious researchers are untouchables, most faculty members are said to be reasonably accessible. All majors offer the co-op option, and senior independent research in biology and life sciences is possible. Most students, however, choose to get classes over with in four years and find a full-time job as quickly as possible.

The majority of FIT students are sun worshippers from the colder and more cosmopolitan regions of the North and Northeast. In addition, the school attracts a substantial number of Asian, South American, and African students. For those willing to settle for less than straight A's, the academic climate can be less than intense. However, as a computer engineering major warns, "Students coming only to surf and go to the beach will not last long at this school." Merit scholarships ranging from $1,000 to full tuition are awarded to all National Merit Scholars and a limited number of other outstanding students. More than forty male and female athletes win scholarships in seven varsity sports.

Like all other buildings on campus, the dormitories are modern, air-conditioned, and well maintained. Freshmen are required to live on campus in single-sex dormitories, and the rooms are adequate "but boring." Apartment units, which can comfortably house up to six students, are available to a small percentage of qualifying upperclassmen, with graduate and married students given first priority. About half the student body eventually moseys off campus and into the many reasonably priced apartments in Melbourne. The meal plan offers ten or twenty meals a week in the huge main cafeteria or two smaller ones, and students regard the food as just on the edible side of terrible. "Institutional food takes on a whole new meaning here," says one. Frat houses produce more appetizing fare.

Bicycles are the favored method for getting around for those who don't have cars or motorcycles; public transportation in Melbourne consists of a minibus system. The beach is only a couple of miles away, and when students are not lounging there, they might be found seeking diversion in Orlando (home of Disney World) or at the Kennedy Space Center. The latter is only forty miles away, and watching space shots from campus with a professional eye and beer in hand is a treasured pastime. Melbourne is not the most stimulating of environments, but at least it has an airport, which comes in handy for out-of-towners.

Campus social life is hampered by the poor male/female ratio, and most men must look elsewhere for dates. About a tenth of the students join fraternities or sororities. Besides partying, students spend weekends shopping, surfing, or going for a Sunday fly with flight school students. Crew is the most successful varsity sport, followed by basketball, baseball and soccer. Intramurals are Greek-only affairs.

Florida Tech best serves competent but low-key science jocks. Since the school "is still in its toddler's stage as universities go," concerned students feel they play a role in making it grow. That feeling of involvement, combined with relatively low tuition and a near guarantee of a decent job, puts FIT high on the list of technically minded students from coast to coast.

Florida State University

Tallahassee, FL 32306

Location City outskirts	**Applicants** 9,920
Total Enrollment 23,140	**Accepted** 75%
Undergraduates 17,640	**Enrolled** 42%
Male/Female 45/55	**Academics** ★ ★ ★
SAT V/M 480/530	**Social** 🐘 🐘 🐘
Financial Aid 33%	**Q of L** ● ● ●
Expense Pub $	**Admissions** (904)644-6200

Warmed by a temperate climate, shaded by moss-draped oaks, and intoxicated by the heavy scent of magnolias (and often the refreshing taste of an afternoon beer), it's no wonder that many Florida State students exist in a state of peaceful bliss. Huge lecture courses have a way of bringing on a wave of drowsiness, as does the lack of air-conditioning in more than one dorm. But for highly motivated students with the mettle to fight off the seductive, sun-drenched air, FSU can turn out to be a surprisingly stimulating place.

"We are not a surfer school" is the angry chorus emanating from within the walls of this attractive Gothic/modern campus, and in many areas, their indignation is justified. FSU has fine programs in music, drama, art, and dance, and its hotel and restaurant administration program has a high job placement rate for its graduates. Five hundred interactive terminals support the growing computer science program, now the most popular major on campus. Communications and business (especially accounting) have strong reputations in the Southeast, and philosophy and policy studies are improving. Since Tallahassee is the state capital, there are plenty of internships and jobs available for future politicos, and FSU's extensive co-op program offers students in everything from accounting to urban and regional planning the chance for on-the-job experience. Though the University of Florida is supposed to be the place to go for serious study of the natural sciences, FSU is moving up fast with a brand-new engineering program and improved equipment and facilities in physics, chemistry and biology. For A students who scored 1200 on their SAT, the honors program offers the enticing reward of smaller classes and closer faculty contact. Unfortunately, courses in popular majors like business and computer science are often hard to get into until the junior and in some cases senior year.

As for the rest, the admissions office reports that "minimum standards" for entrance exist: basically just test scores and high school grades, with recommendations and essays coming into play only in borderline cases. And although there are many academic high spots, "a minimum of effort" is all that is required to drift through the core courses in liberal arts, also known as Liberal Studies. Part of the problem is that Liberal Studies courses often have large enrollments. The administration verifies that courses with 920 students are actually offered at this university (students say some have more than a thousand), and basic chemistry and biology classes never have less than several hundred. Underclassmen also tend to encounter more graduate students than professors at the blackboards. Upperclassmen can expect classes to range from fifteen to fifty in their major field.

Many students say what's even more frustrating than "wasting time" fulfilling basic studies requirements is wasting time in the drop/add line trying to earn a spot in a limited enrollment course, usually in business or computer science. "People have been known to pay big bucks for a spot in the drop/add line," one junior reveals. For a break from these typical large university ordeals, FSU offers study abroad programs for all majors in London and Florence, for hotel administration majors in Switzerland, and for Spanish language students in Costa Rica, just to name a few.

Floridians comprise around 80 percent of the student body, with Georgians and Alabamians making up most of the rest. Most students "are mainly interested in finishing their education so they can start earning money," a senior reports. About a tenth are Hispanic or black, while Asian Americans make up only 1 percent of the student body. By and large students are friendly small-towners and would-be cosmopolitans, with a small but vocal liberal element. "If you're a real intellectual or a party animal, this might not be the place for you," one woman advises. The university assembles a "workable financial-aid package" for those in need, and in addition, over two hundred athletic scholarships, and six hundred academic merit awards, ranging up to $5,000, are given out every year.

About a quarter of the students live in the university dorms, most of which are coed, though three all-women's dorms and one for only men are also available. Students may opt for older halls, typically spacious but not air-conditioned, or newer ones with air-conditioning that tend to be more cramped. Space is limited in the dorms, and rooms are assigned on a first-come, first-served basis. Many who want to live on campus get stuck in temporary housing or wind up without a room altogether. Upperclassmen generally forsake the housing rat race and move into a nearby apartment, house, or trailer. The city and campus bus systems are substantially cheaper and infinitely easier to use than driving and parking a car in FSU's crowded lots. The dorms are equipped with kitchens, and various meal plans that offer "good but expensive" food are available. Each Greek house has its own dining facilities.

While some students go home for the weekend, there are always lots of dorm parties, concerts, and films, and off-campus hangouts are just a block or two away. Beaches and lakes are close at hand (the Gulf of Mexico is thirty miles to the south), and lots of people take advantage of the opportunity to canoe, fish or simply sun themselves at the "Seminole Reservation," a university-owned recreational park. On the rowdier side, about a tenth of the student population, mostly underclassmen, belong to the total of forty fraternities and sororities. Big-time football is also an integral part of the social scene, and the baseball team, runner-up in the 1986 College World Series, draws an enthusiastic following. The well-funded Lady 'Noles also field strong teams. But while Florida State has all of the elements of a party school, the merrymaking at FSU never seems to reach the riotous excesses known at other southern state universities. The FSU style of relaxation is more to "have a beer, be with friends, shoot some pool, and forget the books."

Florida State, in short, is neither for the manic grind nor the maniac partyer. Rather, it's for calmer souls who take life, including the life of the mind, as it comes. Students wanting to soak in the Florida sunshine and learn without burning their brains out will find more than twenty thousand welcoming sympathizers waiting in Tallahassee.

University of Florida

Gainesville, FL 32611

Location Center city	**Applicants** 13,000
Total Enrollment 35,100	**Accepted** 46%
Undergraduates 27,690	**Enrolled** 50%
Male/Female 55/45	**Academics** ★ ★ ★ ★
SAT V/M 520/590	**Social** 🐗 🐗 🐗 🐗
Financial Aid 60%	**Q of L** ● ● ● ●
Expense Pub $ $	**Admissions** (904)392-1365

Compared with most state schools in the South, the University of Florida is like fresh-squeezed orange juice alongside the stuff that comes in a can. With bushels of undergraduate, graduate, and professional programs, as well as sophisticated science and research facilities, it numbers among the academic leaders of the New South. To the typical student, however, that is a curse as well as a blessing; as is the case at many large research universities, the undergraduates all too often get lost in the shuffle.

Florida is set on a pretty tree-lined campus, with traditional collegiate-style brick structures and several modern ones, though recent construction has meant that it is "getting more and more crowded with buildings and sidewalks," a senior notes. Academically, UF is strongest in preprofessional areas. The physical sciences, biological sciences (especially agriculture), business, engineering, and Florida's various other career training schools are all very popular. The well-known School of Journalism was the first to offer students an electronic newsroom, and broadcasting students run their own radio and television stations. The Center for Gerontological Studies certifies undergraduates in several social science and health fields, and an honors program is reserved for students with 3.5 GPAs and SAT scores of at least 600 verbal and 1260 overall. Although the graduate school of education is strong, its undergraduate counterpart suffers from a lack of funding, as do many programs in the social sciences, humanities, and fine arts. Regardless of a student's main interests, he or she has a good chance of finding a major program, since only two universities, Ohio State and Minnesota, offer more degree programs on one campus than Florida.

To counteract the narrow preprofessionalism of many of its students, all are required to take Humanities Perspectives on the Professions as part of their general education requirements. In addition, all BA candidates must study math, English, behavioral and social sciences, physical science and biological science in order to graduate. Volunteer work in Gainesville and cooperative-education options are growing in popularity, as is the rigorous five-year joint-degree program in accounting. Those who want to flee the Sunshine State can study through exchange programs in Brazil, Israel, Colombia, Japan, China or more than a dozen cities in Eastern and Western Europe.

The size of the university poses problems in the form of occasional videotaped lectures and a bureaucracy that is "too big for its own good." Classroom crowding has reached horrific proportions, with lectures enrolling six hundred and seven hundred. Such herds are almost always corralled into smaller discussion sections, but professors must still rely heavily on multiple-choice tests, prompting one senior political science major to complain, "Real knowledge of concepts cannot be gauged in this manner." Academic counseling is "a joke"; "I personally know people who have had graduation delayed because of bad advisers," says a senior in public relations. Academic pressure varies with the major, but most undergraduates tend to engage in the fiercest competition just trying to get the courses they want. A new platoon of academic peer counselors is proving a great help to confused undergraduates, and if all else fails, students "raise holy Hell until somebody listens to you."

More than 90 percent of the students on campus are Floridians, and most finished in the top fifth of their class in one of the state's public high schools. Despite the geographical homogeneity, students claim that they're a diverse bunch, with introverts and people who can't handle being just another "pea-in-the-pod" the only ones who don't fit in. Politically, there is a broad range of persuasions "from Communist to Fascist to Libertarian, with all variations in between," an English major maintains. Most students, however, fit neatly into the laid-back conservative category. Blacks and Hispanics make up about 6 and 5 percent of the student body, respectively. Athletic scholarships are awarded to men and women in all traditional sports, and about 3 percent of undergraduates receive merit scholarships ranging from $100 to $5,000. National Merit Scholars automatically qualify if they list UF as their first choice.

Housing is run by a Social Security number lottery, and there are not enough rooms for everybody. Freshmen are guaranteed space, but after that those with unlucky numbers have to fend for themselves in the off-campus housing market, and many move into a sorority or fraternity house. Only 20 percent of the students can live on campus, in doubles, triples, or suites. Most of the dorms are coed by floor. For meals, students on campus usually eat on the meal plan, which is "pretty bad," or use the dorm kitchens. There are also several student pubs on campus, and it's easy to get to one of the cheap local restaurants. As for parking a car on campus, one student says, "There are 10,000 people who must fit into 3,000 spaces, and it just doesn't work."

Gainesville, a city of about 125,000, is no tourist mecca, but students say it's a livable college town. It has a sports arena and plenty of stores and restaurants that cater to the student population. The beaches of both the Atlantic and the Gulf of Mexico, jai alai frontons, and Walt Disney World are all near enough for road trips. The university owns a nearby lake, which is "great for lazy Sundays," as well as more vigorous water sports, and there are more than enough parks, forests, rivers, and streams close by for backpacking, camping and canoeing. About a quarter of the students join fraternities and sororities, making Florida's Greek system the largest in the nation, but most of the parties are closed to outsiders. Independents needn't fret; with over twenty thousand of them on campus, there's always a party going on somewhere.

Sports are a year-round obsession at Florida. In the fall, Gator football sets the campus on its ear, with a flurry of "big weekend" social events clustered around every home game. Basketball is the biggest winter spectator sport, and in the spring baseball frequently takes the SEC title. Seven gold medals were won by UF swimmers in the last Olympics in L.A., and both the men's and women's teams continue to be powerhouses. Unfortunately, UF's zest for big-time sports goes a little overboard at times. A recent recruiting scandal earned the Gators two years of NCAA probation. Women's sports are generously funded, and also get a fair amount of fan support; after men's football and basketball, women's gymnastics is the third-largest spectator sport. Intramural sports are also big, and everybody takes pride in the university's extensive program and facilities.

Some students insist that the UF's lingering reputation as a party school is dated, while others say the low drinking age (nineteen) is what they like best about their school. It's useless to argue about such things at an enormous but high-quality institution like the University of Florida. For students who don't mind being just another number in a massive bureaucracy, the good academics and great weather can make for a fun-filled yet educational four years.

Fordham University

Bronx, NY 10458

Location Urban
Total Enrollment 12,230
Undergraduates 5,250
Male/Female 47/53
SAT V/M 510/540
Financial Aid 70%
Expense Pr $ $

Applicants 4,010
Accepted 72%
Enrolled 43%
Academics ★ ★ ★
Social ☎ ☎ ☎
Q of L ● ● ●
Admissions (212)579-2133

Fordham University is a Jekyll and Hyde kind of school, a schizophrenic university that can cater to two opposite personality types—those who desire a peaceful, remote campus atmosphere and those who crave an electrified urban education scene. Fordham's main Rose Hill campus is an oasis in the Bronx: a cluster of Gothic buildings set amid lawns, hardy trees, and flowers. Thirty minutes away by subway is the Lincoln Center campus, its sleek high-rise building blending with the rest of Manhattan's cement and glass.

Fordham's dissimilar campuses are united by their common Jesuit heritage and concern for liberal values. Although the university is an independent institution with no formal religious ties, it still has more faculty members who belong to the Society of Jesus than any other American school, and it bills itself as "the Jesuit university of New York." For most students, the Roman Catholic influence, when they choose to acknowledge it, is more of a comfort than a hindrance. As one student puts it, "There's an emphasis on a life worth living, not just making a living." And with an impressive list of creative and individualistic alums (Alan Alda, Vince Lombardi and Charles Osgood to name a few), it's obvious the formula is working.

The eighty-acre Rose Hill campus (aka the *"rus in urbe,"* or countryside in the city) contains Fordham College as well as undergraduate schools of business administration and general studies. Fordham College, the principal liberal arts school, has gone back to basics in the broadest sense. The imaginative core curriculum concentrates on developing this liberal arts foundation in three distinct but interlocking stages: the history of the Western world, study of the contemporary world, and an introduction to the various disciplines scholars choose in studying both the past and the present. Business students take slightly more than half their courses in liberal arts but have no core requirements. The business program is especially strong in marketing, accounting and finance, and it provides hundreds of internships in all areas of Manhattan's business community, many leading to jobs.

The Manhattan campus has its own college at Lincoln Center as well as the law school and other graduate programs. Started as an alternative-style urban institution with no grades, it has become more traditional over the years but still retains much of its original flexibility and innovative spirit. Distribution requirements are more relaxed than uptown, and there is no core curriculum. Incoming students, however, can opt for the Freshman Interdisciplinary Seminar. Other Lincoln Center programs not offered at Rose Hill include January Projects (one month on an individual or group academic endeavor) and the major in medical technology taken in cooperation with Lenox Hill Hospital.

Both colleges have strong humanities departments: Rose Hill's strengths include history, philosophy, psychology and religious studies, while Lincoln Center's forte is, appropriately enough, theater. Communications/media studies are praised at both schools; the natural sciences are not, though the administration promises quick attention. The computer science program, still byte-sized, is growing, and computer facilities have been expanded to provide students with 150 on-line terminals available around the clock. Both colleges offer interdisciplinary majors, including black and Puerto Rican studies, and preprofessionals may enter 3-2 engineering or nursing programs at Columbia.

More than two-thirds of the students are from the New York area, and more than half are from private or parochial high schools. About one-third of Fordham's enrollees are from minority groups—17 percent are Hispanic or Puerto Rican and 10 percent are black. Though the atmosphere at both campuses is less intellectual than at nearby Columbia or New York universities, Fordham students tend to be hard workers. The university still fulfills its historical role as an institution for aspiring first-generation college students. The undergraduates here tend to be liberal, unpretentious, and, as is required of their environment, aggressive. The preppie types tend to gravitate to Rose Hill; the nonconformist types head south. As one woman says, "We have a wild streak that comes out on Manhattan dance floors."

A generous number of students who apply for financial aid on the basis of need receive something. There are also 450 merit scholarships with stipends that range from $1,000 to $8,000 and ten Presidential Scholarships that offer full tuition plus room. Sixty-five full athletic scholarships are awarded to talented students on six men's sports and four women's teams.

The college has been seeking to build up its residential character with new dorms. More than half of the Rose Hill students now live on campus in single-sex or coed dorms. All dorm residents are guaranteed rooms for the next year, but housing space is tight and the administration "politely encourages upperclassmen to move off campus." Though students have earned credit for renovating a burnt-out brownstone, there just isn't much off-campus housing at Rose Hill, so those who don't live in dorms commute. Lincoln Center students who can afford the pricey rents move in nearby; others live at home or on the Rose Hill campus if they can find space. Boarders start off on a mandatory meal plan but may drop it as upperclassmen.

Life at Lincoln Center is not all that different from life anywhere else in the city, particularly as there are no dorms to provide community identity. The school sponsors some extracurricular activities, including a feeble intramurals program in Central Park, but they can't compete with the city's vast cultural smorgasbord. "Everything comes to a standstill on Friday afternoons," reports a media studies major who yearns for more on-campus weekend activities.

Life is a bit different up at Rose Hill, which is adjacent to the Bronx Zoo, the beautiful botanical gardens, and Belmont, the "Little Italy" of the Bronx. Students recommend caution in venturing too far from the "safe" areas. The marvelous Lombardi Athletic Center (named for that famed alumnus) inspires an active program of club sports and intramurals, while "grandstand athletes" especially enjoy rooting for the varsity basketball team. The student pub offers lively midweek activities, but things die down on weekends. The university's cultural affairs program brings the Bronx campus students into the Big Apple for a little high life, and Manhattan is always just minutes away by train, subway, or college shuttle bus.

When you add the advantages of intimate classes and reasonable tuition (about $1,000 less than the competition), Fordham—in both locations—offers a winning combination. If you can't choose between the two separate lives of Fordham students, take advantage of both. You may never have another chance to fully exploit the schizophrenic in you.

Franklin and Marshall College

Lancaster, PA 17604

Location Small city
Total Enrollment 2,000
Undergraduates 2,000
Male/Female 53/47
SAT V/M 570/610
Financial Aid 35%
Expense Pr $ $ $

Applicants 3,900
Accepted 45%
Enrolled 30%
Academics ★ ★ ★
Social 🐻 🐻 🐻
Q of L ● ● ●
Admissions (717)291-3951

Named for two great American statesmen—Benjamin Franklin and former chief justice of the United States John Marshall—Franklin and Marshall College tries to promote the spirit of its namesakes. Indeed, the student body strives to emulate Franklin's industriousness and Marshall's foresight, but don't be fooled. Most "Fummers," as students here are often called, dream not of the pages of history, but rather of the deposit column of checkbooks to come.

Franklin and Marshall is the starting point for many a future lawyer, doctor and business leader. In fact, the administration recently became so worried about F&M undergraduates suffering from preoccupation with their future occupations that it appointed a "humorist in residence" to remind students how to laugh and loosen up their tightly knit preprofessional brows. On a more serious note, F&M also began recommending that all incoming students purchase an Apple Macintosh personal computer to aid them in "applying the appropriate technology to their liberal arts."

The college's location, in the Amish country of pastoral Pennsylvania, provides restless scholars with few cosmopolitan alternatives to *fumming*—a verb that one college publication defines as "engaging in any aspects of life associated with living at Franklin and Marshall College, also known as Camp Fum." Indeed, it's hard to deny the peace and tranquility afforded by the beauty of the surrounding countryside. F&M's mainly colonial brick and Gothic-style campus, with a few modern additions, boasts well-kept grounds, bordered by "some of the most gorgeous farms and rolling hills I've ever seen," according to one senior.

To force a little culture into its self-described "conservative, success-oriented, and preprofessional" students, the school introduced the college studies curriculum, designed to expose students to disciplines outside their major. As far as individual departments go, students seem to agree on F&M's strengths: geology (reportedly one of the best in the nation), experimental psychology, government, business, accounting, economics, English, biology and chemistry. Foreign language offerings are being strengthened through the recruitment of new faculty members and the opening of a campus French house. With the exception of theater, the arts are a F&Mbarrassment. New music professors have been added—the faculty could now field a full quartet.

The quality of teaching is excellent, and the smallness of the student body enables a strong sense of community to flourish among students and faculty members. F&M offers cross-registration with two other small Pennsylvania colleges (Dickinson and Gettysburg) and several domestic exchange and cooperative degree programs. In the summers, F&M sends study-abroad trips to countries such as Japan and the Soviet

Union, and students may take semesters abroad through other colleges' programs. Co-op and 3-2 programs in engineering and forestry are available with half a dozen other institutions.

About 40 percent of F&M's students graduate from private high schools, and more than two-thirds rank in the top fifth of their graduating class. Traditionally, the college has been almost exclusively a regional institution, with Pennsylvania, New York and New Jersey residents making up three-quarters of the student body. There has been a recent influx of students from other regions, especially New England and the West. While one student reports that "conservativism is prevalent, but not overwhelming," a classmate clarifies that "Fummers are, on the average, liberal Republicans—educated to concern themselves with social issues as well as their own professional futures." Still, there remains at F&M a feeling of relaxed assuredness, the kind that goes with wealthy people who know where they're going. School spirit and pride are in no short supply, and a senior says nothing annoys her more than "the myths that circulate which say the Fummers are nothing but a bunch of Ivy League rejects who work under such incredible pressure that they have to blow off weekends in intoxicated stupors." One economics major claims that "if anything, F&M suffers from a superiority complex."

Although F&M attempts to admit students regardless of need, there are no guarantees that those admitted will receive aid. No merit scholarships, athletic or other, are awarded. Student housing ranges from fraternities (home for about two hundred males) and campus dorms, to theme houses, a co-op, or private apartments near the campus. Freshmen, sophomores and seniors are guaranteed rooms on campus. A fair number of juniors content themselves with leftovers; others scrap the whole lottery procedure for more advanced real estate activities. "Apartment hunting is a major spring pastime," notes a prelaw student. Housing opportunities in Lancaster are generally plentiful, though the natives have a reputation for being a bit testy when subjected to off-campus partying. Boarders eat all their meals in the campus cafeteria, and fraternity members take most of their meals with their brothers. The one small sorority provides no residential facilities.

"I am always eager to debate the people who gripe about the poor social life," says one gregarious student. "I always say boring people have boring social lives, and by God, it follows accurately." The administration took a look at the situation on campus and found fraternities dominating social life. The results: a prohibition against first semester freshmen joining fraternities and a tightening up on alcohol policies. A favorite campus meeting place, Ben's Underground, was built to provide an alternative and has become a popular place for students to gather for dance parties and to show off their talents on the open-mike nights.

Lancaster, "a city with a rural flair," offers about a dozen movie theaters and, for the junk food junkie, a plethora of McDonald's-type establishments. Although bars are now supposed to be off-limits to anyone under the age of twenty-one, F&M students still sing the praises of many local watering holes, including The Lancaster Dispensing Company, Quips and Hildey's Tavern. Many students find the Amish culture interesting and frequent the charming farmer's market. Parents can stay at Mennonite guest houses where the truly motivated can rise at dawn to watch the cows be milked, and enjoy other aspects of the traditional, rural life, such as the opportunity to shop for gorgeous handmade Amish quilts. And one enthusiastic senior credits Lancaster with "the best restaurant selection I've seen anywhere—including Philadelphia." For those concerned with more contemporary action, there is a steady fare of concerts, plays, and dances at other area colleges, in town at the Fulton Opera House, and in nearby Harrisburg, Hershey and York. Students can take advantage of a proximity to Philadelphia, Baltimore, Washington and the Susquehanna River for day trips.

The college has a good selection of intramural sports that include the recently initiated and popular coed events. In addition to a Division I wrestling powerhouse, F&M boasts strong Division III men's and women's soccer, lacrosse and track teams. The men's squash team came in second place—behind Harvard—in the intercollegiate championship last year. Varsity squads are called the Diplomats, a name that is irresistibly abbreviated to "the Dips." Yet, one senior, who finds it dispiriting to shout "Go Dips!" in support of his team, reports of an underground student movement to call the athletes the Fighting Amish. "But something tells me the local community won't go for it," he confesses.

F&M attempts to limit the number of intended premeds admitted each year, and that helps to keep it from becoming a factory for preprofessional degrees. The school can rightly boast of strengths in such diverse areas as geology, drama and astronomy and a group of well-rounded students, some of whom value their education not only as a credential but also for its own sake.

Furman University

Greenville, SC 29613

Location City outskirts	**Applicants** 2,510
Total Enrollment 2,610	**Accepted** 56%
Undergraduates 2,430	**Enrolled** 49%
Male/Female 48/52	**Academics** ★ ★ ★
SAT V/M 540/580	**Social** 🍷 🍷 🍷
Financial Aid 23%	**Q of L** ● ● ●
Expense Pr $ $	**Admissions** (803)294-2034

Nestled at the foot of the Blue Ridge Mountains on 750 acres of lush countryside, Furman University is not actually a university but a small liberal arts college strongly influenced and generously funded by the Southern Baptists. Replete with Japanese gardens, abundant oaks and maples, and a man-made lake full of swans and ducks, the remarkable beauty of the campus is one of Furman's most immediately evident attractions. In fact its twenty-odd tennis courts and eighteen-hole golf course have earned the school the nickname, "The Country Club of the South." Country club scenery, perhaps, but the emphasis on academics, community service, and alcoholic abstinence are far from stereotypical country club values.

The red-brick buildings, lolling amid the par threes and fours, are decidedly Williamsburg colonial, and the campus itself, like most of its inhabitants, is unmistakably southern. "There's something to be said for southern hospitality," pipes an English major, "but Furman students take it a step further." The caring, close-knit community allows for emphasis on academic achievement without cutthroat competition. "We're in this together," remarks one student.

A range of liberal arts courses is mandatory, including one religion course. English, chemistry, psychology, history and music are the school's strongest departments, while both sociology and physics are weak. Students note the pleasing aesthetics of the new art building, but have no such praise for the classes offered inside. And renovations for the small, ill-equipped theater facilities are "nowhere in sight." Students also complain that the main library lacks resources, "is a terrible place to study," closes at 5 PM on Saturday, and does not open on Sunday until two in the afternoon.

Furman students take three courses during the fall and spring terms, and two courses during the shorter eight-week winter term, which offends one senior because "we start and end school so late." The low student-to-faculty ratio results in small class size and excellent student-faculty relations. "The faculty members are amazingly available and generous with time outside of class," pronounces one student. Study-abroad options include a special exchange program with Kansai–Gaidai University in Japan and study in the Middle East, Russia, and North Africa.

Most Furman undergrads are bright public school graduates—about three-quarters rank in the top fifth of their high school classes—and most are Caucasian southerners from middle to upper class, politically conservative backgrounds. "Most students are well mannered, friendly and interested in leading productive lives," states a chemistry major. Such motivation toward productivity leads almost 40 percent of Furman graduates to professional schools, where they are accepted at impressive rates: 80 percent into medical and business schools and more than 90 percent into law schools. The college claims it has been able to provide for 85 percent of students' demonstrated financial aid needs, and it annually awards about 160 academic scholarships, which range from $500 to $3,000. Furman also offers 244 athletic scholarships to men and women in a wide variety of sports.

Although many denominations are represented at Furman, the influence of the Southern Baptist Convention is pervasive, even "overpowering." Alcohol and drugs are prohibited on campus (though one student confesses that "there is not 100 percent compliance behind closed doors"), and visitation hours in the single-sex dormitories are limited. Not only are there no coed dorms, but men and women are housed at opposite ends of the campus—"The Furman male has to walk exactly one half mile to the nearest female dorm," complains a senior. As for the separate but decidedly unequal housing, it's the women who draw the long straw. While female quarters are air-conditioned and comfortable, the male dorms lack sufficient air-conditioning and have "lousy plumbing." Freshmen must live on campus and are usually assigned double rooms. Many upperclassmen choose to live off campus, but those who stay can usually finagle a suite. Small cabins adjacent to the lake are available for upperclass women seeking to do their own cooking. Though all dormitory halls have kitchens, students must subscribe to meals for five to seven days a week. These meals, home-cooked in Furman kitchens, are served up in one big, central dining room. Students enjoy the recently installed, palate-pleasing extras such as a soft ice cream machine and a breakfast bar with fresh fruit and waffle irons.

Social life at Furman is described by one student as "adequate, but it tends to leave a milk and cookie aftertaste." The Student Activities Board sponsors movies, dances, coffeehouses, and bowling and skating parties, which are generally less well attended than the off-campus parties thrown by the men's fraternities or the women's social clubs (all local). There are several organizations to join; depending on your degree of tenacity, you could pick the hardworking student government or the free-spirited David Letterman Club. A large number of students also choose to devote spare time to the Collegiate Educational Service Corps, which organizes extensive social service projects in the community.

The city of Greenville, about five miles from campus, is good for a few shopping malls, movie theaters, restaurants and nightclubs. Atlanta is a two-and-a-half-hour drive away; skiers can hit the slopes after a two-hour car trip, and for hearty sojourners, the great South Carolina beaches are about four hours from campus. Football and soccer are the most popular spectator sports, and the golf, tennis and swim teams are strong for both men and women. Almost 70 percent of the students compete for the coveted All Sports Trophy by participating in the well-organized intramural games, which range from flag football to horseshoes.

A community in itself, Furman's atmosphere is what one English major describes as "an enlarged, close southern family"—a family that sometimes finds itself caught between the realities of the outside world and the disciplined, caring atmosphere it works so hard to preserve. But the most content Furmanians are those who seek both spiritual support and a serious academic education. For them, a senior reports, "getting a degree from the Country Club of the South is pure heaven."

George Washington University

Washington, DC 20052

Location Urban	**Applicants** 6,460
Total Enrollment 17,550	**Accepted** 78%
Undergraduates 6,370	**Enrolled** 24%
Male/Female 49/51	**Academics** ★ ★ ★
SAT V/M 530/580	**Social** ☎ ☎ ☎
Financial Aid 38%	**Q of L** ● ● ●
Expense Pr $ $ $	**Admissions** (202)994-6040

If you've ever visited the White House, you may well have walked right past George Washington University without even knowing it. Located only three blocks up Pennsylvania Avenue from the West Wing and the Oval Office, George Washington, often known as "the school without a campus," is barely distinguishable from the urban milieu that surrounds it. But if GW lacks ivy-covered walls and well-trodden courtyards, most students are too busy enjoying the bustle and excitement of the nation's capital to give it a second thought. Never known as a hotbed of intellect, GW attracts career-oriented, street-smart types who know how to take care of themselves, which is just as well since "GW does not hold a student's hand," as one senior warns.

Academically, as goes Washington, so goes GW. When politics was the only game in town, GW sent hordes of political science, history and public affairs majors up to Capitol Hill. Now that Washington is also a financial and international hub, the school's programs in economics, accounting and international affairs are also extremely strong. The School of Engineering and Applied Science is quite popular and offers an honors program that allows students to work one-on-one with a professor on a research project of mutual interest. Programs in art history and American studies benefit from links with the Smithsonian and the Folger Shakespeare Library. Perhaps the ultimate bow to the city is a new, and by all accounts popular, major in political communications, combining political science, journalism and radio/TV programs. About sixty students major in the radio/TV division, which recently moved into new $5-million facilities, and students with an interest in computers will be glad to learn that the university has just installed a new communication system linking dorms, classrooms, laboratories and offices via computer.

GW's old standard-bearer, political science, is still one of the most popular majors. Almost half the department's professors divide their time between the halls of academia and the corridors of power—a good many holding high-level government positions. This assures that their teaching is state-of-the-art, but it also means their loyalties are somewhat divided. Many students get a head start on their careers with internships, part-time and summer jobs in the Congress and along the business corridor of K Street. For those in an even bigger hurry, there is an accelerated program that allows students to graduate in three normal academic years.

Undergrads must take twelve credit hours in each of three areas: humanities, science and math, and social science, which takes up much of the first year and part of the second. They also can take advantage of several interdisciplinary courses, such as politics and values and computers and society. The "700 series" courses are novel interdepartmental classes that encourage innovative teaching and study across a variety of program areas. But don't count on doing much of your studying in the library, which is new and beautiful but, students say, short on necessary materials and long on crowds and noise. As a backup, there's always the Library of Congress, a ten-minute subway ride away. If you prefer to get your information from the tube rather than the books, pick topics that will let you make use of GW's unusual archive of television newscasts.

Like Washington itself, GW draws people from all over America and around the world. There is strong minority representation, and a generous 15 percent of the students come from foreign countries. Among the rest, a large contingent are upper-middle-class easterners who either couldn't or didn't want to get into high-powered northern schools. Most students are "the go out and get 'em type" eager to tap Washington's immense resources. GW has a no-frills admissions policy—based almost solely only on grades and tests—which is a good thing, since the GW admissions office is something akin to a revolving door. For every student who is alienated by GW and decides to transfer out, there is one at another school—usually with an interest in politics—waiting to transfer in. Nearly half the student body began its undergraduate career at another school, while almost a fifth of the undergraduates are older, part-time students. A little less than a quarter were in the top 10 percent of their high school class. Students with a B average and SAT scores above 500 should have little trouble getting in.

The university is need-blind in admissions, and financial aid is awarded to "the neediest and best students first." About 120 of GW's prime recruits—those in the top 10 percent of their high school class with SATs above 1300 (1250 for engineers)—get academic scholarships ranging from $1,000 to half tuition. A roughly equal number get athletic scholarships in eleven sports. Both deferred and prepayment plans are available, perhaps because GW, unlike many private universities, is in excellent shape financially. In recent years the university has put a healthy chunk of its financial resources into adjacent real estate.

About half the students live off campus—near the university if they can afford it, in the Maryland and Virginia suburbs if they can't. On-campus housing in converted apartments or hotels is well maintained and relatively spacious, with private baths the norm and household appliances in many rooms. Most freshmen are booked into suites of up to six roommates in Thurston Hall, which is the biggest and rowdiest dorm on campus. The two single-sex dorms tend to be less crowded but also less fun. Freshmen and transfers are guaranteed a room; upperclassmen take their chances in a lottery that awards seniors first pick and a shot at rooms in a converted apartment building offering all singles. The excellent meal plan, mandatory for freshmen and sophomores, offers a variety of options—including cash credit at the campus pub—in addition to standard dining hall fare. Upperclassmen have the option of cooking in the dorm kitchens or frequenting the many fast-food restaurants and casual eateries nearby.

School spirit, somewhat lacking in general, comes out in force at men's basketball games. Less strongly supported, but no less competitive, are women's basketball and men's and women's tennis and soccer. Other sports are strictly for participants only, and GW students must be content with the NFL's Redskins, since there is no football team on campus. Intramurals enjoy wide popularity, and there is even a special "play all night" event. For early risers, "a morning jog around the White House and the Washington Monument is an uplifting way to start one's day," says a student. Fraternities and sororities, growing in popularity, provide most of the campus social life, though many students forgo campus activities in favor of hitting the bars, stores, movies and plays in small groups of friends. Nearby Georgetown (the area, not the university, as one student smugly points out) is the most popular hangout, and two nearby bars, GG Flip and The 21st Amendment, have been adopted as campus hangouts.

George Washington University isn't the place to linger and smell the roses. Anyone who tried would undoubtedly be trampled underfoot by the eager hordes intent on making their mark in the fast-paced Washington scene. GW offers good programs in many areas, but with no campus to speak of, and little sense of community, GW functions best as a base of operations for those seeking to launch a career in government or economics. Political science majors everywhere are green with envy.

Georgetown University

Washington, DC 20057

Location Center city	**Applicants** 11,860
Total Enrollment 11,970	**Accepted** 21%
Undergraduates 5,770	**Enrolled** 51%
Male/Female 49/51	**Academics** ★ ★ ★ ★
SAT V/M 630/660	**Social** 🐦 🐦 🐦 🐦
Financial Aid 47%	**Q of L** ● ● ● ●
Expense Pr $ $ $	**Admissions** (202)625-3051

When George Washington's nephews enrolled at Georgetown University at the end of the eighteenth century, the college's prospectus was already being printed in French and Spanish as well as English. Today, both the student body and the philosophy are similarly cosmopolitan. Prepoliticos are attracted by Georgetown's prestigious name and faculty, the Washington location, and the rare opportunity to earn an undergraduate degree in foreign affairs. "Power-hungry megalomaniacs" is what one student calls them. But he also assures prospectives that "not everyone at Georgetown interns on Capitol Hill." The school is equally suited to students fiercely determined to succeed in academic and less political professional careers—basketball, for instance. A couple of NCAA championships make nice credentials for the pros.

Situated on a hill overlooking the Potomac River, Georgetown affords its students an excellent vantage point from which to survey the world. The campus is a mishmash of building styles ranging from the collegiate Healy Hall to the modern, bunker-like School of Foreign Service. Though the cobblestone streets are less evocative of the Old World than of old money, Georgetown can boast both charm and wealth. The school is able to enjoy the numerous resources of the nearby city and the relative serenity of a modern suburb. Georgetown is "a city school tucked into a quaint corner all its own," according to a French major.

Georgetown is run by the Society of Jesus, but the Jesuits long ago learned how to combine religious faith with academic freedom, and the religious atmosphere is by no means oppressive. Almost 60 percent of the students are Roman Catholics, but all faiths are respected and practiced on campus. In fact, one student even goes so far as to say, "GU is probably one of the most un-Catholic of the Catholic schools because of its increased competition with academic powerhouses like Duke, Penn, and Princeton." The main way in which the Jesuits express their tradition is through their commitment to high-level intellectual excellence.

Would-be Hoyas must apply separately to one or more of the five undergraduate schools: arts and sciences, nursing, languages and linguistics, business administration and the Edmund A. Walsh School of Foreign Service. The latter is by far the most prominent of the university's divisions and gives future diplomats, journalists, and others a strong "liberal-arts program grounded in the social sciences." Prospective freshmen must declare intended majors on their applications, and their secondary school records are judged accordingly. This means, among other things, intense competition within the College of Arts and Science for the limited number of spaces in Georgetown's popular premedical and predental programs.

Within the liberal arts program, American studies is a strong area, as are history, government, and, of course, theology. The School of Foreign Service stands out for its offerings in international economics, and regional and comparative studies. The business school balances liberal arts with professional training, and, like the nursing school, strongly encourages fieldwork. The School of Nursing cooperates closely with the Georgetown University Hospital. The School of Languages and Linguistics, the only undergraduate program of its kind, offers an intensive language and liberal arts curriculum to enable students "to speak a language effectively and gain a foreign cultural understanding." Students express disappointment with sociology, math and computer science. The small fine arts department is unable to offer much variety.

General education requirements apply to all students regardless of the division in which they have enrolled. These include two semesters each of theology, philosophy, English, history and/or social science, and all students except for those in the School of Foreign Service have requirements in math and/or science. A major academic weakness is the library, which students say is "small and noisy." (A recently completed capital campaign should improve the situation since $15 million is slated for library facilities.) In the meantime, there's always the Library of Congress. That GU views most subjects through an international lens is evidenced by the large portion (one-third) of GU students who study abroad. For the culturally curious, there are more than thirty university-sponsored study programs in Asia, Latin America, Russia, Poland, Israel, France, Germany and at the university's villa in Florence.

The university likes to boast about its faculty, but even when they're not on leave for government assignments, stars like Henry Kissinger and Arthur Burns tend to restrict their services to graduate students. Still, luminaries aside, the overwhelmingly lay faculty is generally respected and available and counts few teaching assistants in its ranks. Regular student-faculty Happy Hours are a treasured tradition.

"Georgetown students are extremely motivated, but in a materialistic way," explains an international affairs student. "They aspire to become as rich as their neighbors in the chic Georgetown suburb." Less than 10 percent come from the Washington area, and many have lived abroad. About one-fourth come from parochial schools, with another 30 percent from private prep schools contributing to Georgetown's strong preppie contingent. Blacks and Hispanics make up 10 percent of the undergraduate body, and there are nearly as many foreign nationals. A huge percentage—80 to 95, the university estimates—pursue advanced study within ten years after graduation. In addition to need-based financial aid, sixty-one athletic scholarships for men and women are offered.

Even students with full-tuition scholarships can have trouble making ends meet in Georgetown, where the cost of living is high and all housing options are particularly expensive. University-owned dorms, town houses and apartments accommodate three-quarters of the students, and fittingly, the university guarantees students housing for three out of four of their years. Freshmen must live on campus, and it's usually juniors or seniors who are forced to fend for themselves. All dorms are coed, and some, like New North, have more activities and community than others. The wait is long for a single room. Four dining halls serve "passable" food for which the Marriott Corporation (in charge of Georgetown's food service) is "to blame." The popular student-run café offers more palatable options.

Jesuits, who know all about secret societies, frown upon fraternities or sororities at their colleges. As a result, Georgetown's social life is somewhat decentralized, which is not necessarily a bad thing. The dozens of bars, nightclubs and restaurants of Washington's most stimulating neighborhood are heavily frequented, though students on a limited budget will soon notice how "ridiculously expensive" Georgetown can be. Washington provides cultural resources ranging from the Smithsonian and the aerospace museum to the Kennedy Center. On campus, there are enough keg parties to prompt one business student to classify GU as "alcohol-intensive." Students flock to the Center Pub, where "a mysterious substance known to Hoyas as 'Pub Scum' always winds up on your shoes." But if it's the close one-on-one male-female relationships you're yearning for, look elsewhere because "there is *no* dating at Georgetown," according to a lonely nursing student. Given Washington's excellent system of public transportation and the absence of on-campus parking, a car is probably more trouble than it's worth.

With the exception of a nationally prominent basketball team that helps provide some of the traditional school spirit, varsity sports arouse little excitement at Georgetown. Most of the thrill of victory and agony of defeat originates in intramural competition in the superb underground Yates Athletic Center. And you best believe there's a wealth of resumé-building clubs, organizations and student government activities at this school of aspiring public leaders.

"GU is a very sophisticated university," says one satisfied senior. "The students are smart, well educated, and worldly." For anyone interested in government and politics, it offers the perfect combination of classroom learning and the chance to observe Congress and the other arms of the federal government at close range. And if you don't like what you see, you always have the option of switching your major to theology.

Georgia Institute of Technology

Atlanta, GA 30332

Location City center
Total Enrollment 11,500
Undergraduates 7,880
Male/Female 80/20
SAT V/M 540/650
Financial Aid 50%
Expense Pub $ $

Applicants 6,100
Accepted 60%
Enrolled 50%
Academics ★ ★ ★ ★
Social ☎ ☎
Q of L ● ●
Admissions (404)894-4154

The word "institute" should be the first clue that Georgia Tech isn't your typical laid-back southern state university. Tech is one of the most intense and competitive schools south of the Mason-Dixon Line, attracting many of the keenest technical minds in the South to tackle any and all aspects of math, science and engineering—from integrals to integrated circuits. Though the work is hard and the social life bad, the promise of a high-paying job after four years keeps Tech's future engineers chugging full speed ahead.

Set in a none-too-attractive neighborhood uncomfortably close to the roaring traffic of I-85, Georgia Tech's 320-acre campus consists mainly of modern buildings, with a few flowers and trees sprinkled in to make it look like a college. Tech academics are as rigorous as they come, and the institute is a national leader in most engineering fields, notably chemical, electrical, aerospace, and industrial systems engineering, as well as in solar energy. Information and computer science attracts large numbers of students, but computers are also used widely in other course work, both in class and out. Besides the standard technical fare, there is an increasingly popular management college, and a school of architecture well known for its work in historic preservation and energy conservation. The liberal arts, however, are uniformly weak. The most heavily frequented building on the Tech campus is undoubtedly the library; it's where students go for "problem-solving sessions," social and academic.

Georgia Tech offers a number of five-year combination programs with units of the University of Georgia and Atlanta University as well as with ten black colleges and twenty women's colleges. Special travel programs include a year in Paris for architects and a summer in London for chemical engineers; others participate in the study-abroad programs run jointly with the University of Georgia. Far more popular is the co-op program, through which about two thousand students finance their education by working one half of a school year and going to classes the other half. Co-op study is available in almost every field.

Georgia Tech is an institution of higher learning, but technically speaking, it is really more like an institution of higher researching. The Tech faculty has turned out volumes of learned tracts over the years, but unfortunately undergraduate teaching has suffered in the process. One student claims, "Most professors could care less about teaching. That's a technicality to doing their research at Tech." Most professors do manage to hold office hours, and some incorporate their research material into lectures or use students as aides in a project. Stringent grading is the rule, and serious students find that the work load sometimes requires what a chemical engineer characterizes as "all-weekers." But others assure prospective students there is time to relax on the weekends.

About 60 percent of the students come from Georgia, the rest from around the country and the world, and almost all are extremely motivated, bright and preprofessional. "Tech is for people who want to work hard, play hard, and reap big money benefits," says one woman. Another student adds, "If you can't take deadline pressures, you shouldn't come at all." Political conservativism is a foregone conclusion, though most students are too busy studying to pay much attention to politics. Southern white males are the overwhelming majority, with blacks and Hispanics accounting for about 8 percent of the students. Technology rules even in the admissions office at Tech, where a computerized formula based on four parts academic average, two parts SAT math score, and one part SAT verbal score is used to determine clear-cut acceptances and rejections. Human judgment intervenes in borderline cases, which are reviewed individually by real people. To limit burgeoning enrollment, out-of-state applicants now must meet slightly higher criteria than their Georgia counterparts.

Those seeking financial aid must have their applications in by February 15, and the university is committed to meeting needs, "although not necessarily the total amount indicated from the need analysis." Approximately two hundred merit scholarships are awarded each year, ranging from $750 to $7,700, depending on need, and over three hundred students get athletic scholarships each year.

Less than half of Tech students live in the dorms, and there's a severe shortage of space. Freshmen are guaranteed a room, but about 20 percent of the upperclassmen are forced off campus each year as a result of a random lottery. Some recent renovation has improved the drab buildings, and the opening of a new dorm has recently eased the crunch somewhat. All the halls are single sex, though visitation rules are lenient. There is little rhyme or reason to rooming assignments, and freshmen can easily wind up with a senior for a roommate. Housing off campus is generally more comfortable and not hard to find close by, but some of the surrounding neighborhood is none too safe. Two large dining halls serve on-campus students; the most common description of the food is "adequate and somewhat overpriced." Many of the dorms do have kitchen facilities, and the fraternities and other organizations offer dining options. Anyway, who can resist the allure of the world's largest drive-in restaurant, the Varsity?

Georgia Tech is on the edge of downtown Atlanta, and public transportation provides an easy link to the city's action. Besides its many cultural and recreational attractions, Atlanta often hosts conventions and seminars that fit the interests of Tech students. Women take advantage of the overwhelming male-female ratio, while for men, it is often necessary to check out some of the local fashion colleges or nursing schools. Those with more intellectual tastes look for companionship at Agnes Scott and Emory. About a quarter of the students belong to one of the dozens of fraternities and sororities, which are responsible for a good deal of campus partying and dating opportunities. Greek or not, students study most of the weekend, and the most diehard geeks fail ever to take time out for a sports event or two. The large student athletic complex provides home base for most intramurals, and Tech's varsity sports have recently become as big time as any in the South. The basketball team, once the laughingstock of the Atlantic Coast Conference, was recently a contender for the national championship, and football is nearly as popular. Techies love to cheer for the "Rambling Wreck," named for a car, especially during their frequent encounters with the much-hated Georgia Bulldogs.

Unless you weigh 225 pounds and have a nickname like Tank or Stretch, Georgia Tech is not a snap, nor is it a particularly pleasant place to be. But many of the students dismiss the negatives as "character-building." They know that their reward is likely to be a gaggle of job offers in practically recession-proof fields.

University of Georgia

Athens, GA 30602

Location Small city
Total Enrollment 25,180
Undergraduates 17,960
Male/Female 49/51
SAT V/M 490/530
Financial Aid 15%
Expense Pub $ $

Applicants 9,780
Accepted 76%
Enrolled 47%
Academics ★ ★ ★
Social 🐗🐗🐗🐗
Q of L ● ● ●
Admissions (404)542-2112

The football stadium at the University of Georgia stands right at the geographic center of the campus—which is a fitting symbol for a place where the most frequently uttered question from preseason practice to New Year's Day is "How 'bout them Dogs?" Bulldogs, that is. Them Dogs have been doing fine on the playing field recently, but unfortunately their performances in the classrooms have been nothing to bark about. Accusations that athletes were being admitted and pushed along without meeting normal academic standards led to NCAA probation, the resignation of the president and the loss of a $2.5-million lawsuit to a faculty whistle-blower. It looks like them Dogs have got their tails between their legs.

The 1986 athletic scandal was all the more unfortunate because it came at the end of a period in which the University of Georgia—under the leadership of the very president who became the scapedog for the Board of Regents—had made great academic strides. Founded in 1785, Georgia was the nation's first chartered state university, and it spent most of its first two centuries getting bigger. Success showed up in a vast array of major programs in ten undergraduate colleges, an impressive 2.2-million-volume library, and nearly six hundred acres of campus. Bigness securely under its belt, UGA then directed its efforts at getting better. Programs across the board have improved, more distinguished faculty members have been hired and the university has emerged as one of the top fifty research schools in the country.

Despite these great strides toward improving the quality of education, UGA undergraduates still, by and large, take a low-key approach to the academic program. "Students are only under the pressure they put on themselves," says one man, and for many the pressure is just to meet requirements, not to excel. Exceptions to the casual academic environment are found mainly in premedical and preveterinary concentrations, and in the honors program, the third largest in the nation. Business and journalism are standout majors, but students have mixed feelings about the arts, physics, education, anthropology and sociology. Courses in the humanities, social sciences, mathematics and natural sciences are required for graduation.

With huge classes commonplace for at least the first year or two, students have little opportunity for individual attention and what they get in the lower-level and lab courses comes from graduate assistants. A huge influx of third-year transfers from junior colleges puts a kink in the course registration process, but generally students report few problems getting the courses they want in all areas except phys ed. First pick for all courses usually goes to honors students and varsity athletes, and the rest follow by seniority. Gut courses abound for those intent upon attending Camp Georgia; serious students may partake of several special programs, such as a five-year business/engineering degree offered in conjunction with Georgia Tech. Business majors may take a year at Nijenrodes, the largest business school in the Netherlands; other foreign study is available in France, Germany, Greece and Italy. Summer courses, night classes, and free tutorial sessions are also offered. "With the right kind of advising, you can get a good education here," counsels one undergrad.

The university's student body is overwhelmingly Georgian in origin—a mixture of "small-town rednecks and big-city sophisticates"—but all fifty states and more than a hundred foreign countries are also represented. Most Bulldogs are public school graduates, and many belong to one of more than a dozen religious organizations on campus (the Baptist Student Union is the largest). The most prevalent characteristic seems to be friendliness; students smile and say "Hi" to strangers. Georgia makes its admissions decisions without regard to student financial need, but it issues no guarantees that any need will be met. Aid is awarded on a first-come, first-served basis. The university meets the needs of nearly three hundred extraordinary male and female athletes, no problem.

Tales of miscreant air-conditioning and elevators in some regular dorms often lure freshmen to the high-rise variety, where they find the smallest rooms on campus and a roommate or two with whom to share. Some dorms have their own swimming pools. Most upperclassmen prefer the roomier low-rise dorms, if they haven't already moved off campus. Students aren't required to buy one of the two meal plans (for five or seven days a week), but most do. There are three dining halls plus the student union's snack bar (called the Bulldog Room, naturally). Every dorm has a kitchen for those who prefer to cook for themselves, but, like the laundry facilities, they are often in poor repair.

The campus itself is pretty, with many large greens and wooded walks. Downtown Athens borders the university and provides free bus service and diversions catalogued by one student as follows: "Many bars and nightclubs, eight movie theaters, restaurants in abundance, and, if we don't feel like going out, four pizza places that deliver." And never mind the lawsuits and NCAA probation, the whole town of Athens still supports the consistently winning football team. UGA has hired a public relations firm to reverse any damage done to the Bulldog image as a result of this scandal, and the athletic office is happy to report that ticket sales have not dropped off in the least. The top-ranked tennis team also draws large crowds. The university has everything the weekend jock could want, including indoor and outdoor tennis and swimming, handball, racquetball and tennis courts, and a jogging and exercise trail.

Georgia's thirty-one fraternities and eighteen sororities provide most of the social activity. Only a deceptively small number of students actually pledge, but most everyone attends at least a couple of Greek bashes each year. "The partying never stops around here," says one student. "Just wander around frat row for five minutes and you'll find one." Those with other tastes in recreation are also well served. "With more than four hundred clubs and organizations, how could you go wrong?" one student asks. Atlanta is only an hour away, and several ski slopes can be found in the nearby Smokies. The whole student population descends on Florida en masse twice a year: first for the Florida football game and then for spring break. If you bring a car, don't count on finding a place to put it.

Georgia may be a "football-crazy school," but it's also big enough to accommodate an enormous range of academic interests and abilities. "People who want a college degree without much effort can find a place here," advises a student (but of course he was not referring to athletes). Serious scholars are also satisfied with the offerings here. In fact, more than ever before, the University of Georgia may be worth a look. As one enthusiastic Bulldog puts it, "Where else can you get an education and have so much fun for so little money?"

Gettysburg College

Gettysburg, PA 17325

Location Small town	**Applicants** 2,930
Total Enrollment 1,850	**Accepted** 59%
Undergraduates 1,850	**Enrolled** 31%
Male/Female 49/51	**Academics** ★★★
SAT V/M 530/570	**Social** 🏛🏛🏛
Financial Aid 37%	**Q of L** ●●●
Expense Pr $ $ $	**Admissions** (717)337-6100

Situated on the edge of one of the nation's most famous Civil War battlefields, 150-year-old Gettysburg College couldn't have a richer past. Abraham Lincoln made history when he gave his you know what here, and nearly a century later Dwight Eisenhower wrote his autobiography in what is now the admissions office. Today, over 125 years after the Union and Confederate armies fired their last rounds, a new battle rages for Gettysburg students—the quest for a high-paying job after graduation.

Plopped down in the midst of southern Pennsylvania's gently rolling hills, Gettysburg's two-hundred-acre campus has a mix of architectural styles, ranging from Victorian brownstones to Greek revival to modern. The battlefield park—though often crowded with tourists—is a spacious playground for outdoorsy types, while the campus itself is blessed with "plenty of trees and squirrels." Indoors, the English department is among the strongest at Gettysburg, as are the natural sciences. The fine psychology department offers opportunities for students to participate in faculty research. Business majors are popular, and so is the excellent history department, which is bolstered by the school's prestigious Civil War Institute. The fine arts department benefits from newly renovated facilities, and a new theater arts complex should appeal to would-be actors and actresses. The library system boasts 300,000 volumes, an on-line computer catalogue search and a new library/learning resource center. Despite the Greek revival architecture on campus, students say classics offerings are weak, as are those in religion.

The small class sizes at the college make for close student-teacher relationships. "How marvelous as a junior," says one, "to be recognized and remembered by a professor from my first freshman semester." A college-wide honor system contributes to the atmosphere of community and mutual trust, but the intellectual climate is by no means scintillating. "Students need to be more responsive to the intellectual atmosphere the faculty is always trying to foster," says a senior history major. About a third of each student's course work is spent on distribution requirements covering many fields, including religion (a remnant of the days when the school's Lutheran affiliation really meant something). The freshman colloquy in liberal learning, also required, aims at strengthening reasoning, writing and speaking skills, using a multidisciplinary theme. Another interesting program is the Area Studies Symposium—each year focusing on a different region of the world—which offers lectures and films for the whole campus in addition to academic credit for participating students. The college recently scrapped its January term and went back to a conventional academic calendar.

Gettysburg sponsors a Washington semester with American University, a United Nations semester through Drew University in New Jersey and cooperative work-study programs in engineering and forestry. Through the Central Pennsylvania Consortium, students may take courses at two nearby colleges, Dickinson and Franklin and Marshall. Outstanding seniors may participate in the Senior Scholars' Seminar, with independent study on a major contemporary issue—Human Sexuality was a recent topic—but all students have a chance to do independent work and/or design their own majors. Study-abroad programs are approved on a case-by-case basis.

Though a conservative, white, middle-class Christian will think Gettysburg is one of the friendliest places imaginable, anyone else may feel outnumbered. Though the administration is trying to lure more minorities, with activities like an Intercultural Awareness Think Tank, black enrollment remains a paltry 1 percent, and Hispanics are even fewer. "Most of the students are from Pennsylvania and New Jersey, and their main interest is to make money," says one of the school's football warriors. Nearly three-quarters come from public high schools, almost a third were in the top 10 percent of their high school class and nearly all were in the top half. Lutherans account for only 16 percent of undergraduates, and several students contend that there are a larger number of Catholics on campus. Many Christian groups—from the campus Chapel Council to the Fellowship of Christian Athletes—draw large followings.

Recent contributions have enabled Gettysburg to upgrade its need-based Presidential Scholarship Program, which now enables about 140 students with high-ranking academic credentials (combined SATs of 1200 and top 10 percent of class) to "have the majority or all their needs met with scholarship assistance." The college carries on an institutionally financed loan program under which parents can borrow up to one-half of tuition per year and repay at favorable interest rates over a period of up to five years. Also, the Lutheran Church funds a scholarship program for its members. No athletic scholarships are available.

Campus housing is guaranteed all four years, and students can choose from coed dorms or single-sex halls with three visitation options. Seniors have first pick and generally opt for a spot in the new Apple apartments, which come fully furnished and have air-conditioning and wall-to-wall carpeting. About a fifth of the men live in frat houses; the sororities are nonresidential. Off-campus apartments lure about 15 percent of the upperclassmen, but freshmen are required to remain in the dorms and take three meals a day in the recently renovated dining hall. Everyone else can pick from a variety of dining options, including the ever-popular Bullet Hole, the campus snack bar/grill room where many students take their regular meals. Upperclassmen can also cook for themselves (the dorms have kitchens).

Social life at "the Burg" revolves around the eleven fraternities—three-quarters of the men belong—and those who don't may feel out of it socially. The seven sororities, which do not have houses, draw about half of the women but play a much smaller role on campus. A student activities committee provides alternative social events, including bus trips to Georgetown, movies, and campus coffeehouses. Those who get the munchies can make the short walk to the Lincoln Diner or take a brief road trip to Stavros, a locally famous pizza parlor. The orchards and rolling countryside surrounding the campus are peaceful and scenic, and there is a small ski slope nearby. "The battlefield is great for jogging, a bike ride or simply laughing at the tourists," a student notes (students get free passes to the historical attractions). Gettysburg, a tiny town of eight thousand geared to the tourist trade, occupies a spot "in the middle of nowhere but not far from anywhere" within an hour and a half of both Baltimore and Washington, D.C.

About a quarter of Gettysburg's students earn varsity letters. Women's field hockey recently took the Division III national championship, and men's football, baseball and lacrosse have won conference titles. Both track and swimming frequently produce all-Americans. Fraternities field the most teams for intramural sports, which generally stir up more excitement among the men than the women. On the varsity level, the college has recently moved to upgrade the women's athletic program.

Though students here stay only four years instead of four score and seven, most find happiness at their own Gettysburg address. "Friendly, rewarding, challenging and supportive" is how one student describes it. Respectable academic and lively social opportunities are available, and between them, says one student, "it's easy to find a livable balance."

Gordon College

Wenham, MA 01984

Location Suburban	**Accepted** 80%
Total Enrollment 1,220	**Enrolled** 60%
Undergraduates 1,220	**Academics** ★ ★ ★
Male/Female 40/60	**Social** ☎ ☎
SAT V/M 510/530	**Q of L** ● ● ● ●
Financial Aid 90%	**Admissions** (800)322-0463
Expense Pr $ $	in Massachusetts,
Applicants 780	(800)343-1379 out of state

Secluded amid the rolling hills and wooded vales of the Massachusetts North Shore, there lies a Christian college that is creating quite a stir on its once-peaceful eight-hundred-acre tract of New England countryside. From humble beginnings as a school for missionaries in 1889, Gordon has grown to become the leading evangelical Christian college in the Northeast. In 1985, Gordon's expansion accelerated dramatically when it absorbed a previously independent evangelical institute, Barrington College, touching off a flurry of new construction and renovation as Gordon worked to assimilate the new arrivals. Today, the college remains in flux. The fall of '87 brought implementation of a new core curriculum and a new academic calendar, plus the completion of a new Learning Resource Center that will double the college's library facilities.

Despite the recent upheaval, Gordon hasn't strayed from its missionary ideals. The college views itself as a community of evangelical Christians—about thirty denominations are represented—and all courses are taught "from a biblical perspective." Chapel attendance twice a week is mandatory, as is the Friday convocation on the "Christian and his world." Drinking, smoking and social dancing are no-no's.

Gordon disavows the term "fundamentalist," and its conviction that faith should be subjected to critical investigation has put the school in some fundamentalists' doghouse.

At Gordon, religious commitment is seen as an enhancement rather than a threat to free and rigorous academic inquiry. "Gordon is a Christian college, but students aren't encouraged to accept everything they are taught without question," says one junior. Education and business are two of the most popular majors, and not surprisingly, the programs in biblical and theological studies are strong and the humanities are for the most part above par. Biology is strong and Gordon graduates have a 90 percent acceptance rate at medical schools. Currently, the weak links academically are foreign languages, fine arts and communications. Although a lecture hall in the library has been converted into a small theater, facilities in this area are still sorely lacking. Since Barrington has more of a professional orientation than Gordon, new programs in accounting, social work and youth ministeries will complement the school's established liberal arts offerings.

Gordon's already demanding core curriculum is currently undergoing revision. The current version includes requirements in thirteen areas, including three in religion, in addition to those in a student's major. Though the changes are still on the drawing board, the administration maintains that the new core will include more interdisciplinary courses, a foreign language requirement, and more emphasis on "active learning" outside the classroom. Fitting all this into a schedule is already a challenge, and many students find they have to set up their four-year study plan when they arrive. Students in the Kenneth Pike honors program are exempt from the core. The college recently abandoned its trimester calendar in favor of twelve-week semesters.

Faculty members—85 percent of whom have their PhDs—are born-again Christians, and they care about their undergraduates. "Profs invite students for meals, have long office hours, allow students to bug them anytime, and attend the same churches as students," a senior notes. The president expects faculty members to be outstanding classroom performers, and they do their best to come up with interesting courses, such as an interdisciplinary course in human sexuality and another in Jewish culture. Gordon offers an interesting array of summer programs, including eight-week European seminars for credit during the summer and jaunts to Israel to visit key biblical and historical sites. Those interested in politics may go to Washington, D.C., with the Christian College Consortium's* American Studies program, or opt for La Vida, a two-week wilderness experience. Throughout the year, about one hundred students are placed in cooperative education jobs that give them experience in area high-tech firms, Boston publishing houses, and local service organizations. Gordon admits students without regard to need, and then tries its best to fill any financial aid gaps of the students who enroll. About 10 percent of the best students get merit scholarships ranging up to $6,200 a year. Gordon also grants a 5 percent discount to families that cough up the full year's cost by August 15.

Students come to Gordon from all over the United States in search of a college that integrates faith and learning, although this regional diversity can be deceiving. Virtually all are white, middle-class and socially conservative, and most are either from Massachusetts or the rest of New England. The college caters to the "zealously Christian," and the "Young Republicans flourish here," one undergraduate reports. No one gets in without a personal reference from a minister or spiritual leader, and students must sign a "statement of faith" affirming their belief in the fundamental tenets of Christianity. But according to one student, a minority "do not live by those tenets, and show disregard for the school's restrictions on the use of alcohol and tobacco."

Gordon is situated on a beautiful campus in the midst of hundreds of acres of forestland and five lakes—one of which students use for swimming in the warmer months. The academic buildings and dorms are in a small area, and it doesn't take more than two or three minutes to walk anywhere. Most of the buildings are institutional red brick, except for an old stone mansion. "Coed dorms" at Gordon means that men and women live in separate wings of the same building separated by a lobby, a lounge and a laundry room. Persons of the opposite sex are allowed to traverse these barriers only at specified times. The dorms are modern and comfortable, and freshmen can count on getting the nicest rooms. The other three classes enter a lottery for the remainder. To cope with the influx of students from Barrington, one new dorm was added and several others renovated. But unfortunately rooms are still scarce by the time sophomores get to pick. Many end up on waiting lists, and since the college sometimes overbooks rooms, there is often crowding for those who do get them. About 10 percent of the student body lives off campus, with permission to move out granted only after all the dorms are filled.

The dining hall is a main focus of social life, and the food is palatable but expensive, with meal plans keyed to whether students are light or heavy eaters. In between chapel services and Bible classes, students find time for sports. The men's varsity soccer team is a powerhouse, and the women's volleyball team has ranked tops in the state and number two in New England. Men's basketball is also strong. For outdoorsy types, Gordon's setting on Cape Ann is ideal, though others might describe it as a bit isolated. The campus offers cross-country ski trails and ponds for swimming, sailing and skating. The ocean is a quick bike ride away, and students frequently ski New Hampshire's nearby White Mountains. For social life, most students are content with weekend excursions to Boston, church-related functions and an occasional square dance. There is some partying off campus, but students seldom work up to more than "mild drinking."

At Gordon, romances are strictly aboveboard, and students can be dismissed for violation of scriptural prohibitions, including anything from sex to dishonesty. But most students don't mind the rules—that's part of why they chose Gordon—and appreciate the shared sense of purpose and community spirit that is fostered among the students, faculty and administration.

Goucher College

Towson, MD 21204

Location Suburban	**Applicants** 590
Total Enrollment 840	**Accepted** 83%
Undergraduates 760	**Enrolled** N/A
Male/Female N/A	**Academics** ★ ★ ★
SAT V/M 500/500	**Social** 🐘 🐘 🐘 🐘
Financial Aid 60%	**Q of L** ● ● ● ●
Expense Pr $ $ $	**Admissions** (301)337-6100

Goucher has seen the handwriting on the wall. Faced with declining enrollments and ominous studies showing that most women prefer coed schools, Goucher decided to begin admitting men in the fall of '87. Many women here feel betrayed by the move, but administrators say it was necessary to avoid a steep decline in academic standards. After a century of helping talented women make it in a man's world, the college must now focus on integrating men into its feminine environment.

Founded in 1885 to "prepare women for an equal place in the working world," Goucher has long been a leader in women's education. Phi Beta Kappa established a chapter on campus only twenty years after the college was founded, and Goucher ranks among the nation's top fifty schools in turning out students destined for PhDs in the sciences. Set on 254 exquisitely landscaped acres in the suburbs of Baltimore, Goucher's wooded campus comes complete with lush lawns, stately sandstone buildings, and rare trees and shrubs from all corners of the globe.

A rigorous general education program forms the foundation of every Goucher student's education. Currently, there are distribution requirements in eight categories, but a new Goucher Plan would reshuffle them into five broad areas: intellectual skills and the application of knowledge, career experience and connections, global awareness, responsibility and leadership, and development of intellectual and physical potential. Present requirements stipulate that students must show proficiency in English composition, computer literacy and a foreign language. Physical education, with an emphasis on learning skills and habits to ensure lifelong good health, is also mandatory. An off-campus internship in the student's major field of study is required and often pursued during the five-week January term in congressional offices, museums, law firms, newspapers or other institutions. The program is well established and widely recognized for its excellence, and most students consider this hands-on experience an invaluable asset come graduation.

Goucher's science departments have an excellent reputation. Facilities include space for research, a greenhouse, an observatory with a six-inch refractor telescope, and a special facility for the observation of primate behavior. English, history, political science, and dance all get high ratings from students, as does the computer science department, which is well equipped. The college has done much to integrate computers into the curriculum—"I think they breed while we sleep," says one student—but demand still outstrips supply. Management is popular but suffers from overcrowding. Students say art history, anthropology and sociology are among the school's weakest departments, and despite the recent addition of a new dance studio, the fine arts departments, notably theater and art, still need improvement. "The professors are fantastic," claims one student, "but the college has not offered them a tremendous amount of support."

Goucher's commitment to international learning, demonstrated by its foreign language requirement and school-sponsored study trips to France, Spain, Germany and the Soviet Union, will increase in view of a new five-year agreement with the Bois Roberts International School, a private French boarding school. The college will rent unused residence hall space to Bois Roberts students and allow them to enroll in freshman-level Goucher courses. The administration hopes this agreement will provide an academic and cultural boost to the international relations and modern languages departments while bringing additional revenue to the college. In addition, Goucher students are free to take courses at nearby Johns Hopkins University and seven smaller colleges in the area. An unusual masters program in art and dance therapy is also offered, to which several graduating seniors are admitted each year. Adults returning to college can enroll in Goucher II, which offers a separate curriculum for those with little or no college experience as well as support services for those in the regular undergraduate program. The campus library facilities were recently renovated, but still draw complaints from some students—mainly because they close at 5 PM on the weekends. Goucher's free access to the library at Johns Hopkins often comes in handy, especially for science majors.

Faculty members devote most of their time and energy to undergraduate teaching and have a good rapport with students. "I had the chair of the English department for a 100 level course my first semester here," brags one junior. Each freshman is assigned a faculty adviser to assist with both academic and overall adjustment to college life. Small classes and individual instruction are the rule rather than the exception, and supportive "you-can-do-it" attitude pervades the campus. Academic pressure is intense but not suffocating, and grading is generally tough but fair. The administration requires a written explanation from professors for each A or F they hand out. Says one student, "If it makes your day when you get your computer science program to run, then you belong at Goucher. If you'd rather read *Mademoiselle* than the recommended text—forget it."

A little over 40 percent of the women at Goucher come from Maryland, and most of the rest hail from Pennsylvania, Virginia, New York and New Jersey. Though 65 percent attended public high schools, most students are well off financially. Blacks and

Hispanics make up a little over 7 percent of the student body. Student assessments of their peers vary. One Goucher woman claims that "the general impression is that of Jewish American Princesses," while another says that "students who are initially somewhat reserved and conservative fit in well at Goucher." A couple of years on campus tends to have a liberalizing effect on many students, who by graduation tend to adopt a more feminist stance. Goucher showed its strident feminist streak during the coed debate in 1986, when many of the women sported T-shirts proclaiming BETTER DEAD THAN COED. Some students are still bitter about an administration they feel is "sneaky and does things behind the students' backs." Goucher is need-blind in admissions and offers a limited number of merit scholarships of up to $6,000. College-sponsored loan programs are available for students from all income brackets. Goucher was founded under Methodist auspices, but is now nondenominational.

Generous grants and gifts recently awarded to Goucher have funded a new student center and renovation costs for converting residence halls into coed facilities. Currently, students can choose to live in one of four dormitories, which are divided into sixteen residential houses that accommodate about fifty students each. Houses are the basic unit of campus social life, and each has its own atmosphere. Rowdy or reserved, every sort of student can find a congenial environment, though as a rule the dorms are quiet and good for studying. Freshmen are doubled up in spacious rooms, while upperclassmen select housing through lotteries; the available singles usually go to juniors and seniors, though lucky sophomores can occasionally get one. Right now, each house votes on its own rules governing male guests, so some houses, observes one student, become "very coed on weekends." The administration limits off-campus living to local students and about 10 percent of the juniors and seniors, but women who want to get an apartment closer to male-dominated Johns Hopkins can usually do so.

Goucher's two dining halls serve average college fare, but the required fifteen- or nineteen-meals-per-week plans displease some students. Other options include a kosher dining hall and a cooperative living house that cooks its own meals as a group. Many students take advantage of the restaurants and bars in Towson, the small but bustling college town which is a five-minute walk away. A frequent shuttle service to Towson's shopping mall and to Johns Hopkins is also available. Baltimore is a twenty-minute drive, Washington forty, and both offer many educational, social and cultural attractions.

Goucher's suburban location is great for nature lovers, but it can make for a slow social life. Access to a car is virtual necessity; according to one woman, "students have to, must, and need to go beyond the college into the city or find other social activities at other colleges." Johns Hopkins and its fraternities give Goucher women a much-needed source of men, while saltier types call on Annapolis and "invite midshipmen over for a six-pack and pizza and football games in the hallways." Goucher has no sororities, but the close-knit housing units hold periodic events, and the college hosts plenty of movies, concerts and lectures on the weekends.

Since Goucher was a women's college for so many years, women's athletics are more highly developed than at many coed schools. The most successful teams include tennis, field hockey, lacrosse, volleyball and equestrian, and a new women's cross-country team recently took to the trails. The fate of men's varsity athletics partly hinges on how successful Goucher proves in attracting them. The college has joined NCAA Division III for both men's and women's sports, and plans to offer men's varsity soccer, cross-country, swimming, basketball, fencing, lacrosse and equestrian. A new physical education complex is in the planning stages. Though intramural sports are presently "all but nonexistent," horseback riding is popular thanks to the stables and beautiful wooded trails on campus. Goucher also has several tennis courts, a driving range, practice fields, a swimming pool and saunas.

Nostalgic alumni will no doubt shed some tears at the passing of old Goucher, but no one really knows yet how different the new coed version will be. The college public relations office faces a monumental task trying to sell a former women's college to high school boys. Goucher's transition from a well-known women's college to one that is fully coed will take years, and it won't be easy.

Grinnell College

Grinnell, IA 50112

Location Small town	**Applicants** 1,770
Total Enrollment 1,250	**Accepted** 58%
Undergraduates 1,250	**Enrolled** 37%
Male/Female 50/50	**Academics** ★ ★ ★
SAT V/M 600/630	**Social** 🕾 🕾
Financial Aid 65%	**Q of L** ● ● ● ●
Expense Pr $ $	**Admissions** (515)236-2100

When Horace Greeley uttered those famous words "Go west, young man. Go west," he was talking to an intelligent businessman, lawyer and clergyman named Josiah Bushnell Grinnell. It was through the enlightened young Grinnell and a group of Congregationalist social reformers that the New England heritage of liberal education was transplanted to the Iowa prairie. Once a stop on the Underground Railroad, Grinnell has for two centuries been a frequent stop for poets, educators and musicians traveling cross-country. Today it's home to a first-rate school system, hospital and community arts program—not to mention its local institution of higher education.

Grinnell College grew up sharing the liberal values of its host town and cultivating a remarkable academic tradition. It was the first college west of the Mississippi to admit blacks and women, and it was the first in the country to establish an undergraduate department of political science. Its graduates include Harry Hopkins, architect of the New Deal, and Robert Noyce, inventor of the integrated circuit—who together have probably had as much influence on the shape of twentieth-century American society as any two people you could think of. Even as social currents change, the school continues to foster the noblest aspects of the pioneer spirit. As Grinnell's president puts it, "Our obligation to the future has been established by the history of the college."

The campus is an attractive blend of Oxford-Cambridge Gothic and modern Bauhaus academic buildings and prairie-style houses. (Architecture buffs should take note of the dazzling Louis Sullivan bank facade right off campus.) The arches and an old-fashioned auditorium also contribute to the Ivy League appeal of this bucolic and spacious campus in the center of rural Iowa—fifty-five miles from Des Moines and sixty from Iowa City. "But you have to walk at least six or seven miles before you hit the cornfields," disclaims a political science major.

Strong departments are those in the sciences and foreign languages. The chemistry department, for example, draws its majors into independent research projects. The Russian major can include a semester program in Moscow, Leningrad or Krasnodar. Anthropology, international relations and Chinese studies also receive high ratings. In contrast, the classics, fine arts, music and theater programs garner negative reviews, primarily due to a shortage of resources. Grinnell maintains an open academic style without structured core or distribution requirements; students determine their own course of study with the aid of a faculty member. The only requirement outside the major field is the freshman tutorial, modeled after Oxford University's program and designed to enhance research, writing and discussion skills and to allow freshmen to work individually with professors. Study abroad is offered in London and Rennes, as well as thirty-two other cities. Co-op and 3-2 engineering and architecture programs are additional options.

No doubt about it, Grinnell's academic standards are high. Nearly half the students move on to graduate and professional schools. Students who don't mind studying, even on weekends, will be happiest at Grinnell—"We do it well and often," says one woman. "During midterms or finals we're all a bunch of walking zombies," reports an English major. Nevertheless, there is relatively little competition between students. Teaching is a higher faculty priority than research, and with a student-teacher ratio of eleven to one, many students are able to develop close friendships with their professors. Classes range from about ten to twenty students in the upper levels to possibly fifty students in the introductory courses.

Called the "most comfortable library in the nation for a liberal-arts college" by *Rolling Stone* magazine, the newly remodeled Burling Library is plush, close to the dorms, and well stocked with periodicals. It also houses the oldest selective depository of government documents in Iowa. Guided by alumnus Robert Noyce, inventor of the microchip, Grinnell has become a national leader in applying computers to arts and science education. More than two hundred terminals are available for student use in several locations around the campus, including the library and residence halls.

The mostly liberal and progressive student body comes from all over the country and twenty-four foreign countries. In fact, there are more transplanted Chicagoans here than home-grown Iowans. But a sophomore warns that all Grinnell students "must be willing to sacrifice seeing the most current movies and frequenting four-star restaurants for a new experience in a rural setting." The financial aid office works overtime to come up with funds for needy students, because, as one aid recipient puts it, "they do care that you stay." There are twenty academic scholarships ranging from $750 to $2,200, and National Merit Scholars who list Grinnell as their first choice are automatic recipients.

The college guarantees four years of housing in recently renovated dorms, but a limited number of upperclassmen can and do live off campus. All but two dorms are coed, and after freshman year students participate in the room draw. Two dining halls, one on each side of the campus, serve surprisingly good food—in fact, there have been rumors that Grinnell serves the best college food in America (aside from the asparagus crepes). Even the pep band is named More Casserole after a common plea made by students. Meal plans range from full board to just dinner, and special dinners are served family-style every other Wednesday night.

Relations between the college and the tiny midwestern town could be better. As one sophomore assesses, "Basically we think the townies are hicks, and they think we're rude and dress weird," but both sides are trying to improve the situation. There are few special resources in town, but students are not lacking for things to do. The area lends itself to biking, running and cross-country skiing. The most popular hangout is the only bar in town, called, appropriately enough, The Bar. A place called Link's has the best pool tables, "if you don't mind the motorcycle gang giving you funny looks." There is a bus station, which leaves some students wondering where they're supposed to go.

With no fraternities or sororities, intramurals and all-campus parties revolve mainly around the dorms. The recent rise of the drinking age has significantly altered social activities, although progressive drinking parties are still enjoyed. For special interests, Grinnell offers a wide variety of social groups and activities, such as the Society for Creative Anachronisms, the Black Culture Center, improvisational workshops, poetry readings and GORP (Grinnell Outdoor Recreational Program). The latter sponsors outdoor trips, for which it will provide tents, canoes, backpacks, cross-country skis, and even kayaks. There is also the Grinnell Experience, which consists of a series of events like Spring Waltz ("Yes, we really waltz"). According to one student, "The college recognizes that we are in the middle of Iowa, so it does its best to bring things to Grinnell for the students (movies, plays, dance troupes, etc.)."

In sports, soccer and basketball draw the best crowds, but cross-country, track, and swimming teams also do well. Women's athletics are strong, although there are fewer women's varsity teams than men's.

Caring and cohesiveness appear to be an integral characteristic of Grinnell. The corn may get "oppressive," and gossip may travel quickly across the campus (all four blocks of it), but the good features far outweigh such disadvantages. Says one student, "Grinnell's facilities and equipment are outstanding for this size college. We also have things money can't buy, like an interested faculty." Writer Tom Wolfe once called Grinnell the Midwest's City of Light, and most students here are inclined to agree.

Hamilton College

Clinton, NY 13323

Location Rural	**Applicants** 3,340
Total Enrollment 1,670	**Accepted** 42%
Undergraduates 1,670	**Enrolled** 32%
Male/Female 55/45	**Academics** ★ ★ ★
SAT V/M 560/610	**Social** ☎ ☎ ☎ ☎
Financial Aid 52%	**Q of L** ● ● ●
Expense Pr $ $ $ $	**Admissions** (315)859-4421

Hamilton College takes its name from Alexander Hamilton, who in the days of the Founding Fathers was the leading champion of America's emerging social and commercial elite. And the appellation is a fitting one. At this liberal arts college in upstate New York the academics are still high-quality, the students upwardly mobile, the values traditional and the pace of change slow. "To make waves at Hamilton is extremely difficult," says one junior.

This prevailing stodginess caused quite a rift back in 1977, when all-male Hamilton absorbed its fledgling sister school across the street, Kirkland College. In fact, the students from the two colleges blended about as well as the traditional nineteenth-century sandstone buildings on the Hamilton side of the road and the brightly decorated modern cube structures of the Kirkland campus. And the opposing moods of each campus—more raucous and social at Hamilton, calmer and more individualistic at Kirkland—didn't help in forming a cohesiveness. But all's quiet, or quieter, these days in the Mohawk Valley, where the two campus separated by a hundred yards of woods have become one on a steep hill between the Catskills and the Adirondacks.

English and history have long been solid subjects in Hamilton's liberal arts curriculum, while the economics and government departments are the younger of the popular subjects. Prelaw, premed, and business concentrations are filled with eager preprofessional students, and interdisciplinary programs in American studies, women's studies and linguistics get good marks. Strongest of the social sciences is psychology, whose faculty is unusually productive in terms of research and publication, sometimes in collaboration with students. For those who have more specific interests, Hamilton recently developed concentrations in biochemistry/molecular biology and ancient Mediterranean civilization. The math, music and physics departments are on the up and up, but students still moan about the art, speech and theater offerings. Construction of a new center for music and the performing arts promises to help out in these areas. A critical languages program features native-speaking instructors in a wide variety of languages, but quality is spotty. As an alternative, check out the special interest housing (French, Russian and Spanish suites). Plans for a new writing and reading center and linguistics facility are under way. The modern Burke Library is impressive—all-night reading room, extensive Ezra Pound collection—but it gets too hot in the winter and often doubles as a social gathering place. "Sometimes it seems more like a cocktail party than a library," says a senior.

"Students are given considerable latitude within a strong faculty advisement system to structure their own academic goals," says an administrator. This is educationese for saying that Hamilton has no general ed requirements. Effective with the class of 1991, however, there will be senior requirements within their concentrations that may take the form of an independent or group study project. Many students opt to spend time off campus or abroad. Hamilton offers yearlong programs in France and Spain and terms in both Washington and Mystic Seaport, Connecticut.* In an extensive six-year program students can earn both a BA degree from Hamilton and a law degree from Columbia University, and premeds may take advantage of the Medical School Early Assurance Plan.

Because Hamilton is not a research university, its faculty members are chosen for their teaching ability, and accessibility is the norm. "Professors really want that one-to-one relationship with the students," notes an English major. Schoolwork is not all-consuming for the majority, although "students are not about to forget they spend a good deal of money to receive a Hamilton education," reprimands one undergrad.

New York residents (most from downstate) make up about half the student body, and almost 80 percent of Hamilton students come from the top fifth of their high school classes. Minorities make up 5 percent. Despite the sixty-to-forty ratio of public to private school enrollees, preppiedom is still prominent at Hamilton. One student describes her peers as "generally attractive, secure but not particularly intellectually challenging or inquisitive." Politically, the majority of students are "staunchly moderate," says an English literature major, who nevertheless acknowledges a recent "blossoming of fringes on both ends of the political spectrum." Fifty-three new need-based scholarships have been created, but, for reasons more philosophical than financial, no athletic or academic merit scholarships are offered.

Housing at Hamilton is plush. Half the rooms in the dorms—most of which are coed—are singles, and some have fireplaces and private bathrooms. Students can live in the elegant stone buildings of the Hamilton campus or the modern cement dorms, with wall-to-wall carpeting and huge plate glass windows of the former Kirkland campus. Rooms are assigned to freshmen, and upperclassmen play a lottery system based on seniority. Although students are guaranteed a roof over their heads for four years, "sophomore housing can be disastrous." Still, a mere 1 percent of the students venture off campus. About one in ten of all students live in fraternities and sororities, which have their own dining facilities and better food than can be found in the three dining halls on campus. A student food co-op gives alternative-life-style types a chance to whole-wheat-and-wok-it on their own.

The male/female ratio is now tilted only slightly in favor of the men, and coeducation has managed to temper the chauvinism a bit. With the closing of two fraternities (they were reborn as sororities) and continued criticism of others, even the once all-powerful Greek system has experienced a setback in popularity. Still, women wish that the merger had brought more "social options." Because the drinking age is twenty-one, parties are strictly "proofed" and underclassmen are required to find nonalcoholic diversions on the weekend.

Substantial amounts of snow fall on Clinton every year, so the skiing, both downhill and cross-country, is excellent. The bucolic Hamilton setting may be a welcome change for jaded city dwellers, but it "can get claustrophobic." There are a lot of cows to look at but little in the form of culture or entertainment apart from what is imported. Clinton, at the bottom of the hill, has four bars and a pizza joint—that's it. The nearest small city, Utica, is twenty minutes away by car and has factory outlets galore for bargain hunters and an Amtrak station for those bent on escape. The intramural program is often dominated by the school's out-of-season athletes, which is unfortunate for those ninety-eight-pound weaklings looking for less-serious competition. At least the extensive sports facilities leave room for solitary endeavors. The basketball team has frequently been ranked nationally in the top ten in Division III, football is good, and the men's and women's swimming teams do well despite poor facilities. An expanded coaching staff and a bigger budget have brought women's athletics closer to a par with men's.

It has been an interesting adjustment period since Hamilton officially became coeducational, but it now appears that the most severe growing pains have passed—with the conservative values for the most part winning out over the more free-wheeling attitudes. Alexander Hamilton would have liked that.

Hampshire College

Amherst, MA 01002

Location City outskirts	**Applicants** 1,120
Total Enrollment 1,010	**Accepted** 70%
Undergraduates 1,010	**Enrolled** 45%
Male/Female 45/55	**Academics** ★ ★ ★ ★
SAT V/M 560/560	**Social** 🛥 🛥 🛥
Financial Aid 48%	**Q of L** ● ● ●
Expense Pr $ $ $ $	**Admissions** (413)549-4600

With a flock of sheep and a pack of dogs in its front yard, Hampshire College appears a bit abnormal at first glance. But those who know the school as the "Frisbee college" (a name that was coined after one student designed his own free-throwing major) understand that this is simply a liberal arts institution minus boring traditional givens like course requirements, grades, academic departments and faculty tenure. (The sheep are from the innovative farm center lab; the dogs represent the uncontrolled group in a canine breeding experiment.)

The idea of Hampshire College was conceived of in the '50s, nurtured in the progressive education movement of the '60s, and became a reality in 1970. Although the anti–status quo New England school has had its ups and downs, its number of applicants is growing and people are realizing the college's lack of structure and demand for active learning is not as off the wall as it sounds. "Hampshire just has a slightly different way of presenting the traditional liberal arts," claims one student.

Everything is a little bit different about Hampshire, but let's start with the academics. You get your degree not by accumulating course credits, but rather by passing a series of examinations and independent studies. The first hurdle, known as Division I, consists of taking a course in each of the four multidisciplinary schools of study: natural science, social science, communications and cognitive sciences, and humanities and arts. In each area it is up to the student to define an academic question and put together a collection of course work, papers and independent projects to answer it. Then the student plans an exam and gives it to two or three professors to conduct. "For natural science, you can write a computer program to assist Spanish children in learning English; for social science you could propose a theory of why southern women have a harder time being lesbians than northern women. . . ." one man explains. Get the idea?

The second hurdle (Division II) comprises a "concentration"—roughly equivalent to a major elsewhere—of independent research and creative work. And the final requirement (Division III) is "advanced study," or some sort of ambitious project along the line of a senior thesis. Instead of grades, professors hand out written evaluations or critiques. As a result of the division system, there are as many curriculums at Hampshire as there are students. The common denominator equals a heavy work load, an emphasis on self-initiated study, close contact with faculty advisers, and the assumption that first-year students can be asked to do what other colleges reserve for graduate students.

Faculty members are selected because they like teaching, and choosing the right professor as an academic adviser is the most important decision a Hampshire student makes. The college requires that every student complete a community service project and encourages internships during the fall, spring or optional January term. Hampshire's bachelor degree could be renamed a pre–grad school degree because close to 100 percent of the students go on to further study (two-thirds to master's or doctoral programs and one-third to professional schools). It's not at all unusual for Hampshire students to end up in businesses that they themselves start in fields such as computer programming, construction or film production.

Hampshire is strong in the social and natural sciences, especially women's studies, cognitive sciences, agriculture and environment technology (a new bioshelter was added to the Science Center for carefully controlled experiments). A new program, Third World Expectation, demands that students relate course projects directly to Third World problems. The school's flexibility is ideal for artists, and the departments of film and photography are dazzling, which is also the reason they are overcrowded. The dance and music faculty are gifted, and the building they occupy is new. On the other hand, one student says, "The pianos really need help."

For quality courses in modern and classical languages, students must travel to another school in the Five College Consortium.* And although Hampshire's library is a quiet and pleasant place to study, it has a limited collection and no archives. But by taking advantage of the library resources at all five colleges, students have ready access to about three million volumes. "Five-College students have more resources available to them than any other college students I know," comments a feminist studies major. She adds that there is no extra cost for use of the other schools' facilities, or the buses to get to them.

Granola and seed-eater stereotypes aside, Hampshire students tend to be bright, self-assured, and intellectually aggressive. "Students who suspect that professors and their textbooks are liars until otherwise proven are prime Hampshirites," proclaims a skeptical junior. They come to Hampshire from all over the country (several from the West Coast) and 8 percent are foreigners. Students are "liberal to one degree or another," according to one undergrad, yet defined as "upper-middle-class prep school types less the patent leather shoes and button-down oxford shirts," by another. But undergrads here still get more involved with social issues than their job-obsessed counterparts elsewhere: "The main interests seem to be lobbying for public interest groups and debating international issues," says one student. And it is generally not a good idea to ask where the Greek houses are at Hampshire because, as one partisan puts it, "fraternities and sororities are considered sexist, elitist organizations, largely detrimental to a healthy campus, and are frowned upon."

Hampshire has stepped up its attempts to offer all eligible students financial aid to meet their needs. The school figures each student's need by subtracting the expected family contribution from the cost of the education and then provides Hampshire grants of up to $2,000. If further aid is needed, it is supplied through loans, work-study and additional grants. Students can also compete for thirty merit awards ranging from $1,000 to $3,000.

Set amid apple orchards and next to a farm, Hampshire's facilities are modern and "not too impressive architecturally," according to one student, who says the campus is "too clean and looks more like a large hotel facility than a school." First-year students live in coed dorms (almost all the rooms are singles and "functional to the point of being spartan"). These dormies eat at the dining hall, where the food is OK by college standards, "but inevitably mediocre by any other." Brunches on Saturdays and Sundays, complete with made-to-order omelettes, and the daily availability of ice cream help. The alternative living situation is "mods"—apartments in which groups of four to ten students share the responsibility for cleaning and cooking as well as less exotic tasks like taking out the garbage. Special quarters are arranged for nonsmokers, veggies, pet owners and others with special preferences. For those in the mods, good, inexpensive food is available from an on-campus cooperative. Only a hundred or so students live off campus, and only with special permission. Campus housing is assigned on a lottery basis, with squatting rights respected.

Hampshire is no place for competitive jocks, since many sports are coed and primarily noncompetitive. There are no paid coaches, so students organize the sports clubs (men's and women's soccer and basketball are the biggies) and intramural teams (including Ultimate Frisbee, volleyball and softball). There is an outstanding outdoors program that offers frequent opportunities for mountaineering, cross-country skiing and kayaking, and all equipment can be borrowed at no cost. Other sports facilities include a jogging/exercise trail, a superb gym with a solar-heated pool and a well-populated coed sauna. On weekends many students head for Boston, New York, Hartford or, in season, the ski trails of Vermont and New Hampshire. But there are plenty of cultural resources within the Five College area, and the free twenty-minute bus rides to Northampton and South Hadley are much used. There's almost always a party going, but if not, don't worry—"Hampshire students know how to have a good time, and are innovative about fulfilling their play-time goals," one student says.

The absence of grades and other standard forms of competition at Hampshire reduces the stress in one sense, but also throws a lot of the responsibility back on the student. Many, if not most, Hampshire scholars go through a period of "creative floundering," and the dropout rate is high. Hampshire requires a tolerance for ambiguity and "the unavoidable moments of isolation inherent to an individual-geared system," according to one coed. But for those who deeply value their independence, this school is a haven from a highly structured education. "College is a time for productive self-indulgence," says one free-spirited senior amid the flocks and packs, "and Hampshire is the perfect place to do this."

Hartwick College

Oneonta, NY 13820

Location Small city
Total Enrollment 1,420
Undergraduates 1,420
Male/Female 44/56
SAT V/M 460/500
Financial Aid 50%
Expense Pr $ $

Applicants 1,830
Accepted 76%
Enrolled 30%
Academics ★ ★
Social 🐾 🐾 🐾
Q of L ● ● ●
Admissions (607)432-4200

Hartwick College has scored some impressive gains over the past several years—and not all of them were on the soccer field. Students report that the academic challenge has improved as professors crack down on easy grading policies, and this liberal arts college has outgrown its party school image. Of course, these fun-loving Hartwickians admit the New York State legislature had something to do with their move toward more rigorous studying—with the drinking age raised to twenty-one, students aren't nearly as tempted to pass up the library on their way to little Oneonta's large selection of watering holes.

Hartwick's ivy-covered, red-brick buildings with white cupolas, gables and trim constitute a more modern version of traditional New England schools. The campus setting on the Oyaron Hill, overlooking the city and the Susquehanna Valley beyond, provides a breathtaking view, which almost makes up for the many steps students must climb to get to class. Likewise, the colorful autumns almost make up for the long, cold winters.

Hartwick's liberal arts framework assures that students are exposed to what one administrator terms "a broad swath of human knowledge," but its best and most popular programs are its career-oriented ones, notably nursing and management. Students are enthusiastic about political science, history, biology and chemistry. The faculty and facilities for art and music are excellent, but students note a lack of interest in these areas and hence a lack of strength. Computer and information science are rapidly growing programs, but students seem to be less than thrilled with some of the behavioral sciences. Many feel that not enough money or administrative support is going into the English, theater arts and foreign languages departments.

Writing competency is required of all undergraduates. Freshmen are given a writing test and assigned to a series of writing classes until they obtain college-level skills. Students must also take courses from three designated areas: humanities, natural sciences and mathematics, social and behavioral sciences—as well as four skill courses in physical education. A Great Books course helps to tie together various liberal arts subjects. The most notable example of Hartwick's academic enrichment is a new honors program for students who complete the freshman year with a grade average of at least

3.5. Honors students can tailor their own more-demanding programs and take honors options in individual courses. A new, tougher Curriculum XXI is in the planning stages, but the faculty hopes the finished product will "better equip students for their lives in the 21st century."

The course offerings are necessarily limited by Hartwick's small size, but the Individual Student Program enables students to create a major dealing with their particular interests, and they may take courses at the nearby State University College at Oneonta (SUCO). Hartwick offers other unconventional learning options—many of them in off-campus locations. "Opportunities abroad are varied, encouraged, cheap and excellent," reports a well-traveled senior who has been to a deserted U.S. Naval base in San Salvador and on a tour of China and Hong Kong, and plans to study politics in the Soviet Union. The biology department uses a field station on an island in the Bahamas, and the college even owns its own 1,100-acre environmental study center, Pine Lake, situated a short drive from campus. An Outward Bound program, offered to freshmen as part of orientation, is now an option for management majors who want to test their leadership skills. Formal internship programs exist for nursing, management and education students, and the four-week January term is a good time to explore new areas.

Hartwick seems to be full of dedicated professors who enjoy teaching more than anything else. "This is not a research school where every professor is writing a book," cites an English major. "Students get the total attention of their professors." Private tutoring and help sessions are offered to those in need, and students are enthusiastic about the strong vocational counseling program. Most student complaints focus on the library, which has been an issue for a long time. "It's not very well supplied, nor is it a great place to study," explains a sophomore. "Unfortunately, it's more of a social gathering place." The administration claims library improvement is number one on their list of priorities, but meanwhile students can usually find what they need at the SUCO library, which is within walking distance.

As Hartwick has begun to upgrade its academics and become better known, its student body has become somewhat more diverse. Most are from "fairly well-to-do" families and tend to be relaxed, sociable, and a bit on the politically sedate side. "The average Hartwickian is probably conservative as far as world issues go," says a biochem major. "But they don't really get involved in heated issues; they seem to be quite sheltered here in Oneonta." Even if politics don't excite Hartwickians, there's always the great outdoors. "Many students look like they just stepped out of an L. L. Bean catalogue," reports a senior. "Wholesome is the adjective that comes to mind. Sports are important to them and when the sun is out, so are they." Over half of the students are from New York State, especially Westchester County and Long Island, and most of the rest come from New England or the Middle Atlantic states. Although a fourth of the students come from the top fifth of their high school class, more than 30 percent are from the bottom half. Each year the financial aid office awards sixty academic scholarships, which range from $300 to full tuition.

The school's seven residence halls (one all-female dorm and the rest coed to varying degrees) provide plenty of spacious rooms, but the new town houses are considered the *"crème de la crème"* of Hartwickian habitation. Freshmen and sophomores are required to live on campus, though the latter may move into one of the fraternity or special-interest houses (biology, music, English and international). Juniors and seniors may choose a new room in the lottery or move into reasonably priced off-campus houses or apartments. Hartwick's second campus at Pine Lake has winterized cabins that are heated by wood stoves and a lodge where environmentally inclined students can live in a rustic style. On-campus students eat at a single dining commons, where the food is decent (Wednesday is Chinese night) and the view is even better ("It's a nice place to scope out guys," according to a senior).

From campus, it's only a short walk (or bus ride) downhill into the small city of Oneonta, with its tantalizing profusion of bars. Since most Hartwick students aren't old enough to get past the front doors, the college's Saturday movies are popular. Also, the four fraternities and three sororities sponsor campus-wide events as well as members-only cocktail parties, but less than a fifth of the students belong. Other diversions include ski areas within an hour's drive, and Pine Lake, which offers cross-country trails, swimming, boating, and fishing. Buses run to Binghamton and Albany, as well as to New York City. Baseball fans can trundle over to nearby Cooperstown to admire their heroes in the Hall of Fame.

But if soccer is your game, then Oneonta is your town—it's home of the national soccer Hall of Fame and often called "soccer town U.S.A."—and Hartwick is your school. The men's soccer team is a perennial contender for the national Division I championship. The eleven athletic scholarships awarded at Hartwick go to the soccer team, and the entire county assembles whenever the Wick Warriors are playing at home. Men's basketball and women's soccer, basketball, and field hockey teams have also been nationally ranked for the past two years. "Everyone is into intramurals," contends an athletic senior who adds that even these nonvarsity sports are played on the Astroturf, underneath the lights.

Hartwick is in a period of transition, striving toward a more scrupulous academic program and a toning down of the play-school image. Intellectual stimulation may still be on the weak side, but students do appreciate the supportive environment at this little school. "The emphasis is on the students here," says a junior. Perhaps that's why a senior reports that "it's hard to leave Hartwick."

Harvard University

Cambridge, MA 02138

Location City outskirts
Total Enrollment 16,870
Undergraduates 6,560
Male/Female 60/40
SAT V/M 680/700
Financial Aid 70%
Expense Pr $ $ $ $

Applicants 13,700
Accepted 16%
Enrolled 71%
Academics ★ ★ ★ ★ ★
Social ☎ ☎ ☎
Q of L ● ● ● ●
Admissions (617)495-1551

Students at ordinary colleges tend to give a wide variety of reasons for having enrolled: attractive campus, a scholarship, unique programs, good social life and the list goes on. For Harvard students, if anyone has the boldness to ask, the answer is often very simple. As one student puts it, "How can you pass up an acceptance?" Fewer people pass up places at Harvard than at any other competitive college in the country.

Three hundred and fifty years after its founding, the nation's first institution of higher education continues to command unequaled respect from graduate schools, Wall Street employers, and the folks back home. While few undergraduates anywhere have the luxury of academic resources as superb as Harvard's, they still must cope with the institutional indifference to their presence that is also part of the Harvard experience. Harvard may be the best school in the nation from which to graduate, but it's not necessarily the best school for every bright high school graduate to attend. Inside the classroom and out, satisfaction and success at Harvard come only to people who would rather blaze a trail than take a relaxed stroll. "Self-motivated students with outgoing personalities and belief in themselves do well here," says a junior. You do not decide to write for Harvard's school newspaper. You try out.

Spiritually as well as geographically, the campus centers on the famed Harvard Yard, a classic quadrangle of Georgian brick structures the walls of which seem to echo with the voices of William James and Henry Adams and other intellectual greats who crossed its shaded paths in decades past. Outside the yard's wrought iron gates, the campus is an architectural mix ranging from the modern ziggurat that calls itself a Science Center to the white towers of residential houses along the Charles River.

Unquestionably, one of the most amazing things about Harvard is the quality of the faculty. Under its star system, Harvard grants tenure only to those scholars who have already made it—almost always at some place other than Harvard—and then gives them free rein to pursue their own research. It seems that every year a Harvard science professor wins a Nobel Prize, and every other year a humanities professor wins a Pulitzer, and every four years half of the Harvard government and economics departments move to Washington to decide national policy. Harvard professorships are perhaps the closest the Boston Brahmins have come to creating royalty, and students must learn to adjust to their status in the university court.

There's a down side to all this that you may have heard about. The rap on Harvard is that students who arrive with expectations of coffee and doughnuts with Stephen Jay Gould or setting John Kenneth Galbraith straight on Keynesian economics in a tiny seminar end up spending an inordinate amount of time with graduate teaching assistants, and some students say the stereotype fits. "Generally, professors tend to concentrate on their grad students and research," grumbles one student. "Even seniors find top professors inaccessible." Class size can also be an impediment; a recent course in economics, notorious for large classes, packed in 811 students. For those undergraduates determined to match wits with the wizards, persistence and initiative are key. Some faculty luminaries do occasionally conduct small undergraduate seminars (including those reserved for freshmen), and in the opinion of one student, "Faculty contact is possible for any student with any modicum of aggressiveness—you just have to make the first move." To help facilitate faculty-student contact, the college has initiated a faculty dining program under which professors dine at the various residential houses and chew over ideas as well as mystery meat.

Harvard's best-known departments are often its largest—economics, biology, history, government and English account for 50 percent of undergraduate majors. But don't overlook smaller departments with equally exciting scholarship. East Asian studies and philosophy are easily tops in the country, and classics, anthropology and applied mathematics are all strong. Harvard's smaller, interdisciplinary honors majors often boast the best instruction and happiest undergraduates. These programs—social studies, history and science, history and literature, and folklore and mythology—are the only majors in which students must write a senior thesis. This traditional exercise in academic research is optional in other departments, though unfortunately it is often overseen by graduate students, not professors. Likewise, math is criticized for relying too heavily on teaching assistants, and fine arts types should be aware that the music department is mainly concerned with theory. Students in drama or women's studies are on their own since Harvard offers no formal programs in either. The university has been slow to jump on the bandwagon of academic computing—one ingenious experiment has been coin-operated word processors—but once the dust has settled on the current debate over the right hardware and software you can be sure that Harvard will buy in on a large scale.

Back in the mid-1970s Harvard helped launch the current curriculum reform movement, and the new core curriculum that emerged ranks as perhaps the most exciting collection of academic offerings in all of American higher education. Students can crowd into Stephen Jay Gould's lectures on the History of Life and of the Earth and hear his environmentally oriented approach to evolution. The next period they can hear them rebutted by his arch-antagonist, E. O. Wilson, who, in his course on evolutionary biology, argues for the genetic basis of social patterns and human behavior. In Justice, Michael Sandel applies the political thought of Aristotle, Locke and Kant to current issues like pornography, affirmative action and creationism, and when he brings in a visiting lecturer it's likely to be a Supreme Court justice. There's also a long-standing tradition that teachers in the more popular general education courses look for ways to entertain as well as enlighten. To demonstrate the relation between mass and velocity, one professor once ended a class by getting into a small rocket-shaped car and propelling himself across the room and out through a pair of hidden doors. Professor Wilson has been known to dress his teaching assistants up as insects and flowers to perform an elaborate pollination dance to the music of the "Dance of the Sugarplum Fairy."

Core courses are taught in a format typical at Harvard; big-name professors do much of the lecturing, with smaller discussion sections usually led by graduate students. That's OK by many students, who say they feel more comfortable addressing their dumb questions to mere mortals rather than demigods. In formal terms, the core requires students to select eight courses, or a quarter of their program, from a list of offerings in six different "modes of inquiry": literature and arts, historical study, social analysis, science, moral reasoning and foreign cultures. In practice, however, students take half again as many core courses on an elective basis. Students can petition for individualized majors but they must choose some sort of major at the end of their freshman year, a year earlier than most schools. The field of concentration can be changed later, but Harvard expects its students to hit the ground running. For many, if not most, students, the most rewarding form of instruction is the sophomore and junior tutorial, a small group-directed study in a student's field of concentration that is required in most humanities and social sciences. Sophomore tutorial is a standard introduction to the academic subject; junior tutorials offer a range of in-depth examinations of a single issue. Teaching of the tutorials is split between professors and graduate students, and the weight of each party's responsibility varies with the subject and the professor. Juniors and seniors may also take graduate seminars taught by professors, while a popular freshman seminars program provides close contact with faculty and hard work on a pass/fail basis.

The oft-made claim that "the hardest thing about Harvard is getting in" is deceptive. It may be difficult to fail a course, but it is just as difficult to get an A. Reports one student, "In hard core science courses, the curve is steep and vicious." Outside the sciences, however, students challenge themselves as little or much as they please. Some grind away at a dizzying pace throughout the semester, but the combination of numerous large lecture-style classes and an academic calendar with fall term exams after New Year's makes it easy to "blow off" for long periods of time. As Harvard's student-produced course critique observes, "The much maligned Harvard calendar is convenient for extracurricular buffs—you can pretty much put academics on the back burner during sports seasons, play rehearsals, or before publication deadlines and catch up during reading period."

The bottom line is that while schools like Yale and Swarthmore have academic climates more serious than Harvard's, few if any can match the intensity of Harvard's extracurricular scene, where 6,500 of the most talented students in the world compete for leadership positions in a galaxy of extracurricular opportunities. Sooner or later, though, everyone ends up in the library, and there they find facilities unparalleled at any American university. Wood chairs, high ceilings and endless objects of fascination make them "a joy to study in, even if you don't like to study." With eleven million volumes in the system, it is topped only by the Library of Congress.

Undoubtedly Harvard's greatest asset is its student body: a diverse, high-powered, competitive and exciting group. You will meet smooth-talking government majors who appear to have begun their senatorial campaigns in kindergarten. You will meet flamboyant fine arts majors who have cultivated an affected accent all their own. You will probably not meet brilliant biochemists, unless you, too, spend all your time in laboratories. "It's a wonderful conglomeration of people whose varied motivations, goals and approaches to life allow you to open your mind to our kaleidoscopic world," one student gushes. Exciting as they may be, all those achievers can be a grueling workout on the ego. "It's hard to adjust to so many leaders and not enough followers," a sophomore says. Those who have difficulties adjusting will find psychological counseling "terribly understaffed."

Harvard undergraduates come from all fifty states and scores of foreign countries, but the student body is weighted toward the Northeast. Massachusetts and New York are the most heavily represented states, with California now registering third. Blacks and Hispanics account for about 13 percent of enrollment, public high school graduates for two-thirds. No one's going to try to tell you exactly what it takes to gain admittance to Harvard (if they do, apply a grain of salt), but here's a hint: 90 percent of the current student body ranked in the top tenth of their high school class. Two-thirds of the undergraduates receive some form of financial aid; admissions are need-blind, and those with financial need get it. Though there are a few of the expected old money types—who probably donned Harvard sweatshirts and argyle socks while they were still spitting up Gerber's—their numbers are smaller than one might imagine on a campus that is actually quite liberal. As is perhaps inevitable at an institution with a $3.5-billion endowment, an undertone of affluence and elegance pervades most Harvard gatherings. Students feel as if they've made it to the top—and have every intention of staying there throughout their professional lives. Harvard's 350th-anniversary gala featured everything from symposia to a six-hundred-foot plastic rainbow across the nearby Charles River—and everyone in Cambridge is quite confident that the next 350 years will pass in equally fine fashion.

Women are something of a special case at Harvard. They started off at Radcliffe. Today, they officially still do, but they are dually enrolled at Harvard. Under a 1977 agreement Harvard has gradually been absorbing most of Radcliffe's undergraduate functions: The admissions process is now sex-blind, and women receive diplomas from both schools. Radcliffe retains its own administration and runs several programs and resource centers, including the largest and best-known library on the history of women. Still a vital force for professional women, researchers and alumnae, Radcliffe speaks to undergraduates as the guardian of a great tradition in women's education. Radcliffe women were making major achievements before most of the prestigious eastern colleges went coed. At Harvard College women have a past to prove they're equals, not trespassers or "the newly admitted."

Freshman year, when all students live in Harvard Yard, is the only time Harvard's class of 1,600 lives, eats, and plays as a single unit. For the next three years students live in one of twelve residential houses, built around their own courtyards with their own dining halls and libraries. All the houses are coed, and most contain about four hundred students—breaking down the size of the student body into manageable groups. Designed to be an intellectual community of sorts, houses come equipped with a complement of resident tutors, affiliated faculty members, and special facilities, from art studios to swimming pools. The lottery system gives more than 80 percent of freshmen one of their top three choices, and in choosing, a student advises, "The personality of the house is more important than its physical appearance." Eliot suits only those who are "blue-blooded and preppie enough," and the Dudley co-ops attract those interested in more active communal living and willing to tough it a bit since, as one student reports, "they are in a sad state of neglect."

The nine houses along the Charles River feature suites of rooms, while the three dorms at the Radcliffe Quad, half a mile away, have single rooms off a hall. Some students value the greater privacy of the Quad houses; others consider it equivalent to Siberian exile, especially during harsh Cambridge winters. The older dorms provide spacious wood-paneled rooms, but all are equipped with original Harvard chairs, which can make valuable if illicit souvenirs. A small number of students elect to move off campus.

Socializing at Harvard tends to be done in small groups, and, with the exception of the annual all-school Freshman Mixer, parties are private affairs. "Gatherings for Trivial Pursuit or cards or some such activity are common on almost every weeknight, and you can always find someone willing to duck work by talking or going for ice cream," a physics major reports. Some consider the key to happiness in Harvard's high-powered environment is finding a niche, a comfortable academic or extracurricular circle around which to build your life. Those in search of all-male niches can try the nine "final clubs," reminders of Harvard's very male, very WASPy past. About 10 percent of upperclass males do. These bastions of elitism "punch" sophomore men, run them through a gamut of cocktail parties, elect those of whom they approve and require them to pay hefty dues, dress up in black tie, and date Wellesley women. Most undergraduates ignore them, although they do own some of the choicest real estate in Harvard Square.

The possibilities of Harvard's social life are increased tenfold by Cambridge and Boston. Harvard Square itself is a legendary gathering place for tourists, shoppers, bearded intellectuals, and café addicts. Performing arts are strictly segregated from academic work at Harvard, although the Visual and Environmental Studies major serves filmmakers, studio artists and urban planners. Nevertheless, drama and music flourish here. Robert Brustein's American Repertory Theater, transplanted from Yale, offers a season of professional productions, while house dining halls and libraries double as theaters for more than sixty shows a year. Cambridge and Harvard have always enjoyed a symbiotic relationship, but town-gown relations have soured a bit recently because Harvard owns much of the town's land but pays no taxes.

Athletic facilities are rapidly improving, with a brand-new pool, hockey rink, track and basketball arena among the recent additions. The women's soccer and lacrosse and men's crew, hockey, squash and swimming teams are among the finest in the country. As for football, the season always boils down to the Yale game, memorable as much for the antics of the spectators and marching band as for the exploits of the players.

When all is said and done, an education at Harvard is unlike that found anywhere else. Nowhere but Harvard does the identity of the school—its history, its presence, its pretense—intrude so much into the details of undergraduate life, for better or for worse. Admission to Harvard opens the door to a world of intellectual wonder, academic challenges, and faculty minds unmatched in the United States—then drops you on the threshold. Progress from there is up to you.

Haverford College

Haverford, PA 19041

Location Suburban	**Applicants** 2,110
Total Enrollment 1,110	**Accepted** 45%
Undergraduates 1,110	**Enrolled** 35%
Male/Female 55/45	**Academics** ★ ★ ★ ★
SAT V/M N/A	**Social** 🍺 🍺 🍺
Financial Aid 45%	**Q of L** ● ● ● ● ●
Expense Pr $ $ $ $	**Admissions** (215)896-1350

Not too long ago, a revealing little incident took place at Haverford College. As one undergraduate tells it: "One morning two students woke up late and found insufficient hot water in the shower. Instead of just waiting for the hot water to come back later, they went to the president's house nearby, wearing their towels. He let them use his own shower, with the stipulation that they clean up the bathroom before they left. Such is life here."

As the above portrayal suggests, Haverford isn't one of the more rigid and formal institutions in American higher education. Founded under Quaker auspices in 1833, Haverford functions more like a family than anything else. Classes are often held in the professor's living room, and the whole college, from the president on down, unites to make Haverford a supportive and stimulating community. Haverford's abiding Quaker influence comes through in the college honor code, and in the healthy respect Haverfordians have for each individual. With only 1,110 students, Haverford is among the most intimate of the nation's topflight colleges.

Situated on 216 secluded acres just off Philadelphia's "Main Line" railroad, Haverford's campus looks like a summer camp. Complete with duck pond, nature trails and over four hundred species of shrubs and trees, it is as densely wooded and self-contained as a college campus could be in the midst of Philadelphia's most prestigious suburb. The architecture, "Quaker-eclectic" to one student, consists mainly of nineteenth- and early twentieth-century stone buildings, with a sprinkling of modern structures added in.

While other institutions are forsaking their liberal arts traditions to meet student demand for professional training, Haverford still puts "emphasis, not just lip service, on a liberal education." Starting with biology and chemistry and continuing through economics, English, history, music and philosophy, Haverford's curriculum is strong from top to bottom. The few weak spots include foreign languages and fine arts, though the latter was recently bolstered by the addition of a new facility. Since there are no graduate students, undergraduates, particularly those in the sciences, often get to assist professors in their research. Perhaps Haverford's biggest selling point is its faculty, who are praised for being teacher-scholars—in that order. "One professor held his class in his living room, and he and his wife made us lunch every Tuesday," says a senior. Most faculty live in the immediate vicinity of campus and play an active role in campus affairs; there is even a directory listing both office and home phone numbers of each professor. Classes are usually small—most have less than twenty students and some as few as five—and the emphasis is on participation from everyone. The library is well stocked and comfortable, and students have assigned carrels where they can leave materials throughout the semester. Thanks to interlibrary loan, students "can get anything in print within two days," and the college is currently working on a joint computerized card catalogue with Bryn Mawr and Swarthmore.

In order to graduate, each student must take one year of writing, be proficient in a foreign language, and take one course either on non-Western peoples, U.S. minorities, women or prejudice in society. Courses also are required in each of the seven curriculum areas, and no more than thirteen of the thirty-two credits required for graduation can be in a student's major field.

One of Haverford's most distinctive features is its honor code, which governs all facets of life. The code, administered entirely by students, helps instill the values of "integrity, honesty and concern for others." Students schedule their own finals, and tests have not been proctored since 1898. "The code *is* Haverford, and Haverford *is* the code," believes one student. The atmosphere of trust it helps generate extends to academic competition, or the lack thereof; while students are bright and highly motivated, there are no class rankings and little in the way of pressure and cutthroat competition. Likewise, the admissions office doesn't release median SAT scores, though a majority of the students score above 600 on both. In good Quaker tradition, the faculty makes decisions by consensus rather than formal voting, and students also play a large role in formulating college policy, through the Honor Council, Student Council and membership on various college committees.

What students can't get at Haverford, they can usually find a mile down the road at Bryn Mawr. The two schools have a unique relationship stemming from the days (less than a decade ago) when Haverford was all male. Students at each institution can take courses, use the facilities, eat and even live in the dormitories of the other. Haverford and Bryn Mawr students cooperate on a weekly newspaper, radio station, orchestra and other clubs and sports, and a free shuttle bus runs between the campuses. Cross-registration is also available at nearby Swarthmore and the University of Pennsylvania. Under a 3-2 engineering program, students can transfer to Penn after their junior year to complete an engineering major in two more years. Haverford encourages students to take time off during their college careers; some work at a job, while others travel or enroll at other colleges for a semester or two. Even while they are going to school, many students participate in a volunteer work program wherein they share in maintenance, security, and other chores.

Haverford admits students without regard to their ability to pay and bases financial aid solely on student need. Some complain that there is a lack of diversity—"a bit too homogeneous" is how one minority student describes Haverford. Partly because it is so small, Haverford doesn't enjoy a reputation proportionate to its quality, which presents problems for recruiting outside the northeastern establishment. Many Haverfordians are from well-to-do families in Pennsylvania, New York and other nearby states, and blacks and Hispanics account for a combined total of about 8 percent of the students. Almost 40 percent come from private and parochial schools, and 90 percent ranked in the top fifth of their high school class. Political liberalism is a staple of life; women's issues, South African apartheid and environmental concerns have all generated student interest in recent years. Nevertheless, according to one student, "We are basically preprofessional, but are loath to reflect that fact." Though the college is nonsectarian, the continuing Quaker influence lives on in the form of an optional Quaker meeting on Thursday between 10 and 11 AM, when no classes are scheduled.

The residence halls, spacious and well maintained, are in harmony with students' privileged background. Many students spend their four years in single rooms, sometimes in a suite with a living room and fireplace. All the dorms are coed, but students can request single-sex floors. Freshmen are guaranteed housing, and even the sophomores, who draw last in the lottery, can usually get a good room. The college-owned Haverford Park Apartments, located on the edge of campus, are becoming a popular option. They include one and two bedroom apartments, each with a living room, kitchen, and bathroom. Students in the apartments can cook for themselves, but all others living on campus must participate in a complete meal plan that covers weekends. There is only one dining hall at Haverford, which serves passable fare, but students also have the option of eating at one of three Bryn Mawr dining halls where the food is more palatable. About eighty students opt to live at Bryn Mawr in any given semester.

Whenever life in the suburbs gets stifling, students can easily hop the train into downtown Philadelphia, twenty minutes away, where they can take advantage of $2 orchestra tickets and Flyers and Phillies games. New York City, Washington, the New Jersey beaches, Poconos ski areas and Atlantic City's casinos are only a couple of hours away by car.

The community spirit at Haverford works well for academics and personal development, but not so well for socializing. "Haverfordians have big ears and big mouths, and secrets are hard to keep under the table," grumbles a senior. Students tend to hang out in small groups of friends and some complain there is not enough romance. With Bryn Mawr down the road, one woman notes, "dating becomes a numerical improbability." In the absence of fraternities and sororities, Haverford and Bryn Mawr hold joint campus parties, while Haverford reimburses students who host smaller affairs. Both colleges frequently sponsor movies, concerts and other activities, usually for free.

Football was dropped, so there are no more Saturday afternoons spent cheering on the "Fighting Quakers." That leaves soccer, a sport Haverford played in the first intercollegiate game more than eighty years ago, as the most popular spectator sport. Men's cross-country and track teams are strong, and though women have only been around since 1980, women's lacrosse, field hockey, and tennis have all won league championships in recent years. The athletic facilities are newly renovated, and include new squash courts. Haverford also boasts the number one college cricket team in the country—mostly because it is the only school that has one. Intramural sports are popular, not least because participation counts toward the six terms of athletic credit Haverford requires during the freshman and sophomore years.

"When you decide to go to Haverford," claims one student, "it's like purchasing wool or cotton over polyester or dacron." With a bright and opinionated student body, a dedicated faculty and a true commitment to the life of the community, Haverford delivers education like it ought to be. Though there are times when the "team Haverford" spirit wears a little thin, students here know they're getting an education that makes most schools—even most good ones—pale in comparison.

Hiram College

Hiram, OH 44234

Location Rural
Total Enrollment 730
Undergraduates 730
Male/Female 49/51
SAT V/M 520/500
ACT 23
Financial Aid 65%
Expense Pr $ $

Applicants 550
Accepted 85%
Enrolled 40%
Academics ★ ★ ★
Social ☎ ☎ ☎
Q of L ● ● ●
Admissions (216)569-5169

Hiram is a small college in rural Ohio whose biggest claim to fame was producing James Garfield. For anyone who flunked American History, Garfield was elected president in 1880 but was assassinated a few months after taking office. Since then, both he and Hiram have faded into obscurity, but a hundred years later the college of which he also served as president is trying to change that situation. With close student-faculty relations, a fine biology program stressing fieldwork and numerous study-abroad options, Hiram at last appears to be making a name for itself.

Set on a charming hilltop campus that occupies the second-highest spot in Ohio, Hiram is blessed with an abundance of flowers and trees as well as a nice view of the valley below. The prevailing architectural motif is New England brick, and many Hiram buildings are restored nineteenth-century homes. Inside those buildings, the liberal arts flourish, with psychology, English, history and religion among the strongest departments. Hiram has excellent computer facilities for a school its size, including a new computer science lab and about forty-five terminals available for use twenty-four hours a day. Sociology and art are weak spots, and course offerings are sparse in physics, political science and philosophy, each of which has only two professors.

With all due respect to the other departments, biology is the undisputed star of Hiram's academic universe, thanks mainly to the many opportunities Hiram provides for fieldwork. Students maintain a 145-acre college-owned field study station a mile from the campus, which comes complete with a greenhouse, four labs, a 70-acre beech and maple forest, and numerous plant and animal species. Five students actually live on the site, and many others assist in its upkeep. During the summer, Hiram offers still more unusual opportunities, most notably the Northwoods Station in northern Michigan, where courses are offered in environmental studies, photography, botany, geology, natural history, philosophy and writing. For those who prefer the sea breeze to Michigan's icy winds, Hiram is an affiliate college of the Shoals Marine Lab, run by Cornell and the University of New Hampshire, which offers summer study in marine science, ecology, coastal and oceanic law and underwater archeology. For stay-at-home types, the university boasts a new Electron Microscopy Center that has a computer software package on using the scope.

Hiram's core curriculum is extensive enough to satisfy even the most diehard liberal arts advocates. Everyone is required to complete four three-course interdisciplinary sequences that are team taught by faculty from different departments. Freshmen must take The Idea of the West, and other recent sequences have included topics such as Science, Values and Technology, and The Woman Writer. These and most other classes at Hiram are small—thirty-five students is the upper limit and some have as few as five—and faculty accessibility is one of Hiram's strong suits. "Many a time I have just stopped by a professor's office and talked," testifies one student. The Institute for Human Effectiveness brings well-known figures to the campus for seminars with students and others in the community. Past participants have included columnist James Kilpatrick, former baseball commissioner Bowie Kuhn and economist John Kenneth Galbraith. Hiram's modest library has only 160,000 volumes, but many students take advantage of interlibrary loans with Kent State University, about twenty minutes away.

While intramurals are popular on many campuses, at Hiram the buzzword is "Extra Murals," the name for the college's study-abroad programs. Hiram offers an array of professor-led trips to all corners of the globe—from Brazil to the Soviet Union—and all participating students win academic credit. Students can also study at Hiram's affiliate in Rome, the John Cabot International College, and transfer credit to Hiram. Since the college is on the quarter system, there is ample opportunity for study abroad and other off-campus opportunities, including the Washington Semester* at American University.

If Hiram sounds to you like the name of a nice boy next door, students here are every bit as friendly, responsible and upstanding as the name suggests. The atmosphere is "warm and family-like," in the words of one student, and pressure to conform is at a minimum. "I like being me and not being ashamed of it," says a senior religion major. Seventy-five percent of the students are in-staters, and most of the rest hail from New York and Pennsylvania. In recent years, Hiram has attracted increasing numbers of top students; the percentage of students in the top 10 percent of their high school class has risen from 25 to 35 in only two years, and median SAT scores are also climbing. Minority enrollment, however, remains low, with blacks making up 3 percent of the students and Hispanics less than 1. Hiram was founded by the Disciples of Christ, and though 5 percent of the students are members, the affiliation has little impact on student life. In addition to need-based financial aid, Hiram awards 141 merit scholarships, ranging from $240 to $5,000, which require a separate application.

Eighty-five percent of Hiram's students live on campus, and everyone who wants a room gets one. Though there is a single-sex option for women, most of the halls are coed, and students choose between twenty-four-hour quiet, twenty-four-hour noise, and a happy medium somewhere in between. Teetotalers can also opt for a dry dorm where alcohol is forbidden. Hiram has two dining halls, one of which was recently renovated, and all students living on campus are required to get a twenty-one-meal plan. The cafeterias dish out average college food, though two special gourmet dinners each term spice up the menu with delicacies such as swordfish and prime rib. A bagel shop, snack bar and pizza oven provide additional alternatives.

"We are not a party school," says one student with a knack for understatement. The surrounding countryside is Nowhere, U.S.A.—there isn't even a fast-food joint in the vicinity—so students must make their own fun. A student activities board plans a variety of campus events, including concerts, comedians, dances and movies, and local fraternities and sororities attract a significant percentage of the students, though they are relatively tame compared to their rabble-rousing counterparts at most universities. For ski buffs, the college has its own cross-country trail, and good slopes are about an hour away. Cleveland is about the same distance, and the college frequently sponsors excursions there, often providing free tickets to concerts, plays, ballets, etc.

Hiram is hardly a mecca for budding all-Americans, but it does have a good sports program. Football, basketball and wrestling are among the most successful men's teams, and student support is widespread. The women's program is also strong, especially in track, rugby, basketball and volleyball. The baseball program was recently enhanced by the addition of a new field.

Hiram could be an excellent choice for green thumbs who want a firsthand look at their genuses and genotypes, or for anyone else who wants to go to school in a tight-knit community. Though four years in the middle of nowhere with 730 of the same old faces may sound like a daunting prospect, there are plenty of off-campus opportunities to break up the monotony. And besides, if Hiram's past graduates are any indication, the odds are only about 23,662 to 1 that you too will grow up to be president of the United States.

Hobart and William Smith Colleges

Geneva, NY 14456

Location Small city	**Applicants** 3,000
Total Enrollment 1,970	**Accepted** 57%
Undergraduates 1,970	**Enrolled** 33%
Male/Female 60/40	**Academics** ★ ★ ★
SAT V/M 540/580	**Social** 🕿 🕿 🕿
Financial Aid 43%	**Q of L** ● ● ●
Expense Pr $ $ $ $	**Admissions** (315)789-5500

Secluded in upstate New York's Finger Lakes region, Hobart and William Smith Colleges have attempted to strike a delicate balance between coeducation and single-sex colleges through their "coordinate" system. The colleges share a single board of trustees, administration, and faculty but retain separate deans, admissions offices, athletic programs and student governments. The women (William Smith) seem to favor the arrangement more than the men (Hobart) and appreciate the attention paid to their separate sports program and the opportunity to become leaders in their own community. "The best of both worlds" is how one woman assesses the coordinate-college system. "It stresses feminism without bitterness toward men," says another. Others call it a formal division that ends up having very little effect on students' lives.

Perched on a 170-acre stretch of ground above the shores of Seneca Lake, HWS's tree-lined campus is the kind of place that was made for crisp fall afternoons. Though the architecture ranges from colonial to postmodern, the curriculum is classic liberal arts. The colleges have traditionally been strong in the humanities and premed areas, and students single out English, religious studies, biology and chemistry for particular praise. Economics also gets kudos, but the arts and languages suffer from a lack of majors and thus a limited number of offerings. Theater and dance facilities are also on the weak side. Students begin studies with a full-year course called Ways of Knowing, team-taught by six professors, that "throws the freshman into the fire of interdisciplinary thinking." Upperclassmen put this knowledge to good use, first through a junior baccalaureate essay and then in the senior baccalaureate colloquium, the latter dealing with an interdisciplinary issue "of global interest." All students must take two courses each in the humanities, social sciences and natural sciences, including a lab science and a course in fine or applied arts. Failing marks are not given at HWS. Students whose work falls below a C receive a slash mark and no credit for the course. Freshmen can receive three slashes before being reviewed by the dean's committee, but the allowance decreases each year, and seniors must pass all courses. While the policy can be a convenient escape hatch, it does permit the more serious student to explore unfamiliar academic areas without jeopardizing the all-important GPA.

In keeping with their "global" approach to education, the colleges strongly encourage students to take the junior year abroad via one of a number of programs in Europe, Asia and Mexico. Washington and United Nations semesters are also available, and future engineers can take a 3-2 program with RPI, Columbia or the University of Rochester. HWS professors are accessible and receive high praise for their teaching. "We share a feeling of learning with them, not from them," says one student. Even so, the academic climate is not overly rigorous, and students consider their schedule one of "fun mixed with work," not the other way around. Only a decade old, the library could use a few more books. In the meantime any extensive research usually requires an hour's drive to either Cornell or the University of Rochester. Hobart and William Smith are among a small group of liberal arts colleges using the trimester system, which divides the year into three terms with a load of three courses in each.

Since most students come from upper-middle-class, northeastern backgrounds and are headed toward professional careers, the campus population is rather homogeneous. Resident New Yorkers make up 45 percent of the students, while blacks and Hispanics account for 8 percent. Some students would like to see that change. "If those students only interested in goals and jobs would go elsewhere, this college would be extraordinary," a senior says. William Smith, established in 1906 by a wealthy nurseryman, tends to attract a slightly higher caliber of student than does Hobart, which was founded as Geneva College in 1822 and renamed for an Episcopalian bishop who took a fancy to the place. The colleges meet the computed financial need of most—though not all—of their accepted applicants, and there are no merit or athletic scholarships.

Most students at HWS live in dorms that are ivy-covered and distinguished on the outside but overcrowded and run-down on the inside. Freshmen are all housed in single-sex dorms; those reserved for Hobart men are said to be especially poor. Nevertheless, freshmen can pick their dorms, so remembering the names of the ones you like best after a campus visit could be a help. Most sophomores live in a large complex known as "Super Dorm," and those who wish to move off campus must enter a lottery to win the privilege. Just over 15 percent of the students opt to move off, while another 10 percent live in fraternity houses. The famous college food service, Saga, now a national multimillion-dollar business, had its humble beginnings at HWS in the 1940s, though HWS students don't brag about the fact to their friends elsewhere. An "absolutely magnificent" new dining center and a much smaller dining room in one of the William Smith dorms are where most students, and all freshmen, eat. All who live on campus are required to partake of the meal plan, either ten or nineteen times a week. Frat brothers eat at their houses, and the small number of students who live in co-ops or apartments usually cook for themselves.

Relative isolation has forced the colleges to become quite self-reliant. Their idyllic lakeside setting is marred by brutal winter storms and spring rains, while nearby Geneva is considered "a wasteland" that adds little to college life. "If you're into long bus rides and beautiful countrysides, you'll be in heaven," one student says. Having a car is a definite social plus, but cheap shuttle buses provide transportation to nearby ski slopes. Ithaca, Syracuse and Rochester, each with its own large student population, are an hour or so away.

The nine Hobart fraternities sponsor most of the college parties, although no one senses any pressure to join. The cachet of going Greek is on the upswing. Those who are old enough—the drinking age went up recently—still frequent nearby bars, and for those who aren't, a student social affairs group sponsors nonalcoholic alternatives, as does the Cellar, which often features a live band. William Smith has no sororities, but any woman can share fraternity activities as a "big sister." Many Hobartians take the search for Miss Right to two nearby women's colleges, Keuka and Wells. The granola crowd has its own coffeehouse, Amaranth, which features wholesome baked goods, nonalcoholic drinks and folksy entertainment. Campus organizations range from Young Entrepreneurs to the Clown Club, but sports are unquestionably the most popular activities. In the spring, the campus comes alive with mania for lacrosse, "our pride and obsession." The men's team has won eight straight Division III championships, setting an NCAA record for consecutive titles. For the annual Hobart-Cornell game, just about the whole campus travels to Ithaca as a cheering squad. Many other sports are popular, and intramurals are extensive.

HWS offers its students a broad-based liberal arts education without making academic achievement an obsession. "Be ready to cope with winter term blues, L. L. Bean boots, monogrammed sweaters, professors who look alike after three months, students who look alike after three months, a sudden snowfall on October 15th, and a sudden snowfall on April 27th," warns one wizened veteran, who adds, "If you get through these you're ready for life."

Hofstra University

Hempstead, NY 11550

Location Suburban
Total Enrollment 11,900
Undergraduates 8,260
Male/Female 50/50
SAT V/M 490/540
Financial Aid 70%
Expense Pr $

Applicants 7,520
Accepted 65%
Enrolled 32%
Academics ★ ★
Social ☎ ☎
Q of L ● ●
Admissions (516)560-6700

Plant a college campus smack in the middle of an old Long Island airfield and you know it's going to be an uphill public image battle from day one. Forget battle—Hofstra University has declared war. With barely a quarter century under its belt as a full-fledged university, this ambitious institution is attempting to discard its reputation as a regional commuter school and earn respect from coast to coast (or at least from the Atlantic to Lake Erie). Armed to the teeth with the latest gadgetry in fields from computers to broadcasting, Hofstra is selling its "hands-on environment" to a generation of job-hungry students. And it's working. Enrollments are up, the endowment has quadrupled in the past decade, and new programs and facilities are multiplying faster than a den of rabbits. Many students are enjoying Hofstra's continuing media blitz and its newfound academic prestige; others gripe about how "the university often seems to be more concerned with image than substance."

The university's image consciousness extends to the campus itself. "Hofstra takes great pride in its 238-acre home," reports one student, "The grounds are always kept in immaculate condition." Those grounds are divided into two parts: Student life is centered on the very modern North Campus, while the more picturesque southern portion is dotted with Jeffersonian-style academic buildings. Over 175 species of trees, 50,000 tulips, and about 20 outdoor sculptures are spread across the flat, green grounds—"a 238-acre art gallery," according to the president. Many of Hofstra's academic programs have also blossomed in recent years, most notably the preprofessional programs. The drama department, one of the school's best, has fostered numerous film and theater talents, including Francis Ford Coppola and Madeline Kahn, and produces a popular Shakespeare festival annually. There is also a resident ballet company, a good music program, and a new television institute that is one of the finest facilities of its kind in the nation, featuring modern broadcast equipment, four studios, a satellite receiver and a mobile van with three cameras. Popular offerings at the other end of the academic spectrum are Long Island's only accredited undergraduate and graduate business programs, where accounting and international trade—which includes study-abroad opportunities—are standouts. Engineering and the natural sciences are not as strong but boast of annual improvement in the number of premeds placed in medical school, while computer science boasts an IBM 4381 Model 13, the largest of its kind. Courses in the College of Liberal Arts and Sciences are generally less demanding than those in preprofessional fields, though history, political science and English are good programs that require more commitment than most.

Hofstra has an abundance of academic creativity to match its ambition. Programs like music merchandising, publishing studies and art appraisal enable students to study the arts with a practical bent. There is also a semester in Washington and an unusual program in technology and public policy. The New College, patterned on the original school of that name in medieval Oxford, offers a more individualized curriculum than the main campus, with flexible requirements, four terms a year instead of two, independent study, and small classes. It has special studies for those who need remedial work as well as a rigorous program for the gifted student. The freshman-level program introduces students to the university and one another through an integrated sequence of general education courses. During the optional January term students take a single course for a month. Overcrowding is usually only a problem in popular business and English courses, but dealing with the administration, in any capacity, can be a nightmare "comparable to dealing with a bureaucracy like the Motor Vehicle Bureau," one man reports. The faculty at Hofstra is very accessible and dedicated to students, but unfortunately its relations with the administration aren't as good. Bitterness lingers from a five-day faculty strike in 1985 over wages and teaching loads.

Hofstra undergraduates are not an especially diverse lot; less than 6 percent are black or Hispanic, most come from nearby Long Island public high schools, and only 15 percent are from out of state. But the commuter population is not as large as it once was, and Hofstra's hustling administrators have managed to attract increasing numbers of top students in recent years. The percentage of freshmen graduating in the top fifth of their high school class is now over 50 percent, and almost all were in the top half. Hofstra's innovation extends to the realm of student aid: It awards $500 a year to students whose families' incomes fall between $10,000 and $25,000. The university also has a substantial number of merit scholarships that range from $700 to full tuition, depending on a student's SAT scores and high school rank.

Looking ahead to the days when it will attract even more out-of-towners, Hofstra has recently expanded residential facilities. Half the full-time students are now spread between six high-rise dormitories, one college apartment building, a freshman living/learning center, and two complexes that offer housing in suites. The dorms have their own kitchen facilities and pool tables, but rooms are small. Students generally prefer the suite complexes and the apartments, the latter having private kitchen and bath. Rooms are assigned by lottery, with those who have lived on campus the longest getting first pick, and most students who live far away guaranteed a room. There are five dining halls on campus and a variety of meal plans, including seven, ten, fourteen, or nineteen meals a week. Only freshmen are required to eat the dining hall fare, which is less than impressive, and fraternities and sororities have tables in the campus pub where they generally eat. There are no Greek houses.

With more and more students living on or near campus, social life is on the upswing. Hofstra USA is reputed to be one of the most swinging campus centers in the state, and a "miracle mile" of bars is within walking distance of campus. Fraternities and sororities, though still few in number, are increasingly popular and host an impressive number of campus parties for their size. The Nassau Coliseum is right next door ("Don't forget your Islanders T-shirt"), and arts groups perform regularly on campus, but much of weekend socializing still involves travel. A half hour on the Long Island Rail Road puts fans of big-time nightlife in Manhattan, and Long Island beaches are in easy reach. A large and well-equipped gym, augmented by a new Olympic-size pool, and an intramural program with everything from horseshoes to horseback riding keep the energetic in shape. Victories by the football team—which went to the Division III playoffs in 1986—no longer go unnoticed now that the Screaming Dutchmen booster club and their mascot duck attend all the games and lead the kick line. Other popular sports include basketball, wrestling, lacrosse and soccer. Women's teams usually do well in field hockey, volleyball, basketball and gymnastics.

Hofstra is an excellent choice for students with career interests in one of its areas of strength, and for Long Islanders who want a school close to home. The academic climate is steadily improving, though a senior maintains that "totally academic, competitive people would be happier in a more stringent environment." Once enrolled, if you ever doubt that Hofstra was the right choice, just tune your radio to any station, wait a minute or two, and you're bound to hear one of the university's ubiquitous PR blurbs telling one and all what a wonderful school you attend.

Hollins College

Roanoke, VA 24020

Location City outskirts	**Applicants** 775
Total Enrollment 960	**Accepted** 75%
Undergraduates 820	**Enrolled** 40%
Male/Female N/A	**Academics** ★ ★ ★
SAT V/M 510/520	**Social** ☎ ☎ ☎
Financial Aid 33%	**Q of L** ● ● ● ●
Expense Pr $ $	**Admissions** (703)362-6401

"Women who are going places start at Hollins," reads a sassy red and yellow brochure. Interestingly enough, Hollins College is the prime place for undergraduates who know they're going somewhere, but aren't quite sure where it is. Supportive is the adjective students think best describes their school. The administration, faculty, and even the strong network of alumni challenge, encourage and counsel students toward fulfilling all their professional potential. As one successful graduate recalls, "Hollins believed in me long before I believed in myself."

An integral part of Hollins' supportive structure is the honor system, a key component of which is the student-administered Independent Exam System, which allows students to take their exams within certain time slots. "The exam system epitomizes the atmosphere of trust and mutual respect," declares an English major. "Signing the honor pledge is required and meaningful to all." Paradoxically, this same trusting institution also enforces an unusual policy requiring undergraduates to submit excuses from the dean's office or infirmary when they have to miss a class. But students happily report that not all professors enforce this stricture.

Nestled in the Roanoke Valley, beneath the shadow of the stately Blue Ridge Mountains, the Hollins campus is fronted by a historical quadrangle of red-brick, neo-classical buildings complete with thick, white columns and rocking chairs on the spacious front porches. Exploration beyond this facade will uncover additional red-brick structures of more modern beginnings. But the huge, willowy trees and plentitude of grass and shade characterize the entire setting.

The school's academic program is typical of a small liberal arts college. The best departments are English, particularly creative writing, and psychology, each with nationally known faculty and coed master's degree programs. Students recommend political science, history, economics and art, while the administration gives itself a pat on the back for the quality of the computer science department. "Computers across the curriculum" is how Hollins bills its newfound love affair with technology, an attachment so strong that the student/computer ratio has been reduced to eleven to one. Students say the science offerings suffer from a lack of student interest, and foreign language and music programs could use some more interest from the administration.

Standard distribution requirements include proven writing competency, and strongly self-motivated students are encouraged to design individualized major programs. Although it does emphasize liberal arts, Hollins offers combined-degree programs in engineering, architecture and nursing as well as Army ROTC (in conjunction with Washington and Lee). Those seeking relief from the Virginia humidity can spend semesters at Hollins' extended campuses in London and Paris. Other travel-abroad options are sought through the Seven College Exchange.* The popular January term renders a midyear break for on-campus projects, travel or internships, with alumnae helping to arrange housing in Washington and other cities. And maybe because, as one creative writer expresses it, "bonds are strong between Hollins women," those busy alumnae seem to keep tabs on all sorts of undergraduate career needs. The college is also noted for its strong counseling, whether it be academic, psychological, career or financial aid. The library's audiovisual departments are good, and the books and reference materials have been expanded, but an efficient interlibrary-loan service with nearby Virginia Tech and Washington and Lee augments Hollins' resources.

The typical Hollins woman is pretty much what she has always been: white, upper-middle-class, southern preppie. Yet an American history major argues that "no one person represents the Hollins woman because this school teaches us to be individuals who represent our own unique ideas." Nearly half the students graduated from private schools, and almost a quarter are from Virginia. Hollins' academic profile has improved in the past decade, and now 86 percent of the students come from the top half of their high school classes. These woman are career-oriented from the word go, and almost everyone is quick to voice disdain for the finishing-school label. "Political conservatism has been a trend among Hollins students for years," says a senior. "However, moderate and liberal views are not squelched."

Hollins' administration remains proud of its willing financial assistance and "anticipates being able to continue meeting the full demonstrated financial need of all admitted applicants." It rewards its ten "most outstanding" freshmen with annually renewable scholarships for one-half of their tuition, based on a minimum combined SAT of 1200, rank in top 10 percent of graduating class, evidence of leadership, and extracurricular involvement.

First-year students are assigned singles or doubles in one of the two modern freshman dorms, complete with kitchens and carpeting. The older upperclass dorms in the Front Quad, where students are almost guaranteed a single, have beautiful rooms with wood floors and brass door knobs. The college-owned apartments across the street cost the same as the dorms and are popular among seniors. "It's difficult to narrow it down to the best dorms," recollects a senior history major. "They are all well liked at different stages of one's undergraduate life." Almost no one lives off campus. The food at Hollins is often described as "better than mom's," and the salad bar "is better than Wendy's." There are frequent international dinners and a make-your-own-sundae bar, and consequently, putting on the dreaded "freshman fifteen" is an accepted fact of life.

Oddly enough, among this contemporary, career-minded group of undergraduates, feminist issues command surprisingly little attention. But that does not mean Hollins women are lazy or apathetic. The campus Coalition for Peace and the Hollins Outlook on Political Education are both popular, and students often get involved in more traditional service organizations, choirs and student government. Frequent outings organized by the established Hollins Outdoor Program give many students opportunities to hike, canoe, raft, bike, spelunk and simply enjoy the beautiful Shenandoah Valley and Blue Ridge Mountains. Hollins' large on-campus horse stable complements the school's extensive equestrian program, and a huge swimming facility has just been completed. Tennis, soccer, lacrosse and field hockey teams win consistently, and basketball, fencing, volleyball and riding are other popular varsity sports. "Since the school is small, most who have interest play varsity or JV sports, so intramurals are not a large part of Hollins," one woman explains. The mile-and-a-half road circling the campus is popular as a jogging track.

Hollins shuns sororities but does organize school-wide mixers and maintains several traditional activities. At the annual Tinker Day festivities, sometime after the first frost, classes are canceled in the morning, and the whole school hikes to the top of Tinker Mountain for picnics, songs, and skits. On Ring Night juniors receive their class rings from senior ring sisters, and on Hundredth Night seniors put on skits to celebrate the hundredth night before graduation. Road trips are often made on the weekends, especially expeditions to Washington and Lee University, forty miles due north. No matter how liberated Hollins women become, a W&L fraternity man is still considered a catch. For male friends visiting Hollins, there is a "men's dorm" in which a guest may stay for a small fee.

Hollins provides its Hollie Collies (a nickname most students abhor) with a friendly, sustaining atmosphere and a nice touch of tradition that most students feel are essential to their continued success. "These four years are only the first few steps toward a lifelong investment," recites a senior. "Hollins will live within me forever."

College of the Holy Cross

Worcester, MA 01610

Location City outskirts
Total Enrollment 2,650
Undergraduates 2,650
Male/Female 49/51
SAT V/M 580/610
Financial Aid 45%
Expense Pr $ $ $

Applicants 4,640
Accepted 32%
Enrolled 32%
Academics ★ ★ ★ ★
Social 🐿 🐿 🐿 🐿
Q of L ● ● ● ●
Admissions (617)793-2443

Holy Cross is a small Jesuit institution that's like a big family. Students here look, talk and act alike and most are Irish Catholic easterners, upper-middle-class, academically motivated, religious, preppie (at least in dress) and destined to keep the beer companies in the black forever.

Located on a hill overlooking the city of Worcester, the campus of Holy Cross, with its mixture of classical and modern architectural styles, is well groomed, picturesque and well planted—it is, in fact, a registered arboretum. An award-winning advising program and an average class size of twenty-two help Holy Cross faculty members keep a close eye on each of their undergraduate dependents. Students study a lot and are even prone to spending some of Friday or Saturday night in the library. Grading is fairly tough, and there just aren't enough A's to go around to those who might get them at less competitive schools. Luckily, these rigorous standards are balanced to some degree by the warm, caring atmosphere. "The spiritual life under the guidance of the Jesuits helps immensely in these years of occasional confusion," contends a classics major.

The premed program is highly rated, as are history, English, religious studies, math, and economics/accounting. Classics is also a standout here, a department where "majors are treated to a very brilliant and demanding faculty." While other departments, such as sociology, political science, modern languages, philosophy and fine arts, are not as strong, carefully chosen seminars in all of them can be excellent. The fine and performing arts departments are young and still in their try-out stage. In all majors the emphasis is on ideas and thinking rather than on preparation for a specific vocation. No business or computing-science major is offered. Students looking for a 3-2 program in engineering are in luck; Worcester Polytechnical Institute is right across the street.

Distribution requirements consist of two courses in the social sciences, two in the natural and mathematical sciences, plus one course each in the arts, language or literature, religious studies, philosophy, history and cross-cultural studies. An interdisciplinary humanities program provides a chance to study a particular topic with three or four different professors. The selective honors program gives special attention to top students, and the Fenwick Scholars Program allows students to design and carry out an independent project. Students may take advantage of internships for credit either in Worcester or other cities, especially Washington. There is a junior year abroad, and Holy Cross is a member of the Worcester Consortium,* which helps make up for the fact that the Holy Cross library is only adequate. A new science library is a much-needed addition, and the music library has everything from rare classical albums and scores to modern rock.

Because Holy Cross is small and isolated, the religious influence is somewhat greater than at some other Jesuit schools. Most students are Catholics from New

England, and about 40 percent went to Catholic high schools. "But we don't have to go to mass each day and we don't carry Bibles around everywhere," clarifies a premed student. It is, however, very common among this tightly knit group to have relatives as classmates and parents who graduated with other students' parents. Four times a year the chaplain's office leads students on a five-day silent retreat in which they follow the spiritual exercises of St. Ignatius. "Most students are fairly conservative, yet a deep concern for social justice motivates many people," reports a psychology major.

Not every student accepted at Holy Cross gets all the financial aid he or she needs, although most do. Of those put on a waiting list for financial aid—no more than 15 percent of the class—"most are offered support within three semesters' time," the college says. Holy Cross awards meritorious awards, including full tuition to two classics majors in each class. Athletic scholarships, 154 of them, are divided among men's football and basketball players, and women athletes across the board.

"Worcester is a GREAT city," exclaims one man, "and anyone who tells you otherwise is ignorant of the many museums and movie theaters we have here." It has other attractions—a symphony, restaurants and a local community that "is in love with Holy Cross and its students." Still, there are some not-so-nice sections of the city, and students who venture off St. James hill at night do so with a degree of caution. Boston is about an hour away, and the Cape Cod beaches and White Mountain ski resorts aren't much farther. Most people, especially underclassmen who are discouraged from having cars, are content to take advantage of the action on campus. The level of student volunteer work among the elderly, handicapped and other disadvantaged people in the Worcester community is high. The dorms are coed by floor and are well maintained but "spartanly furnished." Housing is guaranteed for four years, and most dorm rooms are doubles. Almost everybody lives on campus and on a full meal plan, which comes with no options except a vegetarian alternative.

Movies, student plays, bands and the pub keep things hopping on weekends, but the rallying point is undoubtedly the keg. "Unfortunately, Holy Cross carries the stigma of being a beer-swilling Irish Catholic school," reports a senior who does not deny the validity of this characterization. The drinking age of twenty-one makes public imbibing difficult for underclassmen, and the college is increasingly conscientious about enforcing that law. "Parties are not allowed in dorm rooms," explains a senior. "Consequently, social life has deteriorated over my four years." The dating scene at Holy Cross, once about as exciting as dinner with your grandparents, has picked up a little. "I have noticed a surge in dating," says one student, "but at Holy Cross if 20 percent of the campus is dating, it's a lot." Everyone knows almost everyone else, and students love to socialize in packs. Worcester has joined the new Colonial League, and students attend varsity football and basketball games en masse, and many join in the active intramurals program. The student newspaper and radio station are also well regarded, but there are few minority or political activities on campus.

Holy Cross offers a fine education with a Jesuit twist. Beyond that, it also provides a large but supportive community where, even if you look like everyone else, you'll never be lost in the crowd.

Hood College

Frederick, MD 21701

Location City outskirts
Total Enrollment 1,970
Undergraduates 1,150
Male/Female 10/90
SAT V/M 500/500
Financial Aid 39%
Expense Pr $ $ $

Applicants 600
Accepted 86%
Enrolled 45%
Academics ★ ★ ★
Social ☎ ☎ ☎
Q of L ● ● ●
Admissions (301)663-3131

Founded at the turn of the century, Hood College set out from the very beginning to prepare women for productive work outside as well as within the home, and the same philosophy holds true today. A few men attend Hood as day students, but this is still definitely a women's college. "In all that the college says and does," says the president, "it affirms the importance of women in today's society." With women comprising 65 percent of the faculty and occupying several of the top administrative posts (and the campus chaplaincy), there's no shortage of successful female role models on campus.

The fifty-acre campus, brightened by the traditional Georgian red-brick buildings with white columns, resides in the historic Civil War town of Frederick. Tucked into the foothills of the Blue Ridge Mountains amid chirping birds and darting rabbits, the campus is an easy walk to the downtown area and it's a short bike ride to quiet farmland. Every weekend, students can take chartered buses to Washington and Baltimore, which are only an hour away. Equally important, considering the dearth of male students, Hood is within an hour and a half of nearly thirty colleges, including Georgetown, Gettysburg, the University of Maryland and the Naval Academy at Annapolis.

Months before first semester of freshman year, prospective students can get an idea of Hood's thorough and personalized approach to education during a Saturday admissions seminar. Like Bard College, Hood offers a single-topic morning workshop where applicants can try out college-level work and faculty members can assess a student's academic potential with more than a transcript. Seminar participants receive an indication of Hood's admission decision before they head home that very day. Other innovative Hood programs include a student-run honor system with self-scheduled and unproctored final exams, an artist- and executive-in-residence series, and a law and society major, one of the few preprofessional programs in legal studies at a women's college.

After a decade of no requirements and increasing student specialization, Hood in 1981 moved to bolster its general education program by instituting a flexible liberal arts core curriculum. "Students are given a lot of freedom in designing a program of their choice," says one student, who noted that creative interdepartmental majors are often approved. The twenty-nine standard major programs, however, still have a preprofessional bent. Hood's strengths lie in the areas of biology, management and economics, and mathematics and computer science (which draws on the resources of nearby high-tech companies). Students and administrators also recommend the programs in foreign languages, political science, history, sociology, English and dietetics. Education and home economics remain notable after all these years. Programs in recreation and leisure studies, music and radiologic technology are being phased out due to low enrollments and lack of quality. Communications has never been Hood's forte, and according to students, unless you're into print journalism and don't care about the broadcast fields, forget it. Students praise the competence and accessibility of faculty and say classes are almost never too large or hard to get into.

Hood considers internships an integral part of its students' education and requires them in some majors. More than two hundred regular internship placements are made each year, including overseas jobs for language and business majors, stints in law or accounting firms, or legislative and cultural positions in nearby Washington, D.C. The college also runs a 3-2 engineering program with George Washington University. Structured programs and resource centers aid students whose reading, writing and math skills need to be strengthened through personalized attention. An extensive bilingual program with professional orientation makes Hood attractive to Hispanic students.

Premier facilities on the Hood campus include the renovated Hodson Science Center and the Marx Center, a model residential structure with modular living units, facilities for the handicapped, and a computerized monitoring system that enables students to assess the efficiency of various energy systems. As out-of-date as the Marx Center is modern, the main campus library needs more new books. One senior moans, "The books available are woefully outdated." Fortunately, an extensive interlibrary-loan program is available.

More than one hundred older women are pursuing degrees in the continuing-education program at Hood, half of them full time. Regular undergraduates are predominantly white and middle to upper middle class. A great majority come from Maryland and D.C., most of the rest hail from elsewhere in the Northeast, while a few trickle in from distant areas. "Some students are very preppie, others are punk, but most fall into the jeans-and-T-shirt category," calculates a computer science major. Students recognize that the school demands they be committed to their studies and careers; if "girls just want to have fun," says one, they go somewhere else. Hood provides financial assistance in one form or another to half of its student body. Fifteen percent of the students receive endowed merit scholarships ranging from $1,000 to $4,000. Special tuition reduction for second members of the family attending the school, and loan and payment plans are available.

Hood is the school from which the Roommate Negotiation Workbook comes, so students here are experts in taking an active role in their roommate relationship, i.e., not being afraid to kick out your roommate's visiting boyfriend, without "being abusive." Since men can only be day students, Hood's dorms are for women only, and they're considered better than adequate by most students. In a lottery system based on seniority, women choose between older residence halls with carpeting and grandfather clocks and modern units. Freshmen can expect to be assigned to doubles (generally only seniors get singles), and three small language dorms house students who are expected to speak French, Spanish or German exclusively. A few private apartments and houses are available for rent in the area, and about 40 percent of the students live off campus. The dining hall, with its ceiling fans and chandeliers, offers good interesting fare. There is no such thing as a meal plan here; the price paid for "room and board" includes unlimited quantities of three meals a day.

As at most small women's colleges, there are no sororities, but the dorms at Hood seem to fulfill a similar social function. Each has its own personality, as well as its own house council, rules and social activities. As one woman explains, "Hood is like one big sorority in that most students on campus know each other and attend each other's parties." Social events bring "plenty of men here on the weekend," but day-to-day contact between the sexes is limited. Students find the intramural program well coordinated and extensive in its offerings. Unlike many other women's colleges, Hood has not developed strong varsity sports, though students report that interest in sports is increasing each year.

The founders of Hood would be proud of their school today; not only are students well prepared for their chosen career, but, in the words of a senior, "Hood provides me with the opportunity to prove myself as a person, not a 'woman in a man's world.'"

Hope College

Holland, MI 49423

Location Small city	**Applicants** 1,254
Total Enrollment 2,300	**Accepted** 93%
Undergraduates 2,300	**Enrolled** 51%
Male/Female 45/55	**Academics** ★ ★ ★
SAT V/M 500/550	**Social** ☎ ☎ ☎
ACT 23	**Q of L** ● ● ●
Financial Aid 65%	**Admissions** (616)392-5111
Expense Pr $	

Founded by a group of religious Dutch settlers in 1866 and affiliated with the Reformed Church of America today, Hope College has managed to hold on to what the administration calls "the perspectives and values of historic Christianity." Translated into undergraduatese that means curtailed visitation hours, a faithfully enforced alcohol policy and a rather homogenized student body, but that's not to say that this small midwestern college doesn't have a lot to offer in other, more tangible areas. As one student puts it, "Religion is very important to some; others are just here for academics."

Situated on the edge of a small town just a short drive or bike ride from the beaches and sand dunes of Lake Michigan, Hope College maintains a no-nonsense approach to education. The sciences definitely stand out among academic offerings (chemistry reigns supreme), with excellent, up-dated laboratory facilities and faculty who rank high in the number of grants awarded them by the National Science Foundation. Professors regularly include students in their research projects, and undergraduates have been known to conduct extremely advanced experiments and get their names on published papers. "I have even taken apart and rebuilt a megawatt nitrogen laser," exclaims a chemistry major. Twenty-five to thirty chemistry students are involved in full-time research in the summer, and a large proportion of science majors go on to medical schools and PhD programs. For others, Hope offers good programs in English, religion, education and music.

Students don't hesitate to voice their disappointment in the art, communications and dance departments, but with the DePree Art Center and Gallery as well as a television studio and a young mass media program, there is, shall we say, hope. Business administration and computer science are becoming more popular yet still suffer some growing pains. And unless you absolutely must experience Michigan winters in a small town, don't go to Hope for anthropology, linguistics, journalism or social work. The present library's collection is adequate at best and the building noisy and overcrowded, but a new 93,000-square-foot library is now under construction.

Hope's core curriculum—fifty-seven semester hours—exposes its undergraduates to the whole liberal arts spectrum including two mandatory religion classes. Students choose their majors from one of twenty-four departments or they can design their own composite major or contract curriculum. The capstone course, or senior seminar, allows students to flex their academic muscles on such topics as science and human values and Christianity and contemporary literature.

As a member of the Great Lakes Colleges Association,* Hope offers a score of off-campus programs, including Washington Honors and New York Arts semesters. Students can study abroad in twenty-six countries during the school year or opt for one of Hope's summer programs in places such as Yugoslavia, Japan or the Middle East. Travelers will welcome Hope's adoption of the Dartmouth method of intensive foreign language study.

The Hope faculty plays a large part in sustaining a supportive community atmosphere. "Professors present many different views, not just their own," says one student. "Most professors are very open—giving out their home phone numbers and encouraging an open door policy," adds another. The college offers 160 academic and leadership scholarships ranging from $700 to $2,000. About one-quarter of each freshman class ends up with non-need-based aid, while more than half the school receives some sort of aid for financial reasons.

Less than a third of the students belong to the Reformed Church of America, but the student body is overwhelmingly Christian, white and, for the most part, conservative. "Many students can fit in," reports a senior, "but it helps to be a WASP." Despite administrative claims to work toward a more integrated student body, one junior states: "Gays and freaks meet with a lot of suspicion here." About three-quarters hail from Michigan. The next most-popular home states are New York and New Jersey; many come from other places "out East."

Hope students can live in on-campus apartments or small houses called cottages. Traditional dorms (mainly single sex, with one coed by wing and one coed by floor) are also available. The rooms, mostly doubles, are small but well maintained. Freshmen are assigned to dorms and roommates; thereafter rooms are assigned by lottery, with seniors getting first dibs. Visitation hours for single-sex dorms (midnight on weekdays and 2 AM on weekends) are strictly enforced and about 25 percent of the students beat the system by moving off campus altogether. The five fraternities and five sororities (all local) are housed in a residential complex. On-campus campers eat in one large dining hall where they rarely complain about the food, especially the homemade bread and desserts.

With a luscious pine grove in its center—a good place to go when feeling confined or crowded, according to one source—the campus is situated on four square blocks in Holland (population forty thousand). The eclectic campus incorporates everything from nineteenth-century Flemish to modern architecture, "but it somehow just seems to belong together," says one observer. For most students, life is community oriented, with a heavy emphasis on clean fun. There is chapel three times a week, but attendance is not required. The chaplain's office organizes several popular and visible religious activities. Frats and sororities are nonexclusive, but many of the campus dances are sponsored by the social activities committee. Occasional off-campus parties are a sure way to beat the college ban on alcohol in the dorms, and students often provide their own theater and dance entertainment as well as "spontaneous fun." The school brings thespians and musicians to campus through its Great Performances series.

When campus attractions pale, students head to the beaches of Lake Michigan or drive an hour away to Grand Rapids, which offers some larger-city amenities and good Friday rental deals at the ski slopes. Holland itself, quiet and of Dutch heritage, "is *not* renowned for its exciting night life," according to one source. The town offers little more than a few bars and an annual Tulip Time Spring Festival—a bit of Old

World culture for sure, but hardly a major undergraduate attraction. Several varsity sports, particularly men's football and basketball, and men's and women's swimming, get a bigger Hope turnout than the tulips any day.

Religion at Hope "is a real part of life," a chemistry major says, "but students are given a lot of space to develop their own beliefs." And while some students complain about the homogeneity of the student body and an administration that is "too paternalistic," it seems that for every one who believes the school "needs a more worldly view," there is another who appreciates the individual attention and close-knit, secure community that is Hope College.

Houghton College

Houghton, NY 14744

Location Rural
Total Enrollment 1,140
Undergraduates 1,140
Male/Female 40/60
SAT V/M 530/550
Financial Aid 80%
Expense Pr $

Applicants 610
Accepted 83%
Enrolled 56%
Academics ★ ★ ★
Social 🏛 🏛 🏛
Q of L ● ● ● ●
Admissions (716)567-2211

Houghton is run by the Wesleyan Methodist Church of America, but there's much more to this Christian liberal arts college than mandatory chapel. The college is committed to the integration of faith and learning, which means it fosters academic freedom and scholarly excellence as well as evangelical, social and religious values. In the words of one student, "Most students are Christians who are seeking to think through the faith intelligently."

Set on a hill overlooking a gorgeous valley, the campus is "1,200 acres of rural beauty" surrounded by vast expanses of western New York countryside. The academic buildings are a mix of stone and brick with ivy-covered walls. Though Houghton looks like a typical northeastern liberal arts college, no one is going to mistake it for one of its secular counterparts. Chapel is required Monday through Thursday mornings— some of the faculty members wanted to have it for three days only, but students overruled them. Sunday church and Tuesday prayer meetings are optional. All meals begin with grace, and professors may start classes with devotions. All students sign "the pledge" to abstain from such vices as tobacco, alcohol, drugs, social dancing, cards and swearing.

"Houghton's academic philosophy and program is to provide a Christian liberal arts education in an evangelical context," according to the administration. The biology, chemistry, Bible and theology, psychology, history and music departments are particularly strong, though the latter suffers from the lack of a fine arts center. Virtually all of Houghton's premeds make it into medical school. Houghton's weaker departments include art, communications and foreign languages. The faculty is very accessible, and one student reports "an unusual camaraderie between students and professors." General education requirements are extensive, but the only two required religious courses are biblical literature and ethics (actually an introduction to philosophy). The library, which is adequate enough, closes for meals and chapel services and just plain shuts down on Sundays.

Students at Houghton can spend a semester at any school in the Christian College Consortium,* or take part in an American studies program in Washington, D.C., sponsored by a related group, the Christian College Coalition.* Houghton's own extension campus in Buffalo offers training for secondary-school teaching. Three-two engineering programs with Clarkson College of Technology (New York) or Washington University (Missouri) are also available. About half the students sign up for the optional three-week May term at the end of spring semester, in which they take one course three hours a day. Along with a group of other colleges, Houghton offers joint trips to France, Spain, Mexico, Germany and Austria.

Houghton attracts an able student body with one of the highest proportions of National Merit Scholars in the state. About 28 percent ranked in the top 10 percent of their high school class, and over 90 were in the top half. The majority of students, "strongly conservative on most of the ethical issues of the day," are from upstate New York, but about 40 percent come from other states and foreign countries. Less than a fifth are Wesleyan Methodists, but almost all are evangelical Protestants from lower-middle- or middle-class homes. Not surprisingly, there's a big contingent of MKs (missionary kids).

Students are enthusiastic about the close community atmosphere—"a love and warmth and friendliness that can't be explained." Houghton, though need-blind in admissions, does not guarantee aid awards to students who show need. The college gives about sixty merit scholarships ranging from $400 to $2,000. Students praise Houghton's academic and psychological counseling programs.

Dorms, including two brand-new ones, are well maintained and single sex, with freshmen usually living on their own floors. The dorms are "comfortable" and equipped with kitchens; singles are available but cost more. No visitation in the rooms is allowed, but dorm lounges are open every day to members of the opposite sex—only until curfew, of course. There is plenty of healthy interaction between the sexes, just not much privacy. On-campus students eat twenty-one meals a week in the dining hall, which draws few complaints. After the first two years, almost all males and about half the females move off campus. Many opt for college-approved "outside" houses where regulations are self-imposed, but "the pledge" still applies.

There are no fraternities or sororities at Houghton to sponsor typical college beer bashes. "We have fun in less debilitating ways," a student explains. Houghton choral groups perform regularly with the Rochester Philharmonic, and students run their own radio station. In a town that boasts one country store, a gas station, and a post office, Houghton is about as far out in the boondocks as you can get. When not snowed in, students often take the hour-and-a-half drive to Buffalo or Rochester, or to nearby parks and ski areas. Since the surrounding area is one of the poorest regions in New York State, the college provides many opportunities for volunteer activity. Although more than 70 percent of Houghton graduates go to graduate school, many ultimately enter service-related professions such as the ministry, social work, public health and education.

Soccer is the favorite sport on campus (there is no football), and the varsity team is always a top contender for the championship of the National Christian College Athletic Association. Both men's and women's basketball and volleyball are popular, as is field hockey. A new sports facility opened several years ago that includes three basketball courts, four racquetball courts, a pool and an indoor track. Students use a nearby state park and the college's own ski trails for less formal athletic exertions. Equestrian aficionados will enjoy the indoor riding arena. Intramurals, including pool and Ultimate Frisbee, provide fun competition for just about everyone.

With the nearest stoplight a half hour away, there is no doubt that Houghton students are far from the madding crowd, but many see this as an advantage rather than a problem. As one student puts it, "We draw our strength from within. A student who wants to become a stronger Christian will love it here."

University of Houston

Houston, TX 77004

Location City outskirts	**Applicants** 7,273
Total Enrollment 29,040	**Accepted** 61%
Undergraduates 18,720	**Enrolled** 56%
Male/Female 55/45	**Academics** ★ ★
SAT V/M 460/520	**Social** ☎ ☎
Financial Aid 40%	**Q of L** ● ● ●
Expense Pub $	**Admissions** (713)749-2321

Texas isn't doing so well: Oil has lost its high price tag, multimillionaires have lost some of their millions, and the University of Houston–University Park has lost its University Park. Well, it didn't literally lose the park—it still has over one hundred acres of green lawns, trees, fountains and outdoor sculptures—but the school has changed its name again (the third time in four years) to plain ole University of Houston. But then, what's in a name?

Established sixty years ago, UH didn't become part of the state-supported system of higher education until 1968, when it grew more affordable, but also more dependent on the now-troubled state economy. In spite of it all, UH remains an optimistic, future-oriented school with strong preprofessional programs. Chemical engineering and anything business—marketing, operational behavioral management and finance—are popular and prominent offerings. But the one department that attracts students from all over the country is the hotel and restaurant management school, generously endowed by the Hilton (as in Hilton Hotels) Foundation.

In an attempt to spruce up programs in the College of Technology, the university has hired some world-class faculty members and expanded its programs in emerging technological and scientific fields: computer science, robotics, and cell and molecular biology. The education school has made a name for itself and the adequate drama, art, and music departments contribute to Houston's cultural offerings. Psychology is decent here, and the history department offers unique courses that bridge the technical-humanitarian gap by focusing on contemporary professions in an historical perspective. Houston happens to be home to one of only two creative writing PhD programs in the nation, with novelists Donald Barthelme and Philip Lopate on the faculty. But liberal arts in general tend to be less challenging.

Houston mandates a sturdy fifty-six-hour core curriculum encompassing English, math, cultural heritage and interdisciplinary studies. Some lower and intermediate level lectures are huge, but they generally break down into discussion groups of thirty or fewer students. Freshmen and sophomores quickly get used to the sight of TAs—assuming they get into the crowded required courses. Students may improve their academic lot by becoming one of 610 honors students (a combined SAT score of 1245 helps in this transformation) who enjoy smaller class sizes, more in-depth course work and special study areas. The library has a respectable 1.4 million volumes as well as creative writing and Texana collections. But the new architecture building designed by Philip Johnson has become the conversation piece of the campus with its square skylight, crown of columns and huge floor-to-ceiling atrium. The university operates a surprisingly cheap humanities program in London. (Students pay only low UH tuition and housing rates to attend.) Houstonians can also opt to study architecture in Italy; manage hotels and restaurants in France, Germany or Spain; or work with German corporations.

An overwhelming majority of students are from Houston's Harris County (77 percent commute from home), and another 9 percent hail from other parts of the Longhorn State. A fourth of the student body is either black, Hispanic or Asian, and there is a small contingent of foreign students, mostly from the Middle East and Taiwan. The substantial number of older and married students who drive home in the evening, and the many part-time students, give the university a transitory atmosphere. The average student is over twenty-five years old; "middle-aged" is how one student describes her fellow classmates. They're also middle-income and middle-of-the-road politically, say others. The university provides financial aid on a first-come, first-served basis "with rolling processing as long as funds remain." About five hundred academic scholarships are awarded annually, ranging from $100 to $4,000. More than two hundred male and female athletes in a dozen different sports receive a little financial incentive to make UH their first choice. With that unbelievably low Texas state school tuition, though, even students who don't get a cent of financial aid or scholarship are getting a good deal.

Only 10 percent of the students live on campus, and the university provides two coed living options: a modern tower complex and a group of old, slightly musty low-rise dorms. Each dorm has its own dining facility where "the food is actually good." Those who need a daily fix from each of the four food groups—fried, fast, frozen and fattening—will find relief from one of the vendors who dot the campus. "The infant Greek system," says one student, is composed of generally younger students, "people looking to be more than commuters and to get involved." Though only a fraction of the students join, fraternities and sororities make a significant contribution to the social scene with their frequent parties. The Residence Halls Association and more than 250 student groups sponsor additional activities.

Houston does have several varsity athletic teams, although they are not necessarily permanent fixtures. As of late, the athletic program has been operating at a deficit and the job-minded, middle-aged, transient student body is more worried about building the academic reputation of the school than letting precious funds go to supporting the teams. "Some students want to do away with intercollegiate athletics," reports an undergraduate source. "It's a really big controversy." The administration has decided to hold on to athletics for at least three more years, but the two big-time teams, the Phi Slama Jama fraternity (also known as the Cougar basketball team) and the Cougar gridders, are under pressure to perform and bring in some revenue. Despite deficits, the golf team has won fifteen national championships, which is not bad for a school without a golf course.

Houston is a sprawling city with "very humid weather," smart shops, hotels and restaurants, as well as its own symphony, opera and ballet companies. A great memento of the city's more affluent days is the $31-million Astrodome, which UH's few loyal fans rattle around in when the football Cougars play there. The Houston campus consists mainly of buildings built since the school went public; therefore, most are semimodern, predictably nondescript, government-sponsored-type buildings. But the beautiful, if not notable, University Park is rich with greenery, marvelous greenery—a

291

sharp contrast from the concrete jungle of downtown Houston only three miles away. Although the campus is ringed with bus stops, cars really are a must. Parking on campus is a chore, but handicapped students will find that Houston is a national leader in accommodating their needs.

UH is starting to live up to its own high expectations, building new facilities, hiring new faculty, and hoping inevitable state cuts aren't too deep. And perhaps, if all that prospers is not linked to the oil industry, there is hope for the city of Houston and the school that now bears its name—and *only* its name.

Howard University

Washington, DC 20059

Location Center city	**Applicants** 5,500
Total Enrollment 12,280	**Accepted** 41%
Undergraduates 8,880	**Enrolled** 77%
Male/Female 45/55	**Academics** ★ ★ ★
SAT V/M 430/450	**Social** ☎ ☎ ☎
Financial Aid 82%	**Q of L** ● ● ●
Expense Pr $	**Admissions** (202)686-6200

Since it was founded in 1866 by General Oliver Howard, commissioner of the Freedmen's Bureau, Howard University has been the nation's preeminent black university. Its purpose has always been to serve students who might not otherwise have an opportunity for a university education, although today first-generation college students mingle with the "sons and daughters of important and famous people." (Alumni include the likes of Thurgood Marshall, Vernon Jordan and Andrew Young.) There is no such thing as Afro-American studies at this university where the black experience is central to all instruction.

Since its inception, Howard has promoted the liberal arts, contrary to the advice of early black leaders like Booker T. Washington, who argued in favor of technical training. Within its seventeen schools and colleges, students cite political science, social work and business as outstanding, primarily because of their emphasis on bettering the conditions of black people. Extensive offerings in Afro-American and African art and an institute of jazz studies also emphasize the black cultural heritage. Other popular fields are engineering, chemistry, biology, and special education; accelerated programs offer a BS on the way to a medical, dental or public-management degree. Weaker departments include math, theater management and the communications department, which runs two radio stations and the nation's first black television station but suffers from the lack of a centralized facility.

Academic facilities at Howard, in general, are not the best, though the new college of business and undergraduate library buildings are showpieces. Located in a high-crime, low-income section of Washington, the campus is a tree-shaded combination of historic buildings and sleek modern structures, "serving as a scenic reminder of how we started and how far we have come," one student reflects. All students must complete a general education program that requires courses in math, English, sciences and humanities. In general, the work at Howard is demanding. Although professors are accessible and academic support programs numerous, it is by no means uncommon for students to spend more than four years as an undergraduate at this federally subsidized institution; three out of five freshmen do not graduate from Howard within five years. Academically "there is some pressure, but it's not overwhelming," according to one senior. For students who need a break from the academic grind, internship opportunities are many, and study abroad is available at fifty universities in Africa, Asia, Australia, Canada, Europe and Latin America.

The vast majority of Howard students are black, and many foreign countries have representatives on campus. Howard, says one student, is a place to encounter people "from the South Bronx to Soweto." Adds another, "Whether you're from New Jersey or Jamaica, you are somebody unique." Less than 20 percent graduated in the top tenth of their high school class, though 80 percent were in the top half. Career-minded and highly motivated men and women fit in best, current students say. Most are politically liberal. Howard awards about a hundred merit scholarships to entering freshman, with awards averaging $1,750. Students who maintain a 3.0 grade point average qualify, as do National Merit Scholars. A deferred payment plan is available that allows families to pay each semester's tuition in three installments. About 90 percent of the students apply for need-based aid, and about 90 percent of those get some form of assistance. The university also budgets about 170 athletic scholarships, including awards for women in basketball, volleyball, tennis, track and swimming. Howard is one of a handful of universities in the nation that is supported by federal subsidies.

Housing facilities are limited, and only a third of the students are able to reside on campus. Coed and single-sex options are offered, and renovation has reached a furious pitch. Upperclass room assignments are made by a lottery. No one raves about the dining facilities, but there are few options outside of cooking for yourself. Howard is the home of the nation's first black fraternities and sororities, but these groups do not have their own housing or dining facilities.

Weekends bring an assortment of social happenings to campus, many of which take place in the student center. People usually go to parties and sports events or into downtown Washington, which is easily accessible by public transportation. Only a small percentage are Greek, but as the sponsors of parties, political activities and bus trips, these groups are "an important, integral part of the university." Athletics are also an important presence on campus, particularly varsity basketball, soccer, football and track.

As the most comprehensive of the predominantly black institutions in the country, Howard, says one student, makes "young black individuals aware of their heritage." It is just the place for "a student who is looking to broaden his or her scope, who is interested in being somebody, who is concerned about himself and the future of black people, who is interested in viewing life from a black perspective in order to build a better black tomorrow."

Hunter College, NY
—See CITY UNIVERSITY OF NEW YORK

Idaho State University

Pocatello, ID 83209

Location Small city
Total Enrollment 9,810
Undergraduates 4,970
Male/Female 48/52
ACT V/M N/A
Financial Aid 62%
Expense Pub $

Applicants 1,110
Accepted 100%
Enrolled 70%
Academics ★ ★ ★
Social 🗣 🗣 🗣
Q of L ● ● ●
Admissions (208)236-3277

Idaho State University is a teaching-oriented university situated in Pocatello, the second largest city in the state. For the students, who are mostly from Idaho, both the town and the school are extremely popular. The out-of-staters, too—or at least those who can appreciate breathtaking views and fantastic skiing, climbing and fishing—look around this lovely valley with the Rocky Mountains on three sides and think they've found paradise. The school does not purport to be an intellectual stomping ground, but that isn't what most people come for anyway.

Founded as an agricultural college in 1901, Idaho State was designated as the lead institution in the state in health-related programs and is also strong in science, education, business and engineering. English and philosophy are good, but other nontechnical areas are weak. Everyone takes a general education program that sets out after a dozen "goals" ranging from writing proficiency to "knowledge of other cultures." The campus is open and outdoorsy—"laid-back" is the most common description—with a blend of traditional collegiate brick buildings and newer ones "that look like IBM punchcards." Because the university offers six-month to two-year vocational-technical programs, many older students are attracted to it, and they are granted all the privileges of the typical undergraduate. Students tend to take a casual approach to academics—"There's no real killer instinct," a pharmacy major notes—although certain major programs can be rigorous. The faculty is strong on teaching, extremely available for consultation, and popular with the students. As one student explains, "Profs will nail you on a test and talk with you about it at a bar or up in a hunting camp." Small classes contribute to the coziness, with only biology reaching the 175-student mark.

The school has the second best CPA exam pass rate in the nation, but all that wizardry has not buffered it from the budget traumas of state-supported institutions. Social work, speech, theater, nursing and communications suffer from inadequate funding, and the destination of the next budget-cutting ax is a constant worry. "The budget cutbacks are making ISU's best faculty leave the institution," a senior complains. Even the fairly new library—hailed by locals as "the best in the West"—has suffered cutbacks to its services. The gentle inroads made by computers on the campus are beginning to ring with the hue and cry of "More terminals!"

Ninety percent of the students are from the state, and most are "sick of Californians and easterners making potato jokes." The average age on campus is twenty-five, so many students have responsibilities to families and jobs, as well as to school. Many commute, as there are good bus routes connecting towns as far away as fifty miles. The school, of course, has no religious affiliation, but the dominant religious influence on campus is Mormon.

One distinctive financial aid effort provides tuition waivers to about fifty nonresident students who meet the deadline for application and who demonstrate "extreme" need. There are 230 athletic scholarships and 500 other merit awards of up to $2,000 for less well-coordinated undergrads.

Only about half of the first- and second-year students live on campus, where dorms are single sex, and attractive double rooms are readily available. Adjacent male and female buildings make socializing easy, but upperclassmen tend to choose to live in the on-campus apartments, the single-room senior dorm, or else they move into town. Some say that it is cheaper to live off campus, but then a car becomes important. Either way, students can buy flexible meal plans, which are honored by three dining halls, a snack bar, and a deli. Unfortunately, food quality wins such ratings as "bland" and "blah," and a freshman claims that it "gets worse as the year goes on."

"ISU offers more outside the campus than within," one student notes. Jackson Hole, Sun Valley, Snowbird and the Salmon River beckon students to ski, fish, white-water and climb in some of the most beautiful mountains in the world. A recruiting program one year involved mailing high school students a poster bearing the legend, "Ski the big potato." While Pocatello offers little in the way of cultural enlightenment, there's a ski area only ten minutes from town, and students point out that Salt Lake City is within a three-hour drive. One of the largest collegiate programs of its kind in the country, the Outdoor Program, sponsors numerous films, outings, races and speakers and runs an extensive ski hut system.

A small Greek system is growing more popular, but the fraternities and sororities don't have a tight grip on campus life. The student-run program board attempts to provide an opportunity for fun in eleven specialty social areas. On a typical weekend, lectures, name bands, proms and first-run movies vie with sports, dorm parties and going dancing and barhopping in "town—if you could call it that." Nobody complains about the social life at Idaho State any more than they would complain about the skiing. "This school is a vacation," one man boasts. Women's tennis recently made it into the Big Sky Conference. The new domed stadium and extensive athletic complex has boosted varsity sports incredibly and attracted many jocks. Intramural athletes also have access to the facilities, and practically every sport is available except surfing.

Idaho State is not a school for preppies or activists, and people here are happy about the lack of pretensions. Those interested in the vocational-technical program, or in the health field, or business, might give ISU a second look. A local sign reads, WELCOME TO IDAHO. SET YOUR CLOCK BACK 20 YEARS. It should also say: HOPE YOU BROUGHT YOUR SKIS.

Illinois Institute of Technology

Chicago, IL 60616

Location Urban
Total Enrollment 6,230
Undergraduates 2,150
Male/Female 80/20
ACT 25
Financial Aid 71%
Expense Pr $ $

Applicants 1,570
Accepted 74%
Enrolled 37%
Academics ★ ★ ★
Social ☎ ☎
Q of L ● ●
Admissions (312)567-3025

"Problem solving" and "decision making" are the axioms of the educational philosophy at the Illinois Institute of Technology, and the corollary for graduates is a choice of lucrative jobs at the end of four years. Businesses throughout the country, and especially those in the Midwest and its "capital," Chicago, are more than eager to snap up the engineers, architects and computer scientists turned out by this prestigious technical school.

Ludwig Mies van der Rohe was the director of the architecture school for twenty years, and many of his students, some highly acclaimed themselves, serve on the faculty. As a result, architecture and design, still under his influence, is an important department. All engineering departments—chemical, electrical and computer, environmental, civil, mechanical, and metallurgical—are strong. The sciences, chemistry in particular, are also first-rate, as is math, which has undergone a shift in emphasis from theoretical to applied. The program in business administration offers helpful instruction on increasing productivity through the management of manufacturing operations. Computer science has grown to its natural preeminence at a school that emphasizes meeting industry's needs for graduates trained with up-to-the-minute technology. Computer literacy has been a requirement for all IIT graduates, and the ready availability of computers, except at occasional crunch times, is a happy fact of life. Students say that new interdisciplinary programs, such as bioengineering and computer engineering, are "noteworthy and becoming increasingly popular."

IIT maintains departments in the humanities and social sciences in order to provide a "true university education," and it even offers BA degrees. The administration warns, though, that these departments exist primarily to provide general education to its technically oriented students, all of whom must take twelve semester hours each in the humanities and social sciences. Some students find the courses laughably easy, and, as usual in a technical school, many resent the diversion from their specialized fields. Even so, courses in music appreciation and film analysis are popular respites from programs such as aerospace engineering.

Classes are relatively small, except for introductory courses. Engineering students have extensive use of sophisticated labs and independent research labs in Chicago are also available. Undergraduates have many opportunities to take part in faculty research projects. The five-year co-op program is another possibility for hands-on experience, but who wants to sit around in classes any longer than they have to with all the big bucks out there waiting to be made? As one student notes, "IIT is not the place for 'professional students' [i.e., 'life-ers']. Students here generally graduate on time and find their way into the marketplace." Combined BS/MS degrees in business administration and public administration are available, and there are study programs in France for engineers and Scotland for architects. Internships, co-op education and good old-fashioned jobs are all readily available locally.

IIT students are likely to be products of public or Roman Catholic parochial schools in the local area who graduated in the top fifth of their class. State residents make up three-quarters of the student body. Actually, about 8 percent of the students are foreign, and blacks and Hispanics constitute a fifth of the population, thanks to the splendid job that IIT has done in seeking out talented minority students from high schools in Chicago and elsewhere. The school also has a program to encourage women to become scientists and engineers. Although most students are seriously interested in getting a good education and then a good job, diversity shows up in nonacademic interests. "You can find most any language, religion or ideology on campus," a sophomore has discovered. IIT guarantees to all students a financial aid package that meets their computed need and also offers a variety of non-need scholarships. The latter include renewable awards of up to $8,000 to outstanding freshman applicants.

A little better than half the students commute, which is just as well since, as one student says, "The dorms are pits and should be demolished." Some students opt to live in apartments in the area or up on Chicago's North Side; others inhabit fraternity houses. The dining hall has five- and seven-day meal plans for residents, with a special menu for vegetarians, and the student union serves lunch for commuters. The library's closing at 10 PM drives some students up a wall, but somehow they manage.

IIT's six-block campus with its attractive towers is an architectural and social oasis in this run-down area of Chicago's South Side. Not far away are some ominous-looking public-housing high rises, but a few miles beyond them is downtown. "IIT's most special resource is the city of Chicago," says one student. The glitter of Michigan Avenue and crush of nightlife crowds on Rush Street are within easy reach by car or public transportation. The subway stops right on campus, and there is also a free minibus service. For architecture students, this city that boasts one of the most beautiful skylines in the world is a veritable museum, with buildings designed by the likes of Frank Lloyd Wright, Louis Sullivan, and, of course, Mies. The White Sox play just a few blocks away in Comiskey Park, and Lake Michigan is within jogging distance. Chicago's surprisingly sizable Chinatown is also close by, offering authentic and reasonably priced meals for a break from dorm food.

Most students head home on weekends, so campus life can get slow. Fraternities and sororities, which claim a membership of about a fourth of the students, sponsor most of the campus social events, although there are at least two movies a week. "At my house," says one Greek, "we usually drink and do homework or go downtown and drink or maybe just go drinking. Sometimes we eat as well." Dormies and "frat-rats" tend not to communicate with one another. Traveling is a must for males seeking dates, with local colleges such as Loyola or Northwestern the usual destination. Studying for physics exams leaves little time for extracurricular activities; as one student says, "Academics do come first here, an athlete must also be a good student." But if the basketball team is unlikely to frighten nearby basketball-crazy schools, students praise the basketball, swimming and soccer teams. The intramural program is strong, though students gripe that the facilities close at 3 PM Saturday and 5 PM Sunday.

The work at IIT is hard, and the neighborhood and social life are lousy. But the big city is a tremendous asset. One student chose IIT over other top midwestern technical schools because "IIT is located within the nation's second largest design market." And you don't have to be a philosophy major to understand that kind of logic.

University of Illinois at Urbana–Champaign

Urbana–Champaign, IL 61801

Location Small city	**Applicants** 14,822
Total Enrollment 36,330	**Accepted** 67%
Undergraduates 27,200	**Enrolled** 59%
Male/Female 54/46	**Academics** ★★★★★
SAT V/M 530/600	**Social** 🐒🐒🐒
Financial Aid 64%	**Q of L** ●●●
Expense Pu $ $ $	**Admissions** (217)333-0302

Like the slugger with "broad shoulders" on the edge of the prairie in Carl Sandburg's poem "Chicago," the University of Illinois at Urbana–Champaign is a giant among academic institutions, ranking among the world's great universities. And while it's easy to feel like just another stalk of corn among the school's field of thirty-six thousand, there's little doubt about the fertile opportunities awaiting those students willing to pursue them.

Illinois' campus is centrally located—right in the middle of nowhere that is. Amid the midwestern prairies, between the two twin cities of Champaign and Urbana, and equidistant from Chicago, Indianapolis and St. Louis, Illinois stands alone. A few stately brownstone Gothics and white-columned brick Georgians rise above the green lawns and criss-crossing walkways, but otherwise, the campus is a mishmash of inconsistent architecture ("not the Ivy Look," according to one student), which is rather unspectacular. But physically disabled students tend to have more appreciation for this campus, which is flat and well equipped with ramps and widened doorways.

Illinois boasts twenty-one colleges and schools and 150 degree fields—if you can't find something, you can probably design it on your own. The College of Liberal Arts and Sciences attracts 40 percent of undergrads, and although distribution requirements vary from school to school, they're generally on the light side. Accountancy, agriculture, biological sciences, education, engineering, library and information sciences, physics and psychology are just a sampling of the sixteen university departments that rate highly. Some of the most popular programs among the students are the applied life studies, aviation, commerce and business administration. Since the performing arts facilities and faculty are among the best in the nation, auditions are required for majors, and sometimes to get into courses in theater, dance and music. In fact, excellence leads to demand across the boards at Illinois, and entering freshman may find that getting into popular courses requires performance, dexterity and patience.

Illinois houses the largest state university library (over seven million volumes), which is also the third-largest academic library in the country after Harvard and Yale. The Morrow Plots, the oldest experimental field in the nation, has been preserved in the middle of the campus as testimony not only to the university's origins but also to its continuing strength in the field of agriculture. These days at Illinois, a lot of plotting goes on inside as well, since the university is home base for the PLATO educational computer system and was selected by the National Science Foundation as one of four sites for the $200-million, high-speed "Supercomputer" system. The most notable new development at Illinois is undoubtedly the Beckman Institute for Advanced Science

298

and Technology, an interdisciplinary center to bring together the study of biological and physical sciences in pursuit of new insights into human and artificial intelligence. The university also initiated a new honors program for undergraduates, which includes a faculty mentor program, seminars, advanced sections of regular courses, and access to special resources. More than six hundred undergraduates each year travel and study abroad, roaming everywhere from Canada to Venezuela.

Illinois certainly has its share of award-winning faculty, including a two-time Noble Laureate in physics. "It's great to learn from the authors of your textbooks," states a finance major. Yet there are problems sometimes with such a high-powered faculty in a school where the largest class is just a few dozen short of a thousand students. "Professors are very distant in most courses," says one student. "Some ask for your Social Security number instead of your name," claims another, "and nobody is going to hunt you down and ask if you like what you're learning." In general, the course work is tough, and with 89 percent from the top quarter of their high school class, there's lots of brutal competition.

All but 3 percent of undergrads come from Illinois, including the mass exodus from the suburbs of Chicago. They tend to be conservative, competitive, career-oriented, upper-middle-class and, according to one student, "uninterested in global causes." The most visible faction on the Illinois campus is undoubtedly the Greeks. The university claims to have the largest Greek system anywhere—count 'em. Fifty-two fraternities and twenty-six sororities attract a fifth of the student body.

In addition to more than 150 athletic scholarships, Illinois awards about 600 academic and talent scholarships, which range from $800 to $1,200 per year. They are usually divided among the disciplines, and students should write to specific departments for more information. In addition, the administration claims it is making special efforts to increase the enrollment of high-achieving minority students through a President's Award program of financial support. Despite Illinois' comparative bargain tuition price, beware that in-state juniors and seniors pay $200 extra a year; out-of-state upperclassmen dish out an additional $500.

The twenty-three dorms, which range in size from 150 to 675 beds and come in both single-sex and coed styles, are set in large clusters across the campus. Each quad serves as a mini-neighborhood for its residents, with separate facilities that can include not only dining halls but also darkrooms, libraries, music practice rooms, computer terminals (personal and mainframe) and study carrels. This helps people get to know one another and counteract the negative effects of the school's large size. One-fourth of the students live in the dorms, less than 10 percent in Greek houses, and many upperclassmen move to on- or off-campus apartments and houses (some of which are closer to classrooms than the dorms).

Needless to say, the influence of the Greek organizations is strong, and parties and intramural sports are the most important parts of their domain. "At the beginning of the year there are several all-campus parties," says one business major. "Things keep roaring all year round." The twin cities are surrounded by corn and soybean fields, but that doesn't mean the area's a wasteland. The magnificent Krannert Center for the Performing Arts, with its four theaters and more than 350 performances every year, serves as the cultural center for the entire area. There are plenty of movies, pizza parlors and bars, which have a steady clientele all week long and an increase of business on the weekends. Also, Chicago and Lake Michigan are only a few hours away.

The Illini have resurfaced as national and Big Ten powers in football and basketball, and the women's volleyball team is outstanding to say the least. The intramural program is extensive, mainly because of the university's excellent sports facilities, which include nine full-length basketball courts, four pools, twenty-one handball/racquetball courts, a skating rink and tennis courts.

Illinois students attempt to deal with all the bureaucratic hassles that come with a gargantuan school, and they compensate for their remote location by making a lot of their campus a fun place to be. "But the main interest here," says a senior, "is to excel and be the best."

Indiana University at Bloomington

Bloomington, IN 47401

Location Small city	**Applicants** 13,870
Total Enrollment 32,360	**Accepted** 77%
Undergraduates 24,460	**Enrolled** 54%
Male/Female 50/50	**Academics** ★★★★
SAT V/M 470/520	**Social** 🐿🐿🐿🐿
Financial Aid 60%	**Q of L** ●●●●
Expense Pub $ $	**Admissions** (812)335-0661

When you think of basketball, you might naturally think of Indiana University's Bobby Knight, the bombastic coach of the 1984 Olympic team. But what comes to mind when you think of geology, accounting, foreign languages, opera, ethnomusicology or, in fact, anything to do with music?

Think Indiana again. With more than a hundred degree programs and five thousand courses in everything from African and Asian languages to zoology and the study of zygotes, IU offers massive quantity, but also high quality, in numerous areas. It's a Big Ten powerhouse with everything from Nobel Laureates to concert pianists, scenic landscapes to social extravagance. "Indiana is an endless array of spectacular opportunities," confirms one sophomore business major.

Indiana's attractive, wooded campus is set on 1,800 acres, and buildings are of white limestone in every style, from Gothic to modern. A pretty creek, the Little Jordan River, runs alongside the shaded paths and is topped by wooded bridges. (It will all look familiar if you saw the classic seventies flick *Breaking Away*.) IU's ten schools offer great diversity and flexibility. Multiple majors and minors, cross-disciplinary study, individually designed curriculums, intense honors and research programs and yearlong study in eight countries are readily available. The highly touted business school is currently the most popular on campus—leading of course to overcrowded lectures. That may change soon, though, as the university moves to stiffen requirements for those seeking business majors. Students give high marks to education, international studies, sociology, psychology, optometry, public and environmental administration, health, physical education, history, journalism, biology, chemistry, geology, folklore, telecommunications and foreign languages (forty-four to choose from). The Kinsey Institute for the Study of Human Sexual Behavior is internationally known, and the optometry and music schools are tops in their field.

"Engineering and agriculture are relegated to Purdue," one liberal arts student chuckles. The only departments to receive widespread student criticism are math and computer studies. Long-range plans call for terminals in every dorm, and students currently have twenty-four-hour access to the computer facility.

Indiana prizes a liberal arts education for its students, admitting freshmen not to preprofessional schools but to the "university division." Majors are declared after one or two years, discouraging premature specialization. All undergraduates must fulfill distribution requirements in five areas, and many go beyond the call of duty to be well rounded. "I'm taking piano lessons in the school of music," says a chem major. "I've never played in my life, but I like having this opportunity to learn." Students in the College of Arts and Sciences must take an intensive writing course and show proficiency in a foreign language.

Underclassmen report having extraordinary difficulty with registration and frequently being shut out of desired courses. "The good classes are always filled," a sophomore journalism major complains. As for class size, one woman says succinctly, "IU has many lecture halls and many introductory courses to fill them." Still, by the junior year, enrollment in courses dwindles, and the average class at IU is twenty-seven students. The honors program puts academically motivated students in classes of six to twelve people headed by some of the best minds in their fields. Despite their obligation to perform research, professors are praised for their concern for students. Academic advising, however, has serious gaps, and some students feel they should earn credit just for having to deal with the university's complex bureaucracy.

Sixty-five percent of IU students take advantage of the low in-state tuition rates, while the remainder hail from every state and more than a hundred foreign countries. Less than 30 percent ranked in the top tenth of their high school class, but over 50 percent were in the top half. "We are," says one education major, "liberal, conservative, radical, punk, Greek, sophisticates and hicks. IU is a true melting pot of personalities, cultures and ideas." Other students stress that their school "is nowhere near as wild, drug-infested and liberal as popular legend in the Midwest would have you believe." IU students may be a degree looser than most Hoosiers, but the overall mood is unquestionably conservative. The rolling admissions system enables students to know of their fate only a month after their application is complete.

The university packages financial aid on a first-come, first-served basis. It offers about 300 merit awards, ranging from $500 to $2,000, and applicants must be in the top 10 percent of their graduating class and have a minimum combined SAT score of 1250. There is also an "NCAA maximum" program of over 250 full athletic scholarships, encompassing ten men's sports and eight women's.

Housing ranges from Gothic quads, coed by building, to thirteen-floor high rises, coed by floor or unit. To be assured a room, freshmen should send in their housing requests early, if possible with their application. Incoming males with acceptable high school grades may join a fraternity over the summer and move right in when they arrive, but women must wait until the "tea and crumpets" pledging each spring if they wish to join a sorority. There is one all-women's dorm. Upperclassmen are spared a lottery and simply state their housing preferences, which are usually honored. Academic floors (requiring a GPA of 3.1 or better) are popular with bookworms who find that the high-rise dorms can become a bit zoo-like. Collins Living/Learning Center provides a residential college living option. The food served in each dorm's dining hall is "not as good as Mom makes, but you won't starve either." Students rail, however, at the fact that twenty meals per week is the only option. Half of the student body lives off campus, mostly in apartments or small wooden houses with big front porches, within walking distance either of the campus or of the school bus system, which runs on six different routes around the area.

"Bloomington is known as a party town," says one senior, "but parties are just part of the fun for IU students." There's always a movie being shown somewhere, and about nine hundred musical events are open to the public each year. There are shows in the new art museum, plays in the auditorium, rock and blues bands in the local bars. The state's drinking age (twenty-one) means students need "an awfully good ID" (though not necessarily their own) to get into any Bloomington bar. On-campus drinking must be behind closed doors. The student union is the largest in the nation, and the range of extracurricular organizations is also impressive. Locally, the area offers some of the best rock quarries imaginable (often used as illegal but refreshing swimming pools) and miles of public forests and lakes. Spelunkers will exult in the many nearby caves.

About a quarter of the student body belongs to one of the fifty or so fraternities or sororities, and membership is a status symbol. Since there are fewer sororities than fraternities, competition for pledges is especially keen among the women—about half get cut. Greeks are active in most campus organizations and hold many leadership positions. While "some people feel very left out if they don't make it," others are happy to remain "dormies" or independents (the off-campus students) and face off against the fraternities in an extensive intramural sports rivalry.

Intramurals pale, though, in comparison with varsity athletics. Basketball takes on the status of an established religion in the state of Indiana. The IU gym is the holy of holies and Coach Knight the high priest. Students and faculty members are all eligible for tickets, but get your requests in early. Soccer bumped swimming as the second most popular sport after the team recently won two successive NCAA crowns. But swimming continues to dominate the Big Ten in the water, and the Olympic legacy of Mark Spitz and Johnny Weissmuller lives on. Women's sports get a fair share of attention. The annual Little 500 bike race—"World's Greatest College Weekend"—is a major social event.

"I love IU," one woman confesses unashamedly. "I love the beauty of the campus, the feeling of age and scholarship that prevails among the ivy-covered buildings, the cultural programs, the excitement of IU basketball, the opportunities for involvement and directing your own learning." Neither getting in nor getting through is very difficult at Indiana University, and students could easily mark the year in terms of sports seasons, not academic semesters. But this approach hardly does justice to a state school that prizes nationally ranked academic departments as much as it does championship teams. The size and bureaucracy can be overwhelming at times, but most students don't let it get them down. "It's actually pretty hard to be lonely and friendless here," says a sophomore. "It's a Big Ten university with a small-town heart."

Iowa State University

Ames, IA 50011

Location Small city
Total Enrollment 26,430
Undergraduates 22,560
Male/Female 60/40
ACT 24
Financial Aid 50%
Expense Pub $

Applicants 9,100
Accepted 65%
Enrolled 68%
Academics ★★★
Social ☎☎
Q of L ●●●
Admissions (515)294-5836

If you're an Iowan, you probably know that Iowa State provides a more than respectable education in engineering, agriculture, and several other areas. If you're interested in academic history, you may know Iowa State has the oldest veterinary school in the country and, in 1939, produced the world's first digital computer. If you're looking for a big, friendly, unpretentious school where there's a healthy balance between heavy studying and abundant social life, your search might end in Ames.

Located on a 1,730-acre tract in the middle of a small city, the university's neatly landscaped park-like campus features a mix of preserved historic buildings and hi-tech modern ones. Partially closed to traffic during the school year, the campus has plenty of greenery and its own lake. Created in 1858 as the Iowa Agricultural College and Model Farm and officially listed today as Iowa State University of Science and Technology, the university is divided into eight colleges, each devoted to a particular field of study. The liberal arts program, called the College of Science and the Humanities, is the largest of the eight divisions, but it is not as strong as the more technical or professional programs, which are this school's fortes. The agriculture and home economics colleges are among the university's strong points. Engineering is another highly ranked college; the four others are business, design, education and the graduate school.

Regardless of major, all undergraduates must take two semesters of English composition as freshmen and demonstrate proficiency in English prior to graduation. Other general education requirements vary with major but typically include courses in communications, natural sciences and mathematics, social sciences and humanities, as well as a one-half credit course on the use of the library. Iowa State is one of the few universities in the nation that owns a TV station affiliated with a major network, where it provides professional training for more than 150 students each semester in broadcast journalism, telecommunicative arts, and meteorology. A new campus telecommunications system allows students to plug their personal computers into the university system, and a new $10-million Computation Center soon to be completed will further enhance the facilities. Music instruction likewise benefits from a new facility. An honors program snatches up about a hundred outstanding freshmen each year, and a state summer language program sends interested students to France, Germany or Spain. The library has over 1.6 million volumes and a new addition with comfortable study space.

The faculty draws mixed reviews on accessibility; one student praised the "excellent rapport" with students, while another maintains that the profs are "somewhat distant and sometimes uncaring." Obviously it varies with the prof. The business school is understaffed and overcrowded, and students often find it difficult to get the courses they want or need. The size of the university rightly dismays many students, who complain of long lines and a massive bureaucracy. However, as one student points out,

"Relationships depend on the students. You can be a Social Security number if you want to be, or you can get to know your instructors quite well."

Iowa is a state known for its keen interest in education and willingness to invest resources into the public school system. Consequently, the more than 70 percent of students who are homegrown Iowans are likely to be well prepared for a university education. Out-of-staters usually come from surrounding states, with a healthy cohort from the Chicago area. Students exude wholesomeness, and are "honest, hardworking and fun loving," according to one. Conservatism is the prevailing political bent, though there are some liberals kicking around, usually in the College of Design. Iowa State was the first land-grant institution to be coed from its inception, and in keeping with the homesteading nature of the curriculum, 14 percent of the students are married. In addition to need-based financial aid, about 1,000 merit awards are available, ranging upward from token $100 awards to $2,500. About 250 athletic scholarships are doled out in 11 sports.

About half the students live in on-campus residence halls and apartments. Freshmen seeking a room submit questionnaires outlining their preferences, which are processed on a first-come, first-served basis. Students warn prospective students to get applications in early, since those who are late responding are liable to end up in temporary overflow housing. Single-sex and coed dorms are available, and rooms are for the most part comfortable, if a bit cramped. Special floors are available for married students, internationals, teetotalers, and particularly studious undergraduates. The overwhelming majority of upperclassmen decide to live off campus, usually in nearby apartments. The Greeks remain very strong; there are thirty-two fraternities and sixteen sororities that together house nearly 9 percent of the students. Campus dining rooms come complete with a large salad bar, though a plan for twenty meals a week is the only option available. Greek houses have their own chefs and generally eat family-style.

Iowa State is not simply located in Ames, Iowa. In many respects it *is* Ames, Iowa. A handful of local bars, theaters and night spots cater to students, and there is a local concert hall that has recently hosted groups like Chicago and Loverboy. Des Moines, a medium-size city that is the capital of Iowa, is about forty-five minutes away. For the most part, however, socializing stays on the campus. The big event every spring is a three-day campus festival called VEISHEA (an acronym for the school's academic divisions when the festival first began), which features parades, exhibitions, and canceled classes. During the rest of the year, culture comes to the campus via the Iowa State Center, an impressive complex that attracts major orchestras, rock groups and speakers. The ISU wrestling team, which perennially challenges the U of Iowa for the national championship, has dominated the sports scene for many years, but recently a new kid on the block, varsity basketball, has created a sensation with several outstanding seasons in a row. ISU also fares well in track and women's basketball; football remains popular despite marginal success.

It may have started as a cow college, but Iowa State has grown into a self-described "institution of science and technology complemented by the liberal arts." Involved from the outset in scientific research and the transfer of technology from the laboratory to the world beyond, it offers a "cornucopia of artistic attractions" and a student body with representatives from more than a hundred foreign nations. Students interested in agriculture and at least a few other things in life, no matter where they're from, have good reason to be Iowa bound.

University of Iowa

Iowa City, IA 52242

Location Small city
Total Enrollment 29,500
Undergraduates 21,340
Male/Female 49/51
ACT 24
Financial Aid 60%
Expense Pub $ $

Applicants 8,920
Accepted 83%
Enrolled 50%
Academics ★ ★ ★ ★
Social 🐘 🐘 🐘
Q of L ● ● ●
Admissions (319)335-3847

Most people who have never been to the Midwest would not think to utter the words *Iowa* and *excitement* in the same breath. But people who know better, like admissions officers at the University of Iowa, use the slogan "The excitement of Iowa" on the cover of their brochures. Maybe they're talking about the nationally known programs in medicine and creative writing. Or maybe it's what novelist Nicholas Meyer discovered during his Iowan visit: "What seemed to be serious here was the life of the mind."

The seating capacity of the University of Iowa's football stadium is greater than the entire population of Iowa City, but don't get the wrong idea. With the glistening, gold-domed former state capitol at the center of campus, the University of Iowa looks like the crown of Iowa's fine educational system, and it is. The campus is a mix of old and new buildings, and one student says, "You can't believe how green it gets in the summer or how pretty the Iowa River looks at night." An excellent shuttle bus system connects different parts of the 1,880-acre campus, which runs through downtown Iowa City.

Iowa is distinctive within the Big Ten for its strength in the liberal and creative arts. Students in the liberal arts college (the largest of ten colleges, seven of which offer bachelor's degrees) face numerous core requirements in areas such as rhetoric, natural science, quantitative reasoning, foreign civilization and a foreign language—in addition to the demands of their major. The Unified Program is a good bet for motivated students who want to satisfy all general education requirements in small, seminar-style classes taught by some of the university's best professors.

English is widely regarded as one of Iowa's best departments, in part because of the national reputation of the Writer's Workshop, the university's graduate center for creative writing. Many prominent authors visit the Workshop, and their talent spills over into undergraduate instruction. (Tennessee Williams, Tracy Kidder and John Irving are three of many alumni names students can drop.) Fine arts and music are also solid. Astronomy and astrophysics are star departments in more ways than one, and noted experts in the field are praised for their accessibility to undergraduates. Iowa's college of education is another strong program. The educational tests developed at this school have become standard fare for elementary students across the nation.

Psychology, speech pathology and audiology are other outstanding areas. The university's on-campus hospital is the largest such teaching hospital in the United States, and the Iowa Health Center, affiliated with the hospital, encompasses four colleges—medicine, dentistry, pharmacy and nursing. Medicine and dentistry are primarily graduate programs, but undergraduates may take courses in related health professions, such as physician's assistant or medical technician. Students heap praise upon several of the engineering programs—biomedical, electrical and environmental—but are less enthusiastic about the business school's offerings. And don't even look for

305

agricultural and many other typical farm-related departments here. U of I sticks to its excellent humanities, creative and liberal arts programs and leaves the meat and potatoes for other schools.

Despite the intellectual nature and rigor of its curriculum, the academic climate at Iowa is described by one administrator as "Western-serious; that is, pretty relaxed." A senior engineering major adds that students are competitive, but "the pressure is healthy and mostly derived from trying to learn rather than beating a classmate on a test." Classes are sometimes large (often 250 to 300 students), but occasionally surprisingly small—"I was able to take a course taught by the president of the university in which there were only 15 students," exclaims an astonished undergrad. But getting into popular courses can be a problem because registration is done on a revolving system based on your Social Security number. Professors and teaching assistants are almost always willing to see students outside of class, but students wouldn't mind seeing fewer TAs in the classroom.

More than two-thirds of the undergraduates hail from Iowa, with most of the rest coming from contiguous states, especially Illinois. It's hard to categorize U of I students as conservative or liberal because, as one senior proclaims, "we have both extremes— small-town conservatives, punk rockers, preppies and everything in between." Tolerance and diversity make this campus a comfortable place to be. Besides the 350 athletic scholarships available in ten sports apiece for men and women, there are nearly 2000 merit scholarships with stipends ranging from $100 to $2,500.

If a hen ever saw what the University of Iowa student union cafeteria does to eggs, she'd never lay again. Freshmen fare better, since each dorm has its own dining hall, where the quality of food is generally better than in the main cafeteria. All dormitories are coed by floor or wing except for one female dorm, but housing is only available for a quarter of Iowa's students. Consequently, more than half live in apartments or houses that are adjacent to the campus or more expensive units in Iowa City; virtually all juniors and seniors live off campus. Only 5 percent of Iowa's students live in "frats and sores," so it is not surprising that Greek organizations, while still influential, play less of a role in the social life than they do elsewhere. "Although the Greek system is popular, there isn't any pressure to join or not to join," reports an independent. "The atmosphere is conducive to individualism." Socializing tends to be done in small groups and usually on weekends. Iowa City is nice but limited, and true city lovers head for Chicago, Kansas City, or St. Louis, which are all within a six-hour drive by car—a short road trip by midwestern standards. Skiing is an additional hour away, in Minnesota.

In the state of Iowa, the word *culture* is usually prefixed *agri,* but not so on the university campus. Orchestras, dance companies and Broadway shows that visit the state will probably stop at the university, and theater is strong, again thanks to the Writer's Workshop. "The opportunity to be a spectator to a great variety of fine arts performances" is what one biochemistry major likes best about being here. As for sports, there's that big football stadium, which occasionally houses a strong team. Basketball draws lots of fan support, but the NCAA champion wrestling team, the men's swimming squad and women's field hockey team offer spectators the biggest rewards.

It is the graduate programs that are the real magnets at the University of Iowa, but undergraduate education is solid. In particular, the liberal arts are treated seriously and expertly. Iowa as a state has traditionally been one where education is emphasized and well supported. The University of Iowa is a monument to that educational excitement.

Ithaca College

Ithaca, NY 14850

Location Small city
Total Enrollment 5,760
Undergraduates 5,390
Male/Female 44/56
SAT V/M 500/530
Financial Aid 55%
Expense Pr $ $

Applicants 7,900
Accepted 59%
Enrolled 34%
Academics ★ ★ ★
Social ☎ ☎ ☎ ☎ ☎
Q of L ● ● ●
Admissions (607)274-3124

Founded as a conservatory of music in 1892, Ithaca College has added on so many varied programs over the past century it's hard to think of a professional interest that isn't covered in its curriculum. The administration boasts that "Ithaca offers programs that reflect tomorrow's careers. It's a forward-thinking approach." Like college, like students, they always say, and one corporate organizational media major confirms this belief: "Outgoing, energetic students who have a good sense of where they are going fit in well at Ithaca."

Appropriately, none of the clean, streamlined buildings on campus are more than a few decades old, and the campus grounds are kept in tip-top condition all year round. The college is perched on a hill overlooking the city and Lake Cayuga, the longest of the Finger Lakes. It can get colder than cold in the winter, but "the view of the lake on a nice day is almost intoxicating," says one student. Adds another: "One look and most people are sold."

Today's Ithaca College offers seventy-seven undergraduate degree programs through six schools that vary in format, reputation and requirements: allied-health professions; business; music; communications; health, physical education and recreation; and humanities and sciences. True to its roots, Ithaca retains a fine reputation for music education and boasts many good performance studios. The school of communication is known for its programs in radio and TV and its success in preparing students for careers as broadcast executives, producers and reporters. With a nearly 100 percent placement rate, physical therapy is a standout among allied health offerings. The athletic training concentration found in the school of health and physical education is notable. The business school is young but has grown rapidly in the past decade; accounting continues to be its strongest program. Teacher certification is available in more than a dozen fields. Students voice disappointment in some of the relatively new professionally oriented majors, such as computer science, marketing and community health education. Business/psychology is among the several popular dual majors.

With more than two thousand students, Humanities and Sciences is the largest school on campus—virtually a college within a college—and its more traditional orientation tends to set it apart from the other schools. While all Ithaca College students must take several liberal arts courses, only students in the School of Humanities and Sciences must fulfill specific distribution requirements that include course work in the fine and performing arts, humanities, natural sciences and mathematics, and social and behavioral sciences. Among the strongest of the school's nineteen departments are the natural sciences, which offer students plenty of opportunity to engage in research and even to publish papers. Good acting and technical production programs are solid parts of the theater arts concentration.

The 3-2 program in engineering with Cornell is popular, and Ithaca students in any major can enter that Ivy League castle on the next hill to take courses not offered on their campus (the arrangement is reciprocal). Other opportunities include numerous internships and foreign study options, including programs with the Institute for American Studies in Canterbury, England, and Avignon, France. Freshmen who have yet to settle upon a specific course of study can enroll in the Exploratory Program, which combines career counseling with academic exploration.

Ithaca students generally hail from the Northeast, and about half are from New York. The black community is small (about 2 percent) as are the Hispanic and Asian-American populations, but student opinion persists that the student body is diverse. "We have preps, athletes, granola munchers and designer-jean queens," reports a senior. Yet socioeconomically there appears to be little disparity: "Most come from predominately upper-class families." Students who are self-motivated thrive here, according to one undergraduate. "Students intent on having a super college experience will not be disappointed. If you're willing to do the work, the benefits that you reap are enormous." The administration concedes that it is possible to qualify for financial aid and not get any. Merit scholarships are few and meager ($500 tops), and in accordance with Division III guidelines, the school offers no athletic scholarships.

Dorm facilities are renovated with reasonable frequency, so upkeep is never a problem. However, overcrowding at the beginning of the year usually is. Many arriving freshmen will find themselves squeezed into a double or triple or packed into common room lounges. But don't despair: Many of the lounges have TVs, fireplaces and terraces, and if you're in a triple for more than three weeks you get a rebate. Dorms are either coed by floor or wing, or single sex. And despite the crowded situation, less than a quarter of the students move off campus because housing is neither cheap nor luxurious in Ithaca, and you can't move back on campus once you've deserted. The garden apartments are *the* place to live if you're a junior or senior, and since they come complete with kitchens, their inhabitants don't have to subscribe to the meal plan. Other on-campus dwellers must eat in one of the neat and clean dining halls where students often complain about the food—not because it's bad, you understand, but because "we have to have something to complain about."

You can't spend your free time surfing in the almost ideal college town of Ithaca, but you can do just about anything else. As one undergrad explains, "Everyone here takes his or her studies seriously but realizes that school work is not the only motivational force in life and should not be." On weekends Ithaca students can take advantage of an array of city and college activities, both at IC and at Cornell. Ithaca has all the restaurants, movies, concerts and entertainment that two large institutions can support. Legend says that it also has more bars per square foot than any other college town. Sailing is a favorite warm weather activity, and in the winter skiing at nearby slopes is popular. There's a good city bus system, but a car is convenient for students who want to take advantage of the area's gorgeous state parks.

The Greek scene at Ithaca is low-key but, as one woman says cheerfully, "with Cornell and its dozens of frats we never lack!" Almost all the twenty-four men and women's teams on campus regularly turn in winning seasons, but student turnout for sports events is sparse; this very active student body is more into playing than watching. Students can take physical education for credit as well as exercise, and the athletic facilities on campus are excellent.

The professional nature of Ithaca's separate schools results in a somewhat segregated approach to all extracurricular activities. The two campus theaters, for example, are constantly filled with productions by drama and music students but remain impenetrable to nonmajors. The same is true of the TV and radio stations, which provide a training ground for communications majors but little opportunity for anyone else to play MC or DJ. The atmosphere here is so much like a small university, it's hard to understand why it's called a college.

Ithaca College is still fairly young. It is shedding its past reputation as a party school and, in the absence of long-standing academic traditions, appeals to a generally nouveau-professional crowd. Students here lead very active extracurricular lives, but generally not at the expense of endangering their academic and preprofessional careers. This generation of pragmatic, no-nonsense students are making their mark on Ithaca. And, Ithaca's emphasis on the contemporary nature of its programs and its forward-thinking approach has made a mark on them.

John Jay College of Criminal Justice, NY
—See CITY UNIVERSITY OF NEW YORK

The Johns Hopkins University

Baltimore, MD 21218

Location Urban	**Applicants** 4,590
Total Enrollment 3,720	**Accepted** 53%
Undergraduates 2,580	**Enrolled** 31%
Male/Female 65/35	**Academics** ★ ★ ★ ★ ★
SAT V/M 630/690	**Social** 🏠 🏠 🏠
Financial Aid 66%	**Q of L** ● ● ●
Expense Pr $ $ $ $	**Admissions** (301)338-8171

The Johns Hopkins University is not a school by any other name. And should you have an urge to infuriate some proud undergrads at this most serious and highly rated institution, ask them if they go to *John* Hopkins, the premed factory. Although there is no denying that Hopkins' natural science programs are top-notch, that undergraduate research opportunities abound here, and that students study much more than they play, *"not everyone here wants to be a doctor,"* screams a political science major.

Johns Hopkins is a multicampus, multischool university/hospital that annually enrolls more than 11,700 students. The main undergraduate schools, arts and sciences and engineering, with more than 3,700 students, are located on the predominantly red-brick Homewood campus, walled in between a low-income neighborhood and a wealthy residential area of Baltimore. This well-foliaged, urban campus is dressed in a combination of Georgian, Federalist and "garish-modern-eyesore" architecture. And as much as liberal artsies and future engineers like to deny it, "premeds dominate here," a junior claims, and he's about 33 percent on target. The university's hospital provides excellent research opportunities, and the Graduate School of Hygiene and Public Health now offers a popular undergraduate major. Preengineers, about 15 percent of the student body, also enjoy strong departments.

The quality of Hopkins science offerings is undisputable, but undergraduates reserve some of their highest praise for the outstanding faculty members in the humanities, especially in English, history and art history. The distinguished program in international relations is a favorite among social scientists, as are the departments of psychology and political economy. Here again, students benefit from the well-developed graduate side of Johns Hopkins. The International Studies Program, for example, is enriched by its offering at the university's Bologna Center in Italy and at its School of Advanced International Studies in Washington, D.C. (A new Johns Hopkins Washington Center for the study of American government is in the making.)

On campus, fine arts are weak, but students interested in these fields can take courses at the affiliated Peabody Conservatory of Music, which grants degrees from Johns Hopkins, or the independent Maryland Institute of Art. The foreign language offerings are also weak, and the mathematics department is "the worst department, admitted by students, faculty, and deans (yes deans)," warns one senior. The computer science department, still in its infancy, is expected to double in size over the next few years, but for now leaves a lot to be desired.

Although Johns Hopkins is a firm supporter of rigid and traditional scholarship, there are several surprisingly creative offerings for undergraduates. Students can receive a BA in creative writing through the writing seminars program, in which they study with authors and playwrights such as John Barth and Edward Albee. The Humanities Center, with its casual, interdisciplinary approach, is like a "mini–Hampshire College." With maximum curriculum flexibility allowed them, undergraduates are free to range as broadly or focus as specifically as they want. Students can also take a broad "area major," like social sciences or quantitative studies, and choose from a cluster of related disciplines to design their own program. Even the strictly structured engineering course plan stresses the importance of interdisciplinary and interdepartmental exposure.

The profs, especially those feeling publish-or-perish pressures, are often distracted only by the more assertive students. And all the would-be doctors running around makes for an extremely "throaty" (that's Hopkinsese for cutthroat) academic atmosphere. The curved grading system encourages intense competition, and the absence of plus or minus grades can make life especially harsh. Johns Hopkins generously allows freshmen an entire semester on a pass/fail basis to ease them into the academic rigor of the place. After this honeymoon period, students buckle down to an unavoidable herculean work load: "There's always something due," sighs one student. Some relief is offered, however, by the optional January intersession, during which students can take courses or pursue independent study for one or two credits.

The libraries are excellent, housing nearly two million volumes and utilizing a computerized catalogue system. The main library, the Milton S. Eisenhower, is underground and reported to have a nasty smell and an uninspiring, exceptionally conducive to sleeping, atmosphere. The Hut (Hutzler undergraduate library) has a twenty-four-hour reading room available for those last-minute cram sessions.

The students are remarkably talented, with nine out of ten from the top fifth of their high school classes. "At first it is very humbling to no longer be number one," admits one senior. Such an abundance of academically motivated students cannot help but affect the collegiate community. One student bemoans an epidemic of nerdism among his contemporaries, but optimistically notes an increase in "people with personalities, not just good GPAs." Politically, according to a seasoned senior, "the prime party is Apathy but the close followers are Criticism and Cynicism." Geographically, most students come from the Middle Atlantic states and New England with a remainder "from any and every other place on earth."

Hopkins' endowment is among the top twenty in the country, and the university remains "committed to fully meeting need-based financial aid." Yet student recipients give mixed reviews of the aid program, because packages tend to change drastically from year to year. Prepayment and monthly payment plans help middle-income families, and Hopkins generously rewards the extraordinarily talented with ninety hefty merit scholarships (regardless of need), renewable annually for those who keep a 3.0 GPA.

Freshmen from out of town are guaranteed housing in the newly renovated single-sex or coed-by-floor dormitories. Upperclassmen, on the other hand, are "shoved out the door by the administration to fend for ourselves," says one evicted junior. While some students consider this policy one of worst aspects of JHU, others chalk it up as one more learning experience: "Planning meals, buying toilet paper and paying bills is at first shocking, but well worth it for independence you gain," attests a senior. There is a lottery for apartments in university-owned buildings near campus, where about a third of the upperclassmen live under three-year leases. Floors in nearby turn-of-the-century row houses are easy to come by, though Baltimore's urban renaissance and condo conversions are driving up the rents. Freshmen must join the university's meal plan, which is supposed to have improved in the last few years and now offers such bonuses as a cookie bar, potato-toppings bar and kosher food. That doesn't explain why most freshmen believe "P.B.&J. sandwiches and Cap'n Crunch are life itself." "The other main dining options range from the trek to McD', actual cooking (heaven forbid) to microwaved Stouffer's," says a gourmet senior.

"Your social life is what you make it here, no more, no less," a student explains. "Most students do not worry about a social life; they are too busy with academics," claims another. With students dispersed among the city's apartment buildings, rowdy dorm parties and all-campus events are few and far between. But for those determined to bypass the heavy work load (and the drinking age of twenty-one), traditional college partying can be found—and the seven fraternities are usually the best place to look. (Two sororities formed at the turn of the decade have had moderate success.) Students also tend to hang out in groups that center on a particular interest, usually academic, and get together at someone's apartment. Apart from dollar movies, there are few university-generated social events. The campus "Rat" (rathskeller) features live music or a DJ every Thursday night.

Downtown Baltimore and the famed Inner Harbor are not too distant, and some of the city's best attractions—the art museum, Wyman Park, and the Memorial Stadium (home of the Orioles) are right near campus. Yet students who look beyond the city for fun had best be prepared for a long journey. "Skiing is laughable around here and the beaches are hopeless—full of cloudy water and dirty sand," says a displeased art history major.

Most extracurricular activities suffer from a lack of interest, but "lacrosse is life," and when undergrads come together to cheer on their perennial national championship team and release some study tension, "it's the next best thing to outright violence," brags a senior. Baseball, soccer, fencing and swimming are not embarrassments, either, but the rest of the athletics program is small scale. There are now ten varsity sports teams for women, but in general, women's teams are considered inferior to the men's. Always a welcome alternative to the books, Hopkins' intramural sports program provides some playing time for other students.

Despite an occasional athletic or social diversion, academics come first for nearly everybody at Johns Hopkins. If you can't sit still and study for a few hours, you might be happier somewhere else. At this school of big brains, big ambitions, and big opportunities, they really don't mind if you comment on their reputable premed program, but please don't call them *John*.

Kalamazoo College

Kalamazoo, MI 49007

Location City outskirts	**Applicants** 930
Total Enrollment 1,110	**Accepted** 80%
Undergraduates 1,110	**Enrolled** 40%
Male/Female 45/55	**Academics** ★ ★ ★
SAT V/M 540/580	**Social** ☎ ☎ ☎
ACT 26	**Q of L** ● ● ● ●
Financial Aid 52%	**Admissions** (616)383-8408
Expense Pr $ $	

Some people join the navy to see the world; others go to Kalamazoo College. A small, academically solid, midwestern liberal arts college, Kalamazoo might seem indistinguishable from dozens of like institutions were it not for its unique K (for Kalamazoo) Plan. This approach—which combines teaching, internships, independent research and subsidized foreign study experiences all around the globe—is Kalamazoo's answer to the question of how to produce students who are "curious, open, flexible, and above all, independent."

Life on Kalamazoo's sixty-acre, wooded campus centers about the quad, a green lawn where students ponder their destiny and play Ultimate Frisbee with equal ease. With its rolling hills, Georgian architecture, and cobblestone streets, the campus has a quaint and historic New England look that belies its proximity to the city of Kalamazoo and its eighty thousand residents. This beautiful setting provides a four-year home for the 10 percent of students who choose not to explore the world on the numerous foreign-study programs, and a restorative home base for those who do.

Kalamazoo runs on a ten-week quarter system, and students are required to spend three-quarters of their first year on campus. Many freshmen choose to begin the year with a "land-sea ordeal," sailing an old wooden ship up Lake Michigan into Canada for three weeks of canoeing and climbing in the mountain wilds. By the end, they're convinced they can survive anything, including the rigors of a Kalamazoo education. Back on campus, they start to explore possible majors and begin to fulfill distribution requirements, which include courses in the major academic divisions—as well as art and physical education—and proficiency in a foreign language.

Sophomores select a career area they'd like to know more about and use their spring quarter for a career-development internship in that field. Then they are back on campus for the summer, preparing for two junior year terms abroad in any of thirty-two countries—for the regular tuition price. The final year brings the senior independent project, pursued in either fall or winter term and sometimes both. This can be an internship, directed research, an art project, or a traditional thesis—anything that will cap off each student's education in some meaningful way. Kalamazoo also participates in the Great Lakes Colleges Association,* which provides additional plans and missions.

The K Plan's strength lies not only in the off-campus experience but also in its careful integration into the traditional liberal arts education. The synthesis is designed to guide students through academic and career planning and prepare them for real-life choices. The intensity of a Kalamazoo education doesn't let up once travel journals are shelved and jet lag subsides. The atmosphere inside the classroom is high-powered and competitive, and pressure is increased both by the short ten-week terms and eager pursuit of good grades.

The languages and physical sciences are exceptionally good, and students heap praise on the English and history departments. Interdisciplinary studies in public policy and international commerce are gaining in enrollments and recognition. The computer science major is still young, and the performing arts programs remain quite small. Most professors give students individual attention and are rewarded by some of Michigan's highest faculty salaries.

Formerly associated with the American Baptist Churches, Kalamazoo, founded in 1833, is the oldest college in Michigan. State residents comprise three-quarters of the student body, with midwestern public schools' top students and a sprinkling of easterners and foreign students accounting for the rest. Less than 5 percent are black or Hispanic, and the administration reports that 80 percent of graduates go on to professional or graduate school within five years of leaving Kalamazoo. The common characteristic these students see in themselves is independence accompanied by a willingness to experiment and take chances. "Students who have set their future in stone would probably be happier elsewhere," warns an economics major.

Kalamazoo awards about 225 generous merit scholarships, including competitive scholarships for students who win English writing, social science, science and math, music, art, foreign languages or drama contests. Kalamazoo's in-state students also benefit from Michigan's tuition-differential grants, worth $500 a year and available to all state residents enrolled in a private college. A special Kalamazoo endowment makes foreign study (including travel expenses) available to every student at the cost of regular on-campus tuition and fees.

With so many students off campus because of the K Plan (two to three hundred students each quarter), a certain instability pervades all activities, from athletics to student government. First-year students usually live in one of four predominantly freshman dorms, three coed and one all women. While the quarterly room draw may sound like a collegiate version of musical chairs, it seems to work, and upperclassmen can hold their rooms through squatters' rights. The large dorm rooms come in suites for six, two or one. There are no sororities or frats, but language houses offer a more community-oriented atmosphere that includes family-style dinners. The central dining hall's food is uninspired, but its decor should win some award for originality. The six "motif" rooms are all done up to fit a nationality—the English pub has wood panels and stained glass windows, the Oriental room cushions and knee-high tables.

The city of Kalamazoo, located in southwestern Michigan, is much appreciated for its restaurants, theaters and concerts, and is about two and a half hours from both Chicago and Detroit. The facilities and functions of other colleges in town are all open to Kalamazoo students, who particularly like the library and gym at large Western Michigan University, right across the street. For those who equate college with big-time varsity athletics, though, Kalamazoo will be a disappointment. Except for nationally prominent tennis, swimming, and soccer teams, sports are low-key.

Favorite social activities at Kalamazoo include the theme dance once a quarter, weekly beer blasts, movies and, weather permitting, picnics on Lake Michigan's beautiful beaches about thirty-five minutes away (especially advantageous for those who remain on campus for the summer quarter). Thursday night forum brings prominent speakers to campus to address students on current topics, and there are a wide range of issue-oriented clubs and organizations active on campus.

Kalamazoo is not the place for a high school senior who has already charted the next four years and beyond. "What you think you want will always be questioned here," says one woman approvingly. A unique alternative to the preprofessional grind, Kalamazoo's K Plan expands the liberal arts curriculum with challenges and explorations outside a standard academic setting.

University of Kansas

Lawrence, KS 66045

Location Small city	**Applicants** 9,037
Total Enrollment 25,820	**Accepted** 84%
Undergraduates 19,670	**Enrolled** 87%
Male/Female 55/45	**Academics** ★ ★ ★ ★
ACT V/M 21/21	**Social** 🐷 🐷 🐷 🐷
Financial Aid 20%	**Q of L** ● ● ● ●
Expense Pub $	**Admissions** (913)864-3911

More of the Midwest's best and brightest are turning down invitations to prominent eastern schools (yes, even Harvard) to attend this relatively inexpensive public institution in the middle of Kansas. Such students cite the excellent reputation, the low cost, the down-to-earth student body and of course, the basketball team—"We go crazy over the Hawks"—as big reasons for going to KU. They aren't necessarily attracted by particular courses of study because KU is a comprehensive institution, a cornbelt Berkeley (or wheatbelt, to be more exact).

About half of the undergraduate population is enrolled in the College of Liberal Arts and Sciences, which offers more than fifty majors. A new general education curriculum for this college stresses mathematics and English and requires courses in both Western and non-Western civilization (a proposed university-wide core curriculum is in the planning stages). Standouts are English, languages, chemistry and philosophy. Of the thirteen graduate and professional schools, those most noted for undergraduate programs are architecture and urban design, journalism and mass communications, allied health and engineering. (If you're wondering where the agriculture is, head over to Kansas State, the state's land-grant university.) There is no unanimous condemnation of any academic area at KU, although some of the undergraduate sciences and social sciences, like physics, computer science and psychology, don't have strong reputations. Political science suffers from an overabundance of majors, and a program entitled human development and family living, nicknamed "huddle fuddle," isn't too popular. "But nothing is all *that* weak," advises a senior, "you just have to choose your courses and faculty carefully—the grapevine helps."

Students pretty much regulate their own academic climate at KU. Several walk around in heavy clouds of self-imposed intensity, while others "seem never to study." With eighty endowed chairs, including five new ones in the humanities, the faculty includes numerous eminent professors "who enjoy talking about their own research, but also make an effort to assist students." There is a great range in class size—introductory chemistry takes the prize with nine hundred students—but occasionally you will find yourself in a room with fewer than twenty-nine other people. Numerous teaching assistants do their best to humanize the economy-size intro courses, and students can find ways of avoiding standing-room-only classes and gaining access to top professors. Options include independent study, the honors program (for those with good academic records and/or good board scores), or study abroad in one of thirty-one cities including Seoul, Leningrad, Warsaw, Jerusalem and Barcelona. Kansas provides several area study programs (supported by language instruction in more than twenty languages). The top-ranked Latin American, Spanish and Portuguese studies are three good examples. Undergraduates at KU may receive awards to work with faculty members in publishing papers and poetry. And students are pleased with their library system, which includes a well-equipped main library and two smaller science and engineering libraries. To be completed in the not-too-distant future is a $14-million library facility for science and technology.

The thousand-acre campus is set atop Mount Oread ridge—once a lookout point for pioneer wagon trains—and spreads out on rolling green hills overlooking valleys. Most students describe their surroundings as beautiful, although a few of the mixed modern and traditional buildings leave a great deal to be desired. "They are yellow limestone and some are just plain ugly," according to one observer. The real beauty of the campus lies in the landscape, and anyone with an untested regional prejudice against the midwestern countryside (no, it's not all flat and colorless) should visit Kansas in the fall to witness breathtaking foliage.

Two-thirds of the students are from Kansas, and most of the rest are fellow midwesterners (a lot are from Chicago). Five percent are foreign students lured, along with those from the outer fringes of the nation, by the solid academic program and reasonable nonresident tuition. "There are a lot of conservative students, but for Kansas, this is Red Square," says one chemical engineering student. "No particular group stands out," comments another student. "We've got everybody: homosexuals, minorities, foreigners and even sorority snobs."

Both coed and single-sex dorms are available, and both get overcrowded at the beginning of fall semester, so it is wise to apply early. Students with 2.5 GPAs can live in scholarship halls—"the best of all possible living situations"—where fifty men or women live in a cooperative-type arrangement. These scholars govern themselves regarding chores like cooking and cleaning, and in turn they enjoy an academic-style of fraternizing and reduced board rates. Greek fraternities and sororities are home to about 10 percent of the population. More than half the students (usually upperclassmen) live off campus in Lawrence apartments, which are considered expensive only by Kansas standards. Every dorm has a cafeteria, and the food varies from plain old bad to slightly above average, but nowhere is it "shockingly good." Most fraternities and sororities have their own cooks, and discriminating eaters should consider going Greek. Scholarship dormers claim their menu offers less variety than the cafeteria, but they do enjoy the "more home-cooked taste." In addition to offering housing benefits to top achievers, the university awards approximately seven hundred merit scholarships ranging from $100 to $2,000. Athletic awards are also abundant, with more than two hundred men and nearly one hundred women sharing a big bundle of bucks.

The picturesque campus is a delight for sturdy walkers but a trial for tenderfoots. The university's fine bus system is much appreciated, especially during the cold, windy winters. Lawrence is a quiet university town that is into things like chamber music and jazz, as well as bars and pizza parlors. The university supplements cultural offerings with plays and concerts. City slickers can trundle off to Topeka, the state capital, or to Kansas City, each less than an hour's drive. The KC airport makes for easy long-distance transportation, and the area is served by Amtrak.

The social side of Greek life is hardly overwhelming at the University of Kansas, but it does offer a tempting option for those who want a strong social network. Scholarship halls, dorms and other student groups also sponsor large campus parties and events. There is little boredom, with more than three hundred organized and not-so-organized extracurricular activities available, including movies, poetry readings, concerts by local or visiting performers, trips to the local watering holes—two of which are nonalcoholic—and don't forget Joe's runs (a traditional KU doughnut break at the nearby bakery). For outdoor enthusiasts, there are parks, wooded areas and large water-skiable lakes nearby. KU varsity teams—the only ones in the nation that carry the nickname Jayhawks—compete in the tough Big Eight Conference where the football team is frequently trampled, but the basketball is rarely beat. "KU is *very* attached to its basketball team," says a serious fan. Men's and women's swimming are also frequent champions, and KU women's basketball players have competed in the Olympics. Casual jocks head to the gymnasium where they can participate in a host of intramural sports.

KU's not perfect, but it's been winning the battle against mediocrity for years. This big public university can compete with more expensive eastern schools in a number of areas—excellent faculty, strength in a variety of disciplines and a shortage of campus parking. Yet it's also got some things that money just can't buy—intense school spirit, an all-accepting student body and hair-curling humidity. Perhaps that's why more midwesterners are happy to stay in Kansas—because there's no place like home.

Kent State University

Kent, OH 44242

Location Suburban	**Applicants** 6,950
Total Enrollment 20,830	**Accepted** 93%
Undergraduates 16,640	**Enrolled** 55%
Male/Female 45/55	**Academics** ★
SAT V/M 430/460	**Social** ☎ ☎ ☎
ACT 19	**Q of L** ● ● ●
Financial Aid 65%	**Admissions** (216)672-2444
Expense Pub $ $	

For sixty years Kent State University was a fairly obscure, competent public institution, quietly serving the population of northeastern Ohio. Then on May 4, 1970, four students were shot and killed during an antiwar protest, and suddenly a university whose academics would never merit national attention became the most widely publicized school in the country, the subject matter for a popular Neil Young song, and the symbol of a troubled period in American history. Although the tragedy will never be forgotten, today's Kent State students are more placid than their academic ancestors and more intent on getting an education and a lucrative job. In fact, most students admit they're tired of hearing about the shootings. "It was seventeen years ago. Let it go."

The present-day campus serenity permeates the small college town of Kent, which consists of little more than the university itself. The architecture on the campus changes from old brick colonial to modern high rise as you walk from end to end, but none of the man-made structures can compete with the beauty of the surrounding rural countryside. Broad, well-kept lawns provide ample running and hiding space for the famous black squirrels, who are celebrated members of the campus community and the honoraries of an annual daylong festival.

Most of the school's strongest programs are in professional fields. The admissions policy permits almost all Ohio high school graduates to enroll, but entrance to the better programs, like architecture, nursing, journalism, and arts, is more selective. A futuristic, translucent art building offers architecture students inspiration while they're on campus, and the school's architecture program in Florence, Italy, offers exposure to more classical modes of design. The Schools of Nursing, Speech Pathology and Audiology have strong undergraduate health majors, while two radio stations, a cable television station, and fully equipped studios greatly enhance the potential for hands-on experience in broadcast journalism. Many students heap praise upon the School of Fashion Design and Merchandising, which has also drawn raves from designers and professionals. Among the sciences, geology, aerospace technology, chemistry and physics are relatively solid.

Teacher training, the original program around which the school was founded, is still noted for its quality but not its enrollment figures. The department of social work has been eliminated, and the math department draws criticism from students. Other avoidables at Kent include the psychology and Romance language departments, which "wouldn't even hire their own graduates," according to one student.

Special educational resources include the Center for Peaceful Change, established in the wake of the shootings, and critical-language tutorials, which provide instruction in more than twenty foreign tongues. The Experimental College features offbeat classes in parapsychology and Zen meditation. Combined graduate and bachelor's degree programs are open to qualified students in all graduate fields, and Kent students are exposed to the world through the Center for NATO Studies, the World Music Center, and several study-abroad programs. A prestigious Honors College offers academically motivated students a more intensive educational experience and the scholarships to help pay for it.

An excellent twelve-story library, which includes a fine film-lending facility, provides study motivation. Entry level class sizes can exceed five hundred students, but after students learn their way around the red tape, they can usually carve out as much personalized attention as they want. Kent State makes a considerable financial commitment to highly creative and academically qualified students, by extending nearly 250 merit awards yearly worth $800 to $2,000. There are also nearly 200 athletic scholarships, and need-based aid is provided as long as the money holds out. Students come primarily from public schools in Ohio. "The majority come from middle-class families whose homes are not more than two hours from campus," according to one student. "We have some preppies, some punkers, some hippies, some Vogue and GQ types," says one student, and most seem to agree there's no one stereotype. Contrary to the radical school label Kent State drew after the 1970 incident, today's students tend to lean more to the right, if they lean at all. "Many students work part- or full-time and scrape to get funds to pay for school," contends a junior. "They are serious about getting good grades and getting the most for their money."

The university requires all first- and second-year students to live on campus. After that, you have to get your deposit in early to be guaranteed a room. With twelve coed and seventeen single-sex dorms, living arrangements are available in a variety of shapes and sizes—from an all-singles high rise to several special interest dorms—depending on the amount of money a student can or wants to pay. Some dorms are equipped with pool tables and bowling alleys. The home-style program allows students to decorate and furnish their rooms and residence hall lounges any way they want. A recent rise in enrollment has caused a housing crunch, but the town of Kent has plenty of rentable apartments and group houses to accommodate the pushed-out upperclassmen. Dining facilities on campus are nothing to celebrate, but they could be worse. At least there are a lot of options: Students can use their food coupons at the dining halls, snack bars, sit-down restaurants or on-campus grocery stores. Light eaters can sell them for cash to other students on the black market.

Kent State provides one of the country's biggest and best college bus systems, which makes getting around campus and the nearby area very convenient. Many local students head home on the weekends, but those who stay make sure the campus doesn't suffer from the loss. "We frequent bars frequently," one man sheepishly admits. Stepping out is not restricted to the end of the week, as Monday and Tuesday are bargain nights at several popular watering holes. A portion of Kent Staters join fraternities and sororities, but undergrads stress that you don't have to be Greek to have a social life. Students consider Kent State's rural location a big plus and enjoy the national parks and ski slopes nearby. They also find the hills on campus perfect for "traying" down on food trays "borrowed" from the cafeteria. Cleveland is only an hour's drive when a helping of big city culture is craved, and the Richfield Colosseum, less than an hour away, is a big cultural attraction.

Varsity sports are not too exciting at this school with a "notoriously poor football team," although winning men's basketball and men's and women's gymnastics teams have developed a following. Intramurals flourish here with everything offered from flag football to inner-tube water polo. There's a huge, new gymnasium with four basketball courts, built on the site of the 1970 shootings.

The administration's chosen therapy of determined silence regarding May 4 seems to have paid off, and certainly the rising tide of campus conservatism and student self-involvement has helped erase the memory. It's doubtful that anyone will forget the tragedy completely, but today's students bemoan the idea that "many outsiders only remember this school because of the 1970 shootings" because, as a senior explains, "Kent State is much more than what it was then."

Kenyon College

Gambier, OH 43022

Location Rural	**Applicants** 2,070
Total Enrollment 1,530	**Accepted** 60%
Undergraduates 1,530	**Enrolled** 35%
Male/Female 52/48	**Academics** ★★★★
SAT V/M 560/600	**Social** ☟☟☟
Financial Aid 31%	**Q of L** ●●●
Expense Pr $ $ $	**Admissions** (800)282-2459

Kenyon College was founded on the frontiers of Western civilization in 1824, a fact the administration is still trying to live down. Located in an Ohio village of two thousand, the college grumbles that it "must continually point out that culture and civilization don't end at the Pennsylvania border." Judging from the quality and geographical diversity of the student body, though, the message is coming through loud and clear. Kenyon compensates for its isolation and self-containment with a full complement of its own cultural offerings, a distinguished faculty, and a student body with interests that range far beyond the country roads and cornfields of the surrounding area.

Once students actually arrive at Kenyon's six-hundred-acre campus, they're usually hooked. Set on a wooded hillside with grand Gothic architecture and "a few gargoyles thrown in for effect," Kenyon's campus is as beautiful as they come. "Fall in Gambier is like fall in Heaven, I'm sure," marvels one student. Along with the physical beauty, Kenyon's tight sense of community sets the tone for a learning experience that one student describes as "liberal arts education in a pure form." The strongest programs are in the social sciences and humanities. This is the home of *The Kenyon Review,* a prestigious literary quarterly, and not coincidentally, the English department is exceptionally strong. About a third of the students are majors, and the department offers an exchange program with Exeter University in England. "The diversity within the department is exciting," one major cheers. "Each professor possesses a unique character that must be experienced."

Students also praise the religion, history, economics, psychology and philosophy departments, as well as the Integrated Program of Humane Studies, a three-year seminar sequence in the humanities that draws on all the above departments. Political science is said to be good, though conservative and very much oriented toward philosophy, and a new international studies program allows students to specialize in a particular area of the globe with classes in a number of departments. Studio art is strong, as is drama (ask Paul Newman). Students say math is a weak department, and the computer facilities, though improving, still have a way to go.

The hallmark of Kenyon's academic philosophy is an almost fanatical devotion to the liberal arts. "All innovations are considered with regard to their place in a liberal arts education," an administrator explains. The president recently ruffled the feathers of both students and faculty by backing a program to integrate somewhat radical feminist perspectives into the curriculum, which many saw as an attempt to inflict left-wing politics on the entire campus. Vocational programs are also taboo; other than a 3-2 engineering program with several universities and a five-year joint masters in education with the Teacher's College of Columbia University, there are few if any vocational or professional programs. With a 99 percent acceptance rate to graduate programs of law and business and 92 percent for med school, Kenyon's emphasis on arts and sciences is clearly yielding some relevant results. All students must complete course work in the humanities, fine arts, social sciences and natural sciences. Kenyon is affiliated with the Episcopal church, but no religious study is required. An honors program is available, though standards for admission differ with the department.

Class size is not an issue at Kenyon, partly because the larger introductory courses use a two-part format, where students meet for lectures one week and split up for discussion classes with the professor the next. Only in the popular English department do students report trouble in getting the classes they want. Students say professors are very accessible—partly because they must all live within a ten-mile radius of the college. Once a week the president holds an open house. A new library funded by a $5.5-million grant by the Olin Foundation boasts an art gallery, forty computer terminals, and private carrels for honor students, as well as a sunny atrium where students can take a break from the grind. Another recent addition is the fully equipped $2-million Bolton Theater.

Despite broad geographical diversity, Kenyon students are almost universally upper-middle-class and white. (Blacks and Hispanics each account for a meager 1 percent of the student body.) Less than a third come from prep schools, but those who haven't can find out here what it was like. The homogeneous student body, incessant academic demands, and introverted community lead boarding-school grads to report that Kenyon is "four more years of the same thing." Kenyon prides itself on fostering a self-contained community, but after a year or two it tends to get claustrophobic. Kenyon students share an "East Coast WASP mentality," according to one man, who nevertheless adds, "the college is becoming more tolerant of untraditional groups—liberals, gays/lesbians, etc., but there is still work to be done." Political attitudes generally range from conservative to apathetic, though a restless minority of liberals—most notably a coed group called the "Peeps" that is supposedly a haven for '60s types—continue to press for change. Kenyon remains rife with traditions, the most hallowed of which is renewed each year as incoming freshmen sing college songs to the rest of the community from the steps of Rosse Hall, and departing seniors sing the same songs at graduation time.

Kenyon is need-blind in admissions and offers aid to the majority of students who demonstrate financial need. It also awards fifteen merit scholarships of $2,000 to $5,000 on the basis of test scores, academic achievement and leadership. There are no athletic scholarships. Freshmen occupy five dorms at the north end of the campus and move south to considerably less attractive housing the following September. Most dorms are coed, except for a few of the best—three beautiful old buildings reserved for the brothers of the nine fraternities. Largely because of the frat men, the south end is the campus party scene. Unaffiliated juniors and seniors tend to gravitate toward the college-owned apartment complex on the north end. Everyone, including those in the apartments with kitchens, must eat on the college meal plan. There are dining halls on each end of the campus, and the food has improved recently. There is always a vegetarian entree, as well as ice cream, soup of the day, and freshly popped popcorn. A quick bite can also be had at the three on-campus bars, which serve no liquor other than beer to those under twenty-one.

Kenyon's strong fraternity system draws about 55 percent of the male students, but fraternities provide constant social life for the entire student body, not just their members. Many students, however, purposely shun the Greeks, and some women view them as sexist. Gambier, a town that "looks like a Norman Rockwell painting," provides little of interest. A ten-minute walk in any direction will probably put you in the middle of a farm, but students say this has its advantages. "Kenyon's isolation serves as a catalyst for creative social activities," says one econ major. "We know we must entertain ourselves, so drama, music, film societies and other performing groups flourish." A shuttle bus provides daytime transportation to little Mount Vernon, four miles away, and there are two small ski areas nearby. Columbus and Ohio State University are a forty-five-minute drive to the south.

Traditionally sports-minded, Kenyon was instrumental in establishing the new North Coast Athletic Conference, which involves a number of academically strong midwestern schools. Kenyon swimming teams regularly win the Division III national championship, and lacrosse and men's rugby are popular. Clubs sponsor everything from Frisbee to fencing to water polo.

Kenyon takes the upper crust of the eastern seaboard and introduces it to rural Ohio. Few could take more than four years of the intense academics and introverted community, but many don't want less. The prescription for happiness is simple: "A student who enjoys isolation, farms, strong academics and familiar faces will love Kenyon."

Knox College

Galesburg, IL 61401

Location Small city
Total Enrollment 970
Undergraduates 970
Male/Female 53/47
SAT V/M 530/560
Financial Aid 75%
Expense Pr $ $

Applicants 760
Accepted 79%
Enrolled 45%
Academics ★ ★ ★
Social 🛋 🛋 🛋
Q of L ● ● ●
Admissions (800)255-2255

In 1837, the Reverend George Washington Gale, a Presbyterian minister, packed up his followers and headed west to found an educational institution embodying his utopian views of the spiritual value in manual labor. The result: Knox Manual Labor College, which educational historians like to think of as the original School of Hard Knox. While Gale's utopian vision has seemingly faded and the school's name has thankfully been shortened, vestiges of that pioneer spirit remain.

Located one mile closer to Chicago than St. Louis (166 and 167 miles respectively), the sixty-acre campus mixes modern buildings like the science-math complex with elegant nineteenth-century red-brick buildings like Old Main, a national historic landmark and the site of the fifth Lincoln–Douglas debate. Most buildings face into a large quadrangle, beautifully landscaped with flowering trees and shrubbery. The campus is fragrant in spring, colorful in fall, and even winter has its redeeming qualities, like the chance to slide down into the Knox Bowl on trays from the cafeteria.

In the spirit of cooperation, students, faculty and administrators make decisions about everything from the curriculum to the college's mission, serving on boards together with equal voting power. Exposure to the traditional liberal arts begins with freshman "preceptorials," two mandatory terms of study in seminars that teach students to question givens and probe the meaning of existence. All students must also complete "rock hard" core requirements, including courses in a foreign language, mathematics and the sciences. Strong departments include political science, modern languages, chemistry, biology and English, particularly the writing courses. Poets may find inspiration in the fact that Galesburg is the birthplace of Carl Sandburg. Also, *Catch,* the school's literary journal, has won several national awards. Students give low grades to the departments of fine arts, geology and psychology.

Knox operates on an honor system, illustrating the trust between students and administration. "Typically, a teacher will hand out a test and students will go to their favorite test-taking spot to work on it," explains a chem major. Faculty-student relations are "casual and cordial," and while professors do publish, their main commitment is to teaching. Many classes are limited to ten to fifteen students, and even a large class has only about sixty students. The academic climate is highly demanding without being high pressure. The trimester system packs a great deal of information and studying into a short time period but "faculty try to tame the amount of studying required by creating a more casual and understanding atmosphere," reports a senior. Competition among students is far from cutthroat.

An early identification program selects five Knox freshmen to be admitted automatically to Rush Medical College four years later if they maintain a four-year B average. Knox also offers 3-2 or 3-4 programs in engineering, business, nursing, medical technology, law and architecture, and runs several domestic and international off-campus programs, such as Newberry Library programs in the humanities. The two general libraries are equipped both with Macintosh microcomputers and terminals hooked up to Knox's two large computer systems.

Students are mostly from the Midwest, especially the St. Louis and Chicago areas; 8 percent come from a wide variety of foreign countries. Knox maintains a balance of liberals and conservatives, with perhaps a slight leaning toward the left. "Those looking for a spouse, or those who are used to a very chic and jet-setting life-style would be happier somewhere else," states a political science major. Most students went to public high schools and half managed to graduate in the top fifth of their class. About one hundred scholarships of up to $3,500 are awarded regardless of need, on the basis of academic merit and talent in the arts.

Housing is superb on the Knox campus. Students live in groups of eight to sixteen organized around a common living area and bathroom. With maid service three times a week, the suites are "extremely well kept, despite the plastic furniture." Coed living arrangements are available; freshmen must live in single-sex suites with one or two upperclass residential advisers. Older students may band together friends or form a special interest suite. The five fraternities are residential, although the three sororities are not. Permission to live off campus is rarely given, and, luckily for those thus stuck on campus, food in the dining hall is reasonably good, with the salad bar worth checking out even if you don't have a pet rabbit.

Galesburg is variously described as "an oasis in the middle of the world's biggest cornfield" and "a northern town with a southern (country) feel." At one time, this city of about thirty-five thousand was a center of abolitionism, and the honorary degree that it bestowed on presidential candidate Abraham Lincoln was his first formal degree. It's filled with beautiful, old, slightly run-down mansions, and there are also movie theaters, a shopping mall, and restaurants. Nearby Lake Storey offers boating, waterslides, miniature golf and nature trails, and if things still get boring, students can travel twenty miles and see what it's like to "play in Peoria." Chicago is three and a half hours away.

For obvious reasons, campus activities are the focus of Knox social life, and students are creatively self-sufficient. There is always a dance or fraternity party to attend, although one non-Greek claims that "the Greek system isn't necessary for a good, healthy social life." The Union Board Committee sponsors concerts, shows, and theme nights, and the award-winning Knox/Galesburg Symphony plays once a term. However, according to one premed, "people who don't enjoy drinking beer can sometimes still be left with little to do on weekends." And don't expect to have a lot of privacy on this tiny campus; the grapevine is "absolutely incredible at disseminating information." Sports generate a reasonable degree of enthusiasm, and participation is open to all who are interested. Soccer, tennis and baseball do particularly well. For potential DJs and music enthusiasts, Knox boasts a thousand-watt radio station, rare for a school its size.

Knox provides a lively and supportive atmosphere in which to try your wings. "It's like going to a school that is run by your friends," says one sophomore. Guided by three paradoxical principles—shared learning yet independent thought, rigorous academics within a laid-back atmosphere, and collaboration amid emphasis on individualism—Knox College serves up four friendly years that just might be at the end of your rainbow.

Lafayette College

Easton, PA 18042

Location City outskirts
Total Enrollment 2,030
Undergraduates 2,030
Male/Female 60/40
SAT V/M 560/640
Financial Aid 32%
Expense Pr $ $ $

Applicants 4,670
Accepted 37%
Enrolled 30%
Academics ★ ★ ★
Social ☎ ☎ ☎ ☎ ☎
Q of L ● ● ●
Admissions (215)250-5100

Over a hundred years ago, Lafayette added engineering to its liberal arts curriculum, a combination that continues to win praise despite the high pressure climate it generates. Over fifty years ago, Lafayette's fraternities added a heavy schedule of partying to the social curriculum, another combination that undergrads receive with enthusiasm. If you're ready for a twenty-four-hour campus where involvement in academics and extracurriculars are both top priority, Lafayette may be ready for you.

Its architecture is a combination of "French Renaissance and American inventiveness." The well-landscaped Lafayette campus is located on a hilltop above the Delaware River near a section of Easton full of parks and old houses. The school has won considerable respect for its technical and science program, and all six engineering departments are among the top offerings in the school. The one-third of students who elect engineering have their choice of the traditional BS degree or a BA—the latter perfect for carving out a career in the managerial or marketing sector of the engineering field. Biology and chemistry are also highly praised, and economics recently got a new building courtesy of well-known alumnus William Simon. Professional schools look with favor on Lafayette graduates; acceptance rates at medical and business schools run an impressive 90 and 100 percent respectively. Students say the government and law department is hurt by internal squabbling, but law school applicants show no sign of wear and tear: 94 percent get accepted. Traditionally weak in the fine and performing arts, Lafayette recently built the Morris R. Williams Center for the Arts in an attempt to add an artsy touch to a campus overrun by culturally backward engineers. Though the facility itself is top-notch, the arts departments are still weak and attract only a handful of majors. A new computer science department, with three faculty members, is just getting off the ground.

Lafayette strives to preserve flexibility in its liberal arts, requiring students to achieve "educational goals" that include understanding of symbolic reasoning, appreciation of artistic expression and knowledge of a foreign culture. To meet each goal, students must take two approved courses, and the whole program is capped by an interdisciplinary senior colloquium called An Approach to Synthesis. Students at Lafayette enjoy close and frequent interaction with professors, especially those in the McKelvy Scholars program, which houses selected honor students in a living-learning atmosphere. Independent studies are available, and students can apply for summer research grants that come with a free dorm room. While Lafayette sponsors no long-term study-abroad programs (you go through other schools), shorter doses of the exotic are available through faculty-led trips during the four-week January break. The main library, currently being renovated and expanded, is adequate to most needs, though many students wish it were open past midnight.

Along with the attempt to broaden its cultural base, Lafayette is attempting to

323

increase its geographic diversity and become "national by 1999." As things stand now, Lafayette students are a homogeneous lot, the vast majority hailing from the Northeast. Says one man, "We are a group of conformists, which is not necessarily meant in a bad way. The oxford–Docksides combo is a necessity." Most come from thoroughly conventional suburban backgrounds, and have equally conventional aspirations. "Everyone is a yuppie having his four years of fun before he buys his three-piece suit and his BMW," says a senior computer science major. Lafayette's homogeneity does have its benefits. The student body forms a close, social community that prides itself on its friendliness, and even the admissions director suggests that "interpersonal relations should rank highly" among the interests of Lafayette applicants. Another necessity is top high school grades. Eighty percent of Lafayette students come from the top fifth of their class. The academic atmosphere is intense, especially for engineers, but far from intellectual. Many people work incredibly hard, but it is considered uncool to let it show.

Seven percent of the student body is black or Hispanic, and there is a Black Cultural Center with attached living facilities. There are no academic or athletic merit scholarships at Lafayette, but there is HELP (Higher Education Loans to Parents). Through this program, families whose available resources do not exceed Lafayette's costs by $5,000 can borrow up to $3,000 a year at favorable interest rates. While the student is at Lafayette, the college picks up the interest payments, and family repayment of interest and principal, spread over eight years, begins only after the student leaves the college.

Lafayette shares responsibility for housing and feeding the student body with numerous "self-governing social houses." These include the ever-popular Greek houses as well as independent social dormitories and college-owned apartments that offer a variety of living and eating arrangements. Freshmen are assigned to single-sex or coed college dorms (South, the biggest and most central, is a favorite) where doubles or triples are the rule until senior year. They eat together in an elegant college cafeteria that boasts carpeting, chandeliers and tablecloths. After their freshman year, most students, including women and unaffiliated males, join meal plans at fraternities or the social dorms. Recently, the lack of a campus meal plan for upperclassmen has become an issue on campus, and there is talk of building a new student center that would include a dining alternative for upperclassmen. Excluding the various house dwellers, about 6 percent of the students move off campus.

Three-quarters of the upperclassmen and half of their female counterparts join one of the sixteen fraternities and five sororities, although they do not necessarily live there. Four frats a week share the sponsorship of Wednesday and Thursday pub nights (leading to the oft-heard question, "Who's on tonight?"). A similar division of labor governs the wild weekend parties, which come replete with themes and dancing. Pennsylvania's drinking age, twenty-one, is generally ignored, and the Greeks welcome any and all comers on any night of the week, making for very easy relations between them and the rest of the community.

While everyone appears to enjoy their parties, some voice frustration with the lock fraternities have clamped on the social life. Until the proposed student center is completed, alternatives are likely to remain sparse, though a student coffeehouse does screen free movies on Wednesday nights, and bargain-basement culture can be had in the arts center. A smattering of nearby watering holes, along with a joint known as Campus Pizza, are the only places of interest in the immediate area. Easton holds little attraction for Lafayette's sophisticated suburbanites, but there are reportedly some good eats within a twenty-minute drive. Philadelphia and New York are an hour or two away. The school often sponsors discount trips to shows or exhibits.

The football team is known more for past than present glories, but the Lafayette–

Lehigh rivalry, extending into its second century, still inspires the biggest weekend of the fall. Men's basketball, men's and women's tennis and cross-country are strong, as are men's lacrosse and women's field hockey. For those not up to varsity level, there's an extensive intramural program, again frat dominated.

The premium placed on enthusiastic involvement and achievement in all aspects of college life makes Lafayette the right choice only for those with the requisite academic confidence and social energy. "Students who are not afraid of always being busy and always being challenged are perfect for this campus," says one undergrad. Another Lafayette fan provides a checklist of qualities for prospective Lafayette students: "If you can't handle informal class situations, competition in all areas of life (educational, social, athletic and personal) or hot, crowded fraternities where everyone is screaming and/or dancing, or if you study more than eight hours per day—take a look at Harvard or your local community college. We are *not* for you."

Lake Forest College

Lake Forest, IL 60045

Location Suburban	**Applicants** 1,120
Total Enrollment 1,190	**Accepted** 55%
Undergraduates 1,140	**Enrolled** 48%
Male/Female 50/50	**Academics** ★ ★ ★
SAT V/M 520/540	**Social** 🏠 🏠 🏠 🏠
Financial Aid 55%	**Q of L** ● ● ●
Expense Pr $ $ $	**Admissions** (312)234-3100

The well-groomed town of Lake Forest is an exclusive northern Chicago suburb with gracious homes, trimmed lawns and gardens, numerous expensive clothing stores and affluent citizens who like the idea of a college, but not necessarily the students who come with it. "Lake Forest is a small town which absolutely refuses to cater to the social needs of the college students—except for nice restaurants," says one Lake Forest College sophomore.

Yet with the Windy City only an hour train ride away and the beaches of Lake Michigan less than a mile from the densely wooded campus, Lake Forest collegians aren't complaining too much about their upper-class surroundings. In fact, the if-you-can't-beat-'em-join-'em motto appears to have infiltrated the student body. As one undergrad says, Lake Forest is a good school for cosmopolitan students—"It's sort of a training ground for yuppies."

Career-minded and inquisitive, Lake Forest students are pampered by flexible academic guidelines and large doses of individual attention. In the absence of any core requirements at the college, faculty advisers work with each student individually to plan a well-rounded series of courses. The Independent Scholar Program, which allows undergrads to create their own majors and cross-cut traditional disciplines, is a highly respected and valued program for students who seek more academic autonomy. Lake Forest also encourages academic exploration through a number of unusual interdisciplinary majors, including Humanistic Inquiry, Scientific Inquiry and Local and Regional Studies. With a twelve-to-one student/faculty ratio and a great deal of patience and understanding, LFC is able to custom fit its students with tailor-made degrees to suit personalities and potentials.

About 40 percent of the undergrads participate in the school's strong intern program. Unlike part-time internships at other schools, Lake Forest interns spend up to two terms working full-time in business, education, social and political activities and nonprofit agencies. A newly developed International Internship Program has placed students in several foreign organizations including The Municipal Museum of Madrid, the Spanish Parliament and ITT France.

It's difficult to find a consensus on what the school's best departments are, but art and art history received rave reviews from the artsy and straitlaced alike. The economics, English, history, political science and psychology departments have developed fan clubs among the students who define their majors within them. And, of course, premed students proclaim the credibility of Lake Forest's sciences—chemistry and biology in particular. The moral is, most standard liberal arts departments are strong here, except for music and theater. The administration plans to strengthen the teaching staff and build a new facility for the music department in the next two years; the theater program is to remain primarily an extracurricular activity. But students who don't like what's offered at Lake Forest can create their own classes, provided they find professors to teach them.

Even the academic calendar at Lake Forest is flexible. Courses in the spring semester can be taken in a fifteen-week block or split into two equal blocks, enabling students to take more in-depth study or internship programs in one of the shorter periods of time. Study abroad is available through the Associated Colleges of the Midwest.* Other special programs include a selective sophomore honors seminar, and options for juniors and seniors to complete special independent research projects.

The average freshman class size is twenty-three students, and as one undergrad says, "access to the faculty is above and beyond excellent." In keeping with the prevailing flexibility, student work loads vary. One senior describes the academic climate as "tough and getting tougher." A classmate adds, "It's high pressure for workaholics, but casual if you are here to grow in other ways—good or bad."

Presbyterian-founded Lake Forest prides itself on its interstate appeal. More than 55 percent of the students come from outside the Land of Lincoln, many from the East. Politically, "students are apathetic at best," a senior maintains. "And to say that LFC students are Republican is misleading; their parents are Republican." In another student's opinion, her peers have "very liberal morals and very conservative dress codes."

Minority students make up 9 percent of the population at Lake Forest and according to one undergrad, "they tend to fare the worst because they are few in numbers." Students say that the people who are happiest at Lake Forest are those who are well rounded, outgoing and able to handle a very close, intimate community where privacy is not easy to maintain. "You know everyone on campus and they know you, which can be a little overbearing at times," a senior responds.

The college offers no athletic or merit scholarships, but more than half the students receive some form of need-based aid. Few students have the megabucks to live off campus in Lake Forest, so nine out of ten spend fours years in the dorms, where, save for one all-female dorm, the housing is coed by floor or by quad unit. Freshmen are assigned rooms by the dean of students and upperclassmen fend for themselves by playing a lottery based on seniority. Students are not always satisfied with the small library, which aesthetically fits the petite campus but is unable to house enough material for the diverse, ever-changing areas of undergraduate research. Although Lake Forest takes part in a twenty-six-member interlibrary-loan program, students often wait three or more days to receive needed books. But the campus itself, with its mixture of century-old Gothic and modern glass structures, is storybook beautiful, and one can get away by walking to the magnificent lakefront. Everybody eats in a pleasant central dining hall (the social beehive of the campus) where unlimited helpings are served except on Wednesdays—steak and shrimp night.

Students may find the social life on campus less than exciting. There is a heavy movie schedule and when the weekend parties begin to bore, students head for downtown Chicago or north to Milwaukee. Interest in varsity athletics is hardly obligatory; the most popular sport is football but a few spectators follow the successful men's hockey, lacrosse and soccer teams, not to mention the powerhouse handball team that has won the national championship eleven times in the last thirteen years. A new women's varsity soccer team has been established to complement the strong women's volleyball and softball teams. Intramurals draw a high level of participation, although many extracurricular activities are drowning in apathy. "If you want to be president of a club, just show up for the first meeting," says a disgruntled sophomore. Fraternities and sororities Lake Forest–style are called "purpose units," and, students claim, serve the paradoxical dual purpose of providing the main social functions and fostering elitism. Subsequently, the small school has adopted a sophisticated social structure. "The student body 'cliques' up fast," observes one junior, "but most everyone can find a group." Everyone, that is, except those who want to "blow off four years listening to the Grateful Dead," he adds. "They should not *even* consider Lake Forest."

Although many students are more than generous with the time they allot to the social scene, one student warns, "If all you want to do is party, go to a big university—it's cheaper." This midwestern college, once an unabashed party school, has tightened its policies and turned its students on to learning and career goals through a combination of scheduling freedom, real world working experiences and exposure to those local restaurants.

Lawrence University

Appleton, WI 54912

Location Center city	**Applicants** 870
Total Enrollment 1,090	**Accepted** 81%
Undergraduates 1,090	**Enrolled** 41%
Male/Female 48/52	**Academics** ★ ★ ★
SAT V/M 540/570	**Social** ☎ ☎ ☎
Financial Aid 56%	**Q of L** ● ● ●
Expense Pr $ $	**Admissions** (414)735-6500

Lawrence University has a few public relations problems. The administration admits the school suffers from a lack of name recognition—"We are neither Saint nor Sarah—just Lawrence"—and there are many misperceptions about Appleton, "which is a thriving and dynamic small city." With these two strikes against it, this truly lovable little liberal arts institution doesn't always find it easy to attract prospective students. But then, Lawrence doesn't want just any prospects. As a philosophy major explains, "Students with vocational interests may be happier where they can restrict their studies to one particular area—an attitude to which Lawrence does not cater."

Back in 1847, before Wisconsin's statehood, the first permanent resident in Appleton arrived in a dugout canoe and selected a wooded bluff above the beautiful Fox River as the site for a university. The town and the school have grown up together. Today, Appleton has a population of sixty thousand. The pristine eighty-one-acre hilltop campus not far from the shores of mammoth Lake Winnebago is described as compact ("You can walk across it in ten minutes") but not really small. Lawrence has an "awkward, somewhat bizarre blend of styles," which range from nineteenth-century to modern architecture with no dominant theme. "Most of the new buildings look boxy," notes a senior, "but the campus is beautiful with foliage in the fall and spring, and there's plenty of snow in the winter."

The first students of Lawrence were German immigrants and native Indians. Lawrence was one of the first coeducational colleges in the country, and while there may not be many identifiable Germans and Indians left, students of both sexes with a genuine love for learning come to Lawrence because "Lawrence is nothing if not an advocate of the learning process of the liberal arts," explains a Russian major.

One of its strongest academic drawing cards is the conservatory of music, which adds texture to the campus life, in part because of its first-rate jazz group. It exists alongside the liberal arts college where history, government, English, economics, drama, Slavic studies, political science, physics and biology are consistently praised. But students say an interest in art, geology, education or sociology is not a good reason to come to Lawrence. Psychology has been in a state of flux, though, "in the recent past, this situation has improved considerably," according to a senior. To keep up with the times, the administration has established a program in public policy analysis, and "a well-balanced computer studies program supports and enhances teaching and learning in all divisions." Freshmen are required to take a two-term course focusing primarily (but not exclusively) on great works of the Western tradition. Other general education requirements involve exposure to foreign language, humanities, fine arts, social sciences, mathematics and laboratory sciences.

Students consider the faculty Lawrence's primary asset. "Lawrence profs are committed to teaching first, but they're also respected for research within their fields and being open to all students," contends an anthropology major. "It's not unusual to see them hanging out in the campus pub or playing racquetball with students." And nearly all faculty are credited with creating an excellent atmosphere in those "wonderfully small classrooms." Students report they have little or no trouble getting into necessary and desirable courses. Lawrence encourages its students to take internships or to study off campus, and more than half do. The college maintains its own London Study Center, the Slavic department offers a popular summer tour of Eastern Europe, and there's also a marine biology term in the Caribbean. Through the Associated Colleges of the Midwest students have access to a wide range of domestic and foreign study programs.

The student body at Lawrence is generally bright and well-off. (Lawrence's tuition is one of the highest in the Midwest.) One psych major insists, "We are not all rich snobs, as people seem to want to think we are. The rich are disproportionately represented, but there's plenty of poor kids too." Many come from Illinois, Minnesota and, of course, Wisconsin. While metropolitan areas are well represented, so is "traditional small-town America." Students are said to be "politically informed, but not politically active." Another student opinion contends that "Lawrence takes pride in its liberal approach to education, but both students and professors are more conservative than they like to admit." The administration has begun more active recruitment of minority students, who now make up about 5 percent of the total enrollment. No athletic scholarships are offered, but a number of students may receive merit scholarships if they are National Merit finalists, have superb musical talent or are Green Bay public schools graduates who show academic excellence.

Housing is fine, except for the types who prefer noninstitutional living. The few students granted permission to live off campus each year must come up with convincing reasons why they should. Everyone else lives in one of the seven dorms—two are resolutely for upperclassmen and the other five place freshmen in designated areas. All dorms are coed, either by room or by floor, and all have laundry facilities, kitchens, televisions and lounges. "Dorms are really comfortable and the people in each dorm tend to get really close," reports one woman. On-campus students have a choice of meal plans and eat in one of the two dining halls, where "the menu patterns become somewhat monotonous after a while," and the newly installed microwaves and soft ice cream machines are a welcome change of pace.

The alternative to dorm life is offered by the six fraternity houses. About a quarter of the campus population belongs to a fraternity or sorority, and although the frats are the center of the social scene, one student claims that "there is no pressure to go Greek at Lawrence." Other students view the situation differently: "The Greek system here detracts miserably from the feeling of camaraderie by dividing a small portion of the students into high school–like cliques." For relaxation students usually turn to the plentitude of campus movies and conservatory concerts. The long hard winters are warmed by the inevitable keg, and several students confirm that drinking is the favorite recreational activity. In autumn there's Saturday football, the only sport to which anyone pays much attention. But a new, well-equipped recreation center has added a bit of vim and vigor to intramural sports, which provide a necessary outlet for many winterized students—"A rousing game of broom ball is a good remedy for the winter blahs."

Students rarely leave campus, mainly because there's no place nearby to go. Appleton is two hours from Milwaukee and half an hour from Green Bay. Longer excursions to Chicago are less frequently taken. Those who stick around have to put up with what a biology major describes as "mysterious, Hitchcock-like mayflies (unique to Lawrence), which invade the campus every spring." But spring at Lawrence is worth all the fly swatting in the world if only for the annual festival, Celebrate, which is most popular with the students.

Lawrence may be little, and its small-town surroundings may have condemned it to a certain degree of academic obscurity, but there are distinct advantages to this school. Students genuinely adore LU's friendly community and its liberal arts bent, which, in the words of one student, "blunt the edge of a competitive 'hurry-up-tomorrow' world and give students as many different perspective on life as they are willing to seek."

Lehigh University

Bethlehem, PA 18015

Location City outskirts	**Applicants** 6,410
Total Enrollment 6,440	**Accepted** 60%
Undergraduates 4,480	**Enrolled** 29%
Male/Female 65/35	**Academics** ★ ★ ★ ★
SAT V/M 550/640	**Social** ☎ ☎ ☎ ☎
Financial Aid 32%	**Q of L** ● ●
Expense Pr $ $ $ $	**Admissions** (215)758-3100

Founded as a men's engineering school, Lehigh University has since opened its doors to business students, liberal arts students and women. The percentage of female students is creeping up, and efforts are being made to increase the options for social life. But at heart Lehigh still remains a male preserve—football, fraternities, beery froth and all—and the academic emphasis remains technical.

The Lehigh campus is stunning. Grand old oaks shade ivy-covered stone structures, with a few modern buildings here and there. All of this is tucked into the side of a mountain, though, so don't plan to use your bikes much. "It's so easy to get down to classes," warns a sophomore, "but so hard to get back up to the dorms." Lehigh's picturesque setting more than makes up for the bleak surroundings offered by Bethlehem, a town still dominated by the depressed steel industry.

The college of engineering and physical sciences garners close to half of the undergraduate enrollment; the rest is pretty evenly split between the other two colleges: arts and sciences and business and economics. Everyone agrees that the engineering and physical science departments are outstanding. Strengths in business administration include accounting, finance, economics and an interdisciplinary offering in management and technology. The college of arts and sciences is the weakest, though programs in international relations, government, religion studies, English, journalism and architecture are considered good. Students find the fine arts and foreign languages particularly weak.

The work load is heavy, especially in engineering and business, where a student describes the climate as "very competitive, very pressured, and very serious." A junior adds, "Lehigh is noted [for being] lenient on admittance, but it's a challenge to remain once you get in." Students heap kudos on their professors, who are "always available for extra help." Class size does not present much of a problem, and students claim to have no trouble getting into the courses they want or need.

Distribution and other requirements vary by academic area, with engineers the most limited in their choices. A variety of special degree options are offered: A combined BA/MD or BA/DDS can be achieved in six years through programs with several Pennsylvania medical schools; five-year arts/engineering and engineering/MBA programs are available; and multiple majors, internships and cooperative education arrangements are common. Students are encouraged to spend their summers obtaining field-related work experience (required for engineers the summer before their senior year). Lehigh also has a program for study in England and participates in a consortium for students who wish to study in France or Germany.

The two main libraries receive universally high marks from students, and the newer of the two is especially well equipped. As one student explains, "It contains a computerized card catalogue system that can be accessed by students who have personal computers in their dorm rooms." Coin-operated word processors are popular.

Although the academic offerings at Lehigh are diverse, the students aren't. About a third come from Pennsylvania, and most of the rest hail from other areas of the Northeast. Three-quarters are from public schools, with about the same percentage coming from the top fifth of their graduating class. Minorities make up only 6 percent of the undergraduates. Upper-middle-class conservatism is in the air, and strong career goals cut across all disciplines. According to a senior majoring in journalism, "Most Lehigh students are money conscious." Women have all but stopped complaining about being the second-class citizens as their percentage of the population creeps up. National Merit Scholars automatically receive at least $500 a year, more if their need is demonstrated. Athletes who demonstrate need are in line for hefty student grants courtesy of Lehigh's generous alumni.

Special interest housing, including language dorms, an international house, and a women's honors dorm, sets Lehigh apart from the typical institute of technology. Residential colleges, in which faculty, freshmen and upperclassmen reside together, are a recent (and popular) option. Freshmen are required to live on campus, and are usually placed in the older, less glamorous dorms. The majority of upperclassmen live in Greek houses or off campus. Coed dorms are segregated by section or room. The dining halls have been refurbished recently, and the food is considered above average.

Social life at Lehigh revolves around "the Hill," where the vast majority of the thirty-three fraternities are located. (The six sororities "play almost no role at all" in the social scene.) Few students leave campus on the weekends. Instead, Lehigh's reputation as a party school par excellence draws a hardy group of socializers from other area colleges. Partying begins on Thursday, which is pub night, and continues all weekend. According to a sophomore, "There is too much emphasis on beer and alcohol." A senior adds, "Fraternity parties can become monotonous every weekend." The student union, where comedians and rock bands often perform on Thursday and Friday nights, is one alternative.

Several college-oriented restaurants, bars and shops have opened in Bethlehem recently, but there is little else in the form of entertainment unless students take one-and-a-half to two-hour trips to Philadelphia or New York City. The Poconos and the Jersey shore, which offer ski slopes and beaches, are nearby. For those who are less mobile, the on-campus intramural program is very strong and highly competitive. Wrestling, football and basketball are the biggest men's varsity sports, and lacrosse, field hockey and tennis are the most popular for women.

Life at Lehigh seems to be summed up well by a student-adopted motto: "Work hard and play hard"—two goals that students seem to have little trouble achieving. And if they attack life after college with the same enthusiasm that they exhibit on this campus, Lehigh graduates seem certain to reach their career goals.

Lehman College, NY
—See CITY UNIVERSITY OF NEW YORK

Lewis and Clark College

Portland, OR 97219

Location Suburban
Total Enrollment 2,840
Undergraduates 1,630
Male/Female 47/53
SAT V/M 510/540
Financial Aid 53%
Expense Pr $ $ $

Applicants 1,710
Accepted 76%
Enrolled 36%
Academics ★ ★ ★
Social 🐿 🐿 🐿
Q of L ● ● ●
Admissions (503)293-2679

Appropriately enough, going places is the favored activity at Lewis and Clark College. This relatively young college, which moved to its present site on a hill overlooking Portland less than half a century ago, follows the example set by its two namesakes, explorers Meriwether Lewis and William Clark. Its students always seem to be setting off on expeditions—not only overland but overseas as well.

In the last twenty years, Lewis and Clark students have visited at least fifty-five countries, including Hungary, Indonesia, Kenya, Costa Rica, Japan and Israel. And what's really amazing is that the college picks up the tab for airfare, so the cost of participating in one of the ten annual overseas programs is minimal. As one student points out: "For about the same price you can either be taking classes in Portland or in the Soviet Union." About 60 percent of Lewis and Clark students take advantage of the programs, and some study in two or three countries. The international angle manifests itself in campus life as well. One woman estimates that forty different countries and about forty states are represented by the student body.

At home, Lewis and Clark students get a sound liberal arts education. The core curriculum and general education requirements have been redefined recently to include a three-course Inquiry sequence, as well as Perspectives courses in the humanities, social sciences, natural sciences and fine arts. In Basic Inquiry (a "frustrating and challenging," but mandatory class), freshmen are to take everything they have ever learned about authority—religious, scientific, art and civil—and question it. Not surprisingly, the bachelor of arts degree also has a foreign language requirement, as well as a math proficiency requirement. Departments considered outstanding are international affairs, business and administrative studies, chemistry, political science, history and communications. Courses in gender and gender issues are also popular. Less strong are the departments of physics, philosophy, sociology and computer science. The music program is currently "redefining itself" as a liberal arts major after years of offering a bachelor of music degree. Honors programs are available in selected majors, although not at the time of admission; 3-2 programs in engineering are also offered.

While the course work is challenging, very few majors can be characterized as high pressure, and students do not feel a great sense of competition. Class size averages around two dozen, and a class rarely has more than seventy students. Professors teach and grade their own courses, without TAs. One student says, "I feel very comfortable with most of my professors because I know them as people."

The campus is located on the fir-covered hill of an old estate, complete with elaborate gardens. Cement is almost nonexistent; instead, the roads are paved with brick or cobblestones. Newer structures, intermittently added among the traditional Tudor-style buildings, were designed to reflect Northwest Indian architecture. Lucky dorm residents have views of Mt. St. Helens, Mt. Hood, or the Portland skyline in the distance, and Oregon's breathtaking landscape makes putting up with the accompanying northwestern rain worth it. The relatively new library leaves something to be desired—resources and assistance can be limited, and the top floor is often too noisy to study—but there is an interlibrary-loan program, as well as access to surrounding libraries.

"Students vary in socioeconomic backgrounds as well as personality types: rockers, intellectuals, musicians, preppies and granolas," observes a political scientist. Seventy-six percent graduate from public high schools, and almost a third are in the top tenth of their class. In general, LC students are independent, outgoing, and interesting: "Snobs are almost nonexistent." In addition to regular financial aid packages, Lewis and Clark offers merit scholarships (from $500 to $2,500), based on talent and/or general academic excellence, to about 5 percent of the student body. No athletic scholarships are offered.

Of the eight dorms, seven are coed by room or floor, and one is entirely female. The dorms are comfortable, with ten to twenty residents on a floor, but most popular is the newly renovated Odell (nicknamed "Odell Hotel"). Rooms are assigned by the RAs based on forms filled out by the students. For freshmen and returning dorm residents, getting a room is no problem, but choosing to go off campus usually means staying off. Fields dining room (aka the "airplane hangar" because of its high ceilings and width) caters to students on one of two meal plans: fourteen or twenty meals per week. According to one sophomore, Fields has a real "social atmosphere—you can see everyone at meal time."

When not dining together, fun-seeking Lewis and Clark students rely primarily on a group known as Students Organized for Activities (SOFA), which sponsors parties, contests (like the Love Connection), study breaks, and talent shows. Movies are sometimes shown at the pool (forget the popcorn), and students enjoy the flicks while floating in inner tubes or on rafts. The two tiny fraternities occasionally sponsor parties, but they play a very small role in campus social life, and, as one woman discloses, "people like it that way—in fact, most wish there were no frats at all."

The immediate neighborhood is pleasant, affluent suburbia, which provides a sense of security, but few activities that interest college students. Downtown Portland, however, with its theaters, stores, restaurants, museums, zoo and open-air markets, is only fifteen minutes away on the Portland transit system. Mt. Hood skiing is but an hour away, the Oregon beach less than two hours, and the Williamette River, a mere five minutes. The College Outdoors program sponsors inexpensive trips, which include everything from mountain climbing to spelunking—no previous experience required. The school has excellent athletic facilities, including a jogging trail with exercise stations and a sauna, and the intramural program is extensive and well organized. While lacrosse is not a varsity sport, the team is one of the best on the West Coast; and women's soccer and volleyball teams, and men's baseball and basketball teams generate some excitement for at least a few weeks each year. Yet, according to one student, "The purpose of athletics at LC differs from larger schools, where the only goal is to win. LC athletics encourages participation—then competition."

Many students come to Lewis and Clark because of its tremendous overseas offerings. Once there, however, they find that the trip abroad is only part of the educational journey. Liberal arts courses, personalized attention and the freedom to think and explore for themselves instills in Lewis and Clark students an inquisitive nature and a thirst for new adventure that would do old Meriwether and William proud.

Louisiana State University

Baton Rouge, LA 70803

Location Urban	**Applicants** 7,000
Total Enrollment 27,700	**Accepted** 89%
Undergraduates 23,220	**Enrolled** 74%
Male/Female 52/48	**Academics** ★ ★
ACT V/M 20/18	**Social** 🏺 🏺 🏺 🏺
Financial Aid 59%	**Q of L** ● ● ●
Expense Pub $	**Admissions** (504)388-1175

New Orleans is known for its February Mardi Gras, but at Louisiana State University in Baton Rouge, life is a perennial Mardi Gras. Those hedonistic LSU students always seem to find something to celebrate—a football or basketball victory, the beginning of a new week, a Wednesday afternoon, whatever. Despite the administration's attempts at strengthening academic programs, raising admissions standards, and creating a more serious atmosphere, one student rather tactfully explains that "a lot of students at LSU just don't take their education seriously."

Maybe it's the abundance of azaleas, Japanese roses and other flowers that makes the atmosphere here so casual and relaxed. And there are plenty of lakes, ancient oak trees and Italian Renaissance buildings all around. Or maybe because this beautiful campus resides on a former plantation (sorority women live in mansions), the leisurely souls of past southern belles and gentlemen refuse to be laid to rest. Whatever it is, with 123 undergraduate programs that vary dramatically in quality and academic rigor, individual estimates of study time vary from five to thirty-five hours a week. Students in the schools of engineering, chemistry and physics can expect the heaviest work loads and, not coincidentally, the best educational payback. The two prestige departments are chemical and petroleum engineering, the latter featuring an interdisciplinary degree in petroleum land management. Students also give good marks to architecture and business. As one of the nation's thirteen sea-grant colleges, LSU's offerings in coastal studies and coastal ecology are notable. Within the sphere of liberal arts, geography is strong, as is the program in Latin American studies.

Education and journalism get frequent thumbs-down ratings from students, along with a few other humanities departments, but the administration admits there isn't a department in the school that couldn't use some improvement. In fact, they're gearing up a Quality Thrust program aimed at getting the school into the top thirty universities in the country. Cooperative education and study-abroad programs are available.

The honors program, limited to freshmen arriving with high ACT scores over 27, offers interdisciplinary work and special recitations within basic introductory courses. Another bonus: Honor students will be the only ones allowed into LSU's one coed dorm, which surprisingly, or then again perhaps not surprisingly, is the one with the quiet atmosphere.

Contact with faculty members is average for a large university: a talking head at a lectern facing as many as three hundred students for the first two years and more interaction later when classes shrink to from twenty to thirty students. "Honor students have an extreme advantage," says one honor scholar. "Our classes are much smaller and we have a much closer relationship with professors." Some faculty members' preoccupation with research can be annoying, and signing up for classes has turned to a nasty ritual. Most students warn that you don't always get what you want when you want it.

With good ol' southern hospitality, students insist that "just about anyone could fit in" at LSU, but in the end they do characterize themselves pretty much as politically conservative locals. One student took it a few steps further: "Lots of us are hicks, rednecks, Cajuns or Acadians. This is the deepest of the Deep South universities. Morality is very old-fashioned." One undergrad claims that "a lot of girls at LSU go to school to find a husband." Unfortunately, a small number of students have difficulty extending the region's famed graciousness to the fifteen hundred foreign students who often give stiff competition in the engineering school. "The only students who may feel discriminated against are the many foreign students from the Middle East who are not really accepted by the conservative collegians," says an education major.

LSU's open-admissions policy, which automatically invites Louisiana high school graduates to join the freshman class, will change as of fall 1988. The administration plans to set new criteria for in-state students, requiring them to pass a certain number of English, math, science and foreign language courses before being admitted to LSU. For the approximately two thousand students from out of state, grades and test scores are weighed equally. The university does not guarantee financial aid to all those in need and makes special provisions for "academically strong" students by arranging the package by starting with scholarships first. It also offers a generous number of non-need scholarships (ranging from $500 to $1,200) for National Merit Scholars who indicate LSU as their first choice. Athletes don't do badly either, with more than four hundred scholarships available to them for participation in nine men's and women's sports. Since football is king here, one student grumbles that athletes are coddled to the point where "the best (academic) counseling goes to the biggest asset—the athletes."

About one-quarter of LSU students pack themselves into the campus dorms. Freshmen have their own dorms, filled on a first-come, first-served basis. Sophomores who make the lottery cutoff move to the upperclass dorms and usually settle into one room for the remaining years. The dorms are mostly single sex with a variety of visiting hours, in general more liberal for the men's than the women's. Yet it's the men's dorms that tend to be less inviting—"Most male dorms are very dirty," comments a sophomore. But even when the dorm atmosphere is the pits, the mandatory meal plans that come with them are reported to be inexpensive and the food is categorized as either "wonderful" or "great."

LSU undergraduates are not known for spending a lot of time in their rooms anyway. Bending the elbow at local bars is probably the favorite extracurricular activity, followed by attendance at home football and basketball games. When the Tigers are on the road, the campus tends to empty out as students find their fun elsewhere, often amid the "divine decadence" of New Orleans. The way to assure a nonstop campus social life and a more formal dating scene is to join one of the numerous Greek organizations. "There is a big clash between Greeks and non-Greeks here," reports a broadcast journalism major. Fraternal members tend to think of themselves as campus leaders, but one student notes, "Non-Greeks are as proud of their status as the Greeks are." The student union also offers a wide variety of events, including movies, plays, concerts, fashion shows, lectures and banquets.

Nobody is going to make you spend your years at LSU shuttling between keg parties and the stadium, and if your interests run to academics, the university is competent to meet your needs. But for most who come here the temptation to party outweighs the temptation to study—much to the dismay of the administration. "There is always something going on," says a senior. "Some would argue that there is too much going on."

University of Louisville

Louisville, KY 40292

Location City outskirts	**Applicants** N/A
Total Enrollment 20,080	**Accepted** N/A
Undergraduates 15,440	**Enrolled** N/A
Male/Female 51/49	**Academics** ★ ★
ACT 18	**Social** ☎ ☎
Financial Aid 65%	**Q of L** ● ● ●
Expense Pub $ $	**Admissions** (502)588-6531

No one goes to the University of Louisville for the parties, because there just aren't that many. More than 90 percent of those enrolled commute to the "genteel, relaxed campus" for their classes and, of course, to watch their championship basketball team, the Louisville Cardinals, romp over another rival. But students looking for a highfalutin social life had better turn the page because at UL "the main interests are school, part-time jobs and BASKETBALL!"

Belknap, the school's main campus, is a mixture of sleek modern and old southern-style buildings. It sits five minutes from downtown in Old Louisville, an area that has undergone some recent renovation, although students report it remains a high-risk crime section of the city. There are five hospitals within two minutes of UL, which is appropriate for a university with a competitive nursing program, challenging premed offerings (complemented by good medical and dental schools) and a strong allied health department that renders degrees in medical technology, physical therapy and other health fields.

All in all, undergraduates have a choice of ten different schools, and recommended programs in other areas include justice administration, teacher education and commercial communications. Students at the prestigious Speed School of Engineering, which also offers degrees in computer technology, work even harder than premeds, consider themselves the campus elite and participate in a mandatory three-semester cooperative program which involves on-the-job training in the Louisville community. The School of Business, which resides in a new building, has integrated microcomputers into the curriculum and allows students to send homework via electronic mail.

The faculty is now developing a new general education program to replace current distribution requirements in English, history, humanities and social and natural sciences. Students can take advantage of the active department of theater arts, the national championship debate program, the somewhat "stuffy" music school or opt to study abroad in many European countries. The enlarged library is one of the biggest assets of the campus, and the education school's media center is said to be "first class." Louisville also happens to be one of the few universities in the country with its own planetarium.

Perhaps because the administration encourages research and publication, the faculty is often perceived as being distant and not overly interested in its students. "Some [professors] are absorbed in research, and some are absorbed in themselves," confides a senior. But there are intimate discussion courses (graded pass/fail) just for freshmen that are taught by full professors. Otherwise, classes can be huge, and a student may find himself without a seat in the larger lectures.

You don't have to be a whiz kid to get admitted to UL, because anyone with a Kentucky high school diploma may register in the Preparatory Division (and take advantage of remedial programs in mathematics and reading). Any high school senior can make a smoother transition to undergraduate life at the university by signing up for the educational-survival project and student orientation. These programs, run by the administration and upperclassmen, introduce students to college and campus life, provide special advising sessions both before and after school starts, and, as an extra bonus, permit participants to register early. Because so many of the university's students grew up in Louisville, the student body is fairly homogeneous. Minority representation is about 12 percent, but the majority is white, Christian and conservative. "It's basically an apathetic campus with only a few left-wing students" is how one junior sums it up. Many undergraduates took time off before college, so they are "slightly older than usual and a bit more committed." About 250 full athletic scholarships are handed out each year, along with 400 merit awards.

The dorms house only a fraction of UL's undergraduates, with out-of-staters getting first dibs on rooms, followed by Kentuckians outside of Louisville, and then Louisville residents. "Many in-state students would like to live on campus but can't get a room," complains a political science major, who adds that more dorms would help create more of a campus community. There are usually two students to a room with members of the opposite sex on separate floors. Once into university housing, students enjoy squatters' rights for the next three years. For those living at home or in their own apartment, an efficient transit system makes commuters' lives "bearable and affordable" by preventing them from having to fight for the few, coveted parking spaces. Both commuters and residents may join one of five meal plans.

School always lets out just before the Kentucky Derby (some things are just more important than classes), but even without Churchill Downs, Louisville would be more than a one-horse town. Ranked eighth in the country for best places to live, Louisville boasts an orchestra, theater, ballet and opera for culture cravers, and plenty of bars and discos for everyone else. For the few who stick around campus on weekends, the Red Barn provides daily entertainment ranging from live bands to first-run movies. A good portion of the campus residents (but less than 5 percent of all students) join fraternities or sororities, in which the social life is a bit more structured and school spirit more in evidence.

As for spectator sports, "basketball is a mania," one fan reports. "Students arrange class schedules around games." (The Cardinals were 1980 and 1986 NCAA champions and are becoming regular nesters in the final four.) Football is another popular sport—as long as the parties in the stands and on the tailgates are good. The extensive campus intramural program pits residents and commuters, Greeks, staff and faculty members in fierce competition over everything from softball and balloon races to the popular Turtle Derby. "We have everything from turkey trots to tug-o-wars," testifies one woman. Then, for those who would rather get off campus for their exercise, there are a skating rink, several lakes and numerous golf courses nearby, and ski slopes—"very small ski slopes that is"—just a half hour away.

Louisville students tend to be hardworking, industrious and often too busy with their studies and jobs to be overly social. "The campus life is almost nonexistent," sighs a soon-to-be mechanical engineer. "Students get extracurricularly involved when and if their schedules permit." Yet most Louisville students do find the time to cheer on their much-loved basketball team and appreciate the educational opportunities afforded them right here in their old Kentucky home.

Loyola University

New Orleans, LA 70118

Location City outskirts
Total Enrollment 5,210
Undergraduates 3,750
Male/Female 46/54
SAT V/M 500/500
ACT 24
Financial Aid 43%
Expense Pr $

Applicants 3,890
Accepted 54%
Enrolled 39%
Academics ★ ★
Social ☜ ☜
Q of L ● ● ●
Admissions (504)865-3240

A small institution in New Orleans, Loyola University does its best to keep its students untainted by the city's many temptations. It offers progressive liberal arts and pre-professional programs within the Jesuit educational tradition that emphasizes religious and social values of the individual.

Loyola is the largest Catholic school in the South. Its attractive Gothic buildings and well-kept grounds are located in the historic uptown Garden district of New Orleans, "overlooking acres of Audubon Park and beyond that, the mighty Mississippi," notes a cheerful denizen. The university's nineteen-acre compact campus mixes Tudor-Gothic and modern structures and is nestled next to the larger campus of Tulane University. "Students and professors are often seen jogging together in Audubon Park," one student reports, and they get along famously in class as well.

Sixty undergrad degree programs are offered at Loyola. The college of business administration is a standout, as is the renowned school of music. The premed program is demanding and its grads have a 90 percent admission rate. "The new performing arts/communications complex makes us a national leader," comments a student, and in fact, communications majors at Loyola have some rare opportunities. The university owns and operates one of New Orleans' commercial television stations as well as an AM and FM radio station. Revenues from these operations provide subsidies to the tune of $2,000 per student. Social sciences and education are the least popular programs. A low student/faculty ratio means that help is readily available and "academic pressure is easier to deal with."

All students must take forty-eight hours of liberal arts and interdisciplinary work in the common curriculum, a program initially funded by the National Endowment for the Humanities. "A lot of the common curriculum classes are casual," says a computer science major, "but upper division classes are usually challenging." Nine of the required hours must be in religion. Loyola students benefit from the university's involvement in the New Orleans Consortium with cross-registration and library usage at Tulane, Xavier, the University of New Orleans and other schools. Foreign studies are centered in Rome and Mexico City. The school's honors program receives student praise as well. There's also a 3-2 liberal arts/engineering arrangement with Notre Dame, a thousand miles up the river.

Eighty-five percent of the student body comes from the South, the majority from Louisiana, Florida, Missouri, Texas and Alabama. Three-quarters are recruited from affiliated parochial and other private high schools, and as a group the students tend to be traditional and politically conservative. Nearly 20 percent are blacks and Hispanics. Religion has a significant influence on the tone of the campus, with about 70 percent of the students Roman Catholic, and 15 percent of the faculty members Jesuits. Daily mass is voluntary, and many attend regularly. In addition to need-based financial aid, Loyola makes thirty full-tuition academic grants yearly. There are also 150 merit scholarships, including some for minority students. A low-interest loan program is available for that part of tuition that is not covered by other forms of financial aid, with repayment over five years.

Most of the student body commutes from home or their own apartments. A third of the women and about 15 percent of the men live on campus in single-sex dormitories. The administration imposes a curfew for all first-semester freshmen, and intervisitation rules for dorms last all four years. Loyola recently purchased Dominican College down the block to ease space shortages. The university has no varsity sports (students are step-fans for Tulane); but there is a brand-new gym with racquetball, basketball and other facilities, and the "huge" intramural and outdoor program draws three thousand participants a year. There are several fraternities and sororities on campus (rarities at a Jesuit school), but only a small percentage of the students belong.

Situated on St. Charles Avenue, Loyola is only a streetcar ride away from the French Quarter of New Orleans, with its marvelous restaurants, jazz spots and other forms of nightlife. "The Mississippi River Levee, only a bike ride away, is a quiet spot to catch the sunset over the river after a busy day," a religious studies major reports. Weekends around campus tend to involve the campus pub, local bars and restaurants, and Mardi Gras is the high point of the social season. But the tone of the extracurricular life is, in general, subdued.

Loyola's atmosphere is that of a small liberal arts institution set squarely in the Jesuit tradition. Located in New Orleans—a catholic as well as a Catholic city—Loyola provides a well-rounded, value-centered education both on campus and off. "I look forward to carrying my classroom experience into the real world," says a philosophy major, "because, when it comes down to it, we're all in the same boat, and someone's got to have a decent paddle and a compass that works."

Macalester College

St. Paul, MN 55105

Location City outskirts	**Applicants** 1,690
Total Enrollment 1,770	**Accepted** 66%
Undergraduates 1,770	**Enrolled** 41%
Male/Female 53/47	**Academics** ★★★★
SAT V/M 590/610	**Social** 🐿🐿🐿
Financial Aid 63%	**Q of L** ●●●●
Expense Pr $ $	**Admissions** (612)696-6357

For a tiny midwestern college, Macalester manages to get itself a surprising amount of national publicity. Walter Mondale went here, and Hubert Humphrey taught here. The school's debate team continually does well in national competitions, and whenever a college bagpipe band shows up in a parade, it's probably Macalester's. The football team attracted national attention a few years ago when it ran up a fifty-game losing streak.

Macalester's football coach says he took the job because "I enjoy a challenge," and much the same spirit animates most everyone at Mac. With a range of options for designing one's own curriculum, Macalester turns its bright, energetic students loose to meet their own academic needs. The school emphasizes interdisciplinary majors, and many people major in two or three fields. Though Mac draws its share of driven academic types, many students view Mac as a congenial alternative to more intensely competitive northeastern liberal arts colleges. "We tend to catch a lot of transfer fallout from Ivy League and pseudo–Ivy League schools, which makes me think we are not so high pressure as other schools," says a senior.

Among the popular interdepartmental majors are urban studies, environmental studies, international relations and computer studies, as well as a wide variety of individually designed interdepartmental majors. For students who want to stick to one major field, history, biology and anthropology stand out, "and the economics department, even though it's right wing, is excellent," a student adds. Students also praise political science, physics, music, psychology and English, while education and performing arts are considered to be the weakest departments.

Despite its flexibility, a Mac education does come with a few requirements. Students must take at least two foundation courses in each of three areas—the social sciences, natural sciences and mathematics, and humanities and fine arts—and no more than twenty-four of the thirty-one courses required for graduation can be chosen from any one of the groups. Optional but recommended is Mac's series of freshman seminars, which explore issues like The Life of the Mind and Humans and Their Language. Professors make teaching a priority and are more than willing to spend time with students outside the classroom. Undergraduates often assist their professors on research projects, and since a number of faculty play intramural sports, students may even find professors giving them some assists when basketball season rolls around. Mac boasts impressive facilities for a school its size, including an observatory, a particle accelerator, two electron microscopes, a nuclear physics lab, and computer-mapping equipment. Only the library draws complaints, and while a new one is under construction, students make frequent forays to the libraries of Minneapolis/St. Paul and the University of Minnesota. A required interim term in January offers students a chance to try everything from visiting East European capitals to tracking deer and moose in northern Minnesota, as well as opportunities for internships and study abroad.

Macalester prides itself on its international focus. Almost 10 percent of its denizens come from overseas, representing about sixty countries, so if you're interested in making contacts in Nepal or Bangladesh, this is the place. More students than not do at least some of their studying abroad, either through Mac's own programs or through the Associated Colleges of the Midwest.* The chairman of the geology department even led a student trip to Antarctica. Undergraduates may cross-register with four other St. Paul colleges or enroll in cooperative degree programs in engineering, occupational therapy, nursing or architecture with larger midwestern schools.

Nearly a quarter of Macalester students come from the Twin Cities region, and all areas of the country are represented. The admissions office looks at much more than grades and often gives "high risk, high gain" candidates the benefit of the doubt. According to its president, Macalester welcomes students with "a heightened awareness of social, political, international, and ethical issues," and the school has traditionally been a haven for activists. Explains one student, "We are very much a 'free-speech' style community." Some students complain, however, that recent freshman classes are more conservative and less individualistic than in the past. Despite Mac's long-standing commitment to minority education, black and Hispanic enrollment has declined to less than 5 percent, generating unrest among many students. Though Mac's ability to attract minorities appears to be waning, applications are up overall, and median SAT scores have been steadily on the rise. Macalester is need-blind in admissions and meets each student's full financial need. A separate endowment funds merit scholarships of $500 to $3,000 that go to roughly a quarter of each entering class. National Merit Scholars qualify automatically.

Over two-thirds of Mac students live on campus, and a room is guaranteed to all who want one. Though generally well maintained, the dorms vary widely in quality. Juniors and seniors often luxuriate in posh suites with single bedrooms, while freshmen are generally assigned more cramped quarters. Fittingly for this colony of individualists, singles are plentiful. Many students live in various language houses, and members of the Hebrew House often prepare their own meals. Other students cope with the uninspiring food service, which offers several meal options, though many dorm residents "have a fridge and a hot pot and order a lot of pizzas to keep going."

Macalester has a self-contained campus with architecture ranging from ivy-covered Old Main to the modern chapel. "The grassy areas of the campus are slowly eroding into brick plazas, despite student protest," a history major complains. Located in an attractive residential neighborhood and adjacent to the "longest, best-preserved street of Victorian homes left in the U.S.," Macalester can easily be forgiven for boasting about its location. It's less than twenty minutes by reliable public transportation from not one but two major cities, Minneapolis and St. Paul, which have established themselves as major cultural centers in the Midwest. The euphoria may be tempered a bit when it's below zero outside, but southerners numbed by Minnesota winters can take a measure of comfort: The Mississippi River is only about a mile and half from the campus. Local restaurants range from Italian delis to Vietnamese.

Having no fraternities or sororities, Macalester's social scene is quite diverse. Small parties are popular, as are inexpensive campus movies. Trips to local bars or into the city proper are also frequent. At Macalester, prestige comes not to those who make touchdowns, but to those who toot their own horns well in debate or among other bagpipers. "We are not an athletically inclined school," one student sums up. The women's volleyball team regularly turns in strong seasons, and men's cross-country and women's track and field are also consistent winners. After a tremendous effort to build the once hapless football squad, it has finally achieved at least modest success. "We have a beautiful new swimming pool that may some day have a wonderful team to swim in it," a student reports. Meanwhile extensive intramurals set a tone of easygoing physical recreation in "everything from touch football to inner-tube water polo." Mac students typically have a high social consciousness, and many do volunteer work in community organizations.

At Macalester, one student claims, "we have a tradition of questioning without ridicule, of respecting even when we don't follow the same ideals." Prizing both individualism and tolerance, Macalester trains its students to accept others and at the same time actively pursue personal interests and beliefs.

University of Maine

Orono, ME 04469

Location Rural
Total Enrollment 10,960
Undergraduates 9,724
Male/Female 53/47
SAT V/M 470/520
Financial Aid 60%
Expense Pub $ $

Applicants 4,720
Accepted 63%
Enrolled 49%
Academics ★ ★
Social ☎ ☎ ☎ ☎
Q of L ● ● ●
Admissions (207)581-1561

Most of the students at this school in the woods love the wilderness in the state of Maine more than they love the academic state of mind. "I guess you could say we have a lot of outdoorsmen," notes a junior. Yet by building its reputation on several top-notch, outdoor-oriented courses of study such as forestry and marine life, the University of Maine at Orono is able to dish out an outdoor-style education that could capture the attention of Smokey the Bear himself.

Looking like a winter wonderland for much of the school year, UMO—the flagship school of the state's university system—resides on its own island between the Stillwater and Penobscot rivers. The architectural theme fluctuates from typically New England academic, with ivy-covered red-brick buildings and white clapboard houses, to modern structures "reflecting the smooth lines of the '80s." The campus is arranged in quads and encompasses a large grass mall area with a plentitude of trees (of course). UMO has seven undergraduate colleges on campus: engineering and science, education, life science and agriculture, arts and sciences, forest resources, business administration and Bangor Community College (a two-year technical school). Students apply to only one of these colleges, and transferring from one to another is difficult. Distribution requirements vary from college to college, though all students round off their education with a certain number of mandatory courses in the liberal arts and sciences.

UMO provides a comprehensive array of majors, many of which prepare students to go right into technical or professional jobs. One of the most demanding and highly competitive programs is engineering, which one student refers to as "the feather in UMO's cap." Those claim-to-fame programs—forest resources and wildlife, agriculture, marine science and pulp and paper technology—are predictably strong. And its neighbors to the near north would be happy to know that UMO has the largest Canadian studies program in the country. Business administration "is a tiny but accredited program" that is slowly growing, although there still aren't enough faculty to meet the student demand. Political science and history are offerings that stand out among the humanities. The performing arts are weak, but there is hope that the new Center for the Arts, with two museums and a concert hall, might move this wilderness-loving student body in a more artsy direction. Education, nursing and physical education also receive less than positive student reviews. Although the "academic climate depends on your major and your peers," according to one student, "UMO is becoming more academically oriented," in the opinion of an English major. The library, one of Maine's finest, is the regional depository for American and Canadian government documents and houses a number of alumnus Stephen King's papers.

Seventy freshmen with a minimum combined SAT score of 1200 are admitted to UMO's honors program, the oldest in the nation. Internships and co-op opportunities are available in virtually all fields, although they are particularly emphasized in engineering. Juniors who want a reprieve from the bitterly cold winters can head for Brazil, while heartier types may study abroad in Canada, Scandinavia and Ireland. Most students, however, are immune to the weather, since about three-fourths are from Maine and many of the rest hail from other parts of New England. The student body is almost entirely white and seems to have inherited a conservatively slanted political numbness. "Back in the '60s, while other campuses across the nation were protesting, here it was business as usual," reflects one student who adds that "today, the average student is politically lethargic." For the most part, UMO undergrads are friendly, rugged and down-to-earth.

The university offers 199 athletic scholarships each year in sports ranging from men's football and ice hockey to women's basketball and field hockey. The academically inclined can compete for 303 merit scholarships ranging from $200 to a full ride.

Almost half the students live off campus (either in Orono, nearby Bangor, or the sparsely populated area in between), partly to avoid the administration's stricter rules about alcohol in the dorms. But those who hang their hats in university housing find "some of the cleanest dorms in the nation," according to one denizen. Dorms are available in coed, single-sex and co-op models, and some even come with health clubs and computer terminals. About five hundred men live in the seventeen fraternities; the ten sororities have no housing. The dining halls in each residential area stay open continuously from 7 AM to 6 PM, and students with the unlimited meal plan can eat "pretty good" food all day long if they so desire.

Not surprisingly, UMO students take full advantage of the ski slopes at Sugarloaf, the hiking trails at Mount Katahdin and the beaches near Bar Harbor, depending on the time of year. The college town of Orono, eight miles south of the campus, offers a few bars, fast-food places and other hangouts, but it helps to have a car to get around. As one senior says, "There are no big cities to interfere with your work, but plenty of activities to relax you when your work is through." Bar Harbor and Portland aren't too far away, and Boston—the nearest "big city"—is great for weekends, but too far for day trips. On the sports scene, baseball is tops—UMO's team consistently competes in the College World Series—followed by hockey and men's and women's basketball and swimming. Intramurals, which cover a range of sports—from swimming and wrestling to hoop ball (golf with a basketball) and broomball—are popular, and competition between dorms is fierce.

Then there is the social life. As one student plainly states, "There is an incredible amount of partying that goes on," and apparently, it's the Greek party life that dominates. The University of Maine is definitely "a fun school," which helps keep students from feeling stranded in their rather remote setting. There are over 130 student organizations, including flying and scuba diving clubs. Concerts and dances are found every weekend on campus.

The main UMO prerequisite is a desire to learn both inside and outside the classroom, and that's the least you can expect from a state that puts VACATIONLAND on its license plates. But you don't have to be a Mainiac to go to school here because anyone willing to make the extra effort will get the education he or she wants. And for those whose idea of a good college education means more fun than studying, at the University of Maine, they won't feel alone.

Manhattanville College

Purchase, NY 10577

Location Suburban
Total Enrollment 1,300
Undergraduates 1,050
Male/Female 35/65
SAT V/M 530/530
Financial Aid 60%
Expense Pr $ $ $

Applicants 990
Accepted 65%
Enrolled 40%
Academics ★ ★ ★
Social ☎ ☎ ☎
Q of L ● ● ●
Admissions (914)694-2200

Much of Manhattanville College's claim to fame evolves around three of its most distinguished alums: a mother and her two daughters, or more specifically, Rose Fitzgerald Kennedy, Eunice Kennedy Shriver and Jean Kennedy Smith. This little liberal arts school in the suburbs of New York City (it's not in Manhattan anymore) was responsible for the formal education of three of the lady Gueneveres of Camelot. The ideals of the college have not changed over the years; it still offers a close-knit community and a caring atmosphere while attempting to arm students with "the ability to reach personal moral decisions and the courage to defend those convictions." Today's students find such goals all fine and dandy, but now that the college has gone coed the women here have other matters on their minds. In fact, the biggest complaint you'll hear these days is about the indisputable shortage of Sir Lancelots at "the Ville."

The earliest beginnings of Manhattanville College can be traced back to a humble Roman Catholic academy for girls on Houston Street in New York City. Not until 1917 did the school award bachelor's degrees. By 1952 the college had severed its ties with the Catholic Church, pulled up stakes in Manhattan and plopped itself down on a generous, 125-acre estate about twenty-five miles north of the city in affluent, white Westchester County. The Manhattanville campus is five minutes from White Plains and several major corporation headquarters (great internship hunting grounds) and but a half hour train ride from New York City. The focal point of the campus is the nineteenth-century Gothic castle, which is "the epitome of class and taste with its tremendous rooms, pink marble staircase, and antiques," explains an English literature major who is less impressed with the rest of the buildings—"semimodern and insignificant."

The most distinguishing feature of the Manhattanville curriculum is a portfolio system that allows students to shape their own degree programs, justify and reevaluate their decisions and present the product of their four years at Manhattanville to a six-member faculty committee during their final semester. "It's basically a package presentation of the student," explains a senior. To launch them into the portfolio plan, freshmen are assigned a faculty preceptor who serves as an adviser in preparing a tentative four-year study plan. After students develop their course of study, they compose a rationale, or essay, explaining why they chose their major and second and third areas of study. By the end of their senior year, students' portfolios should contain their study plans, rationale, transcript of satisfactorally completed course work in all areas and annual written evaluations (the student's personal reflections on the strengths and weaknesses of the work accomplished). All undergraduates must complete courses in the humanities, social sciences, performing arts, math and sciences and languages.

Students who are interested in studying psychology, economics, English, political science, music or computer science will be pleased with the offerings at Manhattanville.

The art and art history departments have widely recognized faculty and accessibility to New York's museums for auxiliary instruction. The administration admits that the foreign language departments need to be expanded, and the natural sciences lack depth and laboratory equipment for individual research. Students turn their noses up at much that the religion and management departments have to offer and claim that the communications and journalism programs need to be expanded. For those seeking the most challenging of Manhattanville experiences, there's the two-part honors program: The honors seminar is a freshman course that allows close faculty-student interaction and includes trips to major cultural centers in NYC, and the honors major, reserved for students with a B-plus average and proficiency in at least one foreign language. The college offers student exchange programs with American University and Mills College plus trips abroad to Tokyo, Crete, Oxford and Bath. Special 3-2 programs in engineering with Clarkson University and nursing with Columbia University are popular. The campus library, with its 250,000 volumes, is rated as "adequate for a school this size but not superior," and any necessary material can be obtained through an extensive interlibrary-loan system.

"Most students here are white, Irish-Catholics from upper-middle-class and wealthy families," explains a sophomore. About 55 percent come from the state of New York; many of the rest are from elsewhere in the Northeast, and 12 percent arrive from foreign countries. Half the students attended public schools, and half come from the top fifth of their high school class. "There are some 'pre-weds' girls here," points out one student, but with the women outnumbering men two to one, many a Manhattanville female is intensely career oriented. Student accounts say that a few funky types can be found on campus, but a sophomore biology major believes that "99 percent of the students are conservative Republicans, and the percentage will stay that way." A classmate adds that "most students are politically conservative, but very liberal in social views—a strange, but pleasant combination." Those seeking financial aid compensation for athletic endeavors had best look beyond Manhattanville. The college does dole out a handful of merit scholarships, worth $2,000 to $4,200, for students who have demonstrated excellent leadership abilities or who graduated in the top fifth of their class and have a composite SAT of 1100.

While 14 percent of Manhattanvillers are commuters, almost all of the rest live in one of four dorms. One floor in the freshman dorm is all women, but other floors on campus alternate sexes by room or suite. Freshmen are assigned rooms while upperclassmen enter into the lottery. "All rooms are well maintained, but sometimes the hot water and heating systems fail," explains a psych major. For those who live on campus, there are two meal plans of fifteen or nineteen meals a week, and students can use their meal cards at Café di Ville, a deli-type facility. An on-campus pizzeria stays open late on weekends. There are two dining halls, which students claim are clean and well kept. "The salad bar, baked goods and fresh-baked desserts are the strong points," says one expert.

"Social life is limited, but it can be found," reports a history major. Many students go home on the weekends, and there are no fraternities or sororities. The student programming board works hard to improve the social life by organizing school-sponsored dinners, formals in the castle, parties, comedy and talent shows, plays, concerts and films. Students, however, rely mostly on private parties that are open to everyone. Since the New York drinking age went up to twenty-one, most of the good parties are the illegal ones in the dormitories: "They usually occur in suites, but the hall parties are extremely wild and crowded," divulges a sophomore. Rye Beach is not too far from campus, and heading north for skiing is a popular pastime. During the week, the restaurants and shopping malls in White Plains suffice, but weekends are reserved for "the City." Many take the train into Manhattan to see plays or try to get into nightclubs.

The strongest varsity teams are men's baseball, basketball, and lacrosse and women's field hockey, soccer, swimming and volleyball. "Students have a great time at the games and attendance is high, especially at men's games," claims one fan. Yet, because of the majority of women on campus, female athletics are "far superior to men's." Some students whine that the intramural program suffers greatly from lack of organization, others say the situation is getting better. The creation of a fall field festival helps spur interest in first-of-the-year games. Extracurricular activities abound with clubs for every interest from karate to Latin awareness.

"An archetypal Manhattanville student must be unique and open-minded," explains a sophomore international studies major. "He or she cannot be the kind of person who wants to be behind the scenes." Maybe not all of Manhattanville alums will make a name for themselves the way those Kennedy ladies did, but most will go out of their way to make themselves known to all who grace their campus. And hopefully, according to one restless female, more males will be gracing "the Ville" soon.

Marlboro College

Marlboro, VT 05344

Location Rural	**Applicants** 146
Total Enrollment 180	**Accepted** 94%
Undergraduates 180	**Enrolled** 50%
Male/Female 40/60	**Academics** ★ ★ ★
SAT V/M N/A	**Social** ☎ ☎ ☎
Financial Aid 65%	**Q of L** ● ● ● ●
Expense Pr $ $ $	**Admissions** (800)343-0049

Not long ago, the esteemed Harvard sociologist David Riesman marveled that Marlboro College "is still there when by all the laws of demographics, economics and good sense, it shouldn't be there." Undaunted by mass-market, preprofessional trends in higher education, Marlboro remains firmly committed to its highly individualized approach to the liberal arts.

Founded just after WWII atop a small mountain with a gorgeous view in southern Vermont, Marlboro College certainly has physical beauty on its side. An old barn renovated by returned GIs once contained the whole college, but today a cluster of modern and New England farmhouse-style buildings, many with passive solar heating, sit proudly in the middle of the 350-acre campus. Just as, in the words of one student, "the whiteness of its buildings brings forth the true blueness of the sky," the highly individualized Marlboro Plan of Concentration brings forth the true curiosity and talents of its eager group of learners.

Marlboro students must pass a clear writing requirement by the end of their freshman year. After that hurdle, they don't even take courses, in the traditional sense. The cornerstone of a Marlboro education is the Plan of Concentration, which is developed independently by each student. Juniors and seniors "on plan" take most course work in one-on-one tutorials with the faculty sponsors. Seniors present their thesis or project to their faculty sponsors backed up by outside examiners. Marlboro's flexibility should not be confused with academic flabbiness. Grades are an integral part of the evaluation process, professors are stingy with A's, and most students work hard. Self-motivation is a must, although it doesn't always come easy at first. "After learning to write for teachers in high school, I am finally learning to work for myself," a literature student says. Academic pressure is high, but not in the usual way. "There is an inordinate sense of community, and everyone is expected to carry their work load," explains one student. "It's pretty obvious you haven't read the assignment when there's an hour-long discussion with only two other people in the class."

Luckily, procrastination is not much of a temptation since there is little to do atop the mountain in evenings but curl up in front of one of the nonworking fireplaces in Marlboro's library and study. The library is operated on the honor system where students sign out their own books twenty-four hours a day. Ditto for the computer center, which is tiny but probably has more computers per student than MIT.

As for the academic offerings themselves, the limitations lie not with quality but quantity. Marlboro offers good instruction in literature, history and languages (including Latin and Greek). Natural sciences have recently become quite popular, although facilities are lacking. Art students, however, now enjoy a new studio facility. Because each subject is taught by only one or two professors, a personality conflict may mean problems with a whole department. Students point out, though, that since they are free to pursue their intellectual interests wherever they may lead, smallness should not be confused with lack of variety. A new global studies program in conjunction with the School for International Training can provide an eight-month professional internship and/or study experience abroad. A rare attraction is Morris dancing, a colorful variation on the polka in which teams of dancers dress up in brightly colored medieval costumes with specially tuned bells attached below each knee: It is both an object of study and regular form of evening recreation.

Completely run by a New England town meeting–style government that involves the whole student body and faculty in every aspect of policymaking, Marlboro is, in the words of a history student, "as democratic as any college can be." Students can veto the faculty members on hiring and retention decisions, and it takes a two-thirds vote of the faculty to override them. As in ancient Athens, however, pure democracy can have its problems. Once the town meeting voted to bar smoking in the dining hall during meals. The debate had gone on for weeks, but the actual vote "required a keg to secure a quorum."

Marlboro's nearly two hundred students come mostly from middle-class suburban homes, and an administrator says that the school tends to attract not Ivy League types but their nonconformist siblings. In the 1960s and early 1970s the dominant tone of the college was communal and nonmaterialistic, but even Marlboro has been swept by today's prevailing conservative winds. One denizen notes that while hiking boots are still a necessity, "there are fewer vegetarians and no Indian print skirts and tie-dyed shirts in evidence." Another points to the presence of "four or five Saab Turbos" in the parking lot as a sign of the times. What Marlboro students do share, in addition to their independent spirit, is a distaste for "unnecessary pomposity" and a suspicion of "form-filling education." Many of these students (half from prep schools, half from public) find they can't even handle Marlboro's nonconformist stance, and about 60 percent of those who enroll as freshmen do not graduate. Whether they last or not, the college, which is need-blind in its admission policy, assembles a "workable" financial package for all those in need.

The dorms, mostly coed, are small (about fifteen students each), but rooms are large, and most upperclassmen have singles. Additional housing is available, and highly desired, in eight cottages about ten minutes on foot from campus. The off-campus community is relatively large but well integrated with campus life. Most live twenty minutes away in Brattleboro and shuttle to and from campus in a school van. Boarders gather for home-cooked meals in a converted barn, where the food is wholesome and plentiful but still provides "inherent excuses for leftovers." Students say the best meals tend to coincide with trustee meetings and parent weekends.

The town of Brattleboro offers drama, films, and restaurants and is a fascinating spot in itself—"a combination of local working-class, counterculture holdovers from the '60s and affluent patrons of the summer music festival." There is at least one organized activity on campus each weekend, as well as several spontaneous ones, and snowball fights by the library are serious business. "Marlboro College is the kind of place where on a Saturday night someone will bring music to the Student Center, and there will suddenly be a party," one man explains. However, if you are at all the restless sort, a car is advisable; cabin fever can hit badly at times.

An extensive program of coed sports for novices and experts—soccer, basketball, volleyball, hackeysack, hiking—helps students take advantage of the great outdoors at their doorstep. "Sports are student-arranged so they change yearly." Intercollegiate competition is for the most part limited to volleyball and soccer against other alternative colleges and to cross-country and downhill skiing, where Marlboro holds its own against Ivy competitors. Forty miles of cross-country ski trails radiate from the center campus, and excellent downhill slopes are a few minutes drive away.

The smallness of the college community is a mixed blessing. While students are supportive of anyone with a problem, "People know too much of other people's personal lives," warns one senior. The admissions director agrees that "for those who don't like themselves, life in a small community can be tough."

Marlboro provides an exciting alternative to typical colleges for students following a different tom-tom. The new president, who came to the woods after a quarter century as a *Newsweek* magazine editor, is determined to increase public awareness of what the school has to offer, and he has plenty of young ambassadors ready to help. "My education has been a creative, if often exhausting task," one senior reflects, "but overall, Marlboro has been wonderful for me."

Marquette University

Milwaukee, WI 53233

Location Urban	**Applicants** 5,960
Total Enrollment 11,800	**Accepted** 80%
Undergraduates 8,820	**Enrolled** 39%
Male/Female 52/48	**Academics** ★ ★ ★
SAT V/M 480/540	**Social** 🐻 🐻 🐻
Financial Aid 80%	**Q of L** ● ● ●
Expense Pr $	**Admissions** (414)224-7302

Few disagree that Marquette's basketball team is what put the school on the map. The chance to cheer for a national powerhouse—plus a reputation for having the highest number of bars per capita of any college in the country—has made Marquette attractive to some students. Others come because they know this Roman Catholic school continues to offer a fine education rooted in the Jesuit tradition.

Eighty acres of "concrete with interludes of grass and trees," Marquette's campus is located just a free throw away from the heart of downtown Milwaukee. Although most of the buildings are relatively modern, the Milwaukee campus is the site of the oldest building in the Western hemisphere, the St. Joan of Arc Chapel, which was built in France in 1400 and later transported to Wisconsin. Though the college is "not in the best part of town," students do appreciate the wealth of cultural events, close proximity of Lake Michigan and its beaches, bike trails, botanical gardens and three parks within walking distance.

Marquette has colleges of journalism, nursing, speech, engineering, arts and sciences and business administration, the last three being the best. Engineering grads are "snatched up in the job market," and several other colleges have modeled their nursing programs on Marquette's. The university has the only dental school in the state that offers undergraduates programs in dental hygiene and physical therapy. But the fine and performing arts departments fall short of students' expectations. Co-op programs are offered to students in journalism, speech, business and engineering. Everyone may take advantage of Marquette's own study-abroad options (France, Spain and Germany), and several programs are available through other universities. The school's system of three libraries is adequate for an institution of this size, and an interlibrary-loan program with other Milwaukee libraries makes up for any slack. A brand-new word-processing center in Memorial Library has proven so popular among students that it will probably need expansion.

Faculty members, expected to teach and do research, are reportedly concerned about students and "very flexible with their hours." Although courses can be rather large, students usually manage to get into the ones they want. An honors program is available for highly motivated students, while the Freshman Frontier program offers admission and intensive assistance to students "who did not reach full academic potential in high school."

The "Christian message" is considered an integral part of the school's education, and faculty members are expected to "teach, not to propagandize"; students are expected to develop "disciplined but independent patterns of thought." Every undergraduate program involves a carefully designed core curriculum including courses in the sciences, the social sciences and especially the humanities. The administration encourages students to "put our beliefs into practice" through volunteer activity, student religious organizations, and the dorms' weekly masses. Roman Catholics understandably predominate in the student body but religious practice is left to the individual.

Although the university actively recruits in twenty or so states, most of the student body is from the Midwest, half from Wisconsin itself. Despite the weighted regionalism, "Anyone who is outgoing will probably fit in," one student reports. In general, Marquette boasts a friendly collection of middle-class students who tend to like basketball and did well enough to graduate in the top half of their high school classes. Like their curriculum, Marquette students are vocationally oriented—more than three-quarters of them go straight into the job market on graduation. "Some of us want to set the world on fire," claims a mathematics student. "But most of us just want to make big bucks and drive BMWs." The university accepts students without regard to their financial need and assembles aid packages on a first-come, first-served basis. About 12 percent of the students—those who rank in the top 10 percent of their high school class and have combined SATs of 1100 or ACTs of 24—receive scholarships ranging from $500 to full tuition. Marquette also allots more than $260,000 for athletic scholarships—almost half of this for basketball, men's and women's.

The dorms are filled mostly with freshmen and sophomores for whom residency is required. Five of the eight houses are coed, and the rooms are comfortable if not spacious. Incoming students can pick which they would like to live in. By junior year, students are encouraged to move off campus, which they're usually anxious to do after two years of putting up with strict policies about bringing visitors of either sex into dorms. No one, however, not even a Milwaukee resident, is automatically forced out of the dorms. A student's meal card ensures entrance into any of the dorms' cafeterias, including hamburger and pizza specialty shops.

Wherever students live, they will get a pretty good taste of Milwaukee city life: crime, cold weather and pollution on the negative side, and good bars, restaurants and entertainment centers on the positive. Unfortunately for the beer capital of the country, the state's drinking age has just gone up to twenty-one, kindling a sudden interest in dorm parties and the Student Rec Center. There are fraternities and sororities, but their impact on student life is "minuscule," according to one senior. Fans will find that tickets to the Milwaukee Bucks and Brewers games are easier to come by than those for the school's basketball games. Nature lovers can head just outside the city limits to Lake Michigan or Kettle Moraine, a glaciated region ideal for hiking and cross-country skiing. Milwaukee itself, be warned, can get mighty cold in the winter.

An urban-renewal project spearheaded by Marquette has improved conditions in the so-so neighborhood near the school and has resulted in the addition of a theater, museum of art, and recreational gym that, as one student notes, "impresses the heck out of visitors." The gym, and its five basketball courts, is out of bounds to the Warriors, who have their own courts, but fair game for all in the school's fine intramural program. As the school grows, other varsity sports are gaining a higher profile after years of neglect, and men's and women's track, and men's soccer have turned in recent championship seasons.

Located just ninety miles from Chicago, "Marquette's star does not always shine as brightly as it should," an administrator laments. Nevertheless, school leaders can be credited for knowing it takes more than NCAA titles and a location in one of the nation's most livable cities to make a good university. Serious but spirited, Marquette students are all-Americans to the last.

University of Maryland

College Park, MD 20742

Location Suburban	**Applicants** 14,890
Total Enrollment 38,680	**Accepted** 67%
Undergraduates 30,560	**Enrolled** 46%
Male/Female 53/47	**Academics** ★ ★ ★
SAT V/M 470/540	**Social** 🍺 🍺 🍺
Financial Aid 25%	**Q of L** ● ● ●
Expense Pub $ $ $	**Admissions** (301)454-5550

"Multi" is the prefix of choice at this multiversity whose main goals, according to the administration, are to become "a model multicultural, multiracial, multigenerational institution that provides a quality education for all students." If you're willing to put up with a multiplicity of little frustrations like long lines and quickly filled classes, the University of Maryland can provide a multitude of opportunity.

The town of College Park and the university are synonymous. "The length and width and breadth makes us a city," boasts the admissions director. The campus, covering more than seven hundred prime suburban acres, is just nine miles from downtown D.C. The red-brick and white-pillared Georgian buildings comprise graceful quadrangles that punctuate grassy knolls and valleys. As enormous as the campus itself is the range of academic programs—everything from soil conservation to business law to textiles and clothing. Each student chooses a major from within one of the five academic divisions: arts and humanities; agriculture and life sciences; behavioral and social sciences; mathematics, physical sciences and engineering; and human and community resources.

Engineering (especially electronic) and natural sciences such as astronomy, microbiology and physics ground the university's reputation. Computer science and business (marketing and accounting in particular) come well recommended by students, and economics and home economics are strong. History, political science, art and performing arts are all above average, although humanities in general are not as strong as the sciences. The journalism department is decent (it tends to be more theoretical than practical in focus) but the quality of the radio, television and film department has declined due to outdated equipment. General education requirements, which take up one-third of every student's courses, demand mastery of basic English and mathematic skills, while offering a broad-based sampling of courses in all the major academic divisions.

Maryland provides an honors program as well as an intensive educational development program for students who need tutoring and educational supplements. An individual studies program, which allows students to combine two established majors to create their own programs, plus internships in Washington and Baltimore and study abroad in Israel, London and Sri Lanka, are all escape-from-standard-study options. The seven-branch library system is fittingly vast, and serves as a regional depository for federal documents. Although the administration admits library holdings are not as complete or well maintained as they could be, students do appreciate its seven-day-a-week, twenty-four-hour study room.

Students also report that it would be difficult to get good grades here without hitting the books at least a couple of hours every day, especially in the most competitive majors. Low-level classes tend to be large and impersonal (easy to hide in, even easier to skip), but are broken up into weekly discussion sections led by teaching assistants. Round about junior year the story changes, and classes of thirty or forty students become the norm. The computerized preregistration system has alleviated some course sign-up hassles, but many courses close quickly. Students note that strong teacher-pupil relationships must be student-initiated at this easy-to-get-lost-in-the-shuffle school: "If students don't go to professors, then the relationship will be nil," attests a senior. To help bridge the gap between pedagogues and neophytes there is Faculty Appreciation Week, which includes a take-a-professor-to-lunch day.

Three out of four students here are from Maryland; New York and New Jersey are also well represented. Middle-class backgrounds predominate, and a good job after four years of good fun is not an unusual goal. While many insist it's impossible to stereotype Maryland students, strength and independence are required characteristics for every undergrad at this no-pamper institution. "Someone who has led a sheltered life would be uncomfortable here," says a sophomore, referring to the enormity of the school. "It's an eye-opening experience." Admission for in-state residents from the top third of their high school class is easy; out-of-staters face stiffer competition. Decisions on financial aid and housing are affected by one's acceptance date, so the earlier you apply, the better you are likely to fare in that department. Maryland meets the indicated need of students and offers more than four hundred merit-based scholarships. Outstanding male and female athletes vie for close to three hundred additional awards.

Campus housing accommodates only a quarter of Maryland's students, the majority of them freshmen and sophomores. Choices include single-sex or coed dorms, recently renovated or about to be renovated, limited or unlimited visitation hours. It is often cheaper to live off campus, and about half the students commute from nearby apartments or home. Nearly 20 percent live in fraternities or sororities, and dine there as well. One student says the best eats on campus are the Hillel kosher meals, although standard dining-hall fare is "adequate, often great and offered in a wide variety." For fast meals, there is an endless variety of snack bars and restaurants on campus, including the world's largest Roy Rogers.

Situated right in the Baltimore–Washington corridor, the University of Maryland's location is one of its greatest selling points. If the lure of these two cities isn't enough for you, a host of beaches and other colleges are lurking nearby. With most students native Marylanders, the campus tends to empty out on weekends. For those left behind, partying (at the frats, in the dorms or in D.C.) is the chief social activity. About 10 percent of the student body is Greek and "most of these students have no other interests," reports an accounting major. Since the Greek houses are scattered among the homes in College Park, "the local community is often at odds with the frat-rats."

The athletic program, once the showcase of the school, has recently been the cause of much grief and embarrassment at Maryland. The school lost basketball star Len Bias to drugs, and lost academic esteem to reports that many basketball players were flunking their majors in "eligibility," i.e., taking dopey courses, which they rarely attended. Despite all this, Terrapin fans are unsinkable (in case you're wondering, a terrapin is a water turtle). Students turn out heavily to support football as well as men's and women's basketball. The lacrosse team is a varsity powerhouse, and thousands of students claim their moments of glory on the intramural fields, where "participation is high among all types of campus populations."

The most visible feature—and the most dominant fact of undergraduate life—at the University of Maryland is its size. Largeness can translate into long lines on computer terminals, poor academic advising and hassles everywhere. But it can also be exciting. "I've explored every corner and life-style on this campus, and feel I've gotten an incredible return," an aerospace engineering major says. Students who enjoy challenge and thrive on unlimited opportunities will be right at home in this multitudinous environment. Because, while a lot of colleges claim to prepare you for the real world, Maryland *immerses* you in it.

Massachusetts Institute of Technology

Cambridge, MA 02139

Location Urban
Total Enrollment 9,600
Undergraduates 4,500
Male/Female 75/25
SAT V/M 630/730
Financial Aid 58%
Expense Pr $ $ $ $

Applicants 6,210
Accepted 28%
Enrolled 56%
Academics ★ ★ ★ ★ ★
Social ☎ ☎ ☎
Q of L ● ● ●
Admissions (617)253-4791

Anyone who thinks MIT is populated only by brilliant but boring brains should know about the Harvard–Yale football game of 1982—when the techies released a weather balloon with their school's initials from beneath the forty-yard line during the second half. Lapses into high-technology versions of eating goldfish are a part of what keeps brilliant brains sane at this educational mecca for math whizzes, budding scientists and engineering prodigies. MIT is "a world of toys for the scientist," according to one undergraduate. Freshmen may be daunted at first by the exceptional talent among their ranks, but they soon come to see each other as normal human beings who just happen to score well into the 700s on their math SATs.

MIT's urban campus, massive and imposing, is set between the Charles River and a rather dull area of Cambridge. Its composition ranges from nineteenth-century Gothic Roman architecture carved from stone to more modern designs in brick and glass. All the buildings are familial by pigment: "off-white (from dirt)." The university stresses science and engineering studies with a "concern for human values and social goals." Every science department is superb, and the newly expanded biology department is a leader in the search for designer genes. Nevertheless, pure sciences tend to play second fiddle to the engineering fields. Electrical engineering and computer science are almost universally credited as tops in the nation; physics, chemical and mechanical engineering, and the tiny aeronautics and astronautics department are all highly praised as well. Note that MIT emphasizes the traditional Defense Department engineering fields—"many students are concerned with the possible dilemma of working in the defense industry," one student notes—whereas technical schools in the west tend to focus on energy and earth-science areas.

With such quality in the sciences, most MIT students have yet to discover the school's strength in the humanities, arts and social sciences (known as HASS to the techies). But with the establishment of a new College of Liberal Arts and the initial offering of a bachelor of arts degree, MIT could soon become as attractive to future poets and painters as it is to future technical experts. In addition, the institute will soon beef up liberal arts requirements in order to expose all students to these newly improved departments. MIT has also shelled out the bucks to attract top professors in these areas, including such luminaries as linguist Noam Chomsky and economist Paul Samuelson. Economics, political science, management, urban studies, linguistics, graphics for modern art and holography—plus anything that can be linked to a computer—are strong, and the tiny minority who major in these subjects receive enough personal attention to make any college student envious. A new media technology building is an added attraction for both students and faculty.

One of MIT's most successful innovations is the Undergraduate Research Opportunities Program (UROP), which facilitates student-faculty research projects. Considered one of the best programs of its kind in the nation, it allows students to earn course credit or money for doing research. The experimental study group allows freshmen and sophomores to set a self-paced course of study as they learn through tutorials instead of through the traditional lecture format. With an eight-to-one student/faculty ratio, most students have access to even the top professors, who carry lighter teaching loads to allow them time for students and research. The library facilities are vast: One is even open twenty-four hours a day and "some students spend the majority of their time (awake or asleep) there," one student reports.

Mandatory pass/fail grading for freshmen makes for an easy adjustment to what one biology major terms "MIT brainstretching," and failures are stricken from the record. Grades or not, most MIT students set themselves a breathtaking pace. Even a seasoned senior rates the academic pressure as "HIGH . . . ULTRA HIGH," while another warns that "getting an education at MIT is like getting a drink from a firehose." Some relief is found through the optional January period of independent activities offering noncredit seminars, workshops, and activities in fields outside the regular curriculum. Participation in the engineering co-op program, junior year abroad, or cross-registration at all-female Wellesley College are other helpful ways to get young noses away from the grindstone.

While MIT has somewhat justly earned an image as a "conservative, rich boys' school," there is enough variety to shake up this homogeneity, with significant numbers of foreign and Asian students and faculty members. Virtually all of the students come from the top fifth of their high school class. Nevertheless, in assembling each freshman class, the admissions office looks for evidence of diversity, individuality and creativity, not just the ability to calculate and make good grades. Consequently, MIT students tend to be well rounded, more often than not jocks and sometimes professional-caliber musicians. And while one student claims, "everyone knows Maxwell's equations," another stresses, "Most students are not nerds!" The institute helps financially needy students pay the super-hefty tuition bill (MIT fights it out with Bennington every year to see who will have the highest tuition in the country); however, each undergrad is expected to pick up at least $4,500 of each year's cost. MIT does not give purely academic or athletic scholarships, but it does offer its own parent loan fund with favorable interest rates to augment the federal loan programs available.

Freshmen decide on their housing arrangements during orientation week, a seven-day ordeal that some claim is the most pressure-packed part of the MIT experience. Assigned temporary housing when they first arrive, the confused tenderfoots must, during the first week, either be successfully rushed by a fraternity, join an "independent living group" (sort of like special-interest coed fraternities), or choose a dorm. The guaranteed housing is either single sex or coed, with dorms in the middle of campus, and most of the fraternities and living groups sit a mile or less away across the Charles. Upperclass students can usually rate singles, while freshmen and sophomores may crowd into triples. Freshmen must suffer through a mandatory board plan, with a new food service where "many changes have occurred, but most are not for the better." The frat-rats, however, feast on spreads prepared by their full-time cooks, and the Kosher Kitchen, run by Hillel, provides some refuge for others.

MIT's social life is doubly hexed by an uneven male/female ratio and the torrential work load, not to mention the distinct lack of social graces on the part of some younger students. "Many are academic successes and social failures," one student claims. On the other hand, the student body is so diverse that almost anyone can fit in and find a niche. Many men find their dates at nearby women's schools (Wellesley, Simmons, Lesley) or Boston University. Perhaps the best way to establish a secure social life is to abandon the dorms and join one of the myriad fraternities (some of them coed), an option about a third of the students take. On-campus dances and parties, including semiformals and a Fiji Island party, as well as Thursday night pub runs, are frequent. The multifaceted Boston metropolis lies only a short hike across the Massachusetts Bridge and the New England ski slopes are readily accessible. But mostly, when MIT's students want relief from the pressures of academics, these computer jocks turn into real jocks. While few techies are Arnold Schwarzeneggers, MIT claims to have "more intercollegiate athletic teams than any other college—thirty-six." The fencing, pistol, and women's volleyball teams have captured championships, not to mention the competitive track, cross-country, crew and tennis teams. Even more popular is the extensive and well-organized intramural program—"Virtually every student competes in at least one sport a year"—with sports ranging from Ping-Pong, billiards and bowling to the more traditional basketball and volleyball. Everyone has access to MIT's up-to-date and sumptuous athletic facilities.

Though students often wonder what life at a "real" college would have been like, chances of survival and even satisfaction at MIT are excellent. One student explains, "We all enjoy ourselves, but to us school always—and must—come first." As the top comprehensive technical institute in the nation, MIT is perfect for geniuses searching for anonymity and for any other highly motivated individuals who aren't afraid to check it out. "I was terrified about not meeting anyone normal," says a junior. "I was pleasantly surprised."

University of Massachusetts—Amherst

Amherst, MA 01003

Location Small town	**Applicants** 19,953
Total Enrollment 26,420	**Accepted** 60%
Undergraduates 19,750	**Enrolled** 60%
Male/Female 51/49	**Academics** ★★★★
SAT V/M 490/540	**Social** ☎☎☎☎
Financial Aid 83%	**Q of L** ●●●
Expense Pub $	**Admissions** (413)545-0222

Founded during the Civil War, the University of Massachusetts has for many years waged its own two-front battle for recognition and survival, fighting off the twin plagues of a stingy state legislature and a bad reputation. Anxious to make the bad old days of "Zoo Mass" a distant memory, the university has embarked on an ambitious plan to become the best public university in the Northeast. Though that may be a little much to expect just yet, there's no denying that UMass is improving by leaps and bounds.

Several years ago, the state earmarked $45 million for the renovation of UMass academic buildings, laboratories and residence halls. Crumbling modern and colonial facades on the "haphazardly planned, rather unaesthetic campus" are getting much-needed face-lifts. Meanwhile, academic foundations at UMass seem to have withstood the test of time. Of the seven undergraduate colleges and schools, management and engineering are considered first-rate, and the education school has a reputation for innovation. The large College of Food and Natural Resources offers programs ranging from environmental design to hotel, restaurant and travel administration. Health Sciences offers majors in communication disorders, nursing and public health. Solid programs in the College of Arts and Sciences include art, communication studies, computer and information science, economics, women's studies, English and linguistics and language—especially Chinese and Japanese.

Chemistry and nursing are on a list of programs targeted for improvement by the administration.

An abundance of academic resources and extracurricular opportunities exist for those who are purposeful enough to "manipulate the system for their own ends." Students looking to stand out from the Umasses should look into the interdisciplinary major in Social Thought and Political Economy or consider the bachelor's degree with Individual Concentration program, a design-it-yourself major. An optional January term costs extra but helps some students to catch up on requirements or get into a normally crowded course. For those who don't, classes aren't in session again until February. There are an honors program and well-established exchanges with schools in this country and abroad. Internships for credit are readily available and popular. The summer program is good, especially the drama department's Theater in the Works program, which allows students to stage their works with professional actors in residence, and the English department's summer seminar at Trinity College, Oxford.

What UMass itself can't provide, its neighbors in the Five College Consortium* can. "If you can't afford Amherst, Smith, Hampshire, or Mount Holyoke (the four other consortium members)," says one English major, "you can attend UMass and take courses at the others." Classes on the home campus can be large—most for freshmen and sophomores are in the hundreds. Despite the obvious barriers to student-faculty interaction, at least one senior reports dinner parties with professors. Most of the largest courses are broken down in smaller sections with teaching assistants, and freshman writing classes are limited to eighteen students. Rigorous state core requirements include writing, humanities, social and behavioral sciences, and mathematics and natural sciences. The library, though it houses about a million volumes, has been a campus joke for decades due to shoddy construction. The twenty-eight-story structure opened with fanfare in 1973, only to be closed again six years later when the brick facade began to chip, raining debris near the base of the building in every direction. After seven more years of limited service, the saga apparently has a happy ending, thanks in part to nearly 3,500 student volunteers who put the finishing touches on a long-needed renovation.

The typical UMass student is a white public school graduate heading straight for the job market after graduation. The prevalent 1980s motivation to succeed is much in evidence, but a climate of liberalism remains from earlier decades, especially among administrators. As one student notes, "There is a celebration of diversity here." The celebration is dampened by the fact that blacks and Hispanics together still make up only about 5 percent of the student body. Some five hundred student organizations are registered, ranging from the Women's Leadership Project to the Armenians Club. The student government is one of the most powerful in the country and presides over a $1.7-million budget that finances such activities as free rock concerts and lobbying in Boston and Washington for student financial aid.

Massachusetts residents need only rank in the top 40 percent of their class and record combined SATs of about 900 to be "reasonably confident of admission" to all but the most selective majors. Standards are quickly rising, though, and applications have nearly doubled since 1980. Standards for out-of-state students are tougher (top 25 percent and SATs of 1000), but available spots have recently been increased from 5 percent of each class to 15 percent. Students in other New England states are treated as Massachusetts residents for admission purposes if their own state universities don't offer the programs they want. As a result of heavy application pressure, quotas have been instituted in popular majors like management, engineering, and computer science. UMass runs on rolling admissions, so students looking to these areas should get their applications in early. The university makes no guarantees about financial aid, distributing it to those with the greatest needs until funds are exhausted. Also available are more than three hundred non-need academic scholarships, ranging from $1,296 to $5,000, as well as talent awards in the arts. About 320 athletic scholarships are awarded in a variety of men's and women's sports.

UMass has the sixth-largest residence hall system in the country. Its fifty dorms, situated in five different residential areas, can house eleven thousand students. Freshmen can choose single-sex or coed living and also submit a list of their preferred living areas in descending order. Most end up in the Southwest Area, a "huge, city-like complex" with five high-rise towers and eleven low-rise residence halls. Two dorm areas offer residential college services—counseling, classes, and social activities all in one place—while a third stresses community-style living, with suites housing six to eight students. Half of the dorms are coed. About 40 percent of the students live off campus, including most of the upperclassmen, who generally set up shop in one of the two dozen nearby apartment complexes or in fraternities or sororities. Four large but clean dining halls serve up the usual uninspired fare, although two offer vegetarian meals and one has a kosher food plan. For those who like a more personal touch, one dorm has its own meal plan and serves family style.

Though UMass isn't the party school it once was, students here still know how to have a good time. A relaxed academic atmosphere keeps people out of the library on weekends, when the campus sizzles with student-sponsored concerts, dances, ballets, and movies. The Massachusetts drinking age "has moved much social drinking behind closed doors," but those over twenty years old can patronize one of Amherst's dozen bars or drink at two on-campus spots. About two dozen fraternities and sororities occupy the time of some students, but they are somewhat out of the mainstream and scorned by the "socially aware." A free public transportation system allows maximum mobility not only among the Five Colleges but to nearby towns.

The university's location in the Pioneer Valley is one of its most enticing features. Surrounded by the Berkshire foothills, Amherst is a typically quaint New England college town in close proximity to good skiing, hiking and canoeing areas and only an hour-and-a-half drive to Boston. Varsity sports are low-key but well financed and popular. The strongest of these is the nationally ranked men's lacrosse team, which attracts thousands of fans who for a big game can even muster a "wave" cheer. Men's basketball and soccer are also good, though recently women athletes have begun to upstage the men, with nationally ranked field hockey, soccer and softball teams in the past few years. The two gyms on campus offer excellent facilities for the recreational athlete, and intramurals receive heavy coverage by the campus newspaper, which is the largest college daily in New England.

If you'd love to tiptoe through the ivy of a small, private New England college but aren't ready for the price, isolation and limitations that would probably come along with the deal, take a look at UMass. It's big enough to offer a vast number of academic and extracurricular opportunities, while its participation in the Five College Consortium gives students access to four leading New England private colleges. Through UMass, you can seek out private school atmosphere and opportunities for overachieving at a price that's public all the way.

Miami University

Oxford, OH 45056

Location Rural
Total Enrollment 15,970
Undergraduates 14,330
Male/Female 45/55
SAT V/M 530/600
Financial Aid 51%
Expense Pub $ $ $

Applicants 10,980
Accepted 57%
Enrolled 54%
Academics ★ ★ ★
Social 🙢 🙢 🙢
Q of L ● ● ●
Admissions (513)529-2531

Miami University has a misleading name that perks the ears of surfers and beach bums, but in reality, this school (days away from a decent surf) is a safe, secluded midwestern school that even a mother could love. In fact, MU/Ohio is oft referred to as Mother Miami because it keeps close tabs on its pretty pampered and somewhat sheltered student body. One undergrad admits, "People at this school are unrealistically optimistic and ignorant of many unpleasantries in the world."

The university was staked out on a vast acreage of farmland, "in the middle of one HUGE cornfield." The campus is dressed in a coherent Georgian style, and remains as impeccably groomed as its students. With the luscious green of the trees and salient red of the brick, it's always looking a lot like Christmas in Miami. The school evokes the same staunchly collegiate image as its prestigious private competitors in the East. A pennant-waving, beaver-coated student from yesteryear could stroll across campus tomorrow and feel right at home.

Miami provides a private school environment at a public school price and has been classified as "public ivy." The university's strongest offerings are in the school of business administration. The accounting major is rated highly by the students, and one popular program unites marketing, art, mass communications and advertising majors into teams that promote competing companies. The education department earns high marks for both the elementary and secondary teaching majors, and for those whose inclination runs in this direction, the university's unique pulp and paper science technology degree is hard to match.

The College of Arts and Sciences maintains several notable programs, especially physics, botany, zoology, politics and history. Still, liberal arts students complain they sometimes feel suffocated by the career-oriented preoccupations of those in the professional schools, especially the 40 percent who gravitate to the business school. "They tend to be semishallow and materialistic," says a communications major.

The population at Miami remains predominantly white, conservative and, according to some students, a bit spoiled. The administration claims it would like to attract more minority students, but says the reasons for its lack of success "are not entirely clear." The university maintains an *in loco parentis* philosophy regarding social restrictions, which students view as a major obstacle to an otherwise idyllic four years. What diversity there is can be found in a select group of students enrolled in the Western College of Interdisciplinary Studies. This community of scholars leads a segregated life across the street from the main university, and is home to the "punkish movement on Western campus." Western students design individual programs of study, building on the core courses in social science, natural science and humanities. Miami's European Center in Luxembourg offers a semester- or yearlong program in the fine arts or political science and the opportunity to live with a foreign family. An exchange program with a university in Japan as well as summer workshops in Italy, Germany and China are also available.

Because Miami (the name comes from an Indian tribe) is primarily an undergraduate school, professors concentrate on teaching. All hold regular office hours and teach introductory courses on a rotating basis. Lecture classes are public-university large. Upper-level class sizes in general are not a problem, although getting into them can be a big problem—particularly business and communication courses.

Miami is the only state university in Ohio that receives significantly more applications from high school students than it can admit. Ninety-nine percent of freshmen are from the top half of their classes, and more than a third of Miami graduates continue their schooling and enjoy high placement rates in professional schools. Students are drawn primarily from Ohio (75 percent), Indiana and Illinois. They are 97 percent white and mostly from middle- or upper-middle-class families. Students who fit in best "are stylish, well-mannered, heterosexual conservatives," according to an accounting major. "It's sad to say, but those who vary have a difficult time being happy at Miami." In fact, many students complain about the homogeneous student body and ivory tower atmosphere, which they consider safe but unrealistic. And one senior admits, "Many students are seeking spouses as well as an education."

In addition to need-based financial aid, Miami awards 320 grant-in-aid scholarships for athletes, and more than a thousand academic merit scholarships from $200 to $4,000.

The condition of the dormitories reflects the overall quality of the campus facilities. They are comfortable and squeaky clean. Less than a quarter of the dorms are coed, and freshmen are placed in single-sex dorms where strict visitation rules still apply. Most upperclassmen find good, cheap off-campus pads by their senior year. The fraternities offer members separate housing; sororities are given only blocks of suites in the dorms. Dormies are subjected to institutionalized food, which they concede is not too bad. In fact, the dining hall management is most receptive to students' suggestions and makes a conscious effort to provide diet foods.

Miami is located in the small town of Oxford, where the students outnumber citizens two to one. "Merchants are very responsive to student needs," reports one collegiate shopper. "Nowhere else can you have everything from bagels to cheesecake delivered." Since cars are banned from campus and the local menu is limited, those seeking urban action and romantic dining may have a little trouble finding a ride to Cincinnati, only a half hour away. Travel restrictions mean that social life centers on the campus, and with over a third of the students pledging fraternities and sororities, Greek parties and fund raisers are dominant social forces. "Uptown" Oxford, the brick-laid main street lined with small stores and five bars, poses another entertainment option, with those under twenty-one drinking beer only.

Much of the recreational activity in this rural setting revolves around athletics and the great outdoors. Hueston Woods State Park, with its lake marina, beach, golf course and wilderness trails, is only four miles away. The well-organized recreation program provides teams for just about every sport (including the ever-popular korfball and broomball). The administration emphasizes (some students say overemphasizes) athletics, and the successful men's varsity football, basketball, hockey and soccer teams enjoy superb facilities and adequate spectator support. Although the field hockey program is strong, women's athletics are not on par with men's teams. Miami is sometimes called the Cradle of Coaches and periodic upsets of Big Ten rivals in the major sports have earned Miami a reputation as a giant killer.

With its conservative policies and isolated location, Miami does not offer students much opportunity to diversify or experiment with freedom: "We're hanging on to

'Mother Miami's' apron strings," says one student. But it is a well-respected school, with beautiful grounds and a strenuous academic agenda that is just perfect for a student body one senior defines as "the intelligent side of the 'me' generation."

University of Miami

Coral Gables, FL 33124

Location Suburban	**Applicants** 5,710
Total Enrollment 13,380	**Accepted** 75%
Undergraduates 8,500	**Enrolled** 39%
Male/Female 55/45	**Academics** ★ ★ ★
SAT V/M 530/580	**Social** 🏫 🏫 🏫 🏫
Financial Aid 70%	**Q of L** ● ● ●
Expense Pr $ $ $	**Admissions** (305)284-4323

Set in a tropical paradise of swaying palm trees and blue skies, the University of Miami has all the trappings of a collegiate Shangri-la. Things haven't always been so idyllic, though, for this private college in the posh community of Coral Gables. Over the years it has survived a devastating hurricane and now it has another tough job on its hands: shedding the unhappy nickname of "Suntan U." With characteristic persistence, UM is laboring long and hard to build up its academic programs and let people know that while it's still a great place to catch some rays, it's also a good place to catch some lectures.

The weather may be balmy, but the university itself is on the move. Freshman SAT scores have climbed more than a hundred points in just five years, partly because the administration has been trimming the size of the freshman class in order to emphasize quality over quantity. There is a new six-year medical program for outstanding students, and the school recently received a $56-million gift from a wealthy benefactor—one of the largest in the history of American higher education. The administration, one student notes, is "working to identify and eliminate problem areas in its trek toward excellence."

Miami is best known for its offerings in marine science and music. It has one of the nation's top programs in marine biology and was the first university to offer a degree in music engineering, which remains top-notch. The business school and communications department are also recommended by students, while undergraduates in the departments of art and architecture praise their professors but complain about poor facilities. Majors in the schools of nursing and education and in some of the liberal arts tend to have suspiciously better tans than their science and business counterparts. But on the whole students are satisfied with the programs in the social sciences and humanities, and to a somewhat lesser degree, engineering. Introductory courses can run to several hundred students, but by and large class size is not an issue. Most professors make an effort to be accessible, and large numbers turn out at student-faculty mixers. Distribution requirements vary from school to school. Those with a little extra time on their hands can take Miami's summer or semester program in the Caribbean.

Highly motivated students in any field can apply to the school's extensive honors program, which enrolls over a thousand students who were in the top fifth of their high school class and have a combined SAT score of at least 1200. The overall academic climate is fairly casual, but the honors program "enrolls some of the finest minds in the country," a business major says. To supplement the honors curriculum, the university recently raised the curtain on a new Honors Residential College that is part of a move to convert all the dorms to a residence system modeled on Yale's. It houses 385 students and several faculty members and comes fully equipped with twenty-five computers, a library, and exercise rooms. Despite the high quality of its honor students, UM still attracts its share of sun-addled beach bums, who stumble in for a couple of classes in the morning, spend the rest of the day at the shore, and almost never see the inside of the library—which, by the way, is one of the best in the region.

Nearly half of its students are commuters from the local area, and another quarter are in-state boarders, a group that the university has recently been cultivating. Nevertheless, UM has assembled a student body of surprising diversity, with out-of-staters drawn mainly from the Northeast, Ohio and the Chicago area. UM is one of the few ranking universities in the nation that is less than 60 percent Caucasian; Hispanics account for a substantial 27 percent of the total, blacks and Asian Americans make up a combined total of 15 percent, and foreigners chip in another 6 percent. The large number of Hispanics is due to the influx of Cuban and other Caribbean refugees into southern Florida, and at times it seems that Spanish is the mother tongue on campus. The Latin influence mixes strangely with that of the wealthier New Yorkers—many of whom view their time here as an extended vacation—but the one characteristic everyone seems to share is the hope of getting a high-paying job after graduation.

Students are accepted for admission without regard to their financial need, and those who apply on time receive funds to cover their demonstrated need. Miami has been particularly aggressive in recent years in recruiting top students with healthy scholarships, including a dozen full-tuition renewable awards named for the writer Isaac Bashevis Singer and requiring standing in the top 5 percent of the high school class and combined SATs of 1300 or ACTs of 30. In all, about three hundred merit scholarships ranging up to full tuition are awarded each year. Two hundred and twenty-five athletic scholarships are available in a wide range of men's and women's sports, as is a full-tuition prepayment plan, which allows students to avoid costly fee increases during their upperclass years.

With all dorms on campus soon to be transformed into residential colleges, both the facilities and the sense of community in and around them should increase. All housing at Miami is coed, and students can choose from a variety of campus dwellings, including standard dorm rooms, suites and apartment-style housing. Most freshmen live on campus and can also choose "special interest" floors—catering to studious types, international students and music majors, for instance. Because of all the shuffling around due to the implementation of the college system, some freshmen end up in the University Inn across the street from the campus for their first semester. Most dorms have their own cafeterias, which dish up passable but nondescript food. A variety of plans, from five to twenty meals, are available, and there is a kosher alternative. There are plenty of inexpensive apartments and houses available for rent nearby, and over half the student body lives off campus or in Greek houses.

Ten minutes from Key Biscayne and Miami's beaches, the university is located in upscale Coral Gables, far from what students call the city's war zone (made famous by the likes of Don Johnson). With its own lake in the middle of the campus (and on the cover of most brochures), the campus is architecturally diverse but modern. "No boring ivy-covered brick here," trumpets a biology major. Those who shun sand between their toes can hang out at the campus's outdoor swimming pool or bike down to the boutiques in Coconut Grove, only three miles away. Miami students love to dance, and they spend their weekends hotfooting it at nearby bars or in the Campus

Rat, home also of the popular Fifth Quarter post–football game parties. Public transportation runs right in front of the dorms, but most students recommend a car in order to get "the full Florida effect." An extensive campus beautification program has produced a proliferation of trees and grass on campus and has made it even tougher to find a parking place.

Some students complain that the administration is not supportive of the Greek system, but the fraternities manage to thrive anyway, even if they account for only a small minority of students. Many of the frats and sororities are small (averaging about thirty members) but they often join forces in throwing popular keg parties. The sororities, with no housing of their own, have less of a following. Football is indisputably king on campus, and fall is Hurricane season when the 'Canes, who always rank high in the Top 20, come out in force. The baseball squad is usually a contender for a spot in the College World Series, women's golf is strong, and the swimming and diving teams sent four members to the most recent Olympic games.

Thawed-out northeasterners, or anybody without much motivation, will find that a perpetual spring vacation can easily be arranged here. But most students are excited about Miami's new push for excellence. Says one senior, "The University of Miami is no longer satisfied with being an average school and has undertaken the task of making itself one of the best—it's a place for students willing to step forward and have a voice in influencing their education."

Michigan State University

East Lansing, MI 48824

Location City outskirts	**Applicants** 17,400
Total Enrollment 41,890	**Accepted** 73%
Undergraduates 33,910	**Enrolled** 53%
Male/Female 48/52	**Academics** ★ ★ ★
SAT V/M 480/530	**Social** 🍺 🍺 🍺 🍺
Financial Aid 55%	**Q of L** ● ● ●
Expense Pub $ $	**Admissions** (517)355-8332

It's fitting that Michigan State University is located near the Motor City; wheels are practically essential to get around on this sprawling five-thousand-acre campus, with its thirty-three miles of roadway, ninety-eight miles of walkways, and twelve miles of bike paths. Most students hoof it to class, though, and along the way, they can enjoy some of the sixteen thousand varieties of trees and shrubs that fill the campus. A casual glance through the course catalogue reveals plenty of varieties of undergraduate majors as well: over two hundred at last count, with strengths in such diverse areas as business and agriculture, hotel and restaurant management and the sciences.

Students at Michigan State seem to enjoy going to a school bigger than most of their home towns. The half-modern, half-traditional campus is quite attractive, with the Red Cedar River dividing MSU's Gothic-style original campus from the cement high rises of the newer science and communications section. In addition, there's a three-thousand-acre arboretum, a remnant of the school's land-grant roots. Although students seem to take their school's massiveness in stride, it can at times be disheartening. "It would be nice to be recognized by professors when I see them outside of class," says one woman wistfully.

In an effort to break down the massive university into manageable units, MSU has several "colleges within the college." The two smallest house fewer than a thousand students, one organized around the social sciences, the other around the natural sciences and math. Each is designed to foster the illusion of a small undergraduate institution. Three much bigger living-learning complexes, each with about four residence halls, give resident students access to a library, faculty offices, classrooms, counseling, a cafeteria and a recreation area. Finally, an honors college brings together the brightest students of each freshman class, houses them separately if they wish, and assigns special advisers to guide them through the school's legendary red tape.

In spite of these cozy alternatives, every student must suffer through the massive registration process, and the quarter system means facing it three times a year. Assistance is available to freshmen their first time around, but getting into some courses can still be excruciatingly difficult. Athletes and honors students get first dibs. The exclusive use of teaching assistants instead of professors in some lower-level courses and classes taught only from cassettes or videotapes are no joys either. Those who survive the first two years are rewarded with smaller upper-level courses and more personal attention, this time from the top teachers. Although the academic climate varies, it is "much more casual than other universities of similar academic standing," according to a junior.

Some of MSU's programs have been subjected to budget cuts in recent years, but even slashes to the tune of millions of dollars barely make a dent in the wide variety of university offerings. MSU is traditionally strong in agriculture and preveterinary science, though in the past few decades business, engineering, education and communications have become just as respected. MSU boasts the nation's first school of packaging, and the university hotel is manned by student trainees. More than seven hundred MSU students per year study in about twenty foreign countries, and MSU offers numerous opportunities for individualized learning. There are always thousands of research projects going on at the school, and undergraduates have ample opportunities to get involved. MSU students can also take advantage of the school's proximity to the Michigan state capitol, where there are abundant internship opportunities.

Despite MSU's backwoods heritage, farm-bred students are in the minority, and most undergraduates are much more familiar with plants of the industrial variety than the kind that come out of the ground. Over 90 percent are from Michigan, with a high percentage of those from large public schools in the Detroit area. MSU isn't the place for liberals or agitators, since "most students are conservative and are more worried about their future than political issues," says a senior. Blacks and Hispanics account for about 7 percent of the students, and foreigners a little under 2 percent. Each year, more than six hundred students win awards for outstanding academic performance, ranging from $300 up to full tuition, room and board, and athletes in fourteen sports rake in another 278 scholarships. The university guarantees to "attempt" to meet the demonstrated financial need of students, with its own money or by directing students to outside sources of aid, or a combination of both. MSU sponsors a deferred payment plan available for everyone who lives in university housing.

With a capacity of about seventeen thousand people, MSU's residence system is the largest of any university in the nation. Freshmen and sophomores usually live in residence halls of about fifteen hundred people, which are, in various combinations, single sex or coed, high-rise or low-rise, quiet or rambunctious. After that, apartment living becomes the thing—either in college-owned facilities or in East Lansing, although financial aid is often decreased for nonboarders. Fraternity and sorority members mostly live in their own off-campus houses, though some houses are much too small to handle all their members. Room and board includes three meals a day at any f the cafeterias sprinkled throughout the dorms. "The school does an extremely good job of serving hot, beautifully created meals and of promoting clever, special themes to spice up the daily routine," says a junior (other positive reviews prove she wasn't paid to say it). The Greek houses don't have meal plans, but their residents do have the option of buying into the one on campus. A significant percentage of the students commute, but finding a parking space is a major headache.

An efficient campus bus system is a boon to some students, and when they feel an urge to see people older or younger than college age, East Lansing is a short walk away. Dooley's, Casey's, Mac's and rows of more bars are also just a short stagger from campus. Both the residence halls and the active Greek system sponsor social events—and not just the usual beer bashes. Cedar Village, the site of the on-campus apartments, hosts a semiannual block party dubbed Cedarfest that attracts thousands of revelers from throughout the campus and beyond. Other popular leisure-time fare includes picnics, pizza-eating contests, hall Olympics, hayrides and ice skating outings—and of course movies, dances and concerts. With so many things to do already, it's hard to know how students will be able to work in trips to a new $30-million student events center, now under construction.

Weekends are dominated by Big Ten athletic competitions. More than a few times, MSU has broken from the pack to produce national championship teams in football and basketball. Magic Johnson of the NBA Lakers and Kirk Gibson of the Detroit Tigers are two of the most famous of MSU-spawned all-Americans. In recent years, the hockey team has been the most successful on campus, winning the national championship in 1986. Even when the varsity teams are offering little to cheer about, the marching band is always worth a listen, and the intramural program is ever popular.

Michigan State is a small city unto itself, and once students get over initial intimidation, most thrive on the opportunities offered by its diversity and size—or at least the ones they choose to take advantage of. And they do have to choose. Says one senior, "MSU has more to offer than any student has time to experience."

University of Michigan

Ann Arbor, MI 48109

Location Urban	**Applicants** 17,470
Total Enrollment 34,850	**Accepted** 54%
Undergraduates 22,400	**Enrolled** 49%
Male/Female 52/48	**Academics** ★ ★ ★ ★ ★
SAT V/M 550/630	**Social** ☎ ☎ ☎
Financial Aid 44%	**Q of L** ● ● ●
Expense Pub $ $ $ $	**Admissions** (313)764-7433

Even if a kryptonite meteor smash-landed on its main campus, the University of Michigan couldn't radiate more power. One of the top universities in the country, it produces major research in every field from ancient civilizations to zoology, provides an excellent undergraduate liberal arts education, and crunches offensive lines in front of as many fans as any other school in higher education.

Unfortunately, great power is often accompanied by great volume, and this superuniversity has long lines for just about everything: registration, getting into the popular classes or dorms, buying books, dropping and adding classes, or just eating lunch. Indeed, a humble undergrad can get lost among the maze of superlatives that are the essence of UM. As one microbiology major puts it, "Michigan is a user unfriendly school." But those with persistence can learn how to cope with the unavoidable red tape, and once that's accomplished, a truly diverse world of opportunity lies ready and waiting.

Michigan's campus is so massive that newcomers may want to come equipped with flares and a compass in case they get lost on the way to class. The sprawling grounds are divided into several subcampuses, the most important of which is Central Campus, the heart of the university. Central is centered around the "diag," a lawn where students congregate between classes. Architecturally, Central features a wide range of styles, from Bauhaus to Art Deco to the postmodern undergraduate library, known to detractors as "Ugli." North Campus, a short walk from Central, is relatively new and houses the schools of music and art and architecture, as well as the recently relocated School of Engineering. A third region of the campus, South Quad, is chiefly the domain of athletes, and another residential area lies to the east. While not likely to win any campus beauty awards, Michigan is one of the few schools in the nation with its own 144-acre arboretum, "a hilly paradise" complete with woods, trails, and a river.

Academically, the university ranks among the best in the nation in most fields of study, mainly because it attracts some of the biggest names in academia to teach and conduct research in Ann Arbor. In its largest division, the College of Sciences, Literature, and Art, Michigan's strongest academic suits are considered to be the social sciences—especially psychology, sociology and anthropology—as well as biology, geology, philosophy, classical studies, political science and foreign languages. The colleges of engineering and business administration are highly regarded, and the university's programs in health-related fields are first-rate as well.

On the other hand, a senior reports that the communications department "exists primarily so that football players can major in something," and the education program suffers from declines in interest as well as funding. Because of the emphasis on high quality research at UM and the size of the classes (freshman and sophomore lectures often hit two hundred), it can be hard for students to get personal attention from professors. In fact, unless you're in a special program, one student says, "you may not even see a professor in your freshman or sophomore years."

It is in those special programs, offered mainly through the College of Sciences, Literature, and Art, that Michigan is at its best. The 650-student Residential College and the smaller Pilot Program enable students to enjoy highly personalized instruction with their own special courses and faculty, in programs like the excellent intensive language study offered in the RC. The Collegiate Institute for Values and Science provides an interdisciplinary approach to emerging problems of technology and society, and top incoming freshmen may be invited into the Honors College, which crosses most departmental lines and offers excellent academic advising. Fifty impatient premed students are accepted into the seven-year Interflex program, which allows them simultaneously to work on a BA and an MD without the typical premed pressures. A second program guarantees 150 top high school students admission to Michigan's graduate schools in business, engineering or pharmacy provided that they make satisfactory progress during their undergraduate years. Off-campus experiences include a year abroad in French or German universities, a business program in Paris, summer internships in selected majors, and special trips organized by individual departments.

Michigan is full of ambitious students for whom "studying is always first priority," an economics major says. The competition is stiff and the climate intense. "Even the most socially active are often library bound," a junior notes. During finals week, students line up outside the library before it opens to get a good seat. One compensation for the academic pressure is the policy of ending classes in April, so students have an edge in lining up summer jobs. A somewhat brutal although realistic boot camp for the real world, Michigan, as one senior puts it, "is a place where it is good to know how to toot your own horn."

Michigan's admissions office seeks out some of the best students in the country, with almost 70 percent of the students in the top 10 percent of their high school classes. Recruiting naturally focuses on Michigan but reaches into New England, New York, Ohio and Illinois and has recently been expanded to other areas of the South and Midwest. The aim is to further bolster the quality of the 30 percent who are out-of-staters, who already go up against much stiffer competition than Michigan residents for the right to pay three times as much tuition as the natives do. Admission is always offered to only one of the eight schools at UM, and there are different in-state and out-of-state quotas for each, so chances of admission could be increased by applying to a less popular school.

Although brains and ambition are taken for granted, the student body is remarkably diverse for a state university. Everyone from Young Republicans to bohemians rubs shoulders among UM's 22,400 undergraduates. Many of the Michigan natives hail from the more affluent suburbs of Detroit, but the school also attracts people from Michigan's small towns and farming areas. Blacks and Hispanics combine for about 6 percent of the student body. The university has long received an influx of liberal northeasterners, though the whole student body is more conservative today than it was a decade ago. Did you see *The Big Chill*? Those celluloid romantics were mourning UM radical idealism. But it hasn't all died out, and an art major assures, "There are still plenty of lefties and student activism." Dubbed "Little Berkeley" by some, the RC program is known as one of the biggest liberal hotbeds.

Michigan is the most expensive public university in the nation and really socks it to out-of-staters with a $6,000 surcharge. Michigan residents, however, may get enough aid to cover their total cost of tuition, room and board and expenses. Students can also vie for 850 merit scholarships, ranging from $250 to $3,200, as well as 370 full and partial athletic scholarships for men and women.

Dormitories at UM traditionally have well-defined personalities. Sixties-inspired types and "eccentrics" find the East Quad the "most open-minded dorms" (the RC is here). The Hill dorms are "more sedate and preppie." To the south reside the jocks and their groupies. Freshmen are guaranteed housing and can specify their first three dorm choices and desired number of roommates. A few single-sex dorms are available. On-campus housing is comfortable and well maintained, and each residence hall has its own computer facility, as well as computer jacks in each room that link them to the university's system. Even so, many students, especially upperclassmen, choose to do battle with Ann Arbor's tight housing market to secure an off-campus apartment or group house, which can be expensive. Other alternatives include college-owned cooperatives, and fraternity and sorority houses. Some 7 percent of the students reside in the latter, and though the Greeks are the bane of campus liberals, they seem to be gaining strength. There are dining halls in the dorms that serve average college fare, and anyone with a meal card can sample them all.

Detroit is a little less than an hour away, but most students become quite fond of the picturesque town of Ann Arbor and stay around on weekends to hit the bars and cheap movies. Those with other tastes will enjoy a surprising amount of visual and performing arts, and the newly renovated Michigan Union includes everything from fast-food to a travel agency. Michigan's drinking age, twenty-one, goes practically unnoticed, as does Ann Arbor's penalty for possession of marijuana: $5. Many lakes and swimming holes are within a short drive and seem to keep the large summer term population happy. But the winters are brutal, which may be why, as one premed students says, "parties and bars are the basic components of our social life."

No matter what the social activity, football overshadows everything else—especially if the Wolverines happen to get past Ohio State and into the Rose Bowl. "Attending football games with over 100,000 other fans is an integral part of the UM experience," students say. The trials and tribulations of living in Big Ten football country are that students don't pay as much attention to other high-performance teams, such as the basketball squad, which has recently arrived as a bona fide contender for the national championship. Besides being spectators, Michigan's more informal jocks can enjoy a wealth of recreational facilities, including three intramural gyms.

Few students seem to think that thirty-five thousand classmates are too many to enjoy for four years. "Finding your own niche among a wide range of opportunities and occupations makes college extremely satisfying," one junior says. And on the scattered occasions when a person *wants* to feel like part of the crowd—like when the "Tiger wave" sweeps around the stadium during a Wolverines game—the opportunity is there. "Hardened, self-reliant and resourceful students" who can get through all the lines and fight their way through the bureaucratic mazes usually end up agreeing that the university has everything. Insists one woman: "Boredom is an alien feeling in Ann Arbor."

Middlebury College

Middlebury, VT 05753

Location Small town	**Applicants** 3,450
Total Enrollment 1,900	**Accepted** 37%
Undergraduates 1,900	**Enrolled** 43%
Male/Female 50/50	**Academics** ★ ★ ★ ★
SAT V/M 610/640	**Social** ☎ ☎ ☎
Financial Aid 30%	**Q of L** ● ● ●
Expense Pr $ $ $ $	**Admissions** (802)388-3711

Four years at Middlebury College render the student "body" as fit for success as the student mind. The college has its own ski center, eighteen-hole golf course, and lighted jogging and cross-country ski trail, and access to two of the most inspiring hiking and backpacking ranges in the East. In case all the temptations aren't enough to get you moving, the college requires participation in one of twenty-eight coed "life-sports" programs. Nevertheless, physical exercise is only a secondary form of exertion for most students here. It is primarily Middlebury's solid academic reputation that lures motivated scholars to the heart of Vermont's snowy Green Mountains for four years of top-quality education.

"Heaven on earth" is how one philosophy major describes the small, picturesque and architecturally consistent gray- and brownstone campus nestled in a quaint New England mountainside town. "The campus is always beautiful, even during mud season," an English major adds. Middlebury is one of the few campuses in the nation where you can pick your room based on which mountain range you find most appealing—the

Green Mountains to the east, or the Adirondacks, which loom on the western horizon. It's so peaceful and calm you can hear the snow fall—which it does, a lot, from early November to mid-April.

Academically, Middlebury leaves little doubt where its priorities lie; a fourth of the faculty teaches languages and literature. Every summer, Middlebury banishes English from its campus, and teaches hundreds of would-be linguists a foreign language through its distinctive immersion method, where students live, learn and, they hope, think only in their chosen language. The language departments continue their excellent instruction during the school year, achieving especially notable success in Russian and Chinese. Although there is no foreign language requirement, just about every student studies another tongue, if only to prepare for going abroad. Middlebury has always been strong in international studies, and a new program in international politics and economics should make a good thing even better. Any student can take advantage of Middlebury's campuses in France, Germany, Italy, Spain, England and the Soviet Union, and a whopping 40 percent of each junior class studies abroad for all or part of the year. Of special interest back on campus is the northern studies major, which offers an interdisciplinary examination of countries in the northern hemisphere and includes a year in residence at the Center for Northern Studies in Wolcott, Vermont.

Other highly touted departments include English, history, biology and political science, and the premed track is popular. Psychology is universally declared the weakest department but, according to the administration, is a "target for special efforts in the near future," as are music and environmental studies. Lovers and haters of computers take note: Middlebury has installed fully equipped auxiliary centers in all three freshman dorms, and a spanking new computer center recently opened its doors.

Middlebury's academic rigor and innovative character are reflected in several aspects of its requirements and curriculum. Applicants are able to substitute advanced placement tests for SATs. Freshmen must take special foundations courses in three of the four academic divisions. Upperclassmen choose not only a major but also a concentration in a second, disparate field of knowledge. Professors may be "cordial, understanding and down-to-earth," but they also expect a lot and the curriculum, across-the-board, is challenging. A four-week January term, sandwiched between the rigorous fall and spring semesters, provides time for study on a topic not offered in the regular curriculum. Recent offerings have ranged from a Shakespeare course in England to a seminar on The Waitress in American Life. January term is a welcome respite from the usual academic grind, and many students take the opportunity to head for the nearby ski slopes.

About 60 percent of Middlebury's students graduated in the top 10 percent of their high school class, and almost all were in the top half. Most attended public schools, but minorities account for a scant 4 percent, and diversity is the college's Achilles' heel. Complains one woman, "The campus is too homogeneous—happy students at Middlebury are generally rich, athletic, conservative, good-looking people who are very smart but don't generally talk to each other about their work." Students note a division between academic and social life at "Club Midd"; hard weeks of classes and then all weekend to play is a pattern many adopt. Middlebury is need-blind in its admissions policy and meets the full demonstrated need of everyone it accepts. There are no athletic or merit scholarships, but the college does offer low-interest loans to middle-income families.

Few Middlebury students live off campus because their comprehensive tuition fee includes housing and allows only a meager refund for those not in the dorms. However, the college owns a number of large houses on the periphery of the campus that make up for the restriction somewhat, and a recently completed residence hall has made space plentiful. Students choose among a variety of dorms, most of which are coed. Rooms for upperclassmen are parceled out in a lottery, which is based on seniority. Since classes tend to move into dorms together, it is not unusual to find a dorm filled mostly with seniors or juniors—often with their own singles. Students on the meal plan eat at one of five usually crowded dining halls, where all food aside from the salad bar is considered uninspired at best. "I know it's the in-thing to complain about college food, but we really do have lousy chow," a senior says. Two nearby delis do a brisk business on nights when the food is less than palatable.

Socially, Middlebury's fun-loving student body heats up the arctic climes. Except for a few pockets of resistance where cocktail parties predominate, the common denominator for any campus event is "beer, beer, and more beer"—though a recent rise in the drinking age means that the underaged must now be a little more discreet. Since all fraternities were made coed and house dining clubs were abolished, the role of Greeks has been purely social, a responsibility they happily live up to. The Greek affairs are generally mobbed, and for those who tire of them, the college's Gamut Room provides a mellow weeknight alternative, with dance music every Thursday. A $3-million addition to the student center is in the planning stages and should increase campus social opportunities, but not of the romantic variety. Men and women get along so well as friends in this small community that some students say the idea of dating almost seems incestuous.

There is only so much to do on a small campus in a small town in Vermont, so the college takes responsibility for airlifting or busing in culture and entertainment on a regular basis. February can get a little grim, and road trips have become popular for a brief change. The progressive city of Burlington is only an hour away, Montreal is barely three, and Boston four. Outdoor lovers, however, do just fine. Middlebury's own ski center ($50 for the season) and proximity to most Vermont ski slopes make this a paradise for ski fanatics, a breed Middlebury attracts in predictably large numbers. According to one woman, skiing "seems to be the life philosophy for many Midd kids and their main reason for being here." The varsity ski teams are popular and successful, as are football, ice hockey, and lacrosse. Perhaps the biggest outdoor activity of all is the Winter Carnival, an annual extravaganza of fun in the snow.

Good at "making their own fun (or trouble)," Middlebury students are a congenial, fun-loving, and hardworking group. The number of blond preps per capita may be a little too high for some tastes, but for those seeking excellence in the liberal arts, few schools can match Middlebury's pleasing mix of skiing and scholarship.

Mills College

Oakland, CA 94613

Location City outskirts	**Applicants** 640
Total Enrollment 990	**Accepted** 77%
Undergraduates 740	**Enrolled** 50%
Male/Female N/A	**Academics** ★ ★ ★
SAT V/M 520/530	**Social** ☎ ☎ ☎
Financial Aid 70%	**Q of L** ● ● ●
Expense Pr $ $ $	**Admissions** (415)430-2135

When Mills College was founded in 1852 as a young ladies' seminary, most of the students were the children of California Gold Rush adventurers who were determined to see their daughters raised in an atmosphere of gentility rather than among the rowdiness of mining camps. Today, students on this lush, Spanish-style campus in East Oakland are anything but sequestered. Mills is the premier women's college west of the Rockies (and the second oldest women's college in the nation), and the combination of student diversity and educational opportunity guarantees that no one can graduate without having her horizons well extended.

"Not a girls school without men, but a women's school without boys," is how one Mills student describes her college, and indeed a high level of maturity is expected here. The curriculum emphasizes individual choice, while a recently instituted general education program requires students to take two courses in each of the following areas: natural sciences and math, social sciences, humanities and fine arts. Classes range from small to smaller, and it's not unusual for a woman to find herself in a room with four other students and a department chairman. There's a new "writing across the curriculum" program and a speaking skills requirement in the wings. Professors are friendly and accessible—"one of the most outstanding features of Mills," says one student. With a remarkable 60 percent of them women, there's no shortage of excellent role models. Students consider grading strict but stress the supportive academic atmosphere and the emphasis on personal achievement and excellence. "There's much more of a helpful attitude among students than a competitive one," reports a junior.

Mills' curriculum displays all-around strength. English, economics, history, government, dance and psychology are all praised by students. Sciences are also strong, and premed students enjoy a 75 percent acceptance rate at med schools. Popular among prelaw students is the new interdisciplinary program in administration and legal studies. The Indonesian and North Indian music specializations within the music program are worthy of note, as is the fact that Mills was the first women's college to offer a major in computer science. Mathematics faculty members stand ready to help students overcome any lingering math anxiety and gear up for calculus. No departments are considered shamefully weak, but those that are too small to command much attention on campus include physics, anthropology, drama and math. Communications is also small but boasts a new electronic writing lab. With the life science building and arts center newly renovated, the campus is on its way to becoming extraordinarily well equipped. It's already extraordinarily beautiful, with eucalyptus trees and jasmine bushes clustered around red-roofed, white buildings against the almost always blue California sky.

Mills students are encouraged to explore beyond the bounds of the Oakland campus—the school's motto is "one destination, different roads"—and many take advantage of the many excellent programs abroad and exchanges with other American schools. A year at a women's or coed college in the East is especially popular. Mills has concurrent cross-registration agreements with UC Berkeley and most Bay area universities, and there is also a five-year engineering program with several of the same schools. Opportunities for internships abound. The library includes a twelve-thousand-volume collection of rare books and the otherwise modest holdings are currently marked for expansion. Students also have the privilege of using the huge facilities at Berkeley, via the free shuttle bus that connects the campuses.

About two-thirds of the Mills women are from California. More than 20 percent of the students are from minority groups and about 10 percent from foreign nations. About three-quarters of the students are graduates of public high schools, most ranking in the middle to upper echelons of their graduating classes. An influential subgroup of the student body are "resumers," women returning to college after a break of several years. Everybody appreciates the variety of viewpoints offered by their diverse class-mates. As one woman says, "Anything is accepted, cliques are rare, and the small student body lets everybody recognize one another." Sixty merit scholarships are handed out, ranging from $2,000 to full tuition.

Residential living, required for most undergraduates, is especially attractive. Four Mediterranean-style old dorms and three California modern Hill dorms all have spacious single rooms; only a few freshmen live in doubles. There are also college-owned apartments and French- and Spanish-language wings. Older dorms are more homey, and all function without curfews or visitation regulations. Each of the older dorms has its own dining room, and students living in the three newer dorms eat together at the commons. The food is excellent, and each Wednesday night a sit-down candlelight dinner is served.

While some Mills women may have reservations about their college's single-sex status when entering, fears about a stunted social life are quickly dispelled. On a typical weekend evening, students can choose any one of several options: "going to a film or dance on campus, having a party in their room, going into Berkeley or San Francisco." Frat hops around Berkeley are popular and men frequently show up at Mills functions. "Guys are here quite frequently," reports one woman, "but then there are times when you appreciate the fact that they aren't." With a bus stop on campus, it is easy to get around Oakland and into San Francisco (half an hour away) to take advantage of the dining, dancing and cultural resources of both cities. Farther away, there's the college ski lodge in the Sierra Nevadas. Mills students are also becoming more involved in intercollegiate sports. The college joined the NCAA Division III in 1982 and increased its varsity offerings to six while expanding its intramural program. Tennis, volleyball and a championship crew are the athletic highlights. Participation in student government and other campus organizations is strong, and the Feminist Alliance is one of the most active student groups.

In assessing their undergraduate years, Mills women praise especially the institution's intimacy and diversity. "I really like the other students here," adds one senior. "They are intelligent, creative women who are unafraid of success and achievement." In short, Mills offers a respectable academic education without high pressure or high competition—a place in which students can pursue intellectual growth without missing out on all the delights of California's most beautiful area and a social life miles ahead of that of most women's schools.

371

Millsaps College

Jackson, MS 39210

Location City outskirts
Total Enrollment 1,360
Undergraduates 1,270
Male/Female 48/52
SAT Comp 1100
ACT 24
Financial Aid 51%
Expense Pr $

Applicants 890
Accepted 82%
Enrolled 43%
Academics ★ ★ ★
Social ☎ ☎ ☎
Q of L ● ● ●
Admissions (601)354-5201

From the Mississippi backwoods to the growing capital city of Jackson where it is located, accolades accrue for tiny Millsaps College. By popular acclaim it's the best school in Mississippi. As far as resources and reputation goes, Millsaps is hardly a competitor with small liberal arts colleges above the Mason-Dixon Line. But hour for hour in the library, its undergraduates could take on the best of any Yankee student body. As one student attests, "If you don't study, you're an outcast."

The faculty enjoys a high rating in accessibility and overall ability, and small classes ensure "an unavoidable encounter with teachers." At Millsaps, classroom instruction is "the opposite end of the spectrum from the assembly-line approach to teaching," explains one senior. Millsaps has a rigorous core curriculum with requirements in all the standard liberal arts fields. A popular way for freshmen to satisfy half the core requirements is through the Heritage program, a team-taught, yearlong interdisciplinary study of the cultural heritage of the West. With its four lectures, two discussion seminars, one lab a week, and a companion English writing course, Heritage accounts for two-thirds of a freshman's work load. It's a heavy commitment that makes for a difficult freshman year, but completion of the program allows for more flexibility in scheduling during the next three years. Juniors with at least a 3.0 average may opt for Science and the Human Prospect, a three-semester honors program that carries the Heritage experience over into the natural science requirements. This program requires a special colloquium and research leading to a thesis in the senior year. A recent curriculum change has added a required upper-level course, which is designed to emphasize the development of thinking and writing skills.

The premed and prelaw curricula at Millsaps are highly regarded both by students and by graduate schools. Eighty percent of medical school hopefuls and 90 percent of the lawyers-to-be are accepted into graduate programs. The School of Management, in its newly renovated facility, offers solid bachelor degree programs in accounting, administration, finance and economics. Qualified students can also earn an MBA in five years. Other good programs include music (excellent faculty and strong preprofessional training), history ("Fantastic!") and political science. Art, geology and sociology generate negative reviews.

Students may take the Oak Ridge Science Semester,* complete research in marine sciences at the Gulf Coast Research Laboratory, or gain academic credit for internships in business, government and health. Other options include a semester at Oxford or London and cooperative engineering and medical technology programs with Vanderbilt, Columbia, Georgia Tech and other schools.

Centered around the "Bowl," which, according to legend, is the crater of an extinct volcano, Millsaps' hundred-acre campus near the center of Jackson is a pleasant mix of modern and traditional red-brick buildings. At the bottom of the Bowl is the student union. Millsaps is completely surrounded by a new ten-foot-high fence, and efforts to close the campus off to cars are currently under way. "We spend a lot of time dodging dirt piles right now, but that's only a sign of improvement," reports an English major.

Millsaps is a Methodist-sponsored institution, but the amount of religious influence that trickles down to the student level is debatable. One student reports the affiliation has a "near unnoticeable effect," while another contends it means "we have to act superficially proper." Yet Millsaps has broadened the philosophical and regional roots of its student body in recent years—only 35 percent of the students are Methodist, and approximately half now come from beyond state borders. There's even diversity among the southerners. "Students range from boarding school brats, to small-town country boys, to suntanned, bleached-blond beach bums from the coast," reports one student. Although only half of the students graduated in the top fifth of their class, "the cool thing to do is to make A's, not drink the most beer," one man says.

Millsaps was the first college in the state to adopt voluntarily a policy of open admissions for minority students (now about 7 percent of the student body), and it has developed a special premedical program for the disadvantaged. The college attempts to meet "95 to 100 percent of the demonstrated financial need of all enrolling students." It also offers about forty-seven academic merit scholarships yearly, ranging from $1,000 to $4,000. Tuition may be the highest of any college in Mississippi, but by national standards Millsaps is a bargain.

High-caliber football, basketball and both men's and women's tennis attract a fair number of jocks, but athletics are secondary to learning at Millsaps. "Our football team can go undefeated, and the players walk off the field worrying about tests on Monday," observes one sports fan.

Most of the students live in comfortable air-conditioned campus housing, including the two new dorms, built to accommodate the recent increase in enrollment. The freshmen have their own single-sex dorms and strict visitation regulations. Upperclassmen choose among two women's dorms (one has a kitchen), a men's dorm or four fraternity houses. There is no sorority housing, though a large proportion of the women as well as men are Greek-affiliated. Students buy either a twenty-one- or fourteen-meal plan with tickets redeemable in either the cafeteria or the grill.

Fraternities and sororities, while exclusive, don't dominate campus activities. Each of the eight organizations must throw one open party a year, and most provide more. Any latent animosity between independents and Greeks is resolved on the intramural playing fields or playing tables: backgammon, bridge and Trivial Pursuit are new intramural sports at Millsaps. Thursday nights at CS's, a bar and restaurant directly across the street, is another way the whole campus gets together. Ten miles to the north is a huge reservoir, popular for weekend water sports, and New Orleans, three-and-a-half hours away, makes a nice weekend road trip.

Some of the smartest students in Mississippi attend Millsaps, although one Millsapian notes, "True intellectuals tend to leave the state"—as do many Millsaps graduates. But for those committed to a Sun Belt future, the college is an excellent investment. One accounting major sums his choice to stay in Jackson this way: "We live in a brand-name society and in the South, Millsaps is the best label around."

University of Minnesota—Twin Cities

Minneapolis, MN 55455

Location Urban
Total Enrollment 46,440
Undergraduates 33,000
Male/Female 55/45
SAT V/M 490/570
ACT 23
Financial Aid 66%
Expense Pub $ $

Applicants 11,320
Accepted 73%
Enrolled 62%
Academics ★ ★ ★
Social 🕿 🕿 🕿
Q of L ● ● ●
Admissions (612)625-2008

The University of Minnesota is not just big. It's enormous. More than forty-six thousand students—about thirty-three thousand of them undergraduates—attend classes at the Twin Cities campus, making it one of the largest single campuses in the nation. You know it has to have something for everyone.

Students can choose from more than 250 majors in twenty-eight separate schools, but the president says that "professional education is what the university has focused on and is able to do best." Engineering is notable for the options it offers for tutorials and internships. Mathematics, agriculture and the sciences are also strong, as are geography, astronomy, psychology, political science, journalism and economics. The forestry and Scandinavian studies programs are also excellent—not surprising considering the area and its cultural heritage. Undergraduates also have access to more esoteric fields, from aging studies and biometry to therapeutic recreation and mortuary science. The university's distribution requirements in the liberal arts were recently strengthened—three years of a foreign language are now part of the package—and even undergraduates in the Institute of Technology have to fulfill them. In addition, the university has moved to put more emphasis on writing throughout the curriculum.

"Combining both the beauty of nature and the excitement of a big city," the University of Minnesota's physical setting couldn't be better, one student cheers. There are actually three main sections of the vast Twin Cities campus, and within each the architecture is highly diverse. The St. Paul campus encompasses the colleges of agriculture, forestry and home economics, and the Minneapolis campus is divided by the Mississippi River into an East Bank and a West Bank that are home to the other colleges and most of the dormitories, as well as all but a few of the fraternities and sororities. The two campuses are linked by a free bus service. Academic facilities are excellent, beginning with the 3.8-million-volume library system, which is one of the best in the nation. Every one of the colleges has its own library, many of which are good places to study. There is also a 695-acre arboretum, which is used for research and teaching. The popular computer science major is supported by sophisticated facilities. But while there are even terminals in the dorms, demand still outstrips supply.

Class size can range from ten to twenty-five hundred, with introductory classes normally the biggest and the professor just a talking head on a video screen (one was in reruns for two years after he was fired). The thoughtful student can, however, find ways of rising out of the sea of anonymity. The place is crawling with potentially helpful teaching assistants, and the excellent honors program in the liberal arts college allows close contact with faculty members as well as leeway to enroll in certain graduate courses and seminars. Still, as one engineering major says, "If a student disliked large classes, he wouldn't attend here." Undergraduates have a difficult time enrolling in all the courses they want at registration, but the use of a rotating alphabetical system assures everyone a crack at the courses they really want sometime during their academic careers. Those careers are often four and a half or five years long, since many students take time off to work and others find internship opportunities at the many corporations and government agencies in the Twin Cities area. The university operates on the quarter system, with the summer term interchangeable with the other three. Almost all classes have a pass/fail option, but this can be invoked for no more than a quarter of a student's courses.

Nearly half the students at the university come from the top fifth of their high school class, and all but 20 percent of them are from Minnesota. At a university that has graduates ranging from former Chief Justice Warren Burger to Yankee outfielder Dave Winfield, you can expect to find a diverse group. "It seems that there is a progressive tendency among students, but the fundamentalists scream pretty loud, so it weighs out about equally," a chemistry major comments. In addition to need-based financial aid, a number of academic merit scholarships are awarded, with stipends from $500 to $3,000. National Merit Scholars who specify Minnesota as their first choice qualify automatically. The athletic department hands out over three hundred additional awards to both men and women athletes.

All but about 10 percent of the students live off campus and commute to classes. Since there are only eight residence halls, dorm rooms are very hard to obtain, and parking spaces for all those commuters are almost as dear. Students who have rooms get the chance to keep them for the next year, leaving freshmen to try for what's left, which isn't much. Prospective freshmen should apply for a room early—even before they've been admitted—although an invitation to live on campus does not guarantee admission to the university and vice versa. Dorm residents are required to join a meal plan. About 4 percent of the undergraduates live in the forty-three fraternities and sororities, which provide most of the social life for a significant number of students but by no means all. Partying goes on at a variety of other venues, and most students "try to keep a warm fire burning inside while blizzards are raging outside."

Since so many students live off campus, the school social life is not the only diversion available. The downtown areas of the Twin Cities are easy to get to by bus, and there are scores of good bars, restaurants, night spots and movie theaters. This is an athletically inclined bunch of students, with both intramural and varsity sports popular. Minnesota boasts great hockey and basketball teams, and students are always hoping that the current season will be one in which the gridiron Gophers take home the roses in a bowl victory. Intramural competition can go on well past midnight. More than four hundred extracurricular organizations offer respite from the books—"Myself, I joined the ballroom dancing club," an English major reports.

Minnesota can get brutally cold in the winter, but for those who enjoy skiing or skating that's no hardship. For those who want to avoid the winter winds, many of the campus buildings are linked by underground tunnels. In the summer Minnesota's famed ten thousand lakes offer swimming, boating and fishing.

"The U," as students call it, has everything. It's easy to become a needle in the haystack, but it's also possible to use its riches to your advantage. "I can blend into the crowd if I want to," says one student, "or I can make myself stand out if I feel like it." At the University of Minnesota, the clear blue sky is the limit.

University of Missouri—Columbia

Columbia, MO 65211

Location Rural
Total Enrollment 22,890
Undergraduates 17,260
Male/Female 51/49
SAT V/M 470/520
ACT 23
Financial Aid 55%
Expense Pu $ $

Applicants 7,200
Accepted 84%
Enrolled 60%
Academics ★ ★
Social 🐗🐗🐗🐗
Q of L ●●●
Admissions (314)882-7786

The University of Missouri is the quintessential large public university. The architecture and academic offerings are diverse; the students work hard and party even harder. For years, Mizzou (as the natives lovingly call it) has been tagged as one of the top party schools in the country. Sitting smack dab in the middle of the "Show-Me" state, Mizzou upholds its responsibility to exemplify college life a la American.

Mansion-like fraternity and sorority houses flank the edges of a spacious, tree-filled campus that could double as a history lesson in a century and a half of changes in American architecture. The school's progression from the first public college west of the Mississippi to a sprawling university complex can easily be charted. Divided into a red campus of vine-covered, historical red-brick buildings and a white campus of stone and modern facilities, Mizzou houses everything from a white wooden chicken coop and livestock pavilion to a sleek new engineering complex.

With 250 degree programs and 19 schools and colleges, Mizzou offers a comprehensive set of choices for basic and advanced study. By far the most prestigious of all departments is the school of journalism (the first in the nation), which continues to attract many out-of-staters. Young writers get hands-on experience with the *Columbia Missourian,* the local daily paper, the news department of an NBC affiliate and a National Public Radio station. Missouri boasts an 83 percent job placement record in news-related fields.

The agriculture program is also nationally ranked, especially in the area of applied research for the agribusiness and farm communities. Its strong and diverse offerings include an Animal Science Research Center and a Food for the 21st Century research program. The College of Engineering maintains several notable undergraduate segments, including agricultural, aerospace, civil and nuclear. The College of Business and Public Administration is nationally ranked and highly competitive. Regardless of the school they enter, however, undergrads can expect 60 percent of their study to be in the College of Arts and Sciences, where the departments of history, geology and biology are particularly strong. The recent creation of the School of Fine Arts has bolstered an already impressive speech and dramatic arts department, and a new writing program woven into the curriculum is aimed at shaping coherent undergraduate writing skills. Computer science, education, the classics, allied health sciences and modern languages receive low scores among students.

"Class size is astounding at first," recalls a junior. Lectures can contain five hundred or more students, which obviously limits personal contact between students and professors, and tends to promote the "just-another-number syndrome." Some of these mass-production classes have laboratory sections run by teaching assistants to help the overworked professors and answer student questions. Registration offers the dual certainty of long lines and slim chances of getting into all of the courses you want. "It took me three semesters to get into one mandatory class in the advertising sequence," reports a senior. "The lack of courses being given at different times leaves out a number of students." To complicate matters further, "academic advising is one of the university's weakest points," claims a poli-sci major. "Students are either left on their own or advised into classes they can't handle." Still, students attest to the caring, concerned attitudes of most faculty members, who attempt to make themselves available when needed.

The academic climate at Mizzou is as varied as the huge campus. The school of journalism is said to maintain an almost cutthroat atmosphere, and "is proud to have the most students with stress problems." Yet in other areas, students contend "many would just as soon kick back and take life casually." The study-conscious sorts will find plenty of room and resources in Ellis Library, which is so tremendous that, to reduce the number of lost students, the university offers a course on how to use it. (After the $8-million addition is complete, students can *really* get lost.) Mammoth though they may be, the library and the campus are highly accessible to the handicapped.

About 90 percent of Mizzou's students are native Missourians; the roads from St. Louis and Kansas City are well traveled by cars stuffed with black-and-gold Mizzou paraphernalia at the beginning and end of each summer. Most students are from public schools, and almost half ranked in the top 20 percent of their high school class. Out-of-staters are as eligible for need-based aid as anyone else. One out of six students receives some sort of merit scholarship, from $200 to full tuition. A typical incoming class might have as many as 125 National Merit Scholars, and more than 250 athletes on nine men's and seven women's sports teams receive scholarships.

Dormitories have double rooms and are often crowded and noisy, and many report great fun to live in. Only two dorms are coed by floor, and visitors of the opposite sex must abide by the strictly enforced rules. After a year or two many residents decide to leave the dorms and live in Columbia, where most apartment complexes in this little-more-than-college town are occupied by students. The frat and sorority houses are livable (the frat houses less so) although not all members can fit. Dorm residents are required to take twenty meals a week at their dorm cafeteria, and meal plans are also available to nonresidents. "The food is Grade D but edible," says one student. When all else fails, hamburgers and french fries are obtainable at every meal, and the recently added microwaves make frozen food an option.

Students are generally a "don't-rock-the-boat," traditional crew. Studying is "the thing to do" most every weeknight, which means students must work twice as hard on the weekends to maintain their big party-school image. The great Greek way mesmerizes about 20 percent of Mizzou students and offers an unending good time for those who enjoy homecoming dances or theme parties down at the Lake of the Ozarks. Although "there's a lot of separation between independents and Greeks," the less fraternal type student will find plenty to do.

The town offers a versatile bar scene (comedy, video, progressive music, etc.), and movies, expensive shops and private bashes—all of which provide limitless entertainment. "Columbia is a great place to go to school, but I wouldn't want to live here," says a finance major. Because "education is the main industry of Columbia," many students find they need an occasional change of scenery and head back east to St. Louis, out west to Kansas City (each about an hour and a half away), or wherever—"Everyone likes to road trip and it doesn't matter where as long as it's fun," explains a journalism major.

377

Mizzou has always been a big basketball school, but the football team often has a tough time battling its Big Eight rivals. School spirit tends to fluctuate—"There's a lot of student interest when we win"—but the women's basketball team is consistently something to cheer about. The popular intramural program offers nearly two dozen sports and two divisions of skill, so the bloodthirsty competitors and peace-loving nonjocks can each get what they want out of the program. In fact, it takes extra effort to become bored at this university, which publishes "an entire book of extracurricular activities."

Mizzou is large, but the friendly midwestern atmosphere helps most students find a comfortable niche as well as their own particular balance between the social extravagance and the many academic alternatives. One student notes, "Mizzou is an excellent school at which to have unlimited fun without completely sacrificing educational goals." Now that's higher education the American way.

Montana College of Mineral Science and Technology

Butte, MT 59701

Location City outskirts	**Applicants** 400
Total Enrollment 1,850	**Accepted** 92%
Undergraduates 1,750	**Enrolled** 85%
Male/Female 60/40	**Academics** ★ ★ ★
SAT V/M 470/540	**Social** ☎ ☎
ACT 20	**Q of L** ● ● ●
Financial Aid 66%	**Admissions** (406)486-4178
Expense Pub $	

Montana College of Mineral Science and Technology's motto is *De Re Metallica,* which loosely translated means "concerning metal." This accurately sums up not only the school's reason for being but its academic strengths as well. Situated on a shoulder of "the richest hill on earth" overlooking the once prosperous but now declining mining town of Butte, Tech (formerly called Montana School of Mines) has long existed in order to turn out engineers for mineral and petroleum industries. Consequently, its undergraduates view themselves less as students and more as engineers-in-training.

Tech's degree programs emphasize the study of the world's energy, mineral and environmental problems. Among the school's curriculums in eight engineering fields, departments in mining, metallurgical engineering, mineral processing, petroleum engineering and geology are the standouts, but efforts have been made in recent years to develop work in the basic sciences underlying these engineering programs. Everyone faces general education requirements, much to the dismay of some who would prefer a wider choice of technical electives. But for those with somewhat wider interests, there is a new (although still ill-defined) major in science and technology that attempts to relate liberal arts to today's increasingly technological society. As a hedge against declining job prospects in the energy field, the college has built up its business administration program to the extent that it now has the largest enrollment in the institution. The administration concedes, though, that business offerings still need "refinement" if they are to become academically competitive with the more established courses of study.

Academic work at Tech is rigorous, with gym the only subject that can be taken pass/fail. Courses usually get easier after the freshman year, though, and few people actually sweat over their books late into the night. Faculty members have a genuine interest in teaching and are willing to go out of their way to accommodate students. What the professors may lack in academic training (only 60 percent or so have their PhDs), they make up for in industrial experience—most engineering faculty have spent an average of eight years on the job. They also win praise for the close attention they lavish on students. "If you need help, you'll get it," a senior states.

The small, sixteen-building campus is a blend of old (1900) and new. Unique features include the Museum Building, which houses one of the country's largest mineral collections, the Earthquake Studies Office, which records tremors throughout southwestern Montana, and the Montana Bureau of Mines and Geology, a research arm of the college which produces geological and mineralogical maps and publications. The new library featuring a 260-seat auditorium is well stocked with technical materials but deficient in everything else. The other serious resource gap is the limited lab facilities in a few programs such as environmental engineering and engineering science.

More than 80 percent of the students are from Montana and anyone who graduates from a Montana public high school is guaranteed admission. There is no limit on class size and applications are accepted up to the day of registration. The good number of foreigners and few out-of-staters (who hail from as far away as Florida and Connecticut) must meet slightly more rigorous admissions criteria. Many undergraduates are reportedly the first in their families to go to college. "Hicks who are intelligent but lack knowledge of the world" is how one man describes his classmates. If you're not conservative, be ready to stand on your own.

Freshmen vie for a hefty batch of non-need scholarships, ranging up to $1,800 and awarded on the basis of "academic merit and leadership ability." Registration and incidental fees are waived for any Montana state resident of one-fourth Indian blood or more, for war orphans and for a few others. Twenty percent of the students pack into the dorm, which provides rooms for men on the first three floors, women on the fourth. The school likes freshmen to live on campus, but upperclassmen live either in the many nearby apartments or houses. Dorm students eat in the campus cafeteria, where food is good enough to lure nearly everybody to lunch. A bus service runs into town.

Although the ratio of men to women is three to two, little dating occurs among Tech students, who usually seek entertainment with hometown friends. Fraternity life, attracting but 5 percent of the men, is largely ignored by the bulk of students. On weekends, students fill the time between studying with dinner, a movie, church, or outdoor recreation. Butte's setting is magnificent and areas for skiing, fishing, hunting, hiking, and camping are close by. Athletics are improving—the administration seems to have taken a fancy to it—and football and basketball games are drawing bigger crowds. Women's volleyball brings home the most trophies. Tech students take advantage of the excellent intramural program and facilities in a modern physical education complex. The Student Union features a dining area, game room, bookstore, student-owned FM radio station and television, where students are known to tune in to cartoons in the afternoon.

Montana Tech's goal-oriented students praise their school for the fine technical education they receive. Although employment in the oil and mining industries isn't what it used to be, they remain pleased with the school's job placement statistics. To them, the school is a gem.

Morehouse College, GA
—See ATLANTA UNIVERSITY CENTER

Morris Brown College, GA
—See ATLANTA UNIVERSITY CENTER

Mount Holyoke College

South Hadley, MA 01075

Location Small town	**Applicants** 2,020
Total Enrollment 1,950	**Accepted** 54%
Undergraduates 1,950	**Enrolled** 53%
Male/Female N/A	**Academics** ★ ★ ★ ★
SAT V/M 600/600	**Social** 🐘 🐘 🐘
Financial Aid 60%	**Q of L** ● ● ●
Expense Pr $ $ $ $	**Admissions** (413)538-2023

Mount Holyoke, once the nation's only college for women, stands proudly in the tradition that women's colleges are the best place for women to reach their full potential. Strong academics make this easy to do as far as the mind is concerned. Developing a comparable social life takes a little more resourcefulness. But Mount Holyoke students are convinced that a little inconvenience on the weekends is a small price to pay for the educational riches that abound the other five days of the week.

Eight-hundred acres of rolling hills, lakes and waterfalls soften the stark modern glass and stone buildings so that they seem to blend naturally with the older ivy-covered red-brick structures. Similarly, despite a few modernizations, "the curriculum has remained traditional, which makes it look innovative in the '80s," says one administrator. One noteworthy feature is that all students must take at least one course in non-Western culture, visible proof of the school's commitment to "break away from the strictly Eurocentric focus" of most liberal arts curriculums in the United States. Otherwise, distribution requirements are fairly standard, including courses in a foreign language and physical education. "We take our work seriously," confesses one senior. And so, it seems, do the professors. One student tells of a German professor who made tracks through a New England blizzard on cross-country skis to deliver a scheduled exam on time. "That's serious!"

Mount Holyoke is decidedly strongest in the sciences, boasting some of the best equipped undergraduate chemistry labs in the country. Also well equipped are the students who emerge from these labs—more graduates from this school go on to earn PhDs in chemistry and biology than any other liberal arts college. Mount Holyoke is also a center of research in the field of women's studies, and international relations is the fastest-growing department. Students praise English, history, dance and studio art, but they say astronomy, geography and most languages are not up to par. And even the administration admits sociology offerings are "lackluster."

Although intro courses can have as many as sixty students, most upper-level courses are intimate. Students report they have been in classes of three. With a ten-to-one student/professor ratio at Mount Holyoke, students appreciate their close relationships with the faculty—relationships even a first-semester freshman can enjoy. As one student recalls, "I had the opportunity to take classes with Shirley Chisholm, James Baldwin and Joseph Brodsky my *freshman* year!" There is even a tutorial program set up to allow freshmen and faculty members to study a subject of mutual interest one-on-one. Competition among students is rare, since the emphasis is on individual improvement. Students adhere to an honor system that includes self-scheduled final exams. The January winter term is optional at Mount Holyoke, but students often opt to take a two-credit, nontraditional course or participate in an off-campus internship during the month. The Washington internship program is the most popular of these real-life work experiences. Many students pack their bags junior year and leave Massachusetts for a semester abroad—either with the Twelve-College Exchange* or one of Mount Holyoke's own programs in England, Japan or a Third World country.

Mount Holyoke attracts students from all over the nation and the world, and students value this diversity. Only a quarter of the student body is from Massachusetts, and two-thirds come from public school backgrounds. Minorities make up about 11 percent of the student body, and as one student stresses, "The only thing you need to fit in here is an open mind—a willingness to explore different cultures and accept others with different values, goals and attitudes." A plus in MHC admissions: Sixty to seventy students enter the college from the waiting list in early February. The college attempts to meet the demonstrated need of most students, but no merit or athletic scholarships are tendered.

The nineteen spacious dorms range in size from 65 to 130 students, and all maintain a proportional representation of the classes. Freshmen are included in every dorm and even have a choice of which one they prefer. After this first year of preferential treatment, students endure both a dorm and room lottery. Upperclassmen usually win singles; freshmen and sophomores have large, one-room doubles. Dinner is served in the dorms by student waitresses Monday through Thursday; the rest of the week students eat cafeteria style. Anyone who finds studying at night leads to the hungries need not have a growly stomach at Holyoke because milk and crackers are served at 10 PM each night. Yet with the college's own bakery on the premises, "crackers" really means tempting desserts of all kinds, and the "freshman 10" are a fact of life.

Students find the Five College Consortium* to be one of Mount Holyoke's greatest assets. A free bus service runs every twenty minutes between UMass, Amherst, Smith and Hampshire, multiplying a Holyoke student's access to academic, social, and cultural opportunities. The college encourages athletic participation for everyone and tempts laggards with a demanding golf course, jogging trails and two lakes. An extensive equestrian center is in the soon-to-be-completed stages, and a magnificent new $9-million sports complex houses a pool, courts for half a dozen indoor sports and a state-of-the-arts dance performance center. Varsity teams are strong on the whole; the riding team won the 1986 Nationals. And recently track and field has been added as a varsity sport. The crew regattas take the place of football games; nearly everyone comes out to cheer. Students also crowd the ski slopes of nearby Mount Tom, and during winter term make the trek to mountains near Dartmouth and Williams. Year-round, they trek to Dartmouth for something other than outdoor sports. "Road trips are really the focal point of most social activities," says one woman. And this road tripping is not all one-sided: Mount Holyoke looks like a coed school on the weekends, students report.

Although students admit to having to work for a social life, Mount Holyoke women, perhaps more than their counterparts at Smith and Wellesley, have made a virtue out of their school's most visible "vice": the lack of men. "Being at a single-sex institution, I've had a greater opportunity to become a student leader and really realize my potential," proclaims a chemistry major. Students enjoy the fact that all leadership positions are filled by women, and there's a strong and supportive community spirit. "Like a family, the success of one reflects well on all," says one student.

The traditional college social life is there (or nearby) for the asking, but most MHC women make academics their first priority. "You can be all you want to be," one student claims. "Mount Holyoke instills a belief in your ability, especially as a woman."

Muhlenberg College

Allentown, PA 18104

Location City outskirts	**Applicants** 1,850
Total Enrollment 1,500	**Accepted** 65%
Undergraduates 1,500	**Enrolled** 36%
Male/Female 49/51	**Academics** ★ ★ ★
SAT V/M 520/570	**Social** 🐘 🐘 🐘
Financial Aid 64%	**Q of L** ● ● ● ●
Expense Pr $ $ $	**Admissions** (215)821-3201

One of several colleges in Pennsylvania's Lehigh Valley, Muhlenberg stands out for its combination of a challenging curriculum with a family atmosphere that makes everyone feel at home. Students commend the enthusiasm of their professors, accept the demands of a five-course-per-term work load, and thrive on an environment that leaves little time for relaxation. In the poetic words of one premed: "We have a definite attitude of diligence when it comes down to studying."

Set upon seventy-five acres in a safe, suburban area, overlooking the Lehigh Valley and adjacent to Allentown's public park system, Muhlenberg is in the process of adding more modern buildings to its mix of Gothic and nineteenth-century structures. "The grass and trees are evaporating," complains one student about the common sight of construction sites here. But others see the expansion as positive and necessary. "If Muhlenberg rises in status over the next few decades as it plans to, I can see my diploma appreciating in value," says a visionary science major. The college is also attempting to boost its liberal arts departments up to the standards of its science offerings while keeping the student body small and the student/faculty ratio intimate.

Muhlenberg made its regional reputation on its premedical program, which continues to attract a large proportion of students and to set the campus tone. "Anyone who makes it through is guaranteed a seat in med school," says one hard-at-work student. The science lab equipment is state-of-the-art, including two electron microscopes, and the chemistry department has a major textbook author right on staff. For those who can't choose among the scientific goodies, a comprehensive natural science major enables you to sample all of them. Students also praise the English, math, history and drama departments as well as the smaller programs of environmental, American and Russian studies. Business administration and computer science, popular majors despite student complaints about their quality, have been upgraded and expanded in the past two years. Communications, art and music departments remain weak, although the lavish Center for the Arts (designed by Philip Johnson) is a boon for extracurricular activities. Despite Muhlenberg's Lutheran connection (the college is named for the patriarch of Lutheranism in America), it offers no religion major, only a broad pretheological interdisciplinary program. The college's general education requirements include four courses in the humanities, four courses in the natural sciences and mathematics, a two-semester history course and three courses in the social sciences.

Except for the introductory science lectures, most classes enroll fewer than thirty students, ensuring a close student-teacher interaction. A three-person advising team (one professor and two upperclassmen) adopt groups of ten to fifteen freshmen, providing individual attention that eases the transition from high school. Internships are gaining in popularity, and independent study is easily arranged. Muhlenberg sends study groups to Russia and Washington, D.C., and students may spend semesters abroad in France, Germany or Spain. Cooperative programs with larger universities in dentistry, engineering and forestry are available. The library is described as "stuffy and bleak," insufficient, especially for research, and replete with "lots of obscure German texts." The opening of a technologically modern, $11-million library is anxiously awaited by students and staff.

Muhlenberg draws more than half of its undergraduates from the top fifth of northeastern and Middle Atlantic public school classes. They are a fairly homogeneous bunch, with members of minority groups accounting for less than 5 percent of the total enrollment. There is, however, a touch of religious diversity, with about 15 percent of the students Lutheran and many of the rest either Jewish or Roman Catholic. Muhlenberg attempts to meet the computed financial needs of all its students. Undergraduates of Swedish descent who need financial aid can apply for special scholarships, and children of Lutheran ministers get a 50 percent discount. Only a handful of $500 merit awards are available to others, and there are no athletic scholarships.

Muhlenberg discourages off-campus living and guarantees housing to all undergraduates except transfers. Single-sex and coed dorms are available, and one denizen notes that the housing department is "doing an excellent job of upgrading all the residence halls." As befits a school with a strong sense of community, single rooms are rare, and all houses enjoy round-the-clock visitation rights. Increased enrollment in the past decade resulted in some overcrowding and led to the construction of McGregor Village, a complex of prefabs that has become a popular housing choice.

The dining hall serves either a seven- or five-day meal plan. Freshmen must choose the former, while fraternity members and McGregor Village residents, who have kitchenettes, are excused altogether. The food is decent, varied somewhat by a salad bar, a soup-and-bread line, brown bag lunches, "wellness" entrees and an ever-operative ice cream machine.

Social life at Muhlenberg is low-key, partly because of the work load (study dates are popular) and partly because no parties are allowed on school nights. But when undergrads turn from studies to weekend diversions, they find enough to satisfy every taste. The Muhlenberg Theater Association provides an excellent assortment of drama each season, and the Nite Owl, a campus pub, sponsors talent nights. Buses stop five minutes from campus for trips to Allentown proper and nearby malls.

Muhlenberg's five fraternities provide the focus for dancing and drinking, although dorms have their share of weekend parties. Pennsylvania's drinking age is twenty-one, but one student reports that "Muhlenberg has a type of 'anything goes' attitude as long as it is done on campus." About half of the Muhlenberg men pledge fraternities, which offer housing to some, but not all, of their members. Three sororities have appeared on campus, though as yet they have no housing facilities. To everyone's relief, the Greeks don't dominate Muhlenberg social life, just vary it.

For the athletically minded, intramural sports arouse far more passion than varsity efforts. In fact, the new Life Sports Center is off limits to varsity teams. For those intent on enjoying a little intercollegiate rivalry, football and basketball generate the most enthusiasm. Budding DJs can perfect their rap on the 250-watt radio station, which reaches out about fifty miles.

In any case, Muhlenberg students have more on their minds than wild parties and games all week, or even weekend long. Their focus is largely on success in life after college, and most are willing to put up with dwindling green space, and long hours in the library and laboratory to get it.

University of Nebraska at Lincoln

Lincoln, NE 68588

Location Center city	**Applicants** 5,950
Total Enrollment 23,170	**Accepted** 93%
Undergraduates 17,820	**Enrolled** 65%
Male/Female 56/44	**Academics** ★ ★ ★
ACT V/M 20/21	**Social** ☏ ☏ ☏ ☏
Financial Aid 52%	**Q of L** ● ● ●
Expense Pub $ $	**Admissions** (402)472-3620

Bright high school students who want to stay in the Cornhusker State make a beeline for Lincoln, home of the largest branch of the state's university system and one of the nation's consistently great football teams. The University of Nebraska is a typical land-grant state university: large, rural and somewhat impersonal in tone. Also tied to the land are the university's finances, and the depressed Nebraska farm economy has forced the state government to snip away at the UNL budget four times in the last five years. When students here speak woefully of "cuts," and they do often, they're not talking about skipping classes.

UNL spreads across two campuses. The East Campus with its beautiful arboretums and commons is home to the schools of agriculture and home economics, alongside the schools of law and dentistry. Most entering students end up on the larger City Campus, where concrete is the norm rather than grass and where the architecture is described as a "mish-mash of whatever they had enough money to build at the time."

It is home to six of the eight undergraduate colleges: architecture, arts and sciences, business administration, engineering, technology, and the teacher's college.

Strong undergraduate offerings include electrical and chemical engineering, teacher preparation and journalism, while the agriculture college receives much student approval for its outstanding animal science programs. The liberal arts get somewhat shortchanged amidst the profusion of professional programs, but English, math and chemistry are particular standouts in the college of arts and sciences. As for the college of business, "My God, it's overcrowded," exclaims a junior who is not at all pleased by the use of "low-quality" videotapes in place of living, breathing accounting professors. Innovative offerings include construction management in engineering, franchise management in business and actuarial science. Another bright spot is the university's honors program, which allows students whose interests do not fall within traditional departmental lines to develop their own major under the tutelage of faculty members. If all this sounds confusing, the newly instituted, one-semester get-acquainted-with-UNL course for incoming freshmen is praised by students.

The main library keeps only limited hours on the weekends—those budget cuts again—and part of the building has been sealed off because of staff layoffs. Getting into courses in the most popular areas can be a problem; for all schools, preregistration is a must to ensure a satisfactory schedule. All senior faculty members are required to teach introductory courses, and freshmen are thus assured of contact with top professors, if only in the lecture hall. But until junior or senior year, the most personal instruction is often with graduate teaching assistants. Academic counseling needs improvement; many students say they prefer to get help from upperclassmen. Nebraska offers study abroad in Costa Rica, Mexico, Japan and Great Britain. Students can also immerse themselves in a foreign language by living on campus for five weeks during the summer in a special language house.

This primarily Nebraskan student body is divided, most conspicuously, into two types of students: the elite band of mesomorphs who play on the football team and the remaining majority of mere mortals who root for the Big Red. The whole fall semester revolves around football weekends, and the celebration usually extends to the postseason when the beloved Cornhuskers are almost always in one of the top college bowl games. Other than these two body types, the university rarely challenges the friendly, conservative community. According to one man's perspective, "Our Democrats are like the rest of the country's Republicans, and our Republicans are weird!"

Admissions is carried out on a rolling basis, with class rank, not test scores, considered the most important factor. Nebraska usually accepts 95 percent of applicants from the state and about 80 percent of outsiders. About three-fourths come from the top half of their high school classes. Students are admitted without regard to their ability to pay, and those with their papers in order by April 1 will be considered for need-based aid. But, according to students who've experienced the financial aid fiasco, the staff is usually backlogged. In addition to 120 athletic scholarships, Nebraska offers more than 3000 merit scholarships ranging from $100 to $5,000.

About a quarter of the students live in the university's single-sex or coed dorms. On-campus housing is standardized but comfortable, and dorm lotteries favor those wanting to stay in the same room or on the same floor. The most recommended dorm complex is Harper/Schramm/Smith, but the East Campus, home of the ag school, reputedly serves the best food. Other dining facilities draw lots of complaints. One man's summation: "The food is always cold and tastes old." Freshmen are welcomed to the residence halls through the FINK program, which is friendlier than it sounds. (The acronym stands for Freshman Indoctrination of New Kids.)

The 17 percent of students who belong to the fifteen sororities and twenty-seven fraternities are among the more active and ambitious UNL undergraduates. Tension

385

can run a little high—"vicious" is the way one student puts it—between Greeks and non-Greeks, with therapy coming in the form of student elections and some serious snowball fights between the denizens of frats and residence halls. Nebraska is also a mixture of "preppies and cowboys"; and while they may not mix, there's enough social life for both types. Plenty of bars and movies are within walking distance, and for the culturally enlightened, Nebraska offers more than a hundred musical recitals each year at the Kimball Recital Hall. The Sheldon Gallery, which specializes in modern American art, hosts regular exhibits. Lincoln itself has all the excitement of a big midwestern city. Beyond the sidewalks are miles of flat roads and plains, ideal for biking, skiing and snowmobiling. You can canoe on nearby Holmes Lake, and Omaha is only an hour away. In addition to football, UNL is generally a powerhouse in gymnastics, basketball, swimming and baseball. Women athletes are still somewhat overshadowed, but they regularly turn out outstanding teams in gymnastics, basketball, and volleyball.

Despite severe cuts in its state funding, UNL remains the pride and joy of thousands upon thousands of Nebraskans. And it's still true that on certain Saturday afternoons, in the midst of a crisp midwestern autumn, Cornhusker fans paint the town of Lincoln red—and white. And anyone within a hundred miles can hear their triumphant refrain floating gleefully out of the parked football stadium: "There is no place like Nebraska, / Where we're all true blue. / We'll all stick together / In all kinds of weather, / For dear old Nebraska U!"

New College, FL
—See UNIVERSITY OF SOUTH FLORIDA

University of New Hampshire

Durham, NH 03824

Location Rural	**Applicants** 10,020
Total Enrollment 10,500	**Accepted** 53%
Undergraduates 9,500	**Enrolled** 40%
Male/Female 45/55	**Academics** ★ ★ ★
SAT V/M 490/550	**Social** 🐿🐿🐿🐿
Financial Aid 50%	**Q of L** ●●●●
Expense Pub $ $ $	**Admissions** (603)862-1360

The University of New Hampshire's lovely but rural setting, not far from the Atlantic Coast, serves as a playground for lovers of the outdoors, a laboratory for students of the environment and an increasingly reliable place for preprofessionals to launch their careers. In the past decade UNH's leaders have set out to "counter the notion that a public university in New England has to be considered a second choice." Academic standards have been tightened at this undergraduate-oriented institution, the curriculum has been improved and several facilities have been built or renovated. The state's long-time frozen finances are beginning to thaw, and a dollar or two (or twenty-two million) has trickled down to ole UNH. With all of this enthusiasm—and a strictly enforced new drinking age of twenty-one—happy hour is no longer UNH's most popular extracurricular activity.

In typical rural fashion, the university's campus is sprawled across its wide open grassy campus in a simple blend of modern facilities and New England–style, ivied brick buildings. Amid the stark surroundings, the campus bell's chimes echo off the walls of the White Mountains. It's no wonder that those who reside here consider the New Hampshire sea coast, and even Boston, to be "just down the road a piece."

The university's traditional emphasis on technical education is enriched by a variety of interdisciplinary offerings among its five undergraduate schools. Liberal arts offerings are generally solid, and the English department, headed by several award-winning writers, has a fine creative-writing program. Health, natural and physical sciences all have strong major programs, which are even stronger now because of the new $15-million science and research center. The history department is noted for its exceptional teaching; hotel administration and engineering have excellent reputations. Both the social welfare and nursing programs require an extensive amount of fieldwork. One of the most popular UNH programs, communications, is also one of the weakest due to a faculty shortage.

The university's general education requirements apply to undergraduates in all schools and fill roughly one-third of each student's total credits with courses in writing skills, quantitative reasoning, science, historical perspectives, foreign culture, fine arts, social science or philosophy and works of literature and ideas. But these required courses often have large enrollments, and admittance to entry-level business and communications courses are long shots for nonmajors. New Hampshire keeps class sizes relatively small for a public university; the downside, however, is that students may find themselves on waiting lists for all this personal attention. Waiting is also something students do at the university's computer terminals where lines can be three hours long. But UNH will soon alleviate this problem by installing three microcomputer clusters. To make up for a shortage of study space in the main library, the university installed lounges on every dorm floor and opened classrooms after hours. Students from all fields still vie for leather armchairs and quiet cubicles in the science libraries.

Unusual research opportunities are open to budding scientists and sociologists at the research centers for space science, plants and animals, and family violence. The Isle of Shoals Marine Laboratory, which operates several research projects in conjunction with Cornell University, is located just ten miles from campus. And then there's UNH's new technology, society and values program, which promises to educate students about the ethical implications of the computer age. An honors program has recently been introduced. For students seeking options to traditional undergraduate programs, a five-year master's degree program is offered in business. The Thompson School of Applied Science confers two-year associate degrees in a number of vocational fields. Changes of scenery, for a year or a semester, are available through study-abroad programs in Austria, France, Mexico, England, Germany, Singapore, the U.S.S.R. and Canada as well as domestic exchange programs with San Diego State and the University of California at Santa Cruz.

UNH is New Hampshire's main state school, and it is becoming increasingly popular with out-of-staters, who make up over a third of its students. Most students are from public schools, and minority enrollment is virtually nonexistent. But only at a school like UNH can environmentalist groups exist side by side with the Society Advocating Nuclear Energy. "The interests are so diverse, I couldn't even go into it," sighs one senior. Financial aid is awarded to needy students from both in and out of state. There are 140 athletic scholarships, and merit scholarships are given to 199 National Merit qualifiers from New Hampshire and one very lucky, very qualified out-of-stater.

UNH houses about half of its students. Freshmen are guaranteed rooms; the rest go fast by lottery. Although not superbly maintained, the thirty single-sex and coed dorms offer a variety of extras, including special interest groupings, comfortable lounges, study rooms and saunas. A new apartment complex provides rooms for four hundred juniors and seniors. Still, many upperclassmen choose to find off-campus homes, and because rentals in Durham tend to be expensive, students can be found in everything from studios in nearby Dover to luxury homes on Rye Beach. All residents eat in the three dining halls, which feature nutrition-conscious meals including fare from salad bars. Greeks eat in their own houses.

The town of Durham caters to student tastes, including an adequate supply of bars. Several pubs on and off campus have been divided into two separate sections for legal consumers of alcohol and everyone else. "The Greek system is strong here," notes a leisure management major. "But it's definitely not the only form of social life by any means." SCOPE, the student committee on popular entertainment, brings top acts to campus: George Carlin, Squeeze, Billy Idol. The athletic scene is dominated by the nationally ranked men's and women's lacrosse teams. Many of the women's sports outshine the men's, and fans often show up to cheer for UNH's top-notch female ice hockey team. Men's football and baseball are also notable.

When there's no game to watch or postgame revelry to indulge in, nature provides UNH students with more than enough to do. Skiing, camping, fishing and hiking in the nearby national forest are the favorite seasonal pastimes, and the outing club provides excursions and equipment to its more than five hundred members. Social activists can always pop over to the nearby Seabrook nuclear power plant and join a demonstration. A bus service runs from campus to nearby towns (including the popular Newington Mall), to the beach, and to Boston, an hour to the south. (Preppies take note: L. L. Bean is just an hour and a half away.) Juniors and seniors can have cars for campus getaways but underclassmen need special permission to park on university grounds.

Things aren't getting any easier for the students at this traditionally low-pressure school. With the new and tougher academic requirements, students are curling up with their textbooks on those long New Hampshire winter nights—an idea that makes the administration feel warm all over. But up here where the water is pure and sparkling and the air fresh, even the most serious students still find time to play.

New Jersey Institute of Technology

Newark, NJ 07102

Location Center city
Total Enrollment 7,590
Undergraduates 5,190
Male/Female 85/15
SAT V/M 480/600
Financial Aid 75%
Expense Pub $ $ $

Applicants 1,280
Accepted 48%
Enrolled 55%
Academics ★ ★
Social ☎
Q of L ● ●
Admissions (201)596-3300

Bet you always dreamed of going to school in downtown Newark, New Jersey. Not true? Well, chances are not too many people on the campus of New Jersey Institute of Technology did either. But they're here anyway, thanks to the Institute's fine reputation in engineering and technology-related fields. For those hearty souls willing to look beneath the concrete and tarmac surface, an NJIT education is a ticket to greener pastures and an easier life—preferably in the suburbs.

Located in a not-so-nice area of Newark, NJIT's campus offers mainly modern buildings, with state-of-the-art laboratories and studios that include a new $5-million mechanical engineering center. Students who long for a touch of traditional collegiate atmosphere can gaze fondly at the century-old Eberhardt Hall. NJIT is a state-supported institution that provides what one student calls "a good, economical, technical education with a minimum of frills and partying." Its programs—including majors in engineering technology, surveying, industrial administration and a pseudo-liberal arts major known as science, technology, and society—are a bit more varied than those at nearby Stevens Institute of Technology. Students applaud the math, chemistry and architecture programs, but the universally acknowledged mainstay of the institution is the engineering school (it used to be called the Newark College of Engineering), where the chemical engineering department earns rave reviews. The mechanical engineering department is notoriously tough, and computer science is immensely popular, which stands to reason at a school where every incoming student is provided with his or her own computer. Actuarial science, surveying and applied chemistry haven't yet measured up to other departments, and physics receives wide criticism from students. The quality of the liberal arts offerings also leaves a great deal to be desired (an average of about one course each semester is required), as do those in business. Reasons one junior: "NJIT is a computer and engineering school, not a business school."

Lectures can run as large as 120 students, but most classes average around 30, "small enough so you can't hide if you don't do the work." The library satisfies most student needs within its decidedly specialized scope, but the inside, nearly as run-down as the surrounding neighborhoods, needs repair. If students can't find the book they need, the Newark Public Library, workplace for the hero of Philip Roth's *Goodbye, Columbus,* is a fifteen-minute walk away. Grading is tough here, but almost everyone gets a second chance if he or she runs into academic trouble. The administration is more than happy to arrange for a leave of absence or even extra semesters with a lighter work load.

The faculty members are well liked, and since most have worked in industry, they are willing and able to help students with both academic difficulties and postgraduate plans. "The thing I like best is the ability to communicate with professors on a one-to-one basis," says a junior electrical engineering major. Freshmen are welcomed to the school through the "mini-versity," an orientation program in which upperclassmen and faculty members band together to teach some fun courses. About forty of the new arrivals with SATs over 1200 are invited to take the university honors program, which includes a weekly noncredit colloquium, special seminars in the humanities and social sciences and opportunities to take graduate-level courses. Undoubtedly Jersey Tech's most-favored academic option is the co-op program—available in engineering, computer science and industrial administration—that enables juniors to get paid for two six-month work periods spent with technical companies. They graduate in five years instead of four. Also available are several BA/MA programs and liberal arts–career combinations in which students spend their first three years at Upsala College, Seton Hall University or Lincoln University, then transfer to NJIT, ending up with technical and liberal arts diplomas.

As the state of New Jersey's comprehensive technological university, NJIT attracts a broad cross section of students from the state, including many first-generation college-goers. Only about 2 percent are from states other than Jersey; foreign students account for 3 percent. Black and Hispanic enrollment totals a substantial 18 percent, and the college works with local businesses to recruit qualified minority scholars, offering them scholarships and a series of summer jobs. Though math SATs of students are comparable to scores of applicants at other top technical schools, their class rank often is not, and about 35 percent ranked below the top fifth of their graduating class. Pragmatism and career orientation unite this otherwise heterogeneous student body, and the main attraction is definitely the chance for "a good education at an affordable price." The Institute says it does not anticipate modifying its need-blind admissions policy, and more than three hundred outstanding freshmen and upperclassmen annually earn merit scholarships ranging from $100 to full tuition. Students in the honors program get a $1,000 stipend for each year enrolled.

A new dorm with apartment-style accommodations has more than doubled dorm capacity to over five hundred rooms, but that hasn't been enough to fully alleviate a housing shortage. Freshmen and students living farthest away get first crack at the rooms, and those who make it in are automatically guaranteed space for the next year. Upperclassmen often move into fraternity houses or nearby off-campus apartments. Many commute from home, which can be a cramp in the old collegiate life-style. Says one junior, "Since I live so close, it is ridiculous to live on campus. I don't like the 9-to-5-type atmosphere here." With a growing waiting list for space in the dorms, a third hall is supposedly in the works. A good salad bar is the highlight of the three-hundred-seat dining hall, which is otherwise sufficiently unappealing to encourage some students to try out the Rutgers cafeteria across the street. Fortunately, the new dorm comes equipped with cooking facilities in the rooms, and frats have their own kitchens.

Students pack up their graph paper and flee for home at the end of the week, although the regular Friday dorm or fraternity parties entice some to stay a few hours longer. The Center Tap Pub also whets undergraduate interests. The beach is an hour away, and many students enjoy wind-surfing and sailing—with equipment courtesy of NJIT. Newark's proximity to nearby recreational meccas (New York City, Great Gorge, Atlantic City) and excellent public transportation systems increase the options for weekend entertainment. Even Newark itself, after long years of decline, is showing signs of life as a business and cultural center. Though the institute offers only a modest sports program, men's basketball, men's cross-country and women's volleyball have recently brought home league championships. Varsity hockey, however, was recently dropped, prompting an outcry from a number of disgruntled students. On a more positive note, women's basketball was added to the varsity roster in 1986, and a renovation of the women's locker facilities is planned for the near future. Undergraduates gamely assert that the lopsided male/female ratio "is getting better every year," but, as at every other engineering school, social life is tough. Yet with a large percentage of students holding down part-time jobs, there is little time for much frivolity anyway.

Jersey Tech's ardent apologists declare that they don't find Newark to be the Springsteen-esque urban jungleland they expected, and they can't say enough about their academic experience. "NJIT's technically oriented education makes us more than technicians," says one woman. "We are the people of the future."

New Mexico Institute of Mining and Technology

Socorro, NM 87801

Location Rural	**Applicants** 350
Total Enrollment 1,220	**Accepted** 86%
Undergraduates 780	**Enrolled** 47%
Male/Female 70/30	**Academics** ★ ★ ★
SAT V/M 540/600	**Social** ☎ ☎
Financial Aid 50%	**Q of L** ● ●
Expense Pub $	**Admissions** (505)835-5424

There was a time when a New Mexico Tech education was as good as gold for job-hunting seniors, but with the once-booming petroleum industry now in deep distress, today's students may feel as if they're graduating after the gold rush. Over a third of the class of '86 was jobless in September of that year, and though the industry may recover in the next few years, another era to match the heady days of the late '70s appears unlikely for the moment. Even so, students interested in the natural resources field should take a hard look at New Mexico Tech, a school that offers highly personalized technical training at a bargain price.

Located along the Rio Grande at an elevation of 4,600 feet, Tech enjoys an ideal location for geological study. The tree-lined campus includes picturesque white adobe and red-tiled buildings and plenty of grassy open spaces. Inside those buildings are a number of excellent programs in the school's three areas of expertise: energy, mineral and water resources. The geology department as well as petroleum, mining and geological engineering are among Tech's best. The school claims ownership to Socorro Peak, which contains a working mine and has a mountaintop observatory and lab for atmospheric studies. Although students are required to take liberal arts courses and are even offered majors in history and a catchall social science program, humanities and fine arts at Tech are as barren as the surrounding countryside. The environmental and materials sciences offerings are also reportedly weak. The library, with fifty-five thousand titles, is barely adequate, but computer facilities on this very computer-literate campus are good and getting better. Most courses in the technical fields are offered sequentially, and a student who doesn't take a cluster all the way through may have to wait several semesters before the necessary course is offered again.

Tech's student/faculty ratio is quite low for a technical school, and Tech's distinguished faculty, though research oriented, take their teaching seriously. Introductory courses top out at about one hundred students, and while graduate assistants assume some of the teaching load, what is special about Tech is the fact that undergraduates get to join their professors on research projects, and even do some of their own. Jobs with mineral industries are available during both summers and the academic year for those enrolled in the five-year cooperative work-study program. Undergraduates can also work part-time at the three research divisions on campus: the Government Bureau of Mines and Mineral Resources, the Research and Development Division and the New Mexico Petroleum Recovery Research Center.

Almost half the undergraduates are from out of state, and 5 percent are foreign nationals. About 8 percent of the students are Hispanic or black. Nearly one-third of the population is female, which is high for technical schools but not enough to normalize the social life. With only 780 undergraduates, "you know most everyone or know of them," a junior explains. Although it doesn't guarantee to offer admitted applicants a financial aid package, Tech tries to find aid "for as many students as we can." There are also institutional scholarships ranging from $200 to $3,000 (3.0 GPA and an ACT of 24 or SAT of 1050) and industrial scholarships based on academic performance and major. All together, almost 40 percent of the student body receives some form of merit award. Even without a scholarship, Tech is as cheap as any comparable school in the nation. On the down side, applications have plummeted almost 75 percent and undergraduate enrollment about 25 percent since the early '80s, and Tech is now forced to accept about 86 percent of those who apply.

Housing facilities have expanded since the days when women were housed in the school's trailer park. Nearly half the students live in the six coed and single-sex dorms on campus, one of which is a quiet dorm for very studious men and women. Apartment-style suites are favorites of upperclassmen, who are guaranteed a room. A little legwork can turn up decent and inexpensive accommodations off campus. Those living in the dorms are required to buy the meal plan, but the food is, according to general consensus, less than consistently appealing. "The dining facilities are probably the worst part of the school," one student believes. Luckily, another reports that there is "more Mexican food than you can shake your tailfeathers at in town."

Socorro is a tiny mining-turned-farm town in one of the most sparsely populated areas in the Southwest, but the nearby mountains and desert provide a wealth of outdoor opportunities. If job prospects haven't panned out lately, panning for gold in the peaks close to campus remains a popular extracurricular activity. According to one techie, "In New Mexico, nature dominates the landscape; it can be stark and desolate, but also beautiful." Most students seem to have mixed feelings about their environs. Even those who enjoy the scenery admit a direct correlation between sanity and access to a car, which can provide access to Albuquerque and El Paso, or the Taos ski slopes. There are no varsity sports, but coed lacrosse, Ultimate Frisbee, and cross-country clubs do travel to challenge other schools, as do the men's rugby and soccer teams. Many students also enjoy an extensive intramural competition program and the quality golf course. Sunbathing on the sandy campus or at a nearby lake is another popular activity, and well it should be in a place with an average of 172 days per year of clear sunshine.

With no varsity athletics, two men for every woman, and little of interest in the tiny town of Socorro, it's no wonder that students at Tech have traditionally created their own diversions, though some say it's getting harder. A raucous annual freshman initiation ceremony, complete with greased pole competitions and beer flowing through the night, was recently abolished by the school administration. "The carefree, 'do as you please just don't break anything' attitude is changing," one upperclassman reports. Social life now revolves around the bars and bowling alley in town, and on campus, free movies every Friday and small parties all the time.

When (and if) the natural resources field recovers from its recent catastrophes, applications should stabilize, and Tech's graduates once again should find their sheepskin a highly marketable degree. With fewer than a thousand undergraduates, Tech can boast of one of the most intimate technical educations—and certainly some of the best weather—in the nation. Students admit to occasional bouts of boredom and claustrophobia, but most Techies have the motivation and self-discipline to make it through. "We're hard workers and hard partyers," says one student. In the long run, they wouldn't have it any other way.

University of New Mexico

Albuquerque, NM 87131

Location Urban	**Applicants** 3,540
Total Enrollment 24,100	**Accepted** 86%
Undergraduates 19,750	**Enrolled** N/A
Male/Female 47/53	**Academics** ★ ★
ACT 20	**Social** ☎ ☎ ☎
Financial Aid 70%	**Q of L** ● ● ●
Expense Pub $ $	**Admissions** (505)277-4021

The natural beauty of the Southwest is one of the University of New Mexico's biggest lures. Although located smack in the middle of Albuquerque, the university's sand-colored buildings run the gamut of every style adobe can be molded into, and the gorgeous Sandia Mountains are in view from almost every spot on campus. The scholastic climate—"so relaxed that some mistake academics for dead"—reflects the "Land of Mañana" atmosphere of the state as a whole. With an average student age of twenty-seven, not all UNM students are at college just because it was the next thing to do, though, as a psychology major notes, "The beauty of UNM is that virtually all types of people fit into the college atmosphere."

Founded in 1892 when the state of New Mexico was still a territory, the university has grown to become one of the largest universities in the Southwest, offering over four thousand courses in fourteen colleges and schools. Undergraduates matriculate in one of four areas: arts and sciences, education, engineering or management. Academic and general education requirements vary in number and difficulty depending on the college. Those reluctant to specialize can take a few semesters in the University College while they decide, or they can take the popular bachelor of university studies degree.

More focused students have several attractive options. Anthropologists can root around in the state's many archeological sites, and engineers may join in major solar energy projects. The university is also strong in painting, sculpture and related fields of the arts. UNM is the only institution in the state to offer majors in architectural planning, dentistry and pharmacy, as well as a four-year nursing program. Agriculture and mining are, however, left to other state schools. The business major is popular, but students say it is a good idea to steer clear of education, math and statistics at UNM. Journalism suffers from a lack of funding, and a better bet might be the professional writing program offered in conjunction with the English department. The university has an open-ended exchange program with the National Autonomous University of Mexico as well as more limited study-abroad programs at other universities in Mexico, Ecuador and Spain.

The administration encourages faculty research by providing course-load reductions and leaves for scholarship. According to one student, "Professors are so pressured to produce grant money that sometimes they are not too accessible." Still, given the size of the university, most seem satisfied with faculty availability. "All professors I have come into contact with will go out of their way to help students," a senior reports. Classes can be huge, but most break down into smaller "labs" (run by graduate students) once a week.

UNM enjoys one of the largest enrollments of Hispanic and Native American students of any university in the nation (about 25 percent) and it continues to strive for parity with state population in this respect. A higher than average number of Hispanic and Native American faculty members have also been recruited, and bilingual education (in Native American languages as well as Spanish) is a special emphasis. Latin American studies are correspondingly strong. The administration accommodates a growing number of older and part-time students by offering more than 20 percent of all classes—and several complete degree programs—in the late afternoon and evening.

Nine out of every ten students are state residents, and regional pride is fierce. Northerners or easterners seeking fun in the sun may be disillusioned. One student warns, "Don't come with romantic preconceptions about the West—UNM isn't for anyone accustomed to *The New York Times* and Danish at breakfast." Almost everyone comes from public schools, and, although a C average is required for admission, a good percentage ranked in the bottom half and even the bottom fifth of their class. Excellent remedial programs help those scoring low on the ACT entrance exams or needing extra help to pass the exam in communications skills, a prerequisite for entering many departments. Yet, UNM actively recruits high-ability students. A third come from the top fifth of their class, and about 900 get partial merit scholarships of up to $1,500. About 350 athletic scholarships are parceled out in nine sports.

About three-quarters of the students commute, and with only 8 percent of the students living on campus, the dorms are "mostly a stopover for freshmen before finding off-campus housing." With the addition of a new apartment complex nearby, students no longer have to rely on the "shoddy and high rent" apartments across the street from the campus. Campus food is not worth the wait in line, but more edible fare is available in the campus delis and on "junk-food row" nearby.

Albuquerque is New Mexico's largest city, and, along with the surrounding area, it offers a variety of cultural attractions, including the nation's largest balloon fiesta, a growing artists' colony that provides feasts for the eyes and concert tours to charm the ears. Santa Fe is an hour away, and Las Vegas draws its share of vacationing UNM high rollers. Those with cars or the more popular pickup trucks take advantage of the state's many natural attractions: superb skiing in Taos (less than three hours away), the Carlsbad Caverns, the Sandias and "the world's largest tramway," as well as excellent hiking and camping opportunities. If you have wheels, good luck in trying to find a parking place on campus.

Although alcohol is banned on campus, UNM officials rarely enforce the state's drinking age of twenty-one. Local bars are, however, more strict. In contrast to other large universities, fraternities and sororities play a minimal role in the campus's mellow social life. Most students spend weekends partying at home or nearby campsites,

394

"watching the sunset, starting at about 9 AM, with a cooler of beer stocked to last the day." For those who overdo it, the university's crisis clinic is open twenty-four hours.

Varsity athletics are generally an embarrassment, although most students engage in intramural sports. The Lobos basketball team is back on the rise after being slapped with a three-year suspension and a $36,000 fine for academic violations by the NCAA. Football, women's basketball, women's golf and swimming are also strong. A new gym offers double the space that the old one used to, and the school rents out equipment for almost any athletic activity, including skiing and rafting.

The campus architecture underlines the New Mexican sense of identity and consciously recalls the Indian pueblos that dot the New Mexico landscape. Compared to many American public universities, New Mexico has a rather limited, regional appeal, but it serves its constituency well. Says a political science major, "UNM is friendly, dedicated to southwestern cultural awareness, and lets the individual take responsibility to put as much emphasis as desired on achieving academic excellence."

New School for Social Research

New York, NY 10011

Location City center	**Applicants** 210
Total Enrollment 4,920	**Accepted** 67%
Undergraduates 200	**Enrolled** 47%
Male/Female 65/35	**Academics** ★ ★ ★ ★
SAT V/M 580/530	**Social** ☎
Financial Aid 78%	**Q of L** ● ● ●
Expense Pr $ $ $	**Admissions** (212)741-5665

Question: What college is smack in the middle of Greenwich Village, conducts classes only in seminars, and is a hotbed for liberal and radical intellectuals?

Answer: The Eugene Lang College of the New School for Social Research. And if that doesn't sound like your cup of tea, it probably isn't.

Set amid the brownstones and neon boutique signs in one of New York's most vibrant neighborhoods, the New School is well known for its graduate work in the social sciences and for the vast array of continuing-education courses that have become an integral part of the intellectual life of Manhattan. It was founded in 1919 by a band of progressive scholars that included John Dewey, Charles Beard and Thorstein Veblen, and earned its fame a decade and a half later by sheltering European intellectuals fleeing Nazi persecution. Over the years it became the teaching home of many notable thinkers, including Buckminster Fuller and Hannah Arendt, and it today retains a select graduate faculty in the political and social sciences. Created in 1978, the undergraduate arm was recently renamed after a benefactor who gave $5 million on the condition that the college raise its enrollment to five hundred in the next few years. Now approaching its tenth anniversary, the school is in a period of transition.

The two most distinctive features of Lang College are the small classes—no more than fifteen students—and the practice of having undergraduates design their own program of study with no required majors or distribution of classes. In fact, there aren't even any departments. As freshmen, students choose from a selection of broad-based seminars, before choosing a concentration for their sophomore and junior years. Each concentration is self-designed, though students can pick ones that correspond to conventional majors. A new twist to the curriculum is senior seminars, added in the fall of '87, in which students return to a broad plain of thought for a new perspective on the more specialized work of their middle years. Because each student pursues an individualized educational program, competition between them is minimal. If it's all starting to sound like a piece of cake, you should talk to a few students. "It's really not easy having to make all these decisions for yourself," a junior says. All courses are graded quite strictly, written work is often demanded for each meeting, and participation in discussions is essential—"Students must always be prepared for class, or class doesn't make much sense," a sophomore observes.

Students take at least two seminars a semester on such disparate topics as musical ideals of beauty and order, the nuclear age, or adolescence and systems development. The only requirements apply to faculty members: They must teach one seminar exclusively for freshmen and one for upperclassmen each term, designing these courses from scratch and without guidance from the executive suite. Students say this guarantees invigorating sessions. Seminars meet twice a week for two hours each and work with original texts—at times even reading three or four translations of a particular work. "Sometimes the pressure is absolutely overwhelming," says a junior.

The New School faculty is particularly strong in political and social theory, anthropology, philosophy, literature and literary theory, writing and film. In economics, renowned economist Robert Heilbroner teaches the freshman seminar on capitalism. Math and science are weak spots, mainly due to the lack of courses, but the administration has targeted them for improvement. The college is also planning to beef up its offerings on the history and literature of Third World and minority peoples. Many professors approach their subjects from a left-wing perspective, and the graduate students that cluster around them help raise the political consciousness of the campus. "Teachers usually seem as willing to learn from students as students are from teachers," an undergraduate reports.

The main academic complaint is that the range of seminars is somewhat limited by the small size of the school, and some students eventually transfer to other institutions in search of more variety. Students may, however, enroll in any of the courses offered by the New School—from hot-air ballooning and Taoism in the continuing-education school to the more serious classes at the affiliated Parsons School of Design or in the graduate School of Management and Urban Professions. The New School's library is small, but students have access to the massive Bobst Library at nearby New York University. Sophomores and juniors imbued with wanderlust can spend a year at the American College in Paris.

Lang College attracts a disparate group of undergraduates, but most of them can be described as "young, idealist, independent," says one senior. About one-fifth of the freshman class are technically high school seniors, many of whom move on to more traditional schools after this accelerated year. More and more students, however, are looking to the college for a four-year experience, instead of using it as a stopping off place. Nearly 10 percent of the students are black or Hispanic, 8 percent are foreign, and about a third are from New York City. The rest of the under-thirty set may be swinging toward the right, but Lang College students "tend to be politically liberal, with the flares of radical political change arising in conversation, casually, throughout the day," a sophomore reports. The school is trying slowly to build up the size of the student body, in part by attracting transfer students.

Lang College admits students regardless of their financial need, and is usually able to put together a package of aid that will enable the student to enroll. A select group of twenty are awarded scholarships between $1,200 and $1,500, whether or not they are needy. A deferred payment plan allows students to pay tuition in twelve installments.

About 30 percent of the students live on campus, which means they are housed in suites in an apartment building at Union Square West, or in a YMCA on 34th Street. The Union Square building also houses students from the Parsons School of Design and is laid out in suites with kitchens and bathrooms. (Rumor has it that Lang students will be relocated when the lease runs out.) Freshmen have priority, but a few upperclassmen manage to squeeze in. The dorms are crowded and loud and "nothing to brag about," one resident attests. Nor is the area particularly safe. But the thrill of a place of one's own in the Big Apple obscures such minor annoyances as drug peddlers, dirt and incessant noise. The rest of the students are scattered throughout the city's five boroughs, living nearby if they can afford it, commuting if they can't. There is no meal plan, but students tend to congregate in the New School's cafeteria, pick up sandwiches at delis or go to NYU, where meal plans are available.

Space is at a premium in the Village, and students have no campus to speak of. Nor do they have any organized sports teams. The social life for undergraduates is more a function of individual initiative than college planning—"One is expected to invent one's own extracurricular activities"—although there are occasionally such typical college activities as dances and wine and cheese parties. Underclassmen have dorm parties or drift over to the rock clubs in the vicinity. And for the rest, well, "it's New York City, folks, with all the pluses and minuses that that involves."

It's not surprising that few students are bothered by the lack of a traditional social life. After all, their school also doesn't have the traditional college campus, curriculum or student body, either. These are the things that set Lang College apart from every other school in the country, as well as what its devotees love most about it.

New York City Technical College, NY
—See CITY UNIVERSITY OF NEW YORK

New York University

New York, NY 10003

Location Urban	**Applicants** 9,266
Total Enrollment 28,721	**Accepted** 59%
Undergraduates 14,780	**Enrolled** 35%
Male/Female 45/55	**Academics** ★ ★ ★ ★
SAT V/M 550/590	**Social** 🐘 🐘 🐘
Financial Aid 75%	**Q of L** ● ● ●
Expense Pr $ $ $ $	**Admissions** (212)598-3591

After more than a decade's absence, varsity basketball is back at New York University. And while such a fast-paced sport can't help but bring a bit of the old rah-rah college spirit with it, this cosmopolitan university is in no danger of going the cheerleader and letter-sweater route. The real world—or perhaps super-real describes it better—lies just too tantalizingly close.

A university simply can't get any more urban than NYU. Its modern and historical academic buildings mingle with the nineteenth-century brick town houses of Washington Square—where the peaceful, pot-smoking, anything-goes attitude of the 1960s still prevails and the parade of fire-eaters, breakdancers, punkers and other assorted characters never stops. It might be centered at Washington Square, but NYU actually has all of Greenwich Village as its campus. Avant-garde shops, galleries, clubs, bars and eateries lace the chic Village area, while the ethnic charms—and exquisite food—of Little Italy and Chinatown are just a few blocks away.

NYU contributes to this eclectic atmosphere with a wide range of practical and distinctive academic programs. The renowned Tisch School of the Arts is one of the best in the country, especially its film department. Oliver Stone, the director of *Platoon,* honed his skills there, and today's undergrads annually win the lion's share of national student filmmaker awards. The drama, dance, photography and television departments are also strong. NYU is *the* place for applied math, and its business school is a favorite with students (and with New York corporations), and boasts an excellent accounting department. English, history and political science departments flourish in the college of arts and sciences. Departments of French and art history have national reputations; nursing, social work and computer science are also good. Only the biology department gets uniformly bad grades from students, while special education receives only mixed reviews. A newer program of medieval and Renaissance studies has attracted quite a bit of undergraduate interest. The Gallatin Division provides flexible schedules, course freedom, and independent study for those wishing to develop their own majors.

One thing that everyone agrees on is that this is not a place for students who don't want to work. While the academic climate is "not high pressure, but demanding," this varies among departments. The growing number of preprofessional students aiming for medical, law and business school may find the academics particularly grueling and competitive. Under the new liberal education program, most freshmen and sophomores take a broad distribution of courses, including a foreign language and two semesters of expository writing. Like other large universities, NYU inflicts crowded introductory courses on its freshmen, many of which are "taught by visiting professors or bad teachers," one marketing major claims. But there are also many opportunities to meet professors in smaller, specialized classes and most remain dedicated to their teaching duties.

The variety of degree options here may tempt students to hang around the Village for more than four years. There are joint engineering degree programs with nearby Cooper Union, five-year programs for BA and masters in science, and a seven-year dental program. There are study programs in France, Spain, England, Japan, Turkey and Israel, and freshmen who make it into the University Scholars program alternate semesters of study and travel. NYU has the largest open-stack library in the country, and it's one of the finest, accommodating the needs of the perennial scholar as well as the weekend crammer. Unfortunately, a sophomore reports, many of the many books "are often hidden or stolen," and many students resort to using the mammoth New York Public Library on 42nd Street. Nonliterate types can play with "over a quarter of an acre of computer terminals."

Founded in 1831, NYU is one of the country's largest private universities, with a cast of 4,700 faculty members—more than the number of students at many schools. Sixty percent of students are from New York City itself, and another 15 percent hail from other parts of the state. Blacks and Hispanics make up 14 percent of the student body, and 10 percent are foreign. "There is no typical NYU student," one sociology major observes. What many students do have in common is the ability to adapt and succeed on their own. "It's a city school and students who attend must have a certain 'toughness' to survive and grow," notes a junior.

The university admits students on a need-blind basis, but it does not guarantee to offer a full assistance package. Three-quarters of students get some form of need-based financial aid, and the university offers some merit scholarships. No athletic scholarships are offered.

Self-sufficient types are the most apt to cheerily put up with NYU's size, bureaucracy, and some of its attendant hassles. Chief among these inconveniences is the housing shortage. The university recently has added to its housing stock, and now guarantees four years of housing to all freshmen who seek it. About a quarter of the students live in the dorms, which are known for their partying ways, while the commuting majority are forced either to find their own fun in New York or stick with their circle of high school friends. NYU now has some apartment-style housing, and students who live in these rooms are not required to buy into the meal plan. Freshmen often end up in Weinstein, a modern dorm with small rooms, while upperclassmen mostly live in two converted hotels. Those who can't commute from home will find off-campus housing exorbitantly expensive anywhere in New York, but especially in the Village where $500 a month for a single room is a bargain. There are three cafeterias for those on the meal plan, but most students prefer to take advantage of the nearby delis. As far as services like academic advising and career placement go, many students seem unaware of their existence.

The sporting life has come back in vogue at NYU with the return to varsity basketball and the addition of Coles athletic center, which is one of the best-equipped gyms in the city. Students flock to Coles, but old habits die hard and NYU for the most part "is not a sports-oriented school," one senior notes. There is not much interest in varsity or intramural games, and little in the way of sis-boom-bah. The fraternity population, while small, is "quite active and throws lots of open parties," a sophomore notes. Otherwise, NYU is an individualist's nirvana, full of "motivated students who can function on their own and who go for it."

NYU offers a chance to mix academic work and the urban scene. Its students know they are giving up most of what college life is traditionally held to be to attend a large, bureaucratic institution that sits smack-dab in the city streets. What's in it for them is an incredibly diverse academic program and an eclectic place where almost any student can find a niche—and, of course, a shot at all the riches that New York has to offer.

North Carolina State University

Raleigh, NC 27650

Location Center city
Total Enrollment 24,020
Undergraduates 16,850
Male/Female 60/40
SAT V/M 480/550
Financial Aid 29%
Expense Pub $

Applicants 8,560
Accepted 71%
Enrolled 57%
Academics ★ ★ ★
Social 🐺 🐺 🐺
Q of L ● ● ●
Admissions (919)737-2434

Not that sports is the only thing that matters at North Carolina State University, but students do love to proclaim their allegiance to the Home of the Wolfpack. Besides nurturing a recent NCAA basketball championship, NCSU offers a no-nonsense education—especially in technical fields—to those students who can take the ball and run with it.

The campus consists of red-brick buildings and brick-lined walks dotted with pine trees. "Though it is in the middle of the city, it doesn't have the atmosphere of an urban campus," reports a chemical engineer. NCSU excels in the professional areas of engineering, design, agriculture and forestry—which are the largest and the most demanding divisions. Not surprisingly, given its location in the cotton belt, the school also boasts a first-rate textiles school, one of the largest such programs in the country. Even the most technical of majors requires students to take a broad range of liberal arts courses, although the humanities are far from the biggest game on campus. In fact, one science major notes, "Some students in technical fields look down on humanities majors." An important feature of NC State's hardheaded approach to education is the cooperative education program, through which students in all schools can alternate semesters of on-site work with traditional classroom time. There are also domestic and international exchanges (Germany, Colombia, England, Spain and Mexico) and a scholars program for academic standouts.

Most classes at State are large, but the faculty gets high grades for being accessible and interested in teaching, and "go out of their way to be friendly." The academic atmosphere is noncompetitive. "There is a lot of group work and a feeling of 'we're in this together,'" says one student. Tutoring is offered free in most subjects, thanks to subsidies from state industries. Grading is especially tough in the introductory courses, which weed out underprepared students. Though the library is considered a good place to do research, it is too much of a social center to get much studying done. A current renovation should open up more—and maybe even quieter—study space. The university benefits greatly from its relationship with Duke and the University of North Carolina at Chapel Hill, linked through the state's Research Triangle Park.

The students at NC State are largely hardworking, bright North Carolinians. Some 84 percent are in-state students, and about 12 percent are from minority groups. Students range "from redneck to preppie to punk," a biochemistry majors notes, but even so, "College Republicans is the largest political organization on campus." The school has a rustic, down-home image next to its more polished neighbors at Duke and the University of North Carolina at Chapel Hill, and must endure frequent ribbing as

400

a result. ("If you can't go to college, go to State.") Jocks and sports fans abound, and the university underwrites a million dollars worth of scholarships that support 376 men and women. Those with academic skills can compete for almost six hundred merit scholarships ranging up to $4,500. To be considered for merit awards, students must file a separate application in the early fall of their senior year in high school. The university provides aid for just about anyone with financial need.

The university houses only about a quarter of the students in eighteen residence halls. Freshmen are guaranteed rooms and stay on by the luck of the lottery after that. Dorms are well maintained, and range from spacious, older rooms in East Campus to the newer (and noisier) dorms of West Campus. A small percentage of students are housed in fraternities and sororities, and the international house is also an option. The dining hall feeds all freshmen and anyone else who cares to join the meal plan. It's an all-you-can-eat deal, and students can use their meal cards at numerous campus snack bars and sandwich shops. Off-campus housing is plentiful; many Raleigh landlords rent whole houses to students at dorm rates.

The twenty-one fraternities and five sororities may not dominate the social scene, an engineering major says, "but they do have a role." Adds another student, "The parties on fraternity court are frequent and fun." Dorm and suite parties are also popular, and many students head to downtown Raleigh to hit the bars and dancing places. With home close by for so many students, the campus does tend to thin out on weekends. Those who stay can cheer on the home teams, which do well in men's swimming, soccer and football. The women's cross-country team recently won the national championship, but needless to say, basketball reigns supreme. The Wolfpack plays in the high-powered Atlantic Coast Conference, and usually spends most of each season ranked in the national Top 20. Intramurals also thrive, and a particularly popular event is Big Four Day, when NC State's intramural teams compete against their neighbors at Duke, Wake Forest and UNC–Chapel Hill. The recent addition of a new gym and pool complex has greatly enhanced the facilities.

NC State seems to be well integrated into its host city, Raleigh, which is the state capital. Public transportation affords easy access to downtown, with its shops, restaurants, theaters and night spots, and students take advantage of such cultural and social opportunities. Although the male/female ratio is about sixty to forty, there are three all-women's colleges in the vicinity and few complaints about dating possibilities.

North Carolina State seems to have overcome many of the disabilities associated with large land-grant universities. It has attracted a dedicated and friendly student body—tough enough to deal with the inevitable anonymity of a state school, but eager to avail itself of the university's faculty and resources. A math major sums up the attitude of many on campus by saying, "State is basically just a great place to be."

University of North Carolina at Chapel Hill

Chapel Hill, NC 27514

Location Suburban
Total Enrollment 21,580
Undergraduates 15,270
Male/Female 40/60
SAT V/M 520/570
Financial Aid 63%
Expense Pub $ $

Applicants 13,650
Accepted 39%
Enrolled 64%
Academics ★ ★ ★ ★ ★
Social ☎ ☎ ☎ ☎
Q of L ● ● ● ●
Admissions (919)966-3621

North Carolina's Senator Jesse Helms once remarked that the best way to control the University of North Carolina's students would be to build a fence around Chapel Hill and make it a zoo. Fortunately, leaders of the state university system have fought bravely against such attitudes and have supported Chapel Hill's long tradition of student involvement in politics as well as scholarship. All this, along with high academic standards and an outstanding faculty, places Chapel Hill on par with Virginia as the finest state university in Dixie.

Occupying a 730-acre campus dotted with trees, lawns and walkways, the University of North Carolina at Chapel Hill "looks the way a college should," a sophomore says. The architecture ranges from Palladian to postmodern, but red brick is the prevailing motif. The flagship campus of the state university system, Carolina offers about sixty undergraduate degree programs, the best of which are English, history and political science. Other strong programs include journalism, sociology, business, accounting and art history. Students say that the education, math and computer science programs are not quite up to snuff. Engineering and architecture are not offered at all, and the performing arts are a disappointment to creative types. The drama department, for example, runs a repertory company with professional actors, limiting student involvement.

One of the first state universities in the nation, Carolina is a "national, yet down-homey" institution. "It has high standards in every aspect of college life but it does not project the conceitedness that other universities of its caliber do," one sophomore says. On a more practical note, the Research Triangle Park, a nearby corporate community, employs many students as research assistants (it was also chosen, after an extensive search, to be the home of the National Humanities Center). Foreign study is available in France, England, Germany, Italy, Spain and Japan during the academic year and in more exotic places over the summer, while the most popular on-campus offerings are probably the small honors seminars open to all undergraduates, including freshmen. The low-pressure, low-tension academic atmosphere, unusual at a school of Chapel Hill's caliber, lets students set their own scholarly pace. They are expected to work, but "without driving themselves crazy," the chancellor explains. Academic and social life is governed by a student-run honor system.

The Carolina faculty is, for the most part, top-notch, but "some professors seem to be absorbed in research beyond a level healthy for students," a senior math major complains. Professors keep regular office hours, though, and will welcome those students who seek them out. Introductory classes can be difficult to get into and may enroll as many as four hundred students. Chapel Hill's library system, with more than three million volumes, is one of the best in the region.

Carolina, like many colleges across the country, has beefed up both graduation and admissions requirements. Its general education curriculum, adopted in the early '80s, is a model for big state universities. It requires students to take at least thirteen courses during their first two years in a variety of disciplines, among them English composition, science, art and a foreign language. In addition, UNC has taken a step that has often been discussed in higher education but rarely implemented: It has extended the general education concept to the junior and senior years through capstone courses, designed to help students synthesize what they have learned in various areas.

Under trustee policy, 85 percent of UNC's freshman class must be state residents (though children of alums, no matter where they live, are considered in-staters), and the admissions office has no problem filling this quota with the cream of the North Carolinian crop. "Carolina is, in many opinions, *the* state university, and, as a result, many UNC students *plan* on coming here for many years," one native notes. Chapel Hill also attracts a good number of students who can't afford—or don't want to pay for—an Ivy League or private school education. In light of the quota, though, out-of-state students will find competition for admission especially tough. At times, it seems the southern "preppie business major" dominates the scene, but "non-southerners seem to find each other early and become a tight social group as well," one Yankee says. Despite their other differences, most students enroll to "obtain a marketable degree and prepare for their future," a desire that cuts across state lines. Southern traditions prevail in Tar Heel country, but "anyone can find a comfortable niche at Carolina," one woman reports.

The university tries to assist all students with documented financial need. This sports-minded school awards a whopping 390 athletic scholarships. Students also can vie for more than five hundred merit-based academic scholarships, including the Morehead Foundation Awards, which are modeled on the Rhodes Scholarships and in North Carolina carry just as much prestige. Progue Scholarships worth $3,300 each are awarded to one hundred talented minority students from North Carolina. The university also offers a need-based loan program, with low interest and repayment periods running as long as ten years after a student leaves school. The Student Government Association carries on a part-time employment service, which provides about five hundred student jobs.

Spring at Carolina brings a glorious flowering of azaleas and dogwoods—and a housing lottery that leaves about one thousand students scrambling for homes elsewhere. Only freshmen are guaranteed university housing, and private accommodations are expensive and scarce. But once settled off campus, students can take advantage of buses that run frequently and are reliable. On campus, housing on the north side offers old but comfortable dorms; the south side offers high-rise "cell blocks" of cramped four-room suites, which are further from the center of campus. Freshmen often find themselves tripling up at the beginning of each semester. The food, dished out in a newly remodeled dining hall, is improving, students report, but many students prefer to cook for themselves, frequent the fraternities or sororities or dine out most evenings. For starters, Franklin Street, the main drag in town, offered at last count four Mexican and four Chinese restaurants, five ice-cream parlors, one Greek restaurant, three vegetarian eateries and three bakeries. There is also a generous supply of bars, but now that the drinking age is twenty-one, they are off limits to most undergraduates.

Impressive transcripts aren't the only prerequisites for success at Chapel Hill and boring bookworms will not find many kindred spirits here. Carolina, as one senior puts it, is for "students who want to grow and learn and have fun and live." The town of Chapel Hill is pleasant and attractive—"Looks like something out of *Gone With the*

Wind," one student says. For nighttime entertainment, several bars, a disco and movie theaters are within walking distance of campus. For those willing to go a little farther, North Carolina's beaches and ski slopes are within four hours, and students regularly roadtrip to Washington, D.C., and Atlanta (for Braves' games). A car is a necessity to take advantage of it all, and unfortunately parking is a royal pain.

Anyone wanting a secure handle on a social life should head straight for the fraternities or sororities, some of which date to the 1880s. The Greeks exert an influence far beyond their numbers (about 20 percent of undergraduates), and "their all-campus parties are almost always a big hit," a math major notes. The school newspaper long ago determined that the average Chapel Hill student consumes more beer than the average German. Perhaps the only organizations more important than the Greeks are the varsity teams: especially basketball, football and, well, basketball, which won the national championship in 1982 and placed two squad members on the Olympic team. "The average student loves football and basketball and attends many games," an English major reports. Baseball and lacrosse also are popular, as are the women's soccer, swimming and field hockey teams. A strong intramural program draws heavy participation.

Chapel Hill offers a low-key environment, a place where "one is expected to be social and still maintain above-average grades," as one senior says. Students probably don't begin to exhaust the university's superb academic resources, and those with the least bit of motivation can acquire an excellent education. And for the North Carolina resident, one native attests, "it is the best education buy around."

University of North Carolina at Greensboro

Greensboro, NC 27412

Location Center city	**Applicants** 3,600
Total Enrollment 10,400	**Accepted** 89%
Undergraduates 7,650	**Enrolled** 49%
Male/Female 30/70	**Academics** ★ ★
SAT V/M 440/470	**Social** ☎ ☎
Financial Aid 10%	**Q of L** ● ● ●
Expense Pub $	**Admissions** (919)334-5243

UNC–Greensboro has come a long way from its start almost a century ago as a state women's college devoted to the traditional fields of teaching, nursing and home economics. Women still outnumber men at this school, which has been coed since 1963, but business administration and accounting now rank among the most popular majors. No matter what their interests, Greensboro students can enjoy what one student describes as "everything a large university has to offer with a small college atmosphere."

Set on 167 acres sprinkled with magnolia and dogwood trees, Greensboro's well-landscaped campus features a mix of colonial brick and modern architecture. The

College of Arts and Sciences and the six professional schools—business and economics; education; music; health, physical education, recreation and dance; nursing; home economics—offer a wide range of undergraduate degrees. Other opportunities can be found under Plan II, whereby industrious students can design their own major and program of study. Greensboro also is the only school in the state system other than Chapel Hill with PhD programs and the resultant research opportunities for undergraduates.

The best offerings are in the arts, and the music, drama and dance programs all have reputations that cross state lines. The music school has three ensembles, a symphony orchestra and three choral groups, and top students can audition for the Greensboro Symphony Orchestra. All of the arts programs should benefit from the completion of a new $7.5-million center. The nursing school is the largest in the state, and more than 90 percent of its graduates pass the exam for certification as registered nurses on the first try. Programs in speech pathology and audiology are also highly regarded, and there are some unusual interdisciplinary programs such as therapy training, which combines classes from the dance, education, fine arts and theater departments. Greensboro's program in home economics is North Carolina's largest, and its program in child development and family relations is among the best in the South. Business now eclipses all other programs in the sheer number of majors, and communications is also popular. Science courses tend to be weaker, as are some technical offerings such as data processing.

General education requirements include the college core courses in Western civilization and other courses in the humanities, and natural, social and behavioral sciences. Nearly every faculty member teaches at the undergraduate level. "Greensboro's staff and faculty are very student-oriented," an education major notes. Enrollments in introductory courses sometimes swell to over a hundred, but preregistration is done by mail—no waiting in line. Only in business and communications do students report any trouble in getting the classes they want. Those who make it into the residential college program enjoy the atmosphere of an intimate "academic community" with class sizes usually ranging from fifteen to twenty students. The library is spacious and comfortable, and students also have materials from the entire sixteen-campus system available to them. The honors program allows talented students the opportunity to tackle a broad interdisciplinary program through small seminars.

A third of the students at Greensboro are local, and all but 15 percent come from North Carolina. Most of the out-of-staters are from the South, though there is a sizable contingent from New York and New Jersey. Blacks are a significant minority (about 11 percent), and the Neo-Black Society is very active on campus. Women still outnumber men by a good deal, but the ratios of freshman classes are better than those of the university as a whole. Greensboro is populated by "friendly, open-minded, outgoing students," about 45 percent of whom graduated in the top fifth of their high school class. Politically, most of the campus has liberal leanings, and according to one student, "Students take stands on social issues." The university tries to help all students who demonstrate financial need, but generally does not meet the full need of all applicants. Outstanding students who scored 1200 on the SAT and ranked in the top 10 percent of their high school class can vie for merit scholarships ranging from $100 to $2,850 a year.

Because of the high percentage of local students, less than half the undergraduates live in Greensboro's twenty-two residence halls. Some dorms suffer from leaky roofs; but renovations of the residence halls are slated for the near future, and it is characteristic of the spirit of the place that "students take pride in their housing and have painted rooms and halls themselves." A number of students are forced off campus each year by the annual room lottery, but off-campus housing is plentiful and cheap. Those who stay choose between spacious rooms in the older, more attractive dorms on the quad and more cramped quarters in the modern high rises. Singles are in short supply and cost extra. Most dorms are single sex, and a few have segregated wings that are joined by lounges and other common areas. At the beginning of the year, each residence hall votes on guidelines within the established visitation policy for members of the opposite sex. Students who live on campus must eat fourteen or twenty-one meals a week in one of four huge dining halls, which are currently being renovated to the tune of $6.4 million. Eating options are to include a bakery, pizza parlor, soda shop and fast-food.

Both the campus and the city from which it takes its name are known for their beauty. "Greensboro has all the charm of a small college town," says an English major. You can't beat the location—central North Carolina, midway between its beaches and its mountains. The Coliseum, a scant two miles distant, regularly plays host to respectable rock bands, and lots of bars, restaurants, and stores are within walking distance. Public transportation is reliable and inexpensive, so the rules allowing parking on campus only for juniors, seniors and graduate students don't cause much complaint. Students with cars make road trips to Washington and Atlanta as well as to Chapel Hill, Duke, Wake Forest and other colleges in the area. For women, who outnumber the males more than two-to-one, traveling for dates is especially important.

Since many students pack up and leave on weekends, the place can be pretty dull for those who stay around. "The social life is only 'average' at the university," a senior reports. The seven fraternities and six sororities are a relatively recent addition to campus life, "but they have grown tremendously and now serve as a major social outlet," a student notes. Local bars are now off limits to everyone under twenty-one, but the Student Union Council, which sponsors dances, coffeehouses and movies, has picked up some of the slack.

Greensboro has never had a reputation as a sports powerhouse, but that could change in the near future. The board of trustees recently approved a plan to upgrade the university's National Intercollegiate Athletic Association status from Division III to Division II immediately and then on to Division I by 1991. As part of this upgrading process, several sports will be added and a new $15.7-million physical activities complex will be constructed to complement the already existing Olympic-size pool, nine-hole golf course and three gyms. Meanwhile, the soccer team has managed to take four Division III national titles in the past six years, and both tennis teams were recent conference champions.

Some students complain that Greensboro, living in the shadow of its big sister at Chapel Hill, lacks the reputation it deserves for providing a first-rate education in such diverse fields as the arts, nursing and business. It may not have the rah-rah atmosphere available at many other colleges, but its academic offerings, small-college atmosphere and low cost make it one of North Carolina's least-known assets. "Some students from Chapel Hill transfer *here,*" says one contented undergrad, "because our students get more attention."

Northeastern University

Boston, MA 02115

Location Urban
Total Enrollment 34,090
Undergraduates 15,510
Male/Female 62/38
SAT V/M 440/500
Financial Aid 55%
Expense Pr $ $ $

Applicants 20,900
Accepted 57%
Enrolled 33%
Academics ★ ★
Social ☎ ☎
Q of L ● ●
Admissions (617)437-2200

If you would really rather be at work than at school, try Northeastern. At this huge private university in Boston, just about everyone spends nearly half his college years studying and the other half away from campus working at salaried jobs as part of the school's program of cooperative education. The administration bills Northeastern as the world's leader in cooperative education, and students cite the opportunity to "earn while they learn" as their main reason for coming to this school.

Meshed into the streets of a not-too-terrific section of Boston, Northeastern's gray and concrete campus is basic, not beautiful. "The campus quad—complete with its three or four trees—is something you would never know existed if it weren't for the campus map," observes one student. But then the lack of a typical college setting is fitting; Northeastern doesn't offer a typical college education either.

The academic year, including summer, is divided into four quarters. Freshmen spend their first year, and seniors their last term, on campus; in between, students alternate eight quarters of study with either seven or eight on the job. Except for students in the College of Arts and Sciences, co-oping is mandatory. There's no academic credit for the quarters spent on the job (meaning it takes five years to earn a bachelor's degree), but getting fired twice will lead to suspension or other academic sanctions.

For six months worth of work students average $7,000, which usually goes directly back to the school to pay for their tuition. Students on financial aid complain that the school decreases the amount of need-based aid they receive by the amount of money they earn on co-op. Most of the jobs are in the Boston area and related to the student's major, and about half of Northeastern grads, especially those in the more technical fields, end up taking jobs at one of their co-op employers. On the other hand, some positions can be utterly unfulfilling—a philosophy major can wind up as a cashier in a grocery store or a mail carrier. And students warn against depending on co-op advisers for good jobs.

Northeastern's most career-oriented schools, which readily lend themselves to the co-op approach, are the best academically. This urban university is known for its fine engineering school, and business, physical therapy and nursing are also strong. The new College of Computer Science is, understandably, becoming popular fast, and the undergraduate School of Criminal Justice is good. The arts and sciences are weaker; journalism, sociology, English and economics all generate complaints, and students warn that psychology should be avoided at all costs.

While the ninety-year-old co-op program is a success, the Northeastern campus experience, both in the classroom and out, leaves a great deal to be desired. Although students say that most teachers are concerned with students' needs, getting into their classrooms can be a job in itself. Many courses are crowded and it's a good idea to preregister during the previous term for those you really want to take. Students often find that courses they want, including an occasional required one, are tough to fit into a schedule. Some introductory classes are over three hundred students strong and have multiple-choice exams corrected by computer. The administration concedes that the library is Northeastern's greatest weakness. Students have another word for it: "pathetic." According to one speech communications major, the library functions better as a social center than a repository of knowledge: "Thank God for the Boston Public Library." But the administration claims (students say that it has been claiming this for many years) that a new $35-million facility will be started soon.

Northeastern, which was founded as a YMCA educational program, has traditionally served many local students from working-class backgrounds. There are not many Brooks Brothers and Burberry types here. One of the largest private schools in the nation, Northeastern is full of "down-to-earth and very conservative students," reports a junior, "and these are serious, life-long conservatives—it's not just a trend." Three-quarters of the students are from Massachusetts, and most of the rest are from New England, New York, New Jersey and other Middle Atlantic states. There is also a substantial foreign population representing 105 countries. Blacks are an especially prominent presence on campus, with their own institute, art gallery and newspaper. Besides the money they can earn in co-op programs, outstanding students can compete for one hundred merit scholarships that cover half to full tuition. And there are over three hundred athletic scholarships for men and women in a wide range of sports, including women's ice hockey.

For the four thousand students who live in school dorms and apartments, quarters are cramped. Freshmen, who keep their rooms for the entire year, live in the concrete high-rise dorms, while upperclassmen change rooms each quarter they are at school. "The problem with getting a room is that you can't," complains a criminal justice student. "They always overbook." Some relief may come from the two recently renovated and reopened dorms. Off-campus housing in Boston is difficult to find and never a bargain. Students in the dorms must pay for twenty-one meals a week.

The co-op program puts strains on campus social life. There are many clubs and activities, but the constant flow of students on and off the campus tends to be disruptive. "There's a constant stress with relationships when people are always moving between co-oping or school," one nursing student attests. "It is tough to get back into the swing of school after working a few months," another notes. Fraternities and sororities are small and mostly overlooked as a part of NU social life. Says one student, "Freshman year everyone goes to their first 'frat' party. Usually people don't go to more than one." While social life here is limited, the city of Boston, with its huge student population and wealth of bars, restaurants, museums, theaters, shops, and parks, serves as a fully acceptable substitute. In fact, with the Museum of Fine Arts located on Huntington Avenue alongside the university, students can even take in an exhibit on their way to art history class. And Red Sox fans will be happy to hear that Fenway Park is in Northeastern's backyard. In the winter, students head to the ski slopes of Vermont, and to the beaches of Cape Cod, and the North Shore in balmier weather. A few students on co-op might need a car to get to their jobs, but a Bean Town trolley goes zing, zing, zing down the middle of campus and finding a parking space in Boston is comparable to the old needle in the haystack routine.

"The football team is laughed at; the basketball team is just about worshipped," says one adoring fan. But the biggest sports series of the year is the Beanpot Hockey Tournament, which pits Northeastern against rival teams from Harvard, Boston College and Boston University. Northeastern's female pucksters have prevailed as champs for three years running. And the men came away with the pot in '86.

Northeastern is a place for those who have a good idea of what they want to do

in life, or at least a desire to find out. If their co-op experience does not turn int
permanent job, it certainly helps them in their search. Northeastern has shaky libe
arts offerings, no campus to speak of, and a transient student body. It is not the pl
for a student looking for the traditional collegiate experience. But as one NU'er, w
wouldn't trade the experience, attests, "You learn to be responsible for yourself."

Northwestern University

Evanston, IL 60201

Location Suburban	**Applicants** 9,420
Total Enrollment 10,930	**Accepted** 46%
Undergraduates 6,910	**Enrolled** 42%
Male/Female 51/49	**Academics** ★ ★ ★ ★ ★
SAT V/M 590/640	**Social** 🐿 🐿 🐿
Financial Aid 55%	**Q of L** ● ● ●
Expense Pr $ $ $ $	**Admissions** (312)491-7271

In its first 140 years of existence, to paraphrase the famous Christmas song, Northwestern University gave to us "thirteen Pulitzer Prize winners, five Academy Award recipients, three United Nations ambassadors, two United States Supreme Court justices, one NASA astronaut and the mayor of Chicago Ci-ty." It's a school that's known for its winning academics and losing football team. It was founded in 1851 to give the Northwest Territory an institution of "the highest order of excellence" and it still pursues this goal even though it attracts students from all over the country. Northwestern has been called "the country club by the lake," and while it may have gracious green hills and its own private beach, students here will quickly tell you that Northwestern is no club when it comes to course work and exams.

Running a mile along the shoreline of Lake Michigan with the Chicago skyline shimmering in the distance, Northwestern's eclectic architectural styles range from Gothic to mirrored and modern. Acres of beautiful park provide students with a prime location for fishing, running, cycling, roller skating or just daydreaming and watching the sailboats go by. Students have a love/hate relationship with Lake Michigan. In the spring students study in their swimsuits on the beach. In the winter they pull their overcoats high over their heads to fend off its icy winds.

Northwestern offers those who aren't intimidated by its tough academics a choice of some widely known programs; among the six undergraduate divisions, speech and journalism and the technological institute have national reputations. The school of speech has excellent departments across the board, from theater and radio-TV-film to communicative disorders. Journalism offers ten-week internships at about twenty-five newspapers across the country and a four-year combined bachelor's/master's program. A $25-million campaign is under way to centralize the video facilities of the radio-TV-film department and the news-gathering components of the school of journalism. The technological institute is particularly strong in all aspects of engineering, a program that offers a five-year co-op option. The physical and social sciences are the strongest of the liberal arts. Economics and English's writing major are especially praised, while math and languages are considered only mediocre. Fine programs in the music school enhance that college's offerings. Comments one premed/drama major, "Northwestern's schools are all very strong in their own rights, so it's never too late to change a decision about career or field of study and still receive an excellent education." There are many accelerated and combined-degree programs, like a seven-year honors program in medical education (BA/MD) and a 3-2 program with NU's graduate school of management. Interdisciplinary programs ranging from American culture to integrated sciences are offered in eighteen fields.

Requirements vary from one school to the next, and the widespread practice of grading on a curve, i.e., restricting the percentage of high grades, adds to the fierce academic competition. A transfer student bemoans that "everyone here has been a top student, there's no one to bring the average down." Unlike most schools on a quarter system, Northwesterners take four (not three) courses each quarter, except in the technological institute, where five are permitted. The Primal Scream before each finals period (at the appointed time, everyone opens his window and screams) does help to relieve at least a small bit of the tension, and students can take a break from the campus through any of twenty field study programs and eleven programs abroad.

While a couple of science majors complain that some professors are so devoted to their research that teaching has become a secondary concern, the majority of students find the faculty strongly committed to teaching. Virtually all undergraduate courses, including required freshman seminars (of ten to fifteen students) in arts and sciences, are taught by regular faculty members. Introductory courses are larger than most, but the average class size is about thirty students. Northwestern's library has nine and a half acres of floor space and a fully computerized catalogue. Library use is such a firmly embedded habit of students that a half-hour nine o'clock break in the lounge has become an institution. The university is currently putting the finishing touches on a twenty-six-acre research park contiguous to the campus.

About three-quarters of the ethnically and religiously diverse student body come from out of state, and more than two-thirds graduated in the top tenth of their high school classes. Political organizations on campus run the gamut, from the Conservative Council to the Democratic Socialists Organization, "but most students fall into the decidedly uninterested category," according to a political science major. There are many artsy students in theater, pre–business tycoons in economics and serious science-oriented premeds. The abundance of preprofessionals has added to Northwestern's image as "young corporate America," and the acceptance rate of its graduates at schools of medicine, business and law hovers around 90 percent. No academic merit scholarships are awarded, but NU does provide about 240 scholarships for its athletes. Loans for middle-income families are available through tax-exempt bonds.

Housing is guaranteed to freshmen, while upperclass students must try their luck in a lottery. Dorms range from small single-sex houses to large coed buildings, the most popular of which are organized in suites of eight students around a common living room. One entire building is made up of singles. Students may also join thematic or nonthematic residential colleges, which bring students and faculty members together during faculty "firesides" or simply over meals. Fraternity and sorority housing is another option. Students can eat at any one of the six dining halls, and a variety of meal plans are available, including one that provides Sunday brunch. Evanston offers some comfortable apartments to the 20 percent who live off campus, but rents are high and zoning laws prohibit occupancy of a house or apartment by more than three unrelated people.

Evanston is the national headquarters of the Women's Christian Temperance Union—and the butt of many jokes as a result. City ordinances still prohibit bowling alleys and fast-food restaurants (at the local Burger King you have to bag your own), but recently the old ban on restaurant bars and liquor stores was lifted. Downtown

Chicago is twelve miles away—half an hour by the el train, which runs twenty-four hours a day. Being adjacent to Lake Michigan, while affording a tremendous view, is a mixed blessing. Winters are "a real downer," says one native southerner, with freezing winds off the lake producing what meteorologists call "lake-effect snow," which is more unpleasant than the real thing. "But spring quarter is so much fun you forget the winter ever happened."

Although social life is circumscribed by the academic pressure, "anyone who says he can't find anything to do just isn't looking," declares a student. About a third of the students go Greek (including members of one coed fraternity), but while fraternity and sorority parties are an important part of campus social life, "it's easy to prosper outside the Greek system," say independents. The student government and Activities and Organizations Board sponsor an array of campus-wide events like the thirty-hour dance marathon, Pumpkin Prom, Armadillo Day (an all-day fair that offers face painting, spin art, and earthballs) and a program of concerts, lectures and films. The campus has its own radio station, television studio and award-winning newspaper, and, says one administrator, "certainly any student who wishes to act, produce, direct, conduct, build scenery, or play in a musical ensemble has ample opportunity to do so."

As the only private school in the public-dominated Big Ten athletic conference, Northwestern has spent decades getting creamed in big-time sports, most notably football (which probably saves the university a lot of money, since every time the Wildcats win a home game enthusiastic fans ceremoniously throw the goalposts in the lake). Many students take pride in the fact that the university refuses to lower academic standards to strengthen its teams. Women's teams consistently fare better than the men's, especially in volleyball, softball, field hockey and tennis. With the new sports complex and aquatics center, athletic facilities now rival or surpass most institutions of similar size in the country. The student-sponsored intramural program provides vigorous competition among teams from dorms and rival fraternities.

Freshmen soon learn, as one veteran warns, that "many students will get their first C's at Northwestern," and that a good deal of self-discipline is necessary. Asserts one senior, "The faculty expects a lot from us, because we can give it to them." But serious students who are occasionally willing to divorce themselves from the academic environment of Northwestern and check out the fraternity parties or travel to Chicago will find that if they're not careful, four years in Evanston might turn out to be as fun as it is challenging.

University of Notre Dame

Notre Dame, IN 46556

Location City outskirts
Total Enrollment 9,630
Undergraduates 7,550
Male/Female 70/30
SAT V/M 570/650
Financial Aid 52%
Expense Pr $ $

Applicants 6,710
Accepted 44%
Enrolled 62%
Academics ★ ★ ★ ★
Social 🐻 🐻 🐻
Q of L ● ● ●
Admissions (219)239-7505

While most of America thinks that Notre Dame is where robust Roman Catholic men go to play football, the administration likes to say that Notre Dame is where the Church does its thinking. In reality, Notre Dame is both and more—including the purveyor of a rigorous education to a set of highly motivated, competitive undergraduates.

In 1842, a French priest, the Reverend Edward Sorin, christened a rustic log cabin in the snowy wilderness above a Northern Indiana lake L'Université de Notre Dame du Lac with the vision that it would become a great Catholic institution. Almost a hundred and fifty years after this humble beginning, Notre Dame numbers among the most prestigious universities—Catholic or otherwise—in the nation. The lofty golden dome that rises above the ivy-covered Gothic and modern campus buildings and the old yellowish brick stadium where in the 1920s Knute Rockne made "the Fighting Irish" almost synonymous with college football are not only school buildings, but national symbols. Today, the Notre Dame mystique not only attracts top athletes, but also talented and competitive student scholars to all four university colleges—arts and letters, science, engineering and business.

At Notre Dame, liberal education is more than just a catch phrase. No matter what their major, students must take the Freshman Year of Studies, one of the most extensive—some would say restrictive—core programs of any nontechnical university in the nation. Of the ten courses freshmen enroll in during their first two semesters, only three are electives; the rest include two courses each in math and natural science or foreign language, one semester of English composition and literature, and one of history or social science. The tenth spot is reserved for a freshman seminar with about twelve to fifteen students, and all must also take physical education or ROTC both semesters. The university has numerous academic and peer-counseling programs for freshmen, and, administrators hasten to add, 98 percent of the freshmen make it through and come back the next fall. When they do, they're greeted with more distribution requirements, depending on their major, that include two semesters each of philosophy and theology.

In the College of Arts and Letters, highly regarded departments include history, government, English, chemistry and math. The engineering departments (especially chemical) are also good, and the College of Business Administration and Accountancy is ranked among the nation's best. The fine arts enjoy improved facilities; the campus theater has been renovated, and the art department recently moved into a newly refurbished building. Academic intensity varies depending on the college; engineers, premeds and business majors tend to be more pressured, and more competitive, than their peers in the College of Arts and Letters. A variety of special programs and options are available, including the program of liberal studies that examines "The Great Books." A new computer applications program offers a cross-disciplinary sequence of twenty-four credits in computer application coupled with any liberal arts major. The arts and letters program for administrators combines a second business major with liberal learning, and a five-year arts and letters/engineering program is popular. Students also benefit from research and programs in institutes like the Center for the Study of Man in Contemporary Society, the Center for Civil and Human Rights, the Center for Ethics and Religious Values in Business, the Medieval Institute and the Institute for Peace Studies. A sophomore foreign studies program leads ND students to distant sites like the People's Republic of China.

Despite a predominantly lay board of trustees and faculty, Notre Dame remains committed to "the preservation of a distinctly Catholic community." The president and many top administrators are priests of the Congregation of the Holy Cross, and each dorm has its own chapel, most with daily masses. Students feel Notre Dame nurtures their faith as well as their mind. "There is a genuine feeling of community and concern at ND resulting from the school's religious character," notes one student. The late '80s will be a period of transition for the university due to the recent departure of Reverend Hesburgh, the university's academic and spiritual leader for over three decades.

Over 90 percent of the students are Catholic, and while plenty of them are non-Irish, virtually all are middle- and upper-middle class. "As individualistic as we like to think we are," says one woman, "the reality is that the student population is homogeneous." That could spell trouble for deviants from ND's all-American norm; "radical ideas and life-styles are not well received," a freshman notes. The faculty, more liberal than the students, at times adopts a gadfly role in an attempt to stir the awareness of ND's buttoned-down conservative undergraduates. "One of my profs said that we are the worst-informed student body in the world," relates a freshman. Minorities are likely to find a vast cultural gulf separating them from most at ND. Blacks make up only 2 percent of the student body, and Hispanics comprise less than 4 percent. Almost half the students come from private Catholic high schools, and about a quarter are children of alumni. "Very bright, success-oriented and talented" is how one English major describes the students, three-quarters of whom ranked in the top tenth of their high school class. Despite its cultural homogeneity, Notre Dame recruits a national student body with the largest numbers coming from Indiana, Michigan, Illinois, Ohio, New York, New Jersey and Pennsylvania. Notre Dame is need-blind in admissions and awards almost two hundred athletic scholarships each year.

Except for a group of restless seniors, almost all Notre Dame students live on campus. Freshmen should list their dorm preferences carefully, because once assigned, students are encouraged to stay in the same one until graduation. Fraternities are banned, so the dorms become surrogate fraternities or sororities that breed a similar spirit of togetherness while varying widely in their character and reputation. Some students opt for the hundred-year-old dorms with chipped ceilings; others choose the 1980 cinderblock models in better condition with less atmosphere. Space in the dorms is tight, and students contemplating a transfer should be forewarned that they'll probably end up among the minority living off campus. Parietal rules (midnight on weekdays, 2 AM on weekends) are strictly enforced, though each dorm has a twenty-four-hour lounge that remains in bounds throughout the night. Boarders eat in either the North Quad or South Quad cafeteria and must buy a nineteen-meal plan. For those who tire of institutional cuisine, The Huddle is a pay-as-you-go snack bar. Students can also buy selected items in each dorm, or sign out food and equipment from the kitchen to whip up something of their own.

Notre Dame was strictly a men's school until 1972, which is abundantly clear from the male/female ratio. But the presence of 1,600 women at St. Mary's College across the street does normalize the relations to some degree. Many a "Domer," as ND men are affectionately known, has found a sweetheart and future wife among the

"Smick Chicks" at Saint Mary's. Unfortunately for the party set, ND social life isn't as rambunctious as it once was thanks to the policy that forbids alcohol at campus social events. "The old form of weekend entertainment—big dorms parties—has died," according to one student. Nevertheless, each dorm holds dances about twice a month, and there's always the annual "Screw Your Roommate" weekend where students are paired with blind dates by those with whom they share rooms. A recent addition that has doubled the size of the student center should also help fill the void. South Bend is a small town for which students have few kind words—one student reports that "the campus is like an island." Those who feel marooned often head for Chicago, about ninety minutes away.

While ND has come a long way from its humble frontier beginnings, one thing hasn't changed: "Winter is dead, especially when we're snowed in," laments a student. But even under subarctic conditions, that Fighting Irish spirit always manages to rouse the campus to a fever pitch when ND teams are playing. From the Gipper right on down to modern day greats like Joe Montana, the spirit of Notre Dame football has given the university its special character. Irish rooters have been disheartened in recent years by a string of mediocre teams, but a new coach appears ready to bring them back to the top. It wasn't intentional—at least so they say—but the giant mosaic of Christ on the tower of the library lifts both hands toward the heavens, as if to signal yet another Irish touchdown. Though not nearly so rich in tradition, men's basketball is the most popular winter sport, while the fencing team has recently brought home two national championships. For the women, basketball and volleyball are among the best teams. Diehard jocks who can't make the varsity will find plenty of company in ND's intramural leagues, where "the interhall rivalries are hot!" Notre Dame is one of the few colleges in the nation where intramural football is played with tackling and pads.

Everyone at the university, from administrators to students, is considered part of the Notre Dame family. For some, that could be too close for comfort. But for those who value security and unity over diversity and debate, Notre Dame provides a unique atmosphere that is at once supportive and competitive. "There's really a great spirit at ND," says one senior. "It's a very special place."

Oberlin College

Oberlin, OH 44074

Location Small town	**Applicants** 4,052
Total Enrollment 2,720	**Accepted** 57%
Undergraduates 2,720	**Enrolled** 36%
Male/Female 45/55	**Academics** ★ ★ ★ ★ ★
SAT V/M 610/630	**Social** 🏠 🏠 🏠 🏠
Financial Aid 52%	**Q of L** ● ● ● ●
Expense Pr $ $ $	**Admissions** (216)775-8411

The tiny Ohio town of Oberlin, once a major stop on the Underground Railroad, is the home of one of the most progressive medium-size colleges in the country—and one of the most academically challenging and diverse. Oberlin College was founded in 1833 by independent thinkers with uncommon ideas—it was one of the first schools in the country to admit students regardless of color, race or gender. Today, consistent with this aggressive tradition, Oberlin offers more courses (nine hundred) than institutions twice its size and graduates more BAs who go on to become PhDs than any other predominantly undergraduate institution. The school also boasts an internationally known conservatory of music. Even with such a heavy load of tradition and scholastic distinction, it is mainly the students' interests that keep the college alive.

Although Oberlin remains a bastion of liberal thought and a mecca for the socially and politically aware (yes, there are still some Deadheads and granola munchers), the current national conservative trend has crept in while the rads weren't looking. Incoming classes are increasingly subdued in dress, manner and politics, but more diversity doesn't seem to be upsetting this traditionally supportive community. Lively debating takes place "in dining halls, bars, and even on bathroom walls," one senior notes. Says an English major: "Jill may not like Jack's politics, but she'll defend Jack's right to speak."

The small-town Ohio surroundings come complete with wooded rolling hills. The attractive Oberlin campus "is not the Ivy League style at all; it's very unique," according to a senior. The architecture offers something for everyone with a pleasant mix of Italian Renaissance buildings (four designed by Cass Gilbert), late nineteenth/early twentieth-century organic stone structures, and some less interesting 1950s barracks-type dormitories.

Oberlin was also a leader in efforts to build up science teaching in a liberal arts college. Consequently the departments of biology and chemistry (which produced the discovery that electricity was the key to producing economical aluminum) are two of the strongest. English, performance, history and music history all maintain solid reputations. Standing firm despite the nation's preprofessional trend, the creative-writing program is excellent, and, in fact, the English department still attracts the most majors. Its courses are popular, and consequently, there is an occasional shortage of spots for sophomores and nonconcentrators. Interdisciplinary and self-created majors are popular and include programs in black, Latin American, environmental and women's studies, as well as neuroscience, biopsychology and urban studies. East Asian studies were strong at Oberlin even before they came into vogue nationwide, and the two-year Shansi fellowship in an Asian country is a popular and competitive postgraduate goal. According to students, the psychology and anthropology departments are weak and the facilities for theater and dance, though slated for improvement, are not adequate to meet high student demand. Most agree that Oberlin's professors and courses are extremely accessible.

The academic program at Oberlin tends to be all consuming. "Learning and Labor" is the motto, and heavy work loads and Saturday morning classes are the reality. The college has attempted to minimize the negative side of this academic intensity by allowing students to take an unlimited number of grade-free courses (credit/no entry), and anything below a C-minus is scratched from the student's transcript. Most departments offer group and individual independent-study opportunities and invite selected undergrads to pursue a rigorous honors program. Students praise the faculty's "personal commitment to teaching," a dedication probably increased by the long tradition of faculty governance at Oberlin. Faculty-student friendships are common; if you bring a prof to the Rat on Thursdays, you'll get free mugs of soda or beer.

There are no distribution requirements, but students must participate in three January winter terms during which they pursue monthlong projects, traditional or unique, on or off campus. EXCO is not Oberlin's personal oil company but an experimental college (noncredit) that offers students and interested townsfolk the chance to teach one another anything from American sign language or auto repair to beginning investing—subjects not found in the standard curriculum. Many outstanding opportunities are available beyond the town of Oberlin as well. OC is a member of the Great Lakes Colleges Association* and offers its own programs in London, Spain, France, Germany, Kyoto, and Dublin. In fact, so many people leave Oberlin for a semester or two that the break is practically part of the curriculum.

Oberlin's art museum (often ranked third after Harvard and Yale) is by far the loveliest building on campus, with its brick courtyard, flowering gardens and fountain made from part of a nineteenth-century Japanese incense burner. The Mudd Library is superb, but even more special is the Oberlin Conservatory of Music, perhaps the better-known half of the school. It offers 184 practice rooms, more Steinway grand pianos under one roof than anywhere in the world (two hundred), and daily concerts. Qualified students can earn both a BM and BA in a five-year double-degree program. The majority of students come from public schools where they place in the top tenth of their graduating classes. Approximately half are out of the Northeast and the Middle Atlantic states, a third from the Midwest, and the remainder from other parts of the United States and thirty foreign nations.

Oberlin provides aid packages to all needy students who enroll, and virtually everyone gets the financial help necessary. Special parental loan programs are also available. Minorities have strong support groups at Oberlin and continually hold many of the top positions in student government. Feminist and homosexual groups are comfortable, and the student-run Sexual Information Center is successful in helping students deal with a variety of issues. The location of the school in the heart of downtown Oberlin necessitates interaction with the community, a two-fifths black population of less than ten thousand and unique in its own right. Town-gown relations are good, and increasing contact with business and professional firms (locally and nationwide) means, among other things, more internship possibilities.

Most students choose among twenty-seven dorms, ranging in size from 15 to 235 people, several of which are based around foreign languages. While four are single sex, the remaining dorms have coed floors. In general the dorms, many of which are currently undergoing major renovations, are all open to freshmen. Seniors and lucky juniors can land the preferred singles or move into cheaper off-campus apartments, although only a fraction of the nonboarders are allowed off the meal plan. The dining halls, which are chosen through another lottery, are scheduled for some much-needed revamping. As an alternative, many students enjoy home-style cooking at one of the six student-run co-ops. Here, students can enjoy planning and preparing meals, not to mention lower prices. Only 5 percent of the student body actually live in these houses, but almost twice that number enjoy their meals there. "At its best, co-op dining can be a wonderful experience. At its worst, you may have to subsist on boiled cabbage and carrots before the next food shipment comes in," reports one senior.

Students approach their social life with as much personal commitment as they give their academic and musical studies. A good time is defined as eating out at Selenti's restaurant, going to a movie or concert, dancing at the campus disco, or cooking dinner with friends. People here love to sit around talking or arguing politics, preferably over beer or wine. The school's ultramodern physical education center has superb facilities, and varsity sports draw increasingly enthusiastic followings. The school just joined the North Coast Atlantic Conference which emphasizes scholarship and considers women's sports on a par with the men's. Men's soccer and swimming and women's cross-country are the traditional powerhouses, and participation in intramurals is on the rise. Predictably, fraternities and sororities are taboo, apparently to no one's regret. Popular ventures away from the center of the campus include strolls in the nearby arboretum or skinny dipping at the reservoir. "The quiet back roads are suitable for biking and one is sure to stumble upon an unusual town to explore." If all else fails, there's Cleveland thirty minutes away, now more accessible through the school's new Saturday shuttle bus. "Of course," admits one senior, "Cleveland is . . . well, Cleveland is Cleveland."

Long one of the few radical outposts in Ohio, Oberlin College is not sitting stagnantly in the '60s as the rest of the world moves through the '80s. A new breed of students on campus feel that "liberalism can be a little forced at times," and that "the left is not always right." Today, more than ever, the school must depend on its tradition of tolerance to keep its community united.

Socially, academically and in every way, Oberlin College consistently challenges students and their conditioned beliefs. Immigrants from big eastern cities, common victims of "boondock shock," must make an additional adjustment. But the potential rewards for hardy souls are priceless. Says one senior: "Students who enjoy freedom and independence, as long as they accept the accompanying responsibilities, will do well." If a student likes to search out opportunities to excel, Oberlin, the "oasis" as one theater major suggests, offers an opportunity for a remarkable education.

Occidental College

Los Angeles, CA 90041

Location Urban	**Applicants** 1,740
Total Enrollment 1,670	**Accepted** 68%
Undergraduates 1,660	**Enrolled** 40%
Male/Female 50/50	**Academics** ★ ★ ★ ★
SAT V/M 550/600	**Social** ☎ ☎ ☎
Financial Aid 65%	**Q of L** ● ● ● ●
Expense Pr $ $ $ $	**Admissions** (213)259-2700

When they hear the name, most people probably think that Occidental is an insurance company. That's unfortunate, because Occidental College not only is one of a very few small liberal arts colleges located in a major metropolitan area but is also one of the best colleges on the West Coast.

Oxy's self-contained, Mediterranean-style campus is a secluded enclave of flowers and trees just fifteen minutes from downtown Los Angeles. Inside this urban oasis resides a thriving community of high achievers who don't for a moment believe that the liberal arts are dead. Occidental's core program provides the foundation for the college's commitment to a "total education," emphasizing personal, ethical, social and political growth. All students must take a foreign language, courses in math, science, writing, the arts and world cultures (American, European, and comparative), and later on pass a writing proficiency test and a senior comprehensive examination. Though some students complain that the core courses cut into the number of electives they can take, most agree that they are worth it. Since everyone has to take them, core course classrooms can also be large, as can intro science lectures. But small discussion groups mitigate this problem, and upper-level courses often enroll fewer than a dozen students.

As rigorous as its requirements are, Occidental encourages diverse learning experiences through a number of flexible programs, including individualized majors, internships, independent study and excursions abroad. Capable freshmen can do an end run around the core requirements by enrolling in the Collegium, an intense interdisciplinary program in which seventy students and seven professors spend the year studying patterns in history and culture. A third option for freshmen is Core III, in which a group of about a dozen students spend the year with one professor on a single broad topic. Students also can propose an Independent Pattern of Study program without adhering to a fixed distribution of courses. Under a new college honors program, outstanding students can work independently on special projects. There is a computer science emphasis, but no major. As for quality, Occidental's academic departments are excellent across the board, with economics, political science, chemistry and biology among the strongest. The only department really lacking is physical education, and even that program has been recently revamped. A new science center is in the planning stages.

Faculty members are readily available in and out of the classroom, and teaching is one of Occidental's strong points. "As a sophomore I could call two department chairs as well as a dozen professors by first name," says one student. Despite their friendliness, the profs keep the academic heat on and demand a lot of students, several of whom describe the academic atmosphere as "high-pressure." Occidental operates on a quarter system with the summer session optional. The eleven-week terms allow students to take a wide variety of courses (three per term) each year, but also keep the pace quick and intense. The calendar is ideal for trips abroad—Oxy has programs in Western Europe and Japan—and for politicos, there is "Oxy-in-Washington" and "Oxy-at-the-UN." Though the library is sometimes short on resources, students can journey to UCLA for materials missing at home.

The majority of Occidental's students are from California, two-fifths from the L.A. area. There also are sizable delegations from Washington, Oregon and Arizona. But more and more students from Chicago and especially New York are discovering this hidden liberal arts gold mine in the sunny Southwest. About one-fourth of the students are minorities, mostly Hispanic and Asian, and about 5 percent are foreign. Students, many of whom come from respected public schools in the area, are intellectual and self-confident, and this is one of those places where students still engage in late-night discussions on "politics, economics and even where to buy the best beer," one participant notes. Politically, there is a definite leftward tilt on campus, though some think it's nothing more than an *Oxy-moron;* students "vote Democrat as they enjoy their upper-middle-class Republican life-styles," according to one. Like many of their peers at other colleges, Oxy students are interested in "money and careers," an urban studies major says.

Occidental's admissions policy is need-blind, and most of those accepted are provided for fully. The college provides 142 merit scholarships ranging from $500 to $10,000. There are no athletic scholarships. Dorm living, with its student-run residence staff and many dances, parties, trips and other activities, is an integral part of life at Occidental. Freshmen are required to live on the pleasant, Spanish-style campus and to eat in the dining hall, where Clancy, a woman who has run the cafeteria for almost half of Oxy's hundred-year history, serves up food that is considered good by college standards. There also are plenty of hole-in-the-wall eateries nearby. Dorms are coed by floor, except for one male and one female dorm, and freshmen may live either among other freshmen or with students from all four classes. The housing quality varies, with some dorms boasting balconies, carpets and air-conditioning and others offering "small, inconvenient and very ugly" rooms. What you get depends on how you fare in the housing lottery. One-quarter of the students live off campus, although the surrounding neighborhood of Eagle Rock, a gritty lower-middle-class community, is "unsafe and declining economically and socially," according to one student.

When students weary of the "Oxy fishbowl" social life, they head to the bars, restaurants, museums and the theaters of Los Angeles, where, a senior notes, "you can find almost anything except snow." The beaches of southern California, the ski slopes of the San Gabriel Mountains and Disneyland are not far away by L.A. standards. Yet public transportation is frightful (fortunately the college runs free buses to many locations in the city), and a car (your own or someone else's) is practically a necessity in order to get anywhere. The weather is warm and sunny, but the air is often full of that famous L.A. smog.

Students rave about the friendly and supportive nature of the campus, but also complain that the coziness lends itself to gossip and cliques. "The Oxy grapevine works better than a radio station," muses one student. "When you least desire it, it seems like everyone knows what you're up to," gripes another. Three fraternities and three sororities rustle up a small membership, but they are not selective or exclusive and are required by campus rules to invite everyone to their functions; students choose which one to join, rather than being chosen. The Greek system "is a social option, definitely not a necessity," a sophomore notes. A new student center is on the drawing board, as is an expansion of the athletic facilities. Sports teams compete in Division III and draw a modest following among students. The football team, once quarterbacked by Congressman Jack Kemp, is the most popular, followed by men's basketball, soccer and track, and women's tennis, volleyball and track. The most popular intercollegiate sport of all, according to one student, is studying.

Occidental gives Pomona a run for its money as the best liberal arts college in California. Though Oxy's small campus can sometimes seem too small, most students find the atmosphere challenging and enjoy the close relationships that develop with faculty members and fellow students. One thing's for sure, at Occidental you're never just a number. Which is more than you can say for an insurance company.

Ohio State University

Columbus, OH 43210

Location Center city	**Applicants** 16,730
Total Enrollment 53,200	**Accepted** 81%
Undergraduates 40,830	**Enrolled** 50%
Male/Female 54/46	**Academics** ★ ★ ★
SAT V/M 460/520	**Social** ☎ ☎ ☎ ☎
Financial Aid 35%	**Q of L** ● ● ●
Expense Pub $ $	**Admissions** (614)292-3980

What does author James Thurber have in common with Olympic champion Jesse Owens? Columnist Earl Wilson with golfer Jack Nicklaus? And what do they all have in common with Wayne W. (aka Woody) Hayes? All are Buckeyes, graduates of Ohio State University—but the Who's Who of OSU grads is only one way to gauge the diversity and potential for achievement at this mammoth, unpretentious place.

The mere mention of Ohio State University evokes memories of the Rose Bowl, fast Buckeye running backs, and the now-retired but legendary football coach Woody Hayes. Today, this powerhouse university still grinds out Big Ten championships for

419

its fanatic fans, but when the dust from pounding cleats settles on the turf, Ohio's megauniversity stands on its 3,200 wooded acres, rubbing up to the edge of downtown Columbus, with a lot more to offer students than a Friday night pep rally and a Saturday afternoon game. At Ohio State, a sophomore political science major notes, "you are limited only by yourself."

For those who are bona fide students and not just jocks in sheepskin clothing, this academic colossus on the banks of the Olentangy River has a flabbergasting array of academic programs: nineteen colleges that offer seven thousand courses in 219 undergraduate majors. OSU has a program for every type of engineering imaginable (and some unimaginable) including landscape, mechanical, metallurgical and welding. Accounting, chemistry, economics, education, geography, linguistics and political science are among the school's most celebrated departments. OSU bills itself as *the* place to go for computer graphics, and the school with the largest and most comprehensive black studies program anywhere. (It turns out more black PhDs than any other university in the nation.) The university also has the nation's only programs in audio recording and geodetic science, and the state's only program in medical communications. Outside of a remote mountaintop monastery in Greece, the university houses the only major collection of medieval Slavic manuscripts. If your concerns are of a more extraterrestial nature, be forewarned that OSU's radio telescope is the only continuous monitor for signs of life in outer space.

Such exotica aside, the university's fundamental commitment to liberal arts learning means all undergrads must satisfy basic education requirements in natural sciences, social sciences and humanities. Hundreds of "cake" courses are balanced by an equal number of killers. A newly instated fall quarter selective admission program has replaced OSU's open door policy. Although Ohio residents are still admitted on a continuing basis, some may be wait-listed when the class quota is filled. A conditional/unconditional admissions policy allows some poorly prepared students to play catch up in their designated insufficient areas.

Freshmen, who are grouped together in the University College before entering one of the degree-granting programs, find the size of most introductory lectures huge. Teaching assistants, not professors, hold smaller recitation sections and deal on a personal level with students. "I would say the professors and students have a somewhat distant relationship," says a mathematics major, "but it's not impossible to meet with them." Students find that class sizes whittle down as they continue in their field of study. OSU's honors program allows twenty-five hundred students in eleven colleges to take classes taught by top professors and limited to twenty-five students. Internships are required in some programs and optional in others, and possibilities for study abroad include the People's Republic of China and Japan. A personalized study program enables students to create their own majors.

OSU's architectural style is anything but consistent, yet it's all tied together in one huge red-brick package. "One part of the campus maintains a nostalgic air, while another is relatively modern," observes a senior. The grounds are nicely landscaped, and a centrally located lake provides a peaceful setting for contemplation. Inside the old ivy-covered halls and modern prefab monstrosities are some of the best in up-to-date equipment and facilities, including a "phenomenal" library system with two dozen branches and nearly four million volumes—all coordinated by computer. Those who take the time to figure out how it all works may reserve library materials by phone and either pick them up later or have them delivered to their dormitory rooms. Unfortunately, the school has yet to find a way—through technology, prayer or black magic—to manage its own bureaucracy. "So much of one's time is wasted waiting in lines—cafeteria lines, parking lines, registration lines—it's impossible not to feel insignificant sometimes," a philosophy major muses. "Scheduling is a runaround," says a mechanical engineering major. "In my three years I've never had the exact schedule I turned in." Other students report that to take advantage of the wealth of services, you have to learn to beat the system.

Virtually all of Ohio State's students come from Ohio, adjacent states or foreign countries. There are aggies and city slickers, Greeks and grinds, liberal-artsy types and pre-everythings, all in huge numbers. All this plus a large contingent of part-time or continuing-education students. Paradoxically, with its nationally recognized black studies program, this school has a student body that is less than 5 percent black, and one senior bemoans that there are "separate groups between the blacks and other students on campus."

The dormitories that house most of the Ohio State masses fall into three areas: North, South and Olentangy (i.e., those closest to the Olentangy River). Freshmen, with the lowest housing priority, get stuck in the last of these, the dreaded Towers, which have sixteen-person suites on twenty-two stories and look like they were plucked from the Manhattan skyline. Upperclassmen find the South campus section (it's more sociable, louder, and full of single rooms) the most desirable. All in all, students have a choice of single-sex, coed and married couples dorms if they want to live in the easy-to-obtain campus housing. Dormitory students have a choice of five dining halls, but others cook for themselves or eat in fraternity houses.

Such a large student market has of course produced a strip of bars, fast-food joints, convenience stores, bookstores, vegetarian restaurants and you-name-it along the edge of the campus on High Street, and downtown Columbus is just a few minutes away. The fine public transportation system carries students not only throughout this capital city but also around the sprawling campus. In addition to the usual shopping centers, restaurants, golf courses and movie theaters, Columbus boasts a symphony orchestra, and its central location in the state makes it easily accessible to Cleveland and Cincinnati. Physical fitness buffs can ski in nearby Mansfield, canoe and sail on the Olentangy and Scioto rivers, hike around adjacent quarries or camp in the nearby woods.

Ohio State is a bustling place on weekends. Various social events are planned by on-campus housing groups—floors, dorms or sections of the campus. Two student unions run eateries as well as movies on Friday and Saturday nights, and High Street's zillion bars, saloons, restaurants and discos come to life. Less than a fifth of this vast campus belongs to one of the fifty-five fraternities and sororities. By one account, these students make the Greek system "a way of life and isolate themselves from the rest of the student population." For those who want exercise but aren't 265-pound males, there are plenty of alternatives to football. "You name the sport, and OSU offers it," boasts an agricultural major. There are twenty-six courts for handball, squash or racquetball; twelve courts for basketball; forty-four intramural sports and fifty-one sports clubs— "It rained one day last spring and two hundred softball games were rained out," one student reports. Basketball now rivals football as a focus of school spirit, but there's enough Buckeye support for both. OSU claims to have the largest athletic program in the Big Ten with twelve varsity teams, including golf, synchronized swimming and everything in between.

OSU is sometimes overwhelming to be sure, but students say they "thrive on the challenge and excitement" of a big university. They enjoy "the freedom to pick and choose courses, programs, activities and friends to fit their needs." You certainly don't have to love football or basketball to come here, but you might want to buy a season's pass for the games, anyway—you can always sell the tickets to local fans and live like royalty for the rest of the semester.

Ohio University

Athens, Ohio 45701-2979

Location Rural
Total Enrollment 15,700
Undergraduates 13,500
Male/Female 51/49
SAT V/M 440/470
ACT 20
Financial Aid 65%
Expense Pub $ $ $

Applicants 7,700
Accepted 90%
Enrolled 45%
Academics ★ ★ ★
Social 🐘 🐘 🐘 🐘
Q of L ● ● ●
Admissions (614)593-4100

Ohio University is not your run-of-the-mill public institution. If only there were ivy on the walls, it could easily be mistaken for a small, private school nestled in the classic college town of Athens—Socrates would have loved it here. The university prides itself on its personal approach to education, exemplified in an outstanding honors tutorial college that was modeled after the one-to-one educational system of Oxford and Cambridge universities. But OU sticks out most like a sore thumb among comparable state schools on the football field, where the relatively unsuccessful football team is ungraciously outdone by the spectacular marching band—the Marching 110. It's sad but true that most Ohio fans come to see the halftime show and then promptly adjourn before the third quarter.

Marching 110 tunes are especially smooth resounding off the walls of the winding hills in southeastern Ohio, where the quaint and simplistic but incredibly picturesque Ohio U campus subsists. Georgian architecture, tree-lined, red-brick walkways, and white-columned buildings are clustered on "greens," which are like small neighborhoods. "In the fall, Athens wears its brilliant autumn colors," relates a journalism student. "And I'm not just talking browns and golds, but a beautiful rainbow of yellows, burgundies and maroons." In the center of twelve state parks with dense clusters of trees for as far as the eye can see, the little town of Athens and its university are isolated—"There aren't too many roads in or out of town," says a senior.

The pride and joy of Ohio U is its honors tutorial college, which one public relations major describes as "an especially imaginative and challenging program unique to OU." Students in the honors program take an individualized curriculum in a major field, including weekly tutorials with profs on a one-to-one basis. Most enrollees complete their undergraduate work in three years and go on to leading graduate programs with close to a 100 percent acceptance rate. The university also boasts of the nationally acclaimed college of communication and its three brightest offspring: the schools of telecommunications, visual communications and journalism, the latter of which recently moved into a new home filled with state-of-the-art facilities and equipment— videotex, computer graphics and microcomputers. The most recent addition to this college is the communication systems management program, designed to expose students to business, communications and computers while preparing them to manage a variety of telecom systems. The college of engineering and technology is now housed in a new center furnished with $4.5 million in laboratory instructional and computer equipment. The college of business administration is one of the university's most popular and most selective schools. And physical therapy, one of the youngest programs OU has to offer, is showing signs of becoming one of the strongest. Students applaud the dance department as well as the foreign languages, but they are not pleased

422

with the natural sciences, the fine arts or the anthropology and political science offerings.

All OU undergraduates must complete a three-tiered series of general education requirements. Tier I is made up of freshman writing and mathematics, and a junior-level writing course. Tier II requires students to complete a minimum of four credit hours in four of five areas: applied science and technology, fine arts and humanities, natural science and mathematics, social science, and Third World cultures. Tier III consists of a senior year capstone interdisciplinary course. OU students regularly head over the ocean to study for a semester in Europe, or sometimes they trek north to Canada or south to Mexico. Co-op programs are available for engineering students and nearly anyone can earn credit for an internship. The Extern program, offered through the alumni association, provides weeklong internships in which students stay at the home of an alumnus and work with him or her on a daily basis.

Classes of two hundred students do exist, but they are rare. The majority of the classes have twenty-five students or fewer. "I came here expecting to be treated like a number, but I was wrong—*way* wrong," says a senior. Freshmen and sophomores often have problems getting into courses, but the more credit hours students earn, the simpler class-getting gets. Underclassmen do have access to top professors, but "I would admit that professors are more apt to spend longer periods of time with upperclassmen," admits a public relations major. The library is a seven-story structure that houses four million volumes. Students complain that "some of the materials are a little outdated and some of the floors are a little too noisy." The academic climate is conducive to healthy competition—"There is no breakneck pace," says a senior.

The student body is 78 percent Ohioan and 8 percent foreign. Most come from middle-income families and public schools, and have careers on their minds. Politically, they run the gamut, but, for the most part, "conservative capitalistic bourgeoisie is the trend here," according to a senior. Two hundred athletic scholarships in eight men's and nine women's sports are awarded annually, and eighteen hundred merit scholarships, ranging from $250 to $2,000, are reserved for academically accelerated students with high test scores and class ranks.

Everyone lives on campus for two years; then most everyone moves off. Freshmen and sophomores live in forty-eight dormitories in one of three residential neighborhoods, or greens ("West is full of Techs, East is full of brains, South is a mixture"). Campus housing comes in a mixture of coed and single-sex options, and there are quiet study dorms, academic interest dorms and international dorms. Students report that obtaining housing is becoming more of a problem due to increased enrollments, and undergraduates can be found living in lounges, guest houses and doubles-made-into-triples. Upperclassmen usually end up in well-maintained fraternity or sorority houses or nearby apartments or homes for rent. "Dining facilities are adequate, air-conditioned and not spartan," observes a senior. Four different meal plans are available through the four cafeterias where the fast-food counters are viable alternatives to the regular entrees. Fraternities and sororities have their own private cooks and usually have informal dinners during the week and more formal sit-downs on weekends.

With more and more students going Greek every year (15 percent by the latest count), the fraternities and sororities have been becoming more visible. Still, one student contends, "Ours is not a campus where the entire social life evolves around the Greeks." While many of the students and the administration try to down play OU's party school image, "in truth, the bars are jam-packed Thursday through Saturday," reports a journalism major. "Students here like to live it up." Movies are offered through the school, and OU has a top-notch theater group that performs a variety of plays. "The biggest drawback to OU and Athens is their location one and a half hours from any major city and forty-five minutes from a small size town," complains a senior. "Acceptable ski slopes are four hours away, and last time I checked, Ohio didn't have any beaches unless you count Lake Erie, which nobody does." Other students are more content with the plentitude of state parks and the proximity of Lake Erie. Hiking, swimming, boating, sunbathing and playing Frisbee are favorite activities of some.

OU is known for having one of the best basketball teams in the Mid-American Conference, and a communications management major reports that "it's hard to find a seat thirty minutes before a basketball game." Women's basketball is also on the rise. Thousands of students compete in a host of intramural sports, and the top games are flag football, broomball and softball. Clubs and extracurricular activities abound, but, according to one student, the best events take place in the spring, when each residential green hosts a "green weekend," and it all culminates with springfest, a free, all-campus outdoor party.

"There's a niche for everyone here, but if you're super serious and disappointed Harvard didn't accept you, this is not the place to come," explains a senior. "You've initially got to like the atmosphere before you prosper." Despite the substantial size of the campus and the student body, there is a private-school sense of unity and belonging that is evident—except during the second half of football games.

Ohio Wesleyan University

Delaware, OH 43015

Location Small town	**Accepted** 74%
Total Enrollment 1,500	**Enrolled** 36%
Undergraduates 1,500	**Academics** ★ ★ ★
Male/Female 50/50	**Social** 🐾 🐾 🐾 🐾 🐾
SAT V/M 480/520	**Q of L** ● ● ●
Financial Aid 48%	**Admissions** (800)862-0612
Expense Pr $ $	in Ohio, (800)922-8953 out of state
Applicants 1,760	

Ohio Wesleyan University likes to think of itself as a born-again school. After troubled times back in the '70s, when it seemed more intent on attracting any student with a 98.6 body temperature than these with 1000 cumulative SAT scores, this midwestern school has seen the light and set out to regain its previous standing as a ranking small liberal arts college. Under the leadership of a young and energetic president who at one point moved into the dorms for a firsthand look at "what made students tick," Ohio Wesleyan has tightened policies concerning alcohol and residential life, and taken other visible steps to bridge the chasm that once existed between the social and academic worlds. So forget what your older brother or sister may be telling you. This place no longer guarantees nine-month vacations.

The small-town campus has remained peaceful and quaint, with ivy-covered brick academic buildings clustered on one side of a busy highway and dormitories and fraternities centered a few blocks away on the other, forcing students, in effect, to "commute" between the two. Ohio Wesleyan's 150-year tradition of turning out successful professionals also remains in place. Strong vocational programs range from pre-everything (pre–music therapy, pre-pharmacy) to nursing, computer science and business/accounting. Journalism students, who benefit from one of the oldest college papers in the nation, take double majors that assure solid exposure to the liberal arts, and nursing students get strong doses of basic science. The fine arts and music offer both professional and liberal arts degrees. History, political science, chemistry and life sciences are strong, with the zoology and botany-bacteriology departments offering an interesting alternative to the traditional premedical-science routine. The achievement scholars' program keeps honors students highly stimulated and productive, and an unusual special languages program offers self-directed study and tutoring by native speakers in languages such as Arabic, Chinese, Japanese and modern Greek. Departments of popular foreign languages, however, are in need of improvement, particularly German. Recent retirements have put several departments into flux, including education, music, physics and theater.

Central to the administration's strategy of raising the intellectual climate is the National Colloquium: a yearlong series of forums on timely issues, such as the nuclear arms race or the two hundredth birthday of the U.S. Constitution, that culminates in a capstone spring symposium that brings prestigious speakers from across the nation to the tiny Ohio campus. Apparently the strategy is bearing fruit. "The kind of student who would enjoy it here has drastically changed in the past four years," reflects a senior. "Ambitious students would feel most comfortable."

None of this is to suggest, though, that academic seriousness is getting out of hand. "Students go to classes, study and take tests without making a big melodramatic deal out of it," explains a liberal arts major. Whatever their degree of academic commitment, all students laud the faculty for ability and accessibility. Students take advantage of the top-notch library, the second-largest among Ohio's private colleges. An off-campus studies department oversees an excellent range of study-abroad and internship options, including those sponsored by the Great Lakes Colleges Association.* The school also provides good career and academic advising in its integrated counseling center.

Ohio Wesleyan has several distinct constituencies. About 40 percent are students from Ohio; another big contingent consists of students from Middle Atlantic and New England states, some of whom got into better schools but choose OWU because it showed more personal interest in them. Recruits from Chicago and California are increasing. There are still some not-so-able students from prestigious eastern prep schools, and the rift between these preppies and the more studious public school types is a source of some tension on campus. "Students who wanted to go to an Ivy League school and will miss driving their BMWs as a freshman will suffer and be miserable," proclaims one ferocious junior. All students demonstrating financial deficiencies are offered aid packages to meet the need in full. There are no athletic awards offered, but top entering students with strong records of academic achievement or demonstrating talent in music, theater or art receive $1,500 to $8,525 of their aid in gift money.

All but one of the dorms are coed, and rooms are arranged mostly into either apartment-style suites or singles. Fraternities, unlike sororities, offer a residential option. Special-interest houses, such as Fine Arts House, House of Black Culture and Women's House, are also available. Off-campus permits have been virtually eliminated, but the biggest complaints are with the housing lottery, which is not weighted to favor seniority. "If you get a bad number you're screwed," says one upperclassman.

The meal plan is run on a system in which a certain number of points is subtracted (far too many in the opinion of most students) for each of a number of culinary options: from à la carte or "all you can eat" in the three dining halls to pizza, Chinese food (delivered free) or snacks from the college grocery store.

The men's soccer and lacrosse teams routinely rank near the top of national

Division III rankings and the campus comes out in force to observe their winning ways. The football team is less spectacular—actually quite dismal—and averages only about one win per season. Women's athletics are reported by students to be "just as important as men's." Student athletes praise the sports program both for its openness to all levels of talent and for its excellent coaching. The sports fever carries over into both single-sex and coed intramurals. Rowdy fraternity parties are the social hub of student life (Greek membership hovers around 60 percent for men, 40 percent for women), although part of OWU's commitment to mending its partying ways includes "dry rush" for all fraternities, strict carding at private parties, and rules about drinking in dorms and grandstands. But plenty of good, clean fun opportunities—movies, concerts, clubs, etc.—keep students occupied.

Delaware is no cultural center, "but it serves its purpose," concedes one junior. The small symphony is appealing to many students and the famous Little Brown Jug harness race can provide some offbeat fun. Columbus, about twenty minutes away by car or bus, is a thriving, growing city full of college students and ways to amuse them. As the state capital and one of Ohio's largest cities, it also offers many job and internship opportunities. Lakes, farms, rivers and even ski slopes are all within a few hours drive.

Reborn or not, OWU can still party. "I don't know anyone who doesn't drink," one woman asserts. But the effort has been made to shift toward a more academically conducive climate, and the results are becoming evident. "What I like most about OWU," says one senior, "is that those things I like the least are changing for the better."

University of Oklahoma

Norman, OK 73019

Location Suburban	**Applicants** 4,600
Total Enrollment 20,500	**Accepted** 88%
Undergraduates 15,850	**Enrolled** 70%
Male/Female 55/45	**Academics** ★ ★ ★
ACT 21	**Social** 🏠 🏠 🏠
Financial Aid 30%	**Q of L** ● ● ●
Expense Pub $	**Admissions** (405)325-2251

Ever since the legendary Bud Wilkinson coached the Sooner football team to forty-seven straight wins back in the mid-'50s, OU has been better known for tight ends and linebackers than teaching and learning. Though the athletic department still garners the most number one rankings on campus, many academic departments (particularly those in preprofessional areas) also get high marks. Along with its legions of pro football players, OU can claim a large proportion of the state's geologists, engineers, doctors and business professionals among its alumni.

Tree-lined streets and a mix of Gothic-style and modern buildings make up Oklahoma's attractive campus. A new $45-million Energy Center houses some of the brightest energy-related programs under the sun. The recently established College of Geosciences brings together Oklahoma's strong programs in meteorology, geology and geophysics and geography. All Oklahoma freshmen start out in the University College before choosing one of several degree-granting institutions within the university. These include the colleges of architecture, arts and sciences, education, fine arts and health professions. The last of these offers undergraduate degrees in majors like occupational or physical therapy and nursing as well as a five-year degree in pharmacy. The popular School of Business Administration has an unusual major in petroleum land management, and the respected engineering college has specializations in geological, nuclear, and petroleum engineering. OU has the state's only comprehensive fine arts college, which features one of the nation's oldest collegiate ballet programs and a growing program in baroque music. The School of Music recently moved into a new facility, and the campus art museum was recently refurbished. In the College of Arts and Sciences, the natural sciences, notably chemistry, are strong. Like tumbleweeds scattered across a barren Oklahoma plain, top departments in the humanities and social sciences are few and far between, and the recent oil bust has forced budget cuts that have curtailed course offerings in some areas and meant fewer sections and larger classes.

Each college has its own set of general education requirements. Nearly half the student body is enrolled in a degree program that requires at least one course in computing, and terminals are often crowded. The relatively new Carl Albert Congressional Research and Studies Center is a fertile resource for political science students. Army, Navy and Air Force ROTC are available for men and women, and those who need a break from campus can take advantage of a variety of study-abroad options.

Oklahoma is considered an easy school, but for the academically ambitious, the university has two limited-enrollment honors programs. In the major honors program, students take small classes with outstanding faculty members, do independent reading and research for credit, and participate in interdisciplinary studies. A B average is required to continue with the program. The general honors program "recognizes superior achievements and intellect" on the basis of college entrance exams and GPA. Top students can also apply for admission to the Scholarship-Leadership Enrichment Program, which attracts well-known lecturers from outside the university to give seminars for academic credit. At the other end of the scale, remedial programs provide special guidance counseling and a concerned tutorial staff. Students praise the campus counseling center.

As at any school this size, freshmen "pretty much feel like numbers when they first enter." Class size is not generally a problem, but getting into desired courses can be quite a battle. "Top profs are not necessarily attentive to underclassmen," a public administration major reports, and courses taught by graduate assistants are common.

Such problems are tolerated, though, by an outdoorsy, sports-oriented student body that is not overly concerned with the academic program. More than three-quarters of the students are from within the state, with 18 percent from the immediate area. Minorities account for about a tenth of the student body, and foreign students are especially prominent in the engineering school. Students describe themselves as "close-minded but creative," conservative, "laid-back self-achievers."

OU can provide housing for fewer than half its students, so only freshmen and athletes are required to live on campus. Housing ranges from air-conditioned buildings with color TV lounges and recreation rooms to the basic box with no frills attached. Most halls are coed by floor. Off-campus housing is available but expensive, and about a tenth of the students opt to live in Greek houses.

Besides being a low-cost institution, OU rightfully prides itself on its broad-based financial aid program. Besides the expected bundle of athletic scholarships—about three hundred of them, spanning all intercollegiate men's and women's sports—over six hundred students get merit-based awards ranging from $250 to $3,000. OU also has a loan program under which upperclassmen who maintain a C average can borrow up to $2,200 a year at 6 percent interest. Since it began in 1927, more than 6,500 students have borrowed a total of more than $7 million.

The town of Norman is basically bland, but it offers many student-oriented services and plenty of joints where Sooners can let off steam. Oklahoma City is only half an hour in one direction, and the big, bad "D" (Dallas to the uninitiated) is not far the other way. The campus social scene is transplanted to Padre Island on the Gulf of Mexico for spring break.

A well-developed Greek system draws about a fifth of the student body. According to one student, there is "snobbery between some of the Greeks," and students may feel out of it if they don't belong to fraternities or sororities. Needless to say, athletics are an integral part of the "Sooner spirit," especially on home football weekends when seventy thousand fans jam the stadium. "Football is a cult activity in Oklahoma," says one student. "All students are somehow involved in it." There is a seamier side to all of this. According to the NCAA, OU's list of recruiting infractions, including gifts of free meals, transportation, and clothing to athletic prospects, is long and incriminating.

If you're into football, going to OU almost guarantees you a ticket to the Orange Bowl once or twice. Future oil barons should also consider coming here. And it's a good place for the average student who likes a big university atmosphere and a quiet environment—except on football weekends. Says one student, "It's a super place to get an education and enjoy oneself." Adds a classmate simply: "It's FUN, FUN, FUN!"

Oregon State University

Corvallis, OR 97331

Location Small city	**Applicants** 3,850
Total Enrollment 15,200	**Accepted** 87%
Undergraduates 13,380	**Enrolled** 63%
Male/Female 60/40	**Academics** ★ ★ ★
SAT V/M 450/510	**Social** 🐻 🐻 🐻
Financial Aid 55%	**Q of L** ● ● ●
Expense Pub $ $	**Admissions** (503)754-4411

A land-grant institution since its founding, Oregon State University endured many years of heckling as Moo U by the more glamorous University of Oregon. You can still board your horse on campus, and to celebrate their roots, as it were, OSU's good-natured students continue to hold an annual spring Cow Day festival, during which they don their best bib overalls, drag out bales of straw and hold milking contests—while consuming large quantities of a preferred, grain-based beverage. But don't be deceived. OSU, whose past contributions to the world include the maraschino cherry, is now a major center for research in marine science and aquaculture as well as agriculture—making it as much a fish farm as a cow college. Besides, OSU students, heirs to Oregon's vigorous pioneer spirit of independence, are as impervious to epithets as ever.

Located in the pristine, but rainy, Willamette Valley, Oregon State is a mix of older ivy-covered buildings and more modern additions. The university is beefing up its liberal arts program to the extent that a tight budget allows, but with the exception of history and English, the specialties of the house remain the vocationally oriented physical and life sciences. The administration expects to attract applicants primarily because of its science programs, and engineering, forestry, oceanography, agriculture and home economics are the major drawing cards. Although these programs are strong, resources tend to be stretched thin in the most popular programs.

OSU has the leading business school in the state, and the innovative education school has begun "guaranteeing" the quality of its graduates (schools can send them back for further training if not satisfied). Health programs also are decent offerings. Not surprisingly, the liberal arts (including such standard college fare as sociology, psychology, economics and philosophy) play second fiddle to more technical fields. This is not to say that students can't get a perfectly adequate education in these subjects, but the liberal arts courses are mostly "traditional and do not have much variety," one junior reports.

Distribution requirements exist in all schools, but they are lenient enough to make early specialization quite possible. Academic pressure depends a lot on one's major, but even those in the various honors programs don't feel overworked. Since the school is on a quarter system, however, finals do come around three times a year, making for "a lot to do and little time." Students have good access to professors but classes tend to be crowded and, a senior notes, "many business, engineering and education people are bumped from their courses." In what must be the understatement of the academic year, one student suggests that the library "could use a few more books."

Of particular note is the Experimental College, where undergraduates can spice up a semester with noncredit courses in a range of imaginative subjects—everything from wine tasting to the art of bashing, a medieval war technique. Those who can afford a semester abroad can join organized expeditions to England, France, Australia, Mexico, New Zealand, China and Japan or participate in individual exchange programs in still other countries. (Oregon State returns the favor, playing host to more than a thousand foreign students from more than seventy nations each year.) The small-town location makes it difficult to get much in the way of career-oriented part-time employment, and semester-time internships are hard to come by. Students in almost all majors, however, can participate in the cooperative education program, which allows students to alternate terms of study with several months of work in a job relevant to their field of study.

Statistically, OSU State certainly doesn't boast the most diverse student body. Eighty percent of the students are from Oregon, and almost all are public school graduates. The 12 percent who are minorities are mostly Asian; there are few blacks and Hispanics. Because the legislature limits enrollment (by funding only a certain number of students), admissions are competitive and focus on grades and test scores. If accepted, out-of-state students can expect to pay more than three times as much as Oregonians for the right to attend, but "scholarships" are available that let a lucky few enroll at the same tuition rate as natives.

Within the overall homogeneity of the student population, however, there are many variations. "The college has its intelligentsia, its social butterflies, its determined athletes, and any combination of those," an engineering major reports. Mostly, OSU is home to many "healthy, well-groomed" types who hail from the farms and small towns of Oregon. "Not much here is new wave," a senior says. "Purple hair is rare." Students tend to be conservative, but not obstinately so. Up to eight hundred academic scholarships, ranging from $200 to $2,000, are awarded each year to outstanding students. More than 250 athletic scholarships are awarded to men and women.

Freshmen are expected to live in college housing, although upperclassmen get the best spots. The dorms, which are reasonably comfortable and well maintained, are coed or single sex and house about a quarter of the students. Off-campus apartments are not hard to find, and fraternities, sororities and co-ops round out the housing options. Fraternity-house cooking beats so-so dorm meals ("not enough low-cal or healthy foods") and may be as big a reason for pledging as the much-talked-about Greek party life, which is "the hub of social activities" on campus. The relatively small number of members, spread over more than fifty societies, tend to mix their big parties with lots of community service, creating a good name for themselves on campus but little pressure to join their organizations.

Alcohol is forbidden in the dorms (Oregon has a drinking age of twenty-one) but is very much in evidence elsewhere. Cheering for the nationally ranked basketball team demands a lot of time and energy, as does participation in the well-rounded intramural program. As for in-state rivalries, one student says, "Civil War games between OSU and U of O are a big part of every season."

Another popular student activity is complaining about the Willamette Valley weather: "People in the valley don't tan, they rust," warns one native. One reward for this sogginess, however, are the flowers and trees that bloom in every color and shape. Many students consider Corvallis (population, 42,000) a good-size town but those seeking a quick-paced urban life-style will not find it here (the administration is wont to note it is 3,312.4 miles from New York City). Other than an occasional movie, the arts aren't too much in evidence out here, and city slickers as well as farm boys better cultivate a love for the wet outdoors. Ocean beaches are less than an hour away, and some of the best skiing in the country can be found in the Cascade Mountains, two hours to the west. Hiking and rafting are just around the corner. The town is surrounded by fifteen thousand acres of university forest and agricultural land that constitutes the extended campus for many course offerings.

At OSU, moderation is practiced with care. Students say it's a "nice" college, the professors are "helpful," and Corvallis is "a safe and pleasant little town." Oregon State University doesn't scream out for attention, it just goes along its merry way, doing a good job of serving the students of Oregon. Says one, "This school is for all those who want a good academic education in a warm, open atmosphere."

University of Oregon

Eugene, OR 97403

Location Small city	**Applicants** 4,900
Total Enrollment 16,380	**Accepted** 82%
Undergraduates 12,635	**Enrolled** 55%
Male/Female 50/50	**Academics** ★ ★ ★
SAT V/M 470/500	**Social** 🍺 🍺 🍺
Financial Aid 45%	**Q of L** ● ● ● ●
Expense Pub $ $	**Admissions** (503)686-3201

Blend two vegetarians, one track star, a fraternity brother, two no-nukers, three hikers and one conservative. Add a dash of the smarts and cover with a sturdy umbrella. What have you got? Ten University of Oregon students waiting for a bus.

There is no such thing as a "typical" UO student. The university's one-time image as a radical campus has given way to diversity—some even say the "me decade" has finally hit this haven of activists. But whatever their political orientation, everyone on this wet and lovely campus in western Oregon loves the outdoors. It is perhaps the only school in the country where the administration boasts about the number of bike paths available. People in Eugene are concerned with the quality of life. No one litters, everyone recycles and jogs, and nearly everyone conserves energy.

A strong liberal arts emphasis underlies the entire curriculum, but requirements are not rigorous—nor is pressure. A lot of students find it possible to slide by without much work at all, but many still enjoy their classes. A new program of freshman seminars aims to introduce students to top professors in small class settings. Five of the six professional schools (journalism, architecture and allied arts, education, business and music) are highly regarded, while human development and performance has a less solid reputation. Of the more than thirty-five departments in the college of arts and sciences, psychology, biology and chemistry are nationally known and highly regarded by students. The humanities and social sciences draw less applause, but a new humanities center should improve that situation. Business is another popular major and Asian languages are a specialty. Computer science is still playing catch up.

Highly motivated undergraduates may join the Honors College, which functions as a small liberal arts college with its own courses in the university, and outstanding liberal arts majors may spend five years and earn a master's degree in the Graduate School of Management. Innovators are big on acronyms at UO. The student-run ESCAPE (Every Student Caring About Personalized Education) provides credit for community volunteer work, while SEARCH (which dates to 1967 and stands for something that no one can remember) allows students and faculty members to offer one-time, experimental classes in "anything that has proven of interest." They will also organize on-campus internships that allow students to earn credit for special work with university organizations and academic departments. UO participates in an exchange program with colleges across the country and in a wide variety of study-abroad programs.

Like most state-financed institutions, UO is feeling the budget crunch. Tuition is increasing along with class size as the number of available courses is cut. Journalism and business courses are the hardest to get into. Registration badly needs to be computerized. The libraries also suffer from underfinancing, resulting in limited acquisitions and 11 PM closing times, but nevertheless still qualify as the best system in Oregon. Overall, a popular administration has kept the quality of education from suffering anything much beyond inconvenience.

Students consider UO one of the last collegiate strongholds for people who "are liberal in their life-style preference, and also sexual preference." But even they admit "there has been a swing from the 'herbal' to the more pragmatic students." In general, every part of the white Anglo-Saxon spectrum is well represented, with an especially heavy dose of the athletically inclined. "Anyone who jogs will feel instantly at home in Eugene," one student says. There is a noticeable influx of foreign students and 12 percent more come from out of state (most venturing north from California).

Since there are no residence requirements and few dorms, three of every four students live off campus in nearby apartments. Although some dorms are reserved for upperclassmen, most boarders are freshmen who reserve a spot when they apply to the school (dorm space fills up quickly). Good dorms include Walton, Carlton and University Inn. Students can also consider joining the active Greek program, which provides living space along with social activities. Only dorm residents can sign on for the meal plan in the two main dining halls, while student union restaurants and off-campus fast-food fare give assurance that no one ever goes hungry. The university each year distributes about 115 athletic scholarships to aspiring Ducks—90 of them in football—and 200 academic scholarships.

Eugene is a lovely city, even though it rains and rains and rains. "Students should have webbed feet or a good umbrella," warns one resident. But even the moist climate rarely dampens enthusiasm for the many expeditions available through the university's well-coordinated outdoor program, from rock climbing to skiing. An hour to the west the rain turns to spume on the Pacific Coast; an hour to the east it turns to snow in the Cascade Mountains. A profusion of shops and student-oriented entertainment establishments turns the area around UO into a pleasant and convenient college town. Academic and residential buildings range from nineteenth-century colonials to modern high rises, and as to be expected with the constant precipitation, the campus stays green year round.

Athletic activities and parties head the list of favorite free-time frivolity. When students aren't out on the fields and tracks themselves, they're trooping down to the stadium to join the Quacker Backers cheering on the successful basketball, football and track teams. Alberto Salazar and Mary Decker are among the Olympic notables to have begun careers at UO. Oregon's drinking age of twenty-one means that alcohol is theoretically banned from the college-owned dorms. The student association runs a beer garden on Friday afternoons in the student union.

The university, a hodgepodge of life-styles and differing degrees of academic commitment, manages to create an atmosphere with more than the usual amount of liveliness and zest, and students are easily won over. Pledges one, "I'll always be a Duck."

University of the Pacific

Stockton, CA 95211

Location Suburban	**Applicants** 2,400
Total Enrollment 3,900	**Accepted** 75%
Undergraduates 3,600	**Enrolled** 39%
Male/Female 49/51	**Academics** ★ ★ ★
SAT V/M 480/520	**Social** 🍺 🍺 🍺
Financial Aid 60%	**Q of L** ● ● ● ●
Expenses Pr $ $ $ $	**Admissions** (209)946-2211

When Hollywood film and TV directors need that small-college, Ivy League look and they don't want to pack up crew and equipment for the East Coast, they simply head upstate to Stockton. That medium-size city, about halfway between San Francisco and Lake Tahoe, is home to the University of the Pacific, a relatively small, private university that takes pride in the personal attention and wide range of opportunity it affords both preprofessional and liberal arts–oriented students. It's a favorite not only with budget-conscious film directors, but also with serious students who are willing to pay the price for private school education under the gorgeous California sun.

In the heart of the San Joaquin Valley, surrounded mostly by farms, orchards and ranches, UOP's main Stockton campus is expanding rapidly. In the last few years the university has added a new library, two new music buildings, a new engineering building, and a new computer facility to its 150-acre, ivy-covered, red-brick campus. (At the same time, it has not gotten rid of certain "temporary structures" built around the time of World War II.) The lush green lawns and profusion of flowering trees characterize the Stockton campus, which is home to five undergraduate professional schools and the College of the Pacific, the university's central liberal arts division. The graduate school of law is in Sacramento, and the graduate school of dentistry is in San Francisco.

Although the academic climate varies depending on the school or subject area, in general students find UOP to have a "very hospitable academic environment" in which competition is self-induced. Strong departments are those in the schools of engineering, pharmacy and business (with a special program on the entertainment industry) as well as music education, math, and the sciences. The communications department and the humanities in the College of the Pacific are somewhat weak. Art, drama and religious studies are also less than impressive. The university-wide general education program has two main components: the liberal learning program (interdisciplinary courses) and fundamental skills. A number of internship, co-op, study-abroad and dual-degree programs are available, as are accelerated or honors programs for students with a high GPA and strong SAT scores. Students may also design their own majors with approval from the faculty.

Professors are accessible and easy to talk to, and the majority are "very involved and concerned" with their students' and advisees' academic lives. Classes are generally of medium size, with an average of thirty-five students. Occasionally lower division students have access problems to classes with the top professors, but enough sections are available to eliminate the chance of not getting into a required course. The student-to-student advising center and the academic skills center are very strong, as is the career planning and placement center.

Almost three-quarters of UOP students are Californians, predominantly from public high schools, and about half ranked in the top tenth of their graduating class. Hawaii and Colorado are strongly represented, and foreign students make up nearly 10 percent of the student body. Most are fairly conservative, "not resorting to trends or fads." One senior reports that although UOP is often characterized by a small group of students who come from "very well-to-do families and love to party, most students are actually hard working, serious, and represent many different socioeconomic levels." A mechanical engineering major invites students with an interest in meeting people with different life-styles and pursuits to "come on down."

All underclassmen are required to live on campus, and few complain. The one women's and dozen coed dorms are adequate. "No one will mistake them for Hiltons, but they're very clean and well maintained," says a student. Grace Covell is the wildest and, with 350 people, the largest, but most have no more than 100 residents. Rooms and roommates are assigned by the residential life staff according to cards filled out by students. While plenty of rooms are available, more than half of the upperclassmen choose to move off campus, and about a fifth of the students live in fraternity and sorority houses. For dorm residents, three meal plans, three dining halls and three fast-foodish facilities provide well. In addition to the regular entrees and ubiquitous college salad bar, special theme dinners add flair. Vegetarian options are available but aren't all that great.

"Studying is an obscene word on the weekends," a business administration major reports, since that's when many students head for the slopes or San Francisco, each about an hour and a half away. Sacramento is closer for quick jaunts. Stockton itself has its "very rough spots and pretty nice spots; however, most of it is not what you would want to venture out into," says one woman. Bars and the Bay area provide much of the local social life. The fraternities are a good source of parties although they often limit their social funtions to other Greeks, and this prominent "segretation" is a sore point. The dorms do have social programming, and occasionally the school hosts big-name concerts and other campus-wide events. Movies are shown free three nights a week.

Women's volleyball is by far the most successful of varsity sports, and women's softball is a close second. Students are relatively apathetic toward most other sports, and, as one student points out, "Student interest is 90 percent of the team morale." Intramural sports, on the other hand, are quite active.

Pitted against the state's awesome public university system, tiny UOP's strengths and drawbacks quickly become clear. For those who seek individual attention, a conservative attitude, and a decent learning environment in a picture-perfect ivy-covered campus not too far from the coast, this school may be just the ticket. Bring your own popcorn.

Pennsylvania State University

University Park, PA 16802

Location Small town	**Applicants** 24,472
Total Enrollment 35,170	**Accepted** 43%
Undergraduates 29,440	**Enrolled** 45%
Male/Female 55/45	**Academics** ★★★
SAT V/M 520/580	**Social** 🐘🐘🐘🐘
Financial Aid 78%	**Q of L** ●●●
Expense Pub $ $ $	**Admissions** (814)865-5471

Tucked in a valley amid the rolling Alleghenies in central Pennsylvania, Penn State provides about as pleasant a big-college experience as any all-American teenager could hope for. Every year, thousands of the state's high school graduates flock to the town, actually named State College, for four years of fraternity parties, football games and all around fun.

At this collegiate Shangri-la, most students can even enjoy the time they spend in the classroom. Sporting an eclectic architectural mix, including white-columned brick, stone and some modern apartments thrown in for good measure, this land-grant university maintains strong programs in technical and agricultural fields. The meteorology program is tops (Accu-weather is located here). Engineering is good in all areas, including architectural and environmental, and the astronomy and chemistry departments are also solid. The agriculture college has a wide range of course offerings and extensive facilities that include huge livestock barns. Dairy products from the school's cows are sold at an on-campus store, and you can take courses in the production of ice cream. Penn State has its own Stone Valley recreation area that is used to train students in park maintenance, recreation and horticulture. The business administration college, and especially its undergraduate program in accounting, has a good reputation. The program in graphic design is notable for its "highly charged

434

creative atmosphere" and speech and communications are also praised by students.

The arts and humanities, however, are another story. The career-oriented student population doesn't tend to get very excited about the liberal arts, and neither does the administration. Penn State is underfunded compared with most state universities, and the humanities and social sciences are where it shows. "The administration puts so much emphasis on raising our standards in technical areas that the aesthetic ones are forgotten," says a speech communications major. Penn State's general education requirements are satisfied by taking clusters of core courses followed by related electives. Required subjects include communications, quantification, humanities, arts, natural sciences, social sciences and physical education. Most departments also require a foreign language and an introductory course in computer science. About thirteen hundred of the university's best and brightest are invited to study in the university scholars program, which offers opportunities for independent study and graduate work as well as honors options in regular courses. Best of all, there is a university scholars house that accommodates three hundred students and offers a full slate of after-hours activities including dinner seminars and conferences with visiting scholars. A combined SAT score of 1300 or over and an excellent high school record are required to join the program.

Classes, especially on the intro level, are sometimes very large (two hundred and up) and there can be problems getting into certain courses, especially in the business and phys ed fields. According to one senior, "It's often difficult to take a popular course offered by a popular prof, no matter what standing the student is." Good professors teach in just about every department, but many with national reputations for their research have little time for undergraduates. The library has about two million volumes, but students complain that the hours and study space are limited. A large number of study-abroad and combined undergraduate/graduate degree options are available, as are co-op programs in engineering.

Most undergraduates come from public high schools in the Keystone State, with a smattering from New York, New Jersey, Ohio and Maryland. The largest groups are from the state's two major cities, Philadelphia and Pittsburgh, but there is also a sizable rural contingent. The minority population is only about 6 percent, but it is on the rise thanks to some federal court–inspired recruiting campaigns in Philadelphia and Pittsburgh. "We have very few diehard preps here and almost no punkers," says one student. "But we do have a wide range of people, from '60s leftovers to junior-executive types." A large number of athletic scholarships are available, as are a considerable number of merit awards for academic excellence.

Freshmen must live in the dorms, which are crowded. Single-sex halls still predominate, but coed options are on the rise. Upperclassmen have the option of entering a room lottery, but more than half decide to live off-campus, where options include sharing a house downtown with friends, renting an apartment in one of the many new high rises in the town of State College, or even moving into an isolated farmhouse in the country. Rents are high, however, and a car is recommended. Sorority women live in the dorms, while frat men can opt to live in their houses. The meal plan operates on a point system where you pay only for what you eat. The food is average institutional cuisine, and those who tire of it can frequent one of the many establishments near campus, or join a frat where the house chef does all the cooking.

Penn State's pastoral surroundings are picturesque and peaceful. A ski slope is only fifteen minutes away, and students can sail, canoe, hike and even rent cabins in Stone Valley. If it weren't for the university, State College wouldn't amount to more than a fork in the road, but it nevertheless manages to attract its share of cultural events, usually in the form of visiting theater companies, symphonies and ballets. Says one dent, "It's a lively college town that offers many big-city events without the big-city hassles."

Partying at Penn State is almost as legendary as its football team, which after several near misses has registered two national championships in the '80s. The drinking age in Pennsylvania is twenty-one, but the word apparently hasn't gotten around to the fraternities. Many are housed in rambling old mansions, which are put to good use with keg parties wild enough to rival any campus. "Penn State is like one big Miller-Time ad on weekends," remarks one woman. Sororities have less cachet, since they are housed on campus. For those of age, local bars can be a second home, though on some nights they are so packed you can't even get in. Even more exciting for the typical student are football weekends, when the legendary Joe Paterno's Nittany Lions take to the gridiron. With thousands of alumni converging on State College for the game, the festivities include tailgate parties, pregame parties, postgame parties and victory celebrations.

The school also fields excellent teams in soccer, wrestling, field hockey and men's and women's gymnastics. The men's basketball team, long an embarrassment for the Nittany Lion fans, is still "nowhere," but the women's basketball is doing well. Tennis courts dot the campus, and there are three large gyms and an extensive intramural program.

While in-state tuition is one of the highest in the nation for a state university, Penn State remains a good deal for career-minded undergraduates, many of whom spend their first two years at a less-expensive branch campus near their home before making it to the main one. The State College campus offers a sense of belonging that is unusual for a school its size. "I like the bigness, the spirit, the overflow of activities," says one man. "Never am I bored here." Known as a party school, Penn State can also be a tough, competitive place, as indicated by the students who complain about the library closing at midnight. It is people who like to immerse themselves completely in college life—academically or socially or both—who put State College on the map.

University of Pennsylvania X

Philadelphia, PA 19104

Location Urban	**Applicants** 13,100
Total Enrollment 17,500	**Accepted** 35%
Undergraduates 9,130	**Enrolled** 46%
Male/Female 55/45	**Academics** ★★★★★
SAT V/M 610/680	**Social** 🐘🐘🐘
Financial Aid 45%	**Q of L** ●●●
Expense Pr $ $ $ $	**Admissions** (215)898-7507

The past ten years have been busy at the University of Pennsylvania: This Ben Franklin–founded, Quaker-based, preprofessional institution has been preoccupied with climbing out of the cellar of the Ivy League. After surpassing both Princeton and Yale and riding hot on the heels of Brown and Harvard in the race for highest number of applicants, Penn is strutting like a peacock and pleased to inform its Ivy brethren that not only does it have more applicants, but it has more applicants with higher test scores and class rankings then ever before. How'd they do it? They didn't. The computer did it. Using a Penn-authored computer program (which, by the way, they are willing to share with other schools—for a price), the university is able to profile any region or neighborhood in the country, seek out those most-likely-to-succeed prospective high schoolers, and inundate them with enough Penn paraphernalia and personal attention that they will never, ever confuse this school with Penn State again.

Penn's past popularity problems stemmed from Ben Franklin and other founding fathers, who valued prosperity and practical training over the intellectual values that characterized the earliest New England colleges. While the university developed a series of first-rate graduate and professional schools, it virtually ignored both the liberal arts and its undergraduate population until World War II, and thus lacked the foundation on which to build a national reputation for the university as a whole. Moreover, in contrast to their counterparts in Boston and other cities, Philadelphia's first families never viewed their university as crucial to their self-identity. Indeed, Penn over the years has been characterized by an anti-intellectual, professionally oriented strain. Yet in an era when much emphasis is placed on making money and getting ahead, many prospective students are looking at Penn in a new light. After all, it's the only Ivy League school where in four years you can pick up a degree that applies directly to the business and/or engineering worlds.

The ten graduate schools still dominate the university, including the prestigious Wharton School for business administration, the Annenberg School of Communication, and the well-known law, medical and veterinary schools. Three of four undergraduate schools—engineering, nursing, and the undergraduate division of Wharton—are also professionally oriented and offer an education that's hard to beat anywhere. The College of Arts and Sciences, in which the majority of undergraduates now enroll, may not muster all the big names of top Ivies, but it does offer high-quality instruction as well as the chance to run into a Nobel laureate here and there—teaching freshman econ, for instance.

Economics, psychology, romance languages and the natural sciences are among the strongest departments in Penn's College of Arts and Sciences, and anthropology ranks with Chicago as perhaps the best in the country. Sociology boasts some formidable scholars, and history has traditionally been strong at this institution, which was one of the pioneers in the field of American studies. Penn gives itself a round of applause in the field of cognitive and computer sciences because of its special program linking psychology, linguistics and computers with philosophy. Another popular crème de la crème interdisciplinary major, biological basis of behavior, combines psychology, economics and anthropology. Students also single out English, folklore and the legal studies concentration as good A&S bets and point to astronomy, geology, political science and fine arts as definite weak spots.

Individualized majors and the wonderful opportunity to take courses from all of the undergraduate and professional schools add to the value of the undergraduate experience at Penn. An added plus that comes with a Penn undergraduate education is the opportunity for early entry (submatriculation) into the university's graduate programs. Juniors may apply to any master's program (continuing into the Wharton MBA program is especially popular) and begin completing graduate requirements their senior year. In addition, Penn offers innovative and marketable joint majors. Design and structural technology or management and technology, for example, lead to dual arts and engineering or business and engineering degrees in four years. On the other hand, Penn offers no co-op programs and discourages full-time internships for credit, remaining true to the Ivy League belief that learning is best done in the classroom. Participation in the Sea Semester* is testimony that a floating classroom can count, as can study abroad at Penn's programs in Italy, Scotland, Japan, France and London.

Professors at Penn take their research responsibilities seriously, leaving graduate teaching assistants to manage all but the lectures and office hours for many classes. Freshman seminars and general honors courses (usually more demanding versions of introductory courses) provide exceptions to the rule, and "take a professor to lunch week" is a favored tradition in several departments. Advising in the professional schools receives student praise, but arts and sciences students often turn to peers for advice. The various schools share the more than three million volumes and excellent computerized search system—"mind-boggling"—in Penn's huge and busy main library, which one student describes as "a good place to check books out, a bad place to read them." The first floor is known for socializing: "The Rosengarten Reserve Room is commonly called Rosengossip."

All Penn students fulfill liberal arts distribution requirements. The Wharton, engineering and nursing schools all require students to take a substantial number of liberal arts courses, and the School of Arts and Sciences is now revising and strengthening its distribution requirements. Strict academic policies and demanding professors exacerbate the academic pressure. "Because it's not the most prestigious university," a communications major reasons, "it has to be the toughest." But a history major adds, "I wouldn't term Penn as cutthroat. You can get notes from people if you miss class, but there's not much fellow-student sympathy for someone who won't put in the time and do the work."

Penn claims it is in the midst of a renaissance in terms of student diversity. Less than a fourth of each entering class comes from Pennsylvania, which is testimony to the success of the computerized nationwide recruitment plan. More than three-quarters of the students rank in the top 10 percent of their high school classes, and two-thirds come from public high schools. "Young creative entrepreneurs" abound, as do rather conservative men and women. Penn attempts to admit students regardless of need and does not offer any merit scholarships, athletic or otherwise. Through its innovative Penn Plan, the university has pioneered the idea that virtually every family with a college-bound son or daughter, no matter what their income, can benefit from financial assistance. For some this means scholarships, subsidized loans and other traditional forms of aid. Other possibilities under the Penn Plan, however, include prepayment and borrowing options designed with the rate of inflation in mind and aimed at families in the higher income brackets.

Two-thirds of the students live on campus and enjoy a wide range of living options. Dorms are coed by room, "a system of which I wholeheartedly approve," notes a marketing major. Freshmen live mostly in King's Court, Hill's House, or the Quad, which is voted most popular because of its new paint, butcher block furniture and "overall freshmanness." Upperclassmen reluctantly move to the high rises across campus that look like "prefabricated twenty-four-story monsters" but do offer more space as well as kitchens. Students may also apply for a number of small special-interest dorms that provide a greater community experience. Reportedly in the past the housing lottery was plagued by scalpers who sold good numbers to the highest bidders; so rather than compete for rooms that are already considered overpriced, many juniors and seniors simply head off campus. Some of these nomads end up in nearby renovated three-story houses in the neighborhood. Like housing, the meal plans are optional (though strongly recommended in the freshman year as an important source of social life), and the food "tastes just like Mom's home cooking . . . if she were cooking for nine thousand people." There is no food served on weekends, and students cry about this situation all the way to Chinatown.

The university is situated in a pleasant and largely self-contained nest called University City. Its hundred-plus buildings are a mix of very old structures such as College Hall, with red and green foliage creeping up its facade, and very new ones, such as Wharton's graduate school, which is strung along a 240-acre site just west of the Schuylkill River. The area directly surrounding the university campus is a little grim, and high crime rates concern most students. But downtown Philadelphia, only a few minutes away by foot, cab or public transportation, offers enough social and cultural activities to make up for the less attractive aspects of city living. "As I get older," philosophizes a third-year student, "I find myself exploring Philadelphia's offerings more and more—from soft pretzels and cheesecakes to the famous art museum." Students also frequent sporting events, malls, South Street ("a miniature Greenwich Village") and, of course, a myriad of bars and dancing joints. In fact, a good part of the years at Penn are spent at one party or another.

Undergraduates may work hard during the week, but, in contrast to most Ivy League achievers, they leave it behind them on weekends and thus enjoy one of the most relaxed, typically collegiate social lives in the Ivy League. Despite the state's drinking age of twenty-one, the pubs near the campus serve students with hardly a blink (Doc Watson's and Smokey Joe's are favorites), and even off-campus bars will accept any student ID as valid proof of age. More than two dozen fraternities provide lively parties and "your basic meat-market scene" with enough mixing so that the unequal male/female ratio doesn't seem to bother anyone. Sororities are of little importance here. Alternative entertainment is available at the co-op Eatery, where campus radicals and artists gather to talk and party.

Now that Penn's basketball squad has reached as high as the country's top four and the football team has grown accustomed to sitting on the top of the Ivy League, a widespread revival of school spirit is highly visible. "Maniac loyalists" now sleep outdoors for days in order to purchase season tickets. This dedication should come as no surprise to an administration that once endured an occupation of its offices by students protesting the elimination of five sports, including varsity hockey. Classics majors who don't know a T-formation from a touchdown can now be seen wearing school colors and cheering "Kill 'em, Quakers" from the stands. Men's lacrosse and fencing, and women's lacrosse and field hockey are big with athletes, and nearly two dozen intramural sports bring thousands out to play each year.

Benjamin Franklin, the exile from Boston who founded Penn in 1740, never meant for it to equal the scholarly snobbery of Harvard or Yale—schools he looked down on for their useless emphasis on the classics and liberal arts. Instead, Franklin said an education at his university "should be an education for citizenship, and should lead to mercantile and civic success and usefulness." Penn has followed its founder's prescription faithfully from that day to this. Although it may have been tough to be the East Coast's premier preprofessional institution in the hippie-sixties, in the yuppie-eighties, Penn's sitting in clover.

Pepperdine University

Malibu, CA 90265

Location Suburban	**Applicants** 2,240
Total Enrollment 6,700	**Accepted** 56%
Undergraduates 3,200	**Enrolled** 44%
Male/Female 47/53	**Academics** ★ ★ ★
SAT V/M 510/560	**Social** ☎ ☎
Financial Aid 65%	**Q of L** ● ● ● ●
Expense Pr $ $ $ $	**Admissions** (213)456-4392

Perched on a hill above the beach community of Malibu and flanked by the rugged Santa Monica Mountains, Pepperdine University's campus is, in the words of one student, "absolutely breathtaking." This is a school with a top-ranking surfing team and a setting that can be described as a sun-worshipping party-lover's dream come true. But looks can be deceiving: This Pacific paradise is actually one of the most conservative schools in Southern California.

Pepperdine's modern Spanish-style, stucco campus has a spectacular view of the Pacific coastline, and this location is a strong selling point for potential students. A senior admits, "Frankly, after visiting the gorgeous Malibu campus, to say the aesthetic beauty of the campus didn't affect my decision would be less than honest." The 650-acre campus features fountains, hillside flower gardens, and mountain trails. The weather is usually impeccable except during rainy periods when mud slides can cover the roads.

Pepperdine's affiliation with the staunchly evangelical Church of Christ is apparent in nearly every aspect of campus life. Students at Seaver College, the undergraduate arm of the university, must take two religion courses and show up in their assigned seats at weekly convocations. Campus residents endure both prohibitions against drinking and fairly strict coed visitation rules in the dorms. Few students seem to mind the regulations, though; in fact, most seem to like the "highly moral" atmosphere, and one man sums up, "For the most part, this religious overtone has a positive impact on campus life."

While the emphasis at Seaver is on striving for academic excellence, the atmosphere is casual. "We are spared the high-pressure 'dog eat dog' sense of competition found in the Ivy League schools," notes a business major. While the less intense climate is welcome, some students complain that a certain percentage of students are there primarily for the sunshine. "I'm sure this exists at other schools but it's easier to see at Pepperdine because of the 'Malibu' stereotype that many students have adopted." In order to get a Pepperdine degree students must complete the general studies program, which includes four trimesters of physical education (no wonder everyone's in great shape), two courses in English composition and one class in a foreign language. The Great Books Colloquium has recently been added to the curriculum and is available to eighty freshmen each year.

Business, communications and biology are all strong departments. Computer science, with its recently expanded facilities, is recommended. Sports medicine, a rare offering at the undergraduate level, is a popular major. Brand-new music studios and the promise of a new art building should boost the sagging fine arts department. The undergraduate college's small size and friendly atmosphere encourage independent and interdisciplinary study. Juniors interested in German culture may spend a year at

Pepperdine's own facilities near Heidelberg Castle, and programs in London and Florence are also offered.

The already excellent library has recently been doubled in size, in terms of both space and number of books. Students believe that they "couldn't have a better relationship" with the faculty. Professors in seminars often have students to their homes for class or perhaps even for dinner; teaching assistants are nonexistent. But Pepperdine's goal is to provide more than an academic education. Says one man, the university "teaches you how to deal with people and how you can achieve success while still leading a Christian lifestyle." While personal faith in Christ is not required (only 13 percent of the students belong to the Church of Christ), the university does emphasize the values and ethics of Christianity in every possible area of campus life.

One might expect students at this religiously oriented school to be conservative, and they are very much so politically. "A militant left-wing radical would not find the climate too welcoming and would probably be happier at Berkeley," says a junior. However, an advertising major reports that "the conduct of their personal lives is often a different subject entirely, and many of the students do not share the same views on drinking or religion that the school does, which can be very interesting." Many undergraduates come from well-to-do California families; there is also a relatively high percentage of wealthy international students, and all of this money has led to a large number of Porsches, Ferraris and BMWs on campus.

Student vehicles may fit into the small, very wealthy community of Malibu better than the students themselves. Town/gown relations are not the best, mainly because the town sees the university as a catalyst for development of the area, which most residents oppose. And because the social scene in Malibu is pretty grim, students appreciate their proximity to L.A. and Santa Monica. On campus, fraternities and sororities (all local) are playing an increasingly large entertainment role.

Except for commuters, students are required to live on campus through their sophomore year or their twenty-first birthday, whichever comes first. Twenty-one identical single-sex dorms and apartments house the campus dwellers. The million-dollar views available from about a quarter of the rooms almost compensate for the crowded conditions of the dorms, which are organized into suites of four bedrooms, a bath, and a living room. Rooms are assigned according to resident preference on a first-come, first-served basis. Few upperclassmen choose to live off campus due to the high cost of living in the Malibu area. All dormitory residents must purchase meal tickets, which are good only at the campus cafeteria. This facility serves as the main campus social center, since Pepperdine lacks a student union. The food is pretty tasty, with good variety, and students can eat on a terrace facing the ocean.

Sports receive a lot of attention—both jocks and sports fans abound—and more than 130 athletic scholarships in eleven sports assure quality teams. Men's tennis, basketball, baseball and volleyball teams are all conference champions. Water polo and surfing (of course) are also popular, and two women's teams, golf and tennis, have recently been added. The intramural program is quite active as is the physical education department, which offers surfing, horseback riding and hang gliding.

In addition to athletic scholarships, Pepperdine offers a variety of other ways to help students, whether needful or not, to make ends meet, including sixty-five merit scholarships ranging from $1,500 to $5,000 per year. The best students get the best grants, but financial aid for those in need is readily available.

Pepperdine offers a solid, people-oriented education in an intimate atmosphere, and most students value it as much for its warmth as for its Christian ideals. Being able to tolerate what one student euphemistically calls a "controlled environment," is definitely a must, but the inspirational scenery certainly helps.

University of Pittsburgh

Pittsburgh, PA 15260

Location City center	**Applicants** 7,310
Total Enrollment 28,710	**Accepted** 77%
Undergraduates 19,000	**Enrolled** 47%
Male/Female 52/48	**Academics** ★ ★ ★
SAT V/M 480/530	**Social** ☎ ☎
Financial Aid 60%	**Q of L** ● ●
Expense Pub $ $ $ $	**Admissions** (412)624-PITT

Back in 1787, a gentleman named Hugh Brackenridge helped found a tiny educational academy deep in the forests of the Allegheny Mountains. "Pittsburgh is greatly to be chosen for a seat of learning," he said at the time, "the fresh air, the excellent water, and the plenty and cheapness of provisions, render it highly favorable." Since then, both the city and the university have endured some lean times, but today Mr. Brackenridge is looking more and more like a prophet. Pittsburgh is currently rated the "most livable" city in the nation by Rand McNally, and the university, bolstered by the region's newfound prosperity, has taken to calling itself "the Campus of the Future."

Times have not always been so good. In the late '60s, the private university had financial difficulties before the state of Pennsylvania stepped in and agreed to underwrite a fourth of its operating budget. The deal meant lower tuition for Pennsylvania residents, increased competition for admission and better students. Now entering its bicentennial decade, Pitt has a campus that features everything from a forty-two-story neo-Gothic academic building ("you get nosebleeds on the way up there"), to generic modern office buildings, to light and airy contemporary buildings. Boasting sixteen schools and 139 departments, Pitt rightfully claims to accommodate "students with divergent needs." The academically motivated can take advantage of an excellent university honors college; the career-oriented don't complain about the head start Pitt obligingly gives them in the summer job hunt by ending the academic year in April.

Nestled amid the shops, parks and apartment complexes of Pittsburgh's bustling Oakland section, Pitt's campus has a mix of Gothic and modern buildings. Academically, the university's professional divisions are its showpieces. The schools of engineering and nursing are also excellent and attract high-caliber students. Anything health-related, from physical therapy to pharmacy, is also a good bet. The College of Arts and Sciences is weaker, though academic standards were strengthened in 1982 with the addition of skill requirements in writing, math and foreign language, and distribution requirements in the humanities, social sciences and natural sciences. Among traditional academic departments, philosophy stands head and shoulders above the rest, though most foreign languages are good. However, the biology department is reportedly not up to par, and computer science is having difficulty meeting increased student demand. Those interested in the liberal arts should definitely investigate the frequently praised honors program, which enables students with at least a B-plus average to rise above the mediocrity of many of the regular courses. Honors students publish the *Pittsburgh Undergraduate Review,* which receives submissions from students nationwide. Qualified students in arts and sciences may transfer into four other undergraduate schools after the sophomore year or into the School of Pharmacy after one year. For undergraduates with wanderlust, the university cosponsors a rigorous semester at sea that permits them to sail around the world and take courses at the same time. Closer to home, Pitt is working with major technological and communications firms to equip the university with an integrated fiber-optic system that will transmit voice and video communication and electronic data across campus at the speed of light.

A strong evening program and two short spring and summer sessions give students considerable flexibility in planning their program. Many faculty members are involved in research, but some students see that as a plus, "since they need us to work on their grants." Others would rather have a little more attention, and say the impersonal side of Pitt is especially evident in introductory science courses, where computerized multiple-choice tests are the norm.

Ninety-four percent of the students are native Pennsylvanian's including a substantial number from the Pittsburgh area. Blue collars are as prevalent at the university as in the city proper, though more than half the students graduated in the top fifth of their high school class. Blacks account for just over a tenth of the student body. Pitt admits students without reference to financial need and continues to fill the need of those who meet application deadlines, with the others being aided as long as there are funds. The university also offers more than five hundred merit awards of $500 to $9,900 a year to students who scored over 1200 on the SAT, were in the top 10 percent of their high school class, and maintained at least a B-plus average. Athletic scholarships are offered in every sport except tennis, and a deferred tuition payment plan is also available. The academic and psychological counseling programs are both very strong, with the latter offering rap sessions seven days a week.

Less than a fourth of the students live on campus. Since there are only forty-five hundred beds available, freshmen get priority but no guarantees. Many students live in apartments in nearby residential communities, or simply commute in from home. There are ten coed dorms with liberal visitation hours, and all kinds of rooming situations are available, from singles to seven-person suites. Upperclassmen vie for their rooms in an annual lottery, and since the high-rise dorms seem like "cinder-block prisons," competition for the nicer halls is stiff. The food in the school cafeterias won't kill you, but you probably won't be asking for many recipes.

From the Carnegie Museum to the Pittsburgh Steelers, the city has enough artistic, corporate, historical and athletic offerings to keep any student satisfied for four years. Pitt is situated in Oakland, the cultural center of Pittsburgh, adjacent to Carnegie–Mellon University and about three miles from downtown. Parking is virtually nonexistent unless you get to school before 9 AM, but public transportation is readily accessible. Students also have easy access to shopping malls, fast-food places, and practically every other imaginable staple of life. A huge public park right next to campus is a welcome escape hatch, offering ice-skating, golfing, a pool, jogging trails, and tennis courts. For those who feel the need for a break from the urban setting, ski slopes and mountain trails are not far away.

Anyone at Pitt will be expected to develop a taste for beer and the night spots of Oakland. Since the campus empties out on the weekends, Thursday night is bar night. For those who stick around, the fraternities and sororities keep the parties going and play two major roles on campus: They provide those who feel a little lost with a sense of group identity, and they keep everyone under twenty-one (the legal drinking age) supplied with plenty of booze. As one fraternity brother says, "Bacchus has a hell of a following here." Following close on Bacchus in popularity are the Pittsburgh Panthers, and being in the stands on Saturday afternoons for home games is de rigueur. Though not nearly as popular, other successful teams include men's and women's basketball and swimming and women's volleyball.

Since its reincarnation as a private/public university, Pitt has served the educational needs of western Pennsylvania well. As old as the Constitution, but with its eyes on the future, Pitt manages to be both down-home and dynamic at the same time—and please a wide variety of customers along the way.

Pitzer College, CA—See CLAREMONT COLLEGES

Pomona College, CA—See CLAREMONT COLLEGES

Pratt Institute

Brooklyn, NY 11205

Location Urban	**Applicants** 1,570
Total Enrollment 3,670	**Accepted** 72%
Undergraduates 2,810	**Enrolled** 47%
Male/Female 65/35	**Academics** ★ ★ ★
SAT V/M 430/470	**Social** ☎
Financial Aid 86%	**Q of L** ● ●
Expense Pr $ $ $	**Admissions** (718)636-3669

By most collegiate standards, Pratt students would have a lot to complain about. The Brooklyn neighborhood is unappealing and crime-ridden. Some facilities are outdated or inadequate, and the organized social life is, to put it generously, low key. Students, however, utter few complaints. They chose Pratt for its professional training, mostly in art-related fields, for the dedicated faculty, and for the "creative and freethinking" atmosphere. They soon get so wrapped up in their artistic and professional pursuits that the environment doesn't make much difference.

Charles Pratt opened the institute in 1887 to train immigrants in the fields of drafting, electrical engineering, leather tanning and home economics. The school was also designed to serve as a shoe factory just in case the educational venture failed. Today, the twenty-five-acre campus presents a mix of attractive turn-of-the-century buildings and '50s-style additions. A recent (and welcome) addition is the Rubelle and Norman Schafler art gallery, which doubled the amount of exhibition space available on campus.

The institute is internationally known for the quality of its programs in the fine arts, architecture and design. The engineering school is also strong, but the programs in management, computer science and nutrition and dietetics simply are not in the same academic league. Pratt is especially proud of its faculty members, three-quarters of whom are part-time instructors and practicing professionals who bring into the class-room knowledge of the latest developments in their fields. Pratt has numerous Guggen-heim, Tiffany and Fulbright recipients on its faculty and ranks third in the country in producing National Endowment for the Arts fellows.

A professional school from top to bottom, Pratt does not pretend to serve students interested primarily in the humanities. All students, however, must fulfill liberal arts requirements that comprise at least one quarter of their total course work, a regimen that the administration believes "prepares students for careers and provides them with the ability to advance within their professions." Entering students in Pratt's largest school, art and design, are required to follow a one-year foundation core to develop their "critical visual literacy and understanding of the creative processes." Other special programs include an optional four-week Winterim in January and opportunities for study abroad, including popular semester programs in London, Copenhagen and Italy, and a spring architecture program in Cypress and Rome. Engineering and computer science students in co-op programs spend their entire freshman and senior years at Pratt but for the middle two years alternate semesters of study with semesters of work in a specific field. Students in art, design and architecture are encouraged to take internships in their fields for college credit.

Career-advising and job-placement services are good, and both students and alumni flock to the job referral office. The renovated library has emerged as "the jewel of the campus," but students complain that its hours are inconvenient, closing by 9 PM during the week and before five P.M. on Saturday. But in all fairness, one industrial design major notes, "the demand is not terribly high." At this school, students are more interested in studio time than stack time.

Admission to Pratt depends on a number of variables, which change from one division to the next. For those applying to the schools of architecture and art and design, portfolio evaluation is emphasized. Admissions officers stress that talented students should not rule themselves out because of outwardly inadequate SAT scores. Pratt holds a national talent search for the best and brightest young students in art and design, architecture and fashion, offering more than a million dollars in scholarship money to those chosen. And Pratt's Search for Future Engineers awards more than $350,000 in scholarships to nearly thirty outstanding high school seniors who wish to pursue a career in engineering and are "eager to take a leadership role in the solution of societal problems."

While students are drawn primarily from New York (about 60 percent from the city and an extra 2 percent from elsewhere in the state), there is still a cross section of every color, temperament, sexual preference, nationality and personality at Pratt. On the whole, the artists seem to set the tone, but the conservative-minded engineers are accepted for their quirks and eccentricities. However, students interested in football team rankings, fraternity life, and keg parties should not waste time considering Pratt. The climate is best suited for individualistic, self-motivated types who have already committed themselves to a career in an artistic or technical field and view college as a time "to eat, sleep, and drink their area of interest."

Except for those who commute from home, most of the students live in college dorms or apartments. A seventeen-story coed dorm, a married student dorm, and a women's dorm are the options, and two additional dorms are soon to be completed. Since all suites are equipped with kitchens, there is no meal plan available on campus. There is, however, a convenience store in the main dorm and a pay cafeteria on campus, not to mention a wealth of ethnic eateries both nearby and in Manhattan that can appease just about any appetite. The Clinton Hill/Fort Greene area of Brooklyn, where Pratt's campus is located, is full of run-down but gorgeous brownstones, making it "beautiful but somewhat unsafe." Still, about 8 percent of the students live in off-campus apartments near the school.

Despite some attempts at schoolwide social events, students tend to organize their own free time and use Manhattan, just a half hour away on the other side of the East River, as their playground. Social groups coalesce around the different academic disci-

445

plines. Sports, both varsity and intramural, are only moderately popular. On weekends, "most people either go home or stay and work out in the gym or party in the sauna," notes one art and design major. Despite the lack of structure, social life at Pratt is, in the assessment of one student, "pretty good—for an art school."

Mr. Pratt would probably be pleased to know his institute is now training some of the most talented students in the fields of art, design and architecture, rather than supplying the shoes to take them elsewhere.

Princeton University

Princeton, NJ 08544

Location Small town	**Applicants** 12,660
Total Enrollment 6,200	**Accepted** 17%
Undergraduates 4,550	**Enrolled** 54%
Male/Female 65/35	**Academics** ★ ★ ★ ★ ★
SAT V/M 640/700	**Social** 🐘 🐘 🐘
Financial Aid 43%	**Q of L** ● ● ●
Expense Pr $ $ $ $	**Admissions** (609)452-3060

Like its Big Three rivals, Harvard and Yale, Princeton offers a top-quality education backed up by some of the finest academic resources in the nation. Its uniqueness lies in its scale (among the Ivies, only Dartmouth has a lower total enrollment) and its emphasis on undergraduates. Guardian of two and a half centuries worth of the tried and true in American higher education, Princeton is "imbued with a sense of tradition," one student observes. "Changes aren't considered changes here—they're 'new traditions.'" One recent such revelation was the administration's decision to revise the university's 128-year-old song, "Old Nassau." Almost twenty years after women were first admitted to Princeton, they have finally been included in the alma mater via gender-neutral lyrics that will replace references to "sons" and "boys."

Cloistered in a secluded but upscale New Jersey town, Princeton's architectural trademark is Gothic, from the cavernous and ornate university chapel to the four-pronged Cleveland Tower rising majestically above the treetops. Examples of Colonial architecture are also interspersed, most notably historic Nassau Hall, which served as the temporary home of the Continental Congress in 1783. A host of modern structures, some by the leading American architect Robert Venturi, add variety and distinction to the campus, but the ambience is still quintessentially Ivy League.

Among major research institutions, Princeton offers its students unparalleled faculty contact. With few graduate students to siphon off resources or consume faculty time, undergraduates get the lion's share of both; at last count, about 70 percent of Princeton's department heads taught introductory undergraduate courses. Lovers of literature can study with Joyce Carol Oates or John McPhee, and nearly every other department has a few stars of its own. At least one or two of the small discussion groups that accompany each lecture course are led by senior professors. Every liberal arts student works closely with a faculty member of his or her choice in completing two Junior Papers—about thirty pages of independent work each semester prepared in addition to the normal course load. Princeton is also one of the few colleges in the country to require every graduate to complete a senior thesis—an enterprise that serves as a culmination of their work in their field of concentration.

As one might expect, Princeton's small size means the number of courses offered is smaller than at other Ivies; but lack of quantity does not mean lack of quality. Princeton's math and philosophy departments are among the best in the nation, and English, politics, physics, astrophysics, history, classics, economics, art history, music, German and French are right on their heels. Princeton is one of the few top liberal arts universities with equally strong engineering programs, most notably chemical, mechanical and aerospace engineering. The only departments that draw consistently negative reviews from students are sociology, psychology and anthropology.

One of Princeton's best-known programs is the prestigious Woodrow Wilson School of Public and International Affairs ("Woody Woo" to the students), which admits undergraduates on a selective basis. Freshmen explore various texts and ideas that have shaped Western culture in interdisciplinary seminars taught by senior faculty members. The university has recently undertaken a major new effort to become a national center in the field of molecular biology, with a new $29-million laboratory for teaching and research staffed by eleven new faculty members. A note of interest for computer whizzes: The National Science Foundation recently selected Princeton as a "supercomputer university," one of four schools to be a part of a $200-million computer networking project.

Distribution requirements for BA candidates cover natural sciences, social sciences, arts and humanities and include extensive writing and mastery of a foreign language. Engineering students must also satisfy the writing requirement and a similar set of distribution requirements. Princeton's semester system gives students a two-week reading period before exams in which to catch up, with first-term exams postponed until after New Year's. The university honor code, unique among the Ivies, allows for unproctored exams. Princeton's outstanding library facilities embrace over four million volumes and five hundred private study carrels for seniors working on their theses, as well as another seven hundred enclosed carrels in other parts of the campus. With a major addition to the main library now under way, the facilities can only improve.

Although field study (internships) and foreign study are touted in the catalogue, they aren't encouraged on campus. "Regardless of its rhetoric, Princeton is not very flexible," a senior notes. The administration wants students here for four full years, so the academic standards for outside work are stringent. With exceptions for students with sufficient advanced standing to complete their degree requirements in three and a half years, leaves of absence must be taken by the year, not the semester, another discouragement to "stopping out." A limited number of courses can be taken on the pass/fail option, however, and the University Scholars program provides especially qualified students with what the administration calls "maximum freedom in planning programs of study to fulfill individual needs and interests."

Princeton undergraduates are admitted to the university without regard to their financial need, and those who qualify for aid get an appropriate package of benefits. The majority of these "highly organized, highly competitive, goal-oriented" students are achievers, both in terms of academics—90 percent from the top tenth of their high school classes—and extracurricular activities. Engineers must compete separately for the two hundred or so spots available for them. "It seems that almost everyone plays the piano decently and plays an excellent game of tennis" is how one student describes his classmates, about 40 percent of whom come from private and parochial schools. Princeton may no longer be the exclusive white male playground immortalized by F. Scott Fitzgerald, but Brooks Brothers types are still much in evidence. Princeton has historically drawn more southerners than any other Ivy and has always had trouble attracting women and minorities. Black and Hispanic enrollment now stands at 10

447

percent. Politically, the campus is a mix of liberal and conservative, but counterculture types are in notably short supply. "Artists and individualists, come only if you are fairly thick-skinned and wish to develop some other aspects of who you are," a creative writing major advises. The administration hopes that recent renovations of the arts facilities, coupled with a $5.9-million expansion of the art gallery, will make Princeton more appealing to future Picassos and Baryshnikovs.

The university's turn-of-the-century Gothic dorms may look like crosses between cathedrals and castles, but conditions on the inside are often less glamorous. Some halls have amenities including living rooms, bay windows and working fireplaces, but others are marred by overcrowding and basement bathrooms. A new dorm with space for forty students has helped ease the space crunch somewhat, and two more under construction should alleviate it altogether. The modern and roomy Spelman dorms, which come complete with kitchens, are the best on campus and fill up quickly every year with seniors who do not belong to eating clubs. Real estate in the area is expensive and scarce, so only about 4 percent of the students live off campus.

In an attempt to provide a high quality of life for freshmen and sophomores, Princeton recently grouped many of its dorms into residential colleges, each with its own dining hall, faculty residents and an active social calendar. Under this system, nearly all underclass students live and dine with their residential college unit, alleviating the formerly fragmented social situation. However, by creating a separate social sphere for freshmen and sophomores, the new system can "create a gulf between underclass and upperclass students."

Princeton's most firmly entrenched bastions of tradition are the eating clubs that line Prospect Avenue and have for over a century assumed the role of fraternities in weekend as well as dining activities. Of the thirteen, eight admit members through an open lottery, but the other five still use a controversial selective admissions process called "bicker" (because of the wrangling over whom to admit), to the embarrassment of the administration and most of the students. Catering exclusively to upperclassmen, the clubs provide a secure sense of community for their members. More than half of all sophomores join one of the clubs at the end of the year, becoming full-fledged members by the fall of their junior year. Some students, however, opt for life in independent dormitories, the Third World Center, or Stevenson Hall, and a handful of fraternities and a couple of sororities have sprung up on campus over the past few years.

While the residential colleges have made strides in social programming, the Prospect Avenue eating clubs are still the place for most of Princeton's dating and partying—a source of some grumbling among nonmembers. Each has an identity all its own, and most students seem to find one where they fit in. "You can find just about every type at the clubs—jocks, nerds, BPs (Beautiful People), feminists and everything in between," says one woman. Since they are often invited to the eating club parties, underclass women can expect a more active social life than underclass men.

Princeton's campus is self-contained, but those who venture outside its Gothic walls will find the surroundings quite pleasing. "There are no factories, toxic waste dumps, or smokestacks, contrary to popular belief," assures a junior. One side of the campus abuts quaint Nassau Street, which is increasingly dominated by chic (and overpriced) boutiques. The other side of campus ends with a huge man-made lake (financed by Andrew Carnegie so that Princetonians would not have to forgo crew). Students rarely venture much farther than New York or Philadelphia, each one hour (in opposite directions) on the train. "There isn't much time, except for during the breaks, to do much road-tripping," a student reasons. Few students complain about boredom and many praise the affluent town of Princeton for the parks, woods, bike trails and, most importantly, the quiet and safety it offers students. "After all, who wants to get mugged on a date?" a biology major asks. McCarter Theatre, adjacent to campus, is the nation's seventh busiest performing arts center and houses Princeton's Triangle Show, Jimmy Stewart's launching pad.

Princeton has the oldest licensed college radio station, plenty of journalistic opportunities, a prestigious debating and politics society (Whig-Clio), and a plethora of arts offerings. Although many students believe the athletic programs could use more administration support, such alleged lack of backing has not hampered the success of the men's cross-country and basketball teams and the women's squash, volleyball, ice hockey and softball teams, which consistently take Ivy League championships. But perhaps the most closely followed spectator sport at Princeton is the annual nude olympics in which a group of sixty sophomores (six of them women) streak through the Rockefeller College courtyard to celebrate the first snowfall of the winter. Less exhilarating events are found on the intramural fields where the teams from the eating clubs and residential colleges compete.

The new residential colleges have changed the social life somewhat, but Princeton will still give you a taste of college as it used to be—before the upheavals of the sixties and the preprofessionalism of the seventies. The tenor of the place is unmistakably traditional, and the education harks back to old-fashioned ideals of academic rigor and close student-faculty interaction. In short, Princeton is the prototype of a prestigious—some would say elitist—undergraduate community. It can be a great experience for those who fit into this version of the ivory tower, and rough going for those who don't.

Principia College

Elsah, IL 62028

Location Rural	**Applicants** 214
Total Enrollment 690	**Accepted** 85%
Undergraduates 690	**Enrolled** 83%
Male/Female 45/55	**Academics** ★ ★ ★
SAT V/M 490/530	**Social** ☎ ☎ ☎
Financial Aid 70%	**Q of L** ● ● ● ●
Expense Pr $ $ $	**Admissions** (800)851-1084

High on the bluffs above the mighty, muddy Mississippi River, the Principia College chapel bells ring out every quarter hour across the sprawling but secluded campus. The community of people within hearing distance—students, faculty and staff members—all have one thing in common: They are Christian Scientists. From this shared starting ground, students are encouraged to demonstrate spiritual, intellectual and personal growth, "to unfold individual potential by mastering, not just covering, subject matter." Prin's curriculum emphasizes liberal arts and preprofessionalism in a way that complements the religious foundation of the college. "The 'right' answers are not stressed," says one woman, "but rather the 'right' method of thinking."

The wide openness of the Midwest affords Principians a spectacular view of the river and beyond. "The campus setting is idyllic, truly the most beautiful of many I've seen," says one student. The buildings are mainly English Tudor and Gothic, and many were designed by Bernard Maybeck, a noted architect of the early 1900s who attempted to re-create a small English town—lilacs and orchards and all—on the Principia grounds.

The faculty members are dedicated at this college where teaching ability is seen as much more important than research or publishing. Students praise the no-nonsense departments of business, education, political science, English, studio art and history. Yet because of the school's small size, some programs lack depth (especially earth science, philosophy and the newly added communications department). Whatever their major, students spend a lot of time at the books: "Academics are stressed and considered very important, though it's not a high pressure situation," reports a senior.

Class size is held down to an average of about sixteen students, which means the settings are intimate forums for discussing ideas. "The professors are a godsend," says one recent graduate. "They're more than just teachers—they become your mentors." But the small classes also mean underclassmen sometimes get closed out of courses they want. Requirements include proficiency in at least one foreign language, as well as courses in the fine arts, history, religion and philosophy, and the social sciences. Motivated freshmen and transfer students may enroll in the Falcon program (Freshman Analytic Learning Concentration), which emphasizes analytical thinking as a groundwork for further exploration in the liberal arts and sciences. Those who are underprepared for college receive special tutoring and instruction through the Phoenix program. Principia is on the quarter system, with ten-week fall, winter and spring terms (and time off from Thanksgiving to January).

Each year during one of these terms, or even during the breaks, nearly one in four of Prin's students take advantage of the excellent "Prin Abroad" as well as the "Mini-Abroad" programs. Prin has sent student groups to Africa, Russia, the Orient, Central America, the Middle East, Australia and Europe. Students are also able to design their own majors and connect with the corporate and political world for internships.

Although Principia has never had any formal ties with the Church of Christ, Scientist, from the beginning (1898) everyone who has administered, taught or studied there has been of the Christian Scientist faith. "I feel the unity of thought and purpose adds to a close family-like atmosphere," says a senior, "and it is required that students live by set community standards." Yet these standards are not always happily embraced. "Sometimes the administrators think that because the rules have worked for years, that they will still work," comments a history major. "I wish they were more open to new ideas." Despite their common faith, students are geographically quite diverse. Most are from either the East or West coasts (82 percent are from out of state), and 6 percent are from overseas. Three-quarters are from public schools, and about 15 percent come directly from the upper school of the Principia in St. Louis (and vie for special scholarships along the way). About a quarter of each year's new students have transferred from other colleges, and there is a small but growing contingent of "nontrads," or students over the age of twenty-four returning to school.

The single-sex dorms house about thirty to sixty students and are warm and homey. After their first year, most students elect to become house members and stay in the same building (which serves the same purpose as a frat) for the duration of their time at Prin. Students tend to move frequently within their houses, trying out every set-up from quads to singles. "We change rooms and roommates each quarter to aid in growth and personal expansion," reports one woman. Ironically, the older, Maybek-designed houses, which lack some modern amenities like air-conditioning, are the most popular among the students. "They are very rustic and special to the campus," notes a junior. For less sentimental denizens, the fully air-conditioned newer additions are quite comfortable. Each house has a resident houseparent or two to keep watch over things. Some students feel that the doors-ajar policy when a member of the opposite sex is in the room is unnecessary. Students pick up their meals in the "scramble room," and then eat together in the plush dining hall. "The food's pretty good for school meals," says one senior.

Elsah, a "gravy-and-biscuits midwestern" river town, dates back to the 1800s and now boasts a restaurant, post office and a whopping two hundred inhabitants. The town rates high on charm but low on entertainment potential, so a car is recommended. St Louis is just forty minutes away. Whether near, far or in a motor car, Prin students are never at a loss for weekend fun. There are no fraternities or sororities, but the houses sponsor frequent nonalcoholic parties. The Christian Science organization (aka "the org") is the largest of the abundant extracurricular groups, and it runs the religious services on campus. Dancing is probably the students' favorite activity, though concerts, movies and supporting the often highly successful NCAA Division III varsity athletic program is also popular. Men's soccer and men's and women's swimming have turned out championship teams in recent years, and in 1985 Prin became the first college ever to claim both the men's and women's singles titles in tennis. Intramurals, with competition organized by house, are also "a blast."

While some of the administrative guidelines seem a bit antiquated, Principia offers students a chance to live among others who share their convictions. "It's neither a paradise nor a community of prudes," says another. "We're a group of active young people who are interested in God and good thinking."

University of Puget Sound

Tacoma, WA 98416

Location Suburban	**Applicants** 2,290
Total Enrollment 3,000	**Accepted** 85%
Undergraduates 2,770	**Enrolled** 35%
Male/Female 42/58	**Academics** ★ ★ ★
SAT V/M 500/530	**Social** ☎ ☎ ☎
Financial Aid 60%	**Q of L** ● ● ●
Expense Pr $ $	**Admissions** (206)756-3211

When folks in Tacoma refer to UPS, they mean the university, not the delivery company. But when it comes to a good liberal arts education and personalized attention, few colleges in the Pacific Northwest have a better reputation for delivering the goods than the University of Puget Sound.

Look out just about any window of the university's ivy-covered, red-brick, Tudor-Gothic buildings, and the view will be breathtaking. Mount Rainier looms in the distance, sunlight reflecting off its snow-covered peak. The nearby Cascades, Puget Sound and the ocean coast also offer stunning vistas. And all that famous Washington rain keeps the trees and flowers on the seventy-two-acre campus green and lush. "The campus is like an island of beauty—and I'm totally serious," coos a sophomore.

Founded by Methodist ministers in 1888, Puget Sound sets a dual goal of changing with the times and remaining committed to a broad-based education in the liberal arts. The eleven-course core curriculum, implemented in 1976, requires all students to take one unit each in written communication, oral communication, quantification, a historical and humanistic perspective, the fine arts and comparative values. Under-

451

graduates must also take two courses each in the study of the natural world and society (or political or economic systems).

Once students get through all these requirements, there is a wealth of majors to choose from within the five undergraduate schools. Chemistry, economics, history, math and computer science courses are the pride of the university, along with the occupational and physical therapy programs. While art, sociology, biology, religion and the languages are voted less likely to please by both the administration and the students. The academic climate ranges from casual to intense, depending on one's motivation, but most undergrads agree that close relationships with professors are a big selling point. "I have never had a prof who I didn't get to know on a one-to-one basis," attests one student. Class size is generally small, with only freshman introductory courses going over a hundred students.

The university's intensive honors program centers around the classic texts of Western civilization. "Imagine, giving freshman students a steady foundation in Locke, Marx, Mill, Kant, etc.," says a thoroughly impressed junior. UPS also offers other unique learning programs, such as the Pacific Rim program, which takes students on exciting nine-month jaunts through such countries as Japan, Thailand, Korea, India and Nepal to study the art, architecture, politics, population and philosophies of these other cultures. Other study-abroad programs are offered in the Netherlands, France, Mexico, England and Spain, while back home on campus, four foreign language houses offer a chance for students to immerse themselves as much as possible in their study. The new business leadership program has gained recognition for placing business and related analytical courses into a liberal arts context. And an unusual freshman orientation program called Prelude & Passages combines ungraded literature sessions with fishing and backpacking trips.

UPS students are generally not encouraged to think of their undergraduate education as "pre" anything, and only about a fourth of them stampede toward professional schools upon graduation. In fact, the administration is so sold on the value of a UPS education that, calculating job changes every seven years and three career shifts, it promises that "graduates will have gained the skills and qualities that will benefit them for a period of 40 working years."

Mostly middle- to upper-middle-class whites and mostly from Washington, the students are, according to one, "a bit materialistic and exceedingly conservative." The administration, though, notes that students recently created a scholarship to give a South African student a UPS education, and one politics major reports that "there are a few activists running around." Another explains, "We don't have a lot of diversity, but that doesn't mean we don't like it." In addition to need-based financial aid, UPS offers 103 athletic scholarships and more than 800 merit scholarships, ranging up to $5,000, for achievement and promise in general academics, athletics and specific talent areas.

Freshmen are guaranteed housing on campus but not required to live there. Except for one women's dorm (where sororities can claim a hall), all eight dorms are coed by floor. Students may also choose to live in frat houses or school-owned chalets and A-frames, or move off campus altogether. The student union just received a much needed $2.5-million renovation, giving students more elbow room in the dining area, a new game room, television lounge and the student-run Pizza Cellar.

Fraternities and sororities are becoming more popular at UPS. The administration is fighting back, though, by strengthening the residence hall program and trying to gain greater control over rush and the easy access to alcohol at parties (at official campus functions, the Washington drinking age of twenty-one is strictly enforced). Although the Greeks are a major social force on campus, students appreciate the campus-sponsored alternatives—entertainment by Robin Williams, guest speakers and readings from Claude Bolling and Kurt Vonnegut, among others.

"Location is probably the biggest advantage UPS has over other colleges of equal academic reputations," an economics major assesses. "It's one hour to the ski slopes (five areas), ten minutes to the Sound for sailing, windsurfing and diving, and one-and-a-half hours to the Pacific Ocean." The school rents out all the equipment necessary for a variety of weekend outings, and a large number of students take off on weekends for the mountains or the coast. While UPS's home town, Tacoma, has few cultural and social plusses, Seattle is only an hour away, Olympia even less. Intramurals are popular but unorganized. And, among varsity teams, men's football and basketball and women's tennis are the only notables, but even these aren't crowd pleasers.

For the individual who desires a true liberal arts education, in a particularly beautiful setting, the University of Puget Sound stands ready. Just remember to throw in an umbrella and raincoat with your calculator and hiking boots.

Purdue University

West Lafayette, IN 47907

Location Small city
Total Enrollment 32,240
Undergraduates 26,920
Male/Female 60/40
SAT V/M 470/540
Financial Aid 44%
Expense Pub $ $

Applicants 16,810
Accepted 84%
Enrolled 36%
Academics ★ ★ ★
Social ☎ ☎ ☎
Q of L ● ● ●
Admissions (317)494-1776

Aside from the technological revolution, Purdue University has missed just about every other major upheaval of the last few decades. The atmosphere on this ivy-covered campus is '50s rah-rah college. Students come here because their fathers or grandfathers came here, or their older brothers or sisters came here, or everyone they ever knew came here. This is a university built on tradition, and, as one senior explains, "it's not the right place for outrageous people—most of the students here are not active in anything but conservativeness."

To say that you need to acquire a taste for midwest farmland in order to enjoy Purdue's surroundings is an understatement. "In between Indianapolis (an hour away) and Chicago (two hours), there's nothing except corn, soybeans, and Purdue," according to one West Coast transplant. Lafayette is a small industrial town, and the university is one of its main industries. Most of the campus architecture is, like its students, traditional. Red-brick buildings dominate the condensed campus, which sits daintily on the banks of the Wabash River.

In keeping with Purdue's status as a land-grant university, the curriculum concentrates on agriculture and the mechanical arts. The university has become distinguished for having awarded more bachelor's degrees in engineering than any other university, and students here flock to the five-year co-op program in engineering. Purdue, where Amelia Earhart once taught and numerous space scientists and astronauts (including Neil Armstrong and Gus Grissom) earned BAs, continues to offer a strong undergraduate program in flight technology. Pharmacy, chemistry, computer science, communications and consumer and family sciences are also superior. In contrast to its outstanding sciences, Purdue's offerings in the humanities, still seen as supports for the "practical" disciplines, have weak spots. There is little in the way of classics, languages or the social sciences.

Each of the university's ten schools establishes its own, usually extensive set of curriculum requirements—Purdue students just do *not* dabble in offbeat electives. Although required courses tend to be large, access is usually assured. In fact, with some of the classes scheduled for 7:30 AM on weekdays and even a few offered on Saturday mornings, getting into courses is often less of a problem than getting up for them. Research is a must for science and social science faculty, but it doesn't appear to take away from their time with students. A junior asserts that "Purdue faculty seem to be student-oriented, and they are always willing to answer questions." Laboratory facilities are outstanding but the main library does not meet all the research needs of the student body. With each school running its own departmental library, students take advantage of the university's study options. As one student notes, "There is a library for everyone."

Prospective students should apply early in their senior year of high school in order to beat the cutoff dates for certain programs. As one admissions officer states, "We cannot accommodate all who qualify and wish to attend, especially the out-of-state requests." Since there's no admission fee and numerous athletic and academic scholarships are offered, sending an application to Purdue promptly might turn out to be a good investment. The students, 69 percent of whom are from Indiana, are "intensely family oriented" and conservative. "There is not a lot of bizarre behavior or youth rallies on campus," assures a senior. Purdue students tend to be more "vocationally minded," and only 12 percent of them pursue graduate degrees.

But even these straitlaced undergraduates find their living conditions archaic. Dorm attendants enforce visitation hours between men and women, and a coed dorm here means, as one student explains, that both sexes share a dining hall and a lobby "with 30,000 tons of concrete in between." Freshmen obtain housing on a first-come, first-served basis. While there is generally no problem finding a room on campus, more than half the student body hunts down inexpensive and accessible off-campus housing options. For dorm residents there are meal plans, and partakers carefully describe the food as "sufficient and well balanced." But fraternity and sorority members seem to fare a lot better with food straight from their own kitchens.

The drinking age in Indiana, to the dismay of many an undergraduate, is twenty-one, so local bars have limited patronage. But fraternity and off-campus house parties are more accessible to the underaged. West Lafayette, equal in population to its favorite university, offers little in the way of culture. And although the drive time to Indianapolis or Chicago is not unbearable, most students use weekends for forgetting the books, sleeping in and catching a flick or two. Roughly 20 percent of the students belong to one of the forty-six fraternities and nineteen sororities. Nevertheless, "this is not a party school."

But this is a big sports school with a brand new all-purpose athletic facility. The intramural program fosters intense rivalries and involves a large number of students in a variety of team sports. Attendance at varsity football and basketball games is strong, although the teams themselves, especially football, are not. Purdue recruits women athletes nationwide, offering them as many scholarships as the men. The women's volleyball team boasts championship seasons and growing student attendance over the past four years. But in general women's sports do not get the same attention as the men's.

Students may not graduate from Purdue ready to jump into sophisticated city life, but they will be prepared for good careers and always have strong family ties to their oh-so traditional alma mater. One senior, who did not even consider applying to another school, fondly remembers childhood weekends spent by her father's side at Purdue football games. Another student cheers, "Spirit makes a campus, and here at Purdue, we are PROUD!"

Queens College, NY—See CITY UNIVERSITY OF NEW YORK

Randolph–Macon Woman's College

Lynchburg, VA 24503

Location City outskirts	**Applicants** 1,000
Total Enrollment 750	**Accepted** 50%
Undergraduates 750	**Enrolled** 50%
Male/Female N/A	**Academics** ★ ★ ★
SAT V/M 530/530	**Social** ☎ ☎
Financial Aid 29%	**Q of L** ● ● ● ●
Expense Pr $ $	**Admissions** (804)846-7392

Whatever you do, do not suggest to a Randolph–Macon Woman's College student that her school is a finishing school. The members of this southern college community are extremely proud of their academic tradition (Pearl S. Buck is a graduate). Their school was the first southern women's college to qualify for a Phi Beta Kappa chapter, and it prides itself on its ability to educate each student "in the singular." Believing in the "big, close-knit family" philosophy of R–MWC, professors take a personal interest in their students, as do the president and other top administrators. "We are respected, mature women with class," asserts one student, "with a strong commitment to academics."

The college's old and majestic brick buildings, which stand in a protective, encompassing semicircle, are strewn with purple wisteria vines and surrounded by thick trees that burst into bloom in the spring and melt into colors in the fall. Residential, administrative and academic buildings are interspersed on the compact, hundred-acre campus, and nearly all are linked by glass corridors called trolleys—"a physical reflection of the strong sense of community," notes one school official.

At Randolph–Macon, a feeling of mutual trust allows students a great deal of autonomy. Everyone works under an all-encompassing, student-regulated honor system that includes unproctored, self-scheduled exams. Instead of enforcing formal distribution requirements, the college relies on optional guidelines and the tailoring of individual programs by a faculty adviser. When it comes time to declare a major, a student can choose from among traditional departments or interdisciplinary majors such as communication, international relations or Asian studies. And, if none of these suit, she can design her own. Everyone agrees that economics (including business) is not only the most popular but also the strongest department. English, psychology, languages, history and art also get favorable reviews. Weaknesses tend to lie in the limited offerings of specialties like physics and mathematics.

The school's small size creates a family atmosphere, but it also has its disadvantages. Course offerings are not as abundant or varied as at a larger school. The library closes at midnight, and its stacks are often inadequate for intensive research projects. Most students, however, consider these limitations a modest price to pay for the highly responsive and engaging academic setting. Randolph–Macon's participation in the Seven-College Exchange* gives the women an opportunity to experience another campus for a year or a semester. A junior year abroad at the University of Reading in England and a joint 3-2 engineering program with Vanderbilt are also available. Students can easily arrange for special internships, independent study or study abroad through other schools.

Randolph–Macon women hail from more than forty states and a dozen foreign countries. While a majority come from public schools, there are always enough southern prep school graduates to give the college what some call a "southern-belleish" tone. "Those with liberal points of view may find the R–M attitude stifling," warns one student. A classmate chimes in that "students are basically conservative until it comes to men." Most students take part in the long-standing traditions of R–MWC, which include afternoon teas, a "pumpkin parade" (where seniors, dressed in gowns, march across campus with pumpkins carved for them by sophomores), and a rivalry between Odds and Evens, i.e., those who graduate in odd- or even-numbered years.

Admission depends largely on high school grades and class rank—doing well on your SATs will not make up for an unsatisfactory record. The college admits students regardless of financial need, and the funds needed are provided, with the best scholars getting relatively more in grants as opposed to loans. There are also about twenty-five non-need, renewable awards ranging from $2,500 to $5,000 a year for students with distinguished academic records.

With the exception of a few commuters, all students must live in the college's dormitories, most of which are older buildings with "lots of personality and charm." While Main Hall is hailed as the best dorm, many provide a gorgeous view of the Blue Ridge Mountains. The rooms are wood paneled, spacious and homey, even if the ancient heating system is a bit cranky; the seemingly eternal renovation of the dorms is still under way. Traditionally, underclassmen have doubles, while most older students enjoy singles. In all the dorms, freshmen live alongside upperclassmen, which encourages their integration into the college community. An important focus of R–MWC life is the "slow and enjoyable" family-style dinner. Students sit at tables set with linen tablecloths and dinner china and are served excellent homemade fare by student-waitresses. Between meals, the on-campus bakery offers savory snacks galore, and a snack bar churns out homemade yogurt. "The food is too tasty," assesses one student. "The infamous 'freshmen 20' [pounds] still go around."

Even with the Student Activities Board's increased efforts to provide more attractions, the campus thins out significantly on weekends. "The college sponsors a number of social events, but they are better described as drunken fiascos," says one otherwise-happy student. Traveling to the nearby coeducational and men's colleges is a tradition still well supported. Since Randolph–Macon is rather isolated, its students are to a large extent limited to meeting men in traditional dating setups or at crowded fraternity parties—and almost always on the man's turf. "But if I had come to college to meet a man," observes one student, "I wouldn't have come here." There are no sororities at R–M, but "secret societies," condoned by the administration, "add an aura of excitement and mystery to the college."

Lynchburg itself "is a nice city," says one student, "but doesn't really have enough nightspots." Others concentrate on taking full advantage of the beautiful natural surroundings. Ski slopes—Snow Shoe and Wintergreen—are an hour away, and the school will bus students there for lessons. The Blue Ridge Parkway and the Appalachian Trail, both ideal for camping and hiking excursions, are even closer, and so is a large lake. A van will take students on the fifteen-minute ride to the school riding stables. "We have a wide range of sports to choose from," says one senior, "but overall, they're not that big a deal to the nonathletes on campus." Even coaches give organized athletics less attention than academics, but most teams are at least respectable and a pep club manages to muster decent turnouts for home basketball games.

Randolph–Macon students tend to feel very good about their school—so good that after four years of this supportive atmosphere, they feel ready to take on the world. One graduating senior advises, "A well-rounded girl who wants to be treated as a person, be able to hold leadership positions, and be able to grow as a person before having to compete with men—*that's* who should go to Randolph–Macon."

University of Redlands

Redlands, CA 92373

Location City outskirts	**Applicants** 1,350
Total Enrollment 1,220	**Accepted** 72%
Undergraduates 1,190	**Enrolled** 35%
Male/Female 49/51	**Academics** ★ ★ ★
SAT V/M 500/536	**Social** 🏛 🏛 🏛
Financial Aid 72%	**Q of L** ● ● ●
Expense Pr $ $ $	**Admissions** (714)793-2121

A David battling the twin Goliaths of anonymity and an excellent state university system, the University of Redlands in Southern California offers its students a rich blend of professional and liberal arts programs. About 10 percent of them opt for one of the most unorthodox educations on the West Coast: an experimental college where work is done by student-faculty contracts, not assignments. The others get a more traditional learning environment offering sound academics and lots of individual attention.

The Johnston Center for Individualized Learning was established in 1969 to function as an alternative college within a traditional setting. The program offers unusual academic freedom; there are no departments, majors, distribution requirements or even predetermined courses. Instead, students contract with professors for their entire plan of study. At the beginning of each course students make up the syllabus by consensus and then set their own research and writing goals. Instead of grades, they receive written evaluations. Each student develops four-year goals, reviewed by a student/faculty board for direction and breadth, within one or more broad areas: the social sciences, behavioral sciences, humanities and fine and performing arts. Students must arrange for at least one cross-cultural experience off campus before graduation.

Compared with other Redlands students, Johnston undergrads are a bit older (many transfer in), more geographically diverse, and better qualified academically, with average SATs that are one hundred points above the Redlands median. Johnston students are motivated, creative, "totally liberal," and, as one student explains, "often too individualistic to get along in a traditional setting." Despite their independence all Johnston students manage to live, work and eat together in old but charming Bekins Hall, which also houses faculty offices, classrooms and a meditation room. Unfortunately, the university no longer actively markets Johnston to prospective applicants, and enrollment has dwindled from three hundred in 1973 to fewer than a hundred.

Aside from Johnston, Redlands is distinctive among liberal arts institutions mainly in that it also offers professional programs. The schools of education and music provide strong career training, as does the excellent program in communicative disorders. The business department is popular but overcrowded, though a new 2.7 grade point requirement for students entering the major should cut the numbers down to size. The five-year engineering co-op program is also in demand, despite the fact that the university's engineering department is unaccredited. For older students returning to college, the university sponsors the Whitehead Center for Lifelong Learning, which enrolls about fifteen hundred students on five regional campuses throughout Southern California.

The class of the liberal arts offerings at Redlands is reflected in the English department's superb creative writing program. A solid core curriculum "is designed to ensure that students develop basic skills necessary to function effectively in a complex world and provides exposure to a broad variety of knowledge areas"—eight, to be exact. Redlands recently axed three of its weakest programs—geology, communications and theater arts—and majors in French and physical education were also done away with. An affiliation with the American Baptist denomination has little if any effect on student life, and no religious study is required.

One of the few schools on the West Coast with a 4-1-4 calendar, Redlands has students take one intensive course each January. Students may also choose among twenty-eight study-abroad options, mainly in Europe and Asia. Freshman seminars place small groups of first-year students with some of the school's best professors, while the selective honors program enables outstanding students to work individually with professors who are very accessible outside of class and occasionally even come by the dorms for "fireside chats." According to a junior, "Faculty advisers usually become one of the student's best friends on campus." Classes are hardly ever larger than twenty-five, and students may cross-register between Johnston Center and the university at any time. Whether in academic or extracurricular programs, students say, Redlands makes it possible for anyone with a little initiative and a good idea to become a big fish in their small pond.

About two-thirds of the pond dwellers come from within the state, creating a "mellow, Southern California atmosphere" on campus. Parties are rarely raucous, and work is seldom overwhelming, but grading is tough. Outside of the Johnston Center crowd, "Redlands tends to be very sheltered and conservative." Middle-class whites predominate, though blacks and Hispanics each make up about 9 percent of the student body, and Asian Americans account for another 4 percent. About a third of all seniors go on to graduate or professional schools.

The San Bernardino Mountains serve as the scenic backdrop for Redlands' spacious, well-landscaped campus. "Overall, there's a kind of Ivy League austerity interrupted by flat-topped California-Spanish-style buildings and too much sun and blue (though sometimes grayly smoggy) sky for it to be truly austere," one woman notes. Redlands is one of those rare schools with no housing problem. "I've never known someone not to get the room they want," observes one student. Rooms are parceled

458

out on the basis of points that students accrue for each semester they live in a particular hall. Most of the dorms are coed, though there is an all-women's dorm. Complaints about dorm living center on the blocky "cement-box" structure of the houses and long lines in the school's lone cafeteria. Other housing options include on-campus apartments and student-run co-ops, but don't plan on living off campus; the university doesn't like to make it common practice. In addition to need-based aid, Redlands annually awards over three hundred merit scholarships, ranging from $200 to $9,000, with various awards depending on the student's GPA and SAT score for those with at least 3.7 and 1000, respectively. There are also talent awards in art, music and debate.

The Southern California heat and smog can become unpleasant, especially in early fall, and students with wheels often flee Redlands on weekends for healthier pleasure spots along the California coast or in the mountains. For quick doses of big-city life, L.A. is about two hours away. Road trippers and locals visiting home drain the campus on weekends, although the student government has begun to schedule more activities at school. Local fraternities and sororities claim about a fifth of the undergraduates as members, and their parties are open to all. If the social life is a bit slow, few people complain. "Most of our best times are at unofficial parties with friends," says one student.

The sports program injects a measure of excitement into the social scene, and about seven of every ten students join one intramural team or another. The men's varsity tennis team has long been a national power in Division III, and men's basketball and women's basketball, softball and volleyball are also very competitive. Unfortunately, the football team is, well, "terrible," and would-be all-Americans are advised to take up verbal combat via the debate team, one of the best in the country.

Tiny University of Redlands has mastered what might be called the smorgasbord approach to education. With hardly more than a hundred faculty members, it manages to be a preprofessional institute, a liberal arts college, and an alternative school all in one. Those with an individualist streak can head back to the 1960s and do their own thing at Johnston Center, but others will find that the rest of Redlands is, as one senior notes, "still a conservative, small, and very safe place to get an education."

Reed College

Portland, OR 97202

Location City outskirts	**Accepted** 77%
Total Enrollment 1,230	**Enrolled** 37%
Undergraduates 1,200	**Academics** ★ ★ ★ ★ ★
Male/Female 55/45	**Social** ☎ ☎ ☎
SAT V/M 620/640	**Q of L** ● ● ● ●
Financial Aid 45%	**Admissions** (503)777-7511
Expense Pr $ $ $	in Oregon, (800)547-4750 out of state
Applicants 1,160	

Reed College is a place for young radicals to feel comfortable and for young intellectuals to learn things. Nonconformity is the norm among this sometimes brilliant group of students. Reedies plunge themselves into their books, welcome eccentricity, relish the unconventional—nay, the anticonventional—and hope that they, in their own small way, will change the world.

"Reed wants very much to look as venerable as its East Coast counterparts," explains one woman. And although the architectural style begins in traditional Gothic, it ends in glass and metal, with beautiful lawns, trees, and a wildlife refuge scattered throughout. This handsome campus is situated in a residential part of Portland—"close enough to downtown not to be totally isolated, yet removed enough to be an oasis." And it's easy to get to and from the city by means of the excellent bus service.

Reed offers unsurpassed intellectual opportunities for a school of its size, including a new loan program that allows students to buy personal computers through small monthly payments to the school. But for students who would rather not make computer investments, Reed provides free twenty-four-hour access to its main terminals. In addition, the Triga Research Nuclear Reactor is usually run by students who have passed an eight-hour Atomic Energy Commission examination. Although the college works within a structure of personal freedom, the curriculum is, curiously, highly traditional. Stiff requirements include foreign language proficiency, a course in the humanities and physical education, and two courses in each of four major academic divisions. All juniors must pass a qualifying exam in order to become seniors, and Reed is one of a handful of colleges that requires all of its students to write a senior thesis to graduate. In fact, thesis writing at Reed is such a long and arduous task that on the due-day of these great works, students release their pent-up frustrations in a unique ritual. They march from the library steps to the registrar's office in a Thesis Parade, inscribe their names on a giant thermometer known as the Thesis Meter—and then throw what one participant called "the best party in town."

Most departments—especially history, chemistry, biology and English—are outstanding, but students say that German, the performing arts, sociology and economics are weak. Interdisciplinary programs and opportunities to design an individual major abound, and several 3-2 engineering programs with East and West Coast schools are offered. Many students take leaves of absence, not only as a respite from the constant pressure, but also because, as one explains, "the social milieu here almost demands that one go to Europe, India, Alaska, or wherever for an 'intense' experience." Structured study-abroad programs are available in twenty-three countries, including Germany, Russia, China and Costa Rica.

Studying is a way of life at Reed and students say they have neither time nor inclination to do much else. Most take full advantage of the library's late hours and even turn tables and carrels into their own private desks. The excellent professors are willing to put as much energy into teaching and advising as they demand from their students in class, and students and faculty often work together on research projects. "Grades are de-emphasized," one woman reports, "meaning you go to your adviser or dean to find them out at the end of the semester—if you wish." Faculty regularly write evaluations of students' work, however, and are known for their brutal honesty. Most courses, except for introductory ones, are run as seminars or conferences with enrollments of a dozen or less, and gripes abound when class size reaches twenty. Over the years a quarter of its grads have gone on for PhDs—third highest of any college in the country.

Although Reed has been around for less than eighty years, its offerings currently attract students from all over the nation. Most come directly from high school, often from upper-middle-class backgrounds. And despite the wave of conservatism presently washing over the nation's campuses, Reed seems committed to remaining an island of intellectual independence and diversity. "We have representatives of various subcultures, particularly hippies," remarks a senior. A popular T-shirt proclaims the school's motto to be: "Communism, Atheism and Free Love," and although it's certainly not official, some Reedies think it gives people a good idea of the unorthodoxy for which they strive. Minorities are poorly represented on campus, a situation many students lament. A small percentage of students with demonstrated need are routinely wait-listed for aid, and no merit or athletic scholarships are available.

About half the students live on campus in small, homey dorms that usually house fewer than thirty people, and some of the rooms feature such niceties as fireplaces or balconies. Singles usually go to on-campus seniors, but there is sufficient privacy for all—even most doubles have two rooms. All dorms and most bathrooms are shared by both sexes. Many upperclassmen prefer to live off campus, and houses to share are cheap and plentiful. On-campus students must join the meal plan and eat in the Commons, where the food is edible but bland. A salad bar adds some alimentary diversity, but students are most appreciative of the student-run coffee shop. "I often wonder if Reedies eat," says one woman. "It seems to me they live almost completely on coffee and Camels."

Just about everyone goes to the campus socials, which feature free beer and nonstop dancing and are held about every other week. Movies, coffeehouses, television, and dinner out take up the rest of weekend time. People here lead casual social lives, hanging around mostly in groups, often in the library. The beautiful Oregon coast is only an hour away, and for skiers and outdoorsy types, the school maintains its own ski cabin on nearby Mount Hood, with a kitchen, sauna and sleeping space for thirty. There are no varsity athletics, although some clubs, such as basketball, soccer and rugby, compete with clubs from other colleges in the area. There is wide interest in sports on a casual basis, and the sports center offers beautiful squash and paddleball courts, a swimming pool and other facilities.

"People who find it difficult to fit into mainstream social structures may fit in more easily at Reed than elsewhere," according to a senior. But for all their philosophical and social tolerance, Reed students approach scholarship with almost puritanical fervency and purpose. As one woman explains: "Students here are inquisitive and interested in whatever they learn—from Plato to underwater basket weaving."

Rensselaer Polytechnic Institute

Troy, NY 12181

Location City outskirts	**Applicants** 5,700
Total Enrollment 6,440	**Accepted** 61%
Undergraduates 4,690	**Enrolled** 35%
Male/Female 80/20	**Academics** ★★★★
SAT V/M 570/680	**Social** ☎☎☎
Financial Aid 62%	**Q of L** ●●●
Expense Pr $ $ $ $	**Admissions** (518)266-6216

Each September hundreds of Rensselaer Polytechnic Institute students cart their sleeping bags and textbooks to the front of the Student Union, where they camp out on concrete sidewalks, rain or shine, for more than a week. Why? They want to get good seats for the hockey season. Love of sport and loyalty to the team only partially explain this modern-day pagan ritual, and there's a good reason why the school hasn't used its state-of-the-art computer facilities to conjure up an alternative to the Hockey Line. Living every day with intense academic pressure and the knowledge that an excellent job is less than four years away, RPI students just have to devote body and soul to something ridiculous once in a while.

Situated on a hill overlooking a gritty industrial city in upstate New York, RPI's campus is a mix of modern and ivy-covered brick buildings. It was founded in 1824, making it the oldest science and engineering school in the nation, and it continues to excel in chemical, electrical and systems engineering. Computer science is also among its most respected programs; a $7-million computer center contains one of the largest computer graphics laboratories at an American university, and the nuclear science department has its own accelerator. Just as RPI provided the civil engineering expertise to build bridges and structures during the Industrial Revolution, the institute is today, according to one administrator, "at the forefront of research in computers, graphics, microelectronics, applied mathematics, polymers, composite materials, aeronautics, and studies of the social context of the sciences and engineering." With RPI central to the area's economic growth, corporate contributions are on the rise.

Understandably, the nonscience major at RPI will feel like a fish out of water. While twenty-four hours of courses in the humanities and social sciences are required for graduation, none of the humanities and social sciences programs is on par with those in technical fields. The few that are noteworthy often have a technical slant, such as the department of language, literature and communication, which specializes in scientific and technical communication. One sign of priorities: The Gothic-style computer center used to be a chapel. In addition to humanities, social sciences, natural sciences, math, physical education and communication, the core curriculum includes computing.

Two-thirds of the students at Rensselaer are undergraduates, a high percentage for a top engineering school, and both graduate and undergraduate students are taught by a single faculty. Many professors are renowned researchers in their fields, and although they may be inspirational role models, they're often not the most accessible people in the world. Student descriptions of their relationships with faculty members range from fair to strained. Juniors and seniors enjoy small classes, self-paced course options, and occasionally paid assistantships in faculty research. Freshmen, on the other hand, usually end up taking at least a couple of lecture courses with enrollments of several hundred. The average workload rivals the labors of Hercules. "The atmosphere in the freshman dining hall before an F-test (as they are called) can best be described as high-strung," an aeronautical engineering major reports. But it all pays off in the end: RPI survivors are an extremely employable commodity and the school's preprofessional students enjoy a 90 to 95 percent acceptance rate at graduate school.

For students who can't wait to get out in the working world, popular co-op programs in over a dozen fields provide a chance to work up to a year in science industries for both pay and credits. Six-year dual-degree options in medicine, dentistry and law are available, as are four- and five-year masters programs in biology, geology, mathematical science and architecture. For students eager to explore the world beyond their computer screens, RPI offers exchange programs to several European countries, most notably at Switzerland's renowned Federal Institute of Technology. Students who maintain a 3.0 grade point average have the option of spending a semester at Williams College to broaden their horizons.

RPI students tend to be bright and studious. Sixty-nine percent graduated in the top fifth of their high school class, nearly all in the top half. The student body is fairly diverse, with one out of eight students from minority groups. "Computer nerds" fit in fine, while those looking for "political protests and faddish college traditions" are sure to be disappointed. New Yorkers account for a little under 40 percent of the students, and most of the rest are from the Northeast. Blacks and Hispanics combine for about 7 percent of each class, and a tenth of the students are foreigners. Sixty-two percent of the students receive need-based aid, but RPI is not absolutely need-blind in admissions, and in some cases ability to pay is a factor in admissions decisions. Rensselaer offers ninety merit scholarships yearly, in amounts ranging from $500 to $1,000. RPI is cold on athletic scholarships except for men hockey players, who share the twenty awarded yearly.

Freshmen are sentenced to a year of hard labor in the frosh dorms, and they must buy the meal plan. Upperclassmen can exercise squatters' rights, enter the campus room lottery, or live in college-owned apartments off campus (definitely the preferred choice). Eighteen percent of the students live in fraternity and sorority houses, where they eat meals family-style, and another 28 percent move off campus entirely. Many upperclassmen take full or partial meal plans at the Commons, and when they're not partaking of its bountiful offerings, including salad, deli and pasta bars, they're usually over at the Student Union munching on cheap pizzas and subs.

Free shuttle buses run regularly from campus to downtown Troy, but while gentrification is leading to a proliferation of boutiques, there aren't a lot of good reasons for college students to make the trip. One student explains that Troy "is not among the most beautiful or interesting cities and, in fact, may be the armpit of America." (Troy isn't real hot on RPI, either.) For scenic excursions, Lake George is only an hour away, and major ski slopes in New York, Massachusetts and Vermont are within an hour's drive.

Even women at RPI say the four-to-one male/female ratio is less than desirable. "Sometimes you need to talk to another woman, and one can't be found," a female biology major complains. She'd like the administration to work toward improving the ratio, which has remained about the same for nearly a decade. For a decent social life, the best strategy is to go Greek, as do about 40 percent of the students. On weekends, many lovelorn male engineers haunt the hallowed halls of Russell Sage (next door) or Skidmore (forty minutes away). Campus social life revolves around Greek parties, sporting events, live entertainment, concerts and movies, and the half dozen local pubs. Extracurricular clubs, organized around such interests as chess, dance, judo and skiing, are all chartered and funded through the impressively large Student Union, an organization totally managed and controlled by the students themselves.

Varsity ice hockey, as noted, has a religious following at RPI. While most sports at Rensselaer are Division III, the hockey team was the Division I national champion in 1986. (If you are wondering how the jocks mix hockey with the rigors of an engineering curriculum, they don't. They major in communications.) Among lesser sports, the men's and women's tennis are especially strong, and the swimming program should benefit from a new NCAA regulation pool. Intramural programs are also of good quality and draw many participants, most of whom are frat brothers.

Science and technical programs can bring out the cutthroat tendencies in even the gentlest students, but it happens less at RPI than some other places that offer training of equal quality. At this serious technical institute where the emphasis is on undergrads, "People here look out for themselves and for others," says one student. "We're all in this together and for that reason we should all succeed."

University of Rhode Island

Kingston, RI 02881

Location Small town
Total Enrollment 14,300
Undergraduates 11,420
Male/Female 50/50
SAT V/M 450/500
Financial Aid 55%
Expense Pub $ $ $

Applicants 8,320
Accepted 71%
Enrolled 38%
Academics ★★
Social 🐿🐿🐿
Q of L ●●●
Admissions (401)792-2164

The student newspaper at the University of Rhode Island is *The Good 5-Cent Cigar*— taken from the famous remark by Woodrow Wilson's vice president (OK, all you AP history types, who was he?) in reference to what this country "really needs." Until recently what URI has really needed was more money from the legislature. Under the leadership of a popular new president that situation has been looking up, and word is spreading across state lines that URI is one state university where classes are small, professors are accessible and "students are people, not numbers."

URI's two-thousand-acre campus is located on Kingston Hill, a rural area in the midst of farmland about fifteen minutes from the coast. The main academic buildings, a mixture of modern and old New England granite, surround a central quad, with residential housing on the hillside below. For the first two years, all students enroll in the University College, where they pursue a general education program that includes writing, humanities, science and foreign language requirements. Then they move on to more specialized colleges. Among the latter, pharmacy is nationally ranked, and the engineering (with a new emphasis on robotics), zoology, nursing and accounting programs also are first rate. The graduate school of oceanography, which has its own campus nearby, is best known of all. Computer offerings were recently enhanced by the opening of a new computer center; meanwhile, business is popular but lacks adequate resources. Though applications to the College of Arts and Sciences have been on the rise recently, the humanities and social sciences are not a high priority and still draw only marginal funding. Students interested in public service may intern under the University Year for Action, while others take advantage of study abroad, independent study and field placement in some departments. The pharmacy school offers a much-used five-year work-study option, and Rhode Island residents with a 3.5 GPA may apply for early admission to Brown University's medical school. The honors program offers tiny classes and the chance to work on an individualized senior project.

It is much easier to get accepted at Rhode Island than it is to register for courses once you are there. Required and popular introductory courses and electives are often booked to capacity, and "even pre-registering doesn't assure a class," one junior notes. And while the library is good enough for most everyday needs, a journalism major believes it is "quite inadequate for proper research." On the plus side, Rhode Island's student faculty ratio is one of the lowest you'll find at any state school, and a history major says that "the professors here really seem to care about the students." Profs even take their advising seriously, a rare attitude at a state school. Significantly, the faculty instituted a system of student evaluation of teaching and opened up a small center to help them do it better. URI draws almost two-thirds of its students from Rhode Island, and most of the rest from surrounding states. The university is becoming increasingly popular with out-of-staters, especially those from New York, New Jersey and Connecticut. New Englanders are also attending in growing numbers; any who want to major in a subject not provided at their own state universities pay only 25 percent above in-state tuition, a hefty savings over the regular nonresident charge. Top students can vie for over one hundred academic scholarships, awarded regardless of need and ranging from $130 to $2,375, and 253 athletic scholarships.

Less than half the students live in the dorms, most of which are of the modern, run-down variety. There are traditional dorms—long hallways with bathrooms at the end—and suites, and some dorms have saunas, balconies or weight rooms. All but one dorm for women are coed. Freshmen have first crack at housing, and students not wishing to exercise squatters rights for their current accommodations may find a better room hard to find. Housing has tightened up recently, and some out-of-staters are apt to get bumped. Upperclassmen usually live off campus, and a sizable percentage of the student body commutes from home. Twelve percent of the students live in Greek houses. A meal plan in one of the three dinings halls, which serve standard college fare, is mandatory for those living on campus. The Greek houses have their own kitchens and cooks, and there are numerous restaurants and pizza establishments nearby. Students who tire of institutional cuisine can escape to one of the three pizza parlors on campus, the snack bar or coffeehouse.

Many upperclassmen choose to live "down the line" in empty vacation homes near the beach. It's an attractive and economical alternative, but check the annual heating oil bill before signing your lease. A campus shuttle bus provides ready access to Kingston. Those who drive will find a shortage of parking spaces close to campus, and the campus police don't hesitate to ticket and tow. Fraternities have their own private parking lots, an extra incentive to go Greek.

Kingston is a tiny village that has been restored to its eighteenth-century splendor. The URI student center, run by students, offers everything from a newsstand to flower and dress shops. Rhode Island is famous for its beaches, which lie only a few miles down the road, and in the early fall and spring "everyone goes to the beach after classes." The university is also within striking distance of the major New England ski slopes. Newport, with its heady social scene, is readily accessible, and Boston, Hartford, New Haven and Providence are all an easy drive; and the Amtrak station is on the campus. Many natives of this tight little state where everybody knows everybody else return home on weekends, so Thursday is usually set aside for partying. The administration is working to reduce the suitcase carrying, and for the growing numbers of those who stick around, the Greeks offer beer blasts, off-campus students sponsor beach parties and an organization called Weekenders helps keep the campus busy Saturday and Sunday. But the state drinking age of twenty-one has put a damper on on-campus partying and dorm parties are strictly regulated.

Sports are big at Rhode Island, and the intramural program draws high praise. The pep buses to basketball games at the Civic Center are usually full, and varsity football, a recent conference champion, always attracts a crowd. The sailing team regularly produces all-Americans, and as for the women's teams, volleyball, softball, soccer, and cross-country are consistent winners. Students tend to be "casual and outdoorsy," and the campus in general offers a relaxed, friendly atmosphere.

Many programs at URI still suffer from a lack of resources, and the large number of commuters has hindered URI's development of a strong sense of identity. Unfair comparisons to its prestigious neighbor, Brown, have not helped morale either. But with a little effort and some scouting about for the right programs, you can get a lot more than a nickel's worth at URI.

Rhodes College

Memphis, TN 38112

Location City residential
Total Enrollment 1,220
Undergraduates 1,220
Male/Female 47/53
SAT V/M 550/590
Financial Aid 42%
Expense Pr $ $

Applicants 1,650
Accepted 81%
Enrolled 33%
Academics ★ ★ ★
Social 🐿 🐿 🐿
Q of L ● ● ●
Admissions (901)726-3700

Surprised the name doesn't sound familiar? Don't be: It's just a new name for an old southern favorite. Known as Southwestern at Memphis until 1984, Rhodes College is an ambitious little up-and-comer trying to make a name for itself in the educational world—literally.

Founded as a Presbyterian school in 1848 in Clarksville, Tennessee, and transplanted to Memphis in 1925, Southwestern became Rhodes after college officials gave up trying to distinguish their school from the seventy others in the country with some form of the word "south" in their titles. ("Southwestern" referred to its location within a Presbyterian synod.) Now that the name of a much-loved president emeritus has been adopted, Rhodes is moving on to the task of spreading its reputation as a small but strong college of liberal arts and sciences. In the middle of a region that thinks in terms of large state colleges, Rhodes has refused to accept the limitations of its size—which, by the way, is increasing.

Rhodes sits on a hundred-acre site in midtown Memphis, and one student claims it's "undoubtedly the most beautiful campus in the state." The original Gothic structures of brownish-orange stone, leaded glass windows and slate roofs, have served as models for all forthcoming buildings. Some of the most recent include a new theater, a music building, and two residence halls. Yet, with the exception of its underground science center, Rhodes' elegant, old-fashioned tonality remains in tact, with no steel monstrosities to destroy the architectural consistency. Thirteen of the buildings are listed on the National Register of Historic Places, and the slate for the roofs comes from Rhode's own quarry in Blunt Nose, Arkansas.

Rhodes' rapid physical growth, brash confidence and unabashed ambitions don't always sit well with its students, some of whom complain about the school's self-congratulatory slogan: "Our ivy is in a league by itself." As a biology major puts it, "The push for national recognition by the college has been disconcerting. Putting up new buildings, etc., seems to be overemphasized." But she and others do appreciate Rhodes' commitment to student self-governance, which is manifested in an unbelievably trusting honor system. "The honor code is a set of principles that we must live by," reports a psych major. "We promise not to cheat, steal or lie." And the college takes their word for it. This code enables professors to give take-home tests and unproctored exams.

Degrees are offered in forty-two traditional and interdisciplinary programs. The natural sciences are Rhodes' forte, but strong programs also exist in business administration, economics, foreign languages, English and international relations. The education, media arts, history and some social sciences departments are still subjects of student criticism. In addition to standard distribution requirements and a foreign language mandate, all students must now fulfill a humanities requirement that includes taking one of two four-term courses—Search for Values in the Light of History and Religion (SEARCH for short) or Life: Then and Now. The SEARCH course (previously called MAN) has been a staple of the school's curriculum for forty-five years. It takes students through the whole history and culture of Western civilization with a special emphasis on the Bible.

Other special educational opportunities have been spawned by the school's energetic self-improvement efforts. With lectures, seminars, honors programs, one-on-one tutorials, studies at Oxford, supervised internships, bridge (multiple) majors, and independent directive studies, there are dozens of ways to get an education at Rhodes. And students especially like Rhodes' special 12-12-6 calendar, with its shortened spring term, during which the school offers trips abroad and innovative classes at home. Thanks to the active role they are given in college decision making, students have more than once campaigned to keep the weighted trimester from being axed.

The academic pressure varies among majors, with workload and grade competition highest in the premed and prelaw fields. Across the boards, though, Rhodes' small size and low student faculty ratio keep the learning process informal and intimate. "I've had lunch with the president several times and regularly dine with the faculty," says one English major.

Students are drawn from both public and private schools, with 70 percent from the top fifth of their class. The flavor of Rhodes' student body is definitely southern, with many of the undergraduates coming from both rural and urban areas of Tennessee. Students are predominantly middle- to upper-middle-class and conservative, "and becoming more so as the tuition goes up," concludes a senior. But there's "enough diversity to make Rhodes interesting," a literature major says. She adds, "People are very friendly and receptive to those different from themselves, so no one should feel inhibited." Rhodes is still affiliated with the Presbyterian Church in the U.S., but less than a quarter of its students are Presbyterians, and the religious emphasis, while self-consciously part of the school's identity, is broad. The college has a healthy endowment and is unabashedly able to give 125 merit-based scholarships worth up to $10,000 as a means of building up the academic credentials of the student body. Although there are no financial offerings available for campus jocks, "Scholarships seem to grow on trees," says one senior.

All dorms are air-conditioned and reportedly clean. The two new dorms are quite welcome in the face of increasing enrollments. Freshmen are sprinkled throughout the single-sex residence halls, the majority of which now have twenty-four-hour open visitation hours. Upperclassmen fend for a spot in the yearly lottery. Only 2 percent of the students live off campus, where room and board can be cheaper, but few students recommend the move. "One tends to miss a lot that goes on," one dorm resident warns. There's one main dining hall nicknamed the Rat; there's one twenty-one-meals-a-week plan, and that's that.

Rhodes students are indeed homebodies, reluctant to stray much further than the Overton Zoo, right across the street. During their free time they prefer bopping to the band at the college pub or heading over to the fraternities for their popular beer busts (Wednesday, Friday, and Saturday nights). Although about half the student body pledges a fraternity or sorority, the Greek parties are usually open, keeping tension between Greeks and Freaks within reasonable bounds. The cafeteria, however, still tends to divide regularly into Greek and non-Greek sections. As for sports, "low-key is the word." Intramurals are moderately popular, as are varsity athletics. Except for soccer, women's teams generally outperform the men's.

For those willing to leave the reservation, the sights and sounds of Memphis can be pleasant indeed. The city was the stomping ground of W. C. Handy, "the father of the blues," and Beale Street and The Peabody are continuing attractions. In May the city sponsors a cultural festival, including everything from barbecue cooking contests to the Sunset Symphony, with much of it taking place along the banks of the Mississippi River. Public transportation is good, and one student suggests that "fried chicken and wine at the river at sunset is a cheap dinner date." If everything else fails, you can always join the groupies at Graceland, home of Elvis Presley.

Determined to move beyond a solely regional reputation, Rhodes College has put its heart, and name, into making a national mark. Academically inclined and socially active men and women should take note: There's now more to do in Memphis than sing the blues.

Rice University

Houston, TX 77251

Location Urban	**Applicants** 3,840
Total Enrollment 3,850	**Accepted** 31%
Undergraduates 2,590	**Enrolled** 47%
Male/Female 60/40	**Academics** ★ ★ ★ ★ ★
SAT V/M 630/690	**Social** 🐻 🐻 🐻
Financial Aid 40%	**Q of L** ● ● ● ●
Expense Pr $	**Admissions** (713)527-4036

In a state that prizes bigness and boldness, Rice University has long made a virtue of smallness and caution. In a state where a winning football team is the sign of academic virility, the Owls are known mainly for an audacious marching band that performs half-time parodies about the "professional" players on opposing teams. If denizens of the Lone Star state can be forgiven for finding the world according to Rice a bit mystifying, its students do not. They know they're onto one of the best deals around.

Created under the will of legendary Texas cotton mogul William Marsh Rice nearly a hundred years ago, Rice was modeled after such disparate institutions as progressive, tuition-free Cooper Union and the more traditional Princeton University. Its residential "college" system was imported from Oxford, and one student says the three-hundred-acre campus with oak trees and stone paths reminds him of Stanford— "except our campus is perfectly flat." Despite its semblances to other institutions, Rice maintains distinctive characteristics of its own. The predominant architectural theme of the campus is Spanish Mediterranean, but there is versatility. "For example," explains a behavioral studies major, "the new business school closely resembles argyle socks." Geographically, Rice is situated in the center of Houston and surrounded by a row of hedges—the singular buffer between the quiet campus and the sounds of the city.

The students—a fourth of whom are National Merit Scholars—tend to put a lot of pressure on themselves to succeed. "Most classes are graded on a curve," reports a managerial studies student. "So students are not just competing to get an A but also competing with each other to define what an A is. Competition in the engineering and premed programs is especially intense, and each year a good number of students who start in these fields retreat to the humanities. In fact, Rice has a long tradition of encouraging double, and even triple, majors in such seemingly opposite fields as electrical engineering and art history. Even the admissions office concedes Rice needs students who "don't collapse when they discover others are brighter or more talented."

The university excels in the sciences and engineering, and the SEs (as these students are called) still dominate the student body. Architecture is one of the finest undergraduate programs in the nation, and the space physics program works closely with NASA. English, history and the Shepherd School of Music are all outstanding. Business is almost nonexistent, but students can opt for a concentration in managerial studies. Under a Mellon Foundation grant, humanities majors can spend the spring and summer of their senior years in "responsible" internship positions, mainly with local corporations. Most political, social and computer science offerings draw less favorable reviews; foreign languages aren't recommended either.

Under the area major program students can draw up proposals for independent interdisciplinary majors. Those who want to take their education on the road can visit Swarthmore in Pennsylvania or study in one of fifteen universities in the United Kingdom, and there are internships for engineering and architecture students. School-wide distribution requirements are minimal: eight courses outside of the major.

Class size rarely presents a problem—"One of my classes has four students, and another one has about 100," reports a senior. "And all the others are somewhere in between." Faculty members for the most part are friendly and accessible, sometimes providing upperclassmen with research opportunities. The professors eat with students, attend parties and coach intramural teams, one student reports. Under an extensive advising system, incoming students are assigned two or three student counselors and two professors during the first two years. Everyone operates under the honor system, and most exams go unsupervised. The library, however, is lacking. Students usually find needed materials, but they report that many books are in terrible condition and the atmosphere is the pits—"uncomfortable furnishings and a defective climate control system."

At the time of its founding, Rice was to serve "residents of Houston and the state of Texas," and while Texans still dominate the student body, this may be changing. Today, 45 percent of Rice students come from out of state, with high percentages transplanted from California, Florida, the Northeast and other southern states. About 17 percent of undergraduates are minorities, 2 percent are foreign, and almost all are public school graduates. Interests vary, but Rice students as a rule are in the know, "whether it be book-smart or well-rounded intelligence." Rice requires a rather rigorous course load in high school to prepare for the challenges of freshman year. Although many students claim that, by Texas standards anyway, they are liberal, others report an intense amount of political apathy. "Even a skip-one-meal plan to raise money for Oxfan America was rejected by the student body," wails a disgusted political science major. "The main interests of students here are themselves, their grades and their future salaries."

Because much of the university's $570-million endowment (the eleventh largest in the country) is dedicated to keeping tuition low, Rice costs thousands of dollars less than most other selective, private universities. On top of this built-in bargain, Rice promises to provide for students with financial need. For a university not counted among the athletic leaders in the Southwest, much less the nation, there are a surprisingly high number—220 or so—of athletic scholarships. Of these, about 60 are awarded to women. Rice also sponsors about 500 merit scholarships with stipends that vary from $500 to $8,500.

Fraternities and sororities are forbidden on campus—Mr. Rice did not approve of elitist organizations—but their functions are largely assumed by the eight residential colleges, Rice's version of dorms. Each college houses about 225 students who remain affiliated with it for all four years and develop a strong esprit de corps, even for those who later move off campus. "The residential college system is the basis of the family feeling you get around here," says one denizen. Freshmen are assigned a college randomly, depending on their preference for one of the six coed dorms or two single-sex dorms. (Students report that, due to popular demand, all eight colleges will be going coed in the near future.) Many freshmen enjoy rooms as spacious as their older colleagues, and a dormer contends that "no college is better than another, they're just different." Air-conditioning is a standard weapon against Houston's muggy climate.

To prevent overcrowding, the annual rooming lottery forces about 10 percent of the upperclassmen off campus, but everyone is guaranteed a room for at least three of the four years. In all, about one-quarter of the students go packing, many seeking quieter surroundings and cheaper rents. Students can eat at any of the college dining halls, and cafeteria hopping can be a "great way to meet people," and a great way to develop a chronic case of indigestion. "The food is generally a bone of contention," says a junior.

Houston has plenty of nightlife, but to enjoy it bring a car; mass transit is virtually nonexistent. Luckily, parking on campus is easy. Galveston's beaches on the Gulf of Mexico are only forty-five minutes away, and heading for New Orleans, especially in February, can make a great weekend trip. In fact, there's only one problem with the school's location: It attracts blackbirds—and more than four and twenty. Every year, during the rainy winter, about a million of these squawking creatures roost at Rice. So far even the campus ornithologists have not come up with an explanation for "The Birds."

Ardent fans rip out the goal posts when Rice's football team wins a home game. But considering the team's record, the goalpost budget remains manageable. The Mob, Rice's outrageous marching band, is what half the crowd comes to see. On the brighter side, baseball and women's volleyball are strong. Rice students go wild for intramurals, which gives them a chance to let off the academic steam and express some creativity in naming their teams, e.g., The Throbbing Love Muscles.

Students don't have time to plan anything more formal on weekends than the traditional TGIF parties on Friday afternoon, but parties spring up spontaneously and frequently. Some students complain their on-campus party bubble has been burst by the hike in Texas' drinking age—it's now twenty-one, but drinking age or no, students are expected to unwind on the weekends. "People who study constantly are considered dullards, and people who are negligent about academics aren't taken seriously," a history and English major explains. If nothing else, there's always the campus movie. No one complains too much about the dating scene despite the imbalance of the sexes on campus.

Rice doesn't need a losing football team to prove its emphasis on strong academics, but it does sort of reinforce the point. High-achieving students, strong faculty and excellent resources are other telling signs of what this school's all about. Throw in the pint-sized tuition and ten-gallon endowment, and you have the best academic bargain in American higher education.

University of Richmond

Richmond, VA 23173

Location Suburban
Total Enrollment 4,300
Undergraduates 2,750
Male/Female 50/50
SAT V/M 550/600
Financial Aid 15%
Expense Pr $

Applicants 5,130
Accepted 42%
Enrolled 33%
Academics ★ ★ ★
Social ☎ ☎ ☎
Q of L ● ● ●
Admissions (804)289-8640

If some students would like to see the University of Richmond loosen up a tad and encourage more diversity in life-styles, enough others embrace the conservative southern traditions to ensure their continued dominance. Equally secure is the influence of the Baptist General Association of Virginia, which founded the school 140 years ago. Only 8 percent of the undergraduates are Baptist and no religious study is required, but, as one student says, "The Baptist affiliation sets the mood and reputation for the university."

The Virginia climate produces long falls with colorful leaves, mild winters, and early springs complete with flowering dogwood and azaleas. Visitors seldom fail to remark on the beauty of this campus, which a student describes as the "northernmost southern university." Set on 350 suburban acres of rolling hills and pines, Richmond's Gothic-style campus actually houses three schools in one. First, there are two liberal arts divisions: Richmond College for men and Westhampton College for women. This unusual system of "coordinate education" keeps men and women apart, as does a ten-acre man-made lake between the two campuses (students of both sexes will tell you it takes about ten minutes to walk around). While classes are coed, visiting hours in the single-sex dorms are restricted. The third branch of the university is the coed E. Claiborne Robins School of Business Administration, tactfully named for an alumnus who donated $50 million to its construction.

The business school admits students who have completed two years in the liberal arts colleges, and it's exceptionally popular among ambitious students who would eventually like to be in the position of donating a building with their own name on it. For the majority who follow the liberal arts route, the sciences, particularly chemistry and biology, are among the best departments, largely because of a strong faculty and exceptional facilities. English, history, political science, sociology and psychology are also strong. Computers have been broadly integrated into the curriculum, and sections of English composition are available in a special microcomputer writing classroom. Other noteworthy programs include area studies: criminal justice, Third-World studies and women's studies. Art, theater and speech communications are weaker departments, primarily due to their small size.

For majors in political science, Richmond, as Virginia's capital city, offers many opportunities for internships. The same goes for business students, who benefit from their school's ties with the community, a Winter Business Forum and the Executive-in-Residence program. There are opportunities for joint degrees with accredited law, dental and medical schools, as well as a joint forestry program with Duke University. Qualified undergraduates are eligible to receive research grants.

Grading is considered fair and not overly tough, though faculty members have been on a campaign against grade inflation. Some students say the pressure gauge is rising as many of the school's programs, especially sciences and business, become better known. The pass/fail option is available to upperclassmen in the liberal arts; in the business school, however, a D is forever. All students must complete proficiency and distribution requirements detailed in a rigorous core curriculum. Classes are for the most part small, though registration based on seniority may prevent underclassmen from getting the courses they want. The libraries get crowded in peak hours, but nocturnal types like the 2 AM closing hour during the week.

Vigorous marketing and recruiting efforts have increased Richmond's visibility in metropolitan areas of the Midwest and Northeast and made it a fashionable backup for more prestigious colleges. Thus, only a little over a quarter of the students still come from Virginia. The board of trustees is committed to preserving what it calls the current "balance and diversity of the student body," which is probably not a very good sign on this far from diverse campus. Richmond students are "predominantly conservative, clean cut, and from upper-middle-class families," according to a marketing-finance major. Blacks make up 4 percent of the student body and foreign students, 3 percent. Athletes vie for 132 scholarships, outstanding students for nearly 100 more, ranging in value from $3,800 to a full ride.

"Just about everyone lives on campus," says a senior, but it's not hard to get a room. Most dorms and student apartments are newly built or recently remodeled and blend in tastefully with the older, more typically collegiate Gothic buildings. Dorm rooms are large and well maintained, though the women do better than the men on both counts. Separate eating facilities for men and women was a source of complaint in the past, but dining facilities have now been consolidated.

Dating can be a challenge. Rooted in their own campus, many freshman women remain loyal to their hometown honeys. A dozen fraternities draw nearly half the men and constitute "the nucleus of campus social life," and Greek parties fulfill the essential function of bringing the sexes together. While there are no sororities, the fraternities do have little-sister programs. The administration is not shy about enforcing its rules, especially regarding drinking. "It's virtually impossible to have a party with beer or liquor without prior permission," said a junior. The Baptist Student Union, the Fellowship of Christian Athletes and other service organizations attract the most extracurricular participation. Intramural sports are popular among fraternity rivals; water polo, among myriad other sports, is a favorite. When it comes to varsity athletics, football is undisputed king.

On weekends many students make the ten-minute jaunt to Richmond to shop, see a movie, or go out to eat. Buses run downtown frequently, so cars aren't essential for those who live on campus. Virginia Beach is only an hour and forty-five minutes away for day tripping, and there is the nearby James River where students like to go rafting. The nation's capital and the Atlantic Ocean are within two hours driving distance, as are Virginia's Blue Ridge Mountains.

Richmond is a school dominated by healthy, well-adjusted types who are looking for more than a four-year beer blast and who don't need a lot of extremists around to spice up the intellectual climate. One student likened it to "a scholarly country club," and many stress that it's a good place to grow, develop, and find yourself while getting a firm grounding in business or the liberal arts.

Ripon College

Ripon, WI 54971

Location Small town
Total Enrollment 840
Undergraduates 840
Male/Female 55/45
SAT V/M 520/560
Financial Aid 79%
Expense Pr $ $

Applicants 700
Accepted 86%
Enrolled 42%
Academics ★ ★ ★
Social 🕿 🕿 🕿
Q of L ● ● ●
Admissions (414)748-8102

The size and atmosphere of tiny Ripon College are such that you'd almost have to work at not having friends among students and faculty—and practically hide out if you didn't want help in getting through a tough class. The cordial and "personally involved students, faculty, and staff" make life easy and learning pleasant for those who don't think a cutthroat competitive environment is necessary for a good liberal arts education.

Set on a hill in a tiny Wisconsin town, Ripon's campus features tree-lined walks, plenty of open space, and a mixture of nineteenth- and twentieth-century architecture. Founded as a coed school in 1851, Ripon is a place where the curriculum is based on tradition, and there is little room for dabbling in trendy educational fashions. "Our strength is in the basics, not the exotic or the peripheral," an official says. Academic work takes a high priority among Ripon students, and while the quiet, rural setting has both cultural and down-home midwestern activities for those who seek them out, there isn't much danger of twinkling neon lights distracting anyone from his or her studies.

The chemistry, biology, English and philosophy departments win especially high marks from students; other departments rated highly include history, physics, politics and government, economics, psychology, anthropology and sociology. Foreign languages and religion are weak, mainly because of too little staff, but the administration says it is working on the problem by hiring more staff. Having Spencer Tracy as an alumnus has had little effect on the fine arts and theater programs, although a new art center may give a boost. Business management and leadership studies are two small but interesting programs. The library is a good place to study but does not provide strong resources for research. The pickings are so sparse in some areas that only the twenty-mile trip to the public library in Oshkosh will help you get the information you need. On Saturday night students get an official OK to begin partying when the library closes at five PM.

Distribution requirements cover natural sciences and mathematics, foreign language, writing skills, behavioral and social sciences, fine arts, humanities and physical education studies. Ripon students delight in their small classes. If the student faculty ratio wasn't the reason they applied here, it's one reason they stay. For temporary changes of scenery, study abroad is available through the college's own programs in addition to programs sponsored by the Associated Colleges of the Midwest.*

The Ripon student body comes predominantly from Wisconsin, Illinois and Minnesota, with the second largest group made up of easterners, especially from Connecticut and Massachusetts. The vast majority are upper-middle-class conservatives, with blacks and Hispanics combining for a scant 2 percent of the students. Sixty percent of the students come from the top fifth of their graduating classes, but a solid chunk are admitted with just average high school records. Students eager to finish

473

college in three years should investigate Ripon's accelerated degree program, which allows eager beavers to pick up a degree in three years without summer study. Ripon admits students on a rolling-admissions basis, and applicants can expect a decision on their status in two to four weeks. With a proud record of three decades of balanced budgets, Ripon is generous with financial aid. More than three-quarters of the students receive some financial assistance, and the average award exceeds $8,000. The college also offers about eighty renewable merit awards of $500 to $7,500.

Freshmen are housed together in newly remodeled dorms and are given a choice between coed and single-sex halls, as are the upperclassmen. Those who want singles will have to pay a premium each term, and only 6 percent of students live off campus. All students eat in one large dining hall, and food is described as good and plentiful.

Ripon officials boast that their little town is so safe that many people don't bother to lock their doors or chain their bicycles. Were it not for the friendly atmosphere, the only real danger would be dying of boredom. The bars however are much frequented. Other leisure options include an array of concerts, plays and cultural activities. Fraternities and sororities enroll about half the student body, and with all Greeks living in dorms and eating in the dining hall, there is little tension between them and nonmembers. Fraternity parties are the main form of campus social life, and Ripon is so darned friendly that independents are included in just about all Greek events. According to one student, "Numbing one's ability to contemplate reality seems to be extremely ubiquitous in nature."

The small midwestern town of Ripon is well known to history buffs because it gave birth to the Republican Party—at a meeting on the college campus on February 28, 1854, to be exact. One student describes the town as "the standard midwestern variety: small, relatively quiet, and lots of old people. We have a Main Street, which is a curious architectural mixture of the early 1900s and mid to late 1960s." It's not just the architecture that presents such a mix. For a break from campus life, you can attend tractor pulls or corn roasts or get out to one of the many nearby fast-food places. This is also wonderful north woods territory, a spot in the state where the scattered trees begin to grow thicker and then give way to rugged pine forests. Frozen lakes and a blanket of snow are a natural part of the winter landscape, and students can cross-country and downhill ski, toboggan, skate and attend dogsled and iceboat races. Nearby Green Lake boasts facilities for skiing and, when it's not winter ("for one month during the year," warns one student), facilities for water sports. On campus, athletics (both varsity and intramural) are likewise a favorite student pastime. Strong teams include men's basketball, men's tennis and women's volleyball, and women's soccer was recently upgraded to varsity status.

The population of the town of Ripon is still only seven thousand so smallness is both an asset and a liability of this liberal-arts college. Students appreciate the intimacy of their classes and the attention they get from their professors, but the lack of privacy can be a high price to pay. As one student admits, "At this school you sooner or later know just about everybody or at least something about them. There's no place to hide."

Rochester Institute of Technology

Rochester, NY 14623

Location Suburban
Total Enrollment 14,450
Undergraduates 8,500
Male/Female 65/35
SAT V/M 480/560
Financial Aid 68%
Expense Pr $ $ $

Applicants 4,500
Accepted 76%
Enrolled 44%
Academics ★ ★ ★
Social ☎ ☎ ☎
Q of L ● ● ●
Admissions (716)475-6631

From the endless flow of quarters dropping into vending machines and video games, to the whiz of shuttles running between apartments and campus, to the strains of heavy metal wafting down from open dorm windows, everything at Rochester Institute of Technology is tech, tech, tech. The campus has a clunky, modern look—like the set of a sci-fi movie about a planet where flowers and trees flourish but everything else is made of brick. It's hard to mistake RIT for anything but what it is: one of the most diverse and practically oriented technical institutes in the country.

Majors are offered in more than two hundred fields ranging from basic electrical and mechanical engineering, to rare specialty programs like packaging design and nuclear medicine technology. Fortunately, applicants narrow the range of choices to a manageable size by applying to only one of eight undergraduate colleges: applied science and technology, business, engineering, fine and applied arts, graphic arts and photography, liberal arts, science and the National Technical Institute for the Deaf. (Sign language interpreters are present in every classroom and lab, both to accommodate the 10 percent of student body who are hearing impaired and to "make all students comfortable around the handicapped," says the school's president.)

The most popular and fastest growing areas are printing, graphic arts, photography, computer science and engineering, but excellent facilities assure that all of RIT's technical departments are strong. The new state-of-the-art computer engineering center supports the school's ground-breaking microelectronic engineering and imaging science programs as well as its commitment to require computer literacy of all students. Although poets and philosophers will probably end up climbing a brick wall, RIT is an excellent school for artists and crafts people. The RIT school of American crafts offers excellent programs in ceramics, weaving, textile design, glass, metalcraft and jewelry making, and students have the run of Brevier Gallery, where visiting artists provide firsthand instruction.

All students take general studies requirements, which total a third of their undergraduate work. Offered through the college of liberal arts, these requirements include courses in social science, language, literature and humanities. RIT's academic pressure is not as intense as at some technical colleges, nor are its students as competitive. But no one can coast, especially since the four-quarter academic year speeds up the pace. "The enemy here is time, not your fellow students," attests a senior. The most competitive academic event is probably registration; required introductory courses are crowded and some people are turned away the first time around. Most upper-level classes have forty-five or fewer students.

Many faculty members lead a double life with some kind of commitment to the professional world, and most research is in applied rather than theoretical areas. The administration counts five years of professional experience as the equivalent of a PhD in making faculty appointments, hence the pressure here is to "consult or perish." Professors may not always be available for chitchat with students, but at least they are conversant with the latest advances in their fields. Academic and career counseling programs prompt few complaints, and faculty members' real world connections can help students get internships. These connections, along with RITs' proximity to Xerox and Kodak facilities, also help students find co-op jobs required after their junior year in most majors. And after RIT, a near-universal 90 percent move directly into jobs.

Most students come from New York State, Pennsylvania and Connecticut, and minorities make up a fairly respectable 16 percent of the student body. Preprofessionalism is a common bond, but beyond that interests vary. "Propeller-heads and computer geeks would fit in real well," says one printing major. Students place high value on doing well, but competition rarely gets ugly. RIT admits without regard to student financial need, and it meets the demonstrated need of students for as long as the funds allow. It also has a variety of 110 academic scholarships ranging from $100 to $7,700, made without reference to need.

More than two-thirds of the students live in college dorms and apartments. Freshmen often begin the year three to a room, but first semester attrition usually remedies the situation. Upperclassmen live in doubles and a few singles. Dorms are new, well maintained, and offer a variety of living styles: single-sex, coed-by-room, coed-by-floor or special interest floors. Campus residents choose between several meal plans all of which provide good food from the campus-run food service. For upperclassmen eager for the glamorous apartment life, the university supplies four separate complexes, which are in high demand every year. Others live off campus in areas serviced by the school shuttle bus. Then there are those who choose to go Greek and live and eat in RIT's ten fraternities and three sororities.

Though the academic pressure at RIT probably won't drive students to drink, many indulge anyway. Maybe they're trying to enliven the sedate suburban campus, where the only facility within walking distance is a shopping plaza. Students also drive into Rochester, New York's third largest city, for movies and other cultural events. For those without transportation, there's always something to do on campus. Drama and other creative arts are less common than parties and movies, but a fine jazz ensemble and a chorus perform regularly.

Intramurals attract the more active students, as do several varsity sports. Men's hockey is the overwhelming favorite—a real winter crowd pleaser that draws even the campus commuters and local residents to the rink. Other sports, such as men's soccer and lacrosse and women's tennis and swimming, are strong but not followed. A new recreational complex has added three all-purpose indoor courts, a synthetic track and expanded playing fields to RIT's existing sports facilities. A new bookstore/computer store and a new interfaith chapel have the students talking about RIT's seemingly never-ending state of construction.

RIT operates on a rolling-admissions policy, so students receive acceptances early. Many try to find jobs on campus, and those who have no luck simply have to be patient: They're bound to find one quickly upon graduation. In the meantime, they can take advantage of the many opportunities to have fun in the little world of RIT, while preparing for the big one that lies beyond.

University of Rochester

Rochester, NY 14627

Location Small city
Total Enrollment 8,450
Undergraduates 4,530
Male/Female 60/40
SAT V/M 540/610
ACT 27
Financial Aid 53%
Expense Pr $ $ $ $

Applicants 6,540
Accepted 62%
Enrolled 30%
Academics ★ ★ ★ ★
Social ☎ ☎ ☎
Q of L ● ● ●
Admissions (716)275-3221

The University of Rochester recently received a blow to its ego when it learned 41 percent of high school students think that this small, extremely well-endowed and oh-so-private university is a public institution. It talked about changing its name (few private schools are called University of . . .) but decided instead to combat its unobtrusiveness with an innovative plan to rekindle the curriculum and thereby build up its national image as the warm, intense little snow-covered school that it is.

The head-turning changes at U of R include deleting freshman grades from student transcripts as a way of encouraging more daring academic exploration. The Freshmen Ventures program, in keeping with the experimental first-year philosophy, offers courses based on unconventional perspectives of established themes. The popular Take Five program allows undergrads to stay at Rochester for a tuition-free fifth year if the requirements of their majors don't allow enough breadth of studies for a liberal education. The Rochester Conference, held the week before the spring semester, features seminars, lectures and workshops focusing on a theme. In addition, Rochester has adopted Wednesday as its University Day, when it bans afternoon and evening classes to make time for special "at home" lectures held in residence halls.

The university's 150 traditional degree programs span the standard fields of study, but Rochester takes special pride in its famed Eastman School of Music. It also excels in scientific fields (competition is keen to beat the mean among science majors) and offers a unique major in optics (Rochester is home to Kodak and Bausch and Lomb). The College of Arts and Sciences has a number of strong departments including economics and English. Students and administrators alike brag about the nationally acclaimed political science department. And a cognitive science program—a cooperative venture among faculty in computer science, psychology, philosophy and the Center for Brain Research—is innovative and popular. The nursing program is also praised by undergrads. But, on the other side of the coin, Rochester has shown weaknesses in foreign languages, and the fine arts department is in a rebuilding phase; the sociology department was recently closed.

Flexible distribution requirements are designed to ensure that all students are exposed to the full range of liberal arts, and specific courses must be taken in formal reasoning and writing (plus a foreign language for arts and science students). No matter what their fields of interest, students who are sufficiently advanced may combine undergraduate with graduate study. Students may also study abroad—the university sponsors programs in England and Israel—not to mention what one student calls a "chance of a lifetime" British Parliament internship program, which enables Rochester students to have a ringside seat to British politics. Undergrads also work as interns at nearby high-tech companies or in Washington, D.C. Under the Rochester Plan, qualified juniors can enroll early in the university's outstanding medical school.

Administrators acknowledge the university has an image as a "cold and distant outpost," but anyone who visits will find a bustling community thriving on an almost clandestinely snug little campus that nestles in a bend in the Genesee River. The attractively consistent, Georgian-style buildings and pristine landscaping never let students forget they're on a college campus, and the gray, freezing winter days are perfect for sitting inside and hitting the books. In fact, Rochester looks like "what everyone thinks a college ought to look like," according to one student, "not square and cinder-blocky like some campuses." Although a few buildings are modern—the Witson Commons student center designed by I. M. Pei for one—the red-brick and ivy common denominators create an aesthetically pleasing contrast between old and new.

Nearly three out of five students hail from New York State, with large contingents from Westchester, Long Island and New York City. Many come from Massachusetts, Connecticut, New Jersey and the Great Lakes areas. There appears to be no prototypical U of R undergrad because "many are upper-class, many are not; many are career-minded, but many are not. We have new wave as well as preppy, liberals as well as conservatives," according to a senior. She adds that if there is a political slant, it's toward the conservative, but "trying to impress others with fancy cars and clothes is not popular at the U of R."

The university does not guarantee a workable financial aid package for every applicant, but half the students do receive need-based aid, and several renewable scholarships, ranging from $500 to $2,500, are awarded to freshmen of outstanding academic promise. A new work-study program called Reach for Rochester provides students with on- or off-campus jobs as well as funds for student-run businesses.

As for the housing facilities, "there is always a dorm somewhere being renovated," whines one student. Yet this reworking has brought about such benefits as computer terminals, oak floors and marble trim to some dorm rooms. Freshmen are assigned to rooms, usually doubles, and upperclassmen can get singles or suites. Single-sex, coed-by-floor and coed-by-room dormitories are available. Few students choose to live off campus, since there is no housing within walking distance and living in the city practically mandates a car. Dormitory students may eat seven to twenty meals a week in one of the two cafeterias where a credit system assures they pay per meal, instead of in one lump sum. The fare served in the dining halls receives high ratings from students, especially the à la carte selections such as tacos, burritos and a deli bar. Other meal options available include dining at the fast-food Pit and the Common Ground Café of the frats.

Only about a fourth of Rochester's men belong to fraternities, and even fewer women belong to sororities. "Greeks do a lot for the social life and are nonexclusive," one woman notes. Many students take the free campus shuttle into the city where they may entertain themselves on the beaches of Lake Ontario, in the George Eastman Photography Museum or with the Rochester Philharmonic Orchestra. Other favored activities include campus movies, beer at the student union, frequent ski trips and a spring fling known as Dandelion Day.

While the Division III varsity sports "do not play a huge role in students' lives," according to one senior, Rochester's admittance to the University Athletic Association and renovation of the ice hockey rink should help boost student involvement. For those who like something to cheer about, the football team, men's and women's soccer teams and men's and women's basketball teams are successful. Intramurals are a popular outlet for "ex-jocks from high school who miss their glory days gone by," and inner-tube water polo is especially popular. Even if intramurals aren't your bag, an $8-million sports complex is replete with every kind of facility imaginable.

Many students bemoan the fact that the school doesn't have a more prominent reputation, and some even suffer "a bit of an undeserved inferiority complex regarding their school," admits a senior. Yet few question the excellence and marketability of the education they are receiving. And with the administration battling for a spot among the nation's best private universities by supplying a unique model of an integrated education, Rochester may even become a popular place to go to school. And then, "if there is any confusion about whether it is public or private," says one student, "they should mail out the tuition rates."

Rollins College

Winter Park, FL 32789

Location Suburban	**Applicants** 1,980
Total Enrollment 3,730	**Accepted** 59%
Undergraduates 1,410	**Enrolled** 36%
Male/Female 45/55	**Academics** ★ ★ ★
SAT V/M 500/540	**Social** 🎭 🎭 🎭
Financial Aid 35%	**Q of L** ● ● ● ●
Expense Pr $ $	**Admissions** (305)646-2161

Located amid the lush, tropical landscape of sunny central Florida, the Rollins College campus looks so much like a resort "you almost expect Roarke from Fantasy Island to appear out of the administration building," one student says. It would, however, be a fantasy to view this small, friendly liberal arts college as just a place to play in the sun.

Set on a campus of Spanish Mediterranean buildings "where everything matches," as one student puts it, Rollins comes complete with palm trees and a beautiful lake that borders much of the campus. Rollins' Florida setting puts all sorts of entertainment extras within easy reach, but academically Rollins offers a no-frills liberal arts package. At a time when other colleges are falling all over themselves to attract students with trendy new preprofessional majors, Rollins recently dropped its major in business; it now has only an eight-course minor in business studies that must be combined with a major selected from twenty-six liberal arts offerings. Rollins has also reintroduced the classics and now offers courses in Latin, Greek and classics in translation. All students must complete a general education program, the most unusual element of which is a values requirement that can be met through a number of courses ranging from philosophy to medical ethics. For true liberal arts devotees, Rollins has a new program called the Community of Learners, where twenty students may enroll in three classes and one group seminar that are in some way thematically related. Each of the seminars features a "master learner," a professor who participates as a student "suffering the usual anxieties along with fellow students," according to the administration.

According to the students, the best departments include history, English, chemistry and physics. The premed and preengineering programs are also praised, but art garners criticism. The famous Annie Russell Theater hosts productions staged by the active theater department, which takes pride in alumni Buddy Ebsen and Tony Perkins.

The new, but not-quite-fully computerized, library is a welcome and long-overdue addition to Rollins—that is if you are a student who likes his studies tough and his academics rigorous. Not everyone here does, and according to a senior, "There is a division of people—some take their work very seriously and others are really casual about it." Independent work off campus is popular, thanks to the five-week winter term that gives students the option of doing an internship or participating in a college-sponsored overseas trip. Rollins also operates exchange programs with schools in Australia, Spain and Ireland, and offers five-year master's degree programs in engineering, forestry and business.

Rollins draws more than half its students from outside Florida, mostly from the Northeast. "Wealthy brats who come to the South to play in the sun for eight months," is what one Floridian woman calls them. However, most of her native peers aren't hurting too much financially, either, which is fortunate since Rollins has the highest tuition, room and board costs of any college in Florida. When it comes to politics, Rollins "is a very conservative campus and not real involved in current events," says a junior. Nearly a quarter of Rollins students finish in the top tenth of their high school class, but just as many graduate in the bottom half. The college offers 128 merit scholarships that pay anywhere from $1,000 to full tuition costs. They are awarded to freshmen on the basis of outstanding grades, SATs, activities, recommendations and essays, with some limited to Florida residents. Over fifty athletic scholarships go to male and female standouts in half a dozen different sports.

About three-quarters of the students live on campus in comfortable coed dorms. Freshmen are mixed in with everybody else, and rooms are assigned by class and GPA. About 22 percent live in Greek houses, while a handful opt to move off campus entirely. Meals at Rollins include three food lines: a fast-food grille; an à la carte line for hot meals; and a sandwich and salad line. The kitchen stays open from seven AM to seven PM, and food is charged on a credit card system, which means that students eat when they want and pay only when they eat. The main place to eat at Rollins is the Beanery, which prompts fewer complaints than the name may suggest. There's also a campus pub open to eleven PM, and every dorm has its own kitchen for students to use.

As befits the alma mater of television's Mr. Rogers, Rollins has many a beautiful day in its neighborhood. The quiet little town of Winter Park's main street leads right to the college's door, inviting students to take the ten-minute stroll along its cobblestone streets to downtown. "The local community is like walking down the Lido—quaint shops and romantic parks," one student observes. The area does, however, lack culture—unless your taste runs to the Seven Dwarfs. The nearby amusement parks include Disney World, EPCOT Center, Sea World, Busch Gardens and others. At Rollins there is no lack of social life. The Greeks throw all-campus parties every weekend and nearby Orlando offers popular entertainment complexes such as Rosie O'Grady's Good Time Emporium and the Cheyenne Saloon. Sports are plenty important here, but not the varsity type. Although women's tennis and men's and women's waterskiing are strong intercollegiate teams, the students here are too busy engaging in all those sports themselves to stand still and watch. With beaches close by and the beautiful Lake Virginia in their backyard, students add body surfing, sunbathing and windsurfing to their activity list.

As to who might fit in at Rollins, one student comments, "Those students who think they'll be coming to Club Med can stay home." A serious commitment to academics is expected from every student here and, in the majority of cases, is given. Although future success for most of these well-to-do sons and daughters doesn't hinge upon a perfect transcript, one man assures: "Most students at least know when to put away the lotion and rackets, and pick up the books."

Rose–Hulman Institute of Technology

Terre Haute, IN 47803

Location City outskirts
Total Enrollment 1,320
Undergraduates 1,300
Male/Female NA
SAT V/M 540/670
Financial Aid 90%
Expense Pr $ $

Applicants 2,900
Accepted 50%
Enrolled 25%
Academics ★ ★ ★
Social ☎
Q or L ● ●
Admissions (812)877-1511

According to its wisecracking admissions brochure, Rose–Hulman is "a college for men who take their Tinker Toys seriously." Actually, it's a little more complicated than that—most students have moved up to things like infrared spectrophotometers and Orion digital pH meters—but you get the idea. As one of the few engineering schools in the nation that enrolls only undergraduates, Rose–Hulman offers top-notch technical training in a highly personalized atmosphere.

Established in 1874, Rose–Hulman is the oldest private engineering school west of the Allegheny Mountains. Its 138-acre campus features "solid, sharp-line, down-to-business" architecture in an idyllic setting that boasts two small lakes. Although the admissions office tries to promote a sort of "wild and crazy guy" image for the school, don't be fooled: People here work harder than they play. More shopping lists and telephone messages are fouled by algebraic quotations in the margins than beer bottle rings in the center. Both the curriculum and work load are demanding, and "the academic climate is very competitive and high pressured," one sophomore says. "Freshmen are usually apprehensive because there are a lot of academically talented students and they aren't used to that," another student reports. Class time counts for only a fraction of the work; afternoons are spent in labs, evenings at work on individual projects, and the wee hours puzzling out problems.

There are nine degree programs offered in engineering, chemistry, computer science, math and physics. R–H was the first private college to offer a degree in chemical engineering and this department remains among the strongest. Electrical and mechanical are also tops, and students praise the premed and computer science programs. Freshmen take a structured introductory program, which includes courses in military science. About a fifth of each student's coursework is in the department of humanities, social and life sciences. Rose's library system is excellent in technical fields, but for anything else, students must make the trek to the library at nearby Indiana State University, where they have free access.

There are a number of special programs. One beginning even before freshman year is Operation Catapult, a three-week summer program of intensive problem solving in engineering, physics, chemistry and math for high school juniors. Rose also offers her boys a rare technical translator's certificate program in either Russian or German, as well as double-major and dual options. There are a number of programs, such as Fast Track Calculus, that enable students to accelerate in areas where they demonstrate special aptitude.

A low student/teacher ratio (about 15:1) and an emphasis on teaching rather than

481

research assure personal attention. A junior characterizes the student-professor relationship as extremely positive and says, "I have asked for help from professors I neither had nor knew and received cheerful instruction." There is quite a bit of fancy gear at Rose, including a 60-Mhz nuclear-magnetic resonance spectrometer, neutron howitzers and generators, electron accelerators, holography tables and numerous other appliances not generally found in the modern kitchen. And what is really unusual is that all are accessible to undergraduates.

The boys of Rose–Hulman describe themselves as "academically strong" and conservative. The majority are from working-class white families in rural Indiana and surrounding states, and many are the first in their families to attend college. "White, male, Republicans. That sums it up as succinctly as I can," says a sophomore. Though the administration says it does its best to recruit minorities, blacks and Asian Americans, each account for only 2 percent of the student body. A chemical engineering major characterizes his fellows as "very goal oriented—they want to get a technical degree and then move into management." Self-discipline and the ability to concentrate are also characteristics of these students, who must, after all, go for long periods of time without having contact with members of the opposite sex. One claims that the student body's main activities include "chasing girls, computers, mind-fantasy games (such as Dungeons and Dragons), and classwork," while another is "surprised at the large number of athletes." Nearly half of the students are from the top tenth of their high school classes. Rose–Hulman recruits heavily and the ability to pay is less a factor than academic ability. Only 25 percent of those accepted actually enroll, indicating that Rose is a second choice for many who apply. Seven hundred and fifty no-need scholarships, ranging from $500 to $2,000, supplement a good need-based financial aid program. Even without aid, Rose is a bargain compared to other top-quality private engineering schools.

As one of the last holdouts against coeducation, Rose–Hulman appears determined to remain all male, apparently fearing the loss of the animated sense of male camaraderie that the administration tries so hard to promote. Student opinion is mixed on the issue, though at least one student believes that "the students here need more exposure to women . . . in an academic setting." The admissions office concedes that Rose–Hulman's all-male status is a major liability in attracting students.

Freshmen are required to live on campus. Upperclass halls are air-conditioned, but there are not always enough rooms available. Though seniors who qualify for on-campus housing get the first pick of rooms, they are also the ones who get bumped when there are not enough rooms to go around. Just under half of the student body lives off campus in nearby apartments. There is almost universal praise for the food in the on-campus dining hall, provided by "the official food service of the 1984 Olympics," one man proudly boasts. "There are a wide variety of choices, including hamburgers every night, and unlimited seconds." There are even kind words for the food service staff, who will, as many testify, "go out of their way to accommodate a special diet." Members of any of the seven fraternities eat in their houses.

"Ah," laments one junior, "social life is a bit of a problem; the social life of a freshman is typically boring, and it doesn't get a lot better if the student is somewhat shy." The fraternities provide most of the parties on campus, so it helps if you're among the 40 percent who join. A student activities board also plans events. There is a women's college, St. Mary's in the Woods, about fifteen minutes away (needless to say Rose boys go a-hunting in those woods), as well as Indiana State University. Students often go into the city to take advantage of bars and restaurants.

Lest anyone envision Rose–Hulman students as pale lab dwellers, rest assured that athletics are very popular. Over 90 percent of the students play intramurals, and even the faculty get into the act. Varsity teams play in Division III of the NCAA, with football, basketball, baseball and cross-country among the strongest of these. The student government has a sizable operating budget and sponsors movies, parties, chess, bridge and table tennis tournaments and war games competitions.

Rose–Hulman is an alternative to larger technical schools on both coasts. Nevertheless, the academic climate is just as intense and high-pressured as those of its better-known rivals. And as for the job outlook, Rose–Hulman may have the highest ratio of recruiters to students in the nation. About four hundred companies send representatives annually to fight over 270 seniors. At Rose, students will get more personal attention from faculty and more hands-on use of equipment than they could ever hope for at places like MIT. For all those times when Mommy took away the Tinker Toys, a Rose–Hulman education is sweet revenge.

Rutgers University

New Brunswick, NJ 08903

Location Small city
Total Enrollment 47,650
Undergraduates 35,410
Male/Female 48/52
SAT V/M 500/560
Financial Aid 35%
Expense Pub $ $

Applicants 21,760
Accepted 62%
Enrolled 46%
Academics ★ ★ ★ ★
Social ☎ ☎ ☎
Q of L ● ● ●
Admissions (201)932-3770

Founded in 1766 as a small private institution known as Queens College, Rutgers has since evolved into a comprehensive land-grant university with aims of joining the nation's research supergiants in the not-too-distant future. It has just launched a $338-million fund drive to add or renovate forty-five buildings and create nine brand new high-tech research institutes. Yet in New Jersey, a state where quality higher education is hard to find once you move beyond the likes of Princeton, Rutgers and Drew, a high percentage of its academically talented high school graduates have been sent packing. But today, with the cost of college soaring, a growing number of budding scholars from the Garden State are taking a look at New Jersey's answer to Ann Arbor. And it's about time.

Named for Colonel Henry Rutgers, a Revolutionary War veteran who has to be the last benefactor to parlay $5,000 into a college bearing his name, Rutgers encompasses six residential colleges (four at New Brunswick and one each at Newark and Camden), professional programs in engineering, pharmacy, nursing and the arts, and University College, an undergraduate evening college for adults that has its own faculty. Of the four New Brunswick colleges, the largest is Rutgers College, which is devoted to the liberal arts and sciences. Adjacent to it is Livingston College, which directs itself toward urban youths with demonstrated potential. Across the Raritan River is Douglass College, a smaller liberal arts school exclusively for women, and Cook College that offers the land-grant subjects of agricultural and environmental sciences. You must also trek across the river for all science facilities. The architecturally diverse (mostly colonial and modern) campuses are well landscaped and provide more than a bit of green for concrete-weary New Jersey residents. But carry a map with you—the university's decentralization can be a bit daunting.

Once ensconced at the New Brunswick campus, students may take courses in any of the colleges. Overspecialization is discouraged—even the preprofessional programs are based firmly in the liberal arts—and each school has area requirements that its graduates must meet. Especially strong programs include English, history, economics, political science, psychology, math and chemistry. The work load is steady for most and strenuous for science majors. One habitué warns, "Once the semester is into full swing, you have to get to the library by 5:30 to have a seat for the evening. Reservations are not accepted."

In an effort to reverse New Jersey high school superstars' emigration for college, Rutgers offers a popular four-year honors program, which includes special seminars, internships and independent projects. Merit scholarship winners automatically qualify. Admittance to the George H. Cook Scholars Program is by faculty invitation, and only those who rank in the top 15 percent of their high school class and successfully complete twenty-four hours plus a two-term course of directed study at Rutgers will be considered. Five-year joint-degree programs include a BA/BS degree in engineering, a BA/MS in criminal justice, and a BA/MBA. Rutgers also offers study programs in France, Italy, West Germany and Mexico. Adjacent to the campus is the 370-acre Rutgers Ecological Preserve and Natural Teaching Area, used for science classes, birdwatching, and other outdoor pursuits. As at any big state university, registration can sometimes be a scramble, and computer facilities, while well developed, are often crowded. On the plus side, students find the counseling arrangements, especially for personal problems, quite strong.

Though the administration has been trying to increase the number of out-of-staters, more than 90 percent of Rutgers students are still from New Jersey. Nevertheless, the student population is as diversified as that of the state, with a good proportion of students from suburbs, farms, and seaside communities. Almost two-thirds graduate in the top fifth of their high school classes, and the many who live nearby still hang out with their high school friends. Students are encouraged to apply to up to three colleges on any campus (a simple matter of checking the appropriate boxes on the application). Rutgers attempts to meet the demonstrated financial need of its enrollees, although a small percentage of those with need receive nothing at all. Less than forty students receive athletic scholarships, and only twenty receive awards based on academic merit, ranging from $200 to $4,500.

On-campus housing, which accommodates about 60 percent of full-time students, is "not luxurious, but it is inexpensive." Juniors and seniors with low lottery numbers often search for better housing off campus, but most of the students are somehow squeezed in if they request rooms. Options range from the usual hallways to special-interest areas to apartment complexes with kitchens and living rooms. The wide assortment of meal plans lets students choose to eat in any of the five dining rooms; the best bet is the smaller Cooper Dining Hall. Brower Commons, with seating for one thousand gets the most complaints. Convenient bus and train stations make it easy enough to get to school from home, even without a car, and a free and frequent bus makes getting around campus convenient.

Central New Brunswick has undergone a much-needed revitalization and is now actually an attractive place to go for a drink or dinner on the town. New York and Philadelphia are each only about an hour distant, and students flood the Jersey shore in springtime. Most dorms plan a winter ski trip to the Poconos as well. The regular weekend exodus (except at exam time) makes on-campus social life minimal—Friday and Saturday, that is. Weeknights students enjoy "wild fraternity and dormitory dancing parties," and Tuesday and Thursday are standing room only at the College Avenue

Pub. Each college has its own student center with pinball machines, pool tables, bowling alleys and a snack bar.

Varsity sports fill the gaps that the social life leaves in the undergraduate existence. Rutgers, the site of the first American football game (against arch-rival Princeton), fields strongly competitive men's soccer, lacrosse, football and basketball teams, and women's volleyball and basketball squads. A women's soccer program is a recent addition. Though Princeton has won a good share of its games against Rutgers since 1869, the Tigers are no longer any match for the Scarlet Knights, and in 1980 Princeton bowed out of the oldest football rivalry in the nation.

Rutgers has the plethora of people and programs characteristic of state universities, but it also has a lot more—including loyal support from the state's legislature and private sector. "It should be the jewel of our system," New Jersey's governor was quoted as saying, and the millions his budget is currently directing toward that goal will certainly help Rutgers sparkle.

St. John's College

Annapolis, MD 21404   **Santa Fe, NM 87501**

Location Center city	**Location** City outskirts
Total Enrollment 390	**Total Enrollment** 320
Undergraduates 390	**Undergraduates** 320
Male/Female 58/42	**Male/Female** 55/45
SAT V/M 640/600	**SAT V/M** 590/580
Financial Aid 50%	**Financial** 66%
Expense Pr $ $ $	**Expense** Pr $ $ $
Applicants 270	**Applicants** 190
Accepted 91%	**Accepted** 74%
Enrolled 64%	**Enrolled** 75%
Academics ★★★★★	**Academics** ★★★★★
Social ☎☎☎	**Social** ☎☎☎
Q of L ●●●●	**Q of L** ●●●●
Admissions (301)263-2371	**Admissions** (800)331-5232

St. John's College, with campuses in Maryland and New Mexico, is a haven for extraordinary people who can't resign themselves to the compromises of the typical American college experience. It is a school that caters exclusively to serious students whose single goal is to read, write and philosophize every waking hour of the day.

Physically, the two campuses are more than just time zones away. The old-world traditional brick buildings of the one in Annapolis, with its historic 1744 administration building, are a tight fit on this small urban campus. The other campus, meanwhile, located on the outskirts of Santa Fe, features sun-drenched adobe buildings set against a backdrop of the Sangre de Cristo Mountains. Though near no mass transportation, it provides students with easy access to the wilderness.

Geographically miles apart, the two campuses are of a like mind when it comes to academics. With a history that goes back more than 275 years, they follow a curriculum that would have delighted the poet and educator Matthew Arnold, who argued in an 1882 essay that the goal of education is "to know the best which has been thought and said in the world" and that the best way to meet it is to immerse students in the greatest classical texts. St. John's curriculum, known as the Program, is built around about 150 writings of Western civilization, and every student must read these "great books" in roughly chronological order. There are no registration or scheduling hassles: The daily course of study for all four years is mapped out before a student sets foot on campus. The breakdown is four years of mathematics, two years of ancient Greek, two of French, three years of laboratory science, a year of music and, of course, four years of great-books seminars. Freshmen study the Greeks, sophomores advance to the Renaissance, juniors cover the seventeenth and eighteenth centuries, and seniors the nineteenth and twentieth centuries. Readings are from primary sources only: You learn math from Euclid, physics from Einstein, psychology from Freud and so on for all fields. The assumption is that these books represent the highest achievements of man's intellect. Once they are mastered and analytical abilities are finely tuned, students will be ready to take on anything the world has to offer.

Though the formidable curriculum is far more structured and classical than any other college's, the method of presenting it is as radical as that of any alternative school. Professors, called tutors, are considered only the most advanced students in class ("The book is the teacher" and "Reason is the only recognized authority"). Like true Renaissance men, tutors must be able to teach any subject in the curriculum, and in a few years' time they do. Many never publish at all, and they put teaching above all else. Instruction is entirely by small discussion groups, where the tutor's responsibility is to listen rather than lecture, and there are no exams. Libraries are adequate, unless you are looking for "fun" books. Actually most students have every book they need for study on the shelves in their rooms, and the libraries provide comfortable armchairs and quiet, tucked away study nooks. The few computer terminals on the Annapolis campus are open only ten hours a week, and even then they're not often in use.

The Program is so rigorous that there is a 40 percent attrition rate, but survivors are usually enthusiastic about the experience. "To see a student like myself with a math phobia able to grasp an understanding of calculus by reading directly from Newton's *Principia* is a great accomplishment," raves a student. Still occasional grumblings do surface. Some students don't like the foreign language classes' emphasis on translating, not communicating, and find the music department weak as there are no introductory courses and those students who don't know much about the subject before they begin quickly feel lost and alienated. Another complaint has to do with the solely Western focus. But overall, students who stay to graduate manage to appreciate the Program for what it is without expecting it to be all things.

Many St. John's students find they need a year off between sophomore and junior year. Some decide simply to switch from the Annapolis campus to Santa Fe, or vice versa, not only for a change of scenery but for a change of atmosphere. Santa Fe, founded in 1964 to increase St. John's size without sacrificing the virtues of a small campus, is definitely more relaxed than the comparatively uptight Annapolis campus. "We like bright colors, mountains, and heavy talks," says one Santa Fe student. As dutiful as the cadets at the naval academy across the street, Annapolis "Johnnies" come as close as students possibly can to learning every waking hour of the day.

The reason students choose St. John's is never simple. Says one sophomore, "My search in life is for the essential. I am looking for experiences that impact my moral fabric and from my education I expect to better choose how to spend my life." And just how they spend their lives after St. John's is far from predictable. Many head for graduate school, or take time to teach but few are on the traditional fast track to career and a job. A third of the students have transferred to St. John's from other more conventional colleges—an act of devotion, since St. John's accepts no transfer credits and requires all students to begin as freshmen. But Johnnies must be devoted to do well here and keep up with the reading overload. At St. John's, the books always come first, as a prospective student noticed on a recent visit to campus: "Students at most schools put their books over their heads when it rains, but at St. Johns they put them under their shirts." Qualified students are admitted on a first-come, first-served basis. After all spaces fill up (the school keeps a strict cap on enrollment), admissions begin for the following semester. About half the students on both campuses ranked in the top 10 percent of their high school classes, and blacks and Hispanics account for an evenly divided 8 percent. Operating on a need-blind basis, St. John's expects students to meet the first $3,000 of their documented need through loans and/or part-time employment and then attempts to make up the rest.

Dorms on the Annapolis campus are coed, small and some well worn (dating to the mid–nineteenth century). Freshmen usually live on campus, but a little under 30 percent of the student body have found housing elsewhere in this quiet town. Juniors and seniors on campus usually receive singles. The Santa Fe campus boasts a luxurious collection of small two-story dorms housing twenty students each. The rooms are spacious, mostly singles and, with the campus located at seven thousand feet on the edge of mountains that turn blood-red at sunset, provide a more scenic view than most luxury hotel rooms. Weather permitting, students camp out on their balconies. But food on both campuses is rated "poor" and the college requires a doctor's order at Annapolis and special permission at Santa Fe to be excused from eating it under the mandatory meal plan. Santa Fe undergraduates plunge into the outdoor life encouraged by their location, while Annapolis students limit their adventures to well-organized intramural teams, sporting names such as the Druids, the Spartans and the Furies, for their annual croquet tourney with the U.S. Naval Academy, or trips to Washington, Chesapeake Bay or West Virginia. "It's very strange here," says a student about weekend life, "students study until 10 PM Saturday or Friday and then dance, drink or see a college flick."

While students admit that drinking provides the favored release for Johnnies, there are other popular, more cerebral diversions happening, just not as often. For instance, the tri-weekly formal waltz parties, coffeehouse entertainment, discussion sessions and the annual Seducers and Corrupters parties for incoming freshmen. Two favorite all-campus events on the Annapolis campus are Senior Prank, a twenty-four-hour-long surprise party for the whole college community, and Reality, a weekend-long party that includes a mock Olympics. Even after running out of entertainment, never does a "Johnnie" watch TV—or at least never admits to it. Says one junior, "St. John's students are looking for something to DO on the weekends rather than vegetate in front of a television." And he warns prospectives, "To bring a television to school is considered a rather serious faux pas."

There is an almost mystical reverence for learning at St. John's. Students will tell you they're looking for truth, beauty and other lofty ideals in their education instead of seeking a thorough grounding in something as pedestrian as political science. St. John's rigid adherence to its unusual curriculum can lead to pretentiousness, elitism and intellectual arrogance, the antithesis of the creativity so admired in great thinkers of the past. But these are the hazards that Johnnies are willing to risk for the potential returns of gaining an education that one student describes as "noble in the Aristotelian sense" at this last bastion of classical liberal arts.

St. John's University

Collegeville, MN 56321

Location Rural
Total Enrollment 1,950
Undergraduates 1,780
Male/Female N/A
SAT V/M 490/560
Financial Aid 68%
Expense Pr $

Applicants 1,220
Accepted 69%
Enrolled 58%
Academics ★★★
Social 🐝🐝🐝
Q of L ●●●
Admissions (612)363-2196

St. John's University is owned and operated by the largest Benedictine monastery in the world. It also boasts the fifth winningest football coach in NCAA history. If Roman Catholic monks and rah-rah college spirit strike you as an unlikely combination, welcome to St. John's, a school where students contemplate the life hereafter, but leave plenty of time for having fun in this one.

Set on two thousand gorgeous acres in rural Minnesota, the St. John's campus is an ideal stomping ground for the eighteen hundred men who make up its student body. Forests, lakes and wide open spaces provide ample room for everything from soccer to skiing, crew to croquet. Along with fine academics and an abiding sense of Christian purpose, the campus itself is one of the main reasons why many men choose St. John's. The admissions staff goes so far as to claim that a color aerial photo of the university is its best recruiting tool. Though the isolation might prove too much for some, most students settle comfortably into this friendly, supportive and fun-loving community.

Despite its idyllic setting, the academic focus at St. John's is decidedly real world. The university's chief strengths lie in preprofessional fields, most notably the premedical and prebusiness programs. Students also praise economics, accounting and the natural sciences, and the forests on and around the campus are a boon for the field biology offerings. An innovative management program places majors in control of computer-simulated corporations. Students interested in the liberal arts will find excellent programs in theology, music, English, humanities and medieval studies. There is also a new program in classical studies. Probably the poorest offering at St. John's is computer science. One student summed up the prevailing view when he described it as "god-awfully weak." Unfortunately, the demand for courses in this and other popular subject areas often exceeds the university's ability to staff them. For the most part though, classes are small and professors very accessible. Students and faculty are usually on a first name basis and frequently meet informally through departmental social clubs.

Each January students take a break from regular course work to indulge in the J-term—a month long chance to study a subject outside the regular curriculum in depth, or to go on a college-led trip abroad (also available during the semester). According to one student, "J-term can be a joke unless the student wants to make it worthwhile; either way it's a good break between semesters."

Two of the most popular courses at St. John's are a required freshman writing seminar and a highly respected values analysis course that explores ethical issues in a student's intended field. Despite the strong presence of the monastery, whose brothers make up 30 percent of the St. John's faculty, only one theology course is added to the normal requirements for liberal arts distribution. The Christian Humanism project involves students and faculty in seminars that explore the historical relations between Christian faith and humanism. The school's largest annual academic event is Forum, a series of debates that brings renowned intellectuals and social figures to campus to argue important contemporary social, political and religious issues. An auxiliary event features student-faculty debates. Another academic plus is cross-registration with the College of St. Benedict, St. John's University's sister school four miles down the road in the small town of St. Joseph. A new library at St. Ben's, fully accessible to St. John's students, has expanded study and research facilities in the bi-college area.

Though 80 percent are Catholic, few St. John's undergraduates resemble priests in training. On the contrary, most are gearing up to climb the corporate ladder after graduation. Basically, they're all-American boys from the North Woods who like to study hard all week and then really let loose on the weekend. About a quarter ranked in the top 10 percent of their high school class; 85 percent were in the top half. Three out of four come from Minnesota, while Chicago and other midwestern cities are also well represented. Students are mostly white, middle class and very athletic. "Intelligent, conservative, social jocks is what we are," says one, "and glad to get away from home." The faculty, meanwhile, "are generally very liberal, a fact many of the Young Republicans detest," according to a senior among the liberal minority. Following the monks' example of brotherly love, St. John's students make their campus a congenial and accepting place.

A committed residence staff, including one monk living on each floor, oversees the homey dormitory life. Incoming students are assigned to doubles on freshman floors in one of the six dorms. Other options include small houses off campus for half a dozen students each, an experimental Christian community housing project, and college-owned apartments, including a new earth-sheltered complex on the shore of a lake. About 15 percent of upperclassmen live off campus in the nearest town and commute by car or college bus. All on-campus students must buy a fourteen or nineteen-meal plan for use in the refectory, which offers all-you-can-eat meals, a salad bar, and a delicatessen.

If Catholicism is the dominant religion on campus, football is a close second. The team is a perennial Division III powerhouse, and its followers are every bit as rabid as any at the likes of Notre Dame or Georgetown. Basketball, track, soccer and swimming also field excellent teams and are enthusiastically supported. Those not up to varsity status make frequent use of the university's modern athletic facilities and extensive intramural program. Key intramural matchups are known to attract nearly as much interest as varsity games. The ultimate goal of intramural play is a chance at the coveted "red cotton"—T-shirts that proclaim championship status. All this friendly competition contributes to the distinctly masculine tenor of life at St. John's. As one junior explained, "Being fit and strong is the pride of this place."

Luckily for St. John's men, the feminine touch of St. Benedict's women is always close at hand. Many romantic liaisons—a large number of them permanent—are struck up between "Johnnies" and "Bennies." Freshman floors at each school are paired for social events at the beginning of the school year. Buses run frequently between the two campuses, as do ardent St. John's men from time to time. Between cross-registration and liberal visitation policies, some say that St. John's is practically coed. Still, "not much sex goes on here," according to one student, since "it's not tolerated, and we don't believe in it before marriage for the most part." Some of his classmates would say he's speaking for himself. Since there are no social fraternities—"don't need them," explains one student—the social scene tends toward private or college-sponsored parties at St. John's and bar hopping in nearby St. Cloud, a city of ninety thousand that is fifteen minutes away by car. Large quantities of beer are usually consumed during the course of an evening. For more refined tastes, the Benedicta Arts Center on the St. Benedict campus hosts a wide variety of cultural events.

St. John's is not the most intellectual school in the world, nor the most diverse. But students eager for fine preprofessional training in a community that fosters Catholic ideals are seldom disappointed. The monks set the tone on campus, but the college does not try to impose hard-core religion on its students. A more important factor to consider is the school's location. Anyone who chooses St. John's had better be prepared for four long winters in the boondocks of Minnesota. Armed with a heavy coat and a love of the great outdoors, many men find St. John's an ideal mix of Catholic tradition and college fun.

St. Lawrence University

Canton, NY 13617

Location Village	**Applicants** 2,450
Total Enrollment 2,250	**Accepted** 69%
Undergraduates 2,250	**Enrolled** 35%
Male/Female 52/48	**Academics** ★ ★ ★
SAT V/M 530/580	**Social** 🍸 🍸 🍸
Financial Aid 40%	**Q of L** ● ● ●
Expense Pr $ $ $	**Admissions** (315)379-5261

Only twenty miles from the Canadian border, St. Lawrence University is located in a rural backwater that makes the boondocks look like the inner city. It's a long, cold winter in Canton, but the semi-Siberian weather and isolated atmosphere contrast with an unusually warm and friendly college community. Long considered a haven for "aristocratically casual" rich kids who wanted to flee the world and drink for four years, St. Lawrence has been working on beefing up academic standards. Students now point with pride to their extensive library and solid computer program. They have higher SAT scores, study harder, at least on weekdays, and they have even begun to dream of turning their school into the Middlebury or Williams of upstate New York.

The dream is not impossible. St. Lawrence offers a broad-based, classical liberal arts education. With little to distract them in their surroundings, faculty members give everything to their academic responsibilities. "Even the most formidable profs are easily accessible," says one student. The most highly recommended majors at St. Lawrence are government, psychology and English; economics is also popular, but the administration concedes that the department "has so many students that it cannot always teach them all." But many students prefer less conventional programs, such as Renaissance music or the highly ranked environmental program, which supplements input from faculty in several other departments and makes full use of the ecological riches of the St. Lawrence River area. Other interdisciplinary majors include Canadian studies, which profits from the school's proximity to the border, and the newly instituted math/computer science program. The school admits to a weak art department and finds it difficult to develop or attract student attention to religion or philosophy programs. Students may design their own program across three or more of the twenty-six departments.

The neatly groomed, thousand-acre campus has several old buildings dating back to the school's founding in 1856, combined with nondescript but adequate modern structures. And whoever designed the layout of the campus was smart enough to compact the distance between any two buildings, significantly decreasing students' chances of getting frostbite as they move from class to class. Either despite or because of the location, more than half of St. Lawrence students study abroad for at least a semester before graduation in places such as Nairobi, Japan or Madrid. Students may also take advantage of group-sponsored exchange programs in Denmark, Montreal and Washington or even spend a semester at sea. There are also five-year combined programs with other universities in engineering and nursing. Computers are considered a basic resource, like the library, and are used in most disciplines.

Even with an increasingly serious approach toward academics, St. Lawrence, in the words of an administrator, is "unhampered by debilitating competition among students." No cutthroat atmosphere here. There is an emphasis on shared learning furthered by the school's student-approved college system in which students living in the same dorm take a common interdisciplinary course—"closing the gap between living and learning" is how one administrator sums up the system.

"Larries" are about as diverse as the suburban country clubs where they learned to swim. Almost everyone is white, eastern, outdoorsy and gregarious. "Grade-grubbers and introverts would best apply elsewhere," says one student. According to another student, "Our main interests are socializing, sex, lively sports (squash, tennis, jogging) and career ambition." Two-thirds of the students enter the job market after graduation. Although St. Lawrence students are not financially compensated for their scholastic or athletic endeavors, about 40 percent of them receive need-based aid with average grants of $6,000.

Housing is an unexceptional mixture of traditional and modern buildings, all well maintained. Sykes Hall, the largest dorm, underwent a major renovation and is reported to be the best. Most dorms have coed wings and students generally live in doubles. Rooms are assigned by lottery with priority given to upperclassmen (they get all the singles). Seniors occasionally gain permission to live off campus. Those who do often organize theme cottages such as the French house or the International House. Fortunately, campus living has its rewards: The food served in the two dining halls is cooked on the premises and "can even be imaginative at times." Close to one-fourth of the students live and eat in fraternity and sorority houses. The latest eating option on campus is the pub located in the newly renovated Student Center.

The social and political issues of the far-off world hardly touch the St. Lawrence campus, although there is an extremely active volunteer program and a speakers program. "Those who want to find problems and then have demonstrations or petitions will find that the majority of students here are not too liberally active in this regard," says a sophomore. Concerts, movies and art exhibitions sometimes make it all the way to Canton, but such cultural activities are, to say the least, limited. Most St. Lawrence students enjoy sports and find their amusement in their immediate surroundings. There's the indoor field house, eight squash courts, indoor tennis, a pool and the school's own ski bowl. The on-campus golf course doubles as a cross-country skiing trail during the winter. And complete riding facilities service the school's many national riding champions. Other outdoor activities, from rock climbing and canoeing to "all the skiing you can stand" are available in and around the nearby Adirondacks and St. Lawrence River. In varsity sports men's hockey and skiing are Division I and championships have been won in cross-country, basketball and track. Students characterize their intramural program as super-strong, which is no exaggeration considering there are fifty-two softball teams, thirty-eight hockey teams and twenty-nine volleyball teams that compete.

Many students have cars to take in all these diversions as well as the slightly more distant entertainment in Ottawa (an hour and a half away) or Montreal (two and a half). For those without wheels, the school outing club sponsors bus trips. Most of the big parties blast off at fraternity and sorority houses, and these groups are probably the most conservative on this generally conservative campus. They even promote old-time dating on occasion. Luckily, they are tolerant of non-Greeks. The new drinking age of twenty-one and the corresponding administration crackdown on violators has made for new alternative socializing activities available on campus, usually at the new pub. But students still "flock to frat parties like lemmings."

Some people love St. Lawrence's geographic location and the strong sense of community it fosters; for others it can cause a severe lack-of-culture shock. But, if you're one of those people who is self-motivated academically, loves the outdoors and can live without a cosmopolitan life-style, St. Lawrence might be just the shock you need.

St. Louis University

St. Louis, MO 63103

Location Center city	**Applicants** 2,189
Total Enrollment 10,030	**Accepted** 81%
Undergraduates 6,560	**Enrolled** 45%
Male/Female 52/48	**Academics** ★ ★ ★
SAT V/M 500/520	**Social** 🐿 🐿
Financial Aid 75%	**Q of L** ● ● ●
Expense Pr $	**Admissions** (314)658-2500

Out-of-towners regard St. Louis University as "that *other* school in St. Louis," the second fiddle to prestigious Washington University. But among St. Louisans, this Jesuit institution is as much a part of the city's history and tradition as the Roman Catholic church itself. Hence, SLU is sharing in the present rush of city rejuvenation by doing a bit of its own spiffin' up (more than $100 million worth in the past seven years—Hail Mary!).

SLU is within sight of the famous Gateway Arch (a symbolic portal of the American West), which is fitting because it was the first college west of the Mississippi River and established itself as the gateway to higher knowledge. In keeping with its strong Jesuit commitment to educating the whole person, all undergrads are required to complete a core curriculum of humanities, science and math and social sciences. "A well-rounded Jesuit education helps develop the complete person, not a one-dimensional robot," affirms one American studies major.

Premed and prelaw programs are the biggies at this city school, which turns out a large percentage of St. Louis' doctors and lawyers. Most science and health-related departments are strong, including geophysics, meteorology, avionics, nursing and allied health. Naturally, under Jesuit guidance, philosophy and theology are deemed outstanding. One of the world's most complete microfilm collections of Vatican documents attract scholars from around the globe. Business, psychology and urban affairs programs are considered solid; sociology, anthropology, foreign languages and the fine and

492

preforming arts aren't. Students give the big thumbs down to the math department. "Our computer system is entirely inadequate," says a senior, "and communications is an embarrassingly easy department."

Faculty members tend to be outgoing and accessible. "Freshmen and sophomores get many high-quality professors because department chairmen often teach at least one introductory course," explains a junior. Although there are fewer Jesuits teaching at SLU these days, their influence is still felt. The student volunteer program is one of the most visible, and students can earn class credit or merely self-satisfaction by working for nonprofit organizations. Some students elect to spend their spring break working with the poor in Appalachia or on Indian reservations in the West. Another interesting possibility is Uncommon Classroom, where students spend the summer hiking and camping while studying biology and English in the Ozark Mountains. A small number of topflight sophomores are guaranteed admission to the medical school upon graduation.

Ancient to modern is an accurate assessment of the architectural range on SLU's ever-changing campus. The most impressive of the visions and revisions is the expansion of the Pius XII Library, with a bright, comfortable and much-needed study area. "It makes studying a much more pleasant chore," reports one senior, "and nap taking much more comfortable." Other improvements include a new avionics building, a new gymnasium-convocation center, the refurbishment of older buildings and the addition of greenery and flowers to what used to be a concrete campus. As might be expected at a school where the library is named after a pope, the most outstanding building is a beautiful Gothic church. A street once dividing the campus is now a mall for walkers and bikers only, and the huge recreation-sports complex draws rave reviews.

Stuck between St. Louis's artsy Central West End and a not-so-nice but quickly improving part of town, SLU has all the advantages and problems usually associated with being smack in the middle of the city. "The surroundings are slightly shocking at first," a junior reports. "Most of the people are very poor." Campus security runs an escort service to apartments as well as the dorms and medical campus. SLU is just blocks from commercial St. Louis, which boasts everything from Powell Symphony Hall to Busch Stadium, not to mention the old Union Train Station, now a huge shopping and dining complex.

Sixty percent of SLU students hail from the Show Me state and a large portion of those are commuters. Most of the rest are either from the East or other parts of the Midwest. About 11 percent are black or Hispanic, and 65 percent are Catholic. A majority come from parochial schools, including nearby St. Louis University High School. Mass is celebrated in the basements of dorms every night. "SLU students have a Catholic preppie look and attitude. They like to study, drink and sit in the quad 'scoping,' " says a business major. He adds, however, that the prevailing atmosphere is "a warm, caring and accepting one."

The costs for tuition, fees and housing are kept low, thanks in part to a $120-million endowment. Besides the generous athletic scholarships that usually go to about eighty men and women, the university offers about 550 awards yearly, ranging from $500 to $3,000, for students demonstrating academic excellence.

A variety of living options exist: single-sex, coed-by-floor, coed-by-suite and scholarship dorms. A newly purchased hotel is to be converted into luxury dorms. Noncommuting freshmen must live on campus and are assigned rooms, while upperclassmen adhere to squatter's rights. "Maintenance and housekeeping are less than average," remarks one resident, "which is partly due to the age of the dorms." But a good number of comparably priced, off-campus apartments are within walking distance of the campus. Dorm residents must buy one of three meal contracts and the food is unremarkable, "generally average, sometimes worse," according to one participant.

The high percentage of commuters tends to dampen the campus social life a bit, but formal dances (including one with couples matched up by computer) are popular. Fraternities appear to be gaining in popularity, and their parties are open to everyone. The two bars just off campus, Clark's and Humphrey's, are also favorite partying places. SLU has no varsity football team, but its soccer team more than makes up for this deficit. It is perennially one of the best in the country, and a number of SLU graduates are now playing professionally. Men's basketball and women's field hockey are also excellent, and intramurals are "fantastic."

"There is a sense of unity and a shared Catholic background in SLU students, which makes them very friendly and sympathetic," observes one sophomore. "Yet it's a special school that accepts new people," adds a senior from out of state. SLU is as much of a paradox as the city to which it belongs—rich in provincial and religious traditions, yet welcoming to newcomers; it's a place that is growing rapidly, yet is holding on to its roots. Proud students and alumni will remind you, lest you forget, that this is *THE* University of St. Louis.

St. Mary's College of Maryland

St. Mary's City, MD 20686

Location Rural	**Applicants** 860
Total Enrollment 1,190	**Accepted** 66%
Undergraduates 1,190	**Enrolled** 50%
Male/Female 45/55	**Academics** ★ ★ ★
SAT V/M 510/530	**Social** ☎ ☎
Financial Aid 16%	**Q of L** ● ● ● ●
Expense Pub $ $	**Admissions** (301)862-0292

At first glance, St. Mary's College of Maryland has all the trappings of a thousand other small liberal arts colleges. Her buildings are picturesquely situated on a self-contained campus, and the low student/faculty ratio, close-knit community and academically motivated students might be found on any number of small private college campuses across the country. What makes St. Mary's different is that it's a *public* institution. "I'm receiving a private college education at a state school price," chirps one student. "What a bargain!"

St. Mary's owes its current public-in-price-only status to a peculiar deal struck in the late '60s by St. Mary's county legislators, who vowed to give up the county's lucrative slot machines if the state would finance the expansion of their junior college into a real four-year school. Today, St. Mary's SAT scores are among the highest of all Maryland state schools, and although one student admits "you would have to be pretty dumb to flunk out," several classmates cite an increase in academic pressure.

Situated on a peninsula in southern Maryland, where the Potomac River meets the Chesapeake Bay, the St. Mary's campus is a mixture of modern and colonial architecture. "The buildings are rather ordinary, but they are entirely eclipsed by the

494

beauty of the sunsets on the river," remarks a history major. And the college has taken advantage of its setting by developing certain outstanding programs through judicious exploitation of the natural resources. For instance, the river front has become an outdoor laboratory for the marine biology program, and because the city of St. Mary's has a long lineage (it was the original capital of Maryland), archeological digs dot the campus and provide inspiration and material for a strong program in colonial history.

Other respectable academic programs include English, economics and human development (otherwise known as the grab bag major because it covers everything from philosophy to physical education). In addition, the school has established an excellent music program that is exceptionally strong in modern jazz. Apart from the biology department, however, the natural sciences need improvement, mainly due to inadequate facilities. Foreign languages suffer from a faculty shortage, and students find little in the math program to enthuse them.

A new general education curriculum emphasizes Western heritage, writing and mathematics. Under these new requirements, students must take two upper-level Q and W courses, i.e., classes that emphasize quantitative thinking and writing. St. Mary's also has decided to enter the computer age in a big way by offering more hands-on access to microcomputers than any other college in Maryland. Additional programs of interest include study in England at Oxford's Center for Medieval and Renaissance Studies, an exchange program with a Chinese university, and full-credit faculty-supervised career internships. A respected and quite selective honors program has aided the effort to boost academic standards, as has the requirement that juniors and seniors take only upper-level courses. Students rate the library as okay but also admit that they anxiously await the promised expansion.

Almost all St. Mary's students are from Maryland, and most are from public schools. Although students are adamant about the diversity of the student body, one senior reveals that more and more wealthy, conservative students are sneaking onto campus—"The yuppie scene has finally hit St. Mary's." The petiteness of the college allows many the opportunity to, as one junior says, "be a big fish in a small pond." And while peer pressure pushes more students toward the books than the kegs these days, the atmosphere is far from cutthroat. "Luckily, striving for the GPA doesn't override a genuine interest in classes and learning," states a political science major. Only 4 percent of St. Mary's graduates go on to law, business, or medical school, but for those who apply, the acceptance rate is 90 percent. The college enjoys an unusually high retention rate for the minority students, who make up 8 percent of the student body. St. Mary's offers several fellowships for academic ability and promise (one for non-Caucasians), which range from $500 to full rides. No athletic scholarships are awarded.

Three-quarters of the student body crowd into the five on-campus residence halls, two of which are coed, but the new townhouses under construction promise to relieve some of the housing crunch. Since rooms are assigned on a first-come, first-served basis, prospective freshmen should get their paperwork done early in the summer. Upperclassmen often move off campus into one of the charming old farmhouses or riverside cottages available for rent. Undistinguished food is served in an undistinguished cafeteria. Those who prefer more distinctive fare can join the vegetarian food co-op or head for the river and treat themselves to hand-caught fish and crabs.

The secluded location of St. Mary's (about an hour from Washington or Baltimore) means there's little to do off campus, so St. Mary's students have become adept at making their own fun. Films are shown on campus three nights a week and the programs board makes sure there's something happening every weekend. "We have air band concerts, battles of the bands, Monte Carlo night, etc.," notes a sophomore. Yet a classmate adds that the main source of fun is the beach. "The college has a large number of sailboats, canoes and windsurfers available for students, and life revolves around the water." But the rural setting can become too subdued after a while, and one student moans that "if you don't enjoy beer and the beach you're extremely limited."

More successful than weekend social life are St. Mary's intramurals—everyone's favorite activity. Men's and women's flag football arouses more enthusiasm than many varsity sports, and the annual SMC Spring Olympics, which involves half the student body plus much of the faculty and staff is a definite don't-miss. Intercollegiately St. Mary's holds its own in men's and women's soccer, and the men's lacrosse team is prominent nationally. Both men's and women's sailing teams are among the best in the nation.

St. Mary's is a maverick in the world of higher education: an attempt to provide lower-income families with the benefits of a small, private college. But St. Mary's has only been a four-year college for twenty years, so it's got a lot of catching up to do. The school's funds and facilities could certainly be more extensive, but as any St. Mary's student can tell you, sunsets on the river every evening can make up for a lot.

St. Olaf College

Northfield, MN 55057

Location Small town	**Applicants** 2,120
Total Enrollment 2,290	**Accepted** 66%
Undergraduates 2,290	**Enrolled** 58%
Male/Female 47/53	**Academics** ★★★★
SAT V/M 530/600	**Social** ☎☎☎
Financial Aid 52%	**Q of L** ●●●●
Expense Pr $	**Admissions** (507)663-3025

In good biblical fashion, St. Olaf is "a college set on a hill." Founded a century ago by Lutheran immigrants from Norway and named after that country's patron saint, the college's limestone buildings are spread between clusters of sugar maples on a prospect overlooking a small town in rural Minnesota. The names of the campus buildings— Skoglund Athletic Center, Rolvaag Library, Thorson and Ytterboe dorms—are testimony to the rich Norwegian heritage, and Scandinavian studies and Norwegian language courses are still popular among students, many of whom trace their St. Olaf tie back many generations.

The academic program is strong, with emphasis on the liberal arts in a Christian context. General core courses emphasize a broad, yet selective survey of natural sciences, languages and literature, behavioral sciences and the arts. St. Olaf also requires three courses in religion. Chemistry, physics and biology are highly regarded among liberal arts majors and base the solid premed program. English, music and philosophy are strong departments, and mathematics is an unusually popular field of study here, with math majors comprising a whopping 10 percent of a recent graduating class. The social sciences, on the other hand, are rather weak, though economics is very popular among students. Undersubscription means that Russian and Chinese language courses lack vitality.

496

Supplementing the traditional college format is the Paracollege, which permits students to design their own majors and work with a professor on a one-to-one basis. "It's set up like the British tutorial system," one student explains. Students in another intensive nontraditional program, the two-year-long Great Conversation course in classic works, live together in one dorm to facilitate late-night study sessions. The program in international studies is an important part of the school's curriculum, and about half the students travel abroad at some point during their college careers, often on exchanges through the Associated Colleges of the Midwest).* Foreign excursions and independent study projects are particularly popular during the interim January semester in the school's 4-1-4 calendar. An adequate number of computer terminals sustain constant but manageable traffic. Freshmen must complete a mandatory word-processing assignment for an English class. A major addition to the library, now in the planning stages, will expand facilities that currently draw criticism. Students also have access to nearby Carleton College's library.

The professors are readily accessible and show genuine concern for their students. According to one senior, "Students are encouraged, even invited, to have dinner or share a cup of coffee with faculty." Though many students regard the grading as tough and the academic climate as high pressure, one suggests that it's "pressure put on oneself, not pressure between peers." Students don't mind being frivolous with some of their classroom hours, however, and two of the most popular courses in the school's history are human sexuality and ballroom dancing.

As for the student body, homogeneity is pervasive. All but 2 percent of the students are white—meaning there are only about sixty minority students in the whole school—a situation that the administration says it is working to change. "A typical Ole," says one, "should be Norwegian, a Lutheran, and have blond hair and blue eyes." The homogeneity tends to breed conformity and, some students believe, a high school-ish "in" crowd. Most students are high achievers from midwestern public schools and financially secure families, and the look is healthy and handsome. Sixty percent are from Minnesota, and an equal percentage belong to the American Lutheran Church. Most students take their religion seriously. St. Olaf is need-blind in admissions and meets the computed financial need of its students. With its tuition and room and board fees totaling under $10,000, St. Olaf is widely considered to be one of the best bargains among private colleges in the nation.

For housing, freshmen are assigned double rooms in twenty student "corridors," each of which has two junior counselors. Most upperclassmen also live in the dorms, except for a few each year who find their way into the handful of college-owned houses two blocks away. In part because so many students choose to live on campus, space in the dorms is tight, but a new hall under construction should improve the situation. The dorms are coed by floor, and each has its own personality, ranging from quiet Rand Hall to "Ytterboe, St. Olaf's version of Animal House." Students eat in a large modern cafeteria where the food is considered above average for college fare. Every December the dining hall serves a special meal of traditional Norwegian cuisine. But unsuspecting freshmen beware: The lutefisk can be lethal.

Most of the extracurricular entertainment at St. Olaf is provided by the fine arts departments, with a great many theater, dance and music performances. About half the student body signs up for one of more than a dozen vocal and instrumental organizations, and orchestra members often find themselves preparing for tours of the United States or Europe. "Music at St. Olaf is what sports are at most other schools," says one student. Varsity sports attract little attention, but there is an extensive intra-mural program. Broomball is the sport of choice in the winter—even the president of the college gets into the act. Strong debate and forensic teams turn in better records than almost all varsity except the successful men's swimming team.

In theory, alcohol is prohibited on campus, though many students find ways of getting around the rule. Any large-scale merrymaking is usually done off campus as party-loving students migrate to the two bars in town on the weekend. For others, weekends are usually spent attending the weekly on-campus movie, dropping in at the Lion's Pause (the college coffeehouse that features live local entertainment) or studying. A student activities committee sponsors occasional dances, speakers and cultural events. Daily chapel services, though not mandatory, are heavily attended. The Fellowship of Christian Athletes has a large chapter on campus, and numerous other student-organized Bible studies and fellowship groups draw wide participation.

Northfield, a small town in the midst of farming communities, offers little of interest aside from Carleton, another well-known liberal arts college, where students often go to socialize if boredom sets in at St. Olaf. When Oles really want to get away, Minneapolis and St. Paul are less than an hour's drive, with buses leaving regularly. There is excellent cross-country skiing in the area, and downhill slopes are close by. St. Olaf is situated atop Manitou Heights, which is picturesque in spring and fall, but subject to fierce January winds. "Making it through a Minnesota winter is a true accomplishment," says one man. At least students don't have to waste time digging their cars out of the snow: No vehicles are permitted on campus without special permits. Students report that with only three counselors for three thousand students, campus mental health counseling services are less-than-adequate to deal with student problems during the dark months or, for that matter, any other time.

To get the most out of St. Olaf, a student must value its strong ties with the church and be geared for rigorous academic work and a low-key social life. In the current college marketplace, where the success of hundreds of small private colleges depends on their ability to carve out a distinctive identity, St. Olaf has wisely decided to reemphasize its traditional commitment to "the search for values." The St. Olaf mold is a tight fit, but for those who can handle it, the college provides a competitive, high-quality, broad-based education in an atmosphere of concern and friendship.

University of San Francisco

San Francisco, CA 94117

Location Urban	**Applicants** 3,000
Total Enrollment 4,980	**Accepted** 70%
Undergraduates 2,830	**Enrolled** 19%
Male/Female 48/52	**Academics** ★ ★ ★
SAT V/M 460/510	**Social** ☎ ☎ ☎
Financial Aid 47%	**Q of L** ● ● ● ●
Expense Pr $ $	**Admissions** (415)666-6563

Everyone knows San Francisco is a cosmopolitan town with a diverse population, a strong interest in the arts and above all an atmosphere tolerant of diversity in its midst. The University of San Francisco reflects the character of the city where it is located, and its motto, "For the City and the University," indicates how closely the two are aligned. "Our graduates literally run city hall," says one student, "and I like the idea that the city also supports and likes us."

USF's fifty-two well-kept acres spotted with beautiful basilica-type buildings and modern facilities are, according to one student, "wedged into the heart of San Francisco." The campus stands aloft one of San Francisco's seven hills adjacent to the Golden Gate Park and overlooking the San Francisco Bay and the city skyline. Founded by the Jesuits in 1885, USF today has a diverse student body that includes students from eighty-five foreign nations as well as a good mix of ethnic groups mostly from the West and Northwest. About half of the student body is Roman Catholic, and twelve hours in theology and philosophy are required for graduation; but tolerance is the dominant mood of the campus. "I'm not Catholic," said one business major, "and rarely do I feel any ambivalence directed at me because of it." The theology department includes both a rabbi and a Lutheran minister, and the administration estimates that the Catholics make up only about 60 percent of the faculty.

The academic emphasis at USF is clearly on its excellent preprofessional programs, especially nursing, premed, communications and business. According to critical students, the Jesuit tradition of a strong liberal arts program is not upheld here, and offerings in English and foreign languages are especially disappointing. The forty-five-hour general education curriculum garners mixed reviews—"Some of the courses just don't seem useful to me," says a math major. But one way to avoid the general ed "tedium" is through enrollment in St. Ignatius Institute, which offers an integrated four-year curriculum based on the great books of Western civilization presented in an unusual seminar/lecture combination. Some of the preprofessional majors are demanding, but the academic atmosphere of the campus as a whole is relaxed.

Classes are kept medium in size so that "professors can become your friend as well as your mentor," a student reports. Yet one senior, citing "a contagious shyness among many students," says that access to top profs "needs to be utilized more often." Hours at the two libraries are not extensive enough to satisfy even those who do seem pleased with the collections, and the computer facilities are limited, to say the least.

The university operates on the basis of fall and spring semesters, with seven weeks off at Christmas time, and there are some attractive programs abroad for diversity. Students interested in speeding up their education can enroll in optional four-week courses in January at extra cost.

"Although the school is located in a liberal city, I would classify most of the students as ultraconservative," an economics major says. And most appear unruffled by world news and politics: "Liberals looking for demonstrations and student rebellions won't find them on this campus," warns one senior. While most students are from California, the large foreign student population does spice things up a bit and adds a diversity that everyone here appreciates. Admissions are need-blind, and the university makes an effort to provide financial aid to all accepted students, but late applicants cannot be guaranteed help. Close to fifty athletic scholarships for men and women are awarded, sixty merit scholarships for $1,000 to $2,000 and about fifteen academic superstars receive President's Scholars awards.

Although freshmen and sophomores (or those under twenty-one) are required to live on campus, by and large, USF is a commuting school. Those upperclassmen who don't live at home often leave campus and take on the city's high rents. Students who do want dorm rooms (some with views of San Francisco Bay) have four choices: an all-female dorm, a coed-by-floor dorm that "caters to a younger population," a coed-by-room dorm "for a more liberal life-style," or the quiet coed Lone Mountain Hall for upperclassmen. On-campus students eat in a commons, where various meal plans are offered. "Too bad the Hospitality Management department can't have some input to improve the terrible food," gripes one cranky customer.

USF's greatest asset is, undoubtedly, its location. Students can take advantage of the city's public transportation to get to a large number of cultural attractions, ranging from Chinatown to the symphony. Nightlife is great for those who want to dance in the discos or meet in the bars. The Knights of Columbus, the Greeks, professional groups and international clubs all plan activities to keep students on campus, none of which are too well attended. The freshmen and sophomores are the only loyal fraternity fraternizers, but with the more stringent alcohol policies on campus, even they are not as "fraternal as once observed," notes a senior. There are frequent forays to the California beaches, the wine country in the Napa Valley and even all the way to Lake Tahoe, which is about four hours away by car.

Varsity athletics provide a popular diversion, and USF is a perennial national powerhouse in soccer. Much to the joy of the student body, the basketball program has been reinstated after a three-year hiatus that resulted from charges of recruitment improprieties. The women's teams do well in basketball and volleyball. And everyone anxiously awaits the opening of a new health and recreation center that will house an Olympic-size swimming pool, exercise rooms, courts and a snack bar.

"There's always a sense of peace and tranquility on campus," reports one USF student, and the religious roots may be part of the reason why. Of course, the university is located in San Francisco, which may be reason enough to attend.

Santa Clara University

Santa Clara, CA 95053

Location Suburban	**Applicants** 3,150
Total Enrollment 7,750	**Accepted** 62%
Undergraduates 3,680	**Enrolled** 45%
Male/Female 52/48	**Academics** ★ ★ ★
SAT V/M 510/580	**Social** ☎ ☎ ☎ ☎
Financial Aid 45%	**Q of L** ● ● ●
Expense Pr $ $	**Admissions** (408)554-4700

Situated in the heart of Silicon Valley, the University of Santa Clara was founded as a mission to bring European values and religion to the Indians in 1777. Today the university is high-teching it into the future. And with a decent endowment, generous alumni support, thousands of dollars annually from the Jesuit order and funds from a recent successful fund-raising drive, the university has just the resources to do it. So Santa Clara is building, renovating, adding new faculty, shifting the engineering program into high gear, and rerouting a major highway to expand the campus. It's even flipped its name around—that's Santa Clara University, and don't forget it.

But students still revel in SCU's old world charm—140 acres complete with lush green lawns, palm trees, luscious rose gardens, and authentic Spanish architecture. The famous eighteenth-century classic mission church stands as a reminder of the school's Jesuit tradition, "to educate, not to train." Nevertheless, there's an increasing emphasis on solid professional programs, especially computer science and electrical engineering (mechanical engineering has a strong research department but is weaker in undergraduate instruction). And Santa Clara has even rewarded its aspiring engineers with a shiny new state-of-the-art engineering complex. The business school is renowned along the West Coast, and accounting is a particular strength. The international business program is also distinctive, and Santa Clara has an excellent interdisciplinary media program, designed, according to one student, "to promote serious, intelligent public broadcasting." Retail management and ethnic and women's studies are popular off-the-beaten-track programs.

In good Jesuit fashion, Santa Clara is committed to the humanities and theology, and its curricular approach was described by the United States secretary of education as a model of "coherent and rigorous general education." Requirements include courses in religion, ethics, the social sciences, composition, mathematics and natural sciences and Western culture. Add to this distribution requirements in the major academic divisions, and you're sure to end up well rounded. An honors program puts thirty or forty selected freshmen in special honors classes, and at the end of their freshman year two or three honors students are designated honors scholars and allowed to design their own course of study.

One student calls Santa Clara a "small school with big-school goals and achievements." As at any small school, resources and facilities are limited: The library is not always adequate for research needs, forcing students to nearby Stanford to get the materials they need. But students generally have no problems with getting into SCU's small classes and enjoy a unique rapport with their professors. Besides being on a first-name basis with all their students, professors "spend quality time out of the classroom, giving both academic and career-related advice," reports a finance major. The academic climate is described by one senior as being "at the low end of high pressure," but when the going gets rough just take your nerves over to the Test 'n' Tension sessions offered to combat test anxiety. In conjunction with other institutions, sophomore- and junior-years abroad are offered in Italy, France, Spain, Austria, England, Spain, Germany and Japan.

More than half the students are Roman Catholic, and religion, while not intrusive, is a factor in most aspects of campus life. Campus ministry provides counseling in "family life, dorm life, academic life, marriage and divorce," according to one student, and many students are active in local volunteer organizations. The Jesuit presence is also a contributor to the family atmosphere that most students say is their favorite aspect of SCU.

Half the student body is from California and most of the other half is from the West Coast or at least the West—Oregon, Hawaii, Washington and Arizona. Students are, for the most part, conservative "with little pockets of all different types of people." The student body is equally divided between graduates of public and parochial or other private schools, and two-thirds of the students come from the top fifth of their high school classes. Almost one quarter of them are minority students. Santa Clara attempts to admit students regardless of their financial need and uses a variety of means to help all students pay the bills. Besides more than seventy athletic scholarships, Santa Clara awards a considerable number of merit scholarships ranging from $200 to full tuition. There are other talent awards in debate, music and theater.

Dorms work "by luck freshman year, and by lottery thereafter." Most are coed with small rooms, but the halls are well maintained, and many students make their residences the focus of their social lives. Housing is tight, so after freshman year close to half the students move off campus. The football team is a Division II champion, and the basketball team usually does well, as do women's tennis, volleyball and basketball. On the whole, though, varsity athletics are not a significant force on campus. Intramurals are far more popular and are accessible to all, but one student warns that competition can get "intense to the point of being vicious."

Perhaps somewhat surprising to any tee-totaler observer is the amount of partying that goes on at this religion-oriented university. One reason may be the weather. "We have a lot of BBQs since the weather is mostly sunny," says a senior. The California sun also encourages excursions to the beach at Santa Cruz and even on to San Francisco, forty-five miles away. Another contributing party factor is Santa Clara's academic schedule, which bars classes on Wednesdays. "This effectively gives us two Friday nights a week," says one student. The state's drinking age is twenty-one, but it has had no measurable effect on the behavioral patterns of Santa Clara undergraduates. In fact, what used to be a modest Greek presence on campus has blossomed into four fraternities and two sororities, and both are gaining immense popularity.

Santa Clara University is making every effort to become a top-notch school with an eye toward the future. Even those students who don't warm up to their computers like its friendly and supportive religious spirit. They work hard and play hard, and that keeps them busy night and day, especially Tuesday night and Wednesday.

Sarah Lawrence College

Bronxville, NY 10708

Location Suburban
Total Enrollment 1,080
Undergraduates 940
Male/Female 25/75
SAT V/M 560/550
ACT 25
Financial Aid 47%
Expense Pr $ $ $ $

Applicants 880
Accepted 69%
Enrolled 37%
Academics ★ ★ ★
Social ☎ ☎
Q of L ● ● ●
Admissions (914)793-4242

Sarah Lawrence College was founded in 1926 to offer an individualized alternative to the rigid and arbitrary values dominating mainstream higher education. The challenge of rampant preprofessionalism is still there, and Sarah Lawrence today continues to march to its own drummer. There are no major fields or real grades at Sarah Lawrence, and no subject is out of bounds, including those artsy things that would be strictly extracurricular at other schools. Some students can easily become overwhelmed here, but others find that the combination of close faculty supervision and an endless number of choices brings a kind of personalized education available almost nowhere else.

The quaint thirty-five-acre campus is home to the intertwined English tudor buildings and mansions of converted estates—a setting that might inspire freshmen to take up pen and begin work on a great Victorian novel. Inspired or not, all freshmen must take a writing course—one of the few things that *everyone* is required to do at Sarah Lawrence. Students are "encouraged" to complete work in three of four major subject areas: natural sciences, social science, humanities and creative arts. Other than that, undergraduates write their own academic tickets, with the help of a faculty adviser (who is called a "don" from the Latin for "gift"). Sarah Lawrence students don't have majors. In fact, if you try to pin down what someone's academic concentration is, you may get an answer like "learning how to think, articulate my thoughts and communicate them to others in speech and writing." In each of their four years, students take three yearlong courses (only about one-fourth of the courses are semester-long) and pursue a personal independent study project in coordination with each of these classes. Most students get so involved in their individual projects—or so intimidated by faculty members paying attention to their every move—that they work far beyond requirements. Freshmen meet weekly with their don, and all students must hold biweekly meetings with each of their teachers. Seminar enrollment is strictly limited, and even the largest lecture courses have only around sixty enrollees. Getting into popular classes is a problem for freshmen and sophomores, but the administration assures students of getting at least two of their first three course choices each semester. Special conference courses are available for those who choose to study a topic not covered in the regular curriculum.

The Sarah Lawrence writing program is arguably one of the strongest in the country, and other highly rated fields include visual arts, literature, history, philosophy and women's studies. The strong psychology department offers fieldwork at the college's Early Childhood Center. The premed program, somewhat more structured than other offerings, places a respectable percentage of its graduates into medical schools. The performing arts department, although once indisputably the school's most outstanding program, has undergone many changes and is now either the strongest or the weakest, depending on whom you talk to. Film, however, is considered poor, and computer science is only a byte of what it is slated to become.

Since individual attention is the cornerstone of the Sarah Lawrence educational philosophy, even grading is done personally. Students and teachers give one another written evaluations twice a year, though conventional marks also go on record. The library is a delight, with an area for eating and a pillow room for cozy studying and occasional dozing. Off campus, there are academic years in Oxford, Paris, New York City and Florence.

Some rich and pretentious, most intelligent, and almost all independent, Sarah Lawrence students are not your run-of-the-mill young American men and women. "When someone says, 'You're so Sarah Lawrence,' I take it to mean I'm making some sort of individualistic statement," explains one woman. A third of the students come from New York State—the bulk of those from New York City—and most of the rest are from somewhere along either the East or West Coast. There's also a substantial foreign population, and close to 19 percent of the students are members of minority groups. There is an even split between graduates of private and public schools, and not all students are academic superstars: Fewer than half were in the top fifth of their high school class. The college accepts students without reference to financial need, and its ability to offer aid has increased greatly in the past few years. Still, it is conceivable that a student will not be offered sufficient funds to attend the school. No merit scholarships are awarded and there are no athletic scholarships. Counseling services are particularly suited to the unique student body, prompting one student to exclaim "five shrinks—FREE!" When asked about vocational counseling, she replied, "What's a vocation?"

Seventy-two percent of the students live on campus, where freshmen usually get doubles in the new dorms and upperclassmen usually get singles in the prettier old dorms or college-owned houses. Bronxville is a staid, super-rich suburb, so off-campus students often commute from Westchester County's lower-rent districts or from New York City. The cafeteria cooking is good, and there's also a choice of crunchy natural food from the health food bar or greasy student fare from the college pub. Most dorms also have their own kitchens.

Weekend life often revolves around New York City (a half hour away by train, plus a ten-minute walk to the Bronxville station), but for those who stay there's the pub and plenty of movies, plays and dance and music performances. With the male/female ratio so skewed, SLC's social scene is as complex as its students. It can also be just plain depressing. Observes one: "It's OK to be neurotic, everybody's neurotic. Sarah Lawrence students are competitive about being neurotic." They're certainly not very competitive on athletic playing fields. "I think we have a volleyball team," one senior ventures. While the school does actually field six intercollegiate teams (basketball, volleyball, tennis, softball, soccer and equestrian) nary a "go get 'em" is heard from the students. "SL is not a team sport rah-rah type of place," explains a senior. But students have noticed an increased interest in individual athletics and fitness. One student raves about the school's hydrafitness center and says aerobic classes are always full.

The Sarah Lawrence community, says one member, is not for anyone "dismayed by bohemia, gayness, sarcasm, foreigners, brilliance, fringe lunacy, or any form of mental illness." It is a community where disdain for blatant preprofessionalism is still fashionable, and distance between the academic and the extracurricular is negligible. For students willing to put up with a little excessiveness on the margins, Sarah Lawrence offers an intimate liberal arts education that is becoming increasingly rare in the stodgy upper reaches of academe.

Scripps College, CA—See CLAREMONT COLLEGES

Seton Hall University

South Orange, NJ 07079

Location Suburban	**Applicants** 3,410
Total Enrollment 9,000	**Accepted** 72%
Undergraduates 5,000	**Enrolled** 39%
Male/Female 50/50	**Academics** ★ ★
SAT V/M 450/480	**Social** ☎ ☎
Financial Aid 65%	**Q of L** ● ●
Expense Pr $	**Admissions** (201)761-9332

Named for Mother Elizabeth Seton, the first American sanctified by the Vatican, Seton Hall University is the largest and oldest diocesan college in the country. Following an economic slump in the '70s, the university has staged an energetic comeback by expanding its physical plant and making a bold attempt to upgrade academics. On the other hand, when it comes to the subject of social freedom, it may appear that this still-devoutly Roman Catholic school has entered a time warp. The priests have moved into the residence halls.

Located in the upper-middle-class suburb of South Orange, Seton Hall's ultramodern and Victorian buildings stand shoulder to shoulder on this cozy little fifty-eight-acre campus. The grounds are undergoing "massive relandscaping" to make

Seton Hall, in the words of one administrator, "one of the loveliest campuses in the region" and a welcome sanctuary from nearby New York City. Nevertheless, easy access to the Big Apple means Seton Hall students are able to take advantage of the city through co-op, work/study and internship programs offered in the university's preprofessional departments. These departments tend to be the school's strongest.

Business and nursing earn the highest awards from students. Education gets honorable mention for its in-the-field work opportunities, and communications is noted for its decent TV and radio facilities. The computer science department is growing qualitatively as well as quantitatively, and natural sciences, especially chemistry, provide solid premed foundations. Unfortunately, with the exception of Asian studies, most humanities departments are not so hot, and English and the classics are the biggest disappointments. Religious studies (believe it or not) have been notoriously weak, but the Seminary is moving back onto campus, and the administration has faith this will unify the religion program.

Seton Hall has strengthened the core curriculum for its liberal arts majors and will soon be implementing university-wide requirements. The faculty has a long record of dedicated teaching; many are members of the clergy. "The clergy are cool and in touch with us," says a communications major. Teachers win kudos for being "more concerned with actual learning instead of spitting back information," and the academic pressure is far from taxing. Undergraduates work closely with the campus ministry on a variety of community welfare projects, and students may study in Mexico, China, Israel, Tokyo, Italy or Spain.

Considering Seton Hall's size, students complain a lot about red tape. Registration can be the most trying of experiences, since many courses fill up rapidly. The university uses a random alphabetical process, with freshmen up to bat last, but students note that a heartfelt plea usually persuades professors to expand their class lists. The library is OK for day-to-day needs, but don't plan on intense research or long, into-the-night study hours.

Most students are from New Jersey, and most are Catholics. Just over half graduated from public schools, and almost a fourth come from parochial schools. But that doesn't make for a homogeneous student body. On the contrary, students all agree the SHU student body is a "good cross-section of characters—beach boys, city people, country folk and suburbanites." The university tolerates a wide range of academic achievement, with more than a fifth of the students arriving from the bottom half of their high school class. Sixty percent of the students commute to school, and many hold part-time jobs to pay their way.

Despite a new residence hall that is billed by the administration as "hotel-like," housing is scarce, and fewer than one of every four students live on campus. All dorms are coed, and room assignments are made through the lottery. Residents eat in the Galleon Room on one of the three meal plans, and commuters can eat there on a pay-as-you-go basis. For those who can't stomach any one of the three entrees offered daily, burgers and dogs are found at every dinner.

Students contend SHU is in the best of all possible campus locations. It's an easy bus ride to Newark and the PATH trains for access to Manhattan. Ski slopes lie within an hour's drive, and the Jersey shore is only forty minutes away. The formerly tight parking situation has been eased by the addition of new underground spaces. Still, many commuters and nearly all residential students use public transportation.

Despite increased programming on campus, especially on weekends, the social life at Seton Hall is still something to drive home about. "The exodus begins Friday afternoon at three," one student says. Thanks to New Jersey's drinking age of twenty-one, no alcohol is to be found at most dorm functions. Fraternities don't have houses (they function more as social clubs) but do provide some organized entertainment on campus. The basketball team is a member of the exciting Big East conference, and students turn out faithfully to watch their boys get smeared by Georgetown, St. John's and most of the other schools they come up against. Women sport a more successful basketball squad, as well as good swimming, softball and tennis teams; even so, student support is nonexistent. Intramurals are widely popular. "Seton Hall's 1940 gymnasium was a model for its day; that day has passed," an administrator notes. A new recreation center will soon be open.

The university's caring attitude and focus on self-improvement has caught on among the students. "I love that it's easy to become an active member of the Seton Hall student population," says one senior. "Students have a voice on this campus, and I am proud that I have helped the university grow."

Skidmore College

Saratoga Springs, NY 12866

Location City outskirts	**Applicants** 4,220
Total Enrollment 2,200	**Accepted** 54%
Undergraduates 2,160	**Enrolled** 30%
Male/Female 40/60	**Academics** ★ ★ ★
SAT V/M 530/570	**Social** ☎ ☎ ☎
Financial Aid 50%	**Q of L** ● ● ●
Expense Pr $ $ $ $	**Admissions** (518)587-7569

More than three-quarters of a century after its founding as a women's arts school, Skidmore still excels in the fine and performing arts, but little else remains the same. The college went coed in 1970 and traded its quaint old campus of Victorian splendor in the heart of Saratoga Springs for a modern forty-seven building complex on a six-hundred-acre estate ten minutes from town. Most importantly, the school has revamped its core curriculum and come up with a coherent, interdisciplinary approach to what it means to be an educated person.

Skidmore students describe the new all-college core program as an "imaginative" and relatively painless way to explore the liberal arts. "It's just the intellectual spark we needed," says a junior. Students must now complete a sequence of four liberal studies courses during their freshmen and sophomore years in areas such as "cultural traditions and social change" that cross traditional disciplinary lines. Other requirements include courses in language, writing, quantitative reasoning, non-Western studies, performing arts and lab sciences. Skidmore students of a decade ago would have balked at this rigorous structure, but today's students have embraced the new expectations. "The new requirements have created a more intense academic climate," one senior remarks. "The library is much more crowded than in the past—and the students are studying, not talking."

English, history, government, biology, business and studio art rank as the school's strongest departments. A new fine arts center, which promises to strengthen the theater and music programs, is near completion. The school has matched its liberal arts offerings with an aggressive internship program—one of its few concessions to professionalism. Under the new two-semester system, students may move from a spring internship into a summer job. Another much-praised option is the junior year abroad spent in a Skidmore-run program in France or Spain, or in one of several other countries available through other colleges. And then there's the Skidmore University Without Walls, a nontraditional, nonresidential program offering an unusually flexible and inexpensive route to a bachelor's degree via a combination of course work, internships, independent studies, tutorials and life experiences.

Students at Skidmore typically are well-off and from the Eastern seaboard. Most hail from New York State, the Boston area and Connecticut. More than a decade of extra effort to recruit men has resulted in a male enrollment of more than eight hundred, but prospects for a fifty-fifty ratio seem far in the future. "The men we are getting now are just as good as you'd find elsewhere," observes one student. "The only problem is there's just not enough of them." Students say their peers defy stereotypes. "The athlete is often also politically active and talented in music," reports a biologist.

Skidmore has some of the most luxurious living accommodations in the East. The eight college dorms and the on-campus Scribner Village apartments house over 80 percent of the student body and boast spacious carpeted rooms with air-conditioning and cozy window seats. The dorms are arranged so that four to eight people share a bathroom, and there are lounges and kitchenettes on every floor. All dorms are coed by floor or suite. The favorite rooms—obtained through the lottery—are in the North Quad where freshmen are assured of doubles. Juniors and seniors routinely enjoy singles. With the exception of the students in Scribner Village who prepare their own meals, everyone on campus eats in one of the two dining halls where the meals are above average on the institutional food scale. Falstaff's, the new student-run pub, is fast-becoming a popular change from the dining halls.

With no fraternities or sororities, parties are mostly dorm-generated and well attended only if accompanied by live music. The Trattoria bar is a favorite Friday hangout. One student describes Skidmore's location as "a fantastic synthesis of a charming town and a spectacular countryside"—not that much of an exaggeration if you can handle subzero winter weather. The nearby Adirondacks make the school a backpacker's and skier's heaven. If you can weather the winter, Saratoga, an old summer resort town, offers plenty of civilization for the unreformed urbanite including the Saratoga Performing Arts Center and the country's oldest thoroughbred racetrack. Saratoga is also summer home to the New York City Ballet and the Philadelphia Orchestra.

The sports program has surged ahead from a standing start about a decade ago, finally winning Division III status in 1984. The preppier recreations abound. Men's and women's tennis, golf, riding and—would you believe—polo are the strongest sports, the first three winning regional championships. Intramural sports, especially football, have really caught on, boasting twenty-plus teams, a student commissioner and colorful student cheering sections.

The transition from highly acclaimed women's school to coed liberal arts college has not been an easy one. But Skidmore is giving it the old college try. It continues to win the hearts of its on-the-move students with its flexibility, openness and receptivity to change and grow. As one senior says, "If you want to just float through four years of college, then don't come here. Your peers and Skidmore's curriculum will leave you behind."

507

Smith College

Northampton, MA 01060

Location Small city	**Applicants** 2,140
Total Enrollment 2,500	**Accepted** 61%
Undergraduates 2,500	**Enrolled** 48%
Male/Female N/A	**Academics** ★★★★★
SAT V/M 600/600	**Social** ☎☎☎
Financial Aid 43%	**Q of L** ●●●●
Expense Pr $ $ $ $	**Admissions** (413)584-0515

What do Gloria Steinem and Nancy Reagan have in common? Not much, except that both attended Smith College, a school where students rally for divestment of South African investments by the hundreds yet still sip Friday afternoon tea in the living rooms of their residential houses. A progressive college that is nevertheless steeped in tradition, Smith offers women a unique mix of old-fashioned Seven Sisterhood and 1980s feminism.

Set on a well-manicured stretch of countryside in the foothills of the Berkshire Mountains, Smith's campus is a pleasing blend of clapboard houses and ivy-covered brick buildings. With its own botanical garden and a picturesque "Paradise Pond," Smith's tranquil New England setting belies the intensity of its academic programs. "Smith expects a lot from its women," testifies one sophomore," and its women expect a lot from themselves." Those expectations don't, however, make for cutthroat competition between students; Smith's student-run honor system, which covers everything from exams to library checkout, is widely credited with fostering a community of "warmth and friendliness."

The highly regarded economics program now is the most popular major on campus, although, traditionally, the best and most popular departments at Smith have been art history and government. The Smith Art Museum offers serious students in fine arts a resource usually available only at much larger institutions. Other notable departments include English, history and sociology. Because there are no requirements outside a student's major, women here have more leeway in designing their plan of study than in most colleges. Qualified students may enter the Smith Scholars program and embark on one or two years of independent or extra-college research for full credit. About three hundred Smith undergraduates are enrolled in the Ada Comstock Scholars program for women older than traditional college age.

Although the sciences have traditionally been Smith's weakest suit, they continue to improve. A fledgling computer science major was recently added to the curriculum, and four computer centers are now in operation. Two electron microscopes are available for student use, and through the Five College Consortium* students have access to one of the best radio astronomy facilities in the world. Engineering is available through a five-year program with the University of Massachusetts. New interdisciplinary minors, in areas ranging from neuroscience and public policy, are also an option. In all areas, Smith professors are "enthusiastic, helpful, and always willing to make time for students," a biology major says. One senior says she has shared a meal with three of her four professors every term. Smith's four libraries have almost a million volumes between them, one of the largest collections of any undergraduate school in the country.

Membership in the Five College Consortium—along with UMass, Amherst,

Hampshire and Mount Holyoke—has always been one of Smith's biggest drawing cards. Farther afield, students can study for a semester or two at one of twelve well-known New England colleges through the Twelve College Exchange Program.* Students are also enthusiastic about the opportunity to take part in Smith's well-known junior year away program (which includes an exchange with a university in Shanghai, China, and placements in the Soviet Union and Japan). Students are admitted to these programs by lottery rather than merit, a policy appreciated by everyone.

Despite the stereotypes Smith is saddled with in the outside world, women of all sorts populate the campus. "There are radical feminists and earth mothers, and there are yuppie/preppie/future corporate lawyers," observes one student. Blacks and Hispanics account for 4 and 2 percent of the student body, respectively. Most students are "upwardly motivated women," more than half of whom ranked in the top 10 percent of their high school class. Just over a quarter are natives of Massachusetts and most of the rest are from the Northeast. Political liberalism pervades the campus, which was convulsed in 1986 with heated protests of the college's investments in companies that do business in South Africa. Six months after nearly two hundred student protesters occupied the administration building for six days, Smith's trustee's voted to divest. Smith is need-blind in admissions and provides financial aid to nearly all of its applicants with documented need. If they choose, families have the option of paying for all four years when their daughter first enrolls to avoid costly tuition increases, or paying each semester bill in ten installments. With an endowment in excess of a quarter of a billion dollars, Smith has escaped the financial difficulties that plague many women's colleges today.

Outside of academics, one of Smith's biggest selling points is its extremely popular house system. Students live in a tight-knit residential community that reinforces the supportive climate of the college. Each of the thirty houses, accommodating from sixteen to ninety students, is a self-governing unit, responsible for everything from the menus at meals to weekend parties and concerts. The head resident, appointed by the administration, is the nominal head of the house, but day-to-day affairs are run by the elected dorm council.

The atmosphere is almost unremittingly homey, less that of a sorority than of an extended family. Except for one senior house, classes are not segregated, and freshmen easily mingle with more experienced hands. Upperclassmen are all but guaranteed single rooms if they want them. House living rooms come complete with fireplaces and pianos, and every floor has a kitchenette.

Meals are a variation on the same community theme. "Nothing beats going to breakfast in your pajamas," a senior claims. A buffet replaces the cafeteria line at lunch, and dinner is served family-style at the table. The food, prepared in the dorm's own small kitchens, is highly praised. Thursday dinners, served with tablecloths and candlelight, provide a touch of midweek graciousness to which professors are often invited. In some houses, visitors may be shocked to find cubbyholes with students' own linen napkins and napkin rings, vestiges of Smith's prim and proper past. Incoming freshmen can indicate a preference for size and location of their first house, and switches are possible by entering a lottery. Except for Comstock Scholars, the administration strongly discourages off-campus living but offers two alternatives—cooperatives and an apartment complex—for those unhappy with house life.

In contrast to the convenience of classes or meals, meeting men requires continued and conscientious effort. Nevertheless, "Smith is not a cloister!" insists one woman; indeed, the lure of 2,800 women in one place attracts men by the hundreds every weekend. Each house throws an average of three parties a semester, but while several steps above a typical college beer bash, the atmosphere at these boy-meets-girl functions is not always pleasant. "Sometimes parties can become a meat-market environment," one woman notes. For special weekends a whole fraternity may be invited from Dartmouth or another nearby college, an arrangement that is only slightly more civilized.

If mixers don't suit a student's fancy, there is free bus service to the other four members of the consortium, which between them offer a myriad of social and cultural opportunities. Northampton is a college town of about forty thousand that is surprisingly chic given its location, offering a nice mix of boutiques, shops, and cafés that cater to the collegiate crowd. The New England countryside also has numerous special charms, including ski slopes only ten minutes away. The president reminds Smith students of the beauty of the Berkshires every fall on a traditional "Mountain Day," when classes are canceled. Students are supposed to head for the hills, but, of course, many end up in the library. Boston is two hours away and New York is a three-hour drive.

Smith was the first women's college to join the NCAA and still places a premium on recruiting scholar-athletes. The college averages six all-American swimmers each year, and its crew coach was on the gold medal–winning Olympic team. The soccer, basketball, and cross-country teams are also quite successful, and a new multimillion dollar sports complex includes indoor tennis and track facilities, as well as a riding ring for horse aficionados. Interhouse competitions include everything from kickball to inner-tube waterpolo. For nonathletic types the student government plays an important role in the life of the college, with the president serving as a trustee of the college for two years after graduation. Service Organizations of Smith (SOS) arranges for about 650 students to volunteer for a total of 25,000 hours annually in Northampton and surrounding communities.

If there aren't men around every minute of the day, that suits Smithies just fine. "Smith offers you premium educational opportunities without asking you to be twice as aggressive, twice as smart, etc. as a male counterpart," testifies one political science major. With an intimate housing system that fosters close relationships among all in the college community, Smith is "a great place to learn and grow—and a great place to be a woman."

University of the South —Sewanee

Sewanee, TN 37375

Location Rural	**Applicants** 1,210
Total Enrollment 1,130	**Accepted** 64%
Undergraduates 1,060	**Enrolled** 36%
Male/Female 50/50	**Academics** ★★★
SAT V/M 570/590	**Social** 🐈🐈🐈
Financial Aid 37%	**Q of L** ●●●
Expense Pr $ $	**Admissions** (615)598-5931

You may hear the familiar crooning of "Sewanee, Sewanee, how I love you, how I love you" from the students of this small liberal arts college, but "Sewanee is not a river," students point out; it's a way of life. Perched high above the Tennessee countryside on the Cumberland Plateau, the University of the South (known as Sewanee) is isolated not only by geography but also by attitude. The densely wooded campus of ten thousand acres—that's almost ten acres for each student—provides a haven for values of an older and more aristocratic era and codes of manner and dress that have virtually vanished elsewhere.

The university was founded in 1857 by a group of southern bishops of the Episcopal Church, which has been described as "the Republican party at prayer," and Sewanee might be described as both institutions at study. Its first buildings were destroyed in the Civil War, but classes began in 1868 thanks to generous gifts from English churches and book donations from Oxford and Cambridge. Today, the University of the South's stately Gothic buildings of native mountain sandstone are home to both a college of arts and sciences and a seminary. Owned by twenty-eight dioceses of the Episcopal Church, the university calls its semesters Advent and Easter. The student body is predominantly Christian, but only a rather bland nondenominational introduction to religion course is required. Beyond that, religious values are encouraged but not forced on anyone.

Sewanee's undergraduate curriculum is broad in the classical sense. Students must master a foreign language and take courses in five academic divisions ranging from literature to the sciences. The English department is well known and respected, especially a creative writing program that's due to inherit the $10-million estate of Tennessee Williams after the death of the playwright's sister. *The Sewanee Review* remains one of the nation's foremost literary reviews. History, chemistry, biology, and the vocationally oriented natural resources department are also excellent. Over half of recent graduates in the sciences have gone on to earn doctoral-level degrees. Despite the addition of a new art gallery on campus, most fine arts remain weak. Departments that have only one faculty member include Italian, Russian and geology. For students who wish to specialize in engineering or forestry, joint five-year programs are offered with several universities, and the U.S. Forest Service has a research station on campus. Sewanee also offers an extensive internship program in public affairs and business. Of the many study-abroad opportunities, the summer British studies program at Oxford is especially popular.

Sewanee maintains many old customs and standards that add a quaint veneer to campus life. Typically, women wear dresses and men wear jackets and ties to class. Professors as well as the numerous honor students (members of the Order of Gownsmen) wear black academic gowns to class. An honor code is strictly observed, and lying, cheating or stealing usually results in expulsion. Particularly when the heavy fog rolls in during the winter, Sewanee is not unlike "a bit of Oxford in Tennessee," reflects one junior. However, Sewanee stays atop contemporary issues through the addition of a new women's center, located in a historic Sewanee house. The library facilities are limited, but a loan program with Vanderbilt provides some relief for students. However, "this program is often ineffective due to the time factor involved," explains an English major.

Since faculty members are not pushed to engage in research, they are resolutely dedicated to teaching and advising; some make their homes available for students not living in the dorms. This cordiality persists in the classroom, with introductory-level classes averaging about twenty students and upper-level classes containing as few as six. In fact, one student jokingly complains that "classes are too small, and there's nowhere to hide if you're unprepared." On a per capita basis, the university ranks among the top ten schools for producing Rhodes Scholars. Sewanee's applicants to law and business schools can boast acceptance rates of 93 and 97 percent respectively. Eighty-nine percent of medical school attempts are successful.

Traditional clothes and traditional attitudes go together here. A substantial number of students are socialites from wealthy southern families, while "some proud Yankees" represent New York, New Jersey, Pennsylvania and New England. The student population is 95 percent white, and half of the students identify themselves as Episcopalians. "I will benefit from the Episcopalian old-boy network," one woman wagers. Southern prep is the predominant look, although it has a bohemian edge among the many who, according to one student, "have fuzzy sweaters and fuzzy hair; play hackeysack; and own a puppy, Dead tapes and a mountain bike."

Thirty-seven percent of the students receive need-based aid. Sewanee also awards Wilkins Scholarships of up to $5,000 without regard to need to outstanding students, along with National Merit Scholarships ranging from $250 to the total amount of demonstrated need. A parent loan plan enables families with incomes between $30,000 and $75,000 to borrow up to $5,000 a year for four years at 10 percent interest.

Since the town of Sewanee is almost synonymous with the campus, it's difficult to live off campus without becoming a bush person. Almost all the dorms are single sex, and there are three language houses. Most of the housing is comfortable and spacious, including two renovated inns and a former hospital. "Not only are they architecturally charming, but the plumbing works," remarks a contented denizen. Honor students get first crack at housing, and juniors and seniors may get single rooms. Everyone eats in one of two dining facilities, where the food ranges from "bland" to "horrible."

This school's one concession to populist thinking is its policy that virtually no one gets cut from varsity sports squads; "ordinary students make up the teams," a Latin major says. As a result, "football games are a social event," a sophomore reports, "even when we rot." There is growing administrative and peer support for women's athletics, especially field hockey and soccer. There is also a strong intramural program for all breeds of Sewanee Tigers.

The social life provided by the eleven national fraternities and five local sororities, to which almost two-thirds of the students belong, dominates. Fortunately, nonmembers are also welcome to parties. Sewanee's reputation as a party school has died down somewhat, but parties are still not limited to Friday and Saturday nights. The campus pub is the central spot for socializing when there are no frat parties.

The town offers a Hardee's and a few gas stations. "Sewanee is centrally isolated," claims an English major—and students must trek some fifteen miles down the mountain to reach Egg McMuffins and "civilization." "Most students see it as a sanctuary from the real world," explains one junior, but some students complain of boredom. "It's hard to meet a variety of people," says one. On the other hand, the beautiful rural setting—complete with lakes, waterfalls and even caves and caverns—makes outdoor activities popular. The Sewanee Outing Club provides endless opportunities for students to hike, rappel, kayak or canoe together. Students who occasionally feel a need for the real world can go to nearby Chattanooga (fifty miles) or Nashville (just under a hundred miles). Even Atlanta is within reach for a weekend trip, but there's practically no public transportation available.

For the most part, though, students are in no rush to get away. They seem content with their school's way of life, its concern for safeguarding the past and its gorgeous natural setting. The University of the South's isolation can be stifling, but it can also translate into a feeling of closeness. One man, who, like many of his fellow students, was accepted by several schools larger in reputation and size than Sewanee, explains, "The more relaxed and romantic side of me won out, and I came to Sewanee."

University of South Carolina

Columbia, SC 29208

Location Center city
Total Enrollment 22,690
Undergraduates 14,550
Male/Female 48/52
SAT V/M 450/490
ACT 21
Financial Aid 31%
Expense Pub $ $

Applicants 6,160
Accepted 81%
Enrolled 46%
Academics ★ ★ ★
Social 🐘 🐘 🐘
Q of L ● ● ●
Admissions (803)777-7700

The University of South Carolina at Columbia tries to be all things to all people. It offers a professional and technical as well as a liberal arts education, and its seventeen schools and colleges offer more than one hundred bachelor's degree programs. Its academic repertoire ranges from university 101, which teaches the basic "intellectual and social survival skills" of college life, to the rigorous honors program known as South Carolina College. Many students actively appreciate the rich diversity of academic opportunity, while others are here mainly for what one senior describes as "just plain fun."

Carolina's large modern campus is located right in the heart of Columbia, a city of 400,000 and capital of the state. Government buildings and downtown businesses are all within walking distance of the campus and serve as fertile hunting ground for internship opportunities. The temperature rarely goes below 40°F in the winter, and, as depicted by a biology major, "the landscaping is chock full of dogwoods and grass woven into a metropolitan area." Azaleas and wisteria are abundant, and the old section of the campus, including the glorious oak-lined Horseshoe, has several historic buildings that date back to the school's founding in 1801.

The university's strong preprofessional offerings nearly mirror the job market. The computer science department, with its new computer service center, and the engineering program, which will soon be housed in a spacious new facility, are particularly good. Students in the huge marine science program enjoy a splendid seventeen-thousand-acre facility, about an hour from the main campus, the use of which was given to the school by the daughter of Bernard Baruch. The College of Journalism is the beneficiary of an excellent film library, complete with old Movietone news reels. Much of the economy of South Carolina is tied to foreign trade, and fittingly, the university has developed top-notch international studies programs, some of them geared to future diplomats and international businessmen. The college of education attracted national attention by initiating a five-year program for secondary school teachers. Nursing is another college in transition: The two-year technical program has been phased out, while a doctoral program is now offered. The programs in business administration, pharmacy and hotel, restaurant and tourism win plaudits from students.

Among the liberal arts, English is one of the best departments in the region, and the natural sciences are strong. History and geography are also recommended. While the performing arts have never been outstanding at South Carolina, the administration tells of "an impressive renaissance" underway in this area. The construction of a

$15-million center for the arts and a new cooperative education program with the Shakespeare Theatre at the Folger in Washington, D.C., are two testaments of this rebirth. The foreign language and philosophy departments continue to receive criticism from students.

Many classes are predictably large, and freshmen should not be surprised to find themselves taught by graduate students in "microphone classes" of several hundred where they are known only by their social security numbers. Student relationships with faculty members can develop, one senior explains, "but the student has to make the first move." The addition of a spacious, well-stocked underground library complements the university's impressive library system. Hours are on the short side, however, and the main library closes on Saturday nights. "I think that's stupid," complains one honors college student. Average work loads vary from one to six hours daily, depending on the degree program and the current fortunes of the Gamecocks on the gridiron. Professionally oriented students, whose access to upper-division courses in their major depends on their GPA, tend to be more serious than their liberal arts counterparts.

Carolina, experiencing a recent rise in popularity, has changed its admissions process from rolling to closed. Students apply to separate programs, and for some departments such as engineering, business and journalism, the necessary SAT scores and rank are much higher than for general admission. Honors college hopefuls should have SAT scores of 1200 and be in the top 10 percent of their high school class. The student body overwhelmingly hails from South Carolina public schools, about half from the top fifth of their high school class. Fourteen percent are black, and just 18 percent are out-of-staters, mostly "Yanks" who gravitate toward the nationally known journalism, business and science programs. Diversity can't help showing up in a school of twenty-three thousand, so Carolina has contingents of "preps, beat generation throwbacks, punk rockers, stuffed shirts, extreme conservatives with counterparts on the political left." But overall, admits a nursing student, "students are basically conservative; we have few riots or demonstrations."

Need-based financial aid is available with equal priority to residents and nonresidents who meet the April 15 deadline. Besides the expected bundle of athletic scholarships (235, about a third for women), the university hands out over thirteen hundred scholarships annually to the academically talented, without regard to financial need. Some awards are restricted to state residents who fill out special applications; most students admitted to Carolina are automatically considered for other scholarships. Amounts range up to full tuition for students "who predict at least a 3.0 on a 4.0 scale."

The advice to prospectives: Apply before Christmas if you want a room on campus. Everything here works on a first-come, first-served basis, and with the tight housing situation, freshmen as well as upperclassmen must compete for space. The best rooms in the stately old Horseshoe section of campus cost considerably more than one-room, two-bed arrangements in dorms with bathrooms in the hall—"comfort depends on the amount you pay." Just about every choice of living space is available, and the surest way to beat the housing system is to get into the honors college, which entitles you to some of the best rooms. Just over half the students live off-campus in apartments that are relatively easy to find. On-campus dining options are numerous: "We have a choice of everything from regular cafeteria food to a sub shop, baked potato bar, Mexican food bar, frozen yogurt and a pizza delivery service," one budding restaurant critic explains. There are the all-you-can-eat meal plans and "cashcards" of various denominations.

Fall weekends center on football ("We love our Gamecocks!"), winter weekends on basketball, and spring weekends can be spent at Myrtle Beach, three hours away. For hiking, skiing, camping or just getting away, mountains are located just four hours to the north. Athletic victories and losses are equally good excuses for setting up weekend-long parties on campus, but a raise in the drinking age (to twenty-one) and strict campus policies regarding alcohol have cramped the traditional Carolina style. "Campus life is readjusting," one student explains, and drinking is now "a lot more discreet." One staunchly independent senior claims that "the Greek system is detested and considered far too exclusive by non-Greeks," and only a small percentage of the campus community joins the fraternities and sororities, but these organizations tend to initiate a large percentage of the extracurricular activities. Black students have a separate but equally active Greek system. Club sports have been eclipsed by the varsity teams, but intramurals are still strong. And with more than two hundred political, religious, social clubs and service clubs on campus, everyone can find something to get involved with.

Like other state universities with big-time athletic programs and large graduate schools, the University of South Carolina can sometimes make its undergraduates feel a little lost or neglected. The honor's college offers a supportive intellectual population within the larger university community, but it's not easy to get into. Students who aren't ready to take the initiative, "who don't know how to get themselves involved" would be wise to look elsewhere. But students who enjoy the lively sports-oriented collegiate life and are ready to take responsibility for their academic involvement, or lack thereof, may find a lot to like in Carolina.

University of Southern California

Los Angeles, CA 90089

Location Center city	**Applicants** 10,940
Total Enrollment 30,930	**Accepted** 68%
Undergraduates 16,590	**Enrolled** 43%
Male/Female 57/43	**Academics** ★ ★ ★
SAT V/M 480/540	**Social** 🐗 🐗 🐗 🐗
Financial Aid 41%	**Q of L** ● ● ●
Expense Pr $ $ $ $	**Admissions** (213)743-5122

Whether they're planning to join the two hundred-plus USC graduates who have participated in the Olympic games, or just planning to join daddy down at the firm, everyone at USC seems to be going for the gold in some way. As the colors of their credit cards and suntanned arms prove, many are already there. University of Spoiled Children, is how one freshman interprets her school's acronym. And just because Porsches and BMWs glitter in every aisle of the student parking lot doesn't mean similar levels of quality and excellence can't be reached in the classroom—not to mention on the playing fields or in the career placement office.

Appropriately located within a discus throw of the Coliseum where the 1984 summer Olympics were held, USC is a mere ten-minute drive from the heart of Los Angeles. An immaculate mix of traditional ivy-type and modern structures, the campus provides a richly foliaged and well-shaded refuge from the surrounding city asphalt and

515

glaring Southern California sun. As the oldest independent teaching and research university in the West, USC built its reputation on excellent professional schools of medicine, law, business and engineering. Successful alumni have all but run L.A.'s private sector for the past century, and their loyalty to the school is as fierce as its rivalry with UCLA. "You're a Bruin for four years but you're a Trojan for life," is how the saying goes, and for USC students it translates into the promise of many open doors in the professional world. "USC has extremely strong alumni ties—a plus when it comes to looking for jobs after graduation. The school's reputation for turning out successful professionals is too good to pass up," says one prelaw student.

USC has recently made efforts to push undergraduate academic programs into the same spotlight as the professional schools. Drama and music now shine as brightly as law, business and engineering. With a little help from its friends Steve Spielberg, George Lucas and Johnny Carson, who made possible the recent addition of a high-tech, state-of-the-art new cinema/TV complex, USC is able to boast a stellar cinema/ television department. Journalism, international relations and communication are also good undergraduate bets, as is the fine Thematic Option honors program, which takes the place of general education requirements for outstanding freshmen who pass the school's skill level exams in math, foreign language and composition. The Traumatic Option, as some students call it, is one of the most pressured and rewarding paths through USC, although premeds, business majors and honors students in other departments also can be found closing the libraries. (Of course, closing one of the sixteen libraries here is no major achievement, since most are only open until 5 P.M. on Fridays and Saturdays and midnight during the week.) Foreign languages, math, political science and the freshman writing program are areas most often cited as needing improvement.

Professors at USC are expected to publish, but they are said to be reasonably dedicated to teaching and accessible to undergraduates. General education requirements vary with the schools but are seldom difficult. Getting into courses is also relatively easy, but if you want to drop or add, get ready to endure the longest of this school's long lines. "Be prepared to read a James Michener novel in the process," one man warns. Students can't help but acquire skills needed to survive in the real world as they hustle to find housing and untangle financial aid snarls. Co-op programs and internship options in nearly all majors are available, as are USC-run abroad programs in England, France and Spain.

Students at USC tend to be hardworking, outgoing preprofessionals who know what they want. Affluent, conservative, Reagan-supporting Southern Californians seem to predominate but actually the majority of students are on some form of financial aid, and extremely high minority and foreign student enrollments give the campus an interesting flair. Academic backgrounds run the gamut, with about a third of the students from the top tenth of their high school classes. As the Olympic legacy suggests, some of the best athletes in the country are found on this campus, and nearly 240 of them receive at least a little financial incentive to flex their muscles for USC. More than two thousand academic scholarships ranging from $1,000 to $10,000 are awarded annually without regard to need.

Dorms, both coed and single sex, are large, comfortable, well maintained, and, luxurious beyond the wildest dreams of most American undergraduates. Swimming pools, tennis courts, carpeting, air-conditioning, dishwashers—you name the convenience and you'll find it in a USC dorm. But you pay for what you get, for housing—on or off campus—is expensive. About 20 percent of the students live off campus, but since the surrounding area of Los Angeles is neither particularly attractive nor safe, this usually requires a car. Dining halls are equally upscale, serving croissants, frozen yogurt and gourmet coffee.

Students complain about their location in the heart of L.A.'s low-income area. "You don't walk alone off campus," assures a sophomore, "unless you are either very big, brave, dangerous or stupid." But during the day students see their immediate surroundings in a different light. Many students get involved in the numerous campus volunteer groups reaching into this minority community through food and toy drives and special education programs. And how can anyone complain too much with L.A. just minutes away—Westwood, Chinatown. The entertainment possibilities are endless. Students can also get to any one of several beaches in twenty minutes, or be at a ski slope in an hour and a half.

Back on campus, sports are the biggest thing going. Football reigns supreme at O. J. Simpson's and Marcus Allen's alma mater, but there are a myriad of other sports to patronize or play. Tennis and basketball are the winningest of the women's squads. And with the McDonald Swim Stadium (the hundred-meter swimming and fifty-meter diving pools built for the '84 Games), lots of USC students are in the swim. Socially, fraternities and sororities exert an influence beyond what their numbers indicate. Only about a quarter of students are officially Greek, and about half that group actually live in houses on "the row." But a large number of students show up at the frequent fraternity bashes. The university's film program shows first-run movies twice a week at below-movie-theater rates. The daily student newspaper is an institution, and student-run radio stations, speaker's series, clubs and other organizations seem to satisfy just about every possible extracurricular yen.

USC is a place where everything seems large and prosperous, and getting to be more so all the time. It has a dedicated administration that is keeping academics on the upswing, and an energetic student body that "lives the good life," concentrating simultaneously on studies, careers, parties and football in equal measure.

Southern Methodist University

Dallas, TX 75275

Location Suburban	**Applicants** 4,000
Total Enrollment 8,000	**Accepted** 68%
Undergraduates 5,800	**Enrolled** 42%
Male/Female 50/50	**Academics** ★ ★ ★
SAT V/M 525/575	**Social** 🏛 🏛 🏛 🏛
Financial Aid 48%	**Q of L** ● ● ●
Expense Pr $ $	**Admissions** (214)692-2058

A football team does not a good university make. At least that's the greatest hope of those at Southern Methodist University, the recipient of the harshest penalty in the history of the National Collegiate Athletic Association. The SMU football program is benched for two years because boosters gave too much boost—cash, cars and condos—to the players. Much to the dismay of this southwesternly sweet, public-relations-oriented university, it has become the national symbol of higher education's preoccupation with maintaining big-time college athletic teams at any price.

But who's to say that this most embarrassing punishment is not a blessing in disguise? The two-year absence of football may be just the ticket SMU needs to finally show off its intellectual muscle, which some believe has been overshadowed by Mustang Mania for too long. As one student puts it: "I didn't come here because of the football team; I want to learn."

Totally removed from the glitter and glitz of downtown Dallas, SMU resides in "The Bubble," the local term applied to the plush, tranquil suburb of Highland Park. One student describes it as "Beverly Hills without the palm trees—just beautiful mansions, beautiful cars and the so-called beautiful people." In keeping with the tone of its surrounding neighborhood, the park-like campus is rich with trees, flower beds, fountains, and well-kept and well-watered lawns. The red-brick Georgian architecture has an eastern-institutional feel, and appropriately enough, a beautiful Methodist church is a prominent structure at the campus entrance. Although Methodist is its middle name, the university is "tied to the Church only on paper," according to one senior who has yet to meet a Methodist classmate.

SMU's fine academic reputation, though somewhat obscured, is no accident. The opportunity for a first-rate education does exist. All students spend two years in the Dedman College of Arts and Sciences participating in the Common Educational Experience. As the mainstay of the undergraduate curriculum, these requirements allow students to choose courses from among four categories—English literature, social and political institutions, religious and philosophical thought, and sciences and technology—before selecting their majors. At the end of their sophomore year, those students who get hooked on the liberal arts can stay in Dedman College for their major program, but most venture across campus to the Meadows School of the Arts, the recently expanded Cox School of Business or the College of Engineering and Applied Sciences.

The best that SMU has to offer is found in its art school, where Bob Hope pops in from time to time to teach a course in comedy. The dance programs, especially jazz, are top-rate, and the school's contributions to the art world are dazzling. Theater is prospering, due in part to some big gifts in recent years in the arts and sciences, but English is the standout department, partially because of SMU's nationally acclaimed literary festival that brings well-known poets and authors (like Edward Albee, Joseph Heller and Margaret Atwood) to campus to give readings, participate in classes and be wined and dined by awestruck aspiring writers. History, art history, and anthropology are also popular and have fine professors, but students consider math and natural sciences weak links. The business school offers its students some strong programs and, because of its extremely close ties to the Dallas business community, a guaranteed job for those who wish to stay in town after graduation. The journalism program is up-and-coming, but the communications department as a whole "should be nuked," according to one student.

On the basis of past academic achievement, students can qualify for a three-year program, and internships are available in business, journalism and theater. The engineering school has a cooperative education option. Travel programs to France, Spain, England and Austria are available. The library has more than a million volumes, but an economics student reports that it is somewhat of a "scam joint (a place to scam out members of the opposite sex), and one must retreat to the stacks to get any work done." Classes are small, and students have "complete and total access to all profs, at all levels," attests a pleased political scientist. The academic attitude is fairly relaxed—at the beginning of the semester anyway.

Who goes to SMU? "If you've got a BMW, Mercedes or a Porsche, you will fit right in—but only if your Rolex is genuine," says one social critic. A classmate adds, "A conservative and worldly person does well at SMU. And it helps to be extremely good-looking." Students from private schools and large cities set the tone of the campus, and blacks and Hispanics are few. What variety there is comes from the artsy types drawn by SMU's strong performing and fine arts programs. More than half the students are from outside Texas, primarily from the East and Midwest. Chicagoans and Ohioans, especially, seem to be attracted by the warm climate. The university tries to meet the financial need of all who apply. Besides hundreds of athletic scholarships (legitimate and illegitimate), SMU provides a large number of merit scholarships to academically talented freshmen ranging up to full tuition.

Freshmen and upperclassmen live in separate quads; the freshman dorms are primarily single sex, and singles are a rare commodity for everyone. Campus housing is mandatory for all noncommuting freshmen. Several nearby generic-looking apartment complexes (nicknamed the Honeycomb Hideouts) are populated mostly by SMU-ers, but fast-rising rents are forcing more upperclassmen to try their luck in the room lottery. Coed dorms are available, but those with the worst numbers get stuck in freshman dorms or in the "God quad," i.e., theology school dorms. There are two completely renovated dining halls, and one happy Manhattanite raves, "They look just like New York delis!" A large portion of upperclassmen dine at the fraternity and sorority houses or else try their digestive durability at the multitudinal Tex-Mex fast-food outlets.

The Greek system, to which half the students belong, provides more than a housing option; it is the mainstay of SMU's social life. According to one member of the Interfraternity Council: "I can assure you that the phrase 'Greek or Geek' holds true at SMU." The pressure to go Greek is heavy, since "students outside the system often find themselves excluded," and competition to get into the "elite" organizations is stiff. For those old enough to get in, or clever enough to sneak in, visits to the plentitude of bars and dance clubs that line Greenville Avenue are "almost as much a part of the routine as going to class." The SMU super party school image, though, has been tainted by the rise in the Texas drinking age, and more students are realizing that there are social alternatives to passing out on a soggy fraternity house floor. The SMU theater department puts on several productions each year, and Dallas boasts a fantastic new art museum, a highly touted symphony, and big-time events like the Texas State Fair. The Avon and World Circuit tennis tournaments are also held here.

Despite the heavy blow to the football program, those unsinkable SMU fans continue to cheer for the university's remaining teams. Unfettered by distasteful imbroglios, the tennis, swimming and track teams are all powerhouses. Intramurals are also popular, and SMU's Dedman Center for Lifetime Sports has every conceivable facility. Extracurricular activities tend toward a strong and vocal student government, student-run fund-raisers, symposiums, and volunteer work.

At this institution more widely known for its "Pony Express" than anything else, mere memories of Saturday afternoon football games will have to suffice for the next two years. And with the Mustangs temporarily sacked, perhaps SMU will decide to demonstrate its competitive edge in the academic fields rather than the Cotton Bowl.

University of South Florida (including New College)

Tampa, FL 33620

Location City outskirts
Total Enrollment 29,460
Undergraduates 19,970
Male/Female 46/54
SAT V/M 530/480
Financial Aid 20%
Expense Pub $ $

Applicants 5,770
Accepted 58%
Enrolled 54%
Academics ★ ★ ★
Social ☎ ☎ ☎ ☎
Q of L ● ● ●
Admissions (813)974-3350

There is no middle ground at the University of South Florida. It's either bust your brains for three and a half years in the small, free-wheeling New College for honors students in Sarasota, or enter one of the programs on the main campus in Tampa, where the academic pressure is casual, good grades are much easier to come by than good courses and a main ingredient of survival is a bottle of Coppertone.

Of USF's special resources none is more impressive than New College, which has to rank as one of the best kept secrets in higher education. The campus of over one hundred acres embraces twenty-eight mostly modern buildings, three historic mansions on Sarasota Bay, classrooms with teleconference capabilities, and a comprehensive media center. Formerly a four-year private liberal arts college, New College's merger with USF in 1975 guaranteed its future financial security, and produced one of the most complete high-quality learning environments with a public school price tag in the country. Limited to five hundred honors students, New College, with its own admissions staff and academic standards, offers a flexible, challenging, and personalized education. Applicants tend to have SAT scores around 1200 and must complete both the standard USF and special New College applications. Students, about half of whom are from out of state, work out a contract with their adviser each semester and receive written evaluations of their work. They may major in traditional disciplines or a whole division, like social science; or they may opt for any number of interdepartmental combinations. Graduation requirements include three independent study projects and a thesis. Psychology, math, literature, history and political science are particularly strong.

Most New College students live in a group of dorms set around a courtyard of palm trees and green grass, a convenient site for most of their parties. With such a small student body, everyone tends to socialize together, and a strong and welcoming sense of community flourishes. Small size is the school's greatest asset, yet it's also a limiting factor since professors, while accessible, are not plentiful. With only two professors per department, the narrowness of their specializations can become a problem. Yet it's a small sacrifice considering the personal attention available to students in the close community. Because it's not yet fifteen years old and hasn't become widely known, USF's New College is starving for good students—and that's a tip you might want to follow up on.

USF's Tampa facility is located on the outskirts of the city in a typically Floridian setting: lots of sand, brown grass and palm trees. The buildings are described by one student as "nondescript, cement blocks" and the architectural style, in the words of another student, is "a prison motif, circa 1965."

Business is the most popular of the eighty-five undergraduate programs. Engineering and fine arts, particularly dance and theater, are also strong. USF's programs in computer science and the natural sciences are on the rise, and the bequest of a collection of 850,000 butterflies (complete with a building and library to house them), brings the school's Lepidoptera holdings to 1.5 million specimens. The St. Petersburg campus, located on a deepwater port, boasts an excellent marine science program. The students' loudest criticism is directed at the liberal arts and mass communications programs.

USF provides several opportunities for off-campus study: semester exchanges with other American colleges, a humanities and art term in New York City, a cooperative education program and study-abroad programs in several countries, including Colombia, Spain and Yugoslavia. The main library on the Tampa campus is not particularly well stocked, but few students seem to care. Though the grinds (usually students in engineering or the natural sciences) put in at least two to three hours a day, most students don't spend much time at the library. A core curriculum in the liberal arts is required of all students, but the biggest problem on campus is getting into popular courses, such as upper-level business, science labs and freshman English. Professors are generally accessible and helpful; counseling services are just adequate.

Of the students on the main campus, close to 90 percent are Floridians. Minorities make up just more than 10 percent of the student body, which is about evenly divided between blacks and Hispanics. Two thousand transfers enroll each year and a good proportion of the undergraduates are returning to school after a few years in the working world. "Most students here are business majors who believe they will eventually work for Fortune 500 companies regardless of the fact that they are unable to read or write," explains an American studies student. Shorts and T-shirts are the campus uniform, and attendance is taken at the beach on Saturdays. The university helps underwrite the students in financial need, but those who don't make the February 1 application deadline are usually wait-listed. About five hundred merit scholarships are available to outstanding students, and 140 men's and women's athletic scholarships are offered in more than a dozen sports.

Unlike New College, USF–Tampa is a commuter school, with only one-fourth of the undergraduates living in college housing. Dorms, named after the first twelve letters of the Greek alphabet, are scarce, and students who don't get spaces one semester have priority next term. Freshmen should apply for rooms as soon as they are accepted. Coed and single-sex options are available. Nearby off-campus housing is "either slummy or too expensive" and requires the same advance booking as the dorms, so many students are dispersed around Tampa and its environs. The fraternities and sororities do not have houses, but students hint that this situation may change in the near future. Meal plans are offered to both resident and off-campus students, and there are an endless number of fast-food options close by. "People rarely even stay on campus for lunch," reports a frequent Big Mac attack victim.

Southern Florida's weather can make a body sluggish, but students who can barely drag themselves to classes turn surprisingly lively when the sun goes down. USF social life centers on beer kegs and Greek activities. Though the fraternity and sorority population is still quite small, it is in to be a Greek, and those who don't join still show up at their parties. There is no football team, but basketball packs fans into the modern sports arena known as the Sun Dome, and soccer is also popular. Tennis and volleyball are the winningest women's sports. There are also indoor and outdoor pools—with strong swimming teams to match—a golf course, and an extensive intramural program that includes thirty-five volleyball teams.

USF, in short, has something for everyone. The bright, motivated student wanting a personal and "alternative" approach to a college education can head for New College. And those searching for technical and preprofessional offerings that won't break their backs can head up the coast a bit and settle in at the Tampa campus. Few public universities have managed to combine both these options in a single institution. USF has pulled if off.

Southampton College, NY—See LONG ISLAND UNIVERSITY

Southwestern University

Georgetown, TX 78626

Location Suburban	**Accepted** 77%
Total Enrollment 1,120	**Enrolled** 54%
Undergraduates 1,120	**Academics** ★ ★ ★
Male/Female 44/56	**Social** 🐿 🐿 🐿
SAT V/M 510/550	**Q of L** ● ● ●
Financial Aid 51%	**Admissions** (800)252-3166 in Texas,
Expense Pr $	(800)531-6068 out-of-state
Applicants 730	

Southwestern University is fond of calling itself the Harvard of the South. The slogan is a Texas-size overstatement, but it does underscore this diminutive school's drive to establish and maintain the highest level of combined academic and preprofessional excellence.

Southwestern's campus is, as one student puts it, "quiet and serene, with lots of trees and a minimum of concrete." Most buildings are constructed of native limestone in a turn-of-the-century, Spanish-style architecture, and "the setting can be described as a 'hometown' atmosphere." Southwestern is Texas' oldest university, founded in 1840, only four years after the Alamo fell, when Methodist settlers obtained a charter from the Republic of Texas. True to its original mission, Southwestern still seeks to foster value-centered education, and it has managed to maintain its reputation as one of the best small liberal arts college notched into the lustrous Sun Belt.

Although it may appear limited in comparison to the colossus thirty miles to the south—the University of Texas in Austin—Southwestern boasts some impressive near-perfect grad school placement rates of applicants into law, business and music schools and a 70 percent acceptance rate at medical schools. The student/faculty ratio is less than fourteen to one, and there are more than twenty different major programs in the humanities and natural and social sciences. In addition, bachelor degrees are conferred in music, fine arts, education, business administration and applied science. Strong liberal arts departments include English, history, psychology, sociology, biology and chemistry, and the professionally oriented music offerings are excellent. Students claim the real excitement on campus is found in the growing-by-leaps-and-bounds business department. According to an accounting major, "business course offerings are expanding, and the academic rigor within the department has greatly increased." Computer science is reported to be another up-and-coming department, and computer literacy is a graduation requirement. Physical education, foreign languages and art need improvement, and the political science department receives mixed reviews.

Southwestern's hefty endowment has enabled it to become competitive in attracting top faculty. Professors are committed to teaching rather than research, and the university keeps classes intimate. "Where else can you attend a lecture by a professor and then talk about it with him for another hour outside of class?" asks a political science major. Generally, the academic climate is rigorous. Southwesterners do take their academic studies seriously, and staying in to study is a legitimate excuse every once in a while. But students stress that "this is not Egghead U.—you are in competition with no one but yourself." The library is less than inspiring, although completion of construction that will double its size is in sight. In the meantime, serious research often requires a half-hour trip to Austin to use UT's excellent facilities.

Each spring, classes are canceled for three days for the Brown Symposium, an annual series of discussions and seminars organized around a single topic, such as genetic engineering, computers in everyday life or the achievements of a single scholar or artist like composer Benjamin Britten. A semester-long seminar relating to the subject of a symposium is just one requirement for graduation; students must also complete a forty-two-hour general education program that includes foundation courses in English composition and mathematics as well as perspective courses in various disciplines and a capstone project within their major. Interested students can take advantage of 3-2 engineering or medical technology programs with various schools or study-abroad opportunities in England, France, Austria, Mexico, Greece or the Orient.

Although the increase in numbers of out-of-state and foreign students reflects the administration's vigorous recruitment policy, the majority of Southwestern students remain middle class, white and Texan—with large numbers from the metropolitan areas of Houston, Dallas and San Antonio.

The social and political climate is generally conservative—"Students are career-minded but not blindly practical," observes a philosophy major—and the size and location mean that the place can be a "gossip machine." Southwestern attempts to meet the demonstrated financial need of all students. In addition, more than a fifth of the student body receives merit scholarships, awarded regardless of need and ranging from $1,000 to $7,000. Forty-eight athletic scholarships are awarded equally to men who excel in basketball and baseball and to women who shine in volleyball and basketball. Out-of-state students should also note that tuition here is markedly less than at institutions of similar quality in other parts of the country.

Since Georgetown is a smallish town (pop. 10,000), there is little in the way of off-campus housing available. No problem: Students seem quite content living in the school's coed and single-sex dorms. And a new dormitory for women, Mabee Hall, was recently completed. Comments about the food service are equivocal. "The dining facilities are nice, which sometimes compensates for what is served inside—the food is often good, but just not as often as it is mediocre," one man comments. Okay. Various meal plans are available, and for variety, students can eat in the student union snack bar or one of the frats.

"Goin' south" to Austin (a half-hour drive) seems a natural bent for Southwestern students, and this southern connection provides a veritable wonderland of time-enriching and time-wasting activities to those with wheels: movies, honky-tonks, concerts, Tex-Mex restaurants, shopping, not to mention the Texas legislature, which some consider to be the best show around. Georgetown itself, "where the townspeople and the school enjoy something of a cheerful cohesiveness," is a lovely area and especially beautiful in spring when blooming wildflowers cover the hillsides. There are lakes, hills, and miles and miles of well-kept highway just beyond the campus; "going for a drive" has real meaning in central Texas.

When they're not on the road, many Southwestern students rely on Greek organizations for campus social life. "These are not the animal houses that exist on other campuses," emphasizes a senior. Intramurals are "one of the most important aspects of SU," a junior notes, and a variety of other extracurriculars are available. Because football is not offered (yes, this school is in Texas), other intercollegiate sports have an opportunity to flourish. Baseball and basketball have won championships in recent years.

Southwestern is the kind of personalized university that makes students feel right at home. And for those interested in a solid liberal arts orientation, this is not a bad place to hang your hat for four years. "Students who are people-oriented, who enjoy interpersonal communication and who like to feel they are an important part of the community are happiest here," says one content junior who is all three of the above.

Spelman College, GA—See ATLANTA UNIVERSITY CENTER

Stanford University X

Stanford, CA 94305

Location Suburban	**Applicants** 16,140
Total Enrollment 13,270	**Accepted** 16%
Undergraduates 6,570	**Enrolled** 62%
Male/Female 55/45	**Academics** ★ ★ ★ ★ ★
SAT V/M N/A	**Social** 🐘 🐘 🐘 🐘
Financial Aid 45%	**Q of L** ● ● ● ● ●
Expense Pr $ $ $ $	**Admissions** (415)723-2091

Leland Stanford Jr.'s University provides a quality of education that rivals the best in the East with a quality of life that is California's own. It's a sun-drenched version of prestigious education that is reaching new heights of popularity. The end of the baby boom may mean a decline in the number of college-age students, but at Stanford the number of applications for admissions continues to climb to record highs, along with the academic aspirations of its administrators. Not too long ago Stanford set out to become the first university anywhere to raise $1 billion, a move that undoubtedly has Leland Stanford, the nineteenth-century railroad magnate who established the university in the name of his son, smiling from his grave.

Palm trees, low Mediterranean-style buildings with red roofs and literally thousands of high school valedictorians wearing sandals and riding expensive ten-speed bikes combine to give Stanford an ambience more like a country club than a college. Despite all the outward mellowness, Stanford students are as achievement oriented as they come, and a preprofessional attitude pervades much of the student body. Chemical engineering draws a small, intense group, while the scores of potential electrical engineers spend their college careers "holed up in LOTS," the Low Overhead Time-Sharing computer facility. The "physics tank" reigns as the ugliest building on campus, but the instruction that goes on inside is excellent. Chemistry is an extremely popular department, although, says one student, "it is more geared to weeding people out for medical school than toward helping and encouraging them to understand the subject." An unusual major in human biology proves the sciences are not all drudgery; it combines the biological and behavioral sciences and gets rave reviews. Another distinctive major, product design, combines arts and engineering and teaches students how to create perfect syrup dispensers and toys that will last all through toddlerhood.

Classes are smaller outside the sciences, especially in the humanities, but there is no corresponding decline in quality. English, psychology, political science and history are among the most respected departments. Communications "used to be a joke," says one student, although all agree that renovation of the communications building and addition of state-of-the-art television, radio, photography and typesetting equipment has made a big difference. "It's as well equipped as ABC in San Francisco," says one woman. The undergraduate major in feminist studies requires students to take an introductory core of courses and then focus on a particular topic such as Women in Language and Symbol. In terms of the number of majors, economics is the most popular department on campus.

Stiff distribution requirements mean all students must "cross over the two cultures," according to one dean. "Our engineering students must spend a minimum of one year studying literature, art, etc.," while humanities students must study mathematics, science and technology. In addition to fulfilling requirements in seven different academic areas, students must complete a freshman survey of Western culture and another course in a non-Western culture. "I've learned something from every distribution course I've taken," says a junior. "If you plan it right it doesn't have to be a pain." The only major complaint with the expanded requirements comes from engineering students, who end up having time for only one or two electives each year. However, the administration is aware of the problem and is working to find a solution.

For those students not committed to four years in sun-baked Palo Alto, Stanford's overseas campuses offer a degree of luxury and leisure that few colleges can match. A term in England, Japan, France, Germany or Italy is a Stanford experience not to be missed—unless, of course, you are hung up on doing schoolwork while you're abroad. Besides the overseas campuses, there are exchange programs in such exotic places as Lima, Nairobi and Salamanca.

Stanford's faculty ranks among the best in the nation, with most departments able to boast a nationally known name or two. But considering the number of graduate students running around campus, it should come as no surprise that almost all Stanford undergraduate departments use teaching assistants, especially in introductory courses. "It's often hard to get quality time from a professor because they have so many people pulling on them," says a history major. "You have to compete with grad students and their consulting and committee responsibilities." Adds another student, "You may spot your professors at the pool, but don't plan on playing squash with them every week." You're also sure to spot the president whipping across campus on his bike, or he may turn out to be your freshman adviser. The academic advising system, in general, leaves something to be desired, and committees are working to think of ways to supplement it. "It would be better to have someone who really cares than some big name who doesn't have time for you," one woman wistfully notes.

Competition for grades among determined preprofessionals is fierce, especially in the sciences. The curve is all important, as is partial credit for half-completed test answers. Explains one senior, "Most problems on the tests are so difficult that no one can solve them, so partial credit for trying is the big thing." Stanford has received some criticism for inflating grades, although students report that while C's are a cinch and B's the most common grade on campus, A's are still extremely difficult to earn. Failing marks are not recorded on a student's transcript, and students can take a large number of courses pass/no credit if they desire. "You may be slitting your throat for graduate school if you take too many, but not everyone cares about that," says an Asian languages major.

Stanford is often thought of as an Ivy League school transplanted to California, but anything more than a casual glance reveals that the university has little in common with its eastern counterparts aside from academic quality. Stanford is more preprofessional, less intellectual, and more conservative than the Ivys, where the liberal arts reign supreme and engineers are as scarce as palm trees on the New England countryside. "You don't have to talk about Nietzsche or Keynesian economics at dinner," says a senior. "If the conversation starts getting too intellectual, some one will bring up the latest in sports. I like that." Stanford was once an activist mecca, but in recent years it has become more staid and conventional than most other high-powered academic schools. "The College Republicans have a huge following," a confirmed liberal sadly reports. Although wealth is supposedly "something you have but you don't talk about," one look at the campus and student body shows a spectacular emphasis on easy living: sports cars, fancy stereos and beautiful clothes. "There are more seemingly empty-headed California blonds (male and female) than I expected," sniffs one out-of-stater.

Scratch the surface, though, and you find plenty of low-profile, hard-working achievers. Applicants for a recent freshman class included 2,400 high school valedictorians, or half again as many as there were places. Stanford doesn't release its median SAT scores, though rest assured that both verbal and math are well over 600. More than half the student body is from out of state, and foreigners from one hundred countries account for 4 percent of the undergraduates. Minority enrollment stands at 26 percent, about evenly divided between blacks, Asian Americans, and Hispanics.

A quarter of Stanford students take advantage of the university's liberal stop-out policy, which allows students to take some time out along the way rather than stay in school for four straight years. Stanford is fervently need-blind in its admissions; the only exception, albeit conspicuous, to the university's policy of granting student aid on the basis of demonstrated need are the 335 athletic scholarships awarded annually. Almost 60 percent of the students receive some form of financial aid.

Housing is a weak spot. There are only enough rooms to accommodate 85 percent of the students for three of their four school years. About 350 students per year would like to live on campus, but instead have to try to find an affordable apartment in the extraordinarily expensive Silicon Valley area. Those who are lucky in the annual room lottery can find themselves in spacious rooms, while those who are less fortunate may end up in structures reminiscent of Army barracks, or even one of the trailers in which Stanford houses grad students and undergrad overflow. There is, however, a great amount of diversity, and students can choose between theme houses, apartment-style complexes, and co-ops. The multimillion-dollar Governors' Corner dorm complex, built in the early '80s, is undoubtedly the most luxurious option, with its all-oak fixtures, homey rooms with views into foothills or onto the coast, microwave ovens in the kitchenettes, and Italian leather sofas in the lounges. Cement-block-style Stern Hall is among the liveliest of the dorms, all of which are coed by room or floor.

Those living in residence halls must sign up for a meal plan, but it's far from a punishment. Governor's Corner uses a point-blank system, and computerized meal cards allow students in the other dorm dining halls to take a certain number of meals each week whenever they want them. The food is highly rated.

Even in a state that boasts of its beauty, Stanford stands out. The campus is large (eight thousand acres), and most students find it difficult to commit themselves to the indoors in this climate and environment. The hills are perfect for jogging and biking, and a small lake is great for sailing and windsurfing (which is also the most popular PE class in the spring). Students with cars make weekend forays into San Francisco, and others, if they have patience, can get there in an hour and a half by train or bus. Trips to the Sierra Nevada Mountains (four hours away) or to the Pacific Coast (forty-five minutes) are much more frequent. Palo Alto is a quiet city, with pretty residential streets ("boring," says one Stanford student). A handful of bars in the vicinity of campus cater to the Stanford clientele.

On campus, activities and social life vary a great deal. The student government is described as a "playground for resumé building." Incoming females are advised quickly they aren't "true Stanford women" until they've been kissed at midnight in the quad by a senior. Starry nights will find a bevy of giggling freshwomen eager to receive their initiation. The frats have gained in popularity recently, and sororities, banned in 1944 because of fear that they would create unhealthy social pressures, have been reinstated. Staple Greek events, open to all, include Thursday night happy hours and weekend beer bashes.

Most undergraduates have a streak of the jock in them, but varsity athletics do not dominate the campus consciousness or the scoreboards. Nevertheless, the men's and women's swim teams both do well, and the baseball team was national champion in 1987. Both tennis teams have produced championship performances in years past (John McEnroe lingered here for a year before deciding that his profession did not require Stanford credentials). The football team does fairly well against tough PAC-10 competition, though it has never drawn as many headlines as the notoriously irreverent marching band. The band drew a two-year probation that bars it from marching at football games because of "vulgar and lewd" performances that have been known to include formations spelling out four-letter words and depicting a certain part of the male anatomy. Students find more wholesome sources of diversion in intramural contests in one of the three leagues, which cater to everyone from serious jocks (A league) to weekend athletes (C league).

Although a lot of studying and pencil gnawing goes on behind closed doors, students here still make a conscious effort to steer themselves away from inordinate degrees of intellectual stuffiness. The administration, however, is making an effort in the opposite direction by implementing new honors programs and urging students to stop accepting the stereotype of being "intellectually lazy, as though somewhat addled by the sun." The results of this push for greater, more conspicuous academic intensity remain to be seen. Meanwhile, Stanford continues to provide an excellent education and highly marketable diploma in a location far more beautiful, a climate far more temperate, and an atmosphere far more relaxed than Chicago and the Ivies to its east.

STATE UNIVERSITY
OF NEW YORK

With more than 360,000 students spread across sixty-six campuses, the State University of New York is the largest university system in the world. Whatever your academic interest, from flight training to high energy physics, you can do it somewhere in this remarkable collection of institutions.

The statistics of SUNY (pronounced *SOOney*) are awesome. The university has an annual operating budget of more than $2.5 billion, greater than the gross national product of many countries and larger than the budget of more than a dozen American states. It has 24,500 faculty members and maintains more than 2,200 buildings on 21,000 acres of property, the equivalent of one and a half Manhattan Islands. Every year it awards approximately 63,500 degrees, from associate to PhD, in thousands of different academic fields. And—you're not going to believe this one—it has over a million living graduates.

Such figures are all the more remarkable because until 1948 New York had no state university at all. That year, the legislature created the State University around a cluster of thirty-two existing public institutions to handle the flow of returning World War II veterans. Even then a gentlemen's agreement not to compete with the state's private colleges (which for generations had enjoyed a monopoly on higher education in New York) hindered SUNY's movement into the liberal arts. Not until Nelson A. Rockefeller became governor in 1960 and made the building up of the university his major priority did SUNY begin its dramatic growth.

SUNY has now ripened into a network of four research-oriented university centers, thirteen arts and sciences colleges, six agricultural and technical colleges, five "statutory" colleges, five specialized colleges, thirty locally sponsored community colleges, and four graduate medical schools. Students apply directly to the SUNY unit they seek to attend. Forty-six of the colleges, though, use a common form application that enables a prospective student to apply to as many as four SUNY campuses at the same time. The central administration runs a SUNY Admissions Assistance Service that helps students who are not admitted to colleges where they applied find places at other campuses. Students who earn associate degrees at community or other two-year colleges are guaranteed the chance to continue their education at a four-year institution, though not necessarily that of their first choice. The level of selectivity varies widely. Most community colleges guarantee admission to any local high school student, but the university centers, as well as some specialized colleges, are among the most competitive public institutions in the country. Undergraduates at all liberal arts colleges and university centers pay the same tuition, but the rates at community colleges vary (and are lower). Out-of-state students, who make up only 4 percent of SUNY students, pay about double the amount of in-state tuition.

Mainly for political reasons, the State University of New York chose not to follow the model of other states and build a single flagship campus. Instead, it developed the four university centers with undergraduate, graduate, and professional schools and research facilities. When they were created in the 1960s, each one hoped to become fully comprehensive, but there has been a certain degree of specialization from the beginning. Albany is strongest in education and public policy, Binghamton is best known for undergraduate arts and sciences, and Stony Brook is noted for its hard sciences. Buffalo, formerly a private university, maintains a strong reputation in the life sciences and geography but probably comes the closest of any of the four to being a fully comprehensive university. Critics of the system say that the decision to forgo a flagship campus guarantees this lack of national prominence; others, however, insist that somewhere in the labs and libraries of these four university centers are lurking the Nobel Prize winners of the 1990s. To these supporters, it's only a matter of time before SUNY achieves excellence in depth as well as breadth.

The thirteen colleges of arts and sciences likewise vary widely in size and character. They range from the ten-thousand-student College at Buffalo, whose 125-acre campus reflects the urban flavor of the state's second largest city, to the rural College at Geneseo, where half as many students nearly outnumber the year-round residents of the small local village. Still others are suburban campuses, such as Purchase, which specializes in the performing arts, and Old Westbury, which was started as an experimental institution to serve minority students, older women and other students who had been bypassed by more traditional institutions.

With the exception of these two schools, which were started from scratch, the four-year colleges are all former teachers colleges that have, for the most part, successfully made the transition into liberal arts colleges on the small, private New England model. Now, they face a new problem: the growing desire of students to study business, computer science and other more technically oriented subjects. Some have adjusted to these demands well; others are trying to resist the trend. The colleges are also facing the challenge of the decline in the number of eighteen-year-olds that will continue to occur throughout the 1990s, and since recent high school graduates are the basis of their constituency, they are the most vulnerable of any SUNY institutions. The most vulnerable of all are those out in the boonies, such as Geneseo and Oneonta, which lack a population base to make up the difference with older students. All colleges have beefed up their recruiting efforts, the central administration office says.

SUNY's technical and specialized colleges, while they do not enjoy the prominence of the colleges of arts and sciences, serve the demand for vocational training in a variety of two- and four-year programs. Five of the six agricultural and technical colleges (Alfred, Canton, Cobleskill, Delhi and Morrisville) are concerned primarily with agriculture, but also have engineering, nursing, medical technology, data processing and business administration. The sixth, Farmingdale, offers the widest range of programs, from ornamental horticulture to aerospace technology. A new upper-division technical campus at Utica–Rome now provides graduates of these two-year institutions with an opportunity to finish their education in SUNY, instead of having to head for the University of Georgia, Ohio State or similar destinations.

Four of the five statutory schools are at Cornell (agriculture and life sciences, human ecology, industrial and labor relations and veterinary medicine), while the internationally known College of Ceramics is housed at Alfred University, another private university. In addition to Utica–Rome, the specialized colleges consist of the College of Environmental Sciences and Forestry at Syracuse, the Maritime College at Fort Schuyler in the Bronx, the College of Optometry in New York City and the Fashion Institute of Technology, whose graduates are gobbled up as fast as they emerge by employers in the Manhattan garment district where it is situated.

The twenty-nine community colleges have traditionally been the stepchildren of the system, but the combination of rampant vocationalism and the rising cost of education elsewhere is rapidly turning them into the most robust members of the family. Students once looked to the community colleges for terminal degrees that could be readily applied in the marketplace. Now, with the cost of college soaring, a growing number of students who otherwise would have packed off for a four-year college are saving money by staying home for the first two years and then transferring to a four-year college, or even a university center, to get their bachelor's degree.

By and large, the community colleges are computer institutions offering vocationally oriented programs that are closely tied to the needs of the local economy, and the average age of students is usually in the mid-twenties. They range in size from less than 1,650 at North Country Community College near Lake Placid in the sparsely settled Adirondacks, to up to twenty thousand at Nassau and eighteen thousand at Suffolk on densely populated Long Island. The community colleges draw an average of three-quarters of their students from the sponsoring counties, but—as in anything else one might want to say about SUNY—there are exceptions. Sullivan County Community College, for example, situated in the underpopulated Catskills, imports 60 percent of its students.

Following are full-length descriptions of the college at Purchase, which is the liberal arts institution best known beyond New York's borders, and the four university centers.

SUNY—Albany

Albany, NY 12222

Location Suburban	**Applicants** 14,200
Total Enrollment 16,150	**Accepted** 58%
Undergraduates 11,670	**Enrolled** 30%
Male/Female 49/51	**Academics** ★ ★ ★ ★
SAT V/M 520/590	**Social** 🐿 🐿 🐿
Financial Aid 80%	**Q of L** ● ● ●
Expense Pub $ $	**Admissions** (518)457-3300

The senior university center of the State University system, SUNY–Albany is located on the outskirts of the state capital in a network of futuristic buildings by the late Edward Durell Stone that look like a space station. Hence its nickname: "the moon-based SUNY." Almost all the academic buildings are sandwiched together in the center of the campus, while students are housed in four symmetrically situated quads so similar in appearance that it usually takes a semester to figure out which one is yours. (Hint: The quads are named for periods in New York history—Indian, Dutch, State and Colonial—and progress clockwise around the campus.)

Except for the infamous "wind tunnel design that traps all incoming gales," some students actually like Stone's stones. Others don't. "It's one huge monolithic structure made of concrete," says a public policy major. "It's very uninviting and alienating." But then there's always the older, more Ivy League–looking downtown residential campus, with its red bricks and pillars. Like it or not, Albany's striking architecture is home to some strong academic programs.

Most of the science departments and preprofessional programs are among the finest of any SUNY branch, with the school of criminal justice and the department of atmospheric science particularly outstanding. Students in the public administration and social welfare programs may take advantage of their proximity to the state government to participate in internships. Biology, physics, sociology, psychology and German are other notable majors, while undergrads are clamoring for admittance to the university's business administration program. (Warning: Entrance is highly competitive, and you can't apply until after sophomore year.) The administration is trying to ameliorate supply/demand problems in business and two other popular programs: computer science and education. The New York State Writers' Institute is the newest and least traditional of Albany's offerings. But with the appointments of Pulitzer Prize–winner William Kennedy as head of the Institute and author/editor Toni Morrison as first occupant of an endowed professorship, the university's dream of becoming distinguished for its creative writing has nearly come true.

All undergraduates must fulfill Albany's general education program: six credit hours in each of six areas, including symbolics (e.g., math, foreign language or computer science), values and world culture. Students must also satisfy an intensive writing requirement. If this liberal arts exposure whets your appetite for interdisciplinary study, try your hand at Afro-American, Caribbean, Judaic, Puerto Rican or women's studies. The more career-minded can sign up for one of twenty-six BA/MA programs or opt for a law degree with the bachelor's in only six years. Many students take advantage of SUNY–Albany's superior offerings in foreign study. Don't be surprised if you find yourself sitting in class next to someone named Ivan; the university was one of the first in the nation to develop exchange programs with the Soviet Union (and China, for that matter). Undergraduates may also study in several European countries as well as in Brazil, Costa Rica, Israel, Japan and Singapore.

The student body comprises "bits and pieces of every Long Island high school and a dash of upstate, topped off with a Big Apple or two." Specifically, a quarter of the student body is local and nearly half are transplants from the New York City metropolitan area. While most are in-staters, an increasing number of out-of-staters are finding SUNY–Albany a better academic deal than their local state universities.

SUNY–Albany is one of the most selective public universities in the nation, and it shows. Forty percent of those enrolled are from the top tenth of their high school class; almost half go on to graduate or professional school, an impressive rate for a state school. One undergraduate describes his peers as "intelligent, assertive, hardworking, urban—generally pretty fast company." Albany students tend to spend a lot of time thinking about their future careers. But, lest we get the wrong impression, another adds, "They're also highly motivated to party at every available moment." One prerequisite for being a loyal Albanian is adeptness in the fine art of podiating. The verb *to podiate* means chilling out on the huge campus podium in the middle of the uptown quads and next to a huge phallic fountain dedicated to former Governor Nelson Rockefeller, who was best known for his massive construction programs. (Students call it Rockefeller's Last Erection.)

The housing situation on campus and off campus is tight, and while freshmen are encouraged to live in dorms, the administration makes no promises to upperclassmen looking for rooms. The coed quads are exceptionally friendly, surprisingly quiet and comfortable. Each floor of these dorms is divided into four- to six-person suites. But the word from a senior is the best dorms are in the alumni quad on the downtown campus. "These dorms are more traditional," he claims. "There's a sense of family and going home after class." But getting home after class can present a challenge if you rely on the overcrowded university bus known as the Green Monster. The off-campus "student ghetto" is more desirable than its name suggests; it provides relatively cheap apartments right off the bus line. The off-campus housing office is helpful in finding people places. Students on the main campus take their meals at any of the four dorms or at the Rat, while downtowners haunt the cheap local eateries as well as their own cafeterias. Students admit food has improved and seem further appeased by salad bars, diet lines and special taste-testing nights.

While most people are serious about their work, there is no denying that a SUNY–Albany weekend starts on Thursday night and "belongs to the beer guzzlers and the film buffs." Although the new drinking age of twenty-one has busted their gusto a bit, going to parties, bar hopping about town, and podiating with beer in hand help many students avoid work until Sunday night. The Greek life is experiencing a renaissance at Albany and fraternities and sororities are now the main party throwers on campus. Albany students tend to be traditional, and rites of spring festivals are mandatory after enduring the miserable upstate winters. HAP Day (Human Awareness Program) brings thousands of students together for the spring turn-on of that famous fountain. May Fest is a huge all-school concert party that brings in bands like U-2 and the Squeeze.

The natural resources of the upstate region keep students busy skiing and hiking. Treks to Montreal and the $1-billion Rockefeller Plaza in downtown Albany (home of a performing arts center and the state museum and library) are popular pastimes. Men's basketball, tennis, wrestling, football and women's softball, volleyball and basketball are creditable Division III contenders but nothing to get students excited about. However, intramurals engender a great deal of student enthusiasm and participation numbers in the thousands.

While SUNY–Albany is not the stony, sterile diploma mill it first appears to be, it still is easy to remain anonymous here for four years. Prospective moon walkers should be prepared to come down to earth and work for whatever it is they want from an Albany education. As one alumnus warned, "You can find an outlet here for even the most obscure interest, but this is not a school that will educate you when you're not looking."

SUNY—Binghamton

Binghamton, NY 13901

Location Suburban		**Applicants** 13,080	
Total Enrollment 12,200		**Accepted** 48%	
Undergraduates 9,370		**Enrolled** 29%	
Male/Female 47/53		**Academics** ★ ★ ★ ★	
SAT V/M 530/600		**Social** ☎ ☎ ☎	
Financial Aid 85%		**Q of L** ● ●	
Expense Pub $ $		**Admissions** (607)777-2171	

The first of the SUNY campuses to offer a liberal arts degree, Binghamton has taken full advantage of its head start. From medieval studies to computer science, SUNY–Binghamton continues to offer the strongest undergraduate academic programs. But caveat emptor! As the smallest of the SUNYs, it's also the most selective liberal arts university in New York, and, arguably, the most selective public university in the nation.

The university is situated on six hundred acres of fountains, trails and open grassy areas that include a large nature preserve and pond "The surrounding countryside is breathtaking," one woman notes. The campus itself isn't bad either, if you like modern buildings (all structures have been built since 1946). Some students say that from an aerial view, the circular campus bears a striking resemblance to the human brain—a total coincidence and not a secret plan of the architects, the administration asserts.

The first thing that greets SUNY–Binghamton students who do gain admission is stiff distribution requirements. Each of the four professional schools sets its own requirements within the philosophy of the liberal arts. For example, Harpur College, the liberal arts school, requires students to take course work in each of its three divisions: humanities, social sciences, and science and mathematics. Harpur also mandates students gain proficiency in a foreign language and writing. The engineering school is the newest school at Binghamton; the school of nursing is the smallest. Accounting stands out among programs in the school of management, while biology, chemistry, psychology and political science win rave reviews in Harpur College. And the fine arts have come center stage with the completion of the $15-million Floyd E. Anderson Center for the Arts. Interdisciplinary fields of study include Judaic studies, Afro-American studies, and Latin-American and Caribbean area studies. And if these don't satisfy a student's intellectual cravings, the Innovational Project Board will oversee and help a student design not only his own major but his own courses. Internship possibilities exist, as do eight different study-abroad programs. For students choosing to do their studying on campus, the university provides six different libraries with excellent resources and study areas, as well as 250 conveniently located computer stations throughout the campus.

Professors generally receive high marks from students, although there are complaints that research sometimes receives higher priority than teaching. Graduate teaching assistants hold smaller group meetings to supplement large lecture courses that sometimes seat close to five hundred students. It is not uncommon to be closed out of some classes at first, but upperclassmen can usually get what they want or need to take, provided they know the petitioning procedure. Binghamton's strong academic reputation has been enhanced by a tough grading policy in which students are given an F rather than no credit, and pluses and minuses as well as straight letter grades. The academic climate varies from an "extremely high-pressured, very competitive, cut-throat type of atmosphere" in accounting, engineering and other preprofessional fields to a more relaxed climate in the liberal arts college. There, says one English major, "the pressure is one of curiosity rather than grades."

Though SUNY–Binghamton clearly ranks as one of the best public arts and sciences schools in the nation, word of this has yet to cross state lines. Ninety-five percent of the students are New Yorkers, with the heaviest proportion from New York City and its surroundings, especially Long Island. The traditional upstate/downstate divisions of New York State politics are reflected in the student body, with upstaters complaining about provincial peers who think that "New York City is the only city in the world." But SUNY–Binghamton students are of a kind when it comes to academic prowess; sixty-two percent come from the top tenth of their high school class and 99-plus percent from the top half. Binghamton tries to help all students make ends meet on financial needs, although those with late applications or only moderate need may be placed in a hold category. Less than one hundred freshmen receive the merit scholarships of $1,000 to $4,000, and no athletic awards are given.

To help make the university seem a little smaller, dormitories are grouped into four residential colleges. Newing is the oldest and most stately, College-in-the-Woods is the newest, and each college has its own personality and reputation. Dorms are coed, clean and overcrowded. Most freshmen are tripled, and the majority of students move off campus in their upperclass years; housing is plentiful and bus service to the campus is excellent. They usually find, however, that the move is for good, since it is difficult to get back on. Those who decide to stay in dorms can keep their old rooms as long as they want, but they also have to depend on the cafeteria food. But students buy this "mediocre-to-awful" food on a credi-dine system, which means they only pay for what's on their tray.

Entertainment remains secondary to studying, but cheap movies are a major part of Binghamton life, as are dorm parties, occasional concerts and quiet dinners off campus. A few small fraternities and sororities were organized recently, but very few people belong. Few students leave campus for the weekend, but for those who need an escape, the college towns of Syracuse, Ithaca and Oneonta are about an hour away by car.

An organization of faculty members, students and administrators owns and operates a lake for fishing, swimming and waterskiing about forty-five minutes from campus. Soccer, basketball, wrestling and women's cross-country and tennis teams usually perform well, but few students seem to care. Intramurals generate far more excitement. Most popular is co-recreational football, where teams of three men and three women (always a female quarterback) stir up intense rivalries.

SUNY–Binghamton is eager to cultivate its growing reputation as a public alternative to the Ivy League. "The more selective the school, the more students will seek to gain admission to it," reasons one administrator. Binghamton's educational style is sometimes criticized for being factory-like, and those who pine for personal attention will find the cumulative-average calculators and other student grinds tiresome after a while. Daydreamers and romantics are the minority in this very pragmatic student body, but a few students admit to occasionally pining for a more traditional, classically collegiate atmosphere. Then these fancies pass, and a sense of purpose returns. As one student explains: "There is no ivy on our buildings, and the ghosts of intellectual giants do not chime the great bells of buildings which look like churches. At Binghamton we are creating the future, not holding up the past."

SUNY—Buffalo

Buffalo, NY 14260

Location Suburban	**Applicants** 12,090
Total Enrollment 26,970	**Accepted** 72%
Undergraduates 18,390	**Enrolled** 28%
Male/Female 56/44	**Academics** ★ ★ ★
SAT V/M 500/580	**Social** ☎ ☎
Financial Aid 55%	**Q of L** ● ●
Expense Pub $ $	**Admissions** (716)831-2333

Things are looking up at Buffalo, the largest and most comprehensive of New York's state university centers. There was a time not too long ago when motivated students had to search hard for challenging academic programs, when there was little school spirit, and when construction of an ill-conceived auxiliary campus made life in a troubled metropolitan area a real hassle. But now the city of Buffalo has bounced back, and so has its favorite university.

Part of the problem has been architectural schizophrenia. Buffalo has two campuses: the older downtown Main Street side, with its collegiate ivy buildings, and the sleek new and larger facility on twelve hundred sprawling acres in the suburb of Amherst. Students shuttle between them by bus—a half-hour trip. But now the politically controversial construction program is nearing its end, and by the end of this decade all undergraduate liberal arts students will be clustered at Amherst. In the meantime, UB has pulled itself together academically, with common general education requirements for all undergraduates and expanding programs in technology and health sciences. UB has also established a fine honors program, and even though the president

534

has yet to get his wish to plunge into Division I, school spirit is on the rise. Intelligent changes are being made here; regardless of what you've heard, UB deserves another look.

Fine faculty and a variety of academic programs were always UB's strengths, and that hasn't changed. The engineering and business schools are nationally prominent, and architecture is strong. Occupational and physical therapy programs are also quite good. English, French, physiology, geography and music are highly regarded, but the humanities as a whole have suffered from budget cuts. Art, theater and math are currently on the weak side, and physics is the least impressive among the sciences. Complaints occasionally surface about the lack of a journalism or broadcasting major program, although courses in both disciplines are offered. While UB discourages internships, it has a multitude of special programs, joint degrees, and interdisciplinary majors, as well as opportunities for self-designed majors. Students accepted into the honors program enjoy smaller classes, priority in class registration, individual faculty mentors and special scholarships, regardless of need.

Class size can be a problem, especially for freshmen. "Most introductory courses house about 400 students, which can be quite scary," recalls a junior. Smaller recitation sessions humanize the largest courses. Scheduling conflicts are not unusual, but a desired course can always be picked up the following semester. Students seem to accept that some degree of faculty unavailability is the necessary trade-off for having professors who are experts in the field. However, no instructor is completely inaccessible: "Professors always have office hours and are very receptive to students who visit," one junior says. The general education program requires students to take at least one course in each of six "knowledge areas" outside their majors. The areas are literature and the arts, physical and math sciences and technology, social and behavioral sciences, life and health sciences, historical and philosophical studies, and foreign language or cross-cultural studies. The academically oriented student body spends plenty of time in UB's eleven libraries, which are, for the most part, comfortable and well stocked. "There's even a social library where you can meet people while pretending to study," one biology major confides.

Once upon a time, a large majority of UB's student body went straight into the job market after graduation, but today a third go on to graduate school. Of the 96 percent of New York State students, the biggest contingent apart from the locals are New York City residents. As a large public university, UB has "everything from the all-American coed to the active radical." Diverse is definitely the most frequently used adjective in describing the student body, but independent, motivated and hardworking are also often used. Although UB does not guarantee financial aid to all those with demonstrated need for it, all applications that are received before the deadline "are funded as appropriate." Only 1 percent of the students receive merit scholarships ranging from $1,000 to $2,000, and no Buffalo athletes are financially rewarded for their endeavors.

Only a third of the students live on campus; the rest commute from home or find apartments near the Main Street campus. Students warn that potential renters should shuffle off to Buffalo a couple of months early to secure a place. Most of the on-campus dwellers are housed on the Amherst campus in modern, single-sex dorms that are, in the words of an English major, "unusually designed." The Main Street campus dorms are smaller, older, and of a more traditional collegiate design. Upperclassmen prefer this campus, but either way, "singles are like gold—very scarce and high priced." The food gets so-so reviews, but most dorms are equipped with kitchens. "I can add cooking to the long list of things I've learned in college," says one woman.

The Greek system has been born again at UB and is growing slowly but surely. The large number of commuters and the split campus put a damper on social life, but students seem to manage. "Buffalo is a friendly city, and contrary to national opinion, has a lot to do," says one sophomore who's found her way to the city's many movie theaters, concerts, shopping malls, nightclubs, bars and bowling alleys. Students without cars, however, can get trapped when the inter-campus bus stops running after two AM on weekends. Skiing, snowshoeing, and other outdoor sports are at your doorstep, and the ski club—one of the most prominent of the five hundred student organizations, which range from the math club to the juggling club—provides free transportation to the nearby slopes. Students can get a preview of their honeymoon by darting over to Niagara Falls, just a half hour away.

Students rave about UB's new sports complex: "We have the fourth largest pool in the world, as well as a 10,000-seat arena, squash and racquetball courts, a jogging track, weight rooms. . . ." Varsity teams spark a lot of student interest, especially the football team and the strong Division I baseball team. Intramurals also command student attention and enthusiasm.

The largest of the SUNY university centers, Buffalo sometimes causes its students to lose patience with the crowds, standing in lines and the inconvenience of two campuses. But UB continues to offer the most comprehensive education of all the state schools, and hardy students prosper here. "I had no idea of all the opportunities UB offers" raves a satisfied sophomore. "Because it is a SUNY school, UB can afford facilities and programs that many private schools can't—at about one-fifth of the tuition."

SUNY—Purchase

Purchase, NY 10577

Location Suburban	**Applicants** 2,070
Total Enrollment 3,880	**Accepted** 63%
Undergraduates 3,860	**Enrolled** 33%
Male/Female 45/55	**Academics** ★ ★ ★
SAT V/M 500/500	**Social** 🏠 🏠 🏠
Financial Aid 70%	**Q of L** ● ● ●
Expense Pub $ $	**Admissions** (914)253-5046

Founded in the 1960s as an "alternative" college within the system of the State University of New York, Purchase combines a professionally oriented school of the arts with an innovative college of letters and science. At its best, this intertwining of music and literature, politics and dance produces a rare kind of excitement. Unfortunately, Purchase has not been able to escape the rise of new conservatism in the nation or the limitations of being state controlled. As a result, several unusual programs have been discontinued in the past decade. Even with budget cuts, however, the school remains a model of nontraditional public university education.

"Our school is very open—literally and figuratively," explains a sociology major. Set on a five-hundred-acre wooded estate in an area of Westchester's most scenic suburbia, SUNY–Purchase has a campus described by one student as "sleek, modern, ominous and brick—an architectural marvel, but there's no ivy here." This anything-but-traditional school has earned a national reputation for its instruction in music, dance, visual arts, theater and film. Almost all the faculty members in the School of the Arts are professional artists who perform or exhibit regularly in the New York metropolitan area, and the spacious, dazzling physical facilities rank among the best in the world. Dance students, whose building contains a dozen studios, whirlpool rooms, and a "body-correction" facility, may never again work in such splendid and well-equipped surroundings.

Mingling with highly motivated and talented performers and artists can make some letters and science students feel a little drab and out of place—"Everything gets overshadowed by the artists," proclaims one. But for the most part, their inferiority complexes are unwarranted. The only shaky letters and science programs are in languages and the social sciences (including business and accounting). Purchase is a fine place to study humanities and the natural sciences, particularly literature, art history, political science, biology and chemistry. Letter grades are supplemented by individual narrative evaluations in most courses. These evaluations, usually a full page in length, become part of the students' official record.

All students in the college of letters and sciences, and most students in the arts divisions spend one-third of their time at Purchase fulfilling the general education requirements. Within the general ed curriculum, students must take the yearlong sequence, Revolution in Western Thought, which stresses writing skills and the reading of significant literature—everything from Plato to Dickens. The mandatory curriculum also includes Arts and Liberal Studies, a course to integrate the study of liberal arts and fine arts, and a senior course, Seminar on Moral Issues. Students in the arts divisions usually have many more required courses, culminating in a senior recital or show. The college offers certificate programs in computer science, arts management and environmental management. Purchase's one central library doesn't live up to students' expectations. Some criticize its inadequate hours, one student complains of insensitive front desk personnel, and another bemoans the absence of the traditional collegiate library's dusty volumes.

"At times, this place seems so laid back it's falling over backwards," reports a senior who rates the academic pressure as low-to-nil. Anyone arriving at Purchase should come with an open mind. Many students here are "the misfits from high schools," says a senior who's proud to be one of them. "Everyone wears black, members of both sexes wear dresses, and there may be two or three preppies." Ninety percent of the students are New Yorkers, most from NYC and Westchester County. Others are from Long Island, New Jersey or Connecticut, but all are different, and very political (that means very liberal). Despite relatively high SAT scores, students are drawn from almost all levels of their high school class, with 86 percent coming from the top half. "It seems Purchase is a place to release those inner artistic thrusts in the most peculiar ways possible," explains a new convert. Most financial awards are need-based and, according to students, hard to get "for anyone who is not black, Hispanic or dirt-poor." Some merit scholarships, ranging from $500 to $1,000, are awarded on the basis of academic achievements, auditions and portfolios.

The living facilities have been overhauled in the last year and now rate favorable reviews from most students, although residential freshmen and some unlucky sophomores stuck in the smallest of dorms still feel like canned sardines. The two campus apartment complexes are much sought after by upperclassmen who have earned the academic credits to secure a place in one. The two eating facilities offer average institutionalized fare, which translates into "pretty bad" on a home-cooking scale. But apartment dwellers can cook in their own kitchens or run out to a nearby snack bar that also accepts meal tickets. About 30 percent of the student body commutes from nearby communities, though housing in the suburbs proper is expensive and hard to find.

SUNY–Purchase is neighbor to the world headquarters of IBM, Texaco, AMF,

General Foods and Pepsico. While sharing the "billion-dollar mile" with a few Fortune 500s might excite more prebusiness-oriented student bodies, "it doesn't do much for us except provide convenient antiapartheid demonstration locations," contests a senior. New York City is a SUNY student's most appreciated resource. Only forty-five minutes away, it provides a regular weekend distraction that inhibits the formation of a tight campus community. But parties and dances are sponsored regularly on campus, and students who stick around for the weekend are treated to high-class entertainment. The Center for the Arts is host to at least two student or faculty performances every weekend, and there is a constant flow of New York artists and celebrities. Fraternities and sororities are definitely out. "The closest we come to Greek are the two guys from Athens who go here," says a staunch independent.

Strong men's fencing and women's tennis teams are the closest things to regular powerhouse state school athletics, although the Ultimate Frisbee team is a league champion. Intramural programs and an excellent athletic facility exist, but sports are not the most important thing on this campus. "Our 'teams' are our dancers, our vocalists, our musicians, our theater companies," says a fan. And students turn out enthusiastically to support them.

Despite the institutional schizophrenia that occasionally divides the letters and science from the arts, Purchase is a perfect place to study the arts and still be able to indulge in academics of all kinds, or vice versa. If you're determined enough to explore the possibilities and battle the frustrations of an emerging nontraditional institution, then Purchase offers the opportunity for a personalized, diverse education unique within the SUNY system. The experiment is working, students seem to believe, at this "school where anything is possible."

SUNY—Stony Brook

Stony Brook, NY 11794

Location City outskirts	**Applicants** 11,170
Total Enrollment 16,160	**Accepted** 62%
Undergraduates 11,290	**Enrolled** 27%
Male/Female 50/50	**Academics** ★ ★ ★ ★
SAT V/M 470/560	**Social** 🏛 🏛 🏛
Financial Aid 75%	**Q of L** ● ●
Expense Pub $ $	**Admissions** (516)632-6868

Stony Brook's youth—it is barely a quarter of a century old—works both for and against it. While on the one hand it provides the basis for the school's much-heralded promise, flexibility and willingness to experiment, it is also responsible for the lack of sufficient endowment funds and experience to facilitate new initiatives. Students still rattle off lists of major problems and small quirks that need to be worked out, but their lists of praiseworthy aspects of life at Stony Brook are long as well. With a growing academic reputation and proved ability to weather crises and keep forging ahead, "the Brook's" future definitely looks promising.

Despite its plush location on Long Island's North Shore, Stony Brook's campus buildings are a sterile product of the '60s' institutional architectural style. The vast campus, with its bare, boxy concrete high-rise buildings, is set behind a smattering of trees just outside the small picturesque village of Stony Brook, which has been restored as a kind of mini-Williamsburg. The surrounding area ranges from open fields to typical suburbia, and the beach is just a half hour away.

"A child of the Sputnik generation," as one administrator calls it, Stony Brook quickly became widely known and respected for its science departments. Facilities are, understandably, new and extensive, and the science faculty includes a number of nationally known researchers and a Nobel laureate in physics. The comprehensive university hospital and research center make health sciences strong, especially physical therapy. Students praise the social sciences and report that engineering is also strong, although it lacks civil and chemical concentrations. The administration admits that Stony Brook's business management and teacher training do not keep pace with student demand, and students complain that the emphasis on sciences overshadows the school's arts and humanities programs. But efforts have been made to boost the arts with fine instructors in music and a beautiful three-theater fine arts center. The solid English department is getting mandatory student attention because of a new core curriculum that requires students to take at least one English composition course plus one course from each of six core themes: global thinking, Western history, preparing for future society, perspectives on other cultures, understanding the natural world and technological literacy.

Since 90 percent of Stony Brook's faculty are engaged in research, students must take considerable initiative to have contact with professors outside of class. Such initiative, though, is often rewarded by a responsive attitude. "In general the professors wish to meet more students than they do," assures a senior. Even the most prestigious researchers are required to teach undergraduate courses. Science majors are hardest hit by the academic demands, and humanities are reputed to be more relaxed. Introductory courses can be huge, but they are often broken up into smaller discussion sections led by graduate assistants. Since freshmen are the last to register, they sometimes have to wait a semester or two to get a course they want.

Freshmen do have access to special seminars with more personal instruction. Stony Brook has also established an Undergraduate Research and Creative Activities program (URECA) that offers undergraduates the opportunity to work directly with faculty members from the time they are freshmen until they graduate. Some students take time abroad in Stony Brook's excellent travel programs (China, Poland, Italy and Israel are some possibilities), while others plug into established internships in the fields of policy analysis, political science, psychology and social welfare. Combined BA/MA programs are available in engineering, the teaching of math, policy analysis and public management.

The students who have enrolled here are predominantly from New York State (more than half from Long Island alone). Close to 40 percent graduate in the top tenth of their high school class, and more than half of Stony Brook's graduates go on to graduate and professional schools. The biggest adjustment, says one engineer, is to the fact that they're not "the smartest kid in the class anymore." A physical therapy student admits that many of his classmates are "kinda JAPPY," but he adds that Stony Brook students are also liberal and fun-loving people "who are extroverted and have a New York kind of attitude and interest."

Although Stony Brook has one of the largest residential programs in the SUNY system (43 percent live on campus), dormitory housing is still limited, and thus restricted only to students from outside a ten-mile radius of the school. Resident students end up in one of six quadrangles, or "colleges," and many couldn't be happier. "The atmosphere within the residence halls helps students develop in many areas—social, intellectual, physical, spiritual, etc," says one woman. Things are always happening spontaneously, adds another resident, "anything from arguing about the finer points of Plato's *Republic* to avoiding a bucket of water." Commuters deprived of all this fun

539

are given a social facility of their own, "the commuter college." Cafeterias, delis and pizza shops are located throughout the campus, even in academic buildings. While residential freshmen must take a meal plan, upperclass boarders either opt for a flexible food service plan or pay a nominal fee to cook for themselves. Suites come equipped with a dishwasher and range, and each hall has a lounge and kitchen area, all of which, students say, could be kept a lot cleaner. Kosher and vegetarian food co-ops keep interested students well supplied with cheap food.

While Stony Brook has long since shaken off its druggie reputation of the 1960s, parties still take priority over other free-time pursuits. The longtime ban on fraternities and sororities has been lifted, so a fledgling Greek system, with no houses, is now an option. Current and classic movies are screened during the week, and other entertainment is available in the form of frequent concerts, plays, and other performances.

On the weekends, students often go beachcombing on the nearby North Shore or the Atlantic Ocean shore of Long Island or head into New York City. Cars are desirable, but many students make do with trains, and a station is conveniently located at the edge of campus. The local community is "traditional Long Island—shopping centers, Macys, etc.," yawns one student. Nearby Port Jefferson offers smaller shops and more interesting restaurants. Sports facilities, including a field house, have been upgraded, but varsity teams are less than impressive. Exceptions include men's basketball, lacrosse and swimming and women's basketball and soccer. Intramurals provide one of the school's greatest rallying points, and competition in football is especially fierce. Many teams have their own matching jerseys.

Despite its short history, Stony Brook offers some of the best academic opportunities in the SUNY system, and although students have to maneuver around lots of rough spots, few of them would pass up this "fine and affordable" institution if they had to choose again. "There's a lot to like here," says one man, specifically "the people, the relaxed atmosphere, the feeling that I belong."

Stetson University

DeLand, FL 32720

Location Suburban	**Applicants** 1,500
Total Enrollment 2,860	**Accepted** 73%
Undergraduates 2,000	**Enrolled** 48%
Male/Female 45/55	**Academics** ★ ★ ★
SAT V/M 520/560	**Social** 🐾 🐾 🐾
Financial Aid 48%	**Q of L** ● ● ●
Expense Pr $	**Admissions** (904)734-4121

Stetson University may be named for the maker of the ten-gallon cowboy hat, but don't expect to find the last of the wild, wild West on this sedate little campus. In fact, it's not tumbleweed, but lush vegetation that covers this territory. Located in the quaint, hospitable central Florida town of DeLand, this emphatically Christian university founded by Southern Baptists crossed its final frontier a hundred years ago when it became Florida's first private institution of higher education.

The major structures are stone on this attractive campus with traditional, southern-style architecture, but there are enough eccentric brick buildings scattered about to keep things interesting. The theme is old-fashionedness with modern nuances. Students claim that part of the university's allure lies in the beautiful landscaping and large shady trees.

Whatever draws them to Stetson, all undergraduates will enroll in one of three schools: music, business administration or arts and sciences. Required curriculums for each major build on a foundation in the social sciences, the natural sciences and the humanities—including one mandatory semester of Judeo-Christian heritage—but other requirements vary. The music program is noted for quality instruction in brass instruments, organ and voice. Business types say that accounting is particularly strong. One unusual and unbeatable program for hands-on investment experience is the Roland George Investments program, where students manage an actual cash portfolio worth nearly $1 million. The College of Arts and Science is solid in the social sciences, English and history, but weak in political science, philosophy, and the fine arts.

Aided by short library hours, students generally keep their studying under control—though one student claims that "you *must* study on weekends to stay in the 'B' category." Still, academic and professional aspirations permeate the student body— about 40 percent go on to graduate school—and the school's small size helps people to achieve. The largest class to be found on this campus is intro to psych with a mere eighty students; the average size class is under twenty. "The students are challenged to better themselves, but they are not forced to compete for attention," says one senior.

An honors program in the liberal arts allows the brightest students to replace distribution requirements with interdisciplinary seminars, and many an honors student will undertake an independent contract study with professors of his or her choice. Stetson sandwiches a January term between fall and spring semesters, offering courses on and off campus. To add to the novelty of the special one-month term, the university develops a theme for each year, and departments vary their winter term courses to fit the theme. Favorite January activities have included a trip to the Soviet Union and an international business seminar conducted in Europe. The year-abroad program operates out of centers in France (Dijon), Germany (Freiburg) and Spain (Madrid).

The motto of Stetson is "In God and Truth," with the former taking precedence every Wednesday morning when classes are suspended and chapel services are held. Some of the social regulations—particularly single-sex dorms and rules barring alcohol—suggest a stuffy atmosphere. But Florida Baptists are relatively liberal on social issues, and the school attracts a religiously and socially diverse student body, only a quarter of whom are Baptists. "We have a dry campus, but in reality, it isn't," says one student. "Drinking's just done behind closed doors or on frat row." Nearly three-fourths of the students graduated from public high schools, and 8 percent represent minority groups. About 70 percent of Stetson undergraduates are Floridians, and the rest have migrated south from the North and the Midwest. The tone of the school is conservative: "Not too many girls dress in leather and chains and have a mohawk," reports one junior. In fact, "Democrat is a dirty word," proclaims an English major. Because Stetson is so well supported by Baptist churches, tuition remains low for a school of its type. In addition to need-based aid, the university awards one hundred academic and talent scholarships to freshmen each year, ranging from $500 to $6,500, and most are renewable for four years. Nearly fifty athletic scholarships are awarded in a variety of men's and women's sports.

Stetson is a predominantly residential college, with 70 percent of the undergraduates living on campus. The dorms have all been renovated within the last few years, and students rate them highly. The men's and women's dorms are on opposite ends of the campus and are run with restricted visiting hours. Off-campus living is for upperclassmen only. The food is average by college standards, and three meal plans (twenty-one, fifteen, and seven) are offered. If you've had one day too many of mystery meat entrees, you can spend your meal tickets at the campus coffeeshop, the Hat Rack.

With dorms off-limits to alcohol and DeLand almost as dry as the campus, Stetson's Greek organizations have assumed tremendous importance in undergraduate social life. Weekends find fraternity row (and not much else on campus) buzzing with activity. But students report that there are worse things in life than being a non-Greek at Stetson, and all students are welcome to most of the parties throughout the year. There's also the Stetson Union Board to provide entertainment—movies, concerts, speakers, etc. The university also has ample recreational facilities, including a health and physical education center, playing fields and courts, and an outdoor pool.

With a car, all of Florida is available for weekend jaunts. The nightlife of Daytona or Orlando is often irresistible. Surfing is plentiful, and other favorite destinations include Disney World and EPCOT, and the Space Center. "Without football, our homecoming and all spirit centers around basketball," reports one student. But the most successful varsity teams are baseball and women's tennis, softball and volleyball. Intramurals are extraordinarily competitive and well attended. "More people will go to the intramural football playoffs than most of our intercollegiate games," says one devotee. Another suggests that those so inclined can cheer on the nationally prominent forensic team.

With its demanding curriculum, religious commitment and small size, Stetson has been spared an influx of fun-loving, sun-loving students, leaving it free to cultivate academics in a caring, quality atmosphere. While the subtropical climate is indeed a pleasure. Stetson strives, says the admissions office, "to reverse the image of fun in the sun." Stetson's friendly, serious, professionally oriented students take their hats off to that.

Stevens Institute of Technology

Hoboken, NJ 07030

Location Urban	**Applicants** 1,400
Total Enrollment 3,360	**Accepted** 71%
Undergraduates 1,400	**Enrolled** 35%
Male/Female 83/17	**Academics** ★ ★ ★
SAT V/M 520/640	**Social** ☎ ☎
Financial Aid 70%	**Q of L** ● ● ● ●
Expense Pr $ $ $	**Admissions** (201)420-5194

For those who've always thought they wanted to be engineers, an education at Stevens Institute of Technology is a sure way of learning the field if you've got the mettle. The fourteen hundred undergrads at Stevens face four rigorous years of intense technical learning leavened by only nominal doses of the humanities and social sciences, "You've got to have a large interest in the sciences to be happy here," says a soon-to-be mechanical engineer. "Those who don't find out right away."

Stevens' fifty-five-acre campus, situated on a terrace rising up from the Hudson

River, provides students with a panoramic view of Manhattan Island from the George Washington Bridge to the Statue of Liberty. The campus is small and a bit crowded, populated by old brownstone and modern buildings and plenty of playing fields.

Stevens offers majors in the fields of engineering, science, management and computer science. But engineering—be it mechanical, chemical, materials and metallurgical or computer—is the indisputable king of the campus. The administration admits concern over its management major, saying it needs a more defined academic philosophy, but course offerings are popular among students. No one comes to Stevens for the humanities, which is wise considering what they would find if they did. Computer science has become a major in and of itself, and the school tries to ensure that all students are computer fluent—not just literate—by the time they leave. Hence, all freshmen are required to purchase a $2,000 plus DEC 350 personal computer, a policy that not only adds to the cost of attending Stevens but explains why all the dormitory desks are seven feet long.

For the first two years at Stevens, students must follow a core curriculum stressing foundation courses in the sciences and in broad areas of engineering. This rigid program takes the guesswork out of course selection since students are slotted into classes and sections. In addition to all this technical training, students must complete a total of eight humanities and social science courses over their four years, as well as six semester hours of gym. But never fear, there are a number of ways to get around this predestined course load. For example, students not quite up to the intensity of the Steven's academic prescription may arrange for a five-year program, without extra tuition charges. In addition, the Stevens Technical Enrichment Program (STEP) offers a number of remedial programs for the educationally or economically disadvantaged. The STEP Bridge program lets borderline students test their potential at Stevens through a summer session and conditional admission. Many freshmen take the Personalized System of Instruction (PSI) option, which enables them to study at their own pace for a year or two. Qualified juniors can attend one of the school's programs in Scotland or Berlin, and undergraduates are also allowed to take graduate-level courses. Stevens has initiated a cooperative education program, which offers engineering majors two years of on-the-job training.

Students are satisfied with the teaching ability of most professors and are comfortable in the close-knit environment that develops between students and faculty members. Courses are usually taught in "recitations" of fewer than thirty students. Exams are taken under a successful student-run honor system. Given the subject matter, no one considers the work load unreasonable and tutorial help is readily available at no cost. But the academic challenges can raise stress levels to unpleasant heights, and a computer science major warns that if students "don't take advantage of the free time to unwind, they'll go crazy."

Stevens draws three-quarters of its students from New Jersey and most of the rest from New York and Connecticut. Roughly 60 percent come from public high schools, and almost three-quarters graduated in the top fifth of their class. Minorities make up 23 percent of the student body and foreign students 5 percent. The lopsided proportion of men to women can be a source of irritation to both sexes, but when they do get together they have no trouble finding something to talk about. "Their main interest is engineering or else they wouldn't be here," says one student. Admissions staffers look more closely at high school grades, especially in math and science, than at test scores, and letters of recommendation from teachers are helpful. Students praise the school's financial aid policy, and with over 70 percent of the student body receiving some sort of aid, most speak from experience. In addition to need-based funding, Stevens also awards forty academic merit scholarships for $3,500.

Students say housing at Stevens is adequate and well maintained though nondept. Tech Hall is the exception. An ultramodern dorm with carpets, telephones and throoms in each room, it has "all the conveniences of a modern hotel," says one udent. The only difference is, you can't make reservations at Stevens. Dorms are ssigned by lottery or by squatters rights. After the first year, students can, and often do, move into fraternities, old brownstones off-campus or nearby university-owned apartments. Most students bail out of the meal plan after the obligatory freshman year in favor of dorm kitchens or the frat plans. The only hope for the freshmen is that the cafeteria's view of the Hudson and Manhattan's skyline may make them forget they're eating Steven's highly institutionalized food—"simply vile," says one sufferer.

When weekends roll around, students try to pull themselves away from their computers, and usually they pull themselves away from campus altogether. Those who don't go home can take advantage of the "extensive pleasures" of Manhattan, just a fifteen-minute train ride away, or kill time until the evening fraternity parties, which are just about the only on-campus weekend activities. There are mixers with nearby all-women's schools on Friday nights, but the attendance at these once-popular events has dwindled now that New Jersey's drinking age is up to twenty-one. The drinking age, in fact, has put a crimp in the social life at Stevens, forcing many students out of the campus pub and away from the kegs at parties.

Sports are popular at Stevens—especially intramurals, for which "everyone gets together on ridiculously named teams and blows off steam" in sports such as floor hockey and bombardment. Stevens' competitive academic spirit does not translate to the varsity playing field. But think of the bright side: "You don't have to be a superstar to be on a team." Being at a small school with a lot of engineers also gives students a chance to be editor of the college newspaper or disc jockey on the campus radio station without being edged out by journalism or communication majors. Outside the greenery of the campus, downtown Hoboken doesn't have a lot to offer, but beaches and ski slopes are within a ninety-minute drive.

At Stevens, there are ultimate rewards for suffering through the dining hall, enduring the male-female imbalance, and accepting the rigid schedule and surviving the rigorous work load. The Stevens degree provides graduates with good jobs in a variety of technical fields and the satisfaction that they can handle it. "After graduating from here," predicts one student, "everything else will seem simple."

Swarthmore College

Swarthmore, PA 19081

Location Suburban	**Applicants** 2,450
Total Enrollment 1,340	**Accepted** 38%
Undergraduates 1,340	**Enrolled** 38%
Male/Female 52/48	**Academics** ★ ★ ★ ★ ★
SAT V/M 640/670	**Social** 🏆 🏆 🏆
Financial Aid 47%	**Q of L** ● ● ● ●
Expense Pr $ $ $ $	**Admissions** (215)328-8300

Novelist James Michener recently reimbursed Swarthmore College for the $2,000 it had given him as a scholarship in 1925—and threw in $1,198,000 interest. "That's one thousand to one on the value of a good liberal arts education," he said. "Of course the spiritual value is a lot higher."

Located on three hundred verdant acres on the banks of Crum Creek, with its trees labeled by a local horticultural society, Michener's alma mater looks as much like an arboretum as it does a place of higher learning. But make no mistake: Swarthmore is an academic powerhouse where the minds are as fertile as the soil, and the intellectual atmosphere makes most of the Ivy League look lame by comparison. "Students intellectualize, analyze and cultivate 'consciousness' about everything," one reports.

Swarthmore's old, Oxford-style stone academic buildings house strong departments in just about everything, though standouts include biology, education, economics, political science, history, English, sociology and philosophy. One real gem is engineering, a rare offering at colleges like Swarthmore. It is taught as a liberal art, with students taking more than a third of their courses outside engineering and science. Successful engineers, the administration believes, "must possess a thorough understanding of social and economic forces, and have a deep appreciation of the cultural and humanistic traditions of our society." Poor facilities hamper performing arts, and music and studio art offerings could be better; the faculty, however, is quite good in these areas. Math is not a specialty here, and computer science is still relatively new. Requirements outside the major are flexible: Each student must take two courses from each of four distribution groups. Though faculty advising isn't up to par, students praise professors for both scholarship and accessibility. First names are the only names in most cases, and "even if the student doesn't seek out the faculty, the professors make the effort," says one sought-after student. A recent addition to the curriculum is the Undergraduate Writing Associates program, in which a small group of students take a writing seminar and then are hired by the college as writing tutors for $500 per semester.

Grades for first-semester freshmen are strictly pass/fail, to cut down on academic pressure while students learn the ropes. After that, watch out that you don't get hung. Says one history major: "Academics are far and away the first priority of students here, whatever secret talents or fantasies they may otherwise conceal. A general sense of guilt seems to unite an otherwise hopelessly individualistic student body: No other activity is quite justifiable." Another student was a little more to the point: "Don't come here if you aren't ready to work like hell." As testament to the strident work ethic, Swarthmore is affectionately known among initiates as *Sweat*more. (Former Vice President Spiro Agnew reportedly had a less affectionate name for Swarthmore during its more radical years: "The Kremlin on the Crum.")

Those who like to sweat most can opt for Swarthmore's unique honors program, where candidates pursue learning for learning's sake with a program of eight intense seminars during their last four terms, each with four to eight students. Though honors seminars have readings and papers enough to last a lifetime, there are no exams or grades until the end of senior year. At that point external examiners—faculty members invited from other universities—administer a series of final exams, oral and written. on two years of work. Somewhat less than a third of juniors and seniors enroll in the program (a minimum of a B-plus average in one's major is required) and nonhonors students can try out the seminars when there is room.

Unlike most schools, an eerie quiet reigns inside Swarthmore's comfortable library, which is conducive to intense studying and intermittent catnaps, but not to socializing. Though the library stocks more than 550,000 volumes, it doesn't fully satisfy the needs of Swarthmore's eager scholars, who often resort to the interlibrary-loan system. A similar problem plagues the curriculum: students often outgrow what the school has to offer. Courses, especially in smaller departments, may be offered only once every two or three years. The problem is exacerbated by a generous faculty leave program that allows each professor to take one term in six for research only. Registration has never been a picnic here, and several unexpectedly large freshman classes have recently swelled enrollments, making it difficult for freshmen to get the classes they want. Cross-registration with Bryn Mawr and Haverford colleges and the University of Pennsylvania are partial remedies, as is the semester exchange program with schools in other parts of the country (Pomona, Rice, Middlebury, Mills and Tufts). Abroad, Swarthmore sponsors programs in France, Germany, Spain, Colombia, Italy and Sri Lanka, and programs administered by other schools can also be taken for credit.

A healthy chunk of students come from Pennsylvania, New Jersey and New York, but Swarthmore's reputation attracts them from all over the United States. "An amazing group, intellectually stimulating and spiritually invigorating" is how one student describes her classmates. Many set their sights on the academic world after graduation; Swarthmore leads the nation in the number of PhDs per capita. Swarthmoreans are overwhelmingly liberal and very active politically, and any stray conservatives are likely to feel a bit under siege. The school's Quaker roots foster a spirit of community, open-mindedness, and above all, tolerance. "The college is outspoken in its refusal to tolerate intolerance: If you are a racist or a fagbasher, you will not last two weeks here before you land in the Grievance Office," says an English major. Swarthmore is committed to making decisions by consensus (students have an active voice in many administrative actions) and also committed to equal access: All activities on campus—dances, parties, movies, etc.—are free. With one of the largest endowments per student of any college in the nation, Swarthmore is need-blind in admissions and meets the full demonstrated need of all accepted applicants. Believing that student debt loads are getting out of hand, the socially conscious administration has recently increased the proportion of grant money in standard financial aid packages, and needy students can be sure that no more than $800 per year will be covered with loans. Incoming freshmen are also eligible for awards for full tuition (and more if greater need is indicated) based on character, ability and service to school and community.

The college's eleven dormitories, all but two of which are coed by room, range from spacious and modern to crowded and dilapidated. The rooms are parceled out by lottery, though everyone is guaranteed a room. Freshmen, who are spread throughout the campus, usually live in one-room doubles, while upperclassmen choose among singles or spacious suites. The 7 percent who move off campus avoid the excess of cafeteria food; the full meal plan is the only one offered. The dining hall has three rooms and provides "pretty decent" though unspectacular food. A pleasant touch is the weekend "served meal," a student-run service that turns the smallest dining room into a restaurant, with student cooks, waiters, a maître d', and live entertainment, all at no extra charge.

As for the party scene, well, let's just say it's unlikely that Swarthmore will ever crack the Playboy Top 10. A party or two on the weekends and maybe a quick jaunt into Philadelphia is about the extent of it. Recently refurbished Tarble Social Hall provides a snack bar, games and a rathskeller/cabaret till 2 AM, and several dive bars near campus are an option. While the drinking age in Pennsylvania is twenty-one, "it might as well be six" on campus, because alcohol is easily available at college events and parties. Swarthmore has several fraternities (to the dismay of most students) that draw heavily from the few jocks on the Swarthmore campus. As far as outdoor recreation goes, intramurals and informal Frisbee games are as popular as varsity sports, and the highlight of the year is the Crum Regatta, in which student-made boats float downstream in Swarthmore's answer to the America's Cup. Though sparsely supported, many varsity teams are successful, with football, soccer and women's basketball numbering among recent league championships. Swarthmore is one of the few places where women's athletics don't get short shrift compared to the men's; women actually have more varsity teams (twelve) than the men (eleven). Downtown Philadelphia, with its many cultural, social and artistic offerings, is twenty minutes away on a commuter train that stops right on campus and costs only $2.

A Swarthmore education can be an immensely rewarding experience, but four straight years of constant introspection and self-doubt is sometimes too grueling. "You need to take some time off from this place or the intensity of intellectual activity and emotional relationships will get to you," explains a junior majoring in economics and religion. Once replenished, Swarthmoreans inevitably return with renewed vigor. In their dedication to learning and zest for intellectual activity, Swarthmore students stand second to none.

Sweet Briar College

Sweet Briar, VA 24595

Location Rural	**Accepted** 75%
Total Enrollment 660	**Enrolled** 41%
Undergraduates 660	**Academics** ★ ★ ★
Male/Female N/A	**Social** ☎ ☎
SAT V/M N/A	**Q of L** ● ● ● ●
Financial Aid 33%	**Admissions** (800)533-1593
Expense Pr $ $	in Virginia, (800)537-4300 out of state
Applicants 570	

You can't depend on anything to stay the same anymore—not even Sweet Briar College, the elegant southern school where young Scarlett O'Haras once perfected their antebellum-style charm. Like other revitalized women's colleges, SBC is now gung ho about professional training, career internships and the like. At the same time it remains committed to a quality liberal arts education. The stereotype of "white gloves and snobby southern girls" is crumbling as surely as the walls of Jericho amidst the college's new slogan: "An education for reality."

SBC was founded in 1901 by the bequest of Indiana Fletcher Williams, whose goal, worded as carefully as the Constitution, was to educate young women in a way that would "best fit them to be useful members of society" The latest interpretation has prompted Sweet Briar to lace its curriculum with offerings such as business management, public administration, computer science programs, and a new program in international affairs. While English, with its strong creative writing program, remains the largest department on campus, mathematics and computer science now boast strong faculty and excellent facilities. Students give special praise to the history, foreign languages, art history and the studio art departments. In the sciences, faculty and facilities are improving, but the department has not reached its potential, and students also suggest steering clear of music, the classics and theater. The Asian studies program may be another loser, but the administration prefers to label it "developing."

Set on 3,300 acres of rolling green lawns dotted with traditional old brick charmers and wrapped around by the Blue Ridge Mountains, Sweet Briar's campus is a picture of pastoral beauty. Sometimes the surroundings are a bit too idyllic and removed to suit students for four years. "I get homesick for traffic jams, pollution and tall buildings," whines one cosmopolitan junior. But Sweet Briar has never been a school to keep students down on the farm (despite the working dairy on campus); in fact, it strongly recommends seeing Paris. Sweet Briar's Junior Year in France is one of the oldest and best known of the study abroad programs. SBC-sponsored programs in Spain and England are popular, as are its exchanges with St. Andrews University in Scotland. Students can also spend time on other campuses through the Seven College Exchange,* The Tri-College Exchange, or 3-2 liberal arts and engineering or business programs. January term is a popular time for internships, and SBC's unusually strong alumni network is helpful in arranging positions and housing in large cities across the country. Without taking a step off campus, distribution requirements assure the widening of a student's horizons through courses in foreign language, non-Western civilization, English and physical and social science. Sweet Briar has also introduced required senior seminars to replace the dreaded comprehensive exams.

The isolated campus and favorable nine-to-one student/faculty ratio can't help but appeal to students who want close contact with their professors. "You know the faculty's spouses, kids and dogs," says one woman. Even those instructors "who keep to themselves outside of the classroom" are still willing to bend over backwards to help a motivated or troubled student. Students say courses are all easy to get into, and a classroom with over forty means that there are a lot of visitors. "The only problem with class size here is that if you haven't done your homework, it's hard to hide," warns a freshman. Self-scheduled exams and take-home tests increase the atmosphere of mutual respect, and the absence of cutthroat competition puts academic pressure in an unusual light. "You work," says one economics major, "because professors are friends who really believe in you, and you don't want to disappoint them." An honors program and self-designed majors allow some students to spice up their Sweet Briar studies.

The homogeneous character of the school is changing—a little. Minority enrollment constitutes 4 percent of the student body, but almost all the states and nearly twenty foreign countries are now represented. And an increasing number of older "turning point" students contribute a valued perspective. Students here have a healthy, friendly, peaches-and-cream kind of glow, and good manners and style still command quiet respect. Private and public school graduates are equally represented. Sweet Briar's new admissions policy claims to deemphasize high school rank and SAT scores during its selection process. The most outstanding students can qualify for eighty non-need honors awards that range from $1,000 to $6,000.

The college's vintage dorms, with their polished hardwood floors, sweeping wooden staircases and furnished parlors, have aged gracefully (except for the plumbing). These agreeable surroundings partly compensate for overcrowding and limited visiting hours for male friends. Every dorm has a fair share of each class, with student leaders given the first shot at singles. Housing is guaranteed to all, and no one except for a few commuters lives off campus. All residents eat in the common dining hall, which provides freshly baked bread and milk and yogurt from the Sweet Briar dairy.

Sweet Briar is five miles from Amherst and twelve miles from any city of interest. That is, if Lynchburg—Jerry Falwell's hangout—ranks as interesting. "It isn't the most exciting city, but it does have a few nice restaurants, stores, a mall and movie theaters," reports one veteran. The successful outdoor program has converted hundreds of students to the joys of backpacking, canoeing and white water rafting on weekly expeditions. Organized sports such as swimming, tennis and field hockey teams are strong in Division III. And the equestrienne squad (backed by the largest private indoor ring in the country) regularly snags national championships.

Social life on campus is sparse with a "few black-ties" and social club–sponsored mixers. Sororities are nonexistent, partially because, as one senior admits, "Sweet Briar girls are more into fraternities at Washington and Lee, Hampden–Sydney and the

University of Virginia." Each school is only about one hour away, so the best advice is: Bring a car. It's standard equipment for social survival at Sweet Briar. Students also lovingly nurture traditions—lantern bearing, step singing, "tapping" for clubs—and appreciate the genteel image that clings to the school and its graduates.

The women of Sweet Briar value the excellent education and career preparation they receive. In short, SBC has found a way to pursue the goals of the eighties without shedding the trappings of a traditional women's education. The campaign against "those narrow-minded, archaic attitudes that an all-women's college must be a 'finishing school' and that a beautiful campus and quality life detract from learning" may become more furious in years to come.

Syracuse University

Syracuse, NY 13210

Location Center city	**Applicants** 14,000
Total Enrollment 21,020	**Accepted** 68%
Undergraduates 11,850	**Enrolled** 33%
Male/Female 50/50	**Academics** ★ ★ ★
SAT V/M 550/590	**Social** ☎ ☎ ☎
Financial Aid 70%	**Q of L** ● ● ●
Expense Pr $ $ $	**Admissions** (315)423-3611

Syracuse is a hard university to peg. With nearly twelve thousand undergraduates, a massive domed sports arena that seats fifty thousand people, and long lines to do just about anything, it looks for all the world like a large state university. Actually, Syracuse is a private school, which means, among other things, that its tuition bills are a lot steeper than those at its SUNY neighbors. But Syracuse makes up for it with a grab bag of opportunities, from social work to telecommunications management, in fifteen separate schools and colleges. "It's kind of like the Harrod's of U.S. colleges," says one student, "everything from amazing sports to challenging academics all under one dome."

Set on a hill overlooking the city whose name it bears, Syracuse's spacious campus is "a hodgepodge of old and new," from the stately old hall of languages building to the spanking new student center. The academic programs here are equally diverse, but to avoid getting stuck with a public university education at a private university price, Syracuse students must pick their spots carefully. They might start with the Newhouse School of Public Communications, which is known as the "birthplace of sportscasters" and is undoubtedly Syracuse's best-known division. It boasts leading programs in newspaper, magazine and broadcast journalism, though students say public relations has slipped in recent years. Also well known is the Maxwell Graduate School of Citizenship and Public Affairs, whose faculty members teach undergraduate economics, history, geography, political and social sciences. Syracuse's schools of art and architecture are some of the oldest in their fields, and engineering also garners high praise. Business-minded students should take note of solid retailing and transportation management programs in addition to those in the School of Management. The College of Arts and Sciences is the largest college at Syracuse and also one of the weakest;

students say math and foreign languages are below par. Overcrowding is a pervasive problem, but arts and sciences, management, and the Newhouse School are the hardest hit.

Liberal arts students must complete a distinctive general education program designed to "provide coherence in the midst of pluralism." Requirements include thematic "clusters" of courses in the humanities, social sciences and natural sciences, as well as expository writing and either a year of math or two years of a foreign language. An imaginative cluster of courses designed to promote technological literacy by exploring the dimensions of some basic lab sciences is well worth checking out. Syracuse offers a strong honors program based on seminars and independent research that wins rave reviews from its enrollees, and all students have the chance to take internships or study at overseas centers in England, France, Italy, or Spain.

With so much academic flexibility, individual initiative is the key to getting the most out of Syracuse's offerings, something many students haven't yet figured out. "I often get the feeling that this is more like a camp than a university. Very few students really seem to be into the academics," says an architecture major. Notable exceptions include engineers, computer jocks, architects and policy studies majors, for whom the academic climate is generally intense and competitive. Though underclassmen see quite a few graduate teaching assistants, faculty members are fairly accessible. A new computerized preregistration system has humanized what was previously a ghastly ordeal, but students say they still must wait a semester or two to get into popular courses.

Admissions standards differ among the various schools and are most rigorous in the professional schools, especially architecture, communications and engineering. Nearly half of Syracuse's undergraduates come from the top fifth of their high school class, while blacks and Hispanics account for about 6 and 2 percent of the students, respectively. According to an honors student, "If you want to fit in with the main crowd, dressing trendy, acting rich, and joining a fraternity or a sorority are the first steps." Syracuse has a very cosmopolitan flavor, which is not surprising since New York City and Long Island are the most heavily represented geographic areas. The university is reputedly about a third Protestant, a third Catholic and a third Jewish, though according to one student, "The Jewish community seems to far outweigh any other religious group on campus." As for politics, "The student body is very apathetic. There are those who will take a stand on an issue, but I think that most would choose not to choose, turn away, or just walk by," says a junior in international relations. The university does not count financial circumstances as a factor in its admissions process, nor does it guarantee that it will meet the calculated need of all accepted students. There are about 220 athletic grants-in-aid, and a handful of renewable scholarships of $1,000 are awarded annually to students in art and music, based on their portfolio or audition.

Housing is clean and comfortable but occasionally overcrowded. Freshmen are required to live in the dorms, and most wind up in double rooms in one of two adjacent modern residence halls, which are somewhat isolated from the rest of campus in a bad part of the city. Rooms for upperclassmen are assigned by a lottery, and most everyone who wants a room gets one, though a few unfortunate souls get stuck in extended housing, meaning triples or converted lounges. Upperclassmen can also exercise squatters' rights with their current rooms, but most opt to live in the university's luxurious apartments, nearby town houses or off-campus apartments. Living and dining in fraternity or sorority houses is another popular option, although the food served in the campus dining halls is varied and generally appetizing. Without a doubt, the cold, snowy winter is Syracuse's worst point for many students, but one offers assurance that "the sun does shine more than five days a year."

Syracuse isn't the greatest college town—"a depressing pit," in the words of one student—but downtown is in easy reach by walking or using the fine public transportation system. Once there, the opportunities include an excellent art museum, a resident opera company, a symphony, a civic center and a theater, as well as the usual movie theaters and restaurants. Several quaint country towns, complete with farmland, apple trees, lakes and waterfalls, are just a few miles away, as are two popular ski resorts.

Varsity football and basketball are big at Syracuse—big enough to fill the Carrier Dome for every home game. The latter has done especially well of late and is usually a contender for the Big East basketball crown. Though the Dome seats thirty-three thousand for basketball—enough to shatter NCAA attendance records—tickets must still be parceled out by a lottery. Though it gets less attention, the lacrosse team is a frequent contender for the national championship, and old-time fans still have fond memories of all-American Jimmy Brown, better known for his football feats, running down the field carrying a stick. The Carrier Dome is host to some of the biggest touring rock shows in the country, including Springsteen whenever he's out and about. On campus, there's "always a party to go to somewhere," especially now that the Greek system has made a powerful comeback, with about 20 percent of the students joining. Those over twenty-one spend many an evening bar hopping on Marshall street, a lively strip near campus. Drama productions are frequent, and *The Daily Orange* is one of the best college newspapers in the nation.

At a place as large as Syracuse, innumerable choices become a part of everyday life, and students here must be able to thrive on diversity and flux. As one student put it, "If you want your money's worth, you have to go out and get it—take the harder courses, attend lectures, exhibits, etc. The university has a lot to offer, but they won't hand it to you."

Texas A&M University

College Station, TX 77843

Location Small city	**Applicants** 12,000
Total Enrollment 36,570	**Accepted** 75%
Undergraduates 29,700	**Enrolled** 66%
Male/Female 60/40	**Academics** ★ ★ ★
SAT V/M 480/540	**Social** 🐘 🐘 🐘
ACT 23	**Q of L** ● ● ●
Financial Aid 41%	**Admissions** (409)845-1060
Expense Pub $ $	

"Howdy!" (pronounced *HAHdy,* that is!) Welcome to the world of Texas A&M University! The official language of the land is Aggie-speak, a derivative of standard English. And if you like wearing uniforms, screaming your lungs out at football games, attending a midnight "yell practice" to get in shape, and being a part of a conservative but academically up-and-coming institution, then brush up on your jargon. Otherwise, you're bound to be told that "highway six runs both ways." Translated, that means: "College Station, Texas—love it or leave it. And the last one out, please turn off the lights."

Despite the bleak Texas economic picture and cuts in university funding, despite the countless Aggie jokes depicting A&M students as awkward, unrefined hayseeds, there's no turning off this university's lights. Founded as a public land-grant college, A&M, the state's oldest public college, has evolved from an all-male military academy with a primary emphasis on agriculture and mechanics (yes, that's what the A&M stand for) to a vast, modern training ground for scientists, businessmen and engineers. "Very isolated within itself—not a part of a city but a city within itself" is how a building construction major describes central academic complex on A&M's sprawling five-thousand-acre campus. It's the largest campus of any major university in the country, and with the Texas-size spread of superb facilities, ranging from the eighteen-hole golf course to a library that seats forty-five hundred, few students are complaining about their isolation.

The notable engineering and agricultural colleges (the latter has Nobel Prize–winning Dr. Norman Borlaug on its staff) have traditionally been A&M's strongest, but the sound business school, accounting in particular, is gaining recognition as one of the best in the Southwest. A&M also has good programs in architecture, environmental design, elementary education and the sciences. Because of its excellence in oceanographic research, Texas A&M has also become a sea-grant college. The school does not offer degrees in art or in music and has only a fledgling theater department. In fact, the liberal arts in general suffer from student disinterest.

Special programs include cooperative education in just about every preprofessional major you can think of, numerous study-abroad opportunities, an undergraduate fellows program in which selected students do independent research under the guidance of a faculty member, and an honors program. A&M also boasts a newly instated "mentors" program that involves 325 faculty and staff members volunteering their time to counsel students and help them adjust to the huge campus and the high-school-to-college transition. Computer terminals are easily accessible and adequate in number, and the university has recently launched a major effort to coordinate computing activities throughout the campus.

A&M's most cherished program is the venerable Corps of Cadets, the nation's largest supplier of armed services officers outside of the military schools—and a major influence on student life. Its elite unit, the Ross Volunteers, serves as an honor guard for the governor, and the cadets have their own dining halls and dorms. (All members are guaranteed housing, a privilege not accorded civilian students.) The two thousand men and women (the latter known as Waggies) who make up the corps act as the embodiment of the Aggie spirit and keepers of its most visible traditions.

These rites include Twelfth Man—all students stand for the entirety of every football game as a symbol of their loyalty and readiness to take part—and the Aggie Muster, an annual memorial service for A&M alumni around the world who have died within the year. Every year before the Aggie football game with the University of Texas, there is a huge, hundred-foot-high bonfire "made of logs felled, hewn, transported and stacked by the students," expounds one proud fire builder. And the football traditions continue with the three-hundred-plus member Fightin' Texas Aggie Band, and the senior "boot line" at the end of the halftime show. The two-thousand-member Corps of Cadets (aka "jarheads") are beloved by many students for their remarkable halftime displays, which reinforce the Aggie penchant for buffoonery. "Without the corps," says a business major, "we would be just like all the other universities." Of course, there is a minority opinion. "I'm not fond of the Corps outfits," whispers one woman. "These unique (strange) people have a tendency to make newspaper headlines far too often."

Obviously this strangeness has not inhibited the ever-increasing number of freshmen applicants and a growth spurt that has made A&M one of the fastest-growing institutions in the country. Eighty-six percent of the students are Texans, conservative in their outlook, and friendly. Aggies are not "social climbers, beautiful people, drug users or hippies," assures a student. Most are true believers in manifest destiny: "I was born to be an Aggie," says one. "Like most people, I applied only here." Students are admitted without reference to their financial need, but there is no guarantee of support. There are two hundred guarantees for athletes, including eighty-nine for women, and numerous academic scholarships.

Single-sex dorms with two to a room ("hole") range from the cheap and not-so-comfortable to the expensive and cushy (with air-conditioning and private bathrooms). But because of the growth of the student population, there are not enough holes. Most of the freshmen find places, but many upperclass "Non-Regs" (Aggie-speak for a civilian undergrad) end up fending for themselves. Seventy-four percent live off-campus in one of the many apartment buildings surrounding the campus. Several meal plans are offered in the dining halls, and there are snack shops all over campus.

A&M's home base, College Station, is an uninspiring town in the heart of the Brazos Valley and not far from the Brazos River. Most students enjoy dancing at the several country-and-western and rock 'n' roll clubs in town. "We have fun, but grades come first," says one woman. Major urban areas—Austin and Houston—are about two hours distant. Dallas is about two hours more distant.

Athletics, whether on the varsity level or for recreation, are the number one activity next to drinking beer. "Enthusiasm for sports on this campus is unparalleled ANYWHERE," cheers one enthusiast. The football and basketball teams are regional powers, and the well-organized and extensive intramural program includes hundreds of softball teams. To cater to such a vibrant student body, A&M has constructed a new intramural complex, remodeled the football stadium and added physiology research and a conditioning lab. The recently established fraternities are not recognized by the university—there are no houses on campus. But Greeks are growing in popularity nonetheless—especially Sigma Chi, which has an oil well in its backyard that produces five hundred barrels a day.

"How do you get a one-armed Aggie out of a tree?" a double major in mechanized agriculture and industrial distribution gleefully asks. "Wave at him." Perhaps it's this undaunted Aggie ability to laugh at themselves while simultaneously appreciating their unique spirit that nurtures the strong sense of pride on this campus. Whatever their academic or other interests, says a journalism major, the students are "bound together by one common denominator—they are all Aggies, and they are convinced they are something special." Energetic prospective students who feel special and are intrigued by the eccentric are encouraged to "inroll"—that's Aggie-speak for "Come on down!"

Texas Christian University

Fort Worth, TX 76129

Location Suburban	**Applicants** 3,480
Total Enrollment 6,920	**Accepted** 65%
Undergraduates 5,770	**Enrolled** 51%
Male/Female 45/55	**Academics** ★ ★ ★
SAT V/M 520/550	**Social** ☎ ☎ ☎
Financial Aid 40%	**Q of L** ● ● ●
Expense Pr $	**Admissions** (817)921-7490

There's nothing new about football players taking funds for fancy cars from overly zealous alums, but there aren't many places where they turn themselves in. That's what happened at Texas Christian University where, true to the ideals of the founding fathers, six star players got themselves kicked off the team. The incident was typical of football coach Jim Wacker, a God-fearing man idolized by many students and well respected even by those Horn Frog football fanatics who were crushed to see TCU's few moments of football glory quickly come and go in a puff of Wacker smoke. And such a football coach is perfect for a good Christian school whose philosophy might seem too goody-two-shoes for more hedonistic types, but it's an attitude that suits these conservative undergrads just fine.

TCU's 243-acre campus is wedged between Ft. Worth's downtown business district and a residential neighborhood. The football stadium forms one border, the tennis courts another, and a cluster of low-rise, yellow-brick structures with red-tiled roofs mix with some modern glass buildings in between. "Since TCU is in the city, there is not a whole lot of wide-open space on the main campus," says a lit major, "but there are ample trees and grass to keep a country girl like me happy."

Students are impressed with the versatility of curriculum at TCU. Says one senior, "TCU was one of the few universities that would allow me to obtain a BFA in dance and a BS in science." Students can choose their majors from among sixty-two disciplines, and the liberal arts core curriculum makes up 40 percent of every student's course load. This core is devoted to work in the humanities, social sciences, natural sciences, and writing, and one semester of religious studies is required.

Some of TCU's best programs are in the natural sciences and health sciences, business and religion studies. And here's a university that doesn't tiptoe around the fine arts—dance is very strong here—it also boasts that it was the first to offer a degree in ballet and the only institution in the state with a theater internship program. Communications programs also tend to be good, providing hands-on experience using the school's two fully operational TV studios and five-thousand-watt radio station. Also, "the computer science program is gaining steam," reports a chemistry major. But math and foreign languages receive thumbs down. Finance majors step into the shoes of high rollers managing a $1-million-plus investment portfolio, one of the largest student-run investment funds in the nation.

The library has recently doubled in size, but students say its hours are still inadequate. The overall academic atmosphere here is described as casual, but students admit that it depends on what you're into. The premeds and students in the school's highly praised honors program really feel the pressure.

Over half the student body is from Texas, mostly from affluent and often ultraconservative families. "Those who want to mingle with a rather homogeneous, white, upper-class student body would like TCU," contends a geology major. A classmate adds that "the money is very visible here, but not particularly intimidating." TCU is still affiliated with the Christian Church (Disciples of Christ), but in contrast to competitors such as Baylor, the atmosphere is not heatedly religious. The university offers over two hundred athletic scholarships, and students who rank in the top 15 percent of their high school class and have SAT scores of at least 1100 can receive one of the 750 merit awards ranging from $500 to full tuition.

The majority of students live on campus in dorms. Only one out of the nine dorms is coed, and students agree it's the worst one. Despite some overcrowding, the dorms are reported to be comfortable and well maintained. Many upperclassmen flee to apartments near campus to escape the rules on alcohol (forbidden) and visitation (limited) in the dorms, although neither rule seems to be enforced all too strictly. About a fifth of the students commute from home, and the many fraternity and sorority members can live in their houses after freshman year. Dorm residents must take on a meal plan, and there's also The Pitt, a fast-food joint for those additive addicts and Eden's Greens for those who are not.

"TCU is known for having one of the strongest Greek systems in the nation," boasts one senior. Other students claim that TCU's is not a go-Greek-or-die environment—"If you're an independent there are more than enough activities offered to keep you busy." On weekends those choosing not to go to a fraternity party go home, or into Fort Worth's bars and restaurants, or high-step it to Dallas (forty-five minutes away) to clubs or parties at SMU or UT at Arlington. The student government sponsors movies and other events. One feature of TCU's social scene that draws male praise is "the incredible number of pretty girls—I see a new one just about every day."

Fort Worth is in many ways a perfect college town, "Large enough to provide a lot of things to do but small enough to feel like you belong." Buses run regularly to all parts of the city, where students may take advantage of anything from museums and theaters to the stockyards and rodeo. A not-so-terrific area of the city is a little too close to TCU, according to one student, so the university security has been stepped up considerably. Within half an hour of the city are lakes where students water-ski and sail. Women's golf and men's tennis have won recent national championships, and a women's soccer team has been added to the roster. Intramural sports have long been popular, but mostly among the Greeks. The sports facilities on campus are excellent and include two indoor pools, weight rooms, a track and tennis and racquetball courts, with a new women's locker room and training facility in the works.

"I like the helpful, caring faculty," testifies one student. "I appreciate the friendly, warm-hearted attitude of the student body," proclaims another. But there's no question in anyone's mind (especially those of the six ousted football players) why this school's middle name is Christian.

University of Texas at Austin

Austin, TX 78712

Location Urban
Total Enrollment 46,140
Undergraduates 35,010
Male/Female 54/46
SAT V/M 510/570
Financial Aid 25%
Expense Pub $ $

Applicants 15,242
Accepted 65%
Enrolled 59%
Academics ★ ★ ★ ★
Social 🏺 🏺 🏺 🏺
Q of L ● ● ● ●
Admissions (512)471-7601

Over the years, college students have been known to hold sit-ins to protest wars, nuclear weapons and university investments, but rarely have they staged such an event because they don't get to study enough. At the University of Texas at Austin, students got so upset about library hour cutbacks that they did just that. You see, Texans aren't accustomed to tightening their belts, and at a time when the economy is down and the largest state university is feeling the pinch, there are bound to be repercussions.

The UT–Austin saga began almost seventy years ago with the discovery of the Santa Rita One oil well on state-owned land. The result was a flow of money into a state education endowment that propelled this public institution into a position second only to Harvard among the nation's best-endowed universities. For many years, the university's growth was mainly physical; then it began applying itself to other goals, such as luring academic superstars away from top New England schools, snatching the prestigious Institute for Fusion Studies away from more likely university candidates, installing the world's largest telescope to complement its premier observatory site, coming up with $2.4 million for a Gutenberg Bible and creating endowed faculty chairs like they were going out of style.

Those Texans in Austin were having a grand ole time until the price of oil went down, the state deficit went up, and the budget cutters began to snip away at allotted university funds. Today, this once-generous school finds itself apologizing to faculty members for smaller paychecks and unable to fill several of the endowed professorship positions because of the Sunbelt blues.

In addition to these recent problems, UT faces other long-standing deterring factors that compromise its aim for excellence. For instance, UT has another commitment—to admit a large percentage of students from Texas, not all of whom are well prepared for college. Also, a large number of its undergraduate programs are vocationally oriented. One-fourth of the undergraduate student body majors in business: many in advertising, a few in health spa management.

Overlooking forty wooded acres, the attractive, Spanish renaissance–style campus is sprawled out right next to downtown Austin. The buildings range from "old distinguished" to "contemporary" Southwest architecture, complete with red-clay tiled roofs and the famous UT Tower adorned with a large clock and sweet-sounding chimes. It's what one student calls "a perfect environment—mild winters, lush green grass and plenty of trees."

With sixteen schools, 258 degree programs and sixty-five hundred courses. UT–Austin is one of the nation's largest single-campus universities. But bigger is not always better, even in Texas. A marketing major claims, "In the larger classes, with around five hundred students, people are hesitant to ask worthwhile questions. The lecturer seems so distant." Students must practice patience when trying to get into these huge classes; according to one undergrad, "we continuously get closed out of courses we need to graduate." And because this is a research-oriented institution, professors are often busy in the laboratories. To best deal with the situation, a student must take advantage of professors' mandatory office hours and utilize the excellent academic counseling services.

Any list of academic strengths at a school of this size must necessarily be partial, but undergraduate offerings in architecture, botony, biology, foreign language and accounting are among the best in the country. Engineering (especially chemical and electrical) and computer science are both excellent departments that continue to grow. Although spots of excellence can be found in both the business school and the huge English department (ninety-five tenure-track professors!), both have serious weaknesses as well.

An intense and nationally recognized liberal arts honors program, called Plan II, is composed of an interdisciplinary curriculum that features yearlong, small seminar courses and independent studies. Business and natural sciences honors programs are also available, although less renowned. At the other end of the academic spectrum, a strong reading and study skills lab services students in need of remedial help.

Although premed, engineering and certain business programs are definitely high pressure, the overall academic climate is "relaxed and laid back." Specific academic requirements differ among schools, but every student must complete three courses of English plus two courses with a writing component. Engineering majors can alternate work and study in the co-op program, while education and health majors participate in internships during the school year. Libraries are said to be outstanding, which is one reason why students would like to see more of them.

The university attempts to lure students from all over the country, especially those from the top quarter of their high school classes who have combined SAT scores of 1000, but Texas residents who don't measure up to such standards are usually allowed in the next semester. Out-of-state students—less than 10 percent of the student body—face tougher criteria. Since most students are from Texas, "the student body leans to the conservative side, with most just finding out about liberalism," says a senior. A finance major speculates that "a large portion of the students come from affluent backgrounds, as money seems to be everywhere." Despite such illusions of grandeur and low public school tuition, there are needy students at UT–Austin, and they generally get the financial aid they require. Numerous athletic scholarships are also available and outstanding freshmen can receive up to $4,000 per year through one of many merit scholarship programs.

Though one of the dorms (Jester Center) is big enough to warrant its own zip code, the university can house only 12 percent of the student body. Therefore, renting an apartment is usually easier than hassling with the dorm system. High school seniors who hope to enter UT the following fall are encouraged to apply for housing by November 1. Once in the dorms, students are guaranteed a room for four years. These dormies have a variety of living options based on common social and educational interests such as intensive study, women's privacy, business or the freshman experience. There are also a variety of dining facilities and meal plans—all pretty good and all unlimited, "which leads to fatness." Burritos or burgers-on-the-run are main subsistence for many.

Commuters enjoy a system of free shuttle buses that makes "virtually all areas of Austin easily accessible," and with a huge, hilly and spread-out campus of 110 buildings, such shuttling is often essential. One student attests, "you really need to be in shape to walk the great uphill distances between classes."

Austin is not only a picturesque state capital, it's also one outrageous college town. "The social life around Austin is never lacking," claims a seasoned UTexan. An abundant nightlife centers around the infamous 6th Street, full of discos, restaurants, pubs, country-and-western dance clubs and an excellent music scene—"everyone goes there on weekends," says a premed. The Texas Union sponsors movies, as well as a wide range of other social events, and boasts the world's only collection of orange-topped pool tables. For those more interested in octaves than eight balls, there is always the new Performing Arts Center with its two concert halls. When the weather gets too muggy, students can take advantage of their location in the beautiful Texas hill country and head for off-campus campgrounds, lakes and parks. ("Skiing is only twenty hours away," jokes a junior.) Fraternities and sororities are selective and highly visible.

Athletics mean so much here that the Tower is lit in orange (the school's color) whenever a team wins. "Students border on frenzy for athletics," proclaims one fan. And while football is king, many students contend that many women's sports are better than men's: "They are fantastic!" These Lady Longhorns have recently won national championships in basketball, track and swimming. The sometimes "less-studly" men also do quite well in these sports, as well as in baseball and golf. Texans like to do things in a big way and fittingly, UT–Austin's intramural program is the largest in the country and offers access to the same great facilities that the big-time jocks use.

Despite its recent monetary woes, UT–Austin still offers many students unbeatable value for their education dollar. The university may have problems filling all the endowed faculty positions created during Texas' glory days, but if it would just open the doors, it would not have a problem filling up the library—as long as students bring their own midnight oil.

Trinity College

Hartford, CT 06106

Location Urban	**Applicants** 3,470
Total Enrollment 2,100	**Accepted** 41%
Undergraduates 1,930	**Enrolled** 33%
Male/Female 50/50	**Academics** ★ ★ ★ ★
SAT V/M 590/620	**Social** 🛋 🛋 🛋 🛋
Financial Aid 34%	**Q of L** ● ● ●
Expense Pr $ $ $	**Admissions** (203)527-3151

Trinity, Connecticut's second college, was founded by Episcopalians intent on ending the educational monopoly of Congregationalist-controlled Yale. Since the 1960s, Trinity has set itself apart from most other small, prestigious liberal arts colleges in New England by clinging vigorously to its open-curriculum concept and "eschewing the paternalistic approach to education." Today, the little college is doing less eschewing. Trinity has changed its philosophy and injected a mandatory six-course interdisciplinary minor as well as "strict proficiency requirements in writing and mathematics," all of which sounds suspiciously like Connecticut's first college.

Beautiful Gothic-style stone buildings behind wrought iron fences constitute the Trinity campus. Located in the city of Hartford, the campus has a large, open quadrangle where students throw Frisbees or just hang out on a sunny afternoon. While they do appreciate the "spaciousness and serenity" of Trinity's collegiate setting, students would feel safer if the campus did not border on a low-income neighborhood.

Traditional liberal arts departments win rave reviews from Trinity undergraduates, with almost unanimous student enthusiasm for English, history, philosophy, and religion. Economics and the natural sciences are also strong. Although math and social sciences offerings tend to be weak, Trinity praises its budding new program in psychology, which has elicited interest from both students and faculty. And, even if the students don't mention it, the administration does not want to have its Russian and Soviet studies program overlooked. Also of note: There's been a substantial increase in student enrollment in non-European languages especially Chinese. And the school has added Japanese to its language offerings. The fine arts are traditionally the weakest aspect of the curriculum, although enrollments in classes are on the rise, and the fledgling department of theater and dance now offers an unusual integrated major in those two disciplines. The library, which operates on an open-stack basis, is good but tends to get noisy in the evening. "It's more for socializing than anything," sighs one student.

Still in place, for those looking to be liberally educated, is Trinity's freshman seminars program that lures 90 percent of incoming students. Within these first-semester seminars students and professors work closely on projects of mutual interest, and seminar leaders remain with students as academic advisers until the junior year. In addition, qualified freshmen may enter one of two demanding guided-studies programs: one in the humanities, and the second, newer program in the natural sciences. But don't jump into these; one student warns, "People who enter guided-studies programs generally become total nervous wrecks!"

Upperclassmen may devote a full semester to intensive study of a single, broad theme within their major, taking either three related courses and an integrating seminar or simply setting up a series of group tutorials and independent studies. The age of the computer has brought the computer-coordinate major to Trinity; students in this program learn to apply computer techniques to their chosen fields, which are as varied as French, physics or economics. Proof of this computer aptitude is inscribed on their diploma as an attraction to corporate recruiters. There is also a small engineering program, rare at such an institution. In addition, the school runs an extensive internship program with Hartford businesses and government agencies, a career-exploration program tapping the expertise of more than eighteen hundred parents and alumni, and visiting arrangements through the Twelve-College Exchange.* Trinity students may opt to participate in the Mystic Seaport term,* study Italian language and art history at the college's own campus in Rome or try out their Spanish at the University of Cordoba. There's also the new performing arts semester in New York City in cooperation with Café LaMama Experimental Theater Club.

Despite its high-powered resources, the scholastic climate at Trinity is somewhat mixed. Professors are stern graders, and the student body has its share of overachievers. But undergrads can generally be characterized as "serious about studying but not to the point where it gets in the way of necessary physical or mental relaxation." Adds another student, "You do your work but you don't make a martyr of yourself."

The admissions office concentrates its recruiting among "the more academically oriented public and independent schools along the Eastern seaboard," a policy that brings in smart, conservative students, about 65 percent of whom are in the top fifth of their class. Minorities are eagerly recruited and a growing presence at Trinity; but preppies (in the literal sense) make up about 40 percent of the student body. "The typical Trinity student comes from a lot of money, is very attractive, intelligent, social, tends to be conservative but ends up being rather apathetic," sums up one modest undergrad. Less-typical aspirants will be happy to hear that financial need does not enter into admissions decisions. If you're number one in your class during your first three years at Trinity you don't get a tuition bill for the following year.

Over 90 percent of undergraduates choose to live in dorms; there's a choice between modern and high-rise complexes (another new one is on the rise), or "beautiful old brownstones with super multipaned windows." A poor room during your freshman year can often be translated into a good one the next because lottery numbers are assigned on the basis of both seniority and past room quality. Many upperclassmen end up with singles. Fraternities on the campus periphery house about 4 percent of students, and another 5 percent venture even farther away.

Freshmen must eat in Trinity's expanded but still hectic dining hall. Food is considered average at best, and three meal plans are available. Upperclassmen of both sexes may join fraternities as "eating members," perhaps the most convenient escape from food service. Others hibernate in the Cave, a campus sandwich and grill spot, or simply make do in the dorm kitchens.

When studying is over, or even when it isn't, there's plenty to do for fun. Athletics are a top priority for most students, and women's field hockey and men's and women's crew, squash and tennis are as popular as the more traditional football, basketball and hockey. Trinity's rabid rivalry with Wesleyan makes these game weekends seasonal highlights. Just a few minutes away by bus is downtown Hartford with its symphony and other cultural attractions that make it adequate "unless you try to compare it with New York City." Fraternities, which recently survived a faculty effort to ban them, command the allegiance of a quarter of the men and provide much of the social life for the campus. "Frats are BIG, and students who don't enjoy them may find their social lives rather empty," reports one sophomore. There are three newspapers, a ski club, a theater club, an active Big Brothers/Big Sisters program and other campus organizations in which students can participate.

Despite the party school reputation, Trinity students are generally smart kids out for a good education as well as a good time. It is, says one, "a great place to be before having to face the real world."

Trinity University

San Antonio, TX 78284

Location City outskirts		**Applicants** 2,090	
Total Enrollment 2,770		**Accepted** 75%	
Undergraduates 2,420		**Enrolled** 42%	
Male/Female 47/53		**Academics** ★ ★ ★	
SAT V/M 590/620		**Social** ☎ ☎ ☎	
Financial Aid 39%		**Q of L** ● ● ●	
Expense Pr $ $		**Admissions** (800)874-6839	

Money can't buy you love, but as Trinity University in Texas has discovered, it can sure make a great college. The university began life around the time of the Civil War in the tiny central Texas town of Tehuacana, moved to Waxahachie, and then in 1952, in true pioneer fashion, pulled up stakes and settled in San Antonio, this time for good. Along the way Trinity accumulated modest bequests from benevolent oilmen—resources that gushed during the energy-strapped 1970s into one of the nation's largest and fastest growing educational endowments for a school of its size: about $216 million at last count. Trinity has been unashamedly using this wealth not only to lure capable students with bargain tuition rates but to entice talented professors with Texas-sized salaries. "We buy faculty," explains the president.

At TU "everything fits," from the uniform red-brick buildings right down to the cobblestone pathways that wind along luscious lawns and through immaculate gardens studded with Henry Moore sculpture. One student notes that the beautifully landscaped campus probably has the best gardener-to-student ratio of any school in the country.

In the past decade the school has also spruced up its admission standards, trimmed down its enrollment figures, tightened the grading system and begun energetically recruiting high achievers with the same blitzkrieg of personal attention and scholarships that large universities use to obtain promising athletes. In short, Trinity has set its sights on becoming the premier small liberal arts college in the Southwest—conservative, elitist and academically demanding—and seems well on the way to achieving its goal. Definitely aware of what's going on, students respond to the campaign in various ways. "The administration, in its push for prestige, sometimes overlooks students' concerns," says a senior. But for others this push is good reason to come here. "My sense was that Trinity was an institution on the way up. I chose to come because I wanted to be a part of the excitement that comes through establishing a reputation for excellence," says another student.

The university has its share of vocationally oriented programs, including a highly praised education program, and respectable engineering and business programs. Some of the more traditional liberal arts offerings also make the grade with students. History, biology, chemistry, philosophy, economics and religion departments are all well staffed by big-name professors and well thought of by students. Drama, speech and music have lost faculty recently as well as student interest. An attempt to boost art history has led to the creation of its own department, and TU is now in search of quality faculty to staff it.

General education requirements, which make up a third of every student's curriculum, ensure that every student will take at least three courses in arts and letters, the humanities, social sciences and natural and mathematical sciences. A freshman English composition course is also required. Students praise TU's innovative interdisciplinary programs such as the popular international studies, urban studies, Asian studies and European studies. Trinity approves a number of study-abroad programs in Europe, Asia and Africa, and encourages premed and prelaw students, as well as history and English majors, to take advantage of them.

Many students have never taken a course with more than forty classmates, and few courses employ graduate teaching assistants. But, large or small, all courses demand devoted preparation to win high grades. The atmosphere is serious, but not high pressure; the well-to-do student body understands that there is more to life than academics. "Trinity students work hard and play hard, but the work wins out every time," says one.

"Most students are very much 'me-oriented,' " says one disgruntled senior. "In a lot of ways TU is a yuppie factory for middle- to upper-class success-oriented Anglos." Still 13 percent of the Trinity student body represent minority groups, more than half of them Hispanic. Over 80 percent of the undergraduates come from the top fifth of their high school class, and an ever-decreasing majority are Texans. Need-based financial aid is distributed on a first-come, first-served basis, and a waiting list is sometimes called into play. Male and female tennis players are the only recipients of athletic scholarships, but Trinity makes no bones about how it gets a top-notch student body: More than nine hundred merit awards, ranging from $500 to $5,000, are handed out to academic achievers.

Trinity housing garners rave reviews. The four-person suites, most of which have balconies, are clean, spacious, carpeted and air-conditioned. Dorms come in both the coed and single-sex varieties, and a new housing policy guarantees four years of housing to anyone who wants it. About one-third of the students choose to live off campus, which is not such a bad idea. San Antonio is a pleasant city with fairly inexpensive housing and superb public transportation. A bus serving the downtown areas stops on campus every half hour. Meals are served à la carte, so you pay for only what you eat according to appetite: light, medium or Texas-sized.

The sport to follow at Trinity is not football, but, as scholarship policy suggests, tennis. The team competes in Division I, and national championships are regular occurrences. There are other "very low-key" Division III varsity sports like football, basketball and an improving soccer team, but students get a bigger kick out of intramurals—especially members of the five local fraternities and sororities. With no houses and no places to gather, "the frats and sororities tend to be mostly large intramural teams," says a senior.

Weekends (which begin Thursday nights) find students at local bars, fraternity parties or at other on-campus parties and events. Dating outside the fraternity crowd is rare; students prefer to move in groups, or, as some warn, cliques. Excellent lecture series bring notable politicians and public figures to campus on a regular basis.

The warm weather of San Antonio, "gives you that year-round spring-fever feeling," assures an accounting major. The Texas Hill Country, a beautiful area with trees, rivers, small towns, and festivals, is an hour away and a popular destination for weekend adventures, and Austin is seventy miles distant. San Antonio itself is a big draw for most students, who consider it and its gorgeous river walk and "tourist's delights" (home of the Alamo, remember?) far superior to such urban behemoths as Dallas and Houston. The campus is within easy walking distance of Brackenridge Park, the Japanese-style Sunken Gardens, and the fine city zoo, and you can always go check out its plethora of polo fields.

For years Trinity served Lone Star wealth, a contented bastion of preppiedom amidst the oil derricks. While in Texas all things get bigger, Trinity University is intent on just getting better, especially in terms of academic quality. Some students yearn for more school spirit and miss rowdy Saturday afternoon football games underneath the soothing Texas sun; at Trinity "no one even knows the school song." But such is the price that must be paid to buy top-notch faculty and students. The school is making its bid for national recognition, and more people are starting to know about Trinity University—and not only on the tennis court.

Tufts University

Medford, MA 02155

Location Suburban	**Applicants** 7,430
Total Enrollment 7,430	**Accepted** 34%
Undergraduates 4,430	**Enrolled** 36%
Male/Female 50/50	**Academics** ★ ★ ★ ★
SAT V/M 580/640	**Social** 🏫 🏫 🏫
Financial Aid 40%	**Q of L** ● ● ●
Expense Pr $ $ $ $	**Admissions** (617)381-3170

For many years, higher education types throughout New England held conferences and drew up plans to resolve the problem of the lack of a veterinary school in their area of the world. For a variety of bureaucratic reasons, nothing happened. Then suddenly one day Tufts University announced that it would build one all by itself.

The incident is reflective of the leadership that has propelled Tufts into the academic big leagues. For years it has consistently moved forward in traditional areas of graduate strength—medicine, dentistry, law and diplomacy—as well as with new ventures such as a Nutrition Research Center. Such additions had only a peripheral impact on the liberal arts and engineering colleges but now, thanks to a successful mid-'80s capital fund drive, lowly undergraduates have a new campus center and renovated biology and chemistry facilities. Athletic facilities have also been renovated and include a new field house, soccer and football fields. Another project slated for completion in the next few years is a new fine arts complex, comprising a modern theater, art gallery and renovated main auditorium.

With sprouts of ivy covering many of its academic buildings, Tufts looks like a small New England college, and despite its recent flurry of expansion, undergraduate teaching is still the raison d'être on this hilltop campus in a working-class residential neighborhood. Attentive faculty members continue to lead students through distribution requirements in foreign language, foreign culture, the arts, the humanities and the social and natural sciences, and then encourage them to take advantage of wide freedom to design their own majors, pursue independent study and do research and internships for credit. Strong departments include history, political science, international relations, biology, engineering, drama and languages, and there is an excellent child-study program. Those with a taste for the offbeat will appreciate Tufts' priorities; the most popular course on campus is Yiddish literature. Upper-level courses are challenging and reasonably sized, but intro lectures can be quite large. On the rare occasions when being shut out of a class looks likely, one student testifies, "if you bug the professor enough, nine times out of ten you can get in." Women are technically enrolled in Jackson College, by now an institutional nonentity.

Tufts has two popular programs in which students who need a break from being students can develop and teach courses: the two-decade-old Experimental College, which annually offers over a hundred nontraditional, half-credit courses taught by students, faculty and outside lecturers, and the Freshman Explorations seminars, each taught by two upperclassmen and a faculty member to between ten and fifteen students. With topics ranging from media and politics to juggling, Exploration courses are "an easy way for freshmen to meet other freshmen" and ease into the college experience, since the teachers double as advisers.

Ambitious students may enroll in five-year, joint-degree programs with the university's School of the Museum of Fine Arts, the New England Conservatory of Music and the famed Fletcher School of Law and Diplomacy, or they may pack their suitcases for engineering and liberal arts programs in England, Germany, France, Spain and the U.S.S.R. Back home, Tufts offers the Washington Semester,* the Mystic Seaport program,* an exchange with Swarthmore, and cross-registration at a number of Boston schools. Tufts students also have access to other libraries in the area, which is much-appreciated since their own is short on books and space. The one good thing about the Tufts library is its grass-covered roof, which offers an excellent view of the city for would-be studiers.

The student body includes "everyone from Middlebury preppies to Springfield jocks to MIT geniuses." The biggest draw is from Massachusetts, New Jersey and New York, but all areas of the country are represented. The university's reputation in international relations also attracts a substantial number of foreign students and Americans living abroad. "The majority of students are used to the good life," one remarks, but fittingly for a campus in the Tip O'Neill/Joe Kennedy district of Congress, political liberals outnumber conservatives. Tufts meets the demonstrated financial need of most candidates and offers prepayment and loan options to the families of others. Ten merit scholarships are available to sons, daughters, grandchildren, brothers and sisters of current students or alumni.

Accommodations in the "uphill" and "downhill" campus dorms vary from long hallways of double rooms to apartment-like suites, old houses, and co-ops. A good-natured rivalry exists between the two areas; uphill is closer to the humanities and social sciences classrooms and supposedly a little more social, while downhill is nearer the science facilities. Freshmen must live on campus (in double or triple rooms), and sophomores are also guaranteed housing. The rest is doled out by lottery, and some juniors are forced to move off against their will. "Best advice is to go away one semester junior year, and then you're guaranteed housing again," says one senior. About 15 percent of students move off campus into relatively inexpensive apartments or group houses. All but two of the dorms are coed by floor or suite (that's one each for men and women). Food plans for five, ten, fourteen, or twenty meals a week are offered to everyone, but freshmen must choose one of the last two options. Kosher and vegetarian meals are available, and occasional special meals (e.g., Italian Night and Mexican Night) spice up standard college cuisine.

The university is situated on the town line between Medford and Somerville, two of Boston's less thrilling communities. The "T" metro system has been extended to the Tufts campus, so it's easy to make a quick jaunt to Student City (aka Boston), which is only a few miles away. Harvard Square is even nearer and provides plenty of restaurants, nightlife and record stores. The drinking age of twenty-one is an intrusion at times, but for those with valid IDs, the campus pub has become an in place to hang out—especially Monday through Thursday nights. Tufts, incidentally, has earned a national reputation for its programs to promote the "responsible" use of alcohol.

A small band of fraternities provides many of the on-campus weekend parties, with one particularly enterprising house offering an after-hours bar that usually swings until six Sunday morning. Sororities exist but are held in relatively low esteem. Athletes are sharing in the renaissance at Tufts, with the list of winning and championship teams running longer than a full semester syllabus. Sailing, the lone Division I team and a perennial contender for the national championship, tops the list, followed by tennis, women's field hockey and swimming. Two intramural leagues, one competitive and one not so competitive, draw wide participation.

There was a time when Tufts was known as a haven for Ivy League also-rans, but the school has learned to offer its undergraduates the best of both worlds: small classes and personal attention in the exciting environment of a large and powerful university. And the word is out: A third of Tufts freshman students now enroll under early-decision, meaning that Tufts is their first choice. Even if you don't want to be a veterinarian, it's becoming a better choice all the time.

Tulane University

New Orleans, LA 70118

Location Urban
Total Enrollment 10,300
Undergraduates 6,640
Male/Female 55/45
SAT V/M 560/600
Financial Aid 40%
Expense Pr $ $ $ $

Applicants 6,200
Accepted 74%
Enrolled 42%
Academics ★ ★ ★
Social 🍸 🍸 🍸 🍸
Q of L ● ● ●
Admissions (504)865-5731

After resting on its laurels for years as a regional institution, Tulane University spent the 1970s revamping its curriculum, diversifying its enrollment, raising funds and balancing the budget. A basketball scandal set things back somewhat, but Tulane is now marking its sesquicentennial decade by expanding and renovating facilities with an eye to becoming a national academic force. From the recently completed $7-million School of Business to the dazzling new class studio, from a much needed on-campus student apartment complex to the still-in-the-works $12-million Center for Energy and Biotechnology and the $14-million Student Recreation Center, this lady-like southern research and teaching institution is undergoing a major face-lift.

The university resides in a suburban area known as uptown New Orleans—"We have the advantage of being somewhat removed from downtown and still have easy access," reports a semiurbanite senior. Students comment that the grounds of this condensed campus are immaculate: Madame Tulane "takes pride in her appearance." The buildings are modeled after the "neo-collegiate/creole mixture indigenous to Louisiana institutional-type structures. Variations on this theme are found in the two liberal arts colleges that most undergraduates enter: the red-brick Sophie Newcomb for women and the Gothic-style college of arts and sciences for men. These schools have separate administrations but jointly run all departments and courses. Recently tension has developed over allegations by alumnae and faculty members at Sophie Newcomb that the women's college, said to be the model for Barnard, is losing its identity.

Tulane's strength lies in the natural sciences and the humanities, with international studies in general and Latin-American studies in particular deserving special mention. An interdisciplinary program in political economy stands out among the social sciences. For those ready to focus on a career, Tulane also has respected schools of engineering (especially biomedical engineering), architecture and business. Theater, experimental physics and Asian studies programs are not fully developed, and foreign languages suffer from a shortage of majors. Students have little or nothing positive to say about the communications department.

One of Tulane's selling points is that it offers the resources of a research university to a student body of fewer than ten thousand. The learning environment is enhanced by big league research being done in such areas as robotics, satellite communications,

Mayan anthropology, and tropical diseases. Introductory courses, which tend to have about a hundred students rather than the three to five hundred commonly found at many universities, are always taught by full professors, never just by graduate assistants. "One of the major assets of Tulane is the accessibility of faculty," says one student. Students find the library adequate for research, but they don't recommend it for studying. "It's too noisy," is the complaint that echoes through the uncarpeted second and third floors.

All Tulane liberal arts majors must complete a rigorous set of general education requirements. Besides demonstrating competency in English, math and a foreign language, these requirements mandate that students take courses focusing on the natural world, cultures and societies, aesthetic expression and values. Top preprofessional students who complete both these and the requirements of their major field by their third year may apply to enter Tulane's graduate schools, including the well-regarded law and medical institutions, a year early. Each year the university's highly acclaimed honors program invites about 250 outstanding students, known as Tulane Scholars, to partake of accelerated courses taught by top professors and never exceeding twenty students. These select scholars also have the opportunity to design their own major and spend their junior year abroad.

While it continues to have a southeastern orientation, Tulane is no longer a provincial institution. More than three-fourths of the campus population is from out of state—some from way out of state. There are critical masses of students from California and Florida as well as from New Jersey, Long Island and other parts of New York. These include, reports one undergrad, a number of "rich Ivy League rejects who chose Tulane as a safe school." Whether from Bronxville or the bayous, though, students agree that almost everyone can find a niche at Tulane.

Other than New Orleans locals, freshmen must live on campus and leave their wheels at home. After freshman year housing is by lottery and choices include Stadium Place, a new student apartment complex. But on-campus housing is usually more expensive than off, so close to half of the students choose the latter. Some men live in their fraternity houses, but sororities have social halls only. (A city ordinance, passed during an earlier era when New Orleans was known for nocturnal recreation other than jazz, bans group living by women.) Freshmen who don't know any better are forced to sign up for Tulane's meal plan. After that, most survivors make do with their own cooking, the on-campus Arby's restaurant and a couple of campus snack bars. And for those devout diners, there are the free weekly meals offered by the local churches and synagogues. One student religiously follows her stomach to the Catholic church on Mondays for lasagna; the temple for fish on Tuesdays; and the Baptist church for jambalaya on Wednesdays.

Schoolwork may be taken very seriously during the week, but the Tulane student body busts loose on the weekends. Autumn afternoons are spent cheering on the varsity football team, but not because of any winning record. "It's a drunken social meeting," clarifies one student. Women's basketball and volleyball and men's swimming and baseball are the winningest school teams, although they don't receive much school support. "We're all waiting for basketball to be started again," says one hopeful sophomore. The reason he's waiting is that the varsity competition in the sport was cancelled in the wake of a scandal over point shaving and allegations that some players were being admitted whose SAT scores were not that much larger than their sneaker sizes. Club sports are big at Tulane. This student-funded sports program has put together twenty-two teams, some of which are nationally ranked, including Tulane's prized sailing club.

Fraternities and sororities are the center of social life for many students, especially freshmen and sophomores. But with the jazz-hot nightlife of New Orleans just fifteen minutes away, most students follow the music and head for the many offbeat cafés and clubs in the city's French Quarter. And appropriately enough, everything comes to a grinding halt during Mardi Gras, when classes are suspended for two days. The Mississippi Gulf coast is only an hour away, and serious beach addicts can drive to Florida's Pensacola beach in four hours.

Tulane's decade-plus of fine-tuning, building and renovating has given a boost to the academic aspects of the university and its students. But who comes to the heart of America's Dixieland playground solely to pursue a life of letters? Not the Tulane student, because this school is, in the words of one student, "a very respectable academic institution which has not forgotten how to have fun."

University of Tulsa

Tulsa, OK 74102

Location Suburban
Total Enrollment 5,160
Undergraduates 3,640
Male/Female 55/45
SAT V/M 530/560
ACT 25
Financial Aid 50%
Expense Pr $

Applicants 1,290
Accepted 90%
Enrolled 54%
Academics ★ ★ ★
Social ☎ ☎ ☎
Q of L ● ●
Admissions (800)331-3050

Ooooooooooklahoma, where liberal arts come sweeping down the plain! Well, that's not exactly what most people have in mind when they think of colleges in the Southwest, the land of large public institutions and strong engineering and business programs, where undergraduate education is often seen as a ticket to a specific job and a Sooner football game. But then most people have not been to the University of Tulsa, a small, private institution with a gushing endowment (more than $200 million) and an equally effusive commitment to liberal arts education. TU has raised its admission standards and trimmed its enrollment in search of students who are more academically oriented. So while petroleum engineering and geoscience remain two of TU's strongest programs, a student can now explore a number of academic directions at this pioneer institution, and still come out a winner.

TU's campus, quiet and neatly landscaped, is located just five minutes from downtown Tulsa and offers a striking view of that city's skyline from the steps of the library. TU's buildings run the architectural gamut from Gothic to modern—all variations on a theme of yellow limestone rock dubbed "TU Brick." This consistency has transcended into the school's philosophy, causing students to brag about the warm, caring academic climate and personal attention lavished on them. "Excellent research is being conducted at TU, but every professor I've had will always turn away from a microscope or whatever to give you his undivided attention," a premed relates. Adds a classmate: "Professors go the whole nine yards to help student clubs and activities— they're a very visible lot." Classes, on average, have about twenty-five students, and although students feel pressed to do well, the atmosphere is definitely not one of "study, study, study or you'll flunk, flunk, flunk," one student reports.

In addition to the well-established and internationally recognized oil-related and chemical engineering programs, TU now offers solid majors in psychology, accounting and the health sciences. Students have nothing but praise for the rapidly growing English department—the teaching home of S. E. Hinton, whose young adult books (including *The Outsiders* and *Rumblefish*) have immortalized Tulsa as Oz did Kansas. Another serendipitous advantage English scholars will find at this small southwestern school is the university's renowned collection of works by nineteenth- and twentieth-century American and British authors, including various properties of James Joyce: books, letters, original manuscripts and even articles of clothing.

Foreign language studies are improving, and the communicative disorders department offers impressive programs related to speech and hearing. In an attempt to lure better students into teaching, TU has revamped its education program, allowing students to choose a major in the arts and sciences while fulfilling state requirements for certification. The nursing program, once quite strong, is now experiencing difficulties in keeping its enrollment up. Meanwhile, the business and performing arts curriculums are classified in the "need improvement" category by many students. Two preprofessional programs, criminal justice and social work, were recently abolished.

In accordance with the Tulsa Curriculum—the cornerstone of the school's liberal arts program—all undergraduates must take three writing courses, one computer science course, and two years of either a foreign language or mathematics. In addition, each student completes nine courses distributed throughout the categories of artistic imagination, social inequity, cultural interpretation, scientific investigation and the contemporary experience. An expanded computer resource center with new laser printers, software and sixty computer terminals, has helped TU to physically match its modern-thinking requirements.

Undergraduates in all colleges are encouraged to spend a year abroad through one of the many programs with which TU is affiliated, including the University of England in Keele. Three interdisciplinary programs—classical studies, literature and society, and law and society—allow would-be professionals to follow up on liberal arts interests. Honor students take exclusive seminars, complete a thesis or advanced project and have the option of living in a computer-equipped house. Meanwhile, impatient career-oriented types can take advantage of a strong internship program (especially in accounting) or earn a BA/MBA in five years. "Tulsa is for the type of student who is not waiting until graduation for his or her real life to begin," says one student.

Half of Tulsa's students are from Oklahoma; the other half are predominantly mid- and southwesterners, with many from Kansas City and St. Louis. About 10 percent of the students come from much farther away: the Middle East, the Orient and Scandinavia (oil is, after all, a worldwide concern). Eighty-seven percent of TU's undergrads went to public high schools, and more than a third were ranked in the top tenth of their classes. The Republican party is well represented at TU: "Liberals find themselves in a minority," says an undergrad. And although the school is not affiliated with any one church, religious organizations are popular on campus. "Being located in the Bible Belt means we have a lot of holy rollers," according to one source.

Athletes compete for more than two hundred scholarships, and a whopping 22 percent of the student body receive merit scholarships ranging from $500 to full tuition. Adequate need-based financial aid is made available to most qualified students, but is not guaranteed. Yet Tulsa remains comparatively affordable, with low private-school tuition. One student calls his school a real bargain, advertising it as "one of the best educations at a price that is manageable."

Students have plenty of living options, including two mixed-sex dorms (one coed by wing and the other coed by floor), one female dorm, one male dorm, fraternity and sorority houses, campus apartments and winging it on your own. With 30 percent of the students commuting to class, there is no on-campus housing shortage, and dorm campers usually end up where they want to be—the single-sex dorms are known for being more quiet and attractive to upperclassmen. A student study in McFarlin Library is being renovated to its original 1929 decor and a new $6.6-million student center is due to be completed by summer 1987. There are two large non-Greek dining facilities, which are said to serve typical cafeteria food: "starchy and slightly overcooked." This shortcoming is compensated for by the unadulterated provision of a hot fudge sundae bar. Eating in a Greek house can be better or worse, depending on the cook.

"Dorms are lame socially," one man states. "The Greek system *is* the social life." In addition to sponsoring most of the parties on campus, Greeks dominate in student government, sports and most extracurriculars, but the "good-grade students tend to shy away from the Greek scene," one student reports. It's not that there's a lot of tension between various factions on campus; there's just not a lot of integration. "Foreign students, Greeks and commuters all go their own ways," reports one woman. "Those who want a lot of student unity would be happier elsewhere," adds another. School spirit is, thus, not too spectacular, and illustrates another major difference between little TU and the big OU. One man reports that the perennially successful football team was "not invited to a bowl game when we were ten-and-one because we didn't have enough enthusiastic fans." The basketball team is also strong, and the women's golf team is one of the best in the nation.

Nearby parks, lakes and a huge recreational water park (the big-slide kind) accommodate outdoor enthusiasts. Downtown Tulsa, "with its small-town atmosphere and cosmopolitan overtones," as one student describes it, is just a hop and a skip away. The city offers several activities, including its own ballet and opera, and an ever-increasing supply of shopping malls.

The University of Tulsa has been cited as one of the twenty most progressive, innovative colleges in the country. And while it claims to "embody the optimism and confidence of the Southwest," it clearly enjoys its maverick role—the only place in Oklahoma where Stephen Dedalus is as familiar as Will Rogers and the Sooners.

Tuskegee Institute

Tuskegee Institute, AL 36088

Location Small town	**Applicants** 2,630
Total Enrollment 3,330	**Accepted** 59%
Undergraduates 2,860	**Enrolled** 45%
Male/Female 50/50	**Academics** ★ ★
SAT V/M N/A	**Social** 🏛 🏛 🏛
Financial Aid 85%	**Q of L** ● ● ●
Expense Pr $	**Admissions** (205)727-8500

More than a century ago, Booker T. Washington decided his newly emancipated black brothers needed to learn some trades by which to earn their livings, so he founded Tuskegee Institute. It was a controversial notion at the time, and liberal social thinkers were afraid that too much of an emphasis on technical training would hinder blacks' intellectual development. Today, Tuskegee is one of the largest predominantly black institutions in the country and although it no longer offers majors such as tailoring, it remains a rather conservative preprofessional and premilitary kind of place. Rich in black heritage (much of the campus was built by former slaves) and able to boast of graduates including Lionel Richie, Ralph Ellison and William Dawson, Tuskegee obviously teaches students much more than how to get jobs.

The institute's thesis is to provide an array of "quality education for those who are economically, educationally and culturally disadvantaged." The core curriculum encompasses a medium dose of liberal arts and stresses communication skills. The strongest programs are in engineering (aerospace, electrical, chemical and mechanical, in particular) and the natural sciences (supported in part by the George Washington Carver Foundation). The veterinary medicine department, which offers a combined bachelor's doctoral degree program, is praised by both administrators and students. Agriculture, architecture, allied health and nursing (Tuskegee established the first nursing degree in Alabama) programs rate well, and business and computer science are gaining popularity. The education school is not the most inviting, but the administration vows dynamic improvements.

The academic atmosphere is serious, and grading fairly rigorous, but close student-faculty interaction contributes to the school's friendly and motivating environment. Classes are generally small, and because students get to know their professors, they often take a deeper interest in academic work. A counseling center offers advice on everything from careers to financial aid, but students complain the financial aid process is too slow and assistance in this area not up to par. Future engineers may opt to participate in a cooperative education program, which gives them practical work experience in their fields. There also exist excellent opportunities for independent study, and the remedial and tutorial programs are strong. Both Army and Air Force ROTC programs thrive at this school, which was the first site for the training of black military pilots; more of its graduates became flag officers than from any other institution.

With a tuition rate that's approximately 27 percent below the average cost for a private college, Tuskegee is accessible to students from low-income families. More than 80 percent come from public schools. Less than one fourth hail from Alabama, with sizable contingents from Georgia, Florida and Washington, D.C. A smattering come from the North and Southwest. While white students are welcome to Tuskegee, the school's strong black ties attract an 86 percent black student body. About 8 percent more are foreign—mainly from Latin America, Asia and Africa. Yet with several military-oriented students and all the preprofessional training going on, the general Tuskegee political atmosphere is conservative. In fact, "once a student has reached a certain upperclassman status, he tends to become more conservative on most matters," according to a senior. Three hundred students (generally upperclassmen) qualify each year for academic scholarships ranging from $500 to full tuition. Ninety athletic scholarships are awarded in football and basketball.

All men and women live in separate dorms, which students report to be clean and well maintained. Freshmen and sophomores are required to live in dorms, which might explain why some juniors elect to escape institutionalized living. But overall, 65 percent of the student body lives on campus. Freshmen are isolated from upperclassmen and aren't allowed to have visitors of the opposite sex until the second semester. Those who select a room early should have little problem securing quarters, although singles are reserved for resident assistants.

A combination of finicky eaters and indifferent palates creates a lack of consensus on the quality of the food served. All campus residents and some of the off-campus noncooks eat in the "needs improvement" dining hall (circa 1890 and one of several campus buildings constructed by original Tuskegee students). Today, the campus is a National Historical Site and although there have been numerous renovations made on the century-old buildings, the original early American architecture remains intact. The campus, spread out across two hundred green and arboreous acres in rural Macon County, has plenty of room to expand (a new aerospace science and health education center is in the works).

"Because of the size of the city of Tuskegee, the university is quite conducive to studying," admits a senior. For those who long for a little temptation once in a while, Auburn and Montgomery are not far away and offer everything that Tuskegee doesn't, like movie theaters, roller rinks and good night spots. The region's urban center, Atlanta, is somewhat farther, but still within driving distance, and serious road trippers can make it to Florida's Gulf coast (four hours away) and be back in time for Monday morning classes.

Yet Tuskegee undergraduates are not exactly uncreative when it comes to making their own fun. Parties (fraternity or campus sponsored), game nights, speakouts and pep rallys can be found on this middle-of-nowhere campus. Historically, Tuskegee has operated on volunteer labor, and the tradition of community service remains strong. The Christian Fellowship sponsors Sunday school, Bible-study classes and a choir. Athletics may not have the most splendid facilities, but Tuskegee nevertheless fields good baseball, football and basketball teams for men and volleyball and basketball for women. Intramurals are also popular, and there are tennis courts, a swimming pool and a track.

Tuskegee seeks students who, whatever their high school records, show "high career aspirations and a desire to achieve." The school maintains the high standards that Booker T. Washington set, yet it continues to grow toward the future. As one student explains, "Love and support are the characteristics that uphold the Tuskegee family."

Union College

Schenectady, NY 12308

Location City outskirts	**Applicants** 3,050
Total Enrollment 2,140	**Accepted** 51%
Undergraduates 2,050	**Enrolled** 35%
Male/Female 60/40	**Academics** ★ ★ ★ ★
SAT V/M 560/620	**Social** 🐦 🐦 🐦
Financial Aid 40%	**Q of L** ● ● ●
Expense Pr $ $ $	**Admissions** (518)370-6112

The first college in New York State chartered by the Board of Regents is also America's first nondenominational college—"Union" stands for the "union of all faiths." Established in 1795 (and larger than Harvard until the twentieth century), this small liberal arts/engineering school retains both a sense of history and a passion for innovation. Union prides itself on being a spirited leader in the move to integrate technology into the liberal arts. "This is a roll-up-your-sleeves sort of place," an administrator claims.

Union's was one of the first architecturally planned campuses in the country. French architect and landscaper Joseph Jacques Ramée drew up the plans in 1813, and it took about three decades for his vision in brownstone and red brick, with white arches, pilasters, and rows of lacy trees, to materialize. The final effect is romantic collegiate to the extreme: The Barbara Streisand/Robert Redford movie *The Way We Were* was filmed here.

Union was the first liberal arts college to offer an engineering program, and it continues to make a virtue of combining humanistic and technical instruction. In 1976 the college instituted a comprehensive program of liberal learning that requires classes in six subject areas—about a third of a student's total course load. The program includes courses like technology and its social applications, perspectives on other cultures, and human behavior and institutions, as well as one in engineering. All incoming students must take the freshman preceptorial, in which they read, discuss and write about classic texts. Interdisciplinary majors are a popular option and include comparative Communist studies, industrial economics, law and public policy, managerial economics, Latin American studies and medical education. The engineering programs are highly praised, and the strongest liberal arts departments are generally acknowledged to be math, economics, political science and biology. Language and fine arts are less impressive, although the latter has benefited from a new facility.

There are also legislative internships in Albany and Washington, a Mystic Seaport enterprise in Connecticut,* and cross-registration at sixteen other institutions in upstate New York. One-third of Union students take study abroad at some point in their four undergraduate years. The professionally minded can take advantage of the accelerated degree programs with the Albany School of Law or Medicine and receive a JD or MD at the end of six and seven years, respectively. Five years can earn scientists both a BS and MS and future tycoons a BA/MBA. Sophomore and junior honors students participate in interdisciplinary seminars team-taught by faculty members as well as private meetings with visiting luminaries. For those who want more educational innovation, Union's own Internal Education Foundation funds special academic projects.

Faculty members are remarkably accessible to all students. According to one, "Many encourage students to call them at home and some mingle with students at the on-campus drinking establishments." (Professors can't find much to do in Schenectady, either.) A novel program known as CHUC sounds like a new brand of dog food but is actually the acronym for Computerized Humanities Curriculum, a program that has put Union at the forefront of national efforts to use computers throughout its entire academic spectrum. The college recently built links from nearly seven hundred dorm rooms to its system, and students have used the school's computing facilities for everything from foreign language drills to writing haiku. The library's collection draws a few complaints, but it is adequately supplemented by an efficient program of interlibrary loans.

Students love the quiet sense of dignity and tradition within Union's ivy-covered walls, but lately the campus has been anything but tranquil. Construction continues on a new $6.5-million student center (to include dining facilities, a pub, radio station and theater), which will open soon. Also slated for completion is a new indoor athletic complex. And traditionalists needn't fear; both buildings were designed in Ramee's original style.

About 60 percent of Union's students are New York State residents, with many of them from Long Island. The student body has a mix of liberal and conservative, but according to one student, "No one gets very radical about political issues, though there was a lot of controversy over the football fraternity being kicked off campus." The admissions office is working hard to strengthen minority and prep school representation as well as to promote geographical diversity. Blacks currently comprise only 3 percent of the student body, and prepsters about 25 percent. The number of women has been growing steadily since coeducation was introduced in 1970. Although the admissions office is looking for people "who want Union," the college is still a safety school for many Ivy League hopefuls. Yet Union does attract strong students—about three-quarters are from the top fifth of their high school class—and a large contingent of preprofessionals add to the competitive atmosphere. A small handful of National Merit Scholars receive a $500 stipend and up to $2,000 more for financial need, but no athletic or other merit scholarships are awarded. Union has a healthy need-based financial aid program, and most students are offered viable packages.

Union's picture-perfect campus occupies a hundred-acre plot in the middle of Schenectady, lending a touch of sophisticated grace to this industrial city that, thanks to General Electric and more than a dozen other colleges and universities, is becoming a new high-tech center. Dormitory space, however, is limited, and promises to remain so inasmuch as there is no space on campus for more residence halls. All freshmen are guaranteed rooms, but some end up an unwelcome fifth person in a four-person suite. Sophomores are the last to pick and often end up banished from campus against their will. The majority of upperclassmen unaffiliated with the seventeen fraternities or three sororities move off campus, but housing is relatively inexpensive and obtainable. A few men who seek to remain on campus end up being foster brothers at fraternity houses with extra rooms. Greeks have their own dining rooms, while the rest of the students eat at one of two dining halls. "The food service really aims to please," a woman reports. "Recently they've begun asking students for their favorite recipes and preparing these foods." Only freshmen are required to purchase a full meal plan.

Union was the birthplace of Greek fraternities back in the 1820s, and today social life is still dominated by its fraternities and sororities (added in 1977). Tuesday, Friday and Saturday nights find the biggest bashes. Not everyone, however, is enthusiastically Greek: "Fraternities and sororities encourage conformity, conservatism and sexism," a senior believes. For those whose interests extend elsewhere, "Schenectady is on the upswing after years of socioeconomic decay and now has some fine restaurants and theaters," a sophomore reports. On weekends, many students (especially men) take the forty-five-minute drive north to resort-like Saratoga Springs and Skidmore College. An excellent football team and decent men's hockey and basketball teams are the big spectator sports on campus, but women's tennis and lacrosse and men's soccer also turn in frequent championship seasons. Intramural teams are organized by both Greek and independent groups.

"Serious but spirited, new and innovative in an old, traditional setting, and student-oriented, academically and socially" is how one Union premed describes her school. Although an aesthetic gem, the tiny campus can feel claustrophobic at times, and the Greek ruled social scene could prove stifling for many. But students here are not the type who dwell on potential limitations. They know what they want out of college, in the classroom and on the weekends. And in most cases, Union provides.

Ursinus College

Collegeville, PA 19426

Location Rural
Total Enrollment 1,220
Undergraduates 1,220
Male/Female 49/51
SAT V/M 520/570
Financial Aid 65%
Expense Pr $ $

Applicants 1,150
Accepted 68%
Enrolled 39%
Academics ★ ★ ★
Social ☎ ☎ ☎
Q of L ● ● ●
Admissions (215)489-4111

Members of the German Reformed Church founded Ursinus College in 1869 as a place where young men and women "could be liberally educated under the benign influence of Christianity." Somewhere along the line, women's sports became the school's unofficial object of devotion. This tiny liberal arts school, tucked away in a verdant corner of the Delaware Valley, has become one of the best schools in the country for women with serious ambitions in athletics. When the U.S. field hockey team won a bronze medal in the 1984 Olympics, five of the team members and the head coach were from Ursinus, and more than fifty colleges have hired Ursinus grads to coach their field hockey teams. The lacrosse team won three national championships in four years, and the softball and basketball are championship caliber.

Great women collegiate athletes, like their fellow students, must take courses, and Ursinus offers twenty-one major fields of study, including (in case you haven't guessed by now) a great phys. ed. and health program. But in the classroom the natural sciences reign supreme. Premed and predental are by far the most popular undergraduate paths at Ursinus, though prelaw is close behind. The economics and business departments also garner favorable reviews. Students and administrators agree that, as a rule, the humanities are weaker than the sciences, and psychology and the arts are seen as the most lacking. But the recent addition of art studios and a fully equipped darkroom should be helpful to those artistically inclined Ursinusans. Students say the library is low on research material and hours of operation. But resourceful Ursinusans make use of the interlibrary-loan system or make trips to the University of Pennsylvania's library.

Students find their rapport with faculty members enjoyable and the accessibility of instructors a decided advantage. "Professors let us know on the first day of class that they can and should be contacted at the first sign of trouble," reports an economics major. One of the stated goals of the university is to produce well-rounded individuals, so overspecialization is discouraged. Students can choose from more than forty minors. A core education program emphasizes the development of effective writing and speaking skills and requires everyone to take courses in English, public speaking, humanities, a foreign language, mathematics, science, social sciences and physical education. Those who want to go abroad can do so through Ursinus' programs in France and Japan or programs at other colleges. Prospective engineers can take advantage of numerous 3-2 programs at Penn and elsewhere. Honors students complete an independent research project.

Many Ursinus students are Delaware Valley natives, with most others hailing from New York and New Jersey. More than two-thirds are from public schools and more than one-third ranked in the top tenth of their high school classes. While most UC students enjoy going to a small school and knowing a large proportion of their fellow students, some get a bit antsy. "It is difficult to have privacy—everyone knows your business," one man complains. The college awards fifty to sixty academic merit scholarships a year ranging from $1,000 to full tuition. What's hard to believe is that Ursinus offers no athletic scholarships.

The wooded 140-acre campus is adjacent to a small college town, appropriately called Collegeville, about twenty-five miles northwest of Philadelphia. Wide open spaces and lush green lawns proliferate, and modern structures peacefully and aesthetically coexist amid the predominant late-eighteenth-century architecture. The Residential Village—eleven Ursinus properties across the street from the main campus—has just been renovated to preserve its Victorian and Federal character. One of the residential halls in the village is home to students who wish to enjoy international studies together. Campus housing provides shelter for about 85 percent of the student body, and all but two of the dorms are single sex. The best dorms to get into, provided you get the right lottery number, are the "quaint and homey" ones across the street. Weekly maid service, which includes a good vacuuming, is a part of regular dorm maintenance. All students living on campus must purchase a three-meals-a-day plan, and the frequenters of the dining hall seem satisfied with the variety and quality of meals. Zack's Place, the college restaurant, is a favorite gathering spot.

Fraternity and sorority parties are the main social events on campus, even though, as one student complains, these "definitely lack creativity and become monotonous quickly." Greeks do not have their own residential houses and all weekend parties must be open to the entire campus. So, to retain some aura of exclusivity, Ursinus Greeks plan midweek off-campus formals and only invite their dates. Students bemoan the school's recent "tightening of the alcohol policy" in an attempt to enforce the state's drinking age (twenty-one), thus ending a tradition of class-organized parties. To compensate, the school offers a free movie every night of the week and the student union board arranges lectures, dances and comedy shows to add some excitement to life in this rural setting. "The local community is a big zero," one students says. Philadelphia is half an hour by car, and in the absence of public transportation, it's a good idea to bring one.

Ursinus is truly a sportive haven among small colleges. In addition to the women's field hockey, lacrosse and softball teams, men's soccer and wrestling are strong. PE majors oversee the strong intramural program, which draws a large number of students.

"I made a sudden switch," tells a transfer student, "from two years of a cold, flat, busy institution to a friendly, hilly, tree-shaded, intellectually active college." Although Ursinus may be a bit isolated from the cosmopolitan center that is so near, the gorgeous sylvan setting is conducive to studying, making friends and making goals, on or off the athletic field.

University of Utah

Salt Lake City, UT 84112

Location City outskirts
Total Enrollment 24,770
Undergraduates 20,620
Male/Female 60/40
ACT 22
Financial Aid 40%
Expense Pub $

Applicants 7,090
Accepted 89%
Enrolled 51%
Academics ★ ★ ★
Social ☎ ☎ ☎
Q of L ● ● ●
Admissions (801)581-7281

The University of Utah enjoys a picturesque location in the foothills of the magnificent Wasatch Mountains, within a half-hour drive of eight ski resorts and "the greatest snow on earth." The wide open vistas provide a sharp contrast to the restrictive Mormon influence, which is felt as strongly on the campus of this publicly assisted campus as everywhere else in the state. Utah residents are familiar with the conservative life-style espoused by the Mormon Church—no drinking, smoking or "permissiveness" of any kind—but out-of-staters should be ready for mild culture shock.

Though not the aesthetic equal of its stunning backdrop, the Utah campus is quite attractive. Occupying fifteen hundred well-landscaped acres that are part of a state arboretum, the prevailing architecture is modern, with the buildings coming in all shapes and sizes. Academically, Utah has set its sights on becoming nothing less than "the best university in the western heartland between Chicago and California," but unfortunately the budget ax appears to have deferred that dream for the moment. Six percent was cut out of the most recent state allocation to the U of U, and bleak economic conditions in Utah leave the university's long-term financial outlook in doubt.

Founded in 1850, three years after the pioneers settled in Salt Lake City, U of U is the state's comprehensive institution of nonagricultural higher education. It provides strong professional training as well as a solid program in liberal arts. Traditional areas of expertise include business, communications, fine arts, computer science, engineering and mining and the natural sciences. There is an excellent medical center, known for its innovative research in health engineering (its physicians performed the first mechanical heart operation). The Salt Lake Valley is sometimes called the Bionic Valley, with a plethora of high-technology laboratories that provide research opportunities for undergraduates. The outstanding ballet department recently acquired a new student dance facility, and the Middle East Studies Center is well respected. The English department and its new creative writing program show increasing promise. On a different note, the university recently put its sociology department into "receivership" (i.e., a hiring freeze and a halt to graduate student admission) because of internal squabbling among professors.

Utah's program of liberal education, including a year of basic math and a language, gives students scholastic breadth. The honors program, the third oldest in the nation, features top faculty and small classes. Through the Utah Plan, a selected group of freshmen take a specially integrated course of study, including one class together each quarter, that offers close interaction among students and their professors and a bit of small-college atmosphere in this large university setting. For the average student, the academic climate is relaxed. Those already on top of the material covered by these courses can place out through a series of exams, but the large number of students who enter Utah without adequate language or math skills won't find much help from Utah's undernourished remedial services. The five-story library is packed with books and is a good place to study. But an English major complains, "The collections are in bad shape. The legislature simply refuses to provide the funds to keep current."

Also, getting the classes you need when you need them can be a nightmare. "Many times it will take two or three quarters to get a required course for your major," warns a senior psych major. "Most classes are way oversized," adds a civil engineering junior. Introductory classes can have up to several hundred students, which makes contact with professors rare in the first two years.

Students are predominantly middle-class and public school educated, with over three-quarters from the immediate area. Out-of-staters comprise only 9 percent of the student body, and minorities are also in short supply, with blacks and Hispanics combining for less than 3 percent of the student body. Many at Utah are Mormons of the "returned-missionary" variety, pushing the average age of students over the twenty-one mark. The large number of married students testifies to the church's stress on family life and condemnation of premarital sex. Despite Utah's buttoned-down image, there are, lurking among the Reaganites, at least a handful of liberals who have made South African apartheid a recent issue on campus. Utah's open admissions policy also means that the student body varies widely in its academic ability. But, the U of U is a "big enough and diverse enough place that there is room for almost anyone," insists one senior. In addition to need-based financial aid, the university awards several hundred merit scholarships each year that range from $300 to full tuition. Varsity athletes, meanwhile, garner 275 awards in fourteen sports.

Only 10 percent of the students live on campus, though the few who do will find rooms small and comfortable. Most of the rest commute from home, but there are also rambling Victorian houses and apartment buildings for rent nearby. Students who live on campus have their own dining facility, where a variety of meal plans are available, while the student union has a facility that both boarders and commuters can frequent. The campus sits on a hill overlooking Salt Lake City and its flourishing cultural scene, which includes the respected Utah Symphony and opera company and, of course, the Mormon Tabernacle Choir, as well as professional hockey and basketball teams.

Social life is best described as low key. The Mormon student group and the Greek organizations have a corner on the social market on campus, and those who belong to neither will probably feel a bit left out. Don't expect to drown your sorrows; alcohol is not permitted on campus. The university sponsors symposiums and lectures, and students support a variety of movie houses and clubs with live acts. Next door to the campus, the Mormon Institute of Religion sponsors dances, family-home evenings and fireside get-togethers. Weekends on this predominantly commuter campus are slow—a time when most students head either for the slopes or home.

Football and basketball are the most popular sports on campus, and both draw an enthusiastic following. Utah's ski teams, naturally, have been national champions four times since 1978. Gymnastics—especially women's—is a national power, and the swimming teams are also good. The field house has a number of athletic amenities, including indoor tennis courts and saunas, and a new $5 million athletic complex now under construction should further enhance the facilities. Coed intramurals—in sixty different sports—are an important student activity.

The University of Utah is, according to its students, cosmopolitan and diverse, but "the spirit of the place is mostly drained away by four in the afternoon," due to the the commuter exodus. But there is potential in the midst of this outdoor paradise, and the U of U says it's ready and eager for "challenges ten and twenty years down the road."

Vanderbilt University

Nashville, TN 37212

Location City outskirts
Total Enrollment 8,970
Undergraduates 5,320
Male/Female 50/50
SAT V/M 560/620
Financial Aid 58%
Expense Pr $ $ $

Applicants 7,000
Accepted 54%
Enrolled 38%
Academics ★ ★ ★ ★
Social 🐿 🐿 🐿 🐿
Q of L ● ● ●
Admission (615)322-2561

Located within walking distance of Nashville's Centennial Park, where there's a full replica of the Parthenon, Vanderbilt University may be yet another part of the reason that Nashville is known as the Athens of the South. Strong in a variety of academic disciplines, Vanderbilt aims to create an intellectual atmosphere that will "provide knowledge, skills and understanding" to future productive citizens. Lest anyone get too serious, there's always Opryland to visit. And "Vandy" students know how to keep their cool in traditional southern style—letting off steam in the all-important weekend social life.

A maze of cobblestone paths connects the modern and collegiate Gothic buildings on Vanderbilt's campus. Although the university sits alongside a busy Nashville thoroughfare, the quiet, well-landscaped campus, with its abundance of thick, shady trees and resident squirrels, is "its own little city—and a beautiful one at that." In the city of Vanderbilt, undergraduates choose among four schools: liberal arts, engineering, nursing or education. Specific distribution requirements vary from school to school, but most students get a good dose of writing, math, foreign language and humanities courses. The preprofessional programs are boosted by the presence of Vanderbilt's medical, law and business schools, with which combined-degree programs are available. Departments receiving a favorable nod from students include English, science, mathematics, economics, history and engineering. Vanderbilt's merger with the Blair School of Music has helped fine-tune the melodious offerings, and the George Peabody Teacher's College renders strong programs in special education. Less recommended majors include sociology, speech communications, women's studies, psychology and languages.

Vanderbilt's popular study-abroad program features summer, semester and year-long instruction in England, France, Germany, Spain, Mexico and Israel. An added academic bonus is the optional Maymester, where students concentrate four weeks on one project. Drama classes have been known to tour London theaters during this month; film students can use this term to work full-time on producing a film. Vandy's library, besides providing 1.8 million books, has one of the country's best videotape collections of network evening news broadcasts—a special help to students majoring in history and political science. Some students complain, however, that the library does not have enough resource material, and, even though it's open until midnight (with a reserve room open till 2:00 AM), students protest that the hours are inadequate.

"People take grades fairly seriously," according to one student, "but they don't seem to let grades control their college careers." In fact, when it comes to academic etiquette, Vanderbilt students, with few exceptions, adhere strictly to the school's honor system. First instituted in 1875, this system governs all aspects of a student's academic conduct, and is reported by students to be still a "strong and effective" influence.

Faculty members are praised by students: "Many become mentors and take the time to call," says a senior. "This is what I rave about to prospective students." Freshman seminars provide newcomers quick and easy access to the best of Vanderbilt's teaching talent. But outside these seminars, freshmen and sophomores are often subjected to large lecture classes (with three to four hundred students) and less experienced teaching assistants. The program of academic advising is not comprised of forced faculty labor but of volunteers, and there is a corresponding level of interest and quality.

A mixture of Republicans, fraternity and sorority siblings, and "Bible-thumping Presbyterians" sets the rather traditional tone to the campus. As one denizen observes, "This may be the most conservative campus, politically, in America." Young Life, a Christian fellowship, vies with the fraternities in popularity, causing one student to quickly cite "how ultraconservative it is" as her least favorite aspect of the school. Indeed, this is a rather homogeneous bunch of students—about 92 percent are white and many are wealthy southern preppies from the exclusive schools of Atlanta, Memphis, Dallas and Virginia. Tennessee residents make a strong showing, but about 73 percent are from homes beyond the state. Although there is a substantial northeastern contingent, Vanderbilt has retained more of a southern flavor than Duke, Emory or other popular destinations for academic carpetbaggers. A generous need-based financial aid program is complemented by over three hundred academic and athletic merit scholarships.

Ninety percent of the students reside on campus for the long haul, but not, the students contend, because they like it. Most dorms are described by students as "dilapidated." One senior rates them as "so physically disfunctional that they seriously detract from the college experience." Where quality lets off, however, quantity takes over. Freshmen are guaranteed singles or doubles in their own special dorms, and other accommodations include two-story bungalows, six-room suites, theme dorms (art, philosophy, foreign languages) and apartments. Students try to live off-campus but report that housing is not easy to find. There are three "huge, unpleasant" dining halls on campus, which are improving with renovation. Meals are paid for with transferable meal points. Freshmen must eat on campus, but upperclassmen tend to avoid the cafeteria. Fraternity members have their own cooks, but sorority kitchens are used only once a week. In any case, "a hot plate and a refrigerator are a must."

"Sorority or fraternity membership is necessary for social status, but not social life," says one blunt student. Yet somehow almost half the campus manages to get by without either affiliation. Interaction between the Greeks and non-Greeks is encouraged, although not always successfully, by making many functions open to the whole campus (at least during the first semester) and limiting fraternity residence to officers of the organization. Weekends feature a full complement of Greek functions, for which most women simply must have escorts. In fact, many activities at this oh-so-traditional school all but require dates, causing some to lament the fact that "often, those without an escort are looked down upon"—except for Thursdays, that is. Tradition decrees that parties on Thursday evening are open to the unescorted of both sexes. The student government also sponsors activities such as bands on the lawn on Friday afternoons.

Vanderbilt is on the outskirts of Music City U.S.A., a happy fact of life that offers a rich supply of bluegrass, country and rock music, and an abundance of good restaurants and theaters—all within walking distance of the school. Beyond Nashville's borders are the Smokies, state parks with picnic facilities, beautiful lakes and skiing in the winter. Among the campus sports events, only basketball gets raves from Vanderbilt fans. One student claims that Vandy's "high academic standards are not compatible with the athletic success in the Southeast Conference." The fact is, varsity sports don't receive nearly the enthusiastic response from the students as their more amateur intramural counterparts do, a feature that one senior cites as "one of Vanderbilt's greatest assets."

Vandy students enjoy four years of good schooling and great partying in a traditional setting. "Things need to be stirred up here," believes one student, "but it's not likely to happen." And that suits the majority of loyal students just fine. At Vanderbilt, change, like everything else, proceeds at a leisurely southern pace.

Vassar College

Poughkeepsie, NY 12601

Location Small town		**Applicants** 3,800	
Total Enrollment 2,320		**Accepted** 46%	
Undergraduates 2,320		**Enrolled** 33%	
Male/Female 41/59		**Academics** ★ ★ ★	
SAT V/M 620/620		**Social** 🐿 🐿 🐿	
Financial Aid 60%		**Q of L** ● ● ● ●	
Expense Pr $ $ $ $		**Admissions** (914)452-7000	

Long regarded as the most avant-garde of the Seven Sisters, Vassar has had to put up with a lot of name calling over the years. The college's reputation was built on an unusually diverse and outspoken student body and a rigorous liberal arts tradition stressing independent thought and debate. As at other colleges, the mood at Vassar today is more conservative than in earlier periods, but it has survived both the 1968 transition to coeducation and the financial crunch of the 1970s with its liberal academic and social traditions intact.

The spacious, neo-Gothic campus, located on what was once Matthew Vassar's farm, is beautifully landscaped, boasting seas of daffodils around the two lakes in springtime and gorgeous New England foliage in the autumn. "Basically, it's a beautiful place to wake up to in the morning," sighs one graduating senior. Not quite as idyllic, however, is the area outside the prim brick wall that encircles the campus. Poughkeepsie is "a postindustrial town that has seen better days, but is experiencing a modest renaissance," says one well-read student.

English and art history top everyone's list of best departments, with history and philosophy running close behind. The drama department is also strong—it launched Meryl Streep, after all—and Vassar offers the country's only undergraduate major in cognitive science. The student academic gripe list includes physics (the facilities, not the professors, are inadequate) and economics (the supply of esoteric knowledge exceeds student demand). With distribution requirements kept to a minimum, says one student, "the avenues by which you can progress intellectually are opened wide in all directions." By all accounts, students tear them down at breakneck speed. "It can be all-consuming if you take your academics seriously," says an English major. "Professors are always willing to accommodate eager students with ample amounts of work." Forget about things like business administration or engineering—Vassar is liberal arts all the way.

Small classes and tutorials are the rule, even for introductory courses, and friendships with faculty members develop easily. "Professors do have research interests and projects, but their teaching responsibilities very obviously come first and foremost," says a coddled undergrad. Eighty percent of professors live on campus. Pressure for good grades is high, but competition is not. "We do not compete for grades," asserts a senior. "We thirst for knowledge." Exams are run on an honor system.

Most people study in the Gothic-style library, with its "thoroughly delightful decor and atmosphere," half a million volumes, and, best of all, a twenty-four-hour study room for those all-night crams. Other favorite facilities include the college art gallery, which is among the best anywhere, and the film library with its collections of rare prints and equipment. The biology building houses two electron microscopes, and music students are spoiled by a grand collection of Steinways, their own superb library of scores and books and proximity to Lincoln Center and Carnegie Hall. Study abroad is popular and encouraged, with a large number of programs available under the auspices of other colleges. Vassar also sponsors its own semester in England for education majors and a year in Spain under a joint arrangement with Wesleyan.

Half of Vassar's students come from the top tenth of their class, and not a few turn down Ivy League offers for the special benefits of a Vassar education, as well as for a chance to enjoy the Manhattan-oriented student body. "There is a contingent of urban sophisticates (known as BPs, or Beautiful People), but there are also rugby players, political activists, and many others," reports an English major. But most students agree that there aren't any rigid barriers between the various factions. Campus dances feature the latest music from the East Village, and one student suggests that art is "a valuable topic to be fluent in around here." A philosophy major sums up the student body as "intellectual, cosmopolitan and mature beyond their years—this is a community of young adults."

One student suggests that, given the nature and interests of its undergraduate body, "Vassar should be located in Greenwich Village." It is not, however, and for this reason most weekend activities—films, drama and musical entertainment—are found on campus. One exception to this rule is Peter's Place, a bar often frequented by Vassarites when their own pub—Matthew's Mug—shuts down around two AM. Other worthwhile jaunts in the nearby region, however, are Roosevelt's Hyde Park and the Culinary Institute of America (for cheap gourmet meals). Fifty percent of Vassar students do some kind of fieldwork in the area, assisting in hospitals and schools, and even the local soup kitchen. The Bardavon Theater and Hudson Valley Philharmonic also help slow a student exodus to New York City.

The comfortable surroundings extend to dorm life, where most people get a single after freshman year. Each dorm has its own "white angel," a receptionist left over from the days of parietals, parlors and student kitchens. The one single-sex dorm left is reportedly a bit dull (and not so strictly single sex). Other dorms are coed by floor or room. Housing is guaranteed for all four years and "may even verge on palatial by senior year," according to one student with a bay window in his seventeen-foot-wide single. Juniors and seniors favor the off-campus but college-owned Town Houses (five person suites) or the four-person Terrace Apartments, both with kitchens and living rooms. Dorm dwellers eat in relative splendor in the All Campus Dining Center (aka the ACDC) overlooking pine groves and rolling lawns.

The annual gala formals bring high society to Vassar twice a year, while the only thing approaching a fraternity is the mysterious Royal Order of the Moose, which throws a big party for its successful alumni every year. Vassar has been among the more successful former women's colleges in attracting male students, and there are few complaints about the relaxed relationship between the sexes or the improving but yet-to-even-out ratio. Varsity athletics are experiencing a minor renaissance, and squash, soccer, rugby and cross-country are the strongest offerings, with women's sports being favored by spectators. The up-and-coming crew team works out on the

Hudson River, which, at this distance from Manhattan, is still beautiful. Those who choose to leave their idyllic home on weekends usually head for Manhattan or New Haven (Yale tends to be the site for off-campus matchmaking), each about one and a half hours away.

Vassar is one of the few coeducational schools where women hold top leadership positions—as well as 40 percent of the faculty jobs. Its diploma, whether held by a man or a woman, is well respected in the job market and a strong Vassar GPA highly regarded at graduate schools. But even more important is the experience behind the sheepskin and transcript: Vassar's special brand of education—flexible, personalized, highly rigorous—shared by a bright, motivated, creative student body, all in an atmosphere that is now, as one man notes, "incredibly coed."

University of Vermont

Burlington, VT 05405

Location Small city	**Applicants** 10,020
Total Enrollment 11,100	**Accepted** 52%
Undergraduates 8,150	**Enrolled** 41%
Male/Female 45/55	**Academics** ★ ★ ★
SAT V/M 510/570	**Social** 🐟 🐟 🐟 🐟 🐟
Financial Aid 45%	**Q of L** ● ● ● ● ●
Expense Pub $ $ $ $	**Admissions** (802)656-3370

In the wilderness of northern Vermont, perched high on a hill between scenic Lake Champlain and the Green Mountains on the doorstep of Canada, is a clean, progressive city where the only socialist mayor in the country presides over a flourishing cultural scene: symphonies, art galleries, chic shopping and, by one count, fifty-two bars. The city is Burlington, Vermont's largest, and much of what goes on in this bucolic Boston is geared toward the college students in the area, most notably those of the University of Vermont. UVM, the fifth oldest university in the nation (behind Harvard, Yale, Dartmouth and Brown), is noted for its combination of good academic programs, lively social scene and excellent skiing. Add to this its ideal location for outdoors people and, in the words of one economics major, "You can't go wrong."

UVM is not a typical state university; it's actually a thirty-year-old fusion of two schools: a private college founded in 1791 and a land-grant public university established in 1865. The state legislature puts up only 15 percent of the operating expenses (lowest in the country), so it is, for all practical purposes, a private school. Consequently, Vermont natives make up less than half the student body. "When out-of-staters come, they are coming to a private university," says the president.

Academic pressure varies according to department and student attitude, but as a general rule "students work hard so they can play hard." Among the best and most popular of UVM's hundred-plus majors are those in fields related to the environment and health. The university is also known for its strength in agriculture, forestry, and environmental and Canadian studies. The premedical sciences, nursing and physical therapy all benefit from UVM's fine medical school. Math and engineering are also a good bet here, as are political science and history. UVM's academic weaknesses appear primarily in the liberal arts areas such as sociology, psychology and music. The economics department is about as uncertain as the national economy it studies and, as one senior explains, "the college of education is a popular dumping ground for insults." Computer science offerings are not considered very strong, nor are computer facilities, but a new Department of Electrical Engineering and Computer Science suggests future advancements in this area. Also within the next few years, UVM plans to make a new home for the School of Business Administration, already one of the university's stronger programs.

Distribution requirements vary among the schools, but all students have the option of designing their own majors. Another unusual alternative is the Living and Learning Center, an imaginative residential-academic program. Here, students interested in a particular subject, such as photography, nuclear awareness, cycling or Shakespeare, live together in suites and create their own programs with the help of a faculty adviser. Co-op programs are available in engineering, business, recreation management and agriculture, and there's an Army ROTC on campus. UVM also offers study-abroad programs in Italy, France and Austria.

UVM has some of the usual problems associated with a large school: Introductory classes are huge, and popular courses and programs, such as entry-level business and physical therapy, shut out as many students as they accept. But the administration insists that students are able to get 90 percent of the courses they request (persistence helps) and average upperlevel class enrollment seldom exceeds twenty-five. Even the most prestigious professors are attentive, yet many students will comment on the inadequate faculty-student academic advising. The counseling services offered by the Counseling and Testing Center, however, are reported to be outstanding. The Bailey–Howe Library is the largest in Vermont and students consider it a terrific location for all types of education. "The library can be a good place to socialize, especially on the first and second floors," one junior explains, "but the basement and the third floor are very quiet."

UVM students are primarily outdoorsy, easygoing New Englanders, many from Massachusetts and Connecticut. Prefreshmen who don't know how to ski should be prepared to learn. "Overall, students tend to be active, fun-loving, hardworking and fun to be around," comments one. There's a healthy dose of diversity: "Preps, jocks, beautiful people, granolas, Greeks and squids" can all find others like themselves, one student reports. Yet, in their appreciation for diversity, many students express a desire to increase the minority representation on this almost entirely Caucasian campus. In general, political and social attitudes are liberal, "although there is a growing conservatism," explains one senior. Vermonters tend to gravitate to engineering and business, while out-of-staters, who pay a hefty surcharge of more than $5,000 and need higher SAT scores to get into the school, tend to go for the liberal arts. Another distinguishing characteristic: Non-Vermonters buy their L. L. Bean gear from the catalogue before they arrive. While almost half the students are eligible for need-based financial aid, only state residents are considered for the sixty merit scholarships, which cover all expenses for up to four years.

The school's well-kept dorms are situated in three residential areas separated by ten-minute walks. The varietal campus architecture is exemplified in the choice of old, new or freshly renovated housing units. Freshmen are crammed by twos and threes into modern, unattractive shoebox dorms that are coed by floor and shunned by upperclassmen. The other options include the Living and Learning suites, co-ops and apartments. Redstone Campus is rumored to be the rowdiest area. Freshmen must live on campus and are guaranteed housing, but older students can skip the lottery and start searching for an attractive, probably overpriced, apartment in town. Forty-six percent of the students live off campus, and there is still a slight housing shortage. There are eight dining halls, some of which offer standard, unlimited portions, and some of which operate on an à la carte basis. One senior, who fondly refers to the SAGA food service system as "Sniff and Guess Again," admits that "meals are varied and sometimes even tasty." Weekend dinners are set-table affairs in the dining halls, complete with live music. Independent snack bars on wheels offer everything from sweet rolls to health food tacos, and there's always the easily accessible Burlington, which offers "a plethora of good and inexpensive restaurants, many of which have near-cult followings."

UVM hosts several lecture and music series to complement the endless stream of movies, parties and dances. Although only a small percentage of the students partake of the Greek life, many independents occasionally drop in at the big bashes. Burlington is touted as one of the best college towns in the country, but it too has limits. To cool bouts of big-city fever while brushing up on your French, Montreal is just ninety minutes away (the border is only thirty miles upstate). Not far from campus lies some of the best skiing in the Northeast: Stowe and Mad River Glen are within an hour's drive. Cross-country skiing and ice-skating are also available, and the Green Mountains and the Adirondacks offer excellent hiking and backpacking territory. Cars are convenient but hard to park. The Outing Club, UVM's most popular student organization, does offer transportation for many of its activities.

There is no varsity football, so men's soccer is the most popular spectator sport in the fall. Women's soccer and field hockey are also favorites. In the winter, the championship ski team is the pride of UVM, and one Canadian studies major reports that "the hockey games always sell out, and the crowd is one of the loudest in the nation." UVM's exercise-minded students participate in a wide variety of intramurals, from tennis to the ever-popular broomball. Expanded gym facilities now include a dance studio, six indoor tennis courts, a gymnastic area and weight room.

An oft-heard bit of advice to prospectives is to think twice before coming here if all you want to do is study, yet UVM is not just a ski or party school. As one Econ major explains, "Hardworking fun-lovers will thrive at UVM. Apathetic partiers will fail out freshman year." UVM's friendly atmosphere and the freedom to enjoy a wide range of activity are what sells it. After all, most students will tell you, "If you like it, we got it!"

Villanova University

Villanova, PA 19085

Location Suburban	**Applicants** 8,470
Total Enrollment 12,000	**Accepted** 47%
Undergraduates 6,730	**Enrolled** 40%
Male/Female 55/45	**Academics** ★★★
SAT V/M 530/600	**Social** ☎☎☎
Financial Aid 70%	**Q of L** ●●●
Expense Pr $ $	**Admissions** (215)645-4000

For the longest time, this Roman Catholic university was just another second banana to the likes of Georgetown and Notre Dame. It had some good academics and an able faculty, but with no football team and a basketball squad that was a perennial Big East also-ran, Villanova might as well have been Vanilla-nova to the outside world. That is, until the Wildcats' stunning upset of Georgetown in the 1985 NCAA basketball championship abruptly put the university on the map. Suddenly 'Nova became a household word, and since then the whole sports program, indeed the whole university, has been rejuvenated. Now that Villanova has more name recognition, applications are up, and even median SAT scores are climbing.

With all the recent commotion about sports, it's easy to forget that Villanova has been around since 1842. Founded and still operated by the Augustinians, one of oldest teaching orders in the Roman Catholic Church, Villanova occupies a beautiful suburban campus on Philadelphia's posh Main Line. The centerpiece of the 240-acre expanse is a stately gothic chapel, its twin spires towering high above the grounds that were once the estate of a Revolutionary War officer. Villanova's buildings range from ivy-covered stone to modern, with plenty of secluded, tree-lined walkways connecting them.

Villanova's academic departments haven't won a national championship recently, but the university does have at least one contender, the College of Commerce and Finance. Students universally cite it as the best on campus, with accounting singled out for special praise. The College of Engineering also got thumbs up. Astronomy is the brightest star in the College of Arts and Sciences, though most of the offerings that fall under the arts part of the appellation are less than spectacular. Villanova's fourth academic unit, the College of Nursing, gets mixed reviews. Any hint of innovation is notably absent from the curriculum, but a whole squadron of ROTC options are available.

Depending on your point of view, the faculty at Villanova can be its biggest asset or its greatest drawback. Many students praise their professors for both attentiveness and accessibility. "I was surprised when I learned how much the profs really care," testifies a junior. Others, disillusioned by Villanova's religious focus, are less than complimentary. "The teachers carry on the Catholic tradition of teaching you what they want you to know and grading you on how well you repeat it," claims an international business major. "There is almost no free thinking." Students are required to take at least three semesters of religion in order to graduate; other core requirements vary with the college. Introductory class sizes can run well into the hundreds, and students report occasional difficulty getting into core courses, notably introductory religion. The library is adequate to most needs, though it is often more of a social center than a place to get work done. Villanova has an honors program, with enrollment by invitation only.

About 35 percent of 'Nova students are native Pennsylvanians (many commuting from the greater Philadelphia area) and another 39 percent hail from either New York or New Jersey. Eighty-five percent of the students are Catholic, the majority of whom come from fairly affluent families. "Conservative upper-middle-class students who don't make waves would be happy at Villanova," says a chemical engineering major. 'Nova students are as preprofessional as any you'll find, and many boast of the placement office's impressive track record. Since over half come from private high schools, most are used to homogeneity, and at Villanova they get more of the same. Blacks account for 2 percent of the students and Hispanics only 1 percent. "Students at Villanova do not stand out in a crowd," says one. Many students are hopeful that Villanova's recent national exposure will help the university achieve more diversity. In addition to need-based financial aid, Villanova awards sixty-four merit scholarships, ranging from $500 to $7,200. In addition, athletes in ten sports cop 137 full scholarships.

The housing situation is far from ideal. Less than 40 percent of the students live in the dorms, all of which are single sex. Many of the older dorms feature cramped rooms with bunk beds, though two new ones are said to be much nicer. The biggest problem with the housing is simply that there aren't enough rooms to go around. Freshmen and sophomores can usually get a spot, but upperclassmen seeking a room face long odds in the lottery. To make matters worse, the Greek system has no houses and off-campus housing can be difficult to obtain because of hostility from the neighborhood that surrounds the university. Many students from the Philadelphia area avoid all the hassle by commuting from home. Everyone who lives on campus is required to buy a full meal plan and eat in one of three dining halls.

According to a junior, "You need one of two things to have a good social life here—fake ID or a fraternity affiliation. I suggest both." Either way, most socializing takes place off campus; Villanova's campus is dry, but a handful of local bars cater to students, and partying at the apartments or houses of upperclassmen is frequent. About a third of the students join a Greek organization, especially popular among freshmen and sophomores, which provide a steady flow of beer. The student union does provide nonalcoholic alternatives including movies and dances. Many such events take place in Connelly Center, a multimillion-dollar student activities building completed in the early '80s. Those who tire of Villanova's suburban setting can simply hop the train for a short twelve-mile ride into Philly and there partake of a myriad of cultural and social opportunities, from museums to hockey games. Ski resorts, the Jersey Shore, Atlantic City and the Poconos are all within a two-hour drive.

Along with the frats and bars, sports events are the third leg of 'Nova's social triad. The basketball team, under beloved mentor Rollie Massimino, tops the list and has a throng of over two thousand boosters who follow the team wherever it goes. Men's and women's track are also national powerhouses and are as enthusiastically supported as any track teams in the nation. Football, dropped unexpectedly in 1981, was restored in 1985, much to the delight of frustrated tailgaters. The team has already generated considerable enthusiasm playing Division III opponents, and plans to move up to Division IAA in the near future. Other successful varsity teams include men's swimming and women's basketball and cross-country. The entire athletic program benefits from a massive new athletic complex that includes a swimming center, indoor track, a weight room and a number of multipurpose recreation areas. For ex–high school jocks not up to varsity status, there is a thriving intramural program that offers competition in three different leagues that range from serious to slapstick. Extracurricular activities are as numerous as the intramurals, and university masses frequently have standing room only.

Villanova likes to think of itself as a happy family, but some students feel as if they're treated like spoiled children and resent the university's *in loco parentis* policies. Though free spirits would probably find Villanova's atmosphere overly restrictive and conformist, others might benefit from its friendly and supportive environment. And who knows, with the basketball team an established power, there might even be another national championship.

Virginia Polytechnic Institute and State University

Blacksburg, VA 24061

Location Small town	**Applicants** 13,910
Total Enrollment 24,640	**Accepted** 62%
Undergraduates 18,380	**Enrolled** 47%
Male/Female 58/42	**Academics** ★ ★ ★
SAT V/M 510/590	**Social** ☎ ☎ ☎
Financial Aid 35%	**Q of L** ● ● ● ●
Expenses Pub $	**Admissions** (703)961-6267

Founded to bring agricultural know-how to the pioneers on Virginia's frontier, Virginia Polytechnic Institute has since changed its emphasis from the farms to high technology. With a campus in the scenic Blue Ridge Mountains, surrounded by nature paths, ponds and forest, Virginia Tech students are treated to a setting so idyllic that it hardly seems appropriate to their education as the next generation of engineers and architects.

The campus itself, once you can tear your eyes from the stunning surroundings, is "not breathtakingly beautiful, but nice." The buildings are mainly granite gray, the architecture nondescript. The campus bright spot is the centrally located drill field, a patch of greener-than-green grass that serves as the practice field for the drill team and the playing field for high school athletes turned college intramural stars.

Although it now has a college of arts and sciences, Virginia Tech is better known for the first-rate technical training provided in its six other undergraduate schools. For those who crave a big helping of engineering, Tech has programs of almost every flavor, including mechanical, electrical, biomedical and computer (the newest and most popular). The schools of agriculture and business are also prominent, and the five-year architecture program is considered one of the nation's best. Animal science is the strongest program in the school of agriculture and life sciences, especially since it is now supplemented by the new veterinary medicine grad school labs and resources. The school of human resources has good programs in textile design, human nutrition, home economics and family development. But with all these top-banana technical and pre-professional programs, students have found themselves a bit short-changed in the humanities and performing arts departments.

With over eighteen thousand undergraduates roaming the campus, class size tends to be large—sometimes more than five hundred students—and standing in line becomes a Tech student's least-favorite pastime. There are lines for buying books and supplies, lines for registration, for dropping and adding courses. All these lines form not twice but four times a year since Tech is on a quarter calendar, although the school will switch to the semester system in 1988. Students say that Tech professors are too wrapped up in research, so don't expect much contact with top faculty members before your junior year. The catch-22 of Virginia Tech manifests itself in the difficult-to-get-into freshman introductory courses that are prerequisites for all advanced course work.

"As programs diversify and you finally get into your major, this is much less of a problem," one upperclassman reports.

Computers are more common at Virginia Tech than electric typewriters at a secretarial school. Engineering students are required to own a PC. Other students have access to the three thousand terminals and microcomputers throughout the school, and more sections of the popular computer architecture course have been added to meet student demand. Even the newly renovated Newman Library with its more than one million volumes has plugged into this campuswide disc drive. Its catalogue and search systems are all computerized.

Each year, over a thousand students take advantage of Tech's co-op opportunities, available in more than fifty majors. The nationally acclaimed Small Business Institute program enables faculty-led groups of business majors to work with local merchants, analyze their problems, and make suggestions on how to increase profits. Virginia Tech also offers a Corps of Cadets, essentially a small military college, made up mostly of ROTC students.

Despite a 9 percent tuition increase over the past three years, a VPI education is still inexpensive. "Out-of-state Tech was cheaper for me than most of the in-state schools," says one interloper. The low price means the admissions office is inundated with out-of-state applicants, and competition for the 24 percent of the slots available to non-Virginians is stiff. "Students are very mainstream America," one reports. "There isn't very much extreme behavior—not a big new-wave cult or a whole lot of preppies or political radicals." More than 70 percent of the students come from Virginia, and mostly northern Virginia at that. While it may be commonplace for an in-stater to get into Tech, "it's not so easy to stay in," warns a durable mechanical engineering major. Most of the student fallout occurs during the freshman and sophomore years, especially in engineering. Students with financial need who apply for aid before the March 15 deadline receive priority consideration for the limited funds, and freshmen who apply afterward are likely to be out of luck. There is a sizable number of athletic scholarships (about 275) and over four thousand students, including lots of future engineers, are granted merit awards, regardless of need.

The majority of students keep house off campus in nearby apartment complexes, where they can cook their own meals and escape the dorms' visitation policies, which, students note, are becoming more liberal as more dorms are turning coed. A bus service connects the apartments with the school. Only freshmen, members of the Corps of Cadets, and those upperclassmen who do well in the lottery are guaranteed dormitory housing. But because these dorms have no single rooms or air-conditioning, exile isn't such bad news. Many boarders turn the required food plan into a focus of social life, and meals can last for hours. Weight watchers will be pleased to know that the calorie content of each entree is posted.

With 375 approved extracurricular activities, there is certainly plenty to do, "which can mess up one's academic life, if a student isn't careful." Outdoor activities are popular in every season, and there are facilities nearby for skiing, picnicking, hiking, camping in the Cascades or fishing. Football is the prime crowd attraction on campus, "but we are often pitted against weak teams, which makes for boring games," says one fan. Cross-country and basketball teams also fare well. Virginia Tech has one of the nation's most extensive intramural programs, with everything from football to horseshoes and more than four hundred softball teams each spring, many of them coed.

Less rigorous leisure time is spent attending school-sponsored plays, jazz concerts, arts and crafts fairs and dances. Fraternities and sororities sponsor parties regularly. Picturesque but tiny Blacksburg accommodates students' basic needs, while a bit more excitement can be found in Roanoke, a half-hour drive away. For real big-city action, students swing the five-hour trips to either Washington or Richmond.

Despite its numbers, Virginia Tech is a personable place. You may not
everyone here but those smiling faces make you feel like you do. Surrounded
mountains, plentiful in top tech research and solid programs, and wearing
reasonable price tag, VPI could have you smiling too.

University of Virginia

Charlottesville, VA 22903

Location Small city
Total Enrollment 17,420
Undergraduates 11,200
Male/Female 49/51
SAT V/M 590/650
Financial Aid 25%
Expense Pub $ $ $

Applicants 16,240
Accepted 35%
Enrolled 55%
Academics ★ ★ ★ ★ ★
Social 🕿 🕿 🕿 🕿
Q of L ● ● ● ● ●
Admissions (804)924-7751

The University of Virginia is known to one and all in Charlottesville as "Mister
Jefferson's University." Not just any Mister Jefferson, mind you, but *the* Mister Jefferson, esteemed founder of UVA and sometime author of the Declaration of Independence. Though he passed away over 150 years ago, he is referred to here as if he has
just run down to the apothecary shop for a bit of snuff and will be back momentarily.
Ever mindful of its illustrious past, UVA is as pretentious and tradition-bound as any
university in the nation, which means that for the uninitiated, there are a few things
to get straight. Freshmen at UVA are not freshmen; rather, they are known as first-year
students. Likewise, undergraduates here wouldn't deign to set foot on a campus. At
UVA, one walks on the "Grounds."

Designed by Mister Jefferson himself, those grounds are stunning indeed. At the
core of the university, literally and figuratively, is the original academic village, replete
with majestic white pillars, serpentine walls and extensive brickwork. An English
historian once described the central campus, with the rotunda modeled after the
Pantheon in Rome at its head, as "the most beautiful man-made thing in the United
States."

Extraordinarily elite for a public institution of higher education. "Youveeay"
holds its own against the best of the privates. A lucky handful of students are accepted
into the highly selective four-year schools of engineering and architecture, but the vast
majority enter the liberal arts college, where the best departments are history (especially
American), English, government, religious studies and foreign languages, followed by
biology and chemistry. Math and performing arts, meanwhile, could stand some improvement, and little is offered in the fine arts. Some students praise the economics
department, but others protest the strict monetarist approach. After their second year,
many arts and sciences students transfer into the commerce, nursing or education
schools, but competition is tough, especially for commerce spots. Virginia requires
students in every school to master a foreign language, and take courses in humanities
and fine arts, social sciences and natural sciences. The university does not offer many
organized study-abroad or internship programs, although both may be arranged. Instead, the emphasis is on top-level academic programs taught within nationally recog-

nized departments. Most students are high achievers who are "pre-something," one undergraduate notes. With almost three million volumes, the library is more than adequate, as are most academic facilities—the campus comes complete with a nuclear reactor. Recent additions to the physical plant include a student activity building and a recreation center.

A number of special programs are offered in addition to the regular curriculum. The most prestigious of these is the Echols Scholars Program, which exempts students form distribution and major field requirements and lets them loose to explore the academic disciplines as they see fit. The school invites about 130 top freshmen (plan on a cumulative SAT solidly above 1300) into the program and houses them together for their first year. Other options include Curriculum I, a back-to-basics two-year introduction to the liberal arts, students take calculus, European history, chemistry, literature and special composition classes. A newly christened residential college, recently opening its doors to upperclassmen, offers three hundred students a variety of enrichment programs. An interdisciplinary majors program allows students to combine three disciplines and integrate them into a yearlong senior thesis.

Virginia is noted for its honor system, which was instituted by students in 1842 after no one owned up to shooting a professor on the lawn. Students are expected to "have the moral fortitude to abide by the community's standards of moral conduct," and the only penalty for infractions still is a swift dismissal from campus. A number of controversial cases recently produced a measure of reform, but the honor code is still a way of life here, and students have repeatedly voted to retain the single-sanction system.

Admission for out-of-state students, about 38 percent of the undergraduate body, is more competitive than for in-staters, but nearly everyone who gets in is highly qualified. Just under 70 percent of the students were in the top 10 percent of their high school class, and almost all were in the top half. Many students hail from the Washington, D.C., suburbs of northern Virginia, while most out-of-staters come from New York, Pennsylvania and Maryland. Preprofessionalism is rampant, and many students view their education as "a stepping stone to financial security—definitely not what Mr. Jefferson had in mind." UVA's southern, slightly aristocratic ambience gives it a homey charm, but also a streak of anti-intellectualism and apathy. According to a junior in foreign affairs, "My fellow students are bright, well-read, and ambitious but they are also superficial and shallow; one gets the impression they are more worried about keeping their winter suntans, next week's fraternity mixer, and what's on sale at Ralph Lauren than in political crises and the future of America." Blacks now make up 8 percent of the student body, but they often have a difficult time of it in UVA's alien atmosphere. The university began to admit women in 1970 and rapidly doubled in size as it moved to a one-to-one ratio. Some of the preppier fraternities still follow the hallowed Youveeay tradition of "going down the road" to the nearby women's schools, but the tradition is fading. The only merit scholarships offered at Virginia are about fifteen highly prized (you guessed it) Jefferson Scholarships, which are awarded by alumni associations and are good for full tuition. Fifty black Virginians are given grants of $1,000 each, and over three hundred athletes in fourteen sports get athletic scholarships every year.

A conspicuous exception to the beauty and graciousness of most of the Virginia campus is the dorms, which are done in institutional cinder block and are painted green or yellow. All first-year students live "on grounds," as do top senior honor students, who qualify for coveted singles in the academic village. Several newer dorms have alleviated the housing crunch, but most upperclassmen still opt for apartments in town, which along with the frats and sororities are the liveliest centers of social life. Commuters praise Charlottesville's bus system, especially since campus parking space is limited.

A meal plan is mandatory for first-year students, while upperclassmen either cook for themselves or take meals at their Greek houses.

Mister Jefferson founded UVA as a place where students could come together to "drink the cup of knowledge," but today's undergraduates seem to favor a different sort of brew. Studious Virginians by day metamorphose into the Rowdy Wahoos (a nickname derived from one of the college cheers) by night, with beer the universal lubricant. What's the secret formula that makes such a respected academic institution one of the top party schools in the country? "People don't talk about their studies much—they get work done and then have fun," a senior reveals. The Greek system reigns supreme, and most of the social festivities occur on Rugby Road, where some forty fraternity houses have set up shop. The fraternities assume an obligation to provide social activities not only for their own members, but for the campus at large, and the four big weekends—"drunken-orgy-type things"—are legendary. Needless to say, the honor code somehow doesn't apply to Virginia's minimum drinking age of twenty-one (nineteen for beer), and fake IDs are part of the gentleman's outfit. Those who want a break from the party scene can frequent the University Union, which provides a variety of activities including movies, concerts and social hours.

If the city limits of Charlottesville get too confining, students road-trip two hours to Washington or head to Richmond for concerts and other events. Ski slopes are an hour away and Virginia Beach is less than four hours in the opposite direction. Big time ACC basketball has long been an integral part of UVA life, and the team is a perennial Top-20 contender. After many years as a laughing stock, football has become a consistent winner; other strong teams include lacrosse and women's cross-country.

Mister Jefferson's plan for a "university so broad and liberal and modern, as to be worth patronizing with the public support" was a cherished project, and its achievement a triumph he prized above both the presidency and the Declaration of Independence. Virginians are determined to do their founder proud, and their commitment to "the rich history and traditions embodied in the University of Virginia" has kept this elite institution one of the best public universities in the nation.

Wabash College

Crawfordsville, IN 47933

Location Small town	**Applicants** 540
Total Enrollment 770	**Accepted** 84%
Undergraduates 770	**Enrolled** 45%
Male/Female N/A	**Academics** ★ ★ ★
SAT V/M 510/580	**Social** ☎ ☎
Financial Aid 85%	**Q of L** ● ● ●
Expense Pr $	**Admissions** (317)364-4225

Wabash College was founded by transplanted Ivy Leaguers in 1832 on what was then the American frontier. Since those early days, the men of Wabash, their wagons tightly encircled, have been successfully fighting off coeducation, government meddling, creeping vocationalism and other threats to their brand of liberal education. Wabash men are certainly a distinctive breed: They talk with a disarming intensity about the value of male friendships, the importance of liberal arts education and their desire to be professional successes. Midwestern men searching for a sure ticket into the old-boy network need look no further.

The Wabash educational prescription has proven itself. This little college has comprised quite an impressive list of alumni—executives of major corporations, an abundance of doctors and lawyers, and a large portion of PhDs. Many of these post-Wabash success stories demonstrate their appreciation through generous donations. On a per capita basis, Wabash's $70-million endowment makes it one of the wealthiest schools in the nation. This financial security enables the school to refuse any federal grant money, and thus it remains independent of many federal regulations. Financial aid packages to needy students contain few loans and absolutely no work-study contracts. All but the first $1,000 of the estimated need is met with "gift aid; cash dollars that do not have to be worked for or borrowed," the financial aid office reports. But with 85 percent of the student body receiving an average of $4,800 a year in "gifts," Wabash could pass for Santa Claus. On top of that, approximately 150 generous merit scholarships are awarded to outstanding students regardless of need. When it comes to athletic scholarship offerings, though, the buck stops here.

In preparation for following in alumni footsteps, many Wabash students are preprofessional; half will go on to graduate programs, and placement rates for medical, dental, law and business schools are high. While the computer sciences, music and art departments are not the best, students speak highly of the English, economics, political science, biology, chemistry and speech departments. Excellent science facilities include an electron microscope, a 180-acre biological field station and a mobile aquatic lab.

Students must take courses from a wide variety of fields, including a freshman tutorial that focuses on a particular interest of the individual professor, and a sophomore course on culture and traditions. A new writing center is available for all Wabash students who demonstrate a weakness in written communication skills. Be forewarned that all Wabashers must pass a proficiency exam in a foreign language to graduate. Juniors may study in contingents throughout the world or on various domestic programs through the Great Lake-Colleges Association.* Those who can't suppress their techno-vocational desires at Wabash can opt for a 3-2 program in engineering with Columbia or Washington University.

Surrounded by the gorgeous Fuller Arboretum, the colonial-style, red-brick, white-pillared and ivy-covered campus looks teensy amid an abundance of grass and tall trees. The fittingly small class size—"Sometimes it's only you, the professor and another student in the room"—makes it tough to skip class. Professors are not easy with the A's, and tend to be accessible because "it's not easy for them to hide around here and they know it." Most of Wabash's students come from public high schools in Indiana and "were all-country in sports, president of their class, and drink beer by the case," one reports. About 60 percent were in the top fifth of their high school class. As for politics, "most students are conservative, with a few radical groups on campus," observes a senior, "but this school does not seem to be as trendy as most."

Residential life for the temporary denizens of small-town Crawfordsville revolves around the nine fraternities, which draw more than two-thirds of the students. As an alternative to Greek life, there are three modern dorms (two of which have all single rooms); about 15 percent of the students live off campus. Dorm residents must eat in the dining hall, while fraternities have private cooks who prepare "nutritious meals that are really not that bad." Those who live in the dorms may feel excluded from what there is of campus social life, since it's the fraternities who "ship in" sorority members from other schools for parties. "I would say that on most weekends, there are as many women as men here," exclaims one happy frat man. But of course, there are those occasional dry weekends during which Wabash men hit the road, seeking female companionship at nearby coed schools such as DePaul, Indiana or Purdue. Thus, for the most part, "dating requires a full tank of gas," and young men who can't deal with "the absence of females during the week" would not be content at Wabash.

When students are not out partying or studying, they are likely to be working out in the gym or running. Though many extracurricular activities are offered, athletic activity is the favorite. Most of the nonvarsity athletes participate in intramurals, which encompass twenty-two sports, including pool and horseshoes. The outstanding Wabash teams are football (with the third winningest record in Division III history), basketball and wrestling. School spirit is abundant, if not well intended—"What better way to take out your frustrations than to watch our team smash the opponent?" asks an econ major.

Team smashing aside, one rule governs student behavior at Wabash: "The student is expected to conduct himself at all times, both on and off the campus, as a gentleman and responsible citizen." This simple statement defines the character of the school and a continuing belief in the unique nature of the Wabash experience. Most students here are willing to make a few social sacrifices to be among those who are, as a popular school T-shirt proclaims, "the few, the proud, the well endowed."

Wake Forest University

Winston-Salem, NC 27109

Location Small city	**Applicants** 4,380
Total Enrollment 5,060	**Accepted** 47%
Undergraduates 3,360	**Enrolled** 44%
Male/Female 60/40	**Academics** ★★★
SAT V/M 540/590	**Social** ☎☎☎
Financial Aid 30%	**Q of L** ●●●
Expense Pr $	**Admissions** (919)761-5201

The big news at Wake Forest University is that there now are two coed dorms. That might not have made the headlines at other schools, but at Wake Forest—ruled for 150 years by the social code of the North Carolina Baptist State Convention—it was a step akin to moving a mountain.

More changes could be on the way. After years of bickering between university officials and Baptist fundamentalists over the university's direction and purpose, Wake finally severed its church ties in the fall of '86, making further liberalization all but inevitable. That should suit students just fine, many of whom cite social restrictiveness as Wake's main drawback. Aside from that, students have few complaints at this school that styles itself the "Ivy League of the South."

Blessed with a large endowment, a dedicated faculty and a slot in the Atlantic Coast Conference, Wake combines southern traditionalism with an academic challenge so intense that you can "work forever and then find out you haven't worked enough," one undergraduate says. Unlike many other colleges, Wake Forest students complain of "grade deflation." Except for honors students, freshmen and sophomores must endure a rigorous core curriculum that occupies most of the first two years and includes required courses in English, religion, foreign language and physical education, as well as distribution requirements in four broad categories. Among the strongest departments are history, English and business; future accountants do astonishingly well on the CPA exam. The completion of a $5.3-million music wing of the James R. Scales Fine Arts Center has revitalized the music and art departments, and the university also boasts an unusual cardiac rehabilitation program. Students in the innovative honors program participate in small seminars focusing on major thinkers and artists. Only sophomores, who have low priority at registration, may have trouble getting into the classes they want. Computerization is getting under way here as the recently approved computer science as a major. The library, like so many of the campus buildings, is generously funded with Reynolds tobacco money. Access to the stacks ends at eleven PM, which many students consider too early, but there are study rooms open until two AM.

Although the university seeks to attract a national student body to its Old South campus, one student describes Wake as "a very homogeneous group of people." Nearly two-fifths of the undergraduates are from North Carolina, and only 3 percent are black. The students come mainly from middle- and upper-middle-class families and bring with them "strong, conservative attitudes that tend to leave little room for diversity," one student notes. Alumni children, many from a long line of Wake Forest graduates, are ubiquitous. School spirit runs high and Wake Forest alumni consistently lead the nation in supporting their alma mater with contributions.

Paradoxically, the thing that many students like most about Wake Forest (its tradition) also tops the list of complaints. Despite the recent reforms, students still complain about the strained male-female relationships. While students can now visit in the opposite sex dorms until one AM on weekends, liberalization has proceeded at a snail's pace. "Wake Forest is not exactly receptive to change or radicalism," one student notes. The minimum drinking age for beer was recently raised to nineteen, and the law is strictly enforced at campus parties.

Fraternities and the female societies still account for much of the campus night-life. In fact, "most guys feel that the only way to have a social life is to join a fraternity," one senior says. Women are under less pressure to join, though at least one believes that the Greeks foster "an elitist and somewhat cliquish community." Nevertheless, there are plenty of extracurricular activities and "the danger lies in having too much to do, rather than not enough," one history major asserts.

After freshman year, about 20 percent of the students escape the living regulations by fleeing to off-campus housing. Once gone, however, you can't go home again; the university rescinds the dorm privileges of off-campus students. On-campus students have a choice of housing, and the newer women's dorms are considered far superior to the men's, although the latter are now being renovated. The rooms are assigned by a point system that gives seniors first pick. Students select a meal plan to suit their appetites and are charged only for what they eat, be it a salad or a steak. For meals, students can choose from a fairly typical cafeteria, a snack bar and the Magnolia Room, which dishes out classier food served by student waiters and which is also more expensive than the other options. Students use a "credit card" to pay for meals at all three locations, debiting their yearly account.

The school attempts to meet the full financial need of all accepted applicants. In addition, Wake offers about 200 athletic scholarships and 150 merit scholarships, ranging from $1,500 to full cost. These include up to 40 renewable Guy T. Carswell Scholarships (competing students rank in the top 2 percent of their high school class and average 1380 on their SATs) and four renewable, full-cost Reynolds Scholarships that include three summer projects overseas and are intended as counterparts to the prestigious Morehead scholarships at the University of North Carolina at Chapel Hill.

Situated on 470 acres of flower gardens and wooded trails in central North Carolina, Wake Forest's beautiful red-brick buildings "radiate the pride and tradition

594

that is Wake Forest," one student believes. The city of Winston-Salem offers a fair amount of cultural diversion, including a Carolina Streetscene fair, a Christmastime Moravian love feast, and the well-known North Carolina School of the Arts in the heart of downtown. The Carolina beaches, popular weekend spots during the fall and spring, can be reached in four hours. Spectacular mountains are within a two-hour drive. (Wake offers skiing instruction at one nearby slope.) It can help to have a car at Wake Forest, or at least to have friends who do.

Here in the heart of Atlantic Coast Conference country, basketball is the name of the game, and Wake students support their Demon Deacons with enthusiasm. Although the football squad is seldom a national contender, it nevertheless attracts a rabid following that trashes the campus with toilet paper after a big win. The reaction was undoubtedly a little more restrained when the golf team won the national championship in 1986. The women's golf, tennis and basketball teams are also strong, and all three received recent increases in funding. The university is particularly proud of competing in the ACC since it is by far the smallest school in the conference. Wake Forest's athletic facilities are stunning and include seven playing fields, four gymnasiums, and a fine golf course. The sports coliseum also attracts several big-name concert groups yearly.

At a relatively modest cost for a private school, Wake Forest offers a competitive academic program, outstanding faculty and facilities and a name that "carries weight" in the job market. And while some students feel that tradition has stood in the way of positive changes at the university, most agree that without those traditions "it wouldn't be Wake Forest."

Washington and Jefferson College

Washington, PA 15301

Location Small city
Total Enrollment 1,170
Undergraduates 1,170
Male/Female 60/40
SAT V/M 510/550
ACT 23
Financial Aid 75%
Expense Pr $ $

Applicants 1,170
Accepted 86%
Enrolled 33%
Academics ★ ★ ★
Social ☎ ☎ ☎
Q of L ● ●
Admissions (412)223-6025

Washington and Jefferson College has worked long and hard to build its reputation as a grad school training camp for future doctors, lawyers and corporate chiefs. Four years here should substantially increase your MCAT, LSAT or GMAT score, and, amid this socially competitive and predominantly upper-middle-class student body, you just might learn a thing or two about minding your yuppie P's and Q's.

Even the campus is tight-knit: Thirty buildings sit on thirty-five acres in a small town about thirty miles outside of Pittsburgh. W&J is the eleventh oldest college in the country, and some of its structures date back to Colonial days. Modern buildings are randomly sprinkled here and there, but the well-kept paths and lawns manage to tie everything together quite nicely.

As a traditional liberal arts college, W&J has perfected the art of weeding out the hopeless would-be's and getting its capable if unspectacular graduates into professional schools. The formula for success starts with individual attention in small classes. "Professors are very accessible; they all have posted office hours and many will encourage students to call them at home on the night before a test," says a biology major. Core requirements call for a mandatory English course plus credits earned in cultural and intellectual tradition, fine arts, languages and literature, science and mathematics, and social sciences. A new offering that's caused some excitement among the soon-to-be professionals is the entrepreneurial studies program. Student entrepreneurs may choose from one of five majors (business administration, accounting, economics, computer science and psychology), and supplement their studies with special courses on the importance of ambition, energy, poise and integrity. A thematic major allows students to design his or her own course of study, while double majors produce such types as a biologist well versed in literature. Rare among liberal arts colleges are the 3-4 programs with the Pennsylvania state colleges of optometry and podiatry. More technically minded students can take advantage of the 3-2 engineering programs with Case Western Reserve and Washington University in St. Louis.

Among the standard departments, chemistry, biology, business, political science and history are highly praised and popular. Computer science is one of the smaller, faster growing departments; the fine arts and social sciences suffer from being outside of most people's priorities. The library is adequate for most research needs, and most gaps can be filled by the public library right around the corner or at the University of Pittsburgh.

During the January term, students find brief apprenticeships in prospective career areas, take a school tour abroad (marine biology trips to the Bahamas, English theater trips to London, etc.) or engage in nontraditional course work. "I took a music course one year, and in a month I learned to play the flute," one woman boasts. There is also a junior year–abroad option and a semester exchange program with American University in Washington for economics and politics majors.

Although it can seem like Peyton Place at times—"Students who like privacy might find W&J lacking in refuges"—most students agree the small size promotes an intimate atmosphere. More than two-thirds of the students hail from Pennsylvania (the biggest contingent from "the better areas of Pittsburgh") and many are from neighboring states in the Northeast. "Most students here are wealthy—but I don't think that's a prerequisite," ponders a junior. Not all students share the administration's appreciation for "the unique characteristics of the western Pennsylvania milieu," but they do take advantage of public transportation into Pittsburgh, about a half hour away. The town of Washington is a sleepy little steel-mining community that has hit some hard times. Townies tend to be a bit resentful of dressy W&J undergrads but still offer student discounts in their shops. Excellent students can find an even bigger bargain if they win one of the thirty merit scholarships, which range from $500 to $3,000 and are awarded on the basis of test scores, grades and academic promise. All other financial aid is need based, and there are no athletic scholarships.

Most students live in either the one coed dorm or one of the four that are single sex. Women's dorms, built when the campus went coed in the mid-1970s, are the newest and nicest. "The girls' have their own suites with baths, while guys have community baths," one man laments. Fraternity brothers and a few overflow freshmen reside in renovated houses. Sororities obtain block housing within the dormitories and, like the fraternities, have territorial tables in the dining rooms. The food tends to "get repetitive, with the same meal combinations over and over, week after week." All campus dwellers must subject themselves to this monotony by purchasing a twenty-one-meal plan.

A lingering imbalance in the male/female ratio puts a damper on the social life, which is centered around the Greeks. The less than 20 percent of the students who dodge the Greek system "tend to feel left out quite a bit," according to a chemistry major. Fraternities are said to host most campus parties. Sororities are said to host most campus hostilities. "The Greek women tend to have a high level of animosity toward each other, and the competition is often rough," attests an English major. The student activities board tries to counteract the heavy-duty Greek influence by sponsoring parties, movies and trips. Students also frequent their homes on the weekends or explore dating opportunities at nearby colleges. Off campus, skiing at Seven Springs, an hour away, is popular, as are trips to Pittsburgh for shopping, concerts and cultural events. Students also head in to watch major league sporting events in that famed City of Champions.

Sports also play an important role at W&J, where just about everyone with four functioning limbs has a shot at varsity sports. Football generates the most student enthusiasm, although "it's definitely not like Penn State here." Men's and women's basketball, men's wrestling and lacrosse, and women's tennis are also successful. Intra-mural programs, students claim, are a bit sexist—"The program for women is not as extensive or popular as the men's." For those who want to perfect their managerial and organizational skills, there are a multitude of clubs to join—everything from the barbell to the karate club.

W&J offers a solid education that is one of the best small-school bets for students who are seriously considering a professional graduate school. A W&J degree may not make you famous among many people (other than your nosy classmates), but it almost guarantees a few distinguished initials to tie onto the end of your name.

Washington and Lee University

Lexington, VA 24450

Location Small town	**Applicants** 2,400
Total Enrollment 1,800	**Accepted** 33%
Undergraduates 1,430	**Enrolled** 45%
Male/Female 85/15	**Academics** ★ ★ ★ ★
SAT V/M 590/630	**Social** ☎ ☎ ☎
Financial Aid 34%	**Q of L** ● ● ●
Expense Pr $ $	**Admissions** (703)463-8710

Founded in the mid-eighteenth century, Washington and Lee has finally followed the example of its mid-nineteenth-century president, Robert E. Lee, and surrendered—not to the Union, but to the twentieth century. W&L was one of the last all-male holdouts in the nation until the board of trustees voted to invite women to apply for one hundred spots in the class of 1989. It definitely goes against the grain at this bastion of southern white male traditionalism, but the feminine sex is slowly but surely being integrated into the life of the university. One can only hope that the General—who's entombed in the campus chapel—doesn't crack the walls with his spinning.

Taking its name from George Washington, who donated $50,000 to save the school from bankruptcy in 1796, Washington College was a tiny academy serving the local aristocracy until the Civil War. In 1865, General Lee assumed the presidency of the struggling school, catapulting it to regional and national prominence—both as an academic institution, and as the South's most hallowed shrine of the "Lost Cause." Located at the southern end of Virginia's scenic Shenandoah Valley, W&L's gorgeous wooded campus ("an awesome sight") consists of majestic brick and white-columned buildings along with a smattering of modern ones, most notably the library. With a list of alumni no less impressive, from Supreme Court Justice Lewis Powell to newsman Roger Mudd to evangelist Pat Robertson, W&L has a proven track record of turning out highly qualified graduates. Although a standard liberal arts program remains the foundation of W&L's curriculum, its excellent preprofessional programs—particularly the School of Commerce, Economics, and Politics—are immensely popular among the university's job-oriented students, large numbers of whom go on to top medical, law, and business schools and out into the hub of modern business and industry.

Washington and Lee has maintained its excellent departments in history and English, and added interdisciplinary Russian and East Asian studies, the latter enhanced by links with universities in Taiwan and Japan. Business, economics, public policy and accounting are all very popular majors, as are journalism, biology, and a 3-2 engineering program with several leading universities. Math and physics, meanwhile, could stand some improvement. Fine arts and drama languish in abysmal facilities, and as one student diplomatically testifies, "They are good double majors, but if I were serious about being an actor I wouldn't come here; on the other hand, if I wanted to be an accountant on Broadway, W&L would be perfect." The university recently christened a computer science department, now staffed by three professors.

The distribution requirements at W&L now include proficiency in English composition and another language, and courses in literature, humanities, mathematics, social science, laboratory science and physical education. The academic climate ranges from intense to casual depending on the student, though anyone aiming for more than a gentleman's C will find the work load rigorous. Despite stiff grading, the rapport between students and W&L's fine faculty is excellent; even lowly freshmen have access to prestigious faculty members. Class sizes rarely exceed fifty students, and many have as few as five or ten. The spirit of male camaraderie that permeates W&L is due in part to the student-administered honor system, which dates back to the days of General Lee. Test and final exams are taken without any faculty supervision; doors remain unlocked, with calculators on desks, and library stacks are open twenty-four hours a day. The modern library, like most campus facilities, is superb, boasting eight hundred individual study areas as well as private rooms for honors students. Well-qualified students can apply for the Robert E. Lee Undergraduate Research Program, which offers paid fellowships for students assisting professors in research, or doing some of their own.

The recent admission of women notwithstanding, W&L students today are only slightly more liberal than their Confederate forebears of over a century ago. "W&L has always been ultraconservative," explained one student who cited "Robert E. Lee's influence" as a key reason why he attended. Another modern gentleman-in-training says bluntly that "people who do not like southern preppies and fairly rich, elitist people" should not come to W&L. Minorities are in for a particularly rough time, with blacks numbering a miniscule 1.5 percent of the student body. If not culturally diverse, the university does manage to draw students from all regions of the country; less than a quarter are native Virginians, and a healthy percentage come from as far away as

Texas and New Jersey. The university's geographic diversity has not prompted much other differentiation, although sports jerseys and sweatshirts (official W&L emblem only, please) have joined pink button-downs and penny loafers as variations on the campus uniform. Public school graduates (about 60 percent of the students) soon succumb to the pressure to conform and "turn preppie."

W&L maintains a need-blind admissions policy and fully meets the demonstrated need of most of its students. Also available are about seventy non-need, renewable honors scholarships of up to full tuition for four years. Coeducation has been a godsend for the admissions office; applications have skyrocketed in the past several years, and the median SAT scores of each freshman class are on the rise. Students spend their first year at W&L in coed dorms, and as sophomores generally move to a frat house. Upperclassmen have a variety of options, including nearby apartments and farm houses in the surrounding countryside. Since males monopolize most of the nearby housing, upperclass women have fewer alternatives, though a new residence hall should improve the situation. Freshmen are required to buy the meal plan, which is optional for upperclassmen.

With its scenic location in the midst of the Appalachian Mountains, the university provides an abundance of activities for nature lovers, including hunting, fishing, camping, and tubing in the rivers. Washington, Richmond and ski slopes are easily reached by car for weekend trips. Lexington, a quaint old Virginia town that "just got a McDonald's two years ago," is also home to Virginia Military Institute, creating the odd juxtaposition of a button-down military school next to W&L's casual and at times raucous campus life. A thriving intramural program is a staple of W&L life, bringing fraternities and independents together in friendly rivalry. Football sparks some interest in the fall, but W&L students live for the spring and lacrosse. The team is a perennial contender for the national championship and holds the campus in thrall from March to June. Women's sports are only now getting off the ground.

Ringed by five women's colleges within an hour's drive, W&L has always been one of the rowdiest partying schools in the South. "Work hard, play hard," is an unofficial motto, but students follow it as if it were an amendment to the honor code. Sixty percent of the men join fraternities (which dominate the social scene) and the women are only now beginning to form Greek counterparts. Social life focuses on several big weekends a term including an outrageously expensive, cleverly named Fancy Dress Weekend that lures damsels from all over the East Coast. But special events or no, hundreds of women have always made the trip to W&L every week for fraternity parties, school-run mixers, and Wednesday rendezvouses in the General's Headquarters, the school's pub. "If you don't belong to a frat, you have your favorites to party at or you road-trip a lot," says one man.

Since W&L's male/female ratio is likely to remain lopsided well into the '90s, coeducation isn't expected to make for radical changes, social or otherwise, in the near future. Nevertheless, it will be an exciting time for women at W&L—not least because there are over two males for every female in each class—but also a trying one for those who attempt to assert their intellectual equality in a place that for over two centuries was an exclusively male preserve.

University of Washington

Seattle, WA 98195

Location Urban

Total Enrollment 33,670

Undergraduates 25,080

Male/Female 50/50

SAT V/M 500/580

Financial Aid 34%

Expense Pub $

Applicants 9,720

Accepted 65%

Enrolled 55%

Academics ★ ★ ★ ★

Social 🐾 🐾 🐾

Q of L ● ● ●

Admissions (206)543-9686

The University of Washington owes as much to the federal government as any public school in the nation. Thanks to Uncle Sam's largesse, Washington is one of the foremost research institutions in the nation. But while this Goliath-size proprietor of higher education is, in the words of one administrator, "*the* school in the Pacific Northwest," its prominence is hardly recognized outside state boundaries. Knowledge and admiration of this distinguished university is largely a matter of living in the neighborhood.

Three miles from downtown Seattle, the University of Washington's 680-acre campus is an architectural mélange of "collegiate-Gothic and modern, mostly functional buildings," as described by a computer science major. Beautifully manicured grounds complete with flowering trees and a fountain create a park within a city atmosphere. But with 72 percent of the undergraduates commuting from home, the setting tends to be enjoyed only while rushing between classes.

Many of Washington's diverse undergraduate strengths correspond with its excellent graduate programs. The ultracompetitive business major, for example, benefits from the university's highly regarded business school. Similarly, students majoring in public health, community medicine, pharmacy and nursing profit from access to facilities and some of the faculty in the medical school—an international leader in cancer and heart research, cell biology and the development of artificial kidneys. Also recommended for undergraduates are computer science, math and aero- and astronautical engineering, which receives generous research dollars from Boeing and NASA. Reflecting the natural resources at the heart of Washington's economy, the programs in forestry, marine biology and zoology are excellent. Students complain about the arts programs (except drama), and report that the humanities offerings appear to be lower university priorities than the sciences. The administration points a finger at the recent cuts in state funding for the slump in these areas.

Undergraduates in both the professional and liberal arts programs are expected to complete a general education component and prove proficiency in writing and quantitative reasoning. Many Washington professors are tops in their fields, but students say they only benefit from this faculty expertise in the classroom. One student claims that "you have to *really* want to see a professor" to get an appointment. Freshmen and sophomores do have access to the university's star faculty sometimes—but only in large (as in seven hundred–plus students) lecture classes. Not only are the classes large, they are also hard to get into. A junior reports that some students have "immense difficulty getting their desired classes first time around." The academic atmosphere is relatively relaxed, "although there are people here in every form of academic stress or ease," says a physics major.

About a dozen different study-abroad programs are offered, including those in China, Denmark and the USSR. Students in need of financial aid receive priority consideration for funds if they apply before March 1—after that you hope for leftovers. Five hundred merit scholarships, which range from $100 to full tuition are awarded to Washington residents with good high school records and test scores. Athletic scholarships are awarded to men and women in a wide variety of sports.

Ninety percent of Washington's undergraduates are state residents, and a substantial proportion are over the age of twenty-five. This age factor may contribute to what an in-the-minority liberal labels as "student apathy toward social activism and a preoccupation with getting a job and making lots of money." Sixteen percent of the students live in campus housing and can choose from among seven coed dorms. Housing is also available to married students, and the strong fraternity and sorority organizations are homes to another 12 percent of the campus denizens. The rest live off campus in Seattle or other parts of King's County. Each dorm has its own cafeteria and fast-food line, and a complicated account system takes the place of meal plans. One student, hasty to give his opinion of the edible provisions, says, "Yuck." But on second thought, "well, maybe not that bad—you can get pizzas from 8 PM to midnight."

Given the large number of commuters, it's no surprise that Washington's social life, in the words of one student, lacks cohesion. While it is far from dull here, the University of Washington doesn't even come close to being a party school. The Greeks (members of a combined total of forty-four fraternities and sororities) dominate the social scene on campus, and dorms also sponsor frequent dances, trips and events.

A ten-minute bus ride connects students to a full array of urban offerings. The Seattle Center brings in a good crop of opera, symphonics groups and touring shows, while the Kingdome houses the Seahawks and the Mariners. The university's own athletic teams fare considerably better. An epidemic of "Husky Fever" has quarantined U of W students to the football stadium on Saturdays, when they cheer on their top-rated team. Also strong are men's and women's basketball and crew squads.

More than anything else, the great outdoors characterizes the University of Washington. The campus sits on the shores of Lake Washington in Puget Sound and is surrounded by mountains and water. Outdoor recreation is far and away the dominant pastime for students. Boating, hiking, camping and skiing are close by. The weather is consistently temperate, and natives maintain that the city's reputation for rain is greatly exaggerated—but why does that sports stadium have a roof over it? As one student puts it, "To a lot of people, it's Valhalla."

Washington turns away scores of out-of-state applicants, preferring to keep its vast resources "all in the family" so to speak. Some students wouldn't appreciate its no-nonsense and often impersonal academic programs and lack of a centralized social life. But for an independent, well-motivated Washingtonian, going to the University of Washington is a marvelous way of getting your money's worth from Uncle Sam.

Washington University

St. Louis, MO 63130

Location Suburban	**Applicants** 5,920
Total Enrollment 8,370	**Accepted** 62%
Undergraduates 4,440	**Enrolled** 28%
Male/Female 55/45	**Academics** ★ ★ ★ ★
SAT V/M 560/640	**Social** ☎ ☎ ☎
Financial Aid 60%	**Q of L** ● ● ●
Expense Pr $ $ $	**Admissions** (314)889-6000

Washington University in St. Louis is a medium-size school in the middle of the country that works overtime to avoid mediocrity. So far, it's been successful—especially in the sciences and engineering—and has built itself a hearty endowment and a reputation as one of the nation's most prestigious institutions. Students from all over the nation are now knocking down the door of this research-oriented school. If there were ever such a thing as an upwardly mobile university, Wash U is it.

The campus is a real charmer, nestled between two old-fashioned, sedate St. Louis suburbs, abutting Forest Park, the largest urban park in the country. Traditional Gothic buildings of red Missouri granite and white limestone come complete with ivy, gargoyles and arches. Plenty of grass, tall trees and flowers dress the quiet courtyards. "It looks just like what a college is supposed to look like," reflects a history major, "except for a chunk of cement called the law school."

Undergraduates may enroll in one of five schools—arts and sciences, business and public administration, architecture, fine arts and engineering—and can easily arrange for double majors between the divisions or create specially tailored interdisciplinary majors. (One student majored in peace studies.) Another noteworthy offering is the Scholars Program in Medicine, which simultaneously admits qualified freshmen to the college and medical school, allowing them to pursue their undergraduate studies freed from the pressure of taking only premed courses.

The natural sciences (especially biology, chemistry and physics) have long been notable. This strength is a result of the outstanding medical school, which runs a faculty exchange program with the undergraduate biology department. Engineering, political science and business are some of the most celebrated subjects; sociology is small and unpopular. The English faculty has noted novelists and poets in its ranks—Stanley Elkin and William Gass, to name two—and history professors are appreciated for the quality of their teaching. Among the interdisciplinary programs black studies and urban affairs are praised.

To strike a balance between the drawing-card science and preprofessional programs and the university's desire to provide a broad and deep educational experience, a freshman FOCUS Program option has been installed. In FOCUS, a single theme such as law and society or search for human values is explored in different courses and brought into focus through a weekly seminar. The program lets first-year students work closely with faculty members and sample offerings from the various departments.

Students consider themselves the hardworking achievers that professors expect them to be. "Without a doubt, the work load is pretty intense," says an economics major, "but it's not a cutthroat school, and students usually help each other out." Faculty members, for the most part, "have genuine interests in what they are teaching," and many are easily accessible. "The university is big enough that professors cannot babysit students, but anyone who is willing to knock on a door can see a professor," according to an expert with a triple major.

The admissions office acknowledges that "diversity" has become a hackneyed term claimed by most universities for its student body. "But we really do have it— people from fifty states, seventy foreign countries, and a good mix of Protestants, Catholics, Jews, Hindus, Muslims and nonbelievers." Nevertheless, high percentages come from the East (especially New York and New Jersey) and the Midwest (Illinois and Missouri in particular). "Types of students range from the conservative B-school students at one end of campus to the funky art students at the other end" is an economics major's summation. About 11 percent of the student body is composed of minorities, 60 percent are from the top tenth of their high school classes and more than one-third go on to graduate school. At a time when many colleges are involved in hard-core recruitment, Wash U has recently enjoyed a substantial increase (33 percent) in applications.

Wash U boasts the ninth largest endowment in the country, which enables it to be generous with financial aid. More than half the students receive aid directly from the university in the form of scholarships, fellowships, long-term low-interest loans and campus employment. The Cost Stabilization Plan, pioneered by Wash U in 1978, provides parents with the option of freezing tuition, room and board costs at the freshman-year rate by paying four years worth of expenses when the student first enrolls. The university offers fifty competitive honorary merit scholarships to freshmen. Athletic scholarships are unheard of at this seriously academic school because, as one student puts it, "students who play sports here tend to do it for the fun of it, not because they want to make it their life."

Two high-rise and five low-rise buildings offer comfortable, air-conditioned accommodations all together in an area labeled "south 40," a forty-acre plot adjoining the campus. All dorms are coed, though some have single-sex floors, and all have computer centers for residents' use. Freshmen and sophomores are guaranteed rooms, but virtually all upperclassmen who wish to remain on campus can do so. Reasonably priced apartments can be found in the bordering neighborhood of University City; higher rents are found on the other side of campus in the more uppity Clayton area. The university also rents nearby apartments to students. "The best thing about Wash U is that there are so many places to get your meals," reports a senior—not to mention the real life experience of getting to flash your charge card wherever you dine. Students use their meal-plan credit cards in any of seven dining centers. You can even get late night deliveries and say, "Charge it."

Varsity sports, traditionally weak to the point of invisibility, have generated more interest in recent years. Cradled in one of the big soccer cities of the country, Wash U has adapted by producing a soccer squad that almost always ranks in the top ten of Division III. The women's volleyball team is also nationally ranked. Despite such successes, one student confesses that "intramural sports are more popular than varsity sports," a popularity promoted by the recent addition of a $13-million athletic complex, which includes new playing fields, and an Olympic-size pool, as well as several gymnasiums. These all-important intramural sports run the gamut from badminton, arm wrestling and floor hockey to pocket billiards and Ultimate Frisbee.

With Forest Park in its front yard, Wash U can offer students incredible recreational facilities: a golf course, ice-skating rink, zoo, lake with boat rentals, art and history museums, an outdoor theater and a science center. There are also multiple professional sporting events, and a zillion bars and restaurants, both nearby and downtown, near the mighty Mississippi on Lacledes Landing. St. Louis is also one of the best shopping cities in the country, and home of the infamous, addictive Ted Drewes frozen custard.

The drinking age of twenty-one forces many underclassmen to party on campus. Big bashes are hosted by the fraternities and sororities, which consist of about 30 percent of the student body. "Social life does exist at Wash U, contrary to the belief of many," attests one student. "And there are plenty of extracurricular activities to get involved in, it's just a matter of decidng that you're going to break out of the study mode for a little while each day."

Yet tearing themselves away from their books is not a regular habit of Wash U students. They, like their school, are hardworking and goal oriented. So no matter how popular it becomes and how many eager students apply, this anything-but-mediocre school "intends to remain a medium-size research university devoted to growth in quality rather than in size."

Wellesley College

Wellesley, MA 02181

Location Suburban	**Applicants** 2,420
Total Enrollment 2,260	**Accepted** 52%
Undergraduates 2,260	**Enrolled** 51%
Male/Female N/A	**Academics** ★ ★ ★ ★ ★
SAT V/M 600/630	**Social** 🐘 🐘 🐘
Financial Aid 65%	**Q of L** ● ● ● ●
Expense Pr $ $ $ $	**Admissions** (617)431-1183

Nestled in a corner of a wealthy Boston suburb quaintly known as the Vill, Wellesley College lives in its own little world. Its Gothic dormitories and classroom buildings are veritable castles; its grounds encompass five hundred acres of forest, fields, hills, a nine-hole golf course, even a lake. But don't be fooled by the pastoral effects: Blessed with a $265-million endowment ($120,000 per student) and a privileged exchange status with MIT, it is one of the foremost colleges—let alone women's colleges—in the nation. Wellesley students are bright, competitive, and fiercely devoted to their ability (and ambition) to do anything. One dean's favorite saying, "Not equal opportunity, but every opportunity," is well on its way to becoming a new school creed.

Most departments get high ratings from students, especially history, economics and political science; English and art history are among the top in the nation. The East Asian Studies program is excellent, and new courses in Japanese language and culture and in Jewish studies also enhance the humanities curriculum. A continuing education student refers to the theater department as a "neglected child," but administrators have already earmarked the performing arts as an area to receive near-future attention and support. Research in the natural sciences is often on the cutting edge, particularly in molecular biology, where students and faculty work on new DNA discoveries. A multimillion-dollar high-technology science center ("a modern, *George Pompidou*–type aberration, conspicuously distinct from the otherwise heavy, traditional late-nineteenth-century architecture") houses two electron microscopes, two NMR spectrometers, ultracentrifuges, an X-ray diffractometer, and argon and dye lasers. Other superior academic facilities include an extensive greenhouse, botanical garden, observatory, well-stocked art museum, labs and environmental rooms for psychological research and three libraries "with great librarians." Whatever Wellesley women find lacking in their facilities or curriculum can probably be found at MIT, where Wellesley has full cross-registration privileges.

Academically demanding, Wellesley has distribution requirements that include demonstrated competency in a modern or ancient language, a freshman writing course and three courses in each of three academic areas: humanities, social sciences and natural sciences. The academic pressure is intense and "adrenaline runs high," according to one woman. The fault lies both with heavy demands from professors and the extra pressure students put on themselves. Under the honors system, students may take their finals, unsupervised, at any time during exam week, and most consider the self-scheduled exams a lifesaver. Class size is small, and only two courses—Psych 101 and Oceanography—are consistently closed before freshmen register. The faculty, many of whom are on a first-name basis with students, are "ever accessible, patient, approachable, and, as a rule, understanding."

A five-course technology-studies concentration gives liberal arts students the skills necessary to understand and use technological innovations in their further studies and in the professional world. (Ninety percent of the student body is computer literate.) Another favored interdisciplinary venture is the cluster program, an opportunity for first-year students to live together and devote half their course work to studying the artistic, literary, political and scientific work produced in a specific historic era, such as Renaissance Italy or twentieth-century America. Internships are easily obtainable and include a Washington, D.C., program, an urban politics program in Los Angeles, and an urban legal program in Boston. Semesters abroad can be arranged through the Twelve College Exchange,* the National Theater Institute, the Maritime Studies Program or students can go abroad on one of Wellesley's programs in France, West Germany or Spain.

"Wellesley educates women to be their own masters—*femina sui juris*," declares one junior. "The Wellesley woman" traditionally calls to mind extreme prep and WASP stereotypes, but actually about two-thirds graduate from public high schools, and about one-fifth represent minority groups, the largest contingent being Asian Americans. Although the Northeast is the best-represented geographical area, students also come from nearly every state and more than fifty countries. A whopping 90 percent ranked in the top fifth of their high school class. One economics major attempts to describe the composite Wellesley woman as such: "resourceful, independent, well-adjusted, motivated, broad-minded, multitalented individuals—any combination thereof are encouraged to apply." But a classmate warns that "someone who is shy and withdrawn won't necessarily be pulled out of her shell at Wellesley." The college attempts to meet the total financial need of those who demonstrate it but doesn't offer athletic or merit scholarships.

Fifteen well-staffed dorms provide a welcome support and social system of their own, and high-ceilinged living rooms, fireplaces, television annexes, pianos and kitchenettes make dorm living a little more livable. With the exception of one dorm that houses MIT and male exchange students, all dorms are single sex. By junior year anyone who wants a single may have one. "Sometimes room preference is an issue," explains a dorm resident, "but never space." Two co-ops, one with a feminist bent, present an educational housing option, and few students live off campus. Fourteen- and twenty-meals-a-week plans are available (the latter being by far the better financial deal), and meal cards are valid in every dorm, at the campus snack bar and in the convenience store, which is stocked with everything from milk and flour to Twinkies.

Wellesley's location gives it an advantage over most other Seven Sisters colleges, since Boston provides big-city weekend fun and lots of other students, specifically male students from Harvard and MIT. Cambridge, with Harvard Square, MIT frat parties, and lots of jazz clubs, is forty-five minutes away; an hourly school shuttle is free to MIT on weekdays, but the weekend Luck Truck costs $1.25. There is also a trolley stop a short drive from school. On campus, students enjoy mixers, movies, bands, parties at the student center and just hanging out in Café Hoop, the campus coffeehouse. Having a car is a great advantage, with Cape Cod, Providence and the Vermont and New Hampshire ski slopes all within road-tripping distance. Field hockey, crew, swimming, basketball and fencing are popular varsity sports, and even, for those less competitively inclined, the new $18-million sports "palace" offers an Olympic-size pool; squash, racquetball and tennis courts; dance studios; a weight room; and an indoor track.

"Wellesley allows us to be independent in a very supportive environment," notes a chemistry major. Students cite the abundance of role models and the exceptional alumnae network (whose members include, among others, Madame Chiang Kai-Shek, Ali McGraw and Diane Sawyer) as favored aspects of their college. Although they say they miss male friendships, most Wellesley women wouldn't choose anywhere else if they had to do it again. Says one sophomore, "We have incredible opportunities here—lectures, special events, high-caliber faculty, a beautiful campus and fringe necessities. We're spoiled to be sure."

Wells College

Aurora, NY 13026

Location Small town	**Applicants** 265
Total Enrollment 450	**Accepted** 83%
Undergraduates 450	**Enrolled** 49%
Male/Female N/A	**Academics** ★ ★ ★
SAT V/M 510/520	**Social** ☎ ☎
Financial Aid 70%	**Q of L** ● ● ● ●
Expense Pr $ $ $	**Admissions** (315)364-3264

Wells College was founded in 1868 by Henry Wells, pioneer of the Wells Fargo and American Express companies. "It is commonly said that a woman's mind is not capable of attaining to a high order of discipline," Mr. Wells once remarked. "Not acknowledging this, let me say, give her the opportunity!" Over a hundred years later, tiny Wells College continues to carry out its founder's charge.

A few dramatic new additions have not spoiled the classic collegiate atmosphere conjured up by Wells' massive old brick halls and cheery Victorian detailing and trim. Seniors still ride to graduation in beautiful, old Wells Fargo stagecoaches, and the lovely lakeside campus—in fact the whole town of Aurora—have been named to the National Register of Historic Places. With Cayuga Lake affording not only beautiful sunsets, but also boating and fishing opportunities, the students can juxtapose the rigor of their studies with relaxation in a gorgeous environment. Surrounding the 360-acre campus is the rolling New England farmland that shelters Aurora from the urban spoils of Ithaca, Rochester and Syracuse. Yet Wells' outlook is not so antediluvian. Students are as likely to be found interning at a big oil company as sipping afternoon tea with their professors.

The liberal arts provide the basic framework for a Wells education. Core requirements include courses in English, writing-intensive and formal reasoning (math, computer science or logic), plus two courses in a foreign language and four in physical education. Students report that the strongest academic departments are English, foreign languages, government and economics. They also praise the math department and the natural sciences, especially biology with its refurbished facilities. Biology majors are also able to use the local environment (Cayuga Lake and surrounding lands) for ecology and botany field work. Students are impressed with the rapidly growing computer science department. Music, dance and fine arts at Wells have traditionally been weak, and suffer from a lack of faculty and ready access to outside cultural events. An accredited elementary education program is available, and interdisciplinary minors are offered in such fields as secondary education, communications, public policy and women's studies. Qualified students may design their own majors.

The college operates on a 4-1-4 calendar, with the January term used as a time for internships, independent study projects, or short courses. In addition, the college recently initiated a corporate affairs program that is aimed at preparing women for the business and financial professions through special courses and lectures, portfolio management experience and corporate internships. Foreign study is available for either a semester or a year in France, Spain or Germany. The college offers 3-2 dual-degree programs in community health and business administration with the University of Rochester, and in engineering with Texas A&M and Stanford. For a change of pace, students can take one nonmajor course per semester on a pass/fail basis and cross-register to take up to four courses at Cornell University.

The faculty at Wells is unusually accessible and friendly, even by small college standards. "Most professors will relate to you on your level of understanding without seeming condescending," observes a psych major. And class size is far from a problem at this school of only 450. "You get wonderful attention," reports one senior. "But if you're shy, there's *no way* you can hide with only eight people in a class." In addition, the administration gives students a great deal of responsibility for their own education. An honor system is enforced by the student-run collegiate association, and take-home and self-scheduled tests are the rule rather than the exception. The student government takes an active and effective role in policymaking.

Though the students come from similar economic circumstances, they pride themselves on their open-mindedness and variety of philosophies. "We've got '60s-style flower children, Vogue-style rich girls and a healthy serving of regular types," says one history major. "Getting to know the student body is an education in itself." Almost 60 percent of the students are state residents, with the rest coming from all over the country. One out of five has a prep or parochial school background. Because it is small, Wells lacks some of the facilities and academic programs that large universities can offer, and the social isolation may pose problems for some. "Women who want everything spoon-fed to them better go elsewhere," warns an American studies major. "Wells is not a partying school; you must work for your social life." Students who qualify for financial aid have their full needs met. In addition there are three $5,000-a-year Henry Wells Scholarships, awarded on the basis of academic achievement and scores on a Wells exam, as well as twenty-two other academic merit scholarships.

All students are guaranteed housing on campus. The dorms range from the founder's nineteenth-century homestead to modern facilities, and the spacious and comfortable rooms are cleaned daily by a housekeeping service. Freshmen are assigned a double or, in rare cases, a triple room; upperclassmen draw rooms through a lottery system, and most juniors and seniors get singles. There is virtually no off-campus housing in Aurora, where the total population is less than the tiny student body at Wells. The administration frowns on nonresident students and refuses to grant them financial aid, but in recent years 5 percent of the students have found ways to move

campus. Meals are served in a magnificent Tudor-style dining hall complete with
o working fireplaces. The food is much better than typical college fare, but there is
1e traditional emphasis on carbohydrates," one woman complains.

The college owns a great deal of waterfront property and maintains a dock and
boathouses for its students. Scores of waterfalls and wooded trails provide opportunities
for hiking and camping, and a college-owned stable is open to qualified riders. The ski
slopes of Greek Peak are less than an hour away, and the golf course and tennis and
paddle-ball courts are well used. A field house provides an indoor tennis court, a track,
and other facilities. Though the soccer and field hockey teams do fairly well, sports are
not big at Wells. Intramurals are available for those with the initiative, but they take
a back seat to the more popular and numerous clubs (math, French, dance performance, to name a few). Aurora itself offers almost nothing in the way of entertainment
(it doesn't even have a gas station), but Ithaca to the south and Syracuse to the east
provide more diversions. Campus parties tend to be "few and far between," so often
students flee on weekends, if not to Cornell then to Ithaca College, Colgate, Hamilton
or Hobart.

Students at Wells may occasionally miss big-city thrills; they sometimes wish
there were more men around. But at the same time, they feel inspired. "This is a school
that instills a great self-confidence in young women," explains a senior. "You are
encouraged to do *your* best, not better than the girl next to you." Today's Wells women
would do old Henry proud.

Wesleyan University

Middletown, CT 06457

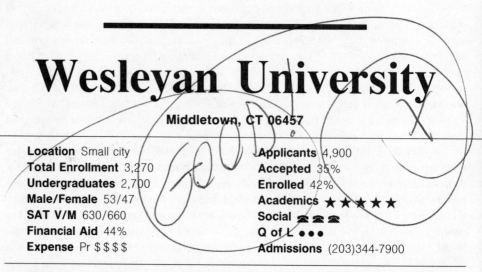

Location Small city
Total Enrollment 3,270
Undergraduates 2,700
Male/Female 53/47
SAT V/M 630/660
Financial Aid 44%
Expense Pr $ $ $ $

Applicants 4,900
Accepted 35%
Enrolled 42%
Academics ★ ★ ★ ★ ★
Social ☎ ☎ ☎
Q of L ● ● ●
Admissions (203)344-7900

Tradition Wesleyan-style centers not as much around the football field as around the
rallies held several times each year on the steps of the administration building. In
between sandwich bites, student and faculty activists let the world know what they
think of U.S. involvement in Central America, apartheid in South Africa or the level
of federal financial aid for higher education. Though Wesleyan's peripatetic protesters
are sometimes branded by skeptical classmates as "liberals without a cause," it is
heartening to see that the conservative eighties have not squelched the spirit of a
first-rate institution that has always been courageous about putting its academic and
social beliefs on the line.

The students of this small, prestigious New England college are marked by an
unusual political, cultural and intellectual sophistication. Wesleyan offers more academic and extracurricular options than almost any school its size, and the Wesleyan
experience means liberal learning in a climate of individual freedom. While most

students thrive in the wide-awake atmosphere, others—at least at first—can be overwhelmed by the amount of independence they are given.

A history/Russian language major notes, "The word *diverse* is used so much at Wesleyan that it's scary. But it is, we are, and hopefully we'll stay that way." Diversity begins with the campus architecture. The core of the campus is a century-old row of lovely ivy-covered brownstones. The rest range from dorms of the '50s and '60s design to the beautiful and modern Center for the Arts. The Wesleyan-owned student residences look freshly plucked from Main Street, U.S.A.

In addition to being considered one of America's hot schools among prospective students, Wesleyan is one of the most richly endowed per capita. It has used its wealth to attract highly rated faculty members who, in accordance with its "little university" philosophy, are expected to be scholar-teachers: academic supermen who do groundbreaking research and exciting teaching at the same time. And they seem to pull it off. "Profs are very approachable," reports one biology major. "They do a lot of research but they really concentrate their energy on teaching classes." There are even opportunities for students to do research with faculty.

Wesleyan students are marked by an unusual commitment to debate—from political to cultural to intellectual—and a high level of restlessness. "This is the only school I know of where the stands will be full at a football game, and in the same weekend an African dance concert will sell out, and the average student will know people at both events," reports one English major.

Among Wesleyan's strongest departments are the natural sciences (including astronomy), history, economics, philosophy and English. Ethnomusicology, including African drumming and dance, is a particular specialty; students can be found reclining on the wide, carpeted bleachers at the Third World Music Hall, watching a dozen musicians play the Indonesian gamelan. The film department is excellent—the annual festival of student-made films is an impressive and popular event—and the music is OK. Art history receives a lot of praise, but students say studio art is shaky, and the drama department is often criticized. Math, sociology and anthropology continue to need improvement.

Wesleyan currently asks that students take a minimum of three courses in each of three areas—humanities and the arts, social and behavioral sciences, and natural sciences and mathematics—but some students can exempt themselves by producing an acceptable rationale. The Freshman Integrated Program offers small interdisciplinary seminars with top professors. At the end of their freshman year, Wesleyan students can apply to major in one of three competitive, interdisciplinary seminar colleges: the College of Letters (literature, politics, history with a leftist bent), the College of Social Studies (politics, economics, history with a conservative bent) and the Science in Society program (concerned with the humane use of scientific knowledge, à la Buckminster Fuller).

Consistent in their praise of the school's academic philosophy ("They treat students as adults here"), Wesleyan students tend to take their work very seriously. The college tries to reduce tension and encourage experimentation by giving extensions to the next semester almost without question, allowing courses to be dropped up to the last day of classes and permitting students to design their own majors. A pass/fail grading option that substitutes a written evaluation for a grade is offered in most classes, and interdisciplinary programs are conducted almost entirely on this basis. Academic advising, a subject of criticism in the past, seems to be on the mend. Says one student, "The deans are really approachable—you don't have to be a disaster to get to know them." Psychological counseling and support programs are well organized and easily available.

While Wesleyan tries to keep its classes small to promote discussion, students claim class size is not what keeps them out of needed courses. The new preregistration system, which was supposed to facilitate signing up for classes, has turned into a nightmare. According to one disgruntled senior, "A lot of students, including seniors, don't get what they want, and the amount of paperwork is horrendous."

One temporary way to avoid the administrative commotion is to study abroad. Programs are available in Israel, Germany, Africa, Japan, Latin America, the USSR and China. Students can also participate in the Venture program,* study at Mystic Seaport,* or take a semester at another Twelve-College Exchange* school. Internships are popular, and students can also take advantage of 3-2 engineering programs with Columbia and Caltech.

Wesleyan likes to describe itself as "a small college with university resources," and at least one undergrad agrees that "we get the best of both worlds." The libraries, among the best in the country for a school this size, include stately and newly enlarged Olin, the main library, on which the administration has just lavished $10 million, and modern SciLi for the sciences. Students claim that whenever you happen to walk past the brightly lit, glass-walled study room of SciLi, you're apt to see numerous students huddled over their books. "Their eyes are bugging out, and it looks like they're in an aquarium," says one Wesleylanite. Hence, at this school, to study is to "squid."

Wesleyan's excellent reputation and strong recruiting network attracts students from all over, assuring the clash of viewpoints that makes it such a vital place. A long-standing commitment to minorities has yielded a 20 percent enrollment of black, Hispanic and Asian-American students. Only 10 percent of the students are from Connecticut, and 5 percent are from outside the United States. No academic or athletic merit scholarships are offered, but Wesleyan does provide need-based financial aid to almost half of its undergrads.

For housing, most freshmen are consigned to singles or doubles in two cinder-block dorm complexes, Foss Hill or Butterfield. Juniors and seniors enjoy numerous housing options: town houses for four or five students, fraternities, college-owned houses and apartments, or special-interest houses organized around concerns such as ecology, feminism or minority-student unity. Sophomores take the brunt of the occasional housing shortage, but often find contentment in ten-person houses in the unique William Street apartment complex, which borders a low-income housing project. Only a limited number of students receive permission to leave university housing. Upperclassmen eat at home, in the school grill, or at the fraternity eating clubs, and everyone else takes meals in Mocon, the glass-walled main dining hall one student likened to "a cathedral in the age of the Jetsons," or two smaller cafeterias.

Middletown is within easy driving distance of Hartford and New Haven but is off the beaten track of the commuter trains. Though many cosmopolitan students find the area provincial, some learn to appreciate Middletown. "It's real life," says one. "People are trying to make ends meet, work, raise a family, or simply stay off the bottle. It helps to maintain a good perspective." And the rural surroundings afford the much-appreciated opportunity to jog through the countryside, swim at nearby Wadsworth Falls, or pick apples in the local orchards. New York and Boston are each two hours away, and decent ski areas and beaches can be reached in just under an hour.

Sports tend to be for scholar-athletes rather than spectators, and the football team has traditionally had more success in building character than winning streaks. Nevertheless, the annual encounters with closest rivals Williams, Amherst and Trinity, muster considerable student enthusiasm. The Ultimate Frisbee club, the Nietzsche Factor, almost always whips challengers; as for varsity teams, wrestling, baseball and men's and women's cross-country and crew usually turn in winning seasons. Intramurals are extremely popular. In fact one student says that "many of my friends live for Sunday afternoons because of intramurals."

Although four former fraternities have turned into coed literary societies, Greek life at the remaining four is a jock preserve. Political and extracurricular organizations serve every imaginable interest. A new student center on Brownstone Row, complete with snack bar, games rooms and lounges, has done much to change the formerly fragmented social life, but one student initiator warns, "You can't sit around and wait for the phone here."

At Wesleyan, the individuality of the students coupled with the scattered living and eating arrangements add up to a variety of social and intellectual challenges. "You have to be willing to struggle a little to find out where you fit," says one veteran. But by the end of their freshmen year, most students fall in with a small circle of friends and discover that this college can not only be mastered but enjoyed. "Career-oriented, one-track students beware," warns one senior. "Not knowing what you want to do for the rest of your life isn't a problem—it's almost a requirement." Proud of its variety and enlivened by its tensions, strong individuals find Wesleyan a good place to grow stronger.

West Virginia University

Morgantown, WV 26506

Location Small city	**Accepted** 87%
Total Enrollment 17,180	**Enrolled** 52%
Undergraduates 12,510	**Academics** ★ ★
Male/Female 55/45	**Social** 🐻 🐻 🐻 🐻
ACT 20	**Q of L** ● ● ●
Financial Aid 38%	**Admissions** (800)344-WVU1
Expense Pub $	in West Virginia, (800)344-WVU2 out of state
Applicants 5,920	

West Virginia University is situated in the heart of the nation's beleaguered coal-mining country, but the energy at WVU doesn't come solely from the coalfields surrounding its Morgantown campuses. If high spirits and football cheers could be hooked up to a generator, the undergraduates at WVU could shut down the nearby mines forever.

As the state's only major university, West Virginia is committed to serving everyone from honor students to those who need remedial help. The university offers undergraduates a total of sixty-four degree programs in fourteen different schools, the best of which are engineering (particularly energy-related fields) and health sciences. WVU also boasts solid programs in journalism, physical education, agriculture and forestry, and the creative arts. About 70 percent of the students opt for the College of Arts and Sciences, where political science is the best department, and the School of Business and Economics is also popular, though understaffed. An honors program, open to students with a 3.5 high school GPA and 1200 on SATs, offers small classes and early registration, allowing students to get spots in the most sought after courses. Freshman honor students are housed in a hall equipped with computer terminals for their use.

All students must complete liberal studies distribution requirements in four areas: humanities, fine arts, social sciences and natural sciences. In addition, everyone must take courses that stress mathematical and writing skills, and there is also an innovative international/minority studies requirement. Though the university accepts practically everyone who could manage a C average in high school, admissions standards vary among particular programs. All are on a rolling-admissions basis, so apply early. Out-of-staters, for whom admissions standards are slightly higher, must be ready to make firm decisions by January 1 of their senior year. After arriving at WVU, the toughest job could be deciding which courses to take. The academic advising system is staffed mainly by graduate students, and not even enough of them. "You have a ten to twenty minute interview, in which time if you can't decide what to take, they decide for you, and you get their signature," says one senior. Outside the honors program, core liberal arts courses are also taught almost exclusively by graduate assistants, though anyone who manages to track down professors outside of class usually finds them willing to help. Overall, the atmosphere "leans toward the casual side," says a charitable honor student. A music education major was more blunt: "Students interested in being surrounded by very serious college students should stay away from WVU."

WVU is located in Morgantown, a college town secluded in the picturesque mountains of north central West Virginia a few miles from the Pennsylvania border. There are two campuses, one in downtown Morgantown, and the other about a mile and half away in a suburb known as Evansdale. The buildings downtown are of ivy-covered brick, dating mainly from the nineteenth century, while the Evansdale campus is more modern. A futuristic driverless rail system connects the two.

Though West Virginia attracts students from all fifty states and eighty-one foreign countries, it is primarily a regional university. "Both of my parents as well as grandparents, aunts, and cousins graduated from WVU," says an engineering major who numbers among the in-state majority. Sizable contingents also hail from western Pennsylvania, lured no doubt by an out-of-state tuition that is cheaper than the in-state fee at most other schools. There aren't many minorities in West Virginia, and the university's enrollment of them is correspondingly small. About 95 percent of the students come from public schools, and three-quarters of the graduates head straight for the job market. Having a good time is a common objective, and one woman characterizes her fellow students as "friendly and fun-loving." To go along with those who are following in the family footsteps, there are significant numbers who are first-generation college attendees. With tuition and fees barely exceeding $1,000 a year for in-staters, the financial demands on students are limited. There is no guarantee that demonstrated need will be met, but it usually is. Athletic scholarships for men and women are plentiful—about 280 in eleven different sports, roughly seventy of which are for women. WVU also gives out four hundred merit awards, for nonresidents as well as residents, ranging from $500 to $6,500. These are offered for strength in creative arts, debate, dance, as well as for general academic achievement. And at West Virginia, you could be better off knowing your pigs and cows than your P's and Q's, since the list of special interests in which merit scholarships are offered includes livestock and animal judging.

All noncommuting freshmen must live in college housing ("to ease their adjustment to university life"), and courses in career options and college-survival skills are offered on a pass/fail basis. For upperclassmen, it's first-come, first-served; most opt for nearby apartments, though about 10 percent choose Greek houses. All dorms are coed, with the older ones known for their character and the newer Towers on the Evansdale campus desirable for those who seek larger rooms and luxuries like air-conditioning. Arnold Hall, which contains the foreign language and honors floors, is probably the choicest of all. Each hall has its own cafeteria offering meal plans to all on- and off-campus students, and fraternities and sororities have their own cooks. The shuttle runs only until midnight, so late-night partyers should bring their own wheels.

West Virginia fields almost two dozen men's and women's varsity teams, including a national champion riflery squad, but football and basketball are the hands-down favorites. "The entire campus are loyal football fans, even students that don't know anything about football," says one woman. When the cheers at WVU's sixty-thousand-seat stadium die down, the action usually moves to fraternity houses, where Homecoming Week and Mountaineer Week highlight the social season. Morgantown supports an active bar scene, though a recent rise in the drinking age to twenty-one has sent underage students scurrying to private parties and fraternities to get their weekly quota of booze. The Mountain Lair, a student center located on the down-town campus, is also a popular hangout. No matter what the venue, the campus stays buzzing on weekends, and most undergraduates find "Mo-town" a great place to spend four years.

Unless you're in engineering or the health-related fields, studies don't figure too prominently in this scenario. Nor do politics, for most students. Says one sophomore of her peers: "Rather than liberal or conservative, they are apathetic." Unburdened by heavy academic pressures or social consciousness, surrounded by friendly and fun-loving peers, it's little wonder WVU undergraduates have energy and enthusiasm to spare.

Wheaton College

Norton, MA 02766

Location Rural	**Applicants** 900
Total Enrollment 1,080	**Accepted** 87%
Undergraduates 1,040	**Enrolled** 40%
Male/Female N/A	**Academics** ★ ★ ★
SAT V/M 510/510	**Social** 🏛 🏛 🏛
Financial Aid 52%	**Q of L** ● ● ● ●
Expense Pr $ $ $	**Admissions** (617)285-7722

It's a women's college's prerogative to change its mind. And that's exactly what Wheaton College did. Citing a waning interest in all-female colleges among high school students, Wheaton caved in against the rush toward coeducation that had already altered the identity of many of its sister institutions. Prospective male students should be pleased to hear that this change allowed Wheaton to fill a gap in the Boston-area college market by becoming a small, personal, liberal arts school that caters to students of both sexes. And women students who might have been shying away from Wheaton because of its notoriously void social scene, may want to consider what the addition of a few good men will do. For future Wheatonians of either sex, the change will be a welcome one, but for advocates of the shrinking number of women's colleges, this development means that another one bit the dust.

Small New England town is the theme of Norton, Massachusetts, despite its inevitable classification as a suburb, albeit a distant one, of Boston. Nestled in these rural surroundings, Wheaton offers an idyllic environment in which to study one's brains out, a pretty blend of ivy-covered Georgian brick (the old campus) and ivy-covered modern architecture (the new) set among beautiful lawns and numerous shady trees. The two halves of the campus are separated by picturesque Peacock Pond, which probably qualifies as the only heated duck pond on any American campus. For outdoor buffs, there is plenty of room for scenic runs or bike trips.

Academically, Wheaton offers much. There are thirty-one major programs in the liberal arts, most of them quite solid, with political science, economics, biology, English and art history considered outstanding. Foreign language departments are small, and as a result majors usually take junior year abroad. Supplementary minors are offered in more career-oriented areas, such as legal studies, computer science, education and management. Independent study courses and individualized majors are encouraged. Wheaton also offers dual degree opportunities in journalism, business administration, engineering and religion in conjunction with other schools, and allows students to take semesters on other campuses through the Twelve-College Exchange.*

For a small college, Wheaton has made many educational innovations. It is recognized as a leader in exploring the relationship between liberal arts and technology. Nationally acclaimed curricular programs in which global issues and works by and about women are integrated into mainstream studies were developed at Wheaton and now serve as models for other programs in the country. Wheaton also has one of the oldest women's studies departments—"It's spectacular, and I urge every student who enters Wheaton to take at least one course in this area," one student raves. The highly praised and well-organized Center for Work and Learning oversees several programs, ranging from the traditional internship (over January break) to an innovative Mentor Program, in which students are matched with a working professional in their chosen career area. Pressure to perform well in academics is strong but largely imposed from within, and "everyone is supportive of each other."

In keeping with Wheaton's attempt to "integrate knowledge across the range of liberal arts disciplines," the college has just revised its general education curriculum to include popular freshman seminars, courses on cultural diversity and global perspectives, and an emphasis on writing. Class enrollment, even in the popular introductory courses, rarely nears one hundred students. The average in upper-level courses rarely exceeds two dozen students, and classes of three, four and five students are not unusual. In addition to being fine teachers, "professors are accessible as friends, mentors, and advisers," one student reports. Academic facilities on the small campus are good and include an expanded library, a science center with an electron microscope, a main computing center, as well as many computer terminals scattered throughout residence halls.

Nearly three-quarters of Wheatonians are from public schools, and about half come from outside Massachusetts. Some of the numerous preppies form cliques, but otherwise there is remarkable harmony in this friendly community. The majority of Wheaton students are hardworking, career-oriented and serious about their studies, but only a few of the women here would consider themselves committed feminists. Rather than force-feed philosophies, Wheaton gives its students "both the encouragement and the resources to set high goals and attain them." The college's aid policy provides some form of assistance to nearly every student whose completed application demonstrates need. Twenty-five merit scholarships, in the form of Apple IIe computers, are available to freshmen, and awarded on the basis of academic performance, leadership qualities, writing ability and extracurricular activities. Loans and payment plans are also offered.

Virtually everyone lives on campus in dorms monitored by teams of upperclass students. Freshmen live in doubles, triples or quadruples, and everyone is guaranteed a single by senior year. Winners in the room lottery head straight for spacious singles with wood floors in the ivy-covered old campus. Losers end up looking at cinder-block walls in the newer, more cramped buildings. Meals in the bright and spacious dining halls are outstanding, at least by the standards of college cuisine. The dining hall staff wins points with imaginative theme dinners, such as Drive-in Movie Night, when a menu of shakes, fries, and burgers is served up along with a popular film. The biggest winners of all are the ducks, who thrive on leftover bread and hang around their Great Society on heated Peacock Pond all winter.

The town is so small that the drugstore, supermarket and pizza joint *(caveat emptor)* are considered hotspots. But the situation is getting better: Norton is rapidly expanding, and the completion of the Great Woods Performing Arts Center is an impressive example of this growth. Just ten minutes from campus, the large center is summer home for the Pittsburgh Symphony as well as the Boston Ballet, and Wheaton provides practice rooms and other facilities year-round for visiting performers. In addition, free bus rides are available to Boston and Providence, nearly an hour and a half hour away, respectively. A car makes for easy escapes to Cape Cod, ski trips, shopping sprees at the area's many malls or road trips to any of the dozens of colleges within dating distance.

Field hockey, lacrosse and tennis teams on campus are traditionally strong, and for the aesthetic sportswoman, synchronized swimming is an option. The TAB (Tackling Abused Bodies) aerobics classes help dissipate some academically induced tension. Athletics, movies and concerts play a significant role in campus happenings, as does the traditional mixer (now called the "social event"). Whatever you call them, they're held just about every weekend, though this frequency is not based on their appeal: Many students consider them forced and awkward. Wheaton women used to complain that meeting men on an intellectual level took too much of an effort, but assuming male students will accept the college's invitation, those days are all but over. Chances are, however, that the male/female ratio will remain skewed in the feminine direction for some time to come, and most Wheaties will continue to find cross-registration programs with Brown helpful in relieving the dating dilemma.

The recently completed $3-million student center should improve social life on campus with its coffee shop, dance studio, radio station, sun deck and terraces. And then there's always the Loft, the student pub that features food, drink and entertainment. The administration and many concerned students are doing everything they can to change the popular refrain, "I love Wheaton during the week and wouldn't want to be anywhere else, but on the weekends. . . ."

Although it may not facilitate a dynamic social life, Wheaton's setting is conducive to the school's goal of developing "a level of confidence, self-reliance, and independence rarely before expected of women." This motto must now be expanded to include the developmental needs of male students as well. But then, the level of confidence and self-reliance of those first few men to tear down the long-standing, women-only tradition at this tightly knit school can't be too low to begin with.

Wheaton College

Wheaton, IL 60187

Location Suburban	**Applicants** 1,460
Total Enrollment 2,570	**Accepted** 78%
Undergraduates 2,200	**Enrolled** 61%
Male/Female 40/60	**Academics** ★ ★ ★
SAT V/M 540/580	**Social** 🐿 🐿 🐿
Financial Aid 55%	**Q of L** ● ● ●
Expense Pr $	**Admissions** (312)260-5005

Wheaton College has been referred to as both the Princeton of Christian schools and the Harvard of Evangelical Protestantism. Prospective Wheatonians must have more than a "strong interest in serving Christ" to attend this school, and they must sign a pledge to stay away from alcohol, drugs, gambling, cheating—even dancing. Bible classes are required, and four times a week everyone files into assigned seats at mandatory chapel services. Faculty members sign a credo declaring that the Bible is "verbally inspired by God and inerrant in the original writing." It's obvious that Wheaton is in a class by itself.

The buildings on Wheaton's eighty-acre campus are interesting in heritage as well as architectural style; Blanchard Hall, built in the middle of the last century, "looks somewhat like a castle perched on top of the front campus hill," explains one student. The wooded, ivy-covered setting is nestled right into the middle of one of Chicago's oldest and most established suburbs—quiet, dignified and quaint.

For all its quiet and quaintness, Wheaton has managed to attract enough National Merit Scholars to put it on a par with the best colleges of its size. It also ranks among the top twelve small colleges in the country in the percentage of graduates who go on for doctorates. The alumni roster reads like a Who's Who among American conservative Protestants, beginning with Billy Graham (BA, anthropology, 1943).

As a Christian liberal arts institution, Wheaton infuses all aspects of campus life with religious overtones. The curriculum is built around traditional distribution requirements but is designed to integrate faith and learning. Sixteen hours of Bible and theology are required of all ("although most students would take them even if they weren't required," attests a Christian education major), and faculty strive to relate this world view to their discipline. This integration of faith is nowhere more evident than in the $13.5-million Billy Graham Center down the hill from the Old Main campus. It has become a cornerstone in research on American evangelicalism.

The once-feared gap between Christianity and science has been overcome at Wheaton, where most of the natural sciences are strong. Medical schools welcome Wheaton grads at a 95 percent rate. History, theology and Bible, economics, social science and psychology departments get high marks, and the conservatory of music produces heavenly harmonics. Students are less devoted to singing the praises of the art and geology offerings. In addition to major programs in the liberal arts and sciences, students can opt for the 3-2 liberal arts/nursing program or liberal arts/engineering double degree.

Studying abroad in East Asia, Ecuador, England, France, Germany or the Holy Land is a possible, even probable, option for Wheaton undergraduates who are also able to take a semester at one of twelve other evangelical schools in the Christian College Consortium. The Human Needs and Global Resources (HNGR) program coordinates studies in Third World development with six-month internships in a development project in a Third World country. The High Road Wilderness program provides an Outward-Bound-type experience in the woods of northern Wisconsin. There is also a Black Hills Science Station for summer study in botany and zoology and Honey Rock Camp for Christian education. The library is small for a college with Wheaton's academic aims, but it has a first-rate collection of modern mythology—Tolkien, C. S. Lewis, etc.—and it even holds born-again Charles Colson's personal Watergate papers.

"I guess to outsiders, Wheaton students would appear to be a lot alike," admits a senior. "The average student is white, from an evangelical Christian background, and a fairly well-off family." Yet this student commonality comes from all corners of the country and several foreign countries. Although most Wheatonians would call themselves political conservatives, one woman reports, "You will find people here who believe that Christ commands us to be interested in the social aspects of society as well." The high-pressured and competitive academic climate is to be expected with 42 percent of the students graduating in the top tenth of their high school classes. The financial aid office tries hard to meet the needs of students qualifying for aid, and about eighty outstanding undergraduates qualify for merit scholarships.

Dorms are clean, comfortable, and well maintained. The only coed dorm, Fischer, is occupied mostly by underclassmen and has large, air-conditioned double rooms with a bathroom between every two. A high percentage of juniors and seniors live in college-owned apartments off campus. All residential students eat in an attractive dining room, with carpets and soft lighting; a new dining hall is in the works. As for the food, a senior remarks that "institutional food never beats Mom's, but the cafeteria here beats most other colleges I've tried."

A quick half-hour train ride transports Wheaton undergrads to Chicago's Loop. Also, the Indiana and Michigan sand dunes are within driving distance. The College Union organizes movies, late-night skating parties and other activities almost every weekend. The best teams on campus are the men's and women's soccer, swimming, tennis and cross-country squads. Intramurals are "exceptionally strong," and locker room facilities have recently been renovated.

Wheaton's motto, "For Christ and His Kingdom," inspires its students not only to excel on the playing field and in the classroom but to live their lives like good Christian soldiers. "We want to make an impact on our world for Jesus Christ," students say. There's little doubt that Wheaton's solid academic program, supportive Christian community and emphasis on worthwhile extracurricular activity offer fine preparation for the task.

Whitman College

Walla Walla, WA 99362

Location Small city	**Applicants** 910
Total Enrollment 1,180	**Accepted** 95%
Undergraduates 1,180	**Enrolled** 41%
Male/Female 50/50	**Academics** ★ ★ ★ ★
SAT V/M 550/590	**Social** 🐗 🐗 🐗
Financial Aid 50%	**Q of L** ● ● ● ●
Expense Pr $ $	**Admissions** (509)527-5176

Whitman has somehow managed to thumb its nose at time. It began as the dream of a husband-and-wife team of medical missionaries on the northwest frontier. Today, it is a close-knit, conservative institution—one that has made the clear choice to hold down the liberal education fort by resisting the temptation to vocationalize its academic offerings, regardless of what other schools are doing. With a high level of alumni support, an endowment of more than $80,000 per student, the only Phi Beta Kappa chapter among Washington's private colleges and a physical plant largely rebuilt in the last two decades, Whitman has no problem maintaining its reputation as one of the best small, liberal arts colleges in the Pacific Northwest.

Everything important, including the main drag of Walla Walla (aka Walla Squared) is within walking or biking distance. The small campus with its ivy-covered brick and few modern buildings, adds a touch of New England to a rolling expanse of northwestern terrain inhabited primarily by wheat farmers and ranch hands. Beyond the town, for as far as the eye can see, are mountains, rivers and forests.

Most students consider Whitman's faculty its biggest asset. Professors are accessible, and dining with them is a frequent occurrence. "A professor gets yelled at if he's not around on a regular basis," observes one student. Whitman's small size means that its course offerings must be relatively simple; but if you want to study something, you can usually find somebody to teach you. Students are serious about their studies and are constantly putting together combination majors such as art and philosophy.

Impressive academic departments are history, psychology, economics and English (especially if you're into Shakespeare). Whitman's historical strength in the natural sciences has been augmented by a new chemistry curriculum and a new major in geology. Both the political science and computer science programs have also been expanded. Music and education suffer from frequent faculty turnovers, and the astronomy, anthropology and religion departments are tiny and do not offer majors. Whitman's general education standards include an interdisciplinary freshman sequence with courses ranging from The Origins of Modernism to Classical Greece. Standard distribution requirements taken throughout the sophomore and junior years ensure students will have a broad-based liberal arts exposure outside of their majors. The senior colloquium serves as a capstone discussion of contemporary issues amongst students specializing in different disciplines.

Whitman boasts a $4-million Asian art collection and expanded Asian studies and art history programs. The library, with 154,000 book titles, is adequate for a school of this size and is as good a place to catch up on the latest campus news as to study. Whitman has 3-2 or 3-3 programs in engineering (with Caltech, Columbia and Duke), forestry (Duke), and law (Columbia), as well as a program of science internships. There are also several organized programs for foreign studies, including a special opportunity for students and recent alumni to teach in China.

Half of Whitman students come from Washington, the rest primarily from California and other western states, including Alaska and Hawaii. Seven percent are Asian Americans, but other minority groups are scarcely a presence, despite recruiting efforts. Also in the minority are jocks and devotees of alternative life-styles. The president frankly admits that Whitman is not geared to serve students "who feel alienated from the mainstream of American life." A sociology major ventures to say, "The term conservative arts institution fits Whitman much better than liberal arts." In its quest for future Horatio Algers, however, Whitman sets aside 10 percent of its freshman places each year for students who will promote diversity or seem to have unusual, if undocumented, potential to succeed. Eighty-five percent of the students come from public high schools, and professional school is an eventual goal for more than half. Future upholders of the peace and the American way will be pleased to know that Whitman is alma mater to Adam West, better known as Batman, the Caped Crusader. Well-endowed Whitman has a financial aid policy wherein every needy student who applies for aid on time will receive a package consisting of 60 percent grant money and 40 percent self-help aid. School-sponsored loans are available to many who no longer qualify for federal loan programs. About 5 percent of the students receive merit scholarships ranging from $500 to $1,500, but athletes get zip.

All freshmen and sophomores must live in the campus housing, which includes some lovely old buildings with large, comfortable rooms that are also sometimes noisy and prone to breakdowns of the heating and water systems. Freshmen are guaranteed assigned rooms; after that they compete with the rest of the student body on the basis of seniority. Most dorms are coed by floor or section; one is reserved for women only. The majority of seniors take advantage of the upperclassmen's privilege to live off campus. Each of the five fraternities has its own house, but the four sororities stake out sections of the women's dorm. Dining halls, situated in several dorms, offer the normal college menu, including a salad bar and vegetarian entrees.

Outdoor attractions are important in this area of the country where the autumns are gorgeous, the winters snowy and the springs warm. Skiing is about forty-five minutes away, and backpacking, canoeing and white-water rafting are popular. Students who get antsy in this remote location say weekend trips to Seattle and Portland can be lifesavers. There is some enthusiasm for varsity sports, but not much (football was booted in the late 1970s). The many intramural activities are popular, and Sherwood Center has extensive facilities for exercise, including a large swimming pool.

About half the students, and the few serious partyers who are attracted to the college, belong to the fraternities and sororities. Being an independent, though, is not tantamount to entering a monastery. The state's minimum drinking-age of twenty-one is honored more in the breach than in the observance. College theater productions are rated excellent; movies are cheap, and a generous special-events budget enables the importing of performers and speakers to make up for Walla Walla's cultural paucity. Three foreign language houses on campus do their thing for the cause of diversity.

Whitman does a good job of serving students who can handle a small community where "gossip flies faster than a sparrow in a power dive." Students value the excellent rapport with faculty, the close-knit sense of community, "the environment of friendship and learning." Whitman, says one student, "would be just like camp if it weren't for all the studying."

Whittier College

Whittier, CA 90608

Location Suburban
Total Enrollment 1,540
Undergraduates 980
Male/Female 50/50
SAT V/M 520/550
Financial Aid 68%
Expense Pr $ $

Applicants 920
Accepted 78%
Enrolled 42%
Academics ★ ★ ★
Social ☎ ☎ ☎
Q of L ● ● ● ●
Admissions (213)693-0771

Whittier College is close enough to L.A. for internships and evenings out, but far enough into the country so you can breathe a bit of air with your smog. Its curriculum is structured around the traditional liberal arts, but offers several vocational and individualized offerings. In a state where the low-cost, public universities rival top-notch private institutions, little Whittier is an enticing alternative for students who seek a caring, supportive and personal atmosphere amid all the comforts of Southern California.

Ideally located less than an hour from white, sandy beaches and no more than two hours from snow skiing, the Whittier campus is a hodgepodge of modern buildings tucked between the red-roofed, white-walled Spanish traditionals. The wooded, 105-acre campus doesn't look much different than it did in the days when the school's most famous alumnus, Richard M. Nixon, strolled along the eucalyptus and palm tree–shaded paths. The college is perched on a hill overlooking the town of Whittier, with the San Gabriel mountains rising up on the side. At night, the lights of L.A. twinkle and glow in the distance.

Founded in 1887 by members of the Society of Friends, Whittier officially ended its affiliation with the Quakers in the 1940s, but the prevailing spirit of community hearkens back to their traditions. Classes tend to be quite small; less than ten students is not unusual, but more than forty is. Faculty win high marks for their concern and accessibility—"You can spend as much time as you want with them"—though several departments are criticized for carrying dead weight. And Whittier courses are generally not so demanding as to stand in the way of enjoying the great location or many extracurricular options.

Two major courses of study are available: the liberal education program and the Whittier scholars program. About 90 percent of the students take the basic liberal arts track, in which they fulfill standard distribution requirements in English composition, math and natural sciences. They then take interdisciplinary courses in the fine arts and humanities, Western and non-Western civilizations, and contemporary society and the individual. These liberally educated Whittierians next choose a major from among twenty-six departments, the strongest of which are economics, political science, biology and chemistry. Students also praise the communications disorders and education departments, but say music, art, physics and geology are too small to be effective. Business administration and accounting are popular, but students have mixed opinions on the quality of the program.

The other 10 percent of the undergraduates choose to bypass the traditional liberal arts program by applying to become Whittier Scholars. They are relieved of most general requirements and start from square one with an educational design process. With the help of an academic adviser, the scholars carve their majors out of standard offerings by taking a bit of this and a bit of that. One woman combined courses from the business and home ec departments and majored in fashion merchandising. Somewhere within their samplings they must include English composition, three scholar seminars and a senior project. The program is highly regarded (even by those who don't elect to take it) because of the more active role it allows students to play and the freedom it affords them in pursuing their interests.

Preprofessional programs—standard or self-designed—are extremely popular, and Whittier boasts 90 percent acceptance rates at schools of law and business, 85 percent at schools of medicine. BA/MBA and cooperative engineering programs are offered, and study-abroad options include programs in Denmark, Mexico and Asia (in fact, Whittier's student exchange with the Beijing Language Institute is one of only a few such programs offered with the People's Republic of China). Undergraduates also may take foreign study tours during the January interim. A new computer center provides students with unlimited access to various systems (there are also terminals in the residence halls), and the writing center offers several microcomputers and printers.

About half the students come from California, and the rest from all over the United States and all over the world (8 percent are foreign). Nearly three-quarters went to public high schools. They tend to be "conservative as far as Southern Californians go, but liberal compared to midwesterners," analyzes a psych major. Yet more than one student points out that the relaxed atmosphere on campus doesn't force people to take a stand or become involved in anything. "There are no intense people here," notes a senior, "they're all laid-back—it's the way it should be." Even the academic climate is casual and noncompetitive: "There are no cutthroats here; we're very supportive of each other's efforts." Hispanic and black enrollment is an impressive 22 percent. Whittier brags about its strong commitment to meet the financial needs of all accepted students. And in addition to need-based aid, the college grants fifteen talent awards of up to $3,650 in art, drama and music, as well as more than forty academic merit scholarships, which range from $1,500 to full rides.

More than a third of the students are forced to seek off-campus shelter, as an increasingly disruptive housing shortage invades the campus with it's two single-sex and four coed dorms. "Most of the dorms are well maintained, but they're getting old," cites a junior. Freshmen are assigned rooms, while Whittier Scholars, athletes and members of the social societies tend to cluster in selected dorms and houses. All campus residents must take at least ten meals at the Campus Inn dining hall, where the food is "probably typical college food—not too good, but fully edible." Small houses and society houses have their own kitchens, and the campus café, The Spot, is popular with off-campus residents. A student-managed coffee shop, Friday's, is great for late night rap sessions and study breaks.

Social societies (local fraternities) attract about half the students and tend to be identified by certain interests. "For instance, the Orthogonian Society is made up mainly of athletes, while the Lancers and Penns tend to be more academically oriented," one man reports. These societies (four men's, four women's and one coed) don't dominate the social scene at Whittier, but their dances, which frequently feature live entertainment, are welcomed by all. The beach is a frequent must (remember it never rains in Southern California), and for nightlife, Los Angeles looms large. "This is California," says one student. "It's tough times if you don't know someone with a car." The local community, known as Uptown Whittier, is pretty but staid. "There aren't many resources—definitely none that are important to social life," says a bio major. Men's and women's basketball are the winningest varsity sports, but Whittier lacrosse, which is a club sport, rules the Western College League. Football, baseball and women's softball and volleyball also do well. Intramurals and the abundant extracurricular organizations are all popular. "Students are encouraged—but not pushed—to get involved," announces an English major.

"The school really wants you to learn," believes a political science major. "They don't just take your money for four years and give you a diploma. They care." Most students agree that, while Whittier is not the most dynamic school on the West Coast, it is a supportive, intimate place where people cooperate and learn from each other. A business student summates: "At Whittier, you can do virtually nothing or virtually everything, or carefully mix and stir the two."

Willamette University

Salem, Oregon 97301

Location Center city	**Applicants** 1,180
Total Enrollment 1,960	**Accepted** 76%
Undergraduates 1,440	**Enrolled** 45%
Male/Female 49/51	**Academics** ★★★
SAT V/M 540/590	**Social** 🕿🕿🕿
Financial Aid 70%	**Q of L** ●●●●
Expense Pr $ $	**Admissions** (503)370-6303

A profusion of trees, ducks, squirrels and other small wildlife and a clean, clear brook running amid old red-brick buildings make the Willamette campus an almost perfect northwestern paradise. The only problem is Guido, the killer goose, who lives in Mill Stream and, when he's irritable, attacks unwary students. But aside from petulant poultry, there is little to frighten seekers of quality higher education at this liberal arts–oriented private university—one of the oldest west of the Mississippi.

Founded in 1842, Willamette offers all the advantages of a small college—low student/faculty ratio, lots of individual attention, a cohesive intellectual community— plus some of the resources of a larger, research-oriented university. It has graduate schools of law and management, and on the undergraduate level it boasts thirty-four degree programs. Willamette also offers opportunities to earn combined liberal arts and professional or master's degrees in conjunction with other institutions in fields such as computer science, forestry, engineering and business management.

The Willamette academic climate, as described by a physics major, comes down to this: "Students are willing to let loose on Friday and Saturday nights, but the pursuit of academic excellence is paramount." Professors are encouraged to do research but still win praise for their accessibility to students. The small size of most classes (none over seventy-five students, most around twenty) promotes "lively discussion and a certain pressure to be prepared and perform well," one student notes.

Among the strongest programs at Willamette are the natural sciences, English, history, math and international studies. Economics and political science benefit from having the state capital complex right across the street, and music has premier facilities and a strong reputation for training performers and music therapists. Computer science is up-and-coming, and is already one of the best departments among schools in the region. Programs in art, sociology, earth science, environmental science and speech communication suffer from a lack of depth both in courses and faculty. Business, premed, and prelaw tracks are popular, and Willamette boasts good rates of acceptance at corresponding professional schools. Students rhapsodize about the new $6.4-million Mark O. Hatfield Library, which boasts a computerized card catalogue system and more than enough study space.

Willamette prides itself on its emphasis on sound liberal arts offerings "with no gimmicky or trendy programs." General education requirements include math and English proficiency, plus courses in the humanities, literature, fine arts, social sciences, natural sciences and interdisciplinary studies. Bachelor of Arts candidates must also show proficiency in a foreign language, while professional degrees in music and drama have other specific core/proficiency requirements. Willamette has its own program for study abroad in France, Japan, China and Italy, and participates in a consortium that provides opportunities for study in Spain, England, Mexico and West Germany.

For the most part, students come to Willamette from the western coastal states— Oregon, Washington, California, Alaska and Hawaii—and more than three-quarters ranked in the top quarter of their high school class. One student refers to his classmates as friendly and supportive, but according to a senior, "There is little ethnic diversity, and although the number of liberals is growing, it's an uphill battle." In addition to need-based financial aid, Willamette offers more than one hundred new talent and academic merit scholarships each year, ranging up to $7,500. Athletes, however, score no points in the scholarship department.

Freshmen and sophomores have to live on campus, but juniors and seniors are moving off in increased numbers. Except for one women's dorm, all residential housing is coed. A large percentage of the students (more than a fourth) live in their own fraternity and sorority houses. Housing generally pleases students, but food is another matter entirely. "Food variety is poor, quality is worse, and they often run out of desired items—and I work for the food service!" exclaims a history major. One interesting feature is the vegetarian Nutritional Awareness Program, and the snack bar is a lifesaver when the cafeteria really strikes out. Sororities have their own kitchens and cooks, and there are restaurants within walking distance of campus.

With nearly half the students belonging to one of the six fraternities and three sororities, Greeks have an undeniable effect on the social scene, but a senior notes that "parties are attended by both Greeks and independent students with no real animosity between the two factions." Movies, dances, Monday night football on the big TV screen, coffeehouses featuring local performers, and just "having intimate gatherings with friends" are all high on one independent's list of favorite leisure-time activities. Then there are the traditional events like Freshman Glee, Spirit Week and the Freshman Leaf Rake.

Although students tend not to become heavily involved in the surrounding community of Salem, most seem to enjoy the activities and resources the state capital city offers—especially the parks, restaurants, and movies. Portland, an hour away, is a popular destination for weekend jaunts, and Mt. Hood and Mt. Bachelor ski areas can be reached in only a couple of hours. Intramural sports are popular, and Willamette fields strong varsity teams in men's and women's basketball, men's baseball, cross-country and track, and women's swimming and diving.

Individuals from the West, or those ready to fall in love with it (remember the rain!), will probably find Willamette a more personalized alternative to some of the larger universities in the area, and a better-endowed alternative to some of the smaller private colleges. "The people—students, faculty, administration—get to know you and really care," insists a chemistry major. "The campus is exceptionally beautiful and— with the exception of Guido the goose—livable. I believe Willamette is the best place for me to live and learn."

College of William and Mary

Williamsburg, VA 23185

Location Small city	**Applicants** 6,510
Total Enrollment 7,010	**Accepted** 40%
Undergraduates 4,990	**Enrolled** 52%
Male/Female 48/52	**Academics** ★ ★ ★ ★ ★
SAT V/M 590/630	**Social** 🍺 🍺 🍺
Financial Aid 46%	**Q of L** ● ● ●
Expense Pub $ $ $ $	**Admissions** (804)253-4228

Maybe

Founded by the decree of King William and Queen Mary in 1693, the College of William and Mary does more than just revere its traditions—it lives them. On the college's picturesque campus in restored Colonial Williamsburg, students "can almost sense what it felt like to attend school in the eighteenth century." Amid the clatter of horses' hoofs on the red-brick and cobblestone streets, one half expects to see Thomas Jefferson hurry by with Locke's Second Treatise under his arm, or John Marshall climbing the worn steps of the Wren Building for another session of English common law. "I love our traditions," says a government major, "the two-hundred-year-old honor code, the Yule log, special candlelight ceremonies at graduation—just the history of it all." Another tradition that lives on at this premiere "public Ivy" is a commitment to old-fashioned academic excellence.

A profusion of azaleas and crape myrtle add splashes of color to William and Mary's finely manicured campus, which is divided into three sections. The Ancient Campus, adjacent to Colonial Williamsburg, is a grouping of three colonial structures, the oldest of which is the Wren Building, which has been in continuous use since 1695 and ranks with Princeton's Nassau Hall as perhaps the loveliest architectural gem on any American campus. The Modern Campus, where the buildings date from the '20s and '30s, is a little farther out, and next to it is New Campus where ground was first broken in the '60s. William and Mary is known—at least in its public relations office—as "the alma mater of a nation," though today its status as a state school deprives it of the national prominence it deserves. The college gave birth to Phi Beta Kappa and the honor code, and still demands much from its students. At least one bemoans "the incredibly high expectations of several professors," and all seem to agree that the academic climate is both rigorous and competitive.

Fittingly, the history department, a joint sponsor with Colonial Williamsburg of the Institute for Early American History and Culture, is among William and Mary's best departments. English, physics, chemistry, religion and government are also praised. The business school is especially rigorous and, according to one student, "recruiters rave about the accounting graduates." Special off-campus attractions include the Venture employment program which allows students to take a semester or a year off in a planned internship. There are also summer and yearlong study-abroad programs in France, the Philippines, Germany, Italy and Mexico and summer field schools in archeology, including one in St. Eustatius in the Caribbean.

Relations between students and professors are said to be excellent and one student reports that William and Mary is one of the few schools in the nation where all classes for undergraduates are taught by full-fledged professors. Most classes include about twenty-five students, though introductory lectures can have as many as three hundred. Though W&M is a relatively small school, preregistration can be a headache, and students must often resort to the drop/add period to get the classes they need. Distribution requirements are thorough and include two years of a foreign language, proficiency requirements in writing and physical education, and a total of eleven other courses in three broad areas: the social sciences, natural sciences and humanities. An expansion project is underway for the library—an upgrading that will be much appreciated, students say. A new Center for Honors and Interdisciplinary Studies will mean the introduction of new majors like women's studies and Afro-American studies, as well as the expansion of an interdisciplinary honors program that currently allows outstanding freshmen two semesters of intensive liberal arts seminars that feature lectures by top scholars from around the country.

By current state policy, two-thirds of the students are Virginians—"Too bad," more than one ambitious out of state applicant has been caught grumbling, because competition for the nonresident spots is stiff. Most of the out-of-staters are from neighboring upper southern states, though significant numbers also hail from the Northeast; about 60 percent of the students were in the top 10 percent of their high school classes. "Your general all-American kid is the norm at William and Mary," says one student. A minority of liberals keep the campus from tilting too far to the right. W&M has its share of eagerly recruited jocks (140 athletic scholarships are offered in all sports). Only a few token academic merit awards are offered for freshmen.

Approximately 80 percent of the students live on campus, in both single-sex and coed housing that ranges from stately old halls with high ceilings to modern buildings equipped with air-conditioning. All freshmen are guaranteed a room on campus, but after that there is a lottery system. Students who do not choose to enter the lottery can either live in special interest housing—there are five language houses and a Creative Arts House—or a fraternity, sorority or off campus. Students praise the two campus cafeterias, where all freshmen must purchase an eighteen-meal plan. Others have a variety of options, including cooking in the dorms; sororities and fraternities have dinner plans open to members and non-Greek friends.

W&M isn't known as a social school, and "sometimes there is a lot of effort required to create a social life for yourself," according to a junior. The Greeks, who claim roughly a third of students as members, provide much of the activity, and when they're not partying, a smattering of local bars and delis pick up the slack. The Student Association sponsors mixers, band parties and tailgate parties and a film series for everyone, and students can always step across the street to Colonial Williamsburg to picnic in the restored area, walk or jog down Duke of Gloucester Street, or study in one of the beautiful gardens. Substantial part-time job opportunities exist for students at Colonial Williamsburg, Busch Gardens, and other tourist-oriented industries in the area. (So be on the lookout: That distinguished-looking gentleman in the powdered wig could be in your English class.) For out-of-town excursions, Richmond and Norfolk, each an hour's drive, are the nearest cities; Virginia Beach, a favorite springtime mecca, is a little farther.

Varsity sports are low-keyed compared to those at most southern state schools, though the football team, which competes in Division I-AA, stirred some enthusiasm recently with a strong season. Basketball and soccer are other popular men's sports, while the women's soccer team, which recently ranked sixth in Division I, spearheads a strong women's athletic program. Intramurals, from skydiving to Ultimate Frisbee, are very popular, and a $4.5-million recreational athletic facility now under construction should make them even more so.

"I chose William and Mary," one student comments, "because it offers the

icy and reputation of the Ivy League at the cost of a public institution." With
d social outlets and a stiff work load, William and Mary can be a pressure cooker,
henever students need to get away, they can always stroll back into the eighteenth
ury and take in a demonstration of candle dipping or horseshoeing. If you're a
M student, admission is free.

Williams College

-> Economics?

Williamstown, MA 01267

Location Small town	**Applicants** 4,660
Total Enrollment 2,020	**Accepted** 25%
Undergraduates 1,970	**Enrolled** 45%
Male/Female 56/44	**Academics** ★ ★ ★ ★ ★
SAT V/M 650/670	**Social** ☎ ☎ ☎
Financial Aid 36%	**Q of L** ● ● ● ●
Expense Pr $ $ $ $	**Admissions** (413)597-2211

During his travels through the Massachusetts wilderness, Henry David Thoreau once
assessed the Berkshire Mountains setting of Williams College as worth "at least one
endowed professorship." While the dramatic beauty of Williams hasn't changed since
its founding in 1793, the quality of the education has improved annually, placing it
among the finest undergraduate liberal arts institutions in the country.

The campus is tucked into the wooded countryside that acts as a perfect backdrop
for the skiing, cycling and backpacking for which Williams students are famous. "This
is no place for Urban Sophisticates who can't bear to walk out the door without
makeup," warns one senior. When there isn't a blanket of snow draped across the
rolling hills and classic New England architecture, the lawns and walks are kept
flawless by a meticulous grounds crew. As one student says, "The whole place is like
a luxurious country club."

Williams' academic reputation stems from a tradition of excellent teaching and
a rigorous curriculum in which active student participation in the classroom is expected. Distribution requirements are few, but the extremely heavy work load within
major programs and the talent and high motivation of the students combine to form
a climate of intense academic pressure. "It can be frightening and overwhelming," notes
one student. "I don't think that I am alone when I feel that I'm in way over my head."
Students are quick to stress, however, that the pressure, although ever present, does
not result in cutthroat competition. Says one, "There is truly a collaborative effort
among the students at Williams—the phrase 'community of scholars' is not inappropri-
ate."

Williams' strengths are in chemistry, political science, English and history, all of
which contribute directly to an acceptance rate of about 90 percent at business, law and
medical schools. Art history and political science are also topflight departments. Anthropology and sociology, weak areas in the past, have seen increased enrollment and
boast new award-winning faculty members. Foreign languages, with the exception of
Russian, are still of questionable quality, but funds have been channeled to develop a
center for foreign languages and improve effectiveness of the program as a whole.

Interdisciplinary programs in Afro-American studies, area studies and women's studies are increasingly popular. Self-paced programs are offered in Arabic, Hebrew, Korean and Swahili. Environmental studies, based in the fourteen-hundred-acre, college-owned Hopkins Forest, make full use of the campus's natural resources. For future engineers a 3-2 BA/BS program is offered in conjunction with Columbia and MIT. Students may design their own courses of study through the contract-major option or cross-register at nearby Bennington College and North Adams State College.

The required winter-study period in January is spent exploring nontraditional course areas, which may be anything from blowing glass to building lasers. One nice way to fill some of the eight required quarters of physical education is by skiing at the fine nearby facilities or engaging in other outdoor activities. In recent years students have explored India, the Soviet Union, West Africa and Western Europe with the college's unusual and relatively inexpensive faculty-guided tours. Opportunities for off-campus study are also available during the fall and spring, the many options including Williams-at–Mystic Seaport, the Twelve-College Exchange,* and an innovative exchange program with Exeter College in Oxford, England.

Williams' faculty is its greatest educational asset, and all students have access to top professors. Most professors live right in Williamstown, giving students the opportunity to see them not just in class, but at the bank, on Main Street, and even in their homes. The computer center is well equipped, and Sawyer Library, according to one man, "may be the most comfortable library in the country—many carrels have lounge chairs that recline, all the stacks are open and food is allowed anywhere." The Williams College Museum of Art and the campus health service building have recently been expanded, and improvements on the athletic center are underway.

The typical Williams student is an enthusiastic, well-rounded extrovert "with an extremely high energy level." In making admissions decisions, Williams tends to prefer a "Renaissance man to the fifteen-year-old who devotes all his free time to the reclassification of butterfly taxonomy and is embraced by Harvard's admissions office," says one in-the-know junior. Almost everyone works hard and plays with a vengeance. ("Madonna/Rambo Night" and "Screw Your Roommate" parties are among those beer bashes known to vie for student brain cells.) Nearly a third of the students are bona fide preppies—the rest just look that way. More than three-quarters graduate in the top 10 percent of their high school class, but other personal accomplishments carry weight for applicants with less competitive grades. New Englanders and New Yorkers tend to dominate the wide geographic makeup. There are no athletic or merit scholarships, but Williams' financial aid policy provides all accepted students with a financial aid package designed to meet their computed need. A campus-based parent-loan program allows families to borrow at low interest rates.

Campus housing at Williams is among the best to be found anywhere. One of the school's dorms was once a fine old inn, and with fireplaces and mahogany paneling, several others look like they should have been. Resumé in hand, one senior frets, "I don't know if I'll ever live this well again." Living options range from two modern complexes to the lovely row houses that were fraternities before Greek organizations were abolished in 1962. Small co-op houses are available for students who want to cook and play house. New arrivals reside in "frosh only" dorms, where the highly praised junior adviser system works to provide advice and support. Upperclassmen, virtually assured a single, may enter the room lottery individually or in groups. The college permits only a handful of students to move off campus. Food is another area where Williams' resident overachievers are pampered. Except for the much-feared tofu pie, the food is considered quite good, and nearly everyone buys the meal plan usable in any of the six campus dining halls.

Though the Berkshire setting is hours from a big city, Williamstown is far from a cultural desert. The Clark Art Museum, within walking distance of campus, possesses one of the finest collections of Renoir and Degas in the nation as well as a fine library. The modern college music center attracts top classical musicians, and the college theater is home to a renowned summer festival that often features Broadway stars. Films, lectures and concerts abound on most weekends, as do the usual number of parties. Relations between the sexes, however, are less than ideal. Basically, everyone's "either 'married' or very, very single," one student reports. And news of a change in status travels fast.

Sports are more like a religion than an extracurricular activity. Everyone seems to play on some team, and any contest with arch-rival Amherst assures a big crowd. Both the men's and women's swim teams are nationally ranked ("They win championships in their sleep"), and the squash team is usually one of the tops in the nation. The Taconic golf course, rated among the best collegiate facilities, has been host to several national college championships. The college helps maintain a fifteen-hundred-foot private alpine ski slope and a ten-kilometer cross-country ski trail located ten miles from town, and both are available to students. Heading to the slopes directly after class is more like an involuntary muscle reflex then a well-thought-out plan. And as if that weren't enough, the organized intramurals are also popular.

Even four long, cold winters in a small New England town fail to chill most Ephs' love for their school (that's pronounced *eefs,* as in school founder Ephraim Williams). Those who survive the wilderness, the work load and the weather can move quite comfortably into loyal Williams alumnihood—a stage of life that comes complete with a respected degree, professional contacts and an ability to do something for their alma mater. "Williams is the type of place," says one graduating senior, "that produces students who are just dying to give something back to the college."

University of Wisconsin—Madison

Madison, WI 53706

Location Center city	**Applicants** 13,120
Total Enrollment 44,580	**Accepted** 82%
Undergraduates 30,670	**Enrolled** 50%
Male/Female 51/49	**Academics** ★ ★ ★ ★ ★
SAT V/M 510/570	**Social** 🐿 🐿 🐿 🐿
ACT 24	**Q of L** ● ● ● ●
Financial Aid 47%	**Admissions** (608)262-3961
Expense Pub $ $	

The state of Wisconsin has fallen on some financially troubled times, and when it comes time for cutting budgets, the University of Wisconsin—Madison, the flagship school of the state's twenty-two-campus system, is the most obtrusive sitting duck. Suddenly a university that prided itself on being all things to all people, has been forced to become fewer things to fewer people. Even so, Wisconsin continues to offer what one journalism major describes as "the most amazing college of personalities and ideas available in any American university."

Professors at UW–Madison are certainly among the nation's best, with Nobel Prize winners, National Academy of Science members, and Guggenheim fellows scattered liberally among the departments. Access to these people isn't always easy, however, since five thousand research projects do take time to carry out and the few introductory courses in which they show their faces may contain as many as five hundred students. "But any student with a little desire and persistence can get in to see a prof one-on-one," reports one student. Despite a recent faculty salary increase passed by the state legislature, some of Wisconsin's academic stars complain of being underpayed, and others have gone on to greener pastures.

UW–Madison's distinctive campus is spread out over 903 hilly, tree-covered acres and across an isthmus between two glacial lakes, Mendota and Minona, named by prehistoric Indians who once lived along their shores. From atop Bascom Hill, at the center of campus, you look east past the statue of Lincoln and the liberal arts buildings, down to a library mall that was the scene of many a political demonstration during the sixties. Further east you see rows of State Street pubs and restaurants and the bleached dome of the Wisconsin state capitol. On the other side of the hill another campus, dedicated to the sciences, twists along Lake Mendota. But students from both sides of the hill drink beer elbow to elbow in the old student union Rathskeller where political arguments and Go games can rage all night. Outside on the union's veranda students can look out at the sailing in summer or ice boating in winter.

The icy wind that blows off the lakes in winter is vicious, and the academic climate is not exactly tropical either. Course work is demanding, and in many ways akin to graduate school elsewhere. Predictably, grading is tough and inflexible and often figured on a strict curve. Students emphasize that it is almost impossible to get through without the self-discipline to study four to five hours a day outside the classroom.

A list of first-rate academic programs at Madison would read like another college's complete course catalogue. Suffice it to say that biological and physical sciences (especially bacteriology and dairy science), engineering, business, history, journalism, sociology, zoology, economics, German, political science and education are among the standouts.

The university recognizes that overcrowding is one of its most serious problems. With enrollments continuing to rise and funds continuing to sink, many students find themselves closed out of high-demand courses particularly in foreign languages, computer sciences, communication arts and economics. In fact, some popular fields, like engineering and business, have had to restrict entry to their majors by requiring high GPAs. As at other large universities, registration lines can be a hassle. One senior reports, "There have been some cutbacks and courses are a lot harder to get, depending on the time at which you register."

Distribution requirements vary among the different schools and academic departments, but they are uniformly "rigorous and unforgiving," with science and math courses required for BA students and a foreign language for virtually everyone. For students who prefer the academic road less traveled, options include the Institute for Environmental Studies and the Integrated Liberal Studies (ILS), which consists of related courses introducing the achievements of Western culture. A variety of internships are available, as are study-abroad programs all over the world—Europe, Brazil, India, Israel and Thailand.

If there is one common characteristic among the thirty thousand-plus undergraduates, it's aggressiveness. "It's easy to get lost in the crowd here, so you have to be fairly strong and confident," declares one student. "No one holds your hand." The plus side is that "you don't have to look or act any certain way." Almost four out of five students are from Wisconsin. Students from all over the country and one of the largest clusters of foreign students at any American university constitute the rest. Wisconsin is the heartland of progressive politics, and the school's reputation as a liberal haven remains intact. "Students here are called liberal because they are eager and willing to change and are continually looking for newer and better ideas," explains an activist. About thirty-six hundred academic merit scholarships of up to $5,700 are awarded to students with outstanding GPAs and/or artistic talent, and more than 250 talented athletes are awarded scholarships for their contributions.

Housing is a problem, and several thousand students are turned down each year. Freshmen who want dorm space are advised to apply even before receiving a decision from the admissions office. Preference is given to in-state students and current dorm residents; out-of-staters usually have to find private housing. In fact, the vast majority of students scour the city for housing, and the sellers' market means that rents can be high. Dorms are either coed or single sex, and each has a cafeteria where residents are required to board. The student union also offers two meal plans, and there are plenty of restaurants and fast-food places nearby.

Madison has been the stomping grounds for many a fine rock and roll or blues band on the road to fame. There are more film clubs than anyone can follow, and everyone has a favorite bar. About one-fourth of the students go Greek. "Frat parties are a very popular break from the bar scene," reports one expert on both options. UW–Madison is notorious among area schools for its Halloween festivities, and there are also lots of private parties. Nature enthusiasts can lose themselves in the university's twelve-thousand-acre nature preserve, and ski slopes are close at hand. But be prepared to confront thermometers that read twenty below zero. The students at this Big Ten school show "tons of interest" in sports, especially football and hockey. Cross-country and track teams are championship winners. The same amount of funding is given to both men's and women's athletics, and both use the same facilities.

All in all, UW–Madison is a nonstop festival that students sum up as "diverse, intellectual, fashionable, and moderately hedonistic." In these days of financial disparity, the university has been forced to cut back quantitatively, but it has yet to scrimp on the qualitative aspects of this ever lively and convivial community. Wisconsin remains, in the words of an administrator, "one of life's great gold mines, for those willing to dig."

Wittenberg University

Springfield, OH 45501

Location City outskirts	**Applicants** 2,050
Total Enrollment 2,140	**Accepted** 80%
Undergraduates 2,140	**Enrolled** 37%
Male/Female 47/53	**Academics** ★ ★ ★
SAT V/M 500/540	**Social** ☎ ☎ ☎
Financial Aid 52%	**Q of L** ● ● ●
Expense Pr $ $	**Admissions** (513)327-6314

Students at this little Ohio college have a tough time finding something to complain about. They love their campus and their professors. They have enough dorm space and enough ice cream. Reports confirm that "not too many are jumping off the top of the library because of their grades," and the people really are friendly. "It's not a pretense; it's geniune."

The love affair begins with the campus itself: seventy rustic acres in hilly southwestern Ohio. At the center stands a grand old nineteenth-century brick administration building with giant white pillars and an open-air dome. An ultramodern physical recreation center is the newest addition. Everything in between is "an architecturally fun mix of old and new, brick and stone," notes an East Asian studies major, "and the many different trees and flowers make the seasons really come alive." The isolation of this idyllic campus in a pleasant Ohio city can sometimes "blind students to the rest of the world," cautions a chem senior. But most students find it to be a warm and friendly environment for living and learning. Springfield itself, with seventy-seven thousand or so content inhabitants, calls itself an all-American city.

Founded in 1845 by German Lutherans, Wittenberg is committed to providing quality liberal arts disciplines stamped with distinctive contemporaneity. This goal is achieved partially through extensive general education requirements that combine skills (writing, mathematics and foreign language) with traditional disciplines (natural science, humanities and social sciences), with a bit of artistic, religious and philosophical appreciation thrown in for good measure. The three eleven-week terms each year can set a brisk pace. Biology, business administration, East Asian studies, English, history, political science and psych are the school's best departments, while health ed, philosophy and geography are weak. Internships are available in all areas and there are a number of 3-2 program options in engineering, forestry and nursing. Acceptance rates into med, law and graduate business schools are above 80 percent, though most students head for the job market.

Class sizes average in the low twenties, which means communication with faculty is almost impossible to avoid. Teaching assistants are unheard of, and "professors are genuinely concerned and aren't hesitant to become involved in the lives of their students," reports a senior. "I sail with one of my professors and play squash regularly with another," one man claims. Wittenberg encourages a year or semester off campus, either in this country or abroad. Options include the international student exchange program, field studies in the Bahamas and Costa Rica, California state hospital semester or a term at the United Nations.

Although half of the students come from Ohio, many are from New York, New Jersey and Pennsylvania. Wittenberg tends to attract a diverse group in terms of both socioeconomic background and world view. "Most students are easygoing, social

631

minded and especially well rounded," according to one student. Despite the school's academic orientation, not all students were whiz kids in high school. In fact, less than half graduated in the top fifth of their class, and more than 10 percent come from the bottom half. Wittenberg awards fifty scholarships of up to $3,000 based only on scholastic merit.

Freshmen and sophomores must live on campus, and accommodations are pleasant and spacious, even if dorm rules are strict. Visitation hours between men and women are as zealously enforced in the three coed dorms as in the single-sex ones. Almost everyone gets a double all four years, but freshman assignments are processed in the order in which room deposits are received. The one upperclass dorm (complete with cooking facilities), and on- or off-campus apartments are favorites with older students. Food service in Witt's dining hall is a cut above normal institutional fare. There's an all-American line (hot dogs and hamburgers), several bars—salad, deli, cereal, soup and ice cream—and theme dinners once a month.

While Hawaiian Night in the dining hall may be the highlight of a Witt work week, Saturdays and Sundays are a bit more exciting. Fraternities and sororities, whose members comprise half of the student population, hold regular bashes, "but they are by no means the only weekend activities." Dorms frequently sponsor weekend trips and outings. When the weather is conducive, a nearby reservoir is popular for swimming and picnics. There is a pub in the Union basement called the Rat, which is a good get-together spot. More highbrow entertainment is available in Springfield proper (about ten minutes by car), where the city orchestra gives free tickets to Witt students. Dayton is half an hour away, Columbus an hour and Cincinnati an hour and a half.

Wittenburg has been known as an athletic powerhouse among NCAA Division III small schools, winning national championships in both football and basketball. Women's tennis, field hockey and swimming teams are also quite successful. For nonvarsity types, the new health and physical education center houses three gyms as well as a pool, racquetball courts and other things that are good for you. "Intramural rivalries between perennial teams is intense," notes an English major. One of the most dynamic groups on campus is the interdenominational Christian fellowship, but organizations have also been formed around political issues and recreational interests.

Even a casual visitor to the campus can't miss the school pride that animates most Wittenberg undergraduates. But what one senior enjoys the most at this college is "being a real live person whom my professors call by name and are concerned about my education and well-being."

College of Wooster

Wooster, OH 44691

Location Small town
Total Enrollment 1,790
Undergraduates 1,780
Male/Female 50/50
SAT V/M 500/530
Financial Aid 55%
Expense Pr $ $

Applicants 1,870
Accepted 82%
Enrolled 32%
Academics ★ ★ ★
Social ☎ ☎ ☎
Q of L ● ●
Admissions (800)262-4010

The College of Wooster—known to its students as the school that's easy to get into but no cinch to stay in—has a habit of surreptitiously snatching up high school ugly ducklings and metamorphosing them into college swans. Deemphasizing students' past records, Wooster has a keen eye for spotting potential. The college holds high expectations for its students, forcing them either to shape up or ship out. More often than not, the Wooster formula works and motivates underachievers. In terms of numbers of alumni granted PhDs since 1920, Wooster ranks eleventh among private colleges (third in chemistry, fifth in geology and sixth in physical sciences).

There are several ingredients in the Wooster recipe for success. First of all, students must complete a freshman seminar composed of classical reading, critical writing and heated discussions. This broad exploration is followed by a more concentrated sophomore seminar, which in turn leads to an intense three-semester independent study (one semester in junior year and two in senior year) called IS. The forty-year-old IS requirement functions as the backbone of the Wooster curriculum, and most students have a love/hate relationship with it—working one-on-one with a professor on an original research project of your choice is "a scary, but important opportunity." The demands of IS account for much academic pressure; but once the deadline is met, students praise the program as well as their own creative endeavors—collections of short stories, dramatic presentations, cutting-edge physics research in fluids, etc. "We trust students," says one administrator.

One-third of each student's transcript will depict an array of liberal arts courses from outside his or her chosen or self-constructed major; proficiency in a foreign language and one religion course are also required. Dedicated professors, refreshed by well-funded study leaves every fifth year, win high praise for their devotion to teaching and advising. Many students operate on a first-name basis with their professors and share in research projects with them: Science majors have been known to co-author faculty papers, while students in economics collaborate with professors in managing a portion of the college's assets. Student-faculty departmental happy hours and dinners at professors' houses are popular.

Chemistry tends to be rated at the top of the academic pyramid by students, along with geology, biology and history. The social sciences tend to be weaker, with psychology showing the most serious problems. The theatre department hasn't broken any legs lately, and the teacher's certification program is purely practical and uninspired. Students who lack sufficient preparation in any area can take advantage of the fact that Wooster offers free tutors in every subject. The college boasts a wide variety of out-of-classroom experiences, ranging from local internships to study tours. A leadership and liberal learning program includes a seminar class and a week-long "acquaintanceship" in which participants attach themselves to a prominent politician or businessman.

Wooster sponsors programs in India, Colombia, Greece and Russia, and students may also participate in dozens of programs abroad sponsored by the Great Lakes Colleges Association* and the Institute of European Study.

Wooster has led the way in the computerization of small colleges. WoosterNet, a broadband cable computer network implemented with the help of computer science students, links every academic and administrative building and residence hall on campus and provides computer freaks with twenty-four-hour access to more than a hundred microcomputers and terminals. Other academic facilities are improving and renovations in two science buildings have produced more classrooms, a drafting laboratory and individual office space for seniors to work on IS projects. With everything from modern to Gothic architecture, the consistently white limestone and brick buildings resemble castles from various eras. Several of the older buildings were recently renovated to near mint condition, which enables them to properly adorn the finely groomed campus. An abundance of flowers and trees provide a calm, attractive setting, and gracefully intertwined among the buildings are brick pathways—nice to look at, though tough to walk on in high heels, according to one report.

The admissions office, with its ultrapersonal recruitment style—"Not one letter was addressed to Dear Prospective Student," says a sophomore—continues to assemble diverse groups of scholars. In fact, an increase in applicants is pushing Wooster toward becoming a more selective school (median SAT scores are up forty points from three years ago), and the academic climate is becoming more intense. But students report that the pressure here is the "good kind"—self-imposed—and not a result of competition between peers. "You are here to get an education, not compete for one," claims a freshman. "There are always people to lend you notes," attests a history major. "We help each other a lot." As for geographical origins, 9 percent are foreign students, the majority are from the Northeast and Midwest, and a lot are from Ohio and proud of it. One man claims Wooster students "tend to have an eastern attitude, being conservative in dress, study habits, and recreation, but fairly liberal in politics"—a trait one of his classmates defines as "pseudo-liberal." Supportive and friendly attitudes prevail, and one man warns that "conceit, selfishness, and a lack of respect are cardinal sins at this small college." Wooster sponsors several merit scholarships awarded by its own examination and faculty interviews. Twenty percent of the student body receives renewable academic and achievement awards ranging from $1,000 to $8,000 a year, including a smattering of awards for music that are automatically halved after freshman year.

Wooster and about one-fourth of its students are affiliated with the Presbyterian Church, and the Scottish heritage is reincarnated in the school band, complete with bagpipes and kilt skirts. Action groups on disarmament and hunger are significant presences, and groups of community service volunteers who wish to live and work together can apply for one of the twenty university-owned program houses where they can plan and organize all night long. Most students are housed in coed and single-sex dorms offering small rooms, but great maid service. Visitation hours on single-sex halls are democratically determined by the residents. An international hall and a humanities hall are available, as are rooming blocks for the men's and women's social clubs. There are two dining halls on campus where, in the opinion of even a finicky diner, "the food is—you won't believe this—good." All the baking is done on campus, and Wooster has several bars—salad bar, fruit bar, dessert bar and yogurt bar—not to mention enormous quantities of ice cream.

Wooster athletes field respectable Division III teams. Particularly strong women's teams are lacrosse, field hockey, and swimming. Men do well in swimming, soccer, baseball and track, but the Scottish band that performs at games is not able to inspire the football team to similar accomplishments. "There are tons of intramural teams," reports an athlete, and soccer is the most popular one. The administration prefers this good, clean fun to beer bashes, but Wooster has its share of both. The college has no national Greek societies, but there are local "sections" for men and "clubs" for women that provide a large part of the weekend social scene. Ohio's drinking age of nineteen for beer, twenty-one for hard liquor is strictly enforced at parties and in Ichabod's, the campus nightclub. Asking a Wooster student about nearby off-campus entertainment deep in the heart of the Amish country solicits a remorseful response: "There is nothing in or near Wooster, Ohio, but this college and the Rubbermaid factory." Fortunately, Cleveland, Akron, skiing and white-water rafting are only a road trip away; unfortunately there is little public transportation to take you there.

Despite its isolation, Wooster continues to attract students. There's a chance it won't be such an easy-to-get-into school for long. People are interested in the little school in Ohio that stresses individual attention and personal growth. Socially and academically, there's something almost magical about the place. In the words of one duckling, "It's too corny to be true."

Worcester Polytechnic Institute

Worcester, MA 01609

Location City outskirts
Total Enrollment 4,030
Undergraduates 2,770
Male/Female 80/20
SAT V/M 540/660
Financial Aid 70%
Expense Pr $ $ $

Applicants 2,380
Accepted 68%
Enrolled 44%
Academics ★ ★ ★ ★
Social ☎ ☎ ☎
Q of L ● ● ● ●
Admissions (617)793-5286

You think going to engineering school automatically means a chain of prerequisites, inhuman grade grubbing and endless hours of problem sets? Well, take a look at Worcester Polytech, the third oldest independent science and engineering school in the nation, and be prepared for a pleasant surprise. With a reputation for high-quality programs, the college has virtually no required courses, an unconventional grading system, and individualized, project-oriented academic programs. At this unique bastion of technology, the emphasis is not on adhering to the rules, but on learning to create your own. WPI turns out engineers and scientists who are not only technically competent but "sensitive to the social context in which their work is carried out."

Situated on the residential outskirts of Worcester, the second largest city in New England, WPI's campus borders on two parks and a historic district. Old English stone buildings, complete with creeping ivy, dominate the architectural tone, but there are also plenty of modern facilities dotting the immaculately kept grounds, which include two large ponds.

At the center of Worcester's academic program is a project-based curriculum identified simply as the Plan. Introduced in 1972, the Plan gives undergraduates both hands-on experience in their chosen field and an awareness of the social impact of technology. To get their degree students must complete the following:

1. The sufficiency requirement: a set of five thematically related humanities courses followed by a research paper or performance that develops the theme—step one in creating a class of "technological humanists."

2. The Interactive Qualifying Project (IQP): a creative application of technical knowledge to one of society's problems, supervised by both a science and a humanities professor.

3. The Major Qualifying Project (MQP): a student's first chance to work as an engineer on a technical problem of his or her own choice. (Worcester Polytech was the first engineering school to integrate practical labs with theoretical education, a commitment preserved in the MQP.)

4. The Competency Exam: a three- to five-day take-home exam for seniors—the supposed culmination of their education—in which they are given a problem they are likely to face in their first year of real-world work.

Most courses are similarly project-oriented, which brings students and professors in close contact as research colleagues. Courses are often a means by which students acquire the information needed to complete their projects, reemphasizing WPI's curriculum as one driven by knowledge and not credit. Information not provided directly through course work can be attained via the library of videotaped lectures on specific topics. There are four terms per academic year at WPI, each lasting about seven weeks. When students are not completing projects, they take three courses per term, making for a high-pressure atmosphere. "Seven weeks does not leave time for unmotivated students," remarks one junior. "You must be self-driven."

Course offerings in the humanities are somewhat limited (German is the only foreign language understood by people rather than computers), but students don't have much criticism for any particular area, with the exception of biology. The most popular departments are, of course, technical and include mechanical, electrical and chemical engineering and computer science. An unusual program in biomedical engineering is offered in conjunction with the University of Massachusetts Medical School, about two-and-a-half miles away. A new program in manufacturing systems engineering is still in the developmental stages.

Many students take advantage of WPI's unusual internships at the school's two project centers in Washington, D.C., and London. These centers provide students with the opportunities to do more than make-work positions in a business or government agency. Instead, participating undergraduates tackle back-burner problems for a company and spend their term working independently on a specific technical assignment, under the direction of two faculty members. Co-op programs offer juniors and seniors two eight-month work experiences and add an extra year onto the degree program. And off-campus study programs let students attend technical schools in England, Germany, Switzerland, Sweden, Scotland or Ireland for full credit, or at another college in the Worcester Consortium.*

Only three grades are given out at WPI: distinction, acceptable, and no record (the last does not appear on the transcript). Students like the elimination of pressure that comes with the system but complain that, since a D-plus comes out the same as a C-minus on the Polytech scale, hard work has less visible results than at schools with traditional grades. Praise for the innovation and flexibility embodied in the plan runs high, but students are also quick to stress that their training is rigorous and traditional. Explains one student, "Worcester Polytech does have steady classroom and lab activity with absolutely strict schedules, like anywhere else, and it has standard exams (about three per term) in every class." Don't worry if this description of the Plan gives you more questions than answers; admissions officers spend a full hour or more explaining every detail of the program to prospective students.

Most Polytech students—affectionately referred to as "Woopies"—come mainly from New England public high schools, and all, naturally, have a scientific bent. Nevertheless, the admissions office considers more than just mathematical and scientific ability; most students are well rounded, and many excel in athletics. "Everyone likes to be involved in at least one interest other than engineering and studying," proclaims a senior. A strong financial aid program provides assistance to nearly three-fourths of the student body, but no academic or athletic merit scholarships are awarded.

Freshmen are not only guaranteed spots in the university dorms, but they are required to occupy one. There are two single-sex and three coed-by-floor or wing units, including a brand new, spacious 220-bed resident hall. After the first year, undergraduates disperse into fraternity housing or apartments, almost all of which are within a mile of the college grounds. The two dining halls offer two different meal plans along with a hot dog and hamburger bar, and an abundance of omelettes.

When students want recreation they turn to the fraternities and sororities, which regularly hold open parties. School-run coffeehouses, a pub and occasional visiting performers brighten the lives of many highly wired WPI students' weeks. Student entertainment committees have recently been successful in promoting campus-wide events, such as air band concerts and a battle of the bands, but leaving campus on the weekend is also an often-employed option. Boston and Hartford are both an hour's drive away, as are both ski resorts and beaches. With a lopsided male/female ratio of five to one, WPI is hardly a dating haven for either sex; both men and women draw on nine other Worcester colleges linked to Polytech (by shuttle buses) in a social as well as academic consortium.

While not particularly scenic, Worcester does offer a large number of clubs and restaurants, as well as a well-endowed shopping mall. A large multipurpose arena, The Centrum, is host to frequent concerts and occasional visits from Boston's Bruins and Celtics. On campus, an extremely large proportion of the student body takes part in intercollegiate activity, which results, one student notes, in "a shortage of spectators." Yet the winning football team is still able to draw loyal student support. The men's soccer, wrestling and club crew regularly turn in respectable records, as do women's basketball and crew. Varsity teams and an active intramural program have benefited from major renovations of outdoor athletic facilities, including a multipurpose, all-weather playing field. The indoor facility, home to a successful basketball program, is still in need of some attention.

Students value the practicality of their education as well as the easy association with professors, the successful job-placement program and the tone of life at WPI. "The school has a very cooperative atmosphere," says one woman. "We realize engineering isn't a one-person field." And don't be put off by the institute's relative anonymity. The main reason WPI is not as well known as other technical schools is because it has chosen to devote its resources to undergraduates, not research—which is just one more reason to consider this unique engineering education.

Xavier University of Louisiana

New Orleans, LA 70125

Location Urban
Total Enrollment 1,910
Undergraduates 1,690
Male/Female 35/65
SAT V/M 400/400
Financial Aid 77%
Expense Pr $

Applicants 1,020
Accepted 72%
Enrolled 45%
Academics ★ ★
Social ☂ ☂ ☂
Q of L ● ● ●
Admissions (504)483-7388

Xavier University of Louisiana is the only black, Roman Catholic university in the Western hemisphere. Non-Catholics now account for about half of the student body, but six hours of theology are still required for graduation, and Mass is said every day on campus. Fortunately, the university's strong commitment to "nurture growth in Christian values" resonates well with its eager undergraduates. As one student espouses, "I enjoy this aspect of Xavier because it helps me maintain a sense of purpose in reaching my academic and career goals."

The Sisters of the Blessed Sacrament founded the school in 1925, and, despite the continual scrambling for dollars that characterizes all black colleges, Xavier has made it, as have many of its graduates. In the past, students walked Xavier's stately stone quadrangle because they had been denied admission to other southern schools. Now they come here because of the school's recognized commitment to serious education. They return as alumni to speak, recruit and serve as role models.

Only minutes away from the heart of New Orleans, next to city parks and the Art Museum, Xavier's campus paints a deceivingly unprogressive picture. A combination of small modern and Gothic structures are scattered around the centralized landmark, the U-shaped administration building. The university's main goals include the addition of new facilities, the first of which is the soon-to-be-completed Science Center that will provide state-of-the-art teaching facilities and a centralization of academic departments for the sciences. Such an expansion is crucial: The Xavier campus is ruled by the natural sciences—the area in which over 50 percent of its students now major. Xavier has one of two colleges of pharmacy in Louisiana, and the university is credited for educating 15 percent of all black pharmacists nationally. In fact, the college of pharmacy attracts most of the nearly 11 percent of nonblack students, and virtually all of its graduates pass the state licensing exam with above average scores. Those who make it through the premed courses at Xavier are well on their way to medical careers, since for the last ten years, about 80 percent of premed students have been accepted at medical schools. The music and education departments have also been traditional strengths. A core curriculum of prescribed courses in philosophy and theology, art and humanities, history and behavioral sciences and math and the natural sciences round out the degree program, which requires intensive work in both a major and minor field.

The average freshman class size is twenty-two, although science and math courses are often larger. Priests and nuns teach and help run the school. "Faculty members strive to help their students succeed," reports one premed. In addition to the many internships available, Xavier offers cooperative education programs in all fields and a

3-2 engineering program in conjunction with Tulane and other schools. Two special six-week summer programs, SOAR for science students and EXCEL for those in other fields, help incoming freshmen prepare for the rigors of higher education through courses on problem-solving skills. The MARC and MBRS programs aim to attract minority students to the biomedical sciences; students chosen for these programs undertake an honors curriculum, participate in research projects and receive stipends (for MARC, full-tuition scholarships). Students complain that Xavier's library is small, and its hours and study areas are inadequate, however, students have access to facilities at three other New Orleans schools.

Students come mostly from the Deep South (76 percent commute) but almost a third of them carry tales of Mardi Gras back to such cities as Chicago and New York. Many are from middle-class families, and half are from parochial schools. A high percentage are second- or third-generation Xavierites whose parents credit their own success to what they carried away from here. Students are characterized as career oriented but supportive of "movements aimed at improving the quality of life for minorities and the underprivileged." SAT scores and class rank are not overly impressive, but the student success record is. "Xavier attempts to assemble a workable financial package for all eligible enrolled students. Incoming students who have a 3.0 GPA and have a 20 ACT score are eligible for academic stipends, ranging from $500 to full tuition.

Since the four contemporary-looking residence halls are single sex, insufficient in number, and "far from ideal," most students move off campus after their first year. Even freshmen may have a hard time getting on-campus housing, although a number from the waiting list will be assigned to them. There are a cafeteria and a snack bar but few compliments for the food or the food service employees. Xavier is conveniently located to take advantage of the active nightlife of New Orleans, and much student recreation takes place off campus. Greek organizations also play a strong role and sponsor some campus-wide activities.

Basketball for men and women is the only varsity sport, and the Gold Nuggets and Gold Rush teams are both enthusiastically supported. Beyond sports, whatever your interest, there is probably an extracurricular activity affiliated with it on campus: Ping-Pong, guitar, Gospel choir and business organizations are among the many complements to academic life.

Xavier is a school where achievement has been the rule and beating the odds against success a routine occurrence. Although this is not the school for those who want the most intense of academic climates or a place that emphasizes social activities, Xavier has continued to put whatever resources it can muster into its original educational mission of educating the eager and deserving students who seek it out. Founded to provide an affordable college education, Xavier's current reputation assures, says one man, "that blacks who could afford to go elsewhere now come here."

Yale University

New Haven, CT 06520

Location Urban
Total Enrollment 10,800
Undergraduates 5,200
Male/Female 55/45
SAT V/M 670/690
Financial Aid 38%
Expense Pr $ $ $ $

Applicants 11,740
Accepted 19%
Enrolled 60%
Academics ★ ★ ★ ★ ★
Social 🐘 🐘 🐘
Q of L ● ● ●
Admissions (203)432-1900

Ask any Yale student what school offers the best undergraduate education in the nation and you're likely to get only a puzzled look. It's a foregone conclusion on this campus that Yale beats the "other" schools, Harvard and Princeton, hands down. The reasoning is simple: Where Harvard offers unmatched resources, and Princeton a highly personalized learning environment, Yale combines the resources of a large research university with a tradition of undergraduate teaching excellence. Though Yale can't always deliver on its promise of the best of both worlds, many a super-achiever looking for a first-rate education in the liberal arts has found Yale the surest bet.

Yale was founded in 1701 by Connecticut Congregationalists who, the story goes, were concerned about "backsliding" tendencies among their counterparts at a certain school in Massachusetts. Though secular liberalism has replaced the strident Puritanism of centuries past, Yale retains a great sense of academic orthodoxy and concern for traditional values, including the work ethic. For students, that means one of the heaviest work loads of any major university: Thirty-six rather than the usual thirty-two courses are required for graduation. Yalies also cover their material in a shorter time; the reading period and exams are compressed into two weeks at the end of each semester, so work can't be left to the end of the term as at Harvard or Princeton. These demands contribute to an academic atmosphere that ranges from intense to manic. "People are intense about their work because people are intense about themselves," notes one student. Incidentally, people at Yale who work *all* rather than *most* of their waking hours are not called nerds, as they are elsewhere. Here they are weenies.

Unlike most other major research universities, Yale views undergraduate education as its primary task. The university has twelve graduate schools, but Yale College, the undergraduate arts and sciences division, remains the heart of the university. Virtually all faculty members teach undergraduate courses, and even the resources of professional schools—especially architecture, fine arts, drama and music—are put at the disposal of undergraduates. Yale's English and history departments are superb, and students have made them the two most popular undergraduate majors. History is also one of the most demanding: a thirty- to fifty-page senior essay is required by the department. Among other things, the Yale English department is noted as a leading center of "deconstructionist" literary criticism, and its offerings in creative writing are also top-notch but oversubscribed. The interdisciplinary American studies major is quite popular, but the political science department, once the finest in the nation, now gets mixed reviews.

One area in which Yale stands out from its competitors is the quality of its arts programs. It has a long-boasted excellence in drama and music at the undergraduate as well as the graduate levels. Architecture (one of Yale's few selective majors), fine arts and modern languages are also good. The natural sciences have traditionally been viewed as Yale's weakest suit, although the steep quarter-mile trek to Science Hill, where most labs and science classrooms are situated, at least guarantees healthy science majors. The biology department is excellent, as is a major called molecular biochemistry and biophysics (known as MB&B), although both fields are overrun by premeds.

Despite its traditionalism, Yale does not have a core curriculum, and students have plenty of leeway in choosing their course of study. The lone requirements are two classes in each of four broad areas by the end of the sophomore year, and two years of a foreign language or the equivalent. In lieu of preregistration, students have what is known as "shopping period"—two weeks at the beginning of each term to sample morsels of the various offerings before handing in their schedules. Strong-willed souls who prefer a broader-based introduction to college academics can apply to Directed Studies—Directed Suicide to those who manage to live through it—an extremely rigorous interdisciplinary program of three full-year seminars taken the freshman year. Yalies' commitment to the liberal arts is perhaps most vividly reflected in the fact that three-quarters of them take at least one course in philosophy.

Introductory classes at Yale are usually large lectures, which are typically broken down into small sections with teaching assistants. Some of the most popular, such as Eastern-bloc defector Wolfgang Leonhard's course on the Soviet Union, or Jonathan Spence's ruminations on China, seem more like theatrical performances than lectures. Upper-level seminars are small and plentiful, though especially popular ones often turn away even juniors and seniors. As elsewhere, Yale's big-name professors are often more interested in personal research than in undergraduates, but even Nobel laureates teach undergraduate seminars, and most are amenable to meal invitations. Some of the university's most popular courses, such as social and American history seminars, are often taught by junior faculty members—who, by the way, face grim prospects for tenure and tend to be even more open to a free lunch. Yale's libraries are second only to Harvard's and contain more than eight million volumes—many of them underground in the Cross Campus Library. Also located in CCL are rows of tiny study carrels, "beige boxes that look like phone booths with desks in them." To Yalies, these are "weenie bins."

Nearly half the student body is from the Northeast, and Yale, which is need-blind in admissions, meets the full demonstrated financial need of all accepted candidates. About 45 percent of its students come from prep schools, and more than 90 percent graduated in the top fifth of their class. Yale began accepting women in 1969, and, by and large, coeducation has gone well. Yale is consistently more popular with women than most of its rivals, notably Princeton. Most of the traditions that make Yale—singing groups like the Whiffenpoofs, drinking "at the tables down at Mory's"—are now either coed or have female counterparts. A strong recruitment program has stabilized annual minority enrollment at about 9 percent black and Hispanic, 7 percent Asian American. Yalies are a predominantly liberal group, though a small but growing band of alienated conservatives keep the William F. Buckley tradition of political dialogue lively. Career and life goals also vary, but one man says the career resources and placement program is "good for investment banking and law school and not a whole lot else."

Undoubtedly Yale's most distinctive feature is its residential college housing system. Endowed by a Yale graduate (who also began the same house system at Harvard) and modeled on those at Oxford and Cambridge, Yale's colleges provide an intimate living and learning community. Much of each college's distinctive identity is drawn from its architecture. Some are fashioned in craggy, fortress-like Gothic, while others are done in the more open Colonial style, with red brick and green shutters the prevailing motif. All have their own special nooks and crannies with cryptic inscriptions that pay tribute to illustrious Yalies of generations past. The colleges also have their own library, dining hall and special facilities such as photographic labs or tree swings—one is even said to have an endowment used solely for whipped cream. About the only major difference in the two systems is that Harvard students choose their house at the end of freshman year in the Harvard yard, while Yalies arrive at school already assigned to one. However, most freshmen live together in the Old Campus, the historic nineteenth-century quadrangle, before moving into their colleges as sophomores. Those who find their college doesn't agree with them can easily transfer to another after their freshman year. The system of residential colleges is designed not only to break down the impersonality of a large university but also to maximize the diversity that exists.

Each residential college has its own affiliated faculty members, or resident fellows, and offers its own seminars. These, along with plays, concerts, lectures and other events sponsored by the colleges, are integral to the cultural life of the university as a whole. Each college also has a dean, which makes for a more decentralized administrative structure and may provide what one observer describes as "a more carefully constructed safety net" for undergraduates struggling to adapt to academic or other rigors. Sophomores and juniors generally live in three-room suites (four to a room), while most seniors can get a single. Yale's food is rated among the best in the Ivy League. Students may charge meals anywhere on campus, including the excellent cafeterias at the graduate schools.

When Yale is winning the annual Harvard-Yale football extravaganza, the Harvard side has been known to taunt them by shouting across the stadium, "You may be winning, but you have to go back to New Haven." Lately, that jeer carries less weight, since downtown New Haven is in the midst of a genuine urban renaissance. A summer jazz festival now brings thousands to the historic Town Green, as do occasional food fairs and performances of Shakespeare comedies. The city's long-standing tradition of theater—it was once *the* place to try-out plays headed for Broadway—has been brought back to mind with the revitalization and reopening of two grand old theater/concert halls just a block from campus. They bring in traveling Broadway shows and several concerts by the likes of James Brown and the Preservation Hall Jazz Band every month. New Haven also has its own symphony, chamber orchestra, upscale boutique district and a Macy's adjacent to the downtown shopping mall, not to mention a lively restaurant scene. Locals will swear that Pepe's on Wooster Street was the first pizza parlor in the country, and Louis' Lunch the first true hamburger joint. Though town/gown relations have historically been strained, they have improved recently, in part because many students volunteer their time in community service organizations.

Located smack in the middle of town and bordering on good and not-so-good neighborhoods, the Yale campus offers some refreshingly modern buildings to go along with the more stately traditional ones. The most eye-catching of these is the Beinecke rare-book library, a boxlike structure with translucent walls that glow with varying amounts of sunlight. Large, grassy courtyards in each of the colleges give students some room to roam and flip Frisbees—an appropriate activity since New Haven was the home of the now-defunct Frisbee Pie Company, whose round baking tins evolved into the omnipresent campus toy. Safety is an issue, at least around the borders of the campus, but the university runs an elaborate mini-van and escort service.

Each weekend on campus brings two or three big parties sponsored by the social committees of the residential colleges. Movies abound—one a night, and five or six on weekends. The Yale Repertory Theater is an excellent, innovative professional company that depends heavily on graduate school talent but always brings in a few top stage stars each season. The large-scale undergraduate theater company, The Yale Dramat, and plenty of productions in the colleges fill out the busy theater schedule. Natural history and art museums on and near campus, especially the British Art Center, are excellent. For those who want more excitement, the typical Yalie refrain on New Haven—"It's halfway between New York and Boston"—tells it all. Metro-North trains run almost hourly to New York, and visiting Boston is nearly as easy.

At Yale, Greek letters have little importance outside the classical language department, though a handful of fraternities and sororities do attract a tiny but growing number of students. Students tend to identify strongly with their extracurricular groups, spending every evening at the newspaper office, radio station or computer center. Particularly clubby are members of a capella singing groups, who do everything from drink together on a certain night of the week to go on tour together during spring vacation. The most famous is the Whiffenpoofs, who regularly hold forth at Mory's while forcing their audience (or at least those over twenty-one, thanks to the new drinking age) to down various alcoholic concoctions called gold cups, green cups or red cups. Those whose social tastes range to the arcane can investigate Yale's secret societies, mysterious clubs for seniors, some with their own mausoleum-like clubhouses. Although the majority have gone coed and favor achievement over family connections when choosing members, the most traditional of these societies are just as elitist as their counterparts at Harvard and Princeton.

Yale also has some of the strongest varsity athletic teams in the Ivy League. Hockey, squash and crew, routinely post winning seasons, though the football team, once the pride of the Ivy League, has been on the skids of late. Women's sports are strong across the board, but especially in gymnastics, fencing and lacrosse. Women's volleyball, demoted to club status several years ago, was recently restored to the varsity ranks. More than four thousand students a year take part in intramural competition among the twelve colleges, and the enormous Payne Whitney gymnasium is the largest indoor athletic facility in the free world.

Life at Yale is never easy. Academic pressure hangs like a cloud over campus, and so does the pressure to maintain or challenge a constellation of traditions. Yale's intensity of experience—in academic programs and social life—makes the college so important a part of the lives of its alumni that they are not simply Yale graduates. They become Yalies, a loyal breed that originated the phrase, "For God, for country, and for Yale." No matter that the *American Heritage Dictionary* uses this motto as an example of "anticlimax." Even cynical Yalies take it to heart.

Yeshiva University

New York, NY 10033

Location Urban	**Applicants** 620
Total Enrollment 4,350	**Accepted** 79%
Undergraduates 1,120	**Enrolled** 48%
Male/Female N/A	**Academics** ★ ★ ★
SAT V/M 560/620	**Social** 🕾 🕾
Financial Aid 75%	**Q of L** ● ● ●
Expense Pr $ $	**Admissions** (212)960-5277

Now entering its second century, Yeshiva University is America's oldest and largest university under Jewish auspices. "We provide a dual program of faith and learning, trying to synthesize the best of the Western and the Jewish heritages," an administrator explains. This unusual goal, along with students' commitment to their common heritage, makes for an intimate, stimulating atmosphere and one of the most close-knit communities of any college in the country. Its two main undergraduate divisions, Yeshiva College for men and Stern College for Women, offer similar experiences in separate Manhattan locations. (The information in the first half of this profile and the data given in the statistics refer mainly to Yeshiva College; Stern is described separately below.)

Located in the less-than-glamorous upper Manhattan neighborhood of Washington Heights (known to many as Spanish Harlem), Yeshiva has no cohesive, self-contained campus—you'll know you're there when everybody you see is wearing a yarmulke. Buildings are either historic oddities or more modern functionals. Students come to Yeshiva University from all around the nation and a few foreign countries, with the largest proportion from parochial schools in the immediate metropolitan area. The university emphasizes preparation for professional careers, and a high percentage of Yeshiva's graduates go on to further study, including about one-fifth to the rabbinate. The acceptance rate at schools of law and medicine is high, at 96 and 90 percent, respectively (including Stern graduates).

Yeshiva offers a full program of Jewish studies (weighted to accommodate varying levels of background in the field) as well as a typical college grounding in the main liberal arts divisions—humanities, social and natural sciences. Among the strongest majors are accounting, English, philosophy, political science, computer science and Jewish studies. Preprofessional programs such as life sciences are also strong, but music, art, classics, sociology, physics and languages are weaker. Aided by a recent $12-million gift from a group of business executives, the university recently opened a fledgling school of business. Students are encouraged to spend a year of study in Israel, and most students see this as a valuable part of their education. Yeshiva also offers independent study, joint BA/MA programs and a joint five-year engineering degree with Columbia University.

The faculty includes some of the foremost rabbinic scholars in the nation. Relations between professors and the administration were scarred several years ago by an extended dispute over the right of the faculty members to unionize, which eventually led to a landmark Supreme Court decision against the professors. But relations between faculty and students are excellent, both in and out of class. "You can speak personally to any teacher, any time," a psychology major emphatically asserts. In addition, the heavy work load is taken into consideration in grading. The university prides itself on "never rejecting an academically qualified student for financial reasons," and twenty no-need scholarships of $5,000 each are awarded every year.

The sense of community is strengthened, though, by the congenial atmosphere in the dorms, where most of the undergraduates live. Housing is available to all who request it, and those who don't live on campus miss out on the dorm-centered social life. There is a kosher cafeteria that offers cheap, tasty meals, but many students make heavy use of the vending machines and fast-food joints in the area.

Varsity and intramural sports are available, but here, too, facilities are limited. "It's more fun to play pick-up basketball with the neighborhood Puerto Ricans," one athlete notes. There is a good variety of extracurricular activities, including three newspapers, one of them in Hebrew. The student council plays a significant role in organizing social events and helping to set academic policy. Clubs made up of students in a particular major are popular, especially the computer society. On weekends, the Yeshiva campus pace slows as most students go home for a little relaxation. The city, of course, is an important focus of weekend activities (midtown and Greenwich Village are only a subway ride away), and most students go to Yeshiva's sister school, Stern, for dates.

Stern College for Women, situated in the exclusive and quiet Murray Hill neighborhood, is a little smaller than Yeshiva, enrolling six hundred women. The offerings at Stern, which is academically separate from Yeshiva, include majors in liberal arts subjects as well as in nursing, accounting, education and social work. Stern, too, has a required core program in Judaic studies, though the class hours are not nearly as long as those at Yeshiva. In contrast to the male college, which is heavily weighted to Talmudic classes, the women's curriculum concentrates more on the Torah, history and codified Jewish law. All students know Hebrew by the time they graduate, and a hefty percentage study in Israel. Classes are small and relations between students and faculty are extremely personalized. Most Stern students plan professional careers, but they take their more traditional role seriously as well. "I believe that family is the future of the Jewish people, not my career in marketing," says one. "I'm very happy with my role as a woman. I don't feel I have to prove to myself that I'm better than a man."

The social connection between Stern and Yeshiva is strong, and there are numerous joint extracurricular activities and social events. Personal messages travel over midtown via the schools' computers. Some women at Stern may be intent upon pursuing an MRS degree, but others are individualists who would scoff at the insinuation. Notes one student, "Many affect a New York style of dressing and dance at the discos until dawn; others keep their subdued, out-of-town clothing and prefer to curl up with a good book." Thursday night is date night, with Yeshiva men usually coming downtown either to date or just to hang around in the Stern dormitory lounge. As at Yeshiva, no members of the opposite sex are allowed upstairs in the dorms.

Though many students are from New York and other nearby eastern states, those at Stern also come from the West, Canada and other foreign countries. Because of a program with its affiliated high school and a large number of early admits, sixteen is not an uncommon age for Stern freshmen. Undergraduates as a group are not as academically strong as their male counterparts, and admissions are not as selective.

A single dormitory, three blocks away from the college and down the street from the Empire State Building, houses the five hundred or so Stern women who choose to live at school. There is a cafeteria in the school building, but most students cook in the dorms, where they are required to keep kosher. Stern women find dorm living friendly and fun, and they say the area couldn't be better. "Museums, theaters, restaurants and Fifth Avenue are all within a stone's throw," says a Canadian, beaming.

Though some students at Yeshiva and Stern question whether the goal of providing a synthesis between religious and secular studies has truly been achieved, all seem to agree on the importance of a Jewish background. The two institutions, they say, represent "a place where the Jew finds his roots, his heritage, and the possibilities for his future." In the process, students also find a supportive atmosphere and a college experience they wouldn't trade for anything.

Acknowledgments

THE *SELECTIVE GUIDE TO COLLEGES* STAFF

Editor: Edward B. Fiske
Associate Editor: Amy Stuart Wells
Managing Editor: Bruce Hammond
Writers: Linda Borchardt, Randy Castleman, Hal Phillips, Kim Ronemus,
    Mary Tabor, Sam Weiss

The *Selective Guide to Colleges* is a team effort, reflecting the ideas and contributions of many persons. Space prohibits acknowledging all of them, but in addition to those listed as writers and editors, I would like to pay special tribute to several.

Joseph Michalak is a colleague and friend who, with his formidable knowledge of American higher education, was a constant source of wisdom.

Warm and heartfelt thanks go to those patient, patient technological geniuses—Howard Angione, Gary Cosimini, Edmond Gravely, Barbara Williams, Judith Willner and, especially, Frank Stankus—who cheerfully and patiently guided us through the intricacies of bits and bytes.

It was a privilege and pleasure working with my two principal associates on the project, Amy Wells and Bruce Hammond. Amy is a talented journalist whose skills were surpassed only by the cheerfulness with which she took on and solved every problem with which she was presented. Bruce gave generously of his considerable talent and experience in the field. I look forward to working with both of them in the future.

In the final analysis the *Selective Guide* is the work of the thousands of students and college administrators who took the time to answer detailed and demanding questionnaires. Their goodwill and candor are deeply appreciated, and while I, of course, accept full responsibility for the final product, the book is ultimately the product of their reflections on the institutions of which they are a part.

Finally, and most important, my thanks to my wife, Dale, whose support and talent for flowcharts kept the project on track, and to our children, Julie and Suzanna, for their patience during evenings and weekends when my nose was buried in questionnaires. Without them, there would be no *Selective Guide*.

E.B.F.